State Estimation for Robotics

A key aspect of robotics today is estimating the state (e.g., position and orientation) of a robot, based on noisy sensor data. This book targets students and practitioners of robotics by presenting not only classical state estimation methods (e.g., the Kalman filter) but also important modern topics such as batch estimation, Bayes filter, sigma-point and particle filters, robust estimation for outlier rejection, and continuous-time trajectory estimation and its connection to Gaussian-process regression. Since most robots operate in a three-dimensional world, common sensor models (e.g., camera, laser rangefinder) are provided, followed by practical advice on how to carry out state estimation for rotational state variables. The book covers robotic applications such as point-cloud alignment, pose-graph relaxation, bundle adjustment, and simultaneous localization and mapping.

Highlights of this expanded second edition include a new chapter on variational inference, a new section on inertial navigation, more introductory material on probability, and a primer on matrix calculus.

TIMOTHY D. BARFOOT is Professor at the University of Toronto Institute for Aerospace Studies. He has been conducting research in the area of navigation of mobile robotics for over 20 years, in both industry and academia, for applications including space exploration, mining, military and transportation. He is a Fellow of the IEEE Robotics and Automation Society.

State Estimation for Robotics

Second Edition

TIMOTHY D. BARFOOT
University of Toronto

Shaftesbury Road, Cambridge CB2 8EA, United Kingdom

One Liberty Plaza, 20th Floor, New York, NY 10006, USA

477 Williamstown Road, Port Melbourne, VIC 3207, Australia

314–321, 3rd Floor, Plot 3, Splendor Forum, Jasola District Centre, New Delhi – 110025, India

103 Penang Road, #05-06/07, Visioncrest Commercial, Singapore 238467

Cambridge University Press is part of Cambridge University Press & Assessment, a department of the University of Cambridge.

We share the University's mission to contribute to society through the pursuit of education, learning and research at the highest international levels of excellence.

www.cambridge.org
Information on this title: www.cambridge.org/9781009299893
DOI: 10.1017/9781009299909

First published 2017

Second Edition 2024

A catalogue record for this publication is available from the British Library

A Cataloging-in-Publication data record for this book is available from the Library of Congress

ISBN 978-1-009-29989-3 Hardback

Cambridge University Press & Assessment has no responsibility for the persistence or accuracy of URLs for external or third-party internet websites referred to in this publication and does not guarantee that any content on such websites is, or will remain, accurate or appropriate.

Contents

Part II   Three-Dimensional Machinery

Part III   Applications

Preface for the First Edition

My interest in state estimation stems from the field of mobile robotics, particularly for space exploration. Within mobile robotics, there has been an explosion of research referred to as *probabilistic robotics*. With computing resources becoming very inexpensive, and the advent of rich new sensing technologies, such as digital cameras and laser rangefinders, robotics has been at the forefront of developing exciting new ideas in the area of state estimation.

In particular, this field was probably the first to find practical applications of the so-called Bayes filter, a much more general technique than the famous Kalman filter. In just the last few years, mobile robotics has even started going beyond the Bayes filter to batch, nonlinear optimization-based techniques, with very promising results. Because my primary area of interest is navigation of robots in outdoor environments, I have often been faced with vehicles operating in three dimensions. Accordingly, I have attempted to provide a detailed look at how to approach state estimation in three dimensions. In particular, I show how to treat rotations and poses in a simple and practical way using matrix Lie groups.

Introductio Geographica by Petrus Apianus (1495–1552), a German mathematician, astronomer, and cartographer. Much of three-dimensional state estimation has to do with *triangulation* and/or *trilateration*; we measure some angles and lengths and infer the others through trigonometry.

The reader should have a background in undergraduate linear algebra and calculus, but otherwise, this book is fairly stand-alone (Appendix A is new in the second edition and serves as a primer/reminder on matrix algebra and calculus). I hope readers of these pages will find something useful; I know I learned a great deal while creating them.

I have provided some historical notes in the margins throughout the book, mostly in the form of biographical sketches of some of the researchers after whom various concepts and techniques are named; I primarily used Wikipedia as the source for this information. Also, the first part of Chapter 7 (up to the alternate rotation parameterizations), which introduces three-dimensional geometry, is based heavily on notes originally produced by Chris Damaren at the University of Toronto Institute for Aerospace Studies.

This book would not have been possible without the collaborations of many fantastic graduate students along the way. Paul Furgale's PhD thesis extended my understanding of matrix Lie groups significantly by introducing me to their use for describing poses; this led us on an interesting journey into the details of transformation matrices and how to use them effectively in estimation problems. Paul's later work led me to become interested in continuous-time estimation. Chi Hay Tong's PhD thesis introduced me to the use of Gaussian processes in estimation theory, and he helped immensely in working out the details of the continuous-time methods presented herein; my knowledge in this area was further improved through collaborations with Simo Särkkä from Aalto University while on sabbatical at the University of Oxford. Additionally, I learned a great deal by working with Sean Anderson, Patrick Carle, Hang Dong, Andrew Lambert, Keith Leung, Colin McManus, and Braden Stenning; each of their projects added to my understanding of state estimation. Colin, in particular, encouraged me several times to turn my notes from my graduate course on state estimation into this book.

I am indebted to Gabriele D'Eleuterio, who set me on the path of studying rotations and reference frames in the context of dynamics; many of the tools he showed me transferred effortlessly to state estimation. He also taught me the importance of clean, unambiguous notation.

Finally, thanks to all those who read and pointed out errors in the drafts of this book, particularly Marc Gallant and Shu-Hua Tsao, who found many typos, and James Forbes, who volunteered to read and provide comments.

Preface for the Second Edition

It has been just over seven years since the first edition of this book was released. I have been delighted with the reception, with many colleagues and students providing useful feedback, comments, and errata over the years. Since publication of the first edition, I have kept a working copy on my personal webpage and attempted to correct any minor problems as they came in. Thank you very much to all those who took the time to give me feedback; please keep it coming for this second edition.

I am also excited that the first edition has been translated into simplified Chinese and has become extremely popular with Chinese readers; 感谢读者对于本书的支持 (thank you for reading the book!). Thanks very much to 高翔 (Gao, Xiang) and 谢晓佳 (Xie, Xiaojia) for their hard work on producing the translation.

The second edition brings about 160 pages of new material. Highlights of the new additions are as follows (chapter numbers refer to the new edition):

- **Chapter 2, Primer on Probability Theory:** expanded to cover several new topics including cumulative distributions, quantifying the difference between probability density functions, and randomly sampling from a probability density function

- **Chapter 3, Linear-Gaussian Estimation:** expanded to include computing the posterior covariance in the Cholesky and Rauch–Tung–Striebel smoothers, and a short section on recursive continuous-time smoothing and filtering

- **Chapter 4, Nonlinear Non-Gaussian Estimation:** added a new section giving some details for sliding-window filters

- **Chapter 5, Handling Nonidealities in Estimation:** expanded the scope and renamed this chapter to include information on what properties a good estimator should have, and a new section on adaptive covariance estimation

- **Chapter 6, Variational Inference:** a new chapter that frames estimation as finding a Gaussian approximation that is closest to the full Bayesian posterior in terms of the Kullback–Leibler divergence; also enables parameter learning from a common data-likelihood objective

- **Chapter 8, Matrix Lie Groups:** expanded to include sections on Riemannian optimization, computing the statistics of compounded and differenced poses with correlations, a discussion of symmetry, invariance, and equivariance

- **Chapter 9, Pose Estimation Problems:** added a large new section on inertial navigation from a matrix Lie group perspective including IMU pre-integration for batch estimation

- **Chapter 11, Continuous-Time Estimation:** rewrote this chapter from scratch to be consistent with the Simultaneous Trajectory Estimation and Mapping framework that my research group uses regularly

- **Appendix A, Matrix Primer:** a new appendix on linear algebra and matrix calculus that can serve as a primer and reference

- **Appendix B, Rotation and Pose Extras:** some extra derivations for rotations and poses including eigen/Jordan decomposition of rotation and pose matrices

- **Appendix C, Miscellaneous Extras:** a collection of useful results including the Fisher information matrix for a multivariate Gaussian, a derivation of Stein's lemma, converting continuous-time models to discrete time, connection to invariant EKF

- **Exercises:** several new exercises added plus solutions to almost all exercises in Appendix D

In addition to those who I thanked in the first edition, the following people were instrumental in this new version. First and foremost I would like to thank Professor James Forbes from McGill University who has been a wonderful collaborator over the years. He gave me several great suggestions for this second edition and provided invaluable advice on the invariant EKF and inertial navigation sections, in particular. The new chapter on variational inference was also a collaboration with James Forbes, and my student David Yoon and I thank them both for their help. Thanks also to Professor Gabriele D'Eleuterio; we worked together on the eigen/Jordan decomposition of rotation and pose matrices. Charles Cossette and Keenan Burnett helped find typos/issues in some new sections; thank you! A big thank you to my postdoc Dr. Johann Laconte who implemented the methods in the new inertial navigation section to make sure they worked as written and provided feedback to improve the readability. Many thanks to Lauren Cowles, my publisher at Cambridge, who encouraged me to put this second edition together.

Acronyms and Abbreviations

Notation

General Notation

a	This font is used for quantities that are real scalars
$\mathbf{a}$	This font is used for quantities that are real column vectors
$\mathbf{A}$	This font is used for quantities that are real matrices
A	This font is used for time-invariant system quantities
$p(\mathbf{a})$	The probability density of $\mathbf{a}$
$p(\mathbf{a}\vert\mathbf{b})$	The probability density of $\mathbf{a}$ given $\mathbf{b}$
$\mathcal{N}(\mathbf{a},\mathbf{B})$	Gaussian probability density with mean $\mathbf{a}$ and covariance $\mathbf{B}$
$\mathcal{GP}(\boldsymbol{\mu}(t),\mathcal{K}(t,t'))$	Gaussian process with mean function, $\boldsymbol{\mu}(t)$, and covariance function, $\mathcal{K}(t,t')$
$\mathcal{O}$	Observability matrix
$(\cdot)_k$	The value of a quantity at timestep k
$(\cdot)_{k_1:k_2}$	The set of values of a quantity from timestep k_1 to timestep k_2, inclusive
$\underrightarrow{\mathcal{F}}_a$	A vectrix representing a reference frame in three dimensions
$\underrightarrow{a}$	A vector quantity in three dimensions
$(\cdot)^\times$	The cross-product operator, which produces a skew-symmetric matrix from a 3×1 column
$\mathbf{1}$	The identity matrix
$\mathbf{0}$	The zero matrix
$\mathbb{R}^{M\times N}$	The vector space of real $M\times N$ matrices
$\hat{(\cdot)}$	A posterior (estimated) quantity
$\check{(\cdot)}$	A prior quantity

Matrix-Lie-Group Notation

$SO(3)$ The special orthogonal group, a matrix Lie group used to represent rotations

$\mathfrak{so}(3)$ The Lie algebra associated with $SO(3)$

$SE(3)$ The special Euclidean group, a matrix Lie group used to represent poses

$\mathfrak{se}(3)$ The Lie algebra associated with $SE(3)$

$(\cdot)^\wedge$ An operator associated with the Lie algebra for rotations and poses

$(\cdot)^\curlywedge$ An operator associated with the adjoint of an element from the Lie algebra for poses

$\mathrm{Ad}(\cdot)$ An operator producing the adjoint of an element from the Lie group for rotations and poses

$\mathrm{ad}(\cdot)$ An operator producing the adjoint of an element from the Lie algebra for rotations and poses

$\mathbf{C}_{ba}$ A 3×3 rotation matrix (member of $SO(3)$) that takes points expressed in $\underrightarrow{\mathcal{F}}_a$ and re-expresses them in $\underrightarrow{\mathcal{F}}_b$, which is rotated with respect to $\underrightarrow{\mathcal{F}}_a$

$\mathbf{T}_{ba}$ A 4×4 transformation matrix (member of $SE(3)$) that takes points expressed in $\underrightarrow{\mathcal{F}}_a$ and re-expresses them in $\underrightarrow{\mathcal{F}}_b$, which is rotated/translated with respect to $\underrightarrow{\mathcal{F}}_a$

$\boldsymbol{\mathcal{T}}_{ba}$ A 6×6 adjoint of a transformation matrix (member of $\mathrm{Ad}(SE(3))$)

1

Introduction

Robotics inherently deals with things that move in the world. We live in an era of rovers on Mars, drones surveying the Earth, and, soon, self-driving cars. And, although specific robots have their subtleties, there are also some common issues we must face in all applications, particularly *state estimation* and *control*.

The *state* of a robot is a set of quantities, such as position, orientation, and velocity, that, if known, fully describe that robot's motion over time. Here we focus entirely on the problem of estimating the state of a robot, putting aside the notion of control. Yes, control is essential, as we would like to make our robots behave in a certain way. But, the first step in doing so is often the process of determining the state. Moreover, the difficulty of state estimation is often underestimated for real-world problems, and thus it is important to put it on an equal footing with control.

In this book, we introduce the classic estimation results for linear systems corrupted by Gaussian measurement noise. We then examine some of the extensions to nonlinear systems with non-Gaussian noise. In a departure from typical estimation texts, we take a detailed look at how to tailor general estimation results to robots operating in three-dimensional space, advocating a particular approach to handling rotations.

The rest of this introduction provides a little history of estimation, discusses types of sensors and measurements, and introduces the problem of state estimation. It concludes with a breakdown of the contents of the book and provides some other suggested reading.

1.1 A Little History

About 4,000 years ago, the early seafarers were faced with a vehicular state estimation problem: how to determine a ship's position while at sea. Primitive charts and observations of the sun allowed local navigation along coastlines. Early instruments also helped with navigation. The astrolabe was a handheld model of the universe that allowed various astronomical problems to be solved; it could be used as an inclinometer to determine latitude, for example. Its origins can be traced to the Hellenistic civilization around 200 BC and was greatly advanced in the Islamic world starting in the eighth century by mathematician Muhammad al-Fazārī and astronomer Abū al-Battǎnī (aka, Albatenius). Also around 100 BC in ancient Greece, the so-called Antikythera mechanism was the world's

Carl Friedrich Gauss
(1777–1855) was a
German
mathematician who
contributed
significantly to many
fields including
statistics and
estimation. Much of
this book his based on
his work.

Rudolf Emil Kálmán
(1930–2016) was a
Hungarian-born
American electrical
engineer,
mathematician, and
inventor. He is famous
for the *Kalman filter*
and introducing the
notions of
controllability and
observability in
systems theory.

first analogue computer capable of predicting astronomical positions and eclipses decades into the future.

Despite these early capabilities, it was not until the fifteenth century that global navigation on the open sea became widespread with the advent of additional key technologies and tools. The mariner's compass, an early form of the magnetic compass, allowed crude measurements of direction to be made. Together with coarse nautical charts, the compass made it possible to sail along rhumb lines between key destinations (i.e., following a compass bearing). A series of instruments was then gradually invented that made it possible to measure the angle between distant points (i.e., cross-staff, astrolabe, quadrant, sextant, theodolite) with increasing accuracy.

These instruments allowed latitude to be determined at sea fairly readily using celestial navigation. For example, in the Northern Hemisphere, the angle between the North Star, Polaris, and the horizon provides the latitude. Longitude, however, was a much more difficult problem. It was known early on that an accurate timepiece was the missing piece of the puzzle for the determination of longitude. The behaviours of key celestial bodies appear differently at different locations on the Earth. Knowing the time of day therefore allows longitude to be inferred. In 1764, British clockmaker John Harrison built the first accurate portable timepiece that effectively solved the longitude problem; a ship's longitude could be determined to within about 10 nautical miles.

Estimation theory also finds its roots in astronomy. The method of least squares was pioneered by Gauss,[1] who developed the technique to minimize the impact of measurement error in the prediction of orbits. Gauss reportedly used least squares to predict the position of the dwarf planet Ceres after it passed behind the Sun, accurate to within half a degree (about nine months after it was last seen). The year was 1801, and Gauss was 23. Later, in 1809, he proved that the least-squares method is optimal under the assumption of normally distributed errors (Gauss, 1809) and later still he removed this assumption (Gauss, 1821, 1823). Most of the classic estimation techniques in use today can be directly related to Gauss' least-squares method.

The idea of fitting models to minimize the impact of measurement error carried forward, but it was not until the middle of the twentieth century that estimation really took off. This was likely correlated with the dawn of the computer age. In 1960, Kalman published two landmark papers that have defined much of what has followed in the field of state estimation. First, he introduced the notion of *observability* (Kalman, 1960a), which tells us when a state can be inferred from a set of measurements in a dynamic system. Second, he introduced an optimal framework for estimating a system's state in the presence of measurement noise (Kalman, 1960b); this classic technique for linear systems (whose measurements are corrupted by Gaussian noise) is famously known as the *Kalman filter*, and has been the workhorse of estimation for the more than 60 years since its inception. Although used in many fields, it has been widely adopted in aerospace

---

[1] There is some debate as to whether Adrien Marie Legendre might have come up with least squares before Gauss.

applications. Researchers at the *National Aeronautics and Space Administration (NASA)* were the first to employ the Kalman filter to aid in the estimation of spacecraft trajectories on the Ranger, Mariner, and Apollo programs. In particular, the on-board computer on the Apollo 11 Lunar Module, the first manned spacecraft to land on the surface of the Moon, employed a Kalman filter to estimate the module's position above the lunar surface based on noisy inertial and radar measurements.

Many incremental improvements have been made to the field of state estimation since these early milestones. Faster and cheaper computers have allowed much more computationally complex techniques to be implemented in practical systems. Today, exciting new sensing technologies are coming along (e.g., digital cameras, laser imaging, the Global Positioning System) that pose new challenges to this old field.

1.2 Sensors, Measurements and Problem Definition

To understand the need for state estimation is to understand the nature of sensors. All sensors have a limited precision. Therefore, all measurements derived from real sensors have associated uncertainty. Some sensors are better at measuring specific quantities than others, but even the best sensors still have a degree of imprecision. When we combine various sensor measurements into a state estimate, it is important to keep track of all the uncertainties involved and therefore (it is hoped) know how confident we can be in our estimate.

Figure 1.3
Theodolite. A better tool to measure angles.

In a way, state estimation is about doing the best we can with the sensors we have. This, however, does not prevent us from, in parallel, improving the quality of our sensors. A good example is the *theodolite* sensor that was developed in 1787 to allow triangulation across the English Channel. It was much more precise than its predecessors and helped show that much of England was poorly mapped by tying measurements to well-mapped France.

It is useful to put sensors into two categories: *interoceptive*[2] and *exteroceptive*. These are actually terms borrowed from human physiology, but they have become somewhat common in engineering. Some definitions follow:[3]

in·tero·cep·tive [int-ə-rō-'sep-tiv], *adjective*: of, relating to, or being stimuli arising within the body.
ex·tero·cep·tive [ek-stə-rō-'sep-tiv], *adjective*: relating to, being, or activated by stimuli received by an organism from outside.

Typical interoceptive sensors are the accelerometer (measures translational acceleration), gyroscope (measures angular rate), and wheel odometer (measures angular rate). Typical exteroceptive sensors are the camera (measures range/bearing to a landmark or landmarks) and time-of-flight transmitter/receiver (e.g., laser rangefinder, pseudolites, *Global Positioning System (GPS)* transmitter/receiver). Roughly speaking, we can think of exteroceptive measurements as being of the

---

[2] Sometimes *proprioceptive* is used synonomously.
[3] *Merriam-Webster's Dictionary*.

position and orientation of a vehicle, whereas interoceptive ones are of a vehicle's velocity or acceleration. In most cases, the best state estimation concepts make use of both interoceptive and exteroceptive measurements. For example, the combination of a GPS receiver (exteroceptive) and an *inertial measurement unit (IMU)* (three linear accelerometers and three rate gyros; interoceptive) is a popular means of estimating a vehicle's position/velocity on Earth. And, the combination of a Sun/star sensor (exteroceptive) and three rate gyros (interoceptive) is commonly used to carry out pose determination on satellites.

Now that we understand a little bit about sensors, we are prepared to define the problem that will be investigated in this book:

EARLY ESTIMATION
MILESTONES

Estimation *is the problem of reconstructing the underlying state of a system given a sequence of measurements as well as a prior model of the system.*

1654	Pascal and Fermat lay foundations of probability theory
1764	Bayes' rule
1801	Gauss uses least-squares to estimate the orbit of the planetoid Ceres
1805	Legendre publishes 'least-squares'
1913	Markov chains
1933	(Chapman)–Kolmogorov equations
1949	Wiener filter
1960	Kalman (Bucy) filter
1965	Rauch–Tung–Striebel smoother
1970	Jazwinski coins 'Bayes filter'

There are many specific versions of this problem and just as many solutions. The goal is to understand which methods work well in which situations, in order to pick the best tool for the job.

1.3 How This Book Is Organized

The book is broken into three main parts:

    I. Estimation Machinery

    II. Three-Dimensional Machinery

    III. Applications

The first part, *Estimation Machinery*, presents classic and state-of-the-art estimation tools, without the complication of dealing with things that live in three-dimensional space (and therefore translate and rotate); the state to be estimated is assumed to be a generic vector. For those not interested in the details of working in three-dimensional space, this first part can be read in a stand-alone manner. It covers both recursive state estimation techniques and batch methods (less common in classic estimation books). As is commonplace in robotics and machine learning today, we adopt a *Bayesian* approach to estimation in this book. We contrast (full) Bayesian methods with *maximum a posteriori (MAP)* methods, and attempt to make clear the difference between these when faced with nonlinear problems. The book also connects continuous-time estimation with Gaussian process regression from the machine-learning world. Finally, it touches on some practical issues, such as determining how well an estimator is performing, and handling outliers and biases.

The second part, *Three-Dimensional Machinery*, provides a basic primer on three-dimensional geometry and gives a detailed but accessible introduction to matrix Lie groups. To represent an object in three-dimensional space, we need to talk about that object's translation and rotation. The rotational part turns out to be a problem for our estimation tools because rotations are not *vectors* in the usual sense and so we cannot naively apply the methods from Part I to three-dimensional robotics problems involving rotations. Part II, therefore, examines the geometry, kinematics, and probability/statistics of rotations and poses (translation plus rotation).

Finally, in the third part, *Applications*, the first two parts of the book are brought together. We look at a number of classic three-dimensional estimation problems involving objects translating and rotating in three-dimensional space. We show how to adapt the methods from Part I based on the knowledge gained in Part II. The result is a suite of easy-to-implement methods for three-dimensional state estimation. The spirit of these examples can also, we hope, be adapted to create other novel techniques moving forward.

Appendix A provides a summary of matrix algebra and calculus that can serve as a primer or reference while reading this book.

1.4 Relationship to Other Books

There are many other books on state estimation and robotics, but very few cover both topics simultaneously. We briefly describe a few works that do cover these topics and their relationships to this book.

Probabilistic Robotics by Thrun et al. (2006) is a great introduction to mobile robotics, with a large focus on state estimation in relation to mapping and localization. It covers the probabilistic paradigm that is dominant in much of robotics today. It mainly describes robots operating in the two-dimensional, horizontal plane. The probabilistic methods described are not necessarily limited to the two-dimensional case, but the details of extending to three dimensions are not provided.

Computational Principles of Mobile Robotics by Dudek and Jenkin (2010) is a great overview book on mobile robotics that touches on state estimation, again in relation to localization and mapping methods. It does not work out the details of performing state estimation in 3D.

Mobile Robotics: Mathematics, Models, and Methods by Kelly (2013) is another excellent book on mobile robotics and covers state estimation extensively. Three-dimensional situations are covered, particularly in relation to satellite-based and inertial navigation. As the book covers all aspects of robotics, it does not delve deeply into how to handle rotational variables within three-dimensional state estimation.

Robotics, Vision, and Control by Corke (2011) is another great and comprehensive book that covers state estimation for robotics, including in three dimensions. Similarly to the previously mentioned book, the breadth of Corke's book necessitates that it not delve too deeply into the specific aspects of state estimation treated herein.

Bayesian Filtering and Smoothing by Särkkä (2013) is a super book focused on recursive Bayesian methods. It covers the recursive methods in far more depth than this book, but does not cover batch methods nor focus on the details of carrying out estimation in three dimensions.

Stochastic Models, Information Theory, and Lie Groups: Classical Results and Geometric Methods by Chirikjian (2009), an excellent two-volume work, is perhaps the closest in content to the current book. It explicitly investigates the consequences of carrying out state estimation on matrix Lie groups (and hence rotational variables). It is quite theoretical in nature and goes beyond the current book in this sense, covering applications beyond robotics.

Engineering Applications of Noncommutative Harmonic Analysis: With Emphasis on Rotation and Motion Groups by Chirikjian and Kyatkin (2001) and the recent update, *Harmonic Analysis for Engineers and Applied Scientists: Updated and Expanded Edition* (Chirikjian and Kyatkin, 2016), also provide key insights to representing probability globally on Lie groups. In the current book, we limit ourselves to approximate methods that are appropriate to the situation where rotational uncertainty is not too high.

Although they are not estimation books per se, it is worth mentioning *Optimization on Matrix Manifolds* by Absil et al. (2009) and *An Introduction to Optimization on Smooth Manifolds* by Boumal (2022), which discuss optimization problems where the quantity being optimized is not necessarily a vector, a concept that is quite relevant to robotics because rotations do not behave like vectors (they form a Lie group).

The current book is somewhat unique in focusing only on state estimation and working out the details of common three-dimensional robotics problems in enough detail to be easily implemented for many practical situations.

Part I

Estimation Machinery

2

Primer on Probability Theory

In what is to follow, we will be using a number of basic concepts from probability and statistics. This chapter serves to provide a review of these concepts. For a classic book on probability and random processes, see Papoulis (1965). For a light read on the history of probability theory, Devlin (2008) provides a wonderful introduction; this book also helps to understand the difference between the *frequentist* and *Bayesian* views of probability. We will primarily adopt the latter in our approach to estimation, although this chapter mentions some basic frequentist statistical concepts in passing. We begin by discussing general *probability density functions (PDFs)* and then focus on the specific case of Gaussian PDFs. The chapter concludes by introducing Gaussian processes, the continuous-time version of Gaussian random variables.

2.1 Probability Density Functions

2.1.1 Definitions

We say that a *random variable*, x, is distributed according to a particular PDF. Let $p(x)$ be a PDF for the random variable, x, over the interval $[a, b]$. This is a nonnegative function that satisfies

$$\int_a^b p(x)\,dx = 1. \tag{2.1}$$

That is, it satisfies the *axiom of total probability*. Note that this is *probability density*, not *probability*.

Probability is given by the area under the density function. For example, the probability that x lies between c and d, $\Pr(c \leq x \leq d)$, is given by

$$\Pr(c \leq x \leq d) = \int_c^d p(x)\,dx. \tag{2.2}$$

We will also make use of the *cumulative distribution function (CDF)*[1] on occasion, which is given by

---

[1] The classical treatment of probability theory starts with CDFs, Kolmogorov's three axioms, and works out the details of probability densities as a consequence of being the derivative of CDFs. As is common in robotics, we will work directly with densities in a Bayesian framework, and therefore we will skip these formalities and present primarily the results we need using densities. We shall be careful to use the term *density*, not *distribution*, as we are working with continuous variables throughout this book.

Figure 2.1
Probability density
over a finite interval
(a). Probability of
being within a
sub-interval (b).

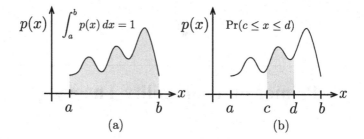

$$P(x) = \Pr(x' \leq x) = \int_{-\infty}^{x} p(x')\,dx', \tag{2.3}$$

the probability that a random variable is less than or equal to x. We have that $P(x)$ is nondecreasing, right-continuous, and $0 \leq P(x) \leq 1$ with $\lim_{x \to -\infty} P(x) = 0$ and $\lim_{x \to \infty} P(x) = 1$.

Figure 2.1 depicts a general PDF over a finite interval as well as the probability of being within a sub-interval. We will use PDFs to represent the *likelihood* of x being in all possible states in the interval, $[a, b]$, given some evidence in the form of data.

We can also introduce a conditioning variable to PDFs. Let $p(x|y)$ be a PDF over $x \in [a, b]$ conditioned on $y \in [r, s]$ such that

$$(\forall y) \qquad \int_{a}^{b} p(x|y)\,dx = 1. \tag{2.4}$$

We may also denote *joint probability densities* for N-dimensional continuous variables in our framework as $p(\mathbf{x})$, where $\mathbf{x} = (x_1, \ldots, x_N)$ with $x_i \in [a_i, b_i]$. Note that we can also use the notation

$$p(x_1, x_2, \ldots, x_N) \tag{2.5}$$

in place of $p(\mathbf{x})$. Sometimes we even mix and match the two and write

$$p(\mathbf{x}, \mathbf{y}) \tag{2.6}$$

for the joint density of $\mathbf{x}$ and $\mathbf{y}$. In the N-dimensional case, the axiom of total probability requires

$$\int_{\mathbf{a}}^{\mathbf{b}} p(\mathbf{x})\,d\mathbf{x} = \int_{a_N}^{b_N} \cdots \int_{a_2}^{b_2} \int_{a_1}^{b_1} p(x_1, x_2, \ldots, x_N)\,dx_1\,dx_2 \cdots dx_N = 1, \tag{2.7}$$

where $\mathbf{a} = (a_1, a_2, \ldots, a_N)$ and $\mathbf{b} = (b_1, b_2, \ldots, b_N)$. In what follows, we will sometimes simplify notation by leaving out the integration limits, $\mathbf{a}$ and $\mathbf{b}$.

2.1.2 Marginalization, Bayes' Rule, Inference

We can always factor a joint probability density into a conditional and a unconditional factor:[2]

---

[2] In the specific case that $\mathbf{x}$ and $\mathbf{y}$ are *statistically independent*, we can factor the joint density as $p(\mathbf{x}, \mathbf{y}) = p(\mathbf{x})p(\mathbf{y})$.

$$p(\mathbf{x}, \mathbf{y}) = p(\mathbf{x}|\mathbf{y})p(\mathbf{y}) = p(\mathbf{y}|\mathbf{x})p(\mathbf{x}). \tag{2.8}$$

This one statement has important ramifications.

First, the process of integrating[3] out one or more variables from a joint density, $p(\mathbf{x}, \mathbf{y})$, is called *marginalization*. For example, integrating the joint density over $\mathbf{x}$ reveals

$$\int p(\mathbf{x}, \mathbf{y}) \, d\mathbf{x} = \int p(\mathbf{x}|\mathbf{y})p(\mathbf{y}) \, d\mathbf{x} = \underbrace{\int p(\mathbf{x}|\mathbf{y}) \, d\mathbf{x}}_{1} \, p(\mathbf{y}) = p(\mathbf{y}). \tag{2.9}$$

The result, $p(\mathbf{y})$, is the *marginal* of the joint density for $\mathbf{y}$. Clearly then, the marginal for $\mathbf{x}$ is $p(\mathbf{x}) = \int p(\mathbf{x}, \mathbf{y}) \, d\mathbf{y}$.

Second, rearranging (2.8) gives *Bayes' rule* (aka Bayes' theorem):

$$p(\mathbf{x}|\mathbf{y}) = \frac{p(\mathbf{y}|\mathbf{x})p(\mathbf{x})}{p(\mathbf{y})}. \tag{2.10}$$

We can use this to *infer* the *posterior* or likelihood of the state given some measurements, $p(\mathbf{x}|\mathbf{y})$, if we have a *prior* PDF over the state, $p(\mathbf{x})$, and the sensor model, $p(\mathbf{y}|\mathbf{x})$. We do this by expanding the denominator so that

$$p(\mathbf{x}|\mathbf{y}) = \frac{p(\mathbf{y}|\mathbf{x})p(\mathbf{x})}{\int p(\mathbf{y}|\mathbf{x})p(\mathbf{x}) \, d\mathbf{x}}. \tag{2.11}$$

We compute the denominator, $p(\mathbf{y})$, by marginalization as follows:

$$p(\mathbf{y}) = \int p(\mathbf{x}, \mathbf{y}) \, d\mathbf{x} = \int p(\mathbf{y}|\mathbf{x})p(\mathbf{x}) \, d\mathbf{x}, \tag{2.12}$$

which can be quite expensive to calculate in the general case. In Bayesian inference, $p(\mathbf{x})$ is known as the *prior* density, while $p(\mathbf{x}|\mathbf{y})$ is known as the *posterior* density. Thus, all a priori information is encapsulated in $p(\mathbf{x})$, while $p(\mathbf{x}|\mathbf{y})$ contains the a posteriori information.

Thomas Bayes (1701–1761) was an English statistician, philosopher and Presbyterian minister, known for having formulated a specific case of the theorem that bears his name. Bayes never published what would eventually become his most famous accomplishment; his notes were edited and published after his death by Richard Price (Bayes, 1764).

2.1.3 Expectations and Moments

The *expectation operator*, $E[\cdot]$, is an important tool when working with probabilities. It allows us to work out the 'average' value of a function of a random variable, $f(\mathbf{x})$, and is defined as

$$E[f(\mathbf{x})] = \int f(\mathbf{x}) \, p(\mathbf{x}) \, d\mathbf{x}, \tag{2.13}$$

where $p(\mathbf{x})$ is the PDF for the random variable, $\mathbf{x}$, and the integration is assumed to be over the domain of $\mathbf{x}$. This is sometimes referred to as the *law of the unconscious statistician (LOTUS)*.[4]

---

[3] When integration limits are not stated, they are assumed to be over the entire allowable domain of the variable; e.g., $\mathbf{x}$ from $\mathbf{a}$ to $\mathbf{b}$.

[4] LOTUS is named so due to the fact that many practitioners apply (2.13) as a definition without realizing that it requires a rigorous proof.

For a general matrix function, $\mathbf{F}(\mathbf{x})$, the expectation is written as

$$E\left[\mathbf{F}(\mathbf{x})\right] = \int \mathbf{F}(\mathbf{x})\,p(\mathbf{x})\,d\mathbf{x}, \tag{2.14}$$

but note that we must interpret this as

$$E\left[\mathbf{F}(\mathbf{x})\right] = \left[E\left[f_{ij}(\mathbf{x})\right]\right] = \left[\int f_{ij}(\mathbf{x})\,p(\mathbf{x})\,d\mathbf{x}\right]. \tag{2.15}$$

When working with mass distributions (aka density functions) in classical mechanics, we often keep track of only a few properties called the *moments* of mass (e.g., mass, center of mass, inertia matrix). The same is true with PDFs. The zeroth probability moment is always 1 since this is exactly the axiom of total probability. The first probability moment is known as the *mean*, $\boldsymbol{\mu}$:

$$\boldsymbol{\mu} = E\left[\mathbf{x}\right] = \int \mathbf{x}\,p(\mathbf{x})\,d\mathbf{x}. \tag{2.16}$$

The second probability moment is known as the *covariance matrix*, $\boldsymbol{\Sigma}$:

$$\boldsymbol{\Sigma} = E\left[(\mathbf{x} - \boldsymbol{\mu})(\mathbf{x} - \boldsymbol{\mu})^T\right]. \tag{2.17}$$

The next two moments are called the *skewness* and *kurtosis*, but for the multivariate case these get quite complicated and require tensor representations. We will not need them here, but it should be mentioned that there is an infinite number of these probability moments.

Finally, we are sometimes interested in the *covariance*, $\mathrm{cov}(\cdot, \cdot)$, of two jointly distributed variables, $\mathbf{x}$ and $\mathbf{y}$, which we denote

$$\mathrm{cov}(\mathbf{x}, \mathbf{y}) = E\left[(\mathbf{x} - E[\mathbf{x}])\,(\mathbf{y} - E[\mathbf{y}])^T\right] = E[\mathbf{x}\mathbf{y}^T] - E[\mathbf{x}]E[\mathbf{y}]^T. \tag{2.18}$$

Here the expectations are taken over $p(\mathbf{x}, \mathbf{y})$, the joint density. The covariance matrix just described is then a special case, $\boldsymbol{\Sigma} = \mathrm{cov}(\mathbf{x}, \mathbf{x})$, or sometimes simply $\boldsymbol{\Sigma} = \mathrm{cov}(\mathbf{x})$.

2.1.4 Statistically Independent, Uncorrelated

If we have two random variables, $\mathbf{x}$ and $\mathbf{y}$, we say that the variables are *statistically independent* if their joint density factors as follows:

$$p(\mathbf{x}, \mathbf{y}) = p(\mathbf{x})\,p(\mathbf{y}). \tag{2.19}$$

We say that the variables are *uncorrelated* if

$$E\left[\mathbf{x}\mathbf{y}^T\right] = E\left[\mathbf{x}\right] E\left[\mathbf{y}\right]^T, \tag{2.20}$$

or equivalently $\mathrm{cov}(\mathbf{x}, \mathbf{y}) = \mathbf{0}$. If the variables are statistically independent, this implies they are also uncorrelated. However, the reverse is not true in general for all types of densities.[5] We will often exploit (or assume) that variables are statistically independent to simplify computations.

---

[5] It is true for Gaussian PDFs, as discussed shortly.

2.1.5 Shannon and Mutual Information

Often we have estimated a PDF for some random variable and then want to quantify how certain we are in, for example, the mean of that PDF. One method of doing this is to look at the *entropy* or *Shannon information*, H, which is given by

$$H(\mathbf{x}) = -E[\ln p(\mathbf{x})] = -\int p(\mathbf{x}) \ln p(\mathbf{x}) \, d\mathbf{x}. \qquad (2.21)$$

Claude Elwood Shannon (1916–2001) was an American mathematician, electronic engineer and cryptographer known as 'the father of information theory' (Shannon, 1948).

We will make this expression specific to Gaussian PDFs shortly.

Another useful quantity is the *mutual information*, $I(\mathbf{x}, \mathbf{y})$, between two random variables, $\mathbf{x}$ and $\mathbf{y}$, given by

$$I(\mathbf{x},\mathbf{y}) = E\left[\ln\left(\frac{p(\mathbf{x},\mathbf{y})}{p(\mathbf{x})p(\mathbf{y})}\right)\right] = \iint p(\mathbf{x},\mathbf{y}) \ln\left(\frac{p(\mathbf{x},\mathbf{y})}{p(\mathbf{x})p(\mathbf{y})}\right) d\mathbf{x}\, d\mathbf{y}. \qquad (2.22)$$

Mutual information measures how much knowing one of the variables reduces uncertainty about the other. When $\mathbf{x}$ and $\mathbf{y}$ are statistically independent, we have

$$I(\mathbf{x},\mathbf{y}) = \iint p(\mathbf{x})\, p(\mathbf{y}) \ln\left(\frac{p(\mathbf{x})p(\mathbf{y})}{p(\mathbf{x})p(\mathbf{y})}\right) d\mathbf{x}\, d\mathbf{y}$$
$$= \iint p(\mathbf{x})\, p(\mathbf{y}) \underbrace{\ln(1)}_{0} \, d\mathbf{x}\, d\mathbf{y} = 0. \quad (2.23)$$

When $\mathbf{x}$ and $\mathbf{y}$ are dependent, we have $I(\mathbf{x},\mathbf{y}) \geq 0$. We also have the useful relationship

$$I(\mathbf{x},\mathbf{y}) = H(\mathbf{x}) + H(\mathbf{y}) - H(\mathbf{x},\mathbf{y}), \qquad (2.24)$$

relating mutual information and Shannon information.

2.1.6 Quantifying the Difference Between PDFs

Given two PDFs (over the same random variable), $p_1(\mathbf{x})$ and $p_2(\mathbf{x})$, we may be interested in quantifying how 'far apart' they are. One method is to compute the *Kullback–Leibler (KL) divergence* (Kullback and Leibler, 1951) between the two:

$$\mathrm{KL}(p_2\|p_1) = -\int p_2(\mathbf{x}) \ln\left(\frac{p_1(\mathbf{x})}{p_2(\mathbf{x})}\right) d\mathbf{x} \geq 0. \qquad (2.25)$$

Kullback–Leibler divergence is a *functional*, meaning its inputs are functions, our two PDFs, and its output is a scalar. Kullback–Leibler is nonnegative and only equals zero when $p_2 = p_1$. It is not a *distance* in the formal sense, partly owing to the fact that the expression is not symmetric in p_1 and p_2. In fact, sometimes the roles of p_1 and p_2 are reversed; see Bishop (2006) for a discussion on the two different KL forms. There are also many other divergences including those of Bregman, Wasserstein (aka Earth-mover's distance), and Rényi.

A more visual way to compare two PDFs (over the same scalar random variable), $p_1(x)$ and $p_2(x)$, is using a *Q–Q (quantile–quantile) plot*. Formally, a *quantile function*, $Q(y) = P^{-1}(y)$, is the inverse (if it exists) of the *cumulative distribution function*. Let $P_1(x)$ be the CDF of $p_1(x)$ and $P_2(x)$ be the CDF of $p_2(x)$. Then, the Q–Q plot is a two-dimensional parametric curve that graphs $Q_2(y)$ versus $Q_1(y)$ as y varies from 0 to 1. If the two PDFs are the same, then the Q–Q plot will be a straight line with unit slope; deviations from this line indicate differences between the PDFs. Quantile–quantile plots can also be generated from experimental data.

2.1.7 Random Sampling

Suppose we have a random variable, $\mathbf{x}$, and an associated PDF, $p(\mathbf{x})$. We can draw random samples from this density, which we denote as

$$\mathbf{x}_{\mathrm{meas}} \leftarrow p(\mathbf{x}). \tag{2.26}$$

A sample is sometimes referred to as a *realization* of the random variable, and we can think of it intuitively as a measurement.

We may be interested in generating such random samples on a computer. In the case of a scalar random variable, x, with CDF, $P(x)$, we can again make use of the quantile function, $Q(y) = P^{-1}(y)$, from the previous section to generate random samples. Assuming our computer is able to already generate random samples from the uniform density over the interval from 0 to 1,

$$y_{\mathrm{meas}} \leftarrow \mathcal{U}[0, 1], \tag{2.27}$$

then we can pass these samples through the quantile function to create random samples for x:

$$x_{\mathrm{meas}} = Q(y_{\mathrm{meas}}). \tag{2.28}$$

For higher-dimensional random variables, generating random samples is a bit more involved; we will see an example later in the section on Gaussian random variables.

Friedrich Wilhelm Bessel (1784–1846) was a German astronomer and mathematician (systematizer of the Bessel functions, which were discovered by Bernoulli). He was the first astronomer to determine the distance from the sun to another star by the method of parallax. The Bessel correction is technically a factor of $N/(N-1)$ that is multiplied in front of the 'biased' formula for covariance that divides by N instead of $N-1$.

2.1.8 Sample Mean and Covariance

If we are given N samples of a random variable, $\mathbf{x}$, from an associated PDF, $p(\mathbf{x})$, we may want to use these samples to estimate the mean and covariance of $\mathbf{x}$. We can use the *sample mean* and *sample covariance* to do so:

$$\boldsymbol{\mu}_{\mathrm{meas}} = \frac{1}{N} \sum_{i=1}^{N} \mathbf{x}_{i,\mathrm{meas}}, \tag{2.29a}$$

$$\boldsymbol{\Sigma}_{\mathrm{meas}} = \frac{1}{N-1} \sum_{i=1}^{N} \left(\mathbf{x}_{i,\mathrm{meas}} - \boldsymbol{\mu}_{\mathrm{meas}} \right) \left(\mathbf{x}_{i,\mathrm{meas}} - \boldsymbol{\mu}_{\mathrm{meas}} \right)^T. \tag{2.29b}$$

Notably, the normalization in the sample covariance uses $N - 1$ rather than N in the denominator, which is referred to as *Bessel's correction*. Intuitively, this is necessary because the sample covariance uses the difference of the measurements with the sample mean, which itself is computed from the same measurements, resulting in a slight correlation. The sample covariance can be shown to be an unbiased estimate of the true covariance, and it is also 'larger' than when N is used in the denominator. It is also worth mentioning that as N becomes large, $N - 1 \approx N$, so the bias effect for which sample covariance compensates becomes less pronounced.

2.1.9 Normalized Product

An operation that is sometimes useful is to take the *normalized product* of two PDFs over the same variable.[6] If $p_1(\mathbf{x})$ and $p_2(\mathbf{x})$ are two PDFs for $\mathbf{x}$, the normalized product, $p(\mathbf{x})$, is formed as

$$p(\mathbf{x}) = \eta \, p_1(\mathbf{x}) \, p_2(\mathbf{x}), \tag{2.30}$$

where

$$\eta = \left(\int p_1(\mathbf{x}) \, p_2(\mathbf{x}) \, d\mathbf{x} \right)^{-1} \tag{2.31}$$

is a normalization constant to ensure $p(\mathbf{x})$ satisfies the axiom of total probability.

In a Bayesian context, the normalized product can be used to fuse independent estimates of a variable (represented as PDFs) under the assumption of a uniform prior:

$$p(\mathbf{x}|\mathbf{y}_1, \mathbf{y}_2) = \eta \, p(\mathbf{x}|\mathbf{y}_1) \, p(\mathbf{x}|\mathbf{y}_2), \tag{2.32}$$

where η is again a normalization constant to enforce the axiom of total probability. To see this, we begin by writing the left-hand side using Bayes' rule:

$$p(\mathbf{x}|\mathbf{y}_1, \mathbf{y}_2) = \frac{p(\mathbf{y}_1, \mathbf{y}_2|\mathbf{x})p(\mathbf{x})}{p(\mathbf{y}_1, \mathbf{y}_2)}. \tag{2.33}$$

Assuming statistical independence of $\mathbf{y}_1$ and $\mathbf{y}_2$ given $\mathbf{x}$ (e.g., measurements corrupted by statistically independent noise), we have

$$p(\mathbf{y}_1, \mathbf{y}_2|\mathbf{x}) = p(\mathbf{y}_1|\mathbf{x}) \, p(\mathbf{y}_2|\mathbf{x}) = \frac{p(\mathbf{x}|\mathbf{y}_1)p(\mathbf{y}_1)}{p(\mathbf{x})} \frac{p(\mathbf{x}|\mathbf{y}_2)p(\mathbf{y}_2)}{p(\mathbf{x})}, \tag{2.34}$$

where we have used Bayes' rule once again on the individual factors. Substituting this into (2.33), we have

$$p(\mathbf{x}|\mathbf{y}_1, \mathbf{y}_2) = \eta \, p(\mathbf{x}|\mathbf{y}_1) \, p(\mathbf{x}|\mathbf{y}_2), \tag{2.35}$$

where

$$\eta = \frac{p(\mathbf{y}_1)p(\mathbf{y}_2)}{p(\mathbf{y}_1, \mathbf{y}_2)p(\mathbf{x})}. \tag{2.36}$$

If we let the prior, $p(\mathbf{x})$, be uniform over all values of $\mathbf{x}$ (i.e., constant), then η is also a constant and (2.35) is an instance of the normalized product described previously.

---

[6] This is quite different than when we are working with a joint density over two variables.

2.1.10 Cramér–Rao Lower Bound and Fisher Information

Suppose we have a deterministic parameter, $\boldsymbol{\theta}$, that influences the outcome of a random variable, $\mathbf{x}$. This can be captured by writing the PDF for $\mathbf{x}$ as depending on $\boldsymbol{\theta}$:

$$p(\mathbf{x}|\boldsymbol{\theta}). \tag{2.37}$$

Furthermore, suppose we now draw a sample, $\mathbf{x}_{\mathrm{meas}}$, from $p(\mathbf{x}|\boldsymbol{\theta})$:

$$\mathbf{x}_{\mathrm{meas}} \leftarrow p(\mathbf{x}|\boldsymbol{\theta}). \tag{2.38}$$

The $\mathbf{x}_{\mathrm{meas}}$ is sometimes called a *realization* of the random variable $\mathbf{x}$; we can think of it as a 'measurement'.[7]

Harald Cramér (1893–1985) was a Swedish mathematician, actuary, and statistician, specializing in mathematical statistics and probabilistic number theory. Calyampudi Radhakrishna Rao, (1920–2023) was an Indian-American mathematician and statistician. Cramér and Rao were amongst the first to derive what is now known as the *Cramér–Rao lower bound (CRLB)*.

Then, the *Cramér–Rao lower bound (CRLB)* says that the covariance of any *unbiased estimate*,[8] $\hat{\boldsymbol{\theta}}$ (based on the measurement, $\mathbf{x}_{\mathrm{meas}}$), of the deterministic parameter, $\boldsymbol{\theta}$, is bounded by the *Fisher information matrix (FIM)*, $\boldsymbol{\mathcal{I}}_{\boldsymbol{\theta}}$ (see Appendix C.1 for a derivation):

$$\mathrm{cov}(\hat{\boldsymbol{\theta}}|\mathbf{x}_{\mathrm{meas}}) = E\left[(\hat{\boldsymbol{\theta}} - \boldsymbol{\theta})(\hat{\boldsymbol{\theta}} - \boldsymbol{\theta})^T\right] \geq \boldsymbol{\mathcal{I}}_{\boldsymbol{\theta}}^{-1}, \tag{2.39}$$

where 'unbiased' implies $E\left[\hat{\boldsymbol{\theta}} - \boldsymbol{\theta}\right] = \mathbf{0}$ and 'bounded' means

$$\mathrm{cov}(\hat{\boldsymbol{\theta}}|\mathbf{x}_{\mathrm{meas}}) - \boldsymbol{\mathcal{I}}_{\boldsymbol{\theta}}^{-1} \geq 0, \tag{2.40}$$

that is, positive-semidefinite. The Fisher information matrix is given by

$$\boldsymbol{\mathcal{I}}_{\boldsymbol{\theta}} = E\left[\frac{\partial^2(-\ln p(\mathbf{x}|\boldsymbol{\theta}))}{\partial \boldsymbol{\theta}^T \partial \boldsymbol{\theta}}\right]. \tag{2.41}$$

The CRLB therefore sets a fundamental limit on how certain we can be about an estimate of a parameter, given our measurements.

2.2 Gaussian Probability Density Functions

2.2.1 Definitions

Ronald Aylmer Fisher (1890–1962) was an English statistician, evolutionary biologist, and geneticist. His contributions to statistics include the analysis of variance, the method of maximum likelihood, fiducial inference, and the derivation of various sampling distributions.

In much of what is to follow, we will be working with Gaussian PDFs. In one dimension, a Gaussian PDF is given by

$$p(x|\mu, \sigma^2) = \frac{1}{\sqrt{2\pi\sigma^2}} \exp\left(-\frac{1}{2}\frac{(x - \mu)^2}{\sigma^2}\right), \tag{2.42}$$

where μ is the *mean* and σ^2 is the *variance* (σ is called the *standard deviation*). Figure 2.2 shows a one-dimensional Gaussian PDF.

The *cumulative distribution function* of a one-dimensional Gaussian is

$$P(x|\mu, \sigma^2) = \frac{1}{2}\left(1 + \mathrm{erf}\left(\frac{x - \mu}{\sqrt{2}\sigma}\right)\right), \tag{2.43}$$

---

[7] We use the subscript, 'meas', to indicate it is a measurement.

[8] We will use $(\hat{\cdot})$ to indicate an *estimated* quantity.

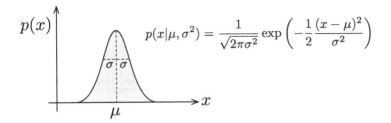

Figure 2.2
One-dimensional Gaussian PDF. A notable property of a Gaussian is that the mean and mode (most likely x) are both at μ.

where $\text{erf}(\cdot)$ is known as the *error function*,

$$\text{erf}(z) = \frac{2}{\sqrt{\pi}} \int_0^z e^{-t^2} dt, \qquad (2.44)$$

and has a sigmoid-like shape. Notably, the domain of $\text{erf}(\cdot)$ is $(-\infty, \infty)$, so that we may evaluate it at negative values, and the range is $(-1, 1)$.

A multivariate Gaussian PDF, $p(\mathbf{x}|\boldsymbol{\mu}, \boldsymbol{\Sigma})$, over the random variable, $\mathbf{x} \in \mathbb{R}^N$, may be expressed as

$$p(\mathbf{x}|\boldsymbol{\mu}, \boldsymbol{\Sigma}) = \frac{1}{\sqrt{(2\pi)^N \det \boldsymbol{\Sigma}}} \exp\left(-\frac{1}{2}(\mathbf{x} - \boldsymbol{\mu})^T \boldsymbol{\Sigma}^{-1}(\mathbf{x} - \boldsymbol{\mu})\right), \quad (2.45)$$

where $\boldsymbol{\mu} \in \mathbb{R}^N$ is the mean and $\boldsymbol{\Sigma} \in \mathbb{R}^{N \times N}$ is the (symmetric positive-definite) covariance matrix. Thus, for a Gaussian we have that

$$\boldsymbol{\mu} = E[\mathbf{x}] = \int_{-\infty}^{\infty} \mathbf{x} \frac{1}{\sqrt{(2\pi)^N \det \boldsymbol{\Sigma}}} \exp\left(-\frac{1}{2}(\mathbf{x} - \boldsymbol{\mu})^T \boldsymbol{\Sigma}^{-1}(\mathbf{x} - \boldsymbol{\mu})\right) d\mathbf{x}, \tag{2.46}$$

and

$$\begin{aligned}
\boldsymbol{\Sigma} &= E\left[(\mathbf{x} - \boldsymbol{\mu})(\mathbf{x} - \boldsymbol{\mu})^T\right] \\
&= \int_{-\infty}^{\infty} (\mathbf{x} - \boldsymbol{\mu})(\mathbf{x} - \boldsymbol{\mu})^T \frac{1}{\sqrt{(2\pi)^N \det \boldsymbol{\Sigma}}} \\
&\quad \times \exp\left(-\frac{1}{2}(\mathbf{x} - \boldsymbol{\mu})^T \boldsymbol{\Sigma}^{-1}(\mathbf{x} - \boldsymbol{\mu})\right) d\mathbf{x}.
\end{aligned} \tag{2.47}$$

In other words, the mean and covariance matrix are as we expected them to be.

We may also write that $\mathbf{x}$ is *normally* (aka Gaussian) distributed using the following notation:

$$\mathbf{x} \sim \mathcal{N}(\boldsymbol{\mu}, \boldsymbol{\Sigma}).$$

We say a random variable is *standard normally* distributed if

$$\mathbf{x} \sim \mathcal{N}(\mathbf{0}, \mathbf{1}),$$

where $\mathbf{1}$ is an $N \times N$ identity matrix.

2.2.2 Joint Gaussian PDFs, Their Factors, and Inference

We can also have a joint Gaussian over a pair of variables, $(\mathbf{x}, \mathbf{y})$, which we write as

$$p(\mathbf{x}, \mathbf{y}) = \mathcal{N}\left(\begin{bmatrix} \boldsymbol{\mu}_x \\ \boldsymbol{\mu}_y \end{bmatrix}, \begin{bmatrix} \boldsymbol{\Sigma}_{xx} & \boldsymbol{\Sigma}_{xy} \\ \boldsymbol{\Sigma}_{yx} & \boldsymbol{\Sigma}_{yy} \end{bmatrix}\right), \tag{2.48}$$

which has the same exponential form as (2.45). Note that $\boldsymbol{\Sigma}_{yx} = \boldsymbol{\Sigma}_{xy}^T$. It is always possible to break a joint density into the product of two factors, $p(\mathbf{x}, \mathbf{y}) = p(\mathbf{x}|\mathbf{y}) \, p(\mathbf{y})$, and we can work out the details for the joint Gaussian case by using the *Schur complement*.[9] We begin by noting that

Issai Schur
(1875–1941) was a
German
mathematician who
worked on group
representations (the
subject with which he
is most closely
associated), but also
in combinatorics and
number theory and
even in theoretical
physics.

$$\begin{bmatrix} \boldsymbol{\Sigma}_{xx} & \boldsymbol{\Sigma}_{xy} \\ \boldsymbol{\Sigma}_{yx} & \boldsymbol{\Sigma}_{yy} \end{bmatrix} = \begin{bmatrix} \mathbf{1} & \boldsymbol{\Sigma}_{xy}\boldsymbol{\Sigma}_{yy}^{-1} \\ \mathbf{0} & \mathbf{1} \end{bmatrix} \begin{bmatrix} \boldsymbol{\Sigma}_{xx} - \boldsymbol{\Sigma}_{xy}\boldsymbol{\Sigma}_{yy}^{-1}\boldsymbol{\Sigma}_{yx} & \mathbf{0} \\ \mathbf{0} & \boldsymbol{\Sigma}_{yy} \end{bmatrix} \begin{bmatrix} \mathbf{1} & \mathbf{0} \\ \boldsymbol{\Sigma}_{yy}^{-1}\boldsymbol{\Sigma}_{yx} & \mathbf{1} \end{bmatrix}, \tag{2.49}$$

where $\mathbf{1}$ is the identity matrix. We then invert both sides to find that

$$\begin{bmatrix} \boldsymbol{\Sigma}_{xx} & \boldsymbol{\Sigma}_{xy} \\ \boldsymbol{\Sigma}_{yx} & \boldsymbol{\Sigma}_{yy} \end{bmatrix}^{-1} = \begin{bmatrix} \mathbf{1} & \mathbf{0} \\ -\boldsymbol{\Sigma}_{yy}^{-1}\boldsymbol{\Sigma}_{yx} & \mathbf{1} \end{bmatrix}$$
$$\times \begin{bmatrix} (\boldsymbol{\Sigma}_{xx} - \boldsymbol{\Sigma}_{xy}\boldsymbol{\Sigma}_{yy}^{-1}\boldsymbol{\Sigma}_{yx})^{-1} & \mathbf{0} \\ \mathbf{0} & \boldsymbol{\Sigma}_{yy}^{-1} \end{bmatrix} \begin{bmatrix} \mathbf{1} & -\boldsymbol{\Sigma}_{xy}\boldsymbol{\Sigma}_{yy}^{-1} \\ \mathbf{0} & \mathbf{1} \end{bmatrix}. \tag{2.50}$$

Looking just to the quadratic part (inside the exponential) of the joint PDF, $p(\mathbf{x}, \mathbf{y})$, we have

$$\left(\begin{bmatrix} \mathbf{x} \\ \mathbf{y} \end{bmatrix} - \begin{bmatrix} \boldsymbol{\mu}_x \\ \boldsymbol{\mu}_y \end{bmatrix}\right)^T \begin{bmatrix} \boldsymbol{\Sigma}_{xx} & \boldsymbol{\Sigma}_{xy} \\ \boldsymbol{\Sigma}_{yx} & \boldsymbol{\Sigma}_{yy} \end{bmatrix}^{-1} \left(\begin{bmatrix} \mathbf{x} \\ \mathbf{y} \end{bmatrix} - \begin{bmatrix} \boldsymbol{\mu}_x \\ \boldsymbol{\mu}_y \end{bmatrix}\right)$$

$$= \left(\begin{bmatrix} \mathbf{x} \\ \mathbf{y} \end{bmatrix} - \begin{bmatrix} \boldsymbol{\mu}_x \\ \boldsymbol{\mu}_y \end{bmatrix}\right)^T \begin{bmatrix} \mathbf{1} & \mathbf{0} \\ -\boldsymbol{\Sigma}_{yy}^{-1}\boldsymbol{\Sigma}_{yx} & \mathbf{1} \end{bmatrix} \begin{bmatrix} (\boldsymbol{\Sigma}_{xx} - \boldsymbol{\Sigma}_{xy}\boldsymbol{\Sigma}_{yy}^{-1}\boldsymbol{\Sigma}_{yx})^{-1} & \mathbf{0} \\ \mathbf{0} & \boldsymbol{\Sigma}_{yy}^{-1} \end{bmatrix}$$
$$\times \begin{bmatrix} \mathbf{1} & -\boldsymbol{\Sigma}_{xy}\boldsymbol{\Sigma}_{yy}^{-1} \\ \mathbf{0} & \mathbf{1} \end{bmatrix} \left(\begin{bmatrix} \mathbf{x} \\ \mathbf{y} \end{bmatrix} - \begin{bmatrix} \boldsymbol{\mu}_x \\ \boldsymbol{\mu}_y \end{bmatrix}\right)$$

$$= (\mathbf{x} - \boldsymbol{\mu}_x - \boldsymbol{\Sigma}_{xy}\boldsymbol{\Sigma}_{yy}^{-1}(\mathbf{y} - \boldsymbol{\mu}_y))^T (\boldsymbol{\Sigma}_{xx} - \boldsymbol{\Sigma}_{xy}\boldsymbol{\Sigma}_{yy}^{-1}\boldsymbol{\Sigma}_{yx})^{-1}$$
$$\times (\mathbf{x} - \boldsymbol{\mu}_x - \boldsymbol{\Sigma}_{xy}\boldsymbol{\Sigma}_{yy}^{-1}(\mathbf{y} - \boldsymbol{\mu}_y)) + (\mathbf{y} - \boldsymbol{\mu}_y)^T \boldsymbol{\Sigma}_{yy}^{-1} (\mathbf{y} - \boldsymbol{\mu}_y), \tag{2.51}$$

which is the sum of two quadratic terms. Since the exponential of a sum is the product of two exponentials, we have that

$$p(\mathbf{x}, \mathbf{y}) = p(\mathbf{x}|\mathbf{y}) \, p(\mathbf{y}), \tag{2.52a}$$
$$p(\mathbf{x}|\mathbf{y}) = \mathcal{N}\left(\boldsymbol{\mu}_x + \boldsymbol{\Sigma}_{xy}\boldsymbol{\Sigma}_{yy}^{-1}(\mathbf{y} - \boldsymbol{\mu}_y), \boldsymbol{\Sigma}_{xx} - \boldsymbol{\Sigma}_{xy}\boldsymbol{\Sigma}_{yy}^{-1}\boldsymbol{\Sigma}_{yx}\right), \tag{2.52b}$$
$$p(\mathbf{y}) = \mathcal{N}\left(\boldsymbol{\mu}_y, \boldsymbol{\Sigma}_{yy}\right). \tag{2.52c}$$

It is important to note that both factors, $p(\mathbf{x}|\mathbf{y})$ and $p(\mathbf{y})$, are Gaussian PDFs. Also, if we happen to know the value of $\mathbf{y}$ (i.e., it is measured), we can work out the likelihood of $\mathbf{x}$ given this value of $\mathbf{y}$ by computing $p(\mathbf{x}|\mathbf{y})$ using (2.52b).

---

[9] In this case, we have that the Schur complement of $\boldsymbol{\Sigma}_{yy}$ is the expression $\boldsymbol{\Sigma}_{xx} - \boldsymbol{\Sigma}_{xy}\boldsymbol{\Sigma}_{yy}^{-1}\boldsymbol{\Sigma}_{yx}$. See also Appendix A.1.8.

This is, in fact, the cornerstone of *Gaussian inference*: we start with a prior about our state, $\mathbf{x} \sim \mathcal{N}(\boldsymbol{\mu}_x, \boldsymbol{\Sigma}_{xx})$, then narrow this down based on some measurements, $\mathbf{y}_{\text{meas}}$. In (2.52b), we see that an adjustment is made to the mean, $\boldsymbol{\mu}_x$, and the covariance, $\boldsymbol{\Sigma}_{xx}$ (it is made smaller).

2.2.3 Statistically Independent, Uncorrelated

In the case of Gaussian PDFs, statistically independent variables are also uncorrelated (true in general) and uncorrelated variables are also statistically independent (not true for all types of PDFs). We can see this fairly easily by looking at (2.52). If we assume statistical independence, $p(\mathbf{x}, \mathbf{y}) = p(\mathbf{x})p(\mathbf{y})$ and so $p(\mathbf{x}|\mathbf{y}) = p(\mathbf{x}) = \mathcal{N}(\boldsymbol{\mu}_x, \boldsymbol{\Sigma}_{xx})$. Looking at (2.52b), this implies

$$\boldsymbol{\Sigma}_{xy}\boldsymbol{\Sigma}_{yy}^{-1}(\mathbf{y} - \boldsymbol{\mu}_y) = \mathbf{0}, \tag{2.53a}$$

$$\boldsymbol{\Sigma}_{xy}\boldsymbol{\Sigma}_{yy}^{-1}\boldsymbol{\Sigma}_{yx} = \mathbf{0}, \tag{2.53b}$$

which further implies that $\boldsymbol{\Sigma}_{xy} = \mathbf{0}$. Since

$$\boldsymbol{\Sigma}_{xy} = E\left[(\mathbf{x} - \boldsymbol{\mu}_x)(\mathbf{y} - \boldsymbol{\mu}_y)^T\right] = E\left[\mathbf{x}\mathbf{y}^T\right] - E\left[\mathbf{x}\right]E\left[\mathbf{y}\right]^T, \tag{2.54}$$

we have the uncorrelated condition:

$$E\left[\mathbf{x}\mathbf{y}^T\right] = E\left[\mathbf{x}\right]E\left[\mathbf{y}\right]^T. \tag{2.55}$$

We can also work through the logic in the other direction by first assuming the variables are uncorrelated, which leads to $\boldsymbol{\Sigma}_{xy} = \mathbf{0}$, and finally to statistical independence. Since these conditions are equivalent, we will often use *statistically independent* and *uncorrelated* interchangeably in the context of Gaussian PDFs.

2.2.4 Information Form of a Gaussian

When working with Gaussians, sometimes it is preferable to express them in *information form*, sometimes called *inverse-covariance form*. If we start with

$$\mathbf{x} \sim \mathcal{N}(\boldsymbol{\mu}, \boldsymbol{\Sigma}) \tag{2.56}$$

and then perform a (linear) change of variables, $\mathbf{y} = \boldsymbol{\Sigma}^{-1}\mathbf{x}$, we have that

$$\mathbf{y} \sim \mathcal{N}(\boldsymbol{\Sigma}^{-1}\boldsymbol{\mu}, \boldsymbol{\Sigma}^{-1}), \tag{2.57}$$

the details of which are a special case of Section 2.2.6. We refer to $\boldsymbol{\Sigma}^{-1}\boldsymbol{\mu}$ as the *information vector* and $\boldsymbol{\Sigma}^{-1}$ as the *information matrix* (aka inverse-covariance matrix or precision matrix).

The advantage of information form is in cases where some component of $\boldsymbol{\Sigma}$ becomes very large (infinite), whereupon that same component of $\boldsymbol{\Sigma}^{-1}$ becomes very small (zero). This can be used to indicate that we know nothing about a particular variable, for example.

2.2.5 Marginals of a Joint Gaussian

The *marginals* of a joint Gaussian,

$$p\left(\mathbf{x}, \mathbf{y}\right) = \mathcal{N}\left(\underbrace{\begin{bmatrix} \boldsymbol{\mu}_x \\ \boldsymbol{\mu}_y \end{bmatrix}}_{\boldsymbol{\mu}}, \underbrace{\begin{bmatrix} \boldsymbol{\Sigma}_{xx} & \boldsymbol{\Sigma}_{xy} \\ \boldsymbol{\Sigma}_{yx} & \boldsymbol{\Sigma}_{yy} \end{bmatrix}}_{\boldsymbol{\Sigma}}\right), \tag{2.58}$$

are simply

$$p(\mathbf{x}) = \int_{-\infty}^{\infty} p(\mathbf{x}, \mathbf{y})\, d\mathbf{y} = \mathcal{N}\left(\boldsymbol{\mu}_x, \boldsymbol{\Sigma}_{xx}\right), \tag{2.59a}$$

$$p(\mathbf{y}) = \int_{-\infty}^{\infty} p(\mathbf{x}, \mathbf{y})\, d\mathbf{x} = \mathcal{N}\left(\boldsymbol{\mu}_y, \boldsymbol{\Sigma}_{yy}\right). \tag{2.59b}$$

In other words, we extract the blocks of the mean and covariance pertaining to the desired marginal.

Sometimes we have our joint Gaussian stored in information form (see previous section) and would like to carry out marginalization. Suppose that the information matrix and information vector are, respectively,

$$\boldsymbol{\Sigma}^{-1} = \begin{bmatrix} \mathbf{A}_{xx} & \mathbf{A}_{xy} \\ \mathbf{A}_{yx} & \mathbf{A}_{yy} \end{bmatrix}, \quad \boldsymbol{\Sigma}^{-1}\boldsymbol{\mu} = \begin{bmatrix} \mathbf{b}_x \\ \mathbf{b}_y \end{bmatrix}. \tag{2.60}$$

The *information-form marginal* for $\mathbf{x}$ is then

$$\boldsymbol{\Sigma}_{xx}^{-1} = \mathbf{A}_{xx} - \mathbf{A}_{xy}\mathbf{A}_{yy}^{-1}\mathbf{A}_{yx}, \quad \boldsymbol{\Sigma}_{xx}^{-1}\boldsymbol{\mu}_x = \mathbf{b}_x - \mathbf{A}_{xy}\mathbf{A}_{yy}^{-1}\mathbf{b}_y, \tag{2.61}$$

and the information-form marginal for $\mathbf{y}$ is

$$\boldsymbol{\Sigma}_{yy}^{-1} = \mathbf{A}_{yy} - \mathbf{A}_{yx}\mathbf{A}_{xx}^{-1}\mathbf{A}_{xy}, \quad \boldsymbol{\Sigma}_{yy}^{-1}\boldsymbol{\mu}_y = \mathbf{b}_y - \mathbf{A}_{yx}\mathbf{A}_{xx}^{-1}\mathbf{b}_x. \tag{2.62}$$

We see again the Schur complement making an appearance (see Appendix A.1.8).

2.2.6 Linear Change of Variables

Suppose that we have a Gaussian random variable,

$$\mathbf{x} \in \mathbb{R}^N \sim \mathcal{N}(\boldsymbol{\mu}_x, \boldsymbol{\Sigma}_{xx}),$$

and that we have a second random variable, $\mathbf{y} \in \mathbb{R}^M$, related to $\mathbf{x}$ through the linear map,

$$\mathbf{y} = \mathbf{G}\mathbf{x}, \tag{2.63}$$

where we assume that $\mathbf{G} \in \mathbb{R}^{M \times N}$ is a constant matrix. We would like to know what the statistical properties of $\mathbf{y}$ are. One way to do this is to simply apply the expectation operator directly:

$$\boldsymbol{\mu}_y = E[\mathbf{y}] = E[\mathbf{G}\mathbf{x}] = \mathbf{G}\,E[\mathbf{x}] = \mathbf{G}\boldsymbol{\mu}_x, \tag{2.64a}$$

$$\begin{aligned} \boldsymbol{\Sigma}_{yy} &= E[(\mathbf{y} - \boldsymbol{\mu}_y)(\mathbf{y} - \boldsymbol{\mu}_y)^T] \\ &= \mathbf{G}\,E[(\mathbf{x} - \boldsymbol{\mu}_x)(\mathbf{x} - \boldsymbol{\mu}_x)^T]\,\mathbf{G}^T = \mathbf{G}\boldsymbol{\Sigma}_{xx}\mathbf{G}^T, \end{aligned} \tag{2.64b}$$

so that we have $\mathbf{y} \sim \mathcal{N}(\boldsymbol{\mu}_y, \boldsymbol{\Sigma}_{yy}) = \mathcal{N}(\mathbf{G}\boldsymbol{\mu}_x, \mathbf{G}\boldsymbol{\Sigma}_{xx}\mathbf{G}^T)$.

Another way to look at this is a change of variables. We assume that the linear map is *injective*, meaning two $\mathbf{x}$ values cannot map to a single $\mathbf{y}$ value; in fact, let us simplify the injective condition by assuming a stricter condition, that $\mathbf{G}$ is invertible (and hence $M = N$). The axiom of total probability lets us write

$$\int_{-\infty}^{\infty} p(\mathbf{x})\, d\mathbf{x} = 1. \tag{2.65}$$

A small volume of $\mathbf{x}$ is related to a small volume of $\mathbf{y}$ by

$$d\mathbf{y} = |\det \mathbf{G}|\, d\mathbf{x}. \tag{2.66}$$

We can then make a substitution of variables to have

$$
\begin{aligned}
1 &= \int_{-\infty}^{\infty} p(\mathbf{x})\, d\mathbf{x} \\
&= \int_{-\infty}^{\infty} \frac{1}{\sqrt{(2\pi)^N \det \boldsymbol{\Sigma}_{xx}}} \exp\left(-\frac{1}{2}(\mathbf{x} - \boldsymbol{\mu}_x)^T \boldsymbol{\Sigma}_{xx}^{-1}(\mathbf{x} - \boldsymbol{\mu}_x)\right) d\mathbf{x} \\
&= \int_{-\infty}^{\infty} \frac{1}{\sqrt{(2\pi)^N \det \boldsymbol{\Sigma}_{xx}}} \\
&\qquad \times \exp\left(-\frac{1}{2}(\mathbf{G}^{-1}\mathbf{y} - \boldsymbol{\mu}_x)^T \boldsymbol{\Sigma}_{xx}^{-1}(\mathbf{G}^{-1}\mathbf{y} - \boldsymbol{\mu}_x)\right) |\det \mathbf{G}|^{-1}\, d\mathbf{y} \\
&= \int_{-\infty}^{\infty} \frac{1}{\sqrt{(2\pi)^N \det \mathbf{G} \det \boldsymbol{\Sigma}_{xx} \det \mathbf{G}^T}} \\
&\qquad \times \exp\left(-\frac{1}{2}(\mathbf{y} - \mathbf{G}\boldsymbol{\mu}_x)^T \mathbf{G}^{-T}\boldsymbol{\Sigma}_{xx}^{-1}\mathbf{G}^{-1}(\mathbf{y} - \mathbf{G}\boldsymbol{\mu}_x)\right) d\mathbf{y} \\
&= \int_{-\infty}^{\infty} \frac{1}{\sqrt{(2\pi)^N \det(\mathbf{G}\boldsymbol{\Sigma}_{xx}\mathbf{G}^T)}} \\
&\qquad \times \exp\left(-\frac{1}{2}(\mathbf{y} - \mathbf{G}\boldsymbol{\mu}_x)^T (\mathbf{G}\boldsymbol{\Sigma}_{xx}\mathbf{G}^T)^{-1}(\mathbf{y} - \mathbf{G}\boldsymbol{\mu}_x)\right) d\mathbf{y},
\end{aligned}
\tag{2.67}
$$

whereupon we have $\boldsymbol{\mu}_y = \mathbf{G}\boldsymbol{\mu}_x$ and $\boldsymbol{\Sigma}_{yy} = \mathbf{G}\boldsymbol{\Sigma}_{xx}\mathbf{G}^T$, as before. If $M < N$, our linear mapping is no longer injective and the change of variable approach cannot be used to map statistics from $\mathbf{x}$ to $\mathbf{y}$.

We can also think about going in the other direction from $\mathbf{y}$ to $\mathbf{x}$, assuming $M < N$ and rank $\mathbf{G} = M$. This is a bit tricky, as the resulting covariance for $\mathbf{x}$ will blow up since we are dilating[10] to a larger space. To get around this, we switch to *information form* from the previous section. Letting

$$\mathbf{u} = \boldsymbol{\Sigma}_{yy}^{-1}\mathbf{y}, \tag{2.68}$$

we have that

$$\mathbf{u} \sim \mathcal{N}(\boldsymbol{\Sigma}_{yy}^{-1}\boldsymbol{\mu}_y, \boldsymbol{\Sigma}_{yy}^{-1}). \tag{2.69}$$

Likewise, letting

$$\mathbf{v} = \boldsymbol{\Sigma}_{xx}^{-1}\mathbf{x}, \tag{2.70}$$

---

[10] *Dilation* is the opposite of *projection*.

we have that

$$\mathbf{v} \sim \mathcal{N}(\Sigma_{xx}^{-1}\boldsymbol{\mu}_x, \Sigma_{xx}^{-1}). \tag{2.71}$$

Since the mapping from $\mathbf{y}$ to $\mathbf{x}$ is not unique, we need to specify what we want to do. One choice is to let

$$\mathbf{v} = \mathbf{G}^T\mathbf{u} \qquad \Leftrightarrow \qquad \Sigma_{xx}^{-1}\mathbf{x} = \mathbf{G}^T\Sigma_{yy}^{-1}\mathbf{y}. \tag{2.72}$$

We then take expectations:

$$\Sigma_{xx}^{-1}\boldsymbol{\mu}_x = E[\mathbf{v}] = E[\mathbf{G}^T\mathbf{u}] = \mathbf{G}^T E[\mathbf{u}] = \mathbf{G}^T\Sigma_{yy}^{-1}\boldsymbol{\mu}_y, \tag{2.73a}$$

$$\begin{aligned}
\Sigma_{xx}^{-1} &= E[(\mathbf{v} - \Sigma_{xx}^{-1}\boldsymbol{\mu}_x)(\mathbf{v} - \Sigma_{xx}^{-1}\boldsymbol{\mu}_x)^T] \\
&= \mathbf{G}^T E[(\mathbf{u} - \Sigma_{yy}^{-1}\boldsymbol{\mu}_y)(\mathbf{u} - \Sigma_{yy}^{-1}\boldsymbol{\mu}_y)^T]\mathbf{G} = \mathbf{G}^T\Sigma_{yy}^{-1}\mathbf{G}.
\end{aligned} \tag{2.73b}$$

Note that if Σ_{xx}^{-1} is not full rank, we cannot actually recover Σ_{xx} and $\boldsymbol{\mu}_x$ and must keep them in information form. However, multiple such estimates can be fused together, which is the subject of Section 2.2.8.

2.2.7 Passing a Gaussian through a Nonlinearity

We now examine the process of passing a Gaussian PDF through a stochastic nonlinearity, namely, computing

$$p(\mathbf{y}) = \int_{-\infty}^{\infty} p(\mathbf{y}|\mathbf{x})p(\mathbf{x})d\mathbf{x}, \tag{2.74}$$

where we have that

$$p(\mathbf{y}|\mathbf{x}) = \mathcal{N}\left(\mathbf{g}(\mathbf{x}), \mathbf{R}\right), \tag{2.75a}$$

$$p(\mathbf{x}) = \mathcal{N}\left(\boldsymbol{\mu}_x, \Sigma_{xx}\right), \tag{2.75b}$$

and $\mathbf{g}(\cdot)$ is a nonlinear map, $\mathbf{g}: \mathbf{x} \mapsto \mathbf{y}$, that is then corrupted by zero-mean Gaussian noise with covariance, $\mathbf{R}$. We will require this type of stochastic nonlinearity when modelling sensors later on. Passing a Gaussian through this type of function is required, for example, in the denominator when carrying out full Bayesian inference.

Scalar Deterministic Case via Change of Variables

Let us first look at a simplified version where x is scalar and the nonlinear function, $g(\cdot)$, is deterministic (i.e., $R = 0$). We begin with a Gaussian random variable, $x \in \mathbb{R}^1$:

$$x \sim \mathcal{N}(0, \sigma^2). \tag{2.76}$$

For the PDF on x we have

$$p(x) = \frac{1}{\sqrt{2\pi\sigma^2}} \exp\left(-\frac{1}{2}\frac{x^2}{\sigma^2}\right). \tag{2.77}$$

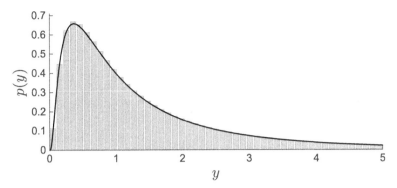

Now consider the nonlinear mapping,

$$y = \exp(x), \tag{2.78}$$

which is invertible:

$$x = \ln(y). \tag{2.79}$$

The infinitesimal integration volumes for x and y are then related by

$$dy = \exp(x)\,dx, \tag{2.80}$$

or

$$dx = \frac{1}{y}\,dy. \tag{2.81}$$

According to the axiom of total probability, we have

$$
\begin{aligned}
1 &= \int_{-\infty}^{\infty} p(x)\,dx \\
&= \int_{-\infty}^{\infty} \frac{1}{\sqrt{2\pi\sigma^2}} \exp\left(-\frac{1}{2}\frac{x^2}{\sigma^2}\right)dx \\
&= \int_{0}^{\infty} \underbrace{\frac{1}{\sqrt{2\pi\sigma^2}} \exp\left(-\frac{1}{2}\frac{(\ln(y))^2}{\sigma^2}\right)\frac{1}{y}}_{p(y)}\,dy \\
&= \int_{0}^{\infty} p(y)\,dy, \tag{2.82}
\end{aligned}
$$

giving us the exact expression for $p(y)$, which is plotted in Figure 2.3 for $\sigma^2 = 1$ as the black curve; the area under this curve, from $y = 0$ to ∞ is 1. The gray histogram is a numerical approximation of the PDF generated by sampling x a large number of times and passing these through the nonlinearity individually, then binning. These approaches agree very well, validating our method of changing variables.

Note that $p(y)$ is no longer Gaussian owing to the nonlinear change of variables. We can verify numerically that the area under this function is indeed 1 (i.e., it is a valid PDF). It is worth noting that had we not been careful about handling the change of variables and including the $\frac{1}{y}$ factor, we would not have a valid PDF.

Figure 2.4 Passing a one-dimensional Gaussian through a deterministic nonlinear function, $g(\cdot)$. Here we linearize the nonlinearity in order to propagate the variance approximately.

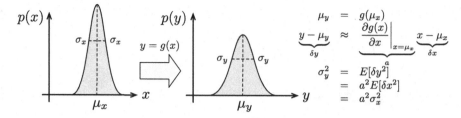

General Case via Linearization

Unfortunately, (2.74) cannot be computed in closed form for every $\mathbf{g}(\cdot)$ and becomes more difficult in the multivariate case than the scalar one. Moreover, when the nonlinearity is stochastic (i.e., $\mathbf{R} > 0$), our mapping will never be invertible due to the extra input coming from the noise, so we need a different way to transform our Gaussian. There are several different ways to do this, and in this section, we look at the most common one, *linearization*.

We linearize the nonlinear map such that

$$\mathbf{g}(\mathbf{x}) \approx \boldsymbol{\mu}_y + \mathbf{G}(\mathbf{x} - \boldsymbol{\mu}_x),$$

$$\mathbf{G} = \left.\frac{\partial \mathbf{g}(\mathbf{x})}{\partial \mathbf{x}}\right|_{\mathbf{x}=\boldsymbol{\mu}_x}, \tag{2.83}$$

$$\boldsymbol{\mu}_y = \mathbf{g}(\boldsymbol{\mu}_x),$$

where $\mathbf{G}$ is the Jacobian of $\mathbf{g}(\cdot)$, with respect to $\mathbf{x}$. This allows us to then pass the Gaussian through the linearized function in closed form; it is an approximation that works well for mildly nonlinear maps.

Figure 2.4 depicts the process of passing a one-dimensional Gaussian PDF through a deterministic nonlinear function, $g(\cdot)$, that has been linearized. In general, we will be making an inference though a stochastic function, one that introduces additional noise.

Returning to (2.74), we have that

$$p(\mathbf{y}) = \int_{-\infty}^{\infty} p(\mathbf{y}|\mathbf{x})p(\mathbf{x})d\mathbf{x}$$

$$= \eta \int_{-\infty}^{\infty} \exp\left(-\frac{1}{2}\left(\mathbf{y} - (\boldsymbol{\mu}_y + \mathbf{G}(\mathbf{x} - \boldsymbol{\mu}_x))\right)^T\right.$$

$$\times \mathbf{R}^{-1}\left(\mathbf{y} - (\boldsymbol{\mu}_y + \mathbf{G}(\mathbf{x} - \boldsymbol{\mu}_x))\right)\Big)$$

$$\times \exp\left(-\frac{1}{2}(\mathbf{x} - \boldsymbol{\mu}_x)^T \boldsymbol{\Sigma}_{xx}^{-1}(\mathbf{x} - \boldsymbol{\mu}_x)\right)d\mathbf{x}$$

$$= \eta \exp\left(-\frac{1}{2}(\mathbf{y} - \boldsymbol{\mu}_y)^T \mathbf{R}^{-1}(\mathbf{y} - \boldsymbol{\mu}_y)\right)$$

$$\times \int_{-\infty}^{\infty} \exp\left(-\frac{1}{2}(\mathbf{x} - \boldsymbol{\mu}_x)^T\left(\boldsymbol{\Sigma}_{xx}^{-1} + \mathbf{G}^T\mathbf{R}^{-1}\mathbf{G}\right)(\mathbf{x} - \boldsymbol{\mu}_x)\right)$$

$$\times \exp\left((\mathbf{y} - \boldsymbol{\mu}_y)^T\mathbf{R}^{-1}\mathbf{G}(\mathbf{x} - \boldsymbol{\mu}_x)\right)d\mathbf{x}, \tag{2.84}$$

where η is a normalization constant. Defining $\mathbf{F}$ such that

$$\mathbf{F}^T \left(\mathbf{G}^T \mathbf{R}^{-1} \mathbf{G} + \boldsymbol{\Sigma}_{xx}^{-1}\right) = \mathbf{R}^{-1}\mathbf{G}, \qquad (2.85)$$

we may complete the square for the part inside the integral such that

$$
\begin{aligned}
&\exp\left(-\frac{1}{2}(\mathbf{x} - \boldsymbol{\mu}_x)^T \left(\boldsymbol{\Sigma}_{xx}^{-1} + \mathbf{G}^T\mathbf{R}^{-1}\mathbf{G}\right)(\mathbf{x} - \boldsymbol{\mu}_x)\right) \\
&\qquad\qquad \times\ \exp\left((\mathbf{y} - \boldsymbol{\mu}_y)^T \mathbf{R}^{-1}\mathbf{G}(\mathbf{x} - \boldsymbol{\mu}_x)\right) \\
&= \quad \exp\left(-\frac{1}{2}\left((\mathbf{x} - \boldsymbol{\mu}_x) - \mathbf{F}(\mathbf{y} - \boldsymbol{\mu}_y)\right)^T\right. \\
&\qquad\qquad \times\ \left.\left(\mathbf{G}^T\mathbf{R}^{-1}\mathbf{G} + \boldsymbol{\Sigma}_{xx}^{-1}\right)\left((\mathbf{x} - \boldsymbol{\mu}_x) - \mathbf{F}(\mathbf{y} - \boldsymbol{\mu}_y)\right)\right) \\
&\qquad\qquad \times\ \exp\left(\frac{1}{2}(\mathbf{y} - \boldsymbol{\mu}_y)^T \mathbf{F}^T \left(\mathbf{G}^T\mathbf{R}^{-1}\mathbf{G} + \boldsymbol{\Sigma}_{xx}^{-1}\right) \mathbf{F}(\mathbf{y} - \boldsymbol{\mu}_y)\right).
\end{aligned}
$$

$$(2.86)$$

The second factor is independent of $\mathbf{x}$ and may be brought outside of the integral. The remaining integral (the first factor) is exactly Gaussian in $\mathbf{x}$ and thus will integrate (over $\mathbf{x}$) to a constant and thus can be absorbed in the constant η. Thus, for $p(\mathbf{y})$, we have

$$
\begin{aligned}
p(\mathbf{y}) &= \rho \exp\left(-\frac{1}{2}(\mathbf{y} - \boldsymbol{\mu}_y)^T\right. \\
&\qquad \times\ \left.\left(\mathbf{R}^{-1} - \mathbf{F}^T\left(\mathbf{G}^T\mathbf{R}^{-1}\mathbf{G} + \boldsymbol{\Sigma}_{xx}^{-1}\right)\mathbf{F}\right)(\mathbf{y} - \boldsymbol{\mu}_y)\right) \\
&= \rho \exp\left(-\frac{1}{2}(\mathbf{y} - \boldsymbol{\mu}_y)^T\right. \\
&\qquad \times\ \left.\underbrace{\left(\mathbf{R}^{-1} - \mathbf{R}^{-1}\mathbf{G}\left(\mathbf{G}^T\mathbf{R}^{-1}\mathbf{G} + \boldsymbol{\Sigma}_{xx}^{-1}\right)^{-1}\mathbf{G}^T\mathbf{R}^{-1}\right)}_{(\mathbf{R}+\mathbf{G}\boldsymbol{\Sigma}_{xx}\mathbf{G}^T)^{-1} \text{ by (2.124)}}(\mathbf{y} - \boldsymbol{\mu}_y)\right) \\
&= \rho \exp\left(-\frac{1}{2}(\mathbf{y} - \boldsymbol{\mu}_y)^T \left(\mathbf{R} + \mathbf{G}\boldsymbol{\Sigma}_{xx}\mathbf{G}^T\right)^{-1}(\mathbf{y} - \boldsymbol{\mu}_y)\right), \qquad (2.87)
\end{aligned}
$$

where ρ is the new normalization constant. This is a Gaussian for $\mathbf{y}$:

$$\mathbf{y} \sim \mathcal{N}\left(\boldsymbol{\mu}_y, \boldsymbol{\Sigma}_{yy}\right) = \mathcal{N}\left(\mathbf{g}(\boldsymbol{\mu}_x), \mathbf{R} + \mathbf{G}\boldsymbol{\Sigma}_{xx}\mathbf{G}^T\right). \qquad (2.88)$$

As we will see later, the two equations (2.91) and (2.87) constitute the observation and predictive steps of the classic discrete-time (extended) Kalman filter (Kalman, 1960b). These two steps may be thought of as the creation and destruction of information in the filter, respectively.

Figure 2.5 The normalized product of two one-dimensional Gaussian PDFs is another one-dimensional Gaussian PDF.

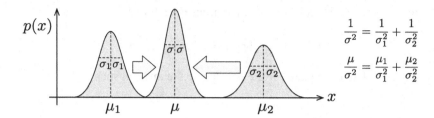

2.2.8 Normalized Product of Gaussians

We now discuss a useful property of Gaussian PDFs; the normalized product (see Section 2.1.9) of K Gaussian PDFs is also a Gaussian PDF:

$$
\exp\left(-\frac{1}{2}(\mathbf{x}-\boldsymbol{\mu})^T\boldsymbol{\Sigma}^{-1}(\mathbf{x}-\boldsymbol{\mu})\right)
$$
$$
\equiv \eta \prod_{k=1}^{K}\exp\left(-\frac{1}{2}(\mathbf{x}-\boldsymbol{\mu}_k)^T\boldsymbol{\Sigma}_k^{-1}(\mathbf{x}-\boldsymbol{\mu}_k)\right), \quad (2.89)
$$

where

$$
\boldsymbol{\Sigma}^{-1} = \sum_{k=1}^{K}\boldsymbol{\Sigma}_k^{-1}, \qquad\qquad (2.90a)
$$

$$
\boldsymbol{\Sigma}^{-1}\boldsymbol{\mu} = \sum_{k=1}^{K}\boldsymbol{\Sigma}_k^{-1}\boldsymbol{\mu}_k, \qquad\qquad (2.90b)
$$

and η is a normalization constant to enforce the axiom of total probability. The normalized product of Gaussians comes up when fusing multiple estimates together. A one-dimensional example is provided in Figure 2.5.

We also have that

$$
\exp\left(-\frac{1}{2}(\mathbf{x}-\boldsymbol{\mu})^T\boldsymbol{\Sigma}^{-1}(\mathbf{x}-\boldsymbol{\mu})\right)
$$
$$
\equiv \eta \prod_{k=1}^{K}\exp\left(-\frac{1}{2}(\mathbf{G}_k\mathbf{x}-\boldsymbol{\mu}_k)^T\boldsymbol{\Sigma}_k^{-1}(\mathbf{G}_k\mathbf{x}-\boldsymbol{\mu}_k)\right), \quad (2.91)
$$

where

$$
\boldsymbol{\Sigma}^{-1} = \sum_{k=1}^{K}\mathbf{G}_k^T\boldsymbol{\Sigma}_k^{-1}\mathbf{G}_k, \qquad\qquad (2.92a)
$$

$$
\boldsymbol{\Sigma}^{-1}\boldsymbol{\mu} = \sum_{k=1}^{K}\mathbf{G}_k^T\boldsymbol{\Sigma}_k^{-1}\boldsymbol{\mu}_k, \qquad\qquad (2.92b)
$$

in the case that the matrices, $\mathbf{G}_k \in \mathbb{R}^{M_k \times N}$, are present, with $M_k \leq N$. Again, η is a normalization constant. We also note that this generalizes a result from the previous section.

2.2.9 Chi-Squared Distribution and Mahalanobis Distance

Suppose we start with a N-dimensional standard normal random variable, $\mathbf{x} \sim \mathcal{N}(\mathbf{0}, \mathbf{1})$. A related distribution is *chi-squared*, $\chi^2(N)$, which is formed by taking the sum of the squares of N standard normal random variables, or

$$y = \mathbf{x}^T \mathbf{x} \sim \chi^2(N). \tag{2.93}$$

The mean and variance of y are then N and $2N$, respectively.

More generally, if we begin with $\mathbf{x} \sim \mathcal{N}(\boldsymbol{\mu}, \boldsymbol{\Sigma})$, we can define

$$y = (\mathbf{x} - \boldsymbol{\mu})^T \boldsymbol{\Sigma}^{-1} (\mathbf{x} - \boldsymbol{\mu}), \tag{2.94}$$

which still has a mean of N and a variance of $2N$. This is known as a squared *Mahalanobis distance*, which is like a squared Euclidean distance but weighted in the middle by the inverse covariance matrix. It is also related to the negative log-likelihood of $\mathbf{x}$ according to the density $\mathcal{N}(\boldsymbol{\mu}, \boldsymbol{\Sigma})$; see the next section for further discussion of this.

Prasanta Chandra Mahalanobis (1893–1972) was an Indian scientist and applied statistician known for this measure of statistical distance (Mahalanobis, 1936).

Squared Mahalanobis distance is a quadratic function, which allows us to rewrite it using the (linear) *trace* operator from linear algebra:

$$(\mathbf{x} - \boldsymbol{\mu})^T \boldsymbol{\Sigma}^{-1} (\mathbf{x} - \boldsymbol{\mu}) = \mathrm{tr} \left(\boldsymbol{\Sigma}^{-1} (\mathbf{x} - \boldsymbol{\mu})(\mathbf{x} - \boldsymbol{\mu})^T \right). \tag{2.95}$$

We can use this observation to help calculate the mean of the squared Mahalanobis distance. Since the expectation is also a linear operator, we may interchange the order of the expectation and trace arriving at

$$
\begin{aligned}
E[y] &= E \left[(\mathbf{x} - \boldsymbol{\mu})^T \boldsymbol{\Sigma}^{-1} (\mathbf{x} - \boldsymbol{\mu}) \right] \\
&= \mathrm{tr} \left(E \left[\boldsymbol{\Sigma}^{-1} (\mathbf{x} - \boldsymbol{\mu})(\mathbf{x} - \boldsymbol{\mu})^T \right] \right) \\
&= \mathrm{tr} \left(\boldsymbol{\Sigma}^{-1} \underbrace{E \left[(\mathbf{x} - \boldsymbol{\mu})(\mathbf{x} - \boldsymbol{\mu})^T \right]}_{\boldsymbol{\Sigma}} \right) \\
&= \mathrm{tr} \left(\boldsymbol{\Sigma}^{-1} \boldsymbol{\Sigma} \right) \\
&= \mathrm{tr} \, \mathbf{1} \\
&= N,
\end{aligned} \tag{2.96}
$$

$$\tag{2.97}$$

which is just the dimension of the variable. The mean-squared Mahalanobis distance is used frequently as a test for whether data conform to a particular Gaussian PDF; see also Section 5.1.2. We leave computing the variance of the squared Mahalanobis distance as an exercise for the reader.

2.2.10 Shannon Information of a Gaussian

In the case of a Gaussian PDF, we have for the Shannon information:

$$
\begin{aligned}
H(\mathbf{x}) &= - \int_{-\infty}^{\infty} p(\mathbf{x}) \ln p(\mathbf{x}) \, d\mathbf{x} \\
&= - \int_{-\infty}^{\infty} p(\mathbf{x}) \left(-\frac{1}{2}(\mathbf{x} - \boldsymbol{\mu})^T \boldsymbol{\Sigma}^{-1}(\mathbf{x} - \boldsymbol{\mu}) - \ln \sqrt{(2\pi)^N \det \boldsymbol{\Sigma}} \right) d\mathbf{x} \\
&= \frac{1}{2} \ln \left((2\pi)^N \det \boldsymbol{\Sigma} \right) + \int_{-\infty}^{\infty} \frac{1}{2}(\mathbf{x} - \boldsymbol{\mu})^T \boldsymbol{\Sigma}^{-1}(\mathbf{x} - \boldsymbol{\mu}) \, p(\mathbf{x}) \, d\mathbf{x} \\
&= \frac{1}{2} \ln \left((2\pi)^N \det \boldsymbol{\Sigma} \right) + \frac{1}{2} \underbrace{E \left[(\mathbf{x} - \boldsymbol{\mu})^T \boldsymbol{\Sigma}^{-1}(\mathbf{x} - \boldsymbol{\mu}) \right]}_{N},
\end{aligned} \tag{2.98}
$$

Figure 2.6
Uncertainty ellipse
for a
two-dimensional
Gaussian PDF. The
geometric area
inside the ellipse is
$A = M^2 \pi \sqrt{\det \Sigma}$.
The Shannon
information
expression is
provided for
comparison.

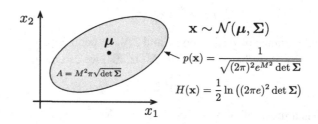

where we see that the second term is (half) of a mean-squared Mahalanobis distance from the previous section. Continuing, we have

$$
\begin{aligned}
H\left(\mathbf{x}\right) &= \frac{1}{2} \ln \left((2\pi)^N \det \Sigma\right) + \frac{1}{2} N \\
&= \frac{1}{2} \left(\ln \left((2\pi)^N \det \Sigma\right) + N \ln e\right) \\
&= \frac{1}{2} \ln \left((2\pi e)^N \det \Sigma\right),
\end{aligned}
\tag{2.99}
$$

which is purely a function of Σ, the covariance matrix of the Gaussian PDF. In fact, geometrically, we may interpret $\sqrt{\det \Sigma}$ as proportional to the volume of the *uncertainty ellipsoid* formed by the Gaussian. Figure 2.6 shows the uncertainty ellipse for a two-dimensional Gaussian.

Note that along the boundary of the uncertainty ellipse, $p(\mathbf{x})$ is constant. To see this, consider that the points along this ellipse must satisfy

$$
(\mathbf{x} - \boldsymbol{\mu})^T \Sigma^{-1} (\mathbf{x} - \boldsymbol{\mu}) = M^2,
\tag{2.100}
$$

where M is a factor applied to scale the nominal covariance so we have the $M = 1, 2, 3, \ldots$ equiprobable contours. In this case we have that

$$
p(\mathbf{x}) = \frac{1}{\sqrt{(2\pi)^N e^{M^2} \det \Sigma}}
\tag{2.101}
$$

on the Mth ellipsoid surface.

2.2.11 Mutual Information of a Joint Gaussian PDF

Assume we have a joint Gaussian for variables $\mathbf{x} \in \mathbb{R}^N$ and $\mathbf{y} \in \mathbb{R}^M$ given by

$$
p\left(\mathbf{x}, \mathbf{y}\right) = \mathcal{N}(\boldsymbol{\mu}, \Sigma) = \mathcal{N}\left(\begin{bmatrix} \boldsymbol{\mu}_x \\ \boldsymbol{\mu}_y \end{bmatrix}, \begin{bmatrix} \Sigma_{xx} & \Sigma_{xy} \\ \Sigma_{yx} & \Sigma_{yy} \end{bmatrix}\right).
\tag{2.102}
$$

By inserting (2.99) into (2.24) we can easily see that the mutual information for the joint Gaussian is given by

$$
\begin{aligned}
I(\mathbf{x}, \mathbf{y}) &= \frac{1}{2} \ln \left((2\pi e)^N \det \Sigma_{xx}\right) + \frac{1}{2} \ln \left((2\pi e)^M \det \Sigma_{yy}\right) \\
&\quad - \frac{1}{2} \ln \left((2\pi e)^{M+N} \det \Sigma\right) \\
&= -\frac{1}{2} \ln \left(\frac{\det \Sigma}{\det \Sigma_{xx} \det \Sigma_{yy}}\right).
\end{aligned}
\tag{2.103}
$$

Looking back to (2.49), we can also note that

$$\det \mathbf{\Sigma} = \det \mathbf{\Sigma}_{xx} \det \left(\mathbf{\Sigma}_{yy} - \mathbf{\Sigma}_{yx}\mathbf{\Sigma}_{xx}^{-1}\mathbf{\Sigma}_{xy}\right)$$
$$= \det \mathbf{\Sigma}_{yy} \det \left(\mathbf{\Sigma}_{xx} - \mathbf{\Sigma}_{xy}\mathbf{\Sigma}_{yy}^{-1}\mathbf{\Sigma}_{yx}\right). \qquad (2.104)$$

Inserting this into the above, we have

$$I(\mathbf{x}, \mathbf{y}) = -\frac{1}{2}\ln\det(\mathbf{1} - \mathbf{\Sigma}_{xx}^{-1}\mathbf{\Sigma}_{xy}\mathbf{\Sigma}_{yy}^{-1}\mathbf{\Sigma}_{yx})$$
$$= -\frac{1}{2}\ln\det(\mathbf{1} - \mathbf{\Sigma}_{yy}^{-1}\mathbf{\Sigma}_{yx}\mathbf{\Sigma}_{xx}^{-1}\mathbf{\Sigma}_{xy}), \qquad (2.105)$$

where the two versions can be seen to be equivalent through *Sylvester's determinant theorem.*

2.2.12 Quantifying the Difference Between Gaussians

In Section 2.1.6 we learned that we could use the *Kullback–Leibler (KL)* divergence to quantify the difference between two PDFs, p_1 and p_2:

$$\mathrm{KL}(p_2\|p_1) = -\int p_2(\mathbf{x})\ln\left(\frac{p_1(\mathbf{x})}{p_2(\mathbf{x})}\right) d\mathbf{x} \geq 0. \qquad (2.106)$$

Consider two Gaussian PDFs with a common dimension of N, $p_1(\mathbf{x}) = \mathcal{N}(\boldsymbol{\mu}_1, \mathbf{\Sigma}_1)$ and $p_2(\mathbf{x}) = \mathcal{N}(\boldsymbol{\mu}_2, \mathbf{\Sigma}_2)$. Then the KL divergence can be shown to be

$$\mathrm{KL}(p_2\|p_1) = \frac{1}{2}\left((\boldsymbol{\mu}_2 - \boldsymbol{\mu}_1)^T\mathbf{\Sigma}_1^{-1}(\boldsymbol{\mu}_2 - \boldsymbol{\mu}_1) + \ln\left|\mathbf{\Sigma}_1\mathbf{\Sigma}_2^{-1}\right| + \mathrm{tr}(\mathbf{\Sigma}_1^{-1}\mathbf{\Sigma}_2) - N\right).$$
$$(2.107)$$

We leave the derivation as an exercise.

2.2.13 Randomly Sampling a Gaussian

We have seen previously in Section 2.1.7 how we can generate random samples from a PDF. For a one-dimensional standard normal PDF, $p(x) = \mathcal{N}(0, 1)$, the associated CDF is

$$P(x) = \frac{1}{2}\left(1 + \mathrm{erf}\left(\frac{x}{\sqrt{2}}\right)\right), \qquad (2.108)$$

so that the quantile function, $Q(y) = P^{-1}(y)$, is

$$Q(y) = \sqrt{2}\,\mathrm{erf}^{-1}(2y - 1). \qquad (2.109)$$

Therefore, to generate a random Gaussian sample, x_{meas}, we can take a sample from the uniform density, $y_{\mathrm{meas}} \leftarrow \mathcal{U}[0, 1]$, and then let $x_{\mathrm{meas}} = Q(y_{\mathrm{meas}})$.

To generate random samples from a N-dimensional Gaussian PDF, $p(\mathbf{z}) = \mathcal{N}(\boldsymbol{\mu}, \mathbf{\Sigma})$, we can leverage the one-dimensional result. First, we need to do a decomposition on the covariance matrix, which is a symmetric, positive-definite

James Joseph Sylvester (1814–1897) was an English mathematician who made fundamental contributions to matrix theory, invariant theory, number theory, partition theory, and combinatorics. This theorem says that $\det(\mathbf{1} - \mathbf{AB}) = \det(\mathbf{1} - \mathbf{BA})$, even when $\mathbf{A}$ and $\mathbf{B}$ are not square.

matrix. All such matrices can be factored as $\boldsymbol{\Sigma} = \mathbf{V}\mathbf{V}^T$, with $\mathbf{V}$ square (see Appendix A.1.10). Then, we can generate N independent one-dimensional samples and stack these into $\mathbf{x}_{\text{meas}}$. A sample from the N-dimensional PDF can then be calculated as

$$\mathbf{z}_{\text{meas}} = \boldsymbol{\mu} + \mathbf{V}\mathbf{x}_{\text{meas}}. \tag{2.110}$$

To see why this *affine* transformation works, we can check the mean and covariance matrix of $\mathbf{z}$. For the mean,

$$E[\mathbf{z}] = E[\boldsymbol{\mu} + \mathbf{V}\mathbf{x}] = \boldsymbol{\mu} + \mathbf{V}\underbrace{E[\mathbf{x}]}_{0} = \boldsymbol{\mu}. \tag{2.111}$$

For the covariance,

$$\begin{aligned}
E\left[(\mathbf{z} - \boldsymbol{\mu})(\mathbf{z} - \boldsymbol{\mu})^T\right] &= E\left[(\boldsymbol{\mu} + \mathbf{V}\mathbf{x} - \boldsymbol{\mu})(\boldsymbol{\mu} + \mathbf{V}\mathbf{x} - \boldsymbol{\mu})^T\right] \\
&= \mathbf{V}\underbrace{E[\mathbf{x}\mathbf{x}^T]}_{1}\mathbf{V}^T = \mathbf{V}\mathbf{V}^T = \boldsymbol{\Sigma}, \tag{2.112}
\end{aligned}$$

as expected. Thus, as long as we can sample from a one-dimensional uniform density, we can sample from a multivariate Gaussian as well.

2.2.14 Cramér–Rao Lower Bound Applied to Gaussians

Suppose that we have K samples (i.e., measurements), $\mathbf{x}_{\text{meas},k} \in \mathbb{R}^N$, drawn from a Gaussian PDF. The K *statistically independent* random variables associated with these measurements are thus

$$(\forall k) \quad \mathbf{x}_k \sim \mathcal{N}(\boldsymbol{\mu}, \boldsymbol{\Sigma}). \tag{2.113}$$

The term *statistically independent* implies that $E\left[(\mathbf{x}_k - \boldsymbol{\mu})(\mathbf{x}_\ell - \boldsymbol{\mu})^T\right] = \mathbf{0}$ for $k \neq \ell$. Now suppose our goal is to estimate the mean of this PDF, $\boldsymbol{\mu}$, from the measurements, $\mathbf{x}_{\text{meas}} = (\mathbf{x}_{\text{meas},1}, \dots, \mathbf{x}_{\text{meas},K})$. For the joint density of all the random variables, $\mathbf{x} = (\mathbf{x}_1, \dots, \mathbf{x}_K)$, we have

$$-\ln p(\mathbf{x}|\boldsymbol{\mu}, \boldsymbol{\Sigma}) = \frac{1}{2}(\mathbf{x} - \mathbf{A}\boldsymbol{\mu})^T\mathbf{B}^{-1}(\mathbf{x} - \mathbf{A}\boldsymbol{\mu}) + \frac{1}{2}\ln\left((2\pi)^{NK}\det\mathbf{B}\right), \tag{2.114}$$

where

$$\mathbf{A} = \underbrace{\begin{bmatrix} \mathbf{1} & \mathbf{1} & \cdots & \mathbf{1} \end{bmatrix}^T}_{K \text{ blocks}}, \quad \mathbf{B} = \text{diag}\underbrace{(\boldsymbol{\Sigma}, \boldsymbol{\Sigma}, \dots, \boldsymbol{\Sigma})}_{K \text{ blocks}}. \tag{2.115}$$

In this case, the Fisher information matrix for the parameter $\boldsymbol{\mu}$ (see Appendix C.1) is

$$\mathcal{I}_{\boldsymbol{\mu}} = E\left[\frac{\partial^2(-\ln p(\mathbf{x}|\boldsymbol{\mu}, \boldsymbol{\Sigma}))}{\partial\boldsymbol{\mu}^T\partial\boldsymbol{\mu}}\right] = E[\mathbf{A}^T\mathbf{B}^{-1}\mathbf{A}] = \mathbf{A}^T\mathbf{B}^{-1}\mathbf{A} = K\boldsymbol{\Sigma}^{-1}, \tag{2.116}$$

which we can see is just K times the inverse covariance of the Gaussian density. The CRLB thus says

$$\text{cov}(\hat{\boldsymbol{\mu}}|\mathbf{x}_{\text{meas}}) \geq \frac{1}{K}\boldsymbol{\Sigma}. \tag{2.117}$$

In other words, the lower limit of the uncertainty in the estimate of the mean, $\hat{\mu}$, becomes smaller and smaller the more measurements we have (as we would expect).

Note that in computing the CRLB, we did not need actually to specify the form of the unbiased estimator at all; the CRLB is the lower bound for any unbiased estimator. In this case, it is not hard to find an estimator that performs right at the CRLB:

$$\hat{\mu} = \frac{1}{K} \sum_{k=1}^{K} \mathbf{x}_{\text{meas},k}. \tag{2.118}$$

For the mean of this estimator we have

$$E[\hat{\mu}] = E\left[\frac{1}{K} \sum_{k=1}^{K} \mathbf{x}_k\right] = \frac{1}{K} \sum_{k=1}^{K} E[\mathbf{x}_k] = \frac{1}{K} \sum_{k=1}^{K} \mu = \mu, \tag{2.119}$$

which shows that the estimator is indeed unbiased. For the covariance we have

$$\begin{aligned}
\text{cov}(\hat{\mu}|\mathbf{x}_{\text{meas}}) &= E\left[(\hat{\mu} - \mu)(\hat{\mu} - \mu)^T\right] \\
&= E\left[\left(\frac{1}{K}\sum_{k=1}^{K}\mathbf{x}_k - \mu\right)\left(\frac{1}{K}\sum_{k=1}^{K}\mathbf{x}_k - \mu\right)^T\right] \\
&= \frac{1}{K^2}\sum_{k=1}^{K}\sum_{\ell=1}^{K}\underbrace{E\left[(\mathbf{x}_k - \mu)(\mathbf{x}_\ell - \mu)^T\right]}_{\Sigma \text{ when } k=\ell, \ \mathbf{0} \text{ otherwise}} \\
&= \frac{1}{K}\Sigma, \tag{2.120}
\end{aligned}$$

which is right at the CRLB.

2.2.15 Sherman–Morrison–Woodbury Identity

We will require the *Sherman–Morrison–Woodbury (SMW)* (Sherman and Morrison, 1949, 1950; Woodbury, 1950) matrix identity (sometimes called the *matrix inversion lemma*) in what follows. There are actually four different identities that come from a single derivation.

We start by noting that we can factor a matrix into either a *lower-diagonal-upper (LDU)* or *upper-diagonal-lower (UDL)* form, as follows:

The SMW formula is named for American statisticians Jack Sherman, Winifred J. Morrison, and Max A. Woodbury, but was independently presented by English mathematician W. J. Duncan, American statisticians L. Guttman and M. S. Bartlett, and possibly others.

$$\begin{aligned}
&\begin{bmatrix} \mathbf{A}^{-1} & -\mathbf{B} \\ \mathbf{C} & \mathbf{D} \end{bmatrix} \\
&= \begin{bmatrix} \mathbf{1} & \mathbf{0} \\ \mathbf{CA} & \mathbf{1} \end{bmatrix} \begin{bmatrix} \mathbf{A}^{-1} & \mathbf{0} \\ \mathbf{0} & \mathbf{D}+\mathbf{CAB} \end{bmatrix} \begin{bmatrix} \mathbf{1} & -\mathbf{AB} \\ \mathbf{0} & \mathbf{1} \end{bmatrix} \quad \text{(LDU)} \\
&= \begin{bmatrix} \mathbf{1} & -\mathbf{BD}^{-1} \\ \mathbf{0} & \mathbf{1} \end{bmatrix} \begin{bmatrix} \mathbf{A}^{-1}+\mathbf{BD}^{-1}\mathbf{C} & \mathbf{0} \\ \mathbf{0} & \mathbf{D} \end{bmatrix} \begin{bmatrix} \mathbf{1} & \mathbf{0} \\ \mathbf{D}^{-1}\mathbf{C} & \mathbf{1} \end{bmatrix}. \quad \text{(UDL)}
\end{aligned}$$
$$\tag{2.121}$$

We then invert each of these forms. For the LDU we have

$$
\begin{bmatrix} \mathbf{A}^{-1} & -\mathbf{B} \\ \mathbf{C} & \mathbf{D} \end{bmatrix}^{-1}
$$

$$
= \begin{bmatrix} 1 & \mathbf{AB} \\ 0 & 1 \end{bmatrix} \begin{bmatrix} \mathbf{A} & 0 \\ 0 & (\mathbf{D}+\mathbf{CAB})^{-1} \end{bmatrix} \begin{bmatrix} 1 & 0 \\ -\mathbf{CA} & 1 \end{bmatrix}
$$

$$
= \begin{bmatrix} \mathbf{A}-\mathbf{AB}(\mathbf{D}+\mathbf{CAB})^{-1}\mathbf{CA} & \mathbf{AB}(\mathbf{D}+\mathbf{CAB})^{-1} \\ -(\mathbf{D}+\mathbf{CAB})^{-1}\mathbf{CA} & (\mathbf{D}+\mathbf{CAB})^{-1} \end{bmatrix}. \tag{2.122}
$$

For the UDL we have

$$
\begin{bmatrix} \mathbf{A}^{-1} & -\mathbf{B} \\ \mathbf{C} & \mathbf{D} \end{bmatrix}^{-1}
$$

$$
= \begin{bmatrix} 1 & 0 \\ -\mathbf{D}^{-1}\mathbf{C} & 1 \end{bmatrix} \begin{bmatrix} (\mathbf{A}^{-1}+\mathbf{BD}^{-1}\mathbf{C})^{-1} & 0 \\ 0 & \mathbf{D}^{-1} \end{bmatrix} \begin{bmatrix} 1 & \mathbf{BD}^{-1} \\ 0 & 1 \end{bmatrix}
$$

$$
= \begin{bmatrix} (\mathbf{A}^{-1}+\mathbf{BD}^{-1}\mathbf{C})^{-1} & (\mathbf{A}^{-1}+\mathbf{BD}^{-1}\mathbf{C})^{-1}\mathbf{BD}^{-1} \\ -\mathbf{D}^{-1}\mathbf{C}(\mathbf{A}^{-1}+\mathbf{BD}^{-1}\mathbf{C})^{-1} & \mathbf{D}^{-1}-\mathbf{D}^{-1}\mathbf{C}(\mathbf{A}^{-1}+\mathbf{BD}^{-1}\mathbf{C})^{-1}\mathbf{BD}^{-1} \end{bmatrix}. \tag{2.123}
$$

Comparing the blocks of (2.122) and (2.123), we have the following identities:

$$
(\mathbf{A}^{-1}+\mathbf{BD}^{-1}\mathbf{C})^{-1} \equiv \mathbf{A}-\mathbf{AB}(\mathbf{D}+\mathbf{CAB})^{-1}\mathbf{CA}, \tag{2.124a}
$$

$$
(\mathbf{D}+\mathbf{CAB})^{-1} \equiv \mathbf{D}^{-1}-\mathbf{D}^{-1}\mathbf{C}(\mathbf{A}^{-1}+\mathbf{BD}^{-1}\mathbf{C})^{-1}\mathbf{BD}^{-1}, \tag{2.124b}
$$

$$
\mathbf{AB}(\mathbf{D}+\mathbf{CAB})^{-1} \equiv (\mathbf{A}^{-1}+\mathbf{BD}^{-1}\mathbf{C})^{-1}\mathbf{BD}^{-1}, \tag{2.124c}
$$

$$
(\mathbf{D}+\mathbf{CAB})^{-1}\mathbf{CA} = \mathbf{D}^{-1}\mathbf{C}(\mathbf{A}^{-1}+\mathbf{BD}^{-1}\mathbf{C})^{-1}. \tag{2.124d}
$$

These are all used frequently when manipulating expressions involving the covariance matrices associated with Gaussian PDFs.

2.2.16 Stein's Lemma

Charles Max Stein (1920–2016) was an American mathematician and professor who made lasting contributions in the area of statistics, including his namesake lemma.

A tool that is sometimes useful when working with Gaussian PDFs is *Stein's lemma* (Stein, 1981). Suppose that $\mathbf{x} \sim \mathcal{N}(\boldsymbol{\mu}, \boldsymbol{\Sigma})$. Stein's lemma tells us that

$$
E[(\mathbf{x}-\boldsymbol{\mu})f(\mathbf{x})] = \boldsymbol{\Sigma}\, E\left[\frac{\partial f(\mathbf{x})}{\partial \mathbf{x}^T}\right], \tag{2.125}
$$

where $f(\mathbf{x})$ is any (once differentiable) scalar function of $\mathbf{x}$. A double application of Stein's lemma also reveals

$$
E[(\mathbf{x}-\boldsymbol{\mu})(\mathbf{x}-\boldsymbol{\mu})^T f(\mathbf{x})] = \boldsymbol{\Sigma}\, E\left[\frac{\partial^2 f(\mathbf{x})}{\partial \mathbf{x}^T \partial \mathbf{x}}\right]\boldsymbol{\Sigma} + \boldsymbol{\Sigma}\, E[f(\mathbf{x})], \tag{2.126}
$$

assuming $f(\cdot)$ is twice differentiable. More generally,

$$
\mathrm{cov}(\mathbf{y}, f(\mathbf{x})) = \mathrm{cov}(\mathbf{y}, \mathbf{x})\, E\left[\frac{\partial f(\mathbf{x})}{\partial \mathbf{x}^T}\right] \tag{2.127}
$$

for two jointly Gaussian variables, $\mathbf{x}$ and $\mathbf{y}$; joint Gaussian distributions are described more fully in the next section. Derivations of all three versions of Stein's lemma are provided in Appendix C.2.

2.2.17 Isserlis' Theorem

Moments of multivariate Gaussian PDFs get a little messy to compute beyond the usual mean and covariance, but there are some specific cases that we will make use of later that are worth discussing. We can use *Isserlis' theorem* to compute higher-order moments of a Gaussian random variable, $\mathbf{x} = (x_1, x_2, \ldots, x_{2M}) \in \mathbb{R}^{2M}$. In general, this theorem says

Leon Isserlis (1881–1966) was a Russian-born British statistician known for his work on the exact distribution of sample moments.

$$E[x_1 x_2 x_3 \cdots x_{2M}] = \sum \prod E[x_i x_j], \quad (2.128)$$

where this implies summing over all distinct ways of partitioning into a product of M pairs. This implies that there are $\frac{(2M)!}{(2^M M!)}$ terms in the sum. With four variables we have

$$E[x_i x_j x_k x_\ell] = E[x_i x_j]E[x_k x_\ell] + E[x_i x_k]E[x_j x_\ell] + E[x_i x_\ell]E[x_j x_k]. \quad (2.129)$$

We can apply this theorem to work out some useful results for matrix expressions.

Assume we have $\mathbf{x} \sim \mathcal{N}(\mathbf{0}, \boldsymbol{\Sigma}) \in \mathbb{R}^N$. We will have occasion to compute expressions of the form

$$E\left[\mathbf{x}\left(\mathbf{x}^T\mathbf{x}\right)^p \mathbf{x}^T\right], \quad (2.130)$$

where p is a nonnegative integer. Trivially, when $p = 0$, we simply have $E[\mathbf{x}\mathbf{x}^T] = \boldsymbol{\Sigma}$. When $p = 1$, we have[11]

$$
\begin{aligned}
E\left[\mathbf{x}\mathbf{x}^T\mathbf{x}\mathbf{x}^T\right] &= E\left[\left[x_i x_j \left(\sum_{k=1}^N x_k^2\right)\right]_{ij}\right] = \left[\sum_{k=1}^N E\left[x_i x_j x_k^2\right]\right]_{ij} \\
&= \left[\sum_{k=1}^N \left(E[x_i x_j]E[x_k^2] + 2E[x_i x_k]E[x_k x_j]\right)\right]_{ij} \\
&= [E[x_i x_j]]_{ij}\sum_{k=1}^N E[x_k^2] + 2\left[\sum_{k=1}^N E[x_i x_k]E[x_k x_j]\right]_{ij} \\
&= \boldsymbol{\Sigma}\operatorname{tr}(\boldsymbol{\Sigma}) + 2\boldsymbol{\Sigma}^2 \\
&= \boldsymbol{\Sigma}\left(\operatorname{tr}(\boldsymbol{\Sigma})\mathbf{1} + 2\boldsymbol{\Sigma}\right). \quad (2.131)
\end{aligned}
$$

Note that in the scalar case we have $x \sim \mathcal{N}(0, \sigma^2)$ and hence $E[x^4] = \sigma^2(\sigma^2 + 2\sigma^2) = 3\sigma^4$, a well-known result. Results for $p > 1$ are possible using a similar approach, but we do not compute them for now.

We also consider the case where

$$\mathbf{x} = \begin{bmatrix} \mathbf{x}_1 \\ \mathbf{x}_2 \end{bmatrix} \sim \mathcal{N}\left(\mathbf{0}, \begin{bmatrix} \boldsymbol{\Sigma}_{11} & \boldsymbol{\Sigma}_{12} \\ \boldsymbol{\Sigma}_{12}^T & \boldsymbol{\Sigma}_{22} \end{bmatrix}\right), \quad (2.132)$$

---

[11] The notation $[\cdot]_{ij}$ implies populating the matrix $\mathbf{A} = [a_{ij}]$ with the appropriate ijth entry in each element.

with $\dim(\mathbf{x}_1) = N_1$ and $\dim(\mathbf{x}_2) = N_2$. We will need to compute expressions of the form

$$E\left[\mathbf{x}(\mathbf{x}_1^T\mathbf{x}_1)^p\mathbf{x}^T\right],\tag{2.133}$$

where p is a nonnegative integer. Again, when $p = 0$, we trivially have $E[\mathbf{x}\mathbf{x}^T] = \boldsymbol{\Sigma}$. When $p = 1$, we have

$$E\left[\mathbf{x}\mathbf{x}_1^T\mathbf{x}_1\mathbf{x}^T\right] = E\left[\left[x_ix_j\left(\sum_{k=1}^{N_1}x_k^2\right)\right]_{ij}\right] = \left[\sum_{k=1}^{N_1}E\left[x_ix_jx_k^2\right]\right]_{ij}$$

$$= \left[\sum_{k=1}^{N_1}\left(E[x_ix_j]E[x_k^2] + 2E[x_ix_k]E[x_kx_j]\right)\right]_{ij}$$

$$= [E[x_ix_j]]_{ij}\sum_{k=1}^{N_1}E[x_k^2] + 2\left[\sum_{k=1}^{N_1}E[x_ix_k]E[x_kx_j]\right]_{ij}$$

$$= \boldsymbol{\Sigma}\operatorname{tr}(\boldsymbol{\Sigma}_{11}) + 2\begin{bmatrix}\boldsymbol{\Sigma}_{11}^2 & \boldsymbol{\Sigma}_{11}\boldsymbol{\Sigma}_{12}\\ \boldsymbol{\Sigma}_{12}^T\boldsymbol{\Sigma}_{11} & \boldsymbol{\Sigma}_{12}^T\boldsymbol{\Sigma}_{12}\end{bmatrix}$$

$$= \boldsymbol{\Sigma}\left(\operatorname{tr}(\boldsymbol{\Sigma}_{11})\mathbf{1} + 2\begin{bmatrix}\boldsymbol{\Sigma}_{11} & \boldsymbol{\Sigma}_{12}\\ \mathbf{0} & \mathbf{0}\end{bmatrix}\right).\tag{2.134}$$

Similarly, we have

$$E\left[\mathbf{x}\mathbf{x}_2^T\mathbf{x}_2\mathbf{x}^T\right] = \boldsymbol{\Sigma}\operatorname{tr}(\boldsymbol{\Sigma}_{22}) + 2\begin{bmatrix}\boldsymbol{\Sigma}_{12}\boldsymbol{\Sigma}_{12}^T & \boldsymbol{\Sigma}_{12}\boldsymbol{\Sigma}_{22}\\ \boldsymbol{\Sigma}_{22}\boldsymbol{\Sigma}_{12}^T & \boldsymbol{\Sigma}_{22}^2\end{bmatrix}$$

$$= \boldsymbol{\Sigma}\left(\operatorname{tr}(\boldsymbol{\Sigma}_{22})\mathbf{1} + 2\begin{bmatrix}\mathbf{0} & \mathbf{0}\\ \boldsymbol{\Sigma}_{12}^T & \boldsymbol{\Sigma}_{22}\end{bmatrix}\right),\tag{2.135}$$

and as a final check,

$$E\left[\mathbf{x}\mathbf{x}^T\mathbf{x}\mathbf{x}^T\right] = E\left[\mathbf{x}(\mathbf{x}_1^T\mathbf{x}_1 + \mathbf{x}_2^T\mathbf{x}_2)\mathbf{x}^T\right] = E\left[\mathbf{x}\mathbf{x}_1^T\mathbf{x}_1\mathbf{x}^T\right] + E\left[\mathbf{x}\mathbf{x}_2^T\mathbf{x}_2\mathbf{x}^T\right].$$
$$\tag{2.136}$$

We furthermore have that

$$E\left[\mathbf{x}\mathbf{x}^T\mathbf{A}\mathbf{x}\mathbf{x}^T\right] = E\left[\left[x_ix_j\left(\sum_{k=1}^{N}\sum_{\ell=1}^{N}x_ka_{k\ell}x_\ell\right)\right]_{ij}\right]$$

$$= \left[\sum_{k=1}^{N}\sum_{\ell=1}^{N}a_{k\ell}E\left[x_ix_jx_kx_\ell\right]\right]_{ij}$$

$$= \left[\sum_{k=1}^{N}\sum_{\ell=1}^{N}a_{k\ell}\left(E[x_ix_j]E[x_kx_\ell] + E[x_ix_k]E[x_jx_\ell]\right.\right.$$

$$\left.\left. + E[x_ix_\ell]E[x_jx_k]\right)\right]_{ij}$$

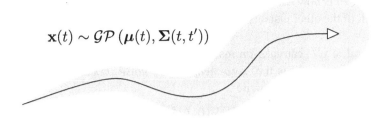

Figure 2.7
Continuous-time
trajectories can be
represented using
Gaussian processes,
which have a mean
function (dark line)
and a covariance
function (shaded
area).

$$
\begin{aligned}
&= [E[x_i x_j]]_{ij} \left(\sum_{k=1}^{N} \sum_{\ell=1}^{N} a_{k\ell} E[x_k x_\ell] \right) \\
&\quad + \left[\sum_{k=1}^{N} \sum_{\ell=1}^{N} E[x_i x_k] a_{k\ell} E[x_\ell x_j] \right]_{ij} \\
&\quad + \left[\sum_{k=1}^{N} \sum_{\ell=1}^{N} E[x_i x_\ell] a_{k\ell} E[x_k x_j] \right]_{ij} \\
&= \boldsymbol{\Sigma} \operatorname{tr}(\mathbf{A}\boldsymbol{\Sigma}) + \boldsymbol{\Sigma}\mathbf{A}\boldsymbol{\Sigma} + \boldsymbol{\Sigma}\mathbf{A}^T\boldsymbol{\Sigma} \\
&= \boldsymbol{\Sigma} \left(\operatorname{tr}(\mathbf{A}\boldsymbol{\Sigma}) \mathbf{1} + \mathbf{A}\boldsymbol{\Sigma} + \mathbf{A}^T\boldsymbol{\Sigma} \right),
\end{aligned}
\tag{2.137}
$$

where $\mathbf{A}$ is a compatible square matrix.

2.3 Gaussian Processes

We have already discussed Gaussian random variables and their associated PDFs. We write

$$
\mathbf{x} \sim \mathcal{N}(\boldsymbol{\mu}, \boldsymbol{\Sigma}),
\tag{2.138}
$$

to say $\mathbf{x} \in \mathbb{R}^N$ is Gaussian. We will use this type of random variable extensively to represent discrete-time quantities. We will also want to talk about state quantities that are continuous functions of time, t. To do so, we need to introduce *Gaussian processes (GPs)* (Rasmussen and Williams, 2006). Figure 2.7 depicts a trajectory represented by a Gaussian process. There is a *mean function*, $\boldsymbol{\mu}(t)$, and a *covariance function*, $\boldsymbol{\Sigma}(t, t')$.

The idea is that the entire trajectory is a single random variable belonging to a class of functions. The closer a function is to the mean function, the more likely it is. The covariance function controls how smooth the function is by describing the correlation between two times, t and t'. We write

$$
\mathbf{x}(t) \sim \mathcal{GP}(\boldsymbol{\mu}(t), \boldsymbol{\Sigma}(t, t'))
\tag{2.139}
$$

to indicate that a continuous-time trajectory is a *Gaussian process (GP)*. The GP concept generalizes beyond one-dimensional functions of time, but we will only have need of this special case.

If we want to consider a variable at a single particular time of interest, τ, then we can write

$$
\mathbf{x}(\tau) \sim \mathcal{N}(\boldsymbol{\mu}(\tau), \boldsymbol{\Sigma}(\tau, \tau)),
\tag{2.140}
$$

where $\Sigma(\tau, \tau)$ is now simply a covariance matrix. We have essentially marginalized out all of the other instants of time, leaving $\mathbf{x}(\tau)$ as a usual Gaussian random variable.

Paul Adrien Maurice
Dirac (1902–1984)
was an English
theoretical physicist
who made
fundamental
contributions to the
early development of
both quantum
mechanics and
quantum
electrodynamics.

In general, a GP can take on many different forms. One particular GP that we will use frequently is the *zero-mean, white noise process*. For $\mathbf{w}(t)$ to be zero-mean, white noise, we write

$$\mathbf{w}(t) \sim \mathcal{GP}(\mathbf{0}, \mathbf{Q}\delta(t - t')), \qquad (2.141)$$

where $\mathbf{Q}$ is a *power spectral density matrix* and $\delta(\cdot)$ is *Dirac's delta function*. This is a *stationary* noise process since it depends only on the difference, $t - t'$.

We will return to GPs when we want to talk about state estimation in continuous time. We will show that estimation in this context can be viewed as an application of *Gaussian process regression* (Rasmussen and Williams, 2006).

2.4 Summary

The main takeaway points from this chapter are as follows:

1. We will be using *probability density functions (PDFs)* over some continuous state space to represent how certain we are that a robot is in each possible state.
2. We often restrict ourselves to Gaussian PDFs to make the calculations easier.
3. We will frequently employ Bayes' rule to carry out so-called Bayesian inference as an approach to state estimation; we begin with a set of possible states (the prior) and narrow the possibilities based on actual measurements (the posterior).

The next chapter will introduce some of the classic linear-Gaussian, state estimation methods.

2.5 Exercises

2.1   Show for any two columns of the same length, $\mathbf{u}$ and $\mathbf{v}$, that

$$\mathbf{u}^T\mathbf{v} = \text{tr}(\mathbf{v}\mathbf{u}^T).$$

2.2   Show that if two random variables, $\mathbf{x}$ and $\mathbf{y}$, are statistically independent, then the Shannon information of the joint density, $p(\mathbf{x}, \mathbf{y})$, is the sum of the Shannon informations of the individual densities, $p(\mathbf{x})$ and $p(\mathbf{y})$:

$$H(\mathbf{x}, \mathbf{y}) = H(\mathbf{x}) + H(\mathbf{y}).$$

2.3   For a Gaussian random variable, $\mathbf{x} \sim \mathcal{N}(\boldsymbol{\mu}, \boldsymbol{\Sigma})$, show that

$$E[\mathbf{x}\mathbf{x}^T] = \boldsymbol{\Sigma} + \boldsymbol{\mu}\boldsymbol{\mu}^T.$$

2.4   For a Gaussian random variable, $\mathbf{x} \sim \mathcal{N}(\boldsymbol{\mu}, \boldsymbol{\Sigma})$, determine expressions for $E[\mathbf{x}^T\mathbf{x}]$ and $E[\mathbf{x}\mathbf{x}^T]$ in terms of the mean, $\boldsymbol{\mu}$, and covariance matrix, $\boldsymbol{\Sigma}$.

2.5   For a joint Gaussian

$$p(\mathbf{x}, \mathbf{y}) = \mathcal{N}\left(\begin{bmatrix} \boldsymbol{\mu}_x \\ \boldsymbol{\mu}_y \end{bmatrix}, \begin{bmatrix} \boldsymbol{\Sigma}_{xx} & \boldsymbol{\Sigma}_{xy} \\ \boldsymbol{\Sigma}_{yx} & \boldsymbol{\Sigma}_{yy} \end{bmatrix}\right),$$

use marginalization to compute $p(\mathbf{x})$ and $p(\mathbf{y})$. Under what conditions does

$$p(\mathbf{x}, \mathbf{y}) = p(\mathbf{x})p(\mathbf{y})$$

hold?

2.6   For a Gaussian random variable, $\mathbf{x} \sim \mathcal{N}(\boldsymbol{\mu}, \boldsymbol{\Sigma})$, show directly that

$$\boldsymbol{\mu} = E[\mathbf{x}] = \int_{-\infty}^{\infty} \mathbf{x}\, p(\mathbf{x})\, d\mathbf{x}.$$

2.7   For a Gaussian random variable, $\mathbf{x} \sim \mathcal{N}(\boldsymbol{\mu}, \boldsymbol{\Sigma})$, show directly that

$$\boldsymbol{\Sigma} = E[(\mathbf{x} - \boldsymbol{\mu})(\mathbf{x} - \boldsymbol{\mu})^T] = \int_{-\infty}^{\infty} (\mathbf{x} - \boldsymbol{\mu})(\mathbf{x} - \boldsymbol{\mu})^T\, p(\mathbf{x})\, d\mathbf{x}.$$

2.8   Show that the normalized product of K statistically independent Gaussian PDFs, $\mathbf{x}_k \sim \mathcal{N}(\boldsymbol{\mu}_k, \boldsymbol{\Sigma}_k)$, is also a Gaussian PDF:

$$\exp\left(-\frac{1}{2}(\mathbf{x} - \boldsymbol{\mu})^T \boldsymbol{\Sigma}^{-1} (\mathbf{x} - \boldsymbol{\mu})\right)$$

$$\equiv \eta \prod_{k=1}^{K} \exp\left(-\frac{1}{2}(\mathbf{x} - \boldsymbol{\mu}_k)^T \boldsymbol{\Sigma}_k^{-1} (\mathbf{x} - \boldsymbol{\mu}_k)\right),$$

where

$$\boldsymbol{\Sigma}^{-1} = \sum_{k=1}^{K} \boldsymbol{\Sigma}_k^{-1}, \quad \boldsymbol{\Sigma}^{-1}\boldsymbol{\mu} = \sum_{k=1}^{K} \boldsymbol{\Sigma}_k^{-1} \boldsymbol{\mu}_k,$$

and η is a normalization constant to enforce the axiom of total probability.

2.9   Show that the weighted sum of K statistically independent random variables, $\mathbf{x}_k$, given by

$$\mathbf{x} = \sum_{k=1}^{K} w_k \mathbf{x}_k,$$

with $\sum_{k=1}^{K} w_k = 1$ and $w_k \geq 0$, has a PDF that satisfies the axiom of total probability and whose mean is given by

$$\boldsymbol{\mu} = \sum_{k=1}^{K} w_k \boldsymbol{\mu}_k,$$

where $\boldsymbol{\mu}_k$ is the mean of $\mathbf{x}_k$. Determine an expression for the covariance. Note that the random variables are not assumed to be Gaussian.

2.10 The random variable

$$y = \mathbf{x}^T \mathbf{x}$$

is *chi-squared* (of order K) when $\mathbf{x} \sim \mathcal{N}(\mathbf{0}, \mathbf{1})$ is length K. Show that the mean and variance are given by K and $2K$, respectively. Hint: use Isserlis' theorem.

2.11 Consider the random variable

$$y = (\mathbf{x} - \boldsymbol{\mu})^T \boldsymbol{\Sigma}^{-1} (\mathbf{x} - \boldsymbol{\mu}),$$

where $\mathbf{x} \sim \mathcal{N}(\boldsymbol{\mu}, \boldsymbol{\Sigma})$ is length K. Show that the variance of y is $2K$. Hint: use Isserlis' theorem.

2.12 Consider two Gaussian PDFs with a common dimension of N, $p_1(\mathbf{x}) = \mathcal{N}(\boldsymbol{\mu}_1, \boldsymbol{\Sigma}_1)$ and $p_2(\mathbf{x}) = \mathcal{N}(\boldsymbol{\mu}_2, \boldsymbol{\Sigma}_2)$. Show that the KL divergence is

$$\mathrm{KL}(p_2 \| p_1) = \frac{1}{2}\left((\boldsymbol{\mu}_2 - \boldsymbol{\mu}_1)^T \boldsymbol{\Sigma}_1^{-1} (\boldsymbol{\mu}_2 - \boldsymbol{\mu}_1) + \ln\left|\boldsymbol{\Sigma}_1 \boldsymbol{\Sigma}_2^{-1}\right| + \mathrm{tr}(\boldsymbol{\Sigma}_1^{-1} \boldsymbol{\Sigma}_2) - N \right).$$

2.13 Suppose that $\mathbf{x}_{k-1} \sim \mathcal{N}(\boldsymbol{\mu}_{k-1}, \boldsymbol{\Sigma}_{k-1})$ and that we update the state through a motion model,

$$\mathbf{x}_k = \mathbf{A}\mathbf{x}_{k-1} + \mathbf{w}_k,$$

where $\mathbf{w}_k = \mathcal{N}(\mathbf{0}, \mathbf{Q})$ is process noise that is statistically independent of $\mathbf{x}_{k-1}$. Show that

$$\mathbf{x}_k \sim \mathcal{N}(\mathbf{A}\boldsymbol{\mu}_{k-1}, \mathbf{A}\boldsymbol{\Sigma}_{k-1}\mathbf{A}^T + \mathbf{Q})$$

by using the usual definitions of mean and covariance.

2.14 Show that the $\mathbf{x}$ marginal for a joint Gaussian

$$p(\mathbf{x}, \mathbf{y}) = \mathcal{N}\left(\begin{bmatrix} \boldsymbol{\mu}_x \\ \boldsymbol{\mu}_y \end{bmatrix}, \begin{bmatrix} \boldsymbol{\Sigma}_{xx} & \boldsymbol{\Sigma}_{xy} \\ \boldsymbol{\Sigma}_{yx} & \boldsymbol{\Sigma}_{yy} \end{bmatrix} \right)$$

is $p(\mathbf{x}) = \mathcal{N}(\boldsymbol{\mu}_x, \boldsymbol{\Sigma}_{xx})$.

2.15 Show that the $\mathbf{x}$ information-form marginal for a joint Gaussian

$$p(\mathbf{x}, \mathbf{y}) = \mathcal{N}(\boldsymbol{\mu}, \boldsymbol{\Sigma}) = \mathcal{N}\left(\begin{bmatrix} \boldsymbol{\mu}_x \\ \boldsymbol{\mu}_y \end{bmatrix}, \begin{bmatrix} \boldsymbol{\Sigma}_{xx} & \boldsymbol{\Sigma}_{xy} \\ \boldsymbol{\Sigma}_{yx} & \boldsymbol{\Sigma}_{yy} \end{bmatrix} \right),$$

$$\boldsymbol{\Sigma}^{-1} = \begin{bmatrix} \mathbf{A}_{xx} & \mathbf{A}_{xy} \\ \mathbf{A}_{yx} & \mathbf{A}_{yy} \end{bmatrix}, \quad \boldsymbol{\Sigma}^{-1}\boldsymbol{\mu} = \begin{bmatrix} \mathbf{b}_x \\ \mathbf{b}_y \end{bmatrix}$$

is

$$\boldsymbol{\Sigma}_{xx}^{-1} = \mathbf{A}_{xx} - \mathbf{A}_{xy}\mathbf{A}_{yy}^{-1}\mathbf{A}_{yx}, \quad \boldsymbol{\Sigma}_{xx}^{-1}\boldsymbol{\mu}_x = \mathbf{b}_x - \mathbf{A}_{xy}\mathbf{A}_{yy}^{-1}\mathbf{b}_y.$$

2.16 One of the key tools that we will use to derive our Bayesian estimators is the so-called 'two-step approach to Bayesian inference'. This question works through that process.

(i) Suppose we have a prior, $p(\mathbf{x}) = \mathcal{N}(\boldsymbol{\mu}, \boldsymbol{\Sigma})$, for a random variable, $\mathbf{x} \in \mathbb{R}^N$. We measure this quantity according to the following measurement model,

$$\mathbf{y} = \mathbf{Cx} + \mathbf{n},$$

where $\mathbf{n} \sim \mathcal{N}(\mathbf{0}, \mathbf{R})$ is measurement noise that is statistically independent from $\mathbf{x}$. Provide an expression for $p(\mathbf{y}|\mathbf{x})$.

(ii) Form the joint likelihood for $\mathbf{x}$ and $\mathbf{y}$ by filling in the following:

$$p(\mathbf{x}, \mathbf{y}) = p(\mathbf{y}|\mathbf{x})p(\mathbf{x}) = \mathcal{N}\left(\begin{bmatrix} ? \\ ? \end{bmatrix}, \begin{bmatrix} ? & ? \\ ? & ? \end{bmatrix} \right).$$

(iii) Now factor the joint likelihood the other way:

$$p(\mathbf{x}, \mathbf{y}) = p(\mathbf{x}|\mathbf{y})p(\mathbf{y}).$$

Provide expressions for $p(\mathbf{x}|\mathbf{y})$ and $p(\mathbf{y})$.

(iv) The Bayesian posterior is $p(\mathbf{x}|\mathbf{y})$. Looking at this expression, will the covariance be larger or smaller than that of $p(\mathbf{x})$? Explain briefly.

3

Linear-Gaussian Estimation

This chapter will introduce some of the classic results from estimation theory for linear models and Gaussian random variables, including the *Kalman filter (KF)* (Kalman, 1960b). We will begin with a batch, discrete-time estimation problem that will provide important insights into the nonlinear extension of the work in subsequent chapters. From the batch approach, we will show how the recursive methods can be developed. Finally, we will examine how to handle continuous-time motion models and connect these to the discrete-time results as well as to Gaussian process regression from the machine-learning world. Classic books that cover linear estimation include Bryson (1975), Maybeck (1994), Stengel (1994), and Bar-Shalom et al. (2001).

3.1 Batch Discrete-Time Estimation

We will begin by setting up the problem that we want to solve and then discuss methods of solution.

3.1.1 Problem Setup

In much of this chapter, we will consider *discrete-time, linear, time-varying* equations (see Appendix C.3 for converting from continuous time). We define the following motion and observation models:

$$\text{motion model:} \quad \mathbf{x}_k = \mathbf{A}_{k-1}\mathbf{x}_{k-1} + \mathbf{v}_k + \mathbf{w}_k, \quad k = 1 \ldots K \quad (3.1\text{a})$$
$$\text{observation model:} \quad \mathbf{y}_k = \mathbf{C}_k\mathbf{x}_k + \mathbf{n}_k, \quad k = 0 \ldots K \quad (3.1\text{b})$$

where k is the discrete-time index and K its maximum. The variables in (3.1) have the following meanings:

$$\begin{aligned}
\text{system state:} \quad & \mathbf{x}_k \in \mathbb{R}^N \\
\text{initial state:} \quad & \mathbf{x}_0 \in \mathbb{R}^N \sim \mathcal{N}\left(\check{\mathbf{x}}_0, \check{\mathbf{P}}_0\right) \\
\text{input:} \quad & \mathbf{v}_k \in \mathbb{R}^N \\
\text{process noise:} \quad & \mathbf{w}_k \in \mathbb{R}^N \sim \mathcal{N}\left(\mathbf{0}, \mathbf{Q}_k\right) \\
\text{measurement:} \quad & \mathbf{y}_k \in \mathbb{R}^M \\
\text{measurement noise:} \quad & \mathbf{n}_k \in \mathbb{R}^M \sim \mathcal{N}\left(\mathbf{0}, \mathbf{R}_k\right)
\end{aligned}$$

These are all *random variables*, except $\mathbf{v}_k$, which is deterministic.[1] The noise variables and initial state knowledge are all assumed to be uncorrelated with one another (and with themselves at different timesteps). The matrix $\mathbf{A}_k \in \mathbb{R}^{N \times N}$ is called the *transition matrix*. The matrix $\mathbf{C}_k \in \mathbb{R}^{M \times N}$ is called the *observation matrix*.

Although we want to know the state of the system (at all times), we only have access to the following quantities and must base our *estimate*, $\hat{\mathbf{x}}_k$, on just this information:

(i) The initial state knowledge, $\check{\mathbf{x}}_0$, and the associated covariance matrix, $\check{\mathbf{P}}_0$; sometimes we do not have this piece of information and must do without.[2]

(ii) The inputs, $\mathbf{v}_k$, which typically come from the output of our controller and so are known;[3] we also have the associated process noise covariance, $\mathbf{Q}_k$.

(iii) The measurements, $\mathbf{y}_{k,\text{meas}}$, which are *realizations* of the associated random variables, $\mathbf{y}_k$, and the associated covariance matrix, $\mathbf{R}_k$.

Based on the models in the previous section, we define the state estimation problem as follows:

The problem of state estimation *is to come up with an estimate, $\hat{\mathbf{x}}_k$, of the true state of a system, at one or more timesteps, k, given knowledge of the initial state, $\check{\mathbf{x}}_0$, a sequence of measurements, $\mathbf{y}_{0:K,\text{meas}}$, a sequence of inputs, $\mathbf{v}_{1:K}$, as well as knowledge of the system's motion and observation models.*

The rest of this chapter will present a suite of techniques for addressing this state estimation problem. Our approach will always be not only to attempt to come up with a state estimate but also to quantify the uncertainty in that estimate.

To set ourselves up for what is to follow in the later chapters on nonlinear estimation, we will begin by formulating a batch *linear-Gaussian (LG)* estimation problem. The batch solution is very useful for computing state estimates after the fact because it uses all the measurements in the estimation of all the states at once (hence the usage of 'batch'). However, a batch method cannot be used in real time since we cannot employ future measurements to estimate past states. For this we will need recursive state estimators, which will be covered later in this chapter.

To show the relationship between various concepts, we will set up the batch LG estimation problem using two different paradigms:

(i) *Bayesian inference*; here we update a prior density over states (based on the initial state knowledge, inputs, and motion model) with our measurements, to produce a posterior (Gaussian) density over states.

---

[1] Sometimes the input is specialized to be of the form $\mathbf{v}_k = \mathbf{B}_k \mathbf{u}_k$, where $\mathbf{u}_k \in \mathbb{R}^U$ is now the input and $\mathbf{B}_k \in \mathbb{R}^{N \times U}$ is called the *control matrix*. We will use this form as needed in our development.

[2] We will use $(\hat{\cdot})$ to indicate *posterior* estimates (including measurements) and $(\check{\cdot})$ to indicate *prior* estimates (not including measurements).

[3] In robotics, this input is sometimes replaced by an interoceptive measurement. This is a bit of a dangerous thing to do since it then conflates two sources of uncertainty: process noise and measurement noise. If this is done, we must be careful to inflate $\mathbf{Q}$ appropriately to reflect the two uncertainties.

(ii) *Maximum A Posteriori (MAP)*; here we employ optimization to find the most likely posterior state given the information we have (initial state knowledge, measurements, inputs).

While these approaches are somewhat different in nature, it turns out that we arrive at the exact same answer for the LG problem. This is because the full Bayesian posterior is exactly Gaussian. Therefore, the optimization approach will find the maximum (i.e., mode) of a Gaussian, and this is the same as the mean. It is important to pursue these two avenues because when we move to nonlinear, non-Gaussian systems in subsequent chapters, the mean and mode of the posterior will no longer be the same and the two methods will arrive at different answers. We will start with the MAP optimization method as it is a bit easier to explain.

3.1.2 Maximum A Posteriori

In batch estimation, our goal is to solve the following MAP problem:

$$\hat{\mathbf{x}} = \arg\max_{\mathbf{x}} p(\mathbf{x}|\mathbf{v}, \mathbf{y}), \qquad (3.2)$$

which is to say that we want to find the best single estimate for the state of the system (at all timesteps), $\hat{\mathbf{x}}$, given the prior information, $\mathbf{v}$, and measurements, $\mathbf{y}$.[4] Note that we have

$$\mathbf{x} = \mathbf{x}_{0:K} = (\mathbf{x}_0, \ldots, \mathbf{x}_K), \quad \mathbf{v} = (\check{\mathbf{x}}_0, \mathbf{v}_{1:K}) = (\check{\mathbf{x}}_0, \mathbf{v}_1, \ldots, \mathbf{v}_K),$$
$$\mathbf{y} = \mathbf{y}_{0:K} = (\mathbf{y}_0, \ldots, \mathbf{y}_K),$$

where the timestep range may be dropped for convenience of notation (when the range is the largest possible for that variable).[5] Note that we have included the initial state information with the inputs to the system; together, these define our prior over the state. The measurements serve to improve this prior information.

We begin by rewriting the MAP estimate using Bayes' rule:

$$\hat{\mathbf{x}} = \arg\max_{\mathbf{x}} p(\mathbf{x}|\mathbf{v}, \mathbf{y}) = \arg\max_{\mathbf{x}} \frac{p(\mathbf{y}|\mathbf{x}, \mathbf{v})p(\mathbf{x}|\mathbf{v})}{p(\mathbf{y}|\mathbf{v})}$$
$$= \arg\max_{\mathbf{x}} p(\mathbf{y}|\mathbf{x})p(\mathbf{x}|\mathbf{v}), \qquad (3.3)$$

where we drop the denominator because it does not depend on $\mathbf{x}$. We also drop $\mathbf{v}$ in $p(\mathbf{y}|\mathbf{x}, \mathbf{v})$ since it does not affect $\mathbf{y}$ in our system if $\mathbf{x}$ is known (see observation model).

A vital assumption that we are making is that all of the noise variables, $\mathbf{w}_k$ and $\mathbf{n}_k$ for $k = 0 \ldots K$, are uncorrelated. This allows us to use Bayes' rule to factor $p(\mathbf{y}|\mathbf{x})$ in the following way:

$$p(\mathbf{y}|\mathbf{x}) = \prod_{k=0}^{K} p(\mathbf{y}_k | \mathbf{x}_k). \qquad (3.4)$$

---

[4] We will be a bit loose on notation here by dropping 'meas' from $\mathbf{y}_{\text{meas}}$.

[5] We will sometimes refer to *lifted form* when discussing variables and equations over the entire trajectory rather than a single timestep. It should be clear when quantities are in lifted form, as they will not have a subscript for the timestep.

Furthermore, Bayes' rule allows us to factor $p(\mathbf{x}|\mathbf{v})$ as

$$p(\mathbf{x}|\mathbf{v}) = p(\mathbf{x}_0 \,|\, \check{\mathbf{x}}_0) \prod_{k=1}^{K} p(\mathbf{x}_k \,|\, \mathbf{x}_{k-1}, \mathbf{v}_k). \tag{3.5}$$

In this linear system, the component (Gaussian) densities are given by

$$p(\mathbf{x}_0 \,|\, \check{\mathbf{x}}_0) = \frac{1}{\sqrt{(2\pi)^N \det \check{\mathbf{P}}_0}}$$
$$\times \exp\left(-\frac{1}{2} (\mathbf{x}_0 - \check{\mathbf{x}}_0)^T \check{\mathbf{P}}_0^{-1} (\mathbf{x}_0 - \check{\mathbf{x}}_0)\right), \tag{3.6a}$$

$$p(\mathbf{x}_k \,|\, \mathbf{x}_{k-1}, \mathbf{v}_k) = \frac{1}{\sqrt{(2\pi)^N \det \mathbf{Q}_k}} \exp\left(-\frac{1}{2} (\mathbf{x}_k - \mathbf{A}_{k-1}\mathbf{x}_{k-1} - \mathbf{v}_k)^T\right.$$
$$\left.\times \mathbf{Q}_k^{-1} (\mathbf{x}_k - \mathbf{A}_{k-1}\mathbf{x}_{k-1} - \mathbf{v}_k)\right), \tag{3.6b}$$

$$p(\mathbf{y}_k \,|\, \mathbf{x}_k) = \frac{1}{\sqrt{(2\pi)^M \det \mathbf{R}_k}} \exp\left(-\frac{1}{2} (\mathbf{y}_k - \mathbf{C}_k\mathbf{x}_k)^T\right.$$
$$\left.\times \mathbf{R}_k^{-1} (\mathbf{y}_k - \mathbf{C}_k\mathbf{x}_k)\right). \tag{3.6c}$$

Note that we must have $\check{\mathbf{P}}_0$, $\mathbf{Q}_k$, and $\mathbf{R}_k$ invertible; they are in fact positive-definite by assumption and therefore invertible. To make the optimization easier, we take the logarithm of both sides:[6]

$$\ln(p(\mathbf{y}|\mathbf{x})p(\mathbf{x}\,|\,\mathbf{v})) = \ln p(\mathbf{x}_0\,|\,\check{\mathbf{x}}_0) + \sum_{k=1}^{K} \ln p(\mathbf{x}_k\,|\,\mathbf{x}_{k-1}, \mathbf{v}_k) + \sum_{k=0}^{K} \ln p(\mathbf{y}_k\,|\,\mathbf{x}_k), \tag{3.7}$$

where

$$\ln p(\mathbf{x}_0\,|\,\check{\mathbf{x}}_0) = -\frac{1}{2} (\mathbf{x}_0 - \check{\mathbf{x}}_0)^T \check{\mathbf{P}}_0^{-1} (\mathbf{x}_0 - \check{\mathbf{x}}_0)$$
$$\underbrace{-\frac{1}{2} \ln\left((2\pi)^N \det \check{\mathbf{P}}_0\right)}_{\text{independent of } \mathbf{x}}, \tag{3.8a}$$

$$\ln p(\mathbf{x}_k\,|\,\mathbf{x}_{k-1}, \mathbf{v}_k) = -\frac{1}{2} (\mathbf{x}_k - \mathbf{A}_{k-1}\mathbf{x}_{k-1} - \mathbf{v}_k)^T$$
$$\times \mathbf{Q}_k^{-1} (\mathbf{x}_k - \mathbf{A}_{k-1}\mathbf{x}_{k-1} - \mathbf{v}_k)$$
$$\underbrace{-\frac{1}{2} \ln\left((2\pi)^N \det \mathbf{Q}_k\right)}_{\text{independent of } \mathbf{x}}, \tag{3.8b}$$

---

[6] A logarithm is a monotonically increasing function and therefore will not affect our optimization problem.

$$\ln p(\mathbf{y}_k \,|\, \mathbf{x}_k) = -\frac{1}{2} \left(\mathbf{y}_k - \mathbf{C}_k \mathbf{x}_k\right)^T \mathbf{R}_k^{-1} \left(\mathbf{y}_k - \mathbf{C}_k \mathbf{x}_k\right)$$

$$\underbrace{-\frac{1}{2} \ln \left((2\pi)^M \det \mathbf{R}_k\right)}_{\text{independent of } \mathbf{x}}. \tag{3.8c}$$

Noticing that there are terms in (3.8) that do not depend on $\mathbf{x}$, we define the following quantities:

$$J_{v,k}(\mathbf{x}) = \begin{cases} \frac{1}{2} \left(\mathbf{x}_0 - \check{\mathbf{x}}_0\right)^T \check{\mathbf{P}}_0^{-1} \left(\mathbf{x}_0 - \check{\mathbf{x}}_0\right), & k = 0 \\ \frac{1}{2} \left(\mathbf{x}_k - \mathbf{A}_{k-1}\mathbf{x}_{k-1} - \mathbf{v}_k\right)^T \\ \quad \times \mathbf{Q}_k^{-1} \left(\mathbf{x}_k - \mathbf{A}_{k-1}\mathbf{x}_{k-1} - \mathbf{v}_k\right), & k = 1 \ldots K \end{cases}, \tag{3.9a}$$

$$J_{y,k}(\mathbf{x}) = \frac{1}{2} \left(\mathbf{y}_k - \mathbf{C}_k \mathbf{x}_k\right)^T \mathbf{R}_k^{-1} \left(\mathbf{y}_k - \mathbf{C}_k \mathbf{x}_k\right), \qquad k = 0 \ldots K, \tag{3.9b}$$

which are all squared *Mahalanobis distances*. We then define an overall *objective function*, $J(\mathbf{x})$, that we will seek to minimize with respect to the *design parameter*, $\mathbf{x}$:

$$J(\mathbf{x}) = \sum_{k=0}^{K} \left(J_{v,k}(\mathbf{x}) + J_{y,k}(\mathbf{x})\right). \tag{3.10}$$

We will work with $J(\mathbf{x})$ as is, but note that it is possible to add all kinds of additional terms to this expression that will influence the solution for the best estimate (e.g., constraints, penalty terms). From an optimization perspective, we seek to solve the following problem:

$$\hat{\mathbf{x}} = \arg \min_{\mathbf{x}} J(\mathbf{x}), \tag{3.11}$$

which will result in the same solution for the best estimate, $\hat{\mathbf{x}}$, as (3.2). In other words, we are still finding the best estimate in order to maximize the likelihood of the state given all the data we have. This is an *unconstrained optimization problem* in that we do not have to satisfy any constraints on the design variable, $\mathbf{x}$.

To further simplify our problem, we make use of the fact that equations (3.9) are quadratic in $\mathbf{x}$. To make this more clear, we stack all the known data into a lifted column, $\mathbf{z}$, and recall that $\mathbf{x}$ is also a tall column consisting of all the states:

$$\mathbf{z} = \begin{bmatrix} \check{\mathbf{x}}_0 \\ \mathbf{v}_1 \\ \vdots \\ \mathbf{v}_K \\ \hline \mathbf{y}_0 \\ \mathbf{y}_1 \\ \vdots \\ \mathbf{y}_K \end{bmatrix}, \quad \mathbf{x} = \begin{bmatrix} \mathbf{x}_0 \\ \vdots \\ \mathbf{x}_K \end{bmatrix}. \tag{3.12}$$

We then define the following block-matrix quantities:

$$
\mathbf{H} = \left[\begin{array}{ccccc|cccc}
1 & & & & \\
-\mathbf{A}_0 & 1 & & & \\
& \ddots & & \ddots & \\
& & & -\mathbf{A}_{K-1} & 1 \\
\hline
\mathbf{C}_0 & & & & \\
& \mathbf{C}_1 & & & \\
& & \ddots & & \\
& & & & \mathbf{C}_K
\end{array}\right],
\tag{3.13a}
$$

$$
\mathbf{W} = \left[\begin{array}{cccc|cccc}
\check{\mathbf{P}}_0 & & & & \\
& \mathbf{Q}_1 & & & \\
& & \ddots & & \\
& & & \mathbf{Q}_K & \\
\hline
& & & & \mathbf{R}_0 & \\
& & & & & \mathbf{R}_1 & \\
& & & & & & \ddots & \\
& & & & & & & \mathbf{R}_K
\end{array}\right],
\tag{3.13b}
$$

where only non-zero blocks are shown. The solid partition lines are used to show the boundaries between the parts of the matrices relevant to the prior, $\mathbf{v}$, and the measurements, $\mathbf{y}$, in the lifted data vector, $\mathbf{z}$. Under these definitions, we find that

$$
J(\mathbf{x}) = \frac{1}{2} (\mathbf{z} - \mathbf{H}\mathbf{x})^T \mathbf{W}^{-1} (\mathbf{z} - \mathbf{H}\mathbf{x}),
\tag{3.14}
$$

which is exactly quadratic in $\mathbf{x}$. We note that we also have

$$
p(\mathbf{z}|\mathbf{x}) = \eta \exp\left(-\frac{1}{2} (\mathbf{z} - \mathbf{H}\mathbf{x})^T \mathbf{W}^{-1} (\mathbf{z} - \mathbf{H}\mathbf{x})\right),
\tag{3.15}
$$

where η is a normalization constant.

Since $J(\mathbf{x})$ is exactly a paraboloid, we can find its minimum in closed form. Simply set the partial derivative with respect to the design variable, $\mathbf{x}$, to zero:

$$
\left.\frac{\partial J(\mathbf{x})}{\partial \mathbf{x}^T}\right|_{\hat{\mathbf{x}}} = -\mathbf{H}^T \mathbf{W}^{-1} (\mathbf{z} - \mathbf{H}\hat{\mathbf{x}}) = 0,
\tag{3.16a}
$$

$$
\Rightarrow \left(\mathbf{H}^T \mathbf{W}^{-1} \mathbf{H}\right) \hat{\mathbf{x}} = \mathbf{H}^T \mathbf{W}^{-1} \mathbf{z}.
\tag{3.16b}
$$

The solution of (3.16b), $\hat{\mathbf{x}}$, is the classic *batch least-squares* solution and is equivalent to the *fixed-interval smoother*[7] from classic estimation theory. The *batch least-squares* solution employs the pseudoinverse.[8] Computationally, to solve this linear system of equations, we would never actually invert $\mathbf{H}^T \mathbf{W}^{-1} \mathbf{H}$

---

[7] The fixed-interval smoother is usually presented in a recursive formulation. We will discuss this in more detail later.

[8] Also called the *Moore–Penrose pseudoinverse*.

Figure 3.1 The batch linear-Gaussian problem is like a mass-spring system. Each term in the objective function represents energy stored in one of the springs, which varies as the carts' (i.e, masses) positions are shifted. The optimal posterior solution corresponds to the minimum energy state.

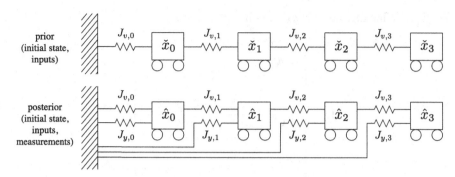

Figure 3.1 The batch linear-Gaussian problem is like a mass-spring system. Each term in the objective function represents energy stored in one of the springs, which varies as the carts' (i.e, masses) positions are shifted. The optimal posterior solution corresponds to the minimum energy state.

(even if it were densely populated). As we will see later, we have a special block-tridiagonal structure to $\mathbf{H}^T\mathbf{W}^{-1}\mathbf{H}$, and hence a sparse-equation solver can be used to solve this system efficiently.[9]

One intuitive explanation of the batch linear-Gaussian problem is that it is like a mass-spring system, as shown in Figure 3.1. Each term in the objective function represents energy stored in one of the springs, which varies as the masses' positions are shifted. The optimal posterior solution corresponds to the minimum-energy state.

3.1.3 Bayesian Inference

Now that we have seen the optimization approach to batch LG estimation, we take a look at computing the full Bayesian posterior, $p(\mathbf{x}|\mathbf{v},\mathbf{y})$, not just the maximum. This approach requires us to begin with a prior density over states, which we will then update based on the measurements.

In our case, a prior can be built up using the knowledge of the initial state, as well as the inputs to the system: $p(\mathbf{x}|\mathbf{v})$. We will use just the motion model to build this prior:

$$\mathbf{x}_k = \mathbf{A}_{k-1}\mathbf{x}_{k-1} + \mathbf{v}_k + \mathbf{w}_k. \tag{3.17}$$

In *lifted matrix form*,[10] we can write this as

$$\mathbf{x} = \mathbf{A}(\mathbf{v}+\mathbf{w}), \tag{3.18}$$

where $\mathbf{w}$ is the lifted form of the initial state and process noise and

$$\mathbf{A} = \begin{bmatrix} \mathbf{1} & & & & & \\ \mathbf{A}_0 & \mathbf{1} & & & & \\ \mathbf{A}_1\mathbf{A}_0 & \mathbf{A}_1 & \mathbf{1} & & & \\ \vdots & \vdots & \vdots & \ddots & & \\ \mathbf{A}_{K-2}\cdots\mathbf{A}_0 & \mathbf{A}_{K-2}\cdots\mathbf{A}_1 & \mathbf{A}_{K-2}\cdots\mathbf{A}_2 & \cdots & \mathbf{1} & \\ \mathbf{A}_{K-1}\cdots\mathbf{A}_0 & \mathbf{A}_{K-1}\cdots\mathbf{A}_1 & \mathbf{A}_{K-1}\cdots\mathbf{A}_2 & \cdots & \mathbf{A}_{K-1} & \mathbf{1} \end{bmatrix}$$

$$\tag{3.19}$$

is the lifted transition matrix, which we see is lower-triangular. The lifted mean is then

---

[9] True for the problem posed; not true for all LG problems.

[10] 'Lifted' here refers to the fact that we are considering what happens at the entire trajectory level.

$$\check{\mathbf{x}} = E[\mathbf{x}] = E[\mathbf{A}(\mathbf{v} + \mathbf{w})] = \mathbf{A}\mathbf{v}, \tag{3.20}$$

and lifted covariance is

$$\check{\mathbf{P}} = E\left[(\mathbf{x} - E[\mathbf{x}])(\mathbf{x} - E[\mathbf{x}])^T\right] = \mathbf{A}\mathbf{Q}\mathbf{A}^T, \tag{3.21}$$

where $\mathbf{Q} = E[\mathbf{w}\mathbf{w}^T] = \text{diag}(\check{\mathbf{P}}_0, \mathbf{Q}_1, \ldots, \mathbf{Q}_K)$. Our prior can then be neatly expressed as

$$p(\mathbf{x}|\mathbf{v}) = \mathcal{N}\left(\check{\mathbf{x}}, \check{\mathbf{P}}\right) = \mathcal{N}\left(\mathbf{A}\mathbf{v}, \mathbf{A}\mathbf{Q}\mathbf{A}^T\right). \tag{3.22}$$

We next turn to the measurements.

The measurement model is

$$\mathbf{y}_k = \mathbf{C}_k\mathbf{x}_k + \mathbf{n}_k. \tag{3.23}$$

This can also be written in lifted form as

$$\mathbf{y} = \mathbf{C}\mathbf{x} + \mathbf{n}, \tag{3.24}$$

where $\mathbf{n}$ is the lifted form of the measurement noise and

$$\mathbf{C} = \text{diag}\left(\mathbf{C}_0, \mathbf{C}_1, \ldots, \mathbf{C}_K\right) \tag{3.25}$$

is the lifted observation matrix.

The joint density of the prior lifted state and the measurements can now be written as

$$p(\mathbf{x}, \mathbf{y}|\mathbf{v}) = \mathcal{N}\left(\begin{bmatrix} \check{\mathbf{x}} \\ \mathbf{C}\check{\mathbf{x}} \end{bmatrix}, \begin{bmatrix} \check{\mathbf{P}} & \check{\mathbf{P}}\mathbf{C}^T \\ \mathbf{C}\check{\mathbf{P}} & \mathbf{C}\check{\mathbf{P}}\mathbf{C}^T + \mathbf{R} \end{bmatrix}\right), \tag{3.26}$$

where $\mathbf{R} = E[\mathbf{n}\mathbf{n}^T] = \text{diag}(\mathbf{R}_0, \mathbf{R}_1, \ldots, \mathbf{R}_K)$. We can factor this according to

$$p(\mathbf{x}, \mathbf{y}|\mathbf{v}) = p(\mathbf{x}|\mathbf{v}, \mathbf{y})p(\mathbf{y}|\mathbf{v}). \tag{3.27}$$

We only care about the first factor, which is the full Bayesian posterior. This can be written, using the approach outlined in Section 2.2.2, as

$$p(\mathbf{x}|\mathbf{v}, \mathbf{y}) = \mathcal{N}\Big(\check{\mathbf{x}} + \check{\mathbf{P}}\mathbf{C}^T(\mathbf{C}\check{\mathbf{P}}\mathbf{C}^T + \mathbf{R})^{-1}(\mathbf{y} - \mathbf{C}\check{\mathbf{x}}),$$
$$\check{\mathbf{P}} - \check{\mathbf{P}}\mathbf{C}^T(\mathbf{C}\check{\mathbf{P}}\mathbf{C}^T + \mathbf{R})^{-1}\mathbf{C}\check{\mathbf{P}}\Big). \tag{3.28}$$

Using the SMW identity from equations (2.124), this can be manipulated into the following form:

$$p(\mathbf{x}|\mathbf{v}, \mathbf{y}) = \mathcal{N}\Big(\underbrace{\left(\check{\mathbf{P}}^{-1} + \mathbf{C}^T\mathbf{R}^{-1}\mathbf{C}\right)^{-1}\left(\check{\mathbf{P}}^{-1}\check{\mathbf{x}} + \mathbf{C}^T\mathbf{R}^{-1}\mathbf{y}\right)}_{\hat{\mathbf{x}}, \text{ mean}},$$
$$\underbrace{\left(\check{\mathbf{P}}^{-1} + \mathbf{C}^T\mathbf{R}^{-1}\mathbf{C}\right)^{-1}}_{\hat{\mathbf{P}}, \text{ covariance}}\Big). \tag{3.29}$$

We can actually implement a batch estimator based on this equation, since it represents the full Bayesian posterior, but this may not be efficient.

To see the connection to the optimization approach discussed earlier, we rearrange the mean expression to arrive at a linear system for $\hat{\mathbf{x}}$,

$$\underbrace{\left(\check{\mathbf{P}}^{-1} + \mathbf{C}^T\mathbf{R}^{-1}\mathbf{C}\right)}_{\hat{\mathbf{P}}^{-1}} \hat{\mathbf{x}} = \check{\mathbf{P}}^{-1}\check{\mathbf{x}} + \mathbf{C}^T\mathbf{R}^{-1}\mathbf{y}, \qquad (3.30)$$

and we see the inverse covariance appearing on the left-hand side. Substituting in $\check{\mathbf{x}} = \mathbf{A}\mathbf{v}$ and $\check{\mathbf{P}}^{-1} = \left(\mathbf{A}\mathbf{Q}\mathbf{A}^T\right)^{-1} = \mathbf{A}^{-T}\mathbf{Q}^{-1}\mathbf{A}^{-1}$ we can rewrite this as

$$\underbrace{\left(\mathbf{A}^{-T}\mathbf{Q}^{-1}\mathbf{A}^{-1} + \mathbf{C}^T\mathbf{R}^{-1}\mathbf{C}\right)}_{\hat{\mathbf{P}}^{-1}} \hat{\mathbf{x}} = \mathbf{A}^{-T}\mathbf{Q}^{-1}\mathbf{v} + \mathbf{C}^T\mathbf{R}^{-1}\mathbf{y}. \qquad (3.31)$$

We see that this requires computing $\mathbf{A}^{-1}$. It turns out this has a beautifully simple form,[11]

$$\mathbf{A}^{-1} = \begin{bmatrix} 1 & & & & & \\ -\mathbf{A}_0 & 1 & & & & \\ & -\mathbf{A}_1 & 1 & & & \\ & & -\mathbf{A}_2 & \ddots & & \\ & & & \ddots & 1 & \\ & & & & -\mathbf{A}_{K-1} & 1 \end{bmatrix}, \qquad (3.32)$$

which is still lower-triangular but also very sparse (only the main diagonal and the one below are non-zero). If we define

$$\mathbf{z} = \begin{bmatrix} \mathbf{v} \\ \mathbf{y} \end{bmatrix}, \quad \mathbf{H} = \begin{bmatrix} \mathbf{A}^{-1} \\ \mathbf{C} \end{bmatrix}, \quad \mathbf{W} = \begin{bmatrix} \mathbf{Q} & \\ & \mathbf{R} \end{bmatrix}, \qquad (3.33)$$

we can rewrite our system of equations as

$$\left(\mathbf{H}^T\mathbf{W}^{-1}\mathbf{H}\right) \hat{\mathbf{x}} = \mathbf{H}^T\mathbf{W}^{-1}\mathbf{z}, \qquad (3.34)$$

which is identical to the optimization solution discussed earlier.

Again, it must be stressed that the reason the Bayesian approach produces the same answer as the optimization solution for our LG estimation problem is that the full Bayesian posterior is exactly Gaussian and the mean and mode (i.e., maximum) of a Gaussian are one and the same.

3.1.4 Existence, Uniqueness, and Observability

Most of the classic LG estimation results can be viewed as a special case of (3.34). It is therefore important to ask when (3.34) has a unique solution, which is the subject of this section.

---

[11] The special sparsity of $\mathbf{A}^{-1}$ is in fact critical to all classic LG results, as we will discuss later. This makes the left-hand side of (3.31) exactly block-tridiagonal. This means we can solve for $\hat{\mathbf{x}}$ in $O(K)$ time instead of the usual $O(K^3)$ time for solving linear systems. This leads to the popular recursive solution known as the Kalman filter/smoother. The sparsity comes from the fact that the system model obeys the Markov property.

Examining (3.34), we have from basic linear algebra that $\hat{\mathbf{x}}$ will exist and be a unique solution if and only if $\mathbf{H}^T\mathbf{W}^{-1}\mathbf{H}$ is invertible, whereupon

$$\hat{\mathbf{x}} = \left(\mathbf{H}^T\mathbf{W}^{-1}\mathbf{H}\right)^{-1}\mathbf{H}^T\mathbf{W}^{-1}\mathbf{z}. \tag{3.35}$$

The question is then, when is $\mathbf{H}^T\mathbf{W}^{-1}\mathbf{H}$ invertible? From linear algebra again, we know that a necessary and sufficient condition for invertibility is

$$\text{rank}\left(\mathbf{H}^T\mathbf{W}^{-1}\mathbf{H}\right) = N(K+1), \tag{3.36}$$

because we have dim $\mathbf{x} = N(K+1)$. Since $\mathbf{W}^{-1}$ is real symmetric positive-definite,[12] we know that it can be dropped from the test so that we only need

$$\text{rank}\left(\mathbf{H}^T\mathbf{H}\right) = \text{rank}\left(\mathbf{H}^T\right) = N(K+1). \tag{3.37}$$

In other words, we need $N(K+1)$ linearly independent rows (or columns) in the matrix $\mathbf{H}^T$.

We now have two cases that should be considered:

(i) We have good prior knowledge of the initial state, $\check{\mathbf{x}}_0$.

(ii) We do not have good prior knowledge of the initial state.

The first case is much easier than the second.

Case (i): Knowledge of Initial State

Writing out $\mathbf{H}^T$ our rank test takes the form

$\text{rank } \mathbf{H}^T$

$$= \text{rank}\begin{bmatrix} 1 & -\mathbf{A}_0^T & & & & \mathbf{C}_0^T & & & & \\ & 1 & -\mathbf{A}_1^T & & & & \mathbf{C}_1^T & & & \\ & & 1 & \ddots & & & & \mathbf{C}_2^T & & \\ & & & \ddots & -\mathbf{A}_{K-1}^T & & & & \ddots & \\ & & & & 1 & & & & & \mathbf{C}_K^T \end{bmatrix}, \tag{3.38}$$

which we see is exactly in row-echelon form. This means the matrix is full rank, $N(K+1)$, since all the block-rows are linearly independent. This means there will always be a unique solution for $\hat{\mathbf{x}}$ provided that

$$\check{\mathbf{P}}_0 > 0, \quad \mathbf{Q}_k > 0, \tag{3.39}$$

where > 0 means a matrix is positive-definite (and hence invertible). The intuition behind this is that the prior already provides a complete solution to the problem. The measurements only serve to adjust the answer. Note that these are sufficient but not necessary conditions.

---

[12] This follows from $\mathbf{Q}$ and $\mathbf{R}$ being real symmetric positive-definite.

Case (ii): No Knowledge of Initial State

Each block-column of $\mathbf{H}^T$ represents some piece of information that we have about the system. The first block-column represents our knowledge about the initial state. Thus, removing knowledge of the initial state results in the rank test considering

$$
\operatorname{rank} \mathbf{H}^T
$$

$$
= \operatorname{rank} \left[\begin{array}{cccc|cccc} -\mathbf{A}_0^T & & & & \mathbf{C}_0^T & & & \\ \hline 1 & -\mathbf{A}_1^T & & & & \mathbf{C}_1^T & & \\ & 1 & \ddots & & & & \mathbf{C}_2^T & \\ & & \ddots & -\mathbf{A}_{K-1}^T & & & & \ddots \\ & & & 1 & & & & \mathbf{C}_K^T \end{array} \right], \quad (3.40)
$$

which we note has $K+1$ block-rows (each of size N). Moving the top block-row to the bottom does not alter the rank:

$$
\operatorname{rank} \mathbf{H}^T
$$

$$
= \operatorname{rank} \left[\begin{array}{cccc|cccc} 1 & -\mathbf{A}_1^T & & & \mathbf{C}_1^T & & & \\ & 1 & \ddots & & & \mathbf{C}_2^T & & \\ & & \ddots & -\mathbf{A}_{K-1}^T & & & \ddots & \\ & & & 1 & & & & \mathbf{C}_K^T \\ \hline -\mathbf{A}_0^T & & & & \mathbf{C}_0^T & & & \end{array} \right]. \quad (3.41)
$$

Except for the bottom block-row, this is in row-echelon form. Again without altering the rank, we can add to the bottom block-row, $\mathbf{A}_0^T$ times the first block-row, $\mathbf{A}_0^T \mathbf{A}_1^T$ times the second block-row, ..., and $\mathbf{A}_0^T \cdots \mathbf{A}_{K-1}^T$ times the Kth block-row, to see that

$$
\operatorname{rank} \mathbf{H}^T
$$

$$
= \operatorname{rank} \left[\begin{array}{cccc|ccccc} 1 & -\mathbf{A}_1^T & & & \mathbf{C}_1^T & & & & \\ & 1 & \ddots & & & \mathbf{C}_2^T & & & \\ & & \ddots & -\mathbf{A}_{K-1}^T & & & \ddots & & \\ & & & 1 & & & & \mathbf{C}_K^T & \\ \hline & & & & \mathbf{C}_0^T & \mathbf{A}_0^T \mathbf{C}_1^T & \mathbf{A}_0^T \mathbf{A}_1^T \mathbf{C}_2^T & \cdots & \mathbf{A}_0^T \cdots \mathbf{A}_{K-1}^T \mathbf{C}_K^T \end{array} \right].
$$

$$(3.42)$$

Examining this last expression, we notice immediately that the lower-left partition is zero. Moreover, the upper-left partition is in row-echelon form and in fact is of full rank, NK, since every row has a 'leading one'. Our overall rank condition for $\mathbf{H}^T$ therefore collapses to showing that the lower-right partition has rank N:

$$
\operatorname{rank} \begin{bmatrix} \mathbf{C}_0^T & \mathbf{A}_0^T \mathbf{C}_1^T & \mathbf{A}_0^T \mathbf{A}_1^T \mathbf{C}_2^T & \cdots & \mathbf{A}_0^T \cdots \mathbf{A}_{K-1}^T \mathbf{C}_K^T \end{bmatrix} = N. \quad (3.43)
$$

If we further assume the system is time-invariant such that for all k we have $\mathbf{A}_k = A$ and $\mathbf{C}_k = C$ (we use italicized symbols to avoid confusion with lifted form) and we make the not-too-restrictive assumption that $K \gg N$, we may further simplify this condition.

To do so, we employ the *Cayley–Hamilton theorem* from linear algebra. Because $\boldsymbol{A}$ is $N \times N$, its characteristic equation has at most N terms, and therefore any power of $\boldsymbol{A}$ greater than or equal to N can be rewritten as a linear combination of $\boldsymbol{1}, \boldsymbol{A}, \ldots, \boldsymbol{A}^{(N-1)}$. By extension, for any $k \geq N$, we can write

Cayley–Hamilton theorem: Every square matrix, $\boldsymbol{A}$, over the real field, satisfies its own characteristic equation, $\det(\lambda\boldsymbol{1} - \boldsymbol{A}) = 0$.

$$\left(\boldsymbol{A}^T\right)^{(k-1)} \boldsymbol{C}^T$$
$$= a_0 \boldsymbol{1}^T \boldsymbol{C}^T + a_1 \boldsymbol{A}^T \boldsymbol{C}^T + a_2 \boldsymbol{A}^T \boldsymbol{A}^T \boldsymbol{C}^T + \cdots + a_{N-1} \left(\boldsymbol{A}^T\right)^{(N-1)} \boldsymbol{C}^T \tag{3.44}$$

for some set of scalars, $a_0, a_1, \ldots, a_{N-1}$, not all zero. Since row-rank and column-rank are the same for any matrix, we can conclude that

$$\mathrm{rank} \begin{bmatrix} \boldsymbol{C}^T & \boldsymbol{A}^T \boldsymbol{C}^T & \boldsymbol{A}^T \boldsymbol{A}^T \boldsymbol{C}^T & \cdots & \left(\boldsymbol{A}^T\right)^K \boldsymbol{C}^T \end{bmatrix}$$
$$= \mathrm{rank} \begin{bmatrix} \boldsymbol{C}^T & \boldsymbol{A}^T \boldsymbol{C}^T & \cdots & \left(\boldsymbol{A}^T\right)^{(N-1)} \boldsymbol{C}^T \end{bmatrix}. \tag{3.45}$$

Defining the *observability matrix*, $\mathcal{O}$, as

$$\mathcal{O} = \begin{bmatrix} \boldsymbol{C} \\ \boldsymbol{C}\boldsymbol{A} \\ \vdots \\ \boldsymbol{C}\boldsymbol{A}^{(N-1)} \end{bmatrix}, \tag{3.46}$$

our rank condition is

$$\mathrm{rank}\, \mathcal{O} = N. \tag{3.47}$$

Readers familiar with linear control theory will recognize this as precisely the test for *observability* (Kalman, 1960a). Thus, we can see the direct connection between observability and invertibility of $\mathbf{H}^T \mathbf{W}^{-1} \mathbf{H}$. The overall conditions for existence and uniqueness of a solution to (3.34) are

A system is *observable* if the initial state can be uniquely inferred based on measurements gathered in a finite amount of time.

$$\mathbf{Q}_k > 0, \quad \mathbf{R}_k > 0, \quad \mathrm{rank}\, \mathcal{O} = N, \tag{3.48}$$

where > 0 means a matrix is positive-definite (and hence invertible). Again, these are sufficient but not necessary conditions.

Interpretation

We can return to the mass-spring analogy to better understand the observability issue. Figure 3.2 shows a few examples. With the initial state and all the inputs (top example), the system is always observable since it is impossible to move any group of carts left or right without altering the length of at least one spring. This means there is a unique minimum-energy state. The same is true for the middle example, even though there is no knowledge of the initial state. The bottom example is unobservable since the entire chain of carts can be moved left or right without changing the amount of energy stored in the springs. This means the minimum-energy state is not unique.

Figure 3.2 In a single dimension, the mass-spring system is observable if there is no group of carts that can be shifted left or right without altering the energy state of at least one spring. The top example uses the initial state and inputs, so this is always observable. The middle example is also observable since any movement changes at least one spring. The bottom example is not observable since the whole chain of carts can be moved left-right together without changing any spring lengths; in one dimension, this only happens with no initial state and no measurements.

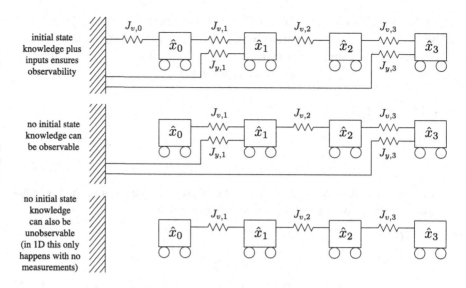

3.1.5 MAP Covariance

Looking back to (3.35), $\hat{\mathbf{x}}$ represents the most likely estimate of $\mathbf{x}$, the true state. One important question to ask is how confident are we in $\hat{\mathbf{x}}$? It turns out we can re-interpret the least-squares solution as a Gaussian estimate for $\mathbf{x}$ in the following way:

$$\underbrace{\left(\mathbf{H}^T\mathbf{W}^{-1}\mathbf{H}\right)}_{\text{inverse covariance}} \underbrace{\hat{\mathbf{x}}}_{\text{mean}} = \underbrace{\mathbf{H}^T\mathbf{W}^{-1}\mathbf{z}}_{\text{information vector}}. \tag{3.49}$$

The right-hand side is referred to as the *information vector*. To see this, we employ Bayes' rule to rewrite (3.15) as

$$p(\mathbf{x}|\mathbf{z}) = \beta \exp\left(-\frac{1}{2}\left(\mathbf{H}\mathbf{x} - \mathbf{z}\right)^T \mathbf{W}^{-1}\left(\mathbf{H}\mathbf{x} - \mathbf{z}\right)\right), \tag{3.50}$$

where β is a new normalization constant. We then substitute (3.35) in and, after a little manipulation, find that

$$p(\mathbf{x}|\hat{\mathbf{x}}) = \kappa \exp\left(-\frac{1}{2}\left(\mathbf{x} - \hat{\mathbf{x}}\right)^T \left(\mathbf{H}^T\mathbf{W}^{-1}\mathbf{H}\right)\left(\mathbf{x} - \hat{\mathbf{x}}\right)\right), \tag{3.51}$$

where κ is yet another normalization constant. We see from this that $\mathcal{N}\left(\hat{\mathbf{x}}, \hat{\mathbf{P}}\right)$ is a Gaussian estimator for $\mathbf{x}$ whose mean is the optimization solution and whose covariance is $\hat{\mathbf{P}} = \left(\mathbf{H}^T\mathbf{W}^{-1}\mathbf{H}\right)^{-1}$.

Another way to explain this is to directly take the expectation of the estimate. We notice that

$$\mathbf{x} - \underbrace{\left(\mathbf{H}^T\mathbf{W}^{-1}\mathbf{H}\right)^{-1}\mathbf{H}^T\mathbf{W}^{-1}\mathbf{z}}_{E[\mathbf{x}]} = \left(\mathbf{H}^T\mathbf{W}^{-1}\mathbf{H}\right)^{-1}\mathbf{H}^T\mathbf{W}^{-1}\underbrace{\left(\mathbf{H}\mathbf{x} - \mathbf{z}\right)}_{\mathbf{s}},$$

$$\tag{3.52}$$

where

$$\mathbf{s} = \begin{bmatrix}\mathbf{w}\\\mathbf{n}\end{bmatrix}. \tag{3.53}$$

In this case we have

$$\hat{\mathbf{P}} = E\left[(\mathbf{x} - E[\mathbf{x}])\,(\mathbf{x} - E[\mathbf{x}])^T\right]$$

$$= \left(\mathbf{H}^T\mathbf{W}^{-1}\mathbf{H}\right)^{-1}\mathbf{H}^T\mathbf{W}^{-1}\underbrace{E\left[\mathbf{s}\,\mathbf{s}^T\right]}_{\mathbf{W}}\mathbf{W}^{-1}\mathbf{H}\left(\mathbf{H}^T\mathbf{W}^{-1}\mathbf{H}\right)^{-1},$$

$$= \left(\mathbf{H}^T\mathbf{W}^{-1}\mathbf{H}\right)^{-1}, \tag{3.54}$$

which is the same result as above.

We will see in the next chapter on nonlinear estimation that the Hessian of the MAP cost function can still be used as an approximation of the inverse covariance matrix of our estimate. In the linear case, the inverse covariance is also equal to the *Fisher information matrix (FIM)* discussed in Sections 2.1.10 and 2.2.14, as we are performing right at the *Cramér–Rao lower bound (CRLB)*.

3.2 Recursive Discrete-Time Smoothing

The batch solution is appealing in that it is fairly easy to set up and understand from a least-squares perspective. However, brute-force solving the resulting system of linear equations will likely not be very efficient for most situations. Fortunately, since the inverse covariance matrix on the left-hand side is sparse (i.e., block-tridiagonal), we can use this to solve the system of equations very efficiently. This typically involves a forward recursion followed by a backward recursion. When the equations are solved in this way, the method is typically referred to as a *fixed-interval smoother*. It is useful to think of smoothers as efficiently implementing the full batch solution, with no approximation. We use the rest of this section to show that this can be done, first by a sparse Cholesky approach and then by the algebraically equivalent classical *Rauch–Tung–Striebel smoother* (Rauch et al., 1965). Särkkä (2013) provides an excellent reference on smoothing and filtering.

3.2.1 Exploiting Sparsity in the Batch Solution

As discussed earlier, the left-hand side of (3.34), $\mathbf{H}^T\mathbf{W}^{-1}\mathbf{H}$, is block-tridiagonal (under our chronological variable ordering for $\mathbf{x}$):

$$\mathbf{H}^T\mathbf{W}^{-1}\mathbf{H} = \begin{bmatrix} * & * & & & & \\ * & * & * & & & \\ & * & * & * & & \\ & & \ddots & \ddots & \ddots & \\ & & & * & * & * \\ & & & & * & * \end{bmatrix}, \tag{3.55}$$

where $*$ indicates a non-zero block. There are solvers that can exploit this structure and therefore solve for $\hat{\mathbf{x}}$ efficiently.

One way to solve the batch equations efficiently is to do a sparse *Cholesky decomposition* (see Appendix A.1.11) followed by forward and backward passes. It turns out we can efficiently factor $\mathbf{H}^T\mathbf{W}^{-1}\mathbf{H}$ into

$$\mathbf{H}^T \mathbf{W}^{-1} \mathbf{H} = \mathbf{L}\mathbf{L}^T, \tag{3.56}$$

where $\mathbf{L}$ is a block-lower-triangular matrix called the Cholesky factor.[13] Owing to the block-tridiagonal structure of $\mathbf{H}^T \mathbf{W}^{-1} \mathbf{H}$, $\mathbf{L}$ will have the form

$$\mathbf{L} = \begin{bmatrix} * & & & & & \\ * & * & & & & \\ & * & * & & & \\ & & \ddots & \ddots & & \\ & & & * & * & \\ & & & & * & * \end{bmatrix}, \tag{3.57}$$

and the decomposition can be computed in $O(N^3(K+1))$ time. Next, we solve

$$\mathbf{L}\mathbf{d} = \mathbf{H}^T \mathbf{W}^{-1} \mathbf{z} \tag{3.58}$$

for $\mathbf{d}$. This can again be done in $O(N^3(K+1))$ time through forward substitution owing to the sparse lower-triangular form of $\mathbf{L}$; this is called the forward pass. Finally, we solve

$$\mathbf{L}^T \hat{\mathbf{x}} = \mathbf{d} \tag{3.59}$$

for $\hat{\mathbf{x}}$, which again can be done in $O(N^3(K+1))$ time through backward substitution owing to the sparse upper-triangular form of $\mathbf{L}^T$; this is called the backward pass. Thus, the batch equations can be solved in computation time that scales linearly with the size of the state. The next section will make the details of this sparse Cholesky approach specific.

3.2.2 Cholesky Smoother

In this section, we work out the details of the sparse Cholesky solution to the batch estimation problem. The result will be a set of forward-backward recursions that we will refer to as the *Cholesky smoother*. There are several similar square-root information smoothers described in the literature, and Bierman (1974) is a classic reference on the topic.

Let us begin by defining the non-zero sub-blocks of $\mathbf{L}$ as

$$\mathbf{L} = \begin{bmatrix} \mathbf{L}_0 & & & & & \\ \mathbf{L}_{10} & \mathbf{L}_1 & & & & \\ & \mathbf{L}_{21} & \mathbf{L}_2 & & & \\ & & \ddots & \ddots & & \\ & & & \mathbf{L}_{K-1,K-2} & \mathbf{L}_{K-1} & \\ & & & & \mathbf{L}_{K,K-1} & \mathbf{L}_K \end{bmatrix}. \tag{3.60}$$

Using the definitions of $\mathbf{H}$ and $\mathbf{W}$ from (3.13), when we multiply out $\mathbf{H}^T \mathbf{W}^{-1} \mathbf{H} = \mathbf{L}\mathbf{L}^T$ and compare at the block level, we have

---

[13] We could just as easily factor into $\mathbf{H}^T \mathbf{W}^{-1} \mathbf{H} = \mathbf{U}\mathbf{U}^T$ with $\mathbf{U}$ upper-triangular and then carry out backward and forward passes.

$$\mathbf{L}_0\mathbf{L}_0^T = \underbrace{\check{\mathbf{P}}_0^{-1} + \mathbf{C}_0^T\mathbf{R}_0^{-1}\mathbf{C}_0}_{\mathbf{I}_0} + \mathbf{A}_0^T\mathbf{Q}_1^{-1}\mathbf{A}_0, \tag{3.61a}$$

$$\mathbf{L}_{10}\mathbf{L}_0^T = -\mathbf{Q}_1^{-1}\mathbf{A}_0, \tag{3.61b}$$

$$\mathbf{L}_1\mathbf{L}_1^T = \underbrace{-\mathbf{L}_{10}\mathbf{L}_{10}^T + \mathbf{Q}_1^{-1} + \mathbf{C}_1^T\mathbf{R}_1^{-1}\mathbf{C}_1}_{\mathbf{I}_1} + \mathbf{A}_1^T\mathbf{Q}_2^{-1}\mathbf{A}_1, \tag{3.61c}$$

$$\mathbf{L}_{21}\mathbf{L}_1^T = -\mathbf{Q}_2^{-1}\mathbf{A}_1, \tag{3.61d}$$

$$\vdots$$

$$\mathbf{L}_{K-1}\mathbf{L}_{K-1}^T = \underbrace{-\mathbf{L}_{K-1,K-2}\mathbf{L}_{K-1,K-2}^T + \mathbf{Q}_{K-1}^{-1} + \mathbf{C}_{K-1}^T\mathbf{R}_{K-1}^{-1}\mathbf{C}_{K-1}}_{\mathbf{I}_{K-1}}$$
$$+ \mathbf{A}_{K-1}^T\mathbf{Q}_K^{-1}\mathbf{A}_{K-1}, \tag{3.61e}$$

$$\mathbf{L}_{K,K-1}\mathbf{L}_{K-1}^T = -\mathbf{Q}_K^{-1}\mathbf{A}_{K-1}, \tag{3.61f}$$

$$\mathbf{L}_K\mathbf{L}_K^T = \underbrace{-\mathbf{L}_{K,K-1}\mathbf{L}_{K,K-1}^T + \mathbf{Q}_K^{-1} + \mathbf{C}_K^T\mathbf{R}_K^{-1}\mathbf{C}_K}_{\mathbf{I}_K}, \tag{3.61g}$$

where the underbraces allow us to define the $\mathbf{I}_k$ quantities,[14] whose purpose will be revealed shortly. From these equations, we can first solve for $\mathbf{L}_0$ by doing a small (dense) Cholesky decomposition in the first equation, then substitute this into the second to solve for $\mathbf{L}_{10}$, then substitute this into the third to solve for $\mathbf{L}_1$, and so on all the way down to $\mathbf{L}_K$. This confirms that we can work out all the blocks of $\mathbf{L}$ in a single forward pass in $O(N^3(K+1))$ time.

Next, we solve $\mathbf{L}\mathbf{d} = \mathbf{H}^T\mathbf{W}^{-1}\mathbf{z}$ for $\mathbf{d}$, where

$$\mathbf{d} = \begin{bmatrix} \mathbf{d}_0 \\ \mathbf{d}_1 \\ \vdots \\ \mathbf{d}_K \end{bmatrix}. \tag{3.62}$$

Multiplying out and comparing at the block level, we have

$$\mathbf{L}_0\mathbf{d}_0 = \underbrace{\check{\mathbf{P}}_0^{-1}\check{\mathbf{x}}_0 + \mathbf{C}_0^T\mathbf{R}_0^{-1}\mathbf{y}_0}_{\mathbf{q}_0} - \mathbf{A}_0^T\mathbf{Q}_1^{-1}\mathbf{v}_1, \tag{3.63a}$$

$$\mathbf{L}_1\mathbf{d}_1 = \underbrace{-\mathbf{L}_{10}\mathbf{d}_0 + \mathbf{Q}_1^{-1}\mathbf{v}_1 + \mathbf{C}_1^T\mathbf{R}_1^{-1}\mathbf{y}_1}_{\mathbf{q}_1} - \mathbf{A}_1^T\mathbf{Q}_2^{-1}\mathbf{v}_2, \tag{3.63b}$$

$$\vdots$$

$$\mathbf{L}_{K-1}\mathbf{d}_{K-1} = \underbrace{-\mathbf{L}_{K-1,K-2}\mathbf{d}_{K-2} + \mathbf{Q}_{K-1}^{-1}\mathbf{v}_{K-1} + \mathbf{C}_{K-1}^T\mathbf{R}_{K-1}^{-1}\mathbf{y}_{K-1}}_{\mathbf{q}_{K-1}}$$
$$- \mathbf{A}_{K-1}^T\mathbf{Q}_K^{-1}\mathbf{v}_K, \tag{3.63c}$$

$$\mathbf{L}_K\mathbf{d}_K = \underbrace{-\mathbf{L}_{K,K-1}\mathbf{d}_{K-1} + \mathbf{Q}_K^{-1}\mathbf{v}_K + \mathbf{C}_K^T\mathbf{R}_K^{-1}\mathbf{y}_K}_{\mathbf{q}_K}, \tag{3.63d}$$

---

[14] In this book, $\mathbf{1}$ is the identity matrix, which should not be confused with the use of $\mathbf{I}$, which in this instance stands for *information matrix* (i.e., inverse covariance matrix).

where again the underbraces allow us to define the $\mathbf{q}_k$ quantities, which will be used shortly. From these equations, we can solve for $\mathbf{d}_0$ in the first equation, then substitute this into the second to solve for $\mathbf{d}_1$, and so on all the way down to $\mathbf{d}_K$. This confirms that we can work out all of the blocks of $\mathbf{d}$ in a single forward pass in $O(N^3(K+1))$ time.

The last step in the Cholesky approach is to solve $\mathbf{L}^T\hat{\mathbf{x}} = \mathbf{d}$ for $\hat{\mathbf{x}}$, where

$$\hat{\mathbf{x}} = \begin{bmatrix} \hat{\mathbf{x}}_0 \\ \hat{\mathbf{x}}_1 \\ \vdots \\ \hat{\mathbf{x}}_K \end{bmatrix}. \tag{3.64}$$

Multiplying out and comparing at the block level, we have

$$\mathbf{L}_K^T\hat{\mathbf{x}}_K = \mathbf{d}_K, \tag{3.65a}$$

$$\mathbf{L}_{K-1}^T\hat{\mathbf{x}}_{K-1} = -\mathbf{L}_{K,K-1}^T\hat{\mathbf{x}}_K + \mathbf{d}_{K-1}, \tag{3.65b}$$

$$\vdots$$

$$\mathbf{L}_1^T\hat{\mathbf{x}}_1 = -\mathbf{L}_{21}^T\hat{\mathbf{x}}_2 + \mathbf{d}_1, \tag{3.65c}$$

$$\mathbf{L}_0^T\hat{\mathbf{x}}_0 = -\mathbf{L}_{10}^T\hat{\mathbf{x}}_1 + \mathbf{d}_0. \tag{3.65d}$$

From these equations, we can solve for $\hat{\mathbf{x}}_K$ in the first equation, then substitute this into the second to solve for $\hat{\mathbf{x}}_{K-1}$, and so on all the way down to $\hat{\mathbf{x}}_0$. This confirms that we can work out all of the blocks of $\hat{\mathbf{x}}$ in a single backward pass in $O(N^3(K+1))$ time.

In terms of the $\mathbf{I}_k$ and $\mathbf{q}_k$ quantities, we can combine the two forward passes (to solve for $\mathbf{L}$ and $\mathbf{d}$) and also write the backward pass as

forward:

$(k = 1 \ldots K)$

$$\mathbf{L}_{k-1}\mathbf{L}_{k-1}^T = \mathbf{I}_{k-1} + \mathbf{A}_{k-1}^T\mathbf{Q}_k^{-1}\mathbf{A}_{k-1}, \tag{3.66a}$$

$$\mathbf{L}_{k-1}\mathbf{d}_{k-1} = \mathbf{q}_{k-1} - \mathbf{A}_{k-1}^T\mathbf{Q}_k^{-1}\mathbf{v}_k, \tag{3.66b}$$

$$\mathbf{L}_{k,k-1}\mathbf{L}_{k-1}^T = -\mathbf{Q}_k^{-1}\mathbf{A}_{k-1}, \tag{3.66c}$$

$$\mathbf{I}_k = -\mathbf{L}_{k,k-1}\mathbf{L}_{k,k-1}^T + \mathbf{Q}_k^{-1} + \mathbf{C}_k^T\mathbf{R}_k^{-1}\mathbf{C}_k, \tag{3.66d}$$

$$\mathbf{q}_k = -\mathbf{L}_{k,k-1}\mathbf{d}_{k-1} + \mathbf{Q}_k^{-1}\mathbf{v}_k + \mathbf{C}_k^T\mathbf{R}_k^{-1}\mathbf{y}_k, \tag{3.66e}$$

backward:

$(k = K \ldots 1)$

$$\mathbf{L}_{k-1}^T\hat{\mathbf{x}}_{k-1} = -\mathbf{L}_{k,k-1}^T\hat{\mathbf{x}}_k + \mathbf{d}_{k-1}, \tag{3.66f}$$

which are initialized with

$$\mathbf{I}_0 = \check{\mathbf{P}}_0^{-1} + \mathbf{C}_0^T\mathbf{R}_0^{-1}\mathbf{C}_0, \tag{3.67a}$$

$$\mathbf{q}_0 = \check{\mathbf{P}}_0^{-1}\check{\mathbf{x}}_0 + \mathbf{C}_0^T\mathbf{R}_0^{-1}\mathbf{y}_0, \tag{3.67b}$$

$$\hat{\mathbf{x}}_K = \mathbf{L}_K^{-T}\mathbf{d}_K. \tag{3.67c}$$

The forward pass maps $\{\mathbf{q}_{k-1}, \mathbf{I}_{k-1}\}$ to the same pair at the next time, $\{\mathbf{q}_k, \mathbf{I}_k\}$.

The backward pass maps $\hat{\mathbf{x}}_k$ to the same quantity at the previous timestep, $\hat{\mathbf{x}}_{k-1}$. In the process, we solve for all the blocks of $\mathbf{L}$ and $\mathbf{d}$. The only linear algebra operations required to implement this smoother are Cholesky decomposition, multiplication, addition, and solving a linear system via forward/backward substitution.

As we will see in Section 3.2.4, these six recursive equations are algebraically equivalent to the canonical *Rauch–Tung–Striebel smoother*; the five equations forming the forward pass are algebraically equivalent to the famous *Kalman filter*.

3.2.3 Posterior Covariance in the Cholesky Smoother

In the development of the Cholesky smoother in the previous section, we did not explicitly solve for the posterior marginal covariance of the estimate at each timestep. We use this section to show how to do this without brute-force inverting the full inverse-covariance matrix only to extract the few blocks in which we are interested, which would be very inefficient.

We had defined the block-tridiagonal inverse of the posterior covariance as

$$\hat{\mathbf{P}}^{-1} = \mathbf{L}\mathbf{L}^T, \tag{3.68}$$

where the non-zero sub-blocks of $\mathbf{L}$ were

$$\mathbf{L} = \begin{bmatrix} \mathbf{L}_0 & & & & & \\ \mathbf{L}_{10} & \mathbf{L}_1 & & & & \\ & \mathbf{L}_{21} & \mathbf{L}_2 & & & \\ & & \ddots & \ddots & & \\ & & & \mathbf{L}_{K-1,K-2} & \mathbf{L}_{K-1} & \\ & & & & \mathbf{L}_{K,K-1} & \mathbf{L}_K \end{bmatrix}. \tag{3.69}$$

The covariance is therefore

$$\hat{\mathbf{P}} = \mathbf{L}^{-T}\mathbf{L}^{-1}, \tag{3.70}$$

where

$$\mathbf{L}^{-1} = \begin{bmatrix} \mathbf{L}_0^{-1} & & & & & \\ -\mathbf{L}_1^{-1}\mathbf{L}_{10}\mathbf{L}_0^{-1} & & & & & \\ \ddots & \ddots & & & & \\ \ddots & \ddots & & \mathbf{L}_{K-2}^{-1} & & \\ \ddots & \ddots & -\mathbf{L}_{K-1}^{-1}\mathbf{L}_{K-1,K-2}\mathbf{L}_{K-2}^{-1} & & \mathbf{L}_{K-1}^{-1} & \\ \ddots & \ddots & \mathbf{L}_K^{-1}\mathbf{L}_{K,K-1}\mathbf{L}_{K-1}^{-1}\mathbf{L}_{K-1,K-2}\mathbf{L}_{K-2}^{-1} & & -\mathbf{L}_K^{-1}\mathbf{L}_{K,K-1}\mathbf{L}_{K-1}^{-1} & \mathbf{L}_K^{-1} \end{bmatrix}. \tag{3.71}$$

Unfortunately, the lower triangle of $\mathbf{L}^{-1}$ is now dense and so is $\hat{\mathbf{P}}$.

Luckily, we can still solve for only the main block diagonal (and additional diagonals up to some block bandwidth) in $O(K)$ time using a backward recursion. We will show this for the main diagonal and one additional diagonal, which is necessary for the covariance interpolation formula in (3.209b).

The blocks of $\hat{\mathbf{P}}$ are

$$
\hat{\mathbf{P}} = \begin{bmatrix}
\hat{\mathbf{P}}_0 & \hat{\mathbf{P}}_{10}^T & \ddots & & \ddots & & \ddots \\
\hat{\mathbf{P}}_{10} & \hat{\mathbf{P}}_1 & \hat{\mathbf{P}}_{21}^T & \ddots & & \ddots & & \ddots \\
\ddots & \hat{\mathbf{P}}_{21} & \ddots & & \ddots & & \ddots \\
& & & \hat{\mathbf{P}}_{K-2} & \hat{\mathbf{P}}_{K-1,K-2}^T & \ddots \\
\ddots & \ddots & \ddots & \hat{\mathbf{P}}_{K-1,K-2} & \hat{\mathbf{P}}_{K-1} & \hat{\mathbf{P}}_{K,K-1}^T \\
\ddots & \ddots & \ddots & \ddots & \hat{\mathbf{P}}_{K,K-1} & \hat{\mathbf{P}}_K
\end{bmatrix}, \tag{3.72}
$$

where we note the matrix is in general dense but we have only assigned symbols to the blocks we will use. Multiplying out $\mathbf{L}^{-T}\mathbf{L}^{-1}$ and comparing to $\hat{\mathbf{P}}$, we can establish a backward recursive relationship:

$$
\hat{\mathbf{P}}_{k-1} = \mathbf{L}_{k-1}^{-T}\left(1 + \mathbf{L}_{k,k-1}^T \hat{\mathbf{P}}_k \mathbf{L}_{k,k-1}\right)\mathbf{L}_{k-1}^{-1}, \tag{3.73a}
$$

$$
\hat{\mathbf{P}}_{k,k-1} = -\hat{\mathbf{P}}_k \mathbf{L}_{k,k-1}\mathbf{L}_{k-1}^{-1}, \tag{3.73b}
$$

which we initialize with

$$
\hat{\mathbf{P}}_K = \mathbf{L}_K^{-T}\mathbf{L}_K^{-1}. \tag{3.74}
$$

As we have already computed all of the blocks of $\mathbf{L}$ in the Cholesky smoother, we can simply include this calculation in the backward pass if we want the posterior covariance associated with our estimate. This does not change the complexity of the overall algorithm, which remains at $O(K)$, albeit with a slightly higher coefficient.

3.2.4 Rauch–Tung–Striebel Smoother

Herbert E. Rauch (1935–2011) was a pioneer in the area of control and estimation. Frank F. Tung (1933–2006) was a research scientist working in the area of computing and control. Charlotte T. Striebel (1929–2014) was a statistician and professor of mathematics. All three co-developed the Rauch–Tung–Striebel smoother while working at Lockheed Missiles and Space Company in order to estimate spacecraft trajectories.

While the Cholesky smoother is a convenient implementation and is easy to understand when starting from the batch solution, it does not represent the canonical form of the smoothing equations. It is, however, algebraically equivalent to the canonical Rauch–Tung–Striebel (RTS) *smoother*, which we now show. This requires several uses of the different forms of the SMW identity in (2.124).

We begin by working on the forward pass. Solving for $\mathbf{L}_{k,k-1}$ in (3.66c) and substituting this and (3.66a) into (3.66d), we have

$$
\mathbf{I}_k = \underbrace{\mathbf{Q}_k^{-1} - \mathbf{Q}_k^{-1}\mathbf{A}_{k-1}\left(\mathbf{I}_{k-1} + \mathbf{A}_{k-1}^T\mathbf{Q}_k^{-1}\mathbf{A}_{k-1}\right)^{-1}\mathbf{A}_{k-1}^T\mathbf{Q}_k^{-1}}_{\left(\mathbf{A}_{k-1}\mathbf{I}_{k-1}^{-1}\mathbf{A}_{k-1}^T + \mathbf{Q}_k\right)^{-1},\text{ by (2.124)}} + \mathbf{C}_k^T\mathbf{R}_k^{-1}\mathbf{C}_k,
$$

$$\tag{3.75}$$

where we have used a version of the SMW identity to get to the expression in the underbrace. By letting $\hat{\mathbf{P}}_{k,f} = \mathbf{I}_k^{-1}$, this can be written in two steps as

$$
\check{\mathbf{P}}_{k,f} = \mathbf{A}_{k-1}\hat{\mathbf{P}}_{k-1,f}\mathbf{A}_{k-1}^T + \mathbf{Q}_k, \tag{3.76a}
$$

$$
\hat{\mathbf{P}}_{k,f}^{-1} = \check{\mathbf{P}}_{k,f}^{-1} + \mathbf{C}_k^T\mathbf{R}_k^{-1}\mathbf{C}_k, \tag{3.76b}
$$

where $\check{\mathbf{P}}_{k,f}$ represents a 'predicted' covariance and $\hat{\mathbf{P}}_{k,f}$ a 'corrected' one. We have added the subscript, $(\cdot)_f$, to indicate these quantities come from the forward pass (i.e., a filter). The second of these equations is written in *information* (i.e., inverse covariance) form. To reach the canonical version, we define the *Kalman gain matrix*, $\mathbf{K}_k$, as

$$\mathbf{K}_k = \hat{\mathbf{P}}_{k,f} \mathbf{C}_k^T \mathbf{R}_k^{-1}. \qquad (3.77)$$

Substituting in (3.76b), this can also be written as

$$\mathbf{K}_k = \left(\check{\mathbf{P}}_{k,f}^{-1} + \mathbf{C}_k^T \mathbf{R}_k^{-1} \mathbf{C}_k\right)^{-1} \mathbf{C}_k^T \mathbf{R}_k^{-1}$$
$$= \check{\mathbf{P}}_{k,f} \mathbf{C}_k^T \left(\mathbf{C}_k \check{\mathbf{P}}_{k,f} \mathbf{C}_k^T + \mathbf{R}_k\right)^{-1}, \quad (3.78)$$

where the last expression requires a use of the SMW identity from (2.124). Then (3.76b) can be rewritten as

$$\check{\mathbf{P}}_{k,f}^{-1} = \hat{\mathbf{P}}_{k,f}^{-1} - \mathbf{C}_k^T \mathbf{R}_k^{-1} \mathbf{C}_k = \hat{\mathbf{P}}_{k,f}^{-1} \big(1 - \underbrace{\hat{\mathbf{P}}_{k,f} \mathbf{C}_k^T \mathbf{R}_k^{-1}}_{\mathbf{K}_k} \mathbf{C}_k \big)$$
$$= \hat{\mathbf{P}}_{k,f}^{-1} \left(1 - \mathbf{K}_k \mathbf{C}_k\right), \quad (3.79)$$

and finally, rearranging for $\hat{\mathbf{P}}_{k,f}$, we have

$$\hat{\mathbf{P}}_{k,f} = \left(1 - \mathbf{K}_k \mathbf{C}_k\right) \check{\mathbf{P}}_{k,f}, \qquad (3.80)$$

which is the canonical form for the covariance correction step.

Next, solving for $\mathbf{L}_{k,k-1}$ in (3.66c) and $\mathbf{d}_{k-1}$ in (3.66b), we have

$$\mathbf{L}_{k,k-1} \mathbf{d}_{k-1} = -\mathbf{Q}_k^{-1} \mathbf{A}_{k-1} \left(\mathbf{L}_{k-1} \mathbf{L}_{k-1}^T\right)^{-1} \left(\mathbf{q}_{k-1} - \mathbf{A}_{k-1}^T \mathbf{Q}_k^{-1} \mathbf{v}_k\right). \quad (3.81)$$

Substituting (3.66a) into $\mathbf{L}_{k,k-1} \mathbf{d}_{k-1}$ and then this into (3.66e), we have

$$\mathbf{q}_k = \underbrace{\mathbf{Q}_k^{-1} \mathbf{A}_{k-1} \left(\mathbf{I}_{k-1} + \mathbf{A}_{k-1}^T \mathbf{Q}_k^{-1} \mathbf{A}_{k-1}\right)^{-1}}_{\left(\mathbf{A}_{k-1} \mathbf{I}_{k-1}^{-1} \mathbf{A}_{k-1}^T + \mathbf{Q}_k\right)^{-1} \mathbf{A}_{k-1} \mathbf{I}_{k-1}^{-1}, \text{ by } (2.124)} \mathbf{q}_{k-1}$$
$$+ \underbrace{\left(\mathbf{Q}_k^{-1} - \mathbf{Q}_k^{-1} \mathbf{A}_{k-1} \left(\mathbf{I}_{k-1} + \mathbf{A}_{k-1}^T \mathbf{Q}_k^{-1} \mathbf{A}_{k-1}\right)^{-1} \mathbf{A}_{k-1}^T \mathbf{Q}_k^{-1}\right)}_{\left(\mathbf{A}_{k-1} \mathbf{I}_{k-1}^{-1} \mathbf{A}_{k-1}^T + \mathbf{Q}_k\right)^{-1}, \text{ by } (2.124)} \mathbf{v}_k$$
$$+ \mathbf{C}_k^T \mathbf{R}_k^{-1} \mathbf{y}_k, \quad (3.82)$$

where we have used two versions of the SMW identity to get to the expressions in the underbraces. By letting $\hat{\mathbf{P}}_{k,f}^{-1} \hat{\mathbf{x}}_{k,f} = \mathbf{q}_k$, this can be written in two steps as

$$\check{\mathbf{x}}_{k,f} = \mathbf{A}_{k-1} \hat{\mathbf{x}}_{k-1,f} + \mathbf{v}_k, \qquad (3.83a)$$
$$\hat{\mathbf{P}}_{k,f}^{-1} \hat{\mathbf{x}}_{k,f} = \check{\mathbf{P}}_{k,f}^{-1} \check{\mathbf{x}}_{k,f} + \mathbf{C}_k^T \mathbf{R}_k^{-1} \mathbf{y}_k, \qquad (3.83b)$$

where $\check{\mathbf{x}}_{k,f}$ represents a 'predicted' mean and $\hat{\mathbf{x}}_{k,f}$ a 'corrected' one. Again, the second of these is in *information* (i.e., inverse covariance) form. To get to the canonical form, we rewrite it as

$$\hat{\mathbf{x}}_{k,f} = \underbrace{\hat{\mathbf{P}}_{k,f}\check{\mathbf{P}}_{k,f}^{-1}}_{\mathbf{1}-\mathbf{K}_k\mathbf{C}_k}\check{\mathbf{x}}_{k,f} + \underbrace{\hat{\mathbf{P}}_{k,f}\mathbf{C}_k^T\mathbf{R}_k^{-1}}_{\mathbf{K}_k}\mathbf{y}_k, \tag{3.84}$$

or

$$\hat{\mathbf{x}}_{k,f} = \check{\mathbf{x}}_{k,f} + \mathbf{K}_k\left(\mathbf{y}_k - \mathbf{C}_k\check{\mathbf{x}}_{k,f}\right), \tag{3.85}$$

which is the canonical form for the mean correction step.

The last step is to resolve the backward pass into its canonical form. We start with the backward pass for the mean. We begin by premultiplying (3.66f) by $\mathbf{L}_{k-1}$ and solving for $\hat{\mathbf{x}}_{k-1}$:

$$\hat{\mathbf{x}}_{k-1} = \left(\mathbf{L}_{k-1}\mathbf{L}_{k-1}^T\right)^{-1}\mathbf{L}_{k-1}\left(-\mathbf{L}_{k,k-1}^T\hat{\mathbf{x}}_k + \mathbf{d}_{k-1}\right). \tag{3.86}$$

Substituting in (3.66a), (3.66b), and (3.66c), we have

$$\hat{\mathbf{x}}_{k-1} = \underbrace{\left(\mathbf{I}_{k-1} + \mathbf{A}_{k-1}^T\mathbf{Q}_k^{-1}\mathbf{A}_{k-1}\right)^{-1}\mathbf{A}_{k-1}^T\mathbf{Q}_k^{-1}}_{\mathbf{I}_{k-1}^{-1}\mathbf{A}_{k-1}^T\left(\mathbf{A}_{k-1}\mathbf{I}_{k-1}^{-1}\mathbf{A}_{k-1}^T + \mathbf{Q}_k\right)^{-1},\text{ by (2.124)}}\left(\hat{\mathbf{x}}_k - \mathbf{v}_k\right)$$
$$+ \underbrace{\left(\mathbf{I}_{k-1} + \mathbf{A}_{k-1}^T\mathbf{Q}_k^{-1}\mathbf{A}_{k-1}\right)^{-1}}_{\mathbf{I}_{k-1}^{-1} - \mathbf{I}_{k-1}^{-1}\mathbf{A}_{k-1}^T\left(\mathbf{A}_{k-1}\mathbf{I}_{k-1}^{-1}\mathbf{A}_{k-1}^T + \mathbf{Q}_k\right)^{-1}\mathbf{A}_{k-1}\mathbf{I}_{k-1}^{-1},\text{ by (2.124)}}\mathbf{q}_{k-1}. \tag{3.87}$$

Using our symbols from above, this can be written as

$$\hat{\mathbf{x}}_{k-1} = \hat{\mathbf{x}}_{k-1,f} + \hat{\mathbf{P}}_{k-1,f}\mathbf{A}_{k-1}^T\check{\mathbf{P}}_{k,f}^{-1}\left(\hat{\mathbf{x}}_k - \check{\mathbf{x}}_{k,f}\right), \tag{3.88}$$

which is the canonical form for the backward smoothing equation.

We can also manipulate the covariance backward recursion from Section 3.2.3 into the canonical RTS form as follows. First, we note that

$$\mathbf{L}_{k,k-1}\mathbf{L}_{k-1}^{-1} = \underbrace{\mathbf{L}_{k,k-1}\mathbf{L}_{k-1}^T}_{-\mathbf{Q}_k^{-1}\mathbf{A}_{k-1}}\underbrace{\mathbf{L}_{k-1}^{-T}\mathbf{L}_{k-1}^{-1}}_{\left(\mathbf{I}_{k-1} + \mathbf{A}_{k-1}^T\mathbf{Q}_k^{-1}\mathbf{A}_{k-1}\right)^{-1}}$$
$$= -\underbrace{\left(\mathbf{A}_{k-1}\hat{\mathbf{P}}_{k-1,f}\mathbf{A}_{k-1}^T + \mathbf{Q}_k\right)^{-1}}_{\check{\mathbf{P}}_{k,f}}\mathbf{A}_{k-1}\hat{\mathbf{P}}_{k-1,f}$$
$$= -\left(\hat{\mathbf{P}}_{k-1,f}\mathbf{A}_{k-1}^T\check{\mathbf{P}}_{k,f}^{-1}\right)^T. \tag{3.89}$$

Also, we have that

$$\mathbf{L}_{k-1}^{-T}\mathbf{L}_{k-1}^{-1} = \left(\mathbf{I}_{k-1} + \mathbf{A}_{k-1}^T\mathbf{Q}_k^{-1}\mathbf{A}_{k-1}\right)^{-1}$$
$$= \hat{\mathbf{P}}_{k-1,f} - \hat{\mathbf{P}}_{k-1,f}\mathbf{A}_{k-1}^T\underbrace{\left(\mathbf{A}_{k-1}\hat{\mathbf{P}}_{k-1,f}\mathbf{A}_{k-1}^T + \mathbf{Q}_k\right)^{-1}}_{\check{\mathbf{P}}_{k,f}}\mathbf{A}_{k-1}\hat{\mathbf{P}}_{k-1,f}$$
$$= \hat{\mathbf{P}}_{k-1,f} - \left(\hat{\mathbf{P}}_{k-1,f}\mathbf{A}_{k-1}^T\check{\mathbf{P}}_{k,f}^{-1}\right)\check{\mathbf{P}}_{k,f}\left(\hat{\mathbf{P}}_{k-1,f}\mathbf{A}_{k-1}^T\check{\mathbf{P}}_{k,f}^{-1}\right)^T. \tag{3.90}$$

Plugging these two results into (3.73a), we have

$$\hat{\mathbf{P}}_{k-1} = \hat{\mathbf{P}}_{k-1,f} + \left(\hat{\mathbf{P}}_{k-1,f}\mathbf{A}_{k-1}^T\check{\mathbf{P}}_{k,f}^{-1}\right)\left(\hat{\mathbf{P}}_k - \check{\mathbf{P}}_{k,f}\right)\left(\hat{\mathbf{P}}_{k-1,f}\mathbf{A}_{k-1}^T\check{\mathbf{P}}_{k,f}^{-1}\right)^T, \tag{3.91}$$

which we initialize with $\hat{\mathbf{P}}_K = \hat{\mathbf{P}}_{K,f}$ and iterate backward. Finally, we can also plug the same two results into (3.73b) to obtain

$$\hat{\mathbf{P}}_{k,k-1} = \hat{\mathbf{P}}_k \left(\hat{\mathbf{P}}_{k-1,f} \mathbf{A}_{k-1}^T \check{\mathbf{P}}_{k,f}^{-1} \right)^T, \tag{3.92}$$

for the blocks above and below the main diagonal of the full covariance matrix, $\hat{\mathbf{P}}$; these are needed, for example, when interpolating for additional times of interest using (3.209b).

Together, equations (3.76a), (3.78), (3.80), (3.83a), (3.85), (3.88), and (3.91) constitute the Rauch–Tung–Striebel smoother:

forward:

$(k = 1 \ldots K)$

$$\check{\mathbf{P}}_{k,f} = \mathbf{A}_{k-1} \hat{\mathbf{P}}_{k-1,f} \mathbf{A}_{k-1}^T + \mathbf{Q}_k, \tag{3.93a}$$

$$\check{\mathbf{x}}_{k,f} = \mathbf{A}_{k-1} \hat{\mathbf{x}}_{k-1,f} + \mathbf{v}_k, \tag{3.93b}$$

$$\mathbf{K}_k = \check{\mathbf{P}}_{k,f} \mathbf{C}_k^T \left(\mathbf{C}_k \check{\mathbf{P}}_{k,f} \mathbf{C}_k^T + \mathbf{R}_k \right)^{-1}, \tag{3.93c}$$

$$\hat{\mathbf{P}}_{k,f} = (\mathbf{1} - \mathbf{K}_k \mathbf{C}_k) \check{\mathbf{P}}_{k,f}, \tag{3.93d}$$

$$\hat{\mathbf{x}}_{k,f} = \check{\mathbf{x}}_{k,f} + \mathbf{K}_k \left(\mathbf{y}_k - \mathbf{C}_k \check{\mathbf{x}}_{k,f} \right), \tag{3.93e}$$

backward:

$(k = K \ldots 1)$

$$\hat{\mathbf{x}}_{k-1} = \hat{\mathbf{x}}_{k-1,f} + \left(\hat{\mathbf{P}}_{k-1,f} \mathbf{A}_{k-1}^T \check{\mathbf{P}}_{k,f}^{-1} \right) \left(\hat{\mathbf{x}}_k - \check{\mathbf{x}}_{k,f} \right), \tag{3.93f}$$

$$\hat{\mathbf{P}}_{k-1} = \hat{\mathbf{P}}_{k-1,f} + \left(\hat{\mathbf{P}}_{k-1,f} \mathbf{A}_{k-1}^T \check{\mathbf{P}}_{k,f}^{-1} \right) \left(\hat{\mathbf{P}}_k - \check{\mathbf{P}}_{k,f} \right)$$
$$\times \left(\hat{\mathbf{P}}_{k-1,f} \mathbf{A}_{k-1}^T \check{\mathbf{P}}_{k,f}^{-1} \right)^T, \tag{3.93g}$$

which are initialized with

$$\hat{\mathbf{P}}_{0,f} = (\mathbf{1} - \mathbf{K}_0 \mathbf{C}_0) \check{\mathbf{P}}_0, \tag{3.94a}$$

$$\hat{\mathbf{x}}_{0,f} = \check{\mathbf{x}}_0 + \mathbf{K}_0 (\mathbf{y}_0 - \mathbf{C}_0 \check{\mathbf{x}}_0), \tag{3.94b}$$

$$\hat{\mathbf{x}}_K = \hat{\mathbf{x}}_{K,f}, \tag{3.94c}$$

$$\hat{\mathbf{P}}_K = \hat{\mathbf{P}}_{K,f}, \tag{3.94d}$$

and $\mathbf{K}_0 = \check{\mathbf{P}}_0 \mathbf{C}_0^T \left(\mathbf{C}_0 \check{\mathbf{P}}_0 \mathbf{C}_0^T + \mathbf{R}_0 \right)^{-1}$.

As will be discussed in more detail in the next section, the five equations in the forward pass are known as the *Kalman filter*. However, the important message to take away from this section on smoothing is that these seven[15] equations representing the RTS smoother can be used to solve the original batch problem that we set up in a very efficient manner, with no approximation. This is possible

---

[15] Technically (3.93g), used to calculate the posterior marginal covariance for each timestep, is optional with respect to solving the original batch problem but it is employed frequently enough that we include it in the RTS proper. We choose not to include the cross-covariances from (3.92), as these are used less commonly.

Figure 3.3 The batch LG solution is a *smoother*. To develop an estimator appropriate to online estimation, we require a *filter*.

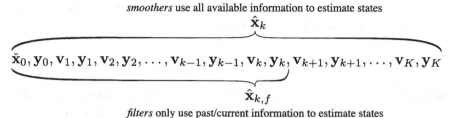

precisely because of the block-tridiagonal sparsity pattern in the left-hand side of the batch problem.

3.3 Recursive Discrete-Time Filtering

The batch solution (and the corresponding smoother implementations) outlined above is really the best we can do. It makes use of all the data in the estimate of every state. However, it has one major drawback: it cannot be used online[16] because it employs future data to estimate past states (i.e., it is not *causal*). To be used online, the estimate of the current state can only employ data up to the current timestep. Figure 3.3 depicts the difference between smoothers and filters. The *Kalman filter* is the classical solution to this problem. We have already seen a preview of the KF; it is the forward pass of the Rauch–Tung–Striebel smoother. However, there are several other ways of deriving it, some of which we provide in this section.

3.3.1 Factoring the Batch Solution

We do not need to start from scratch in our search for a recursive LG estimator. It turns out we can re-use the batch solution and exactly factor it into two recursive estimators, one that runs forward in time and the other backward. The backward pass is a little different than the one presented in the smoother section, as it is not correcting the forward pass, but rather producing an estimate using only future measurements.

To set things up for our development of the recursive solutions, we will reorder some of our variables from the batch solution. We redefine $\mathbf{z}$, $\mathbf{H}$, and $\mathbf{W}$ as

$$
\mathbf{z} =
\begin{bmatrix}
\check{\mathbf{x}}_0 \\
\mathbf{y}_0 \\
\mathbf{v}_1 \\
\mathbf{y}_1 \\
\mathbf{v}_2 \\
\mathbf{y}_2 \\
\vdots \\
\mathbf{v}_K \\
\mathbf{y}_K
\end{bmatrix},
\quad
\mathbf{H} =
\begin{bmatrix}
\mathbf{1} & & & & \\
\mathbf{C}_0 & & & & \\
-\mathbf{A}_0 & \mathbf{1} & & & \\
& \mathbf{C}_1 & & & \\
& -\mathbf{A}_1 & \mathbf{1} & & \\
& & \mathbf{C}_2 & & \\
& & \ddots & \ddots & \\
& & & -\mathbf{A}_{K-1} & \mathbf{1} \\
& & & & \mathbf{C}_K
\end{bmatrix},
$$

[16] It is preferable to say 'online' rather than 'real-time' in this context.

$$
\mathbf{W} = \left[\begin{array}{cc|cc|cc|c|cc}
\check{\mathbf{P}}_0 & & & & & & & & \\
& \mathbf{R}_0 & & & & & & & \\
\hline
& & \mathbf{Q}_1 & & & & & & \\
& & & \mathbf{R}_1 & & & & & \\
\hline
& & & & \mathbf{Q}_2 & & & & \\
& & & & & \mathbf{R}_2 & & & \\
\hline
& & & & & & \ddots & & \\
\hline
& & & & & & & \mathbf{Q}_K & \\
& & & & & & & & \mathbf{R}_K
\end{array}\right], \quad (3.95)
$$

where the partition lines now show divisions between timesteps. This re-ordering does not change the ordering of $\mathbf{x}$, so $\mathbf{H}^T\mathbf{W}^{-1}\mathbf{H}$ is still block-tridiagonal.

We now consider the factorization at the probability density level. As discussed in Section 3.1.5, we have an expression for $p(\mathbf{x}|\mathbf{v}, \mathbf{y})$. If we want to consider only the state at time k, we can marginalize out the other states by integrating over all possible values:

$$
p(\mathbf{x}_k|\mathbf{v}, \mathbf{y}) = \int_{\mathbf{x}_{i,\forall i \neq k}} p(\mathbf{x}_0, \ldots, \mathbf{x}_K|\mathbf{v}, \mathbf{y}) \, d\mathbf{x}_{i,\forall i \neq k}. \quad (3.96)
$$

It turns out that we can factor this probability density into two parts:

$$
p(\mathbf{x}_k|\mathbf{v}, \mathbf{y}) = \eta \, p(\mathbf{x}_k|\check{\mathbf{x}}_0, \mathbf{v}_{1:k}, \mathbf{y}_{0:k}) \, p(\mathbf{x}_k|\mathbf{v}_{k+1:K}, \mathbf{y}_{k+1:K}), \quad (3.97)
$$

where η is a normalization constant to enforce the axiom of total probability. In other words, we can take our batch solution and factor it into the normalized product of two Gaussian PDFs, as was discussed in Section 2.2.8.

To carry out this factorization, we exploit the sparse structure of $\mathbf{H}$ in (3.3.1). We begin by partitioning $\mathbf{H}$ into 12 blocks (only six of which are non-zero):

$$
\mathbf{H} = \left[\begin{array}{ccc}
\mathbf{H}_{11} & & \\
\mathbf{H}_{21} & \mathbf{H}_{22} & \\
& \mathbf{H}_{32} & \mathbf{H}_{33} \\
& & \mathbf{H}_{43}
\end{array}\right]
\begin{array}{l}
\text{information from } 0 \ldots k-1 \\
\text{information from } k \\
\text{information from } k+1 \\
\text{information from } k+2 \ldots K
\end{array}
$$

$$
\begin{array}{l}
\text{states from } k+1 \ldots K \\
\text{states from } k \\
\text{states from } 0 \ldots k-1
\end{array} \quad (3.98)
$$

The sizes of each block-row and block-column are indicated in the preceding math. For example, with $k = 2$ and $K = 4$, the partitions are

$$H = \begin{bmatrix} \begin{matrix} 1 \\ C_0 \\ -A_0 & 1 \\ & C_1 \\ & -A_1 & 1 \\ & & C_2 \\ & & -A_2 & 1 \\ & & & C_3 \\ & & & -A_3 & 1 \\ & & & & C_4 \end{matrix} \end{bmatrix}. \tag{3.99}$$

We use compatible partitions for $\mathbf{z}$ and $\mathbf{W}$:

$$\mathbf{z} = \begin{bmatrix} \mathbf{z}_1 \\ \mathbf{z}_2 \\ \mathbf{z}_3 \\ \mathbf{z}_4 \end{bmatrix}, \quad \mathbf{W} = \begin{bmatrix} \mathbf{W}_1 & & & \\ & \mathbf{W}_2 & & \\ & & \mathbf{W}_3 & \\ & & & \mathbf{W}_4 \end{bmatrix}. \tag{3.100}$$

For $\mathbf{H}^T\mathbf{W}^{-1}\mathbf{H}$ we then have

$$\mathbf{H}^T\mathbf{W}^{-1}\mathbf{H}$$
$$= \begin{bmatrix} \mathbf{H}_{11}^T\mathbf{W}_1^{-1}\mathbf{H}_{11} + \mathbf{H}_{21}^T\mathbf{W}_2^{-1}\mathbf{H}_{21} & \mathbf{H}_{21}^T\mathbf{W}_2^{-1}\mathbf{H}_{22} \\ \mathbf{H}_{22}^T\mathbf{W}_2^{-1}\mathbf{H}_{21} & \mathbf{H}_{22}^T\mathbf{W}_2^{-1}\mathbf{H}_{22} + \mathbf{H}_{32}^T\mathbf{W}_3^{-1}\mathbf{H}_{32} \\ & \mathbf{H}_{33}^T\mathbf{W}_3^{-1}\mathbf{H}_{32} \end{bmatrix}$$

$$\begin{bmatrix} \cdots & & \mathbf{H}_{32}^T\mathbf{W}_3^{-1}\mathbf{H}_{33} \\ & \mathbf{H}_{33}^T\mathbf{W}_3^{-1}\mathbf{H}_{33} + \mathbf{H}_{43}^T\mathbf{W}_4^{-1}\mathbf{H}_{43} \end{bmatrix}$$

$$= \begin{bmatrix} \mathbf{L}_{11} & \mathbf{L}_{12} & \\ \mathbf{L}_{12}^T & \mathbf{L}_{22} & \mathbf{L}_{32}^T \\ & \mathbf{L}_{32} & \mathbf{L}_{33} \end{bmatrix}, \tag{3.101}$$

where we have assigned the blocks to some useful intermediate variables, $\mathbf{L}_{ij}$. For $\mathbf{H}^T\mathbf{W}^{-1}\mathbf{z}$ we have

$$\mathbf{H}^T\mathbf{W}^{-1}\mathbf{z} = \begin{bmatrix} \mathbf{H}_{11}^T\mathbf{W}_1^{-1}\mathbf{z}_1 + \mathbf{H}_{21}^T\mathbf{W}_2^{-1}\mathbf{z}_2 \\ \mathbf{H}_{22}^T\mathbf{W}_2^{-1}\mathbf{z}_2 + \mathbf{H}_{32}^T\mathbf{W}_3^{-1}\mathbf{z}_3 \\ \mathbf{H}_{33}^T\mathbf{W}_3^{-1}\mathbf{z}_3 + \mathbf{H}_{43}^T\mathbf{W}_4^{-1}\mathbf{z}_4 \end{bmatrix} = \begin{bmatrix} \mathbf{r}_1 \\ \mathbf{r}_2 \\ \mathbf{r}_3 \end{bmatrix}, \tag{3.102}$$

where we have the assigned the blocks to some useful intermediate variables, $\mathbf{r}_i$. Next, we partition the states, $\mathbf{x}$, in the following way:

$$\mathbf{x} = \begin{bmatrix} \mathbf{x}_{0:k-1} \\ \mathbf{x}_k \\ \mathbf{x}_{k+1:K} \end{bmatrix} \quad \begin{matrix} \text{states from } 0 \ldots k-1 \\ \text{states from } k \\ \text{states from } k+1 \ldots K. \end{matrix} \tag{3.103}$$

Our overall batch system of equations now looks like the following:

$$\begin{bmatrix} \mathbf{L}_{11} & \mathbf{L}_{12} & \\ \mathbf{L}_{12}^T & \mathbf{L}_{22} & \mathbf{L}_{32}^T \\ & \mathbf{L}_{32} & \mathbf{L}_{33} \end{bmatrix} \begin{bmatrix} \hat{\mathbf{x}}_{0:k-1} \\ \hat{\mathbf{x}}_k \\ \hat{\mathbf{x}}_{k+1:K} \end{bmatrix} = \begin{bmatrix} \mathbf{r}_1 \\ \mathbf{r}_2 \\ \mathbf{r}_3 \end{bmatrix}, \tag{3.104}$$

where we have added the $\hat{(\cdot)}$ to indicate this is the solution to the optimization estimation problem considered earlier. Our short-term goal, in making progress toward a recursive LG estimator, is to solve for $\hat{\mathbf{x}}_k$. To isolate $\hat{\mathbf{x}}_k$, we left-multiply both sides of (3.104) by

$$\begin{bmatrix} 1 & & \\ -\mathbf{L}_{12}^T\mathbf{L}_{11}^{-1} & 1 & -\mathbf{L}_{32}^T\mathbf{L}_{33}^{-1} \\ & & 1 \end{bmatrix}, \tag{3.105}$$

which can be viewed as performing an elementary row operation (and therefore will not change the solution to (3.104)). The resulting system of equations is

$$\begin{bmatrix} \mathbf{L}_{11} & \mathbf{L}_{12} & \\ & \mathbf{L}_{22} - \mathbf{L}_{12}^T\mathbf{L}_{11}^{-1}\mathbf{L}_{12} - \mathbf{L}_{32}^T\mathbf{L}_{33}^{-1}\mathbf{L}_{32} & \\ & \mathbf{L}_{32} & \mathbf{L}_{33} \end{bmatrix} \begin{bmatrix} \hat{\mathbf{x}}_{0:k-1} \\ \hat{\mathbf{x}}_k \\ \hat{\mathbf{x}}_{k+1:K} \end{bmatrix}$$
$$= \begin{bmatrix} \mathbf{r}_1 \\ \mathbf{r}_2 - \mathbf{L}_{12}^T\mathbf{L}_{11}^{-1}\mathbf{r}_1 - \mathbf{L}_{32}^T\mathbf{L}_{33}^{-1}\mathbf{r}_3 \\ \mathbf{r}_3 \end{bmatrix}, \tag{3.106}$$

and the solution for $\hat{\mathbf{x}}_k$ is therefore given by

$$\underbrace{\left(\mathbf{L}_{22} - \mathbf{L}_{12}^T\mathbf{L}_{11}^{-1}\mathbf{L}_{12} - \mathbf{L}_{32}^T\mathbf{L}_{33}^{-1}\mathbf{L}_{32}\right)}_{\hat{\mathbf{P}}_k^{-1}} \hat{\mathbf{x}}_k = \underbrace{\left(\mathbf{r}_2 - \mathbf{L}_{12}^T\mathbf{L}_{11}^{-1}\mathbf{r}_1 - \mathbf{L}_{32}^T\mathbf{L}_{33}^{-1}\mathbf{r}_3\right)}_{\mathbf{q}_k},$$
$$\tag{3.107}$$

where we have defined $\hat{\mathbf{P}}_k$ (by its inverse) as well as $\mathbf{q}_k$. We have essentially marginalized out $\hat{\mathbf{x}}_{0:k-1}$ and $\hat{\mathbf{x}}_{k+1:K}$ just as in (3.96). We can now substitute the values of the $\mathbf{L}_{ij}$ blocks back into $\hat{\mathbf{P}}_k^{-1}$ to see that

$$\hat{\mathbf{P}}_k^{-1} = \mathbf{L}_{22} - \mathbf{L}_{12}^T\mathbf{L}_{11}^{-1}\mathbf{L}_{12} - \mathbf{L}_{32}^T\mathbf{L}_{33}^{-1}\mathbf{L}_{32}$$
$$= \underbrace{\mathbf{H}_{22}^T\left(\mathbf{W}_2^{-1} - \mathbf{W}_2^{-1}\mathbf{H}_{21}\left(\mathbf{H}_{11}^T\mathbf{W}_1^{-1}\mathbf{H}_{11} + \mathbf{H}_{21}^T\mathbf{W}_2^{-1}\mathbf{H}_{21}\right)^{-1}\mathbf{H}_{21}^T\mathbf{W}_2^{-1}\right)\mathbf{H}_{22}}_{\hat{\mathbf{P}}_{k,f}^{-1} = \mathbf{H}_{22}^T\left(\mathbf{W}_2 + \mathbf{H}_{21}\left(\mathbf{H}_{11}^T\mathbf{W}_1^{-1}\mathbf{H}_{11}\right)^{-1}\mathbf{H}_{21}^T\right)^{-1}\mathbf{H}_{22}, \text{ by (2.124)}}$$
$$+ \underbrace{\mathbf{H}_{32}^T\left(\mathbf{W}_3^{-1} - \mathbf{W}_3^{-1}\mathbf{H}_{33}\left(\mathbf{H}_{33}^T\mathbf{W}_3^{-1}\mathbf{H}_{33} + \mathbf{H}_{43}^T\mathbf{W}_4^{-1}\mathbf{H}_{43}\right)^{-1}\mathbf{H}_{33}^T\mathbf{W}_3^{-1}\right)\mathbf{H}_{32}}_{\hat{\mathbf{P}}_{k,b}^{-1} = \mathbf{H}_{32}^T\left(\mathbf{W}_3 + \mathbf{H}_{33}\left(\mathbf{H}_{43}^T\mathbf{W}_4^{-1}\mathbf{H}_{43}\right)^{-1}\mathbf{H}_{33}^T\right)^{-1}\mathbf{H}_{32}, \text{ by (2.124)}}$$
$$= \underbrace{\hat{\mathbf{P}}_{k,f}^{-1}}_{\text{forward}} + \underbrace{\hat{\mathbf{P}}_{k,b}^{-1}}_{\text{backward}}, \tag{3.108}$$

where the term labelled 'forward' depends only on the blocks of $\mathbf{H}$ and $\mathbf{W}$ up to time k and the term labelled 'backward' depends only on the blocks of $\mathbf{H}$ and

$\mathbf{W}$ from $k+1$ to K. Turning now to $\mathbf{q}_k$, we substitute in the values of the $\mathbf{L}_{ij}$ and $\mathbf{r}_i$ blocks:

$$\begin{aligned}
\mathbf{q}_k &= \mathbf{r}_2 - \mathbf{L}_{12}^T \mathbf{L}_{11}^{-1} \mathbf{r}_1 - \mathbf{L}_{32}^T \mathbf{L}_{33}^{-1} \mathbf{r}_3 \\
&= \underbrace{\mathbf{q}_{k,f}}_{\text{forward}} + \underbrace{\mathbf{q}_{k,b}}_{\text{backward}} ,
\end{aligned} \tag{3.109}$$

where again the term labelled 'forward' depends only on quantities up to time k and the term labelled 'backward' depends only on quantities from time $k+1$ to K. We made use of the following definitions:

$$\mathbf{q}_{k,f} = -\mathbf{H}_{22}^T \mathbf{W}_2^{-1} \mathbf{H}_{21} \left(\mathbf{H}_{11}^T \mathbf{W}_1^{-1} \mathbf{H}_{11} + \mathbf{H}_{21}^T \mathbf{W}_2^{-1} \mathbf{H}_{21} \right)^{-1} \mathbf{H}_{11}^T \mathbf{W}_1^{-1} \mathbf{z}_1 \tag{3.110a}$$
$$+ \mathbf{H}_{22}^T \left(\mathbf{W}_2^{-1} - \mathbf{W}_2^{-1} \mathbf{H}_{21} \left(\mathbf{H}_{11}^T \mathbf{W}_1^{-1} \mathbf{H}_{11} + \mathbf{H}_{21}^T \mathbf{W}_2^{-1} \mathbf{H}_{21} \right)^{-1} \mathbf{H}_{21}^T \mathbf{W}_2^{-1} \right) \mathbf{z}_2,$$

$$\mathbf{q}_{k,b} = \mathbf{H}_{32}^T \left(\mathbf{W}_3^{-1} - \mathbf{W}_3^{-1} \mathbf{H}_{33} \left(\mathbf{H}_{33}^T \mathbf{W}_3^{-1} \mathbf{H}_{33} + \mathbf{H}_{43}^T \mathbf{W}_4^{-1} \mathbf{H}_{43} \right)^{-1} \mathbf{H}_{33}^T \mathbf{W}_3^{-1} \right) \mathbf{z}_3$$
$$- \mathbf{H}_{32}^T \mathbf{W}_3^{-1} \mathbf{H}_{33} \left(\mathbf{H}_{43}^T \mathbf{W}_4^{-1} \mathbf{H}_{43} + \mathbf{H}_{33}^T \mathbf{W}_3^{-1} \mathbf{H}_{33} \right)^{-1} \mathbf{H}_{43}^T \mathbf{W}_4^{-1} \mathbf{z}_4. \tag{3.110b}$$

Now let us define the following two 'forward' and 'backward' estimators, $\hat{\mathbf{x}}_{k,f}$ and $\hat{\mathbf{x}}_{k,b}$, respectively:

$$\hat{\mathbf{P}}_{k,f}^{-1} \hat{\mathbf{x}}_{k,f} = \mathbf{q}_{k,f}, \tag{3.111a}$$
$$\hat{\mathbf{P}}_{k,b}^{-1} \hat{\mathbf{x}}_{k,b} = \mathbf{q}_{k,b}, \tag{3.111b}$$

where $\hat{\mathbf{x}}_{k,f}$ depends only on quantities up to time k and $\hat{\mathbf{x}}_{k,b}$ depends only on quantities from time $k+1$ to K. Under these definitions we have that

$$\hat{\mathbf{P}}_k^{-1} = \hat{\mathbf{P}}_{k,f}^{-1} + \hat{\mathbf{P}}_{k,b}^{-1}, \tag{3.112}$$
$$\hat{\mathbf{P}}_k^{-1} \hat{\mathbf{x}}_k = \hat{\mathbf{P}}_{k,f}^{-1} \hat{\mathbf{x}}_{k,f} + \hat{\mathbf{P}}_{k,b}^{-1} \hat{\mathbf{x}}_{k,b}, \tag{3.113}$$

which is precisely the normalized product of two Gaussian PDFs, as was discussed in Section 2.2.8. Referring back to (3.97), we have that

$$p(\mathbf{x}_k | \mathbf{v}, \mathbf{y}) \rightarrow \mathcal{N} \left(\hat{\mathbf{x}}_k, \hat{\mathbf{P}}_k \right), \tag{3.114a}$$

$$p(\mathbf{x}_k | \check{\mathbf{x}}_0, \mathbf{v}_{1:k}, \mathbf{y}_{0:k}) \rightarrow \mathcal{N} \left(\hat{\mathbf{x}}_{k,f}, \hat{\mathbf{P}}_{k,f} \right), \tag{3.114b}$$

$$p(\mathbf{x}_k | \mathbf{v}_{k+1:K}, \mathbf{y}_{k+1:K}) \rightarrow \mathcal{N} \left(\hat{\mathbf{x}}_{k,b}, \hat{\mathbf{P}}_{k,b} \right). \tag{3.114c}$$

where $\hat{\mathbf{P}}_k$, $\hat{\mathbf{P}}_{k,f}$, and $\hat{\mathbf{P}}_{k,b}$ are the covariances associated with $\hat{\mathbf{x}}_k$, $\hat{\mathbf{x}}_{k,f}$, and $\hat{\mathbf{x}}_{k,b}$. In other words we have Gaussian estimators with the MAP estimators as the means.

In the next section, we will examine how we can turn the forward Gaussian estimator, $\hat{\mathbf{x}}_{k,f}$, into a recursive filter.[17]

---

[17] A similar thing can be done for the backwards estimator, but the recursion is backwards in time rather than forwards.

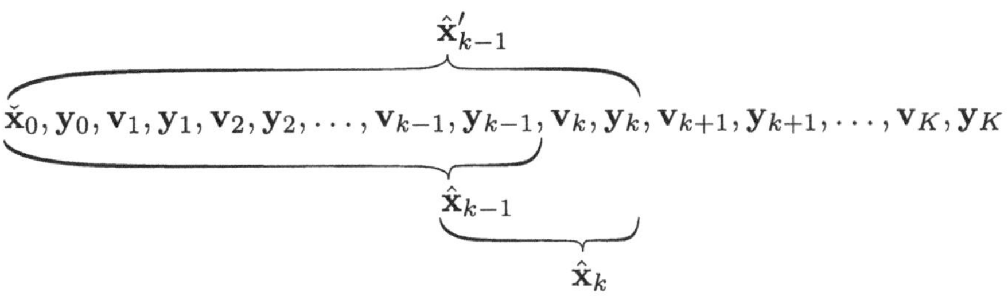

Figure 3.4
Recursive filter
replaces past data
with an estimate.

3.3.2 Kalman Filter via MAP

In this section, we will show how to turn the forward estimator from the last section into a recursive filter called the *Kalman filter* (Kalman, 1960b) using our MAP approach. To simplify the notation slightly, we will use $\hat{\mathbf{x}}_k$ instead of $\hat{\mathbf{x}}_{k,f}$ and $\hat{\mathbf{P}}_k$ instead of $\hat{\mathbf{P}}_{k,f}$, but these new symbols should not be confused with the batch/smoothed estimates discussed previously. Let us assume we already have a forwards estimate and the associated covariance at some time $k - 1$:

$$\left\{\hat{\mathbf{x}}_{k-1}, \hat{\mathbf{P}}_{k-1}\right\}. \tag{3.115}$$

Recall that these estimates are based on all the data up to and including those at time $k - 1$. Our goal will be to compute

$$\left\{\hat{\mathbf{x}}_k, \hat{\mathbf{P}}_k\right\}, \tag{3.116}$$

using all the data up to and including those at time k. It turns out we do not need to start all over again, but rather can simply incorporate the new data at time k, $\mathbf{v}_k$ and $\mathbf{y}_k$, into the estimate at time $k - 1$:

$$\left\{\hat{\mathbf{x}}_{k-1}, \hat{\mathbf{P}}_{k-1}, \mathbf{v}_k, \mathbf{y}_k\right\} \mapsto \left\{\hat{\mathbf{x}}_k, \hat{\mathbf{P}}_k\right\}. \tag{3.117}$$

To see this, we define

$$\mathbf{z} = \begin{bmatrix} \hat{\mathbf{x}}_{k-1} \\ \mathbf{v}_k \\ \mathbf{y}_k \end{bmatrix}, \quad \mathbf{H} = \begin{bmatrix} \mathbf{1} \\ -\mathbf{A}_{k-1} & \mathbf{1} \\ & \mathbf{C}_k \end{bmatrix}, \quad \mathbf{W} = \begin{bmatrix} \hat{\mathbf{P}}_{k-1} \\ & \mathbf{Q}_k \\ & & \mathbf{R}_k \end{bmatrix}, \tag{3.118}$$

where $\left\{\hat{\mathbf{x}}_{k-1}, \hat{\mathbf{P}}_{k-1}\right\}$ serve as substitutes for all the data up to time $k - 1$.[18] Figure 3.4 depicts this graphically.

Our usual MAP solution to the problem is $\hat{\mathbf{x}}$ given by

$$\left(\mathbf{H}^T \mathbf{W}^{-1} \mathbf{H}\right) \hat{\mathbf{x}} = \mathbf{H}^T \mathbf{W}^{-1} \mathbf{z}. \tag{3.119}$$

We then define

$$\hat{\mathbf{x}} = \begin{bmatrix} \hat{\mathbf{x}}'_{k-1} \\ \hat{\mathbf{x}}_k \end{bmatrix}, \tag{3.120}$$

where we carefully distinguish $\hat{\mathbf{x}}'_{k-1}$ from $\hat{\mathbf{x}}_{k-1}$. The addition of the $'$ indicates that $\hat{\mathbf{x}}'_{k-1}$ is the estimate at time $k-1$ incorporating data up to and including time

---

[18] To do this, we have actually employed something called the *Markov property*. Further discussion of this will be left to Chapter 4 on nonlinear non-Gaussian estimation techniques. For now it suffices to say that for LG estimation, this assumption is valid.

k, whereas $\hat{\mathbf{x}}_{k-1}$ is the estimate at time $k-1$ using data up to and including time $k-1$. Substituting in our quantities from (3.118) to the least-squares solution, we have

$$
\begin{bmatrix} \hat{\mathbf{P}}_{k-1}^{-1} + \mathbf{A}_{k-1}^T \mathbf{Q}_k^{-1} \mathbf{A}_{k-1} & -\mathbf{A}_{k-1}^T \mathbf{Q}_k^{-1} \\ -\mathbf{Q}_k^{-1} \mathbf{A}_{k-1} & \mathbf{Q}_k^{-1} + \mathbf{C}_k^T \mathbf{R}_k^{-1} \mathbf{C}_k \end{bmatrix} \begin{bmatrix} \hat{\mathbf{x}}_{k-1}' \\ \hat{\mathbf{x}}_k \end{bmatrix}
$$
$$
= \begin{bmatrix} \hat{\mathbf{P}}_{k-1}^{-1} \hat{\mathbf{x}}_{k-1} - \mathbf{A}_{k-1}^T \mathbf{Q}_k^{-1} \mathbf{v}_k \\ \mathbf{Q}_k^{-1} \mathbf{v}_k + \mathbf{C}_k^T \mathbf{R}_k^{-1} \mathbf{y}_k \end{bmatrix}. \quad (3.121)
$$

We do not really care what $\hat{\mathbf{x}}_{k-1}'$ is in this context, because we seek a recursive estimator appropriate to online estimation, and this quantity incorporates future data; we can marginalize this out by left-multiplying both sides by

$$
\begin{bmatrix} \mathbf{1} & \mathbf{0} \\ \mathbf{Q}_k^{-1} \mathbf{A}_{k-1} \left(\hat{\mathbf{P}}_{k-1}^{-1} + \mathbf{A}_{k-1}^T \mathbf{Q}_k^{-1} \mathbf{A}_{k-1} \right)^{-1} & \mathbf{1} \end{bmatrix}, \quad (3.122)
$$

which is just an elementary row operation and will not alter the solution to the linear system of equations.[19] Equation (3.121) then becomes

$$
\begin{bmatrix} \hat{\mathbf{P}}_{k-1}^{-1} + \mathbf{A}_{k-1}^T \mathbf{Q}_k^{-1} \mathbf{A}_{k-1} & -\mathbf{A}_{k-1}^T \mathbf{Q}_k^{-1} \\ \mathbf{0} & \mathbf{Q}_k^{-1} - \mathbf{Q}_k^{-1} \mathbf{A}_{k-1} \left(\hat{\mathbf{P}}_{k-1}^{-1} + \mathbf{A}_{k-1}^T \mathbf{Q}_k^{-1} \mathbf{A}_{k-1} \right)^{-1} \\ & \times \mathbf{A}_{k-1}^T \mathbf{Q}_k^{-1} + \mathbf{C}_k^T \mathbf{R}_k^{-1} \mathbf{C}_k \end{bmatrix} \begin{bmatrix} \hat{\mathbf{x}}_{k-1}' \\ \hat{\mathbf{x}}_k \end{bmatrix}
$$
$$
= \begin{bmatrix} \hat{\mathbf{P}}_{k-1}^{-1} \hat{\mathbf{x}}_{k-1} - \mathbf{A}_{k-1}^T \mathbf{Q}_k^{-1} \mathbf{v}_k \\ \mathbf{Q}_k^{-1} \mathbf{A}_{k-1} \left(\hat{\mathbf{P}}_{k-1}^{-1} + \mathbf{A}_{k-1}^T \mathbf{Q}_k^{-1} \mathbf{A}_{k-1} \right)^{-1} \left(\hat{\mathbf{P}}_{k-1}^{-1} \hat{\mathbf{x}}_{k-1} - \mathbf{A}_{k-1}^T \mathbf{Q}_k^{-1} \mathbf{v}_k \right) \\ + \mathbf{Q}_k^{-1} \mathbf{v}_k + \mathbf{C}_k^T \mathbf{R}_k^{-1} \mathbf{y}_k \end{bmatrix}.
$$
$$(3.123)$$

The solution for $\hat{\mathbf{x}}_k$ is given by

$$
\left(\underbrace{\mathbf{Q}_k^{-1} - \mathbf{Q}_k^{-1} \mathbf{A}_{k-1} \left(\hat{\mathbf{P}}_{k-1}^{-1} + \mathbf{A}_{k-1}^T \mathbf{Q}_k^{-1} \mathbf{A}_{k-1} \right)^{-1} \mathbf{A}_{k-1}^T \mathbf{Q}_k^{-1}}_{\left(\mathbf{Q}_k + \mathbf{A}_{k-1} \hat{\mathbf{P}}_{k-1} \mathbf{A}_{k-1}^T \right)^{-1} \text{ by } (2.124)} \right.
$$
$$
\left. + \mathbf{C}_k^T \mathbf{R}_k^{-1} \mathbf{C}_k \right) \hat{\mathbf{x}}_k
$$
$$
= \left(\mathbf{Q}_k^{-1} \mathbf{A}_{k-1} \left(\hat{\mathbf{P}}_{k-1}^{-1} + \mathbf{A}_{k-1}^T \mathbf{Q}_k^{-1} \mathbf{A}_{k-1} \right)^{-1} \right.
$$
$$
\times \left(\hat{\mathbf{P}}_{k-1}^{-1} \hat{\mathbf{x}}_{k-1} - \mathbf{A}_{k-1}^T \mathbf{Q}_k^{-1} \mathbf{v}_k \right)
$$
$$
\left. + \mathbf{Q}_k^{-1} \mathbf{v}_k + \mathbf{C}_k^T \mathbf{R}_k^{-1} \mathbf{y}_k \right). \quad (3.124)
$$

We then define the following helpful quantities:

$$
\check{\mathbf{P}}_k = \mathbf{Q}_k + \mathbf{A}_{k-1} \hat{\mathbf{P}}_{k-1} \mathbf{A}_{k-1}^T, \quad (3.125a)
$$
$$
\hat{\mathbf{P}}_k = \left(\check{\mathbf{P}}_k^{-1} + \mathbf{C}_k^T \mathbf{R}_k^{-1} \mathbf{C}_k \right)^{-1}. \quad (3.125b)
$$

---

[19] This is also sometimes called the *Schur complement*.

Equation (3.124) then becomes

$$
\begin{aligned}
\hat{\mathbf{P}}_k^{-1}\hat{\mathbf{x}}_k &= \mathbf{Q}_k^{-1}\mathbf{A}_{k-1}\left(\hat{\mathbf{P}}_{k-1}^{-1} + \mathbf{A}_{k-1}^T\mathbf{Q}_k^{-1}\mathbf{A}_{k-1}\right)^{-1} \\
&\quad \times \left(\hat{\mathbf{P}}_{k-1}^{-1}\hat{\mathbf{x}}_{k-1} - \mathbf{A}_{k-1}^T\mathbf{Q}_k^{-1}\mathbf{v}_k\right) + \mathbf{Q}_k^{-1}\mathbf{v}_k + \mathbf{C}_k^T\mathbf{R}_k^{-1}\mathbf{y}_k \\
&= \underbrace{\mathbf{Q}_k^{-1}\mathbf{A}_{k-1}\left(\hat{\mathbf{P}}_{k-1}^{-1} + \mathbf{A}_{k-1}^T\mathbf{Q}_k^{-1}\mathbf{A}_{k-1}\right)^{-1}\hat{\mathbf{P}}_{k-1}^{-1}}_{\check{\mathbf{P}}_k^{-1}\mathbf{A}_{k-1}\ \text{by logic below}}\hat{\mathbf{x}}_{k-1} \\
&\quad + \underbrace{\left(\mathbf{Q}_k^{-1} - \mathbf{Q}_k^{-1}\mathbf{A}_{k-1}\left(\hat{\mathbf{P}}_{k-1}^{-1} + \mathbf{A}_{k-1}^T\mathbf{Q}_k^{-1}\mathbf{A}_{k-1}\right)^{-1}\mathbf{A}_{k-1}^T\mathbf{Q}_k^{-1}\right)}_{\check{\mathbf{P}}_k^{-1}}\mathbf{v}_k \\
&\hspace{7cm} + \mathbf{C}_k^T\mathbf{R}_k^{-1}\mathbf{y}_k \\
&= \check{\mathbf{P}}_k^{-1}\underbrace{\left(\mathbf{A}_{k-1}\hat{\mathbf{x}}_{k-1} + \mathbf{v}_k\right)}_{\check{\mathbf{x}}_k} + \mathbf{C}_k^T\mathbf{R}_k^{-1}\mathbf{y}_k, \qquad (3.126)
\end{aligned}
$$

where we have defined $\check{\mathbf{x}}_k$ as the 'predicted' value of the state. We also made use of the following logic in simplifying the preceding math:

$$
\begin{aligned}
\mathbf{Q}_k^{-1}\mathbf{A}_{k-1}&\underbrace{\left(\hat{\mathbf{P}}_{k-1}^{-1} + \mathbf{A}_{k-1}^T\mathbf{Q}_k^{-1}\mathbf{A}_{k-1}\right)^{-1}\hat{\mathbf{P}}_{k-1}^{-1}}_{\text{apply (2.124) again}} \\
&= \mathbf{Q}_k^{-1}\mathbf{A}_{k-1}\Big(\hat{\mathbf{P}}_{k-1} - \hat{\mathbf{P}}_{k-1}\mathbf{A}_{k-1}^T\underbrace{\left(\mathbf{Q}_k + \mathbf{A}_{k-1}\hat{\mathbf{P}}_{k-1}\mathbf{A}_{k-1}^T\right)^{-1}}_{\check{\mathbf{P}}_k^{-1}} \\
&\hspace{4cm} \times\ \mathbf{A}_{k-1}\hat{\mathbf{P}}_{k-1}\Big)\hat{\mathbf{P}}_{k-1}^{-1} \\
&= \left(\mathbf{Q}_k^{-1} - \mathbf{Q}_k^{-1}\underbrace{\mathbf{A}_{k-1}\hat{\mathbf{P}}_{k-1}\mathbf{A}_{k-1}^T}_{\check{\mathbf{P}}_k-\mathbf{Q}_k}\check{\mathbf{P}}_k^{-1}\right)\mathbf{A}_{k-1} \\
&= \left(\mathbf{Q}_k^{-1} - \mathbf{Q}_k^{-1} + \check{\mathbf{P}}_k^{-1}\right)\mathbf{A}_{k-1} \\
&= \check{\mathbf{P}}_k^{-1}\mathbf{A}_{k-1}. \qquad (3.127)
\end{aligned}
$$

Bringing together all of these parts, we have for the recursive filter update the following:

$$
\begin{aligned}
\text{predictor:} \quad & \check{\mathbf{P}}_k = \mathbf{A}_{k-1}\hat{\mathbf{P}}_{k-1}\mathbf{A}_{k-1}^T + \mathbf{Q}_k, && (3.128a) \\
& \check{\mathbf{x}}_k = \mathbf{A}_{k-1}\hat{\mathbf{x}}_{k-1} + \mathbf{v}_k, && (3.128b) \\
\text{corrector:} \quad & \hat{\mathbf{P}}_k^{-1} = \check{\mathbf{P}}_k^{-1} + \mathbf{C}_k^T\mathbf{R}_k^{-1}\mathbf{C}_k, && (3.128c) \\
& \hat{\mathbf{P}}_k^{-1}\hat{\mathbf{x}}_k = \check{\mathbf{P}}_k^{-1}\check{\mathbf{x}}_k + \mathbf{C}_k^T\mathbf{R}_k^{-1}\mathbf{y}_k, && (3.128d)
\end{aligned}
$$

which we will refer to as *inverse covariance* or information form for the Kalman filter. Figure 3.5 depicts the predictor-corrector form of the Kalman filter graphically.

Figure 3.5 The Kalman filter works in two steps: prediction then correction. The prediction step propagates the old estimate, $\hat{x}_{k-1}$, forward in time using the measurement model and latest input, v_k, to arrive at the prediction, $\check{x}_k$. The correction step fuses the prediction with the latest measurement, y_k, to arrive at the new estimate, $\hat{x}_k$; this step is carried out using a normalized product of Gaussians (clear from inverse covariance version of KF).

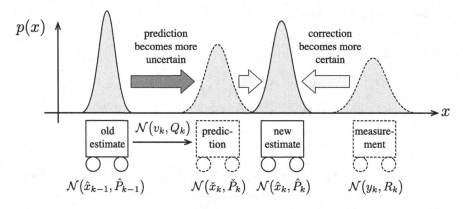

To get to *canonical form*, we manipulate these equations slightly. Begin by defining the *Kalman gain*, $\mathbf{K}_k$, as

$$\mathbf{K}_k = \hat{\mathbf{P}}_k \mathbf{C}_k^T \mathbf{R}_k^{-1}. \tag{3.129}$$

We then manipulate:

$$1 = \hat{\mathbf{P}}_k \left(\check{\mathbf{P}}_k^{-1} + \mathbf{C}_k^T \mathbf{R}_k^{-1} \mathbf{C}_k \right)$$

$$= \hat{\mathbf{P}}_k \check{\mathbf{P}}_k^{-1} + \mathbf{K}_k \mathbf{C}_k, \tag{3.130a}$$

$$\hat{\mathbf{P}}_k = \left(1 - \mathbf{K}_k \mathbf{C}_k \right) \check{\mathbf{P}}_k, \tag{3.130b}$$

$$\underbrace{\hat{\mathbf{P}}_k \mathbf{C}_k^T \mathbf{R}_k^{-1}}_{\mathbf{K}_k} = \left(1 - \mathbf{K}_k \mathbf{C}_k \right) \check{\mathbf{P}}_k \mathbf{C}_k^T \mathbf{R}_k^{-1}, \tag{3.130c}$$

$$\mathbf{K}_k \left(1 + \mathbf{C}_k \check{\mathbf{P}}_k \mathbf{C}_k^T \mathbf{R}_k^{-1} \right) = \check{\mathbf{P}}_k \mathbf{C}_k^T \mathbf{R}_k^{-1}. \tag{3.130d}$$

Solving for $\mathbf{K}_k$ in this last expression, we can rewrite the recursive filter equations as

$$\text{predictor:} \quad \begin{aligned} \check{\mathbf{P}}_k &= \mathbf{A}_{k-1} \hat{\mathbf{P}}_{k-1} \mathbf{A}_{k-1}^T + \mathbf{Q}_k, & (3.131a) \\ \check{\mathbf{x}}_k &= \mathbf{A}_{k-1} \hat{\mathbf{x}}_{k-1} + \mathbf{v}_k, & (3.131b) \end{aligned}$$

$$\text{Kalman gain:} \quad \mathbf{K}_k = \check{\mathbf{P}}_k \mathbf{C}_k^T \left(\mathbf{C}_k \check{\mathbf{P}}_k \mathbf{C}_k^T + \mathbf{R}_k \right)^{-1}, \quad (3.131c)$$

$$\text{corrector:} \quad \begin{aligned} \hat{\mathbf{P}}_k &= \left(1 - \mathbf{K}_k \mathbf{C}_k \right) \check{\mathbf{P}}_k, & (3.131d) \\ \hat{\mathbf{x}}_k &= \check{\mathbf{x}}_k + \mathbf{K}_k \underbrace{\left(\mathbf{y}_k - \mathbf{C}_k \check{\mathbf{x}}_k \right)}_{\text{innovation}}, & (3.131e) \end{aligned}$$

where the *innovation* has been highlighted; it is the difference between the actual and expected measurements. The role of the Kalman gain is to properly weight the innovation's contribution to the estimate (in comparison to the prediction). In this form, these five equations (and their extension to nonlinear systems) have been the workhorse of estimation since Kalman's initial paper (Kalman, 1960b). These are identical to the forward pass of the Rauch–Tung–Striebel smoother discussed previously (with the $(\cdot)_f$ subscripts dropped).

3.3.3 Kalman Filter via Bayesian Inference

A cleaner, simpler derivation of the Kalman filter can be had using our Bayesian inference approach.[20] Our Gaussian prior estimate at $k - 1$ is

$$p(\mathbf{x}_{k-1}|\check{\mathbf{x}}_0, \mathbf{v}_{1:k-1}, \mathbf{y}_{0:k-1}) = \mathcal{N}\left(\hat{\mathbf{x}}_{k-1}, \hat{\mathbf{P}}_{k-1}\right). \qquad (3.132)$$

First, for the *prediction step*, we incorporate the latest input, $\mathbf{v}_k$, to write a 'prior' at time k:

$$p(\mathbf{x}_k|\check{\mathbf{x}}_0, \mathbf{v}_{1:k}, \mathbf{y}_{0:k-1}) = \mathcal{N}\left(\check{\mathbf{x}}_k, \check{\mathbf{P}}_k\right), \qquad (3.133)$$

where

$$\check{\mathbf{P}}_k = \mathbf{A}_{k-1}\hat{\mathbf{P}}_{k-1}\mathbf{A}_{k-1}^T + \mathbf{Q}_k, \qquad (3.134a)$$

$$\check{\mathbf{x}}_k = \mathbf{A}_{k-1}\hat{\mathbf{x}}_{k-1} + \mathbf{v}_k. \qquad (3.134b)$$

These are identical to the prediction equations from the previous section. These last two expressions can be found by exactly passing the prior at $k - 1$ through the linear motion model. For the mean we have

$$\begin{aligned}
\check{\mathbf{x}}_k = E\left[\mathbf{x}_k\right] &= E\left[\mathbf{A}_{k-1}\mathbf{x}_{k-1} + \mathbf{v}_k + \mathbf{w}_k\right] \\
&= \mathbf{A}_{k-1}\underbrace{E\left[\mathbf{x}_{k-1}\right]}_{\hat{\mathbf{x}}_{k-1}} + \mathbf{v}_k + \underbrace{E\left[\mathbf{w}_k\right]}_{\mathbf{0}} = \mathbf{A}_{k-1}\hat{\mathbf{x}}_{k-1} + \mathbf{v}_k, \quad (3.135)
\end{aligned}$$

and for the covariance we have

$$\begin{aligned}
\check{\mathbf{P}}_k &= E\left[(\mathbf{x}_k - E[\mathbf{x}_k])(\mathbf{x}_k - E[\mathbf{x}_k])^T\right] \\
&= E\big[(\mathbf{A}_{k-1}\mathbf{x}_{k-1} + \mathbf{v}_k + \mathbf{w}_k - \mathbf{A}_{k-1}\hat{\mathbf{x}}_{k-1} - \mathbf{v}_k) \\
&\qquad\quad \times (\mathbf{A}_{k-1}\mathbf{x}_{k-1} + \mathbf{v}_k + \mathbf{w}_k - \mathbf{A}_{k-1}\hat{\mathbf{x}}_{k-1} - \mathbf{v}_k)^T\big] \\
&= \mathbf{A}_{k-1}\underbrace{E\left[(\mathbf{x}_{k-1} - \hat{\mathbf{x}}_{k-1})(\mathbf{x}_{k-1} - \hat{\mathbf{x}}_{k-1})^T\right]}_{\hat{\mathbf{P}}_{k-1}}\mathbf{A}_{k-1}^T + \underbrace{E\left[\mathbf{w}_k\mathbf{w}_k^T\right]}_{\mathbf{Q}_k} \\
&= \mathbf{A}_{k-1}\hat{\mathbf{P}}_{k-1}\mathbf{A}_{k-1}^T + \mathbf{Q}_k. \qquad (3.136)
\end{aligned}$$

Next, for the *correction step*, we express the joint density of our state and latest measurement, at time k, as a Gaussian:

$$\begin{aligned}
p(\mathbf{x}_k, \mathbf{y}_k|\check{\mathbf{x}}_0, \mathbf{v}_{1:k}, \mathbf{y}_{0:k-1}) &= \mathcal{N}\left(\begin{bmatrix}\boldsymbol{\mu}_x \\ \boldsymbol{\mu}_y\end{bmatrix}, \begin{bmatrix}\boldsymbol{\Sigma}_{xx} & \boldsymbol{\Sigma}_{xy} \\ \boldsymbol{\Sigma}_{yx} & \boldsymbol{\Sigma}_{yy}\end{bmatrix}\right) \qquad (3.137) \\
&= \mathcal{N}\left(\begin{bmatrix}\check{\mathbf{x}}_k \\ \mathbf{C}_k\check{\mathbf{x}}_k\end{bmatrix}, \begin{bmatrix}\check{\mathbf{P}}_k & \check{\mathbf{P}}_k\mathbf{C}_k^T \\ \mathbf{C}_k\check{\mathbf{P}}_k & \mathbf{C}_k\check{\mathbf{P}}_k\mathbf{C}_k^T + \mathbf{R}_k\end{bmatrix}\right).
\end{aligned}$$

---

[20] In the next chapter, we will generalize this section to present the *Bayes filter*, which can handle non-Gaussian PDFs as well as nonlinear motion and observation models. We can think of this section as a special case of the Bayes filter, one that requires no approximations to be made.

Looking back to Section 2.2.2, where we introduced Bayesian inference, we can then directly write the conditional density for $\mathbf{x}_k$ (i.e., the posterior) as

$$p(\mathbf{x}_k | \check{\mathbf{x}}_0, \mathbf{v}_{1:k}, \mathbf{y}_{0:k})$$
$$= \mathcal{N}\Big(\underbrace{\boldsymbol{\mu}_x + \boldsymbol{\Sigma}_{xy} \boldsymbol{\Sigma}_{yy}^{-1} (\mathbf{y}_k - \boldsymbol{\mu}_y)}_{\hat{\mathbf{x}}_k}, \underbrace{\boldsymbol{\Sigma}_{xx} - \boldsymbol{\Sigma}_{xy} \boldsymbol{\Sigma}_{yy}^{-1} \boldsymbol{\Sigma}_{yx}}_{\hat{\mathbf{P}}_k}\Big), \quad (3.138)$$

where we have defined $\hat{\mathbf{x}}_k$ as the mean and $\hat{\mathbf{P}}_k$ as the covariance. Substituting in the moments from the preceding math, we have

$$\mathbf{K}_k = \check{\mathbf{P}}_k \mathbf{C}_k^T \left(\mathbf{C}_k \check{\mathbf{P}}_k \mathbf{C}_k^T + \mathbf{R}_k\right)^{-1}, \quad (3.139a)$$

$$\hat{\mathbf{P}}_k = (\mathbf{1} - \mathbf{K}_k \mathbf{C}_k) \check{\mathbf{P}}_k, \quad (3.139b)$$

$$\hat{\mathbf{x}}_k = \check{\mathbf{x}}_k + \mathbf{K}_k (\mathbf{y}_k - \mathbf{C}_k \check{\mathbf{x}}_k), \quad (3.139c)$$

which are identical to the correction equations from the previous section on MAP. Again, this is because the motion and measurement models are *linear* and the noises and prior are Gaussian. Under these conditions, the posterior density is exactly Gaussian. Thus, the *mean* and *mode* of the posterior are one and the same. This property does not hold if we switch to a *nonlinear* measurement model, which we discuss in the next chapter.

3.3.4 Kalman Filter via Gain Optimization

The Kalman filter is often referred to as being *optimal*. We did indeed perform an optimization to come up with the recursive relations earlier in the MAP derivation. There are also several other ways to look at the optimality of the KF. We present one of these.

Assume we have an estimator with the correction step taking the form

$$\hat{\mathbf{x}}_k = \check{\mathbf{x}}_k + \mathbf{K}_k (\mathbf{y}_k - \mathbf{C}_k \check{\mathbf{x}}_k), \quad (3.140)$$

but we do not yet know the gain matrix, $\mathbf{K}_k$, to blend the corrective measurements with the prediction. If we define the error in the state estimate to be

$$\hat{\mathbf{e}}_k = \hat{\mathbf{x}}_k - \mathbf{x}_k, \quad (3.141)$$

then we have[21]

$$E[\hat{\mathbf{e}}_k \hat{\mathbf{e}}_k^T] = (\mathbf{1} - \mathbf{K}_k \mathbf{C}_k) \check{\mathbf{P}}_k (\mathbf{1} - \mathbf{K}_k \mathbf{C}_k)^T + \mathbf{K}_k \mathbf{R}_k \mathbf{K}_k^T. \quad (3.142)$$

We then define a cost function of the form

$$J(\mathbf{K}_k) = \frac{1}{2} \text{tr}\, E[\hat{\mathbf{e}}_k \hat{\mathbf{e}}_k^T] = E\left[\frac{1}{2} \hat{\mathbf{e}}_k^T \hat{\mathbf{e}}_k\right], \quad (3.143)$$

---

[21] This is sometimes referred to as the *Joseph form* of the covariance update.

which quantifies (in some sense) the magnitude of the covariance of $\hat{\mathbf{e}}_k$. We can minimize this cost directly with respect to $\mathbf{K}_k$, to generate the *minimum mean-squared error (MMSE)* estimate. We will make use of the identities

$$\frac{\partial \mathrm{tr}\, \mathbf{XY}}{\partial \mathbf{X}} \equiv \mathbf{Y}^T, \qquad \frac{\partial \mathrm{tr}\, \mathbf{XZX}^T}{\partial \mathbf{X}} \equiv 2\mathbf{XZ}, \qquad (3.144)$$

where $\mathbf{Z}$ is symmetric. Then we have

$$\frac{\partial J(\mathbf{K}_k)}{\partial \mathbf{K}_k} = -(1 - \mathbf{K}_k \mathbf{C}_k)\, \check{\mathbf{P}}_k \mathbf{C}_k^T + \mathbf{K}_k \mathbf{R}_k. \qquad (3.145a)$$

Setting this to zero and solving for $\mathbf{K}_k$, we have

$$\mathbf{K}_k = \check{\mathbf{P}}_k \mathbf{C}_k^T \left(\mathbf{C}_k \check{\mathbf{P}}_k \mathbf{C}_k^T + \mathbf{R}_k \right)^{-1}, \qquad (3.146)$$

which is our usual expression for the Kalman gain.

This is also an appropriate place to mention that weighted least-squares in general is optimal in the MMSE sense so long as the measurement errors are independent, zero mean, and of finite variance (which we assume is known in order to weigh each measurement appropriately). Critically, the errors need not be Gaussian distributed, yet no other unbiased estimator can perform better. This is why least-squares is sometimes referred to as the *best linear unbiased estimate (BLUE)*. Least-squares was pioneered by Gauss (1809) who later showed it to be optimal without any assumptions regarding the distribution errors (Gauss, 1821, 1823). This result was rediscovered by Markov (1912), leading to the more commonly known Gauss–Markov theorem (Bjorck, 1996).

Andrey Andreyevich Markov (1856–1922) was a Russian mathematician known for his work on stochastic processes, particularly Markov chains and the Markov property, which bear his name.

3.3.5 Kalman Filter Discussion

There are a few points worth mentioning:

(i) For a linear system with Gaussian noise, the Kalman filter equations are the *best linear unbiased estimate (BLUE)*; this means they are performing right at the Cramér–Rao lower bound.

(ii) Initial conditions must be provided, $\{\check{\mathbf{x}}_0, \check{\mathbf{P}}_0\}$.

(iii) The covariance equations can be propagated independently of the mean equations. Sometimes a steady-state value of $\mathbf{K}_k$ is computed and used for all timesteps to propagate the mean; this is known as the 'steady-state Kalman filter'.

(iv) At implementation, we must use $\mathbf{y}_{k,\mathrm{meas}}$, the actual readings we receive from our sensors, in the filter.

(v) A similar set of equations can be developed for the backwards estimator that runs backwards in time.

It is worth reminding ourselves that we have arrived at the Kalman filter equations through both an optimization paradigm and a full Bayesian paradigm. The difference between these two will be significant when we consider what happens in the nonlinear case (and why the extension of the Kalman filter, the *extended Kalman filter (EKF)*, does not perform well in many situations).

3.3.6 Error Dynamics

It is useful to look at the difference between the estimated state and the actual state. We define the following errors:

$$\check{\mathbf{e}}_k = \check{\mathbf{x}}_k - \mathbf{x}_k, \tag{3.147a}$$

$$\hat{\mathbf{e}}_k = \hat{\mathbf{x}}_k - \mathbf{x}_k. \tag{3.147b}$$

Using (3.1) and (3.131), we can then write out the 'error dynamics':

$$\check{\mathbf{e}}_k = \mathbf{A}_{k-1}\hat{\mathbf{e}}_{k-1} - \mathbf{w}_k, \tag{3.148a}$$

$$\hat{\mathbf{e}}_k = (\mathbf{1} - \mathbf{K}_k\mathbf{C}_k)\,\check{\mathbf{e}}_k + \mathbf{K}_k\mathbf{n}_k, \tag{3.148b}$$

where we note that $\hat{\mathbf{e}}_0 = \hat{\mathbf{x}}_0 - \mathbf{x}_0$. From this system it is not hard to see that $E[\hat{\mathbf{e}}_k] = \mathbf{0}$ for $k > 0$ so long as $E[\hat{\mathbf{e}}_0] = \mathbf{0}$. This means our estimator is *unbiased*. We can use proof by induction. It is true for $k = 0$ by assertion. Assume it is also true for $k - 1$. Then

$$E[\check{\mathbf{e}}_k] = \mathbf{A}_{k-1}\underbrace{E[\hat{\mathbf{e}}_{k-1}]}_{0} - \underbrace{E[\mathbf{w}_k]}_{0} = \mathbf{0}, \tag{3.149a}$$

$$E[\hat{\mathbf{e}}_k] = (\mathbf{1} - \mathbf{K}_k\mathbf{C}_k)\underbrace{E[\check{\mathbf{e}}_k]}_{0} + \mathbf{K}_k\underbrace{E[\mathbf{n}_k]}_{0} = \mathbf{0}. \tag{3.149b}$$

It is therefore true for all k. It is less obvious that

$$E[\check{\mathbf{e}}_k\check{\mathbf{e}}_k^T] = \check{\mathbf{P}}_k, \tag{3.150a}$$

$$E[\hat{\mathbf{e}}_k\hat{\mathbf{e}}_k^T] = \hat{\mathbf{P}}_k, \tag{3.150b}$$

for $k > 0$ so long as $E[\hat{\mathbf{e}}_0\hat{\mathbf{e}}_0^T] = \hat{\mathbf{P}}_0$. This means our estimator is *consistent*. We again use proof by induction. It is true for $k = 0$ by assertion. Assume $E[\hat{\mathbf{e}}_{k-1}\hat{\mathbf{e}}_{k-1}^T] = \hat{\mathbf{P}}_{k-1}$. Then

$$E[\check{\mathbf{e}}_k\check{\mathbf{e}}_k^T] = E\left[(\mathbf{A}_{k-1}\hat{\mathbf{e}}_{k-1} - \mathbf{w}_k)(\mathbf{A}_{k-1}\hat{\mathbf{e}}_{k-1} - \mathbf{w}_k)^T\right]$$

$$= \mathbf{A}_{k-1}\underbrace{E[\hat{\mathbf{e}}_{k-1}\hat{\mathbf{e}}_{k-1}^T]}_{\hat{\mathbf{P}}_{k-1}}\mathbf{A}_{k-1}^T - \mathbf{A}_{k-1}\underbrace{E[\hat{\mathbf{e}}_{k-1}\mathbf{w}_k^T]}_{\mathbf{0}\text{ by independence}}$$

$$- \underbrace{E[\mathbf{w}_k\hat{\mathbf{e}}_{k-1}^T]}_{\mathbf{0}\text{ by independence}}\mathbf{A}_{k-1}^T + \underbrace{E[\mathbf{w}_k\mathbf{w}_k^T]}_{\mathbf{Q}_k}$$

$$= \check{\mathbf{P}}_k, \tag{3.151}$$

and

$$
\begin{aligned}
E\left[\hat{\mathbf{e}}_k\hat{\mathbf{e}}_k^T\right] &= E\left[\left((\mathbf{1}-\mathbf{K}_k\mathbf{C}_k)\,\check{\mathbf{e}}_k+\mathbf{K}_k\mathbf{n}_k\right)\left((\mathbf{1}-\mathbf{K}_k\mathbf{C}_k)\,\check{\mathbf{e}}_k+\mathbf{K}_k\mathbf{n}_k\right)^T\right] \\
&= (\mathbf{1}-\mathbf{K}_k\mathbf{C}_k)\underbrace{E\left[\check{\mathbf{e}}_k\check{\mathbf{e}}_k^T\right]}_{\check{\mathbf{P}}_k}(\mathbf{1}-\mathbf{K}_k\mathbf{C}_k)^T \\
&\quad + (\mathbf{1}-\mathbf{K}_k\mathbf{C}_k)\underbrace{E\left[\check{\mathbf{e}}_k\mathbf{n}_k^T\right]}_{\text{0 by independence}}\mathbf{K}_k^T \\
&\quad + \mathbf{K}_k\underbrace{E\left[\mathbf{n}_k\check{\mathbf{e}}_k^T\right]}_{\text{0 by independence}}(\mathbf{1}-\mathbf{K}_k\mathbf{C}_k)^T+\mathbf{K}_k\underbrace{E\left[\mathbf{n}_k\mathbf{n}_k^T\right]}_{\mathbf{R}_k}\mathbf{K}_k^T \\
&= (\mathbf{1}-\mathbf{K}_k\mathbf{C}_k)\,\check{\mathbf{P}}_k\underbrace{-\hat{\mathbf{P}}_k\mathbf{C}_k^T\mathbf{K}_k^T+\mathbf{K}_k\mathbf{R}_k\mathbf{K}_k^T}_{\text{0 because }\mathbf{K}_k=\hat{\mathbf{P}}_k\mathbf{C}_k^T\mathbf{R}_k^{-1}} \\
&= \hat{\mathbf{P}}_k. \tag{3.152}
\end{aligned}
$$

It is therefore true for all k. This means that the true uncertainty in the system (i.e., the covariance of the error, $E\left[\hat{\mathbf{e}}_k\hat{\mathbf{e}}_k^T\right]$) is perfectly modelled by our estimate of the covariance, $\hat{\mathbf{P}}_k$. In this sense, the Kalman filter is an optimal filter. This is why it is sometimes referred to as *best linear unbiased estimate (BLUE)*. Yet another way of saying this is that the covariance of the Kalman filter is right at the Cramér–Rao Lower Bound; we cannot be any more certain in our estimate given the uncertainty in the measurements we have used in that estimate.

A final important point to make is that the expectations we have employed in this section are over the possible outcomes of the random variables. They are not time averages. If we were to run an infinite number of trials and average over the trials (i.e., an ensemble average), then we should see an average performance of zero error (i.e., an unbiased estimator). This does not imply that within a single trial (i.e., a realization) the error will be zero or decay to zero over time. Further discussion of bias and consistency can be found in Section 5.1.1.

3.3.7 Existence, Uniqueness, and Observability

A sketch of the stability proof of the KF is provided (Simon, 2006). We consider only the time-invariant case and use italicized symbols to avoid confusion with the lifted form: $\mathbf{A}_k=A,\mathbf{C}_k=C,\mathbf{Q}_k=Q,\mathbf{R}_k=R$. The sketch proceeds as follows:

(i) The covariance equation of the KF can be iterated to convergence prior to computing the equations for the mean. A big question is whether the covariance will converge to a steady-state value and, if so, whether it will be unique. Writing P to mean the steady-state value for $\check{\mathbf{P}}_k$, we have (by combining the predictive and corrective covariance equations) that the following must be true at steady state:

$$
P = A\left(1-KC\right)P\left(1-KC\right)^T A^T + AKRK^T A^T + Q, \tag{3.153}
$$

which is one form of the Discrete Algebraic Riccati Equation (DARE). Note that K depends on P in the preceding equation. The DARE has a unique positive-semidefinite solution, P, if and only if the following conditions hold:

- $R > 0$; note that we already assume this in the batch LG case,
- $Q \geq 0$; in the batch LG case, we actually assumed that $Q > 0$, whereupon the next condition is redundant,
- (A, V) is stabilizable with $V^T V = Q$; this condition is redundant when $Q > 0$,
- (A, C) is detectable; same as 'observable' except any unobservable eigenvalues are stable; we saw a similar observability condition in the batch LG case.

The proof of the preceding statement is beyond the scope of this book.

(ii) Once the covariance evolves to its steady-state value, P, so does the Kalman gain. Let K be the steady-state value of K_k. We have

$$K = PC^T \left(CPC^T + R \right)^{-1} \qquad (3.154)$$

for the steady-state Kalman gain.

(iii) The error dynamics of the filter are then stable:

$$E[\check{e}_k] = \underbrace{A \left(1 - KC \right)}_{\text{eigs. } < 1 \text{ in mag.}} E[\check{e}_{k-1}]. \qquad (3.155)$$

We can see this by noting that for any eigenvector, $\mathbf{v}$, corresponding to an eigenvalue, λ, of $(1 - KC)^T A^T$, we have

$$\mathbf{v}^T P \mathbf{v} = \underbrace{\mathbf{v}^T A \left(1 - KC \right)}_{\lambda \mathbf{v}^T} P \underbrace{\left(1 - KC \right)^T A^T \mathbf{v}}_{\lambda \mathbf{v}}$$
$$+ \mathbf{v}^T \left(AKRK^T A^T + Q \right) \mathbf{v}, \qquad (3.156a)$$

$$(1 - \lambda^2) \underbrace{\mathbf{v}^T P \mathbf{v}}_{>0} = \mathbf{v}^T \underbrace{\left(AKRK^T A^T + Q \right) \mathbf{v}}_{>0}, \qquad (3.156b)$$

which means that we must have $|\lambda| < 1$, and thus the steady-state error dynamics are stable. Technically the right-hand side could be zero, but after N repetitions of this process, we build up a copy of the observability Grammian on the right-hand side, making it invertible (if the system is observable).

3.4 Batch Continuous-Time Estimation

In this section, we circle back to consider a more general problem than the discrete-time setup in the earlier part of this chapter. In particular, we consider what happens when we choose to use a continuous-time motion model as the

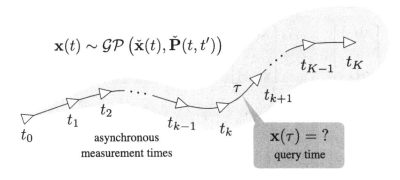

Figure 3.6 State estimation with a continuous-time prior can be viewed as a one-dimensional Gaussian process regression with time as the independent variable. We have data about the trajectory at a number of asynchronous measurement times and would like to query the state at some other time of interest.

prior. We approach the problem from a *Gaussian process regression* perspective (Rasmussen and Williams, 2006). We show that for linear-Gaussian systems, the discrete-time formulation is implementing the continuous-time one exactly, under certain special conditions (Barfoot et al., 2014; Tong et al., 2013).

3.4.1 Gaussian Process Regression

We take a *Gaussian process regression* approach to state estimation.[22] This allows us (i) to represent trajectories in continuous time (and therefore query the solution at any time of interest) and, (ii) for the nonlinear case that we will treat in the next chapter, to optimize our solution by iterating over the entire trajectory (it is difficult to do this in the recursive formulation, which typically iterates at just one timestep at a time). We will show that under a certain special class of prior motion models, GP regression enjoys a sparse structure that allows for very efficient solutions.

We will consider systems with a continuous-time GP process model prior and a discrete-time, linear measurement model:

$$\mathbf{x}(t) \sim \mathcal{GP}(\check{\mathbf{x}}(t), \check{\mathbf{P}}(t, t')), \qquad t_0 < t, t', \qquad (3.157)$$

$$\mathbf{y}_k = \mathbf{C}_k \mathbf{x}(t_k) + \mathbf{n}_k, \qquad t_0 < t_1 < \cdots < t_K, \qquad (3.158)$$

where $\mathbf{x}(t)$ is the state, $\check{\mathbf{x}}(t)$ is the mean function, $\check{\mathbf{P}}(t, t')$ is the covariance function, $\mathbf{y}_k$ are measurements, $\mathbf{n}_k \sim \mathcal{N}(\mathbf{0}, \mathbf{R}_k)$ is Gaussian measurement noise, and $\mathbf{C}_k$ is the measurement model coefficient matrix.

We consider that we want to query the state at a number of times ($\tau_0 < \tau_1 < \ldots < \tau_J$) that may or may not be different from the measurement times ($t_0 < t_1 < \ldots < t_K$). Figure 3.6 depicts our problem setup. The joint density between the state (at the query times) and the measurements (at the measurement times) is written as

$$p\left(\begin{bmatrix} \mathbf{x}_\tau \\ \mathbf{y} \end{bmatrix}\right) = \mathcal{N}\left(\begin{bmatrix} \check{\mathbf{x}}_\tau \\ \mathbf{C}\check{\mathbf{x}} \end{bmatrix}, \begin{bmatrix} \check{\mathbf{P}}_{\tau\tau} & \check{\mathbf{P}}_\tau \mathbf{C}^T \\ \mathbf{C}\check{\mathbf{P}}_\tau^T & \mathbf{R} + \mathbf{C}\check{\mathbf{P}}\mathbf{C}^T \end{bmatrix}\right), \qquad (3.159)$$

---

[22] There are other ways to represent continuous-time trajectories such as temporal basis functions; see Furgale et al. (2015) for a detailed review.

where

$$\mathbf{x} = \begin{bmatrix} \mathbf{x}(t_0) \\ \vdots \\ \mathbf{x}(t_K) \end{bmatrix}, \quad \check{\mathbf{x}} = \begin{bmatrix} \check{\mathbf{x}}(t_0) \\ \vdots \\ \check{\mathbf{x}}(t_K) \end{bmatrix}, \quad \mathbf{x}_\tau = \begin{bmatrix} \mathbf{x}(\tau_0) \\ \vdots \\ \mathbf{x}(\tau_J) \end{bmatrix}, \quad \check{\mathbf{x}}_\tau = \begin{bmatrix} \check{\mathbf{x}}(\tau_0) \\ \vdots \\ \check{\mathbf{x}}(\tau_J) \end{bmatrix},$$

$$\mathbf{y} = \begin{bmatrix} \mathbf{y}_0 \\ \vdots \\ \mathbf{y}_K \end{bmatrix}, \quad \mathbf{C} = \mathrm{diag}\,(\mathbf{C}_0, \ldots, \mathbf{C}_K), \quad \mathbf{R} = \mathrm{diag}\,(\mathbf{R}_0, \ldots, \mathbf{R}_K),$$

$$\check{\mathbf{P}} = \left[\check{\mathbf{P}}(t_i, t_j)\right]_{ij}, \quad \check{\mathbf{P}}_\tau = \left[\check{\mathbf{P}}(\tau_i, t_j)\right]_{ij}, \quad \check{\mathbf{P}}_{\tau\tau} = \left[\check{\mathbf{P}}(\tau_i, \tau_j)\right]_{ij}.$$

In GP regression, the matrix, $\check{\mathbf{P}}$, is known as the *kernel matrix*. Based on the factoring discussed in Section 2.2.2, we then have that

$$p(\mathbf{x}_\tau | \mathbf{y}) = \mathcal{N}\bigg(\underbrace{\check{\mathbf{x}}_\tau + \check{\mathbf{P}}_\tau \mathbf{C}^T (\mathbf{C}\check{\mathbf{P}}\mathbf{C}^T + \mathbf{R})^{-1}(\mathbf{y} - \mathbf{C}\check{\mathbf{x}})}_{\hat{\mathbf{x}}_\tau,\,\text{mean}},$$

$$\underbrace{\check{\mathbf{P}}_{\tau\tau} - \check{\mathbf{P}}_\tau \mathbf{C}^T (\mathbf{C}\check{\mathbf{P}}\mathbf{C}^T + \mathbf{R})^{-1}\mathbf{C}\check{\mathbf{P}}_\tau^T}_{\hat{\mathbf{P}}_{\tau\tau},\,\text{covariance}}\bigg), \tag{3.160}$$

for the density of the predicted state at the query times, given the measurements.

The expression simplifies further if we take the query times to be exactly the same as the measurement times (i.e., $\tau_k = t_k, K = J$). This implies that

$$\check{\mathbf{P}} = \check{\mathbf{P}}_\tau = \check{\mathbf{P}}_{\tau\tau}, \tag{3.161}$$

and then we can write

$$p(\mathbf{x}|\mathbf{y}) = \mathcal{N}\bigg(\underbrace{\check{\mathbf{x}} + \check{\mathbf{P}}\mathbf{C}^T (\mathbf{C}\check{\mathbf{P}}\mathbf{C}^T + \mathbf{R})^{-1}(\mathbf{y} - \mathbf{C}\check{\mathbf{x}})}_{\hat{\mathbf{x}},\,\text{mean}},$$

$$\underbrace{\check{\mathbf{P}} - \check{\mathbf{P}}\mathbf{C}^T (\mathbf{C}\check{\mathbf{P}}\mathbf{C}^T + \mathbf{R})^{-1}\mathbf{C}\check{\mathbf{P}}^T}_{\hat{\mathbf{P}},\,\text{covariance}}\bigg). \tag{3.162}$$

Or, after an application of the SMW identity in (2.124), we can write this as

$$p(\mathbf{x}|\mathbf{y}) = \mathcal{N}\bigg(\underbrace{\left(\check{\mathbf{P}}^{-1} + \mathbf{C}^T\mathbf{R}^{-1}\mathbf{C}\right)^{-1}\left(\check{\mathbf{P}}^{-1}\check{\mathbf{x}} + \mathbf{C}^T\mathbf{R}^{-1}\mathbf{y}\right)}_{\hat{\mathbf{x}},\,\text{mean}},$$

$$\underbrace{\left(\check{\mathbf{P}}^{-1} + \mathbf{C}^T\mathbf{R}^{-1}\mathbf{C}\right)^{-1}}_{\hat{\mathbf{P}},\,\text{covariance}}\bigg). \tag{3.163}$$

Rearranging the mean expression, we have a linear system for $\hat{\mathbf{x}}$:

$$\left(\check{\mathbf{P}}^{-1} + \mathbf{C}^T\mathbf{R}^{-1}\mathbf{C}\right)\hat{\mathbf{x}} = \check{\mathbf{P}}^{-1}\check{\mathbf{x}} + \mathbf{C}^T\mathbf{R}^{-1}\mathbf{y}. \tag{3.164}$$

This can be viewed as the solution to the following optimization problem:

$$\hat{\mathbf{x}} = \arg\min_{\mathbf{x}} \frac{1}{2}(\check{\mathbf{x}} - \mathbf{x})^T \check{\mathbf{P}}^{-1}(\check{\mathbf{x}} - \mathbf{x}) + \frac{1}{2}(\mathbf{y} - \mathbf{C}\mathbf{x})^T \mathbf{R}^{-1}(\mathbf{y} - \mathbf{C}\mathbf{x}). \tag{3.165}$$

Note that at implementation we must be careful to use $\mathbf{y}_{\text{meas}}$, the actual measurements received from our sensors.

If, after solving for the estimate at the measurement times, we later want to query the state at some other times of interest ($\tau_0 < \tau_1 < \ldots < \tau_J$), we can use the GP interpolation equations to do so:

$$\hat{\mathbf{x}}_\tau = \check{\mathbf{x}}_\tau + \left(\check{\mathbf{P}}_\tau \check{\mathbf{P}}^{-1}\right)(\hat{\mathbf{x}} - \check{\mathbf{x}}), \tag{3.166a}$$

$$\hat{\mathbf{P}}_{\tau\tau} = \check{\mathbf{P}}_{\tau\tau} + \left(\check{\mathbf{P}}_\tau \check{\mathbf{P}}^{-1}\right)\left(\hat{\mathbf{P}} - \check{\mathbf{P}}\right)\left(\check{\mathbf{P}}_\tau \check{\mathbf{P}}^{-1}\right)^T. \tag{3.166b}$$

This is linear interpolation in the state variable (but not necessarily in time). To arrive at these interpolation equations, we return to (3.162) and rearrange both the mean and covariance expressions:

$$\check{\mathbf{P}}^{-1}(\hat{\mathbf{x}} - \check{\mathbf{x}}) = \mathbf{C}^T(\mathbf{C}\check{\mathbf{P}}\mathbf{C}^T + \mathbf{R})^{-1}(\mathbf{y} - \mathbf{C}\check{\mathbf{x}}), \tag{3.167a}$$

$$\check{\mathbf{P}}^{-1}\left(\hat{\mathbf{P}} - \check{\mathbf{P}}\right)\check{\mathbf{P}}^{-T} = -\mathbf{C}^T(\mathbf{C}\check{\mathbf{P}}\mathbf{C}^T + \mathbf{R})^{-1}\mathbf{C}. \tag{3.167b}$$

These can then be substituted back into (3.160),

$$\hat{\mathbf{x}}_\tau = \check{\mathbf{x}}_\tau + \check{\mathbf{P}}_\tau \underbrace{\mathbf{C}^T(\mathbf{C}\check{\mathbf{P}}\mathbf{C}^T + \mathbf{R})^{-1}(\mathbf{y} - \mathbf{C}\check{\mathbf{x}})}_{\check{\mathbf{P}}^{-1}(\hat{\mathbf{x}} - \check{\mathbf{x}})}, \tag{3.168a}$$

$$\hat{\mathbf{P}}_{\tau\tau} = \check{\mathbf{P}}_{\tau\tau} - \check{\mathbf{P}}_\tau \underbrace{\mathbf{C}^T(\mathbf{C}\check{\mathbf{P}}\mathbf{C}^T + \mathbf{R})^{-1}\mathbf{C}}_{-\check{\mathbf{P}}^{-1}(\hat{\mathbf{P}} - \check{\mathbf{P}})\check{\mathbf{P}}^{-T}}\check{\mathbf{P}}_\tau^T, \tag{3.168b}$$

to produce (3.166).

In general, this GP approach has complexity $O(K^3 + K^2 J)$ since the initial solve is $O(K^3)$ and the query is $O(K^2 J)$; this is quite expensive, and next we will seek to improve the cost by exploiting the structure of the matrices involved.

3.4.2 A Class of Exactly Sparse Gaussian Process Priors

Next, we will develop a special class of GP priors that lead to very efficient implementation. These priors are based on *linear time-varying (LTV) stochastic differential equations (SDEs)*:

$$\dot{\mathbf{x}}(t) = \mathbf{A}(t)\mathbf{x}(t) + \mathbf{v}(t) + \mathbf{L}(t)\mathbf{w}(t), \tag{3.169}$$

with

$$\mathbf{w}(t) \sim \mathcal{GP}(\mathbf{0}, \mathbf{Q}\,\delta(t - t')), \tag{3.170}$$

a (stationary) zero-mean GP with (symmetric, positive-definite) *power spectral density matrix*, $\mathbf{Q}$. In what follows, we will use an engineering approach that avoids introducing *Itō calculus*; we hope that what our treatment lacks in formality it makes up for in accessibility. For a more formal treatment of stochastic differential equations in estimation, see Särkkä (2006).

The general solution to this LTV ordinary differential equation is

$$\mathbf{x}(t) = \mathbf{\Phi}(t, t_0)\mathbf{x}(t_0) + \int_{t_0}^{t} \mathbf{\Phi}(t, s)\left(\mathbf{v}(s) + \mathbf{L}(s)\mathbf{w}(s)\right)\, ds, \tag{3.171}$$

Kiyoshi Itō (1915–2008) was a Japanese mathematician who pioneered the theory of stochastic integration and stochastic differential equations, now known as the *Itō calculus*.

where $\boldsymbol{\Phi}(t, s)$ is known as the *transition function* and has the following properties:

$$\boldsymbol{\Phi}(t, t) = \mathbf{1}, \tag{3.172}$$

$$\dot{\boldsymbol{\Phi}}(t, s) = \mathbf{A}(t)\boldsymbol{\Phi}(t, s), \tag{3.173}$$

$$\boldsymbol{\Phi}(t, s) = \boldsymbol{\Phi}(t, r)\boldsymbol{\Phi}(r, s). \tag{3.174}$$

It is usually straightforward to work out the transition function for systems in practice, but there is no general formula. See Appendix C.3 for further discussion of discretizing continuous-time models.

Mean Function

For the mean function we have

$$\underbrace{E[\mathbf{x}(t)]}_{\check{\mathbf{x}}(t)} = \boldsymbol{\Phi}(t, t_0)\underbrace{E[\mathbf{x}(t_0)]}_{\check{\mathbf{x}}_0} + \int_{t_0}^{t} \boldsymbol{\Phi}(t, s)\Big(\mathbf{v}(s) + \mathbf{L}(s)\underbrace{E[\mathbf{w}(s)]}_{0}\Big)\, ds,$$

$$\tag{3.175}$$

where $\check{\mathbf{x}}_0$ is the initial value of the mean at t_0. Thus, the mean function is

$$\check{\mathbf{x}}(t) = \boldsymbol{\Phi}(t, t_0)\check{\mathbf{x}}_0 + \int_{t_0}^{t} \boldsymbol{\Phi}(t, s)\mathbf{v}(s)\, ds. \tag{3.176}$$

If we now have a sequence of times, $t_0 < t_1 < t_2 < \cdots < t_K$, then we can write the mean at these times as

$$\dot{\mathbf{x}}(t_k) = \boldsymbol{\Phi}(t_k, t_0)\check{\mathbf{x}}_0 + \sum_{n=1}^{k} \boldsymbol{\Phi}(t_k, t_n)\mathbf{v}_n, \tag{3.177}$$

where

$$\mathbf{v}_k = \int_{t_{k-1}}^{t_k} \boldsymbol{\Phi}(t_k, s)\mathbf{v}(s)\, ds, \qquad k = 1\ldots K. \tag{3.178}$$

Or we can write our system in *lifted form*,

$$\check{\mathbf{x}} = \mathbf{A}\mathbf{v}, \tag{3.179}$$

where

$$\check{\mathbf{x}} = \begin{bmatrix} \check{\mathbf{x}}(t_0) \\ \check{\mathbf{x}}(t_1) \\ \vdots \\ \check{\mathbf{x}}(t_K) \end{bmatrix}, \quad \mathbf{v} = \begin{bmatrix} \check{\mathbf{x}}_0 \\ \mathbf{v}_1 \\ \vdots \\ \mathbf{v}_K \end{bmatrix},$$

$$\mathbf{A} = \begin{bmatrix} \mathbf{1} & & & & & \\ \boldsymbol{\Phi}(t_1, t_0) & \mathbf{1} & & & & \\ \boldsymbol{\Phi}(t_2, t_0) & \boldsymbol{\Phi}(t_2, t_1) & \mathbf{1} & & & \\ \vdots & \vdots & \vdots & \ddots & & \\ \boldsymbol{\Phi}(t_{K-1}, t_0) & \boldsymbol{\Phi}(t_{K-1}, t_1) & \boldsymbol{\Phi}(t_{K-1}, t_2) & \cdots & \mathbf{1} & \\ \boldsymbol{\Phi}(t_K, t_0) & \boldsymbol{\Phi}(t_K, t_1) & \boldsymbol{\Phi}(t_K, t_2) & \cdots & \boldsymbol{\Phi}(t_K, t_{K-1}) & \mathbf{1} \end{bmatrix}.$$

$$\tag{3.180}$$

Notably, $\mathbf{A}$, the *lifted transition matrix*, is lower-triangular.

If we assume that $\mathbf{v}(t) = \mathbf{B}(t)\mathbf{u}(t)$ with $\mathbf{u}(t)$ constant between measurement times, we can further simplify the expression. Let $\mathbf{u}_k$ be the constant input when $t \in (t_{k-1}, t_k]$. Then we can define

$$\mathbf{B} = \text{diag}\,(\mathbf{1}, \mathbf{B}_1, \dots \mathbf{B}_K), \quad \mathbf{u} = \begin{bmatrix} \check{\mathbf{x}}_0 \\ \mathbf{u}_1 \\ \vdots \\ \mathbf{u}_K \end{bmatrix}, \quad (3.181)$$

and

$$\mathbf{B}_k = \int_{t_{k-1}}^{t_k} \mathbf{\Phi}(t_k, s)\mathbf{B}(s)\, ds, \qquad k = 1 \dots K. \quad (3.182)$$

This allows us to write

$$\check{\mathbf{x}}(t_k) = \mathbf{\Phi}(t_k, t_{k-1})\check{\mathbf{x}}(t_{k-1}) + \mathbf{B}_k\mathbf{u}_k, \quad (3.183)$$

and

$$\check{\mathbf{x}} = \mathbf{ABu}, \quad (3.184)$$

for the vector of means.

Covariance Function

For the covariance function we have

$$\underbrace{E\left[(\mathbf{x}(t) - E[\mathbf{x}(t)])(\mathbf{x}(t') - E[\mathbf{x}(t')])^T\right]}_{\check{\mathbf{P}}(t,t')}$$

$$= \mathbf{\Phi}(t, t_0) \underbrace{E\left[(\mathbf{x}(t_0) - E[\mathbf{x}(t_0)])(\mathbf{x}(t_0) - E[\mathbf{x}(t_0)])^T\right]}_{\check{\mathbf{P}}_0} \mathbf{\Phi}(t', t_0)^T$$

$$+ \int_{t_0}^{t} \int_{t_0}^{t'} \mathbf{\Phi}(t, s)\mathbf{L}(s) \underbrace{E[\mathbf{w}(s)\mathbf{w}(s')^T]}_{\mathbf{Q}\,\delta(s-s')} \mathbf{L}(s')^T \mathbf{\Phi}(t', s')^T\, ds'\, ds, \quad (3.185)$$

where $\check{\mathbf{P}}_0$ is the initial covariance at t_0 and we have made the assumption that $E[\mathbf{x}(t_0)\mathbf{w}(t)^T] = \mathbf{0}$. Putting this together, we have the following expression for the covariance:

$$\check{\mathbf{P}}(t, t') = \mathbf{\Phi}(t, t_0)\check{\mathbf{P}}_0\mathbf{\Phi}(t', t_0)^T$$

$$+ \int_{t_0}^{t} \int_{t_0}^{t'} \mathbf{\Phi}(t, s)\mathbf{L}(s)\mathbf{Q}\mathbf{L}(s')^T \mathbf{\Phi}(t', s')^T\, \delta(s - s')\, ds'\, ds. \quad (3.186)$$

Focusing on the second term, we integrate once to see that it is

$$\int_{t_0}^{t} \mathbf{\Phi}(t, s)\mathbf{L}(s)\mathbf{Q}\mathbf{L}(s)^T \mathbf{\Phi}(t', s)^T\, H(t' - s)\, ds, \quad (3.187)$$

where $H(\cdot)$ is the *Heaviside step function*. There are now three cases to worry about: $t < t'$, $t = t'$, and $t > t'$. In the first case, the upper integration limit terminates the integration, while in the last, the Heaviside step function does the same job. The result is that the second term in the covariance function can be written as

$$
\int_{t_0}^{\min(t,t')} \boldsymbol{\Phi}(t,s)\mathbf{L}(s)\boldsymbol{Q}\mathbf{L}(s)^T\boldsymbol{\Phi}(t',s)^T \, ds
$$

$$
= \begin{cases}
\boldsymbol{\Phi}(t,t')\left(\int_{t_0}^{t'}\boldsymbol{\Phi}(t',s)\mathbf{L}(s)\boldsymbol{Q}\mathbf{L}(s)^T\boldsymbol{\Phi}(t',s)^T \, ds\right) & t' < t \\
\int_{t_0}^{t}\boldsymbol{\Phi}(t,s)\mathbf{L}(s)\boldsymbol{Q}\mathbf{L}(s)^T\boldsymbol{\Phi}(t,s)^T \, ds & t = t' \\
\left(\int_{t_0}^{t}\boldsymbol{\Phi}(t,s)\mathbf{L}(s)\boldsymbol{Q}\mathbf{L}(s)^T\boldsymbol{\Phi}(t,s)^T \, ds\right)\boldsymbol{\Phi}(t',t)^T & t < t'
\end{cases} \quad . \quad (3.188)
$$

If we now have a sequence of times, $t_0 < t_1 < t_2 < \cdots < t_K$, then we can write the covariance between two of these times as

$$
\check{\mathbf{P}}(t_i,t_j) = \begin{cases}
\boldsymbol{\Phi}(t_i,t_j)\left(\sum_{n=0}^{j}\boldsymbol{\Phi}(t_j,t_n)\mathbf{Q}_n\boldsymbol{\Phi}(t_j,t_n)^T\right) & t_j < t_i \\
\sum_{n=0}^{i}\boldsymbol{\Phi}(t_i,t_n)\mathbf{Q}_n\boldsymbol{\Phi}(t_i,t_n)^T & t_i = t_j \\
\left(\sum_{n=0}^{i}\boldsymbol{\Phi}(t_i,t_n)\mathbf{Q}_n\boldsymbol{\Phi}(t_i,t_n)^T\right)\boldsymbol{\Phi}(t_j,t_i)^T & t_i < t_j
\end{cases} \quad ,
$$

$$(3.189)$$

where

$$
\mathbf{Q}_k = \int_{t_{k-1}}^{t_k} \boldsymbol{\Phi}(t_k,s)\mathbf{L}(s)\boldsymbol{Q}\mathbf{L}(s)^T\boldsymbol{\Phi}(t_k,s)^T \, ds, \qquad k = 1\ldots K, \quad (3.190)
$$

and we let $\mathbf{Q}_0 = \check{\mathbf{P}}_0$ to keep the notation in (3.188) clean.

Given this preparation, we are now ready to state the main result of this section. Let $t_0 < t_1 < t_2 < \cdots < t_K$ be a monotonically increasing sequence of time values. Define the *kernel matrix* to be

$$
\check{\mathbf{P}} = \Bigg[\boldsymbol{\Phi}(t_i,t_0)\check{\mathbf{P}}_0\boldsymbol{\Phi}(t_j,t_0)^T
$$

$$
+ \int_{t_0}^{\min(t_i,t_j)} \boldsymbol{\Phi}(t_i,s)\mathbf{L}(s)\boldsymbol{Q}\mathbf{L}(s)^T\boldsymbol{\Phi}(t_j,s)^T \, ds\Bigg]_{ij}, \quad (3.191)
$$

where $\boldsymbol{Q} > 0$ is symmetric. Note that $\check{\mathbf{P}}$ has $(K+1)\times(K+1)$ blocks. Then, we can factor $\check{\mathbf{P}}$ according to a block-lower-diagonal-upper decomposition:

$$
\check{\mathbf{P}} = \mathbf{A}\mathbf{Q}\mathbf{A}^T, \qquad\qquad (3.192)
$$

where $\mathbf{A}$ is the lower-triangular matrix given in (3.180) and

$$
\mathbf{Q}_k = \int_{t_{k-1}}^{t_k} \boldsymbol{\Phi}(t_k,s)\mathbf{L}(s)\boldsymbol{Q}\mathbf{L}(s)^T\boldsymbol{\Phi}(t_k,s)^T \, ds, \quad k = 1\ldots K, \quad (3.193)
$$

$$
\mathbf{Q} = \mathrm{diag}\left(\check{\mathbf{P}}_0, \mathbf{Q}_1, \mathbf{Q}_2, \ldots, \mathbf{Q}_K\right). \qquad (3.194)
$$

It follows that $\check{\mathbf{P}}^{-1}$ is block-tridiagonal and is given by

$$
\check{\mathbf{P}}^{-1} = (\mathbf{A}\mathbf{Q}\mathbf{A}^T)^{-1} = \mathbf{A}^{-T}\mathbf{Q}^{-1}\mathbf{A}^{-1}, \qquad (3.195)
$$

where

$$\mathbf{A}^{-1} = \begin{bmatrix} \mathbf{1} & & & & & \\ -\boldsymbol{\Phi}(t_1, t_0) & \mathbf{1} & & & & \\ & -\boldsymbol{\Phi}(t_2, t_1) & \mathbf{1} & & & \\ & & -\boldsymbol{\Phi}(t_3, t_2) & \ddots & & \\ & & & \ddots & \mathbf{1} & \\ & & & & -\boldsymbol{\Phi}(t_K, t_{K-1}) & \mathbf{1} \end{bmatrix}.$$

$$(3.196)$$

Since $\mathbf{A}^{-1}$ has only the main diagonal and the one below non-zero, and $\mathbf{Q}^{-1}$ is block-diagonal, the block-tridiagonal structure of $\check{\mathbf{P}}^{-1}$ can be verified by carrying out the multiplication. This is precisely the structure we had at the start of the chapter for the batch discrete-time case.

Summary of Prior

We can write our final GP for $\mathbf{x}(t)$ as

$$\mathbf{x}(t) \sim \mathcal{GP}\bigg(\underbrace{\boldsymbol{\Phi}(t, t_0)\check{\mathbf{x}}_0 + \int_{t_0}^{t} \boldsymbol{\Phi}(t, s)\mathbf{v}(s)\, ds}_{\check{\mathbf{x}}(t)},$$

$$\underbrace{\boldsymbol{\Phi}(t, t_0)\check{\mathbf{P}}_0\boldsymbol{\Phi}(t', t_0)^T + \int_{t_0}^{\min(t,t')} \boldsymbol{\Phi}(t, s)\mathbf{L}(s)\mathbf{Q}\mathbf{L}(s)^T\boldsymbol{\Phi}(t', s)^T\, ds}_{\check{\mathbf{P}}(t,t')} \bigg).$$

$$(3.197)$$

At the measurement times, $t_0 < t_1 < \cdots < t_K$, we can also then write

$$\mathbf{x} \sim \mathcal{N}(\check{\mathbf{x}}, \check{\mathbf{P}}) = \mathcal{N}\left(\mathbf{A}\mathbf{v}, \mathbf{A}\mathbf{Q}\mathbf{A}^T \right), \qquad (3.198)$$

and we can further substitute $\mathbf{v} = \mathbf{B}\mathbf{u}$ in the case that the inputs are constant between measurement times.

Querying the GP

As just discussed, if we solve for the trajectory at the measurement times, we may want to query it at other times of interest as well. This can be done through the GP linear interpolation equations in (3.166). Without loss of generality, we consider a single query time, $t_k \leq \tau < t_{k+1}$, and so in this case we write

$$\hat{\mathbf{x}}(\tau) = \check{\mathbf{x}}(\tau) + \check{\mathbf{P}}(\tau)\check{\mathbf{P}}^{-1}(\hat{\mathbf{x}} - \check{\mathbf{x}}), \qquad (3.199a)$$

$$\hat{\mathbf{P}}(\tau, \tau) = \check{\mathbf{P}}(\tau, \tau) + \check{\mathbf{P}}(\tau)\check{\mathbf{P}}^{-1}\left(\hat{\mathbf{P}} - \check{\mathbf{P}} \right)\check{\mathbf{P}}^{-T}\check{\mathbf{P}}(\tau)^T. \qquad (3.199b)$$

For the mean function at the query time, we simply have

$$\check{\mathbf{x}}(\tau) = \boldsymbol{\Phi}(\tau, t_k)\check{\mathbf{x}}(t_k) + \int_{t_k}^{\tau} \boldsymbol{\Phi}(\tau, s)\mathbf{v}(s)\, ds, \qquad (3.200)$$

which has complexity $O(1)$ to evaluate. For the covariance function at the query time we have

$$\check{\mathbf{P}}(\tau, \tau) = \boldsymbol{\Phi}(\tau, t_k)\check{\mathbf{P}}(t_k, t_k)\boldsymbol{\Phi}(\tau, t_k)^T + \int_{t_k}^{\tau} \boldsymbol{\Phi}(\tau, s)\mathbf{L}(s)\mathbf{Q}\mathbf{L}(s)^T\boldsymbol{\Phi}(\tau, s)^T \, ds,$$

(3.201)

which is also $O(1)$ to evaluate.

We now examine the sparsity of the product $\check{\mathbf{P}}(\tau)\check{\mathbf{P}}^{-1}$ in the case of a general LTV process model. The matrix, $\check{\mathbf{P}}(\tau)$, can be written as

$$\check{\mathbf{P}}(\tau) = \begin{bmatrix} \check{\mathbf{P}}(\tau, t_0) & \check{\mathbf{P}}(\tau, t_1) & \cdots & \check{\mathbf{P}}(\tau, t_K) \end{bmatrix}. \quad (3.202)$$

The individual blocks are given by

$$\check{\mathbf{P}}(\tau, t_j) = \begin{cases} \boldsymbol{\Phi}(\tau, t_k)\boldsymbol{\Phi}(t_k, t_j)\left(\sum_{n=0}^{j} \boldsymbol{\Phi}(t_j, t_n)\mathbf{Q}_n\boldsymbol{\Phi}(t_j, t_n)^T\right) & t_j < t_k \\ \boldsymbol{\Phi}(\tau, t_k)\left(\sum_{n=0}^{k} \boldsymbol{\Phi}(t_k, t_n)\mathbf{Q}_n\boldsymbol{\Phi}(t_k, t_n)^T\right) & t_k = t_j \\ \boldsymbol{\Phi}(\tau, t_k)\left(\sum_{n=0}^{k} \boldsymbol{\Phi}(t_k, t_n)\mathbf{Q}_n\boldsymbol{\Phi}(t_k, t_n)^T\right)\boldsymbol{\Phi}(t_{k+1}, t_k)^T & t_{k+1} = t_j \\ \quad + \mathbf{Q}_\tau\boldsymbol{\Phi}(t_{k+1}, \tau)^T & \\ \boldsymbol{\Phi}(\tau, t_k)\left(\sum_{n=0}^{k} \boldsymbol{\Phi}(t_k, t_n)\mathbf{Q}_n\boldsymbol{\Phi}(t_k, t_n)^T\right)\boldsymbol{\Phi}(t_j, t_k)^T & t_{k+1} < t_j \\ \quad + \mathbf{Q}_\tau\boldsymbol{\Phi}(t_{k+1}, \tau)^T\boldsymbol{\Phi}(t_j, t_{k+1})^T & \end{cases},$$

(3.203)

where

$$\mathbf{Q}_\tau = \int_{t_k}^{\tau} \boldsymbol{\Phi}(\tau, s)\mathbf{L}(s)\mathbf{Q}\mathbf{L}(s)^T\boldsymbol{\Phi}(\tau, s)^T \, ds. \quad (3.204)$$

Although this looks difficult to work with, we may write

$$\check{\mathbf{P}}(\tau) = \mathbf{V}(\tau)\mathbf{A}^T, \quad (3.205)$$

where $\mathbf{A}$ was defined before and

$$\mathbf{V}(\tau) = \Big[\boldsymbol{\Phi}(\tau, t_k)\boldsymbol{\Phi}(t_k, t_0)\check{\mathbf{P}}_0 \quad \boldsymbol{\Phi}(\tau, t_k)\boldsymbol{\Phi}(t_k, t_1)\mathbf{Q}_1 \quad \cdots$$

$$\cdots \quad \boldsymbol{\Phi}(\tau, t_k)\boldsymbol{\Phi}(t_k, t_{k-1})\mathbf{Q}_{k-1} \quad \boldsymbol{\Phi}(\tau, t_k)\mathbf{Q}_k \quad \mathbf{Q}_\tau\boldsymbol{\Phi}(t_{k+1}, \tau)^T \quad \cdots$$

$$\cdots \quad \mathbf{0} \quad \cdots \quad \mathbf{0} \Big]. \quad (3.206)$$

Returning to the desired product, we have

$$\check{\mathbf{P}}(\tau)\check{\mathbf{P}}^{-1} = \mathbf{V}(\tau)\underbrace{\mathbf{A}^T\mathbf{A}^{-T}}_{\mathbf{1}}\mathbf{Q}^{-1}\mathbf{A}^{-1} = \mathbf{V}(\tau)\mathbf{Q}^{-1}\mathbf{A}^{-1}. \quad (3.207)$$

Since $\mathbf{Q}^{-1}$ is block-diagonal and $\mathbf{A}^{-1}$ has only the main diagonal and the one below it non-zero, we can evaluate the product very efficiently. Working it out, we have

$$\check{\mathbf{P}}(\tau)\check{\mathbf{P}}^{-1} = \Big[\mathbf{0} \quad \cdots \quad \mathbf{0} \quad \underbrace{\boldsymbol{\Phi}(\tau, t_k) - \mathbf{Q}_\tau\boldsymbol{\Phi}(t_{k+1}, \tau)^T\mathbf{Q}_{k+1}^{-1}\boldsymbol{\Phi}(t_{k+1}, t_k)}_{\boldsymbol{\Lambda}(\tau), \text{ block column } k}$$

$$\cdots \quad \underbrace{\mathbf{Q}_\tau\boldsymbol{\Phi}(t_{k+1}, \tau)^T\mathbf{Q}_{k+1}^{-1}}_{\boldsymbol{\Psi}(\tau), \text{ block column } k+1} \quad \mathbf{0} \quad \cdots \quad \mathbf{0} \Big], \quad (3.208)$$

which has exactly two non-zero block columns. Inserting this into (3.199), we have

$$\hat{\mathbf{x}}(\tau) = \check{\mathbf{x}}(\tau) + \begin{bmatrix} \boldsymbol{\Lambda}(\tau) & \boldsymbol{\Psi}(\tau) \end{bmatrix} \left(\begin{bmatrix} \hat{\mathbf{x}}_k \\ \hat{\mathbf{x}}_{k+1} \end{bmatrix} - \begin{bmatrix} \check{\mathbf{x}}(t_k) \\ \check{\mathbf{x}}(t_{k+1}) \end{bmatrix} \right), \qquad (3.209a)$$

$$\hat{\mathbf{P}}(\tau, \tau) = \check{\mathbf{P}}(\tau, \tau) + \begin{bmatrix} \boldsymbol{\Lambda}(\tau) & \boldsymbol{\Psi}(\tau) \end{bmatrix} \left(\begin{bmatrix} \hat{\mathbf{P}}_{k,k} & \hat{\mathbf{P}}_{k,k+1} \\ \hat{\mathbf{P}}_{k+1,k} & \hat{\mathbf{P}}_{k+1,k+1} \end{bmatrix} \right. \qquad (3.209b)$$
$$\left. - \begin{bmatrix} \check{\mathbf{P}}(t_k, t_k) & \check{\mathbf{P}}(t_k, t_{k+1}) \\ \check{\mathbf{P}}(t_{k+1}, t_k) & \check{\mathbf{P}}(t_{k+1}, t_{k+1}) \end{bmatrix} \right) \begin{bmatrix} \boldsymbol{\Lambda}(\tau)^T \\ \boldsymbol{\Psi}(\tau)^T \end{bmatrix},$$

which is a simple combination of just the two terms from t_k and t_{k+1}. Thus, to query the trajectory at a single time of interest is $O(1)$ complexity.

Example 3.1   As a simple example, consider the system

$$\dot{\mathbf{x}}(t) = \mathbf{w}(t), \qquad (3.210)$$

which can be written as

$$\dot{\mathbf{x}}(t) = \mathbf{A}(t)\mathbf{x}(t) + \mathbf{v}(t) + \mathbf{L}(t)\mathbf{w}(t), \qquad (3.211)$$

with $\mathbf{A}(t) = \mathbf{0}, \mathbf{v}(t) = \mathbf{0}, \mathbf{L}(t) = \mathbf{1}$. In this case, the query equation becomes

$$\hat{\mathbf{x}}_\tau = (1 - \alpha)\,\hat{\mathbf{x}}_k + \alpha\,\hat{\mathbf{x}}_{k+1}, \qquad (3.212)$$

assuming the mean function is zero everywhere and where

$$\alpha = \frac{\tau - t_k}{t_{k+1} - t_k} \in [0, 1], \qquad (3.213)$$

which is a familiar interpolation scheme that is linear in τ. More complicated process models lead to more complicated interpolation equations.

3.4.3 Linear Time-Invariant Case

Naturally, the equations simplify considerably in the *linear time-invariant (LTI)* case:

$$\dot{\mathbf{x}}(t) = \boldsymbol{A}\mathbf{x}(t) + \boldsymbol{B}\mathbf{u}(t) + \boldsymbol{L}\mathbf{w}(t), \qquad (3.214)$$

with $\boldsymbol{A}, \boldsymbol{B}$, and $\boldsymbol{L}$ constant.[23] The transition function is simply

$$\boldsymbol{\Phi}(t, s) = \exp\left(\boldsymbol{A}(t - s)\right), \qquad (3.215)$$

which we note depends only on the difference of the two times (i.e., it is stationary). We can therefore write

$$\Delta t_{k:k-1} = t_k - t_{k-1}, \qquad k = 1 \ldots K, \qquad (3.216)$$

$$\boldsymbol{\Phi}(t_k, t_{k-1}) = \exp\left(\boldsymbol{A}\,\Delta t_{k:k-1}\right), \qquad k = 1 \ldots K, \qquad (3.217)$$

$$\boldsymbol{\Phi}(t_k, t_j) = \boldsymbol{\Phi}(t_k, t_{k-1})\boldsymbol{\Phi}(t_{k-1}, t_{k-2}) \cdots \boldsymbol{\Phi}(t_{j+1}, t_j), \qquad (3.218)$$

to simplify matters.

---

[23] We use italicized symbols for the time-invariant system matrices to avoid confusion with the lifted-form quantities.

Mean Function

For the mean function we have the following simplification:

$$\mathbf{v}_k = \int_0^{\Delta t_{k:k-1}} \exp\left(\boldsymbol{A}(\Delta t_{k:k-1} - s)\right) \boldsymbol{B} \mathbf{u}(s)\, ds, \qquad k = 1 \dots K. \quad (3.219)$$

If we assume that $\mathbf{u}(t)$ is constant between each pair of consecutive measurement times, we can further simplify the expression. Let $\mathbf{u}_k$ be the constant input when $t \in (t_{k-1}, t_k]$. Then we can define

$$\mathbf{B} = \mathrm{diag}\left(\mathbf{1}, \mathbf{B}_1, \dots \mathbf{B}_M\right), \quad \mathbf{u} = \begin{bmatrix} \check{\mathbf{x}}_0 \\ \mathbf{u}_1 \\ \vdots \\ \mathbf{u}_M \end{bmatrix}, \qquad (3.220)$$

and

$$\begin{aligned}
\mathbf{B}_k &= \int_0^{\Delta t_{k:k-1}} \exp\left(\boldsymbol{A}(\Delta t_{k:k-1} - s)\right) ds\, \boldsymbol{B} \\
&= \boldsymbol{\Phi}(t_k, t_{k-1}) \left(\mathbf{1} - \boldsymbol{\Phi}(t_k, t_{k-1})^{-1}\right) \boldsymbol{A}^{-1} \boldsymbol{B}, \quad k = 1 \dots K. \quad (3.221)
\end{aligned}$$

This allows us to write

$$\check{\mathbf{x}} = \mathbf{A}\mathbf{B}\mathbf{u} \qquad (3.222)$$

for the vector of means.

Covariance Function

For the covariance function, we have the simplification

$$\mathbf{Q}_k = \int_0^{\Delta t_{k:k-1}} \exp\left(\boldsymbol{A}(\Delta t_{k:k-1} - s)\right) \boldsymbol{L}\boldsymbol{Q}\boldsymbol{L}^T \exp\left(\boldsymbol{A}(\Delta t_{k:k-1} - s)\right)^T ds \qquad (3.223)$$

for $k = 1 \dots K$. This is relatively straightforward to evaluate, particularly if $\boldsymbol{A}$ is nilpotent. Letting

$$\mathbf{Q} = \mathrm{diag}(\check{\mathbf{P}}_0, \mathbf{Q}_1, \mathbf{Q}_2, \dots, \mathbf{Q}_K), \qquad (3.224)$$

we then have

$$\check{\mathbf{P}} = \mathbf{A}\mathbf{Q}\mathbf{A}^T \qquad (3.225)$$

for the covariance matrix.

Querying the GP

To query the GP, we need the following quantities:

$$\boldsymbol{\Phi}(t_{k+1}, \tau) = \exp\left(\boldsymbol{A}\,\Delta t_{k+1:\tau}\right), \qquad \Delta t_{k+1:\tau} = t_{k+1} - \tau, \quad (3.226)$$
$$\boldsymbol{\Phi}(\tau, t_k) = \exp\left(\boldsymbol{A}\,\Delta t_{\tau:k}\right), \qquad \Delta t_{\tau:k} = \tau - t_k, \quad (3.227)$$

$$\mathbf{Q}_\tau = \int_0^{\Delta t_{\tau:k}} \exp\left(A(\Delta t_{\tau:k} - s)\right) LQL^T \exp\left(A(\Delta t_{\tau:k} - s)^T\right) ds. \tag{3.228}$$

Our interpolation equation is still

$$\hat{\mathbf{x}}(\tau) = \check{\mathbf{x}}(\tau) + \left(\mathbf{\Phi}(\tau, t_k) - \mathbf{Q}_\tau \mathbf{\Phi}(t_{k+1}, \tau)^T \mathbf{Q}_{k+1}^{-1} \mathbf{\Phi}(t_{k+1}, t_k)\right)(\hat{\mathbf{x}}_k - \check{\mathbf{x}}_k)$$
$$+ \mathbf{Q}_\tau \mathbf{\Phi}(t_{k+1}, \tau)^T \mathbf{Q}_{k+1}^{-1}(\hat{\mathbf{x}}_{k+1} - \check{\mathbf{x}}_{k+1}), \tag{3.229}$$

which is a linear combination of just the two terms from t_k and t_{k+1}.

Example 3.2 Consider the case

$$\ddot{\mathbf{p}}(t) = \mathbf{w}(t), \tag{3.230}$$

where $\mathbf{p}(t)$ corresponds to position and

$$\mathbf{w}(t) \sim \mathcal{GP}(\mathbf{0}, \mathbf{Q}\,\delta(t - t')) \tag{3.231}$$

is white noise as before. This corresponds to white noise on acceleration (i.e., the 'constant velocity' model). We can cast this in the form

$$\dot{\mathbf{x}}(t) = A\mathbf{x}(t) + B\mathbf{u}(t) + L\mathbf{w}(t) \tag{3.232}$$

by taking

$$\mathbf{x}(t) = \begin{bmatrix} \mathbf{p}(t) \\ \dot{\mathbf{p}}(t) \end{bmatrix}, \quad A = \begin{bmatrix} 0 & 1 \\ 0 & 0 \end{bmatrix}, \quad B = 0, \quad L = \begin{bmatrix} 0 \\ 1 \end{bmatrix}. \tag{3.233}$$

In this case we have

$$\exp\left(A\Delta t\right) = 1 + A\Delta t + \frac{1}{2}\underbrace{A^2}_{0}\Delta t^2 + \cdots = 1 + \begin{bmatrix} 0 & 1 \\ 0 & 0 \end{bmatrix}\Delta t = \begin{bmatrix} 1 & \Delta t 1 \\ 0 & 1 \end{bmatrix}, \tag{3.234}$$

since A is nilpotent. Therefore, we have

$$\mathbf{\Phi}(t_k, t_{k-1}) = \begin{bmatrix} 1 & \Delta t_{k:k-1} 1 \\ 0 & 1 \end{bmatrix}. \tag{3.235}$$

For the $\mathbf{Q}_k$ we have

$$\mathbf{Q}_k = \int_0^{\Delta t_{k:k-1}} \begin{bmatrix} 1 & (\Delta t_{k:k-1} - s)1 \\ 0 & 1 \end{bmatrix} \begin{bmatrix} 0 \\ 1 \end{bmatrix} Q \begin{bmatrix} 0 & 1 \end{bmatrix} \begin{bmatrix} 1 & 0 \\ (\Delta t_{k:k-1} - s)1 & 1 \end{bmatrix} ds$$
$$= \int_0^{\Delta t_{k:k-1}} \begin{bmatrix} (\Delta t_{k:k-1} - s)^2 Q & (\Delta t_{k:k-1} - s)Q \\ (\Delta t_{k:k-1} - s)Q & Q \end{bmatrix} ds$$
$$= \begin{bmatrix} \frac{1}{3}\Delta t_{k:k-1}^3 Q & \frac{1}{2}\Delta t_{k:k-1}^2 Q \\ \frac{1}{2}\Delta t_{k:k-1}^2 Q & \Delta t_{k:k-1} Q \end{bmatrix}, \tag{3.236}$$

which we note is positive-definite even though LQL^T is not. The inverse is

$$\mathbf{Q}_k^{-1} = \begin{bmatrix} 12\,\Delta t_{k:k-1}^{-3}\mathbf{Q}^{-1} & -6\,\Delta t_{k:k-1}^{-2}\mathbf{Q}^{-1} \\ -6\,\Delta t_{k:k-1}^{-2}\mathbf{Q}^{-1} & 4\,\Delta t_{k:k-1}^{-1}\mathbf{Q}^{-1} \end{bmatrix}, \qquad (3.237)$$

which is needed to construct $\check{\mathbf{P}}^{-1}$. For the mean function we have

$$\check{\mathbf{x}}_k = \boldsymbol{\Phi}(t_k, t_0)\check{\mathbf{x}}_0, \qquad k = 1 \ldots K, \qquad (3.238)$$

which can be stacked and written as

$$\check{\mathbf{x}} = \mathbf{A} \begin{bmatrix} \check{\mathbf{x}}_0 \\ \mathbf{0} \\ \vdots \\ \mathbf{0} \end{bmatrix} \qquad (3.239)$$

for convenience.

For trajectory queries, we also need

$$\boldsymbol{\Phi}(\tau, t_k) = \begin{bmatrix} \mathbf{1} & \Delta t_{\tau:k}\mathbf{1} \\ \mathbf{0} & \mathbf{1} \end{bmatrix}, \quad \boldsymbol{\Phi}(t_{k+1}, \tau) = \begin{bmatrix} \mathbf{1} & \Delta t_{k+1:\tau}\mathbf{1} \\ \mathbf{0} & \mathbf{1} \end{bmatrix},$$

$$\check{\mathbf{x}}_\tau = \boldsymbol{\Phi}(\tau, t_k)\check{\mathbf{x}}_k, \quad \mathbf{Q}_\tau = \begin{bmatrix} \frac{1}{3}\Delta t_{\tau:k}^3\mathbf{Q} & \frac{1}{2}\Delta t_{\tau:k}^2\mathbf{Q} \\ \frac{1}{2}\Delta t_{\tau:k}^2\mathbf{Q} & \Delta t_{\tau:k}\mathbf{Q} \end{bmatrix}, \qquad (3.240)$$

which we see will result in a scheme that is not linear in τ. Substituting these into the interpolation equation, we have

$$\hat{\mathbf{x}}_\tau = \check{\mathbf{x}}_\tau + \left(\boldsymbol{\Phi}(\tau, t_k) - \mathbf{Q}_\tau\boldsymbol{\Phi}(t_{k+1}, \tau)^T\mathbf{Q}_{k+1}^{-1}\boldsymbol{\Phi}(t_{k+1}, t_k)\right)(\hat{\mathbf{x}}_k - \check{\mathbf{x}}_k)$$
$$+ \mathbf{Q}_\tau\boldsymbol{\Phi}(t_{k+1}, \tau)^T\mathbf{Q}_{k+1}^{-1}(\hat{\mathbf{x}}_{k+1} - \check{\mathbf{x}}_{k+1}) \qquad (3.241)$$
$$= \check{\mathbf{x}}_\tau + \begin{bmatrix} (1 - 3\alpha^2 + 2\alpha^3)\mathbf{1} & T(\alpha - 2\alpha^2 + \alpha^3)\mathbf{1} \\ \frac{1}{T}6(-\alpha + \alpha^2)\mathbf{1} & (1 - 4\alpha + 3\alpha^2)\mathbf{1} \end{bmatrix}(\hat{\mathbf{x}}_k - \check{\mathbf{x}}_k)$$
$$+ \begin{bmatrix} (3\alpha^2 - 2\alpha^3)\mathbf{1} & T(-\alpha^2 + \alpha^3)\mathbf{1} \\ \frac{1}{T}6(\alpha - \alpha^2)\mathbf{1} & (-2\alpha + 3\alpha^2)\mathbf{1} \end{bmatrix}(\hat{\mathbf{x}}_{k+1} - \check{\mathbf{x}}_{k+1}),$$

where

$$\alpha = \frac{\tau - t_k}{t_{k+1} - t_k} \in [0, 1], \qquad T = \Delta t_{k+1:k} = t_{k+1} - t_k. \qquad (3.242)$$

Charles Hermite (1822–1901) was a French mathematician who did research on a variety of topics, including orthogonal polynomials.

Remarkably, the top row (corresponding to position) is precisely a *cubic Hermite polynomial* interpolation:

$$\hat{\mathbf{p}}_\tau - \check{\mathbf{p}}_\tau = h_{00}(\alpha)(\hat{\mathbf{p}}_k - \check{\mathbf{p}}_k) + h_{10}(\alpha)T(\dot{\hat{\mathbf{p}}}_k - \dot{\check{\mathbf{p}}}_k)$$
$$+ h_{01}(\alpha)(\hat{\mathbf{p}}_{k+1} - \check{\mathbf{p}}_{k+1}) + h_{11}(\alpha)T(\dot{\hat{\mathbf{p}}}_{k+1} - \dot{\check{\mathbf{p}}}_{k+1}), \qquad (3.243)$$

where

$$h_{00}(\alpha) = 1 - 3\alpha^2 + 2\alpha^3, \quad h_{10}(\alpha) = \alpha - 2\alpha^2 + \alpha^3, \qquad (3.244a)$$
$$h_{01}(\alpha) = 3\alpha^2 - 2\alpha^3, \quad h_{11}(\alpha) = -\alpha^2 + \alpha^3, \qquad (3.244b)$$

are the *Hermite basis functions*. The bottom row (corresponding to velocity) is only quadratic in α, and the basis functions are the derivatives of the ones used to interpolate position. It is very important to note that this Hermite interpolation scheme arises automatically from using the GP regression approach and our choice of prior motion model. At implementation, we may work directly with the general matrix equations and avoid working out the details of the resulting interpolation scheme.

It is also easy to verify that when $\alpha = 0$, we have

$$\hat{\mathbf{x}}_\tau = \check{\mathbf{x}}_\tau + (\hat{\mathbf{x}}_k - \check{\mathbf{x}}_k), \qquad (3.245)$$

and when $\alpha = 1$, we have

$$\hat{\mathbf{x}}_\tau = \check{\mathbf{x}}_\tau + (\hat{\mathbf{x}}_{k+1} - \check{\mathbf{x}}_{k+1}), \qquad (3.246)$$

which seem to be sensible boundary conditions.

3.4.4 Relationship to Batch Discrete-Time Estimation

Now that we have seen how to efficiently represent the prior, we can revisit the GP optimization problem described by (3.165). Substituting in our prior terms, the problem becomes

$$\hat{\mathbf{x}} = \arg \min_{\mathbf{x}} \frac{1}{2} (\underbrace{\mathbf{A}\mathbf{v}}_{\check{\mathbf{x}}} - \mathbf{x})^T \underbrace{\mathbf{A}^{-T} \mathbf{Q}^{-1} \mathbf{A}^{-1}}_{\check{\mathbf{P}}^{-1}} (\underbrace{\mathbf{A}\mathbf{v}}_{\check{\mathbf{x}}} - \mathbf{x})$$
$$+ \frac{1}{2} (\mathbf{y} - \mathbf{C}\mathbf{x})^T \mathbf{R}^{-1} (\mathbf{y} - \mathbf{C}\mathbf{x}). \quad (3.247)$$

Rearranging, we have

$$\hat{\mathbf{x}} = \arg \min_{\mathbf{x}} \frac{1}{2} (\mathbf{v} - \mathbf{A}^{-1} \mathbf{x})^T \mathbf{Q}^{-1} (\mathbf{v} - \mathbf{A}^{-1} \mathbf{x})$$
$$+ \frac{1}{2} (\mathbf{y} - \mathbf{C}\mathbf{x})^T \mathbf{R}^{-1} (\mathbf{y} - \mathbf{C}\mathbf{x}). \quad (3.248)$$

The solution to this optimization problem is given by

$$\underbrace{\left(\mathbf{A}^{-T} \mathbf{Q}^{-1} \mathbf{A}^{-1} + \mathbf{C}^T \mathbf{R}^{-1} \mathbf{C}\right)}_{\text{block-tridiagonal}} \hat{\mathbf{x}} = \mathbf{A}^{-T} \mathbf{Q}^{-1} \mathbf{v} + \mathbf{C}^T \mathbf{R}^{-1} \mathbf{y}. \qquad (3.249)$$

Because the left-hand side is block-tridiagonal, we can solve this system of equations in $O(K)$ time with a sparse solver (e.g., sparse Cholesky decomposition followed by sparse forward-backward passes). To query the trajectory at J extra times will be $O(J)$ since each query is $O(1)$. This means that we can solve for the state at the measurement and query times in $O(K + J)$ time. This is a big improvement over the $O(K^3 + K^2 J)$ cost when we did not exploit the sparse structure of our particular class of GP priors.

This is identical to the system of equations we had to solve in the discrete-time approach earlier. Thus, the discrete-time approach can *exactly* capture the continuous-time approach (at the measurement times), and both can be viewed as carrying out Gaussian process regression.

Figure 3.7
Relationships
between various
linear-Gaussian state
estimation
paradigms.

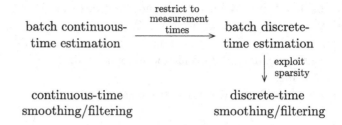

3.5 Recursive Continuous-Time Smoothing and Filtering

3.5.1 Turning Batch Estimation into a Smoother/Filter

Section 3.4 discussed batch continuous-time estimation and at the end, in Section 3.4.4, we showed that our continuous-time approach exactly captures the batch discrete-time approach at the measurement times. This requires that we construct the $\mathbf{A}$ and $\mathbf{Q}$ matrices appropriately for our chosen motion model (see also Appendix C.3). Given this connection, it means that we can solve (3.249) efficiently (and exactly) using the (discrete-time) Cholesky smoother of Section 3.2.2 or the RTS smoother of Section 3.2.4, the forward pass being the Kalman filter; these recursive methods make use of the block-tridiagonal sparsity pattern in the batch problem to make the solution highly efficient.

Figure 3.7 summarizes this discussion and the relationships between the various linear-Gaussian estimation paradigms considered in this chapter. The only topic we have not specifically covered is in the bottom-left corner: continuous-time smoothing/filtering; the next section briefly touches on this. We refer the reader to Särkkä (2013) for additional details on filtering and smoothing.

Richard Snowden
Bucy (1935–2019)
was an American
professor of aerospace
engineering known
for his contributions
to the filter that bears
his name.

3.5.2 Kalman–Bucy Filter

We have not directly covered continuous-time smoothing or filtering. However, one of the classic results in estimation theory is the continuous-time *Kalman–Bucy filter* (Kalman and Bucy, 1961); we will describe it briefly due to its historical significance.

Like in our batch continuous-time estimation in Section 3.4.2, we select the motion model to be an LTV SDE:

$$\dot{\mathbf{x}}(t) = \mathbf{A}(t)\mathbf{x}(t) + \mathbf{B}(t)\mathbf{u}(t) + \mathbf{L}(t)\mathbf{w}(t), \tag{3.250}$$

with

$$\mathbf{w}(t) \sim \mathcal{GP}(\mathbf{0}, \mathbf{Q}(t)), \tag{3.251}$$

a zero-mean GP with (symmetric, positive-definite) power spectral density matrix, $\mathbf{Q}(t)$.

Unlike our batch continuous-time estimation, the observation model is also assumed to take measurements continuously over time:

$$\mathbf{y}(t) = \mathbf{C}(t)\mathbf{x}(t) + \mathbf{n}(t), \tag{3.252}$$

with

$$\mathbf{n}(t) \sim \mathcal{GP}(\mathbf{0}, \mathbf{R}(t)), \tag{3.253}$$

a zero-mean GP with (symmetric, positive-definite) power spectral density matrix, $\mathbf{R}(t)$.

The Kalman–Bucy filter then consists of two differential equations for the estimated mean, $\hat{\mathbf{x}}(t)$, and covariance, $\hat{\mathbf{P}}(t)$:

$$\dot{\hat{\mathbf{x}}}(t) = \mathbf{A}(t)\mathbf{x}(t) + \mathbf{B}(t)\mathbf{u}(t) + \mathbf{K}(t)\left(\mathbf{y}(t) - \mathbf{C}(t)\hat{\mathbf{x}}(t)\right), \tag{3.254a}$$

$$\dot{\hat{\mathbf{P}}}(t) = \mathbf{A}(t)\hat{\mathbf{P}}(t) + \hat{\mathbf{P}}(t)\mathbf{A}(t)^T + \mathbf{L}(t)\mathbf{Q}(t)\mathbf{L}(t)^T - \mathbf{K}(t)\mathbf{R}(t)\mathbf{K}(t)^T, \tag{3.254b}$$

where $\mathbf{K}(t) = \hat{\mathbf{P}}(t)\mathbf{C}(t)^T\mathbf{R}(t)$ is the (continuous-time) Kalman gain. The initial conditions are naturally $\hat{\mathbf{x}}(0)$ and $\hat{\mathbf{P}}(0)$ and the equations must be integrated either numerically or analytically over time. We refer the reader to Stengel (1994, p. 367) for a derivation.

Despite the fact that most sensors can be considered to be producing measurements discretely rather than continuously in time, the Kalman–Bucy filter remains an elegant landmark in the history of estimation theory.

3.6 Summary

The main takeaway points from this chapter are as follows:

1. When the motion and observation models are linear, and the measurement and process noises are zero-mean Gaussian, the batch and recursive solutions to state estimation are straightforward, requiring no approximation.
2. The Bayesian posterior of a linear-Gaussian estimation problem is *exactly* Gaussian. This implies that the MAP solution is the same as the mean of the full Bayesian solution, since the mode and the mean of a Gaussian are one and the same.
3. The batch, discrete-time, linear-Gaussian solution can exactly implement (at the measurement times) the case where a continuous-time motion model is employed; appropriate prior terms must be used for this to be true.

The next chapter will investigate what happens when the motion and observation models are nonlinear.

3.7 Exercises

3.1 Consider the discrete-time system,

$$x_k = x_{k-1} + v_k + w_k, \qquad w_k \sim \mathcal{N}(0, Q),$$
$$y_k = x_k + n_k, \qquad\qquad n_k \sim \mathcal{N}(0, R),$$

which could represent a cart moving back and forth along the x-axis. The initial state, $\check{x}_0$, is unknown. Set up the system of equations for the batch least-squares estimation approach:

$$\left(\mathbf{H}^T\mathbf{W}^{-1}\mathbf{H}\right)\hat{\mathbf{x}} = \mathbf{H}^T\mathbf{W}^{-1}\mathbf{z}.$$

In other words, work out the details of $\mathbf{H}$, $\mathbf{W}$, $\mathbf{z}$, and $\hat{\mathbf{x}}$ for this system. Take the maximum timestep to be $K = 5$. Assume all the noises are uncorrelated with one another. Will a unique solution exist to the problem?

3.2   Using the same system as the first question, set $Q = R = 1$ and show that

$$
\mathbf{H}^T\mathbf{W}^{-1}\mathbf{H} = \begin{bmatrix} 2 & -1 & & & & \\ -1 & 3 & -1 & & & \\ & -1 & 3 & -1 & & \\ & & -1 & 3 & -1 & \\ & & & -1 & 3 & -1 \\ & & & & -1 & 2 \end{bmatrix}.
$$

What will be the sparsity pattern of the Cholesky factor, $\mathbf{L}$, such that $\mathbf{LL}^T = \mathbf{H}^T\mathbf{W}^{-1}\mathbf{H}$?

3.3   Using the same system as the first question, modify the least-squares solution for the case in which the measurements noises are correlated with one another in the following way:

$$
E[y_k y_\ell] = \begin{cases} R & |k - \ell| = 0 \\ R/2 & |k - \ell| = 1 \\ R/4 & |k - \ell| = 2 \\ 0 & \text{otherwise} \end{cases}.
$$

Will a unique least-squares solution still exist?

3.4   Using the same system as the first question, work out the details of the Kalman filter solution. In this case, assume that the initial conditions for the mean and covariance are $\check{x}_0$ and $\check{P}_0$, respectively. Show that the steady-state values for the prior and posterior covariances, $\check{P}$ and $\hat{P}$, as $K \to \infty$ are the solutions to the following quadratics:

$$
\check{P}^2 - Q\check{P} - QR = 0,
$$
$$
\hat{P}^2 + Q\hat{P} - QR = 0,
$$

which are two versions of the discrete algebraic Riccati equations. Explain why only one of the two roots to each quadratic is physically possible.

3.5   Using the MAP approach of Section 3.3.2, derive a version of the Kalman filter that recurses backward in time rather than forward.

3.6 Show that

$$
\begin{bmatrix}
1 & & & & & \\
A & 1 & & & & \\
A^2 & A & 1 & & & \\
\vdots & \vdots & \vdots & \ddots & & \\
A^{K-1} & A^{K-2} & A^{K-3} & \cdots & 1 & \\
A^K & A^{K-1} & A^{K-2} & \cdots & A & 1
\end{bmatrix}^{-1}
$$

$$
=
\begin{bmatrix}
1 & & & & & \\
-A & 1 & & & & \\
& -A & 1 & & & \\
& & -A & \ddots & & \\
& & & \ddots & 1 & \\
& & & & -A & 1
\end{bmatrix}.
$$

3.7 We have seen that for the batch least-squares solution, the posterior covariance is given by

$$\hat{\mathbf{P}} = \left(\mathbf{H}^T \mathbf{W}^{-1} \mathbf{H}\right)^{-1}.$$

We have also seen that the computational cost of performing a Cholesky decomposition,

$$\mathbf{L}\mathbf{L}^T = \mathbf{H}^T \mathbf{W}^{-1} \mathbf{H},$$

is $O(N^3(K+1))$, owing to the sparsity of the system. Inverting, we have

$$\hat{\mathbf{P}} = \mathbf{L}^{-T} \mathbf{L}^{-1}.$$

Comment on the computational cost of computing $\hat{\mathbf{P}}$ by this approach.

3.8 Consider the simple one-dimensional problem in the diagram; all quantities live on the x-axis.

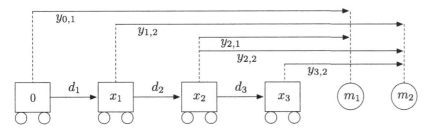

The x_k are robot poses, the d_k are odometry measurements, the m_ℓ are landmark positions, and the $y_{k,\ell}$ are landmark measurements. It is an example of *simultaneous localization and mapping (SLAM)* since we are going to estimate the robot and landmark positions.

(i) Define (linear) error terms for the odometric and landmark measurements:

$$e_k = ?, \qquad e_{k,\ell} = ?$$

(ii) Organize these errors into a stacked error for all the measurements,

$$\mathbf{e} = \begin{bmatrix} e_1 & e_2 & e_3 & e_{0,1} & e_{2,1} & e_{1,2} & e_{2,2} & e_{3,2} \end{bmatrix}^T = ?$$

in terms of the measurements and the state,

$$\mathbf{y} = \begin{bmatrix} d_1 & d_2 & d_3 & y_{0,1} & y_{2,1} & y_{1,2} & y_{2,2} & y_{3,2} \end{bmatrix}^T,$$

$$\mathbf{x} = \begin{bmatrix} x_1 & x_2 & x_3 & m_1 & m_2 \end{bmatrix}^T.$$

(iii) Assuming both the odometric and landmark measurements are corrupted by zero-mean Gaussian noise with covariance, $\mathbf{1}$, define a cost function that we can minimize to find the state that is most likely given the measurements.

$$J = ?$$

(iv) Take the derivative of the cost function, J, with respect to the state, $\mathbf{x}$, and set this to zero to find an equation for the optimal state, $\mathbf{x}^\star$.

$$\frac{\partial J}{\partial \mathbf{x}^T} = ?$$

(v) Will $\mathbf{x}^\star$ be unique in this problem? Why/why not?

3.9   Consider the following one-dimensional *simultaneous localization and mapping (SLAM)* setup with K robot positions and one landmark. There are odometry measurements, d_k, between each pair of positions as well as landmark range measurements, y_k, from the first and last robot positions.

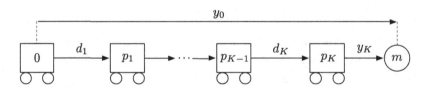

The motion and observation models are as follows:

$$\begin{bmatrix} p_k \\ m_k \end{bmatrix} = \begin{bmatrix} 1 & 0 \\ 0 & 1 \end{bmatrix} \begin{bmatrix} p_{k-1} \\ m_{k-1} \end{bmatrix} + \begin{bmatrix} 1 \\ 0 \end{bmatrix} (d_k + w_k), \qquad w_k \sim \mathcal{N}(0, 2/K),$$

$$y_k = \begin{bmatrix} -1 & 1 \end{bmatrix} \begin{bmatrix} p_k \\ m_k \end{bmatrix} + n_k, \qquad\qquad n_k \sim \mathcal{N}(0, 1),$$

where p_k is the position of the robot and m_k is the position of the (stationary) landmark, both at time k. We will use the Kalman filter approach to carry out the simultaneous estimation of the robot and landmark positions.

(i) The Kalman filter mean and covariance will be initialized as

$$\hat{\mathbf{x}}_0 = \begin{bmatrix} \hat{p}_0 \\ \hat{m}_0 \end{bmatrix} = \begin{bmatrix} 0 \\ ? \end{bmatrix}, \qquad \hat{\mathbf{P}}_0 = \begin{bmatrix} 0 & ? \\ ? & ? \end{bmatrix},$$

where we have set $\hat{p}_0 = 0$ to make the problem observable and also set the robot position covariance to zero (i.e., totally certain). Use the first landmark range measurement, y_0, to help initialize the ? entries.

(ii) Apply the prediction step of the Kalman filter K times in a row (with no correction) to determine expressions for the mean and covariance at time K, just before applying the correction step associated with y_K:

$$\check{\mathbf{x}}_K = ?, \qquad \check{\mathbf{P}}_K = ?$$

(iii) Apply the final correction step of the Kalman filter (associated with y_K) to determine final expressions for the mean and covariance at time K:

$$\hat{\mathbf{x}}_K = ?, \qquad \hat{\mathbf{P}}_K = ?$$

(iv) If we had used the batch approach (see previous question), would our estimate for the positions of the robot and landmark at time K be different or the same? Explain.

3.10 Consider a mobile robot that is estimating its one-dimensional motion using landmarks. It operates by observing a landmark, then moving, then reobserving the same landmark again. This is repeated K times, each time using a different landmark.

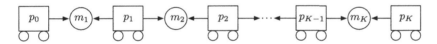

The robot is equipped with a range sensor to measure its distance to the landmarks. Thus, the sensor model for the observation between landmark ℓ and position k is

$$y_{k\ell} = m_\ell - p_k + n_{k\ell}, \quad n_{k\ell} \sim \mathcal{N}(0, \sigma^2),$$

where $n_{k\ell}$ is zero-mean, Gaussian noise corrupting the measurement. Assume that all measurement noises are uncorrelated with one another.

(i) Define an estimator, $\hat{p}_{k,k-1}$, for the incremental distance from p_{k-1} to p_k.

(ii) Show that $\hat{p}_{k,k-1}$ is unbiased and that its variance is $2\sigma^2$.

(iii) Define an estimator, $\hat{p}_{K0}$, for the combined distance from p_0 to p_K.

(iv) Show that $\hat{p}_{K0}$ is unbiased and that its variance is $2K\sigma^2$.

(v) We see that the variance of our estimate is increasing with distance travelled, which is characteristic of odometry methods. If we introduce one extra 'corrective' measurement from p_0 to p_K (not shown on the preceding diagram),

$$y_{K0} = p_K - p_0 + n_{K0}, \quad n_{K0} \sim \mathcal{N}(0, \sigma^2),$$

what is the minimum variance estimator for the distance from p_0 to p_K? Again assume that this measurement noise is not correlated with any of the others. Hint: use the corrective step of the Kalman filter to incorporate this extra measurement.

(vi) What is the variance of the estimator in (v) in the limit as $K \rightarrow \infty$?

Nonlinear Non-Gaussian Estimation

This chapter is one of the most important ones contained in this book. Here we examine how to deal with the fact that in the real world, there are no linear-Gaussian systems. It should be stated up front that *nonlinear, non-Gaussian (NLNG)* estimation is very much still an active research topic. The ideas in this chapter provide only some of the more common approaches to dealing with non-linear and/or non-Gaussian systems.[1] We begin by contrasting full Bayesian to *maximum a posteriori (MAP)* estimation for nonlinear systems. We then introduce a general theoretical framework for recursive filtering problems called the *Bayes filter*. Several of the more common filtering techniques are shown to be approximations of the Bayes filter: extended Kalman filter, sigmapoint Kalman filter, particle filter. We then return to batch estimation for nonlinear systems, both in discrete and continuous time. Some books that address nonlinear estimation include Jazwinski (1970), Maybeck (1994), and Simon (2006).

4.1 Introduction

In the linear-Gaussian chapter, we discussed two perspectives to estimation: *full Bayesian* and *maximum a posteriori*. We saw that for linear motion and observation models driven by Gaussian noise, these two paradigms come to the same answer (i.e., the MAP point was the mean of the full Bayesian approach); this is because the full posterior is exactly Gaussian and therefore the mean and mode (i.e., maximum) are the same point.

This is not true once we move to nonlinear models, since the full Bayesian posterior is no longer Gaussian. To provide some intuition on this topic, this section considers a simplified, one-dimensional, nonlinear estimation problem: estimating the position of a landmark from a stereo camera.

4.1.1 Full Bayesian Estimation

To gain some intuition, consider a simple estimation problem using a nonlinear, camera model:

$$y = \frac{fb}{x} + n. \tag{4.1}$$

This is the type of nonlinearity present in a *stereo camera* (see Figure 4.1), where the state, x, is the position of a landmark (in metres), the measurement, y, is the

---

[1] Even most of the methods in this chapter actually assume the noise is Gaussian.

Figure 4.1 Idealized
stereo camera model
relating the
landmark depth, x,
to the (noise-free)
disparity
measurement, y.

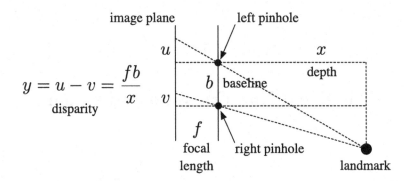

$$y = u - v = \frac{fb}{x}$$

disparity between the horizontal coordinates of the landmark in the left and right images (in pixels), f is the focal length (in pixels), b is the baseline (horizontal distance between left and right cameras; in metres), and n is the measurement noise (in pixels).

To perform Bayesian inference,

$$p(x|y) = \frac{p(y|x)p(x)}{\int_{-\infty}^{\infty} p(y|x)p(x)\,dx}, \tag{4.2}$$

we require expressions for $p(y|x)$ and $p(x)$. We meet this requirement by making two assumptions. First, we assume that the measurement noise is zero-mean Gaussian, $n \sim \mathcal{N}(0, R)$, such that

$$p(y|x) = \mathcal{N}\left(\frac{fb}{x}, R\right) = \frac{1}{\sqrt{2\pi R}} \exp\left(-\frac{1}{2R}\left(y - \frac{fb}{x}\right)^2\right), \tag{4.3}$$

and second, we assume that the prior is Gaussian, where

$$p(x) = \mathcal{N}\left(\check{x}, \check{P}\right) = \frac{1}{\sqrt{2\pi \check{P}}} \exp\left(-\frac{1}{2\check{P}}\left(x - \check{x}\right)^2\right). \tag{4.4}$$

Before we continue, we note that the Bayesian framework provides an implied order of operations that we would like to make explicit:

$$\text{assign prior} \rightarrow \text{draw } x_{\text{true}} \rightarrow \text{draw } y_{\text{meas}} \rightarrow \text{compute posterior.}$$

In words, we start with a prior. The 'true' state is then drawn from the prior, and the measurement is generated by observing the true state through the camera model and adding noise. The estimator then reconstructs the posterior from the measurement and prior, without knowing x_{true}. This process is necessary to ensure 'fair' comparison between state estimation algorithms.

To put these mathematical models into practical terms, let us assign the following numerical values to the problem:

$$\check{x} = 20 \text{ [m]}, \quad \check{P} = 9 \text{ [m}^2\text{]}, \tag{4.5}$$
$$f = 400 \text{ [pixel]}, \quad b = 0.1 \text{ [m]}, \quad R = 0.09 \text{ [pixel}^2\text{]}.$$

As discussed earlier, the true state, x_{true}, and (noise-corrupted) measurement, y_{meas}, are drawn randomly from $p(x)$ and $p(y|x)$, respectively. Each time we

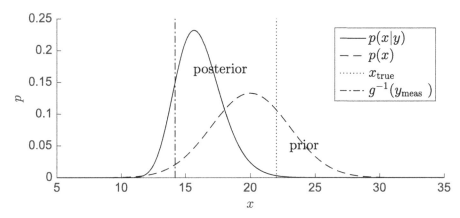

Figure 4.2 Example of Bayesian inference on a one-dimensional stereo camera example. We see that the full posterior is not Gaussian, owing to the nonlinear measurement model.

repeat the experiment, these values will change. In order to plot the posterior for a single experiment, we used the particular values

$$x_{\text{true}} = 22 \; [\text{m}], \quad y_{\text{meas}} = \frac{fb}{x_{\text{true}}} + 1 \; [\text{pixel}],$$

which are fairly typical given the noise characteristics.

Figure 4.2 plots the prior and posterior for this example. Since we are considering a one-dimensional scenario, the denominator integral in (4.2) was computed numerically, and thus we effectively have a view of the full Bayesian posterior with no approximation. We can observe that even though the prior and measurement densities are Gaussian, the posterior is asymmetrical; it is skewed to one side by the nonlinear observation model. However, since the posterior is still unimodal (a single peak), we might still be justified in approximating it as Gaussian. This idea is discussed later in the chapter. We also see that the incorporation of the measurement results in a posterior that is more concentrated (i.e., more 'certain') about the state than the prior; this is the main idea behind Bayesian state estimation: *we want to incorporate measurements into the prior to become more certain about the posterior state.*

Unfortunately, while we were able to effectively compute the exact Bayesian posterior in our simple stereo camera example, this is typically not tractable for real problems. As a result, a variety of tactics have been built up over the years to compute an approximate posterior. For example, the MAP approach is concerned with finding only the most likely state, or in other words the *mode* or 'peak' of the posterior. We discuss this next.

4.1.2 Maximum a Posteriori Estimation

As mentioned earlier, computing the full Bayesian posterior can be intractable in general. A very common approach is to seek out only the value of the state that maximizes the true posterior. This is called *maximum a posteriori (MAP)* estimation and is depicted graphically in Figure 4.3.

In other words, we want to compute

$$\hat{x}_{\text{map}} = \arg \max_{x} p(x|y). \tag{4.6}$$

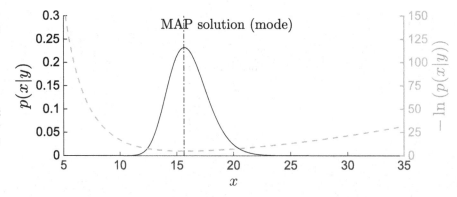

Figure 4.3 Posterior from a stereo camera example, $p(x|y)$, as well as the negative log likelihood of the posterior, $-\ln(p(x|y)$ (dashed). We see that the MAP solution is simply the value of x that maximizes (or minimizes) either of these functions. In other words, the MAP solution is the *mode* of the posterior, which is not generally the same as the *mean*.

Equivalently, we can try minimizing the negative log likelihood:

$$\hat{x}_{\text{map}} = \arg\min_x \left(-\ln(p(x|y))\right), \qquad (4.7)$$

which can be easier when the PDFs involved are from the exponential family. As we are seeking only the most likely state, we can use Bayes' rule to write

$$\hat{x}_{\text{map}} = \arg\min_x \left(-\ln(p(y|x)) - \ln(p(x))\right), \qquad (4.8)$$

which drops $p(y)$ since it does not depend on x.

Relating this back to the stereo camera example presented earlier, we can write

$$\hat{x}_{\text{map}} = \arg\min_x J(x), \qquad (4.9)$$

with

$$J(x) = \frac{1}{2R}\left(y - \frac{fb}{x}\right)^2 + \frac{1}{2\check{P}}\left(\check{x} - x\right)^2, \qquad (4.10)$$

where we have dropped any further normalization constants that do not depend on x. We can then find $\hat{x}_{\text{map}}$ using any number of numerical optimization techniques.

Since the MAP estimator, $\hat{x}_{\text{map}}$, finds the most likely state given the data and prior, a question we might ask is, *how well does this estimator actually capture* x_{true}? In robotics, we often report the average performance of our estimators, $\hat{x}$ with respect to some 'ground truth'. In other words, we compute

$$\hat{e}_{\text{mean}}(\hat{x}) = E_{XN}[\hat{x} - x_{\text{true}}], \qquad (4.11)$$

where $E_{XN}[\cdot]$ is the *expectation operator*; we explicitly include the subscripts XN to indicate that we are averaging over both the random draw of x_{true} from the prior and the random draw of n from the measurement noise. Since x_{true} is assumed to be independent of n, we have $E_{XN}[x_{\text{true}}] = E_X[x_{\text{true}}] = \check{x}$, and so

$$\hat{e}_{\text{mean}}(\hat{x}) = E_{XN}[\hat{x}] - \check{x}. \qquad (4.12)$$

It may be surprising to learn that under this performance measure, MAP estimation is *biased* (i.e., $\hat{e}_{\text{mean}}(\hat{x}_{\text{map}}) \neq 0$). This can be attributed to the presence of a nonlinear measurement model, $g(\cdot)$, and the fact that the mode and mean of

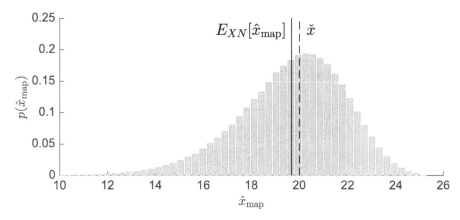

Figure 4.4
Histogram of
estimator values for
1,000,000 trials of
the stereo camera
experiment where
each time a new
x_{true} is randomly
drawn from the prior
and a new y_{meas} is
randomly drawn
from the
measurement model.
The dashed line
marks the mean of
the prior, $\check{x}$, and the
solid line marks the
expected value of the
MAP estimator,
$\hat{x}_{\text{map}}$, over all the
trials. The gap
between dashed and
solid is
$\hat{e}_{\text{mean}} \approx -33.0$ cm,
which indicates a
bias. The average
squared error is
$\hat{e}_{\text{sq}} \approx 4.41$ m^2.

the posterior PDF are not the same. As discussed in the previous chapter, when $g(\cdot)$ is linear, then $\hat{e}_{\text{mean}}(\hat{x}_{\text{map}}) = 0$.

However, since we can trivially set the estimate to the prior, $\hat{x} = \check{x}$, and obtain $\hat{e}_{\text{mean}}(\check{x}) = 0$, we need to define a secondary performance metric. This metric is typically the average squared error, $\hat{e}_{\text{sq}}$, where

$$\hat{e}_{\text{sq}}(\hat{x}) = E_{XN}[(\hat{x} - x_{\text{true}})^2]. \tag{4.13}$$

In other words, the first metric, $\hat{e}_{\text{mean}}$, captures the mean of the estimator error, while the second, $\hat{e}_{\text{sq}}$, captures the combined effects of bias and variance. Performing well on these two metrics results in the bias-variance trade-off in the machine learning literature (Bishop, 2006). Good performance on both metrics is necessary for a practical state estimator. Section 5.1.1 provides additional discussion on assessing the performance of an estimator.

Figure 4.4 shows the MAP bias for the stereo camera example. We see that over a large number of trials (using the parameters in (4.5)), the average difference between the estimator, $\hat{x}_{\text{map}}$, and the ground-truth, $x_{\text{true}} = 20$ m, is $\hat{e}_{\text{mean}} \approx -33.0$ cm, demonstrating a small bias. The average squared error is $\hat{e}_{\text{sq}} \approx 4.41$ m^2.

Note that in this experiment we have drawn the true state from the prior used in the estimator, and we still see a bias. The bias can be worse in practice, as we often do not really know from which prior the true state is drawn and must invent one.

In the rest of this chapter, we will be discussing various estimation approaches for nonlinear, non-Gaussian systems. We must be careful to try to understand what aspect of the full Bayesian posterior each method captures: mean, mode, something else? We prefer to make distinctions in these terms rather than saying one method is more accurate than another. Accuracy can only really be compared fairly if two methods are trying to obtain the same answer.

4.2 Recursive Discrete-Time Estimation

4.2.1 Problem Setup

Just as in the chapter on linear-Gaussian estimation, we require a set of motion and observation models upon which to base our estimator. We will consider

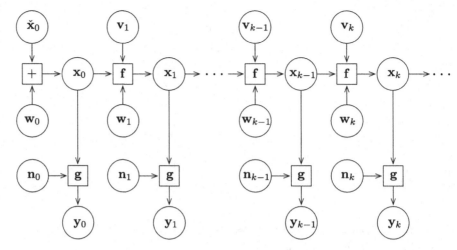

discrete-time, time-invariant equations, but this time we will allow nonlinear equations (we will return to continuous time at the end of this chapter). We define the following motion and observation models:

$$\text{motion model:} \quad \mathbf{x}_k = \mathbf{f}\left(\mathbf{x}_{k-1}, \mathbf{v}_k, \mathbf{w}_k\right), \quad k = 1 \ldots K \quad (4.14a)$$

$$\text{observation model:} \quad \mathbf{y}_k = \mathbf{g}\left(\mathbf{x}_k, \mathbf{n}_k\right), \quad k = 0 \ldots K \quad (4.14b)$$

where k is again the discrete-time index and K its maximum. The function $\mathbf{f}(\cdot)$ is the nonlinear motion model and the function $\mathbf{g}(\cdot)$ is the nonlinear observation model. The variables take on the same meanings as in the linear-Gaussian chapter. For now we do not make any assumption about any of the random variables being Gaussian.

Figure 4.5 provides a graphical representation of the temporal evolution of the system described by (4.14). From this picture we can observe a very important characteristic of the system, the *Markov property*:

In the simplest sense, a stochastic process has the Markov *property if the conditional probability density functions (PDFs) of future states of the process, given the present state, depend only upon the present state, but not on any other past states, that is, they are conditionally independent of these older states. Such a process is called Markovian or a Markov process.*

Our system is such a Markov process. For example, once we know the value of $\mathbf{x}_{k-1}$, we do not need to know the value of any previous states to evolve the system forward in time to compute $\mathbf{x}_k$. This property was exploited fully in the section on linear-Gaussian estimation. There it was assumed that we could employ this property in our estimator design, and this led to an elegant recursive estimator, the Kalman filter. But what about NLNG systems? Can we still have a recursive solution? The answer is yes, but only approximately. The next few sections will examine this claim.

4.2.2 Bayes Filter

In the chapter on linear-Gaussian estimation, we started with a batch estimation technique and worked down to the recursive Kalman filter. In this section, we will start by deriving a recursive filter, the Bayes filter (Jazwinski, 1970), and return to batch methods near the end of the chapter. This order reflects the historical sequence of events in the estimation world and will allow us to highlight exactly where the limiting assumptions and approximations have been made.

The Bayes filter seeks to come up with an entire PDF to represent the likelihood of the state, $\mathbf{x}_k$, using only measurements up to and including the current time. Using our notation from before, we want to compute

$$p(\mathbf{x}_k|\check{\mathbf{x}}_0, \mathbf{v}_{1:k}, \mathbf{y}_{0:k}), \qquad (4.15)$$

which is also sometimes called the *belief* for $\mathbf{x}_k$. Recall from Section 3.3.1 on factoring the batch linear-Gaussian solution that

$$p(\mathbf{x}_k|\mathbf{v}, \mathbf{y}) = \eta \underbrace{p(\mathbf{x}_k|\check{\mathbf{x}}_0, \mathbf{v}_{1:k}, \mathbf{y}_{0:k})}_{\text{forwards}} \underbrace{p(\mathbf{x}_k|\mathbf{v}_{k+1:K}, \mathbf{y}_{k+1:K})}_{\text{backwards}}. \qquad (4.16)$$

Thus, in this section, we will focus on turning the 'forwards' PDF into a recursive filter (for nonlinear non-Gaussian systems). By employing the independence of all the measurements,[2] we may factor out the latest measurement to have

$$p(\mathbf{x}_k|\check{\mathbf{x}}_0, \mathbf{v}_{1:k}, \mathbf{y}_{0:k}) = \eta\, p(\mathbf{y}_k|\mathbf{x}_k)\, p(\mathbf{x}_k|\check{\mathbf{x}}_0, \mathbf{v}_{1:k}, \mathbf{y}_{0:k-1}), \qquad (4.17)$$

where we have employed Bayes' rule to reverse the dependence, and η serves to preserve the axiom of total probability. Turning our attention to the second factor, we introduce the hidden state, $\mathbf{x}_{k-1}$, and integrate over all possible values:

$$p(\mathbf{x}_k|\check{\mathbf{x}}_0, \mathbf{v}_{1:k}, \mathbf{y}_{0:k-1}) = \int p(\mathbf{x}_k, \mathbf{x}_{k-1}|\check{\mathbf{x}}_0, \mathbf{v}_{1:k}, \mathbf{y}_{0:k-1})\, d\mathbf{x}_{k-1}$$

$$= \int p(\mathbf{x}_k|\mathbf{x}_{k-1}, \check{\mathbf{x}}_0, \mathbf{v}_{1:k}, \mathbf{y}_{0:k-1})\, p(\mathbf{x}_{k-1}|\check{\mathbf{x}}_0, \mathbf{v}_{1:k}, \mathbf{y}_{0:k-1})\, d\mathbf{x}_{k-1}. \qquad (4.18)$$

The introduction of the hidden state can be viewed as the opposite of marginalization. So far we have not introduced any approximations. The next step is subtle and is the cause of many limitations in recursive estimation. Since our system enjoys the Markov property, we use this property (on the estimator) to say that

$$p(\mathbf{x}_k|\mathbf{x}_{k-1}, \check{\mathbf{x}}_0, \mathbf{v}_{1:k}, \mathbf{y}_{0:k-1}) = p(\mathbf{x}_k|\mathbf{x}_{k-1}, \mathbf{v}_k), \qquad (4.19a)$$

$$p(\mathbf{x}_{k-1}|\check{\mathbf{x}}_0, \mathbf{v}_{1:k}, \mathbf{y}_{0:k-1}) = p(\mathbf{x}_{k-1}|\check{\mathbf{x}}_0, \mathbf{v}_{1:k-1}, \mathbf{y}_{0:k-1}), \qquad (4.19b)$$

---

[2] We will continue to assume all the measurements are statistically independent as in the *linear-Gaussian (LG)* case.

Figure 4.6
Graphical depictions of the Bayes filter. Here the dashed line indicates that in practice a hint could be passed to the 'correction step' about the states in which the probability mass of the belief function is concentrated. This can be used to reduce the need to work out the full density for the observation, $\mathbf{y}_k$, given the state, $\mathbf{x}_k$.

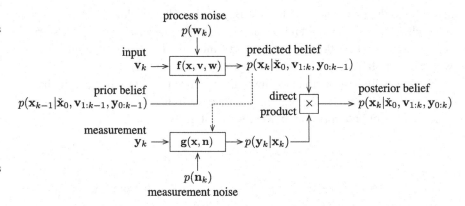

which seems entirely reasonable given the depiction in Figure 4.5. However, we will come back to examine (4.19) later in this chapter. Substituting (4.19) and (4.18) into (4.17), we have the Bayes filter:[3]

$$
\underbrace{p(\mathbf{x}_k|\check{\mathbf{x}}_0, \mathbf{v}_{1:k}, \mathbf{y}_{0:k})}_{\text{posterior belief}}
$$

$$
= \eta \underbrace{p(\mathbf{y}_k|\mathbf{x}_k)}_{\substack{\text{observation} \\ \text{correction} \\ \text{using } \mathbf{g}(\cdot)}} \int \underbrace{p(\mathbf{x}_k|\mathbf{x}_{k-1}, \mathbf{v}_k)}_{\substack{\text{motion} \\ \text{prediction} \\ \text{using } \mathbf{f}(\cdot)}} \underbrace{p(\mathbf{x}_{k-1}|\check{\mathbf{x}}_0, \mathbf{v}_{1:k-1}, \mathbf{y}_{0:k-1})}_{\text{prior belief}} \, d\mathbf{x}_{k-1}.
$$

$$(4.20)$$

We can see that (4.20) takes on a predictor-corrector form. In the prediction step, the prior[4] belief, $p(\mathbf{x}_{k-1}|\check{\mathbf{x}}_0, \mathbf{v}_{1:k-1}, \mathbf{y}_{0:k-1})$, is propagated forward in time using the input, $\mathbf{v}_k$, and the motion model, $\mathbf{f}(\cdot)$. In the correction step, the predicted estimate is then updated using the measurement, $\mathbf{y}_k$, and the measurement model, $\mathbf{g}(\cdot)$. The result is the posterior belief, $p(\mathbf{x}_k|\check{\mathbf{x}}_0, \mathbf{v}_{1:k}, \mathbf{y}_{0:k})$. Figure 4.6 provides a graphical depiction of the information flow in the Bayes filter. The important message to take away from these diagrams is that we require methods of passing PDFs through the nonlinear functions, $\mathbf{f}(\cdot)$ and $\mathbf{g}(\cdot)$.

Although exact, the Bayes filter is really nothing more than a mathematical artifact; it can never be implemented in practice, except for the linear-Gaussian case. There are two primary reasons for this, and as such we need to make appropriate approximations:

(i) Probability density functions live in an infinite-dimensional space (as do all continuous functions) and as such an infinite amount of memory (i.e., infinite number of parameters) would be needed to completely represent the belief, $p(\mathbf{x}_k|\check{\mathbf{x}}_0, \mathbf{v}_{1:k}, \mathbf{y}_{0:k})$. To overcome this memory issue, the belief is approximately represented. One approach is to

---

[3] There is a special case at the first timestep, $k = 0$, that only involves the observation correction with $\mathbf{y}_0$, but we omit it to avoid complexity. We assume the filter is initialized with $p(\mathbf{x}_0|\check{\mathbf{x}}_0, \mathbf{y}_0)$.

[4] To be clear, the Bayes filter is using Bayesian inference, but just at a single timestep. The batch methods discussed in the previous chapter performed inference over the whole trajectory at once. We will return to the batch situation later in this chapter.

approximate this function as a Gaussian PDF (i.e., keep track of the first two moments, mean and covariance). Another approach is to approximate the PDF using a finite number of random samples. We will look into both of these later on.

(ii) The integral in the Bayes filter is computationally very expensive; it would require infinite computing resources to evaluate exactly. To overcome this computational resource issue, the integral must be evaluated approximately. One approach is to linearize the motion and observation models and then evaluate the integrals in closed form. Another approach is to employ *Monte Carlo integration*. We will look into both of these later on as well.

Much of the research in recursive state estimation has focused on better and better approximations to handle these two issues. Considerable gains have been made that are worth examining in more detail. As such, we will look at some of the classic and modern approaches to approximate the Bayes filter in the next few sections. However, we must keep in mind the assumption on which the Bayes filter is predicated: the Markov property. A question we must ask ourselves is, what happens to the Markov property when we start making these approximations to the Bayes filter? We will return to this later. For now, let us assume it holds.

4.2.3 Extended Kalman Filter

We now show that if the belief is constrained to be Gaussian, the noise is Gaussian, and we linearize the motion and observation models in order to carry out the integral (and also the normalized product) in the Bayes filter, we arrive at the famous *extended Kalman filter (EKF)*.[5] The EKF is still the mainstay of estimation and data fusion in many circles, and can often be effective for mildly nonlinear, non-Gaussian systems. For a good reference on the EKF, see Maybeck (1994).

The EKF was a key tool used to estimate spacecraft trajectories on the NASA Apollo program. Shortly after Kalman's original paper (Kalman, 1960b) was published, he met with Stanley F. Schmidt of NASA Ames Research Center. Schmidt was impressed with Kalman's filter and his team went on to modify it to work for their task of spacecraft navigation. In particular, they (i) extended it to work for nonlinear motion and observation models, (ii) came up with the idea of linearizing about the best current estimate to reduce nonlinear effects, and (iii) reformulated the original filter to the now-standard separate prediction and correction steps (McGee and Schmidt, 1985). For these significant contributions, the EKF was sometimes called the Schmidt–Kalman filter, but this name has fallen out of favour due to confusion with another similarly named contribution later made by Schmidt (to account for unobservable biases while keeping state dimension low). Schmidt also went on to work on the square-root formulation of the EKF to improve numerical stability (Bierman, 1974). Later, at Lockheed Missiles and Space Company, Schmidt's popularization of Kalman's work also inspired Charlotte Striebel to begin work on connecting the KF to other types of

Stanley F. Schmidt (1926–2015) was an American aerospace engineer who adapted Kalman's filter early on to estimate spacecraft trajectories on the Apollo program. It was his work that led to what is now called the extended Kalman filter.

---

[5] The EKF is called 'extended' because it is the extension of the Kalman filter to nonlinear systems.

trajectory estimation, which ultimately led to the Rauch–Tung–Striebel smoother discussed in the previous chapter.

To derive the EKF, we first limit (i.e., constrain) our belief function for $\mathbf{x}_k$ to be Gaussian:

$$p\big(\mathbf{x}_k | \check{\mathbf{x}}_0, \mathbf{v}_{1:k}, \mathbf{y}_{0:k}\big) = \mathcal{N}\left(\hat{\mathbf{x}}_k, \hat{\mathbf{P}}_k\right), \tag{4.21}$$

where $\hat{\mathbf{x}}_k$ is the mean and $\hat{\mathbf{P}}_k$ the covariance. Next, we assume that the noise variables, $\mathbf{w}_k$ and $\mathbf{n}_k$ ($\forall k$), are in fact Gaussian as well:

$$\mathbf{w}_k \sim \mathcal{N}(\mathbf{0}, \mathbf{Q}_k), \tag{4.22a}$$

$$\mathbf{n}_k \sim \mathcal{N}(\mathbf{0}, \mathbf{R}_k). \tag{4.22b}$$

Note that a Gaussian PDF can be transformed through a nonlinearity to be non-Gaussian. In fact, we will look at this in more detail a bit later in this chapter. We assume this is the case for the noise variables; in other words, the nonlinear motion and observation models may affect $\mathbf{w}_k$ and $\mathbf{n}_k$. They are not necessarily added after the nonlinearities, as in

$$\mathbf{x}_k = \mathbf{f}\left(\mathbf{x}_{k-1}, \mathbf{v}_k\right) + \mathbf{w}_k, \tag{4.23a}$$

$$\mathbf{y}_k = \mathbf{g}\left(\mathbf{x}_k\right) + \mathbf{n}_k, \tag{4.23b}$$

but rather appear inside the nonlinearities as in (4.14). The equations in (4.23) are in fact a special case of (4.14). However, we can recover additive noise (approximately) through linearization, which we show next.

With $\mathbf{g}(\cdot)$ and $\mathbf{f}(\cdot)$ nonlinear, we still cannot compute the integral in the Bayes filter in closed form, so we turn to linearization. We linearize the motion and observation models about the current state estimate mean:

$$\mathbf{f}\left(\mathbf{x}_{k-1}, \mathbf{v}_k, \mathbf{w}_k\right) \approx \check{\mathbf{x}}_k + \mathbf{F}_{k-1}\left(\mathbf{x}_{k-1} - \hat{\mathbf{x}}_{k-1}\right) + \mathbf{w}'_k, \tag{4.24a}$$

$$\mathbf{g}\left(\mathbf{x}_k, \mathbf{n}_k\right) \approx \check{\mathbf{y}}_k + \mathbf{G}_k\left(\mathbf{x}_k - \check{\mathbf{x}}_k\right) + \mathbf{n}'_k, \tag{4.24b}$$

where

$$\check{\mathbf{x}}_k = \mathbf{f}\left(\hat{\mathbf{x}}_{k-1}, \mathbf{v}_k, \mathbf{0}\right), \quad \mathbf{F}_{k-1} = \left.\frac{\partial \mathbf{f}(\mathbf{x}_{k-1}, \mathbf{v}_k, \mathbf{w}_k)}{\partial \mathbf{x}_{k-1}}\right|_{\hat{\mathbf{x}}_{k-1}, \mathbf{v}_k, \mathbf{0}}, \tag{4.25a}$$

$$\mathbf{w}'_k = \left.\frac{\partial \mathbf{f}(\mathbf{x}_{k-1}, \mathbf{v}_k, \mathbf{w}_k)}{\partial \mathbf{w}_k}\right|_{\hat{\mathbf{x}}_{k-1}, \mathbf{v}_k, \mathbf{0}} \mathbf{w}_k, \tag{4.25b}$$

and

$$\check{\mathbf{y}}_k = \mathbf{g}\left(\check{\mathbf{x}}_k, \mathbf{0}\right), \quad \mathbf{G}_k = \left.\frac{\partial \mathbf{g}(\mathbf{x}_k, \mathbf{n}_k)}{\partial \mathbf{x}_k}\right|_{\check{\mathbf{x}}_k, \mathbf{0}}, \tag{4.26a}$$

$$\mathbf{n}'_k = \left.\frac{\partial \mathbf{g}(\mathbf{x}_k, \mathbf{n}_k)}{\partial \mathbf{n}_k}\right|_{\check{\mathbf{x}}_k, \mathbf{0}} \mathbf{n}_k. \tag{4.26b}$$

From here the statistical properties of the current state, $\mathbf{x}_k$, given the old state and latest input, are

$$\mathbf{x}_k \approx \check{\mathbf{x}}_k + \mathbf{F}_{k-1} \left(\mathbf{x}_{k-1} - \hat{\mathbf{x}}_{k-1}\right) + \mathbf{w}'_k, \tag{4.27a}$$

$$E\left[\mathbf{x}_k\right] \approx \check{\mathbf{x}}_k + \mathbf{F}_{k-1} \left(\mathbf{x}_{k-1} - \hat{\mathbf{x}}_{k-1}\right) + \underbrace{E\left[\mathbf{w}'_k\right]}_{\mathbf{0}}, \tag{4.27b}$$

$$E\left[\left(\mathbf{x}_k - E\left[\mathbf{x}_k\right]\right)\left(\mathbf{x}_k - E\left[\mathbf{x}_k\right]\right)^T\right] \approx \underbrace{E\left[\mathbf{w}'_k \mathbf{w}'^T_k\right]}_{\mathbf{Q}'_k}, \tag{4.27c}$$

$$p(\mathbf{x}_k|\mathbf{x}_{k-1}, \mathbf{v}_k) \approx \mathcal{N}\left(\check{\mathbf{x}}_k + \mathbf{F}_{k-1}\left(\mathbf{x}_{k-1} - \hat{\mathbf{x}}_{k-1}\right), \mathbf{Q}'_k\right). \tag{4.27d}$$

For the statistical properties of the current measurement, $\mathbf{y}_k$, given the current state, we have

$$\mathbf{y}_k \approx \check{\mathbf{y}}_k + \mathbf{G}_k \left(\mathbf{x}_k - \check{\mathbf{x}}_k\right) + \mathbf{n}'_k, \tag{4.28a}$$

$$E\left[\mathbf{y}_k\right] \approx \check{\mathbf{y}}_k + \mathbf{G}_k \left(\mathbf{x}_k - \check{\mathbf{x}}_k\right) + \underbrace{E\left[\mathbf{n}'_k\right]}_{\mathbf{0}}, \tag{4.28b}$$

$$E\left[\left(\mathbf{y}_k - E\left[\mathbf{y}_k\right]\right)\left(\mathbf{y}_k - E\left[\mathbf{y}_k\right]\right)^T\right] \approx \underbrace{E\left[\mathbf{n}'_k \mathbf{n}'^T_k\right]}_{\mathbf{R}'_k}, \tag{4.28c}$$

$$p(\mathbf{y}_k|\mathbf{x}_k) \approx \mathcal{N}\left(\check{\mathbf{y}}_k + \mathbf{G}_k(\mathbf{x}_k - \check{\mathbf{x}}_k), \mathbf{R}'_k\right). \tag{4.28d}$$

Substituting in these results, the Bayes filter becomes

$$\underbrace{p(\mathbf{x}_k|\check{\mathbf{x}}_0, \mathbf{v}_{1:k}, \mathbf{y}_{0:k})}_{\mathcal{N}\left(\hat{\mathbf{x}}_k, \hat{\mathbf{P}}_k\right)} = \eta \quad \underbrace{p(\mathbf{y}_k|\mathbf{x}_k)}_{\mathcal{N}\left(\check{\mathbf{y}}_k + \mathbf{G}_k(\mathbf{x}_k - \check{\mathbf{x}}_k), \mathbf{R}'_k\right)}$$

$$\times \int \underbrace{p(\mathbf{x}_k|\mathbf{x}_{k-1}, \mathbf{v}_k)}_{\mathcal{N}\left(\check{\mathbf{x}}_k + \mathbf{F}_{k-1}(\mathbf{x}_{k-1} - \hat{\mathbf{x}}_{k-1}), \mathbf{Q}'_k\right)} \underbrace{p(\mathbf{x}_{k-1}|\check{\mathbf{x}}_0, \mathbf{v}_{1:k-1}, \mathbf{y}_{0:k-1})}_{\mathcal{N}\left(\hat{\mathbf{x}}_{k-1}, \hat{\mathbf{P}}_{k-1}\right)} d\mathbf{x}_{k-1}. \tag{4.29}$$

Using our formula (2.88) for passing a Gaussian through a (stochastic) nonlinearity, we can see that the integral is also Gaussian:

$$\underbrace{p(\mathbf{x}_k|\check{\mathbf{x}}_0, \mathbf{v}_{1:k}, \mathbf{y}_{0:k})}_{\mathcal{N}\left(\hat{\mathbf{x}}_k, \hat{\mathbf{P}}_k\right)} = \eta \quad \underbrace{p(\mathbf{y}_k|\mathbf{x}_k)}_{\mathcal{N}\left(\check{\mathbf{y}}_k + \mathbf{G}_k(\mathbf{x}_k - \check{\mathbf{x}}_k), \mathbf{R}'_k\right)}$$

$$\times \underbrace{\int p(\mathbf{x}_k|\mathbf{x}_{k-1}, \mathbf{v}_k)\, p(\mathbf{x}_{k-1}|\check{\mathbf{x}}_0, \mathbf{v}_{1:k-1}, \mathbf{y}_{0:k-1})\, d\mathbf{x}_{k-1}}_{\mathcal{N}\left(\check{\mathbf{x}}_k, \mathbf{F}_{k-1}\hat{\mathbf{P}}_{k-1}\mathbf{F}^T_{k-1} + \mathbf{Q}'_k\right)}. \tag{4.30}$$

We are now left with the normalized product of two Gaussian PDFs, which we also discussed previously in Section 2.2.8. Applying (2.91), we find that

$$\underbrace{p(\mathbf{x}_k|\check{\mathbf{x}}_0, \mathbf{v}_{1:k}, \mathbf{y}_{0:k})}_{\mathcal{N}(\hat{\mathbf{x}}_k, \hat{\mathbf{P}}_k)}$$

$$= \eta \, p(\mathbf{y}_k|\mathbf{x}_k) \underbrace{\int p(\mathbf{x}_k|\mathbf{x}_{k-1}, \mathbf{v}_k) \, p(\mathbf{x}_{k-1}|\check{\mathbf{x}}_0, \mathbf{v}_{1:k-1}, \mathbf{y}_{0:k-1}) \, d\mathbf{x}_{k-1}}_{\mathcal{N}\left(\check{\mathbf{x}}_k + \mathbf{K}_k(\mathbf{y}_k - \check{\mathbf{y}}_k), (1 - \mathbf{K}_k\mathbf{G}_k)(\mathbf{F}_{k-1}\hat{\mathbf{P}}_{k-1}\mathbf{F}_{k-1}^T + \mathbf{Q}_k')\right)}, \quad (4.31)$$

where $\mathbf{K}_k$ is known as the Kalman gain matrix (given in what follows). Getting to this last line takes quite a bit of tedious algebra and is left to the reader. Comparing the left and right sides of our posterior expression, we have

$$\text{predictor:} \quad \begin{aligned} \check{\mathbf{P}}_k &= \mathbf{F}_{k-1}\hat{\mathbf{P}}_{k-1}\mathbf{F}_{k-1}^T + \mathbf{Q}_k', & (4.32a) \\ \check{\mathbf{x}}_k &= \mathbf{f}(\hat{\mathbf{x}}_{k-1}, \mathbf{v}_k, \mathbf{0}), & (4.32b) \end{aligned}$$

$$\text{Kalman gain:} \quad \mathbf{K}_k = \check{\mathbf{P}}_k\mathbf{G}_k^T\left(\mathbf{G}_k\check{\mathbf{P}}_k\mathbf{G}_k^T + \mathbf{R}_k'\right)^{-1}, \quad (4.32c)$$

$$\text{corrector:} \quad \begin{aligned} \hat{\mathbf{P}}_k &= (1 - \mathbf{K}_k\mathbf{G}_k)\check{\mathbf{P}}_k, & (4.32d) \\ \hat{\mathbf{x}}_k &= \check{\mathbf{x}}_k + \mathbf{K}_k\underbrace{(\mathbf{y}_k - \mathbf{g}(\check{\mathbf{x}}_k, \mathbf{0}))}_{\text{innovation}}. & (4.32e) \end{aligned}$$

The equations of (4.32) are known as the classic recursive update equations for the EKF. The update equations allow us to compute $\left\{\hat{\mathbf{x}}_k, \hat{\mathbf{P}}_k\right\}$ from $\left\{\hat{\mathbf{x}}_{k-1}, \hat{\mathbf{P}}_{k-1}\right\}$. We notice immediately the similar structure to (3.131) for linear-Gaussian estimation. There are two main differences here:

(i) The nonlinear motion and observation models are used to propagate the mean of our estimate.

(ii) There are Jacobians embedded in the $\mathbf{Q}_k'$ and $\mathbf{R}_k'$ covariances for the noise. This comes from the fact that we allowed the noise to be applied within the nonlinearities in (4.14).

It should be noted that there is no guarantee that the EKF will perform adequately for a general nonlinear system. To gauge the performance of the EKF on a particular nonlinear system, it often comes down to simply trying it out. The main problem with the EKF is that the operating point of the linearization is the mean of our estimate of the state, not the true state. This seemingly small difference can cause the EKF to diverge wildly in some cases. Sometimes the result is less dramatic, with the estimate being *biased* or *inconsistent* or, most often, both.

4.2.4 Generalized Gaussian Filter

The Bayes filter is appealing because it can be written out exactly. We can then reach a number of implementable filters through different approximations on the form of the estimated PDF and handling methods. There is, however, a cleaner approach to deriving those filters that assume up front that the estimated PDF is Gaussian. We have actually already seen this in practice in Section 3.3.3, where we derived the Kalman filter using Bayesian inference.

In general, we begin with a Gaussian prior at time $k-1$:

$$p(\mathbf{x}_{k-1}|\check{\mathbf{x}}_0, \mathbf{v}_{1:k-1}, \mathbf{y}_{0:k-1}) = \mathcal{N}\left(\hat{\mathbf{x}}_{k-1}, \hat{\mathbf{P}}_{k-1}\right). \tag{4.33}$$

We pass this forwards in time through the nonlinear motion model, $\mathbf{f}(\cdot)$, to propose a Gaussian prior at time k:

$$p(\mathbf{x}_k|\check{\mathbf{x}}_0, \mathbf{v}_{1:k}, \mathbf{y}_{0:k-1}) = \mathcal{N}\left(\check{\mathbf{x}}_k, \check{\mathbf{P}}_k\right). \tag{4.34}$$

This is the *prediction step* and incorporates the latest input, $\mathbf{v}_k$.

For the *correction step*, we employ the method from Section 2.2.2 and write a joint Gaussian for the state and latest measurement, at time k:

$$p(\mathbf{x}_k, \mathbf{y}_k|\check{\mathbf{x}}_0, \mathbf{v}_{1:k}, \mathbf{y}_{0:k-1}) = \mathcal{N}\left(\begin{bmatrix}\boldsymbol{\mu}_{x,k} \\ \boldsymbol{\mu}_{y,k}\end{bmatrix}, \begin{bmatrix}\boldsymbol{\Sigma}_{xx,k} & \boldsymbol{\Sigma}_{xy,k} \\ \boldsymbol{\Sigma}_{yx,k} & \boldsymbol{\Sigma}_{yy,k}\end{bmatrix}\right). \tag{4.35}$$

We then write the conditional Gaussian density for $\mathbf{x}_k$ (i.e., the posterior) directly as

$$\begin{aligned}&p(\mathbf{x}_k|\check{\mathbf{x}}_0, \mathbf{v}_{1:k}, \mathbf{y}_{0:k}) \\ &= \mathcal{N}\Big(\underbrace{\boldsymbol{\mu}_{x,k} + \boldsymbol{\Sigma}_{xy,k}\boldsymbol{\Sigma}_{yy,k}^{-1}(\mathbf{y}_k - \boldsymbol{\mu}_{y,k})}_{\hat{\mathbf{x}}_k}, \underbrace{\boldsymbol{\Sigma}_{xx,k} - \boldsymbol{\Sigma}_{xy,k}\boldsymbol{\Sigma}_{yy,k}^{-1}\boldsymbol{\Sigma}_{yx,k}}_{\hat{\mathbf{P}}_k}\Big),\end{aligned} \tag{4.36}$$

where we have defined $\hat{\mathbf{x}}_k$ as the mean and $\hat{\mathbf{P}}_k$ as the covariance. The nonlinear observation model, $\mathbf{g}(\cdot)$, is used in the computation of $\boldsymbol{\mu}_{y,k}$. From here, we can write the generalized Gaussian correction-step equations as

$$\mathbf{K}_k = \boldsymbol{\Sigma}_{xy,k}\boldsymbol{\Sigma}_{yy,k}^{-1}, \tag{4.37a}$$

$$\hat{\mathbf{P}}_k = \check{\mathbf{P}}_k - \mathbf{K}_k\boldsymbol{\Sigma}_{xy,k}^T, \tag{4.37b}$$

$$\hat{\mathbf{x}}_k = \check{\mathbf{x}}_k + \mathbf{K}_k\left(\mathbf{y}_k - \boldsymbol{\mu}_{y,k}\right), \tag{4.37c}$$

where we have let $\boldsymbol{\mu}_{x,k} = \check{\mathbf{x}}_k$, $\boldsymbol{\Sigma}_{xx,k} = \check{\mathbf{P}}_k$, and $\mathbf{K}_k$ is still known as the Kalman gain. Unfortunately, unless the motion and observation models are linear, we cannot compute all the remaining quantities required exactly: $\boldsymbol{\mu}_{y,k}$, $\boldsymbol{\Sigma}_{yy,k}$, and $\boldsymbol{\Sigma}_{xy,k}$. This is because putting a Gaussian PDF into a nonlinearity generally results in something non-Gaussian coming out the other end. We therefore need to consider approximations at this stage.

The next section will revisit linearizing the motion and observation models to complete this cleaner derivation of the EKF. After that, we will discuss other methods of passing PDFs through nonlinearities, which lead to other flavours of the Bayes and Kalman filters.

4.2.5 Iterated Extended Kalman Filter

Continuing on from the previous section, we complete our alternate derivation of the *iterated extended Kalman filter (IEKF)*. The *prediction step* is fairly straightforward and essentially the same as Section 4.2.3. We therefore omit it but note that the prior, at time k, is

$$p(\mathbf{x}_k | \check{\mathbf{x}}_0, \mathbf{v}_{1:k}, \mathbf{y}_{0:k-1}) = \mathcal{N}\left(\check{\mathbf{x}}_k, \check{\mathbf{P}}_k\right),\tag{4.38}$$

which incorporates $\mathbf{v}_k$.

The *correction step* is where things become a little more interesting. Our *non-linear* measurement model is given by

$$\mathbf{y}_k = \mathbf{g}(\mathbf{x}_k, \mathbf{n}_k).\tag{4.39}$$

We linearize about an arbitrary operating point, $\mathbf{x}_{\mathrm{op},k}$:

$$\mathbf{g}\left(\mathbf{x}_k, \mathbf{n}_k\right) \approx \mathbf{y}_{\mathrm{op},k} + \mathbf{G}_k\left(\mathbf{x}_k - \mathbf{x}_{\mathrm{op},k}\right) + \mathbf{n}_k',\tag{4.40}$$

where

$$\mathbf{y}_{\mathrm{op},k} = \mathbf{g}\left(\mathbf{x}_{\mathrm{op},k}, \mathbf{0}\right), \quad \mathbf{G}_k = \left.\frac{\partial \mathbf{g}(\mathbf{x}_k, \mathbf{n}_k)}{\partial \mathbf{x}_k}\right|_{\mathbf{x}_{\mathrm{op},k},\mathbf{0}},\tag{4.41a}$$

$$\mathbf{n}_k' = \left.\frac{\partial \mathbf{g}(\mathbf{x}_k, \mathbf{n}_k)}{\partial \mathbf{n}_k}\right|_{\mathbf{x}_{\mathrm{op},k},\mathbf{0}} \mathbf{n}_k.\tag{4.41b}$$

Note that the observation model and Jacobians are evaluated at $\mathbf{x}_{\mathrm{op},k}$.

Using this linearized model, we can then express the joint density for the state and the measurement at time k as approximately Gaussian:

$$p(\mathbf{x}_k, \mathbf{y}_k | \check{\mathbf{x}}_0, \mathbf{v}_{1:k}, \mathbf{y}_{0:k-1}) \approx \mathcal{N}\left(\begin{bmatrix} \boldsymbol{\mu}_{x,k} \\ \boldsymbol{\mu}_{y,k} \end{bmatrix}, \begin{bmatrix} \boldsymbol{\Sigma}_{xx,k} & \boldsymbol{\Sigma}_{xy,k} \\ \boldsymbol{\Sigma}_{yx,k} & \boldsymbol{\Sigma}_{yy,k} \end{bmatrix}\right)$$

$$= \mathcal{N}\left(\begin{bmatrix} \check{\mathbf{x}}_k \\ \mathbf{y}_{\mathrm{op},k} + \mathbf{G}_k(\check{\mathbf{x}}_k - \mathbf{x}_{\mathrm{op},k}) \end{bmatrix}, \begin{bmatrix} \check{\mathbf{P}}_k & \check{\mathbf{P}}_k \mathbf{G}_k^T \\ \mathbf{G}_k \check{\mathbf{P}}_k & \mathbf{G}_k \check{\mathbf{P}}_k \mathbf{G}_k^T + \mathbf{R}_k' \end{bmatrix}\right).\tag{4.42}$$

Once again, if the measurement, $\mathbf{y}_k$, is known, we can use (2.52b) to write the Gaussian conditional density for $\mathbf{x}_k$ (i.e., the posterior) as

$$p(\mathbf{x}_k | \check{\mathbf{x}}_0, \mathbf{v}_{1:k}, \mathbf{y}_{0:k})$$
$$= \mathcal{N}\left(\underbrace{\boldsymbol{\mu}_{x,k} + \boldsymbol{\Sigma}_{xy,k}\boldsymbol{\Sigma}_{yy,k}^{-1}(\mathbf{y}_k - \boldsymbol{\mu}_{y,k})}_{\hat{\mathbf{x}}_k}, \underbrace{\boldsymbol{\Sigma}_{xx,k} - \boldsymbol{\Sigma}_{xy,k}\boldsymbol{\Sigma}_{yy,k}^{-1}\boldsymbol{\Sigma}_{yx,k}}_{\hat{\mathbf{P}}_k}\right),\tag{4.43}$$

where again we have defined $\hat{\mathbf{x}}_k$ as the mean and $\hat{\mathbf{P}}_k$ as the covariance. As shown in the previous section, the generalized Gaussian correction-step equations are

$$\mathbf{K}_k = \boldsymbol{\Sigma}_{xy,k}\boldsymbol{\Sigma}_{yy,k}^{-1},\tag{4.44a}$$

$$\hat{\mathbf{P}}_k = \check{\mathbf{P}}_k - \mathbf{K}_k\boldsymbol{\Sigma}_{xy,k}^T,\tag{4.44b}$$

$$\hat{\mathbf{x}}_k = \check{\mathbf{x}}_k + \mathbf{K}_k\left(\mathbf{y}_k - \boldsymbol{\mu}_{y,k}\right).\tag{4.44c}$$

Substituting in the moments $\boldsymbol{\mu}_{y,k}$, $\boldsymbol{\Sigma}_{yy,k}$, and $\boldsymbol{\Sigma}_{xy,k}$ from the preceding equations, we have

$$\mathbf{K}_k = \check{\mathbf{P}}_k\mathbf{G}_k^T\left(\mathbf{G}_k\check{\mathbf{P}}_k\mathbf{G}_k^T + \mathbf{R}_k'\right)^{-1},\tag{4.45a}$$

$$\hat{\mathbf{P}}_k = \left(\mathbf{1} - \mathbf{K}_k\mathbf{G}_k\right)\check{\mathbf{P}}_k,\tag{4.45b}$$

$$\hat{\mathbf{x}}_k = \check{\mathbf{x}}_k + \mathbf{K}_k\left(\mathbf{y}_k - \mathbf{y}_{\mathrm{op},k} - \mathbf{G}_k(\check{\mathbf{x}}_k - \mathbf{x}_{\mathrm{op},k})\right).\tag{4.45c}$$

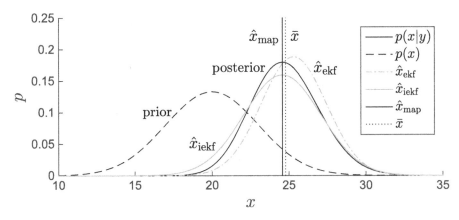

Figure 4.7 Stereo camera example, comparing the inference (i.e., 'corrective') step of the EKF and IEKF to the full Bayesian posterior, $p(x|y)$. We see that the mean of the IEKF matches up against the MAP solution, $\hat{x}_{\mathrm{map}}$, while the EKF does not. The actual mean of the posterior is denoted $\bar{x}$.

These equations are very similar to the Kalman gain and corrector equations in (4.32); the only difference is the operating point of the linearization. If we set the operating point of the linearization to be the mean of the predicted prior, $\mathbf{x}_{\mathrm{op},k} = \check{\mathbf{x}}_k$, then (4.45) and (4.32) are identical.

However, it turns out that we can do much better if we iteratively recompute (4.45), each time setting the operating point to be the mean of the posterior at the last iteration:

$$\mathbf{x}_{\mathrm{op},k} \leftarrow \hat{\mathbf{x}}_k. \tag{4.46}$$

At the first iteration we take $\mathbf{x}_{\mathrm{op},k} = \check{\mathbf{x}}_k$. This allows us to be linearizing about better and better estimates, thereby improving our approximation each iteration. We terminate the process when the change to $\mathbf{x}_{\mathrm{op},k}$ from one iteration to the next is sufficiently small. Note that the covariance equation need only be computed once, after the other two equations converge.

4.2.6 IEKF Is a MAP Estimator

A great question to ask at this point is, *what is the relationship between the EKF/IEKF estimate and the full Bayesian posterior?* It turns out that the IEKF estimate corresponds to a (local) maximum of the full posterior;[6] in other words, it is a MAP estimate. On the other hand, since the EKF is not iterated, it can be very far from a local maximum; there is actually very little we can say about its relationship to the full posterior.

These relations are illustrated in Figure 4.7, where we compare the correction steps of the IEKF and EKF to the full Bayesian posterior on our stereo camera example introduced in Section 4.1.2. In this version of the example, we used

$$x_{\mathrm{true}} = 26 \ [\mathrm{m}], \quad y_{\mathrm{meas}} = \frac{fb}{x_{\mathrm{true}}} - 0.6 \ [\mathrm{pixel}],$$

to exaggerate the difference between the methods. As discussed above, the mean of the IEKF corresponds to the MAP (i.e., mode) solution, while the EKF is not easily relatable to the full posterior.

---

[6] To be clear, this is only true for the correction step at a single timestep.

Figure 4.8 Monte Carlo method to transform a PDF through a nonlinearity. A large number of random samples are drawn from the input density, passed through the nonlinearity, and then used to form the output density.

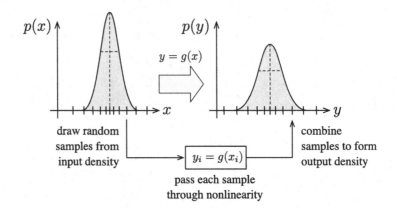

To understand why the IEKF is the same as the MAP estimate, we require some optimization tools that we will introduce later in the chapter. For now, the important takeaway message from this section is that our choice to iteratively relinearize about our best guess leads to a MAP solution. Thus, the 'mean' of our IEKF Gaussian estimator does not actually match the mean of the full Bayesian posterior; it matches the mode.

4.2.7 Alternatives for Passing PDFs through Nonlinearities

In our derivation of the EKF/IEKF, we used one particular technique to pass a PDF through a nonlinearity. Specifically, we linearized the nonlinear model about an operating point and then passed our Gaussian PDFs through the linearized model analytically. This is certainly one approach, but there are others. This section will discuss three common approaches: the Monte Carlo method (brute force), linearization (as in the EKF), and the *sigmapoint* or *unscented*[7] transformation. Our motivation is to introduce some tools that can be used within our Bayes filter framework to derive alternatives to the EKF/IEKF.

Monte Carlo Method

The Monte Carlo method of transforming a PDF through a nonlinearity is essentially the 'brute force' approach. The process is depicted in Figure 4.8. We draw a large number of samples from the input density, transform each one of these samples through the nonlinearity exactly, and then build the output density from the transformed samples (e.g., by computing the statistical moments). Loosely, the *law of large numbers* ensures this procedure will converge to the correct answer as the number of samples used approaches infinity.

The obvious problem with this method is that it can be terribly inefficient, particularly in higher dimensions. Aside from this obvious disadvantage, there are actually some advantages to this method:

(i) It works with any PDF, not just Gaussian.
(ii) It handles any type of nonlinearity (no requirement for differentiable or even continuous).

---

[7] This name lives on in the literature; apparently, Simon Julier named it after an unscented deodorant to make the point that often we take names for granted without knowing their origins.

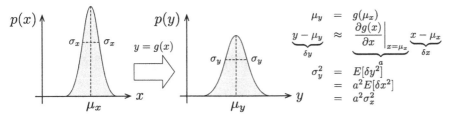

Figure 4.9
One-dimensional Gaussian PDF transformed through a deterministic nonlinear function, $g(\cdot)$. Here we linearize the nonlinearity to propagate the variance approximately.

(iii) We do not need to know the mathematical form of the nonlinear function – in practice the nonlinearity could be any software function.

(iv) It is an 'anytime' algorithm – we can easily trade off accuracy against speed by choosing the number of samples appropriately.

Because we can make this method highly accurate, we can also use it to gauge the performance of other methods.

The other point worth mentioning at this stage is that the mean of the output density is not the same as the mean of the input density after being passed through the nonlinearity. This can be seen by way of a simple example. Consider the input density for x to be uniform over the interval $[0, 1]$; in other words, $p(x) = 1$, $x \in [0, 1]$. Let the nonlinearity be $y = x^2$. The mean of the input is $\mu_x = 1/2$, and passing this through the nonlinearity gives $\mu_y = 1/4$. However, the actual mean of the output is $\mu_y = \int_0^1 p(x)\, x^2\, dx = 1/3$. Similar things happen to the higher statistical moments. The Monte Carlo method is able to approach the correct answer with a large number of samples, but as we will see, some of the other methods cannot.

Linearization

The most popular method of transforming a Gaussian PDF through a nonlinearity is linearization, which we have already used to derive the EKF/IEKF. Technically, the mean is actually passed through the nonlinearity exactly, while the covariance is approximately passed through a linearized version of the function. Typically, the operating point of the linearization process is the mean of the PDF. This procedure is depicted in Figure 4.9 (repeat of Figure 2.4 for convenience). This procedure is highly inaccurate for the following reasons:

(i) The outcome of passing a Gaussian PDF through a nonlinear function will not be another Gaussian PDF. By keeping only the mean and covariance of the posterior PDF, we are approximating the posterior (by throwing away higher statistical moments).

(ii) We are approximating the covariance of the true output PDF by linearizing the nonlinear function.

(iii) The operating point about which we linearize the nonlinear function is often not the true mean of the prior PDF, but rather our estimate of the mean of the input PDF. This is an approximation that introduces error.

Figure 4.10
One-dimensional
Gaussian PDF
transformed through
a deterministic
nonlinear function,
$g(\cdot)$. Here the basic
sigmapoint
transformation is
used in which only
two deterministic
samples (one on
either side of the
mean) approximate
the input density.

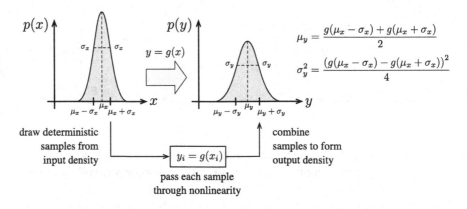

(iv) We are approximating the mean of the true output PDF by simply passing the mean of the prior PDF through the nonlinear function. This does not represent the true mean of the output.

Another disadvantage of linearization is that we need to be able to either calculate the Jacobian of the nonlinearity in closed form, or compute it numerically (which introduces yet another approximation).

Despite all these approximations and disadvantages, if the function is only slightly nonlinear, and the input PDF is Gaussian, the linearization method is very simple to understand and quick to implement. One advantage[8] is that the procedure is actually reversible (if the nonlinearity is locally invertible). That is, we can recover the input PDF exactly by passing the output PDF through the inverse of the nonlinearity (using the same linearization procedure). This is not true for all methods of passing PDFs through nonlinearities since they do not all make the same approximations as linearization. For example, the sigmapoint transformation is not reversible in this way.

Sigmapoint Transformation

In a sense, the *sigmapoint (SP)* or *unscented* transformation (Julier and Uhlmann, 1996) is the compromise between the Monte Carlo and linearization methods when the input density is roughly a Gaussian PDF. It is more accurate than linearization, but for a comparable computational cost to linearization. Monte Carlo is still the most accurate method, but the computational cost is prohibitive in most situations.

It is actually a bit misleading to refer to 'the' sigmapoint transformation, as there is actually a whole family of such transformations; see Section 6.3.3 for a more comprehensive discussion. Figure 4.10 depicts the very simplest version in one dimension. In general, a version of the SP transformation is used that includes one additional sample beyond the basic version at the mean of the input density. The steps are as follows:

---

[8] It might be more accurate to say this is a by-product than an advantage, since it is a direct result of the specific approximations made in linearization.

1. A set of $2L+1$ *sigmapoints* is computed from the input density, $\mathcal{N}\left(\boldsymbol{\mu}_x, \boldsymbol{\Sigma}_{xx}\right)$, according to

$$\mathbf{L}\mathbf{L}^T = \boldsymbol{\Sigma}_{xx}, \quad \text{(Cholesky decomposition, } \mathbf{L} \text{ lower-triangular)} \quad (4.47\text{a})$$

$$\mathbf{x}_0 = \boldsymbol{\mu}_x, \quad (4.47\text{b})$$

$$\mathbf{x}_i = \boldsymbol{\mu}_x + \sqrt{L+\kappa}\,\text{col}_i\mathbf{L}, \quad (4.47\text{c})$$

$$\mathbf{x}_{i+L} = \boldsymbol{\mu}_x - \sqrt{L+\kappa}\,\text{col}_i\mathbf{L}, \quad i=1\ldots L \quad (4.47\text{d})$$

where $L = \dim(\boldsymbol{\mu}_x)$. We note that

$$\boldsymbol{\mu}_x = \sum_{i=0}^{2L} \alpha_i\,\mathbf{x}_i, \quad (4.48\text{a})$$

$$\boldsymbol{\Sigma}_{xx} = \sum_{i=0}^{2L} \alpha_i\left(\mathbf{x}_i - \boldsymbol{\mu}_x\right)\left(\mathbf{x}_i - \boldsymbol{\mu}_x\right)^T, \quad (4.48\text{b})$$

where

$$\alpha_i = \left\{ \begin{array}{ll} \frac{\kappa}{L+\kappa} & i=0 \\ \frac{1}{2}\frac{1}{L+\kappa} & \text{otherwise} \end{array} \right., \quad (4.49)$$

which we note sums to 1. The user-definable parameter, κ, will be explained in the next section.

2. Each of the sigmapoints is individually passed through the nonlinearity, $\mathbf{g}(\cdot)$:

$$\mathbf{y}_i = \mathbf{g}\left(\mathbf{x}_i\right), \quad i=0\ldots 2L. \quad (4.50)$$

3. The mean of the output density, $\boldsymbol{\mu}_y$, is computed as

$$\boldsymbol{\mu}_y = \sum_{i=0}^{2L} \alpha_i\,\mathbf{y}_i. \quad (4.51)$$

4. The covariance of the output density, $\boldsymbol{\Sigma}_{yy}$, is computed as

$$\boldsymbol{\Sigma}_{yy} = \sum_{i=0}^{2L} \alpha_i\left(\mathbf{y}_i - \boldsymbol{\mu}_y\right)\left(\mathbf{y}_i - \boldsymbol{\mu}_y\right)^T. \quad (4.52)$$

5. The output density, $\mathcal{N}\left(\boldsymbol{\mu}_y, \boldsymbol{\Sigma}_{yy}\right)$, is returned.

This method of transforming a PDF through a nonlinearity has a number of advantages over linearization:

(i) By approximating the input density instead of linearizing, we avoid the need to compute the Jacobian of the nonlinearity (either in closed form or numerically). Figure 4.11 provides an example of the sigma-points for a two-dimensional Gaussian.

(ii) We employ only standard linear algebra operations (Cholesky decomposition, outer products, matrix summations).

(iii) The computation cost is similar to linearization (when a numerical Jacobian is used).

Figure 4.11
Two-dimensional
($L = 2$) Gaussian
PDF, whose
covariance is
displayed using
elliptical
equiprobable
contours of 1, 2, and
3 standard
deviations, and the
corresponding
$2L + 1 = 5$
sigmapoints for
$\kappa = 2$.

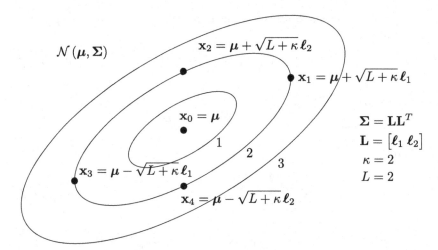

(iv) There is no requirement that the nonlinearity be smooth and differentiable.

The next section will furthermore show that the unscented transformation can also more accurately capture the posterior density than linearization (by way of an example).

Example 4.1   We will use a simple one-dimensional nonlinearity, $f(x) = x^2$, as an example and compare the various transformation methods. Let the prior density be $\mathcal{N}(\mu_x, \sigma_x^2)$.

Monte Carlo Method

In fact, for this particularly nonlinearity, we can essentially use the Monte Carlo method in closed form (i.e., we do not actually draw any samples) to get the exact answer for transforming the input density through the nonlinearity. An arbitrary sample (aka realization) of the input density is given by

$$x_i = \mu_x + \delta x_i, \qquad \delta x_i \leftarrow \mathcal{N}(0, \sigma_x^2). \tag{4.53}$$

Transforming this sample through the nonlinearity, we get

$$y_i = f(x_i) = f(\mu_x + \delta x_i) = (\mu_x + \delta x_i)^2 = \mu_x^2 + 2\mu_x \delta x_i + \delta x_i^2. \tag{4.54}$$

Taking the expectation of both sides, we arrive at the mean of the output:

$$\mu_y = E\left[y_i\right] = \mu_x^2 + 2\mu_x \underbrace{E\left[\delta x_i\right]}_{0} + \underbrace{E\left[\delta x_i^2\right]}_{\sigma_x^2} = \mu_x^2 + \sigma_x^2. \tag{4.55}$$

We do a similar thing for the variance of the output:

$$\sigma_y^2 = E\left[(y_i - \mu_y)^2\right] \tag{4.56a}$$

$$= E\left[(2\mu_x \delta x_i + \delta x_i^2 - \sigma_x^2)^2\right] \tag{4.56b}$$

$$= \underbrace{E\left[\delta x_i^4\right]}_{3\sigma_x^4} + 4\mu_x \underbrace{E\left[\delta x_i^3\right]}_{0} + (4\mu_x^2 - 2\sigma_x^2)\underbrace{E\left[\delta x_i^2\right]}_{\sigma_x^2}$$

$$\qquad\qquad - 4\mu_x \sigma_x^2 \underbrace{E\left[\delta x_i\right]}_{0} + \sigma_x^4 \tag{4.56c}$$

$$= 4\mu_x^2 \sigma_x^2 + 2\sigma_x^4, \tag{4.56d}$$

where $E[\delta x_i^3] = 0$ and $E[\delta x_i^4] = 3\sigma_x^4$ are the well-known third and fourth moments for a Gaussian PDF.

In truth, the resulting output density is not Gaussian. We could go on to compute higher moments of the output (and they would not all match a Gaussian). However, if we want to approximate the output as Gaussian by not considering the moments beyond the variance, we can. In this case, the resulting output density is $\mathcal{N}(\mu_y, \sigma_y^2)$. We have effectively used the Monte Carlo method with an infinite number of samples to carry out the computation of the first two moments of the posterior exactly in closed form. Let us now see how linearization and the sigmapoint transformation perform.

Linearization

Linearizing the nonlinearity about the mean of the input density, we have

$$y_i = f(\mu_x + \delta x_i) \approx \underbrace{f(\mu_x)}_{\mu_x^2} + \underbrace{\left.\frac{\partial f}{\partial x}\right|_{\mu_x}}_{2\mu_x} \delta x_i = \mu_x^2 + 2\mu_x \delta x_i. \qquad (4.57)$$

Taking the expectation, we arrive at the mean of the output:

$$\mu_y = E[y_i] = \mu_x^2 + 2\mu_x \underbrace{E[\delta x_i]}_{0} = \mu_x^2, \qquad (4.58)$$

which is just the mean of the input passed through the nonlinearity: $\mu_y = f(\mu_x)$. For the variance of the output we have

$$\sigma_y^2 = E\left[(y_i - \mu_y)^2\right] = E\left[(2\mu_x \delta x_i)^2\right] = 4\mu_x^2 \sigma_x^2. \qquad (4.59)$$

Comparing (4.55) with (4.58), and (4.56) with (4.59), we see there are some discrepancies. In fact, the linearized mean has a bias and the variance is too small (i.e., overconfident). Let us see what happens with the sigmapoint transformation.

Sigmapoint Transformation

There are $2L + 1 = 3$ sigmapoints in dimension $L = 1$:

$$x_0 = \mu_x, \quad x_1 = \mu_x + \sqrt{1 + \kappa}\, \sigma_x, \quad x_2 = \mu_x - \sqrt{1 + \kappa}\, \sigma_x, \qquad (4.60)$$

where κ is a user-definable parameter that we discuss in the following material. We pass each sigmapoint through the nonlinearity:

$$y_0 = f(x_0) = \mu_x^2, \qquad (4.61a)$$

$$y_1 = f(x_1) = \left(\mu_x + \sqrt{1 + \kappa}\, \sigma_x\right)^2$$
$$= \mu_x^2 + 2\mu_x\sqrt{1 + \kappa}\, \sigma_x + (1 + \kappa)\sigma_x^2, \qquad (4.61b)$$

$$y_2 = f(x_2) = \left(\mu_x - \sqrt{1 + \kappa}\, \sigma_x\right)^2$$
$$= \mu_x^2 - 2\mu_x\sqrt{1 + \kappa}\, \sigma_x + (1 + \kappa)\sigma_x^2. \qquad (4.61c)$$

The mean of the output is given by

$$\mu_y = \frac{1}{1+\kappa}\left(\kappa y_0 + \frac{1}{2}\sum_{i=1}^{2} y_i\right) \tag{4.62a}$$

$$= \frac{1}{1+\kappa}\Big(\kappa\mu_x^2 + \frac{1}{2}\big(\mu_x^2 + 2\mu_x\sqrt{1+\kappa}\,\sigma_x + (1+\kappa)\sigma_x^2 + \mu_x^2$$
$$- 2\mu_x\sqrt{1+\kappa}\,\sigma_x + (1+\kappa)\sigma_x^2\big)\Big) \tag{4.62b}$$

$$= \frac{1}{1+\kappa}\left(\kappa\mu_x^2 + \mu_x^2 + (1+\kappa)\sigma_x^2\right) \tag{4.62c}$$

$$= \mu_x^2 + \sigma_x^2, \tag{4.62d}$$

which is independent of κ and exactly the same as (4.55). For the variance we have

$$\sigma_y^2 = \frac{1}{1+\kappa}\left(\kappa\left(y_0 - \mu_y\right)^2 + \frac{1}{2}\sum_{i=1}^{2}\left(y_i - \mu_y\right)^2\right) \tag{4.63a}$$

$$= \frac{1}{1+\kappa}\left(\kappa\sigma_x^4 + \frac{1}{2}\left(\left(2\mu_x\sqrt{1+\kappa}\,\sigma_x + \kappa\sigma_x^2\right)^2\right.\right.$$
$$\left.\left. + \left(-2\mu_x\sqrt{1+\kappa}\,\sigma_x + \kappa\sigma_x^2\right)^2\right)\right) \tag{4.63b}$$

$$= \frac{1}{1+\kappa}\left(\kappa\sigma_x^4 + 4(1+\kappa)\mu_x^2\sigma_x^2 + \kappa^2\sigma_x^4\right) \tag{4.63c}$$

$$= 4\mu_x^2\sigma_x^2 + \kappa\sigma_x^4, \tag{4.63d}$$

which can be made to be identical to (4.56) by selecting the user-definable parameter, κ, to be 2. Thus, for this nonlinearity, the unscented transformation can exactly capture the correct mean and variance of the output.

To understand why we should pick $\kappa = 2$, we need look no further than the input density. The parameter κ scales how far away the sigmapoints are from the mean. This does not affect the first three moments of the sigmapoints (i.e., μ_x, σ_x^2, and the zero *skewness*). However, changing κ does influence the fourth moment, *kurtosis*. We already used the fact that for a Gaussian PDF, the fourth moment is $3\sigma_x^4$. We can choose κ to make the fourth moment of the sigmapoints match the true kurtosis of the Gaussian input density:

$$3\sigma_x^4 = \frac{1}{1+\kappa}\left(\kappa\underbrace{\left(x_0 - \mu_x\right)^4}_{0} + \frac{1}{2}\sum_{i=1}^{2}\left(x_i - \mu_x\right)^4\right) \tag{4.64a}$$

$$= \frac{1}{2(1+\kappa)}\left(\left(\sqrt{1+\kappa}\sigma_x\right)^4 + \left(-\sqrt{1+\kappa}\sigma_x\right)^4\right) \tag{4.64b}$$

$$= (1+\kappa)\sigma_x^4. \tag{4.64c}$$

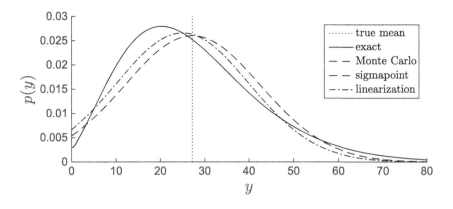

Figure 4.12
Graphical depiction
of passing a
Gaussian PDF,
$p(x) =$
$\mathcal{N}\left(5, (3/2)^2\right)$,
through the
nonlinearity, $y = x^2$,
using various
methods. We see that
the Monte Carlo and
sigmapoint methods
match the true mean,
while linearization
does not. We also
show the exact
transformed PDF,
which is not
Gaussian and
therefore does not
have its mean at its
mode.

Comparing the desired and actual kurtosis, we should pick $\kappa = 2$ to make them match exactly. Not surprisingly, this has a positive effect on the accuracy of the transformation.

In summary, this example shows that linearization is an inferior method of transforming a PDF through a nonlinearity if the goal is to capture the true mean of the output. Figure 4.12 provides a graphical depiction of this example.

In the next few sections, we return to the Bayes filter and use our new knowledge about the different methods of passing PDFs through nonlinearities to make some useful improvements to the EKF. We will begin with the particle filter, which makes use of the Monte Carlo method. We will then try to implement a Gaussian filter using the SP transformation.

4.2.8 Particle Filter

We have seen that drawing a large number of samples is one way to approximate a PDF. We further saw that we could pass each sample through a nonlinearity and recombine them on the other side to get an approximation of the transformation of a PDF. In this section, we extend this idea to an approximation of the Bayes filter, called the *particle filter* (Thrun et al., 2001).

The particle filter is one of the only practical techniques able to handle non-Gaussian noise and nonlinear observation and motion models. It is practical in that it is very easy to implement; we do not even need to have analytical expressions for $\mathbf{f}(\cdot)$ and $\mathbf{g}(\cdot)$, nor for their derivatives.

There are actually many different flavours of the particle filter; we will outline a basic version and indicate where the variations typically occur. The approach taken here is based on *sample importance resampling* where the so-called *proposal* PDF is the prior PDF in the Bayes filter, propagated forward using the motion model and the latest motion measurement, $\mathbf{v}_k$. This version of the particle filter is sometimes called the *bootstrap algorithm*, the *condensation algorithm*, or the *survival-of-the-fittest algorithm*.

PF Algorithm

Using the notation from the section on the Bayes filter, the main steps in the particle filter are as follows:

1. Draw M samples from the joint density comprising the prior and the motion noise:

$$\begin{bmatrix} \hat{\mathbf{x}}_{k-1,m} \\ \mathbf{w}_{k,m} \end{bmatrix} \leftarrow p\left(\mathbf{x}_{k-1}|\check{\mathbf{x}}_0, \mathbf{v}_{1:k-1}, \mathbf{y}_{1:k-1}\right) p(\mathbf{w}_k), \qquad (4.65)$$

where m is the unique particle index. In practice we can just draw from each factor of this joint density separately.

2. Generate a prediction of the posterior PDF by using $\mathbf{v}_k$. This is done by passing each prior particle/noise sample through the nonlinear motion model:

$$\check{\mathbf{x}}_{k,m} = \mathbf{f}\left(\hat{\mathbf{x}}_{k-1,m}, \mathbf{v}_k, \mathbf{w}_{k,m}\right). \qquad (4.66)$$

These new 'predicted particles' together approximate the density, $p\left(\mathbf{x}_k|\check{\mathbf{x}}_0, \mathbf{v}_{1:k}, \mathbf{y}_{1:k-1}\right)$.

3. Correct the posterior PDF by incorporating $\mathbf{y}_k$. This is done indirectly in two steps:

   – First, assign a scalar weight, $w_{k,m}$, to each predicted particle based on the divergence between the desired posterior and the predicted posterior for each particle:

$$w_{k,m} = \frac{p\left(\check{\mathbf{x}}_{k,m}|\check{\mathbf{x}}_0, \mathbf{v}_{1:k}, \mathbf{y}_{1:k}\right)}{p\left(\check{\mathbf{x}}_{k,m}|\check{\mathbf{x}}_0, \mathbf{v}_{1:k}, \mathbf{y}_{1:k-1}\right)} = \eta\, p\left(\mathbf{y}_k|\check{\mathbf{x}}_{k,m}\right), \qquad (4.67)$$

   where η is a normalization constant. This is typically accomplished in practice by simulating an expected sensor reading, $\check{\mathbf{y}}_{k,m}$, using the nonlinear observation model:

$$\check{\mathbf{y}}_{k,m} = \mathbf{g}\left(\check{\mathbf{x}}_{k,m}, \mathbf{0}\right). \qquad (4.68)$$

   We then assume $p\left(\mathbf{y}_k|\check{\mathbf{x}}_{k,m}\right) = p\left(\mathbf{y}_k|\check{\mathbf{y}}_{k,m}\right)$, where the right-hand side is a known density (e.g., Gaussian).

   – Resample the posterior based on the weight assigned to each predicted posterior particle:

$$\hat{\mathbf{x}}_{k,m} \stackrel{\text{resample}}{\longleftarrow} \{\check{\mathbf{x}}_{k,m}, w_{k,m}\}. \qquad (4.69)$$

   This can be done in several different ways. Madow provides a simple systematic technique to do resampling, which we describe below.

Figure 4.13 captures these steps in a block diagram.

Some additional comments should be made at this point to help get this basic version of the particle filter working in practical situations:

   (i) How do we know how many particles to use? It depends very much on the specific estimation problem. Typically hundreds of particles are used for low-dimensional problems (e.g., $\mathbf{x} = (x, y, \theta)$).

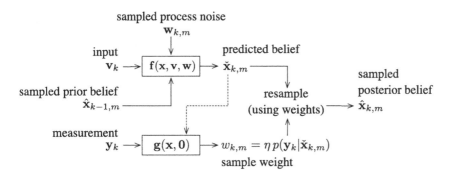

Figure 4.13
Block-diagram
representation of a
particle filter.

(ii) We can dynamically pick the number of particles online using a heuristic such as $\sum w_{k,m} \geq w_{\text{thresh}}$, a threshold. In other words, we keep adding particles/samples and repeating steps 1 through 3 until the sum of the weights exceeds an experimentally determined threshold.

(iii) We do not necessarily need to resample every time we go through the algorithm. We can delay resampling, but we then need to carry the weights forward to the next iteration of the algorithm.

(iv) To be on the safe side, it is wise to add a small percentage of samples in during Step 1 that are uniformly drawn from the entire state sample space. This protects against outlier sensor measurements/vehicle movements.

(v) For high-dimensional state estimation problems, the particle filter can become computationally intractable. If too few particles are used, the densities involved are undersampled and give highly skewed results. The number of samples needed goes up exponentially with the dimension of the state space. Thrun et al. (2001) offer some alternative flavours of the particle filter to combat sample impoverishment.

(vi) The particle filter is an 'anytime' algorithm. That is, we can just keep adding particles until we run out of time, then resample and give an answer. Using more particles always helps but comes with a computational cost.

(vii) The *Cramér–Rao lower bound (CRLB)* is set by the uncertainty in the measurements that we have available. Using more samples does not allow us to do better than the CRLB. See Section 2.2.14 for some discussion of the CRLB.

Resampling

A key aspect of particle filters is the need to resample the posterior density according to weights assigned to each current sample. One way to do this is to use the systematic resampling method described by Madow (1949). We assume we have M samples and that each of these is assigned an unnormalized weight, $w_m \in \mathbb{R} > 0$. From the weights, we create bins with boundaries, β_m, according to

$$\beta_m = \frac{\sum_{n=1}^{m} w_n}{\sum_{\ell=1}^{M} w_\ell}. \tag{4.70}$$

The β_m define the boundaries of M bins on the interval $[0, 1]$:

$$0 \leq \beta_1 \leq \beta_2 \leq \ldots \leq \beta_{M-1} \leq 1,$$

where we note that we will have $\beta_M \equiv 1$. We then select a random number, ρ, sampled from a uniform density on $[0, 1)$. For M iterations we add to the new list of samples, the sample whose bin contains ρ. At each iteration we step ρ forward by $1/M$. The algorithm guarantees that all bins whose size is greater than $1/M$ will have a sample in the new list.

4.2.9 Sigmapoint Kalman Filter

Another way we can attempt to improve on the basic EKF is to get rid of the idea of linearizing altogether and instead use the sigmapoint transformation to pass PDFs through the nonlinear motion and observation models. The result is the *sigmapoint Kalman filter (SPKF)*, also sometimes called the *unscented Kalman filter (UKF)*. We will discuss the prediction and correction steps separately:[9]

Prediction Step

The prediction step is a fairly straightforward application of the sigmapoint transformation since we are simply trying to bring our prior forward in time through the motion model. We employ the following steps to go from the prior belief, $\{\hat{\mathbf{x}}_{k-1}, \hat{\mathbf{P}}_{k-1}\}$, to the predicted belief, $\{\check{\mathbf{x}}_k, \check{\mathbf{P}}_k\}$:

1. Both the prior belief and the motion noise have uncertainty, so these are stacked together in the following way:

$$\boldsymbol{\mu}_z = \begin{bmatrix} \hat{\mathbf{x}}_{k-1} \\ \mathbf{0} \end{bmatrix}, \qquad \boldsymbol{\Sigma}_{zz} = \begin{bmatrix} \hat{\mathbf{P}}_{k-1} & \mathbf{0} \\ \mathbf{0} & \mathbf{Q}_k \end{bmatrix}, \tag{4.71}$$

where we see that $\{\boldsymbol{\mu}_z, \boldsymbol{\Sigma}_{zz}\}$ is still a Gaussian representation. We let $L = \dim \boldsymbol{\mu}_z$.

2. Convert $\{\boldsymbol{\mu}_z, \boldsymbol{\Sigma}_{zz}\}$ to a sigmapoint representation:

$$\mathbf{L}\mathbf{L}^T = \boldsymbol{\Sigma}_{zz}, \quad \text{(Cholesky decomposition, } \mathbf{L} \text{ lower-triangular)} \tag{4.72a}$$

$$\mathbf{z}_0 = \boldsymbol{\mu}_z, \tag{4.72b}$$

$$\mathbf{z}_i = \boldsymbol{\mu}_z + \sqrt{L + \kappa}\, \mathrm{col}_i \mathbf{L}, \tag{4.72c}$$

$$\mathbf{z}_{i+L} = \boldsymbol{\mu}_z - \sqrt{L + \kappa}\, \mathrm{col}_i \mathbf{L}. \qquad i = 1 \ldots L \tag{4.72d}$$

3. Unstack each sigmapoint into state and motion noise,

$$\mathbf{z}_i = \begin{bmatrix} \hat{\mathbf{x}}_{k-1,i} \\ \mathbf{w}_{k,i} \end{bmatrix}, \tag{4.73}$$

---

[9] These are sometimes handled together in a single step, but we prefer to think of each of these as a separate application of the sigmapoint transformation.

and then pass each sigmapoint through the nonlinear motion model exactly:

$$\check{\mathbf{x}}_{k,i} = \mathbf{f}\left(\hat{\mathbf{x}}_{k-1,i}, \mathbf{v}_k, \mathbf{w}_{k,i}\right), \qquad i = 0 \ldots 2L. \tag{4.74}$$

Note that the latest input, $\mathbf{v}_k$, is required.

4. Recombine the transformed sigmapoints into the predicted belief, $\{\check{\mathbf{x}}_k, \check{\mathbf{P}}_k\}$, according to

$$\check{\mathbf{x}}_k = \sum_{i=0}^{2L} \alpha_i \check{\mathbf{x}}_{k,i}, \tag{4.75a}$$

$$\check{\mathbf{P}}_k = \sum_{i=0}^{2L} \alpha_i \left(\check{\mathbf{x}}_{k,i} - \check{\mathbf{x}}_k\right)\left(\check{\mathbf{x}}_{k,i} - \check{\mathbf{x}}_k\right)^T, \tag{4.75b}$$

where

$$\alpha_i = \begin{cases} \frac{\kappa}{L+\kappa} & i = 0 \\ \frac{1}{2}\frac{1}{L+\kappa} & \text{otherwise} \end{cases}. \tag{4.76}$$

Next we will look at a second application of the sigmapoint transformation to implement the correction step.

Correction Step

This step is a little more complicated. We look back to Section 4.2.4 and recall that the conditional Gaussian density for $\mathbf{x}_k$ (i.e., the posterior) is

$$p(\mathbf{x}_k|\check{\mathbf{x}}_0, \mathbf{v}_{1:k}, \mathbf{y}_{0:k})$$
$$= \mathcal{N}\left(\underbrace{\boldsymbol{\mu}_{x,k} + \boldsymbol{\Sigma}_{xy,k}\boldsymbol{\Sigma}_{yy,k}^{-1}(\mathbf{y}_k - \boldsymbol{\mu}_{y,k})}_{\hat{\mathbf{x}}_k}, \underbrace{\boldsymbol{\Sigma}_{xx,k} - \boldsymbol{\Sigma}_{xy,k}\boldsymbol{\Sigma}_{yy,k}^{-1}\boldsymbol{\Sigma}_{yx,k}}_{\hat{\mathbf{P}}_k}\right), \tag{4.77}$$

where we have defined $\hat{\mathbf{x}}_k$ as the mean and $\hat{\mathbf{P}}_k$ as the covariance. In this form, we can write the generalized Gaussian correction-step equations as

$$\mathbf{K}_k = \boldsymbol{\Sigma}_{xy,k}\boldsymbol{\Sigma}_{yy,k}^{-1}, \tag{4.78a}$$

$$\hat{\mathbf{P}}_k = \check{\mathbf{P}}_k - \mathbf{K}_k\boldsymbol{\Sigma}_{xy,k}^T, \tag{4.78b}$$

$$\hat{\mathbf{x}}_k = \check{\mathbf{x}}_k + \mathbf{K}_k\left(\mathbf{y}_k - \boldsymbol{\mu}_{y,k}\right). \tag{4.78c}$$

We will use the SP transformation to come up with better versions of $\boldsymbol{\mu}_{y,k}$, $\boldsymbol{\Sigma}_{yy,k}$, and $\boldsymbol{\Sigma}_{xy,k}$. We employ the following steps:

1. Both the predicted belief and the observation noise have uncertainty, so these are stacked together in the following way:

$$\boldsymbol{\mu}_z = \begin{bmatrix} \check{\mathbf{x}}_k \\ \mathbf{0} \end{bmatrix}, \qquad \boldsymbol{\Sigma}_{zz} = \begin{bmatrix} \check{\mathbf{P}}_k & \mathbf{0} \\ \mathbf{0} & \mathbf{R}_k \end{bmatrix}, \tag{4.79}$$

where we see that $\{\boldsymbol{\mu}_z, \boldsymbol{\Sigma}_{zz}\}$ is still a Gaussian representation. We let $L = \dim \boldsymbol{\mu}_z$.

2. Convert $\{\boldsymbol{\mu}_z, \boldsymbol{\Sigma}_{zz}\}$ to a sigmapoint representation:

$$\mathbf{L}\mathbf{L}^T = \boldsymbol{\Sigma}_{zz}, \quad \text{(Cholesky decomposition, } \mathbf{L} \text{ lower-triangular)} \quad (4.80\text{a})$$

$$\mathbf{z}_0 = \boldsymbol{\mu}_z, \quad (4.80\text{b})$$

$$\mathbf{z}_i = \boldsymbol{\mu}_z + \sqrt{L + \kappa} \, \text{col}_i \mathbf{L}, \quad (4.80\text{c})$$

$$\mathbf{z}_{i+L} = \boldsymbol{\mu}_z - \sqrt{L + \kappa} \, \text{col}_i \mathbf{L}. \qquad i = 1 \ldots L \quad (4.80\text{d})$$

3. Unstack each sigmapoint into state and observation noise,

$$\mathbf{z}_i = \begin{bmatrix} \check{\mathbf{x}}_{k,i} \\ \mathbf{n}_{k,i} \end{bmatrix}, \quad (4.81)$$

and then pass each sigmapoint through the nonlinear observation model exactly:

$$\check{\mathbf{y}}_{k,i} = \mathbf{g}\left(\check{\mathbf{x}}_{k,i}, \mathbf{n}_{k,i}\right). \quad (4.82)$$

4. Recombine the transformed sigmapoints into the desired moments:

$$\boldsymbol{\mu}_{y,k} = \sum_{i=0}^{2L} \alpha_i \, \check{\mathbf{y}}_{k,i}, \quad (4.83\text{a})$$

$$\boldsymbol{\Sigma}_{yy,k} = \sum_{i=0}^{2L} \alpha_i \left(\check{\mathbf{y}}_{k,i} - \boldsymbol{\mu}_{y,k}\right)\left(\check{\mathbf{y}}_{k,i} - \boldsymbol{\mu}_{y,k}\right)^T, \quad (4.83\text{b})$$

$$\boldsymbol{\Sigma}_{xy,k} = \sum_{i=0}^{2L} \alpha_i \left(\check{\mathbf{x}}_{k,i} - \check{\mathbf{x}}_k\right)\left(\check{\mathbf{y}}_{k,i} - \boldsymbol{\mu}_{y,k}\right)^T, \quad (4.83\text{c})$$

where

$$\alpha_i = \begin{cases} \frac{\kappa}{L+\kappa} & i = 0 \\ \frac{1}{2}\frac{1}{L+\kappa} & \text{otherwise} \end{cases}. \quad (4.84)$$

These are plugged into the generalized Gaussian correction-step equations (presented earlier) to complete the correction step.

Two advantages of the SPKF are that it (i) does not require any analytical derivatives and (ii) uses only basic linear algebra operations in the implementation. Moreover, we do not even need the nonlinear motion and observation models in closed form; they could just be black-box software functions.

Comparing Terms to EKF

We see in the correction step that the matrix $\boldsymbol{\Sigma}_{yy,k}$ takes on the role of $\mathbf{G}_k \check{\mathbf{P}}_k \mathbf{G}_k^T + \mathbf{R}'_k$ in the EKF. We can see this more directly by linearizing the observation model (about the predicted state) as in the EKF:

$$\check{\mathbf{y}}_{k,i} = \mathbf{g}\left(\check{\mathbf{x}}_{k,i}, \mathbf{n}_{k,i}\right) \approx \mathbf{g}(\check{\mathbf{x}}_k, \mathbf{0}) + \mathbf{G}_k\left(\check{\mathbf{x}}_{k,i} - \check{\mathbf{x}}_k\right) + \mathbf{n}'_{k,i}. \quad (4.85)$$

Substituting this approximation into (4.83a), we can see that

$$\check{\mathbf{y}}_{k,i} - \boldsymbol{\mu}_{y,k} \approx \mathbf{G}_k\left(\check{\mathbf{x}}_{k,i} - \check{\mathbf{x}}_k\right) + \mathbf{n}'_{k,i}. \quad (4.86)$$

Substituting this into (4.83b), we have that

$$\boldsymbol{\Sigma}_{yy,k} \approx \mathbf{G}_k \underbrace{\sum_{i=0}^{2L} \alpha_i \left(\check{\mathbf{x}}_{k,i} - \check{\mathbf{x}}_k\right)\left(\check{\mathbf{x}}_{k,i} - \check{\mathbf{x}}_k\right)^T}_{\check{\mathbf{P}}_k} \mathbf{G}_k^T + \underbrace{\sum_{i=0}^{2L} \alpha_i \mathbf{n}'_{k,i} \mathbf{n}'^T_{k,i}}_{\mathbf{R}'_k}$$

$$+ \mathbf{G}_k \underbrace{\sum_{i=0}^{2L} \alpha_i \left(\check{\mathbf{x}}_{k,i} - \check{\mathbf{x}}_k\right) \mathbf{n}'^T_{k,i}}_{0} + \underbrace{\sum_{i=0}^{2L} \alpha_i \mathbf{n}'_{k,i} \left(\check{\mathbf{x}}_{k,i} - \check{\mathbf{x}}_k\right)^T}_{0} \mathbf{G}_k^T, \quad (4.87)$$

where some of the terms are zero owing to the block-diagonal structure of $\boldsymbol{\Sigma}_{zz}$. For $\boldsymbol{\Sigma}_{xy,k}$, by substituting our approximation into (4.83c), we have

$$\boldsymbol{\Sigma}_{xy,k} \approx \underbrace{\sum_{i=0}^{2L} \alpha_i \left(\check{\mathbf{x}}_{k,i} - \check{\mathbf{x}}_k\right)\left(\check{\mathbf{x}}_{k,i} - \check{\mathbf{x}}_k\right)^T}_{\check{\mathbf{P}}_k} \mathbf{G}_k^T + \underbrace{\sum_{i=0}^{2L} \alpha_i \left(\check{\mathbf{x}}_{k,i} - \check{\mathbf{x}}_k\right) \mathbf{n}'^T_{k,i}}_{0},$$

$$(4.88)$$

so that

$$\mathbf{K}_k = \boldsymbol{\Sigma}_{xy,k} \boldsymbol{\Sigma}_{yy,k}^{-1} \approx \check{\mathbf{P}}_k \mathbf{G}_k^T \left(\mathbf{G}_k \check{\mathbf{P}}_k \mathbf{G}_k^T + \mathbf{R}'_k\right)^{-1}, \quad (4.89)$$

which is what we had in the EKF.

Special Case of Linear Dependence on Measurement Noise

In the case that our nonlinear observation model has the special form

$$\mathbf{y}_k = \mathbf{g}(\mathbf{x}_k) + \mathbf{n}_k, \quad (4.90)$$

the SPKF correction step can be greatly sped up. Without loss of generality, we can break the sigmapoints into two categories based on the block-diagonal partitioning in the matrix, $\boldsymbol{\Sigma}_{zz}$; we say there are $2N + 1$ sigmapoints coming from the dimension of the state and $2(L - N)$ additional sigmapoints coming from the dimension of the measurements. To make this convenient, we will re-order the indexing on the sigmapoints accordingly:

$$\check{\mathbf{y}}_{k,j} = \begin{cases} \mathbf{g}\left(\check{\mathbf{x}}_{k,j}\right) & j = 0 \ldots 2N \\ \mathbf{g}\left(\check{\mathbf{x}}_k\right) + \mathbf{n}_{k,j} & j = 2N + 1 \ldots 2L + 1 \end{cases}. \quad (4.91)$$

We can then write our expression for $\boldsymbol{\mu}_{y,k}$ as

$$\boldsymbol{\mu}_{y,k} = \sum_{j=0}^{2N} \alpha_j \check{\mathbf{y}}_{k,j} + \sum_{j=2N+1}^{2L+1} \alpha_j \check{\mathbf{y}}_{k,j} \quad (4.92a)$$

$$= \sum_{j=0}^{2N} \alpha_j \check{\mathbf{y}}_{k,j} + \sum_{j=2N+1}^{2L+1} \alpha_j \left(\mathbf{g}\left(\check{\mathbf{x}}_k\right) + \mathbf{n}_{k,j}\right) \quad (4.92b)$$

$$= \sum_{j=0}^{2N} \alpha_j \check{\mathbf{y}}_{k,j} + \mathbf{g}\left(\check{\mathbf{x}}_k\right) \sum_{j=2N+1}^{2L+1} \alpha_j \quad (4.92c)$$

$$= \sum_{j=0}^{2N} \beta_j \check{\mathbf{y}}_{k,j}, \quad (4.92d)$$

where

$$\beta_i = \begin{cases} \alpha_i + \sum_{j=2N+1}^{2L+1} \alpha_j & i = 0 \\ \alpha_i & \text{otherwise} \end{cases} \qquad (4.93a)$$

$$= \begin{cases} \frac{(\kappa+L-N)}{N+(\kappa+L-N)} & i = 0 \\ \frac{1}{2}\frac{1}{N+(\kappa+L-N)} & \text{otherwise} \end{cases} . \qquad (4.93b)$$

This is the same form as the original weights (and they still sum to 1). We can then easily verify that

$$\boldsymbol{\Sigma}_{yy,k} = \sum_{j=0}^{2N} \beta_j \left(\check{\mathbf{y}}_{k,j} - \boldsymbol{\mu}_{y,k}\right)\left(\check{\mathbf{y}}_{k,j} - \boldsymbol{\mu}_{y,k}\right)^T + \mathbf{R}_k, \qquad (4.94)$$

with no approximation. This is already helpful in that we do not really need all $2L+1$ sigmapoints but only $2N+1$ of them. This means we do not need to call $\mathbf{g}(\cdot)$ as many times, which can be expensive in some situations.

We still have a problem, however. It is still necessary to invert $\boldsymbol{\Sigma}_{yy,k}$, which is size $(L-N) \times (L-N)$, to compute the Kalman gain matrix. If the number of measurements, $L-N$, is large, this could be very expensive. We can make further gains if we assume that the inverse of $\mathbf{R}_k$ can be computed cheaply. For example, if $\mathbf{R}_k = \sigma^2 \mathbf{1}$ then $\mathbf{R}_k^{-1} = \sigma^{-2}\mathbf{1}$. We proceed by noting that $\boldsymbol{\Sigma}_{yy,k}$ can be conveniently written as

$$\boldsymbol{\Sigma}_{yy,k} = \mathbf{Z}_k\mathbf{Z}_k^T + \mathbf{R}_k, \qquad (4.95)$$

where

$$\text{col}_j \mathbf{Z}_k = \sqrt{\beta_j} \left(\check{\mathbf{y}}_{k,j} - \boldsymbol{\mu}_{y,k}\right). \qquad (4.96)$$

By the SMW identity from Section 2.2.15, we can then show that

$$\boldsymbol{\Sigma}_{yy,k}^{-1} = \left(\mathbf{Z}_k\mathbf{Z}_k^T + \mathbf{R}_k\right)^{-1} \qquad (4.97a)$$

$$= \mathbf{R}_k^{-1} - \mathbf{R}_k^{-1}\mathbf{Z}_k \underbrace{\left(\mathbf{Z}_k^T\mathbf{R}_k^{-1}\mathbf{Z}_k + \mathbf{1}\right)^{-1}}_{(2N+1)\times(2N+1)} \mathbf{Z}_k^T\mathbf{R}_k^{-1}, \qquad (4.97b)$$

where we now only need to invert a $(2N+1) \times (2N+1)$ matrix (assuming $\mathbf{R}_k^{-1}$ is known).

4.2.10 Iterated Sigmapoint Kalman Filter

An *iterated sigmapoint Kalman filter (ISPKF)* has been proposed by Sibley et al. (2006) that does better than the one-shot version. In this case, we compute input sigmapoints around an operating point, $\mathbf{x}_{\text{op},k}$, at each iteration. At the first iteration, we let $\mathbf{x}_{\text{op},k} = \check{\mathbf{x}}_k$, but this is then improved with each subsequent iteration. We show all the steps to avoid confusion:

1. Both the predicted belief and the observation noise have uncertainty, so these are stacked together in the following way:

$$\boldsymbol{\mu}_z = \begin{bmatrix} \mathbf{x}_{\text{op},k} \\ \mathbf{0} \end{bmatrix}, \qquad \boldsymbol{\Sigma}_{zz} = \begin{bmatrix} \check{\mathbf{P}}_k & \mathbf{0} \\ \mathbf{0} & \mathbf{R}_k \end{bmatrix}, \qquad (4.98)$$

where we see that $\{\boldsymbol{\mu}_z, \boldsymbol{\Sigma}_{zz}\}$ is still a Gaussian representation. We let $L = \dim \boldsymbol{\mu}_z$.

2. Convert $\{\boldsymbol{\mu}_z, \boldsymbol{\Sigma}_{zz}\}$ to a sigmapoint representation:

$$\mathbf{L}\mathbf{L}^T = \boldsymbol{\Sigma}_{zz}, \quad \text{(Cholesky decomposition, } \mathbf{L} \text{ lower-triangular)} \quad (4.99\text{a})$$
$$\mathbf{z}_0 = \boldsymbol{\mu}_z, \qquad (4.99\text{b})$$
$$\mathbf{z}_i = \boldsymbol{\mu}_z + \sqrt{L + \kappa}\, \text{col}_i \mathbf{L}, \qquad\qquad (4.99\text{c})$$
$$\mathbf{z}_{i+L} = \boldsymbol{\mu}_z - \sqrt{L + \kappa}\, \text{col}_i \mathbf{L}. \qquad i = 1 \ldots L \qquad (4.99\text{d})$$

3. Unstack each sigmapoint into state and observation noise,

$$\mathbf{z}_i = \begin{bmatrix} \mathbf{x}_{\text{op},k,i} \\ \mathbf{n}_{k,i} \end{bmatrix}, \qquad (4.100)$$

and then pass each sigmapoint through the nonlinear observation model exactly:

$$\mathbf{y}_{\text{op},k,i} = \mathbf{g}\left(\mathbf{x}_{\text{op},k,i}, \mathbf{n}_{k,i}\right). \qquad (4.101)$$

4. Recombine the transformed sigmapoints into the desired moments:

$$\boldsymbol{\mu}_{y,k} = \sum_{i=0}^{2L} \alpha_i\, \mathbf{y}_{\text{op},k,i}, \qquad (4.102\text{a})$$

$$\boldsymbol{\Sigma}_{yy,k} = \sum_{i=0}^{2L} \alpha_i \left(\mathbf{y}_{\text{op},k,i} - \boldsymbol{\mu}_{y,k}\right)\left(\mathbf{y}_{\text{op},k,i} - \boldsymbol{\mu}_{y,k}\right)^T, \qquad (4.102\text{b})$$

$$\boldsymbol{\Sigma}_{xy,k} = \sum_{i=0}^{2L} \alpha_i \left(\mathbf{x}_{\text{op},k,i} - \mathbf{x}_{\text{op},k}\right)\left(\mathbf{y}_{\text{op},k,i} - \boldsymbol{\mu}_{y,k}\right)^T, \qquad (4.102\text{c})$$

$$\boldsymbol{\Sigma}_{xx,k} = \sum_{i=0}^{2L} \alpha_i \left(\mathbf{x}_{\text{op},k,i} - \mathbf{x}_{\text{op},k}\right)\left(\mathbf{x}_{\text{op},k,i} - \mathbf{x}_{\text{op},k}\right)^T, \qquad (4.102\text{d})$$

where

$$\alpha_i = \begin{cases} \frac{\kappa}{L+\kappa} & i = 0 \\ \frac{1}{2}\frac{1}{L+\kappa} & \text{otherwise} \end{cases}. \qquad (4.103)$$

At this point, Sibley et al. use the relationships between the SPKF and EKF quantities to update the IEKF correction equations, (4.45), using the statistical rather than the analytical Jacobian quantities:

Figure 4.14 Stereo camera example, comparing the inference (i.e., 'corrective') step of the IEKF, SPKF, and ISPKF to the full Bayesian posterior, $p(x|y)$. We see that neither of the sigmapoint methods matches up against the MAP solution, $\hat{x}_{\mathrm{map}}$. Superficially, the ISPKF seems to come closer to the mean of the full posterior, $\bar{x}$.

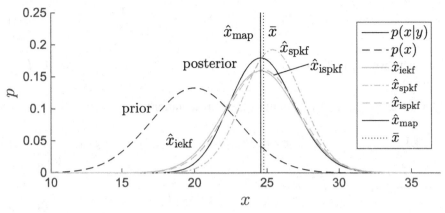

$$\mathbf{K}_k = \underbrace{\check{\mathbf{P}}_k \mathbf{G}_k^T}_{\boldsymbol{\Sigma}_{xy,k}} \underbrace{\left(\mathbf{G}_k \check{\mathbf{P}}_k \mathbf{G}_k^T + \mathbf{R}_k'\right)^{-1}}_{\boldsymbol{\Sigma}_{yy,k}}, \tag{4.104a}$$

$$\hat{\mathbf{P}}_k = \left(\mathbf{1} - \mathbf{K}_k \underbrace{\mathbf{G}_k}_{\boldsymbol{\Sigma}_{yx,k}\boldsymbol{\Sigma}_{xx,k}^{-1}}\right) \underbrace{\check{\mathbf{P}}_k}_{\boldsymbol{\Sigma}_{xx,k}}, \tag{4.104b}$$

$$\hat{\mathbf{x}}_k = \check{\mathbf{x}}_k + \mathbf{K}_k \left(\mathbf{y}_k - \underbrace{\mathbf{g}(\mathbf{x}_{\mathrm{op},k}, \mathbf{0})}_{\boldsymbol{\mu}_{y,k}} - \underbrace{\mathbf{G}_k}_{\boldsymbol{\Sigma}_{yx,k}\boldsymbol{\Sigma}_{xx,k}^{-1}} (\check{\mathbf{x}}_k - \mathbf{x}_{\mathrm{op},k})\right), \tag{4.104c}$$

which results in

$$\mathbf{K}_k = \boldsymbol{\Sigma}_{xy,k}\boldsymbol{\Sigma}_{yy,k}^{-1}, \tag{4.105a}$$

$$\hat{\mathbf{P}}_k = \boldsymbol{\Sigma}_{xx,k} - \mathbf{K}_k\boldsymbol{\Sigma}_{yx,k}, \tag{4.105b}$$

$$\hat{\mathbf{x}}_k = \check{\mathbf{x}}_k + \mathbf{K}_k \left(\mathbf{y}_k - \boldsymbol{\mu}_{y,k} - \boldsymbol{\Sigma}_{yx,k}\boldsymbol{\Sigma}_{xx,k}^{-1}(\check{\mathbf{x}}_k - \mathbf{x}_{\mathrm{op},k})\right). \tag{4.105c}$$

Initially, we set the operating point to be the mean of the prior: $\mathbf{x}_{\mathrm{op},k} = \check{\mathbf{x}}_k$. At subsequent iterations we set it to be the best estimate so far:

$$\mathbf{x}_{\mathrm{op},k} \leftarrow \hat{\mathbf{x}}_k. \tag{4.106}$$

The process terminates when the change from one iteration to the next becomes sufficiently small.

We have seen that the first iteration of the IEKF results in the EKF method, and this is also true for the SPKF/ISPKF. Setting $\mathbf{x}_{\mathrm{op},k} = \check{\mathbf{x}}_k$ in (4.105c) results in

$$\hat{\mathbf{x}}_k = \check{\mathbf{x}}_k + \mathbf{K}_k \left(\mathbf{y}_k - \boldsymbol{\mu}_{y,k}\right), \tag{4.107}$$

which is the same as the one-shot method in (4.78c).

4.2.11 ISPKF Seeks the Posterior Mean

Now, the question we must ask ourselves is, *how do the sigmapoint estimates relate to the full posterior?* Figure 4.14 compares the sigmapoint methods to the full posterior and iterated linearization (i.e., MAP) on our stereo camera example where we used

$$x_{\mathrm{true}} = 26 \ [\mathrm{m}], \quad y_{\mathrm{meas}} = \frac{fb}{x_{\mathrm{true}}} - 0.6 \ [\mathrm{pixel}],$$

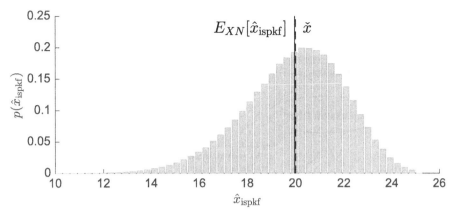

Figure 4.15
Histogram of estimator values for 1,000,000 trials of the stereo camera experiment where each time a new x_{true} is randomly drawn from the prior and a new y_{meas} is randomly drawn from the measurement model. The dashed line marks the mean of the prior, $\check{x}$, and the solid line marks the expected value of the iterated sigmapoint estimator, $\hat{x}_{\text{ispkf}}$, over all the trials. The gap between dashed and solid is $\hat{e}_{\text{mean}} \approx -3.84$ cm, which indicates a small bias, and the average squared error is $\hat{e}_{\text{sq}} \approx 4.32$ m^2.

again to exaggerate the differences between the various methods. Our implementations of the sigmapoint methods used $\kappa = 2$, which is appropriate for a Gaussian prior.

Much like the EKF, we see that the one-shot SPKF method bears no obvious relationship to the full posterior. However, the ISPKF method appears to come closer to the *mean*, $\bar{x}$, rather than the mode (i.e., MAP) value, $\hat{x}_{\text{map}}$. Numerically, the numbers of interest are:

$$\hat{x}_{\text{map}} = 24.5694, \quad \bar{x} = 24.7770,$$
$$\hat{x}_{\text{iekf}} = 24.5694, \quad \hat{x}_{\text{ispkf}} = 24.7414.$$

We see that the IEKF solution matches the MAP one and that the ISPKF solution is close to (but not exactly) the mean.

Now, we consider the question, *how well does the iterated sigmapoint method capture* x_{true}*?* Once again, we compute the performance over a large number of trials (using the parameters in (4.5)). The results are shown in Figure 4.15. We see that the average difference of the estimator, $\hat{x}_{\text{ispkf}}$, and the ground-truth, x_{true}, is $\hat{e}_{\text{mean}} \approx -3.84$ cm, demonstrating a small bias. This is significantly better than the MAP estimator, which had a bias of -33.0 cm on this same metric. The average squared error is approximately the same, with $\hat{e}_{\text{sq}} \approx 4.32$ m^2.

Although it is difficult to show analytically, it is plausible to think that the iterated sigmapoint method is trying to converge to the mean of the full posterior rather than the mode. If what we care about is matching up against groundtruth, matching the mean of the full posterior could be an interesting avenue.

4.2.12 Taxonomy of Filters

Figure 4.16 provides a summary of the methods we have discussed in this section on nonlinear recursive state estimation. We can think of each of the methods having a place in a larger taxonomy, with the Bayes filter at the top position. Depending on the approximations made, we wind up with the different filters discussed.

It is also worth recalling the role of iteration in our filter methods. Without iteration, both the EKF and SPKF were difficult to relate back to the full Bayesian posterior. However, we saw that the 'mean' of the IEKF converges to the MAP

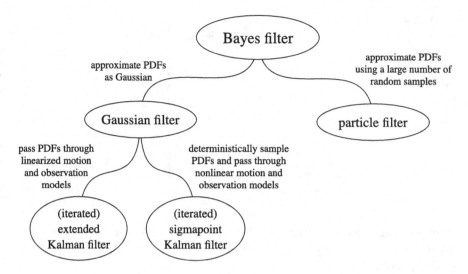

Figure 4.16
Taxonomy of the
different filtering
methods, showing
their relationships to
the Bayes filter.

solution, while the mean of the ISPKF comes quite close to the mean of the full posterior. We will use these lessons in the next section on batch estimation, where we will attempt to estimate entire trajectories at once.

4.3 Batch Discrete-Time Estimation

In this section, we take a step back and question how valid the Bayes filter really is given the fact that we always have to implement it approximately and therefore are violating the Markov assumption on which it is predicated. We propose that a much better starting point in deriving nonlinear filters (i.e., better than the Bayes filter) is the nonlinear version of the batch estimator we first introduced in the chapter on linear-Gaussian estimation. Setting the estimation problem up as an optimization problem affords a different perspective that helps explain the shortcomings of all variants of the EKF.

4.3.1 *Maximum A Posteriori*

In this section, we revisit our approach to linear-Gaussian estimation problems and batch optimization, and we introduce the Gauss–Newton method to solve our nonlinear version of this estimation problem. This optimization approach can be viewed as the MAP approach once again. We first set up our objective function that we seek to minimize, then consider methods to solve it.

Objective Function

We seek to construct an objective function that we will minimize with respect to

$$\mathbf{x} = \begin{bmatrix} \mathbf{x}_0 \\ \mathbf{x}_1 \\ \vdots \\ \mathbf{x}_K \end{bmatrix}, \tag{4.108}$$

which represents the entire trajectory that we want to estimate.

Recall the linear-Gaussian objective function given by Equations (3.10) and (3.9). It took the form of a squared Mahalanobis distance and was proportional to the negative log likelihood of the state given all the data. For the nonlinear case, we define the errors with respect to the prior and measurements to be

$$
\mathbf{e}_{v,k}(\mathbf{x}) = \begin{cases} \check{\mathbf{x}}_0 - \mathbf{x}_0, & k = 0 \\ \mathbf{f}\left(\mathbf{x}_{k-1}, \mathbf{v}_k, \mathbf{0}\right) - \mathbf{x}_k, & k = 1 \dots K \end{cases}, \tag{4.109a}
$$

$$
\mathbf{e}_{y,k}(\mathbf{x}) = \mathbf{y}_k - \mathbf{g}\left(\mathbf{x}_k, \mathbf{0}\right), \qquad k = 0 \dots K, \tag{4.109b}
$$

so that the contributions to the objective function are

$$
J_{v,k}(\mathbf{x}) = \frac{1}{2}\mathbf{e}_{v,k}(\mathbf{x})^T \mathbf{W}_{v,k}^{-1} \mathbf{e}_{v,k}(\mathbf{x}), \tag{4.110a}
$$

$$
J_{y,k}(\mathbf{x}) = \frac{1}{2}\mathbf{e}_{y,k}(\mathbf{x})^T \mathbf{W}_{y,k}^{-1} \mathbf{e}_{y,k}(\mathbf{x}). \tag{4.110b}
$$

The overall objective function is then

$$
J(\mathbf{x}) = \sum_{k=0}^{K} \left(J_{v,k}(\mathbf{x}) + J_{y,k}(\mathbf{x})\right). \tag{4.111}
$$

Note that we can generally think of $\mathbf{W}_{v,k}$ and $\mathbf{W}_{y,k}$ simply as symmetric positive-definite matrix weights. By choosing these to be related to the covariances of the measurement noises, minimizing the objective function is equivalent to maximizing the joint likelihood of the state given all the data.

We further define

$$
\mathbf{e}(\mathbf{x}) = \begin{bmatrix} \mathbf{e}_v(\mathbf{x}) \\ \mathbf{e}_y(\mathbf{x}) \end{bmatrix}, \quad \mathbf{e}_v(\mathbf{x}) = \begin{bmatrix} \mathbf{e}_{v,0}(\mathbf{x}) \\ \vdots \\ \mathbf{e}_{v,K}(\mathbf{x}) \end{bmatrix}, \quad \mathbf{e}_y(\mathbf{x}) = \begin{bmatrix} \mathbf{e}_{y,0}(\mathbf{x}) \\ \vdots \\ \mathbf{e}_{y,K}(\mathbf{x}) \end{bmatrix},
$$

$$
\tag{4.112a}
$$

$$
\mathbf{W} = \operatorname{diag}\left(\mathbf{W}_v, \mathbf{W}_y\right), \quad \mathbf{W}_v = \operatorname{diag}\left(\mathbf{W}_{v,0}, \dots, \mathbf{W}_{v,K}\right), \tag{4.112b}
$$

$$
\mathbf{W}_y = \operatorname{diag}\left(\mathbf{W}_{y,0}, \dots, \mathbf{W}_{y,K}\right), \tag{4.112c}
$$

so that the objective function can be written as

$$
J(\mathbf{x}) = \frac{1}{2}\mathbf{e}(\mathbf{x})^T \mathbf{W}^{-1} \mathbf{e}(\mathbf{x}). \tag{4.113}
$$

We can further define the modified error term,

$$
\mathbf{u}(\mathbf{x}) = \mathbf{L}\,\mathbf{e}(\mathbf{x}), \tag{4.114}
$$

where $\mathbf{L}^T \mathbf{L} = \mathbf{W}^{-1}$ (i.e., from a Cholesky decomposition since $\mathbf{W}$ is symmetric positive-definite). Using these definitions, we can write the objective function simply as

$$
J(\mathbf{x}) = \frac{1}{2}\mathbf{u}(\mathbf{x})^T \mathbf{u}(\mathbf{x}). \tag{4.115}
$$

This is precisely in a quadratic form, but not with respect to the design variables, $\mathbf{x}$. Our goal is to determine the optimum design parameter, $\hat{\mathbf{x}}$, that minimizes the objective function:

$$\hat{\mathbf{x}} = \arg \min_{\mathbf{x}} J(\mathbf{x}). \tag{4.116}$$

We can apply many nonlinear optimization techniques to minimize this expression due to its quadratic nature. A typical technique to use is Gauss–Newton optimization, but there are many other possibilities. The more important issue is that we are considering this as a nonlinear optimization problem. We will derive the Gauss–Newton algorithm by way of Newton's method.

Newton's Method

Newton's method works by iteratively approximating the (differentiable) objective function by a quadratic function and then jumping to (or moving towards) the minimum. Suppose we have an initial guess, or operating point, for the design parameter, $\mathbf{x}_{\mathrm{op}}$. We use a three-term Taylor-series expansion to approximate J as a quadratic function,

$$J(\mathbf{x}_{\mathrm{op}} + \delta\mathbf{x}) \approx J(\mathbf{x}_{\mathrm{op}}) + \underbrace{\left(\frac{\partial J(\mathbf{x})}{\partial \mathbf{x}}\bigg|_{\mathbf{x}_{\mathrm{op}}}\right)}_{\text{Jacobian}} \delta\mathbf{x} + \frac{1}{2}\delta\mathbf{x}^T \underbrace{\left(\frac{\partial^2 J(\mathbf{x})}{\partial \mathbf{x}\partial \mathbf{x}^T}\bigg|_{\mathbf{x}_{\mathrm{op}}}\right)}_{\text{Hessian}} \delta\mathbf{x},$$

$$\tag{4.117}$$

of $\delta\mathbf{x}$, a 'small' change to the initial guess, $\mathbf{x}_{\mathrm{op}}$. We note that the symmetric Hessian matrix needs to be positive-definite for this method to work (otherwise there is no well-defined minimum to the quadratic approximation).

The next step is to find the value of $\delta\mathbf{x}$ that minimizes this quadratic approximation. We can do this by taking the derivative with respect to $\delta\mathbf{x}$ and setting to zero to find a critical point:

$$\frac{\partial J(\mathbf{x}_{\mathrm{op}} + \delta\mathbf{x})}{\partial \delta\mathbf{x}} = \left(\frac{\partial J(\mathbf{x})}{\partial \mathbf{x}}\bigg|_{\mathbf{x}_{\mathrm{op}}}\right) + \delta\mathbf{x}^{*T}\left(\frac{\partial^2 J(\mathbf{x})}{\partial \mathbf{x}\partial \mathbf{x}^T}\bigg|_{\mathbf{x}_{\mathrm{op}}}\right) = \mathbf{0}$$

$$\Rightarrow \quad \left(\frac{\partial^2 J(\mathbf{x})}{\partial \mathbf{x}\partial \mathbf{x}^T}\bigg|_{\mathbf{x}_{\mathrm{op}}}\right)\delta\mathbf{x}^* = -\left(\frac{\partial J(\mathbf{x})}{\partial \mathbf{x}}\bigg|_{\mathbf{x}_{\mathrm{op}}}\right)^T. \tag{4.118}$$

The last line is just a linear system of equations and can be solved when the Hessian is invertible (which it must be, since it was assumed to be positive-definite above). We may then update our operating point according to

$$\mathbf{x}_{\mathrm{op}} \leftarrow \mathbf{x}_{\mathrm{op}} + \delta\mathbf{x}^*. \tag{4.119}$$

This procedure iterates until $\delta\mathbf{x}^*$ becomes sufficiently small. A few comments about Newton's method:

(i) It is 'locally convergent', which means the successive approximations are guaranteed to converge to a solution when the initial guess is already close enough to the solution. For a complex nonlinear objective function, this is really the best we can expect (i.e., global convergence is difficult to achieve).

(ii) The rate of convergence is quadratic (i.e., it converges much faster than simple gradient descent).

(iii) It can be difficult to implement because the Hessian must be computed.

The Gauss–Newton method approximates Newton's method further, in the case of a special form of objective function.

Gauss–Newton Method

Let us now return to the nonlinear quadratic objective function we have in Equation (4.115). In this case, the Jacobian and Hessian matrices are

$$\text{Jacobian:} \quad \left. \frac{\partial J(\mathbf{x})}{\partial \mathbf{x}} \right|_{\mathbf{x}_{\mathrm{op}}} = \mathbf{u}(\mathbf{x}_{\mathrm{op}})^T \left(\left. \frac{\partial \mathbf{u}(\mathbf{x})}{\partial \mathbf{x}} \right|_{\mathbf{x}_{\mathrm{op}}} \right), \tag{4.120a}$$

$$\text{Hessian:} \quad \left. \frac{\partial^2 J(\mathbf{x})}{\partial \mathbf{x} \partial \mathbf{x}^T} \right|_{\mathbf{x}_{\mathrm{op}}} = \left(\left. \frac{\partial \mathbf{u}(\mathbf{x})}{\partial \mathbf{x}} \right|_{\mathbf{x}_{\mathrm{op}}} \right)^T \left(\left. \frac{\partial \mathbf{u}(\mathbf{x})}{\partial \mathbf{x}} \right|_{\mathbf{x}_{\mathrm{op}}} \right)$$
$$+ \sum_{i=1}^{M} u_i(\mathbf{x}_{\mathrm{op}}) \left(\left. \frac{\partial^2 u_i(\mathbf{x})}{\partial \mathbf{x} \partial \mathbf{x}^T} \right|_{\mathbf{x}_{\mathrm{op}}} \right), \tag{4.120b}$$

where $\mathbf{u}(\mathbf{x}) = \big(u_1(\mathbf{x}), \dots, u_i(\mathbf{x}), \dots, u_M(\mathbf{x}) \big)$. We have so far not made any approximations.

Looking to the expression for the Hessian, we assert that near the minimum of J, the second term is small relative to the first. One intuition behind this is that near the optimum, we should have $u_i(\mathbf{x})$ small (and ideally zero). We thus approximate the Hessian according to

$$\left. \frac{\partial^2 J(\mathbf{x})}{\partial \mathbf{x} \partial \mathbf{x}^T} \right|_{\mathbf{x}_{\mathrm{op}}} \approx \left(\left. \frac{\partial \mathbf{u}(\mathbf{x})}{\partial \mathbf{x}} \right|_{\mathbf{x}_{\mathrm{op}}} \right)^T \left(\left. \frac{\partial \mathbf{u}(\mathbf{x})}{\partial \mathbf{x}} \right|_{\mathbf{x}_{\mathrm{op}}} \right), \tag{4.121}$$

which does not involve any second derivatives. Substituting (4.120a) and (4.121) into the Newton update represented by (4.118), we have

$$\left(\left. \frac{\partial \mathbf{u}(\mathbf{x})}{\partial \mathbf{x}} \right|_{\mathbf{x}_{\mathrm{op}}} \right)^T \left(\left. \frac{\partial \mathbf{u}(\mathbf{x})}{\partial \mathbf{x}} \right|_{\mathbf{x}_{\mathrm{op}}} \right) \delta \mathbf{x}^\star = - \left(\left. \frac{\partial \mathbf{u}(\mathbf{x})}{\partial \mathbf{x}} \right|_{\mathbf{x}_{\mathrm{op}}} \right)^T \mathbf{u}(\mathbf{x}_{\mathrm{op}}), \tag{4.122}$$

which is the classic Gauss–Newton update method. Again, this is iterated to convergence.

Gauss–Newton Method: Alternative Derivation

The other way to think about the Gauss–Newton method is to start with a Taylor expansion of $\mathbf{u}(\mathbf{x})$, instead of $J(\mathbf{x})$. The approximation in this case is

$$\mathbf{u}(\mathbf{x}_{\mathrm{op}} + \delta \mathbf{x}) \approx \mathbf{u}(\mathbf{x}_{\mathrm{op}}) + \left(\left. \frac{\partial \mathbf{u}(\mathbf{x})}{\partial \mathbf{x}} \right|_{\mathbf{x}_{\mathrm{op}}} \right) \delta \mathbf{x}. \tag{4.123}$$

Substituting into J, we have

$$J(\mathbf{x}_{\text{op}} + \delta\mathbf{x})$$

$$\approx \frac{1}{2}\left(\mathbf{u}(\mathbf{x}_{\text{op}}) + \left(\left.\frac{\partial\mathbf{u}(\mathbf{x})}{\partial\mathbf{x}}\right|_{\mathbf{x}_{\text{op}}}\right)\delta\mathbf{x}\right)^T\left(\mathbf{u}(\mathbf{x}_{\text{op}}) + \left(\left.\frac{\partial\mathbf{u}(\mathbf{x})}{\partial\mathbf{x}}\right|_{\mathbf{x}_{\text{op}}}\right)\delta\mathbf{x}\right).$$

$$(4.124)$$

Minimizing with respect to $\delta\mathbf{x}$ gives

$$\frac{\partial J(\mathbf{x}_{\text{op}} + \delta\mathbf{x})}{\partial\delta\mathbf{x}} = \left(\mathbf{u}(\mathbf{x}_{\text{op}}) + \left(\left.\frac{\partial\mathbf{u}(\mathbf{x})}{\partial\mathbf{x}}\right|_{\mathbf{x}_{\text{op}}}\right)\delta\mathbf{x}^*\right)^T\left(\left.\frac{\partial\mathbf{u}(\mathbf{x})}{\partial\mathbf{x}}\right|_{\mathbf{x}_{\text{op}}}\right) = \mathbf{0}$$

$$\Rightarrow \left(\left.\frac{\partial\mathbf{u}(\mathbf{x})}{\partial\mathbf{x}}\right|_{\mathbf{x}_{\text{op}}}\right)^T\left(\left.\frac{\partial\mathbf{u}(\mathbf{x})}{\partial\mathbf{x}}\right|_{\mathbf{x}_{\text{op}}}\right)\delta\mathbf{x}^* = -\left(\left.\frac{\partial\mathbf{u}(\mathbf{x})}{\partial\mathbf{x}}\right|_{\mathbf{x}_{\text{op}}}\right)^T\mathbf{u}(\mathbf{x}_{\text{op}}),$$

$$(4.125)$$

which is the same update as in (4.122). We will employ this shortcut to the Gauss–Newton method in later chapters when confronted with dealing with nonlinearities in the form of rotations.

Practical Patches to Gauss–Newton

Since the Gauss–Newton method is not guaranteed to converge (owing to the approximate Hessian matrix), we can make two practical patches to help with convergence:

(i) Once the optimal update is computed, $\delta\mathbf{x}^*$, we perform the actual update according to

$$\mathbf{x}_{\text{op}} \leftarrow \mathbf{x}_{\text{op}} + \alpha\,\delta\mathbf{x}^*, \qquad (4.126)$$

where $\alpha \in [0,1]$ is a user-definable parameter. Performing a line search for the best value of α works well in practice. This works because $\delta\mathbf{x}^*$ is a descent direction; we are just adjusting how far we step in this direction to be a bit more conservative towards robustness (rather than speed).

(ii) We can use the Levenberg–Marquardt modification to the Gauss–Newton method:

$$\left(\left(\left.\frac{\partial\mathbf{u}(\mathbf{x})}{\partial\mathbf{x}}\right|_{\mathbf{x}_{\text{op}}}\right)^T\left(\left.\frac{\partial\mathbf{u}(\mathbf{x})}{\partial\mathbf{x}}\right|_{\mathbf{x}_{\text{op}}}\right) + \lambda\mathbf{D}\right)\delta\mathbf{x}^*$$

$$= -\left(\left.\frac{\partial\mathbf{u}(\mathbf{x})}{\partial\mathbf{x}}\right|_{\mathbf{x}_{\text{op}}}\right)^T\mathbf{u}(\mathbf{x}_{\text{op}}), \quad (4.127)$$

where $\mathbf{D}$ is a positive diagonal matrix. When $\mathbf{D} = \mathbf{1}$, we can see that as $\lambda \geq 0$ becomes very big, the Hessian is relatively small, and we have

$$\delta\mathbf{x}^* \approx -\frac{1}{\lambda}\left(\left.\frac{\partial\mathbf{u}(\mathbf{x})}{\partial\mathbf{x}}\right|_{\mathbf{x}_{\text{op}}}\right)^T\mathbf{u}(\mathbf{x}_{\text{op}}), \qquad (4.128)$$

which corresponds to a very small step in the direction of steepest descent (i.e., the negative gradient). When $\lambda = 0$, we recover the usual Gauss–Newton update. The Levenberg–Marquardt method can work well in situations when the Hessian approximation is poor or is poorly conditioned by slowly increasing λ to improve conditioning.

We can also combine both of these patches to give us the most options in controlling convergence.

Gauss–Newton Update in Terms of Errors

Recalling that

$$\mathbf{u}(\mathbf{x}) = \mathbf{L}\,\mathbf{e}(\mathbf{x}), \tag{4.129}$$

with $\mathbf{L}$ a constant, we substitute this into the Gauss–Newton update to see that, in terms of the error, $\mathbf{e}(\mathbf{x})$, we have

$$\left(\mathbf{H}^T\mathbf{W}^{-1}\mathbf{H}\right)\delta\mathbf{x}^* = \mathbf{H}^T\mathbf{W}^{-1}\,\mathbf{e}(\mathbf{x}_{\mathrm{op}}), \tag{4.130}$$

with

$$\mathbf{H} = -\left.\frac{\partial\mathbf{e}(\mathbf{x})}{\partial\mathbf{x}}\right|_{\mathbf{x}_{\mathrm{op}}}, \tag{4.131}$$

and where we have used $\mathbf{L}^T\mathbf{L} = \mathbf{W}^{-1}$.

Another way to view this is to notice that

$$J(\mathbf{x}_{\mathrm{op}} + \delta\mathbf{x}) \approx \frac{1}{2}\left(\mathbf{e}(\mathbf{x}_{\mathrm{op}}) - \mathbf{H}\,\delta\mathbf{x}\right)^T\mathbf{W}^{-1}\left(\mathbf{e}(\mathbf{x}_{\mathrm{op}}) - \mathbf{H}\,\delta\mathbf{x}\right), \tag{4.132}$$

where $\mathbf{e}(\mathbf{x}_{\mathrm{op}}) = \mathbf{L}^{-1}\mathbf{u}(\mathbf{x}_{\mathrm{op}})$, is the quadratic approximation of the objective function in terms of the error. Minimizing this with respect to $\delta\mathbf{x}$ yields the Gauss–Newton update.

Laplace Approximation

Even though we are discussing MAP estimation in this section, it would still be desirable to obtain an uncertainty estimate along with our point estimate, $\mathbf{x}_{\mathrm{op}}$. For this we can turn to the *Laplace approximation*, which aims to approximate the full Bayesian posterior with a Gaussian centered at the MAP estimate. If this Gaussian takes the form $\mathcal{N}(\hat{\mathbf{x}}, \hat{\mathbf{P}})$, then after MAP has converged we let $\hat{\mathbf{x}} = \mathbf{x}_{\mathrm{op}}$ and $\hat{\mathbf{P}}$ is taken as the inverse of the Hessian of the cost function, evaluated at the MAP estimate, $\mathbf{x}_{\mathrm{op}}$.

In the case of Gauss–Newton MAP estimation, the left-hand side of the update equation is taken as the inverse covariance matrix, $\hat{\mathbf{P}}^{-1}$, of the Laplace approximation:

$$\underbrace{\left(\mathbf{H}^T\mathbf{W}^{-1}\mathbf{H}\right)}_{\hat{\mathbf{P}}^{-1}}\delta\mathbf{x}^* = \mathbf{H}^T\mathbf{W}^{-1}\,\mathbf{e}(\mathbf{x}_{\mathrm{op}}). \tag{4.133}$$

This is also a direct extension of the discussion in Section 3.1.5, where in the linear-Gaussian batch MAP case we took the left-hand side of (3.49) as the inverse covariance matrix.

Pierre-Simon Laplace (1749–1827) was was French polymath who contributed to such diverse fields as mathematics, statistics, physics, astronomy, and philosophy. He was an early adopter of calculus and was the main developer of what is now known as the Bayesian interpretation of probability.

Batch Estimation

We now return to our specific estimation problem and apply the Gauss–Newton optimization method. We will use the 'shortcut' approach and thus begin by approximating our error expressions:

$$\mathbf{e}_{v,k}(\mathbf{x}_{\text{op}} + \delta\mathbf{x}) \approx \begin{cases} \mathbf{e}_{v,0}(\mathbf{x}_{\text{op}}) - \delta\mathbf{x}_0, & k = 0 \\ \mathbf{e}_{v,k}(\mathbf{x}_{\text{op}}) + \mathbf{F}_{k-1}\delta\mathbf{x}_{k-1} - \delta\mathbf{x}_k, & k = 1\ldots K \end{cases},$$

(4.134)

$$\mathbf{e}_{y,k}(\mathbf{x}_{\text{op}} + \delta\mathbf{x}) \approx \mathbf{e}_{y,k}(\mathbf{x}_{\text{op}}) - \mathbf{G}_k\delta\mathbf{x}_k, \quad k = 0\ldots K,$$

(4.135)

where

$$\mathbf{e}_{v,k}(\mathbf{x}_{\text{op}}) \approx \begin{cases} \check{\mathbf{x}}_0 - \mathbf{x}_{\text{op},0}, & k = 0 \\ \mathbf{f}\left(\mathbf{x}_{\text{op},k-1}, \mathbf{v}_k, \mathbf{0}\right) - \mathbf{x}_{\text{op},k}, & k = 1\ldots K \end{cases}, \quad (4.136)$$

$$\mathbf{e}_{y,k}(\mathbf{x}_{\text{op}}) \approx \mathbf{y}_k - \mathbf{g}\left(\mathbf{x}_{\text{op},k}, \mathbf{0}\right), \quad k = 0\ldots K,$$

(4.137)

and we require definitions of the Jacobians of the nonlinear motion and observations models given by

$$\mathbf{F}_{k-1} = \left.\frac{\partial\mathbf{f}(\mathbf{x}_{k-1}, \mathbf{v}_k, \mathbf{w}_k)}{\partial\mathbf{x}_{k-1}}\right|_{\mathbf{x}_{\text{op},k-1}, \mathbf{v}_k, \mathbf{0}}, \quad \mathbf{G}_k = \left.\frac{\partial\mathbf{g}(\mathbf{x}_k, \mathbf{n}_k)}{\partial\mathbf{x}_k}\right|_{\mathbf{x}_{\text{op},k}, \mathbf{0}}.$$

(4.138)

Then, if we let the matrix weights be given by

$$\mathbf{W}_{v,k} = \mathbf{Q}'_k, \quad \mathbf{W}_{y,k} = \mathbf{R}'_k,$$

(4.139)

we can define

$$\delta\mathbf{x} = \begin{bmatrix} \delta\mathbf{x}_0 \\ \delta\mathbf{x}_1 \\ \delta\mathbf{x}_2 \\ \vdots \\ \delta\mathbf{x}_K \end{bmatrix}, \quad \mathbf{H} = \left[\begin{array}{c} \begin{matrix} \mathbf{1} \\ -\mathbf{F}_0 & \mathbf{1} \\ & -\mathbf{F}_1 & \ddots \\ & & \ddots & \mathbf{1} \\ & & & -\mathbf{F}_{K-1} & \mathbf{1} \end{matrix} \\ \hline \begin{matrix} \mathbf{G}_0 \\ & \mathbf{G}_1 \\ & & \mathbf{G}_2 \\ & & & \ddots \\ & & & & \mathbf{G}_K \end{matrix} \end{array}\right], \quad (4.140a)$$

$$\mathbf{e}(\mathbf{x}_{\text{op}}) = \left[\begin{array}{c} \mathbf{e}_{v,0}(\mathbf{x}_{\text{op}}) \\ \mathbf{e}_{v,1}(\mathbf{x}_{\text{op}}) \\ \vdots \\ \mathbf{e}_{v,K}(\mathbf{x}_{\text{op}}) \\ \hline \mathbf{e}_{y,0}(\mathbf{x}_{\text{op}}) \\ \mathbf{e}_{y,1}(\mathbf{x}_{\text{op}}) \\ \vdots \\ \mathbf{e}_{y,K}(\mathbf{x}_{\text{op}}) \end{array}\right], \quad (4.140b)$$

and

$$\mathbf{W} = \mathrm{diag}\left(\check{\mathbf{P}}_0, \mathbf{Q}'_1, \ldots, \mathbf{Q}'_K, \mathbf{R}'_0, \mathbf{R}'_1, \ldots, \mathbf{R}'_K\right), \qquad (4.141)$$

which are identical in structure to the matrices in the linear batch case, summarized in (3.3.1), with a few extra subscripts to show time dependence as well as the Jacobians of the motion/observation models with respect to the noise variables. Under these definitions, our Gauss–Newton update is given by

$$\underbrace{\left(\mathbf{H}^T\mathbf{W}^{-1}\mathbf{H}\right)}_{\text{block-tridiagonal}} \delta\mathbf{x}^* = \mathbf{H}^T\mathbf{W}^{-1}\mathbf{e}(\mathbf{x}_{\mathrm{op}}). \qquad (4.142)$$

This is very comparable to the linear-Gaussian batch case. The key difference to remember here is that we are in fact iterating our solution for the entire trajectory, $\mathbf{x}$. We could at this point recover the recursive EKF from our batch solution using similar logic to the linear-Gaussian case.

4.3.2 Bayesian Inference

We can also get to the same batch update equations from a Bayesian-inference perspective. Assume we begin with an initial guess for the entire trajectory, $\mathbf{x}_{\mathrm{op}}$. We can linearize the motion model about this guess and construct a prior over the whole trajectory using all the inputs. The linearized motion model is

$$\mathbf{x}_k \approx \mathbf{f}(\mathbf{x}_{\mathrm{op},k-1}, \mathbf{v}_k, \mathbf{0}) + \mathbf{F}_{k-1}\left(\mathbf{x}_{k-1} - \mathbf{x}_{\mathrm{op},k-1}\right) + \mathbf{w}'_k, \qquad (4.143)$$

where the Jacobian, $\mathbf{F}_{k-1}$, is the same as the previous section. After a bit of manipulation, we can write this in lifted form as

$$\mathbf{x} = \mathbf{F}\left(\boldsymbol{\nu} + \mathbf{w}'\right), \qquad (4.144)$$

where

$$\boldsymbol{\nu} = \begin{bmatrix} \check{\mathbf{x}}_0 \\ \mathbf{f}(\mathbf{x}_{\mathrm{op},0}, \mathbf{v}_1, \mathbf{0}) - \mathbf{F}_0\mathbf{x}_{\mathrm{op},0} \\ \mathbf{f}(\mathbf{x}_{\mathrm{op},1}, \mathbf{v}_2, \mathbf{0}) - \mathbf{F}_1\mathbf{x}_{\mathrm{op},1} \\ \vdots \\ \mathbf{f}(\mathbf{x}_{\mathrm{op},K-1}, \mathbf{v}_K, \mathbf{0}) - \mathbf{F}_{K-1}\mathbf{x}_{\mathrm{op},K-1} \end{bmatrix}, \qquad (4.145a)$$

$$\mathbf{F} = \begin{bmatrix} \mathbf{1} & & & & \\ \mathbf{F}_0 & \mathbf{1} & & & \\ \mathbf{F}_1\mathbf{F}_0 & \mathbf{F}_1 & \mathbf{1} & & \\ \vdots & \vdots & \vdots & \ddots & \\ \mathbf{F}_{K-2}\cdots\mathbf{F}_0 & \mathbf{F}_{K-2}\cdots\mathbf{F}_1 & \mathbf{F}_{K-2}\cdots\mathbf{F}_2 & \cdots & \mathbf{1} \\ \mathbf{F}_{K-1}\cdots\mathbf{F}_0 & \mathbf{F}_{K-1}\cdots\mathbf{F}_1 & \mathbf{F}_{K-1}\cdots\mathbf{F}_2 & \cdots & \mathbf{F}_{K-1} & \mathbf{1} \end{bmatrix},$$
$$(4.145b)$$

$$\mathbf{Q}' = \mathrm{diag}\left(\check{\mathbf{P}}_0, \mathbf{Q}'_1, \mathbf{Q}'_2, \ldots, \mathbf{Q}'_K\right), \qquad (4.145c)$$

and $\mathbf{w}' \sim \mathcal{N}\left(\mathbf{0}, \mathbf{Q}'\right)$. For the mean of the prior, $\check{\mathbf{x}}$, we then simply have

$$\check{\mathbf{x}} = E\left[\mathbf{x}\right] = E\left[\mathbf{F}\left(\boldsymbol{\nu} + \mathbf{w}'\right)\right] = \mathbf{F}\boldsymbol{\nu}. \qquad (4.146)$$

For the covariance of the prior, $\check{\mathbf{P}}$, we have

$$\check{\mathbf{P}} = E\left[(\mathbf{x} - E[\mathbf{x}])(\mathbf{x} - E[\mathbf{x}])^T\right] = \mathbf{F}\,E\left[\mathbf{w}'\mathbf{w}'^T\right]\mathbf{F}^T = \mathbf{F}\mathbf{Q}'\mathbf{F}^T. \quad (4.147)$$

Thus, the prior can be summarized as $\mathbf{x} \sim \mathcal{N}\left(\mathbf{F}\boldsymbol{\nu}, \mathbf{F}\mathbf{Q}'\mathbf{F}^T\right)$. The $(\cdot)'$ notation is used to indicate that the Jacobian with respect to the noise is incorporated into the quantity.

The linearized observation model is

$$\mathbf{y}_k \approx \mathbf{g}\left(\mathbf{x}_{\mathrm{op},k}, \mathbf{0}\right) + \mathbf{G}_k\left(\mathbf{x}_{k-1} - \mathbf{x}_{\mathrm{op},k-1}\right) + \mathbf{n}'_k, \qquad (4.148)$$

which can be written in lifted form as

$$\mathbf{y} = \mathbf{y}_{\mathrm{op}} + \mathbf{G}\left(\mathbf{x} - \mathbf{x}_{\mathrm{op}}\right) + \mathbf{n}', \qquad (4.149)$$

where

$$\mathbf{y}_{\mathrm{op}} = \begin{bmatrix} \mathbf{g}(\mathbf{x}_{\mathrm{op},0}, \mathbf{0}) \\ \mathbf{g}(\mathbf{x}_{\mathrm{op},1}, \mathbf{0}) \\ \vdots \\ \mathbf{g}(\mathbf{x}_{\mathrm{op},K}, \mathbf{0}) \end{bmatrix}, \qquad (4.150a)$$

$$\mathbf{G} = \mathrm{diag}\left(\mathbf{G}_0, \mathbf{G}_1, \mathbf{G}_2, \ldots, \mathbf{G}_K\right), \qquad (4.150b)$$

$$\mathbf{R} = \mathrm{diag}\left(\mathbf{R}'_0, \mathbf{R}'_1, \mathbf{R}'_2, \ldots, \mathbf{R}'_K\right), \qquad (4.150c)$$

and $\mathbf{n}' \sim \mathcal{N}(\mathbf{0}, \mathbf{R}')$. It is fairly easy to see that

$$E\left[\mathbf{y}\right] = \mathbf{y}_{\mathrm{op}} + \mathbf{G}\left(\check{\mathbf{x}} - \mathbf{x}_{\mathrm{op}}\right), \qquad (4.151a)$$

$$E\left[(\mathbf{y} - E[\mathbf{y}])(\mathbf{y} - E[\mathbf{y}])^T\right] = \mathbf{G}\check{\mathbf{P}}\mathbf{G}^T + \mathbf{R}', \qquad (4.151b)$$

$$E\left[(\mathbf{y} - E[\mathbf{y}])(\mathbf{x} - E[\mathbf{x}])^T\right] = \mathbf{G}\check{\mathbf{P}}. \qquad (4.151c)$$

Again, the $(\cdot)'$ notation is used to indicate that the Jacobian with respect to the noise is incorporated into the quantity.

With these quantities in hand, we can write a joint density for the lifted trajectory and measurements as

$$p(\mathbf{x}, \mathbf{y}|\boldsymbol{\nu}) = \mathcal{N}\left(\begin{bmatrix} \check{\mathbf{x}} \\ \mathbf{y}_{\mathrm{op}} + \mathbf{G}\left(\check{\mathbf{x}} - \mathbf{x}_{\mathrm{op}}\right) \end{bmatrix}, \begin{bmatrix} \check{\mathbf{P}} & \check{\mathbf{P}}\mathbf{G}^T \\ \mathbf{G}\check{\mathbf{P}} & \mathbf{G}\check{\mathbf{P}}\mathbf{G}^T + \mathbf{R}' \end{bmatrix}\right), \quad (4.152)$$

which is quite similar to the expression for the IEKF situation in (4.42), but now for the whole trajectory rather than just one timestep. Using the usual relationship from (2.52b), we can immediately write the Gaussian posterior as

$$p(\mathbf{x}|\boldsymbol{\nu}, \mathbf{y}) = \mathcal{N}\left(\hat{\mathbf{x}}, \hat{\mathbf{P}}\right), \qquad (4.153)$$

where

$$\mathbf{K} = \check{\mathbf{P}}\mathbf{G}^T\left(\mathbf{G}\check{\mathbf{P}}\mathbf{G}^T + \mathbf{R}'\right)^{-1}, \qquad (4.154a)$$

$$\hat{\mathbf{P}} = \left(\mathbf{1} - \mathbf{K}\mathbf{G}\right)\check{\mathbf{P}}, \qquad (4.154b)$$

$$\hat{\mathbf{x}} = \check{\mathbf{x}} + \mathbf{K}\left(\mathbf{y} - \mathbf{y}_{\mathrm{op}} - \mathbf{G}(\check{\mathbf{x}} - \mathbf{x}_{\mathrm{op}})\right). \qquad (4.154c)$$

Using the SMW identity from (2.124), we can rearrange the equation for the posterior mean to be

$$\left(\check{\mathbf{P}}^{-1} + \mathbf{G}^T\mathbf{R}'^{-1}\mathbf{G}\right)\delta\mathbf{x}^* = \check{\mathbf{P}}^{-1}\left(\check{\mathbf{x}} - \mathbf{x}_{\mathrm{op}}\right) + \mathbf{G}^T\mathbf{R}'^{-1}\left(\mathbf{y} - \mathbf{y}_{\mathrm{op}}\right), \quad (4.155)$$

where $\delta\mathbf{x}^* = \hat{\mathbf{x}} - \mathbf{x}_{\mathrm{op}}$. Inserting the details of the prior, this becomes

$$\underbrace{\left(\mathbf{F}^{-T}\mathbf{Q}'^{-1}\mathbf{F}^{-1} + \mathbf{G}^T\mathbf{R}'^{-1}\mathbf{G}\right)}_{\text{block-tridiagonal}}\delta\mathbf{x}^*$$

$$= \mathbf{F}^{-T}\mathbf{Q}'^{-1}\left(\boldsymbol{\nu} - \mathbf{F}^{-1}\mathbf{x}_{\mathrm{op}}\right) + \mathbf{G}^T\mathbf{R}'^{-1}\left(\mathbf{y} - \mathbf{y}_{\mathrm{op}}\right). \quad (4.156)$$

Then, under the definitions

$$\mathbf{H} = \begin{bmatrix} \mathbf{F}^{-1} \\ \mathbf{G} \end{bmatrix}, \quad \mathbf{W} = \mathrm{diag}\left(\mathbf{Q}', \mathbf{R}'\right), \quad \mathbf{e}(\mathbf{x}_{\mathrm{op}}) = \begin{bmatrix} \boldsymbol{\nu} - \mathbf{F}^{-1}\mathbf{x}_{\mathrm{op}} \\ \mathbf{y} - \mathbf{y}_{\mathrm{op}} \end{bmatrix}, \quad (4.157)$$

we can rewrite this as

$$\underbrace{\left(\mathbf{H}^T\mathbf{W}^{-1}\mathbf{H}\right)}_{\text{block-tridiagonal}}\delta\mathbf{x}^* = \mathbf{H}^T\mathbf{W}^{-1}\mathbf{e}(\mathbf{x}_{\mathrm{op}}), \quad (4.158)$$

which is identical to the update equation from the previous section. As usual, we iterate to convergence. The difference between the Bayesian and MAP approaches basically comes down to on which side of the SMW identity one begins; plus, the Bayesian approach produces a covariance explicitly, although we have shown that the same thing can be extracted from the MAP approach. Note that it was our choice to iteratively relinearize about the mean of the best estimate so far, which caused the Bayesian approach to have the same 'mean' as the MAP solution. We saw this phenomenon previously in the IEKF section. We could also imagine making different choices than linearization in the batch case (e.g., particles, sigmapoints) to compute the required moments for the update equations, but we will not explore these possibilities here.

4.3.3 Maximum Likelihood

In this section, we consider a simplified version of our batch estimation problem, where we throw away the prior and use only the measurements for our solution.

Maximum Likelihood via Gauss–Newton

We will assume the observation model takes on a simplified form in which the measurement noise is purely additive (i.e., outside the nonlinearity):

$$\mathbf{y}_k = \mathbf{g}_k(\mathbf{x}) + \mathbf{n}_k, \quad (4.159)$$

where $\mathbf{n}_k \sim \mathcal{N}(\mathbf{0}, \mathbf{R}_k)$. Note that in this case, we allow for the possibility that the measurement function is changing with k and that it could depend on an arbitrary portion of the state, $\mathbf{x}$. We need no longer think of k as a time index, simply as a measurement index.

Without the prior, our objective function takes the form

$$J(\mathbf{x}) = \frac{1}{2} \sum_k \left(\mathbf{y}_k - \mathbf{g}_k(\mathbf{x})\right)^T \mathbf{R}_k^{-1} \left(\mathbf{y}_k - \mathbf{g}_k(\mathbf{x})\right) = -\log p(\mathbf{y}|\mathbf{x}) + C,$$

(4.160)

where C is a constant. Without the prior term in the objective function, we refer to this as a *maximum likelihood (ML)* problem because finding the solution that minimizes the objective function also maximizes the likelihood of the measurements:[10]

$$\hat{\mathbf{x}} = \arg\min_{\mathbf{x}} J(\mathbf{x}) = \arg\max_{\mathbf{x}} p(\mathbf{y}|\mathbf{x}).$$

(4.161)

We can still use the Gauss–Newton algorithm to solve the ML problem, just as in the MAP case. We begin with an initial guess for the solution, $\mathbf{x}_{\text{op}}$. We then compute an optimal update, $\delta\mathbf{x}^*$, by solving

$$\left(\sum_k \mathbf{G}_k(\mathbf{x}_{\text{op}})^T \mathbf{R}_k^{-1} \mathbf{G}_k(\mathbf{x}_{\text{op}})\right) \delta\mathbf{x}^* = \sum_k \mathbf{G}_k(\mathbf{x}_{\text{op}})^T \mathbf{R}_k^{-1} \left(\mathbf{y}_k - \mathbf{g}_k(\mathbf{x}_{\text{op}})\right),$$

(4.162)

where

$$\mathbf{G}_k(\mathbf{x}) = \frac{\partial \mathbf{g}_k(\mathbf{x})}{\partial \mathbf{x}}$$

(4.163)

is the Jacobian of the observation model with respect to the state. Finally, we apply the optimal update to our guess,

$$\mathbf{x}_{\text{op}} \leftarrow \mathbf{x}_{\text{op}} + \delta\mathbf{x}^*,$$

(4.164)

and iterate to convergence. Once converged, we take $\hat{\mathbf{x}} = \mathbf{x}_{\text{op}}$ as our estimate. At convergence, we should have that

$$\left.\frac{\partial J(\mathbf{x})}{\partial \mathbf{x}^T}\right|_{\hat{\mathbf{x}}} = -\sum_k \mathbf{G}_k(\hat{\mathbf{x}})^T \mathbf{R}_k^{-1} \left(\mathbf{y}_k - \mathbf{g}_k(\hat{\mathbf{x}})\right) = \mathbf{0}$$

(4.165)

for a minimum.

We will come back to this ML setup when discussing a problem called *bundle adjustment* in later chapters.

Maximum Likelihood Bias Estimation

We have already seen in the simple example at the start of this chapter that the MAP method is biased with respect to average mean error. It turns out that the ML method is biased as well (unless the measurement model is linear). A classic paper by Box (1971) derives an approximate expression for the bias in ML, and we use this section to present it.

We will see below that we need a second-order Taylor expansion of $\mathbf{g}(\mathbf{x})$ while only a first-order expansion of $\mathbf{G}(\mathbf{x})$. Thus, we have the following approximate expressions:

---

[10] This is because the logarithm is a monotonically increasing function. Another way of looking at ML is that it is MAP with a uniform prior over all possible solutions.

$$\mathbf{g}_k(\hat{\mathbf{x}}) = \mathbf{g}_k(\mathbf{x} + \delta\mathbf{x}) \approx \mathbf{g}_k(\mathbf{x}) + \mathbf{G}_k(\mathbf{x})\,\delta\mathbf{x} + \frac{1}{2}\sum_j \mathbf{1}_j\,\delta\mathbf{x}^T \boldsymbol{\mathcal{G}}_{jk}(\mathbf{x})\,\delta\mathbf{x},$$

$$(4.166a)$$

$$\mathbf{G}_k(\hat{\mathbf{x}}) = \mathbf{G}_k(\mathbf{x} + \delta\mathbf{x}) \approx \mathbf{G}_k(\mathbf{x}) + \sum_j \mathbf{1}_j\,\delta\mathbf{x}^T \boldsymbol{\mathcal{G}}_{jk}(\mathbf{x}), \qquad (4.166b)$$

where

$$\mathbf{g}_k(\mathbf{x}) = [g_{jk}(\mathbf{x})]_j, \quad \mathbf{G}_k(\mathbf{x}) = \frac{\partial \mathbf{g}_k(\mathbf{x})}{\partial \mathbf{x}}, \quad \boldsymbol{\mathcal{G}}_{jk} = \frac{\partial g_{jk}(\mathbf{x})}{\partial \mathbf{x}\partial \mathbf{x}^T}, \qquad (4.167)$$

and $\mathbf{1}_j$ is the jth column of the identity matrix. We have indicated whether each Jacobian/Hessian is evaluated at $\mathbf{x}$ (the true state) or $\hat{\mathbf{x}}$ (our estimate). In this section, the quantity $\delta\mathbf{x} = \hat{\mathbf{x}} - \mathbf{x}$ will be the difference between our estimate and the true state on a given trial. Each time we change the measurement noise, we will get a different value for the estimate and hence $\delta\mathbf{x}$. We will seek an expression for the expected value of this difference, $E[\delta\mathbf{x}]$, over all possible realizations of the measurement noise; this represents the systematic error or *bias*.

As discussed above, after convergence of Gauss–Newton, the estimate, $\hat{\mathbf{x}}$, will satisfy the following optimality criterion:

$$\sum_k \mathbf{G}_k(\hat{\mathbf{x}})^T \mathbf{R}_k^{-1}\left(\mathbf{y}_k - \mathbf{g}_k(\hat{\mathbf{x}})\right) = \mathbf{0}, \qquad (4.168)$$

or

$$\sum_k \left(\mathbf{G}_k(\mathbf{x}) + \sum_j \mathbf{1}_j\,\delta\mathbf{x}^T \boldsymbol{\mathcal{G}}_{jk}(\mathbf{x})\right)^T \mathbf{R}_k^{-1}$$

$$\times \left(\underbrace{\mathbf{y}_k - \mathbf{g}_k(\mathbf{x})}_{\mathbf{n}_k} - \mathbf{G}_k(\mathbf{x})\,\delta\mathbf{x} - \frac{1}{2}\sum_j \mathbf{1}_j\,\delta\mathbf{x}^T \boldsymbol{\mathcal{G}}_{jk}(\mathbf{x})\,\delta\mathbf{x}\right) \approx \mathbf{0}, \quad (4.169)$$

after substituting (4.166a) and (4.166b). We will assume that $\delta\mathbf{x}$ has up to quadratic dependence[11] on the stacked noise variable, $\mathbf{n} \sim \mathcal{N}(\mathbf{0}, \mathbf{R})$:

$$\delta\mathbf{x} = \mathbf{A}(\mathbf{x})\,\mathbf{n} + \mathbf{b}(\mathbf{n}), \qquad (4.170)$$

where $\mathbf{A}(\mathbf{x})$ is an unknown coefficient matrix and $\mathbf{b}(\mathbf{n})$ is an unknown quadratic function of $\mathbf{n}$. We will use $\mathbf{P}_k$, a projection matrix, to extract the kth noise variable from the stacked version: $\mathbf{n}_k = \mathbf{P}_k\mathbf{n}$. Substituting (4.170), we have that

$$\sum_k \left(\mathbf{G}_k(\mathbf{x}) + \sum_j \mathbf{1}_j\,(\mathbf{A}(\mathbf{x})\,\mathbf{n} + \mathbf{b}(\mathbf{n}))^T \boldsymbol{\mathcal{G}}_{jk}(\mathbf{x})\right)^T$$

$$\times \mathbf{R}_k^{-1}\left(\mathbf{P}_k\,\mathbf{n} - \mathbf{G}_k(\mathbf{x})\,(\mathbf{A}(\mathbf{x})\,\mathbf{n} + \mathbf{b}(\mathbf{n}))\right.$$

$$\left. - \frac{1}{2}\sum_j \mathbf{1}_j\,(\mathbf{A}(\mathbf{x})\,\mathbf{n} + \mathbf{b}(\mathbf{n}))^T \boldsymbol{\mathcal{G}}_{jk}(\mathbf{x})\,(\mathbf{A}(\mathbf{x})\,\mathbf{n} + \mathbf{b}(\mathbf{n}))\right) \approx \mathbf{0}. \quad (4.171)$$

---

[11] In reality, there are an infinite number of terms, so this expression is a big approximation but may work for mildly nonlinear observation models.

Multiplying out and keeping terms up to quadratic in $\mathbf{n}$, we have

$$\underbrace{\sum_k \mathbf{G}_k(\mathbf{x})^T \mathbf{R}_k^{-1} \left(\mathbf{P}_k - \mathbf{G}_k(\mathbf{x})\mathbf{A}(\mathbf{x}) \right) \mathbf{n}}_{\mathbf{L}\,\mathbf{n} \quad \text{(linear in } \mathbf{n})}$$

$$\underbrace{+ \sum_k \mathbf{G}_k(\mathbf{x})^T \mathbf{R}_k^{-1} \left(-\mathbf{G}_k(\mathbf{x})\,\mathbf{b}(\mathbf{n}) - \frac{1}{2} \sum_j \mathbf{1}_j \underbrace{\mathbf{n}^T \mathbf{A}(\mathbf{x})^T \boldsymbol{\mathcal{G}}_{jk}(\mathbf{x})\mathbf{A}(\mathbf{x})\,\mathbf{n}}_{\text{scalar}} \right)}_{\mathbf{q}_1(\mathbf{n}) \quad \text{(quadratic in } \mathbf{n})}$$

$$\underbrace{+ \sum_{j,k} \boldsymbol{\mathcal{G}}_{jk}(\mathbf{x})^T \mathbf{A}(\mathbf{x})\,\mathbf{n}\ \underbrace{\mathbf{1}_j^T \mathbf{R}_k^{-1} \left(\mathbf{P}_k - \mathbf{G}_k(\mathbf{x})\mathbf{A}(\mathbf{x}) \right) \mathbf{n}}_{\text{scalar}} \approx \mathbf{0}.}_{\mathbf{q}_2(\mathbf{n}) \quad \text{(quadratic in } \mathbf{n})} \qquad (4.172)$$

To make the expression identically zero (up to second order in $\mathbf{n}$),

$$\mathbf{L}\,\mathbf{n} + \mathbf{q}_1(\mathbf{n}) + \mathbf{q}_2(\mathbf{n}) = \mathbf{0}, \qquad (4.173)$$

we must have $\mathbf{L} = \mathbf{0}$. This follows by considering the case of the opposing sign of $\mathbf{n}$,

$$-\mathbf{L}\,\mathbf{n} + \mathbf{q}_1(-\mathbf{n}) + \mathbf{q}_2(-\mathbf{n}) = \mathbf{0}, \qquad (4.174)$$

and then noting that $\mathbf{q}_1(-\mathbf{n}) = \mathbf{q}_1(\mathbf{n})$ and $\mathbf{q}_2(-\mathbf{n}) = \mathbf{q}_2(\mathbf{n})$ owing to the quadratic nature of these terms. Subtracting the second case from the first, we have $2\,\mathbf{L}\,\mathbf{n} = \mathbf{0}$, and since $\mathbf{n}$ can take on any value, it follows that $\mathbf{L} = \mathbf{0}$ and thus

$$\mathbf{A}(\mathbf{x}) = \mathbf{W}(\mathbf{x})^{-1} \sum_k \mathbf{G}_k(\mathbf{x})^T \mathbf{R}_k^{-1} \mathbf{P}_k, \qquad (4.175)$$

where

$$\mathbf{W}(\mathbf{x}) = \sum_k \mathbf{G}_k(\mathbf{x})^T \mathbf{R}_k^{-1} \mathbf{G}_k(\mathbf{x}). \qquad (4.176)$$

Choosing this value for $\mathbf{A}(\mathbf{x})$ and taking the expectation (over all values of $\mathbf{n}$), we are left with

$$E\left[\mathbf{q}_1(\mathbf{n})\right] + E\left[\mathbf{q}_2(\mathbf{n})\right] = \mathbf{0}. \qquad (4.177)$$

Fortunately, it turns out that $E\left[\mathbf{q}_2(\mathbf{n})\right] = \mathbf{0}$. To see this, we need two identities:

$$\mathbf{A}(\mathbf{x})\mathbf{R}\mathbf{A}(\mathbf{x})^T \equiv \mathbf{W}(\mathbf{x})^{-1}, \qquad (4.178\text{a})$$

$$\mathbf{A}(\mathbf{x})\mathbf{R}\mathbf{P}_k^T \equiv \mathbf{W}(\mathbf{x})^{-1}\mathbf{G}_k(\mathbf{x})^T. \qquad (4.178\text{b})$$

The proofs of these are left to the reader. We then have

$$
\begin{aligned}
E\left[\mathbf{q}_2(\mathbf{n})\right] &= E\left[\sum_{j,k} \boldsymbol{\mathcal{G}}_{jk}(\mathbf{x})^T \mathbf{A}(\mathbf{x})\, \mathbf{n}\, \mathbf{1}_j^T \mathbf{R}_k^{-1}\left(\mathbf{P}_k - \mathbf{G}_k(\mathbf{x})\mathbf{A}(\mathbf{x})\right)\mathbf{n}\right] \\
&= \sum_{j,k} \boldsymbol{\mathcal{G}}_{jk}(\mathbf{x})^T \mathbf{A}(\mathbf{x}) \underbrace{E\left[\mathbf{n}\,\mathbf{n}^T\right]}_{\mathbf{R}} \left(\mathbf{P}_k^T - \mathbf{A}(\mathbf{x})^T \mathbf{G}_k(\mathbf{x})^T\right) \mathbf{R}_k^{-1}\, \mathbf{1}_j \\
&= \sum_{j,k} \boldsymbol{\mathcal{G}}_{jk}(\mathbf{x})^T \left(\underbrace{\mathbf{A}(\mathbf{x})\mathbf{R}\mathbf{P}_k^T}_{\mathbf{W}(\mathbf{x})^{-1}\mathbf{G}_k(\mathbf{x})^T} - \underbrace{\mathbf{A}(\mathbf{x})\mathbf{R}\mathbf{A}(\mathbf{x})^T}_{\mathbf{W}(\mathbf{x})^{-1}} \mathbf{G}_k(\mathbf{x})^T \right) \mathbf{R}_k^{-1}\, \mathbf{1}_j \\
&= \mathbf{0},
\end{aligned}
\tag{4.179}
$$

where we have employed the preceding identities. We are thus left with

$$
E\left[\mathbf{q}_1(\mathbf{n})\right] = \mathbf{0},
\tag{4.180}
$$

or

$$
\begin{aligned}
&E[\mathbf{b}(\mathbf{n})] \\
&= -\frac{1}{2}\mathbf{W}(\mathbf{x})^{-1} \sum_k \mathbf{G}_k(\mathbf{x})^T \mathbf{R}_k^{-1} \sum_j \mathbf{1}_j\, E\left[\mathbf{n}^T \mathbf{A}(\mathbf{x})^T \boldsymbol{\mathcal{G}}_{jk}(\mathbf{x})\, \mathbf{A}(\mathbf{x})\, \mathbf{n}\right] \\
&= -\frac{1}{2}\mathbf{W}(\mathbf{x})^{-1} \sum_k \mathbf{G}_k(\mathbf{x})^T \mathbf{R}_k^{-1} \sum_j \mathbf{1}_j\, E\left[\mathrm{tr}\left(\boldsymbol{\mathcal{G}}_{jk}(\mathbf{x})\, \mathbf{A}(\mathbf{x})\, \mathbf{n}\, \mathbf{n}^T \mathbf{A}(\mathbf{x})^T\right)\right] \\
&= -\frac{1}{2}\mathbf{W}(\mathbf{x})^{-1} \sum_k \mathbf{G}_k(\mathbf{x})^T \mathbf{R}_k^{-1} \sum_j \mathbf{1}_j\, \mathrm{tr}\big(\boldsymbol{\mathcal{G}}_{jk}(\mathbf{x})\, \mathbf{A}(\mathbf{x})\, \underbrace{E\left[\mathbf{n}\,\mathbf{n}^T\right]}_{\mathbf{R}}\, \mathbf{A}(\mathbf{x})^T\big) \\
&\qquad\qquad\qquad\qquad\qquad\qquad\qquad\qquad\qquad \underbrace{\phantom{\boldsymbol{\mathcal{G}}_{jk}(\mathbf{x})\, \mathbf{A}(\mathbf{x})\, E[nn]\, A}}_{\mathbf{W}(\mathbf{x})^{-1}} \\
&= -\frac{1}{2}\mathbf{W}(\mathbf{x})^{-1} \sum_k \mathbf{G}_k(\mathbf{x})^T \mathbf{R}_k^{-1} \sum_j \mathbf{1}_j\, \mathrm{tr}\big(\boldsymbol{\mathcal{G}}_{jk}(\mathbf{x})\, \mathbf{W}(\mathbf{x})^{-1}\big),
\end{aligned}
\tag{4.181}
$$

where $\mathrm{tr}(\cdot)$ indicates the trace of a matrix. Looking back to (4.170), we see that

$$
E[\delta\mathbf{x}] = \mathbf{A}(\mathbf{x})\, \underbrace{E[\mathbf{n}]}_{\mathbf{0}} + E[\mathbf{b}(\mathbf{n})],
\tag{4.182}
$$

and so our final expression for the systematic part of the bias is

$$
E[\delta\mathbf{x}] = -\frac{1}{2}\mathbf{W}(\mathbf{x})^{-1} \sum_k \mathbf{G}_k(\mathbf{x})^T \mathbf{R}_k^{-1} \sum_j \mathbf{1}_j\, \mathrm{tr}\big(\boldsymbol{\mathcal{G}}_{jk}(\mathbf{x})\, \mathbf{W}(\mathbf{x})^{-1}\big).
\tag{4.183}
$$

To use this expression in operation, we will need to substitute our estimate, $\hat{\mathbf{x}}$, in place of $\mathbf{x}$ when computing (4.183). Then we can update our estimate according to

$$
\hat{\mathbf{x}} \leftarrow \hat{\mathbf{x}} - E[\delta\mathbf{x}],
\tag{4.184}
$$

to subtract off the bias. Note that this expression is only approximate and may only work well in mildly nonlinear situations.

Figure 4.17
Comparison of the
iterative schemes
used in various
estimation
paradigms.

Gauss–Newton iterates over the entire trajectory, but runs offline and not in constant time

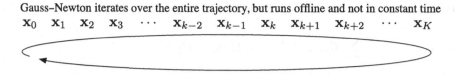

Sliding-window filters iterate over several timesteps at once, run online and in constant time

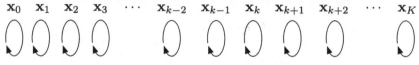

IEKF iterates at only one timestep at a time, but runs online and in constant time

4.3.4 Sliding-Window Filters

If we think of the EKF as an approximation of the full nonlinear Gauss–Newton (or even Newton) method applied to our estimation problem, we can see that it is really quite inferior, mainly because it does not iterate to convergence. The Jacobians are evaluated only once (at the best estimate so far). In truth, the EKF can do better than just one iteration of Gauss–Newton because the EKF does not evaluate all the Jacobians at once, but the lack of iteration is its main downfall. This is obvious from an optimization perspective; we need to iterate to converge. However, the EKF was originally derived from the Bayes filter earlier in this chapter, which applied the Markov property to achieve its recursive form. Once approximations are introduced in the form of a Gaussian assumption or linearization, the validity of assuming the Markov property holds is questionable. The problem with this application of the Markov propoerty is that once it is built into the estimator, we cannot get rid of it. It is a fundamental constraint that cannot be overcome.

There have been many attempts to patch the EKF, including the Iterated EKF described earlier in this chapter. However, for very nonlinear systems, these may not help much. The problem with the IEKF is that it still clings to the assumption that the Markov property holds. It is iterating at a single timestep, not over the whole trajectory at once. The difference between Gauss–Newton and the IEKF can be seen plainly in Figure 4.17.

Batch estimation via the Gauss–Newton method has its own problems. In particular, it must be run offline and is not a constant-time algorithm, whereas the EKF is both online and a constant-time method. So-called *sliding-window filters (SWFs)* (Sibley, 2006) seek the best of both worlds by iterating over a window of timesteps and sliding this window along to allow for online/constant-time implementation. When viewed from an optimization perspective, it is hard to imagine that SWFs do not offer a drastic improvement over the EKF and its variants. We will provide a sketch of how SWFs work.

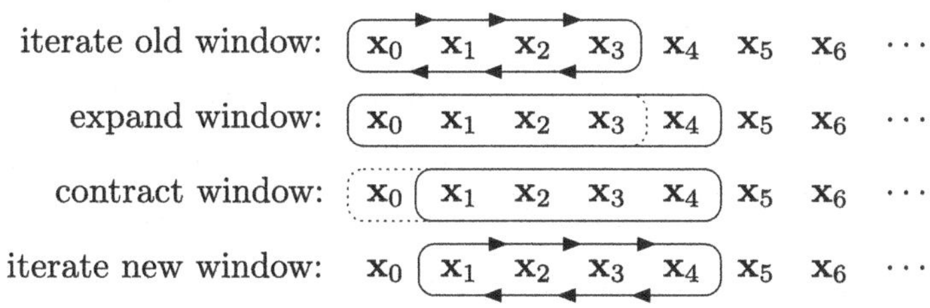

iterate old window: $\boxed{\mathbf{x}_0 \quad \mathbf{x}_1 \quad \mathbf{x}_2 \quad \mathbf{x}_3} \quad \mathbf{x}_4 \quad \mathbf{x}_5 \quad \mathbf{x}_6 \quad \cdots$

expand window: $\boxed{\mathbf{x}_0 \quad \mathbf{x}_1 \quad \mathbf{x}_2 \quad \mathbf{x}_3 \ \vdots \ \mathbf{x}_4} \quad \mathbf{x}_5 \quad \mathbf{x}_6 \quad \cdots$

contract window: $\mathbf{x}_0 \boxed{\mathbf{x}_1 \quad \mathbf{x}_2 \quad \mathbf{x}_3 \quad \mathbf{x}_4} \quad \mathbf{x}_5 \quad \mathbf{x}_6 \quad \cdots$

iterate new window: $\mathbf{x}_0 \boxed{\mathbf{x}_1 \quad \mathbf{x}_2 \quad \mathbf{x}_3 \quad \mathbf{x}_4} \quad \mathbf{x}_5 \quad \mathbf{x}_6 \quad \cdots$

Figure 4.18
Example of a SWF
sliding its window
along.

For the purpose of illustration, suppose that we have a window size of four. Figure 4.18 shows the procedure for sliding the window along. We start by setting up a small batch estimation problem in the usual way for the initial window and iterate it to convergence. We then temporarily expand the window size by one on the right to include the next timestep, followed by a contraction by one timestep on the left to keep the window size constant. We iterate the new window to convergence and continue to repeatedly slide along. Typically, the leftmost estimated state is output from the algorithm before the window slides, but this is not the only possibility.

Using the notation from Section 4.3.1, the batch estimation equations for the initial window will be of the form

$$
\underbrace{\begin{bmatrix} \mathbf{A}_{00} & \mathbf{A}_{10}^T & & \\ \mathbf{A}_{10} & \mathbf{A}_{11} & \mathbf{A}_{21}^T & \\ & \mathbf{A}_{21} & \mathbf{A}_{22} & \mathbf{A}_{32}^T \\ & & \mathbf{A}_{32} & \mathbf{A}_{33} \end{bmatrix}}_{\mathbf{H}^T \mathbf{W}^{-1} \mathbf{H}} \underbrace{\begin{bmatrix} \delta\mathbf{x}_0^\star \\ \delta\mathbf{x}_1^\star \\ \delta\mathbf{x}_2^\star \\ \delta\mathbf{x}_3^\star \end{bmatrix}}_{\delta\mathbf{x}^\star} = \underbrace{\begin{bmatrix} \mathbf{b}_0 \\ \mathbf{b}_1 \\ \mathbf{b}_2 \\ \mathbf{b}_3 \end{bmatrix}}_{\mathbf{H}^T \mathbf{W}^{-1} \mathbf{e}}, \tag{4.185}
$$

where the $\mathbf{A}_{k\ell}$ and $\mathbf{b}_k$ blocks are dependent on the current estimate for the trajectory in the window, $\mathbf{x}_{\mathrm{op}} = \begin{bmatrix} \mathbf{x}_{\mathrm{op},0}^T & \mathbf{x}_{\mathrm{op},1}^T & \mathbf{x}_{\mathrm{op},2}^T & \mathbf{x}_{\mathrm{op},3}^T \end{bmatrix}^T$. We iterate this small batch problem to convergence.

Expanding the window is fairly easy. We increase the state to include the next timestep and incorporate the latest input and measurement so that our batch equations become

$$
\underbrace{\left[\begin{array}{c|ccccc} \mathbf{A}_{00} & \mathbf{A}_{10}^T & & & \\ \hline \mathbf{A}_{10} & \mathbf{A}_{11} & \mathbf{A}_{21}^T & & \\ & \mathbf{A}_{21} & \mathbf{A}_{22} & \mathbf{A}_{32}^T & \\ & & \mathbf{A}_{32} & \mathbf{A}_{33} & \mathbf{A}_{43}^T \\ & & & \mathbf{A}_{43} & \mathbf{A}_{44} \end{array}\right]}_{\mathbf{H}^T \mathbf{W}^{-1} \mathbf{H}} \underbrace{\left[\begin{array}{c} \delta\mathbf{x}_0^\star \\ \delta\mathbf{x}_1^\star \\ \delta\mathbf{x}_2^\star \\ \delta\mathbf{x}_3^\star \\ \delta\mathbf{x}_4^\star \end{array}\right]}_{\delta\mathbf{x}^\star} = \underbrace{\left[\begin{array}{c} \mathbf{b}_0 \\ \mathbf{b}_1 \\ \mathbf{b}_2 \\ \mathbf{b}_3 \\ \mathbf{b}_4 \end{array}\right]}_{\mathbf{H}^T \mathbf{W}^{-1} \mathbf{e}}, \tag{4.186}
$$

where the partition lines now indicate the portions we would like to remove in order to contract the window back to the desired size. Blocks $\mathbf{A}_{44}$, $\mathbf{A}_{43}$, and $\mathbf{b}_4$ are new while $\mathbf{A}_{33}$ and $\mathbf{b}_3$ must be updated from the previous window.

Naively, we could contract the window by simply deleting all the rows and columns in the batch equations related to the first state, $\mathbf{x}_0$, to produce

$$\underbrace{\begin{bmatrix} \mathbf{A}_{11} & \mathbf{A}_{21}^T & & \\ \mathbf{A}_{21} & \mathbf{A}_{22} & \mathbf{A}_{32}^T & \\ & \mathbf{A}_{32} & \mathbf{A}_{33} & \mathbf{A}_{43}^T \\ & & \mathbf{A}_{43} & \mathbf{A}_{44} \end{bmatrix}}_{\mathbf{H}^T\mathbf{W}^{-1}\mathbf{H}} \underbrace{\begin{bmatrix} \delta\mathbf{x}_1^\star \\ \delta\mathbf{x}_2^\star \\ \delta\mathbf{x}_3^\star \\ \delta\mathbf{x}_4^\star \end{bmatrix}}_{\delta\mathbf{x}^\star} = \underbrace{\begin{bmatrix} \mathbf{b}_1 \\ \mathbf{b}_2 \\ \mathbf{b}_3 \\ \mathbf{b}_4 \end{bmatrix}}_{\mathbf{H}^T\mathbf{W}^{-1}\mathbf{e}}. \tag{4.187}$$

However, this is not the best thing to do, as we are throwing away useful information. For example, the initial state knowledge no longer factors into the solution.

A better approach is to view the batch solution as a joint Gaussian density over the whole window and to *marginalize* out the state we no longer want to keep. This is very similar to the Kalman filter derivation in Section 3.3.2, only now we are keeping around a larger window as we are working with a nonlinear system. Section 2.2.5 explained how to compute the marginals of a joint Gaussian. Here our Gaussian is expressed in *information form* (see Section 2.2.4) since $\mathbf{H}^T\mathbf{W}^{-1}\mathbf{H}$ is an information matrix and $\mathbf{H}^T\mathbf{W}^{-1}\mathbf{e}$ is an information vector. Marginalizing out $\mathbf{x}_0$ therefore results in

$$\underbrace{\begin{bmatrix} \mathbf{A}_{11} - \mathbf{A}_{10}\mathbf{A}_{00}^{-1}\mathbf{A}_{10}^T & \mathbf{A}_{21}^T & & \\ \mathbf{A}_{21} & \mathbf{A}_{22} & \mathbf{A}_{32}^T & \\ & \mathbf{A}_{32} & \mathbf{A}_{33} & \mathbf{A}_{43}^T \\ & & \mathbf{A}_{43} & \mathbf{A}_{44} \end{bmatrix}}_{\mathbf{H}^T\mathbf{W}^{-1}\mathbf{H}} \underbrace{\begin{bmatrix} \delta\mathbf{x}_1^\star \\ \delta\mathbf{x}_2^\star \\ \delta\mathbf{x}_3^\star \\ \delta\mathbf{x}_4^\star \end{bmatrix}}_{\delta\mathbf{x}^\star} = \underbrace{\begin{bmatrix} \mathbf{b}_1 - \mathbf{A}_{10}\mathbf{A}_{00}^{-1}\mathbf{b}_0 \\ \mathbf{b}_2 \\ \mathbf{b}_3 \\ \mathbf{b}_4 \end{bmatrix}}_{\mathbf{H}^T\mathbf{W}^{-1}\mathbf{e}}.$$
$$\tag{4.188}$$

We see that as compared to (4.187), the blocks $\mathbf{A}_{00}$, $\mathbf{A}_{10}$, and $\mathbf{b}_0$ now still play a role in the solution. Thankfully, $\mathbf{H}^T\mathbf{W}^{-1}\mathbf{H}$ is still block-tridiagonal, meaning we can exploit the sparsity to make the solution more efficient even though the window size might not be large.

Since $\mathbf{x}_0$ is no longer in the window, it is held constant for the purpose of iterating the batch solution to convergence. Looking into the details of the blocks we have

$$\mathbf{A}_{00} = \check{\mathbf{P}}_0^{-1} + \mathbf{F}_0^T\mathbf{Q}_1'^{-1}\mathbf{F}_0 + \mathbf{G}_0^T\mathbf{R}_0'^{-1}\mathbf{G}_0, \quad \mathbf{A}_{10} = -\mathbf{Q}_1'^{-1}\mathbf{F}_0, \tag{4.189}$$

$$\mathbf{b}_0 = \check{\mathbf{P}}_0^{-1}\mathbf{e}_{v,0} - \mathbf{F}_0^T\mathbf{Q}_1'^{-1}\mathbf{e}_{v,1} + \mathbf{G}_0^T\mathbf{R}_0'^{-1}\mathbf{e}_{y,0}, \tag{4.190}$$

where the definitions of the symbols can be found in Section 4.3.1. The blocks $\mathbf{A}_{00}$ and $\mathbf{A}_{10}$ only depend on $\mathbf{x}_{\text{op},0}$, while $\mathbf{b}_0$ also has a dependence on $\mathbf{x}_{\text{op},1}$ through the error $\mathbf{e}_{v,1}$.

Since we have that

$$\mathbf{A}_{11} = \mathbf{Q}_1'^{-1} + \mathbf{F}_1^T\mathbf{Q}_2'^{-1}\mathbf{F}_1 + \mathbf{G}_1^T\mathbf{R}_1'^{-1}\mathbf{G}_1, \tag{4.191}$$

we can notice that

$$\mathbf{A}_{11} - \mathbf{A}_{10}\mathbf{A}_{00}^{-1}\mathbf{A}_{10}^T = \check{\mathbf{P}}_1^{-1} + \mathbf{F}_1^T\mathbf{Q}_2'^{-1}\mathbf{F}_1 + \mathbf{G}_1^T\mathbf{R}_1'^{-1}\mathbf{G}_1, \tag{4.192}$$

where constant $\check{\mathbf{P}}_1^{-1} = \mathbf{Q}_1'^{-1} - \mathbf{A}_{10}\mathbf{A}_{00}^{-1}\mathbf{A}_{10}^T$ takes on the same role as $\check{\mathbf{P}}_0^{-1}$ (in $\mathbf{A}_{00}$) in the first window.

Similarly, since

$$\mathbf{b}_1 = \mathbf{Q}_1'^{-1}\mathbf{e}_{v,1} - \mathbf{F}_1^T\mathbf{Q}_2'^{-1}\mathbf{e}_{v,2} + \mathbf{G}_1^T\mathbf{R}_1'^{-1}\mathbf{e}_{y,1} \qquad (4.193)$$

we can notice that

$$\mathbf{b}_1 - \mathbf{A}_{10}\mathbf{A}_{00}^{-1}\mathbf{b}_0 = \mathbf{c}_1 + \check{\mathbf{P}}_1^{-1}\mathbf{e}_{v,1} - \mathbf{F}_1^T\mathbf{Q}_2'^{-1}\mathbf{e}_{v,2} + \mathbf{G}_1^T\mathbf{R}_1'^{-1}\mathbf{e}_{y,1}, \quad (4.194)$$

where $\mathbf{c}_1 + \check{\mathbf{P}}_1^{-1}\mathbf{e}_{v,1}$ takes on the same role that $\mathbf{c}_0 + \check{\mathbf{P}}_0^{-1}\mathbf{e}_{v,0}$ does (in $\mathbf{b}_0$, with $\mathbf{c}_0 = \mathbf{0}$) in the first window. The constant, $\mathbf{c}_1$, is given by

$$\mathbf{c}_1 = -\mathbf{A}_{10}\mathbf{A}_{00}^{-1}\left(\check{\mathbf{P}}_0^{-1}\mathbf{e}_{v,0} + \mathbf{G}_0^T\mathbf{R}_0'^{-1}\mathbf{e}_{y,0}\right). \qquad (4.195)$$

In general, after expansion and contraction our batch equations for the window at timestep k will be

$$\underbrace{\begin{bmatrix} \bar{\mathbf{A}}_{kk} & \mathbf{A}_{k+1,k}^T & & \\ \mathbf{A}_{k+1,k} & \mathbf{A}_{k+1,k+1} & \mathbf{A}_{k+2,k+1}^T & \\ & \mathbf{A}_{k+2,k+1} & \mathbf{A}_{k+2,k+2} & \mathbf{A}_{k+3,k+2}^T \\ & & \mathbf{A}_{k+3,k+2} & \mathbf{A}_{k+3,k+3} \end{bmatrix}}_{\mathbf{H}^T\mathbf{W}^{-1}\mathbf{H}} \underbrace{\begin{bmatrix} \delta\mathbf{x}_k^\star \\ \delta\mathbf{x}_{k+1}^\star \\ \delta\mathbf{x}_{k+2}^\star \\ \delta\mathbf{x}_{k+3}^\star \end{bmatrix}}_{\delta\mathbf{x}^\star} = \underbrace{\begin{bmatrix} \bar{\mathbf{b}}_k \\ \mathbf{b}_{k+1} \\ \mathbf{b}_{k+2} \\ \mathbf{b}_{k+3} \end{bmatrix}}_{\mathbf{H}^T\mathbf{W}^{-1}\mathbf{e}},$$
$$(4.196)$$

where the blocks $\bar{\mathbf{A}}_{kk}$ and $\bar{\mathbf{b}}_k$ are computed recursively as

$$\bar{\mathbf{A}}_{kk} = \check{\mathbf{P}}_k^{-1} + \mathbf{F}_k^T\mathbf{Q}_{k+1}'^{-1}\mathbf{F}_k + \mathbf{G}_k^T\mathbf{R}_k'^{-1}\mathbf{G}_k, \qquad (4.197\text{a})$$

$$\bar{\mathbf{b}}_k = \mathbf{c}_k + \check{\mathbf{P}}_k^{-1}\mathbf{e}_{v,k} - \mathbf{F}_k^T\mathbf{Q}_{k+1}'^{-1}\mathbf{e}_{v,k+1} + \mathbf{G}_k^T\mathbf{R}_k'^{-1}\mathbf{e}_{y,k}, \qquad (4.197\text{b})$$

$$\check{\mathbf{P}}_k^{-1} = \mathbf{Q}_k'^{-1} - \mathbf{Q}_k'^{-1}\mathbf{F}_{k-1}\bar{\mathbf{A}}_{k-1,k-1}^{-1}\mathbf{F}_{k-1}^T\mathbf{Q}_k'^{-1}, \qquad (4.197\text{c})$$

$$\mathbf{c}_k = \mathbf{Q}_k'^{-1}\mathbf{F}_{k-1}\bar{\mathbf{A}}_{k-1,k-1}^{-1}\left(\mathbf{c}_{k-1} + \check{\mathbf{P}}_{k-1}^{-1}\mathbf{e}_{v,k-1} + \mathbf{G}_{k-1}^T\mathbf{R}_{k-1}'^{-1}\mathbf{e}_{y,k-1}\right),$$
$$(4.197\text{d})$$

initialized in the first window with $\mathbf{c}_0 = \mathbf{0}$ and $\check{\mathbf{P}}_0^{-1}$, the provided initial information matrix. Notably, at timestep k the quantities $\mathbf{c}_k$ and $\check{\mathbf{P}}_k^{-1}$ are constant (with respect to the variables in the window) so that they need not be updated when iterating the window to convergence.

Once the batch equations are constructed for the new window, we iterate these to convergence, output the converged state estimate for the earliest time in the window, slide the window along, and repeat. Outputting the converged state estimate at the first time gives the benefit of future information being incorporated but does introduce some latency. If latency is of concern, the estimate can be taken from a later point in the window.

The most important thing is that we are iterating over more than one timestep. We only lock in the operating points of linearizations that have exited the window, which allows us to converge to something closer to the full batch solution than the Iterated EKF. The IEKF is actually similar to a SWF of window size one, but it only iterates the correction step while our derivation in this section iterates both the prediction and correction steps over a window of any size.

4.4 Batch Continuous-Time Estimation

We saw in the previous chapter how to handle continuous-time priors through Gaussian process regression. Our priors were generated by linear stochastic differential equations of the form

$$\dot{\mathbf{x}}(t) = \mathbf{A}(t)\mathbf{x}(t) + \mathbf{v}(t) + \mathbf{L}(t)\mathbf{w}(t), \tag{4.198}$$

with

$$\mathbf{w}(t) \sim \mathcal{GP}(\mathbf{0}, \mathbf{Q}\,\delta(t - t')), \tag{4.199}$$

and $\mathbf{Q}$ the usual power spectral density matrix.

In this section, we show how we can extend our results to nonlinear, continuous-time motion models of the form

$$\dot{\mathbf{x}}(t) = \mathbf{f}(\mathbf{x}(t), \mathbf{v}(t), \mathbf{w}(t), t), \tag{4.200}$$

where $\mathbf{f}(\cdot)$ is a nonlinear function. We will still receive observations at discrete times,

$$\mathbf{y}_k = \mathbf{g}(\mathbf{x}(t_k), \mathbf{n}_k, t), \tag{4.201}$$

where $\mathbf{g}(\cdot)$ is a nonlinear function and

$$\mathbf{n}_k \sim \mathcal{N}(\mathbf{0}, \mathbf{R}_k). \tag{4.202}$$

We will begin by linearizing both models and constructing their lifted forms, then carry out *Gaussian process (GP)* regression (Bayesian inference). See Anderson et al. (2015) for applications of this section.

4.4.1 Motion Model

We will linearize the motion model about an operating point, $\mathbf{x}_{\mathrm{op}}(t)$, which we note is an entire continuous-time trajectory. We will then construct our motion prior (mean and covariance) in lifted form at the measurement times.

Linearization

Linearizing our motion model about this trajectory, we have

$$
\begin{aligned}
\dot{\mathbf{x}}(t) &= \mathbf{f}(\mathbf{x}(t), \mathbf{v}(t), \mathbf{w}(t), t) \\
&\approx \mathbf{f}(\mathbf{x}_{\mathrm{op}}(t), \mathbf{v}(t), \mathbf{0}, t) + \left.\frac{\partial \mathbf{f}}{\partial \mathbf{x}}\right|_{\mathbf{x}_{\mathrm{op}}(t),\mathbf{v}(t),\mathbf{0},t} (\mathbf{x}(t) - \mathbf{x}_{\mathrm{op}}(t)) \\
&\quad + \left.\frac{\partial \mathbf{f}}{\partial \mathbf{w}}\right|_{\mathbf{x}_{\mathrm{op}}(t),\mathbf{v}(t),\mathbf{0},t} \mathbf{w}(t) \\
&= \underbrace{\mathbf{f}(\mathbf{x}_{\mathrm{op}}(t), \mathbf{v}(t), \mathbf{0}, t) - \left.\frac{\partial \mathbf{f}}{\partial \mathbf{x}}\right|_{\mathbf{x}_{\mathrm{op}}(t),\mathbf{v}(t),\mathbf{0},t} \mathbf{x}_{\mathrm{op}}(t)}_{\boldsymbol{\nu}(t)} \\
&\quad + \underbrace{\left.\frac{\partial \mathbf{f}}{\partial \mathbf{x}}\right|_{\mathbf{x}_{\mathrm{op}}(t),\mathbf{v}(t),\mathbf{0},t}}_{\mathbf{F}(t)} \mathbf{x}(t) + \underbrace{\left.\frac{\partial \mathbf{f}}{\partial \mathbf{w}}\right|_{\mathbf{x}_{\mathrm{op}}(t),\mathbf{v}(t),\mathbf{0},t}}_{\mathbf{L}(t)} \mathbf{w}(t),
\end{aligned} \tag{4.203}
$$

where $\boldsymbol{\nu}(t)$, $\mathbf{F}(t)$, and $\mathbf{L}(t)$ are now known functions of time (since $\mathbf{x}_{\mathrm{op}}(t)$ is known). Thus, approximately, our process model is of the form

$$\dot{\mathbf{x}}(t) \approx \mathbf{F}(t)\mathbf{x}(t) + \boldsymbol{\nu}(t) + \mathbf{L}(t)\mathbf{w}(t). \qquad (4.204)$$

Thus, after linearization, this is in the *linear time-varying (LTV)* form we studied in the linear-Gaussian chapter.

Mean and Covariance Functions

Since the SDE for the motion model is approximately in the LTV form studied earlier, we can go ahead and write

$$\mathbf{x}(t) \sim \mathcal{GP}\bigg(\underbrace{\boldsymbol{\Phi}(t, t_0)\check{\mathbf{x}}_0 + \int_{t_0}^{t} \boldsymbol{\Phi}(t, s)\boldsymbol{\nu}(s)\, ds}_{\check{\mathbf{x}}(t)},$$

$$\underbrace{\boldsymbol{\Phi}(t, t_0)\check{\mathbf{P}}_0\boldsymbol{\Phi}(t', t_0)^T + \int_{t_0}^{\min(t, t')} \boldsymbol{\Phi}(t, s)\mathbf{L}(s)\mathbf{Q}\mathbf{L}(s)^T\boldsymbol{\Phi}(t', s)^T\, ds}_{\check{\mathbf{P}}(t, t')} \bigg),$$

$$(4.205)$$

where $\boldsymbol{\Phi}(t, s)$ is the transition function associated with $\mathbf{F}(t)$. At the measurement times, $t_0 < t_1 < \cdots < t_K$, we can also then write

$$\mathbf{x} \sim \mathcal{N}(\check{\mathbf{x}}, \check{\mathbf{P}}) = \mathcal{N}\left(\mathbf{F}\boldsymbol{\nu}, \mathbf{F}\mathbf{Q}'\mathbf{F}^T \right), \qquad (4.206)$$

for the usual lifted form of the prior where

$$\mathbf{F} = \begin{bmatrix} \mathbf{1} & & & & & \\ \boldsymbol{\Phi}(t_1, t_0) & \mathbf{1} & & & & \\ \boldsymbol{\Phi}(t_2, t_0) & \boldsymbol{\Phi}(t_2, t_1) & \mathbf{1} & & & \\ \vdots & \vdots & \vdots & \ddots & & \\ \boldsymbol{\Phi}(t_{K-1}, t_0) & \boldsymbol{\Phi}(t_{K-1}, t_1) & \boldsymbol{\Phi}(t_{K-1}, t_2) & \cdots & \mathbf{1} & \\ \boldsymbol{\Phi}(t_K, t_0) & \boldsymbol{\Phi}(t_K, t_1) & \boldsymbol{\Phi}(t_K, t_2) & \cdots & \boldsymbol{\Phi}(t_K, t_{K-1}) & \mathbf{1} \end{bmatrix},$$

$$(4.207a)$$

$$\boldsymbol{\nu} = \begin{bmatrix} \check{\mathbf{x}}_0 \\ \boldsymbol{\nu}_1 \\ \vdots \\ \boldsymbol{\nu}_K \end{bmatrix}, \qquad (4.207b)$$

$$\boldsymbol{\nu}_k = \int_{t_{k-1}}^{t_k} \boldsymbol{\Phi}(t_k, s)\boldsymbol{\nu}(s)\, ds, \qquad k = 1 \ldots K, \qquad (4.207c)$$

$$\mathbf{Q}' = \mathrm{diag}\left(\check{\mathbf{P}}_0, \mathbf{Q}'_1, \mathbf{Q}'_2, \ldots, \mathbf{Q}'_K \right), \qquad (4.207d)$$

$$\mathbf{Q}'_k = \int_{t_{k-1}}^{t_k} \boldsymbol{\Phi}(t_k, s)\mathbf{L}(s)\mathbf{Q}\mathbf{L}(s)^T\boldsymbol{\Phi}(t_k, s)^T\, ds, \qquad k = 1 \ldots K. \qquad (4.207e)$$

Unfortunately, we have a bit of a problem. To compute $\check{\mathbf{x}}$ and $\check{\mathbf{P}}$, we require an expression for $\mathbf{x}_{\mathrm{op}}(s)$ for all $s \in [t_0, t_M]$. This is because $\boldsymbol{\nu}(s)$, $\mathbf{F}(s)$ (through $\boldsymbol{\Phi}(t, s)$), and $\mathbf{L}(s)$ appear inside the integrals for $\check{\mathbf{x}}(t)$ and $\check{\mathbf{P}}(t, t')$, and these depend in turn on $\mathbf{x}_{\mathrm{op}}(s)$. If we are performing iterated GP regression, as discussed earlier, we will only have $\mathbf{x}_{\mathrm{op}}$ from the previous iteration, which is evaluated only at the measurement times.

Fortunately, the whole point of GP regression is that we can query the state at any time of interest. Moreover, we showed previously that this can be done very efficiently (i.e., $O(1)$ time) for our particular choice of process model:

$$\mathbf{x}_{\mathrm{op}}(s) = \check{\mathbf{x}}(s) + \check{\mathbf{P}}(s)\check{\mathbf{P}}^{-1}(\mathbf{x}_{\mathrm{op}} - \check{\mathbf{x}}). \tag{4.208}$$

Because we are making use of this inside an iterative process, we use the $\check{\mathbf{x}}(s)$, $\check{\mathbf{P}}(s)$, $\check{\mathbf{x}}$, and $\check{\mathbf{P}}$ from the previous iteration to evaluate this expression.

The biggest challenge will be to identify $\boldsymbol{\Phi}(t, s)$, which is problem specific. As we will already be carrying out numerical integration in our scheme, we can compute the transition function numerically as well, via a normalized *fundamental matrix* (of control theory),[12] $\boldsymbol{\Upsilon}(t)$. In other words, we will integrate

$$\dot{\boldsymbol{\Upsilon}}(t) = \mathbf{F}(t)\boldsymbol{\Upsilon}(t), \quad \boldsymbol{\Upsilon}(0) = \mathbf{1}, \tag{4.209}$$

ensuring to save $\boldsymbol{\Upsilon}(t)$ at all the times of interest in our GP regression. The transition function is then given by

$$\boldsymbol{\Phi}(t, s) = \boldsymbol{\Upsilon}(t)\,\boldsymbol{\Upsilon}(s)^{-1}. \tag{4.210}$$

For specific systems, analytical expressions for the transition function will be possible.

4.4.2 Observation Model

The linearized observation model is

$$\mathbf{y}_k \approx \mathbf{g}\left(\mathbf{x}_{\mathrm{op},k}, \mathbf{0}\right) + \mathbf{G}_k\left(\mathbf{x}_k - \mathbf{x}_{\mathrm{op},k}\right) + \mathbf{n}'_k, \tag{4.211}$$

which can be written in lifted form as

$$\mathbf{y} = \mathbf{y}_{\mathrm{op}} + \mathbf{G}\left(\mathbf{x} - \mathbf{x}_{\mathrm{op}}\right) + \mathbf{n}', \tag{4.212}$$

where

$$\mathbf{y}_{\mathrm{op}} = \begin{bmatrix} \mathbf{g}(\mathbf{x}_{\mathrm{op},0}, \mathbf{0}) \\ \mathbf{g}(\mathbf{x}_{\mathrm{op},1}, \mathbf{0}) \\ \vdots \\ \mathbf{g}(\mathbf{x}_{\mathrm{op},K}, \mathbf{0}) \end{bmatrix}, \tag{4.213a}$$

$$\mathbf{G} = \mathrm{diag}\left(\mathbf{G}_0, \mathbf{G}_1, \mathbf{G}_2, \ldots, \mathbf{G}_K\right), \tag{4.213b}$$

$$\mathbf{R} = \mathrm{diag}\left(\mathbf{R}'_0, \mathbf{R}'_1, \mathbf{R}'_2, \ldots, \mathbf{R}'_K\right), \tag{4.213c}$$

---

[12] Not to be confused with the fundamental matrix of computer vision.

and $\mathbf{n}' \sim \mathcal{N}(\mathbf{0}, \mathbf{R}')$. It is fairly easy to see that

$$E\left[\mathbf{y}\right] = \mathbf{y}_{\text{op}} + \mathbf{G}\left(\check{\mathbf{x}} - \mathbf{x}_{\text{op}}\right), \quad (4.214\text{a})$$

$$E\left[(\mathbf{y} - E[\mathbf{y}])(\mathbf{y} - E[\mathbf{y}])^T\right] = \mathbf{G}\check{\mathbf{P}}\mathbf{G}^T + \mathbf{R}', \quad (4.214\text{b})$$

$$E\left[(\mathbf{y} - E[\mathbf{y}])(\mathbf{x} - E[\mathbf{x}])^T\right] = \mathbf{G}\check{\mathbf{P}}. \quad (4.214\text{c})$$

4.4.3 Bayesian Inference

With these quantities in hand, we can write a joint density for the lifted trajectory and measurements as

$$p(\mathbf{x}, \mathbf{y}|\mathbf{v}) = \mathcal{N}\left(\begin{bmatrix} \check{\mathbf{x}} \\ \mathbf{y}_{\text{op}} + \mathbf{G}\left(\check{\mathbf{x}} - \mathbf{x}_{\text{op}}\right) \end{bmatrix}, \begin{bmatrix} \check{\mathbf{P}} & \check{\mathbf{P}}\mathbf{G}^T \\ \mathbf{G}\check{\mathbf{P}} & \mathbf{G}\check{\mathbf{P}}\mathbf{G}^T + \mathbf{R}' \end{bmatrix}\right), \quad (4.215)$$

which is quite similar to the expression for the IEKF situation in (4.42), but now for the whole trajectory rather than just one timestep. Using the usual relationship from (2.52b), we can immediately write the Gaussian posterior as

$$p(\mathbf{x}|\mathbf{v}, \mathbf{y}) = \mathcal{N}\left(\hat{\mathbf{x}}, \hat{\mathbf{P}}\right), \quad (4.216)$$

where

$$\mathbf{K} = \check{\mathbf{P}}\mathbf{G}^T\left(\mathbf{G}\check{\mathbf{P}}\mathbf{G}^T + \mathbf{R}'\right)^{-1}, \quad (4.217\text{a})$$

$$\hat{\mathbf{P}} = (\mathbf{1} - \mathbf{K}\mathbf{G})\check{\mathbf{P}}, \quad (4.217\text{b})$$

$$\hat{\mathbf{x}} = \check{\mathbf{x}} + \mathbf{K}\left(\mathbf{y} - \mathbf{y}_{\text{op}} - \mathbf{G}(\check{\mathbf{x}} - \mathbf{x}_{\text{op}})\right). \quad (4.217\text{c})$$

Using the SMW identity from (2.124), we can rearrange the equation for the posterior mean to be

$$\left(\check{\mathbf{P}}^{-1} + \mathbf{G}^T\mathbf{R}'^{-1}\mathbf{G}\right)\delta\mathbf{x}^* = \check{\mathbf{P}}^{-1}\left(\check{\mathbf{x}} - \mathbf{x}_{\text{op}}\right) + \mathbf{G}^T\mathbf{R}'^{-1}\left(\mathbf{y} - \mathbf{y}_{\text{op}}\right), \quad (4.218)$$

where $\delta\mathbf{x}^* = \hat{\mathbf{x}} - \mathbf{x}_{\text{op}}$. Inserting the details of the prior, this becomes

$$\underbrace{\left(\mathbf{F}^{-T}\mathbf{Q}'^{-1}\mathbf{F}^{-1} + \mathbf{G}^T\mathbf{R}'^{-1}\mathbf{G}\right)}_{\text{block-tridiagonal}}\delta\mathbf{x}^*$$

$$= \mathbf{F}^{-T}\mathbf{Q}'^{-1}\left(\boldsymbol{\nu} - \mathbf{F}^{-1}\mathbf{x}_{\text{op}}\right) + \mathbf{G}^T\mathbf{R}'^{-1}\left(\mathbf{y} - \mathbf{y}_{\text{op}}\right). \quad (4.219)$$

This result is identical in form to the nonlinear, discrete-time batch solution discussed earlier in this chapter. The only difference is that we started with a continuous-time motion model and integrated it directly to evaluate the prior at the measurement times.

4.4.4 Summary

We summarize the steps needed to carry out GP regression with a nonlinear motion model and/or measurement model:

1. Start with an initial guess for the posterior mean over the whole trajectory, $\mathbf{x}_{op}(t)$. We will only need this over the whole trajectory to initialize the process. We will only be updating our estimate at the measurement times, $\mathbf{x}_{op}$, then using the GP interpolation to fill in the other times.

2. Calculate the $\boldsymbol{\nu}$, $\mathbf{F}^{-1}$, and $\mathbf{Q'}^{-1}$ for the new iteration. This will likely be done numerically and will involve determining $\boldsymbol{\nu}(s)$, $\mathbf{F}(s)$ (through $\boldsymbol{\Phi}(t, s)$), and $\mathbf{L}(s)$, which in turn will require $\mathbf{x}_{op}(s)$ and hence $\check{\mathbf{x}}(s)$, $\check{\mathbf{P}}(s)$, $\check{\mathbf{x}}$, $\check{\mathbf{P}}$ from the previous iteration to do the interpolation inside the required integrals.

3. Calculate the $\mathbf{y}_{op}$, $\mathbf{G}$, $\mathbf{R'}^{-1}$ for the new iteration.

4. Solve for $\delta\mathbf{x}^*$ in the following equation:

$$\underbrace{\left(\mathbf{F}^{-T}\mathbf{Q'}^{-1}\mathbf{F}^{-1} + \mathbf{G}^T\mathbf{R'}^{-1}\mathbf{G}\right)}_{\text{block-tridiagonal}} \delta\mathbf{x}^*$$

$$= \mathbf{F}^{-T}\mathbf{Q'}^{-1}\left(\boldsymbol{\nu} - \mathbf{F}^{-1}\mathbf{x}_{op}\right) + \mathbf{G}^T\mathbf{R'}^{-1}\left(\mathbf{y} - \mathbf{y}_{op}\right). \quad (4.220)$$

In practice, we will prefer to build only the non-zero blocks in the products of matrices that appear in this equation.

5. Update the guess at the measurement times using

$$\mathbf{x}_{op} \leftarrow \mathbf{x}_{op} + \delta\mathbf{x}^*, \quad (4.221)$$

and check for convergence. If not converged, return to Step 2. If converged, output $\hat{\mathbf{x}} = \mathbf{x}_{op}$.

6. If desired, compute the covariance at the measurement times, $\hat{\mathbf{P}}$.

7. Use the GP interpolation equation[13] also to compute the estimate at other times of interest, $\hat{\mathbf{x}}_\tau$, $\hat{\mathbf{P}}_{\tau\tau}$.

The most expensive step in this whole process is building $\boldsymbol{\nu}$, $\mathbf{F}^{-1}$, and $\mathbf{Q'}^{-1}$. However, the cost (at each iteration) will still be linear in the length of the trajectory and therefore should be manageable.

4.5 Summary

The main takeaway points from this chapter are as follows:

1. Unlike the linear-Gaussian case, the Bayesian posterior is not, in general, a Gaussian PDF when the motion and observation models are nonlinear and/or the measurement and process noises are non-Gaussian.

2. To carry out nonlinear estimation, some form of approximation is required. The different techniques vary in their choices of (i) how to approximate the posterior (Gaussian, mixture of Gaussians, set of samples), and (ii) how to approximately carry out inference (linearization, Monte Carlo, sigmapoint transformation) or MAP estimation.

---

[13] We did not work this out for the nonlinear case, but it should follow from the GP section in the linear-Gaussian chapter.

3. There are a variety of methods, both batch and recursive, that approximate the posterior as a Gaussian. Some of these methods, particularly the ones that iterate the solution (i.e., batch MAP, IEKF), converge to a 'mean' that is actually at the maximum of the Bayesian posterior (which is not the same as the true mean of the Bayesian posterior). This can be a point of confusion when comparing different methods since, depending on the approximations made, we may be asking the methods to find different answers.

4. Batch methods are able to iterate over the whole trajectory, whereas recursive methods can only iterate at one timestep at a time, meaning they will converge to different answers on most problems. Sliding-window filters are a compromise between classic recursive methods and full batch methods.

The next chapter will look briefly at how to handle estimator bias, measurement outliers, and data correspondences.

4.6 Exercises

4.1 Consider the discrete-time system,

$$\begin{bmatrix} x_k \\ y_k \\ \theta_k \end{bmatrix} = \begin{bmatrix} x_{k-1} \\ y_{k-1} \\ \theta_{k-1} \end{bmatrix} + T \begin{bmatrix} \cos\theta_{k-1} & 0 \\ \sin\theta_{k-1} & 0 \\ 0 & 1 \end{bmatrix} \left(\begin{bmatrix} v_k \\ \omega_k \end{bmatrix} + \mathbf{w}_k \right),$$

$$\mathbf{w}_k \sim \mathcal{N}(\mathbf{0}, \mathbf{Q}),$$

$$\begin{bmatrix} r_k \\ \phi_k \end{bmatrix} = \begin{bmatrix} \sqrt{x_k^2 + y_k^2} \\ \mathrm{atan2}(-y_k, -x_k) - \theta_k \end{bmatrix} + \mathbf{n}_k, \qquad \mathbf{n}_k \sim \mathcal{N}(\mathbf{0}, \mathbf{R}),$$

which could represent a mobile robot moving around on the xy-plane and measuring the range and bearing to the origin. Set up the EKF equations to estimate the pose of the mobile robot. In particular, work out expressions for the Jacobians, $\mathbf{F}_{k-1}$ and $\mathbf{G}_k$, and modified covariances, $\mathbf{Q}_k'$ and $\mathbf{R}_k'$.

4.2 Consider transforming the prior Gaussian density, $\mathcal{N}(\mu_x, \sigma_x^2)$, through the nonlinearity, $f(x) = x^3$. Use the Monte Carlo, linearization, and sigma-point methods to determine the transformed mean and covariance and comment on the results. Hint: use Isserlis' theorem to compute the higher-order Gaussian moments.

4.3 Consider transforming the prior Gaussian density, $\mathcal{N}(\mu_x, \sigma_x^2)$, through the nonlinearity, $f(x) = x^4$. Use the Monte Carlo, linearization, and sigma-point methods to determine the transformed mean (and optionally covariance) and comment on the results. Hint: use Isserlis' theorem to compute the higher-order Gaussian moments.

4.4 Consider the simplified (planar) stereo camera model shown in the following figure:

(i) Show that the camera model mapping the Euclidean feature coordinates to image coordinates can be written in the form

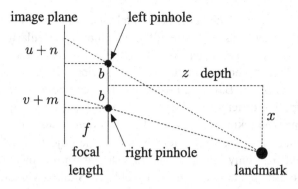

$$\begin{bmatrix} u \\ v \end{bmatrix} = \mathbf{K} \frac{1}{z} \begin{bmatrix} x \\ z \\ 1 \end{bmatrix} - \begin{bmatrix} n \\ m \end{bmatrix},$$

where $\mathbf{K}$ is a 2×3 camera matrix and $n, m \sim \mathcal{N}(0, \sigma^2)$ are independent left and right measurement noises. You must work out $\mathbf{K}$ explicitly.

(ii) Show that the inverse camera model can be written as

$$x = g(u + n, v + m) = b \frac{u + v + n + m}{u - v + n - m},$$

$$z = h(u + n, v + m) = 2fb \frac{1}{u - v + n - m},$$

where the measurement noise has been kept explicit.

(iii) Work out a linearized inverse camera model:

$$x \approx g(u, v) + \left. \frac{\partial g}{\partial u} \right|_{u,v} n + \left. \frac{\partial g}{\partial v} \right|_{u,v} m,$$

$$z \approx h(u, v) + \left. \frac{\partial h}{\partial u} \right|_{u,v} n + \left. \frac{\partial h}{\partial v} \right|_{u,v} m.$$

(iv) Using the linearized inverse camera model, show that

$$\begin{bmatrix} x \\ z \end{bmatrix} \sim \mathcal{N} \left(\underbrace{\frac{b}{u - v} \begin{bmatrix} u + v \\ 2f \end{bmatrix}}_{\text{mean}}, \underbrace{\frac{4b^2\sigma^2}{(u - v)^4} \begin{bmatrix} u^2 + v^2 & (u + v)f \\ (u + v)f & 2f^2 \end{bmatrix}}_{\text{covariance}} \right).$$

(v) Show that for a feature on the optical axis (i.e., $x = 0$), the uncertainties (i.e., standard deviations) in the depth (i.e., z) and lateral (i.e., x) directions are

$$\frac{1}{\sqrt{2}} \frac{z^2}{fb} \sigma \quad \text{and} \quad \frac{1}{\sqrt{2}} \frac{z}{f} \sigma,$$

respectively.

4.5 From the section on the sigmapoint Kalman filter, we learned that the measurement covariance could be written as

$$\boldsymbol{\Sigma}_{yy,k} = \sum_{j=0}^{2N} \beta_j \left(\check{\mathbf{y}}_{k,j} - \boldsymbol{\mu}_{y,k} \right) \left(\check{\mathbf{y}}_{k,j} - \boldsymbol{\mu}_{y,k} \right)^T + \mathbf{R}_k,$$

when the measurement model has linear dependence on the measurement noise. Verify that this can also be written as

$$\mathbf{\Sigma}_{yy,k} = \mathbf{Z}_k \mathbf{Z}_k^T + \mathbf{R}_k,$$

where

$$\mathrm{col}_j \mathbf{Z}_k = \sqrt{\beta_j} \left(\mathbf{\check{y}}_{k,j} - \boldsymbol{\mu}_{y,k} \right).$$

4.6 Show that the following two identities used in the section on ML bias estimation are true:

$$\mathbf{A}(\mathbf{x})\mathbf{R}\mathbf{A}(\mathbf{x})^T \equiv \mathbf{W}(\mathbf{x})^{-1},$$
$$\mathbf{A}(\mathbf{x})\mathbf{R}\mathbf{P}_k^T \equiv \mathbf{W}(\mathbf{x})^{-1}\mathbf{G}_k(\mathbf{x})^T.$$

4.7 Consider the following one-dimensional robot localization setup with just one landmark. There are odometry measurements, u_k, between each pair of positions, x_{k-1} and x_k, as well as landmark range measurements, y_k, from each position, x_k, to the known landmark at position, ℓ.

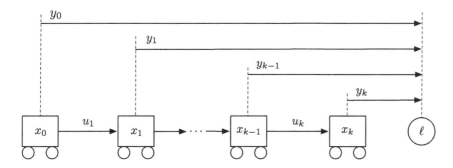

The motion and observation models for this setup are

$$\text{motion:} \quad x_k = h(x_{k-1}, u_k, w_k) = x_{k-1} + u_k + w_k,$$
$$\text{observation:} \quad y_k = g(x_k, \ell, n_k) = \ell - x_k + n_k,$$

where $w_k \sim \mathcal{N}(0, Q)$ and $n_k \sim \mathcal{N}(0, R)$. We will use the EKF to estimate the position of the robot as it moves. Let the estimate (mean and covariance) at time $k - 1$ be $\{\hat{x}_{k-1}, \hat{P}_{k-1}\}$.

(i) Show that after the prediction step of the EKF, our estimate is

$$\check{P}_k = \hat{P}_{k-1} + Q,$$
$$\check{x}_k = \hat{x}_{k-1} + u_k.$$

(ii) Show that the Kalman gain for this simple problem is

$$K_k = -\frac{\check{P}_k}{\check{P}_k + R}.$$

(iii) Show that the corrected estimate at time k is

$$\hat{P}_k = \frac{R}{\check{P}_k + R}\check{P}_k,$$

$$\hat{x}_k = \frac{R}{\check{P}_k + R}\check{x}_k + \frac{\check{P}_k}{\check{P}_k + R}(\ell - y_k).$$

(iv) We see that the expression for the corrected mean, $\hat{x}_k$, is just a weighted sum of the prediction, $\check{x}_k$, and the measured position, $\ell - y_k$. Explain what the weights chosen by the EKF are trying to do.

4.8   Consider the discrete-time system,

$$x_k = x_{k-1} + v_k + w_k, \qquad w_k \sim \mathcal{N}(0, Q),$$

$$y_k = \sqrt{x_k^2 + h^2} + n_k, \qquad n_k \sim \mathcal{N}(0, R),$$

which could represent a cart moving along the x-axis while measuring its distance to the top of a flagpole located at the origin with height, h. Take $h = 1$, $v_1 = v_2 = \cdots = v_k = 1$, $Q = 1$, and $R = 1/2$. We will use EKF to estimate the position of the cart.

(i) Fill in the unknown quantities at $k = 0$:

$$\check{P}_0 = 0, \quad \check{x}_0 = 0, \quad G_0 = ?, \quad K_0 = ?, \quad \hat{P}_0 = ?, \quad \hat{x}_0 = ?,$$

where G_k is the Jacobian of the measurement model with respect to the state, K_k is the Kalman gain, and take $y_0 = 1$ as the received measurement.

(ii) Fill in the unknown quantities at $k = 1$:

$$\check{P}_1 = ?, \quad \check{x}_1 = ?, \quad G_1 = ?, \quad K_1 = ?, \quad \hat{P}_1 = ?, \quad \hat{x}_1 = ?,$$

where $y_1 = \sqrt{2}$.

(iii) Fill in the unknown quantities at $k = 2$:

$$\check{P}_2 = ?, \quad \check{x}_2 = ?, \quad G_2 = ?, \quad K_2 = ?, \quad \hat{P}_2 = ?, \quad \hat{x}_2 = ?,$$

where $y_2 = \sqrt{6}$.

(iv) Comment on the trend of $\hat{P}_k$ in your results. If the cart moves far enough away from the flagpole what do you think will happen to $\hat{P}_k$?

5

Handling Nonidealities in Estimation

In the last chapter, we learned that our estimation machinery can be biased, particularly when our motion/observation models are nonlinear. In our simple stereo camera example, we saw that MAP estimation is biased with respect to the mean of the full posterior. We also saw that the batch ML method is biased with respect to the groundtruth and derived an expression to try to quantify that bias. Unfortunately, these are not the only sources of bias.

In many of our estimation techniques, we make the assumption that the noise corrupting the inputs or the measurements is zero-mean Gaussian. In reality, our inputs and/or measurements may also be corrupted with unknown biases. If we do not account for these, our estimate will also be biased. The classic example of this is the typical accelerometer, which can have temperature-dependent biases that change over time.

Another huge issue in many estimation problems is determining correspondences between measurements and a model. For example, if we are measuring the range to a landmark, we might assume we know which landmark is being measured. This is a very big assumption. Another good example is a star tracker, which detects points of lights; how do we know which point of light corresponds to which star in our star chart? The pairing of a measurement with a part of a model/map is termed *determining correspondences* or *data association*.

Finally, despite our best efforts to negate the effects of biases and find proper correspondences, something deleterious can always happen to our measurements so that we are stuck with a datum that is highly improbable according to our noise model; we call this an *outlier* measurement. If we do not properly detect and remove outliers, many of our estimation techniques will fail, often catastrophically.

This chapter will investigate how to deal with inputs/measurements that are not well behaved. It will present some of the classic tactics for handling these types of biases, determining correspondences, detecting/rejecting outliers, and estimating the covariances required in our estimators.

5.1 Estimator Performance

Before delving into some of the details around biases, correspondence, outliers, and covariances, it is worthwhile to discuss what properties we would like our estimator to have. Sections 3.3.6 and 4.1.2 already began this discussion, which

157

Figure 5.1 A typical
error plot used to
visualize estimator
performance. We
compare the
estimated state to the
true state over time
and also plot
uncertainty
envelopes, $\pm 3\sigma_k$,
derived from the
estimated
covariance.
Specifically,
$\sigma_k = \sqrt{\hat{P}_k}$ is the
square root of the
estimated variance
(i.e., the standard
deviation). We are
looking to see if the
error hovers around
zero (unbiased) and
stays mostly inside
the uncertainty
envelope
(consistent).

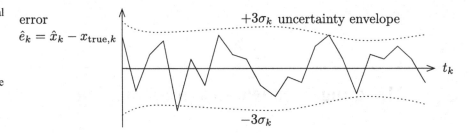

we now continue in more general terms. Our aim is to provide tangible means to evaluate an estimator's health.

5.1.1 Unbiased and Consistent

The two most fundamental properties that we would like our estimator to have are to be *unbiased* and *consistent*. Imagine that we have used one of the discrete-time estimators from the earlier chapters to produce a Gaussian estimate, $\mathcal{N}\left(\hat{x}_k, \hat{P}_k\right)$ for $k = 1 \ldots K$, where we note these are actually the marginals of the full-trajectory estimate at each timestep. Suppose we also have a source of groundtruth, the correct answer for our estimator at each timestep, $x_{\text{true},k}$. The single-timestep estimation error, $\hat{e}_k$, can be simply computed as

$$\hat{e}_k = \hat{x}_k - x_{\text{true},k}. \tag{5.1}$$

Figure 5.1 shows a typical error plot used to visualize the performance of an estimator over a single trajectory estimate. The error is plotted as well as an uncertainty envelope, which comes from the covariance that our estimator computes. Loosely, the estimator is *unbiased* if the error hovers around zero and it is *consistent* if the error (mostly) stays within the $3\sigma_k$ uncertainty envelope; σ_k, the standard deviation, is the square root of the estimated variance, $\hat{P}_k$. Our error should be within the $3\sigma_k$ uncertainty envelope 99.7 per cent of the time.

This brings up an important point. Ideally, we could do a large number of identical trials so that we could compute an average of the error over these many trials at each timestep. In practice, this is usually not possible and we satisfy ourselves by computing the average over all the timesteps instead of trials; this is sometimes referred to as the *ergodic hypothesis*.

While Figure 5.1 allows us to qualitatively determine if the estimator is unbiased and consistent, we can also be quantitative in this regard. For unbiased we require that

The *ergodic
hypothesis* states that
the average of a
process parameter
over time and the
average over the
statistical ensemble
(i.e., many trials) are
the same.

$$E[\hat{e}_k] = 0. \tag{5.2}$$

For consistent we require that

$$E\left[\hat{e}_k^2 / \hat{P}_k\right] = 1. \tag{5.3}$$

If our covariance estimate is a constant over all timesteps, $\hat{P}$, then consistency amounts to $E\left[\hat{e}_k^2\right] = \hat{P}$.

Of course, these relations will never hold exactly since we are using a finite amount of data, so we must use our judgement to determine if they hold well enough for our purpose. We can also use statistics to help in this regard. For example, the sample mean, $\hat{e}_{\text{mean}} = \frac{1}{K} \sum_{k=1}^{K} \hat{e}_k$, is itself a random variable and has the distribution

$$\hat{e}_{\text{mean}} \sim \mathcal{N}\left(\mu, \frac{\sigma^2}{K}\right), \tag{5.4}$$

where $\mu = E[\hat{e}_k]$ and $\sigma^2 = E\left[(\hat{e}_k - \hat{e}_{\text{mean}})^2\right]$ (assuming the errors, $\hat{e}_k$, are independent and normal). As the true variance of the errors, σ^2, is not known, we can substitute the sample variance (see Section 2.1.8)

$$\sigma^2 \approx \frac{1}{K-1} \sum_{k=1}^{K} (\hat{e}_k - \hat{e}_{\text{mean}})^2, \tag{5.5}$$

and then our criterion in (5.2) can be reformulated statistically as

$$Q_{\mathcal{N}(0,\sigma^2/K)}(\ell) \le \hat{e}_{\text{mean}} \le Q_{\mathcal{N}(0,\sigma^2/K)}(u), \tag{5.6}$$

where ℓ and u are lower and upper confidence bounds, respectively, and $Q_{\mathcal{N}(0,\sigma^2/K)}(\cdot)$ is the quantile function for a Gaussian with zero mean (our hypothesis) and variance, σ^2/K. As we have more data, K will increase, and in the limit of $K \to \infty$ we reproduce the exact criterion in (5.2). Typically we might set $\ell = 0.025$ and $u = 0.975$ to create a 95 per cent two-sided confidence interval.

The consistency criterion of (5.3) can also be turned into a statistical test. If each of the errors is independent and normal, $\hat{e}_k \sim \mathcal{N}(\mu, \sigma^2)$, then the quantity $\sum_{k=1}^{K} (\hat{e}_k - \mu)^2/\sigma^2$ will be chi-squared with mean K and variance $2K$ (see Section 2.2.9). If we assume that our estimator is unbiased, $\mu = 0$, and replace the unknown variance, σ^2, with our estimate of variance, $\hat{P}_k$, our consistency criterion in (5.3) can be verified statistically according to

$$Q_{\chi^2(K)}(\ell) \le \sum_{k=1}^{K} \frac{\hat{e}_k^2}{\hat{P}_k^2} \le Q_{\chi^2(K)}(u), \tag{5.7}$$

where ℓ and u are lower and upper confidence bounds, respectively, and $Q_{\chi^2(K)}(\cdot)$ is the quantile function (see Section 2.1.6) for the chi-squared distribution with K degrees of freedom.

When K is large (e.g., greater than 100), we can use an approximation to the chi-squared quantile function (Bar-Shalom et al., 2001, p. 83):

$$Q_{\chi^2(K)}(y) \approx \frac{1}{2}\left(Q_{\mathcal{N}(0,1)}(y) + \sqrt{2K-1}\right)^2, \tag{5.8}$$

where $Q_{\mathcal{N}(0,1)}(\cdot)$ is the quantile function for the standard, normal Gaussian distribution (see Section 2.2.13).

If our estimator is both unbiased and consistent, we would also generally like $\hat{P}_k$ to be as small as possible since this means that our errors do not stray very far from zero. This was our motivation for the derivation of the *Kalman filter (KF)* in Section 3.3.4 where we sought to find the *best linear unbiased estimate (BLUE)*.

When the state is N-dimensional, our estimate will then be $\mathcal{N}\left(\hat{\mathbf{x}}_k, \hat{\mathbf{P}}_k\right)$ and the groundtruth will be $\mathbf{x}_{\text{true},k}$. In this case, our single-timestep error will be

$$\hat{\mathbf{e}}_k = \begin{bmatrix} \hat{e}_{1,k} \\ \vdots \\ \hat{e}_{N,k} \end{bmatrix} = \hat{\mathbf{x}}_k - \mathbf{x}_{\text{true},k}. \tag{5.9}$$

We can then make a plot of the type in Figure 5.1 for each $\hat{e}_{n,k}$ with $n = 1 \ldots N$. The standard deviation for the uncertainty envelope is taken as $\sigma_{n,k} = \sqrt{\hat{P}_{nn,k}}$ where $\hat{P}_{nn,k}$ is the (n, n) entry of $\hat{\mathbf{P}}_k$. Put another way, $\mathcal{N}(\hat{x}_{n,k}, \hat{P}_{nn,k})$, with $\hat{x}_{n,k}$ being the nth row of $\hat{\mathbf{x}}_k$, is the marginal for the nth state variable and we are plotting our estimator performance one marginal at a time. To be unbiased in the N-dimensional case, we extend (5.2) to require

$$E[\hat{\mathbf{e}}_k] = \frac{1}{K} \sum_{k=1}^{K} \hat{\mathbf{e}}_k = \mathbf{0}. \tag{5.10}$$

Again, we can reformulate this into a statistical test, recycling the test of (5.6) for each state variable.

The N-dimensional version of (5.3) for consistency takes a bit more discussion and we therefore devote the next section to this topic.

5.1.2 NEES and NIS

The previous section discussed the conditions for an estimator to be unbiased and consistent in general. In this section, we look specifically at two ways to test for consistency of a multivariate Gaussian estimator.

Suppose that our N-dimensional estimate is $\mathcal{N}\left(\hat{\mathbf{x}}_k, \hat{\mathbf{P}}_k\right)$ for $k = 1 \ldots K$ and the groundtruth is $\mathbf{x}_{\text{true},k}$. We define the *normalized estimation error squared (NEES)*, $\epsilon_{\text{nees},k}$, to be

$$\epsilon_{\text{nees},k} = \hat{\mathbf{e}}_k^T \hat{\mathbf{P}}_k^{-1} \hat{\mathbf{e}}_k, \tag{5.11}$$

where $\hat{\mathbf{e}}_k$ is defined in (5.9). We recognize that (5.11) is a squared Mahalanobis distance, discussed in Section 2.2.9. The mean of $\epsilon_{\text{nees},k}$ should simply be the dimension of the state, N. Our criterion for consistency then becomes

$$E[\epsilon_{\text{nees},k}] = N, \tag{5.12}$$

which we see to be the N-dimensional generalization of (5.3). We say the estimator is underconfident if $E[\epsilon_{\text{nees},k}] < N$ and overconfident if $E[\epsilon_{\text{nees},k}] > N$.

As mentioned in the previous section, ideally we could compute $E[\epsilon_{\text{nees},k}]$ over a large number of independent trials (for each timestep). This could be possible, for example, in simulation where we can run many experiments with random draws of the measurement noise. With real data, we do not usually have the luxury of a large number of random trials and again could turn to the *ergodic hypothesis* where we compute the expectation over many timesteps within a single trial. To do this, we need to use a long trajectory with K big enough to make the test meaningful. It is worth noting that if the estimates are indeed highly correlated at different times (usually the case), the ergodic version of our test can be problematic since the bounds assume independence.[1]

In reality, we will always have a finite amount of data and then (5.12) can be reformulated statistically as

$$Q_{\chi^2(NK)}(\ell) \leq \sum_{k=1}^{K} \epsilon_{\text{nees},k} \leq Q_{\chi^2(NK)}(u), \tag{5.13}$$

where, as in (5.7), ℓ and u are lower and upper confidence bounds, respectively, and $Q_{\chi^2(NK)}(\cdot)$ is the quantile function for the chi-squared distribution with NK degrees of freedom.

While NEES is the preferred quantity to use in consistency tests, our ability to use it depends on the availability of a dataset with groundtruth, $\mathbf{x}_{\text{true},k}$. If we do not have groundtruth, we can instead perform a test based on the *normalized innovation squared (NIS)*, $\epsilon_{\text{nis},y,k}$, which is defined as

$$\epsilon_{\text{nis},y,k} = \mathbf{e}_{y,k}^T \mathbf{S}_{y,k}^{-1} \mathbf{e}_{y,k}, \tag{5.14}$$

with

$$\mathbf{e}_{y,k} = \mathbf{y}_k - \mathbf{g}(\hat{\mathbf{x}}_k), \quad \mathbf{S}_{y,k} = \mathbf{G}_k \hat{\mathbf{P}}_k \mathbf{G}_k^T + \mathbf{R}_k, \tag{5.15}$$

and where we recall the symbols from Section 4.3.1. This is another squared Mahalanobis distance, this time for the *innovation*, $\mathbf{e}_{y,k}$, which is the difference between the measurements, $\mathbf{y}_k$, and a prediction of those measurements based on the estimate, $\mathbf{g}(\hat{\mathbf{x}}_k)$. The covariance, $\mathbf{S}_{y,k}$, accounts for both the estimate uncertainty and the measurement uncertainty. Here we assume the measurement model is of the form

$$\mathbf{y}_k = \mathbf{g}(\mathbf{x}_k) + \mathbf{n}_k, \quad \mathbf{n}_k \sim \mathcal{N}(\mathbf{0}, \mathbf{R}_k), \tag{5.16}$$

where the measurement noise is additive. The Jacobian of the measurement model, $\mathbf{G}_k$, is evaluated at $\hat{\mathbf{x}}_k$. Our consistency criterion then becomes

$$E[\epsilon_{\text{nis},y,k}] = M, \tag{5.17}$$

where M is the dimension of the measurement, $\mathbf{y}_k$. As a statistical test we can formulate this as

$$Q_{\chi^2(M(K+1))}(\ell) \leq \sum_{k=0}^{K} \epsilon_{\text{nis},y,k} \leq Q_{\chi^2(M(K+1))}(u), \tag{5.18}$$

where ℓ and u are lower and upper confidence bounds, respectively, and $Q_{\chi^2(M(K+1))}(\cdot)$ is the quantile function for the chi-squared distribution with $M(K+1)$ degrees of freedom.

---

[1] In this case, we may prefer to look at an aggregate NEES for the whole trajectory at once, $\epsilon_{\text{nees}} = \hat{\mathbf{e}}^T \hat{\mathbf{P}}^{-1} \hat{\mathbf{e}}$, where $\hat{\mathbf{e}}$ is the vector of errors over the whole trajectory and $\hat{\mathbf{P}}$ is the full (possibly correlated) covariance for the whole trajectory. Our consistency criterion becomes $\epsilon_{\text{nees}} = NK$ since we only have one full-trajectory sample.

We have to be a bit careful when testing for the NIS criterion in (5.17). In the case of a batch state estimator (or smoother), we should use measurements, $\mathbf{y}_k$, that were not involved in the calculation of the estimate, $\hat{\mathbf{x}}_k$. These could be from a sensor reserved just for evaluation, or we could separate the measurements into a portion for estimation and a portion for evaluation. Alternatively, we could modify $\mathbf{S}_{y,k}$ to account for correlations between the measurement noise and the estimate.

In the case of the EKF, we can modify the test slightly so that the *innovation* and its covariance are

$$\mathbf{e}_{y,k} = \mathbf{y}_k - \mathbf{g}(\check{\mathbf{x}}_k), \quad \mathbf{S}_{y,k} = \mathbf{G}_k \check{\mathbf{P}}_k \mathbf{G}_k^T + \mathbf{R}_k. \tag{5.19}$$

We have replaced the batch estimate at time k, $\mathcal{N}(\hat{\mathbf{x}}_k, \hat{\mathbf{P}}_k)$, with the EKF-predicted estimate at time k, $\mathcal{N}(\check{\mathbf{x}}_k, \check{\mathbf{P}}_k)$. Since $\mathbf{y}_k$ has not yet been incorporated into the predicted estimate, we are safe to use it to evaluate consistency. The NIS test in (5.17) can then be applied on all the measurements, even online. The measurement model Jacobian, $\mathbf{G}_k$, is evaluated at $\check{\mathbf{x}}_k$.

In the case of the EKF, we can also define a similar NIS quantity based on the motion model, not just the observation model. Suppose the motion model has the form

$$\mathbf{x}_k = \mathbf{f}(\mathbf{x}_{k-1}, \mathbf{u}_k) + \mathbf{w}_k, \quad \mathbf{w}_k \sim \mathcal{N}(\mathbf{0}, \mathbf{Q}_k), \tag{5.20}$$

where the process noise is additive. Then the *prediction error* and its covariance are

$$\mathbf{e}_{v,k} = \mathbf{f}(\hat{\mathbf{x}}_{k-1}, \mathbf{u}_k) - \hat{\mathbf{x}}_k, \quad \mathbf{S}_{v,k} = \mathbf{F}_{k-1} \hat{\mathbf{P}}_{k-1} \mathbf{F}_{k-1}^T + \mathbf{Q}_k, \tag{5.21}$$

with the motion model Jacobian, $\mathbf{F}_{k-1}$, evaluated at $\hat{\mathbf{x}}_{k-1}$. We can define a NIS term based on these as

$$\epsilon_{\text{nis},v,k} = \mathbf{e}_{v,k}^T \mathbf{S}_{v,k}^{-1} \mathbf{e}_{v,k}, \tag{5.22}$$

whereupon our consistency criterion is

$$E[\epsilon_{\text{nis},v,k}] = N. \tag{5.23}$$

As a statistical test we can formulate this as

$$Q_{\chi^2(NK)}(\ell) \le \sum_{k=1}^{K} \epsilon_{\text{nis},v,k} \le Q_{\chi^2(NK)}(u), \tag{5.24}$$

where ℓ and u are lower and upper confidence bounds, respectively, and $Q_{\chi^2(NK)}(\cdot)$ is the quantile function for the chi-squared distribution with NK degrees of freedom.

Naturally, we could combine our two NIS tests using the observation and motion models into a single statistical test if so desired. Finally, if we have nonlinear observation and/or motion models, the criteria in (5.17) and (5.23) will never be met exactly (even if we had an infinite number of data points) as we have linearized the model in the derivation of the test. If the models are actually linear, the tests we have devised are more reliable. Chen et al. (2018) provide a nice introduction to NEES and NIS and how they can be used to tune key parameters in the Kalman filter.

5.2 Bias Estimation

In this section, we will investigate the impact of a bias on both the inputs and measurements. We will see that the case of the input bias is less difficult to deal with than the measurement bias, but both can be handled. We will use linear, time-invariant motion and observation models with non-zero-mean Gaussian noise for the purpose of our discussion, but many of the concepts to be discussed can also be extended to nonlinear systems.

5.2.1 Bias Effects on the Kalman Filter

As an example of the effect of a input/measurement bias, we return to the error dynamics discussed in Section 3.3.6 and see what happens to the Kalman filter (if we do not explicitly account for bias) when we introduce non-zero-mean noise. In particular, we will now assume that

$$\mathbf{x}_k = \boldsymbol{A}\mathbf{x}_{k-1} + \boldsymbol{B}(\mathbf{u}_k + \bar{\mathbf{u}}) + \mathbf{w}_k, \tag{5.25a}$$

$$\mathbf{y}_k = \boldsymbol{C}\mathbf{x}_k + \bar{\mathbf{y}} + \mathbf{n}_k, \tag{5.25b}$$

where $\bar{\mathbf{u}}$ is an input bias and $\bar{\mathbf{y}}$ a measurement bias. We will continue to assume that all measurements are corrupted with zero-mean Gaussian noise,

$$\mathbf{w}_k \sim \mathcal{N}(\mathbf{0}, \boldsymbol{Q}), \quad \mathbf{n}_k \sim \mathcal{N}(\mathbf{0}, \boldsymbol{R}), \tag{5.26}$$

that is statistically independent, so that

$$E[\mathbf{w}_k \mathbf{w}_\ell^T] = \mathbf{0}, \quad E[\mathbf{n}_k \mathbf{n}_\ell^T] = \mathbf{0}, \quad E[\mathbf{w}_k \mathbf{n}_k^T] = \mathbf{0}, \quad E[\mathbf{w}_k \mathbf{n}_\ell^T] = \mathbf{0}, \tag{5.27}$$

for all $k \neq \ell$, but this could be another source of filter inconsistency. We earlier defined the estimation errors,

$$\check{\mathbf{e}}_k = \check{\mathbf{x}}_k - \mathbf{x}_k, \tag{5.28a}$$

$$\hat{\mathbf{e}}_k = \hat{\mathbf{x}}_k - \mathbf{x}_k, \tag{5.28b}$$

and constructed the 'error dynamics', which in this case are

$$\check{\mathbf{e}}_k = \boldsymbol{A}\hat{\mathbf{e}}_{k-1} - (\boldsymbol{B}\bar{\mathbf{u}} + \mathbf{w}_k), \tag{5.29a}$$

$$\hat{\mathbf{e}}_k = (\mathbf{1} - \mathbf{K}_k \boldsymbol{C})\,\check{\mathbf{e}}_k + \mathbf{K}_k(\bar{\mathbf{y}} + \mathbf{n}_k), \tag{5.29b}$$

where $\hat{\mathbf{e}}_0 = \hat{\mathbf{x}}_0 - \mathbf{x}_0$. Furthermore, as discussed earlier, for our estimator to be *unbiased* and *consistent* we would like to have for all $k = 1 \dots K$ that

$$E\left[\hat{\mathbf{e}}_k\right] = \mathbf{0}, \quad E\left[\check{\mathbf{e}}_k\right] = \mathbf{0}, \quad E\left[\hat{\mathbf{e}}_k \hat{\mathbf{e}}_k^T\right] = \hat{\mathbf{P}}_k, \quad E\left[\check{\mathbf{e}}_k \check{\mathbf{e}}_k^T\right] = \check{\mathbf{P}}_k, \tag{5.30}$$

which we showed was true in the case that $\bar{\mathbf{u}} = \bar{\mathbf{y}} = \mathbf{0}$. Let us see what happens when this zero-bias condition does not necessarily hold. We will still assume that

$$E\left[\hat{\mathbf{e}}_0\right] = \mathbf{0}, \quad E\left[\hat{\mathbf{e}}_0 \hat{\mathbf{e}}_0^T\right] = \hat{\mathbf{P}}_0, \tag{5.31}$$

although this initial condition is another place a bias could be introduced. At $k = 1$ we have

$$E\left[\check{\mathbf{e}}_1\right] = \mathbf{A}\underbrace{E\left[\hat{\mathbf{e}}_0\right]}_{0} - \left(\mathbf{B}\bar{\mathbf{u}} + \underbrace{E\left[\mathbf{w}_1\right]}_{0}\right) = -\mathbf{B}\bar{\mathbf{u}}, \qquad (5.32a)$$

$$E\left[\hat{\mathbf{e}}_1\right] = (1 - \mathbf{K}_1 C)\underbrace{E\left[\check{\mathbf{e}}_1\right]}_{-\mathbf{B}\bar{\mathbf{u}}} + \mathbf{K}_1\left(\bar{\mathbf{y}} + \underbrace{E\left[\mathbf{n}_1\right]}_{0}\right)$$

$$= -(1 - \mathbf{K}_1 C)\mathbf{B}\bar{\mathbf{u}} + \mathbf{K}_1\bar{\mathbf{y}}, \qquad (5.32b)$$

which are already biased in the case that $\bar{\mathbf{u}} \neq \mathbf{0}$ and/or $\bar{\mathbf{y}} \neq \mathbf{0}$. For the covariance of the 'predicted error' we have

$$E\left[\check{\mathbf{e}}_1\check{\mathbf{e}}_1^T\right] = E\left[\left(A\hat{\mathbf{e}}_0 - (\mathbf{B}\bar{\mathbf{u}} + \mathbf{w}_1)\right)\left(A\hat{\mathbf{e}}_0 - (\mathbf{B}\bar{\mathbf{u}} + \mathbf{w}_1)\right)^T\right]$$

$$= \underbrace{E\left[(A\hat{\mathbf{e}}_0 - \mathbf{w}_1)(A\hat{\mathbf{e}}_0 - \mathbf{w}_1)^T\right]}_{\check{\mathbf{P}}_1} + (-\mathbf{B}\bar{\mathbf{u}})\underbrace{E\left[(A\hat{\mathbf{e}}_0 - \mathbf{w}_1)^T\right]}_{0}$$

$$+ \underbrace{E\left[(A\hat{\mathbf{e}}_0 - \mathbf{w}_1)\right]}_{0}(-\mathbf{B}\bar{\mathbf{u}})^T + (-\mathbf{B}\bar{\mathbf{u}})(-\mathbf{B}\bar{\mathbf{u}})^T$$

$$= \check{\mathbf{P}}_1 + (-\mathbf{B}\bar{\mathbf{u}})(-\mathbf{B}\bar{\mathbf{u}})^T. \qquad (5.33)$$

Rearranging, we see that

$$\check{\mathbf{P}}_1 = E\left[\check{\mathbf{e}}_1\check{\mathbf{e}}_1^T\right] - \underbrace{E[\check{\mathbf{e}}_1]\,E[\check{\mathbf{e}}_1]^T}_{\text{bias effect}}, \qquad (5.34)$$

and therefore the KF will 'underestimate' the true uncertainty in the error and become inconsistent. For the covariance of the 'corrected error' we have

$$E\left[\hat{\mathbf{e}}_1\hat{\mathbf{e}}_1^T\right] = E\left[\left((1 - \mathbf{K}_1 C)\check{\mathbf{e}}_1 + \mathbf{K}_1(\bar{\mathbf{y}} + \mathbf{n}_1)\right)\right.$$

$$\left. \times \left((1 - \mathbf{K}_1 C)\check{\mathbf{e}}_1 + \mathbf{K}_1(\bar{\mathbf{y}} + \mathbf{n}_1)\right)^T\right]$$

$$= \underbrace{E\left[\left((1 - \mathbf{K}_1 C)\check{\mathbf{e}}_1 + \mathbf{K}_1\mathbf{n}_1\right)\left((1 - \mathbf{K}_1 C)\check{\mathbf{e}}_1 + \mathbf{K}_1\mathbf{n}_1\right)^T\right]}_{\hat{\mathbf{P}}_1 + (1-\mathbf{K}_1 C)\mathbf{B}\bar{\mathbf{u}}\bar{\mathbf{u}}^T\mathbf{B}^T(1-\mathbf{K}_1 C)^T}$$

$$+ (\mathbf{K}_1\bar{\mathbf{y}})\underbrace{E\left[\left((1 - \mathbf{K}_1 C)\check{\mathbf{e}}_1 + \mathbf{K}_1\mathbf{n}_1\right)^T\right]}_{(-(1-\mathbf{K}_1 C)\mathbf{B}\bar{\mathbf{u}})^T}$$

$$+ \underbrace{E\left[\left((1 - \mathbf{K}_1 C)\check{\mathbf{e}}_1 + \mathbf{K}_1\mathbf{n}_1\right)\right]}_{-(1-\mathbf{K}_1 C)\mathbf{B}\bar{\mathbf{u}}}(\mathbf{K}_1\bar{\mathbf{y}})^T + (\mathbf{K}_1\bar{\mathbf{y}})(\mathbf{K}_1\bar{\mathbf{y}})^T$$

$$= \hat{\mathbf{P}}_1 + (-(1 - \mathbf{K}_1 C)\mathbf{B}\bar{\mathbf{u}} + \mathbf{K}_1\bar{\mathbf{y}})$$

$$\times (-(1 - \mathbf{K}_1 C)\mathbf{B}\bar{\mathbf{u}} + \mathbf{K}_1\bar{\mathbf{y}})^T, \qquad (5.35)$$

and so

$$\hat{\mathbf{P}}_1 = E\left[\hat{\mathbf{e}}_1\hat{\mathbf{e}}_1^T\right] - \underbrace{E[\hat{\mathbf{e}}_1]\,E[\hat{\mathbf{e}}_1]^T}_{\text{bias effect}}, \qquad (5.36)$$

where we can see again that the KF's estimate of the covariance is overconfident and thus inconsistent. It is interesting to note that the KF will become overconfident, regardless of the sign of the bias. Moreover, it is not hard to see that as k gets bigger, the effects of the biases grow without bound. It is tempting to modify the KF to be

$$\text{predictor:} \quad \begin{aligned} \check{\mathbf{P}}_k &= A\hat{\mathbf{P}}_{k-1}A^T + Q, & \text{(5.37a)} \\ \check{\mathbf{x}}_k &= A\hat{\mathbf{x}}_{k-1} + B\mathbf{u}_k + \underbrace{B\bar{\mathbf{u}}}_{\text{bias}}, & \text{(5.37b)} \end{aligned}$$

$$\text{Kalman gain:} \quad \mathbf{K}_k = \check{\mathbf{P}}_k C^T \left(C\check{\mathbf{P}}_k C^T + R\right)^{-1}, \quad \text{(5.37c)}$$

$$\text{corrector:} \quad \begin{aligned} \hat{\mathbf{P}}_k &= (1 - \mathbf{K}_k C)\check{\mathbf{P}}_k, & \text{(5.37d)} \\ \hat{\mathbf{x}}_k &= \check{\mathbf{x}}_k + \mathbf{K}_k\left(\mathbf{y}_k - C\check{\mathbf{x}}_k - \underbrace{\bar{\mathbf{y}}}_{\text{bias}}\right), & \text{(5.37e)} \end{aligned}$$

whereupon we recover an unbiased and consistent estimate. The problem is that we must know the value of the bias exactly for this to be a viable means of counteracting its effects. In most cases we do not know the exact value of the bias (it may even change with time). Section 5.5.1 provides a simple scheme to estimate bias (and covariances) if we have access to a dataset with high-quality groundtruth. However, given that we already have an estimation problem, another possibility is to include estimation of the bias directly into our problem. The next few sections will investigate this possibility for both inputs and measurements.

5.2.2 Unknown Input Bias

Continuing from the previous section, suppose we had $\bar{\mathbf{y}} = \mathbf{0}$ but not necessarily $\bar{\mathbf{u}} \neq \mathbf{0}$. Rather than estimating just the state of the system, $\mathbf{x}_k$, we augment the state to be

$$\mathbf{x}'_k = \begin{bmatrix} \mathbf{x}_k \\ \bar{\mathbf{u}}_k \end{bmatrix}, \quad \text{(5.38)}$$

where we have made the bias now a function of time as we want it to be part of our state. As the bias is now a function of time, we need to define a motion model for it. A typical one is to assume that

$$\bar{\mathbf{u}}_k = \bar{\mathbf{u}}_{k-1} + \mathbf{s}_k, \quad \text{(5.39)}$$

where $\mathbf{s}_k \sim \mathcal{N}(\mathbf{0}, W)$; this corresponds to Brownian motion (aka random walk) of the bias. In some sense, we are simply pushing the problem back through an integrator as we now have zero-mean Gaussian noise influencing the motion of the interoceptive bias. In practice, this type of trick can be effective. Other motion models for the bias could also be assumed, but often we do not have a lot of information as to their temporal behaviour. Under this bias motion model, we have for the motion model for our augmented state that

$$\mathbf{x}'_k = \underbrace{\begin{bmatrix} A & B \\ 0 & 1 \end{bmatrix}}_{A'} \mathbf{x}'_{k-1} + \underbrace{\begin{bmatrix} B \\ 0 \end{bmatrix}}_{B'} \mathbf{u}_k + \underbrace{\begin{bmatrix} \mathbf{w}_k \\ \mathbf{s}_k \end{bmatrix}}_{\mathbf{w}'_k}, \quad \text{(5.40)}$$

where we have defined several new symbols for convenience. We note that

$$\mathbf{w}'_k \sim \mathcal{N}\left(\mathbf{0}, \boldsymbol{Q}'\right), \quad \boldsymbol{Q}' = \begin{bmatrix} \boldsymbol{Q} & \mathbf{0} \\ \mathbf{0} & \boldsymbol{W} \end{bmatrix}, \tag{5.41}$$

so we are back to an unbiased system. The observation model is simply

$$\mathbf{y}_k = \underbrace{\begin{bmatrix} \boldsymbol{C} & \mathbf{0} \end{bmatrix}}_{\boldsymbol{C}'} \mathbf{x}'_k + \mathbf{n}_k, \tag{5.42}$$

in terms of the augmented state.

A critical question to ask is whether or not this augmented-state filter will converge to the correct answer. Will the preceding trick really work? The conditions we saw for existence and uniqueness of the linear-Gaussian batch estimation earlier (with no prior on the initial condition) were

$$\boldsymbol{Q} > 0, \quad \boldsymbol{R} > 0, \quad \text{rank } \mathcal{O} = N. \tag{5.43}$$

Let us assume these conditions do indeed hold for the system in the case that the bias is zero, namely $\bar{\mathbf{u}} = \mathbf{0}$. Defining

$$\mathcal{O}' = \begin{bmatrix} \boldsymbol{C}' \\ \boldsymbol{C}'\boldsymbol{A}' \\ \vdots \\ \boldsymbol{C}'\boldsymbol{A}'^{(N+U-1)} \end{bmatrix}, \tag{5.44}$$

we are required to show that

$$\underbrace{\boldsymbol{Q}' > 0, \quad \boldsymbol{R} > 0,}_{\text{true by definitions}} \quad \text{rank } \mathcal{O}' = N + U, \tag{5.45}$$

for existence and uniqueness of the solution to the batch estimation problem for the augmented-state system. The first two conditions are true by the definitions of these covariance matrices. For the last condition, the rank needs to be $N + U$ since the augmented state now includes the bias, where $U = \dim \bar{\mathbf{u}}_k$. In general this condition does not hold. The next two examples will illustrate this.

Example 5.1   Take the system matrices to be

$$\boldsymbol{A} = \begin{bmatrix} 1 & 1 \\ 0 & 1 \end{bmatrix}, \quad \boldsymbol{B} = \begin{bmatrix} 0 \\ 1 \end{bmatrix}, \quad \boldsymbol{C} = \begin{bmatrix} 1 & 0 \end{bmatrix}, \tag{5.46}$$

such that $N = 2$ and $U = 1$. This example roughly corresponds to a simple one-dimensional unit-mass cart, whose state is its position and velocity. The input is the acceleration and the measurement is the distance back to the origin. The bias is on the input. See Figure 5.2 for an illustration. We have

$$\mathcal{O} = \begin{bmatrix} \boldsymbol{C} \\ \boldsymbol{C}\boldsymbol{A} \end{bmatrix} = \begin{bmatrix} 1 & 0 \\ 1 & 1 \end{bmatrix} \quad \Rightarrow \quad \text{rank } \mathcal{O} = 2 = N, \tag{5.47}$$

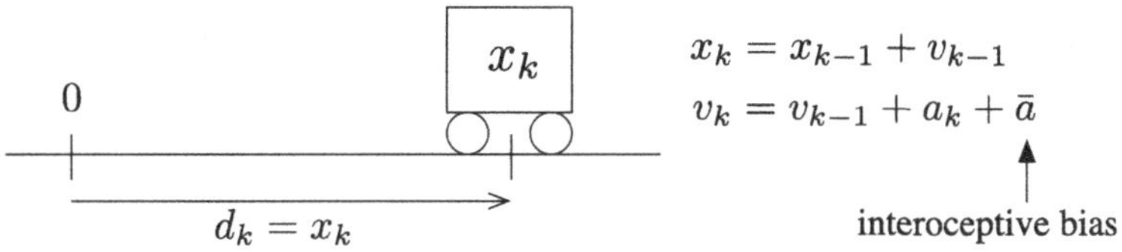

Figure 5.2 Input bias on acceleration. In this case we can successfully estimate the bias as part of our state estimation problem.

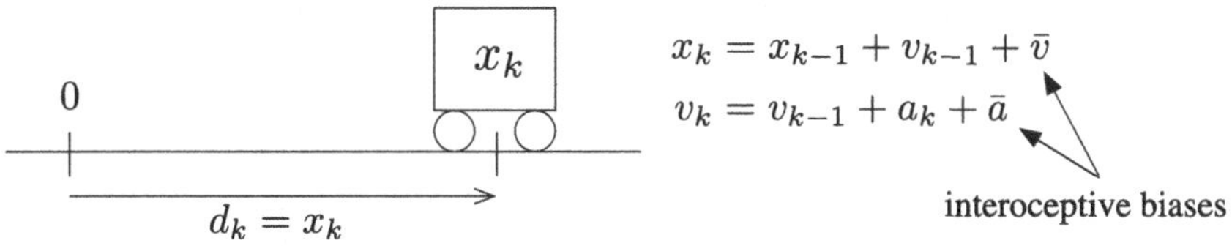

$$x_k = x_{k-1} + v_{k-1}$$
$$v_k = v_{k-1} + a_k + \bar{a}$$

interoceptive bias

Figure 5.3 Input biases on both speed and acceleration. In this case we cannot estimate the bias as the system is unobservable.

$$x_k = x_{k-1} + v_{k-1} + \bar{v}$$
$$v_k = v_{k-1} + a_k + \bar{a}$$

interoceptive biases

so the unbiased system is observable.[2] For the augmented-state system we have

$$\mathcal{O}' = \begin{bmatrix} C' \\ C'A' \\ C'A'^2 \end{bmatrix} = \begin{bmatrix} C & 0 \\ CA & CB \\ CA^2 & CAB + CB \end{bmatrix} = \begin{bmatrix} 1 & 0 & 0 \\ 1 & 1 & 0 \\ 1 & 2 & 1 \end{bmatrix}$$

$$\Rightarrow \quad \text{rank } \mathcal{O}' = 3 = N + U, \quad (5.48)$$

so it, too, is observable. Note that taking $B = \begin{bmatrix} 1 \\ 0 \end{bmatrix}$ is observable, too.[3]

Example 5.2 Take the system matrices to be

$$A = \begin{bmatrix} 1 & 1 \\ 0 & 1 \end{bmatrix}, \quad B = \begin{bmatrix} 1 & 0 \\ 0 & 1 \end{bmatrix}, \quad C = \begin{bmatrix} 1 & 0 \end{bmatrix}, \quad (5.49)$$

such that $N = 2$ and $U = 2$. This is a strange system wherein the command to the system is a function of both speed and acceleration, and we have biases on both of these quantities. See Figure 5.3 for an illustration. We still have that the unbiased system is observable since A and C are unchanged. For the augmented-state system we have

$$\mathcal{O}' = \begin{bmatrix} C' \\ C'A' \\ C'A'^2 \\ C'A'^3 \end{bmatrix} = \begin{bmatrix} C & 0 \\ CA & CB \\ CA^2 & C(A+1)B \\ CA^3 & C(A^2 + A + 1)B \end{bmatrix} = \begin{bmatrix} 1 & 0 & 0 & 0 \\ 1 & 1 & 1 & 0 \\ 1 & 2 & 2 & 1 \\ 1 & 3 & 3 & 3 \end{bmatrix}$$

$$\Rightarrow \quad \text{rank } \mathcal{O}' = 3 < 4 = N + U, \quad (5.50)$$

so it is not observable (since columns 2 and 3 are the same).

5.2.3 Unknown Measurement Bias

Suppose now we have $\bar{\mathbf{u}} = \mathbf{0}$ but not necessarily $\bar{\mathbf{y}} \neq \mathbf{0}$. The augmented state is

$$\mathbf{x}'_k = \begin{bmatrix} \mathbf{x}_k \\ \bar{\mathbf{y}}_k \end{bmatrix}, \quad (5.51)$$

---

[2] It is also *controllable*.
[3] But now the unbiased system is not *controllable*.

Figure 5.4
Measurement bias
on position. In this
case we cannot
estimate the bias as
the system is
unobservable.

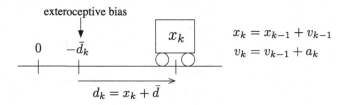

where we have again made the bias a function of time. We again assume a random-walk motion model

$$\bar{\mathbf{y}}_k = \bar{\mathbf{y}}_{k-1} + \mathbf{s}_k, \tag{5.52}$$

where $\mathbf{s}_k \sim \mathcal{N}(\mathbf{0}, \mathbf{W})$. Under this bias motion model, we have for the motion model for our augmented state that

$$\mathbf{x}'_k = \underbrace{\begin{bmatrix} A & 0 \\ 0 & 1 \end{bmatrix}}_{A'} \mathbf{x}'_{k-1} + \underbrace{\begin{bmatrix} B \\ 0 \end{bmatrix}}_{B'} \mathbf{u}_k + \underbrace{\begin{bmatrix} \mathbf{w}_k \\ \mathbf{s}_k \end{bmatrix}}_{\mathbf{w}'_k}, \tag{5.53}$$

where we have defined several new symbols for convenience. We note that

$$\mathbf{w}'_k \sim \mathcal{N}\left(\mathbf{0}, \mathbf{Q}'\right), \quad \mathbf{Q}' = \begin{bmatrix} Q & 0 \\ 0 & W \end{bmatrix}. \tag{5.54}$$

The observation model is

$$\mathbf{y}_k = \underbrace{\begin{bmatrix} C & 1 \end{bmatrix}}_{C'} \mathbf{x}'_k + \mathbf{n}_k, \tag{5.55}$$

in terms of the augmented state. We again examine the observability of the system in the context of an example.

Example 5.3 Take the system matrices to be

$$A = \begin{bmatrix} 1 & 1 \\ 0 & 1 \end{bmatrix}, \quad B = \begin{bmatrix} 0 \\ 1 \end{bmatrix}, \quad C = \begin{bmatrix} 1 & 0 \end{bmatrix}, \tag{5.56}$$

such that $N = 2$ and $U = 1$. This corresponds to our cart measuring its distance from a landmark (whose position it does not know – see Figure 5.4). In the context of mobile robotics this is a very simple example of *simultaneous localization and mapping (SLAM)*, a popular estimation research area. The 'localization' is the cart state and the 'map' is the landmark position (here the negative of the bias).
We have

$$\mathcal{O} = \begin{bmatrix} C \\ CA \end{bmatrix} = \begin{bmatrix} 1 & 0 \\ 1 & 1 \end{bmatrix} \quad \Rightarrow \quad \text{rank } \mathcal{O} = 2 = N, \tag{5.57}$$

so the unbiased system is observable. For the augmented-state system we have

$$\mathcal{O}' = \begin{bmatrix} C' \\ C'A' \\ C'A'^2 \end{bmatrix} = \begin{bmatrix} C & 1 \\ CA & 1 \\ CA^2 & 1 \end{bmatrix} = \begin{bmatrix} 1 & 0 & 1 \\ 1 & 1 & 1 \\ 1 & 2 & 1 \end{bmatrix}$$

$$\Rightarrow \quad \text{rank } \mathcal{O}' = 2 < 3 = N + U, \tag{5.58}$$

so it is not observable (since columns 1 and 3 are the same). Since we are rank-deficient by 1, this means that $\dim(\text{null } \mathcal{O}') = 1$; the nullspace of the observability matrix corresponds to those vectors that produce outputs of zero. Here we see that

$$\text{null } \mathcal{O}' = \text{span} \left\{ \begin{bmatrix} 1 \\ 0 \\ -1 \end{bmatrix} \right\}, \tag{5.59}$$

which means that we can shift the cart and landmark together (left or right) and the measurement will not change. Does this mean our estimator will fail? Not if we are careful to interpret the solutions properly; we do so for both batch LG estimation and the KF:

(i) In the batch LG estimator, the left-hand side cannot be inverted, but recalling basic linear algebra, every system of the form $\mathbf{Ax} = \mathbf{b}$ can have zero, one, or infinitely many solutions. In this case we have infinitely many solutions rather than a single unique solution.

(ii) In the KF, we need to start with an initial guess for the state. The final answer we get will depend on the initial conditions selected. In other words, the value of the bias will remain at its initial guess.

In both cases, we have a way forward.

5.3 Data Association

As discussed earlier, the *data association* problem has to do with figuring out which measurements correspond to which parts of a model. Virtually all real estimation techniques, particularly for robotics, employ some form of model or map to determine a vehicle's state, and in particular its position/orientation. Some common examples of these models/maps are as follows:

(i) Positioning using GPS satellites. Here the positions of the GPS satellites are assumed to be known (as a function of time) in a reference frame attached to the Earth (e.g., using their orbital elements). A GPS receiver on the ground measures range to the satellites (e.g., using time of flight based on a timing message sent by the satellite) and then trilaterates for position. In this case, it is easy to know which range measurement is associated with which satellite because the whole system is engineered and therefore unique codes are embedded in the timing messages to indicate which satellite has sent which message.

(ii) Attitude determination using celestial observation. A map (or chart) of all the brightest stars in the sky is used by a star sensor to determine which direction the sensor is pointing. Here the natural world is being used as a map (surveyed in advance) and thus data association, or knowing which star you are looking at, is much more difficult than in the GPS case. Because the star chart can be generated in advance, this system becomes practical.

Figure 5.5 A
measurement and
point-cloud model
with two possible
data associations
shown.

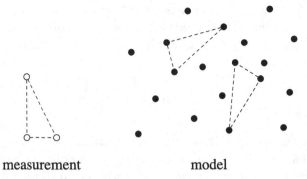

measurement   model

There are essentially two main approaches to data association: external and internal.

5.3.1 External Data Association

In external data association, specialized knowledge of the model/measurements is used for association. This knowledge is 'external' to the estimation problem. This is sometimes called 'known data association' because from the perspective of the estimation problem, the job has been done.

For example, a bunch of targets could be painted with unique colours; a stereo camera could be used to observe the targets and the colour information used to do data association. The colour information would not be used in the estimation problem. Other examples of external data association include visual bar codes and unique transmission frequencies/codes (e.g., GPS satellites).

External data association can work well if the model can be modified in advance to be cooperative; this makes the estimation problem a lot easier. However, cutting-edge computer vision techniques can be used as external data association on unprepared models, too, although the results are more prone to misassociations.

5.3.2 Internal Data Association

In internal data association, only the measurements/model are used to do data association. This is sometimes called 'unknown data association'. Typically, association is based on the likelihood of a given measurement, given the model. In the simplest version, the most likely association is accepted and the other possibilities are ignored. More sophisticated techniques allow multiple data association hypotheses to be carried forward into the estimation problem.

In the case of certain types of models, such as three-dimensional landmarks or star charts, 'constellations' of landmarks are sometimes used to help perform data association (see Figure 5.5). The *data-aligned rigidity-constrained exhaustive search (DARCES)* algorithm (Chen et al., 1999) is an example of a constellation-based data association method. The idea is that the distances between pairs of points in a constellation can be used as a type of unique identifier for data association.

Regardless of the type of data association employed, it is highly likely that if an estimation technique fails, the blame can be squarely placed on bad data

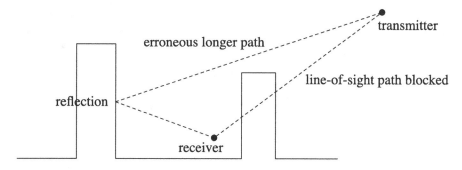

Figure 5.6 A pathological configuration of buildings can trick a GPS system into using an incorrect range measurement.

association. For this reason, it is very important to acknowledge that misassociations will occur in practice, and therefore to design techniques to make the estimation problem robust to these occurrences. The next section, on outlier detection and rejection, will discuss some methods to help deal with this type of problem.

5.4 Handling Outliers

Data misassociation can certainly lead to an estimator completely diverging. However, data association is not the only cause of divergence. There are other factors that can cause any particular measurement to be very poor/incorrect. A classic example is multipath reflections of GPS timing signals near tall buildings. Figure 5.6 illustrates this point. A reflected signal can give a range measurement that is too long. In the absence of additional information, when the line-of-sight path is blocked the receiver has no way of knowing the longer path is incorrect.

We call measurements that are extremely improbable (according to our measurement model), *outliers*. Just how improbable is a matter of choice, but a common approach (in one-dimensional data) is to consider measurements that are more than three standard deviations away from the mean to be outliers.

If we accept that a portion (possibly large) of our measurements could be outliers, we need to devise a means to detect and reduce/remove the influence of outliers on our estimators. We will discuss the two most common techniques to handle outliers:

(i) Random sample consensus (Fischler and Bolles, 1981)
(ii) M-Estimation (Zhang, 1997)

These can be used separately or in tandem. We will also touch on *adaptive estimation* (i.e., covariance estimation) and its connection to M-estimation.

5.4.1 RANSAC

Random sample consensus (RANSAC) is an iterative method to fit a parameterized model to a set of observed data containing outliers. *Outliers* are measurements that do not 'fit' a model, while *inliers* do 'fit'. RANSAC is a probabilistic algorithm in the sense that its ability to find a reasonable answer can only be guaranteed to occur with a certain probability that improves with more time spent in

Figure 5.7
Line-fitting example.
If a line is fit to all
the data, the outliers
will have a large
impact on the result.
The *random sample
consensus
(RANSAC)*
approach is to
classify the data as
either an inlier or an
outlier and then only
use the inliers in the
line fit.

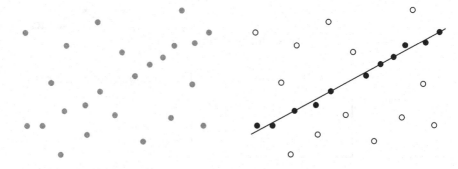

example dataset with inliers and outliers   RANSAC finds line with most inliers

the search. Figure 5.7 provides a classic line-fitting example in the presence of outliers.

RANSAC proceeds in an iterative manner. In the basic version, each iteration consists of the following five steps:

1. Select a (small) random subset of the original data to be hypothesized inliers (e.g., pick two points if fitting a line to xy-data).
2. Fit a model to the hypothesized inliers (e.g., a line is fit to two points).
3. Test the rest of the original data against the fitted model and classify as either inliers or outliers. If too few inliers are found, the iteration is labelled invalid and aborted.
4. Refit the model using both the hypothesized and classified inliers.
5. Evaluate the refit model in terms of the residual error of all the inlier data.

This is repeated for a large number of iterations, and the hypothesis with the lowest residual error is selected as the best.

A critical question to ask is how many iterations, k, are needed to ensure a subset is selected comprised solely of inliers, with probability p? In general, this is difficult to answer. However, if we assume that each measurement is selected independently, and each has probability w of being an inlier, then the following relation holds:

$$1 - p = (1 - w^n)^k, \tag{5.60}$$

where n is the number of data points in the random subset and k is the number of iterations. Solving for k gives

$$k = \frac{\ln(1 - p)}{\ln\left(1 - w^n\right)}. \tag{5.61}$$

In reality, this can be thought of as an upper bound, as the data points are typically selected sequentially, not independently. There can also be constraints between the data points that complicate the selection of random subsets.

5.4.2 M-Estimation

Many of our earlier estimation techniques were shown to be minimizing a sum-of-squared-error cost function. The trouble with sum-of-squared-error cost

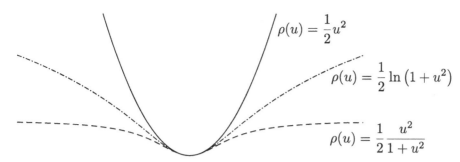

Figure 5.8
Comparison of quadratic, Cauchy, and Geman–McClure cost functions for scalar inputs.

functions is that they are highly sensitive to outliers. A single large outlier can exercise a huge influence on the estimate because it dominates the quadratic cost. *M-estimation*[4] modifies the shape of the cost function so that outliers do not dominate the solution.

We have seen previously that our overall nonlinear MAP objective function (for batch estimation) can be written in the form

$$J(\mathbf{x}) = \frac{1}{2} \sum_{i=1}^{N} \mathbf{e}_i(\mathbf{x})^T \mathbf{W}_i^{-1} \mathbf{e}_i(\mathbf{x}), \tag{5.62}$$

which is quadratic. The gradient of this objective function is

$$\frac{\partial J(\mathbf{x})}{\partial \mathbf{x}} = \sum_{i=1}^{N} \mathbf{e}_i(\mathbf{x})^T \mathbf{W}_i^{-1} \frac{\partial \mathbf{e}_i(\mathbf{x})}{\partial \mathbf{x}}, \tag{5.63}$$

which will be zero at a minimum. Let us now generalize this objective function and write it as

$$J'(\mathbf{x}) = \sum_{i=1}^{N} \alpha_i \, \rho \left(u_i(\mathbf{x}) \right), \tag{5.64}$$

where $\alpha_i > 0$ is a scalar weight,

$$u_i(\mathbf{x}) = \sqrt{\mathbf{e}_i(\mathbf{x})^T \mathbf{W}_i^{-1} \mathbf{e}_i(\mathbf{x})}, \tag{5.65}$$

and $\rho(u)$ is some nonlinear cost function; assume it is bounded, has a unique zero at $u = 0$, and increases monotonically with $u > 0$.

There are many possible cost functions, including

$$\underbrace{\rho(u) = \frac{1}{2} u^2}_{\text{quadratic}}, \quad \underbrace{\rho(u) = \frac{1}{2} \ln \left(1 + u^2 \right)}_{\text{Cauchy}}, \quad \underbrace{\rho(u) = \frac{1}{2} \frac{u^2}{1 + u^2}}_{\text{Geman–McClure}}. \tag{5.66}$$

We refer to those that increase more slowly than quadratic as *robust cost functions*. This means that large errors will not carry as much weight and have little power on the solution due to a reduced gradient. Figure 5.8 depicts these options. Refer to Zhang (1997) for a more complete list of cost functions and MacTavish and Barfoot (2015) for a comparison study.

---

[4] 'M' stands for 'maximum likelihood-type', that is, a generalization of maximum likelihood (which we saw earlier was equivalent to the least-squares solution).

The gradient of our new objective function is simply

$$\frac{\partial J'(\mathbf{x})}{\partial \mathbf{x}} = \sum_{i=1}^{N} \alpha_i \frac{\partial \rho}{\partial u_i} \frac{\partial u_i}{\partial \mathbf{e}_i} \frac{\partial \mathbf{e}_i}{\partial \mathbf{x}}, \tag{5.67}$$

using the chain rule. Again, we want the gradient to go to zero if we are seeking a minimum. Substituting

$$\frac{\partial u_i}{\partial \mathbf{e}_i} = \frac{1}{u_i(\mathbf{x})} \mathbf{e}_i(\mathbf{x})^T \mathbf{W}_i^{-1}, \tag{5.68}$$

the gradient can be written as

$$\frac{\partial J'(\mathbf{x})}{\partial \mathbf{x}} = \sum_{i=1}^{N} \mathbf{e}_i(\mathbf{x})^T \mathbf{Y}_i(\mathbf{x})^{-1} \frac{\partial \mathbf{e}_i(\mathbf{x})}{\partial \mathbf{x}}, \tag{5.69}$$

where

$$\mathbf{Y}_i(\mathbf{x})^{-1} = \frac{\alpha_i}{u_i(\mathbf{x})} \left.\frac{\partial \rho}{\partial u_i}\right|_{u_i(\mathbf{x})} \mathbf{W}_i^{-1} \tag{5.70}$$

is a new (inverse) covariance matrix that depends on $\mathbf{x}$; we see that (5.69) is identical to (5.63), except that $\mathbf{W}_i$ is now replaced with $\mathbf{Y}_i(\mathbf{x})$.

We are already using an iterative optimizer due to the nonlinear dependence of $\mathbf{e}_i(\mathbf{x})$ on $\mathbf{x}$, so it makes sense to evaluate $\mathbf{Y}_i(\mathbf{x})$ at the value of the state from the previous iteration, $\mathbf{x}_{\mathrm{op}}$. This means we can simply work with the cost function

$$J''(\mathbf{x}) = \frac{1}{2} \sum_{i=1}^{N} \mathbf{e}_i(\mathbf{x})^T \mathbf{Y}_i(\mathbf{x}_{\mathrm{op}})^{-1} \mathbf{e}_i(\mathbf{x}), \tag{5.71}$$

where

$$\mathbf{Y}_i(\mathbf{x}_{\mathrm{op}})^{-1} = \frac{\alpha_i}{u_i(\mathbf{x}_{\mathrm{op}})} \left.\frac{\partial \rho}{\partial u_i}\right|_{u_i(\mathbf{x}_{\mathrm{op}})} \mathbf{W}_i^{-1}. \tag{5.72}$$

At each iteration, we solve the original least-squares problem, but with a modified covariance matrix that updates as $\mathbf{x}_{\mathrm{op}}$ updates. This is referred to as *iteratively reweighted least squares (IRLS)* (Holland and Welsch, 1977).

To see why this iterative scheme works, we can examine the gradient of $J''(\mathbf{x})$:

$$\frac{\partial J''(\mathbf{x})}{\partial \mathbf{x}} = \sum_{i=1}^{N} \mathbf{e}_i(\mathbf{x})^T \mathbf{Y}_i(\mathbf{x}_{\mathrm{op}})^{-1} \frac{\partial \mathbf{e}_i(\mathbf{x})}{\partial \mathbf{x}}. \tag{5.73}$$

If the iterative scheme converges, we will have $\hat{\mathbf{x}} = \mathbf{x}_{\mathrm{op}}$, so

$$\left.\frac{\partial J'(\mathbf{x})}{\partial \mathbf{x}}\right|_{\hat{\mathbf{x}}} = \left.\frac{\partial J''(\mathbf{x})}{\partial \mathbf{x}}\right|_{\hat{\mathbf{x}}} = \mathbf{0}, \tag{5.74}$$

and thus the two systems will have the same minimum (or minima). To be clear, however, the path taken to get to the optimum will differ if we minimize $J''(\mathbf{x})$ rather than $J'(\mathbf{x})$.

As an example, consider the case of the Cauchy robust cost function described above. The objective function becomes

$$J'(\mathbf{x}) = \frac{1}{2} \sum_{i=1}^{N} \alpha_i \ln \left(1 + \mathbf{e}_i(\mathbf{x})^T \mathbf{W}_i^{-1} \mathbf{e}_i(\mathbf{x})\right), \tag{5.75}$$

and we have

$$\mathbf{Y}_i(\mathbf{x}_{\text{op}})^{-1} = \frac{\alpha_i}{u_i(\mathbf{x}_{\text{op}})} \left.\frac{\partial \rho}{\partial u_i}\right|_{u_i(\mathbf{x}_{\text{op}})} \mathbf{W}_i^{-1} = \frac{\alpha_i}{u_i(\mathbf{x}_{\text{op}})} \frac{u_i(\mathbf{x}_{\text{op}})}{1 + u_i(\mathbf{x}_{\text{op}})^2} \mathbf{W}_i^{-1}, \tag{5.76}$$

and so

$$\mathbf{Y}_i(\mathbf{x}_{\text{op}}) = \frac{1}{\alpha_i} \left(1 + \mathbf{e}_i(\mathbf{x}_{\text{op}})^T \mathbf{W}_i^{-1} \mathbf{e}_i(\mathbf{x}_{\text{op}})\right) \mathbf{W}_i, \tag{5.77}$$

which we see is just an inflated version of the original (non-robust) covariance matrix, $\mathbf{W}_i$; it gets bigger as the quadratic error, namely, $\mathbf{e}_i(\mathbf{x}_{\text{op}})^T \mathbf{W}_i^{-1} \mathbf{e}_i(\mathbf{x}_{\text{op}})$, gets bigger. This makes sense because less trust is being assigned to cost terms that are very large (i.e., they are outliers).

Finally, an obvious question is to ask which robust cost function should be used in a given situation? While there is no definitive answer, Barron (2019) shows that it is possible to generalize many of the common robust cost functions into a parametric family and then adaptively determine the parameters (thereby choosing the best robust cost) during the estimation process itself. Yang et al. (2020) also discuss how robust cost functions can be applied gradually through a procedure known as graduated non-convexity; this helps prevent the IRLS procedure from becoming trapped in poor local minima, which are often introduced by robust cost functions.

5.5 Covariance Estimation

In the MAP estimation we have discussed so far, we have been dealing with cost functions of the form

$$J(\mathbf{x}) = \frac{1}{2} \sum_{i=1}^{N} \mathbf{e}_i(\mathbf{x})^T \mathbf{W}_i^{-1} \mathbf{e}_i(\mathbf{x}), \tag{5.78}$$

where we have assumed that the covariance associated with the inputs and measurements, $\mathbf{W}_i$, is known. A big question is where does knowledge of these covariances come from? We can try to use sensor datasheets, but often we resort to tuning by trial and error. This is partly why robust cost functions, as discussed in the previous section, are necessary: our noise models are just not that good.

The next three subsections will discuss three different ways to try to estimate covariances from data. Chen et al. (2018) provide another.

5.5.1 Supervised Covariance Estimation

Perhaps the easiest way to estimate covariances is using a dataset with groundtruth. We can refer to this as *supervised* covariance estimation since we require the groundtruth as a supervisory signal. Consider that we are carrying out batch discrete-time state estimation as described in Section 4.3.1. Our cost function will be of the form

$$J(\mathbf{x}) = \frac{1}{2}\mathbf{e}_{v,0}(\mathbf{x})^T \, \check{\mathbf{P}}^{-1} \, \mathbf{e}_{v,0}(\mathbf{x}) + \frac{1}{2}\sum_{k=1}^{K} \mathbf{e}_{v,k}(\mathbf{x})^T \, \mathbf{Q}^{-1} \, \mathbf{e}_{v,k}(\mathbf{x})$$

$$+ \frac{1}{2}\sum_{k=0}^{K} \mathbf{e}_{y,k}(\mathbf{x})^T \, \mathbf{R}^{-1} \, \mathbf{e}_{y,k}(\mathbf{x}), \quad (5.79)$$

where for the purpose of this discussion we assume that the process noise covariance, $\mathbf{Q}$, and measurement noise covariance, $\mathbf{R}$, are constants. The errors in our cost function could actually be biased; let us assume these biases are also constant. If we have a training dataset from an environment that is very similar to our intended application and that has high-quality (i.e., very low noise) groundtruth for the entire trajectory, $\mathbf{x}_{\text{true}}$, we can estimate the bias on the process terms, $\bar{\mathbf{e}}_v$, and the bias on the measurement terms, $\bar{\mathbf{e}}_y$, as

$$\bar{\mathbf{e}}_v = \frac{1}{K}\sum_{k=1}^{K} \mathbf{e}_{v,k}(\mathbf{x}_{\text{true}}), \quad \bar{\mathbf{e}}_y = \frac{1}{K+1}\sum_{k=0}^{K} \mathbf{e}_{y,k}(\mathbf{x}_{\text{true}}), \quad (5.80)$$

where we use the groundtruth to evaluate the errors, $\mathbf{e}_{v,k}(\mathbf{x}_{\text{true}})$ and $\mathbf{e}_{y,k}(\mathbf{x}_{\text{true}})$. Note, there is one more datapoint used for $\mathbf{e}_y$ than $\mathbf{e}_v$, resulting in $K+1$ rather than K in the denominator.

A covariance is supposed to represent the expected value of the outer product of a quantity (minus its mean) with itself. We can therefore estimate $\mathbf{Q}$ and $\mathbf{R}$ as

$$\mathbf{Q} = \frac{1}{K-1}\sum_{k=1}^{K} (\mathbf{e}_{v,k}(\mathbf{x}_{\text{true}}) - \bar{\mathbf{e}}_v)(\mathbf{e}_{v,k}(\mathbf{x}_{\text{true}}) - \bar{\mathbf{e}}_v)^T, \quad (5.81a)$$

$$\mathbf{R} = \frac{1}{K}\sum_{k=0}^{K} (\mathbf{e}_{y,k}(\mathbf{x}_{\text{true}}) - \bar{\mathbf{e}}_y)(\mathbf{e}_{y,k}(\mathbf{x}_{\text{true}}) - \bar{\mathbf{e}}_y)^T, \quad (5.81b)$$

where Bessel's correction has been applied as we are using a sample covariance (see Section 2.1.8). Once $\bar{\mathbf{e}}_v$, $\bar{\mathbf{e}}_y$, $\mathbf{Q}$, and $\mathbf{R}$ are estimated, we can use them in a real operational scenario where we do not have any groundtruth. The initial covariance, $\check{\mathbf{P}}_0$, and any bias on the initial state mean are more difficult to estimate in this way as there is only a single datapoint per trajectory. We can also validate the quality of the estimated covariances with the consistency tests in Section 5.1.2, using a separate validation dataset.

5.5.2 Adaptive Covariance Estimation

We have already seen in Section 5.2 one approach to estimating biases, which was to include the unknown bias into the main state estimation problem. Here we look at another classic approach, known as *adaptive estimation* (aka noise-adaptive filtering). We follow the treatment of Stengel (1994, p. 400). The idea will be to use a trailing window of errors to estimate both biases and covariances.

The method is typically used alongside a traditional filter (i.e., KF or EKF) but could be repurposed to also function with SWFs. The method is unsupervised, meaning we do not need any source of groundtruth for the state, in contrast to the previous section.

Consider the case where the observation model has additive noise of the form

$$\mathbf{y}_k = \mathbf{g}(\mathbf{x}_k) + \mathbf{n}_k, \quad \mathbf{n}_k \sim \mathcal{N}(\mathbf{0}, \mathbf{R}_k), \tag{5.82}$$

where $\mathbf{g}(\cdot, \cdot)$ is the observation model, $\mathbf{y}_k$ is the measurement at time k, $\mathbf{n}_k$ is the measurement noise, and $\mathbf{R}_k$ is the measurement noise covariance. Then the *innovation* in the EKF (see Section 4.2.3) is

$$\mathbf{e}_{y,k} = \mathbf{y}_k - \mathbf{g}(\check{\mathbf{x}}_k), \tag{5.83}$$

with $\check{\mathbf{x}}_k$ the predicted state mean at time k. The mean associated with this error is hopefully near zero and the covariance is

$$E[\mathbf{e}_{y,k}\mathbf{e}_{y,k}^T] \approx \mathbf{G}_k\check{\mathbf{P}}_k\mathbf{G}_k^T + \mathbf{R}_k, \tag{5.84}$$

where $\check{\mathbf{P}}_k$ is the predicted state covariance and $\mathbf{G}_k$ is the observation model Jacobian, both at time k. The covariance expression in (5.84) an approximation since we have linearized the observation model to compute it.

Using a trailing window of L datapoints from the current time, we can use a sample mean and covariance to estimate the true mean and covariance of the innovation as

$$\bar{\mathbf{e}}_{y,k} = \frac{1}{L} \sum_{\ell=k-1}^{k-L} \mathbf{e}_{y,\ell}, \tag{5.85a}$$

$$\mathbf{S}_{y,k} = \frac{1}{L-1} \sum_{\ell=k-1}^{k-L} (\mathbf{e}_{y,\ell} - \bar{\mathbf{e}}_{y,k})(\mathbf{e}_{y,\ell} - \bar{\mathbf{e}}_{y,k})^T, \tag{5.85b}$$

where we use Bessel's correction in the calculation of the sample covariance (see Section 2.1.8). Equating $\mathbf{S}_{y,k}$ with (5.84), we can rearrange for $\mathbf{R}_k$ as

$$\mathbf{R}_k = \mathbf{S}_{y,k} - \frac{1}{L} \sum_{\ell=k-1}^{k-L} \mathbf{G}_\ell\check{\mathbf{P}}_\ell\mathbf{G}_\ell^T. \tag{5.86}$$

The second term subtracts uncertainty that comes from the state estimate (averaged over the trailing window) leaving hopefully only an estimate of the measurement noise. We can compute this estimate of the covariance, $\mathbf{R}_k$, using past data and employ it within the EKF. We slide the trailing window along from one timestep to the next to update the estimate at each new timestep.

A similar approach can be taken to estimating the process noise covariance if we assume the motion model has additive noise of the form

$$\mathbf{x}_k = \mathbf{f}(\mathbf{x}_{k-1}, \mathbf{u}_k) + \mathbf{w}_k, \quad \mathbf{w}_k \sim \mathcal{N}(\mathbf{0}, \mathbf{Q}_k), \tag{5.87}$$

where $\mathbf{f}(\cdot, \cdot)$ is the motion model, $\mathbf{u}_k$ is the input at time k, $\mathbf{w}_k$ is the process noise, and $\mathbf{Q}_k$ is the process noise covariance. We define the *prediction error*, $\mathbf{e}_{v,k}$, as

$$\mathbf{e}_{v,k} = \mathbf{f}(\hat{\mathbf{x}}_{k-1}, \mathbf{u}_k) - \hat{\mathbf{x}}_k, \tag{5.88}$$

where $\hat{\mathbf{x}}_{k-1}$ is the corrected state estimate at time $k - 1$ and $\hat{\mathbf{x}}_k$ is the corrected state estimate at time k (Stengel, 1994, p. 402). The prediction error hopefully has mean near zero with covariance

$$E[\mathbf{e}_{v,k}\mathbf{e}_{v,k}^T] \approx \mathbf{F}_{k-1}\hat{\mathbf{P}}_{k-1}\mathbf{F}_{k-1}^T + \mathbf{Q}_k, \tag{5.89}$$

where $\hat{\mathbf{P}}_{k-1}$ is the corrected state covariance and $\mathbf{F}_{k-1}$ is the motion model Jacobian, both at time $k - 1$. Again, the covariance expression in (5.89) is an approximation since we have linearized the motion model to compute it.

Using a trailing window of L datapoints from the current time, we can use a sample mean and covariance to estimate the true mean and covariance of the error as

$$\bar{\mathbf{e}}_{v,k} = \frac{1}{L} \sum_{\ell=k-1}^{k-L} \mathbf{e}_{v,\ell}, \tag{5.90a}$$

$$\mathbf{S}_{v,k} = \frac{1}{L-1} \sum_{\ell=k-1}^{k-L} (\mathbf{e}_{v,\ell} - \bar{\mathbf{e}}_{v,k})(\mathbf{e}_{v,\ell} - \bar{\mathbf{e}}_{v,k})^T. \tag{5.90b}$$

Equating $\mathbf{S}_{v,k}$ with (5.89), we can rearrange for $\mathbf{Q}_k$ as

$$\mathbf{Q}_k = \mathbf{S}_{v,k} - \frac{1}{L} \sum_{\ell=k-1}^{k-L} \mathbf{F}_{\ell-1}\hat{\mathbf{P}}_{\ell-1}\mathbf{F}_{\ell-1}^T. \tag{5.91}$$

The second term subtracts uncertainty that comes from the state estimate (averaged over the trailing window), leaving hopefully only an estimate of the process noise. We can again compute this estimate of the covariance, $\mathbf{Q}_k$, using past data and employ it within the EKF. We slide the trailing window along from one timestep to the next to update the estimate at each new timestep.

This approach can work well if the covariances, $\mathbf{R}_k$ and $\mathbf{Q}_k$, do not change too quickly and the noise is additive in the observation and motion models. It also makes the assumption that the filter is performing well (unbiased and consistent) up to the time that the covariances are being estimated. Looking back to the NIS test in Section 5.1.2, we see there is a strong connection to adaptive covariance estimation; adaptive covariance estimation is attempting to make the filter consistent according to the NIS test.

5.5.3 MAP Covariance Estimation

Another possibility for estimating covariances is to fold them into the MAP estimation problem itself. We can modify our MAP estimation problem to be

$$\left\{\hat{\mathbf{x}}, \hat{\mathbf{M}}\right\} = \arg \min_{\{\mathbf{x},\mathbf{M}\}} J'(\mathbf{x}, \mathbf{M}), \tag{5.92}$$

where $\mathbf{M} = \{\mathbf{M}_1, \ldots, \mathbf{M}_N\}$ is a convenient way to denote all of the unknown covariance matrices. This is similar to the idea of estimating a bias, as discussed earlier in this chapter; we simply include $\mathbf{M}_i$ in the set of variables to be estimated. To make this work, we need to provide the estimator some guidance in the form of a prior over the possible values that $\mathbf{M}_i$ is likely to have. Without a prior, the estimator can overfit to the data.

One possible prior is to assume that the covariance is distributed according to the *inverse-Wishart distribution*, which is defined over the real-valued, positive-definite matrices:

$$\mathbf{M}_i \sim \mathcal{W}^{-1}\left(\boldsymbol{\Psi}_i, \nu_i\right),\tag{5.93}$$

where $\boldsymbol{\Psi}_i > 0$ is called the *scale matrix*, $\nu_i > M_i - 1$ is the *degrees-of-freedom* parameter, and $M_i = \dim \mathbf{M}_i$. The inverse-Wishart PDF has the form

$$p(\mathbf{M}_i) = \frac{\det(\boldsymbol{\Psi}_i)^{\frac{\nu_i}{2}}}{2^{\frac{\nu_i M_i}{2}}\Gamma_{M_i}\left(\frac{\nu_i}{2}\right)}\det(\mathbf{M}_i)^{-\frac{\nu_i+M_i+1}{2}}\exp\left(-\frac{1}{2}\operatorname{tr}\left(\boldsymbol{\Psi}_i\mathbf{M}_i^{-1}\right)\right),\tag{5.94}$$

where $\Gamma_{M_i}\left(\cdot\right)$ is the *multivariate Gamma function*.

Under the MAP paradigm, the objective function is

$$J'(\mathbf{x}, \mathbf{M}) = -\ln p\left(\mathbf{x}, \mathbf{M} \,|\, \mathbf{z}\right),\tag{5.95}$$

where $\mathbf{z} = (\mathbf{z}_1, \ldots, \mathbf{z}_N)$ represents all of our input and measurement data, respectively. Factoring the posterior,

$$p\left(\mathbf{x}, \mathbf{M} \,|\, \mathbf{z}\right) = p\left(\mathbf{x} \,|\, \mathbf{z}, \mathbf{M}\right) p(\mathbf{M}) = \prod_{i=1}^{N} p\left(\mathbf{x} \,|\, \mathbf{z}_i, \mathbf{M}_i\right) p(\mathbf{M}_i),\tag{5.96}$$

and plugging in the inverse-Wishart PDF, the objective function becomes

$$J'(\mathbf{x}, \mathbf{M}) = \frac{1}{2}\sum_{i=1}^{N}\left(\mathbf{e}_i(\mathbf{x})^T\mathbf{M}_i^{-1}\mathbf{e}_i(\mathbf{x}) - \alpha_i \ln\left(\det\left(\mathbf{M}_i^{-1}\right)\right) + \operatorname{tr}\left(\boldsymbol{\Psi}_i\mathbf{M}_i^{-1}\right)\right),\tag{5.97}$$

with $\alpha_i = \nu_i + M_i + 2$. We have dropped terms that do not depend on $\mathbf{x}$ or $\mathbf{M}$.

Our strategy[5] will be to first find the optimal $\mathbf{M}_i$ (in terms of $\mathbf{x}$) so that we can eliminate it from the expression altogether. We do this by setting the derivative of $J'(\mathbf{x}, \mathbf{M})$ with respect to $\mathbf{M}_i^{-1}$ to zero, since it is $\mathbf{M}_i^{-1}$ that appears in the expression. Using some fairly standard matrix identities, we have

$$\frac{\partial J'(\mathbf{x}, \mathbf{M})}{\partial \mathbf{M}_i^{-1}} = \frac{1}{2}\mathbf{e}_i(\mathbf{x})\mathbf{e}_i(\mathbf{x})^T - \frac{1}{2}\alpha_i\mathbf{M}_i + \frac{1}{2}\boldsymbol{\Psi}_i.\tag{5.98}$$

Setting this to zero for a critical point and solving for $\mathbf{M}_i$, we have

$$\mathbf{M}_i(\mathbf{x}) = \underbrace{\frac{1}{\alpha_i}\boldsymbol{\Psi}_i}_{\text{constant}} + \underbrace{\frac{1}{\alpha_i}\mathbf{e}_i(\mathbf{x})\mathbf{e}_i(\mathbf{x})^T}_{\text{inflation}},\tag{5.99}$$

which is quite an interesting expression. It shows that the optimal covariance, $\mathbf{M}_i(\mathbf{x})$, will be inflated from a constant wherever the residual errors in the

---

[5] An alternate strategy is to marginalize out $\mathbf{M}$ from $p(\mathbf{x}, \mathbf{M} \,|\, \mathbf{z})$ from the beginning, which arrives at the same Cauchy-like final expression (Peretroukhin et al., 2016).

trajectory estimate, $\mathbf{e}_i(\mathbf{x})$, are large. This inflated expression is similar to the IRLS covariance in (5.77) from the section on M-estimation, implying a connection.

We can strengthen the connection to M-estimation by plugging the expression for the optimal $\mathbf{M}_i(\mathbf{x})$ back into $J'(\mathbf{x}, \mathbf{M})$, thereby eliminating it from the cost function. The resulting expression (after dropping factors that do not depend on $\mathbf{x}$) is

$$J'(\mathbf{x}) = \frac{1}{2} \sum_{i=1}^{N} \alpha_i \ln\left(1 + \mathbf{e}_i(\mathbf{x})^T \boldsymbol{\Psi}_i^{-1} \mathbf{e}_i(\mathbf{x})\right). \qquad (5.100)$$

This is exactly the form of a weighted Cauchy robust cost function discussed in the previous section when the scale matrix is chosen to be our usual (nonrobust) covariance: $\boldsymbol{\Psi}_i = \mathbf{W}_i$. Thus, the original problem defined in (5.92) can be implemented as an M-estimation problem using IRLS.

It is not the case that the inflated covariance, $\mathbf{M}_i(\mathbf{x})$, from (5.99) is exactly the same as $\mathbf{Y}_i(\mathbf{x})$ from (5.77), although they are similar. This is because $\mathbf{M}_i(\mathbf{x})$ is the exact covariance needed to minimize our desired objective function, $J'(\mathbf{x})$, whereas $\mathbf{Y}_i(\mathbf{x})$ is an approximation used in our iterative scheme to minimize $J''(\mathbf{x})$. At convergence (i.e., when $\hat{\mathbf{x}} = \mathbf{x}_{\mathrm{op}}$), the two methods have the same gradient and therefore the same minima, although they get there by slightly different paths.

It is quite appealing that in this specific case, the covariance estimation approach results in an equivalent M-estimation problem. It shows that the robust estimation approach can be explained from a MAP perspective, rather than simply being an ad hoc patch. It may be the case that this holds more generally, that all robust cost functions result from a particular choice of prior distribution over covariance matrices, $p(\mathbf{M})$. Black and Rangarajan (1996) provide a starting point for further investigation.

5.6 Summary

The main takeaway points from this chapter are as follows:

1. There are always nonidealities (e.g., biases, outliers) that make the real estimation problem different from the clean mathematical setups discussed in this book. Sometimes these deviations result in performance reductions that are the main source of error in practice.
2. In some situations, we can fold the estimation of a bias into our estimation framework, and in others we cannot. This comes down to the question of observability.
3. In most practical estimation problems, outliers are a reality, and thus using some form of preprocessing (e.g., RANSAC) as well as a robust cost function that downplays the effect of outliers is a necessity.
4. Measurement covariances can be estimated effectively from data, removing the need to tune them by trial and error.

The next part of the book will introduce techniques for handling state estimation in a three-dimensional world where objects are free to translate and rotate.

5.7 Exercises

5.1   Consider the discrete-time system

$$x_k = x_{k-1} + v_k + \bar{v},$$
$$d_k = x_k,$$

where $\bar{v}$ is an unknown input bias. Set up the augmented-state system and determine if this system is observable.

5.2   Consider the discrete-time system

$$x_k = x_{k-1} + v_{k-1},$$
$$v_k = v_{k-1} + a_k,$$
$$d_{1,k} = x_k,$$
$$d_{2,k} = x_k + \bar{d},$$

where $\bar{d}$ is an unknown input bias (on just one of the two measurement equations). Set up the augmented-state system and determine if this system is observable.

5.3   How many RANSAC iterations, k, would be needed to pick a set of $n = 3$ inlier points with probability $p = 0.999$, given that each point has probability $w = 0.1$ of being an inlier?

5.4   How many RANSAC iterations, k, would be needed to pick a set of $n = 2$ inlier points with probability $p = 0.99999$, given that each point has probability $w = 0.75$ of being an inlier?

5.5   What advantage might the robust cost function,

$$\rho(u) = \begin{cases} \frac{1}{2}u^2 & u^2 \leq 1 \\ \frac{2u^2}{1+u^2} - \frac{1}{2} & u^2 \geq 1 \end{cases},$$

have over the Geman–McClure cost function?

6

Variational Inference

In this first part of the book, we have learned about classic linear-Gaussian state estimation and some of the common extensions to nonlinear motion and observation models. We also learned about bias and covariance estimation by a few different techniques. Our development has been 'bottom-up' in the sense that we started with linear-Gaussian estimation and *extended* the classic results to more complicated situations. In this chapter on *variational inference*, we take another look at estimation from a 'top-down' perspective. We will start with a single data-likelihood objective and show how it is possible to not only carry out nonlinear state estimation but also parameter identification that can include system matrices, biases, covariances, and more. Put another way, variational inference provides a single framework in which we can interpret and understand many of the results from earlier chapters.

6.1 Introduction

If we adopt a Bayesian perspective (Bayes, 1764), our goal is to compute the full posterior, $p(\mathbf{x}|\mathbf{z})$, by refining a prior, $p(\mathbf{x})$, not just a point estimate, based on some measurements, $\mathbf{z}$:

$$p(\mathbf{x}|\mathbf{z}) = \frac{p(\mathbf{z}|\mathbf{x})p(\mathbf{x})}{p(\mathbf{z})} = \frac{p(\mathbf{x}, \mathbf{z})}{p(\mathbf{z})}. \tag{6.1}$$

The full posterior is not a Gaussian PDF for nonlinear measurement models, $p(\mathbf{z}|\mathbf{x})$. We are therefore often satisfied with finding the maximum of the Bayesian posterior, which is called the *maximum a posteriori (MAP)* approach. We have seen MAP several times in earlier chapters of this book.

Rather than finding the maximum of the Bayesian posterior, our approach in this chapter will be to find the best Gaussian approximation, in terms of the mean and (inverse) covariance, to the full posterior that is 'closest' in terms of the *Kullback–Leibler (KL)* divergence between the two (Kullback and Leibler, 1951) (see Section 2.1.6). This approach is referred to as *variational inference* or *variational Bayes* (Jordan et al., 1999; Bishop, 2006). As we will restrict ourselves to Gaussian approximations of the posterior, we will refer to this as *Gaussian variational inference (GVI)*. GVI is not commonly used in batch estimation problems, where the state size, N, can be very large. We will discuss how to make GVI tractable for large-scale estimation problems. Specifically, we will show how to exploit a joint likelihood for the state and measurements that can be factored,

$$p(\mathbf{x}, \mathbf{z}) = \prod_{k=1}^{K} p(\mathbf{x}_k, \mathbf{z}_k), \qquad (6.2)$$

where $\mathbf{x}_k$ is a subset of the variables in $\mathbf{x}$. This type of factorization is very common in real-world robotics problems, for example, since each measurement typically only involves a small subset of the state variables and we have already exploited this factorization in earlier chapters in the MAP approach for efficient solution. We can extend this exploit to the GVI approach by identifying that the inverse covariance matrix is *exactly sparse* when the likelihood factors, and most importantly, that we never actually need to compute the entire covariance matrix, which is typically dense and of size $N \times N$. As a by-product of our approach, we also show how to use cubature points (e.g., sigmapoints) for some of the required calculations, resulting in an efficient derivative-free implementation for large-scale batch estimation.

This chapter is primarily based on the work of Barfoot et al. (2020). Opper and Archambeau (2009) also discuss a similar GVI approach in machine learning. They begin with the same KL divergence and show how to calculate the derivatives of this functional with respect to the Gaussian parameters. They go on to apply the method to Gaussian process regression problems (Rasmussen and Williams, 2006), of which batch trajectory estimation can be viewed as a special case (Barfoot et al., 2014; Anderson et al., 2015). Kokkala et al. (2014, 2016), Ala-Luhtala et al. (2015), García-Fernández et al. (2015), Gašperin and Juričić (2011), and Schön et al. (2011) discuss a very similar approach to our GVI scheme in the context of nonlinear smoothers and filters; some of these works also carry out parameter estimation of the motion and observation models, which we also discuss as it fits neatly into the variational approach (Neal and Hinton, 1998; Ghahramani and Roweis, 1999). These works start from the same KL divergence, show how to exploit factorization of the joint likelihood, and discuss how to apply sigmapoints (Kokkala et al., 2014, 2016; Gašperin and Juričić, 2011) or particles (Schön et al., 2011) to avoid the need to compute derivatives. García-Fernández et al. (2015) is a filtering paper that follows a similar philosophy to the current chapter by statistically linearizing about an iteratively improved posterior.

6.2 Gaussian Variational Inference

This section poses the problem we are going to solve and proposes a general solution. Exploiting application-specific structure is discussed later, in Section 6.3. We first define the loss functional that we seek to minimize, then derive an optimization scheme in order to minimize it with respect to the parameters of a Gaussian. As an aside, we show that our optimization scheme is equivalent to so-called *natural gradient descent (NGD)*. Following this, we work our optimization scheme into a different form in preparation for exploiting application-specific structure and finally show that we can recover the classic batch solution in the linear case.

6.2.1 Loss Functional

As is common in variational inference (Bishop, 2006), we seek to minimize the KL divergence (Kullback and Leibler, 1951) between the true Bayesian posterior, $p(\mathbf{x}|\mathbf{z})$, and an approximation of the posterior, $q(\mathbf{x})$, which in our case will be a multivariate Gaussian PDF,

$$q(\mathbf{x}) = \mathcal{N}(\boldsymbol{\mu}, \boldsymbol{\Sigma}) = \frac{1}{\sqrt{(2\pi)^N |\boldsymbol{\Sigma}|}} \exp\left(-\frac{1}{2}(\mathbf{x} - \boldsymbol{\mu})^T \boldsymbol{\Sigma}^{-1}(\mathbf{x} - \boldsymbol{\mu})\right), \quad (6.3)$$

where $|\cdot|$ is the determinant. For practical robotics and computer vision problems, the dimension of the state, N, can become very large and so it is important to show how to carry out GVI in an efficient manner for large-scale problems.

As KL divergence is not symmetrical, we have a choice of using $\mathrm{KL}(p\|q)$ or $\mathrm{KL}(q\|p)$. Bishop (2006, p. 467) provides a good discussion of the differences between these two functionals. The former expression is given by

$$\mathrm{KL}(p\|q) = -\int_{-\infty}^{\infty} p(\mathbf{x}|\mathbf{z}) \ln\left(\frac{q(\mathbf{x})}{p(\mathbf{x}|\mathbf{z})}\right) d\mathbf{x}$$
$$= E_p\left[\ln p(\mathbf{x}|\mathbf{z}) - \ln q(\mathbf{x})\right], \quad (6.4)$$

while the latter is

$$\mathrm{KL}(q\|p) = -\int_{-\infty}^{\infty} q(\mathbf{x}) \ln\left(\frac{p(\mathbf{x}|\mathbf{z})}{q(\mathbf{x})}\right) d\mathbf{x}$$
$$= E_q\left[\ln q(\mathbf{x}) - \ln p(\mathbf{x}|\mathbf{z})\right], \quad (6.5)$$

where $\mathbf{x} \in \mathbb{R}^N$ is the latent state that we seek to infer from data, $\mathbf{z} \in \mathbb{R}^D$, and $E[\cdot]$ is the expectation operator with the subscript denoting over which density the expectation is computed. The key practical difference that leads us to choose $\mathrm{KL}(q\|p)$ is that the expectation is over our Gaussian estimate, $q(\mathbf{x})$, rather than the true posterior, $p(\mathbf{x}|\mathbf{z})$. We will show that we can use this fact to devise an efficient iterative scheme for $q(\mathbf{x})$ that best approximates the posterior. Moreover, our choice of $\mathrm{KL}(q\|p)$ leads naturally to also estimating parameters of the system (Neal and Hinton, 1998), which we discuss in Section 6.4.2.

We observe that our chosen KL divergence can be written as

$$\mathrm{KL}(q\|p) = E_q[-\ln p(\mathbf{x}, \mathbf{z})] \underbrace{-\frac{1}{2}\ln\left((2\pi e)^N |\boldsymbol{\Sigma}|\right)}_{\text{entropy}} + \underbrace{\ln p(\mathbf{z})}_{\text{constant}}, \quad (6.6)$$

where we have used the expression for the *entropy*, $-\int q(\mathbf{x}) \ln q(\mathbf{x}) d\mathbf{x}$, for a Gaussian (see Section 2.2.10). Noticing that the final term is a constant (i.e., it does not depend on $q(\mathbf{x})$), we define the following loss functional that we seek to minimize with respect to $q(\mathbf{x})$:

$$V(q) = E_q[\phi(\mathbf{x})] + \frac{1}{2}\ln\left(|\boldsymbol{\Sigma}^{-1}|\right), \quad (6.7)$$

with $\phi(\mathbf{x}) = -\ln p(\mathbf{x}, \mathbf{z})$. We deliberately switch from $\boldsymbol{\Sigma}$ (covariance matrix) to $\boldsymbol{\Sigma}^{-1}$ (inverse covariance matrix, also known as the *information matrix* or *precision matrix*) in (6.7) as the latter enjoys sparsity that the former does not; we will carry this forward and use $\boldsymbol{\mu}$ and $\boldsymbol{\Sigma}^{-1}$ as a complete description of $q(\mathbf{x})$. The first term in $V(q)$ encourages the solution to match the data while the second penalizes it for being too certain; a relative weighting (i.e., a metaparameter) between these two terms could be used to tune performance on other metrics of interest although then we would not be using KL divergence proper. It is also worth mentioning that $V(q)$ is the negative of the so-called *evidence lower bound (ELBO)*, which we will consequently minimize.

6.2.2 Optimization Scheme

Our next task is to define an optimization scheme to minimize the loss functional with respect to the mean, $\boldsymbol{\mu}$, and inverse covariance, $\boldsymbol{\Sigma}^{-1}$. Our approach will be similar to a Newton-style optimizer.

After a bit of calculus, the derivatives of our loss functional, $V(q)$, with respect to our Gaussian parameters, $\boldsymbol{\mu}$ and $\boldsymbol{\Sigma}^{-1}$, are given by (Opper and Archambeau, 2009)

$$\frac{\partial V(q)}{\partial \boldsymbol{\mu}^T} = \boldsymbol{\Sigma}^{-1} E_q[(\mathbf{x} - \boldsymbol{\mu})\phi(\mathbf{x})], \tag{6.8a}$$

$$\frac{\partial^2 V(q)}{\partial \boldsymbol{\mu}^T \partial \boldsymbol{\mu}} = \boldsymbol{\Sigma}^{-1} E_q[(\mathbf{x} - \boldsymbol{\mu})(\mathbf{x} - \boldsymbol{\mu})^T \phi(\mathbf{x})]\boldsymbol{\Sigma}^{-1} - \boldsymbol{\Sigma}^{-1} E_q[\phi(\mathbf{x})], \tag{6.8b}$$

$$\frac{\partial V(q)}{\partial \boldsymbol{\Sigma}^{-1}} = -\frac{1}{2} E_q[(\mathbf{x} - \boldsymbol{\mu})(\mathbf{x} - \boldsymbol{\mu})^T \phi(\mathbf{x})] + \frac{1}{2}\boldsymbol{\Sigma} E_q[\phi(\mathbf{x})] + \frac{1}{2}\boldsymbol{\Sigma}, \tag{6.8c}$$

where, comparing (6.8b) and (6.8c), we notice that

$$\frac{\partial^2 V(q)}{\partial \boldsymbol{\mu}^T \partial \boldsymbol{\mu}} = \boldsymbol{\Sigma}^{-1} - 2\boldsymbol{\Sigma}^{-1} \frac{\partial V(q)}{\partial \boldsymbol{\Sigma}^{-1}} \boldsymbol{\Sigma}^{-1}. \tag{6.9}$$

This relationship is critical to defining our optimization scheme, which we do next.

To find extrema, we could attempt to set the first derivatives to zero, but it is not (in general) possible to isolate for $\boldsymbol{\mu}$ and $\boldsymbol{\Sigma}^{-1}$ in closed form. Hence, we will define an iterative update scheme. We begin by writing out a Taylor series expansion of $V(q)$ that is second order in $\delta\boldsymbol{\mu}$ but only first order in $\delta\boldsymbol{\Sigma}^{-1}$ (second order would be difficult to calculate and covariance quantities are already quadratic in $\mathbf{x}$):

$$V\left(q^{(i+1)}\right) \approx V\left(q^{(i)}\right) + \left(\frac{\partial V(q)}{\partial \boldsymbol{\mu}^T}\bigg|_{q^{(i)}}\right)^T \delta\boldsymbol{\mu}$$

$$+ \frac{1}{2}\delta\boldsymbol{\mu}^T \left(\frac{\partial^2 V(q)}{\partial \boldsymbol{\mu}^T \partial \boldsymbol{\mu}}\bigg|_{q^{(i)}}\right) \delta\boldsymbol{\mu} + \mathrm{tr}\left(\frac{\partial V(q)}{\partial \boldsymbol{\Sigma}^{-1}}\bigg|_{q^{(i)}} \delta\boldsymbol{\Sigma}^{-1}\right), \tag{6.10}$$

where $\delta\boldsymbol{\mu} = \boldsymbol{\mu}^{(i+1)} - \boldsymbol{\mu}^{(i)}$ and $\delta\boldsymbol{\Sigma}^{-1} = \left(\boldsymbol{\Sigma}^{-1}\right)^{(i+1)} - \left(\boldsymbol{\Sigma}^{-1}\right)^{(i)}$ with i the iteration index of our scheme. We now want to choose $\delta\boldsymbol{\mu}$ and $\delta\boldsymbol{\Sigma}^{-1}$ to force $V(q)$ to get smaller.

For the inverse covariance, $\boldsymbol{\Sigma}^{-1}$, if we set the derivative, $\frac{\partial V(q)}{\partial \boldsymbol{\Sigma}^{-1}}$, to zero (for an extremum) in (6.9) we immediately have

$$\boldsymbol{\Sigma}^{-1(i+1)} = \left.\frac{\partial^2 V(q)}{\partial \boldsymbol{\mu}^T \partial \boldsymbol{\mu}}\right|_{q^{(i)}}, \tag{6.11}$$

where we place an index of $(i+1)$ on the left and (i) on the right in order to define an iterative update. Inserting (6.9) again on the right, we see that the change to the inverse covariance by using this update can also be written as

$$\delta\boldsymbol{\Sigma}^{-1} = -2\left(\boldsymbol{\Sigma}^{-1}\right)^{(i)} \left.\frac{\partial V(q)}{\partial \boldsymbol{\Sigma}^{-1}}\right|_{q^{(i)}} \left(\boldsymbol{\Sigma}^{-1}\right)^{(i)}. \tag{6.12}$$

Convergence of this scheme will be discussed below.[1]

For the mean, $\boldsymbol{\mu}$, we will take inspiration from the MAP approach to Gaussian nonlinear batch estimation and employ a Newton-style update (see Section 4.3.1). Since our loss approximation (6.10) is locally quadratic in $\delta\boldsymbol{\mu}$, we take the derivative with respect to $\delta\boldsymbol{\mu}$ and set this to zero (to find the minimum). This results in a linear system of equations for $\delta\boldsymbol{\mu}$:

$$\underbrace{\left(\left.\frac{\partial^2 V(q)}{\partial \boldsymbol{\mu}^T \partial \boldsymbol{\mu}}\right|_{q^{(i)}}\right)}_{\left(\boldsymbol{\Sigma}^{-1}\right)^{(i+1)}} \delta\boldsymbol{\mu} = -\left(\left.\frac{\partial V(q)}{\partial \boldsymbol{\mu}^T}\right|_{q^{(i)}}\right), \tag{6.13}$$

where we note the convenient reappearance of $\boldsymbol{\Sigma}^{-1}$ as the left-hand side.

Inserting our chosen scheme for $\delta\boldsymbol{\mu}$ and $\delta\boldsymbol{\Sigma}^{-1}$ into the loss approximation (6.10), we have

$$V\left(q^{(i+1)}\right) - V\left(q^{(i)}\right) \approx -\frac{1}{2} \underbrace{\delta\boldsymbol{\mu}^T \left(\boldsymbol{\Sigma}^{-1}\right)^{(i+1)} \delta\boldsymbol{\mu}}_{\geq 0}$$

$$\text{with equality iff } \delta\boldsymbol{\mu} = \mathbf{0}$$

$$-\frac{1}{2} \underbrace{\text{tr}\left(\boldsymbol{\Sigma}^{(i)} \delta\boldsymbol{\Sigma}^{-1} \boldsymbol{\Sigma}^{(i)} \delta\boldsymbol{\Sigma}^{-1}\right)}_{\geq 0} \leq 0, \tag{6.14}$$

$$\text{with equality iff } \delta\boldsymbol{\Sigma}^{-1} = \mathbf{0}$$

---

[1] It is worth mentioning that (6.8c) ignores the fact that $\boldsymbol{\Sigma}^{-1}$ is actually a symmetric matrix. Magnus and Neudecker (2019) discuss how to calculate the derivative of a function with respect to a matrix while accounting for its symmetry; see also Appendix A.2.4 for a summary. They show that if $\mathbf{A}$ is the derivative of a function (with respect to a symmetric matrix, $\mathbf{B}$) that ignores symmetry, then $\mathbf{A} + \mathbf{A}^T - \mathbf{A} \circ \mathbf{1}$ is the derivative accounting for the symmetry of $\mathbf{B}$, where $\circ$ is the Hadamard (element-wise) product and $\mathbf{1}$ is the identity matrix. It is not too difficult to see that $\mathbf{A} = \mathbf{0}$ if and only if $\mathbf{A} + \mathbf{A}^T - \mathbf{A} \circ \mathbf{1} = \mathbf{0}$ in the case of a symmetric $\mathbf{A}$. Therefore, if we want to find an extremum by setting the derivative to zero, we can simply set $\mathbf{A} = \mathbf{0}$ as long as $\mathbf{A}$ is symmetric and this will account for the symmetry of $\mathbf{B}$ correctly.

which shows that we will reduce our loss, $V(q)$, so long as $\delta\boldsymbol{\mu}$ and $\delta\boldsymbol{\Sigma}^{-1}$ are not both zero; this is true when the derivatives with respect to $\boldsymbol{\mu}$ and $\boldsymbol{\Sigma}^{-1}$ are not both zero, which occurs only at a local minimum of $V(q)$. This is a local convergence guarantee only as the expression is based on our Taylor series expansion in (6.10).

We observe that

$$\text{tr}\left(\boldsymbol{\Sigma}^{(i)}\,\delta\boldsymbol{\Sigma}^{-1}\,\boldsymbol{\Sigma}^{(i)}\,\delta\boldsymbol{\Sigma}^{-1}\right) \geq 0, \tag{6.15}$$

with equality if and only if $\delta\boldsymbol{\Sigma}^{-1} = \mathbf{0}$ in our local convergence guarantee in (6.14). To show this, it is sufficient to show for $\mathbf{A}$ real, positive-definite and $\mathbf{B}$ real, symmetric that

$$\text{tr}(\mathbf{ABAB}) \geq 0, \tag{6.16}$$

with equality if and only if $\mathbf{B} = \mathbf{0}$. We can write

$$\text{tr}(\mathbf{ABAB}) = \text{vec}(\mathbf{ABA})^T \text{vec}(\mathbf{B})$$
$$= \text{vec}(\mathbf{B})^T \underbrace{(\mathbf{A} \otimes \mathbf{A})}_{>0} \text{vec}(\mathbf{B}) \geq 0, \tag{6.17}$$

using basic properties of $\text{vec}(\cdot)$ and the Kronecker product, $\otimes$ (see Appendix A.1.14). The matrix in the middle is symmetric positive definite owing to our assumptions on $\mathbf{A}$. Therefore the quadratic form is positive-semidefinite with equality if and only if $\text{vec}(\mathbf{B}) = \mathbf{0}$ if and only if $\mathbf{B} = \mathbf{0}$.

6.2.3 Natural Gradient Descent Interpretation

As an aside, we can interpret our update for $\delta\boldsymbol{\mu}$ and $\delta\boldsymbol{\Sigma}^{-1}$ as carrying out so-called *natural gradient descent (NGD)* (Amari, 1998; Hoffman et al., 2013), which exploits the information geometry to make the update more efficient than regular gradient descent. To see this, we stack our variational parameters into a single column, $\boldsymbol{\alpha}$, using the $\text{vec}(\cdot)$ operator, which converts a matrix to a vector by stacking its columns (see Appendix A.1.14):

$$\boldsymbol{\alpha} = \begin{bmatrix} \boldsymbol{\mu} \\ \text{vec}\left(\boldsymbol{\Sigma}^{-1}\right) \end{bmatrix}, \quad \delta\boldsymbol{\alpha} = \begin{bmatrix} \delta\boldsymbol{\mu} \\ \text{vec}\left(\delta\boldsymbol{\Sigma}^{-1}\right) \end{bmatrix},$$
$$\frac{\partial V(q)}{\partial\boldsymbol{\alpha}^T} = \begin{bmatrix} \frac{\partial V(q)}{\partial\boldsymbol{\mu}^T} \\ \text{vec}\left(\frac{\partial V(q)}{\partial\boldsymbol{\Sigma}^{-1}}\right) \end{bmatrix}. \tag{6.18}$$

The last expression is the gradient of the loss functional with respect to $\boldsymbol{\alpha}$.

The NGD update scheme can then be defined as

$$\delta\boldsymbol{\alpha} = -\mathcal{I}_{\boldsymbol{\alpha}}^{-1}\frac{\partial V(q)}{\partial\boldsymbol{\alpha}^T}, \tag{6.19}$$

where $\mathcal{I}_{\boldsymbol{\alpha}}$ is the FIM (Fisher, 1922) for the variational parameter, $\boldsymbol{\alpha}$, and its calculation can be found in Appendix C.1. Inserting the details of the components of the preceding we have

$$\begin{bmatrix} \delta\boldsymbol{\mu} \\ \text{vec}\left(\delta\boldsymbol{\Sigma}^{-1}\right) \end{bmatrix} = -\begin{bmatrix} \boldsymbol{\Sigma}^{-1} & \mathbf{0} \\ \mathbf{0} & \frac{1}{2}\left(\boldsymbol{\Sigma}\otimes\boldsymbol{\Sigma}\right) \end{bmatrix}^{-1}\begin{bmatrix} \frac{\partial V(q)}{\partial\boldsymbol{\mu}^T} \\ \text{vec}\left(\frac{\partial V(q)}{\partial\boldsymbol{\Sigma}^{-1}}\right) \end{bmatrix}, \qquad (6.20)$$

where $\otimes$ is the Kronecker product (see Appendix A.1.14). Extracting the individual updates, we see

$$\delta\boldsymbol{\mu} = -\boldsymbol{\Sigma}\frac{\partial V(q)}{\partial\boldsymbol{\mu}^T}, \qquad (6.21a)$$

$$\text{vec}\left(\delta\boldsymbol{\Sigma}^{-1}\right) = -2\left(\boldsymbol{\Sigma}^{-1}\otimes\boldsymbol{\Sigma}^{-1}\right)\text{vec}\left(\frac{\partial V(q)}{\partial\boldsymbol{\Sigma}^{-1}}\right). \qquad (6.21b)$$

Finally, using that $\text{vec}(\mathbf{ABC}) = \left(\mathbf{C}^T\otimes\mathbf{A}\right)\text{vec}(\mathbf{B})$, we have

$$\boldsymbol{\Sigma}^{-1}\delta\boldsymbol{\mu} = -\frac{\partial V(q)}{\partial\boldsymbol{\mu}^T}, \qquad (6.22a)$$

$$\delta\boldsymbol{\Sigma}^{-1} = -2\boldsymbol{\Sigma}^{-1}\frac{\partial V(q)}{\partial\boldsymbol{\Sigma}^{-1}}\boldsymbol{\Sigma}^{-1}, \qquad (6.22b)$$

which is the same set of updates as in the previous subsection.

6.2.4 Stein's Lemma

While our iterative scheme could be implemented as is, it will be expensive (i.e., $O(N^3)$ per iteration) for large problems. The next section will show how to exploit sparsity to make the scheme efficient and, in preparation for that, we will manipulate our update equations into a slightly different form using *Stein's lemma* (Stein, 1981) (see Section 2.2.16).

We can apply Stein's lemma from (2.125) and (2.126) to our optimization scheme in (6.11) and (6.13) to write the iterative updates compactly as

$$\left(\boldsymbol{\Sigma}^{-1}\right)^{(i+1)} = E_{q^{(i)}}\left[\frac{\partial^2}{\partial\mathbf{x}^T\partial\mathbf{x}}\phi(\mathbf{x})\right], \qquad (6.23a)$$

$$\left(\boldsymbol{\Sigma}^{-1}\right)^{(i+1)}\delta\boldsymbol{\mu} = -E_{q^{(i)}}\left[\frac{\partial}{\partial\mathbf{x}^T}\phi(\mathbf{x})\right], \qquad (6.23b)$$

$$\boldsymbol{\mu}^{(i+1)} = \boldsymbol{\mu}^{(i)} + \delta\boldsymbol{\mu}. \qquad (6.23c)$$

Ala-Luhtala et al. (2015, appendix C) also make use of Stein's lemma in this way in the context of Gaussian variational smoothers. In general, this iterative scheme will still be expensive for large problems and so we will look to exploit structure to make GVI more efficient. As only the first and second derivatives of $\phi(\mathbf{x})$ are required, we can drop any constant terms (i.e., the normalization constant of $p(\mathbf{x}, \mathbf{z})$).

Notably, our optimization scheme in (6.23) is identical to MAP Newton's method from Section 4.3.1 (with the Laplace covariance approximation) if we approximate the expectations using only the mean of $q(\mathbf{x})$. Thus, MAP Newton with Laplace can be viewed as an approximation of the more general approach we discuss in this chapter.

Additionally, we can combine Stein's lemma with our loss derivatives in (6.8a), (6.8b) and (6.8c) to show the useful identities

$$\frac{\partial}{\partial \boldsymbol{\mu}^T} E_q[f(\mathbf{x})] \equiv E_q\left[\frac{\partial f(\mathbf{x})}{\partial \mathbf{x}^T}\right], \tag{6.24a}$$

$$\frac{\partial^2}{\partial \boldsymbol{\mu}^T \partial \boldsymbol{\mu}} E_q[f(\mathbf{x})] \equiv E_q\left[\frac{\partial^2 f(\mathbf{x})}{\partial \mathbf{x}^T \partial \mathbf{x}}\right] \tag{6.24b}$$

$$\equiv -2\boldsymbol{\Sigma}^{-1}\left(\frac{\partial}{\partial \boldsymbol{\Sigma}^{-1}} E_q[f(\mathbf{x})]\right)\boldsymbol{\Sigma}^{-1},$$

which we will have occasion to use later on. To show (6.24a), we can use (6.8a) to write

$$\frac{\partial}{\partial \boldsymbol{\mu}^T} E_q[f(\mathbf{x})] = \boldsymbol{\Sigma}^{-1} E_q[(\mathbf{x} - \boldsymbol{\mu})f(\mathbf{x})], \tag{6.25}$$

which can also be found in Opper and Archambeau (2009). Applying Stein's lemma from (2.125), we immediately have

$$\frac{\partial}{\partial \boldsymbol{\mu}^T} E_q[f(\mathbf{x})] = E_q\left[\frac{\partial f(\mathbf{x})}{\partial \mathbf{x}^T}\right], \tag{6.26}$$

the desired result. To show (6.24b), we can use (6.8b) to write

$$\frac{\partial^2}{\partial \boldsymbol{\mu}^T \partial \boldsymbol{\mu}} E_q[f(\mathbf{x})] = \boldsymbol{\Sigma}^{-1} E_q[(\mathbf{x} - \boldsymbol{\mu})(\mathbf{x} - \boldsymbol{\mu})^T f(\mathbf{x})]\boldsymbol{\Sigma}^{-1} - \boldsymbol{\Sigma}^{-1} E_q[f(\mathbf{x})], \tag{6.27}$$

again due to Opper and Archambeau (2009). Applying Stein's lemma from (2.126), we have

$$\frac{\partial^2}{\partial \boldsymbol{\mu}^T \partial \boldsymbol{\mu}} E_q[f(\mathbf{x})] = E_q\left[\frac{\partial^2 f(\mathbf{x})}{\partial \mathbf{x}^T \partial \mathbf{x}}\right], \tag{6.28}$$

the desired result. Similarly to (6.8c), we have

$$\frac{\partial}{\partial \boldsymbol{\Sigma}^{-1}} E_q[f(\mathbf{x})] = -\frac{1}{2} E_q[(\mathbf{x} - \boldsymbol{\mu})(\mathbf{x} - \boldsymbol{\mu})^T f(\mathbf{x})] + \frac{1}{2}\boldsymbol{\Sigma}\, E_q[f(\mathbf{x})], \tag{6.29}$$

which is again confirmed by Opper and Archambeau (2009). Comparing the right-hand side of this to the right-hand side of (6.27), we have

$$-2\boldsymbol{\Sigma}^{-1}\left(\frac{\partial}{\partial \boldsymbol{\Sigma}^{-1}} E_q[f(\mathbf{x})]\right)\boldsymbol{\Sigma}^{-1} = \frac{\partial^2}{\partial \boldsymbol{\mu}^T \partial \boldsymbol{\mu}} E_q[f(\mathbf{x})] = E_q\left[\frac{\partial^2 f(\mathbf{x})}{\partial \mathbf{x}^T \partial \mathbf{x}}\right], \tag{6.30}$$

which shows the second part of (6.24b).

6.3 Exact Sparsity

This section shows how to exploit application-specific structure to make the optimization scheme of the previous section efficient for large-scale problems. We first show that when the joint likelihood of the state and data can be factored, the calculation of the required expectations in our optimization scheme is exactly sparse, meaning we only need the marginals of the covariance associated with each factor. We then discuss how we can calculate these marginals efficiently from the inverse covariance, for any GVI problem. Finally, we show how to use sigmapoints drawn from these marginals to implement the full optimization scheme.

6.3.1 Factored Joint Likelihood

We have seen in the previous section that the iterative update scheme relies on calculating three expectations:

$$
\underbrace{E_q[\phi(\mathbf{x})]}_{\text{scalar}}, \quad \underbrace{E_q\left[\frac{\partial}{\partial \mathbf{x}^T}\phi(\mathbf{x})\right]}_{\text{column}}, \quad \underbrace{E_q\left[\frac{\partial^2}{\partial \mathbf{x}^T \partial \mathbf{x}}\phi(\mathbf{x})\right]}_{\text{matrix}}, \tag{6.31}
$$

where we drop the iteration index for now. Let us now assume that the joint state/data likelihood can be factored such that we can write its negative log-likelihood as

$$
\phi(\mathbf{x}) = \sum_{k=1}^{K} \phi_k(\mathbf{x}_k), \tag{6.32}
$$

where $\phi_k(\mathbf{x}_k) = -\ln p(\mathbf{x}_k, \mathbf{z}_k)$ is the kth (negative log) factor expression, $\mathbf{x}_k$ is a *subset* of variables in $\mathbf{x}$ associated with the kth factor, and $\mathbf{z}_k$ is a subset of the data in $\mathbf{z}$ associated with the kth factor.

Let us consider the first (scalar) expectation in (6.31). We can insert the factored likelihood and see what happens:

$$
E_q[\phi(\mathbf{x})] = E_q\left[\sum_{k=1}^{K} \phi_k(\mathbf{x}_k)\right] = \sum_{k=1}^{K} E_q[\phi_k(\mathbf{x}_k)] = \sum_{k=1}^{K} E_{q_k}[\phi_k(\mathbf{x}_k)], \tag{6.33}
$$

where the last step is subtle but paramount: the expectation simplifies from being over $q = q(\mathbf{x})$, the full Gaussian estimate, to being over $q_k = q_k(\mathbf{x}_k)$, the *marginal* of the estimate for just the variables in each factor. This is not an approximation, and the implications are many.

The other two expectations (column and matrix) in (6.31) enjoy similar simplifications and more, but require a bit more explanation. Let $\mathbf{P}_k$ be a projection matrix such that it extracts $\mathbf{x}_k$ from $\mathbf{x}$:

$$
\mathbf{x}_k = \mathbf{P}_k \mathbf{x}. \tag{6.34}
$$

Then, inserting the factored expression into the second (column) expectation, we have

$$E_q\left[\frac{\partial}{\partial \mathbf{x}^T}\phi(\mathbf{x})\right] = E_q\left[\frac{\partial}{\partial \mathbf{x}^T}\sum_{k=1}^{K}\phi_k(\mathbf{x}_k)\right]$$

$$= \sum_{k=1}^{K}E_q\left[\frac{\partial}{\partial \mathbf{x}^T}\phi_k(\mathbf{x}_k)\right]$$

$$= \sum_{k=1}^{K}\mathbf{P}_k^T E_q\left[\frac{\partial}{\partial \mathbf{x}_k^T}\phi_k(\mathbf{x}_k)\right]$$

$$= \sum_{k=1}^{K}\mathbf{P}_k^T E_{q_k}\left[\frac{\partial}{\partial \mathbf{x}_k^T}\phi_k(\mathbf{x}_k)\right]. \tag{6.35}$$

For factor k, we are able to simplify the derivative from being with respect to $\mathbf{x}$, to being with respect to $\mathbf{x}_k$, since there is no dependence on the variables not in $\mathbf{x}_k$ and hence the derivative with respect to those variables is zero; we use the projection matrix (as a dilation matrix) to map the derivative back into the appropriate rows of the overall result. After this, the expectation again simplifies to being with respect to $q_k = q_k(\mathbf{x}_k)$, the marginal of the estimate for just the variables in factor k. For the last (matrix) expectation we have a similar result:

$$E_q\left[\frac{\partial^2}{\partial \mathbf{x}^T\partial \mathbf{x}}\phi(\mathbf{x})\right] = E_q\left[\frac{\partial^2}{\partial \mathbf{x}^T\partial \mathbf{x}}\sum_{k=1}^{K}\phi_k(\mathbf{x}_k)\right]$$

$$= \sum_{k=1}^{K}E_q\left[\frac{\partial^2}{\partial \mathbf{x}^T\partial \mathbf{x}}\phi_k(\mathbf{x}_k)\right]$$

$$= \sum_{k=1}^{K}\mathbf{P}_k^T E_q\left[\frac{\partial^2}{\partial \mathbf{x}_k^T\partial \mathbf{x}_k}\phi_k(\mathbf{x}_k)\right]\mathbf{P}_k$$

$$= \sum_{k=1}^{K}\mathbf{P}_k^T E_{q_k}\left[\frac{\partial^2}{\partial \mathbf{x}_k^T\partial \mathbf{x}_k}\phi_k(\mathbf{x}_k)\right]\mathbf{P}_k. \tag{6.36}$$

The simplified expectations in (6.33), (6.35), and (6.36) are the key tools that enable our *exactly sparse Gaussian variational inference (ESGVI)* approach and we now make several remarks about them:

– We do not require the full Gaussian estimate, $q(\mathbf{x})$, to evaluate the three expectations involved in our iterative scheme but rather we only require the marginals associated with each factor, $q_k(\mathbf{x}_k)$. This can represent a huge computational and storage savings in practical problems because it means that we never need to fully construct and store the (usually dense) covariance matrix, $\mathbf{\Sigma}$. Schön et al. (2011), Gašperin and Juričić (2011), and Kokkala et al. (2016) also show how the required expectations are simplified to being over the marginals specifically for the smoother problem, but here we have generalized that result to any factorization of the joint likelihood.

– Looking to the covariance update in (6.23a) and now the simplification in (6.36), we know that $\mathbf{\Sigma}^{-1}$ will be exactly sparse (with the pattern depending on the nature of the factors) and that *the sparsity pattern will remain constant as we iterate*. A fixed sparsity pattern ensures that we can build a custom sparse solver for the mean (6.23b) and use it safely at each iteration; for example, in the batch state estimation problem, $\boldsymbol{\Sigma}^{-1}$ is block-tridiagonal (under a chronological variable ordering).

– As a reminder, marginalization of a Gaussian (see Section 2.2.5) amounts to projection such that

$$q_k(\mathbf{x}_k) = \mathcal{N}\left(\boldsymbol{\mu}_k, \boldsymbol{\Sigma}_{kk}\right) = \mathcal{N}\left(\mathbf{P}_k\boldsymbol{\mu}, \mathbf{P}_k\boldsymbol{\Sigma}\mathbf{P}_k^T\right), \qquad (6.37)$$

so that it is just specific sub-blocks of the full covariance matrix that are ever required.

– The *only* sub-blocks of $\boldsymbol{\Sigma}$ that we require are precisely the ones corresponding to the non-zero sub-blocks of $\boldsymbol{\Sigma}^{-1}$ (which is typically highly sparse). We can see this more plainly by writing

$$\boldsymbol{\Sigma}^{-1} = \sum_{k=1}^{K} \mathbf{P}_k^T E_{q_k}\left[\frac{\partial^2}{\partial \mathbf{x}_k^T \partial \mathbf{x}_k}\phi_k(\mathbf{x}_k)\right]\mathbf{P}_k, \qquad (6.38)$$

where we can see that each factor uses some sub-blocks, $\boldsymbol{\Sigma}_{kk} = \mathbf{P}_k\boldsymbol{\Sigma}\mathbf{P}_k^T$, to evaluate the expectation, and then the results are inserted back into the same elements of $\boldsymbol{\Sigma}^{-1}$.

– It turns out that we can extract the required sub-blocks of $\boldsymbol{\Sigma}$ very efficiently. For example, for batch state estimation, with a block-tridiagonal $\boldsymbol{\Sigma}^{-1}$, we can piggyback the calculation of the required blocks (i.e., the three main block diagonals of $\boldsymbol{\Sigma}$) onto the solution for the mean in (6.23b) (Meurant, 1992) while keeping the complexity of the solver the same. However, we can also compute the required blocks of $\boldsymbol{\Sigma}$ efficiently in the general case (Takahashi et al., 1973), and the next section is devoted to discussion of this topic.

Some of these remarks may seem familiar to those used to working with a MAP approach to batch state estimation (e.g., the sparsity pattern of $\boldsymbol{\Sigma}^{-1}$ exists and is constant across iterations). But now we are performing GVI that iterates over a full Gaussian PDF (i.e., mean and covariance) not just a point estimate (i.e., mean only).

At this point, the only approximation that we have made is that our estimate of the posterior is Gaussian. However, to implement the scheme in practice, we need to choose a method to actually compute the (marginal) expectations in (6.33), (6.35), and (6.36). There are many choices including linearization, Monte Carlo sampling, and also deterministic sampling. We will show how to use sampling methods in a later section.

6.3.2 Partial Computation of the Covariance

We next discuss how it is possible to compute the blocks of $\boldsymbol{\Sigma}$ (typically dense) corresponding to the non-zero sub-blocks of $\boldsymbol{\Sigma}^{-1}$ (typically very sparse) in an efficient manner. This idea was first proposed by Takahashi et al. (1973) in the context of circuit theory and was later used by Broussolle (1978) in a state estimation context where the matrix of interest was a covariance matrix like ours. Erisman and Tinney (1975) provide a proof of the closure of the Takahashi et al. procedure and also discuss algorithmic complexity. More recently, Triggs et al. (2000, App. B.4) and Kaess and Dellaert (2009) discuss methods to calculate specific blocks of the covariance matrix efficiently from the inverse covariance for computer vision and robotics applications, but do not discuss doing so for the complete set of covariance blocks corresponding to the non-zero blocks of the inverse covariance matrix.

At each iteration of our GVI approach, we are required to solve a system of linear equations for the change in the mean:

$$\boldsymbol{\Sigma}^{-1}\delta\boldsymbol{\mu} = \mathbf{r}, \tag{6.39}$$

where $\mathbf{r}$ is the right-hand side in (6.23b). We start by carrying out a sparse lower-diagonal-upper decomposition,

$$\boldsymbol{\Sigma}^{-1} = \mathbf{L}\mathbf{D}\mathbf{L}^T, \tag{6.40}$$

where $\mathbf{D}$ is diagonal and $\mathbf{L}$ is lower-triangular with ones on the main diagonal (and sparse). The cost of this decomposition will depend on the nature of the prior and measurement factors. The key thing is that the sparsity pattern of $\mathbf{L}$ is a direct function of the factors' variable dependencies and can be determined in advance; more on this in the following discussion. We can then solve the following two systems of equations for the change in the mean:

$$(\mathbf{L}\mathbf{D})\,\mathbf{v} = \mathbf{r}, \quad \text{(sparse forward substitution)} \tag{6.41}$$
$$\mathbf{L}^T\delta\boldsymbol{\mu} = \mathbf{v}. \quad \text{(sparse backward substitution)} \tag{6.42}$$

To solve for the required blocks of $\boldsymbol{\Sigma}$, we notice that

$$\mathbf{L}\mathbf{D}\mathbf{L}^T\boldsymbol{\Sigma} = \mathbf{1}, \tag{6.43}$$

where $\mathbf{1}$ is the identity matrix. We can premultiply by the inverse of $\mathbf{L}\mathbf{D}$ to arrive at

$$\mathbf{L}^T\boldsymbol{\Sigma} = \mathbf{D}^{-1}\mathbf{L}^{-1}, \tag{6.44}$$

where $\mathbf{L}^{-1}$ will in general no longer be sparse. Taking the transpose and adding $\boldsymbol{\Sigma} - \boldsymbol{\Sigma}\mathbf{L}$ to both sides, we have (Takahashi et al., 1973)

$$\boldsymbol{\Sigma} = \mathbf{L}^{-T}\mathbf{D}^{-1} + \boldsymbol{\Sigma}\left(\mathbf{1} - \mathbf{L}\right). \tag{6.45}$$

Since $\boldsymbol{\Sigma}$ is symmetric, we only require (at most) calculation of the main diagonal and the lower-half blocks and, as it turns out, this can also be done through a backward substitution pass. To see this, we expand the lower-half blocks as follows:

Figure 6.1 Example sparsity patterns of Σ^{-1} and the corresponding sparsity patterns of factor $\mathbf{L}$, where $*$ indicates non-zero. The set of zero entries of the lower half of $\mathbf{L}$ is a subset of the zero entries of the lower half of Σ^{-1}. There are some extra non-zero entries of $\mathbf{L}$, shown as $+$, that arise from completing the 'four corners of a box'. The box rule is shown in light grey for the leftmost example; the bottom-right corner of the box is zero in Σ^{-1} but non-zero in $\mathbf{L}$.

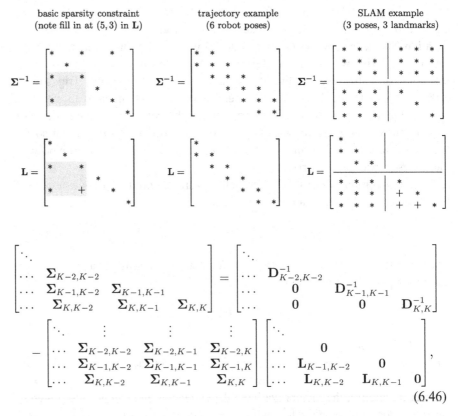

$$
\begin{bmatrix}
\ddots & & & \\
\cdots & \Sigma_{K-2,K-2} & & \\
\cdots & \Sigma_{K-1,K-2} & \Sigma_{K-1,K-1} & \\
\cdots & \Sigma_{K,K-2} & \Sigma_{K,K-1} & \Sigma_{K,K}
\end{bmatrix}
=
\begin{bmatrix}
\ddots & & & \\
\cdots & \mathbf{D}_{K-2,K-2}^{-1} & & \\
\cdots & 0 & \mathbf{D}_{K-1,K-1}^{-1} & \\
\cdots & 0 & 0 & \mathbf{D}_{K,K}^{-1}
\end{bmatrix}
$$
$$
-
\begin{bmatrix}
\ddots & \vdots & \vdots & \vdots \\
\cdots & \Sigma_{K-2,K-2} & \Sigma_{K-2,K-1} & \Sigma_{K-2,K} \\
\cdots & \Sigma_{K-1,K-2} & \Sigma_{K-1,K-1} & \Sigma_{K-1,K} \\
\cdots & \Sigma_{K,K-2} & \Sigma_{K,K-1} & \Sigma_{K,K}
\end{bmatrix}
\begin{bmatrix}
\ddots & & & \\
\cdots & 0 & & \\
\cdots & \mathbf{L}_{K-1,K-2} & 0 & \\
\cdots & \mathbf{L}_{K,K-2} & \mathbf{L}_{K,K-1} & 0
\end{bmatrix},
$$
$$\tag{6.46}$$

where we only show the blocks necessary for the calculation of the lower half of Σ; critically, $\mathbf{L}^{-T}$ is unnecessary since it only affects the upper-half blocks of Σ and is therefore dropped. Temporarily ignoring the need to exploit sparsity, we see that we can calculate the lower-half blocks of Σ through backward substitution:

$$\Sigma_{K,K} = \mathbf{D}_{K,K}^{-1}, \tag{6.48a}$$

$$\Sigma_{K,K-1} = -\Sigma_{K,K}\mathbf{L}_{K,K-1}, \tag{6.48b}$$

$$\Sigma_{K-1,K-1} = \mathbf{D}_{K-1,K-1}^{-1} - \Sigma_{K-1,K}\mathbf{L}_{K,K-1}, \tag{6.48c}$$

$$\vdots$$

$$\Sigma_{j,k} = \delta(j,k)\,\mathbf{D}_{j,k}^{-1} - \sum_{\ell=k+1}^{K} \Sigma_{j,\ell}\mathbf{L}_{\ell,k},\ (j \geq k), \tag{6.48d}$$

where $\delta(\cdot,\cdot)$ is the Kronecker delta function.

In general, blocks that are zero in $\mathbf{L}$ will also be zero in Σ^{-1}, but not the other way around. Therefore, it is sufficient (but not necessary) to calculate the blocks of Σ that are non-zero in $\mathbf{L}$, and it turns out this can always be done. Figure 6.1 shows some example sparsity patterns for Σ^{-1} and the corresponding sparsity pattern of $\mathbf{L}$. The sparsity of the lower half of $\mathbf{L}$ is the same as the sparsity of the lower half of Σ^{-1} except that $\mathbf{L}$ can have a few more non-zero entries to ensure that when multiplied together the sparsity of Σ^{-1} is produced. Specifically, if

$\mathbf{L}_{k,i} \neq \mathbf{0}$ and $\mathbf{L}_{j,i} \neq \mathbf{0}$, then we must have $\mathbf{L}_{j,k} \neq \mathbf{0}$ (Erisman and Tinney, 1975); this can be visualized as completing the 'four corners of a box', as shown in the example in the first column of Figure 6.1.

Figure 6.1 also shows some typical robotics examples. In batch trajectory estimation, $\boldsymbol{\Sigma}^{-1}$ is block-tridiagonal, and in this case the $\mathbf{L}$ matrix requires no extra non-zero entries. In SLAM, $\boldsymbol{\Sigma}^{-1}$ is an 'arrowhead' matrix with the upper-left partition (corresponding to the robot's trajectory) as block-tridiagonal and the lower-right partition (corresponding to landmarks) as block-diagonal. Using an $\mathbf{LDL}^T$ decomposition, we can exploit the sparsity of the upper-left partition, as shown in the example. If we wanted to exploit the sparsity of the lower-right, we could reverse the order of the variables or do a $\mathbf{L}^T\mathbf{DL}$ decomposition instead. In this SLAM example, each of the three landmarks is observed from each of the three poses so the upper-right and lower-left partitions are dense, and this causes some extra entries of $\mathbf{L}$ to be non-zero.

Finally, to understand why we do not need to calculate all of the blocks of $\boldsymbol{\Sigma}$, we follow the explanation of Erisman and Tinney (1975). We aim to compute all the blocks of the lower-half of $\boldsymbol{\Sigma}$ corresponding to the non-zero blocks of $\mathbf{L}$. Looking to (6.48d), we see that if $\mathbf{L}_{p,k}$ is non-zero, then we require $\boldsymbol{\Sigma}_{j,p}$ for the calculation of non-zero block $\boldsymbol{\Sigma}_{j,k}$. But if $\boldsymbol{\Sigma}_{j,k}$ is non-zero, so must be $\mathbf{L}_{j,k}$ and then using our 'four corners of a box' rule, this implies $\mathbf{L}_{j,p}$ must be non-zero and so we will have $\boldsymbol{\Sigma}_{j,p}$ and $\boldsymbol{\Sigma}_{p,j} = \boldsymbol{\Sigma}_{j,p}^T$ on our list of blocks to compute already. This shows the calculation of the desired blocks is closed under the scheme defined by (6.48d), which in turn implies there will always exist an efficient algorithm to calculate the blocks of $\boldsymbol{\Sigma}$ corresponding to the non-zero blocks of $\boldsymbol{\Sigma}^{-1}$, plus a few more according to the 'four corners of a box' rule.

It is worth noting that variable reordering and other schemes such as Givens rotations (Golub and Van Loan, 1996) can be combined with the Takahashi et al. approach to maximize the benefit of sparsity in $\boldsymbol{\Sigma}^{-1}$ (Kaess et al., 2008). In this section, we have simply shown that in general, the calculation of the required blocks of $\boldsymbol{\Sigma}$ (corresponding to the non-zero block of $\boldsymbol{\Sigma}^{-1}$) can be piggybacked efficiently onto the solution of (6.23b), with the details depending on the specific problem. In fact, the bottleneck in terms of computational complexity is the original lower-diagonal-upper decomposition, which is typically required even for MAP approaches. We therefore claim that our ESGVI approach has the same order of computational cost (as a function of the state size, N) as MAP for a given problem, but will have a higher coefficient due to the extra burden of using the marginals to compute expectations.

6.3.3 Marginal Sampling

We have seen in the previous section that we actually only need to calculate the marginal expectations (for each factor),

$$\underbrace{E_{q_k}[\phi_k(\mathbf{x}_k)]}_{\text{scalar}}, \quad \underbrace{E_{q_k}\left[\frac{\partial}{\partial \mathbf{x}_k^T}\phi_k(\mathbf{x}_k)\right]}_{\text{column}}, \quad \underbrace{E_{q_k}\left[\frac{\partial^2}{\partial \mathbf{x}_k^T \partial \mathbf{x}_k}\phi_k(\mathbf{x}_k)\right]}_{\text{matrix}}, \qquad (6.49)$$

which can then be reassembled back into the larger expectations of (6.31).

As a quick aside, an additional use for the preceding 'scalar' expression is to evaluate the loss functional,

$$V(q) = \underbrace{\sum_{k=1}^{K} E_{q_k}[\phi_k(\mathbf{x}_k)]}_{V_k(q_k)} + \underbrace{\frac{1}{2}\ln\left(|\mathbf{\Sigma}^{-1}|\right)}_{V_0}, \tag{6.50}$$

which is used to test for convergence and to perform backtracking during optimization. The V_0 term can be evaluated by noting that

$$\ln\left(|\mathbf{\Sigma}^{-1}|\right) = \ln\left(|\mathbf{LDL}^T|\right) = \ln\left(|\mathbf{D}|\right) = \sum_{i=1}^{N} \ln(d_{ii}), \tag{6.51}$$

where d_{ii} are the diagonal elements of $\mathbf{D}$; this exploits the lower-diagonal-upper decomposition from (6.40) that we already computed during the optimization.

The computation of each expectation in (6.49) looks, on the surface, rather intimidating. The first and second derivatives suggest each factor must be twice differentiable, and somehow the expectation over $q_k(\mathbf{x}_k)$ must be computed. So far we have made no assumptions on the specific form of the factors ϕ_k, and we would like to keep it that way, avoiding the imposition of differentiability requirements. Additionally, recalling how sampling-based filters, such as the unscented Kalman filter (Julier and Uhlmann, 1996), the cubature Kalman filter (Arasaratnam and Haykin, 2009), and the Gauss–Hermite Kalman filter (Ito and Xiong, 2000)(Wu et al., 2006), approximate terms involving expectations, a cubature approximation of the associated expectations in (6.49) appears appropriate. This section considers the use of Stein's lemma and cubature methods to derive an alternative means to compute the terms in (6.49) that is derivative-free.

To avoid the need to compute derivatives of ϕ_k, we can once again apply Stein's lemma, but in the opposite direction from our previous use. Using (2.125), we have

$$E_{q_k}\left[\frac{\partial}{\partial\mathbf{x}_k^T}\phi_k(\mathbf{x}_k)\right] = \mathbf{\Sigma}_{kk}^{-1} E_{q_k}[(\mathbf{x}_k - \boldsymbol{\mu}_k)\phi_k(\mathbf{x}_k)], \tag{6.52}$$

and using (2.126) we have

$$E_{q_k}\left[\frac{\partial^2}{\partial\mathbf{x}_k^T\partial\mathbf{x}_k}\phi_k(\mathbf{x}_k)\right] = \mathbf{\Sigma}_{kk}^{-1} E_{q_k}[(\mathbf{x}_k - \boldsymbol{\mu}_k)(\mathbf{x}_k - \boldsymbol{\mu}_k)^T\phi_k(\mathbf{x}_k)]\mathbf{\Sigma}_{kk}^{-1}$$
$$- \mathbf{\Sigma}_{kk}^{-1} E_{q_k}[\phi_k(\mathbf{x}_k)]. \tag{6.53}$$

Thus, an alternative means to compute the three expectations in (6.49), without explicit computation of derivatives, involves first computing

$$\underbrace{E_{q_k}[\phi_k(\mathbf{x}_k)]}_{\text{scalar}}, \quad \underbrace{E_{q_k}[(\mathbf{x}_k - \boldsymbol{\mu}_k)\phi_k(\mathbf{x}_k)]}_{\text{column}},$$
$$\underbrace{E_{q_k}[(\mathbf{x}_k - \boldsymbol{\mu}_k)(\mathbf{x}_k - \boldsymbol{\mu}_k)^T\phi_k(\mathbf{x}_k)]}_{\text{matrix}}, \tag{6.54}$$

then computing (6.52) and (6.53) using the results of (6.54). The reverse application of Stein's lemma has not destroyed the sparsity that we unveiled earlier because we have now applied it at the marginal level, not the global level.

Of interest next is how to actually compute the three expectations given in (6.54) in an efficient yet accurate way. As integrals, the expectations in (6.54) are

$$E_{q_k}[\phi_k(\mathbf{x}_k)] = \int_{-\infty}^{\infty} \phi_k(\mathbf{x}_k) q_k(\mathbf{x}_k) d\mathbf{x}_k, \tag{6.55a}$$

$$E_{q_k}[(\mathbf{x}_k - \boldsymbol{\mu}_k)\phi_k(\mathbf{x}_k)] = \int_{-\infty}^{\infty} (\mathbf{x}_k - \boldsymbol{\mu}_k)\phi_k(\mathbf{x}_k) q_k(\mathbf{x}_k) d\mathbf{x}_k, \tag{6.55b}$$

$$E_{q_k}[(\mathbf{x}_k - \boldsymbol{\mu}_k)(\mathbf{x}_k - \boldsymbol{\mu}_k)^T \phi_k(\mathbf{x}_k)]$$
$$= \int_{-\infty}^{\infty} (\mathbf{x}_k - \boldsymbol{\mu}_k)(\mathbf{x}_k - \boldsymbol{\mu}_k)^T \phi_k(\mathbf{x}_k) q_k(\mathbf{x}_k) d\mathbf{x}_k, \tag{6.55c}$$

where $q_k(\mathbf{x}_k) = \mathcal{N}(\boldsymbol{\mu}_k, \boldsymbol{\Sigma}_{kk})$. Computing these integrals analytically is generally not possible, and as such, a numerical approximation is sought. There are many ways of approximating the integrals in (6.55), the most popular type being multi-dimensional *Gaussian quadrature*, commonly referred to as Gaussian cubature or simply *cubature* (Cools, 1997; Sarmavuori and Särkkä, 2012; Kokkala et al., 2016; Särkkä et al., 2016; Särkkä, 2013, §6, p. 100). Using cubature, each of the integrals in (6.55) is approximated as (Kokkala et al., 2016; Särkkä et al., 2016; Särkkä, 2013, §6, p. 99–106)

$$E_{q_k}[\phi_k(\mathbf{x}_k)] \approx \sum_{\ell=1}^{L} w_{k,\ell}\, \phi_k(\mathbf{x}_{k,\ell}), \tag{6.56a}$$

$$E_{q_k}[(\mathbf{x}_k - \boldsymbol{\mu}_k)\phi_k(\mathbf{x}_k)] \approx \sum_{\ell=1}^{L} w_{k,\ell}\, (\mathbf{x}_{k,\ell} - \boldsymbol{\mu}_k)\phi_k(\mathbf{x}_{k,\ell}), \tag{6.56b}$$

$$E_{q_k}[(\mathbf{x}_k - \boldsymbol{\mu}_k)(\mathbf{x}_k - \boldsymbol{\mu}_k)^T \phi_k(\mathbf{x}_k)]$$
$$\approx \sum_{\ell=1}^{L} w_{k,\ell}\, (\mathbf{x}_{k,\ell} - \boldsymbol{\mu}_k)(\mathbf{x}_{k,\ell} - \boldsymbol{\mu}_k)^T \phi_k(\mathbf{x}_{k,\ell}), \tag{6.56c}$$

where $w_{k,\ell}$ are weights, $\mathbf{x}_{k,\ell} = \boldsymbol{\mu}_k + \sqrt{\boldsymbol{\Sigma}_{kk}}\boldsymbol{\xi}_{k,\ell}$ are sigmapoints, and $\boldsymbol{\xi}_{k,\ell}$ are unit sigmapoints. Both the weights and unit sigmapoints are specific to the cubature method. For example, the popular unscented transformation (Julier and Uhlmann, 1996; Särkkä et al., 2016; Särkkä, 2013, §6, p. 109–110) uses weights

$$w_{k,0} = \frac{\kappa}{N_k + \kappa}, \quad w_{k,\ell} = \frac{1}{2(N_k + \kappa)}, \quad \ell = 1, \dots, 2N_k \tag{6.57}$$

and sigmapoints

$$\boldsymbol{\xi}_{k,\ell} = \begin{cases} \mathbf{0} & \ell = 0 \\ \sqrt{N_k + \kappa}\mathbf{1}_\ell & \ell = 1, \dots, N_k \\ -\sqrt{N_k + \kappa}\mathbf{1}_{\ell - N_k} & \ell = N_k + 1, \dots, 2N_k \end{cases}, \tag{6.58}$$

where N_k is the dimension of $\mathbf{x}_k$. On the other hand, the spherical-cubature rule (Arasaratnam and Haykin, 2009; Kokkala et al., 2016; Särkkä, 2013, §6, p. 106–109) uses weights

$$w_{k,\ell} = \frac{1}{2N_k}, \quad \ell = 1, \ldots, 2N_k, \tag{6.59}$$

and sigmapoints

$$\boldsymbol{\xi}_{k,\ell} = \begin{cases} \sqrt{N_k}\mathbf{1}_\ell & \ell = 1, \ldots, N_k \\ -\sqrt{N_k}\mathbf{1}_{\ell - N_k} & \ell = N_k + 1, \ldots, 2N_k \end{cases}, \tag{6.60}$$

where $\mathbf{1}_i$ is a $N_k \times 1$ column matrix with 1 at row i and zeros everywhere else. Gauss–Hermite cubature is yet another method that can be used to compute the approximations in (6.56) (Ito and Xiong, 2000; Wu et al., 2006; Särkkä, 2013, §6 p. 99–106). As discussed in Särkkä (2013, §6 p. 103), given an integrand composed of a linear combination of monomials of the form $x_1^{d_1}, x_2^{d_2}, \ldots, x_{N_k}^{d_{N_k}}$, the Mth order Gauss–Hermite cubature rule is exact when $d_i \leq 2M - 1$. However, for an Mth-order Gauss–Hermite cubature approximation, M^{N_k} sigmapoints are needed, which could be infeasible in practice when N_k is large (Särkkä, 2013, §6 p. 103). Fortunately, the approximations of (6.55) given in (6.56) are at the factor level (i.e., at the level of $\mathbf{x}_k$, not $\mathbf{x}$), and at the factor level N_k is often a manageable size in most robotics problems. For this reason, Gauss–Hermite cubature is a reasonable choice, yielding accurate yet reasonably efficient approximations of (6.55).

Some additional remarks are as follows:

– The accuracy of the cubature approximations in (6.56) will depend on the specific method and the severity of the nonlinearity in ϕ_k. Alternative means to approximate (6.56), such as cubature methods that are exact for specific algebraic and trigonometric polynomials (Cools, 1997; Kokkala et al., 2016), Gaussian-process cubature (O'Hagan, 1991; Särkkä et al., 2016), or even adaptive cubature methods (Press et al., 2007, §4, p. 194), can be employed. In the case where computational complexity is of concern, a high-degree cubature rule that is an efficient alternative to Gauss–Hermite cubature is presented in Jia et al. (2013).

– We are proposing quite a different way of using a cubature method (or any sampling method) than is typical in the state estimation literature; we consider the entire factor expression, ϕ_k, to be the nonlinearity, not just the observation or motion models, as is common. This means, for example, that if there is a robust cost function incorporated in our factor expression (see Section 5.4.2), it is handled automatically and does not need to be implemented as iteratively reweighted least squares (Holland and Welsch, 1977).

– Because we have 'undone' Stein's lemma at this point (it was a temporary step to exploit the sparsity only), it may not even be necessary to have ϕ_k differentiable anymore. The next section shows how to get to the derivative-free version of ESGVI directly without the double application of Stein's lemma.

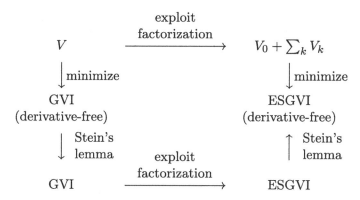

Figure 6.2
Commutative
diagram showing
two paths to get to
the derivative-free
version of ESGVI
starting from the loss
functional, V.

- We see in (6.56) that the scalars, ϕ_k, serve to reweight each sample, but that otherwise the expressions are simply those for the first three moments of a distribution.

- We also use cubature to evaluate $V(q)$ according to (6.50). This is required to test for convergence of the optimization scheme.

The approach that we have presented up to this point is extremely general and can benefit any GVI problem where $p(\mathbf{x}, \mathbf{z})$ can be factored. In computer vision and robotics, some examples include *bundle adjustment (BA)* (Brown, 1958) and *simultaneous localization and mapping (SLAM)* (Durrant-Whyte and Bailey, 2006), which are discussed in Sections 10.1 and 10.2 later on in the book.

6.3.4 Direct Derivation of Derivative-Free Method

In our main ESGVI derivation, we chose to (i) define a scheme to minimize $V(q)$ with respect to q and then (ii) exploit $\phi(\mathbf{x}) = \sum_{k=1}^{K} \phi_k(\mathbf{x}_k)$ to make the scheme efficient. Here we show that we can carry out (i) and (ii) in the opposite order to streamline the derivation of the derivative-free version of ESGVI, avoiding the need for Stein's lemma.

Figure 6.2 shows two paths to get to the derivative-free version of ESGVI starting from our loss functional, V. We originally took the counterclockwise path that goes down, across to the right, and then up. We will now demonstrate the clockwise path that goes right and then down.

Inserting $\phi(\mathbf{x}) = \sum_{k=1}^{K} \phi_k(\mathbf{x}_k)$, the loss functional becomes

$$V(q) = \sum_{k=1}^{K} \underbrace{E_{q_k}[\phi_k(\mathbf{x}_k)]}_{V_k(q_k)} + \underbrace{\frac{1}{2} \ln \left(|\mathbf{\Sigma}^{-1}| \right)}_{V_0}, \tag{6.61}$$

where the expectations are now over the marginal, $q_k(\mathbf{x}_k) = \mathcal{N}(\boldsymbol{\mu}_k, \mathbf{\Sigma}_{kk})$ with

$$\boldsymbol{\mu}_k = \mathbf{P}_k \boldsymbol{\mu}, \quad \mathbf{\Sigma}_{kk} = \mathbf{P}_k \mathbf{\Sigma} \mathbf{P}_k^T, \tag{6.62}$$

and where $\mathbf{P}_k$ is a projection matrix. We then take the first derivative with respect to $\boldsymbol{\mu}$:

$$\frac{\partial V(q)}{\partial \boldsymbol{\mu}^T} = \frac{\partial}{\partial \boldsymbol{\mu}^T} \left(\sum_{k=1}^{K} E_{q_k}[\phi_k(\mathbf{x}_k)] + \frac{1}{2} \ln \left(|\boldsymbol{\Sigma}^{-1}| \right) \right)$$

$$= \sum_{k=1}^{K} \frac{\partial}{\partial \boldsymbol{\mu}^T} E_{q_k}[\phi_k(\mathbf{x}_k)]$$

$$= \sum_{k=1}^{K} \mathbf{P}_k^T \frac{\partial}{\partial \boldsymbol{\mu}_k^T} E_{q_k}[\phi_k(\mathbf{x}_k)]$$

$$= \sum_{k=1}^{K} \mathbf{P}_k^T \boldsymbol{\Sigma}_{kk}^{-1} \underbrace{E_{q_k}\left[(\mathbf{x}_k - \boldsymbol{\mu}_k)\phi_k(\mathbf{x}_k) \right]}_{\text{cubature}}. \tag{6.63}$$

The last step comes from (6.8a) applied at the marginal level. Similarly, we have for the second derivative with respect to $\boldsymbol{\mu}$ that

$$\frac{\partial^2 V(q)}{\partial \boldsymbol{\mu}^T \partial \boldsymbol{\mu}} = \frac{\partial^2}{\partial \boldsymbol{\mu}^T \partial \boldsymbol{\mu}} \left(\sum_{k=1}^{K} E_{q_k}[\phi_k(\mathbf{x}_k)] + \frac{1}{2} \ln \left(|\boldsymbol{\Sigma}^{-1}| \right) \right)$$

$$= \sum_{k=1}^{K} \frac{\partial^2}{\partial \boldsymbol{\mu}^T \partial \boldsymbol{\mu}} E_{q_k}[\phi_k(\mathbf{x}_k)]$$

$$= \sum_{k=1}^{K} \mathbf{P}_k^T \left(\frac{\partial^2}{\partial \boldsymbol{\mu}_k^T \partial \boldsymbol{\mu}_k} E_{q_k}[\phi_k(\mathbf{x}_k)] \right) \mathbf{P}_k$$

$$= \sum_{k=1}^{K} \mathbf{P}_k^T \left(\boldsymbol{\Sigma}_{kk}^{-1} \underbrace{E_{q_k}\left[(\mathbf{x}_k - \boldsymbol{\mu}_k)(\mathbf{x}_k - \boldsymbol{\mu}_k)^T \phi_k(\mathbf{x}_k) \right] \boldsymbol{\Sigma}_{kk}^{-1}}_{\text{cubature}} \right.$$

$$\left. - \boldsymbol{\Sigma}_{kk}^{-1} \underbrace{E_{q_k}[\phi_k(\mathbf{x}_k)]}_{\text{cubature}} \right) \mathbf{P}_k, \tag{6.64}$$

where we made use of (6.8b) at the marginal level in the last step.

The update scheme is then

$$\left(\boldsymbol{\Sigma}^{-1} \right)^{(i+1)} = \left. \frac{\partial^2 V(q)}{\partial \boldsymbol{\mu}^T \partial \boldsymbol{\mu}} \right|_{q^{(i)}}, \tag{6.65a}$$

$$\left(\boldsymbol{\Sigma}^{-1} \right)^{(i+1)} \delta \boldsymbol{\mu} = - \left. \frac{\partial V(q)}{\partial \boldsymbol{\mu}^T} \right|_{q^{(i)}}, \tag{6.65b}$$

$$\boldsymbol{\mu}^{(i+1)} = \boldsymbol{\mu}^{(i)} + \delta \boldsymbol{\mu}, \tag{6.65c}$$

which is identical to the derivative-free ESGVI approach from earlier. The sparsity of the left-hand side comes from the use of the projection matrices. We did not require the use of Stein's lemma (Stein, 1981) using this derivation, which also means that we have made no assumptions about the differentiability of $\phi_k(\mathbf{x}_k)$ with respect to $\mathbf{x}_k$.

6.4 Extensions

There are a number of extensions to the basic ESGVI framework that we can consider. First, we discuss an alternate loss functional that leads to a modified optimization scheme similar to a Gauss–Newton solver and offers some computational savings. Second, we discuss how to extend our approach beyond estimation of the latent state to include estimation of unknown parameters in our models.

6.4.1 Alternate Loss Functional

We can consider an alternate variational problem that may offer computational advantages over the main ESGVI approach. We consider the special case where the negative-log-likelihood takes the form

$$\phi(\mathbf{x}) = \frac{1}{2}\mathbf{e}(\mathbf{x})^T\mathbf{W}^{-1}\mathbf{e}(\mathbf{x}). \qquad (6.66)$$

Substituting this into the loss functional, we have

$$V(q) = \frac{1}{2}E_q\left[\mathbf{e}(\mathbf{x})^T\mathbf{W}^{-1}\mathbf{e}(\mathbf{x})\right] + \frac{1}{2}\ln(|\mathbf{\Sigma}^{-1}|). \qquad (6.67)$$

Owing to the convexity of the quadratic expression, $\mathbf{e}^T\mathbf{W}^{-1}\mathbf{e}$, we can apply *Jensen's inequality* (Jensen, 1906) directly to write

$$E_q[\mathbf{e}(\mathbf{x})]^T\mathbf{W}^{-1}E_q[\mathbf{e}(\mathbf{x})] \le E_q\left[\mathbf{e}(\mathbf{x})^T\mathbf{W}^{-1}\mathbf{e}(\mathbf{x})\right]. \qquad (6.68)$$

The *Jensen gap* is the (positive) difference between the right and left sides of this inequality and will generally tend to be larger the more nonlinear is $\mathbf{e}(\mathbf{x})$ and less concentrated is $q(\mathbf{x})$. Motivated by this relationship, we can define a new loss functional as

$$V'(q) = \frac{1}{2}E_q[\mathbf{e}(\mathbf{x})]^T\mathbf{W}^{-1}E_q[\mathbf{e}(\mathbf{x})] + \frac{1}{2}\ln(|\mathbf{\Sigma}^{-1}|), \qquad (6.69)$$

which may be thought of as a (conservative) approximation of $V(q)$ that is appropriate for mild nonlinearities and/or concentrated posteriors; the conservative aspect will be discussed a bit later on. We will now show that we can minimize $V'(q)$ by iteratively updating $q(\mathbf{x})$ and continue to exploit problem sparsity arising from a factored likelihood.

We begin by noting that we can directly approximate the expected error as

$$E_{q^{(i+1)}}[\mathbf{e}(\mathbf{x})] \approx E_{q^{(i)}}[\mathbf{e}(\mathbf{x})] + \frac{\partial}{\partial\boldsymbol{\mu}}E_{q^{(i)}}[\mathbf{e}(\mathbf{x})]\underbrace{\left(\boldsymbol{\mu}^{(i+1)} - \boldsymbol{\mu}^{(i)}\right)}_{\delta\boldsymbol{\mu}}$$

$$= \underbrace{E_{q^{(i)}}[\mathbf{e}(\mathbf{x})]}_{\bar{\mathbf{e}}^{(i)}} + \underbrace{E_{q^{(i)}}\left[\frac{\partial}{\partial\mathbf{x}}\mathbf{e}(\mathbf{x})\right]}_{\bar{\mathbf{E}}^{(i)}}\delta\boldsymbol{\mu}$$

$$= \bar{\mathbf{e}}^{(i)} + \bar{\mathbf{E}}^{(i)}\,\delta\boldsymbol{\mu}, \qquad (6.70)$$

where we have employed the derivative identity in (6.24a).

We can then approximate the loss functional as

$$V'(q) \approx \frac{1}{2} \left(\bar{\mathbf{e}}^{(i)} + \bar{\mathbf{E}}^{(i)} \, \delta\boldsymbol{\mu} \right)^T \mathbf{W}^{-1} \left(\bar{\mathbf{e}}^{(i)} + \bar{\mathbf{E}}^{(i)} \, \delta\boldsymbol{\mu} \right) + \frac{1}{2} \ln(|\boldsymbol{\Sigma}^{-1}|), \quad (6.71)$$

which is now exactly quadratic in $\delta\boldsymbol{\mu}$. This specific approximation leads directly to a Gauss–Newton estimator, bypassing Newton's method, as we have implicitly approximated the Hessian (see Section 4.3.1). Taking the first and second derivatives with respect to $\delta\boldsymbol{\mu}$, we have

$$\frac{\partial V'(q)}{\partial \, \delta\boldsymbol{\mu}^T} = \bar{\mathbf{E}}^{(i)^T} \mathbf{W}^{-1} \left(\bar{\mathbf{e}}^{(i)} + \bar{\mathbf{E}}^{(i)} \, \delta\boldsymbol{\mu} \right), \quad (6.72a)$$

$$\frac{\partial^2 V'(q)}{\partial \, \delta\boldsymbol{\mu}^T \partial \, \delta\boldsymbol{\mu}} = \bar{\mathbf{E}}^{(i)^T} \mathbf{W}^{-1} \bar{\mathbf{E}}^{(i)}. \quad (6.72b)$$

For the derivative with respect to $\boldsymbol{\Sigma}^{-1}$, we have

$$\frac{\partial V'(q)}{\partial \boldsymbol{\Sigma}^{-1}} \approx -\frac{1}{2} \boldsymbol{\Sigma} \, \bar{\mathbf{E}}^{(i)^T} \mathbf{W}^{-1} \bar{\mathbf{E}}^{(i)} \, \boldsymbol{\Sigma} + \frac{1}{2} \boldsymbol{\Sigma}, \quad (6.73)$$

where the approximation enforces the relationship in (6.24b), which does not hold exactly anymore due to the altered nature of $V'(q)$. Setting this to zero for a critical point, we have

$$\left(\boldsymbol{\Sigma}^{-1} \right)^{(i+1)} = \bar{\mathbf{E}}^{(i)^T} \mathbf{W}^{-1} \bar{\mathbf{E}}^{(i)}, \quad (6.74)$$

where we have created an iterative update analogous to that in the main ESGVI approach.

For the mean, we set (6.72a) to zero and then for the optimal update we have

$$\underbrace{\bar{\mathbf{E}}^{(i)^T} \mathbf{W}^{-1} \bar{\mathbf{E}}^{(i)}}_{(\boldsymbol{\Sigma}^{-1})^{(i+1)}} \, \delta\boldsymbol{\mu} = -\bar{\mathbf{E}}^{(i)^T} \mathbf{W}^{-1} \bar{\mathbf{e}}^{(i)}. \quad (6.75)$$

Solving for $\delta\boldsymbol{\mu}$ provides a *Gauss–Newton (GN)* update, which we will refer to as ESGVI-GN. This is identical to how Gauss–Newton is normally carried out, but now we calculate $\bar{\mathbf{e}}$ and $\bar{\mathbf{E}}$ not just at a single point but rather as an expectation over our Gaussian posterior estimate. We again make a number of remarks about the approach:

- The sparsity of the inverse covariance matrix, $\boldsymbol{\Sigma}^{-1}$, will be identical to the full ESGVI approach. This can be seen by noting that

$$\phi(\mathbf{x}) = \sum_{k=1}^K \phi_k(\mathbf{x}_k) = \frac{1}{2} \sum_{k=1}^K \mathbf{e}_k(\mathbf{x}_k)^T \mathbf{W}_k^{-1} \mathbf{e}_k(\mathbf{x}_k)$$

$$= \frac{1}{2} \mathbf{e}(\mathbf{x})^T \mathbf{W}^{-1} \mathbf{e}(\mathbf{x}), \quad (6.76)$$

where

$$\mathbf{e}(\mathbf{x}) = \begin{bmatrix} \mathbf{e}_1(\mathbf{x}_1) \\ \vdots \\ \mathbf{e}_K(\mathbf{x}_K) \end{bmatrix}, \quad \mathbf{W} = \text{diag}(\mathbf{W}_1, \dots, \mathbf{W}_K). \quad (6.77)$$

Then we have

$$\boldsymbol{\Sigma}^{-1} = E_q \left[\frac{\partial}{\partial \mathbf{x}} \mathbf{e}(\mathbf{x}) \right]^T \mathbf{W}^{-1} E_q \left[\frac{\partial}{\partial \mathbf{x}} \mathbf{e}(\mathbf{x}) \right]$$

$$= \sum_{k=1}^{K} \mathbf{P}_k^T E_{q_k} \left[\frac{\partial}{\partial \mathbf{x}_k} \mathbf{e}_k(\mathbf{x}_k) \right]^T \mathbf{W}_k^{-1} E_{q_k} \left[\frac{\partial}{\partial \mathbf{x}_k} \mathbf{e}_k(\mathbf{x}_k) \right] \mathbf{P}_k, \quad (6.78)$$

which will have zeros wherever an error term does not depend on the variables. We also see, just as before, that the expectations can be reduced to being over the marginal, $q_k(\mathbf{x}_k)$, meaning we still only require the blocks of $\boldsymbol{\Sigma}$ corresponding to the non-zero blocks of $\boldsymbol{\Sigma}^{-1}$.

– We can still use Stein's lemma to avoid the need to compute any derivatives:

$$E_{q_k} \left[\frac{\partial}{\partial \mathbf{x}_k} \mathbf{e}_k(\mathbf{x}_k) \right] = E_{q_k} \left[\mathbf{e}_k(\mathbf{x}_k)(\mathbf{x}_k - \boldsymbol{\mu}_k)^T \right] \boldsymbol{\Sigma}_{kk}^{-1}. \quad (6.79)$$

This is sometimes referred to as a statistical Jacobian and this usage is very similar to the filtering and smoothing approaches described by Särkkä (2013), amongst others, as cubature can be applied at the measurement model level rather than the factor level. Because we are iteratively recomputing the statistical Jacobian about our posterior estimate, this is most similar to Sibley et al. (2006) and García-Fernández et al. (2015), although some details are different as well as the fact that we started from our loss functional, $V'(q)$.

– The number of cubature points required to calculate the expectation $E_{q_k}[\mathbf{e}_k(\mathbf{x}_k)(\mathbf{x}_k - \boldsymbol{\mu}_k)^T]$ will be lower than our full ESGVI approach described earlier, as the order of the expression in the integrand is half that of $E_{q_k}[(\mathbf{x}_k - \boldsymbol{\mu}_k)(\mathbf{x}_k - \boldsymbol{\mu}_k)^T \phi_k(\mathbf{x}_k)]$. Since the number of cubature points goes up as M^{N_k}, cutting M in half is significant and could be the difference between tractable and not for some problems. This was the main motivation for exploring this alternate approach.

– It is known that minimizing $\text{KL}(q||p)$, which our $V(q)$ is effectively doing, can result in a Gaussian that is too confident (i.e., inverse covariance is too large) (Bishop, 2006; Ala-Luhtala et al., 2015). A side benefit of switching from $V(q)$ to $V'(q)$ is that the resulting inverse covariance will be more conservative. This follows from Jensen's inequality once again. For an arbitrary non-zero vector, $\mathbf{a}$, we have

$$0 < \mathbf{a}^T \underbrace{E_q \left[\frac{\partial \mathbf{e}(\mathbf{x})}{\partial \mathbf{x}} \right]^T \mathbf{W}^{-1} E_q \left[\frac{\partial \mathbf{e}(\mathbf{x})}{\partial \mathbf{x}} \right]}_{\boldsymbol{\Sigma}^{-1} \text{ from } V'(q)} \mathbf{a}$$

$$\overset{\text{Jensen}}{\leq} \mathbf{a}^T E_q \left[\frac{\partial \mathbf{e}(\mathbf{x})}{\partial \mathbf{x}}^T \mathbf{W}^{-1} \frac{\partial \mathbf{e}(\mathbf{x})}{\partial \mathbf{x}} \right] \mathbf{a}$$

$$\overset{\text{Gauss–Newton}}{\approx} \mathbf{a}^T \underbrace{E_q \left[\frac{\partial^2 \phi(\mathbf{x})}{\partial \mathbf{x}^T \partial \mathbf{x}} \right]}_{\boldsymbol{\Sigma}^{-1} \text{ from } V(q)} \mathbf{a}, \quad (6.80)$$

which ensures that not only do we have a positive definite inverse covariance but that it is conservative compared to the full ESGVI approach.

Due to the extra approximations made in ESGVI-GN compared to ESGVI, it remains to be seen whether it offers an improvement over MAP approaches. However, as ESGVI-GN provides a batch option that does not require any derivatives, it can be used as a less expensive preprocessor for the derivative-free version of full ESGVI.

6.4.2 Parameter Estimation

We use this section to provide a sketch of how parameters may also be estimated using our ESGVI framework. We introduce some unknown parameters, $\boldsymbol{\theta}$, so that the negative log-likelihood of the data is $-\ln(p(\mathbf{z}|\boldsymbol{\theta})$. This can be decomposed as

$$
-\ln(p(\mathbf{z}|\boldsymbol{\theta}) = \underbrace{\int_{-\infty}^{\infty} q(\mathbf{x}) \ln\left(\frac{p(\mathbf{x}|\mathbf{z}, \boldsymbol{\theta})}{q(\mathbf{x})}\right) dx}_{-\mathrm{KL}(q||p)\leq 0}
$$
$$
\underbrace{-\int_{-\infty}^{\infty} q(\mathbf{x}) \ln\left(\frac{p(\mathbf{x}, \mathbf{z}|\boldsymbol{\theta})}{q(\mathbf{x})}\right) dx}_{V(q|\boldsymbol{\theta})} \quad (6.81)
$$

where

$$
V(q|\boldsymbol{\theta}) = E_q[\phi(\mathbf{x}|\boldsymbol{\theta})] + \frac{1}{2}\ln(|\boldsymbol{\Sigma}^{-1}|), \quad (6.82)
$$

is the negative of the so-called *evidence lower bound (ELBO)* (i.e., an upper bound). In order to minimize $-\ln(p(\mathbf{z}|\boldsymbol{\theta})$, we can employ an *expectation minimization (EM)* approach to estimate parameters when there is a latent state, $q(\mathbf{x})$ (Neal and Hinton, 1998; Ghahramani and Roweis, 1999). The expectation, or E-step, is already accomplished by ESGVI; we simply hold $\boldsymbol{\theta}$ fixed and run the inference to convergence to solve for $q(\mathbf{x})$, our Gaussian approximation to the posterior. In the M-step, which is actually a minimization in our case, we hold $q(\mathbf{x})$ fixed and find the value of $\boldsymbol{\theta}$ that minimizes the loss functional. By alternating between the E- and M-steps, we can solve for the best value of the parameters to minimize $-\ln p(\mathbf{z}|\boldsymbol{\theta})$, the negative log-likelihood of the measurements given the parameters. The EM procedure will converge to a local minimum, not necessarily a global one.

As we have done already in this chapter, we assume the joint likelihood of the state and measurements (given the parameters) factors so that

$$
\phi(\mathbf{x}|\boldsymbol{\theta}) = \sum_{k=1}^{K} \phi_k(\mathbf{x}_k|\boldsymbol{\theta}), \quad (6.83)
$$

where for generality we have each factor being affected by the entire parameter set, $\boldsymbol{\theta}$, but in practice it could be a subset. Taking the derivative of the loss functional with respect to $\boldsymbol{\theta}$, we have

$$\frac{\partial V(q|\boldsymbol{\theta})}{\partial \boldsymbol{\theta}} = \frac{\partial}{\partial \boldsymbol{\theta}} E_q[\phi(\mathbf{x}|\boldsymbol{\theta})]$$

$$= \frac{\partial}{\partial \boldsymbol{\theta}} E_q \left[\sum_{k=1}^{K} \phi_k(\mathbf{x}_k|\boldsymbol{\theta}) \right]$$

$$= \sum_{k=1}^{K} E_{q_k} \left[\frac{\partial}{\partial \boldsymbol{\theta}} \phi_k(\mathbf{x}_k|\boldsymbol{\theta}) \right], \tag{6.84}$$

where in the last expression the expectation simplifies to being over the marginal, $q_k(\mathbf{x}_k)$, rather than the full Gaussian, $q(\mathbf{x})$. As with the main ESGVI approach, this means that we only need the blocks of the covariance, $\boldsymbol{\Sigma}$, corresponding to the non-zero blocks of $\boldsymbol{\Sigma}^{-1}$, which we are already calculating as part of the E-step. Furthermore, we can easily evaluate the marginal expectations using cubature.

To make this more tangible, consider the example of

$$\phi(\mathbf{x}|\mathbf{W}) = \frac{1}{2} \sum_{k=1}^{K} \left(\mathbf{e}_k(\mathbf{x}_k)^T \mathbf{W}^{-1} \mathbf{e}_k(\mathbf{x}_k) - \ln(|\mathbf{W}^{-1}|) \right), \tag{6.85}$$

where the unknown parameter is $\mathbf{W}$, the measurement covariance matrix. Then taking the derivative with respect to $\mathbf{W}^{-1}$, we have

$$\frac{\partial V(q|\mathbf{W})}{\partial \mathbf{W}^{-1}} = \frac{1}{2} \sum_{k=1}^{K} E_{q_k} \left[\mathbf{e}_k(\mathbf{x}_k) \mathbf{e}_k(\mathbf{x}_k)^T \right] - \frac{K}{2} \mathbf{W}. \tag{6.86}$$

Setting this to zero for a minimum, we have

$$\mathbf{W} = \frac{1}{K} \sum_{k=1}^{K} E_{q_k} \left[\mathbf{e}_k(\mathbf{x}_k) \mathbf{e}_k(\mathbf{x}_k)^T \right], \tag{6.87}$$

where we can use cubature to evaluate the marginal expectations. Reiterating, we never require the full covariance matrix, $\boldsymbol{\Sigma}$, implying that our exactly sparse framework extends to parameter estimation.

6.4.3 Constraining Covariance to be Positive Definite

Our GVI optimization problem has been posed as an unconstrained optimization. This means, in particular, that we do not constrain the estimated inverse covariance matrix, $\boldsymbol{\Sigma}^{-1}$, to be positive definite. In practice, if we are close to an optimum, positive-definiteness occurs naturally. However, if our initial guess is quite poor, it is possible for our GVI approach to produce an inverse covariance that is not positive definite. We mention two ways to overcome this limitation.

First, we can run MAP estimation to convergence first (with the Laplace approximation for the inverse covariance) and then use this result to initialize our GVI method. This works extremely well in practice and is computationally efficient since we are only using the full expectations in the later stages of the optimization to refine the results.

Second, we can modify the GVI approach to be a constrained optimization, with the estimated inverse covariance compelled to be positive definite. This can be accomplished through the connection to NGD (see Section 6.2.3) as described by Goudar et al. (2022). This has the advantage of not having to switch from one algorithm to another as in our first approach.

6.5 Linear Systems

In this section, we first show that if the true posterior is Gaussian, the GVI approach is able to recover the discrete-time batch estimation solution described in Section 3.1.3. We then go on to show that the system parameters can be learned from data using the parameter estimation feature described in Section 6.4.2, which is one approach to system identification.

6.5.1 Recovery of the Batch Solution

Recalling Section 3.1.3, the batch linear state estimation problem can be written in *lifted form* (i.e., at the trajectory level):

$$\mathbf{x} = \mathbf{A}(\mathbf{Bu} + \mathbf{w}), \tag{6.88a}$$

$$\mathbf{y} = \mathbf{Cx} + \mathbf{n}, \tag{6.88b}$$

where $\mathbf{x}$ is the entire trajectory (states over time), $\mathbf{u}$ are the control inputs, $\mathbf{y}$ are the sensor outputs, $\mathbf{w} \sim \mathcal{N}(\mathbf{0}, \mathbf{Q})$ is process noise, $\mathbf{n} \sim \mathcal{N}(\mathbf{0}, \mathbf{R})$ is measurement noise, $\mathbf{A}$ is the lifted transition matrix, $\mathbf{B}$ is the lifted control matrix, and $\mathbf{C}$ is the lifted observation matrix. We then have

$$\phi(\mathbf{x}) = \frac{1}{2} \left(\mathbf{Bu} - \mathbf{A}^{-1}\mathbf{x} \right)^T \mathbf{Q}^{-1} \left(\mathbf{Bu} - \mathbf{A}^{-1}\mathbf{x} \right)$$
$$+ \frac{1}{2} \left(\mathbf{y} - \mathbf{Cx} \right)^T \mathbf{R}^{-1} \left(\mathbf{y} - \mathbf{Cx} \right). \tag{6.89}$$

The expected derivatives can be calculated analytically for this linear problem where $q(\mathbf{x}) = \mathcal{N}(\hat{\mathbf{x}}, \hat{\mathbf{P}})$:

$$E_q \left[\frac{\partial^2}{\partial \mathbf{x}^T \partial \mathbf{x}} \phi(\mathbf{x}) \right] = \mathbf{A}^{-T} \mathbf{Q}^{-1} \mathbf{A}^{-1} + \mathbf{C}^T \mathbf{R}^{-1} \mathbf{C}, \tag{6.90a}$$

$$E_q \left[\frac{\partial}{\partial \mathbf{x}^T} \phi(\mathbf{x}) \right] = -\mathbf{A}^{-T} \mathbf{Q}^{-1} \left(\mathbf{Bu} - \mathbf{A}^{-1}\hat{\mathbf{x}} \right) - \mathbf{C}^T \mathbf{R}^{-1} \left(\mathbf{y} - \mathbf{C}\hat{\mathbf{x}} \right). \tag{6.90b}$$

At convergence, (6.90b) must be zero, so we have

$$\hat{\mathbf{P}}^{-1} = \underbrace{\mathbf{A}^{-T} \mathbf{Q}^{-1} \mathbf{A}^{-1} + \mathbf{C}^T \mathbf{R}^{-1} \mathbf{C}}_{\text{block-tridiagonal}}, \tag{6.91a}$$

$$\hat{\mathbf{P}}^{-1}\hat{\mathbf{x}} = \mathbf{A}^{-T} \mathbf{Q}^{-1} \mathbf{Bu} + \mathbf{C}^T \mathbf{R}^{-1} \mathbf{y}, \tag{6.91b}$$

which can be solved efficiently for $\hat{\mathbf{x}}$ due to the block-tridiagonal nature of $\hat{\mathbf{P}}^{-1}$; from here, Section 3.2 shows the algebraic equivalence of this form to the canonical RTS smoother. Thus, our GVI approach still reproduces the classic linear results. In the case of nonlinear systems, GVI provides a different solution than MAP.

6.5.2 System Identification

Consider the discrete-time LTI system of the form

$$\mathbf{x}_k = \mathbf{A}\mathbf{x}_{k-1} + \mathbf{B}\mathbf{u}_k + \mathbf{w}_k, \qquad \mathbf{w}_k \sim \mathcal{N}(\mathbf{0}, \mathbf{Q}) \tag{6.92a}$$

$$\mathbf{y}_k = \mathbf{C}\mathbf{x}_k + \mathbf{n}_k, \qquad \mathbf{n}_k \sim \mathcal{N}(\mathbf{0}, \mathbf{R}) \tag{6.92b}$$

where $k = 0 \ldots K$ is the time index, $\mathbf{x}_k$ is the state, $\mathbf{u}_k$ is the control input, $\mathbf{y}_k$ is the sensor output, $\mathbf{A}, \mathbf{B}, \mathbf{C}$ are the usual constant matrices describing the system, and $\mathbf{Q}, \mathbf{R}$ are the process and measurement covariances, respectively. We may or may not have some knowledge of the initial state of the system,

$$\check{\mathbf{x}}_0 = \mathbf{x}_0 + \mathbf{w}_0, \qquad \mathbf{w}_0 \sim \mathcal{N}(\mathbf{0}, \check{\mathbf{P}}_0), \tag{6.93}$$

where $\check{\mathbf{P}}_0$ is the initial state covariance.

In Chapter 3 and the previous section, we assumed that the system model parameters, $\boldsymbol{\theta} = \{\mathbf{A}, \mathbf{B}, \mathbf{C}, \check{\mathbf{P}}_0, \mathbf{Q}, \mathbf{R}\}$, were known, but what if they are not? Classically, this amounts to solving the system identification problem. While there are several approaches to system identification in the literature, we choose to look at this from a structured learning perspective where we introduce the latent trajectory (Shumway and Stoffer, 1982; Ghahramani and Hinton, 1996). This approach is identical in spirit to the Baum–Welch algorithm for training parameters in a discrete-state *hidden Markov model (HMM)* (Baum and Petrie, 1966). We will use EM as described in Section 6.4.2. The E-step is completed using the procedure in the previous section with $\boldsymbol{\theta}$ held fixed. This leaves the details of the M-step to be worked out here.

In terms of the single-timestep quantities, (6.89) can be written as

$$\phi(\mathbf{x}|\boldsymbol{\theta}) = \frac{1}{2}(\mathbf{x}_0 - \check{\mathbf{x}}_0)^T \check{\mathbf{P}}_0^{-1}(\mathbf{x}_0 - \check{\mathbf{x}}_0)$$

$$+ \frac{1}{2}\sum_{k=1}^{K}(\mathbf{x}_k - \mathbf{A}\mathbf{x}_{k-1} - \mathbf{B}\mathbf{u}_k)^T \mathbf{Q}^{-1}(\mathbf{x}_k - \mathbf{A}\mathbf{x}_{k-1} - \mathbf{B}\mathbf{u}_k)$$

$$+ \frac{1}{2}\sum_{k=0}^{K}(\mathbf{y}_k - \mathbf{C}\mathbf{x}_k)^T \mathbf{R}^{-1}(\mathbf{y}_k - \mathbf{C}\mathbf{x}_k)$$

$$+ \frac{1}{2}\ln|\check{\mathbf{P}}_0| + \frac{1}{2}K\ln|\mathbf{Q}| + \frac{1}{2}(K+1)\ln|\mathbf{R}|, \tag{6.94}$$

which now depends on $\boldsymbol{\theta}$. Following the steps in Section 6.4.2, we next need to compute

$$\frac{\partial V(q|\boldsymbol{\theta})}{\partial \boldsymbol{\theta}} = \frac{\partial}{\partial \boldsymbol{\theta}} E_q[\phi(\mathbf{x}|\boldsymbol{\theta})] = E_q\left[\frac{\partial \phi(\mathbf{x}|\boldsymbol{\theta})}{\partial \boldsymbol{\theta}}\right] = \mathbf{0}, \tag{6.95}$$

to complete the minimization in the M-step.

The derivatives of $\phi(\mathbf{x}|\boldsymbol{\theta})$ with respect to the model matrices (or their inverses where simpler) are as follows:

$$\frac{\partial \phi(\mathbf{x}|\boldsymbol{\theta})}{\partial \boldsymbol{A}} = -\boldsymbol{Q}^{-1} \sum_{k=1}^{K} (\mathbf{x}_k - \boldsymbol{A}\mathbf{x}_{k-1} - \boldsymbol{B}\mathbf{u}_k) \, \mathbf{x}_{k-1}^T, \tag{6.96a}$$

$$\frac{\partial \phi(\mathbf{x}|\boldsymbol{\theta})}{\partial \boldsymbol{B}} = -\boldsymbol{Q}^{-1} \sum_{k=1}^{K} (\mathbf{x}_k - \boldsymbol{A}\mathbf{x}_{k-1} - \boldsymbol{B}\mathbf{u}_k) \, \mathbf{u}_k^T, \tag{6.96b}$$

$$\frac{\partial \phi(\mathbf{x}|\boldsymbol{\theta})}{\partial \boldsymbol{C}} = -\boldsymbol{R}^{-1} \sum_{k=0}^{K} (\mathbf{y}_k - \boldsymbol{C}\mathbf{x}_k) \, \mathbf{x}_k^T, \tag{6.96c}$$

$$\frac{\partial \phi(\mathbf{x}|\boldsymbol{\theta})}{\partial \check{\mathbf{P}}_0^{-1}} = \frac{1}{2}(\mathbf{x}_0 - \check{\mathbf{x}}_0)(\mathbf{x}_0 - \check{\mathbf{x}}_0)^T - \frac{1}{2}\check{\mathbf{P}}_0, \tag{6.96d}$$

$$\frac{\partial \phi(\mathbf{x}|\boldsymbol{\theta})}{\partial \boldsymbol{Q}^{-1}} = \frac{1}{2}\sum_{k=1}^{K} (\mathbf{x}_k - \boldsymbol{A}\mathbf{x}_{k-1} - \boldsymbol{B}\mathbf{u}_k)(\mathbf{x}_k - \boldsymbol{A}\mathbf{x}_{k-1} - \boldsymbol{B}\mathbf{u}_k)^T - \frac{1}{2}K\boldsymbol{Q}, \tag{6.96e}$$

$$\frac{\partial \phi(\mathbf{x}|\boldsymbol{\theta})}{\partial \boldsymbol{R}^{-1}} = \frac{1}{2}\sum_{k=0}^{K} (\mathbf{y}_k - \boldsymbol{C}\mathbf{x}_k)(\mathbf{y}_k - \boldsymbol{C}\mathbf{x}_k)^T - \frac{1}{2}(K+1)\boldsymbol{R}. \tag{6.96f}$$

We require the expectations of these derivatives over the latent trajectory distribution, $q(\mathbf{x}) = \mathcal{N}(\hat{\mathbf{x}}, \hat{\mathbf{P}})$. Taking the expectations of the first three we arrive at

$$E_q\left[\frac{\partial \phi(\mathbf{x}|\boldsymbol{\theta})}{\partial \boldsymbol{A}}\right] = -\boldsymbol{Q}^{-1}\sum_{k=1}^{K}\left(\left(\hat{\mathbf{x}}_k\hat{\mathbf{x}}_{k-1}^T + \hat{\mathbf{P}}_{k,k-1}\right) - \boldsymbol{A}\left(\hat{\mathbf{x}}_{k-1}\hat{\mathbf{x}}_{k-1}^T + \hat{\mathbf{P}}_{k-1}\right)\right. $$
$$\left. - \boldsymbol{B}\mathbf{u}_k\hat{\mathbf{x}}_{k-1}^T\right), \tag{6.97a}$$

$$E_q\left[\frac{\partial \phi(\mathbf{x}|\boldsymbol{\theta})}{\partial \boldsymbol{B}}\right] = -\boldsymbol{Q}^{-1}\sum_{k=1}^{K}\left(\hat{\mathbf{x}}_k\mathbf{u}_k^T - \boldsymbol{A}\hat{\mathbf{x}}_{k-1}\mathbf{u}_k^T - \boldsymbol{B}\mathbf{u}_k\mathbf{u}_k^T\right), \tag{6.97b}$$

$$E_q\left[\frac{\partial \phi(\mathbf{x}|\boldsymbol{\theta})}{\partial \boldsymbol{C}}\right] = -\boldsymbol{R}^{-1}\sum_{k=0}^{K}\left(\mathbf{y}_k\hat{\mathbf{x}}_k^T - \boldsymbol{C}\left(\hat{\mathbf{x}}_k\hat{\mathbf{x}}_k^T + \hat{\mathbf{P}}_k\right)\right), \tag{6.97c}$$

where the blocks of $\hat{\mathbf{x}}$ and $\hat{\mathbf{P}}$ are defined as

$$\hat{\mathbf{x}} = \begin{bmatrix} \hat{\mathbf{x}}_0 \\ \hat{\mathbf{x}}_1 \\ \vdots \\ \hat{\mathbf{x}}_{K-1} \\ \hat{\mathbf{x}}_K \end{bmatrix}, \quad \hat{\mathbf{P}} = \begin{bmatrix} \hat{\mathbf{P}}_0 & \hat{\mathbf{P}}_{10}^T & \ddots & & \ddots & & \ddots \\ \hat{\mathbf{P}}_{10} & \hat{\mathbf{P}}_1 & \hat{\mathbf{P}}_{21}^T & \ddots & & \ddots & \ddots \\ \ddots & \hat{\mathbf{P}}_{21} & \ddots & \ddots & & \ddots & \ddots \\ \ddots & \ddots & \ddots & \hat{\mathbf{P}}_{K-2} & \hat{\mathbf{P}}_{K-1,K-2}^T & \ddots \\ \ddots & \ddots & \ddots & \hat{\mathbf{P}}_{K-1,K-2} & \hat{\mathbf{P}}_{K-1} & \hat{\mathbf{P}}_{K,K-1}^T \\ \ddots & \ddots & \ddots & \ddots & \hat{\mathbf{P}}_{K,K-1} & \hat{\mathbf{P}}_K \end{bmatrix}.$$
$$\tag{6.98}$$

The covariance estimate, $\hat{\mathbf{P}}$, is in general dense but we have only assigned symbols to the blocks that we will use (main diagonal and one above/below). These can be computed in the process of running the RTS or Cholesky smoother (see Section 3.2.3).

Setting each of the expected gradients in (6.97) to zero, we have the following, where we note the A and B updates are coupled:

$$
\begin{bmatrix} A & B \end{bmatrix} = \begin{bmatrix} \sum_{k=1}^{K} \left(\hat{\mathbf{x}}_k \hat{\mathbf{x}}_{k-1}^T + \hat{\mathbf{P}}_{k,k-1} \right) & \sum_{k=1}^{K} \hat{\mathbf{x}}_k \mathbf{u}_k^T \end{bmatrix}
$$

$$
\times \begin{bmatrix} \sum_{k=1}^{K} \left(\hat{\mathbf{x}}_{k-1} \hat{\mathbf{x}}_{k-1}^T + \hat{\mathbf{P}}_{k-1} \right) & \sum_{k=1}^{K} \hat{\mathbf{x}}_{k-1} \mathbf{u}_k^T \\ \sum_{k=1}^{K} \mathbf{u}_k \hat{\mathbf{x}}_{k-1}^T & \sum_{k=1}^{K} \mathbf{u}_k \mathbf{u}_k^T \end{bmatrix}^{-1}, \tag{6.99a}
$$

$$
C = \left(\sum_{k=0}^{K} \mathbf{y}_k \hat{\mathbf{x}}_k^T \right) \left(\sum_{k=0}^{K} \left(\hat{\mathbf{x}}_k \hat{\mathbf{x}}_k^T + \hat{\mathbf{P}}_k \right) \right)^{-1}. \tag{6.99b}
$$

Once we have solved for A, B, and C, we can solve for the remaining parameters, $\check{\mathbf{P}}_0$, Q, and R.

The expectations of the gradients of the remaining parameters are

$$
E_q \left[\frac{\partial \phi(\mathbf{x}|\boldsymbol{\theta})}{\partial \check{\mathbf{P}}_0^{-1}} \right] = \frac{1}{2} (\hat{\mathbf{x}}_0 - \check{\mathbf{x}}_0)(\hat{\mathbf{x}}_0 - \check{\mathbf{x}}_0)^T + \frac{1}{2} \left(\hat{\mathbf{P}}_0 - \check{\mathbf{P}}_0 \right), \tag{6.100a}
$$

$$
E_q \left[\frac{\partial \phi(\mathbf{x}|\boldsymbol{\theta})}{\partial Q^{-1}} \right] = \frac{1}{2} \sum_{k=1}^{K} \left((\hat{\mathbf{x}}_k - A\hat{\mathbf{x}}_{k-1} - B\mathbf{u}_k)(\hat{\mathbf{x}}_k - A\hat{\mathbf{x}}_{k-1} - B\mathbf{u}_k)^T \right.
$$

$$
\left. + \hat{\mathbf{P}}_k - \hat{\mathbf{P}}_{k,k-1} A^T - A\hat{\mathbf{P}}_{k,k-1}^T + A\hat{\mathbf{P}}_{k-1} A^T \right) - \frac{1}{2} K Q, \tag{6.100b}
$$

$$
E_q \left[\frac{\partial \phi(\mathbf{x}|\boldsymbol{\theta})}{\partial R^{-1}} \right] = \frac{1}{2} \sum_{k=0}^{K} \left((\mathbf{y}_k - C\hat{\mathbf{x}}_k)(\mathbf{y}_k - C\hat{\mathbf{x}}_k)^T + C\hat{\mathbf{P}}_k C^T \right)
$$

$$
- \frac{1}{2} (K+1) R. \tag{6.100c}
$$

Setting these to zero to complete the minimization, we have

$$
\check{\mathbf{P}}_0 = (\hat{\mathbf{x}}_0 - \check{\mathbf{x}}_0)(\hat{\mathbf{x}}_0 - \check{\mathbf{x}}_0)^T + \hat{\mathbf{P}}_0, \tag{6.101a}
$$

$$
Q = \frac{1}{K} \sum_{k=1}^{K} \left((\hat{\mathbf{x}}_k - A\hat{\mathbf{x}}_{k-1} - B\mathbf{u}_k)(\hat{\mathbf{x}}_k - A\hat{\mathbf{x}}_{k-1} - B\mathbf{u}_k)^T \right.
$$

$$
\left. + \hat{\mathbf{P}}_k - \hat{\mathbf{P}}_{k,k-1} A^T - A\hat{\mathbf{P}}_{k,k-1}^T + A\hat{\mathbf{P}}_{k-1} A^T \right), \tag{6.101b}
$$

$$
R = \frac{1}{K+1} \sum_{k=0}^{K} \left((\mathbf{y}_k - C\hat{\mathbf{x}}_k)(\mathbf{y}_k - C\hat{\mathbf{x}}_k)^T + C\hat{\mathbf{P}}_k C^T \right), \tag{6.101c}
$$

where we note that A, B, and C are already known. With all the parameters, $\boldsymbol{\theta} = \{A, B, C, \check{\mathbf{P}}_0, Q, R\}$, now known, the M-step is complete and we can return to the E-step (see previous section) and iterate to convergence.

It is interesting to compare the updates for Q and R in (6.101a) to the adaptive covariance updates in (5.91) and (5.86). Both provide methods for estimating Q

and R using data and both have similar forms to the equations in that they make use of outer products of errors. However, they are different in the details. The adaptive covariance approach is using a filtered state estimate that is uncorrelated with the error being computed, and therefore deflates the estimated covariance based on the covariance of the state estimate. The EM approach of this section uses a smoothed state estimate to compute the errors, to which it is correlated, but this is accounted for in the expressions through inflation based on the covariance of the state estimate.

6.6 Nonlinear Systems

In this section, we further show the relationship between the GVI approach and some of the other nonlinear estimators that we encountered in Chapter 4. First, we will examine the GVI approach as applied to the correction step of the Kalman filter. Second, we will revisit the nonlinear stereo camera running example first introduced in Section 4.1.1.

6.6.1 Kalman Filter Correction Step

At the batch level, we have seen there is a strong connection between GVI and the MAP approach: evaluating the expectations using only the estimated mean recovers the standard MAP Newton update (see Section 4.3.1) with the Laplace approximation for the covariance. In this section, we further examine what the GVI approach looks like when applied only to the correction step in a filtering problem.

If we only want to apply GVI to the correction step of a filter we can still set this up as a small optimization problem (see Section 3.3.2). In this case we have a prior term from the prediction step of the filter, $\phi_p(\mathbf{x})$, and a corrective measurement term, $\phi_m(\mathbf{x})$:

$$\phi_p(\mathbf{x}) = \frac{1}{2}(\mathbf{x} - \check{\mathbf{x}})^T \check{\mathbf{P}}^{-1}(\mathbf{x} - \check{\mathbf{x}}), \tag{6.102a}$$

$$\phi_m(\mathbf{x}) = \frac{1}{2}(\mathbf{y} - \mathbf{g}(\mathbf{x}))^T \mathbf{R}^{-1}(\mathbf{y} - \mathbf{g}(\mathbf{x})), \tag{6.102b}$$

where $\mathcal{N}\left(\check{\mathbf{x}}, \check{\mathbf{P}}\right)$ is the output of the prediction step, $\mathbf{y}$ is the measurement, $\mathbf{R}$ is the measurement noise covariance, $\mathbf{g}(\cdot)$ is the observation model, and we have dropped the time subscript, k, on all quantities to keep the notation clean.

The full GVI update in (6.23) requires the first and second derivatives of $\phi(\mathbf{x}) = \phi_p(\mathbf{x}) + \phi_m(\mathbf{x})$:

$$\frac{\partial \phi(\mathbf{x})}{\partial \mathbf{x}^T} = \check{\mathbf{P}}^{-1}(\mathbf{x} - \check{\mathbf{x}}) - \mathbf{G}^T \mathbf{R}^{-1}(\mathbf{y} - \mathbf{g}(\mathbf{x})), \tag{6.103a}$$

$$\frac{\partial^2 \phi(\mathbf{x})}{\partial \mathbf{x}^T \partial \mathbf{x}} \approx \check{\mathbf{P}}^{-1} + \mathbf{G}^T \mathbf{R}^{-1} \mathbf{G}, \tag{6.103b}$$

where $\mathbf{G} = \frac{\partial \mathbf{g}}{\partial \mathbf{x}}$. The second derivative takes the usual Gauss–Newton approximation for simplicity but the full derivative could also be used. Let $q(\mathbf{x}) =$

$\mathcal{N}(\mathbf{x}_{\text{op}}, \mathbf{P}_{\text{op}})$ be our current GVI posterior estimate. Then the required expectations are

$$E_q\left[\frac{\partial\phi(\mathbf{x})}{\partial\mathbf{x}^T}\right] = \check{\mathbf{P}}^{-1}(\mathbf{x}_{\text{op}} - \check{\mathbf{x}}) - E_q\left[\mathbf{G}^T\mathbf{R}^{-1}(\mathbf{y} - \mathbf{g}(\mathbf{x}))\right], \quad (6.104a)$$

$$E_q\left[\frac{\partial^2\phi(\mathbf{x})}{\partial\mathbf{x}^T\partial\mathbf{x}}\right] \approx \check{\mathbf{P}}^{-1} + E_q\left[\mathbf{G}^T\mathbf{R}^{-1}\mathbf{G}\right], \quad (6.104b)$$

and the updates are

$$\mathbf{P}_{\text{op}} \leftarrow \left(\check{\mathbf{P}}^{-1} + E_q\left[\mathbf{G}^T\mathbf{R}^{-1}\mathbf{G}\right]\right)^{-1}, \quad (6.105a)$$

$$\mathbf{x}_{\text{op}} \leftarrow \mathbf{x}_{\text{op}} + \mathbf{P}_{\text{op}}\left(E_q\left[\mathbf{G}^T\mathbf{R}^{-1}(\mathbf{y} - \mathbf{g}(\mathbf{x}))\right] + \check{\mathbf{P}}^{-1}(\check{\mathbf{x}} - \mathbf{x}_{\text{op}})\right). \quad (6.105b)$$

The expectations need to be evaluated using cubature, as discussed in Section 6.3.3. We can also apply Stein's lemma to evaluate them in a derivative-free way.

If we switch over to the alternate loss approach of Section 6.4.1, then the updates become

$$\mathbf{P}_{\text{op}} \leftarrow \left(\check{\mathbf{P}}^{-1} + \bar{\mathbf{G}}^T\mathbf{R}^{-1}\bar{\mathbf{G}}\right)^{-1}, \quad (6.106a)$$

$$\mathbf{x}_{\text{op}} \leftarrow \mathbf{x}_{\text{op}} + \mathbf{P}_{\text{op}}\left(\bar{\mathbf{G}}^T\mathbf{R}^{-1}(\mathbf{y} - \bar{\mathbf{g}}) + \check{\mathbf{P}}^{-1}(\check{\mathbf{x}} - \mathbf{x}_{\text{op}})\right), \quad (6.106b)$$

where $\bar{\mathbf{G}} = E_q\left[\frac{\partial\mathbf{g}}{\partial\mathbf{x}}\right]$ and $\bar{\mathbf{g}} = E_q[\mathbf{g}(\mathbf{x})]$. With this formulation, we can now apply the usual SMW identities to manipulate it into a more standard Kalman form:

$$\mathbf{K} = \check{\mathbf{P}}\bar{\mathbf{G}}^T\left(\mathbf{R} + \bar{\mathbf{G}}\check{\mathbf{P}}\bar{\mathbf{G}}^T\right)^{-1}, \quad (6.107a)$$

$$\mathbf{P}_{\text{op}} \leftarrow \left(1 - \mathbf{K}\bar{\mathbf{G}}\right)\check{\mathbf{P}}, \quad (6.107b)$$

$$\mathbf{x}_{\text{op}} \leftarrow \check{\mathbf{x}} + \mathbf{K}\left(\mathbf{y} - \bar{\mathbf{g}} - \bar{\mathbf{G}}\left(\check{\mathbf{x}} - \mathbf{x}_{\text{op}}\right)\right). \quad (6.107c)$$

If we want to go derivative free, we can use Stein's lemma (see Appendix C.2) to approximate the required expectations. For the expected Jacobian (aka statistical Jacobian) we have

$$\bar{\mathbf{G}} = E_q\left[\frac{\partial\mathbf{g}}{\partial\mathbf{x}}\right] = E_q\left[(\mathbf{g}(\mathbf{x}) - \bar{\mathbf{g}})(\mathbf{x} - \mathbf{x}_{\text{op}})^T\right]\mathbf{P}_{\text{op}}^{-1}, \quad (6.108)$$

which can again be evaluated using Gaussian cubature (e.g., sigmapoints). The expected measurement is

$$\bar{\mathbf{g}} = E_q[\mathbf{g}(\mathbf{x})], \quad (6.109)$$

which can also be easily evaluated using Gaussian cubature.

Looking back to Section 4.2.10 where we discussed the *iterated sigmapoint Kalman filter (ISPKF)*, there are some strong similarities to the derivative-free GVI correction step discussed here, but the two are not identical. The difference primarily lies in which PDF is being used to construct the sigmapoints used to evaluate the expectations. In the ISPKF, the prior covariance, $\check{\mathbf{P}}$, is used while in the GVI approach of this section we use the (iteratively improving) posterior

Figure 6.3 Contour plots of $V(q)$ as a function of μ and σ^{-2} with optimizer steps overlaid for the stereo camera example. The white circle indicates the initial guess (the prior) and the dark circle indicates the converged posterior estimate. The plot in (a) is MAP (same as IEKF) and the plot in (b) is GVI. We see that GVI is able to get closer to the minimum of $V(q)$.

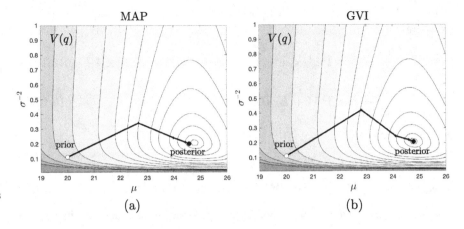

covariance, $\mathbf{P}_{\mathrm{op}}$. The ISPKF can therefore be referred to as a *prior statistical lineariation method* while GVI is a *posterior statistical linearization method* (García-Fernández et al., 2015).

6.6.2 Stereo Camera Example Revisited

To better understand what the GVI estimator is doing, we return to the running example of a nonlinear stereo camera first introduced in Section 4.1.1. We again use

$$x_{\text{true}} = 26 \ [\text{m}], \quad y_{\text{meas}} = \frac{fb}{x_{\text{true}}} - 0.6 \ [\text{pixel}],$$

to make the comparison to our other methods easy. As a reminder, this problem is equivalent to one correction step in a Kalman filter and we have used it to compare the different approaches to handling nonlinear measurement models. The previous section showed the details of applying the GVI approach to a filter correction step.

With GVI, we are optimizing our chosen cost functional, $V(q)$, with respect to both the mean and the (inverse) variance of our Gaussian estimator. Figure 6.3 shows a contour plot of $V(q)$ along with the steps both the GVI and MAP estimators took to arrive at their respective estimates of the posterior. In this simple example, we are fusing a Gaussian prior and a nonlinear measurement term so the MAP estimate is the same as the IEKF; it is also the same as GVI when the expectations are evaluated only at the estimated mean (i.e., $M = 1$ sigmapoint). For the GVI approach we used $M = 3$ sigmapoints with analytical derivatives to evaluate the expectations, as discussed in Section 6.3.3.

Figure 6.4 plots the final GVI posterior estimate as well as the true posterior, the MAP/IEKF estimate, and the ISPKF estimate. Of all the estimators, GVI is visually 'closest' to the true posterior, which is not surprising since this is exactly what we were trying to do: find the Gaussian that is closest to the true posterior in terms of the KL divergence. Numerically, the means of each Gaussian and the true posterior are:

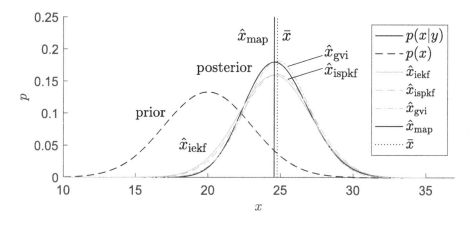

Figure 6.4 Stereo camera example, comparing the inference (i.e., 'corrective') step of the IEKF, GVI, and ISPKF to the full Bayesian posterior, $p(x|y)$. We see that the GVI approach seems to come 'closest' to the shape of the full posterior and very close to matching its mean, $\bar{x}$.

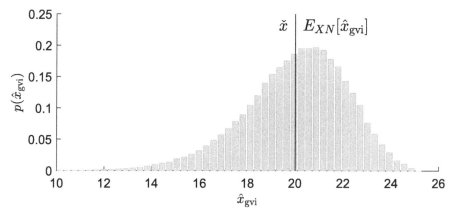

Figure 6.5 Histogram of estimator values for 100,000 trials of the stereo camera experiment where each time a new x_{true} is randomly drawn from the prior and a new y_{meas} is randomly drawn from the measurement model. The dashed line (extremely close to the solid line) marks the mean of the prior, $\check{x}$, and the solid line marks the expected value of the GVI estimator, $\hat{x}_{\mathrm{esgvi}}$, over all the trials. The gap between dashed and solid is $\hat{e}_{\mathrm{mean}} \approx 0.28$ cm, which indicates a very small bias, and the average squared error is $\hat{e}_{\mathrm{sq}} \approx 4.28$ m^2.

$$\hat{x}_{\mathrm{map}} = 24.5694, \quad \bar{x} = 24.7770,$$
$$\hat{x}_{\mathrm{iekf}} = 24.5694, \quad \hat{x}_{\mathrm{ispkf}} = 24.7414, \quad \hat{x}_{\mathrm{gvi}} = 24.7792.$$

As noted before, the IEKF solution matches the MAP one and the ISPKF and GVI solutions are close to (but not exactly) the mean of the true posterior.

Now, we consider the question, *how well does the GVI method capture* x_{true}? Once again, we compute the performance over a large number of trials (using the parameters in (4.5)). The results are shown in Figure 6.5. We see that the average difference of the estimator, $\hat{x}_{\mathrm{gvi}}$, and the ground-truth, x_{true}, is $\hat{e}_{\mathrm{mean}} \approx 0.28$ cm, demonstrating a very small bias. This is significantly better than the MAP estimator (bias of -33.0 cm) and even the ISPKF estimator (bias of -3.84 cm) on this same metric. The average squared error is approximately the same as other methods, with $\hat{e}_{\mathrm{sq}} \approx 4.28$ m^2.

As a final comment, it is interesting to note that GVI and MAP/IEKF are quite similar, the only difference being the number of sigmapoints used to compute the expectations. In this sense, GVI is simply less of an approximation than MAP and this allows it to better capture the true posterior.

Part II

Three-Dimensional Machinery

7

Primer on Three-Dimensional Geometry

This chapter will introduce three-dimensional geometry and specifically the concept of a *rotation* and some of its representations. It pays particular attention to the establishment of *reference frames*. Sastry (1999) is a comprehensive reference on control for robotics that includes a background on three-dimensional geometry. Hughes (1986) also provides a good first-principles background.

7.1 Vectors and Reference Frames

Vehicles (e.g., robots, satellites, aircraft) are typically free to translate and rotate. Mathematically, they have six degrees of freedom: three in translation and three in rotation. This six-degree-of-freedom geometric configuration is known as the *pose* (position and orientation) of the vehicle. Some vehicles may have multiple bodies connected together; in this case each body has its own pose. We will consider only the single-body case here.

7.1.1 Reference Frames

The position of a point on a vehicle can be described with a vector, $\underrightarrow{r}^{vi}$, consisting of three components. Rotational motion is described by expressing the orientation of a reference frame on the vehicle, $\underrightarrow{\mathcal{F}}_v$, with respect to another frame, $\underrightarrow{\mathcal{F}}_i$. Figure 7.1 shows the typical setup for a single-body vehicle.

We will take a *vector* to be a quantity $\underrightarrow{r}$ having length and direction. This vector can be expressed in a reference frame as

$$
\begin{aligned}
\underrightarrow{r} &= r_1 \underrightarrow{1}_1 + r_2 \underrightarrow{1}_2 + r_3 \underrightarrow{1}_3 \\
&= [r_1 \ \ r_2 \ \ r_3] \begin{bmatrix} \underrightarrow{1}_1 \\ \underrightarrow{1}_2 \\ \underrightarrow{1}_3 \end{bmatrix} \\
&= \mathbf{r}_1^T \underrightarrow{\mathcal{F}}_1.
\end{aligned} \tag{7.1}
$$

The quantity

$$
\underrightarrow{\mathcal{F}}_1 = \begin{bmatrix} \underrightarrow{1}_1 \\ \underrightarrow{1}_2 \\ \underrightarrow{1}_3 \end{bmatrix}
$$

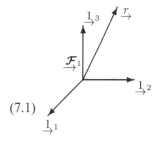

Figure 7.1 Vehicle and typical reference frames.

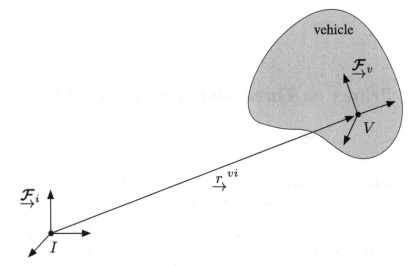

is a column containing the basis vectors forming the reference frame $\underset{\rightarrow}{\mathcal{F}}_1$; we will always use basis vectors that are unit length, orthogonal, and arranged in a dextral (right-handed) fashion. We shall refer to $\underset{\rightarrow}{\mathcal{F}}_1$ as a *vectrix* (Hughes, 1986). The quantity

$$\mathbf{r}_1 = \begin{bmatrix} r_1 \\ r_2 \\ r_3 \end{bmatrix}$$

is a column matrix containing the *components* or *coordinates* of $\underset{\rightarrow}{r}$ in reference frame $\underset{\rightarrow}{\mathcal{F}}_1$.

The vector can also be written as

$$\underset{\rightarrow}{r} = \begin{bmatrix} \underset{\rightarrow}{1}_1 & \underset{\rightarrow}{1}_2 & \underset{\rightarrow}{1}_3 \end{bmatrix} \begin{bmatrix} r_1 \\ r_2 \\ r_3 \end{bmatrix}$$

$$= \underset{\rightarrow}{\mathcal{F}}_1^T \mathbf{r}_1.$$

7.1.2 Dot Product

Consider two vectors, $\underset{\rightarrow}{r}$ and $\underset{\rightarrow}{s}$, expressed in the same reference frame $\underset{\rightarrow}{\mathcal{F}}_1$:

$$\underset{\rightarrow}{r} = \begin{bmatrix} r_1 & r_2 & r_3 \end{bmatrix} \begin{bmatrix} \underset{\rightarrow}{1}_1 \\ \underset{\rightarrow}{1}_2 \\ \underset{\rightarrow}{1}_3 \end{bmatrix} , \quad \underset{\rightarrow}{s} = \begin{bmatrix} \underset{\rightarrow}{1}_1 & \underset{\rightarrow}{1}_2 & \underset{\rightarrow}{1}_3 \end{bmatrix} \begin{bmatrix} s_1 \\ s_2 \\ s_3 \end{bmatrix} .$$

The *dot product* (a.k.a., inner product) is given by

$$\underset{\rightarrow}{r} \cdot \underset{\rightarrow}{s} = \begin{bmatrix} r_1 & r_2 & r_3 \end{bmatrix} \begin{bmatrix} \underset{\rightarrow}{1}_1 \\ \underset{\rightarrow}{1}_2 \\ \underset{\rightarrow}{1}_3 \end{bmatrix} \cdot \begin{bmatrix} \underset{\rightarrow}{1}_1 & \underset{\rightarrow}{1}_2 & \underset{\rightarrow}{1}_3 \end{bmatrix} \begin{bmatrix} s_1 \\ s_2 \\ s_3 \end{bmatrix}$$

$$= \begin{bmatrix} r_1 & r_2 & r_3 \end{bmatrix} \begin{bmatrix} \underset{\rightarrow}{1}_1 \cdot \underset{\rightarrow}{1}_1 & \underset{\rightarrow}{1}_1 \cdot \underset{\rightarrow}{1}_2 & \underset{\rightarrow}{1}_1 \cdot \underset{\rightarrow}{1}_3 \\ \underset{\rightarrow}{1}_2 \cdot \underset{\rightarrow}{1}_1 & \underset{\rightarrow}{1}_2 \cdot \underset{\rightarrow}{1}_2 & \underset{\rightarrow}{1}_2 \cdot \underset{\rightarrow}{1}_3 \\ \underset{\rightarrow}{1}_3 \cdot \underset{\rightarrow}{1}_1 & \underset{\rightarrow}{1}_3 \cdot \underset{\rightarrow}{1}_2 & \underset{\rightarrow}{1}_3 \cdot \underset{\rightarrow}{1}_3 \end{bmatrix} \begin{bmatrix} s_1 \\ s_2 \\ s_3 \end{bmatrix} .$$

But

$$\vec{1}_1 \cdot \vec{1}_1 = \vec{1}_2 \cdot \vec{1}_2 = \vec{1}_3 \cdot \vec{1}_3 = 1,$$

and

$$\vec{1}_1 \cdot \vec{1}_2 = \vec{1}_2 \cdot \vec{1}_3 = \vec{1}_3 \cdot \vec{1}_1 = 0.$$

Therefore,

$$\vec{r} \cdot \vec{s} = \mathbf{r}_1{}^T \mathbf{1} \mathbf{s}_1 = \mathbf{r}_1{}^T \mathbf{s}_1 = r_1 s_1 + r_2 s_2 + r_3 s_3.$$

The notation $\mathbf{1}$ will be used to designate the *identity matrix*. Its dimension can be inferred from the context.

7.1.3 Cross Product

The *cross product* of two vectors expressed in the same reference frame is given by

$$
\vec{r} \times \vec{s} = [r_1 \; r_2 \; r_3] \begin{bmatrix} \vec{1}_1 \times \vec{1}_1 & \vec{1}_1 \times \vec{1}_2 & \vec{1}_1 \times \vec{1}_3 \\ \vec{1}_2 \times \vec{1}_1 & \vec{1}_2 \times \vec{1}_2 & \vec{1}_2 \times \vec{1}_3 \\ \vec{1}_3 \times \vec{1}_1 & \vec{1}_3 \times \vec{1}_2 & \vec{1}_3 \times \vec{1}_3 \end{bmatrix} \begin{bmatrix} s_1 \\ s_2 \\ s_3 \end{bmatrix}
$$

$$
= [r_1 \; r_2 \; r_3] \begin{bmatrix} 0 & \vec{1}_3 & -\vec{1}_2 \\ -\vec{1}_3 & 0 & \vec{1}_1 \\ \vec{1}_2 & -\vec{1}_1 & 0 \end{bmatrix} \begin{bmatrix} s_1 \\ s_2 \\ s_3 \end{bmatrix}
$$

$$
= \begin{bmatrix} \vec{1}_1 & \vec{1}_2 & \vec{1}_3 \end{bmatrix} \begin{bmatrix} 0 & -r_3 & r_2 \\ r_3 & 0 & -r_1 \\ -r_2 & r_1 & 0 \end{bmatrix} \begin{bmatrix} s_1 \\ s_2 \\ s_3 \end{bmatrix}
$$

$$
= \vec{\mathcal{F}}_1^T \mathbf{r}_1{}^\times \mathbf{s}_1,
$$

where the fact that the basis vectors are orthogonal and arranged in a dextral fashion has been exploited. Hence, if $\vec{r}$ and $\vec{s}$ are expressed in the same reference frame, the 3×3 matrix

$$
\mathbf{r}_1{}^\times = \begin{bmatrix} 0 & -r_3 & r_2 \\ r_3 & 0 & -r_1 \\ -r_2 & r_1 & 0 \end{bmatrix} \tag{7.2}
$$

can be used to construct the components of the cross product. This matrix is skew-symmetric;[1] that is,

$$(\mathbf{r}_1{}^\times)^T = -\mathbf{r}_1{}^\times.$$

It is easy to verify that

$$\mathbf{r}_1{}^\times \mathbf{r}_1 = \mathbf{0},$$

---

[1] There are many equivalent notations in the literature for this skew-symmetric definition: $\mathbf{r}_1^\times = \hat{\mathbf{r}}_1 = \mathbf{r}_1^\wedge = -[[\mathbf{r}_1]] = [\mathbf{r}_1]_\times$. For now, we use the first one, since it makes an obvious connection to the cross product; later we will also use $(\cdot)^\wedge$, as this is in common use in robotics.

where $\mathbf{0}$ is a column matrix of zeros and

$$\mathbf{r}_1{}^\times \mathbf{s}_1 = -\mathbf{s}_1{}^\times \mathbf{r}_1.$$

7.2 Rotations

Critical to our ability to estimate how objects are moving in the world is the ability to parameterize the orientation, or rotation, of those objects. We begin by introducing rotation matrices and then provide some alternative representations.

7.2.1 Rotation Matrices

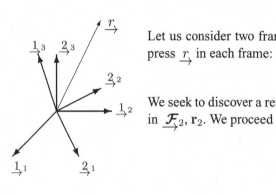

Let us consider two frames $\underrightarrow{\mathcal{F}}_1$ and $\underrightarrow{\mathcal{F}}_2$ with a common origin, and let us express $\underrightarrow{r}$ in each frame:

$$\underrightarrow{r} = \underrightarrow{\mathcal{F}}_1^T \mathbf{r}_1 = \underrightarrow{\mathcal{F}}_2^T \mathbf{r}_2.$$

We seek to discover a relationship between the components in $\underrightarrow{\mathcal{F}}_1$, $\mathbf{r}_1$, and those in $\underrightarrow{\mathcal{F}}_2$, $\mathbf{r}_2$. We proceed as follows:

$$\underrightarrow{\mathcal{F}}_2^T \mathbf{r}_2 = \underrightarrow{\mathcal{F}}_1^T \mathbf{r}_1,$$
$$\underrightarrow{\mathcal{F}}_2 \cdot \underrightarrow{\mathcal{F}}_2^T \mathbf{r}_2 = \underrightarrow{\mathcal{F}}_2 \cdot \underrightarrow{\mathcal{F}}_1^T \mathbf{r}_1,$$
$$\mathbf{r}_2 = \mathbf{C}_{21} \mathbf{r}_1.$$

We have defined

$$\mathbf{C}_{21} = \underrightarrow{\mathcal{F}}_2 \cdot \underrightarrow{\mathcal{F}}_1^T$$

$$= \begin{bmatrix} \underrightarrow{2}_1 \\ \underrightarrow{2}_2 \\ \underrightarrow{2}_3 \end{bmatrix} \cdot \begin{bmatrix} \underrightarrow{1}_1 & \underrightarrow{1}_2 & \underrightarrow{1}_3 \end{bmatrix}$$

$$= \begin{bmatrix} \underrightarrow{2}_1 \cdot \underrightarrow{1}_1 & \underrightarrow{2}_1 \cdot \underrightarrow{1}_2 & \underrightarrow{2}_1 \cdot \underrightarrow{1}_3 \\ \underrightarrow{2}_2 \cdot \underrightarrow{1}_1 & \underrightarrow{2}_2 \cdot \underrightarrow{1}_2 & \underrightarrow{2}_2 \cdot \underrightarrow{1}_3 \\ \underrightarrow{2}_3 \cdot \underrightarrow{1}_1 & \underrightarrow{2}_3 \cdot \underrightarrow{1}_2 & \underrightarrow{2}_3 \cdot \underrightarrow{1}_3 \end{bmatrix}.$$

The matrix $\mathbf{C}_{21}$ is called a *rotation matrix*. It is sometimes referred to as a 'direction cosine matrix' since the dot product of two unit vectors is just the cosine of the angle between them.

The unit vectors in $\underrightarrow{\mathcal{F}}_2$ can be related to those in $\underrightarrow{\mathcal{F}}_1$:

$$\underrightarrow{\mathcal{F}}_1^T = \underrightarrow{\mathcal{F}}_2^T \mathbf{C}_{21}. \tag{7.3}$$

Rotation matrices possess some special properties:

$$\mathbf{r}_1 = \mathbf{C}_{21}^{-1} \mathbf{r}_2 = \mathbf{C}_{12} \mathbf{r}_2.$$

But, $\mathbf{C}_{21}^T = \mathbf{C}_{12}$. Hence,

$$\mathbf{C}_{12} = \mathbf{C}_{21}^{-1} = \mathbf{C}_{21}^T. \tag{7.4}$$

We say that $\mathbf{C}_{21}$ is an *orthonormal* matrix because its inverse is equal to its transpose.

Consider three reference frames $\vec{\mathcal{F}}_1$, $\vec{\mathcal{F}}_2$, and $\vec{\mathcal{F}}_3$. The components of a vector $\vec{r}$ in these three frames are $\mathbf{r}_1$, $\mathbf{r}_2$, and $\mathbf{r}_3$. Now,

$$\mathbf{r}_3 = \mathbf{C}_{32}\mathbf{r}_2 = \mathbf{C}_{32}\mathbf{C}_{21}\mathbf{r}_1.$$

But, $\mathbf{r}_3 = \mathbf{C}_{31}\mathbf{r}_1$, and therefore

$$\mathbf{C}_{31} = \mathbf{C}_{32}\mathbf{C}_{21}.$$

7.2.2 Principal Rotations

Before considering more general rotations, it is useful to consider rotations about one basis vector. The situation where $\vec{\mathcal{F}}_2$ has been rotated from $\vec{\mathcal{F}}_1$ through a rotation about the 3-axis is shown in the figure. The rotation matrix in this case is

$$\mathbf{C}_3 = \begin{bmatrix} \cos\theta_3 & \sin\theta_3 & 0 \\ -\sin\theta_3 & \cos\theta_3 & 0 \\ 0 & 0 & 1 \end{bmatrix}. \tag{7.5}$$

For a rotation about the 2-axis, the rotation matrix is

$$\mathbf{C}_2 = \begin{bmatrix} \cos\theta_2 & 0 & -\sin\theta_2 \\ 0 & 1 & 0 \\ \sin\theta_2 & 0 & \cos\theta_2 \end{bmatrix}. \tag{7.6}$$

For a rotation about the 1-axis, the rotation matrix is

$$\mathbf{C}_1 = \begin{bmatrix} 1 & 0 & 0 \\ 0 & \cos\theta_1 & \sin\theta_1 \\ 0 & -\sin\theta_1 & \cos\theta_1 \end{bmatrix}. \tag{7.7}$$

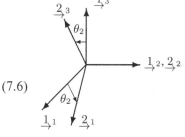

7.2.3 Alternate Rotation Representations

We have seen one way of discussing the orientation of one reference frame with respect to another: the *rotation matrix*. The rotation matrix describes orientation both globally and uniquely. This requires nine parameters (they are not independent). There are a number of other alternatives.

The key thing to realize about the different representations of rotations is that there are always only three underlying degrees of freedom. The representations that have more than three parameters must have associated constraints to limit the number of degrees of freedom to three. The representations that have exactly three parameters have associated singularities. There is no perfect representation that is minimal (i.e., having only three parameters) and that is also free of singularities (Stuelpnagel, 1964).

Euler Angles

Leonhard Euler (1707–1783) is considered to be the preeminent mathematician of the eighteenth century and one of the greatest mathematicians to have ever lived. He made important discoveries in fields as diverse as infinitesimal calculus and graph theory. He also introduced much of the modern mathematical terminology and notation, particularly for mathematical analysis, such as the notion of a mathematical function. He is also renowned for his work in mechanics, fluid dynamics, optics, astronomy, and music theory.

The orientation of one reference frame with respect to another can also be specified by a sequence of three principal rotations. One possible sequence is as follows:

  (i) A rotation ψ about the original 3-axis
 (ii) A rotation γ about the intermediate 1-axis
(iii) A rotation θ about the transformed 3-axis

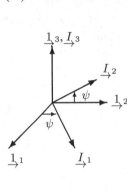 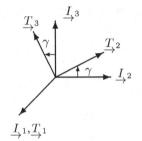 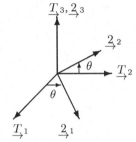

This is called a 3-1-3 sequence and is the one originally used by Euler. In the classical mechanics literature, the angles are referred to by the following names:

$$\theta : \text{ spin angle}$$
$$\gamma : \text{ nutation angle}$$
$$\psi : \text{ precession angle}$$

The rotation matrix from frame 1 to frame 2 is given by

$$
\begin{aligned}
\mathbf{C}_{21}(\theta,\gamma,\psi) &= \mathbf{C}_{2T}\mathbf{C}_{TI}\mathbf{C}_{I1} \\
&= \mathbf{C}_3(\theta)\mathbf{C}_1(\gamma)\mathbf{C}_3(\psi) \\
&= \begin{bmatrix} c_\theta c_\psi - s_\theta c_\gamma s_\psi & s_\psi c_\theta + c_\gamma s_\theta c_\psi & s_\gamma s_\theta \\ -c_\psi s_\theta - c_\theta c_\gamma s_\psi & -s_\psi s_\theta + c_\theta c_\gamma c_\psi & s_\gamma c_\theta \\ s_\psi s_\gamma & -s_\gamma c_\psi & c_\gamma \end{bmatrix}.
\end{aligned} \quad (7.8)
$$

We have made the abbreviations $s = \sin$, $c = \cos$.

Another possible sequence that can be used is as follows:

  (i) A rotation θ_1 about the original 1-axis ('roll' rotation)
 (ii) A rotation θ_2 about the intermediate 2-axis ('pitch' rotation)
(iii) A rotation θ_3 about the transformed 3-axis ('yaw' rotation)

This sequence, which is very common in aerospace applications, is called the 1-2-3 attitude sequence or the 'roll-pitch-yaw' convention. In this case, the rotation matrix from frame 1 to frame 2 is given by

$$\mathbf{C}_{21}(\theta_3, \theta_2, \theta_1) = \mathbf{C}_3(\theta_3)\mathbf{C}_2(\theta_2)\mathbf{C}_1(\theta_1)$$

$$= \begin{bmatrix} c_2 c_3 & c_1 s_3 + s_1 s_2 c_3 & s_1 s_3 - c_1 s_2 c_3 \\ -c_2 s_3 & c_1 c_3 - s_1 s_2 s_3 & s_1 c_3 + c_1 s_2 s_3 \\ s_2 & -s_1 c_2 & c_1 c_2 \end{bmatrix}, \quad (7.9)$$

where $s_i = \sin \theta_i$, $c_i = \cos \theta_i$.

All Euler sequences have singularities. For instance, if $\gamma = 0$ for the 3-1-3 sequence, then the angles θ and ψ become associated with the same degree of freedom and cannot be uniquely determined.

For the 1-2-3 sequence, a singularity exists at $\theta_2 = \pi/2$. In this case,

$$\mathbf{C}_{21}\left(\theta_3, \frac{\pi}{2}, \theta_1\right) = \begin{bmatrix} 0 & \sin(\theta_1 + \theta_3) & -\cos(\theta_1 + \theta_3) \\ 0 & \cos(\theta_1 + \theta_3) & \sin(\theta_1 + \theta_3) \\ 1 & 0 & 0 \end{bmatrix}.$$

Therefore, θ_1 and θ_3 are associated with the same rotation. However, this is only a problem if we want to recover the rotation angles from the rotation matrix.

Infinitesimal Rotations

Consider the 1-2-3 transformation when the angles θ_1, θ_2, θ_3 are small. In this case, we make the approximations $c_i \approx 1$, $s_i \approx \theta_i$ and neglect products of small angles, $\theta_i \theta_j \approx 0$. Then we have

$$\mathbf{C}_{21} \approx \begin{bmatrix} 1 & \theta_3 & -\theta_2 \\ -\theta_3 & 1 & \theta_1 \\ \theta_2 & -\theta_1 & 1 \end{bmatrix}$$

$$\approx \mathbf{1} - \boldsymbol{\theta}^\times, \quad (7.10)$$

where

$$\boldsymbol{\theta} = \begin{bmatrix} \theta_1 \\ \theta_2 \\ \theta_3 \end{bmatrix},$$

which is referred to as a *rotation vector*.

It is easy to show that the form of the rotation matrix for infinitesimal rotations (i.e., 'small angle approximation') does not depend on the order in which the rotations are performed. For example, we can show that the same result is obtained for a 2-1-3 Euler sequence.

Euler Parameters

Euler's rotation theorem says that the most general motion of a rigid body with one point fixed is a rotation about an axis through that point.

Let us denote the *axis of rotation* by $\mathbf{a} = [a_1 \ a_2 \ a_3]^T$ and assume that it is a unit vector:

$$\mathbf{a}^T \mathbf{a} = a_1^2 + a_2^2 + a_3^2 = 1. \quad (7.11)$$

The *angle of rotation* is ϕ. We state, without proof, that the rotation matrix in this case is given by

$$\mathbf{C}_{21} = \cos\phi\mathbf{1} + (1 - \cos\phi)\mathbf{aa}^T - \sin\phi\mathbf{a}^\times. \qquad (7.12)$$

It does not matter in which frame $\mathbf{a}$ is expressed because

$$\mathbf{C}_{21}\mathbf{a} = \mathbf{a}. \qquad (7.13)$$

The combination of variables,

$$\eta = \cos\frac{\phi}{2}, \quad \boldsymbol{\varepsilon} = \mathbf{a}\sin\frac{\phi}{2} = \begin{bmatrix} a_1\sin(\phi/2) \\ a_2\sin(\phi/2) \\ a_3\sin(\phi/2) \end{bmatrix} = \begin{bmatrix} \varepsilon_1 \\ \varepsilon_2 \\ \varepsilon_3 \end{bmatrix}, \qquad (7.14)$$

is particularly useful. The four parameters $\{\boldsymbol{\varepsilon}, \eta\}$ are called the *Euler parameters* associated with a rotation.[2] They are not independent because they satisfy the constraint

$$\eta^2 + \varepsilon_1^2 + \varepsilon_2^2 + \varepsilon_3^2 = 1.$$

The rotation matrix can be expressed in terms of the Euler parameters as

$$\mathbf{C}_{21} = (\eta^2 - \boldsymbol{\varepsilon}^T\boldsymbol{\varepsilon})\mathbf{1} + 2\boldsymbol{\varepsilon}\boldsymbol{\varepsilon}^T - 2\eta\boldsymbol{\varepsilon}^\times$$
$$= \begin{bmatrix} 1 - 2(\varepsilon_2^2 + \varepsilon_3^2) & 2(\varepsilon_1\varepsilon_2 + \varepsilon_3\eta) & 2(\varepsilon_1\varepsilon_3 - \varepsilon_2\eta) \\ 2(\varepsilon_2\varepsilon_1 - \varepsilon_3\eta) & 1 - 2(\varepsilon_3^2 + \varepsilon_1^2) & 2(\varepsilon_2\varepsilon_3 + \varepsilon_1\eta) \\ 2(\varepsilon_3\varepsilon_1 + \varepsilon_2\eta) & 2(\varepsilon_3\varepsilon_2 - \varepsilon_1\eta) & 1 - 2(\varepsilon_1^2 + \varepsilon_2^2) \end{bmatrix}. \qquad (7.15)$$

Euler parameters are useful in many spacecraft applications. There are no singularities associated with them, and the calculation of the rotation matrix does not involve trigonometric functions, which is a significant numerical advantage. The only drawback is the use of four parameters instead of three, as is the case with Euler angles; this makes it challenging to perform some estimation problems because the constraint must be enforced.

Quaternions

We will use the notation of Barfoot et al. (2011) for this section. A *quaternion* will be a 4×1 column that may be written as

$$\mathbf{q} = \begin{bmatrix} \boldsymbol{\varepsilon} \\ \eta \end{bmatrix}, \qquad (7.16)$$

where $\boldsymbol{\varepsilon}$ is a 3×1 and η is a scalar. The quaternion left-hand compound operator, $+$, and the right-hand compound operator, $\oplus$, will be defined as

$$\mathbf{q}^+ = \begin{bmatrix} \eta\mathbf{1} - \boldsymbol{\varepsilon}^\times & \boldsymbol{\varepsilon} \\ -\boldsymbol{\varepsilon}^T & \eta \end{bmatrix}, \quad \mathbf{q}^\oplus = \begin{bmatrix} \eta\mathbf{1} + \boldsymbol{\varepsilon}^\times & \boldsymbol{\varepsilon} \\ -\boldsymbol{\varepsilon}^T & \eta \end{bmatrix}. \qquad (7.17)$$

Quaternions were first described by Sir William Rowan Hamilton (1805–1865) in 1843 and applied to mechanics in three-dimensional space. Hamilton was an Irish physicist, astronomer, and mathematician, who made important contributions to classical mechanics, optics, and algebra. His studies of mechanical and optical systems led him to discover new mathematical concepts and techniques. His best known contribution to mathematical physics is the reformulation of Newtonian mechanics, now called Hamiltonian mechanics. This work has proven central to the modern study of classical field theories such as electromagnetism, and to the development of quantum mechanics. In pure mathematics, he is best known as the inventor of quaternions.

---

[2] These are sometimes referred to as *unit-length quaternions* when stacked as $\mathbf{q} = \begin{bmatrix} \boldsymbol{\varepsilon} \\ \eta \end{bmatrix}$. These are discussed in more detail in what follows.

The inverse operator, -1, will be defined by

$$\mathbf{q}^{-1} = \begin{bmatrix} -\boldsymbol{\varepsilon} \\ \eta \end{bmatrix}. \tag{7.18}$$

Let $\mathbf{u}$, $\mathbf{v}$, and $\mathbf{w}$ be quaternions. Then some useful identities are

$$\mathbf{u}^+ \mathbf{v} \equiv \mathbf{v}^\oplus \mathbf{u}, \tag{7.19}$$

and

$$
\begin{aligned}
(\mathbf{u}^+)^T &\equiv (\mathbf{u}^+)^{-1} \equiv (\mathbf{u}^{-1})^+, & (\mathbf{u}^\oplus)^T &\equiv (\mathbf{u}^\oplus)^{-1} \equiv (\mathbf{u}^{-1})^\oplus, \\
(\mathbf{u}^+\mathbf{v})^{-1} &\equiv \mathbf{v}^{-1+}\mathbf{u}^{-1}, & (\mathbf{u}^\oplus\mathbf{v})^{-1} &\equiv \mathbf{v}^{-1\oplus}\mathbf{u}^{-1}, \\
(\mathbf{u}^+\mathbf{v})^+\mathbf{w} &\equiv \mathbf{u}^+(\mathbf{v}^+\mathbf{w}) \equiv \mathbf{u}^+\mathbf{v}^+\mathbf{w}, & (\mathbf{u}^\oplus\mathbf{v})^\oplus\mathbf{w} &\equiv \mathbf{u}^\oplus(\mathbf{v}^\oplus\mathbf{w}) \equiv \mathbf{u}^\oplus\mathbf{v}^\oplus\mathbf{w}, \\
\alpha\mathbf{u}^+ + \beta\mathbf{v}^+ &\equiv (\alpha\mathbf{u} + \beta\mathbf{v})^+, & \alpha\mathbf{u}^\oplus + \beta\mathbf{v}^\oplus &\equiv (\alpha\mathbf{u} + \beta\mathbf{v})^\oplus,
\end{aligned}
\tag{7.20}
$$

where α and β are scalars. We also have

$$\mathbf{u}^+\mathbf{v}^\oplus \equiv \mathbf{v}^\oplus\mathbf{u}^+. \tag{7.21}$$

The proofs are left to the reader.

Quaternions form a *non-commutative group*[3] under both the $+$ and $\oplus$ operations. Many of the identities above are prerequisites to showing this fact. The identity element of this group, $\iota = \begin{bmatrix} 0 & 0 & 0 & 1 \end{bmatrix}^T$, is such that

$$\iota^+ = \iota^\oplus = \mathbf{1}, \tag{7.22}$$

where $\mathbf{1}$ is the 4×4 identity matrix.

Rotations may be represented in this notation by using a unit-length quaternion, $\mathbf{q}$, such that

$$\mathbf{q}^T\mathbf{q} = 1. \tag{7.23}$$

These form a *sub-group* that can be used to represent rotations.

To rotate a point (in homogeneous form)

$$\mathbf{v} = \begin{bmatrix} x \\ y \\ z \\ 1 \end{bmatrix} \tag{7.24}$$

to another frame using the rotation, $\mathbf{q}$, we compute

$$\mathbf{u} = \mathbf{q}^+\mathbf{v}^+\mathbf{q}^{-1} = \mathbf{q}^+\mathbf{q}^{-1\oplus}\mathbf{v} = \mathbf{R}\mathbf{v}, \tag{7.25}$$

where

$$\mathbf{R} = \mathbf{q}^+\mathbf{q}^{-1\oplus} = \mathbf{q}^{-1\oplus}\mathbf{q}^+ = \mathbf{q}^{\oplus T}\mathbf{q}^+ = \begin{bmatrix} \mathbf{C} & \mathbf{0} \\ \mathbf{0}^T & 1 \end{bmatrix}, \tag{7.26}$$

---

[3] The next chapter will discuss group theory as it pertains to rotations in much more detail.

and $\mathbf{C}$ is the 3×3 rotation matrix with which we are now familiar. We have included various forms for $\mathbf{R}$ to show the different structures this transformation can take.

Gibbs Vector

Josiah Willard Gibbs (1839–1903) was an American scientist who made important theoretical contributions to physics, chemistry, and mathematics. As a mathematician, he invented modern vector calculus (independently of the British scientist Oliver Heaviside, who carried out similar work during the same period). The Gibbs vector is also sometimes known as the *Cayley–Rodrigues parameters*.

Yet another way that we can parameterize rotations is through the *Gibbs vector*. In terms of axis/angle parameters discussed earlier, the Gibbs vector, $\mathbf{g}$, is given by

$$\mathbf{g} = \mathbf{a} \tan \frac{\phi}{2}, \tag{7.27}$$

which we note has a singularity at $\phi = \pi$, so this parameterization does not work well for all angles. The rotation matrix, $\mathbf{C}$, can then be written in terms of the Gibbs vector as

$$\mathbf{C} = \left(1 + \mathbf{g}^{\times}\right)^{-1}\left(1 - \mathbf{g}^{\times}\right) = \frac{1}{1 + \mathbf{g}^T \mathbf{g}}\left((1 - \mathbf{g}^T \mathbf{g})\mathbf{1} + 2\mathbf{g}\mathbf{g}^T - 2\mathbf{g}^{\times}\right). \tag{7.28}$$

Substituting in the Gibbs vector definition, the right-hand expression becomes

$$\mathbf{C} = \frac{1}{1 + \tan^2 \frac{\phi}{2}}\left(\left(1 - \tan^2 \frac{\phi}{2}\right)\mathbf{1} + 2\tan^2 \frac{\phi}{2}\mathbf{a}\mathbf{a}^T - 2\tan \frac{\phi}{2}\mathbf{a}^{\times}\right), \tag{7.29}$$

where we have used that $\mathbf{a}^T \mathbf{a} = 1$. Utilizing that $\left(1 + \tan^2 \frac{\phi}{2}\right)^{-1} = \cos^2 \frac{\phi}{2}$, we have

$$\mathbf{C} = \underbrace{\left(\cos^2 \frac{\phi}{2} - \sin^2 \frac{\phi}{2}\right)}_{\cos \phi}\mathbf{1} + \underbrace{2\sin^2 \frac{\phi}{2}}_{1-\cos \phi}\mathbf{a}\mathbf{a}^T - \underbrace{2\sin \frac{\phi}{2}\cos \frac{\phi}{2}}_{\sin \phi}\mathbf{a}^{\times}$$

$$= \cos \phi\, \mathbf{1} + (1 - \cos \phi)\mathbf{a}\mathbf{a}^T - \sin \phi\, \mathbf{a}^{\times}, \tag{7.30}$$

which is our usual expression for the rotation matrix in terms of the axis/angle parameters.

To relate the two expressions for $\mathbf{C}$ in terms of $\mathbf{g}$ given in (7.28), we first note that

$$\left(1 + \mathbf{g}^{\times}\right)^{-1} = 1 - \mathbf{g}^{\times} + \mathbf{g}^{\times}\mathbf{g}^{\times} - \mathbf{g}^{\times}\mathbf{g}^{\times}\mathbf{g}^{\times} + \cdots = \sum_{n=0}^{\infty}\left(-\mathbf{g}^{\times}\right)^n. \tag{7.31}$$

Then we observe that

$$\mathbf{g}^T \mathbf{g}\left(1 + \mathbf{g}^{\times}\right)^{-1}$$
$$= (\mathbf{g}^T \mathbf{g})\mathbf{1} - \underbrace{(\mathbf{g}^T \mathbf{g})\mathbf{g}^{\times}}_{-\mathbf{g}^{\times}\mathbf{g}^{\times}\mathbf{g}^{\times}} + \underbrace{(\mathbf{g}^T \mathbf{g})\mathbf{g}^{\times}\mathbf{g}^{\times}}_{-\mathbf{g}^{\times}\mathbf{g}^{\times}\mathbf{g}^{\times}\mathbf{g}^{\times}} - \underbrace{(\mathbf{g}^T \mathbf{g})\mathbf{g}^{\times}\mathbf{g}^{\times}\mathbf{g}^{\times}}_{-\mathbf{g}^{\times}\mathbf{g}^{\times}\mathbf{g}^{\times}\mathbf{g}^{\times}\mathbf{g}^{\times}} + \cdots$$
$$= 1 + \mathbf{g}\mathbf{g}^T - \mathbf{g}^{\times} - \left(1 + \mathbf{g}^{\times}\right)^{-1}, \tag{7.32}$$

where we have used the following manipulation several times:

$$\left(\mathbf{g}^T\mathbf{g}\right)\mathbf{g}^\times = \left(-\mathbf{g}^\times\mathbf{g}^\times + \mathbf{g}\mathbf{g}^T\right)\mathbf{g}^\times = -\mathbf{g}^\times\mathbf{g}^\times\mathbf{g}^\times + \mathbf{g}\underbrace{\mathbf{g}^T\mathbf{g}^\times}_{0} = -\mathbf{g}^\times\mathbf{g}^\times\mathbf{g}^\times.$$

$$(7.33)$$

Therefore we have that

$$\left(1 + \mathbf{g}^T\mathbf{g}\right)\left(1 + \mathbf{g}^\times\right)^{-1} = 1 + \mathbf{g}\mathbf{g}^T - \mathbf{g}^\times, \qquad (7.34)$$

and thus

$$\left(1 + \mathbf{g}^T\mathbf{g}\right)\underbrace{\left(1 + \mathbf{g}^\times\right)^{-1}\left(1 - \mathbf{g}^\times\right)}_{\mathbf{C}} = \left(1 + \mathbf{g}\mathbf{g}^T - \mathbf{g}^\times\right)\left(1 - \mathbf{g}^\times\right)$$

$$= 1 + \mathbf{g}\mathbf{g}^T - 2\mathbf{g}^\times - \mathbf{g}\underbrace{\mathbf{g}^T\mathbf{g}^\times}_{0} + \underbrace{\mathbf{g}^\times\mathbf{g}^\times}_{-\mathbf{g}^T\mathbf{g}\mathbf{1}+\mathbf{g}\mathbf{g}^T} = \left(1 - \mathbf{g}^T\mathbf{g}\right)\mathbf{1} + 2\mathbf{g}\mathbf{g}^T - 2\mathbf{g}^\times.$$

$$(7.35)$$

Dividing both sides by $\left(1 + \mathbf{g}^T\mathbf{g}\right)$ provides the desired result.

7.2.4 Rotational Kinematics

In the last section, we showed that the orientation of one frame $\underrightarrow{\mathcal{F}}_2$ with respect to another $\underrightarrow{\mathcal{F}}_1$ could be parameterized in different ways. In other words, the rotation matrix could be written as a function of Euler angles or Euler parameters. However, in most applications the orientation changes with time and thus we must introduce the vehicle *kinematics*, which form an important part of the vehicle's motion model.

We will first introduce the concept of angular velocity, then acceleration in a rotating frame. We will finish with expressions that relate the rate of change of the orientation parameterization to angular velocity.

Angular Velocity

Let frame $\underrightarrow{\mathcal{F}}_2$ rotate with respect to frame $\underrightarrow{\mathcal{F}}_1$. The angular velocity of frame 2 with respect to frame 1 is denoted by $\underrightarrow{\omega}_{21}$. The angular velocity of frame 1 with respect to 2 is $\underrightarrow{\omega}_{12} = -\underrightarrow{\omega}_{21}$.

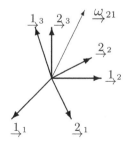

The magnitude of $\underrightarrow{\omega}_{21}$, $|\underrightarrow{\omega}_{21}| = \sqrt{(\underrightarrow{\omega}_{21} \cdot \underrightarrow{\omega}_{21})}$, is the rate of rotation. The direction of $\underrightarrow{\omega}_{21}$ (i.e., the unit vector in the direction of $\underrightarrow{\omega}_{21}$, which is $|\underrightarrow{\omega}_{21}|^{-1}\underrightarrow{\omega}_{21}$) is the *instantaneous* axis of rotation.

Observers in the frames $\underrightarrow{\mathcal{F}}_2$ and $\underrightarrow{\mathcal{F}}_1$ do not see the same motion because of their own relative motions. Let us denote the *vector time derivative* as seen in $\underrightarrow{\mathcal{F}}_1$ by $(\cdot)^{\bullet}$ and that seen in $\underrightarrow{\mathcal{F}}_2$ by $(\cdot)^{\circ}$. Therefore,

$$\underrightarrow{\mathcal{F}}_1^{\bullet} = \underrightarrow{0}, \quad \underrightarrow{\mathcal{F}}_2^{\circ} = \underrightarrow{0}.$$

It can be shown that

$$\underrightarrow{2}_1^{\bullet} = \underrightarrow{\omega}_{21} \times \underrightarrow{2}_1, \quad \underrightarrow{2}_2^{\bullet} = \underrightarrow{\omega}_{21} \times \underrightarrow{2}_2, \quad \underrightarrow{2}_3^{\bullet} = \underrightarrow{\omega}_{21} \times \underrightarrow{2}_3,$$

or equivalently

$$\begin{bmatrix} \underrightarrow{2}_1^{\bullet} & \underrightarrow{2}_2^{\bullet} & \underrightarrow{2}_3^{\bullet} \end{bmatrix} = \underrightarrow{\omega}_{21} \times \begin{bmatrix} \underrightarrow{2}_1 & \underrightarrow{2}_2 & \underrightarrow{2}_3 \end{bmatrix},$$

or

$$\underrightarrow{\mathcal{F}}_2^{\bullet T} = \underrightarrow{\omega}_{21} \times \underrightarrow{\mathcal{F}}_2^{T}. \tag{7.36}$$

We want to determine the time derivative of an arbitrary vector expressed in both frames:

$$\underrightarrow{r} = \underrightarrow{\mathcal{F}}_1^{T}\mathbf{r}_1 = \underrightarrow{\mathcal{F}}_2^{T}\mathbf{r}_2.$$

Therefore, the time derivative as seen in $\underrightarrow{\mathcal{F}}_1$ is

$$\underrightarrow{r}^{\bullet} = \underrightarrow{\mathcal{F}}_1^{\bullet T}\mathbf{r}_1 + \underrightarrow{\mathcal{F}}_1^{T}\dot{\mathbf{r}}_1 = \underrightarrow{\mathcal{F}}_1^{T}\dot{\mathbf{r}}_1. \tag{7.37}$$

In a similar way,

$$\underrightarrow{r}^{\circ} = \underrightarrow{\mathcal{F}}_2^{\circ T}\mathbf{r}_2 + \underrightarrow{\mathcal{F}}_2^{T}\overset{\circ}{\mathbf{r}}_2 = \underrightarrow{\mathcal{F}}_2^{T}\overset{\circ}{\mathbf{r}}_2 = \underrightarrow{\mathcal{F}}_2^{T}\dot{\mathbf{r}}_2. \tag{7.38}$$

(Note that for nonvectors, $(\dot{}) = (\circ)$, i.e., $\overset{\circ}{\mathbf{r}}_2 = \dot{\mathbf{r}}_2$.)

Alternatively, the time derivative as seen in $\underrightarrow{\mathcal{F}}_1$, but expressed in $\underrightarrow{\mathcal{F}}_2$, is

$$\begin{aligned}
\underrightarrow{r}^{\bullet} &= \underrightarrow{\mathcal{F}}_2^{T}\dot{\mathbf{r}}_2 + \underrightarrow{\mathcal{F}}_2^{\bullet T}\mathbf{r}_2 \\
&= \underrightarrow{\mathcal{F}}_2^{T}\dot{\mathbf{r}}_2 + \underrightarrow{\omega}_{21} \times \underrightarrow{\mathcal{F}}_2^{T}\mathbf{r}_2 \\
&= \underrightarrow{r}^{\circ} + \underrightarrow{\omega}_{21} \times \underrightarrow{r}.
\end{aligned} \tag{7.39}$$

The preceding is true for any vector $\underrightarrow{r}$. The most important application occurs when $\underrightarrow{r}$ denotes position, $\underrightarrow{\mathcal{F}}_1$ is a nonrotating inertial reference frame, and $\underrightarrow{\mathcal{F}}_2$ is a frame that rotates with a body or vehicle. In this case, (7.39) expresses the velocity in the inertial frame in terms of the motion in the second frame.

Now, express the angular velocity in $\underrightarrow{\mathcal{F}}_2$:

$$\underrightarrow{\omega}_{21} = \underrightarrow{\mathcal{F}}_2^T \boldsymbol{\omega}_2^{21}. \qquad (7.40)$$

Therefore,

$$
\begin{aligned}
\underrightarrow{r}^{\bullet} = \underrightarrow{\mathcal{F}}_1^T \dot{\mathbf{r}}_1 &= \underrightarrow{\mathcal{F}}_2^T \dot{\mathbf{r}}_2 + \underrightarrow{\omega}_{21} \times \underrightarrow{r} \\
&= \underrightarrow{\mathcal{F}}_2^T \dot{\mathbf{r}}_2 + \underrightarrow{\mathcal{F}}_2^T \boldsymbol{\omega}_2^{21^\times} \mathbf{r}_2 \\
&= \underrightarrow{\mathcal{F}}_2^T (\dot{\mathbf{r}}_2 + \boldsymbol{\omega}_2^{21^\times} \mathbf{r}_2).
\end{aligned} \qquad (7.41)
$$

If we want to express the 'inertial time derivative' (that seen in $\underrightarrow{\mathcal{F}}_1$) in $\underrightarrow{\mathcal{F}}_1$, then we can use the rotation matrix $\mathbf{C}_{12}$:

$$\dot{\mathbf{r}}_1 = \mathbf{C}_{12}(\dot{\mathbf{r}}_2 + \boldsymbol{\omega}_2^{21^\times} \mathbf{r}_2). \qquad (7.42)$$

Acceleration

Let us denote the *velocity* by

$$\underrightarrow{v} = \underrightarrow{r}^{\bullet} = \underrightarrow{r}^{\circ} + \underrightarrow{\omega}_{21} \times \underrightarrow{r}.$$

The *acceleration* can be calculated by applying (7.39) to $\underrightarrow{v}$:

$$
\begin{aligned}
\underrightarrow{r}^{\bullet\bullet} = \underrightarrow{v}^{\bullet} &= \underrightarrow{v}^{\circ} + \underrightarrow{\omega}_{21} \times \underrightarrow{v} \\
&= (\underrightarrow{r}^{\circ\circ} + \underrightarrow{\omega}_{21} \times \underrightarrow{r}^{\circ} + \underrightarrow{\omega}^{\circ}_{21} \times \underrightarrow{r}) \\
&\quad + (\underrightarrow{\omega}_{21} \times \underrightarrow{r}^{\circ} + \underrightarrow{\omega}_{21} \times (\underrightarrow{\omega}_{21} \times \underrightarrow{r})) \\
&= \underrightarrow{r}^{\circ\circ} + 2\underrightarrow{\omega}_{21} \times \underrightarrow{r}^{\circ} + \underrightarrow{\omega}^{\circ}_{21} \times \underrightarrow{r} + \underrightarrow{\omega}_{21} \times (\underrightarrow{\omega}_{21} \times \underrightarrow{r}).
\end{aligned} \qquad (7.43)
$$

The matrix equivalent in terms of components can be had by making the following substitutions:

$$\underrightarrow{r}^{\bullet\bullet} = \underrightarrow{\mathcal{F}}_1^T \ddot{\mathbf{r}}_1 , \quad \underrightarrow{r}^{\circ\circ} = \underrightarrow{\mathcal{F}}_2^T \ddot{\mathbf{r}}_2 , \quad \underrightarrow{\omega}^{\circ}_{21} = \underrightarrow{\mathcal{F}}_2^T \dot{\boldsymbol{\omega}}_2^{21}.$$

The result for the components is

$$\ddot{\mathbf{r}}_1 = \mathbf{C}_{12} \left[\ddot{\mathbf{r}}_2 + 2\boldsymbol{\omega}_2^{21^\times} \dot{\mathbf{r}}_2 + \dot{\boldsymbol{\omega}}_2^{21^\times} \mathbf{r}_2 + \boldsymbol{\omega}_2^{21^\times} \boldsymbol{\omega}_2^{21^\times} \mathbf{r}_2 \right]. \qquad (7.44)$$

The various terms in the expression for the acceleration have been given special names:

$$
\begin{aligned}
\underrightarrow{r}^{\circ\circ} &: \text{ acceleration with respect to } \underrightarrow{\mathcal{F}}_2 \\
2\underrightarrow{\omega}_{21} \times \underrightarrow{r}^{\circ} &: \text{ Coriolis acceleration} \\
\underrightarrow{\omega}^{\circ}_{21} \times \underrightarrow{r} &: \text{ angular acceleration} \\
\underrightarrow{\omega}_{21} \times \left(\underrightarrow{\omega}_{21} \times \underrightarrow{r} \right) &: \text{ centripetal acceleration}
\end{aligned}
$$

Angular Velocity Given Rotation Matrix

Begin with (7.3), which relates two reference frames via the rotation matrix:

$$\underset{\rightarrow}{\mathcal{F}}_1^T = \underset{\rightarrow}{\mathcal{F}}_2^T \mathbf{C}_{21}.$$

Now take the time derivative of both sides as seen in $\underset{\rightarrow}{\mathcal{F}}_1$:

$$\underset{\rightarrow}{0} = \underset{\rightarrow}{\mathcal{F}}_2^{\cdot T} \mathbf{C}_{21} + \underset{\rightarrow}{\mathcal{F}}_2^T \dot{\mathbf{C}}_{21}.$$

Substitute (7.36) for $\underset{\rightarrow}{\mathcal{F}}_2^{\cdot T}$:

$$\underset{\rightarrow}{0} = \underset{\rightarrow}{\omega}_{21} \times \underset{\rightarrow}{\mathcal{F}}_2^T \mathbf{C}_{21} + \underset{\rightarrow}{\mathcal{F}}_2^T \dot{\mathbf{C}}_{21}.$$

Now use (7.40) to get

$$\underset{\rightarrow}{0} = \omega_2^{21^T} \underset{\rightarrow}{\mathcal{F}}_2 \times \underset{\rightarrow}{\mathcal{F}}_2^T \mathbf{C}_{21} + \underset{\rightarrow}{\mathcal{F}}_2^T \dot{\mathbf{C}}_{21}$$
$$= \underset{\rightarrow}{\mathcal{F}}_2^T \left(\omega_2^{21^\times} \mathbf{C}_{21} + \dot{\mathbf{C}}_{21} \right).$$

Therefore, we conclude that

$$\dot{\mathbf{C}}_{21} = -\omega_2^{21^\times} \mathbf{C}_{21}, \tag{7.45}$$

Siméon Denis Poisson (1781–1840) was a French mathematician, geometer, and physicist.

which is known as *Poisson's equation*. Given the angular velocity as measured in the frame $\underset{\rightarrow}{\mathcal{F}}_2$, the rotation matrix relating $\underset{\rightarrow}{\mathcal{F}}_1$ to $\underset{\rightarrow}{\mathcal{F}}_2$ can be determined by integrating the above expression.[4]

We can also rearrange to obtain an explicit function of ω_2^{21}:

$$\omega_2^{21^\times} = -\dot{\mathbf{C}}_{21} \mathbf{C}_{21}^{-1}$$
$$= -\dot{\mathbf{C}}_{21} \mathbf{C}_{21}^T, \tag{7.46}$$

which gives the angular velocity when the rotation matrix is known as a function of time.

Euler Angles

Consider the 1-2-3 Euler angle sequence and its associated rotation matrix. In this case, (7.46) becomes

$$\omega_2^{21^\times} = -\mathbf{C}_3 \mathbf{C}_2 \dot{\mathbf{C}}_1 \mathbf{C}_1^T \mathbf{C}_2^T \mathbf{C}_3^T - \mathbf{C}_3 \dot{\mathbf{C}}_2 \mathbf{C}_2^T \mathbf{C}_3^T - \dot{\mathbf{C}}_3 \mathbf{C}_3^T. \tag{7.47}$$

Then, using

$$-\dot{\mathbf{C}}_i \mathbf{C}_i^T = \mathbf{1}_i^\times \dot{\theta}_i, \tag{7.48}$$

for each principal axis rotation (where $\mathbf{1}_i$ is column i of $\mathbf{1}$) and the identity

$$(\mathbf{C}_i \mathbf{r})^\times \equiv \mathbf{C}_i \mathbf{r}^\times \mathbf{C}_i^T, \tag{7.49}$$

we can show that

$$\omega_2^{21^\times} = \left(\mathbf{C}_3 \mathbf{C}_2 \mathbf{1}_1 \dot{\theta}_1 \right)^\times + \left(\mathbf{C}_3 \mathbf{1}_2 \dot{\theta}_2 \right)^\times + \left(\mathbf{1}_3 \dot{\theta}_3 \right)^\times, \tag{7.50}$$

---

[4] This is termed 'strapdown navigation' because the sensors that measure ω_2^{21} are strapped down in the rotating frame, $\underset{\rightarrow}{\mathcal{F}}_2$.

which can be simplified to

$$\boldsymbol{\omega}_2^{21} = \underbrace{\begin{bmatrix} \mathbf{C}_3(\theta_3)\mathbf{C}_2(\theta_2)\mathbf{1}_1 & \mathbf{C}_3(\theta_3)\mathbf{1}_2 & \mathbf{1}_3 \end{bmatrix}}_{\mathbf{S}(\theta_2,\theta_3)} \underbrace{\begin{bmatrix} \dot{\theta}_1 \\ \dot{\theta}_2 \\ \dot{\theta}_3 \end{bmatrix}}_{\dot{\boldsymbol{\theta}}}$$

$$= \mathbf{S}(\theta_2, \theta_3)\dot{\boldsymbol{\theta}}, \tag{7.51}$$

which gives the angular velocity in terms of the Euler angles and the *Euler rates*, $\dot{\boldsymbol{\theta}}$. In scalar detail we have

$$\mathbf{S}(\theta_2, \theta_3) = \begin{bmatrix} \cos\theta_2\cos\theta_3 & \sin\theta_3 & 0 \\ -\cos\theta_2\sin\theta_3 & \cos\theta_3 & 0 \\ \sin\theta_2 & 0 & 1 \end{bmatrix}. \tag{7.52}$$

By inverting the matrix $\mathbf{S}$, we arrive at a system of differential equations that can be integrated to yield the Euler angles, assuming $\boldsymbol{\omega}_2^{21}$ is known:

$$\dot{\boldsymbol{\theta}} = \mathbf{S}^{-1}(\theta_2, \theta_3)\boldsymbol{\omega}_2^{21}$$

$$= \begin{bmatrix} \sec\theta_2\cos\theta_3 & -\sec\theta_2\sin\theta_3 & 0 \\ \sin\theta_3 & \cos\theta_3 & 0 \\ -\tan\theta_2\cos\theta_3 & \tan\theta_2\sin\theta_3 & 1 \end{bmatrix} \boldsymbol{\omega}_2^{21}. \tag{7.53}$$

Note that $\mathbf{S}^{-1}$ does not exist at $\theta_2 = \pi/2$, which is precisely the singularity associated with the 1-2-3 sequence.

It should be noted that the above developments hold true in general for any Euler sequence. If we pick an α-β-γ set,

$$\mathbf{C}_{21}(\theta_1, \theta_2, \theta_3) = \mathbf{C}_\gamma(\theta_3)\mathbf{C}_\beta(\theta_2)\mathbf{C}_\alpha(\theta_1), \tag{7.54}$$

then

$$\mathbf{S}(\theta_2, \theta_3) = \begin{bmatrix} \mathbf{C}_\gamma(\theta_3)\mathbf{C}_\beta(\theta_2)\mathbf{1}_\alpha & \mathbf{C}_\gamma(\theta_3)\mathbf{1}_\beta & \mathbf{1}_\gamma \end{bmatrix}, \tag{7.55}$$

and $\mathbf{S}^{-1}$ does not exist at the singularities of $\mathbf{S}$.

7.2.5 Perturbing Rotations

Now that we have some basic notation built up for handling quantities in three-dimensional space, we will turn our focus to an issue that is often handled incorrectly or simply ignored altogether. We have shown in the previous section that the state of a single-body vehicle involves a translation, which has three degrees of freedom, as well as a rotation, which also has three degrees of freedom. The problem is that the degrees of freedom associated with rotations are a bit unique and must be handled carefully. The reason is that rotations do not live in a *vector space*;[5] rather, they form the *non-commutative group* called $SO(3)$.

As we have seen above, there are many ways of representing rotations mathematically, including rotation matrices, axis-angle formulations, Euler angles, and

---

[5] Here we mean a vector space in the sense of linear algebra.

Euler parameters/unit-length quaternions. The most important fact to remember is that all these representations have the same underlying rotation, which only has three degrees of freedom. A 3×3 rotation matrix has nine elements, but only three are independent. Euler parameters have four scalar parameters, but only three are independent. Of all the common rotation representations, Euler angles are the only ones that have exactly three parameters; the problem is that Euler sequences have singularities, so for some problems, one must choose an appropriate sequence that avoids the singularities.

The fact that rotations do not live in a vector space is actually quite fundamental when it comes to linearizing motion and observation models involving rotations. What are we to do about linearizing rotations? Fortunately, there is a way forwards. The key is to consider what is happening on a small, in fact infinitesimal, level. We will begin by deriving a few key identities and then turn to linearizing a rotation matrix built from a sequence of Euler angles.

Some Key Identities

Euler's rotation theorem allows us to write a rotation matrix, $\mathbf{C}$, in terms of a rotation about an axis, $\mathbf{a}$, through an angle, ϕ:

$$\mathbf{C} = \cos\phi \mathbf{1} + (1 - \cos\phi)\mathbf{a}\mathbf{a}^T - \sin\phi \mathbf{a}^\times. \tag{7.56}$$

We now take the partial derivative of $\mathbf{C}$ with respect to the angle, ϕ:

$$\frac{\partial \mathbf{C}}{\partial \phi} = -\sin\phi \mathbf{1} + \sin\phi \mathbf{a}\mathbf{a}^T - \cos\phi \mathbf{a}^\times \tag{7.57a}$$

$$= \sin\phi \underbrace{\left(-\mathbf{1} + \mathbf{a}\mathbf{a}^T\right)}_{\mathbf{a}^\times \mathbf{a}^\times} - \cos\phi \mathbf{a}^\times \tag{7.57b}$$

$$= -\cos\phi \mathbf{a}^\times - (1 - \cos\phi)\underbrace{\mathbf{a}^\times \mathbf{a}}_{\mathbf{0}}\mathbf{a}^T + \sin\phi \mathbf{a}^\times \mathbf{a}^\times \tag{7.57c}$$

$$= -\mathbf{a}^\times \underbrace{\left(\cos\phi \mathbf{1} + (1 - \cos\phi)\mathbf{a}\mathbf{a}^T - \sin\phi \mathbf{a}^\times\right)}_{\mathbf{C}}. \tag{7.57d}$$

Thus, our first important identity is

$$\frac{\partial \mathbf{C}}{\partial \phi} \equiv -\mathbf{a}^\times \mathbf{C}. \tag{7.58}$$

An immediate application of this is that for any principal-axis rotation, about axis α, we have

$$\frac{\partial \mathbf{C}_\alpha(\theta)}{\partial \theta} \equiv -\mathbf{1}_\alpha^\times \mathbf{C}_\alpha(\theta), \tag{7.59}$$

where $\mathbf{1}_\alpha$ is column α of the identity matrix.

Let us now consider an α-β-γ Euler sequence:

$$\mathbf{C}(\boldsymbol{\theta}) = \mathbf{C}_\gamma(\theta_3)\mathbf{C}_\beta(\theta_2)\mathbf{C}_\alpha(\theta_1), \tag{7.60}$$

where $\boldsymbol{\theta} = (\theta_1, \theta_2, \theta_3)$. Furthermore, we select an arbitrary constant vector, $\mathbf{v}$. Applying (7.59), we have

$$\frac{\partial \left(\mathbf{C}(\boldsymbol{\theta})\mathbf{v}\right)}{\partial \theta_3} = -\mathbf{1}_\gamma^\times \mathbf{C}_\gamma(\theta_3)\mathbf{C}_\beta(\theta_2)\mathbf{C}_\alpha(\theta_1)\mathbf{v} = \left(\mathbf{C}(\boldsymbol{\theta})\mathbf{v}\right)^\times \mathbf{1}_\gamma, \qquad (7.61a)$$

$$\frac{\partial \left(\mathbf{C}(\boldsymbol{\theta})\mathbf{v}\right)}{\partial \theta_2} = -\mathbf{C}_\gamma(\theta_3)\mathbf{1}_\beta^\times \mathbf{C}_\beta(\theta_2)\mathbf{C}_\alpha(\theta_1)\mathbf{v} = \left(\mathbf{C}(\boldsymbol{\theta})\mathbf{v}\right)^\times \mathbf{C}_\gamma(\theta_3)\mathbf{1}_\beta,$$

$$(7.61b)$$

$$\frac{\partial \left(\mathbf{C}(\boldsymbol{\theta})\mathbf{v}\right)}{\partial \theta_1} = -\mathbf{C}_\gamma(\theta_3)\mathbf{C}_\beta(\theta_2)\mathbf{1}_\alpha^\times \mathbf{C}_\alpha(\theta_1)\mathbf{v} = \left(\mathbf{C}(\boldsymbol{\theta})\mathbf{v}\right)^\times \mathbf{C}_\gamma(\theta_3)\mathbf{C}_\beta(\theta_2)\mathbf{1}_\alpha,$$

$$(7.61c)$$

where we have made use of the two general identities

$$\mathbf{r}^\times \mathbf{s} \equiv -\mathbf{s}^\times \mathbf{r}, \qquad (7.62a)$$

$$(\mathbf{Rs})^\times \equiv \mathbf{Rs}^\times \mathbf{R}^T \qquad (7.62b)$$

for any vectors $\mathbf{r}$, $\mathbf{s}$ and any rotation matrix $\mathbf{R}$. Combining the results in (7.61), we have

$$\frac{\partial \left(\mathbf{C}(\boldsymbol{\theta})\mathbf{v}\right)}{\partial \boldsymbol{\theta}} = \left[\frac{\partial (\mathbf{C}(\boldsymbol{\theta})\mathbf{v})}{\partial \theta_1} \quad \frac{\partial (\mathbf{C}(\boldsymbol{\theta})\mathbf{v})}{\partial \theta_2} \quad \frac{\partial (\mathbf{C}(\boldsymbol{\theta})\mathbf{v})}{\partial \theta_3}\right]$$

$$= \left(\mathbf{C}(\boldsymbol{\theta})\mathbf{v}\right)^\times \underbrace{\left[\mathbf{C}_\gamma(\theta_3)\mathbf{C}_\beta(\theta_2)\mathbf{1}_\alpha \quad \mathbf{C}_\gamma(\theta_3)\mathbf{1}_\beta \quad \mathbf{1}_\gamma\right]}_{\mathbf{S}(\theta_2, \theta_3)}, \qquad (7.63)$$

and thus another very important identity that we can state is

$$\frac{\partial \left(\mathbf{C}(\boldsymbol{\theta})\mathbf{v}\right)}{\partial \boldsymbol{\theta}} \equiv \left(\mathbf{C}(\boldsymbol{\theta})\mathbf{v}\right)^\times \mathbf{S}(\theta_2, \theta_3), \qquad (7.64)$$

which we note is true regardless of the choice of Euler set. This will prove critical in the next section, when we discuss linearization of a rotation matrix.

Perturbing a Rotation Matrix

Let us return to first principles and consider carefully how to linearize a rotation. If we have a function, $\mathbf{f}(\mathbf{x})$, of some variable, $\mathbf{x}$, then perturbing $\mathbf{x}$ slightly from its nominal value, $\bar{\mathbf{x}}$, by an amount $\delta\mathbf{x}$ will result in a change in the function. We can express this in terms of a Taylor-series expansion of $\mathbf{f}$ about $\bar{\mathbf{x}}$:

$$\mathbf{f}(\bar{\mathbf{x}} + \delta\mathbf{x}) = \mathbf{f}(\bar{\mathbf{x}}) + \left.\frac{\partial \mathbf{f}(\mathbf{x})}{\partial \mathbf{x}}\right|_{\bar{\mathbf{x}}} \delta\mathbf{x} + \text{(higher-order terms)} \qquad (7.65)$$

and so if $\delta\mathbf{x}$ is small, a 'first-order' approximation is

$$\mathbf{f}(\bar{\mathbf{x}} + \delta\mathbf{x}) \approx \mathbf{f}(\bar{\mathbf{x}}) + \left.\frac{\partial \mathbf{f}(\mathbf{x})}{\partial \mathbf{x}}\right|_{\bar{\mathbf{x}}} \delta\mathbf{x}. \qquad (7.66)$$

This presupposes that $\delta\mathbf{x}$ is not constrained in any way. The trouble with carrying out the same process with rotations is that most of the representations involve constraints and thus are not easily perturbed (without enforcing the constraint). The notable exceptions are the Euler angle sets. These contain exactly three parameters, and thus each can be varied independently. For this reason, we choose to use Euler angles in our perturbation of functions involving rotations.

Consider perturbing $\mathbf{C}(\boldsymbol{\theta})\mathbf{v}$ with respect to Euler angles $\boldsymbol{\theta}$, where $\mathbf{v}$ is an arbitrary constant vector. Letting $\bar{\boldsymbol{\theta}} = (\bar{\theta}_1, \bar{\theta}_2, \bar{\theta}_3)$ and $\delta\boldsymbol{\theta} = (\delta\theta_1, \delta\theta_2, \delta\theta_3)$, then applying a first-order Taylor-series approximation, we have

$$
\begin{aligned}
\mathbf{C}(\bar{\boldsymbol{\theta}} + \delta\boldsymbol{\theta})\mathbf{v} &\approx \mathbf{C}(\bar{\boldsymbol{\theta}})\mathbf{v} + \left.\frac{\partial\left(\mathbf{C}(\boldsymbol{\theta})\mathbf{v}\right)}{\partial\boldsymbol{\theta}}\right|_{\bar{\boldsymbol{\theta}}} \delta\boldsymbol{\theta} \\
&= \mathbf{C}(\bar{\boldsymbol{\theta}})\mathbf{v} + \left.\left(\left(\mathbf{C}(\boldsymbol{\theta})\mathbf{v}\right)^{\times}\mathbf{S}(\theta_2, \theta_3)\right)\right|_{\bar{\boldsymbol{\theta}}} \delta\boldsymbol{\theta} \\
&= \mathbf{C}(\bar{\boldsymbol{\theta}})\mathbf{v} + \left(\mathbf{C}(\bar{\boldsymbol{\theta}})\mathbf{v}\right)^{\times}\mathbf{S}(\bar{\theta}_2, \bar{\theta}_3)\,\delta\boldsymbol{\theta} \\
&= \mathbf{C}(\bar{\boldsymbol{\theta}})\mathbf{v} - \left(\mathbf{S}(\bar{\theta}_2, \bar{\theta}_3)\,\delta\boldsymbol{\theta}\right)^{\times}\left(\mathbf{C}(\bar{\boldsymbol{\theta}})\mathbf{v}\right) \\
&= \left(\mathbf{1} - \left(\mathbf{S}(\bar{\theta}_2, \bar{\theta}_3)\,\delta\boldsymbol{\theta}\right)^{\times}\right)\mathbf{C}(\bar{\boldsymbol{\theta}})\mathbf{v},
\end{aligned}
\tag{7.67}
$$

where we have used (7.64) to get to the second line. Observing that $\mathbf{v}$ is arbitrary, we can drop it from both sides and write

$$
\mathbf{C}(\bar{\boldsymbol{\theta}} + \delta\boldsymbol{\theta}) \approx \underbrace{\left(\mathbf{1} - \left(\mathbf{S}(\bar{\theta}_2, \bar{\theta}_3)\,\delta\boldsymbol{\theta}\right)^{\times}\right)}_{\text{infinitesimal rot. mat.}}\mathbf{C}(\bar{\boldsymbol{\theta}}),
\tag{7.68}
$$

which we see is the product (not the sum) of an infinitesimal rotation matrix and the unperturbed rotation matrix, $\mathbf{C}(\bar{\boldsymbol{\theta}})$. Notationally, it is simpler to write

$$
\mathbf{C}(\bar{\boldsymbol{\theta}} + \delta\boldsymbol{\theta}) \approx \left(\mathbf{1} - \delta\boldsymbol{\phi}^{\times}\right)\mathbf{C}(\bar{\boldsymbol{\theta}}),
\tag{7.69}
$$

with $\delta\boldsymbol{\phi} = \mathbf{S}(\bar{\theta}_2, \bar{\theta}_3)\,\delta\boldsymbol{\theta}$. Equation (7.68) is extremely important. It tells us exactly how to perturb a rotation matrix (in terms of perturbations to its Euler angles) when it appears inside any function.

Example 7.1 The following example shows how we can apply our linearized rotation expression in an arbitrary expression. Suppose we have a scalar function, J, given by

$$
J(\boldsymbol{\theta}) = \mathbf{u}^T\mathbf{C}(\boldsymbol{\theta})\mathbf{v},
\tag{7.70}
$$

where $\mathbf{u}$ and $\mathbf{v}$ are arbitrary vectors. Applying our approach to linearizing rotations, we have

$$
J(\bar{\boldsymbol{\theta}} + \delta\boldsymbol{\theta}) \approx \mathbf{u}^T\left(\mathbf{1} - \delta\boldsymbol{\phi}^{\times}\right)\mathbf{C}(\bar{\boldsymbol{\theta}})\mathbf{v} = \underbrace{\mathbf{u}^T\mathbf{C}(\bar{\boldsymbol{\theta}})\mathbf{v}}_{J(\bar{\boldsymbol{\theta}})} + \underbrace{\mathbf{u}^T\left(\mathbf{C}(\bar{\boldsymbol{\theta}})\mathbf{v}\right)^{\times}\delta\boldsymbol{\phi}}_{\delta J(\delta\boldsymbol{\theta})},
\tag{7.71}
$$

so that the linearized function is

$$
\delta J(\delta\boldsymbol{\theta}) = \underbrace{\left(\mathbf{u}^T\left(\mathbf{C}(\bar{\boldsymbol{\theta}})\mathbf{v}\right)^{\times}\mathbf{S}(\bar{\theta}_2, \bar{\theta}_3)\right)}_{\text{constant}}\delta\boldsymbol{\theta},
\tag{7.72}
$$

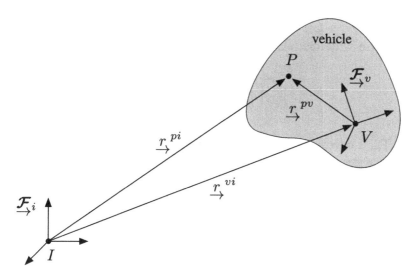

Figure 7.2 Pose estimation problems are often concerned with transforming the coordinates of a point, P, between a moving vehicle frame, and a stationary frame.

where we see that the factor in front of $\delta\boldsymbol{\theta}$ is indeed constant; in fact, it is $\frac{\partial J}{\partial\boldsymbol{\theta}}\big|_{\bar{\boldsymbol{\theta}}}$, the Jacobian of J with respect to $\boldsymbol{\theta}$.

7.3 Poses

We have spent considerable effort discussing the *rotational* aspect of a moving body. We now introduce the notation of *translation*. Together, the translation and rotation of a body are referred to as the *pose*. Pose estimation problems are often concerned with transforming the coordinates of a point, P, between a moving (in translation and rotation) vehicle frame, and a stationary frame, as depicted in Figure 7.2.

We can relate the vectors in Figure 7.2 as follows:

$$\underrightarrow{r}^{pi} = \underrightarrow{r}^{pv} + \underrightarrow{r}^{vi}, \tag{7.73}$$

where we have not yet selected any particular reference frame in which to express the relationship. Writing the relationship in the stationary frame, $\underrightarrow{\mathcal{F}}_i$, we have

$$\mathbf{r}_i^{pi} = \mathbf{r}_i^{pv} + \mathbf{r}_i^{vi}. \tag{7.74}$$

If the point, P, is attached to the vehicle, we typically know its coordinates in $\underrightarrow{\mathcal{F}}_v$, which is rotated with respect to $\underrightarrow{\mathcal{F}}_i$. Letting $\mathbf{C}_{iv}$ represent this rotation, we can rewrite the relationship as

$$\mathbf{r}_i^{pi} = \mathbf{C}_{iv}\mathbf{r}_v^{pv} + \mathbf{r}_i^{vi}, \tag{7.75}$$

which tells us how to convert the coordinates of P in $\underrightarrow{\mathcal{F}}_v$ to its coordinates in $\underrightarrow{\mathcal{F}}_i$, given knowledge of the translation, $\mathbf{r}_i^{vi}$, and rotation, $\mathbf{C}_{iv}$, between the two frames. We will refer to

$$\{\mathbf{r}_i^{vi}, \mathbf{C}_{iv}\}, \tag{7.76}$$

as the *pose* of the vehicle.

7.3.1 Transformation Matrices

We can also write the relationship expressed in (7.75) in another convenient form:

$$\begin{bmatrix} \mathbf{r}_i^{pi} \\ 1 \end{bmatrix} = \underbrace{\begin{bmatrix} \mathbf{C}_{iv} & \mathbf{r}_i^{vi} \\ \mathbf{0}^T & 1 \end{bmatrix}}_{\mathbf{T}_{iv}} \begin{bmatrix} \mathbf{r}_v^{pv} \\ 1 \end{bmatrix}, \tag{7.77}$$

where $\mathbf{T}_{iv}$ is referred to as a 4×4 *transformation matrix*.

To make use of a transformation matrix, we must augment the coordinates of a point with a 1,

$$\begin{bmatrix} x \\ y \\ z \\ 1 \end{bmatrix}, \tag{7.78}$$

which is referred to as a *homogeneous* point representation. An interesting property of homogeneous point representations is that each entry can be multiplied by a *scale factor*, s:

$$\begin{bmatrix} sx \\ sy \\ sz \\ s \end{bmatrix}. \tag{7.79}$$

To recover the original (x, y, z) coordinates, one needs only to divide the first three entires by the fourth. In this way, as the scale factor approaches 0, we can represent points arbitrarily far away from the origin. Hartley and Zisserman (2000) discuss the use of homogeneous coordinates at length for computer-vision applications.

To transform the coordinates back the other way, we require the inverse of a transformation matrix:

$$\begin{bmatrix} \mathbf{r}_v^{pv} \\ 1 \end{bmatrix} = \mathbf{T}_{iv}^{-1} \begin{bmatrix} \mathbf{r}_i^{pi} \\ 1 \end{bmatrix}, \tag{7.80}$$

where

$$\mathbf{T}_{iv}^{-1} = \begin{bmatrix} \mathbf{C}_{iv} & \mathbf{r}_i^{vi} \\ \mathbf{0}^T & 1 \end{bmatrix}^{-1} = \begin{bmatrix} \mathbf{C}_{iv}^T & -\mathbf{C}_{iv}^T \mathbf{r}_i^{vi} \\ \mathbf{0}^T & 1 \end{bmatrix} = \begin{bmatrix} \mathbf{C}_{vi} & -\mathbf{r}_v^{vi} \\ \mathbf{0}^T & 1 \end{bmatrix}$$

$$= \begin{bmatrix} \mathbf{C}_{vi} & \mathbf{r}_v^{iv} \\ \mathbf{0}^T & 1 \end{bmatrix} = \mathbf{T}_{vi}, \tag{7.81}$$

where we have used that $\mathbf{r}_v^{iv} = -\mathbf{r}_v^{vi}$, which simply flips the direction of the vector.

We can also compound transformation matrices:

$$\mathbf{T}_{iv} = \mathbf{T}_{ia} \mathbf{T}_{ab} \mathbf{T}_{bv}, \tag{7.82}$$

which makes it easy to chain an arbitrary number of pose changes together:

$$\underrightarrow{\mathcal{F}}_i \overset{\mathbf{T}_{iv}}{\underleftarrow{\quad}} \underrightarrow{\mathcal{F}}_v = \underrightarrow{\mathcal{F}}_i \overset{\mathbf{T}_{ia}}{\underleftarrow{\quad}} \underrightarrow{\mathcal{F}}_a \overset{\mathbf{T}_{ab}}{\underleftarrow{\quad}} \underrightarrow{\mathcal{F}}_b \overset{\mathbf{T}_{bv}}{\underleftarrow{\quad}} \underrightarrow{\mathcal{F}}_v. \tag{7.83}$$

Homogeneous coordinates were introduced by Augustus Ferdinand Möbius (1790–1868) in his work entitled *Der Barycentrische Calcul*, published in 1827. Möbius parameterized a point on a plane, (x, y), by considering masses, m_1, m_2, and m_3, that must be placed at the vertices of a fixed triangle to make the point the triangle's center of mass. The coordinates (m_1, m_2, m_3) are not unique, as scaling the three masses equally does not change the point location. When the equation of a curve is written in this coordinate system, it becomes homogeneous in (m_1, m_2, m_3). For example, a circle centered at (a, b) with radius r is: $(x-a)^2 + (y-b)^2 = r^2$. Written in homogeneous coordinates with $x = m_1/m_3$ and $y = m_2/m_3$, the equation becomes $(m_1 - m_3 a)^2 + (m_2 - m_3 b)^2 = m_3^2 r^2$, where every term is now quadratic in the homogeneous coordinates (Furgale, 2011).

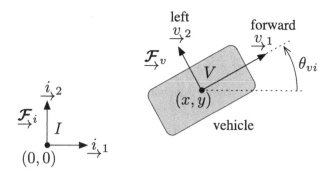

Figure 7.3 Simple planar example with a mobile vehicle whose state is given by position, (x, y), and orientation, θ_{vi}. It is standard for 'forward' to be the 1-axis of the vehicle frame and 'left' to be the 2-axis. Note that the 3-axis is coming out of the page.

For example, each frame could represent the pose of a mobile vehicle at a different instant in time, and this relation tells us how to combine relative motions into a global one.

Transformation matrices are very appealing because they tell us to first apply the translation and then the rotation. This is often a source of ambiguity when working with poses because the subscripts and superscripts are typically dropped in practice, and then it is difficult to know the exact meaning of each quantity.

7.3.2 Robotics Conventions

There is an important subtlety that must be mentioned to conform with standard practice in robotics. We can understand this in the context of a simple example. Imagine a vehicle travelling in the xy-plane, as depicted in Figure 7.3.

The position of the vehicle can be written in a straightforward manner as

$$
\mathbf{r}_i^{vi} = \begin{bmatrix} x \\ y \\ 0 \end{bmatrix} . \tag{7.84}
$$

The z-coordinate is zero for this planar example.

The rotation of $\underset{\rightarrow}{\mathcal{F}}_v$ with respect to $\underset{\rightarrow}{\mathcal{F}}_i$ is a principal-axis rotation about the 3-axis, through an angle θ_{vi} (we add the subscript to demonstrate a point). Following our convention from before, the angle of rotation is positive (according to the right-hand rule). Thus, we have

$$
\mathbf{C}_{vi} = \mathbf{C}_3(\theta_{vi}) = \begin{bmatrix} \cos\theta_{vi} & \sin\theta_{vi} & 0 \\ -\sin\theta_{vi} & \cos\theta_{vi} & 0 \\ 0 & 0 & 1 \end{bmatrix} . \tag{7.85}
$$

It makes sense to use θ_{vi} for orientation; it naturally describes the heading of the vehicle since it is $\underset{\rightarrow}{\mathcal{F}}_v$ that is moving with respect to $\underset{\rightarrow}{\mathcal{F}}_i$. However, as discussed in the previous section, the rotation matrix that we really care about when constructing the pose is $\mathbf{C}_{iv} = \mathbf{C}_{vi}^T = \mathbf{C}_3(-\theta_{vi}) = \mathbf{C}_3(\theta_{iv})$. Importantly, we note that $\theta_{iv} = -\theta_{vi}$. We do not want to use θ_{iv} as the heading, as that will be quite confusing.

Sticking with θ_{vi}, the pose of the vehicle can then be written in transformation matrix form as

$$\mathbf{T}_{iv} = \begin{bmatrix} \mathbf{C}_{iv} & \mathbf{r}_i^{vi} \\ \mathbf{0}^T & 1 \end{bmatrix} = \begin{bmatrix} \cos\theta_{vi} & -\sin\theta_{vi} & 0 & x \\ \sin\theta_{vi} & \cos\theta_{vi} & 0 & y \\ 0 & 0 & 1 & 0 \\ 0 & 0 & 0 & 1 \end{bmatrix}, \qquad (7.86)$$

which is perfectly fine. In general, even when the axis of rotation, $\mathbf{a}$, is not $\underrightarrow{i}_3$, we are free to write

$$\begin{aligned} \mathbf{C}_{iv} = \mathbf{C}_{vi}^T &= \left(\cos\theta_{vi}\mathbf{1} + (1 - \cos\theta_{vi})\mathbf{a}\mathbf{a}^T - \sin\theta_{vi}\mathbf{a}^\times\right)^T \\ &= \cos\theta_{vi}\mathbf{1} + (1 - \cos\theta_{vi})\mathbf{a}\mathbf{a}^T + \sin\theta_{vi}\mathbf{a}^\times, \qquad (7.87) \end{aligned}$$

where we note the change in sign of the third term due to the skew-symmetric property, $\mathbf{a}^{\times^T} = -\mathbf{a}^\times$. In other words, we are free to use θ_{vi} rather than θ_{iv} to construct $\mathbf{C}_{iv}$.

Confusion arises, however, when all the subscripts are dropped and we simply write

$$\mathbf{C} = \cos\theta\mathbf{1} + (1 - \cos\theta)\mathbf{a}\mathbf{a}^T + \sin\theta\,\mathbf{a}^\times, \qquad (7.88)$$

which is very common in robotics. There is absolutely nothing wrong with this expression; we must simply realize that when written in this form, the rotation is the other way around from our earlier development.[6]

There is another slight change in notation that is common in robotics as well. Often, the $(\cdot)^\times$ symbol is replaced with the $(\cdot)^\wedge$ symbol (Murray et al., 1994), particularly when dealing with transformation matrices. The expression for a rotation matrix is then written as

$$\mathbf{C} = \cos\theta\mathbf{1} + (1 - \cos\theta)\mathbf{a}\mathbf{a}^T + \sin\theta\,\mathbf{a}^\wedge. \qquad (7.89)$$

We need to be quite careful with angular velocity as well, since this should in some way match the convention we are using for the angle of rotation.

Finally, the pose is written as

$$\mathbf{T} = \begin{bmatrix} \mathbf{C} & \mathbf{r} \\ \mathbf{0}^T & 1 \end{bmatrix}, \qquad (7.90)$$

with all the subscripts removed. We simply need to be careful to remember what all of the quantities actually mean when using them in practice.

In an effort to be relevant to robotics, we will adopt the conventions in (7.89) moving forward in this book. However, we believe it has been worthwhile to begin at first principles to better understand what all the quantities associated with pose really mean.

7.3.3 Frenet–Serret Frame

It is worth drawing the connection between our pose variables (represented as transformation matrices) and the classical *Frenet–Serret* moving frame. Figure 7.4

---

[6] Our goal in this section is to make things clear, rather than to argue in favour of one convention over another. However, it is worth noting that this convention, with the third term in (7.88) positive, is conforming to a left-hand rotation rather than a right-hand one.

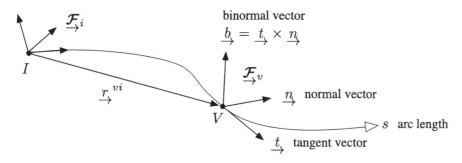

Figure 7.4 The classical Frenet–Serret moving frame can be used to describe the motion of a point. The frame axes point in the tangent, normal, and binormal directions of the curve traced out by the point. This frame and its motion equations are named after the two French mathematicians who independently discovered them: Jean Frédéric Frenet, in his thesis of 1847, and Joseph Alfred Serret in 1851.

depicts a point, V, moving smoothly through space. The Frenet–Serret frame is attached to the point with the first axis in the direction of motion (the curve tangent), the second axis pointing in the direction of the tangent derivative with respect to arc length (the curve normal), and the third axis completing the frame (the binormal).

The Frenet–Serret equations describe how the frame axes change with arc length:

$$\frac{d}{ds}\underrightarrow{t} = \kappa\,\underrightarrow{n}, \tag{7.91a}$$

$$\frac{d}{ds}\underrightarrow{n} = -\kappa\,\underrightarrow{t} + \tau\,\underrightarrow{b}, \tag{7.91b}$$

$$\frac{d}{ds}\underrightarrow{b} = -\tau\,\underrightarrow{n}, \tag{7.91c}$$

where κ is called the *curvature* of the path and τ is called the *torsion* of the path. Stacking the axes into a frame, $\underrightarrow{\mathcal{F}}_v$,

$$\underrightarrow{\mathcal{F}}_v = \begin{bmatrix} \underrightarrow{t} \\ \underrightarrow{n} \\ \underrightarrow{b} \end{bmatrix}, \tag{7.92}$$

we can write the Frenet–Serret equations as

$$\frac{d}{ds}\underrightarrow{\mathcal{F}}_v = \begin{bmatrix} 0 & \kappa & 0 \\ -\kappa & 0 & \tau \\ 0 & -\tau & 0 \end{bmatrix} \underrightarrow{\mathcal{F}}_v. \tag{7.93}$$

Multiplying both sides by the speed along the path, $v = ds/dt$, and right-multiplying by $\underrightarrow{\mathcal{F}}_i^T$, we have

$$\underbrace{\frac{d}{dt}\left(\underrightarrow{\mathcal{F}}_v \cdot \underrightarrow{\mathcal{F}}_i^T\right)}_{\dot{\mathbf{C}}_{vi}} = \underbrace{\begin{bmatrix} 0 & v\kappa & 0 \\ -v\kappa & 0 & v\tau \\ 0 & -v\tau & 0 \end{bmatrix}}_{-\boldsymbol{\omega}_v^{vi\wedge}} \underbrace{\left(\underrightarrow{\mathcal{F}}_v \cdot \underrightarrow{\mathcal{F}}_i^T\right)}_{\mathbf{C}_{vi}}, \tag{7.94}$$

where we have applied the chain rule. We see that this has recovered Poisson's equation for rotational kinematics as given previously in (7.45); the angular velocity expressed in the moving frame,

$$\boldsymbol{\omega}_v^{vi} = \begin{bmatrix} v\tau \\ 0 \\ v\kappa \end{bmatrix}, \tag{7.95}$$

is constrained to only two degrees of freedom since the middle entry is zero. We also have the translational kinematics,

$$\dot{\mathbf{r}}_i^{vi} = \mathbf{C}_{vi}^T \boldsymbol{\nu}_v^{vi}, \quad \boldsymbol{\nu}_v^{vi} = \begin{bmatrix} v \\ 0 \\ 0 \end{bmatrix}. \tag{7.96}$$

To express this in the body frame, we note that

$$\dot{\mathbf{r}}_v^{iv} = \frac{d}{dt}\left(-\mathbf{C}_{vi}\mathbf{r}_i^{vi}\right) = -\dot{\mathbf{C}}_{vi}\mathbf{r}_i^{vi} - \mathbf{C}_{vi}\dot{\mathbf{r}}_i^{vi}$$

$$= \boldsymbol{\omega}_v^{vi\wedge}\mathbf{C}_{vi}\mathbf{r}_i^{vi} - \mathbf{C}_{vi}\mathbf{C}_{vi}^T\boldsymbol{\nu}_v^{vi} = -\boldsymbol{\omega}_v^{vi\wedge}\mathbf{r}_v^{iv} - \boldsymbol{\nu}_v^{vi}. \tag{7.97}$$

We can then combine the translational and rotational kinematics into transformation-matrix form as follows:

$$\dot{\mathbf{T}}_{vi} = \frac{d}{dt}\begin{bmatrix} \mathbf{C}_{vi} & \mathbf{r}_v^{iv} \\ \mathbf{0}^T & 1 \end{bmatrix} = \begin{bmatrix} \dot{\mathbf{C}}_{vi} & \dot{\mathbf{r}}_v^{iv} \\ \mathbf{0}^T & 0 \end{bmatrix} = \begin{bmatrix} -\boldsymbol{\omega}_v^{vi\wedge}\mathbf{C}_{vi} & -\boldsymbol{\omega}_v^{vi\wedge}\mathbf{r}_v^{iv} - \boldsymbol{\nu}_v^{vi} \\ \mathbf{0}^T & 0 \end{bmatrix}$$

$$= \begin{bmatrix} -\boldsymbol{\omega}_v^{vi\wedge} & -\boldsymbol{\nu}_v^{vi} \\ \mathbf{0}^T & 0 \end{bmatrix} \begin{bmatrix} \mathbf{C}_{vi} & \mathbf{r}_v^{iv} \\ \mathbf{0}^T & 1 \end{bmatrix} = \begin{bmatrix} 0 & v\kappa & 0 & -v \\ -v\kappa & 0 & v\tau & 0 \\ 0 & -v\tau & 0 & 0 \\ 0 & 0 & 0 & 0 \end{bmatrix} \mathbf{T}_{vi}. \tag{7.98}$$

Integrating this forward in time provides both the translation and rotation of the moving frame. We can think of (v, κ, τ) as three inputs in this case as they determine the shape of the curve that is traced out. We will see in the next chapter that these kinematic equations can be generalized to the form

$$\dot{\mathbf{T}} = \begin{bmatrix} \boldsymbol{\omega}^{\wedge} & \boldsymbol{\nu} \\ \mathbf{0}^T & 0 \end{bmatrix} \mathbf{T}, \tag{7.99}$$

where

$$\boldsymbol{\varpi} = \begin{bmatrix} \boldsymbol{\nu} \\ \boldsymbol{\omega} \end{bmatrix} \tag{7.100}$$

is a (slightly differently defined) generalized six-degree-of-freedom velocity vector (expressed in the moving frame) that allows for all possible curves for $\mathbf{T}$ to be traced out. The Frenet–Serret equations can be viewed as a special case of this general kinematic formula.

If we want to use $\mathbf{T}_{iv}$ (for reasons described in the previous section) instead of $\mathbf{T}_{vi}$, we can either integrate the preceding and then output $\mathbf{T}_{iv} = \mathbf{T}_{vi}^{-1}$, or we can instead integrate

$$\dot{\mathbf{T}}_{iv} = \mathbf{T}_{iv} \begin{bmatrix} 0 & -v\kappa & 0 & v \\ v\kappa & 0 & -v\tau & 0 \\ 0 & v\tau & 0 & 0 \\ 0 & 0 & 0 & 0 \end{bmatrix}, \tag{7.101}$$

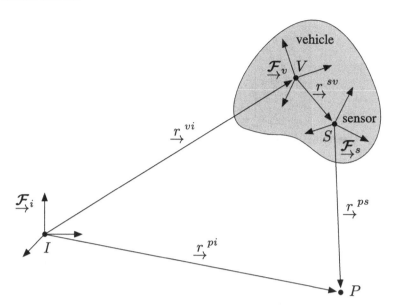

Figure 7.5
Reference frames for
a moving vehicle
with a sensor
on-board that
observes a point, P,
in the world.

which will achieve the same result (proof left as an exercise). If we constrain the motion to the xy-plane, which can be achieved by setting the initial condition to

$$\mathbf{T}_{iv}(0) = \begin{bmatrix} \cos\theta_{vi}(0) & -\sin\theta_{vi}(0) & 0 & x(0) \\ \sin\theta_{vi}(0) & \cos\theta_{vi}(0) & 0 & y(0) \\ 0 & 0 & 1 & 0 \\ 0 & 0 & 0 & 1 \end{bmatrix}, \tag{7.102}$$

and then forcing $\tau = 0$ for all time, the kinematics simplify to

$$\dot{x} = v\cos\theta, \tag{7.103a}$$

$$\dot{y} = v\sin\theta, \tag{7.103b}$$

$$\dot{\theta} = \omega, \tag{7.103c}$$

where $\omega = v\kappa$ and it is understood that $\theta = \theta_{vi}$. This last model is sometimes referred to as the 'unicycle model' for a differential-drive mobile robot. The inputs are the longitudinal speed, v, and the rotational speed, ω. The robot is unable to translate sideways due to the nonholonomic constraint associated with its wheels; it can only roll forwards and turn.

7.4 Sensor Models

Now that we have some three-dimensional tools, we will introduce a few three-dimensional sensor models that can be used inside our state estimation algorithms. In general, we will be interested in sensors that are on-board our robot. This situation is depicted in Figure 7.5.

We have an inertial frame, $\underrightarrow{\mathcal{F}}_i$, a vehicle frame, $\underrightarrow{\mathcal{F}}_v$, and a sensor frame, $\underrightarrow{\mathcal{F}}_s$. The pose change between the sensor frame and the vehicle frame, $\mathbf{T}_{sv}$, called the *extrinsic sensor parameters*, is typically fixed and is either determined through some form of separate calibration method or is folded directly into the state estimation procedure. In the sensor-model developments to follow, we will focus solely on how a point, P, is observed by a sensor attached to $\underrightarrow{\mathcal{F}}_s$.

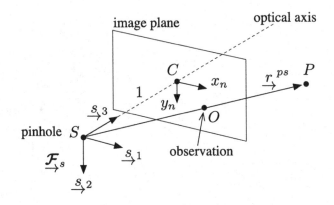

7.4.1 Perspective Camera

One of the most important sensors is the perspective camera. It is cheap yet can be used to infer motion of a vehicle and also the shape of the world.

Normalized Image Coordinates

Figure 7.6 depicts the observation, O, of a point, P, in an ideal perspective camera. In reality, the image plane is behind the pinhole, but showing it in front avoids the mental effort of working with a flipped image. This is called the *frontal projection model*. The $\underrightarrow{s}_3$ axis of $\underrightarrow{\mathcal{F}}_s$, called the *optical axis*, is orthogonal to the image plane, and the distance between the pinhole, S, and the image plane center, C, called the *focal length*, is 1 for this idealized camera model.

If the coordinates of P in $\underrightarrow{\mathcal{F}}_s$ are

$$\rho = \mathbf{r}_s^{ps} = \begin{bmatrix} x \\ y \\ z \end{bmatrix}, \tag{7.104}$$

with the $\underrightarrow{s}_3$ axis orthogonal to the image plane, then the coordinates of O in the image plane are

$$x_n = x/z, \tag{7.105a}$$
$$y_n = y/z. \tag{7.105b}$$

These are called the (two-dimensional) *normalized image coordinates* and are sometimes provided in a homogeneous form as

$$\mathbf{p} = \begin{bmatrix} x_n \\ y_n \\ 1 \end{bmatrix}. \tag{7.106}$$

Essential Matrix

If a point, P, is observed by a camera, the camera is moved, and then the same point is observed again, the two normalized image coordinates corresponding to the observations, $\mathbf{p}_a$ and $\mathbf{p}_b$ (see Figure 7.7), are related to one another through the following constraint:

$$\mathbf{p}_a^T \mathbf{E}_{ab} \mathbf{p}_b = 0, \tag{7.107}$$

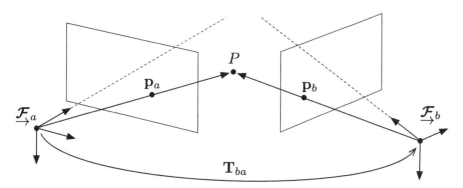

Figure 7.7 Two camera observations of the same point, P.

where $\mathbf{E}_{ab}$ is called the *essential matrix* (of computer vision),

$$\mathbf{E}_{ab} = \mathbf{C}_{ba}^T \mathbf{r}_b^{ab\wedge} \tag{7.108}$$

and is related to the pose change of the camera,

$$\mathbf{T}_{ba} = \begin{bmatrix} \mathbf{C}_{ba} & \mathbf{r}_b^{ab} \\ \mathbf{0}^T & 1 \end{bmatrix}. \tag{7.109}$$

To see that the constraint is true, we let

$$\mathbf{p}_j = \frac{1}{z_j}\boldsymbol{\rho}_j, \quad \boldsymbol{\rho}_j = \begin{bmatrix} x_j \\ y_j \\ z_j \end{bmatrix} \tag{7.110}$$

for $j = a, b$. We also have

$$\boldsymbol{\rho}_a = \mathbf{C}_{ba}^T \left(\boldsymbol{\rho}_b - \mathbf{r}_b^{ab} \right) \tag{7.111}$$

for the change in coordinates of P due to the camera moving. Then, returning to the constraint, we see

$$
\begin{aligned}
\mathbf{p}_a^T \mathbf{E}_{ab} \mathbf{p}_b &= \frac{1}{z_a z_b} \boldsymbol{\rho}_a^T \mathbf{E}_{ab} \boldsymbol{\rho}_b \\
&= \frac{1}{z_a z_b} \left(\boldsymbol{\rho}_b - \mathbf{r}_b^{ab} \right)^T \underbrace{\mathbf{C}_{ba} \mathbf{C}_{ba}^T}_{\mathbf{1}} \mathbf{r}_b^{ab\wedge} \boldsymbol{\rho}_b \\
&= \frac{1}{z_a z_b} \big(-\underbrace{\boldsymbol{\rho}_b^T \boldsymbol{\rho}_b^\wedge \mathbf{r}_b^{ab}}_{\mathbf{0}} - \underbrace{\mathbf{r}_b^{ab^T} \mathbf{r}_b^{ab\wedge}}_{\mathbf{0}} \boldsymbol{\rho}_b \big) = 0.
\end{aligned} \tag{7.112}
$$

The essential matrix can be useful in some pose estimation problems, including camera calibration.

Lens Distortion

In general, lens effects can distort camera images so that the normalized image coordinate equations are only approximately true. A variety of analytical models of this distortion are available, and these can be used to correct the raw images such that the resulting images appear as though they come from an idealized pinhole camera, and thus the normalized image coordinate equations hold. We will assume this undistortion procedure has been applied to the images and avoid elaborating on the distortion models.

Figure 7.8 Camera
model showing
intrinsic parameters:
f is the focal length,
(c_u, c_v) is the
optical axis
intersection.

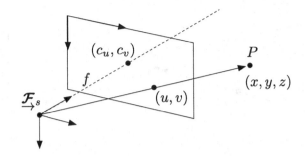

Intrinsic Parameters

The normalized image coordinates are really associated with a hypothetical camera with unit focal length and image origin at the optical axis intersection. We can map the normalized image coordinates, (x_n, y_n), to the actual *pixel coordinates*, (u, v), through the following relation:

$$\begin{bmatrix} u \\ v \\ 1 \end{bmatrix} = \underbrace{\begin{bmatrix} f_u & 0 & c_u \\ 0 & f_v & c_v \\ 0 & 0 & 1 \end{bmatrix}}_{\mathbf{K}} \begin{bmatrix} x_n \\ y_n \\ 1 \end{bmatrix}, \qquad (7.113)$$

where $\mathbf{K}$ is called the *intrinsic parameter matrix* and contains the actual camera focal length expressed in horizontal pixels, f_u, and vertical pixels, f_v, as well as the actual offset of the image origin from the optical axis intersection, (c_u, c_v), also expressed in horizontal, vertical pixels.[7] These intrinsic parameters are typically determined during the calibration procedure used to remove the lens effects, so that we can assume $\mathbf{K}$ is known.

Fundamental Matrix

Similarly to the essential matrix constraint, there is a constraint that can be expressed between the homogeneous pixel coordinates of two observations of a point from different camera perspectives (and possibly even different cameras). Let

$$\mathbf{q}_i = \mathbf{K}_i \mathbf{p}_i, \qquad (7.114)$$

with $i = a, b$ for the pixel coordinates of two camera observations with different intrinsic parameter matrices. Then the following constraint holds:

$$\mathbf{q}_a^T \mathbf{F}_{ab} \mathbf{q}_b = 0, \qquad (7.115)$$

where

$$\mathbf{F}_{ab} = \mathbf{K}_a^{-T} \mathbf{E}_{ab} \mathbf{K}_b^{-1} \qquad (7.116)$$

is called the *fundamental matrix* (of computer vision). It is fairly easy to see the constraint is true by substitution:

$$\mathbf{q}_a^T \mathbf{F}_{ab} \mathbf{q}_b = \mathbf{p}_b^T \underbrace{\mathbf{K}_a^T \mathbf{K}_a^{-T}}_{\mathbf{1}} \mathbf{E}_{ab} \underbrace{\mathbf{K}_b^{-1} \mathbf{K}_b}_{\mathbf{1}} \mathbf{p}_b = 0, \qquad (7.117)$$

---

[7] On many imaging sensors, the pixels are not square, resulting in different units in the horizontal and vertical directions.

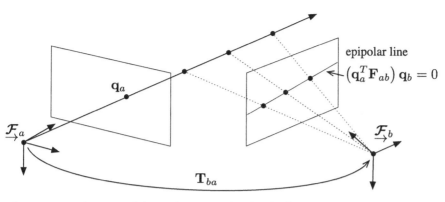

Figure 7.9 If a point is observed in one image, $\mathbf{q}_a$, and the fundamental matrix, $\mathbf{F}_{ab}$, is known, this can be used to define a line in the second image along which the second observation, $\mathbf{q}_b$, must lie.

where we use the essential-matrix constraint for the last step.

The constraint associated with the fundamental matrix is also sometimes called the *epipolar constraint* and is depicted geometrically in Figure 7.9. If a point is observed in one camera, $\mathbf{q}_a$, and the fundamental matrix between the first and a second camera is known, the constraint describes a line, called the *epipolar line*, along which the observation of the point in the second camera, $\mathbf{q}_b$, must lie. This property can be used to limit the search for a matching point to just the epipolar line. This is possible because the camera model is an *affine transformation*, implying that a straight line in Euclidean space projects to a straight line in image space. The fundamental matrix is also useful in developing methods to determine the intrinsic parameter matrix, for example.

Complete Model

Combining everything but the lens effects, the perspective camera model can be written as

$$\begin{bmatrix} u \\ v \end{bmatrix} = \mathbf{s}(\boldsymbol{\rho}) = \mathbf{P}\,\mathbf{K}\,\frac{1}{z}\boldsymbol{\rho}, \tag{7.118}$$

where

$$\mathbf{P} = \begin{bmatrix} 1 & 0 & 0 \\ 0 & 1 & 0 \end{bmatrix}, \quad \mathbf{K} = \begin{bmatrix} f_u & 0 & c_u \\ 0 & f_v & c_v \\ 0 & 0 & 1 \end{bmatrix}, \quad \boldsymbol{\rho} = \begin{bmatrix} x \\ y \\ z \end{bmatrix}. \tag{7.119}$$

$\mathbf{P}$ is simply a projection matrix to remove the bottom row from the homogeneous point representation. This form of the model makes it clear that with a single camera, there is a loss of information as we are going from three parameters in $\boldsymbol{\rho}$ to just two in (u, v); we are unable to determine depth from just one camera.

Homography

Although we cannot determine depth from just one camera, if we assume that the point a camera is observing lies on the surface of a plane whose geometry is known, we can work out the depth and then how that point will look to another camera. The geometry of this situation is depicted in Figure 7.10.

The homogeneous observations for the two cameras can be written as

$$\mathbf{q}_i = \mathbf{K}_i \frac{1}{z_i}\boldsymbol{\rho}_i, \quad \boldsymbol{\rho}_i = \begin{bmatrix} x_i \\ y_i \\ z_i \end{bmatrix}, \tag{7.120}$$

Figure 7.10 If the
point observed by a
camera lies on a
plane whose
geometry is known,
it is possible to work
out what that point
will look like after
the camera makes a
pose change using a
transform called a
homography.

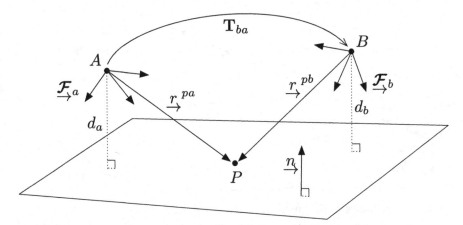

where ρ_i are the coordinates of P in each camera frame with $i = a, b$. Let us assume we know the equation of the plane containing P, expressed in both camera frames; this can be parameterized as

$$\{\mathbf{n}_i, d_i\}, \tag{7.121}$$

where d_i is the distance of camera i from the plane and $\mathbf{n}_i$ are the coordinates of the plane normal in frame i. This implies that

$$\mathbf{n}_i^T \boldsymbol{\rho}_i + d_i = 0, \tag{7.122}$$

since P is in the plane. Solving for $\boldsymbol{\rho}_i$ in (7.120) and substituting into the plane equation, we have

$$z_i \mathbf{n}_i^T \mathbf{K}_i^{-1} \mathbf{q}_i + d_i = 0, \tag{7.123}$$

or

$$z_i = -\frac{d_i}{\mathbf{n}_i^T \mathbf{K}_i^{-1} \mathbf{q}_i} \tag{7.124}$$

for the depth of point P in each camera, $i = a, b$. This further implies that we can write the coordinates of P, expressed in each camera frame, as

$$\boldsymbol{\rho}_i = -\frac{d_i}{\mathbf{n}_i^T \mathbf{K}_i^{-1} \mathbf{q}_i} \mathbf{K}_i^{-1} \mathbf{q}_i. \tag{7.125}$$

This shows that the knowledge of the plane parameters, $\{\mathbf{n}_i, d_i\}$, allows us to recover the coordinates of P even though a single camera cannot determine depth on its own.

Let us also assume we know the pose change, $\mathbf{T}_{ba}$, from $\underset{\rightarrow}{\mathcal{F}}_a$ to $\underset{\rightarrow}{\mathcal{F}}_b$ so that

$$\begin{bmatrix} \boldsymbol{\rho}_b \\ 1 \end{bmatrix} = \underbrace{\begin{bmatrix} \mathbf{C}_{ba} & \mathbf{r}_b^{ab} \\ \mathbf{0}^T & 1 \end{bmatrix}}_{\mathbf{T}_{ba}} \begin{bmatrix} \boldsymbol{\rho}_a \\ 1 \end{bmatrix}, \tag{7.126}$$

or

$$\boldsymbol{\rho}_b = \mathbf{C}_{ba} \boldsymbol{\rho}_a + \mathbf{r}_b^{ab}. \tag{7.127}$$

Inserting (7.120), we have that

$$z_b \mathbf{K}_b^{-1} \mathbf{q}_b = z_a \mathbf{C}_{ba} \mathbf{K}_a^{-1} \mathbf{q}_a + \mathbf{r}_b^{ab}. \tag{7.128}$$

We can then isolate for $\mathbf{q}_b$ in terms of $\mathbf{q}_a$:

$$\mathbf{q}_b = \frac{z_a}{z_b}\mathbf{K}_b\mathbf{C}_{ba}\mathbf{K}_a^{-1}\mathbf{q}_a + \frac{1}{z_b}\mathbf{K}_b\mathbf{r}_b^{ab}. \tag{7.129}$$

Then, substituting z_b from (7.124), we have

$$\mathbf{q}_b = \frac{z_a}{z_b}\mathbf{K}_b\mathbf{C}_{ba}\left(1 + \frac{1}{d_a}\mathbf{r}_a^{ba}\mathbf{n}_a^T\right)\mathbf{K}_a^{-1}\mathbf{q}_a, \tag{7.130}$$

where we used that $\mathbf{r}_b^{ab} = -\mathbf{C}_{ba}\mathbf{r}_a^{ba}$. Finally, we can write

$$\mathbf{q}_b = \mathbf{K}_b\mathbf{H}_{ba}\mathbf{K}_a^{-1}\mathbf{q}_a, \tag{7.131}$$

where

$$\mathbf{H}_{ba} = \frac{z_a}{z_b}\mathbf{C}_{ba}\left(1 + \frac{1}{d_a}\mathbf{r}_a^{ba}\mathbf{n}_a^T\right) \tag{7.132}$$

is called the *homography matrix*. Since the factor z_a/z_b just scales $\mathbf{q}_b$, it can be dropped in practice owing to the fact that $\mathbf{q}_b$ are homogeneous coordinates and the true pixel coordinates can always be recovered by dividing the first two entries by the third; doing so means that $\mathbf{H}_{ba}$ is only a function of the pose change and the plane parameters.

It is worth noting that in the case of a pure rotation, $\mathbf{r}_a^{ba} = \mathbf{0}$, so that the homography matrix simplifies to

$$\mathbf{H}_{ba} = \mathbf{C}_{ba} \tag{7.133}$$

when the z_a/z_b factor is dropped.

The homography matrix is invertible and its inverse is given by

$$\mathbf{H}_{ba}^{-1} = \mathbf{H}_{ab} = \frac{z_b}{z_a}\mathbf{C}_{ab}\left(1 + \frac{1}{d_b}\mathbf{r}_b^{ab}\mathbf{n}_b^T\right). \tag{7.134}$$

This allows us to transform observations in the other direction.

7.4.2 Stereo Camera

Another common three-dimensional sensor is a stereo camera, which consists of two perspective cameras rigidly connected to one another with a known transformation between them. Figure 7.11 depicts one of the most common stereo configurations where the two cameras are separated along the x-axis by a *stereo baseline* of b. Unlike a single camera, it is possible to determine depth to a point from a stereo observation.

Midpoint Model

If we express the coordinates of the point, P, in $\underrightarrow{\mathcal{F}}_s$ as

$$\rho = \mathbf{r}_s^{ps} = \begin{bmatrix} x \\ y \\ z \end{bmatrix}, \tag{7.135}$$

Figure 7.11 Stereo camera rig. Two cameras are mounted pointing in the same direction but with a known separation of b along the x-axis. We choose the sensor frame to be located at the midpoint between the two cameras.

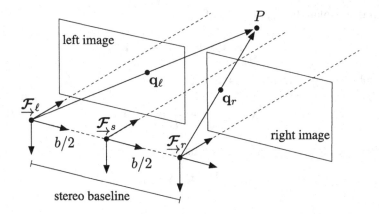

then the model for the left camera is

$$\begin{bmatrix} u_\ell \\ v_\ell \end{bmatrix} = \mathbf{P}\,\mathbf{K}\,\frac{1}{z} \begin{bmatrix} x + \frac{b}{2} \\ y \\ z \end{bmatrix}, \tag{7.136}$$

and the model for the right camera is

$$\begin{bmatrix} u_r \\ v_r \end{bmatrix} = \mathbf{P}\,\mathbf{K}\,\frac{1}{z} \begin{bmatrix} x - \frac{b}{2} \\ y \\ z \end{bmatrix}, \tag{7.137}$$

where we assume the two cameras have the same intrinsic parameter matrix. Stacking the two observations together, we can write the stereo camera model as

$$\begin{bmatrix} u_\ell \\ v_\ell \\ u_r \\ v_r \end{bmatrix} = \mathbf{s}(\boldsymbol{\rho}) = \underbrace{\begin{bmatrix} f_u & 0 & c_u & f_u\frac{b}{2} \\ 0 & f_v & c_v & 0 \\ f_u & 0 & c_u & -f_u\frac{b}{2} \\ 0 & f_v & c_v & 0 \end{bmatrix}}_{\mathbf{M}} \frac{1}{z} \begin{bmatrix} x \\ y \\ z \\ 1 \end{bmatrix}, \tag{7.138}$$

where $\mathbf{M}$ is now a combined parameter matrix for the stereo rig. It is worth noting that $\mathbf{M}$ is not invertible since two of its rows are the same. In fact, because of the stereo setup, the vertical coordinates of the two observations will always be the same; this corresponds to the fact that epipolar lines in this configuration are horizontal such that if a point is observed in one image, the observation in the other image can be found by searching along the line with the same vertical pixel coordinate. We can see this using the fundamental matrix constraint; for this stereo setup, we have $\mathbf{C}_{r\ell} = \mathbf{1}$ and $\mathbf{r}_r^{\ell r} = \begin{bmatrix} -b & 0 & 0 \end{bmatrix}^T$ so that the constraint is

$$\begin{bmatrix} u_\ell & v_\ell & 1 \end{bmatrix} \underbrace{\begin{bmatrix} f_u & 0 & 0 \\ 0 & f_v & 0 \\ c_u & c_v & 1 \end{bmatrix}}_{\mathbf{K}_\ell{}^T} \underbrace{\begin{bmatrix} 0 & 0 & 0 \\ 0 & 0 & b \\ 0 & -b & 0 \end{bmatrix}}_{\mathbf{E}_{\ell r}} \underbrace{\begin{bmatrix} f_u & 0 & c_u \\ 0 & f_v & c_v \\ 0 & 0 & 1 \end{bmatrix}}_{\mathbf{K}_r} \begin{bmatrix} u_r \\ v_r \\ 1 \end{bmatrix} = 0. \tag{7.139}$$

Multiplying this out, we see that it simplifies to $v_r = v_\ell$.

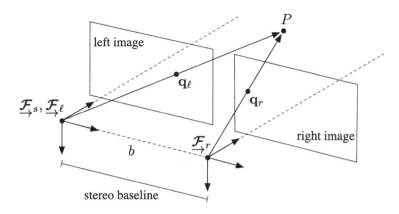

Figure 7.12
Alternate stereo
model with the
sensor frame located
at the left camera.

Left Model

We could also choose to locate the sensor frame at the left camera rather than the midpoint between the two cameras. In this case, the camera model becomes

$$
\begin{bmatrix} u_\ell \\ v_\ell \\ u_r \\ v_r \end{bmatrix} = \begin{bmatrix} f_u & 0 & c_u & 0 \\ 0 & f_v & c_v & 0 \\ f_u & 0 & c_u & -f_u b \\ 0 & f_v & c_v & 0 \end{bmatrix} \frac{1}{z} \begin{bmatrix} x \\ y \\ z \\ 1 \end{bmatrix}.
\tag{7.140}
$$

Typically, in this form, the v_r equation is dropped and the u_r equation is replaced with one for the disparity,[8] d, given by

$$
d = u_\ell - u_r = \frac{1}{z} f_u b,
\tag{7.141}
$$

so that we can write

$$
\begin{bmatrix} u_\ell \\ v_\ell \\ d \end{bmatrix} = \mathbf{s}(\boldsymbol{\rho}) = \begin{bmatrix} f_u & 0 & c_u & 0 \\ 0 & f_v & c_v & 0 \\ 0 & 0 & 0 & f_u b \end{bmatrix} \frac{1}{z} \begin{bmatrix} x \\ y \\ z \\ 1 \end{bmatrix}
\tag{7.142}
$$

for the stereo model. This form has the appealing property that we are going from three point parameters, (x, y, z), to three observations, (u_ℓ, v_ℓ, d). A similar model can be developed for the right camera.

7.4.3 Range-Azimuth-Elevation

Some sensors, such as lidar (light detection and ranging), can be modelled as a *range-azimuth-elevation (RAE)*, which essentially observes a point, P, in spherical coordinates. For lidar, which can measure distance by reflecting laser pulses off a scene, the azimuth and elevation are the angles of the mirrors that are used to steer the laser beam and the range is the reported distance determined by time of flight. The geometry of this sensor type is depicted in Figure 7.13.

---

[8] The disparity equation can be used as a one-dimensional stereo camera model, as we have already seen in Chapter 4 on nonlinear estimation.

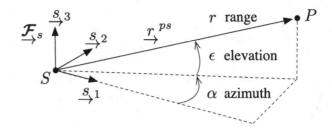

The coordinates of point P in the sensor frame, $\mathcal{F}_s$, are

$$\rho = \mathbf{r}_s^{ps} = \begin{bmatrix} x \\ y \\ z \end{bmatrix}. \tag{7.143}$$

These can also be written as

$$\rho = \mathbf{C}_3^T(\alpha)\,\mathbf{C}_2^T(-\epsilon) \begin{bmatrix} r \\ 0 \\ 0 \end{bmatrix}, \tag{7.144}$$

where α is the azimuth, ϵ is the elevation, r is the range, and $\mathbf{C}_i$ is the principal rotation about axis i. The elevation rotation indicated in Figure 7.13 is negative according to the right-hand rule. Inserting the principal-axis rotation formulas and multiplying out, we find that

$$\begin{bmatrix} x \\ y \\ z \end{bmatrix} = \begin{bmatrix} r\cos\alpha\cos\epsilon \\ r\sin\alpha\cos\epsilon \\ r\sin\epsilon \end{bmatrix}, \tag{7.145}$$

which are the common spherical-coordinate expressions. Unfortunately, this is the inverse of the sensor model we desire. We can invert this expression to show that the RAE sensor model is

$$\begin{bmatrix} r \\ \alpha \\ \epsilon \end{bmatrix} = \mathbf{s}(\rho) = \begin{bmatrix} \sqrt{x^2 + y^2 + z^2} \\ \tan^{-1}(y/x) \\ \sin^{-1}\left(z/\sqrt{x^2 + y^2 + z^2}\right) \end{bmatrix}. \tag{7.146}$$

In the case that the point P lies in the xy-plane, we have $z = 0$ and hence $\epsilon = 0$, so that the RAE model simplifies to the range-bearing model:

$$\begin{bmatrix} r \\ \alpha \end{bmatrix} = \mathbf{s}(\rho) = \begin{bmatrix} \sqrt{x^2 + y^2} \\ \tan^{-1}(y/x) \end{bmatrix}, \tag{7.147}$$

which is commonly used in mobile robotics.

7.4.4 Inertial Measurement Unit

Another common sensor that functions in three-dimensional space is the *inertial measurement unit (IMU)*. An ideal IMU comprises three orthogonal linear accelerometers and three orthogonal rate gyros.[9] All quantities are measured in a

---

[9] Typically, calibration is required, as the axes are never perfectly orthogonal due to manufacturing tolerances.

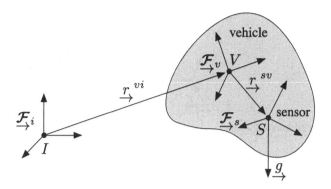

Figure 7.14 An inertial measurement unit has three linear accelerometers and three rate gyros that measure quantities in the sensor frame, which is typically not coincident with the vehicle frame.

sensor frame, $\underset{\rightarrow}{\mathcal{F}}_s$, which may or may not be located at the vehicle frame, $\underset{\rightarrow}{\mathcal{F}}_v$, as shown in Figure 7.14.

To model an IMU, we assume that the state of the vehicle can be captured by the quantities

$$\underbrace{\mathbf{r}_i^{vi}, \quad \mathbf{C}_{vi},}_{\text{pose}} \qquad \underbrace{\boldsymbol{\omega}_v^{vi},}_{\text{angular velocity}} \qquad \underbrace{\ddot{\mathbf{r}}_i^{vi},}_{\text{trans. accel.}} \qquad \underbrace{\dot{\boldsymbol{\omega}}_v^{vi},}_{\text{angular accel.}} \qquad (7.148)$$

and that we know the fixed pose change between the vehicle and sensor frames given by $\mathbf{r}_v^{sv}$ and $\mathbf{C}_{sv}$, which is typically determined by calibration.

The gyro sensor model is simpler than the accelerometers, so we will discuss this first. Essentially, the measured angular rates, $\boldsymbol{\omega}$, are the body rates of the vehicle, expressed in the sensor frame:

$$\boldsymbol{\omega} = \mathbf{C}_{sv}\boldsymbol{\omega}_v^{vi}. \qquad (7.149)$$

This exploits the fact that the sensor frame is fixed with respect to the vehicle frame so that $\dot{\mathbf{C}}_{sv} = \mathbf{0}$.

Because accelerometers typically use test masses as part of the measurement principle, the resulting observations, $\mathbf{a}$, can be written as

$$\mathbf{a} = \mathbf{C}_{si}\left(\ddot{\mathbf{r}}_i^{si} - \mathbf{g}_i\right), \qquad (7.150)$$

where $\ddot{\mathbf{r}}_i^{si}$ is the inertial acceleration of the sensor point, S, and $\mathbf{g}_i$ is gravity. Notably, in free fall, the accelerometers will measure $\mathbf{a} = \mathbf{0}$, whereas at rest, they will measure only gravity (in the sensor frame). Unfortunately, this accelerometer model is not in terms of the vehicle state quantities that we identified earlier, and must be modified to account for the offset between the sensor and vehicle frames. To do this, we note that

$$\mathbf{r}_i^{si} = \mathbf{r}_i^{vi} + \mathbf{C}_{vi}^T\mathbf{r}_v^{sv}. \qquad (7.151)$$

Differentiating twice (and using Poisson's equation from (7.45) and that $\dot{\mathbf{r}}_v^{sv} = \mathbf{0}$) provides

$$\ddot{\mathbf{r}}_i^{si} = \ddot{\mathbf{r}}_i^{vi} + \mathbf{C}_{vi}^T\dot{\boldsymbol{\omega}}_v^{vi\wedge}\mathbf{r}_v^{sv} + \mathbf{C}_{vi}^T\boldsymbol{\omega}_v^{vi\wedge}\boldsymbol{\omega}_v^{vi\wedge}\mathbf{r}_v^{sv}, \qquad (7.152)$$

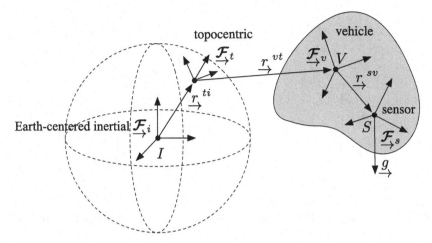

where the right-hand side is now in terms of our state quantities[10] and known
calibration parameters. Inserting this into (7.150) gives our final model for the
accelerometers:

$$\mathbf{a} = \mathbf{C}_{sv}\left(\mathbf{C}_{vi}\left(\ddot{\mathbf{r}}_i^{vi} - \mathbf{g}_i\right) + \dot{\boldsymbol{\omega}}_v^{vi\wedge}\mathbf{r}_v^{sv} + \boldsymbol{\omega}_v^{vi\wedge}\boldsymbol{\omega}_v^{vi\wedge}\mathbf{r}_v^{sv}\right). \qquad (7.153)$$

Naturally, if the offset between the sensor and vehicle frames, $\mathbf{r}_v^{sv}$, is sufficiently
small, we may choose to neglect the last two terms.

To summarize, we can stack the accelerometer and gyro models into the following combined IMU sensor model:

$$\begin{bmatrix}\mathbf{a} \\ \boldsymbol{\omega}\end{bmatrix} = \mathbf{s}\left(\mathbf{r}_i^{vi}, \mathbf{C}_{vi}, \boldsymbol{\omega}_v^{vi}, \ddot{\mathbf{r}}_i^{vi}, \dot{\boldsymbol{\omega}}_v^{vi}\right)$$

$$= \begin{bmatrix}\mathbf{C}_{sv}\left(\mathbf{C}_{vi}\left(\ddot{\mathbf{r}}_i^{vi} - \mathbf{g}_i\right) + \dot{\boldsymbol{\omega}}_v^{vi\wedge}\mathbf{r}_v^{sv} + \boldsymbol{\omega}_v^{vi\wedge}\boldsymbol{\omega}_v^{vi\wedge}\mathbf{r}_v^{sv}\right) \\ \mathbf{C}_{sv}\boldsymbol{\omega}_v^{vi}\end{bmatrix}, \qquad (7.154)$$

where $\mathbf{C}_{sv}$ and $\mathbf{r}_v^{sv}$ are the (known) pose change between the vehicle and sensor
frames and $\mathbf{g}_i$ is gravity in the inertial frame.

For some high-performance inertial-measurement-unit applications, the preceding model is insufficient since it assumes an inertial reference frame can be
located conveniently on the Earth's surface, for example. High-end IMU units,
however, are sensitive enough to detect the rotation of the Earth, and thus a
more elaborate model of the sensor is required. The typical setup is depicted in
Figure 7.15, where the inertial frame is located at the Earth's center of mass (but
not rotating) and then a convenient (non-inertial) reference frame (used to track
the vehicle's motion) is located on the Earth's surface. This requires generalizing
the sensor model to account for this more sophisticated setup (not shown).

7.5 Summary

The main takeaway points from this chapter are as follows:

1. Objects that are able to rotate in three dimensions pose a problem for our state
   estimation techniques in the first part of the book. This is because we cannot,

---

[10] If the angular acceleration quantity, $\dot{\boldsymbol{\omega}}_v^{vi}$, is not actually part of the state, it could be estimated from
two or more measurements from the gyro at previous times.

in general, use a vector space to describe the three-dimensional orientation of an object.

2. There are several ways to parameterize rotations (e.g., rotation matrix, Euler angles, unit-length quaternions). They all have advantages and disadvantages; some have singularities while the others have constraints. Our choice in this book is to favour the use of the rotation matrix since this is the quantity that is most commonly used to rotate vectors from one reference frame to another.

3. There are many different notational conventions in use in different fields (i.e., robotics, computer vision, aerospace). Coupled with the variety of rotational parameterizations, this can often lead to a source of miscommunication in practice. Our goal in this book is only to attempt to explain three-dimensional state estimation consistently and clearly in just one of the notational possibilities.

The next chapter will explore more deeply the mathematics of rotations and poses by introducing matrix Lie groups.

7.6 Exercises

7.1 Show that $\mathbf{u}^\wedge \mathbf{v} \equiv -\mathbf{v}^\wedge \mathbf{u}$ for any two 3×1 columns $\mathbf{u}$ and $\mathbf{v}$.

7.2 Show that $\mathbf{C}^{-1} = \mathbf{C}^T$ starting from

$$\mathbf{C} = \cos\theta \mathbf{1} + (1 - \cos\theta)\mathbf{a}\mathbf{a}^T + \sin\theta\, \mathbf{a}^\wedge.$$

7.3 Show that $(\mathbf{C}\mathbf{v})^\wedge \equiv \mathbf{C}\mathbf{v}^\wedge \mathbf{C}^T$ for any 3×1 column $\mathbf{v}$ and rotation matrix, $\mathbf{C}$.

7.4 Show that

$$\dot{\mathbf{T}}_{iv} = \mathbf{T}_{iv} \begin{bmatrix} 0 & -v\kappa & 0 & v \\ v\kappa & 0 & -v\tau & 0 \\ 0 & v\tau & 0 & 0 \\ 0 & 0 & 0 & 0 \end{bmatrix}.$$

7.5 Show that if we constrain the motion to the xy-plane, the Frenet–Serret equations simplify to

$$\dot{x} = v\cos\theta,$$
$$\dot{y} = v\sin\theta,$$
$$\dot{\theta} = \omega,$$

where $\omega = v\kappa$.

7.6 Show that for the single-camera model, straight lines in Euclidean space project to straight lines in image space.

7.7 Show directly that the inverse of the homography matrix,

$$\mathbf{H}_{ba} = \frac{z_a}{z_b}\mathbf{C}_{ba}\left(\mathbf{1} + \frac{1}{d_a}\mathbf{r}_a^{ba}\mathbf{n}_a^T\right),$$

is

$$\mathbf{H}_{ba}^{-1} = \frac{z_b}{z_a} \mathbf{C}_{ab} \left(1 + \frac{1}{d_b} \mathbf{r}_b^{ab} \mathbf{n}_b^T \right).$$

7.8 Work out the stereo camera model for the case when the sensor frame is located at the right camera instead of the left or the midpoint.

7.9 Work out the inverse of the left stereo camera model. In other words, how can we go from (u_ℓ, v_ℓ, d) back to the point coordinates, (x, y, z)?

7.10 A mobile robot is moving through a (planar) corridor environment. It stops periodically and measures the wall profile (solid black lines) using a perfect laser rangefinder attached to its body. To simplify the sensor model, assume it can see everything in a 3×3 grid centered at its current location.

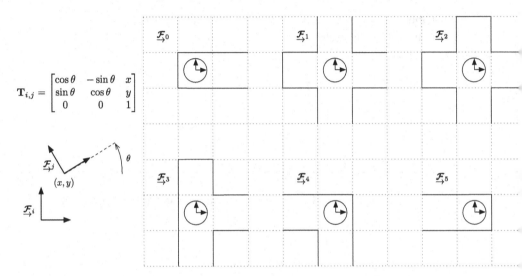

(i) A perfect wheel odometry system provides the following relative transforms:

$$\mathbf{T}_{0,1} = \begin{bmatrix} 0 & -1 & 3 \\ 1 & 0 & 0 \\ 0 & 0 & 1 \end{bmatrix}, \quad \mathbf{T}_{1,2} = \begin{bmatrix} 0 & 1 & 2 \\ -1 & 0 & 0 \\ 0 & 0 & 1 \end{bmatrix},$$

$$\mathbf{T}_{2,3} = \begin{bmatrix} 0 & 1 & 2 \\ -1 & 0 & 0 \\ 0 & 0 & 1 \end{bmatrix}, \quad \mathbf{T}_{4,5} = \begin{bmatrix} 0 & 1 & 0 \\ -1 & 0 & -5 \\ 0 & 0 & 1 \end{bmatrix}.$$

Assuming $\underset{\rightarrow}{\mathcal{F}}_5$ is coincident with $\underset{\rightarrow}{\mathcal{F}}_0$ but facing the opposite direction, determine the following quantities:

$$\mathbf{T}_{0,2}, \quad \mathbf{T}_{0,3}, \quad \mathbf{T}_{0,4}, \quad \mathbf{T}_{0,5}.$$

(ii) Draw the map of the robot's environment using the laser rangefinder readings and the poses computed in the previous question.

(iii) Draw what the robot's laser rangefinder will measure after applying the following transform from $\underset{\rightarrow}{\mathcal{F}}_2$:

$$\mathbf{T}_{2,6} = \begin{bmatrix} -1 & 0 & 2 \\ 0 & -1 & -1 \\ 0 & 0 & 1 \end{bmatrix}.$$

(iv) Given the map and a single laser rangefinder reading, will it always be possible to uniquely determine the robot's pose? Explain.

7.11 Work out an IMU model for the situation depicted in Figure 7.15, where it is necessary to account for the rotation of the Earth about its axis.

8

Matrix Lie Groups

We have already introduced *rotations* and *poses* in the previous chapter on three-dimensional geometry. In this chapter, we look more deeply into the nature of these quantities. It turns out that rotations are quite different from the usual vector quantities with which we are familiar. The set of rotations is not a *vector space* in the sense of linear algebra. However, rotations do form another mathematical object called a *non-commutative group*, which possesses some, but not all, of the usual vector space properties.

Marius Sophus Lie (1842–1899) was a Norwegian mathematician. He largely created the theory of continuous symmetry and applied it to the study of geometry and differential equations.

We will focus our efforts in this chapter on two sets known as *matrix Lie groups*. Stillwell (2008) provides an accessible account of Lie theory, and Chirikjian (2009) is an excellent reference from the robotics perspective.

8.1 Geometry

We will work with two specific matrix Lie groups in this chapter: the *special orthogonal group*, denoted $SO(3)$, which can represent rotations, and the *special Euclidean group*, $SE(3)$, which can represent poses.

8.1.1 Special Orthogonal and Special Euclidean Groups

The *special orthogonal group*, representing rotations, is simply the set of valid rotation matrices:

Note, $SO(3)$ is 'special' because of the extra constraint that $\det \mathbf{C} = 1$, without which it is simply the orthogonal group, $O(3)$.

$$SO(3) = \left\{ \mathbf{C} \in \mathbb{R}^{3 \times 3} \mid \mathbf{C}\mathbf{C}^T = \mathbf{1}, \det \mathbf{C} = 1 \right\}. \tag{8.1}$$

The $\mathbf{C}\mathbf{C}^T = \mathbf{1}$ orthogonality condition is needed to impose six constraints on the nine-parameter rotation matrix, thereby reducing the number of degrees of freedom to three. Noticing that

$$(\det \mathbf{C})^2 = \det \left(\mathbf{C}\mathbf{C}^T \right) = \det \mathbf{1} = 1, \tag{8.2}$$

we have that

$$\det \mathbf{C} = \pm 1, \tag{8.3}$$

allowing for two possibilities. Choosing $\det \mathbf{C} = 1$ ensures that we have a *proper rotation*.[1]

---

[1] There is another case in which $\det \mathbf{C} = -1$, sometimes called an *improper rotation* or *rotary reflection*, but we shall not be concerned with it here.

Although the set of all matrices can be shown to be a vector space, $SO(3)$ is not a valid subspace.[2] For example, $SO(3)$ is not closed under addition, so adding two rotation matrices does not result in a valid rotation matrix:

$$\mathbf{C}_1, \mathbf{C}_2 \in SO(3) \not\Rightarrow \mathbf{C}_1 + \mathbf{C}_2 \in SO(3). \qquad (8.4)$$

Also, the zero matrix is not a valid rotation matrix: $\mathbf{0} \notin SO(3)$. Without these properties (and some others), $SO(3)$ cannot be a vector space (at least not a subspace of $\mathbb{R}^{3 \times 3}$).

The *special Euclidean group*, representing poses (i.e., translation and rotation), is simply the set of valid transformation matrices:

$$SE(3) = \left\{ \mathbf{T} = \begin{bmatrix} \mathbf{C} & \mathbf{r} \\ \mathbf{0}^T & 1 \end{bmatrix} \in \mathbb{R}^{4 \times 4} \ \middle| \ \mathbf{C} \in SO(3), \mathbf{r} \in \mathbb{R}^3 \right\}. \qquad (8.5)$$

By similar arguments to $SO(3)$, we can show that $SE(3)$ is not a vector space (at least not a subspace of $\mathbb{R}^{4 \times 4}$).

While $SO(3)$ and $SE(3)$ are not vector spaces, they can be shown to be *matrix Lie groups*.[3] We next show what this means. In mathematics, a *group* is a set of elements together with an operation that combines any two of its elements to form a third element also in the set, while satisfying four conditions called the group axioms, namely closure, associativity, identity, and invertibility. A *Lie* group is a group that is also a *differential manifold*, with the property that the group operations are smooth.[4] A *matrix* Lie group further specifies that the elements of the group are matrices, the combination operation is matrix multiplication, and the inversion operation is matrix inversion.

The four group properties are then as shown in Table 8.1 for our two candidate matrix Lie groups. Closure for $SO(3)$ actually follows directly from Euler's rotation theorem, which says a compounding of rotations can be replaced by a single rotation. Or, we can note that

$$(\mathbf{C}_1 \mathbf{C}_2)(\mathbf{C}_1 \mathbf{C}_2)^T = \mathbf{C}_1 \underbrace{\mathbf{C}_2 \mathbf{C}_2^T}_{1} \mathbf{C}_1^T = \underbrace{\mathbf{C}_1 \mathbf{C}_1^T}_{1} = 1, \qquad (8.6a)$$

$$\det(\mathbf{C}_1 \mathbf{C}_2) = \underbrace{\det(\mathbf{C}_1)}_{1} \underbrace{\det(\mathbf{C}_2)}_{1} = 1, \qquad (8.6b)$$

such that $\mathbf{C}_1 \mathbf{C}_2 \in SO(3)$ if $\mathbf{C}_1, \mathbf{C}_2 \in SO(3)$. Closure for $SE(3)$ can be seen simply by multiplying,

$$\mathbf{T}_1 \mathbf{T}_2 = \begin{bmatrix} \mathbf{C}_1 & \mathbf{r}_1 \\ \mathbf{0}^T & 1 \end{bmatrix} \begin{bmatrix} \mathbf{C}_2 & \mathbf{r}_2 \\ \mathbf{0}^T & 1 \end{bmatrix} = \begin{bmatrix} \mathbf{C}_1 \mathbf{C}_2 & \mathbf{C}_1 \mathbf{r}_2 + \mathbf{r}_1 \\ \mathbf{0}^T & 1 \end{bmatrix} \in SE(3), \qquad (8.7)$$

---

[2] A subspace of a vector space is also a vector space.

[3] They are actually *non-Abelian* (or non-commutative) groups since the order in which we compound elements matters.

[4] Smoothness implies that we can use differential calculus on the manifold; or, roughly, if we change the input to any group operation by a little bit, the output will only change by a little bit.

Table 8.1 Matrix Lie group properties for $SO(3)$ (rotations) and $SE(3)$ (poses).

property	$SO(3)$	$SE(3)$
closure	$\mathbf{C}_1, \mathbf{C}_2 \in SO(3)$ $\Rightarrow \mathbf{C}_1 \mathbf{C}_2 \in SO(3)$	$\mathbf{T}_1, \mathbf{T}_2 \in SE(3)$ $\Rightarrow \mathbf{T}_1 \mathbf{T}_2 \in SE(3)$
associativity	$\mathbf{C}_1 (\mathbf{C}_2 \mathbf{C}_3) = (\mathbf{C}_1 \mathbf{C}_2) \mathbf{C}_3$ $= \mathbf{C}_1 \mathbf{C}_2 \mathbf{C}_3$	$\mathbf{T}_1 (\mathbf{T}_2 \mathbf{T}_3) = (\mathbf{T}_1 \mathbf{T}_2) \mathbf{T}_3$ $= \mathbf{T}_1 \mathbf{T}_2 \mathbf{T}_3$
identity	$\mathbf{C}, \mathbf{1} \in SO(3)$ $\Rightarrow \mathbf{C1} = \mathbf{1C} = \mathbf{C}$	$\mathbf{T}, \mathbf{1} \in SE(3)$ $\Rightarrow \mathbf{T1} = \mathbf{1T} = \mathbf{T}$
invertibility	$\mathbf{C} \in SO(3)$ $\Rightarrow \mathbf{C}^{-1} \in SO(3)$	$\mathbf{T} \in SE(3)$ $\Rightarrow \mathbf{T}^{-1} \in SE(3)$

since $\mathbf{C}_1 \mathbf{C}_2 \in SO(3)$ and $\mathbf{C}_1 \mathbf{r}_2 + \mathbf{r}_1 \in \mathbb{R}^3$. Associativity follows for both groups from the properties of matrix multiplication.[5] The identity matrix is the identity element of both groups, which again follows from the properties of matrix multiplication. Finally, since $\mathbf{C}^{-1} = \mathbf{C}^T$, which follows from $\mathbf{C}\mathbf{C}^T = \mathbf{1}$, we know that the inverse of an element of $SO(3)$ is still in $SO(3)$. This can be seen through

$$\left(\mathbf{C}^{-1}\right) \left(\mathbf{C}^{-1}\right)^T = \left(\mathbf{C}^T\right) \left(\mathbf{C}^T\right)^T = \underbrace{\mathbf{C}^T \mathbf{C}}_{1} = \mathbf{1}, \tag{8.8a}$$

$$\det\left(\mathbf{C}^{-1}\right) = \det\left(\mathbf{C}^T\right) = \underbrace{\det \mathbf{C}}_{1} = 1. \tag{8.8b}$$

The inverse of an element of $SE(3)$ is

$$\mathbf{T}^{-1} = \begin{bmatrix} \mathbf{C} & \mathbf{r} \\ \mathbf{0}^T & 1 \end{bmatrix}^{-1} = \begin{bmatrix} \mathbf{C}^T & -\mathbf{C}^T \mathbf{r} \\ \mathbf{0}^T & 1 \end{bmatrix} \in SE(3); \tag{8.9}$$

since $\mathbf{C}^T \in SO(3)$, $-\mathbf{C}^T \mathbf{r} \in \mathbb{R}^3$, so this also holds. Other than the smoothness criterion, this establishes $SO(3)$ and $SE(3)$ as matrix Lie groups.

8.1.2 Lie Algebras

With every matrix Lie group is associated a *Lie algebra*, which consists of a vector space,[6] $\mathbb{V}$ over some field,[7] $\mathbb{F}$, together with a binary operation, $[\cdot, \cdot]$, called the *Lie bracket* (of the algebra) and that satisfies four properties:

$$
\begin{aligned}
\text{closure:} \quad & [\mathbf{X}, \mathbf{Y}] \in \mathbb{V}, \\
\text{bilinearity:} \quad & [a\mathbf{X} + b\mathbf{Y}, \mathbf{Z}] = a[\mathbf{X}, \mathbf{Z}] + b[\mathbf{Y}, \mathbf{Z}], \\
& [\mathbf{Z}, a\mathbf{X} + b\mathbf{Y}] = a[\mathbf{Z}, \mathbf{X}] + b[\mathbf{Z}, \mathbf{Y}], \\
\text{alternating:} \quad & [\mathbf{X}, \mathbf{X}] = \mathbf{0}, \\
\text{Jacobi identity:} \quad & [\mathbf{X}, [\mathbf{Y}, \mathbf{Z}]] + [\mathbf{Y}, [\mathbf{Z}, \mathbf{X}]] + [\mathbf{Z}, [\mathbf{X}, \mathbf{Y}]] = \mathbf{0},
\end{aligned}
$$

---

[5] The set of all real matrices can be shown to be an *algebra* and associativity of matrix multiplication is a required property.

[6] We can take this to be a subspace of the square real matrices, which is a vector space.

[7] We can take this to be the field of real numbers, $\mathbb{R}$.

for all $\mathbf{X}, \mathbf{Y}, \mathbf{Z} \in \mathbb{V}$ and $a, b \in \mathbb{F}$. The vector space of a Lie algebra is the *tangent space* of the associated Lie group at the identity element of the group, and it completely captures the local structure of the group.

Rotations

The Lie algebra associated with $SO(3)$ is given by

$$
\begin{aligned}
\text{vector space:} \quad & \mathfrak{so}(3) = \left\{ \boldsymbol{\Phi} = \boldsymbol{\phi}^{\wedge} \in \mathbb{R}^{3\times 3} \mid \boldsymbol{\phi} \in \mathbb{R}^3 \right\}, \\
\text{field:} \quad & \mathbb{R}, \\
\text{Lie bracket:} \quad & [\boldsymbol{\Phi}_1, \boldsymbol{\Phi}_2] = \boldsymbol{\Phi}_1 \boldsymbol{\Phi}_2 - \boldsymbol{\Phi}_2 \boldsymbol{\Phi}_1,
\end{aligned}
$$

where

$$
\boldsymbol{\phi}^{\wedge} = \begin{bmatrix} \phi_1 \\ \phi_2 \\ \phi_3 \end{bmatrix}^{\wedge} = \begin{bmatrix} 0 & -\phi_3 & \phi_2 \\ \phi_3 & 0 & -\phi_1 \\ -\phi_2 & \phi_1 & 0 \end{bmatrix} \in \mathbb{R}^{3\times 3}, \quad \boldsymbol{\phi} \in \mathbb{R}^3. \tag{8.10}
$$

We already saw this linear, skew-symmetric operator in the previous chapter during our discussion of cross products and rotations. Later, we will also make use of the inverse of this operator, denoted $(\cdot)^{\vee}$, so that

$$
\boldsymbol{\Phi} = \boldsymbol{\phi}^{\wedge} \;\Rightarrow\; \boldsymbol{\phi} = \boldsymbol{\Phi}^{\vee}. \tag{8.11}
$$

We will omit proving that $\mathfrak{so}(3)$ is a vector space, but will briefly show that the four Lie bracket properties hold. Let $\boldsymbol{\Phi}, \boldsymbol{\Phi}_1 = \boldsymbol{\phi}_1^{\wedge}, \boldsymbol{\Phi}_2 = \boldsymbol{\phi}_2^{\wedge} \in \mathfrak{so}(3)$. Then, for the closure property, we have

$$
[\boldsymbol{\Phi}_1, \boldsymbol{\Phi}_2] = \boldsymbol{\Phi}_1 \boldsymbol{\Phi}_2 - \boldsymbol{\Phi}_2 \boldsymbol{\Phi}_1 = \boldsymbol{\phi}_1^{\wedge} \boldsymbol{\phi}_2^{\wedge} - \boldsymbol{\phi}_2^{\wedge} \boldsymbol{\phi}_1^{\wedge} = \left(\underbrace{\boldsymbol{\phi}_1^{\wedge} \boldsymbol{\phi}_2}_{\in \mathbb{R}^3} \right)^{\wedge} \in \mathfrak{so}(3). \tag{8.12}
$$

Bilinearity follows directly from the fact that $(\cdot)^{\wedge}$ is a linear operator. The alternating property can be seen easily through

$$
[\boldsymbol{\Phi}, \boldsymbol{\Phi}] = \boldsymbol{\Phi}\boldsymbol{\Phi} - \boldsymbol{\Phi}\boldsymbol{\Phi} = \mathbf{0} \in \mathfrak{so}(3). \tag{8.13}
$$

Finally, the Jacobi identity can be verified by substituting and applying the definition of the Lie bracket. Informally, we will refer to $\mathfrak{so}(3)$ as the Lie algebra, although technically this is only the associated vector space.

Carl Gustav Jacob Jacobi (1804–1851) was a German mathematician who made fundamental contributions to elliptic functions, dynamics, differential equations, and number theory.

Poses

The Lie algebra associated with $SE(3)$ is given by

$$
\begin{aligned}
\text{vector space:} \quad & \mathfrak{se}(3) = \left\{ \boldsymbol{\Xi} = \boldsymbol{\xi}^{\wedge} \in \mathbb{R}^{4\times 4} \mid \boldsymbol{\xi} \in \mathbb{R}^6 \right\}, \\
\text{field:} \quad & \mathbb{R}, \\
\text{Lie bracket:} \quad & [\boldsymbol{\Xi}_1, \boldsymbol{\Xi}_2] = \boldsymbol{\Xi}_1 \boldsymbol{\Xi}_2 - \boldsymbol{\Xi}_2 \boldsymbol{\Xi}_1,
\end{aligned}
$$

where

$$
\boldsymbol{\xi}^{\wedge} = \begin{bmatrix} \boldsymbol{\rho} \\ \boldsymbol{\phi} \end{bmatrix}^{\wedge} = \begin{bmatrix} \boldsymbol{\phi}^{\wedge} & \boldsymbol{\rho} \\ \mathbf{0}^T & 0 \end{bmatrix} \in \mathbb{R}^{4\times 4}, \quad \boldsymbol{\rho}, \boldsymbol{\phi} \in \mathbb{R}^3. \tag{8.14}
$$

This is an overloading of the $(\cdot)^\wedge$ operator (Murray et al., 1994) from before to take elements of $\mathbb{R}^6$ and turn them into elements of $\mathbb{R}^{4\times4}$; it is still linear. We will also make use of the inverse of this operator, denoted $(\cdot)^\vee$, so that

$$\Xi = \xi^\wedge \;\Rightarrow\; \xi = \Xi^\vee. \tag{8.15}$$

Again, we will omit showing that $\mathfrak{se}(3)$ is a vector space, but will briefly show that the four Lie bracket properties hold. Let $\Xi, \Xi_1 = \xi_1^\wedge, \Xi_2 = \xi_2^\wedge \in \mathfrak{se}(3)$. Then, for the closure property, we have

$$[\Xi_1, \Xi_2] = \Xi_1\Xi_2 - \Xi_2\Xi_1 = \xi_1^\wedge\xi_2^\wedge - \xi_2^\wedge\xi_1^\wedge = \left(\underbrace{\xi_1^\wedge\xi_2}_{\in\mathbb{R}^6}\right)^\wedge \in \mathfrak{se}(3), \tag{8.16}$$

where

$$\xi^\lambda = \begin{bmatrix} \rho \\ \phi \end{bmatrix}^\lambda = \begin{bmatrix} \phi^\wedge & \rho^\wedge \\ 0 & \phi^\wedge \end{bmatrix} \in \mathbb{R}^{6\times6}, \quad \rho, \phi \in \mathbb{R}^3. \tag{8.17}$$

Bilinearity follows directly from the fact that $(\cdot)^\wedge$ is a linear operator. The alternating property can be seen easily through

$$[\Xi, \Xi] = \Xi\Xi - \Xi\Xi = 0 \in \mathfrak{se}(3). \tag{8.18}$$

Finally, the Jacobi identity can be verified by substituting and applying the definition of the Lie bracket. Again, we will refer to $\mathfrak{se}(3)$ as the Lie algebra, although technically, this is only the associated vector space.

In the next section, we will make clear the relationships between our matrix Lie groups and their associated Lie algebras:

$$SO(3) \;\leftrightarrow\; \mathfrak{so}(3),$$
$$SE(3) \;\leftrightarrow\; \mathfrak{se}(3).$$

For this we require the *exponential map*.

8.1.3 Exponential Map

It turns out that the *exponential map* is the key to relating a matrix Lie group to its associated Lie algebra. The matrix exponential is given by

$$\exp(\mathbf{A}) = 1 + \mathbf{A} + \frac{1}{2!}\mathbf{A}^2 + \frac{1}{3!}\mathbf{A}^3 + \cdots = \sum_{n=0}^\infty \frac{1}{n!}\mathbf{A}^n, \tag{8.19}$$

where $\mathbf{A} \in \mathbb{R}^{M\times M}$ is a square matrix. There is also a matrix logarithm,

$$\ln(\mathbf{A}) = \sum_{n=1}^\infty \frac{(-1)^{n-1}}{n} (\mathbf{A} - 1)^n, \tag{8.20}$$

which again mimics the scalar series expansion.

Rotations

For rotations, we can relate elements of $SO(3)$ to elements of $\mathfrak{so}(3)$ through the exponential map:[8]

$$\mathbf{C} = \exp\left(\boldsymbol{\phi}^\wedge\right) = \sum_{n=0}^{\infty} \frac{1}{n!}\left(\boldsymbol{\phi}^\wedge\right)^n, \tag{8.21}$$

where $\mathbf{C} \in SO(3)$ and $\boldsymbol{\phi} \in \mathbb{R}^3$ (and hence $\boldsymbol{\phi}^\wedge \in \mathfrak{so}(3)$). We can also go in the other direction (but not uniquely) using

$$\boldsymbol{\phi} = \ln\left(\mathbf{C}\right)^\vee. \tag{8.22}$$

Mathematically, the exponential map from $\mathfrak{so}(3)$ to $SO(3)$ is *surjective-only* (or *surjective/onto* and *non-injective/many-to-one*). This means that we can generate every element of $SO(3)$ from multiple elements of $\mathfrak{so}(3)$.[9]

It is useful to examine the surjective-only property a little deeper. We begin by working out the forwards (exponential) mapping in closed form to go from a $\boldsymbol{\phi} \in \mathbb{R}^3$ to a $\mathbf{C} \in SO(3)$. Let $\boldsymbol{\phi} = \phi\,\mathbf{a}$, where $\phi = |\boldsymbol{\phi}|$ is the angle of rotation and $\mathbf{a} = \boldsymbol{\phi}/\phi$ is the unit-length axis of rotation. For the matrix exponential, we then have

$$\exp(\boldsymbol{\phi}^\wedge) = \exp(\phi\,\mathbf{a}^\wedge)$$

$$= \underbrace{\mathbf{1}}_{\mathbf{a}\mathbf{a}^T - \mathbf{a}^\wedge\mathbf{a}^\wedge} + \phi\,\mathbf{a}^\wedge + \frac{1}{2!}\phi^2\mathbf{a}^\wedge\mathbf{a}^\wedge + \frac{1}{3!}\phi^3\underbrace{\mathbf{a}^\wedge\mathbf{a}^\wedge\mathbf{a}^\wedge}_{-\mathbf{a}^\wedge}$$

$$+ \frac{1}{4!}\phi^4\underbrace{\mathbf{a}^\wedge\mathbf{a}^\wedge\mathbf{a}^\wedge\mathbf{a}^\wedge}_{-\mathbf{a}^\wedge\mathbf{a}^\wedge} - \cdots$$

$$= \mathbf{a}\mathbf{a}^T + \underbrace{\left(\phi - \frac{1}{3!}\phi^3 + \frac{1}{5!}\phi^5 - \cdots\right)}_{\sin\phi}\mathbf{a}^\wedge$$

$$- \underbrace{\left(1 - \frac{1}{2!}\phi^2 + \frac{1}{4!}\phi^4 - \cdots\right)}_{\cos\phi}\underbrace{\mathbf{a}^\wedge\mathbf{a}^\wedge}_{-\mathbf{1}+\mathbf{a}\mathbf{a}^T}$$

$$= \underbrace{\cos\phi\,\mathbf{1} + (1 - \cos\phi)\mathbf{a}\mathbf{a}^T + \sin\phi\,\mathbf{a}^\wedge}_{\mathbf{C}}, \tag{8.23}$$

which we see is the canonical axis-angle form of a rotation matrix presented earlier. We have used the useful identities (for unit-length $\mathbf{a}$),

$$\mathbf{a}^\wedge\mathbf{a}^\wedge \equiv -\mathbf{1} + \mathbf{a}\mathbf{a}^T, \tag{8.24a}$$

$$\mathbf{a}^\wedge\mathbf{a}^\wedge\mathbf{a}^\wedge \equiv -\mathbf{a}^\wedge, \tag{8.24b}$$

---

[8] Solà Ortega et al. (2018) have a nice way of streamlining notation by using capital letters as in $\mathrm{Exp}(\boldsymbol{\phi}) = \exp(\boldsymbol{\phi}^\wedge)$ and $\mathrm{Ln}(\mathbf{C}) = \ln(\mathbf{C})^\vee$; this is clearly convenient but we forgo adoption in the interest of consistency with the first edition.

[9] The many-to-one mapping property is related to the concept of singularities (or nonuniqueness) in rotation parameterizations. We know that every three-parameter representation of a rotation cannot represent orientation both globally and uniquely. Nonuniqueness implies that given a $\mathbf{C}$, we cannot uniquely find a single $\boldsymbol{\phi} \in \mathbb{R}^3$ that generated it; there is an infinite number of them.

the proofs of which are left to the reader. The second of these is also the *minimal polynomial* for $\mathfrak{so}(3)$ (see Appendix B.3.1). This shows that every $\phi \in \mathbb{R}^3$ will generate a valid $\mathbf{C} \in SO(3)$. It also shows that if we add a multiple of 2π to the angle of rotation, we will generate the same $\mathbf{C}$. In detail, we have

$$\mathbf{C} = \exp((\phi + 2\pi m) \, \mathbf{a}^\wedge), \tag{8.25}$$

with m any positive integer, since $\cos(\phi + 2\pi m) = \cos\phi$ and $\sin(\phi + 2\pi m) = \sin\phi$. If we limit the angle of rotation, $|\phi| < \pi$, of the input, then each $\mathbf{C}$ can only be generated by one ϕ.

Additionally, we would like to show that every $\mathbf{C} \in SO(3)$ can be generated by some $\phi \in \mathbb{R}^3$, and for that we need the inverse (logarithmic) mapping: $\phi = \ln(\mathbf{C})^\vee$. We can also work this out in closed form. Since a rotation matrix applied to its own axis does not alter the axis,

$$\mathbf{C}\mathbf{a} = \mathbf{a}, \tag{8.26}$$

this implies that $\mathbf{a}$ is a (unit-length) eigenvector of $\mathbf{C}$ corresponding to an eigenvalue of 1. Thus, by solving the eigenproblem associated with $\mathbf{C}$, we can find $\mathbf{a}$.[10] The angle can be found by exploiting the trace (sum of the diagonal elements) of a rotation matrix:

$$\begin{aligned}
\mathrm{tr}(\mathbf{C}) &= \mathrm{tr}\left(\cos\phi\,\mathbf{1} + (1 - \cos\phi)\mathbf{a}\mathbf{a}^T + \sin\phi\,\mathbf{a}^\wedge\right) \\
&= \cos\phi\,\underbrace{\mathrm{tr}(\mathbf{1})}_{3} + (1 - \cos\phi)\,\underbrace{\mathrm{tr}\left(\mathbf{a}\mathbf{a}^T\right)}_{\mathbf{a}^T\mathbf{a}=1} + \sin\phi\,\underbrace{\mathrm{tr}\left(\mathbf{a}^\wedge\right)}_{0} = 2\cos\phi + 1.
\end{aligned} \tag{8.27}$$

Solving, we have

$$\phi = \cos^{-1}\left(\frac{\mathrm{tr}(\mathbf{C}) - 1}{2}\right) + 2\pi m, \tag{8.28}$$

which indicates there are many solutions for ϕ. By convention, we will pick the one such that $|\phi| < \pi$. To complete the process, we combine $\mathbf{a}$ and ϕ according to $\phi = \phi\mathbf{a}$. It is noteworthy that there is an ambiguity in the sign of ϕ since $\cos\phi$ is an even function; we can test for the correct one by going the other way to see that ϕ produces the correct $\mathbf{C}$ and, if not, reversing the sign of ϕ. This shows that every $\mathbf{C} \in SO(3)$ can be built from at least one $\phi \in \mathbb{R}^3$.

Figure 8.1 provides a simple example of the relationship between the Lie group and Lie algebra for the case of rotation constrained to the plane. We see that in a neighbourhood near the zero-rotation point, $\theta_{vi} = 0$, the Lie algebra vector space is just a line that is tangent to the circle of rotation. We see that, indeed, near zero rotation, the Lie algebra captures the local structure of the Lie group. It should be pointed out that this example is constrained to the plane (i.e., a single rotational degree of freedom), but in general the dimension of the Lie algebra vector space is three. Put another way, the line in the figure is a one-dimensional subspace of the full three-dimensional Lie algebra vector space.

---

[10] There are some subtleties that occur when there is more than one eigenvalue equal to 1. For example, $\mathbf{C} = \mathbf{1}$, whereupon $\mathbf{a}$ is not unique and can be any unit vector.

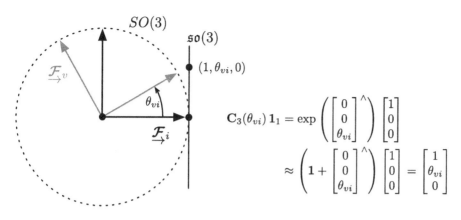

Figure 8.1 Example of the relationship between the Lie group and Lie algebra for the case of rotation constrained to the plane. In a small neighbourhood around the $\theta_{vi} = 0$ point, the vector space associated with the Lie algebra is a line tangent to the circle.

Connecting rotation matrices with the exponential map makes it easy to show that $\det(\mathbf{C}) = 1$ using *Jacobi's formula*, which, for a general square complex matrix, $\mathbf{A}$, says

$$\det\left(\exp\left(\mathbf{A}\right)\right) = \exp\left(\operatorname{tr}(\mathbf{A})\right). \tag{8.29}$$

In the case of rotations, we have

$$\det(\mathbf{C}) = \det\left(\exp\left(\boldsymbol{\phi}^{\wedge}\right)\right) = \exp\left(\operatorname{tr}(\boldsymbol{\phi}^{\wedge})\right) = \exp(0) = 1, \tag{8.30}$$

since $\boldsymbol{\phi}^{\wedge}$ is skew-symmetric and therefore has zeros on its diagonal, making its trace zero.

Poses

For poses, we can relate elements of $SE(3)$ to elements of $\mathfrak{se}(3)$, again through the exponential map:

$$\mathbf{T} = \exp\left(\boldsymbol{\xi}^{\wedge}\right) = \sum_{n=0}^{\infty} \frac{1}{n!}\left(\boldsymbol{\xi}^{\wedge}\right)^{n}, \tag{8.31}$$

where $\mathbf{T} \in SE(3)$ and $\boldsymbol{\xi} \in \mathbb{R}^6$ (and hence $\boldsymbol{\xi}^{\wedge} \in \mathfrak{se}(3)$). We can also go in the other direction,[11] using

$$\boldsymbol{\xi} = \ln\left(\mathbf{T}\right)^{\vee}. \tag{8.32}$$

The exponential map from $\mathfrak{se}(3)$ to $SE(3)$ is also surjective-only: every $\mathbf{T} \in SE(3)$ can be generated by many $\boldsymbol{\xi} \in \mathbb{R}^6$.

To show the surjective-only property of the exponential map, we first examine the forwards direction. Starting with $\boldsymbol{\xi} = \begin{bmatrix} \boldsymbol{\rho} \\ \boldsymbol{\phi} \end{bmatrix} \in \mathbb{R}^6$, we have

---

[11] Again, not uniquely.

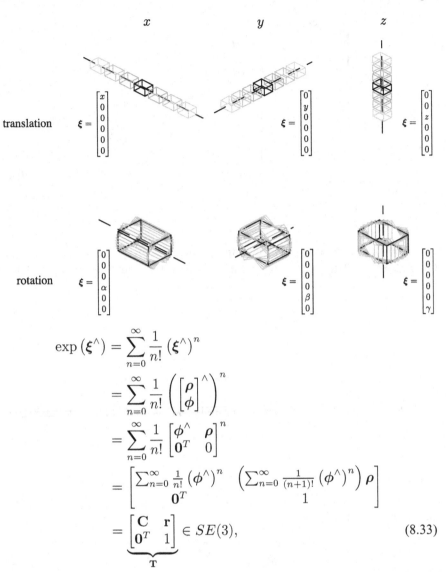

Figure 8.2 By varying each of the components of $\boldsymbol{\xi}$, constructing $\mathbf{T} = \exp(\boldsymbol{\xi}^\wedge)$, and then using this to transform the points composing the corners of a rectangular prism, we see that the prism's pose can be translated and rotated. Combining these basic movements can result in any arbitrary pose change of the prism.

$$\exp(\boldsymbol{\xi}^\wedge) = \sum_{n=0}^{\infty} \frac{1}{n!} (\boldsymbol{\xi}^\wedge)^n$$

$$= \sum_{n=0}^{\infty} \frac{1}{n!} \left(\begin{bmatrix} \boldsymbol{\rho} \\ \boldsymbol{\phi} \end{bmatrix}^\wedge \right)^n$$

$$= \sum_{n=0}^{\infty} \frac{1}{n!} \begin{bmatrix} \boldsymbol{\phi}^\wedge & \boldsymbol{\rho} \\ \mathbf{0}^T & 0 \end{bmatrix}^n$$

$$= \begin{bmatrix} \sum_{n=0}^{\infty} \frac{1}{n!} (\boldsymbol{\phi}^\wedge)^n & \left(\sum_{n=0}^{\infty} \frac{1}{(n+1)!} (\boldsymbol{\phi}^\wedge)^n \right) \boldsymbol{\rho} \\ \mathbf{0}^T & 1 \end{bmatrix}$$

$$= \underbrace{\begin{bmatrix} \mathbf{C} & \mathbf{r} \\ \mathbf{0}^T & 1 \end{bmatrix}}_{\mathbf{T}} \in SE(3), \tag{8.33}$$

where

$$\mathbf{r} = \mathbf{J}\boldsymbol{\rho} \in \mathbb{R}^3, \quad \mathbf{J} = \sum_{n=0}^{\infty} \frac{1}{(n+1)!} (\boldsymbol{\phi}^\wedge)^n. \tag{8.34}$$

This shows that every $\boldsymbol{\xi} \in \mathbb{R}^6$ will generate a valid $\mathbf{T} \in SE(3)$. We will discuss the matrix, $\mathbf{J}$, in greater detail in what follows. Figure 8.2 provides a visualization of how each of the six components of $\boldsymbol{\xi}$ can be varied to alter the pose of a rectangular prism. By combining these basic translations and rotations, an arbitrary pose change can be achieved.

Next we would like to go in the inverse direction. Starting with $\mathbf{T} = \begin{bmatrix} \mathbf{C} & \mathbf{r} \\ \mathbf{0}^T & 1 \end{bmatrix}$, we want to show this can be generated by some $\boldsymbol{\xi} = \begin{bmatrix} \boldsymbol{\rho} \\ \boldsymbol{\phi} \end{bmatrix} \in \mathbb{R}^6$; we need the inverse mapping, $\boldsymbol{\xi} = \ln(\mathbf{T})^\vee$. We have already seen how to go from $\mathbf{C} \in SO(3)$ to $\boldsymbol{\phi} \in \mathbb{R}^3$ in the previous section. Next, we can compute

$$\boldsymbol{\rho} = \mathbf{J}^{-1}\mathbf{r}, \tag{8.35}$$

where $\mathbf{J}$ is built from $\boldsymbol{\phi}$ (already computed). Finally, we assemble $\boldsymbol{\xi} \in \mathbb{R}^6$ from $\boldsymbol{\rho}, \boldsymbol{\phi} \in \mathbb{R}^3$. This shows that every $\mathbf{T} \in SE(3)$ can be generated by at least one $\boldsymbol{\xi} \in \mathbb{R}^6$.

Jacobian

The matrix, $\mathbf{J}$, plays an important role in allowing us to convert the translation component of pose in $\mathfrak{se}(3)$ into the translation component of pose in $SE(3)$ through $\mathbf{r} = \mathbf{J}\boldsymbol{\rho}$. This quantity appears in other situations as well when dealing with our matrix Lie groups, and we will learn later on in this chapter that this is called the (left) *Jacobian* of $SO(3)$. In this section, we will derive some alternate forms of this matrix that are sometimes useful.

We have defined $\mathbf{J}$ as

$$\mathbf{J} = \sum_{n=0}^{\infty} \frac{1}{(n+1)!} \left(\boldsymbol{\phi}^\wedge \right)^n . \tag{8.36}$$

By expanding this series and manipulating, we can show the following closed-form expressions for $\mathbf{J}$ and its inverse:

$$\mathbf{J} = \frac{\sin\phi}{\phi}\mathbf{1} + \left(1 - \frac{\sin\phi}{\phi}\right)\mathbf{aa}^T + \frac{1 - \cos\phi}{\phi}\mathbf{a}^\wedge, \tag{8.37a}$$

$$\mathbf{J}^{-1} = \frac{\phi}{2}\cot\frac{\phi}{2}\mathbf{1} + \left(1 - \frac{\phi}{2}\cot\frac{\phi}{2}\right)\mathbf{aa}^T - \frac{\phi}{2}\mathbf{a}^\wedge, \tag{8.37b}$$

where $\phi = |\boldsymbol{\phi}|$ is the angle of rotation and $\mathbf{a} = \boldsymbol{\phi}/\phi$ is the unit-length axis of rotation. Owing to the nature of the $\cot(\phi/2)$ function, there are singularities associated with $\mathbf{J}$ (i.e., the inverse does not exist) at $\phi = 2\pi m$ with m a non-zero integer.

Occasionally, we will come across the matrix $\mathbf{J}\mathbf{J}^T$ and its inverse. Starting with (8.37a), we can manipulate to show

$$\mathbf{J}\mathbf{J}^T = \gamma\mathbf{1} + (1 - \gamma)\mathbf{aa}^T,$$

$$\left(\mathbf{J}\mathbf{J}^T\right)^{-1} = \frac{1}{\gamma}\mathbf{1} + \left(1 - \frac{1}{\gamma}\right)\mathbf{aa}^T,$$

$$\gamma = 2\frac{1 - \cos\phi}{\phi^2}. \tag{8.38}$$

It turns out that $\mathbf{J}\mathbf{J}^T$ is positive-definite. There are two cases to consider, $\phi = 0$ and $\phi \neq 0$. For $\phi = 0$, we have $\mathbf{J}\mathbf{J}^T = \mathbf{1}$, which is positive-definite. For $\phi \neq 0$, we have for $\mathbf{x} \neq \mathbf{0}$ that

$$\mathbf{x}^T \mathbf{JJ}^T \mathbf{x} = \mathbf{x}^T \left(\gamma \mathbf{1} + (1 - \gamma) \mathbf{aa}^T \right) \mathbf{x} = \mathbf{x}^T \left(\mathbf{aa}^T - \gamma \mathbf{a}^\wedge \mathbf{a}^\wedge \right) \mathbf{x}$$

$$= \mathbf{x}^T \mathbf{aa}^T \mathbf{x} + \gamma (\mathbf{a}^\wedge \mathbf{x})^T (\mathbf{a}^\wedge \mathbf{x})$$

$$= \underbrace{(\mathbf{a}^T \mathbf{x})^T (\mathbf{a}^T \mathbf{x})}_{\geq 0} + \underbrace{2 \frac{1 - \cos \phi}{\phi^2}}_{> 0} \underbrace{(\mathbf{a}^\wedge \mathbf{x})^T (\mathbf{a}^\wedge \mathbf{x})}_{\geq 0} > 0, \qquad (8.39)$$

since the first term is only zero when $\mathbf{a}$ and $\mathbf{x}$ are perpendicular and the second term is only zero when $\mathbf{x}$ and $\mathbf{a}$ are parallel (these cannot happen at the same time). This shows that $\mathbf{JJ}^T$ is positive-definite.

It turns out that we can also write $\mathbf{J}$ in terms of the rotation matrix, $\mathbf{C}$, associated with ϕ in the following way:

$$\mathbf{J} = \int_0^1 \mathbf{C}^\alpha \, d\alpha. \qquad (8.40)$$

This can be seen through the following sequence of manipulations:

$$\int_0^1 \mathbf{C}^\alpha \, d\alpha = \int_0^1 \exp\left(\phi^\wedge\right)^\alpha \, d\alpha = \int_0^1 \exp\left(\alpha \, \phi^\wedge\right) \, d\alpha$$

$$= \int_0^1 \left(\sum_{n=0}^\infty \frac{1}{n!} \alpha^n \left(\phi^\wedge\right)^n \right) d\alpha = \sum_{n=0}^\infty \frac{1}{n!} \left(\int_0^1 \alpha^n \, d\alpha \right) \left(\phi^\wedge\right)^n$$

$$= \sum_{n=0}^\infty \frac{1}{n!} \left(\frac{1}{n+1} \alpha^{n+1} \Big|_{\alpha=0}^{\alpha=1} \right) \left(\phi^\wedge\right)^n = \sum_{n=0}^\infty \frac{1}{(n+1)!} \left(\phi^\wedge\right)^n, \quad (8.41)$$

which is the original series form of $\mathbf{J}$ defined above.

Finally, we can also relate $\mathbf{J}$ and $\mathbf{C}$ through

$$\mathbf{C} = \mathbf{1} + \phi^\wedge \mathbf{J}, \qquad (8.42)$$

but it is not possible to solve for $\mathbf{J}$ in this expression since $\phi^\wedge$ is not invertible.

Direct Series Expression

We can also develop a direct series expression for $\mathbf{T}$ from the exponential map by using the *minimal polynomial* for $\mathfrak{se}(3)$ (see Appendix B.3.2),

$$\left(\xi^\wedge\right)^4 + \phi^2 \left(\xi^\wedge\right)^2 = \mathbf{0}, \qquad (8.43)$$

where $\xi = \begin{bmatrix} \rho \\ \phi \end{bmatrix}$ and $\phi = |\phi|$. Expanding the series and using the minimal polynomial to rewrite all terms quartic and higher in terms of lower-order terms, we have

$$\mathbf{T} = \exp\left(\boldsymbol{\xi}^{\wedge}\right)$$

$$= \sum_{n=0}^{\infty} \frac{1}{n!}\left(\boldsymbol{\xi}^{\wedge}\right)^n$$

$$= 1 + \boldsymbol{\xi}^{\wedge} + \frac{1}{2!}(\boldsymbol{\xi}^{\wedge})^2 + \frac{1}{3!}(\boldsymbol{\xi}^{\wedge})^3 + \frac{1}{4!}(\boldsymbol{\xi}^{\wedge})^4 + \frac{1}{5!}(\boldsymbol{\xi}^{\wedge})^5 + \cdots$$

$$= 1 + \boldsymbol{\xi}^{\wedge} + \underbrace{\left(\frac{1}{2!} - \frac{1}{4!}\phi^2 + \frac{1}{6!}\phi^4 - \frac{1}{8!}\phi^6 + \cdots\right)}_{\frac{1-\cos\phi}{\phi^2}}(\boldsymbol{\xi}^{\wedge})^2$$

$$+ \underbrace{\left(\frac{1}{3!} - \frac{1}{5!}\phi^2 + \frac{1}{7!}\phi^4 - \frac{1}{9!}\phi^6 + \cdots\right)}_{\frac{\phi-\sin\phi}{\phi^3}}(\boldsymbol{\xi}^{\wedge})^3$$

$$= 1 + \boldsymbol{\xi}^{\wedge} + \left(\frac{1-\cos\phi}{\phi^2}\right)(\boldsymbol{\xi}^{\wedge})^2 + \left(\frac{\phi-\sin\phi}{\phi^3}\right)(\boldsymbol{\xi}^{\wedge})^3. \qquad (8.44)$$

Calculating $\mathbf{T}$ using this approach avoids the need to deal with its constituent blocks.

8.1.4 Adjoints

The *adjoint* of a Lie group is a way of describing the elements of that group as linear transformations of its Lie algebra, which we recall is a vector space. For $SO(3)$, the adjoint representation is the same as the group itself, so we omit the details. For $SE(3)$, the adjoint differs from the group's primary representation and so we use this section to provide some details. The adjoint will prove to be an essential tool when setting up state estimation problems, particularly for $SE(3)$.

The *adjoint map* of $SE(3)$ transforms an element $\mathbf{x}^{\wedge} \in \mathfrak{se}(3)$ to another element of $\mathfrak{se}(3)$ according to a map known as the *inner automorphism* or *conjugation*:

$$\mathrm{Ad}_{\mathbf{T}}\mathbf{x}^{\wedge} = \mathbf{T}\mathbf{x}^{\wedge}\mathbf{T}^{-1}. \qquad (8.45)$$

We can equivalently express the output of this map as

$$\mathrm{Ad}_{\mathbf{T}}\mathbf{x}^{\wedge} = (\boldsymbol{\mathcal{T}}\mathbf{x})^{\wedge}, \qquad (8.46)$$

where $\boldsymbol{\mathcal{T}}$ linearly transforms $\mathbf{x} \in \mathbb{R}^6$ to $\mathbb{R}^6$. We will refer to $\boldsymbol{\mathcal{T}}$ as the *adjoint representation* of $SE(3)$.

The 6×6 transformation matrix, $\boldsymbol{\mathcal{T}}$, can be constructed directly from the components of the 4×4 transformation matrix:

$$\boldsymbol{\mathcal{T}} = \mathrm{Ad}(\mathbf{T}) = \mathrm{Ad}\left(\begin{bmatrix} \mathbf{C} & \mathbf{r} \\ \mathbf{0}^T & 1 \end{bmatrix}\right) = \begin{bmatrix} \mathbf{C} & \mathbf{r}^{\wedge}\mathbf{C} \\ \mathbf{0} & \mathbf{C} \end{bmatrix}. \qquad (8.47)$$

We will abuse notation a bit and say that the set of adjoints of all the elements of $SE(3)$ is denoted

$$\mathrm{Ad}(SE(3)) = \{\boldsymbol{\mathcal{T}} = \mathrm{Ad}(\mathbf{T}) \mid \mathbf{T} \in SE(3)\}. \qquad (8.48)$$

It turns out that $\mathrm{Ad}(SE(3))$ is also a matrix Lie group, which we show next.

Lie Group

For closure we let $\boldsymbol{\mathcal{T}}_1 = \mathrm{Ad}(\mathbf{T}_1), \boldsymbol{\mathcal{T}}_2 = \mathrm{Ad}(\mathbf{T}_2) \in \mathrm{Ad}(SE(3))$, and then

$$
\boldsymbol{\mathcal{T}}_1 \boldsymbol{\mathcal{T}}_2 = \mathrm{Ad}(\mathbf{T}_1)\mathrm{Ad}(\mathbf{T}_2) = \mathrm{Ad}\left(\begin{bmatrix} \mathbf{C}_1 & \mathbf{r}_1 \\ \mathbf{0}^T & 1 \end{bmatrix}\right) \mathrm{Ad}\left(\begin{bmatrix} \mathbf{C}_2 & \mathbf{r}_2 \\ \mathbf{0}^T & 1 \end{bmatrix}\right)
$$

$$
= \begin{bmatrix} \mathbf{C}_1 & \mathbf{r}_1^\wedge \mathbf{C}_1 \\ \mathbf{0} & \mathbf{C}_1 \end{bmatrix} \begin{bmatrix} \mathbf{C}_2 & \mathbf{r}_2^\wedge \mathbf{C}_2 \\ \mathbf{0} & \mathbf{C}_2 \end{bmatrix}
$$

$$
= \begin{bmatrix} \mathbf{C}_1 \mathbf{C}_2 & \mathbf{C}_1 \mathbf{r}_2^\wedge \mathbf{C}_2 + \mathbf{r}_1^\wedge \mathbf{C}_1 \mathbf{C}_2 \\ \mathbf{0} & \mathbf{C}_1 \mathbf{C}_2 \end{bmatrix}
$$

$$
= \begin{bmatrix} \mathbf{C}_1 \mathbf{C}_2 & (\mathbf{C}_1 \mathbf{r}_2 + \mathbf{r}_1)^\wedge \mathbf{C}_1 \mathbf{C}_2 \\ \mathbf{0} & \mathbf{C}_1 \mathbf{C}_2 \end{bmatrix}
$$

$$
= \mathrm{Ad}\left(\begin{bmatrix} \mathbf{C}_1 \mathbf{C}_2 & \mathbf{C}_1 \mathbf{r}_2 + \mathbf{r}_1 \\ \mathbf{0}^T & 1 \end{bmatrix}\right) \in \mathrm{Ad}(SE(3)), \tag{8.49}
$$

where we have used the nice property that

$$
\mathbf{C}\mathbf{v}^\wedge \mathbf{C}^T = (\mathbf{C}\mathbf{v})^\wedge, \tag{8.50}
$$

for any $\mathbf{C} \in SO(3)$ and $\mathbf{v} \in \mathbb{R}^3$. Associativity follows from basic properties of matrix multiplication, and the identity element of the group is the 6×6 identity matrix. For invertibility, we let $\boldsymbol{\mathcal{T}} = \mathrm{Ad}(\mathbf{T}) \in \mathrm{Ad}(SE(3))$, and then we have

$$
\boldsymbol{\mathcal{T}}^{-1} = \mathrm{Ad}(\mathbf{T})^{-1} = \mathrm{Ad}\left(\begin{bmatrix} \mathbf{C} & \mathbf{r} \\ \mathbf{0}^T & 1 \end{bmatrix}\right)^{-1} = \begin{bmatrix} \mathbf{C} & \mathbf{r}^\wedge \mathbf{C} \\ \mathbf{0} & \mathbf{C} \end{bmatrix}^{-1}
$$

$$
= \begin{bmatrix} \mathbf{C}^T & -\mathbf{C}^T \mathbf{r}^\wedge \\ \mathbf{0} & \mathbf{C}^T \end{bmatrix} = \begin{bmatrix} \mathbf{C}^T & (-\mathbf{C}^T \mathbf{r})^\wedge \mathbf{C}^T \\ \mathbf{0} & \mathbf{C}^T \end{bmatrix}
$$

$$
= \mathrm{Ad}\left(\begin{bmatrix} \mathbf{C}^T & -\mathbf{C}^T \mathbf{r} \\ \mathbf{0}^T & 1 \end{bmatrix}\right) = \mathrm{Ad}\left(\mathbf{T}^{-1}\right) \in \mathrm{Ad}(SE(3)). \tag{8.51}
$$

Other than smoothness, these four properties show that $\mathrm{Ad}(SE(3))$ is a matrix Lie group.

Lie Algebra

We can also talk about the *adjoint* of an element of $\mathfrak{se}(3)$. The *adjoint map* of $\mathfrak{se}(3)$ transforms an element $\mathbf{x}^\wedge \in \mathfrak{se}(3)$ to $\mathfrak{se}(3)$ according to

$$
\mathrm{ad}_{\boldsymbol{\xi}^\wedge} \mathbf{x}^\wedge = \boldsymbol{\xi}^\wedge \mathbf{x}^\wedge - \mathbf{x}^\wedge \boldsymbol{\xi}^\wedge = [\boldsymbol{\xi}^\wedge, \mathbf{x}^\wedge], \tag{8.52}
$$

which we recognize as the Lie bracket.

As an aside, there is a deep connection between the two maps, $\mathrm{Ad}_{\mathbf{T}}\mathbf{x}^\wedge$ and $\mathrm{ad}_{\boldsymbol{\xi}^\wedge}\mathbf{x}^\wedge$. The Lie algebra adjoint map is essentially the (Lie) derivative of the Lie group adjoint map, evaluated at the identity element of the group. In particular, it can be shown that

$$\frac{d}{dt}\mathrm{Ad}_{\exp(t\boldsymbol{\xi}^\wedge)}\mathbf{x}^\wedge\bigg|_{t=0} = \frac{d}{dt}\exp(t\boldsymbol{\xi}^\wedge)\mathbf{x}^\wedge\exp(-t\boldsymbol{\xi}^\wedge)\bigg|_{t=0} = \mathrm{ad}_{\boldsymbol{\xi}^\wedge}\mathbf{x}^\wedge, \quad (8.53)$$

where we must take care to properly differentiate the exponential map.

We can equivalently express the output of the adjoint map of $\mathfrak{se}(3)$ as

$$\mathrm{ad}_{\boldsymbol{\xi}^\wedge}\mathbf{x}^\wedge = \left(\boldsymbol{\xi}^\curlywedge\mathbf{x}\right)^\wedge, \quad (8.54)$$

where $\boldsymbol{\xi}^\curlywedge$ transforms $\mathbf{x} \in \mathbb{R}^6$ to $\mathbb{R}^6$. We will refer to $\boldsymbol{\xi}^\curlywedge$ as the *adjoint representation* of $\mathfrak{se}(3)$.

Let $\boldsymbol{\Xi} = \boldsymbol{\xi}^\wedge \in \mathfrak{se}(3)$; then the adjoint representation of this element is

$$\mathrm{ad}(\boldsymbol{\Xi}) = \mathrm{ad}\left(\boldsymbol{\xi}^\wedge\right) = \boldsymbol{\xi}^\curlywedge, \quad (8.55)$$

where

$$\boldsymbol{\xi}^\curlywedge = \begin{bmatrix}\boldsymbol{\rho}\\\boldsymbol{\phi}\end{bmatrix}^\curlywedge = \begin{bmatrix}\boldsymbol{\phi}^\wedge & \boldsymbol{\rho}^\wedge\\\mathbf{0} & \boldsymbol{\phi}^\wedge\end{bmatrix} \in \mathbb{R}^{6\times 6}, \quad \boldsymbol{\rho}, \boldsymbol{\phi} \in \mathbb{R}^3. \quad (8.56)$$

Note that we have used uppercase, $\mathrm{Ad}(\cdot)$, for the adjoint of $SE(3)$ and lowercase, $\mathrm{ad}(\cdot)$, for the adjoint of $\mathfrak{se}(3)$.

The Lie algebra associated with $\mathrm{Ad}(SE(3))$ is given by

$$
\begin{aligned}
\text{vector space:}\quad & \mathrm{ad}(\mathfrak{se}(3)) = \{\boldsymbol{\Psi} = \mathrm{ad}(\boldsymbol{\Xi}) \in \mathbb{R}^{6\times 6} \mid \boldsymbol{\Xi} \in \mathfrak{se}(3)\},\\
\text{field:}\quad & \mathbb{R},\\
\text{Lie bracket:}\quad & [\boldsymbol{\Psi}_1, \boldsymbol{\Psi}_2] = \boldsymbol{\Psi}_1\boldsymbol{\Psi}_2 - \boldsymbol{\Psi}_2\boldsymbol{\Psi}_1.
\end{aligned}
$$

Again, we will omit showing that $\mathrm{ad}(\mathfrak{se}(3))$ is a vector space, but will briefly show that the four Lie bracket properties hold. Let $\boldsymbol{\Psi}, \boldsymbol{\Psi}_1 = \boldsymbol{\xi}_1^\curlywedge, \boldsymbol{\Psi}_2 = \boldsymbol{\xi}_2^\curlywedge \in \mathrm{ad}(\mathfrak{se}(3))$. Then, for the closure property, we have

$$[\boldsymbol{\Psi}_1, \boldsymbol{\Psi}_2] = \boldsymbol{\Psi}_1\boldsymbol{\Psi}_2 - \boldsymbol{\Psi}_2\boldsymbol{\Psi}_1 = \boldsymbol{\xi}_1^\curlywedge\boldsymbol{\xi}_2^\curlywedge - \boldsymbol{\xi}_2^\curlywedge\boldsymbol{\xi}_1^\curlywedge = \left(\underbrace{\boldsymbol{\xi}_1^\curlywedge\boldsymbol{\xi}_2}_{\in\mathbb{R}^6}\right)^\curlywedge \in \mathrm{ad}(\mathfrak{se}(3)).$$

$$(8.57)$$

Bilinearity follows directly from the fact that $(\cdot)^\curlywedge$ is a linear operator. The alternating property can be seen easily through

$$[\boldsymbol{\Psi}, \boldsymbol{\Psi}] = \boldsymbol{\Psi}\boldsymbol{\Psi} - \boldsymbol{\Psi}\boldsymbol{\Psi} = \mathbf{0} \in \mathrm{ad}(\mathfrak{se}(3)). \quad (8.58)$$

Finally, the Jacobi identity can be verified by substituting and applying the definition of the Lie bracket. Again, we will refer to $\mathrm{ad}(\mathfrak{se}(3))$ as the Lie algebra, although technically this is only the associated vector space.

Exponential Map

Another issue to discuss is the relationship between $\mathrm{Ad}(SE(3))$ and $\mathrm{ad}(\mathfrak{se}(3))$ through the exponential map. Not surprisingly, we have that

$$\mathcal{T} = \exp\left(\boldsymbol{\xi}^{\curlywedge}\right) = \sum_{n=0}^{\infty} \frac{1}{n!}\left(\boldsymbol{\xi}^{\curlywedge}\right)^n, \tag{8.59}$$

where $\mathcal{T} \in \mathrm{Ad}(SE(3))$ and $\boldsymbol{\xi} \in \mathbb{R}^6$ (and hence $\boldsymbol{\xi}^{\curlywedge} \in \mathrm{ad}(\mathfrak{se}(3))$). We can go in the other direction, using

$$\boldsymbol{\xi} = \ln\left(\mathcal{T}\right)^{\curlyvee}, \tag{8.60}$$

where $\curlyvee$ undoes the $\curlywedge$ operation. The exponential mapping is again surjective-only, which we discuss in what follows.

First, however, we note that here is a nice commutative relationship between the various Lie groups and algebras associated with poses:

$$
\begin{array}{ccc}
& \text{Lie algebra} & \text{Lie group} \\[4pt]
4 \times 4 & \boldsymbol{\xi}^{\wedge} \in \mathfrak{se}(3) \xrightarrow{\ \exp\ } & \mathbf{T} \in SE(3) \\[2pt]
& \Big\downarrow \mathrm{ad} & \Big\downarrow \mathrm{Ad} \\[2pt]
6 \times 6 & \boldsymbol{\xi}^{\curlywedge} \in \mathrm{ad}(\mathfrak{se}(3)) \xrightarrow{\ \exp\ } & \mathcal{T} \in \mathrm{Ad}(SE(3))
\end{array}
\tag{8.61}
$$

We could draw on this commutative relationship to claim the surjective-only property of the exponential map from $\mathrm{ad}(\mathfrak{se}(3))$ to $\mathrm{Ad}(SE(3))$ by going the long way around the loop, since we have already shown that this path exists. However, it is also possible to show it directly, which amounts to showing that

$$\underbrace{\mathrm{Ad}\left(\exp\left(\boldsymbol{\xi}^{\wedge}\right)\right)}_{\mathcal{T}} = \exp\Big(\underbrace{\mathrm{ad}\left(\boldsymbol{\xi}^{\wedge}\right)}_{\boldsymbol{\xi}^{\curlywedge}}\Big), \tag{8.62}$$

since this implies that we can go from $\boldsymbol{\xi} \in \mathbb{R}^6$ to $\mathcal{T} \in \mathrm{Ad}(SE(3))$ and back.

To see this, let $\boldsymbol{\xi} = \begin{bmatrix} \boldsymbol{\rho} \\ \boldsymbol{\phi} \end{bmatrix}$, and then starting from the right-hand side, we have

$$\exp\left(\mathrm{ad}\left(\boldsymbol{\xi}^{\wedge}\right)\right) = \exp\left(\boldsymbol{\xi}^{\curlywedge}\right) = \sum_{n=0}^{\infty} \frac{1}{n!}\left(\boldsymbol{\xi}^{\curlywedge}\right)^n$$

$$= \sum_{n=0}^{\infty} \frac{1}{n!} \begin{bmatrix} \boldsymbol{\phi}^{\wedge} & \boldsymbol{\rho}^{\wedge} \\ \mathbf{0} & \boldsymbol{\phi}^{\wedge} \end{bmatrix}^n = \begin{bmatrix} \mathbf{C} & \mathbf{K} \\ \mathbf{0} & \mathbf{C} \end{bmatrix}, \tag{8.63}$$

where $\mathbf{C}$ is the usual expression for the rotation matrix in terms of $\boldsymbol{\phi}$ and

$$\mathbf{K} = \sum_{n=0}^{\infty} \sum_{m=0}^{\infty} \frac{1}{(n+m+1)!} \left(\boldsymbol{\phi}^\wedge\right)^n \boldsymbol{\rho}^\wedge \left(\boldsymbol{\phi}^\wedge\right)^m,$$

which can be found through careful manipulation. Starting from the left-hand side, we have

$$\mathrm{Ad}\left(\exp\left(\boldsymbol{\xi}^\wedge\right)\right) = \mathrm{Ad}\left(\begin{bmatrix} \mathbf{C} & \mathbf{J}\boldsymbol{\rho} \\ \mathbf{0}^T & 1 \end{bmatrix}\right) = \begin{bmatrix} \mathbf{C} & (\mathbf{J}\boldsymbol{\rho})^\wedge \mathbf{C} \\ \mathbf{0} & \mathbf{C} \end{bmatrix}, \qquad (8.64)$$

where $\mathbf{J}$ is given in (8.36). Comparing (8.63) and (8.64), what remains to be shown is the equivalence of the top-right block: $\mathbf{K} = (\mathbf{J}\boldsymbol{\rho})^\wedge \mathbf{C}$. To see this, we use the following sequence of manipulations:

$$\begin{aligned}
(\mathbf{J}\boldsymbol{\rho})^\wedge \mathbf{C} &= \left(\int_0^1 \mathbf{C}^\alpha \, d\alpha \, \boldsymbol{\rho}\right)^\wedge \mathbf{C} = \int_0^1 (\mathbf{C}^\alpha \boldsymbol{\rho})^\wedge \mathbf{C} \, d\alpha \\
&= \int_0^1 \mathbf{C}^\alpha \boldsymbol{\rho}^\wedge \mathbf{C}^{1-\alpha} \, d\alpha = \int_0^1 \exp\left(\alpha\boldsymbol{\phi}^\wedge\right) \boldsymbol{\rho}^\wedge \exp\left((1-\alpha)\boldsymbol{\phi}^\wedge\right) \, d\alpha \\
&= \int_0^1 \left(\sum_{n=0}^{\infty} \frac{1}{n!}(\alpha\boldsymbol{\phi}^\wedge)^n\right) \boldsymbol{\rho}^\wedge \left(\sum_{m=0}^{\infty} \frac{1}{m!}((1-\alpha)\boldsymbol{\phi}^\wedge)^m\right) \, d\alpha \\
&= \sum_{n=0}^{\infty} \sum_{m=0}^{\infty} \frac{1}{n!\,m!} \left(\int_0^1 \alpha^n (1-\alpha)^m \, d\alpha\right) \left(\boldsymbol{\phi}^\wedge\right)^n \boldsymbol{\rho}^\wedge \left(\boldsymbol{\phi}^\wedge\right)^m, \quad (8.65)
\end{aligned}$$

where we have used that $\wedge$ is linear and that $(\mathbf{C}\mathbf{v})^\wedge = \mathbf{C}\mathbf{v}^\wedge \mathbf{C}^T$. After several integrations by parts we can show that

$$\int_0^1 \alpha^n (1-\alpha)^m \, d\alpha = \frac{n!\,m!}{(n+m+1)!}, \qquad (8.66)$$

and therefore, $\mathbf{K} = (\mathbf{J}\boldsymbol{\rho})^\wedge \mathbf{C}$, which is the desired result.

Direct Series Expression

Similarly to the direct series expression for $\mathbf{T}$, we can also work one out for $\mathcal{T} = \mathrm{Ad}(\mathbf{T})$ by using the *minimal polynomial* for $\mathrm{ad}(\mathfrak{se}(3))$ (see Appendix B.3.3),

$$\left(\boldsymbol{\xi}^\curlywedge\right)^5 + 2\phi^2 \left(\boldsymbol{\xi}^\curlywedge\right)^3 + \phi^4 \boldsymbol{\xi}^\curlywedge = \mathbf{0}, \qquad (8.67)$$

where $\boldsymbol{\xi} = \begin{bmatrix} \boldsymbol{\rho} \\ \boldsymbol{\phi} \end{bmatrix}$ and $\phi = |\boldsymbol{\phi}|$. Expanding the series and using the minimal polynomial to rewrite all terms quintic and higher in lower-order terms, we have

$$\mathcal{T} = \exp\left(\boldsymbol{\xi}^{\wedge}\right)$$

$$= \sum_{n=0}^{\infty} \frac{1}{n!}\left(\boldsymbol{\xi}^{\wedge}\right)^n$$

$$= \mathbf{1} + \boldsymbol{\xi}^{\wedge} + \frac{1}{2!}(\boldsymbol{\xi}^{\wedge})^2 + \frac{1}{3!}(\boldsymbol{\xi}^{\wedge})^3 + \frac{1}{4!}(\boldsymbol{\xi}^{\wedge})^4 + \frac{1}{5!}(\boldsymbol{\xi}^{\wedge})^5 + \cdots$$

$$= \mathbf{1} + \underbrace{\left(1 - \frac{1}{5!}\phi^4 + \frac{2}{7!}\phi^6 - \frac{3}{9!}\phi^8 + \frac{4}{11!}\phi^{10} - \cdots\right)}_{\frac{3\sin\phi - \phi\cos\phi}{2\phi}} \boldsymbol{\xi}^{\wedge}$$

$$+ \underbrace{\left(\frac{1}{2!} - \frac{1}{6!}\phi^4 + \frac{2}{8!}\phi^6 - \frac{3}{10!}\phi^8 + \frac{4}{12!}\phi^{10} - \cdots\right)}_{\frac{4 - \phi\sin\phi - 4\cos\phi}{2\phi^2}} (\boldsymbol{\xi}^{\wedge})^2$$

$$+ \underbrace{\left(\frac{1}{3!} - \frac{2}{5!}\phi^2 + \frac{3}{7!}\phi^4 - \frac{4}{9!}\phi^6 + \frac{5}{11!}\phi^8 - \cdots\right)}_{\frac{\sin\phi - \phi\cos\phi}{2\phi^3}} (\boldsymbol{\xi}^{\wedge})^3$$

$$+ \underbrace{\left(\frac{1}{4!} - \frac{2}{6!}\phi^2 + \frac{3}{8!}\phi^4 - \frac{4}{10!}\phi^6 + \frac{5}{12!}\phi^8 - \cdots\right)}_{\frac{2 - \phi\sin\phi - 2\cos\phi}{2\phi^4}} (\boldsymbol{\xi}^{\wedge})^4$$

$$= \mathbf{1} + \left(\frac{3\sin\phi - \phi\cos\phi}{2\phi}\right)\boldsymbol{\xi}^{\wedge} + \left(\frac{4 - \phi\sin\phi - 4\cos\phi}{2\phi^2}\right)(\boldsymbol{\xi}^{\wedge})^2$$

$$+ \left(\frac{\sin\phi - \phi\cos\phi}{2\phi^3}\right)(\boldsymbol{\xi}^{\wedge})^3 + \left(\frac{2 - \phi\sin\phi - 2\cos\phi}{2\phi^4}\right)(\boldsymbol{\xi}^{\wedge})^4.$$

$$(8.68)$$

As in the 4×4 case, this last expression allows us to evaluate $\mathcal{T}$ without working with its constituent blocks.

8.1.5 Baker–Campbell–Hausdorff

We can combine two scalar exponential functions as follows:

$$\exp(a)\exp(b) = \exp(a + b), \tag{8.69}$$

where $a, b \in \mathbb{R}$. Unfortunately, this is not so easy for the matrix case. To compound two matrix exponentials, we use the *Baker–Campbell–Hausdorff (BCH)* formula:

$$\ln\left(\exp(\mathbf{A})\exp(\mathbf{B})\right)$$
$$= \sum_{n=1}^{\infty} \frac{(-1)^{n-1}}{n} \sum_{\substack{r_i + s_i > 0, \\ 1 \le i \le n}} \frac{\left(\sum_{i=1}^{n}(r_i + s_i)\right)^{-1}}{\prod_{i=1}^{n} r_i! s_i!} \left[\mathbf{A}^{r_1}\mathbf{B}^{s_1}\mathbf{A}^{r_2}\mathbf{B}^{s_2}\cdots\mathbf{A}^{r_n}\mathbf{B}^{s_n}\right],$$

$$(8.70)$$

Henry Frederick Baker (1866–1956) was a British mathematician, working mainly in algebraic geometry, but also remembered for contributions to partial differential equations and Lie groups. John Edward Campbell (1862–1924) was a British mathematician, best known for his contribution to the BCH formula and a 1903 book popularizing the ideas of Sophus Lie. Felix Hausdorff (1868–1942) was a German mathematician who is considered to be one of the founders of modern topology and who contributed significantly to set theory, descriptive set theory, measure theory, function theory, and functional analysis. Henri Poincaré (1854–1912) is also said to have had a hand in the BCH formula.

where

$$[\mathbf{A}^{r_1}\mathbf{B}^{s_1}\mathbf{A}^{r_2}\mathbf{B}^{s_2}\cdots\mathbf{A}^{r_n}\mathbf{B}^{s_n}]$$
$$= [\underbrace{\mathbf{A},\ldots[\mathbf{A}}_{r_1},\underbrace{[\mathbf{B},\ldots,[\mathbf{B}}_{s_1},\cdots\underbrace{[\mathbf{A},\ldots[\mathbf{A}}_{r_n},\underbrace{[\mathbf{B},\ldots[\mathbf{B},\mathbf{B}}_{s_n}\ldots]]\cdots]\cdots]\cdots]]\cdots],$$

(8.71)

which is zero if $s_n > 1$ or if $s_n = 0$ and $r_n > 1$. The Lie bracket is the usual

$$[\mathbf{A},\mathbf{B}] = \mathbf{A}\mathbf{B} - \mathbf{B}\mathbf{A}. \qquad (8.72)$$

Note that the BCH formula is an infinite series. In the event that $[\mathbf{A},\mathbf{B}] = \mathbf{0}$, the BCH formula simplifies to

$$\ln\left(\exp(\mathbf{A})\exp(\mathbf{B})\right) = \mathbf{A} + \mathbf{B}, \qquad (8.73)$$

but this case is not particularly useful to us, except as an approximation. The first several terms of the general BCH formula are

$$\ln\left(\exp(\mathbf{A})\exp(\mathbf{B})\right) = \mathbf{A} + \mathbf{B} + \frac{1}{2}\left[\mathbf{A},\mathbf{B}\right]$$
$$+ \frac{1}{12}\left[\mathbf{A},\left[\mathbf{A},\mathbf{B}\right]\right] - \frac{1}{12}\left[\mathbf{B},\left[\mathbf{A},\mathbf{B}\right]\right] - \frac{1}{24}\left[\mathbf{B},\left[\mathbf{A},\left[\mathbf{A},\mathbf{B}\right]\right]\right]$$
$$- \frac{1}{720}\left(\left[\left[\left[\left[\mathbf{A},\mathbf{B}\right],\mathbf{B}\right],\mathbf{B}\right],\mathbf{B}\right] + \left[\left[\left[\left[\mathbf{B},\mathbf{A}\right],\mathbf{A}\right],\mathbf{A}\right],\mathbf{A}\right]\right)$$
$$+ \frac{1}{360}\left(\left[\left[\left[\left[\mathbf{A},\mathbf{B}\right],\mathbf{B}\right],\mathbf{B}\right],\mathbf{A}\right] + \left[\left[\left[\left[\mathbf{B},\mathbf{A}\right],\mathbf{A}\right],\mathbf{A}\right],\mathbf{B}\right]\right)$$
$$+ \frac{1}{120}\left(\left[\left[\left[\left[\mathbf{A},\mathbf{B}\right],\mathbf{A}\right],\mathbf{B}\right],\mathbf{A}\right] + \left[\left[\left[\left[\mathbf{B},\mathbf{A}\right],\mathbf{B}\right],\mathbf{A}\right],\mathbf{B}\right]\right) + \cdots. \quad (8.74)$$

If we keep only terms linear in $\mathbf{A}$, the general BCH formula becomes (Klarsfeld and Oteo, 1989)

$$\ln\left(\exp(\mathbf{A})\exp(\mathbf{B})\right) \approx \mathbf{B} + \sum_{n=0}^{\infty}\frac{B_n}{n!}\underbrace{[\mathbf{B},[\mathbf{B},\ldots[\mathbf{B},\mathbf{A}]\ldots]]}_{n}. \qquad (8.75)$$

If we keep only terms linear in $\mathbf{B}$, the general BCH formula becomes

$$\ln\left(\exp(\mathbf{A})\exp(\mathbf{B})\right) \approx \mathbf{A} + \sum_{n=0}^{\infty}(-1)^n\frac{B_n}{n!}\underbrace{[\mathbf{A},[\mathbf{A},\ldots[\mathbf{A},\mathbf{B}]\ldots]]}_{n}. \qquad (8.76)$$

The B_n are the *Bernoulli numbers*,[12]

$$B_0 = 1, B_1 = -\frac{1}{2}, B_2 = \frac{1}{6}, B_3 = 0, B_4 = -\frac{1}{30}, B_5 = 0, B_6 = \frac{1}{42},$$
$$B_7 = 0, B_8 = -\frac{1}{30}, B_9 = 0, B_{10} = \frac{5}{66}, B_{11} = 0, B_{12} = -\frac{691}{2730},$$
$$B_{13} = 0, B_{14} = \frac{7}{6}, B_{15} = 0, \ldots, \quad (8.77)$$

[12] Technically, the sequence shown is the *first* Bernoulli sequence. There is also a *second* sequence in which $B_1 = \frac{1}{2}$, but we will not need it here.

The Bernoulli numbers were discovered around the same time by the Swiss mathematician Jakob Bernoulli (1655–1705), after whom they are named, and independently by Japanese mathematician Seki Kōwa (1642–1708). Seki's discovery was posthumously published in 1712 in his work *Katsuyo Sampo*; Bernoulli's, also posthumously, in his *Ars Conjectandi (The Art of Conjecture)* of 1713. Ada Lovelace's *Note G* on the analytical engine from 1842 describes an algorithm for generating Bernoulli numbers with Babbage's machine. As a result, the Bernoulli numbers have the distinction of being the subject of the first computer program.

which appear frequently in number theory (Larson, 2019). It is also worth noting that $B_n = 0$ for all odd $n > 1$, which reduces the number of terms that need to be implemented in approximations of some of our infinite series.

The *Lie product formula*,

$$\exp\left(\mathbf{A} + \mathbf{B}\right) = \lim_{\alpha \to \infty} \left(\exp\left(\mathbf{A}/\alpha\right) \exp\left(\mathbf{B}/\alpha\right)\right)^{\alpha}, \qquad (8.78)$$

provides another way of looking at compounding matrix exponentials; compounding is effectively slicing each matrix exponential into an infinite number of infinitely thin slices and then interleaving the slices. We next discuss application of the general BCH formula to the specific cases of rotations and poses.

Rotations

In the particular case of $SO(3)$, we can show that

$$\ln\left(\mathbf{C}_1 \mathbf{C}_2\right)^{\vee} = \ln\left(\exp(\phi_1^{\wedge}) \exp(\phi_2^{\wedge})\right)^{\vee}$$

$$= \phi_1 + \phi_2 + \frac{1}{2}\phi_1^{\wedge}\phi_2 + \frac{1}{12}\phi_1^{\wedge}\phi_1^{\wedge}\phi_2 + \frac{1}{12}\phi_2^{\wedge}\phi_2^{\wedge}\phi_1 + \cdots, \qquad (8.79)$$

where $\mathbf{C}_1 = \exp(\phi_1^{\wedge})$, $\mathbf{C}_2 = \exp(\phi_2^{\wedge}) \in SO(3)$. Alternatively, if we assume that ϕ_1 or ϕ_2 is small, then, using the approximate BCH formulas, we can show that

$$\ln\left(\mathbf{C}_1 \mathbf{C}_2\right)^{\vee} = \ln\left(\exp(\phi_1^{\wedge}) \exp(\phi_2^{\wedge})\right)^{\vee}$$

$$\approx \begin{cases} \mathbf{J}_{\ell}(\phi_2)^{-1} \phi_1 + \phi_2 & \text{if } \phi_1 \text{ small} \\ \phi_1 + \mathbf{J}_r(\phi_1)^{-1} \phi_2 & \text{if } \phi_2 \text{ small} \end{cases}, \qquad (8.80)$$

where

$$\mathbf{J}_r(\phi)^{-1} = \sum_{n=0}^{\infty} \frac{B_n}{n!} \left(-\phi^{\wedge}\right)^n = \frac{\phi}{2}\cot\frac{\phi}{2}\mathbf{1} + \left(1 - \frac{\phi}{2}\cot\frac{\phi}{2}\right)\mathbf{a}\mathbf{a}^T + \frac{\phi}{2}\mathbf{a}^{\wedge},$$

$$\qquad (8.81a)$$

$$\mathbf{J}_{\ell}(\phi)^{-1} = \sum_{n=0}^{\infty} \frac{B_n}{n!} \left(\phi^{\wedge}\right)^n = \frac{\phi}{2}\cot\frac{\phi}{2}\mathbf{1} + \left(1 - \frac{\phi}{2}\cot\frac{\phi}{2}\right)\mathbf{a}\mathbf{a}^T - \frac{\phi}{2}\mathbf{a}^{\wedge}.$$

$$\qquad (8.81b)$$

In Lie group theory, $\mathbf{J}_r$ and $\mathbf{J}_{\ell}$ are referred to as the *right* and *left Jacobians* of $SO(3)$, respectively. As noted earlier, due to the nature of the $\cot(\phi/2)$ function, there are singularities associated with $\mathbf{J}_r, \mathbf{J}_{\ell}$ at $\phi = 2\pi m$ with m a non-zero integer. Inverting, we have the following expressions for the Jacobians:

$$\mathbf{J}_r(\phi) = \sum_{n=0}^{\infty} \frac{1}{(n+1)!} \left(-\phi^\wedge\right)^n = \int_0^1 \mathbf{C}^{-\alpha} \, d\alpha$$

$$= \frac{\sin\phi}{\phi} \mathbf{1} + \left(1 - \frac{\sin\phi}{\phi}\right) \mathbf{a}\mathbf{a}^T - \frac{1-\cos\phi}{\phi} \mathbf{a}^\wedge, \qquad (8.82\text{a})$$

$$\mathbf{J}_\ell(\phi) = \sum_{n=0}^{\infty} \frac{1}{(n+1)!} \left(\phi^\wedge\right)^n = \int_0^1 \mathbf{C}^\alpha \, d\alpha$$

$$= \frac{\sin\phi}{\phi} \mathbf{1} + \left(1 - \frac{\sin\phi}{\phi}\right) \mathbf{a}\mathbf{a}^T + \frac{1-\cos\phi}{\phi} \mathbf{a}^\wedge, \qquad (8.82\text{b})$$

where $\mathbf{C} = \exp\left(\phi^\wedge\right)$, $\phi = |\phi|$, and $\mathbf{a} = \phi/\phi$. We draw attention to the fact that

$$\mathbf{J}_\ell(\phi) = \mathbf{C}\,\mathbf{J}_r(\phi), \qquad (8.83)$$

which allows us to relate one Jacobian to the other. To show this is fairly straight-forward, using the definitions:

$$\mathbf{C}\,\mathbf{J}_r(\phi) = \mathbf{C} \int_0^1 \mathbf{C}^{-\alpha} \, d\alpha = \int_0^1 \mathbf{C}^{1-\alpha} \, d\alpha$$

$$= -\int_1^0 \mathbf{C}^\beta \, d\beta = \int_0^1 \mathbf{C}^\beta \, d\beta = \mathbf{J}_\ell(\phi). \quad (8.84)$$

Another relationship between the left and right Jacobians is

$$\mathbf{J}_\ell(-\phi) = \mathbf{J}_r(\phi), \qquad (8.85)$$

which is again fairly easy to see:

$$\mathbf{J}_r(\phi) = \int_0^1 \mathbf{C}(\phi)^{-\alpha} \, d\alpha = \int_0^1 \left(\mathbf{C}(\phi)^{-1}\right)^\alpha \, d\alpha$$

$$= \int_0^1 \left(\mathbf{C}(-\phi)\right)^\alpha \, d\alpha = \mathbf{J}_\ell(-\phi). \qquad (8.86)$$

We next look at $SE(3)$.

Poses

In the particular cases of $SE(3)$ and $\mathrm{Ad}(SE(3))$, we can show that

$$\ln\left(\mathbf{T}_1\mathbf{T}_2\right)^\vee = \ln\left(\exp(\boldsymbol{\xi}_1^\wedge)\exp(\boldsymbol{\xi}_2^\wedge)\right)^\vee$$

$$= \boldsymbol{\xi}_1 + \boldsymbol{\xi}_2 + \frac{1}{2}\boldsymbol{\xi}_1^\curlywedge\boldsymbol{\xi}_2 + \frac{1}{12}\boldsymbol{\xi}_1^\curlywedge\boldsymbol{\xi}_1^\curlywedge\boldsymbol{\xi}_2 + \frac{1}{12}\boldsymbol{\xi}_2^\curlywedge\boldsymbol{\xi}_2^\curlywedge\boldsymbol{\xi}_1 + \cdots, \qquad (8.87\text{a})$$

$$\ln\left(\boldsymbol{\mathcal{T}}_1\boldsymbol{\mathcal{T}}_2\right)^\curlyvee = \ln\left(\exp(\boldsymbol{\xi}_1^\curlywedge)\exp(\boldsymbol{\xi}_2^\curlywedge)\right)^\curlyvee$$

$$= \boldsymbol{\xi}_1 + \boldsymbol{\xi}_2 + \frac{1}{2}\boldsymbol{\xi}_1^\curlywedge\boldsymbol{\xi}_2 + \frac{1}{12}\boldsymbol{\xi}_1^\curlywedge\boldsymbol{\xi}_1^\curlywedge\boldsymbol{\xi}_2 + \frac{1}{12}\boldsymbol{\xi}_2^\curlywedge\boldsymbol{\xi}_2^\curlywedge\boldsymbol{\xi}_1 + \cdots, \qquad (8.87\text{b})$$

where $\mathbf{T}_1 = \exp(\boldsymbol{\xi}_1^\wedge)$, $\mathbf{T}_2 = \exp(\boldsymbol{\xi}_2^\wedge) \in SE(3)$, and $\boldsymbol{\mathcal{T}}_1 = \exp(\boldsymbol{\xi}_1^\curlywedge)$, $\boldsymbol{\mathcal{T}}_2 = \exp(\boldsymbol{\xi}_2^\curlywedge) \in \mathrm{Ad}(SE(3))$. Alternatively, if we assume that $\boldsymbol{\xi}_1$ or $\boldsymbol{\xi}_2$ is small, then using the approximate BCH formulas, we can show that

$$\ln\left(\mathbf{T}_1\mathbf{T}_2\right)^{\vee} = \ln\left(\exp(\boldsymbol{\xi}_1^{\wedge})\exp(\boldsymbol{\xi}_2^{\wedge})\right)^{\vee}$$

$$\approx \begin{cases} \boldsymbol{\mathcal{J}}_\ell(\boldsymbol{\xi}_2)^{-1}\boldsymbol{\xi}_1 + \boldsymbol{\xi}_2 & \text{if } \boldsymbol{\xi}_1 \text{ small} \\ \boldsymbol{\xi}_1 + \boldsymbol{\mathcal{J}}_r(\boldsymbol{\xi}_1)^{-1}\boldsymbol{\xi}_2 & \text{if } \boldsymbol{\xi}_2 \text{ small} \end{cases}, \quad (8.88a)$$

$$\ln\left(\boldsymbol{\mathcal{T}}_1\boldsymbol{\mathcal{T}}_2\right)^{\curlyvee} = \ln\left(\exp(\boldsymbol{\xi}_1^{\curlywedge})\exp(\boldsymbol{\xi}_2^{\curlywedge})\right)^{\curlyvee}$$

$$\approx \begin{cases} \boldsymbol{\mathcal{J}}_\ell(\boldsymbol{\xi}_2)^{-1}\boldsymbol{\xi}_1 + \boldsymbol{\xi}_2 & \text{if } \boldsymbol{\xi}_1 \text{ small} \\ \boldsymbol{\xi}_1 + \boldsymbol{\mathcal{J}}_r(\boldsymbol{\xi}_1)^{-1}\boldsymbol{\xi}_2 & \text{if } \boldsymbol{\xi}_2 \text{ small} \end{cases}, \quad (8.88b)$$

where

$$\boldsymbol{\mathcal{J}}_r(\boldsymbol{\xi})^{-1} = \sum_{n=0}^{\infty} \frac{B_n}{n!}\left(-\boldsymbol{\xi}^{\curlywedge}\right)^n, \quad (8.89a)$$

$$\boldsymbol{\mathcal{J}}_\ell(\boldsymbol{\xi})^{-1} = \sum_{n=0}^{\infty} \frac{B_n}{n!}\left(\boldsymbol{\xi}^{\curlywedge}\right)^n. \quad (8.89b)$$

In Lie group theory, $\boldsymbol{\mathcal{J}}_r$ and $\boldsymbol{\mathcal{J}}_\ell$ are referred to as the *right* and *left Jacobians* of $SE(3)$, respectively. Inverting, we have the following expressions for the Jacobians:

$$\boldsymbol{\mathcal{J}}_r(\boldsymbol{\xi}) = \sum_{n=0}^{\infty} \frac{1}{(n+1)!}\left(-\boldsymbol{\xi}^{\curlywedge}\right)^n = \int_0^1 \boldsymbol{\mathcal{T}}^{-\alpha}\,d\alpha = \begin{bmatrix} \mathbf{J}_r & \mathbf{Q}_r \\ \mathbf{0} & \mathbf{J}_r \end{bmatrix}, \quad (8.90a)$$

$$\boldsymbol{\mathcal{J}}_\ell(\boldsymbol{\xi}) = \sum_{n=0}^{\infty} \frac{1}{(n+1)!}\left(\boldsymbol{\xi}^{\curlywedge}\right)^n = \int_0^1 \boldsymbol{\mathcal{T}}^{\alpha}\,d\alpha = \begin{bmatrix} \mathbf{J}_\ell & \mathbf{Q}_\ell \\ \mathbf{0} & \mathbf{J}_\ell \end{bmatrix}, \quad (8.90b)$$

where

$$\mathbf{Q}_\ell(\boldsymbol{\xi}) = \sum_{n=0}^{\infty}\sum_{m=0}^{\infty} \frac{1}{(n+m+2)!}\left(\phi^{\wedge}\right)^n \rho^{\wedge}\left(\phi^{\wedge}\right)^m$$

$$= \frac{1}{2}\rho^{\wedge} + \left(\frac{\phi - \sin\phi}{\phi^3}\right)\left(\phi^{\wedge}\rho^{\wedge} + \rho^{\wedge}\phi^{\wedge} + \phi^{\wedge}\rho^{\wedge}\phi^{\wedge}\right)$$

$$+ \left(\frac{\phi^2 + 2\cos\phi - 2}{2\phi^4}\right)\left(\phi^{\wedge}\phi^{\wedge}\rho^{\wedge} + \rho^{\wedge}\phi^{\wedge}\phi^{\wedge} - 3\phi^{\wedge}\rho^{\wedge}\phi^{\wedge}\right)$$

$$+ \left(\frac{2\phi - 3\sin\phi + \phi\cos\phi}{2\phi^5}\right)\left(\phi^{\wedge}\rho^{\wedge}\phi^{\wedge}\phi^{\wedge} + \phi^{\wedge}\phi^{\wedge}\rho^{\wedge}\phi^{\wedge}\right), \quad (8.91a)$$

$$\mathbf{Q}_r(\boldsymbol{\xi}) = \mathbf{Q}_\ell(-\boldsymbol{\xi}) = \mathbf{C}\,\mathbf{Q}_\ell(\boldsymbol{\xi}) + (\mathbf{J}_\ell\rho)^{\wedge}\mathbf{C}\,\mathbf{J}_\ell, \quad (8.91b)$$

and $\boldsymbol{\mathcal{T}} = \exp\left(\boldsymbol{\xi}^{\curlywedge}\right)$, $\mathbf{T} = \exp\left(\boldsymbol{\xi}^{\wedge}\right)$, $\mathbf{C} = \exp\left(\phi^{\wedge}\right)$, $\boldsymbol{\xi} = \begin{bmatrix}\rho \\ \phi\end{bmatrix}$. The expression for $\mathbf{Q}_\ell$ comes from expanding the series and grouping terms into the series forms of the trigonometric functions.[13] The relations for $\mathbf{Q}_r$ come from the relationships between the left and right Jacobians:

$$\boldsymbol{\mathcal{J}}_\ell(\boldsymbol{\xi}) = \boldsymbol{\mathcal{T}}\,\boldsymbol{\mathcal{J}}_r(\boldsymbol{\xi}), \qquad \boldsymbol{\mathcal{J}}_\ell(-\boldsymbol{\xi}) = \boldsymbol{\mathcal{J}}_r(\boldsymbol{\xi}). \quad (8.92)$$

---

[13] This is a very lengthy derivation, but the result is exact.

The first can be seen to be true from

$$
\begin{aligned}
\boldsymbol{\mathcal{T}} \boldsymbol{\mathcal{J}}_r(\boldsymbol{\xi}) = \boldsymbol{\mathcal{T}} \int_0^1 \boldsymbol{\mathcal{T}}^{-\alpha}\, d\alpha &= \int_0^1 \boldsymbol{\mathcal{T}}^{1-\alpha}\, d\alpha \\
&= -\int_1^0 \boldsymbol{\mathcal{T}}^{\beta}\, d\beta = \int_0^1 \boldsymbol{\mathcal{T}}^{\beta}\, d\beta = \boldsymbol{\mathcal{J}}_\ell(\boldsymbol{\xi}),
\end{aligned}
\tag{8.93}
$$

and the second from

$$
\begin{aligned}
\boldsymbol{\mathcal{J}}_r(\boldsymbol{\xi}) = \int_0^1 \boldsymbol{\mathcal{T}}(\boldsymbol{\xi})^{-\alpha}\, d\alpha &= \int_0^1 \left(\boldsymbol{\mathcal{T}}(\boldsymbol{\xi})^{-1}\right)^{\alpha}\, d\alpha \\
&= \int_0^1 \left(\boldsymbol{\mathcal{T}}(-\boldsymbol{\xi})\right)^{\alpha}\, d\alpha = \boldsymbol{\mathcal{J}}_\ell(-\boldsymbol{\xi}).
\end{aligned}
\tag{8.94}
$$

We can also work out a direct series expression for $\boldsymbol{\mathcal{J}}_\ell$ using the results of Section 8.1.4. From the form of the series expressions, we have that

$$
\boldsymbol{\mathcal{T}} \equiv 1 + \boldsymbol{\xi}^{\wedge} \boldsymbol{\mathcal{J}}_\ell.
\tag{8.95}
$$

Expanding the expression for the Jacobian, we see that

$$
\boldsymbol{\mathcal{J}}_\ell = \sum_{n=0}^{\infty} \frac{1}{(n+1)!} \left(\boldsymbol{\xi}^{\wedge}\right)^n = 1 + \alpha_1 \boldsymbol{\xi}^{\wedge} + \alpha_2 \left(\boldsymbol{\xi}^{\wedge}\right)^2 + \alpha_3 \left(\boldsymbol{\xi}^{\wedge}\right)^3 + \alpha_4 \left(\boldsymbol{\xi}^{\wedge}\right)^4,
\tag{8.96}
$$

where α_1, α_2, α_3, and α_4 are unknown coefficients. We know that the series can be expressed using only terms up to quartic through the use of the minimal polynomial for $\mathrm{ad}(\mathfrak{se}(3))$ in (8.67). Inserting this into (8.95), we have that

$$
\boldsymbol{\mathcal{T}} = 1 + \boldsymbol{\xi}^{\wedge} + \alpha_1 \left(\boldsymbol{\xi}^{\wedge}\right)^2 + \alpha_2 \left(\boldsymbol{\xi}^{\wedge}\right)^3 + \alpha_3 \left(\boldsymbol{\xi}^{\wedge}\right)^4 + \alpha_4 \left(\boldsymbol{\xi}^{\wedge}\right)^5.
\tag{8.97}
$$

Using (8.67) to rewrite the quintic term using the lower-order terms, we have

$$
\boldsymbol{\mathcal{T}} = 1 + \left(1 - \phi^4 \alpha_4\right) \boldsymbol{\xi}^{\wedge} + \alpha_1 \left(\boldsymbol{\xi}^{\wedge}\right)^2 + \left(\alpha_2 - 2\phi^2 \alpha_4\right) \left(\boldsymbol{\xi}^{\wedge}\right)^3 + \alpha_3 \left(\boldsymbol{\xi}^{\wedge}\right)^4.
\tag{8.98}
$$

Comparing the coefficients to those in (8.68), we can solve for α_1, α_2, α_3, and α_4 such that

$$
\begin{aligned}
\boldsymbol{\mathcal{J}}_\ell = 1 &+ \left(\frac{4 - \phi \sin\phi - 4\cos\phi}{2\phi^2}\right) \boldsymbol{\xi}^{\wedge} + \left(\frac{4\phi - 5\sin\phi + \phi\cos\phi}{2\phi^3}\right) \left(\boldsymbol{\xi}^{\wedge}\right)^2 \\
&+ \left(\frac{2 - \phi\sin\phi - 2\cos\phi}{2\phi^4}\right) \left(\boldsymbol{\xi}^{\wedge}\right)^3 + \left(\frac{2\phi - 3\sin\phi + \phi\cos\phi}{2\phi^5}\right) \left(\boldsymbol{\xi}^{\wedge}\right)^4.
\end{aligned}
\tag{8.99}
$$

This avoids the need to work out $\mathbf{J}_\ell$ and $\mathbf{Q}_\ell$ individually and then assemble them into $\boldsymbol{\mathcal{J}}_\ell$.

Alternate expressions for the inverses are

$$
\boldsymbol{\mathcal{J}}_r^{-1} = \begin{bmatrix} \mathbf{J}_r^{-1} & -\mathbf{J}_r^{-1}\mathbf{Q}_r\mathbf{J}_r^{-1} \\ \mathbf{0} & \mathbf{J}_r^{-1} \end{bmatrix},
\tag{8.100a}
$$

$$
\boldsymbol{\mathcal{J}}_\ell^{-1} = \begin{bmatrix} \mathbf{J}_\ell^{-1} & -\mathbf{J}_\ell^{-1}\mathbf{Q}_\ell\mathbf{J}_\ell^{-1} \\ \mathbf{0} & \mathbf{J}_\ell^{-1} \end{bmatrix}.
\tag{8.100b}
$$

We see that the singularities of $\mathcal{J}_r$ and $\mathcal{J}_\ell$ are precisely the same as the singularities of $\mathbf{J}_r$ and $\mathbf{J}_\ell$, respectively, since

$$\det(\mathcal{J}_r) = (\det(\mathbf{J}_r))^2, \quad \det(\mathcal{J}_\ell) = (\det(\mathbf{J}_\ell))^2, \tag{8.101}$$

and having a non-zero determinant is a necessary and sufficient condition for invertibility (and therefore no singularity).

We also have that

$$\mathbf{T} = \begin{bmatrix} \mathbf{C} & \mathbf{J}_\ell\rho \\ \mathbf{0}^T & 1 \end{bmatrix} = \begin{bmatrix} \mathbf{C} & \mathbf{C}\mathbf{J}_r\rho \\ \mathbf{0}^T & 1 \end{bmatrix}, \tag{8.102a}$$

$$\mathcal{T} = \begin{bmatrix} \mathbf{C} & (\mathbf{J}_\ell\rho)^\wedge\,\mathbf{C} \\ \mathbf{0} & \mathbf{C} \end{bmatrix} = \begin{bmatrix} \mathbf{C} & \mathbf{C}\,(\mathbf{J}_r\rho)^\wedge \\ \mathbf{0} & \mathbf{C} \end{bmatrix}, \tag{8.102b}$$

which tells us how to relate the ρ variable to the translational component of $\mathbf{T}$ or $\mathcal{T}$.

It is also worth noting that $\mathcal{J}\mathcal{J}^T > 0$ (positive-definite) for either the left or right Jacobian. We can see this through the following factorization:

$$\mathcal{J}\mathcal{J}^T = \underbrace{\begin{bmatrix} 1 & \mathbf{Q}\mathbf{J}^{-1} \\ 0 & 1 \end{bmatrix}}_{>0} \underbrace{\begin{bmatrix} \mathbf{J}\mathbf{J}^T & 0 \\ 0 & \mathbf{J}\mathbf{J}^T \end{bmatrix}}_{>0} \underbrace{\begin{bmatrix} 1 & 0 \\ \mathbf{J}^{-T}\mathbf{Q}^T & 1 \end{bmatrix}}_{>0} > 0, \tag{8.103}$$

where we have used that $\mathbf{J}\mathbf{J}^T > 0$, which was shown previously.

Choosing the Left

In later sections and chapters, we will (arbitrarily) work with the left Jacobian, and it will therefore be useful to write out the BCH approximations in (8.80) and (8.88) using only the left Jacobian. For $SO(3)$, we have

$$\ln\left(\mathbf{C}_1\mathbf{C}_2\right)^\vee = \ln\left(\exp(\boldsymbol{\phi}_1^\wedge)\exp(\boldsymbol{\phi}_2^\wedge)\right)^\vee$$
$$\approx \begin{cases} \mathbf{J}(\boldsymbol{\phi}_2)^{-1}\boldsymbol{\phi}_1 + \boldsymbol{\phi}_2 & \text{if } \boldsymbol{\phi}_1 \text{ small} \\ \boldsymbol{\phi}_1 + \mathbf{J}(-\boldsymbol{\phi}_1)^{-1}\boldsymbol{\phi}_2 & \text{if } \boldsymbol{\phi}_2 \text{ small} \end{cases}, \tag{8.104}$$

where it is now implied that $\mathbf{J} = \mathbf{J}_\ell$, by convention.[14]

Similarly, for $SE(3)$, we have

$$\ln\left(\mathbf{T}_1\mathbf{T}_2\right)^\vee = \ln\left(\exp(\boldsymbol{\xi}_1^\wedge)\exp(\boldsymbol{\xi}_2^\wedge)\right)^\vee$$
$$\approx \begin{cases} \mathcal{J}(\boldsymbol{\xi}_2)^{-1}\boldsymbol{\xi}_1 + \boldsymbol{\xi}_2 & \text{if } \boldsymbol{\xi}_1 \text{ small} \\ \boldsymbol{\xi}_1 + \mathcal{J}(-\boldsymbol{\xi}_1)^{-1}\boldsymbol{\xi}_2 & \text{if } \boldsymbol{\xi}_2 \text{ small} \end{cases}, \tag{8.105a}$$

$$\ln\left(\mathcal{T}_1\mathcal{T}_2\right)^\curlyvee = \ln\left(\exp(\boldsymbol{\xi}_1^\wedge)\exp(\boldsymbol{\xi}_2^\wedge)\right)^\curlyvee$$
$$\approx \begin{cases} \mathcal{J}(\boldsymbol{\xi}_2)^{-1}\boldsymbol{\xi}_1 + \boldsymbol{\xi}_2 & \text{if } \boldsymbol{\xi}_1 \text{ small} \\ \boldsymbol{\xi}_1 + \mathcal{J}(-\boldsymbol{\xi}_1)^{-1}\boldsymbol{\xi}_2 & \text{if } \boldsymbol{\xi}_2 \text{ small} \end{cases}, \tag{8.105b}$$

where it is now implied that $\mathcal{J} = \mathcal{J}_\ell$, by convention.

---

[14] We will use this convention throughout the book and only show the subscript on the Jacobian when making specific points.

8.1.6 Distance, Volume, Integration

We need to think about the concepts of distance, volume, and integration differently for Lie groups than for vector spaces. This section quickly covers these topics for both rotations and poses.

Rotations

There are two common ways to define the difference of two rotations:

$$\phi_{12} = \ln \left(\mathbf{C}_1^T \mathbf{C}_2 \right)^\vee, \tag{8.106a}$$

$$\phi_{21} = \ln \left(\mathbf{C}_2 \mathbf{C}_1^T \right)^\vee, \tag{8.106b}$$

where $\mathbf{C}_1, \mathbf{C}_2 \in SO(3)$. One can be thought of as the right difference and the other the left. We can define the inner product for $\mathfrak{so}(3)$ as

$$\langle \phi_1^\wedge, \phi_2^\wedge \rangle = \frac{1}{2} \mathrm{tr} \left(\phi_1^\wedge \phi_2^{\wedge T} \right) = \phi_1^T \phi_2. \tag{8.107}$$

The metric *distance* between two rotations can be thought of in two ways: (i) the square root of the inner product of the difference with itself or (ii) the Euclidean norm of the difference:

$$\phi_{12} = \sqrt{\langle \ln \left(\mathbf{C}_1^T \mathbf{C}_2 \right), \ln \left(\mathbf{C}_1^T \mathbf{C}_2 \right) \rangle} = \sqrt{\langle \phi_{12}^\wedge, \phi_{12}^\wedge \rangle} = \sqrt{\phi_{12}^T \phi_{12}} = |\phi_{12}|, \tag{8.108a}$$

$$\phi_{21} = \sqrt{\langle \ln \left(\mathbf{C}_2 \mathbf{C}_1^T \right), \ln \left(\mathbf{C}_2 \mathbf{C}_1^T \right) \rangle} = \sqrt{\langle \phi_{21}^\wedge, \phi_{21}^\wedge \rangle} = \sqrt{\phi_{21}^T \phi_{21}} = |\phi_{21}|. \tag{8.108b}$$

This can also be viewed as the magnitude of the angle of the rotation difference.

To consider integrating functions of rotations, we parametrize $\mathbf{C} = \exp \left(\phi^\wedge \right) \in SO(3)$. Perturbing ϕ by a little bit results in the new rotation matrix, $\mathbf{C}' = \exp \left((\phi + \delta\phi)^\wedge \right) \in SO(3)$. We have that the right and left differences (relative to $\mathbf{C}$) are

$$\ln(\delta\mathbf{C}_r)^\vee = \ln \left(\mathbf{C}^T \mathbf{C}' \right)^\vee = \ln \left(\mathbf{C}^T \exp \left((\phi + \delta\phi)^\wedge \right) \right)^\vee$$
$$\approx \ln \left(\mathbf{C}^T \mathbf{C} \exp \left((\mathbf{J}_r \delta\phi)^\wedge \right) \right)^\vee = \mathbf{J}_r \delta\phi, \tag{8.109a}$$

$$\ln(\delta\mathbf{C}_\ell)^\vee = \ln \left(\mathbf{C}' \mathbf{C}^T \right)^\vee = \ln \left(\exp \left((\phi + \delta\phi)^\wedge \right) \mathbf{C}^T \right)^\vee$$
$$\approx \ln \left(\exp \left((\mathbf{J}_\ell \delta\phi)^\wedge \right) \mathbf{C} \mathbf{C}^T \right)^\vee = \mathbf{J}_\ell \delta\phi, \tag{8.109b}$$

where $\mathbf{J}_r$ and $\mathbf{J}_\ell$ are evaluated at ϕ. To compute the infinitesimal volume element, we want to find the volume of the parallelepiped formed by the columns of $\mathbf{J}_r$ or $\mathbf{J}_\ell$, which is simply the corresponding determinant:[15]

$$d\mathbf{C}_r = |\det(\mathbf{J}_r)| \, d\phi, \tag{8.110a}$$

$$d\mathbf{C}_\ell = |\det(\mathbf{J}_\ell)| \, d\phi. \tag{8.110b}$$

---

[15] We are slightly abusing notation here by writing $d\mathbf{C}$, but hopefully it is clear from context what is meant.

We note that

$$\det(\mathbf{J}_\ell) = \det(\mathbf{C}\,\mathbf{J}_r) = \underbrace{\det(\mathbf{C})}_{1}\det(\mathbf{J}_r) = \det(\mathbf{J}_r), \tag{8.111}$$

which means that regardless of which distance metric we use, right or left, the infinitesimal volume element is the same. This is true for all *unimodular* Lie groups, such as $SO(3)$. Therefore, we can write

$$d\mathbf{C} = |\det(\mathbf{J})|\,d\boldsymbol{\phi}, \tag{8.112}$$

for the calculation of an infinitesimal volume element.

It turns out that

$$|\det(\mathbf{J})| = 2\frac{1-\cos\phi}{\phi^2} = \frac{2}{\phi^2}\left(1 - 1 + \frac{\phi^2}{2!} - \frac{\phi^4}{4!} + \frac{\phi^6}{6!} - \frac{\phi^8}{8!} + \cdots\right)$$

$$= 1 - \frac{1}{12}\phi^2 + \frac{1}{360}\phi^4 - \frac{1}{20160}\phi^6 + \cdots, \tag{8.113}$$

where $\phi = |\boldsymbol{\phi}|$. For most practical situations we can safely use just the first two or even one term of this expression.

Integrating functions of rotations can then be carried out like this:

$$\int_{SO(3)} f(\mathbf{C})\,d\mathbf{C} \;\rightarrow\; \int_{|\boldsymbol{\phi}|<\pi} f(\boldsymbol{\phi})\,|\det(\mathbf{J})|\,d\boldsymbol{\phi}, \tag{8.114}$$

where we are careful to ensure $|\boldsymbol{\phi}| < \pi$ so as to sweep out all of $SO(3)$ just once (due to the surjective-only nature of the exponential map).

Poses

We briefly summarize the $SE(3)$ and $\mathrm{Ad}(SE(3))$ results as they are very similar to $SO(3)$. We can define right and left distance metrics:

$$\boldsymbol{\xi}_{12} = \ln\left(\mathbf{T}_1^{-1}\mathbf{T}_2\right)^\vee = \ln\left(\boldsymbol{\mathcal{T}}_1^{-1}\boldsymbol{\mathcal{T}}_2\right)^{\curlyvee}, \tag{8.115a}$$

$$\boldsymbol{\xi}_{21} = \ln\left(\mathbf{T}_2\mathbf{T}_1^{-1}\right)^\vee = \ln\left(\boldsymbol{\mathcal{T}}_2\boldsymbol{\mathcal{T}}_1^{-1}\right)^{\curlyvee}. \tag{8.115b}$$

The 4×4 and 6×6 inner products are

$$\langle\boldsymbol{\xi}_1^\wedge,\boldsymbol{\xi}_2^\wedge\rangle = \mathrm{tr}\left(\boldsymbol{\xi}_1^\wedge\begin{bmatrix}\frac{1}{2}\mathbf{1} & \mathbf{0}\\ \mathbf{0}^T & 1\end{bmatrix}\boldsymbol{\xi}_2^{\wedge^T}\right) = \boldsymbol{\xi}_1^T\boldsymbol{\xi}_2, \tag{8.116a}$$

$$\langle\boldsymbol{\xi}_1^\curlywedge,\boldsymbol{\xi}_2^\curlywedge\rangle = \mathrm{tr}\left(\boldsymbol{\xi}_1^\curlywedge\begin{bmatrix}\mathbf{0} & \mathbf{0}\\ \mathbf{0} & \frac{1}{2}\mathbf{1}\end{bmatrix}\boldsymbol{\xi}_2^{\curlywedge^T}\right) = \boldsymbol{\xi}_1^T\boldsymbol{\xi}_2. \tag{8.116b}$$

Note that we could adjust the weighting matrix in the middle to weight rotation and translation differently if we so desired. The right and left distances are

$$\xi_{12} = \sqrt{\langle\boldsymbol{\xi}_{12}^\wedge,\boldsymbol{\xi}_{12}^\wedge\rangle} = \sqrt{\langle\boldsymbol{\xi}_{12}^\curlywedge,\boldsymbol{\xi}_{12}^\curlywedge\rangle} = \sqrt{\boldsymbol{\xi}_{12}^T\boldsymbol{\xi}_{12}} = |\boldsymbol{\xi}_{12}|, \tag{8.117a}$$

$$\xi_{21} = \sqrt{\langle\boldsymbol{\xi}_{21}^\wedge,\boldsymbol{\xi}_{21}^\wedge\rangle} = \sqrt{\langle\boldsymbol{\xi}_{21}^\curlywedge,\boldsymbol{\xi}_{21}^\curlywedge\rangle} = \sqrt{\boldsymbol{\xi}_{21}^T\boldsymbol{\xi}_{21}} = |\boldsymbol{\xi}_{21}|. \tag{8.117b}$$

Using the parametrization

$$\mathbf{T} = \exp\left(\boldsymbol{\xi}^\wedge\right) \tag{8.118}$$

and the perturbation

$$\mathbf{T}' = \exp\left(\left(\boldsymbol{\xi} + \delta\boldsymbol{\xi}\right)^\wedge\right), \tag{8.119}$$

the differences (relative to $\mathbf{T}$) are

$$\ln\left(\delta\mathbf{T}_r\right)^\vee = \ln\left(\mathbf{T}^{-1}\mathbf{T}'\right)^\vee \approx \boldsymbol{\mathcal{J}}_r\,\delta\boldsymbol{\xi}, \tag{8.120a}$$

$$\ln\left(\delta\mathbf{T}_\ell\right)^\vee = \ln\left(\mathbf{T}'\mathbf{T}^{-1}\right)^\vee \approx \boldsymbol{\mathcal{J}}_\ell\,\delta\boldsymbol{\xi}. \tag{8.120b}$$

The right and left infinitesimal volume elements are

$$d\mathbf{T}_r = |\det(\boldsymbol{\mathcal{J}}_r)|\,d\boldsymbol{\xi}, \tag{8.121a}$$

$$d\mathbf{T}_\ell = |\det(\boldsymbol{\mathcal{J}}_\ell)|\,d\boldsymbol{\xi}. \tag{8.121b}$$

We have that

$$\det(\boldsymbol{\mathcal{J}}_\ell) = \det(\boldsymbol{\mathcal{T}}\boldsymbol{\mathcal{J}}_r) = \det(\boldsymbol{\mathcal{T}})\det(\boldsymbol{\mathcal{J}}_r) = \det(\boldsymbol{\mathcal{J}}_r), \tag{8.122}$$

since $\det(\boldsymbol{\mathcal{T}}) = \left(\det(\mathbf{C})\right)^2 = 1$. We can therefore write

$$d\mathbf{T} = |\det(\boldsymbol{\mathcal{J}})|\,d\boldsymbol{\xi} \tag{8.123}$$

for our integration volume. Finally, we have that

$$|\det(\boldsymbol{\mathcal{J}})| = |\det(\mathbf{J})|^2 = \left(2\frac{1-\cos\phi}{\phi^2}\right)^2$$
$$= 1 - \frac{1}{6}\phi^2 + \frac{1}{80}\phi^4 - \frac{17}{30240}\phi^6 + \cdots, \tag{8.124}$$

and again we probably will never need more than two terms of this expression.

To integrate functions over $SE(3)$, we can now use our infinitesimal volume in the calculation:

$$\int_{SE(3)} f(\mathbf{T})\,d\mathbf{T} = \int_{\mathbb{R}^3,|\boldsymbol{\phi}|<\pi} f(\boldsymbol{\xi})\,|\det(\boldsymbol{\mathcal{J}})|\,d\boldsymbol{\xi}, \tag{8.125}$$

where we limit ϕ to the ball of radius π (due to the surjective-only nature of the exponential map) but let $\boldsymbol{\rho} \in \mathbb{R}^3$.

8.1.7 Interpolation

We will have occasion later to interpolate between two elements of a matrix Lie group. Unfortunately, the typical linear interpolation scheme,

$$x = (1-\alpha)\,x_1 + \alpha\,x_2, \quad \alpha \in [0,1], \tag{8.126}$$

will not work because this interpolation scheme does not satisfy closure (i.e., the result is no longer in the group). In other words,

$$(1-\alpha)\,\mathbf{C}_1 + \alpha\,\mathbf{C}_2 \notin SO(3), \tag{8.127a}$$

$$(1-\alpha)\,\mathbf{T}_1 + \alpha\,\mathbf{T}_2 \notin SE(3) \tag{8.127b}$$

for some values of $\alpha \in [0,1]$ with $\mathbf{C}_1, \mathbf{C}_2 \in SO(3)$, $\mathbf{T}_1, \mathbf{T}_2 \in SE(3)$. We must rethink what interpolation means for Lie groups.

Rotations

There are many possible interpolation schemes that we could define. One of these is the following:

$$\mathbf{C} = \left(\mathbf{C}_2 \mathbf{C}_1^T\right)^\alpha \mathbf{C}_1, \quad \alpha \in [0, 1], \tag{8.128}$$

where $\mathbf{C}, \mathbf{C}_1, \mathbf{C}_2 \in SO(3)$. We see that when $\alpha = 0$, we have $\mathbf{C} = \mathbf{C}_1$, and when $\alpha = 1$, we have $\mathbf{C}_2$. The nice thing about this scheme is that we guarantee closure, meaning $\mathbf{C} \in SO(3)$ for all $\alpha \in [0, 1]$. This is because we know that $\mathbf{C}_{21} = \exp\left(\phi^\wedge\right) = \mathbf{C}_2 \mathbf{C}_1^T$ is still a rotation matrix due to closure of the Lie group. Exponentiating by the interpolation variable keeps the result in $SO(3)$,

$$\mathbf{C}_{21}^\alpha = \exp\left(\phi^\wedge\right)^\alpha = \exp\left(\alpha\,\phi^\wedge\right) \in SO(3), \tag{8.129}$$

and finally, compounding with $\mathbf{C}_1$ results in a member of $SO(3)$, again due to closure of the group. We can also see that we are essentially just scaling the rotation angle of $\mathbf{C}_{21}$ by α, which is appealing intuitively.

Our scheme in (8.128) is actually similar to (8.126), if we rearrange it a bit:

$$x = \alpha(x_2 - x_1) + x_1. \tag{8.130}$$

Or, letting $x = \ln(y)$, $x_1 = \ln(y_1)$, $x_2 = \ln(y_2)$, we can rewrite it as

$$y = \left(y_2\, y_1^{-1}\right)^\alpha y_1, \tag{8.131}$$

which is very similar to our proposed scheme. Given our understanding of the relationship between $\mathfrak{so}(3)$ and $SO(3)$ (i.e., through the exponential map), it is therefore not a leap to understand that (8.128) is somehow defining linear-like interpolation in the Lie algebra, where we can treat elements as vectors.

To examine this further, we let $\mathbf{C} = \exp\left(\varphi^\wedge\right)$, $\mathbf{C}_1 = \exp\left(\phi_1^\wedge\right)$, $\mathbf{C}_2 = \exp\left(\phi_2^\wedge\right) \in SO(3)$ with $\varphi, \phi_1, \phi_2 \in \mathbb{R}^3$. If we are able to make the assumption that ϕ is small (in the sense of distance from the previous section), then we have

$$\begin{aligned}
\varphi = \ln\left(\mathbf{C}\right)^\vee &= \ln\left(\left(\mathbf{C}_2 \mathbf{C}_1^T\right)^\alpha \mathbf{C}_1\right)^\vee \\
&= \ln\left(\exp\left(\alpha\,\phi^\wedge\right)\exp\left(\phi_1^\wedge\right)\right)^\vee \approx \alpha\, \mathbf{J}(\phi_1)^{-1}\phi + \phi_1,
\end{aligned} \tag{8.132}$$

which is comparable to (8.130) and is a form of linear interpolation. Another case worth noting is when $\mathbf{C}_1 = \mathbf{1}$, whereupon

$$\mathbf{C} = \mathbf{C}_2^\alpha, \quad \varphi = \alpha\,\phi_2, \tag{8.133}$$

with no approximation.

Another way to interpret our interpolation scheme is that it is enforcing a constant angular velocity, $\boldsymbol{\omega}$. If we think of our rotation matrix as being a function of time, $\mathbf{C}(t)$, then the scheme is

$$\mathbf{C}(t) = \left(\mathbf{C}(t_2)\mathbf{C}(t_1)^T\right)^\alpha \mathbf{C}(t_1), \quad \alpha = \frac{t - t_1}{t_2 - t_1}. \tag{8.134}$$

Defining the constant angular velocity as

$$\boldsymbol{\omega} = \frac{1}{t_2 - t_1}\boldsymbol{\phi}, \qquad (8.135)$$

the scheme becomes

$$\mathbf{C}(t) = \exp\left((t - t_1)\,\boldsymbol{\omega}^\wedge\right)\,\mathbf{C}(t_1). \qquad (8.136)$$

This is exactly the solution to Poisson's equation, (7.45),

$$\dot{\mathbf{C}}(t) = \boldsymbol{\omega}^\wedge\,\mathbf{C}(t), \qquad (8.137)$$

with constant angular velocity.[16] Thus, while other interpolation schemes are possible, this one has a strong physical connection.

Perturbed Rotations

Another thing that will be very useful to investigate is what happens to $\mathbf{C}$ if we perturb $\mathbf{C}_1$ and/or $\mathbf{C}_2$ a little bit. Suppose now that $\mathbf{C}', \mathbf{C}_1', \mathbf{C}_2' \in SO(3)$ are the perturbed rotation matrices with the (left) differences[17] given as

$$\delta\boldsymbol{\varphi} = \ln\left(\mathbf{C}'\mathbf{C}^T\right)^\vee, \quad \delta\boldsymbol{\phi}_1 = \ln\left(\mathbf{C}_1'\mathbf{C}_1^T\right)^\vee, \quad \delta\boldsymbol{\phi}_2 = \ln\left(\mathbf{C}_2'\mathbf{C}_2^T\right)^\vee. \tag{8.138}$$

The interpolation scheme must hold for the perturbed rotation matrices:

$$\mathbf{C}' = \left(\mathbf{C}_2'\mathbf{C}_1'^T\right)^\alpha \mathbf{C}_1', \quad \alpha \in [0, 1]. \qquad (8.139)$$

We are interested in finding a relationship between $\delta\boldsymbol{\varphi}$ and $\delta\boldsymbol{\phi}_1, \delta\boldsymbol{\phi}_2$. Substituting in our perturbations, we have

$$\exp\left(\delta\boldsymbol{\varphi}^\wedge\right)\mathbf{C} = \underbrace{\left(\exp\left(\delta\boldsymbol{\phi}_2^\wedge\right)\mathbf{C}_2\mathbf{C}_1^T\exp\left(-\delta\boldsymbol{\phi}_1^\wedge\right)\right)}_{\approx\ \exp((\boldsymbol{\phi}+\mathbf{J}(\boldsymbol{\phi})^{-1}(\delta\boldsymbol{\phi}_2-\mathbf{C}_{21}\,\delta\boldsymbol{\phi}_1))^\wedge)}{}^\alpha \exp\left(\delta\boldsymbol{\phi}_1^\wedge\right)\mathbf{C}_1, \quad (8.140)$$

where we have assumed the perturbations are small to make the approximation hold inside the brackets. Bringing the interpolation variable inside the exponential, we have

$$\exp\left(\delta\boldsymbol{\varphi}^\wedge\right)\mathbf{C}$$
$$\approx \underbrace{\exp\left(\left(\alpha\,\boldsymbol{\phi} + \alpha\,\mathbf{J}(\boldsymbol{\phi})^{-1}(\delta\boldsymbol{\phi}_2 - \mathbf{C}_{21}\,\delta\boldsymbol{\phi}_1)\right)^\wedge\right)}_{\approx\ \exp((\alpha\,\mathbf{J}(\alpha\boldsymbol{\phi})\mathbf{J}(\boldsymbol{\phi})^{-1}(\delta\boldsymbol{\phi}_2-\mathbf{C}_{21}\,\delta\boldsymbol{\phi}_1))^\wedge)\,\mathbf{C}_{21}^\alpha} \exp\left(\delta\boldsymbol{\phi}_1^\wedge\right)\mathbf{C}_1$$
$$\approx \exp\left(\left(\alpha\,\mathbf{J}(\alpha\boldsymbol{\phi})\mathbf{J}(\boldsymbol{\phi})^{-1}(\delta\boldsymbol{\phi}_2 - \mathbf{C}_{21}\,\delta\boldsymbol{\phi}_1)\right)^\wedge\right)$$
$$\times\ \exp\left((\mathbf{C}_{21}^\alpha\,\delta\boldsymbol{\phi}_1)^\wedge\right)\underbrace{\mathbf{C}_{21}^\alpha\,\mathbf{C}_1}_{\mathbf{C}}. \qquad (8.141)$$

---

[16] Kinematics will be discussed in further detail later in this chapter.

[17] In anticipation of how we will use this result, we will consider perturbations on the left, but we saw in the previous section that there are equivalent perturbations on the right and in the middle.

Dropping the $\mathbf{C}$ from both sides, expanding the matrix exponentials, distributing the multiplication, and then keeping only first-order terms in the perturbation quantities, we have

$$\delta\varphi = \alpha\,\mathbf{J}(\alpha\phi)\mathbf{J}(\phi)^{-1}(\delta\phi_2 - \mathbf{C}_{21}\,\delta\phi_1) + \mathbf{C}_{21}^{\alpha}\,\delta\phi_1. \qquad (8.142)$$

Manipulating a little further (using several identities involving the Jacobians), we can show that this simplifies to

$$\delta\varphi = (\mathbf{1} - \mathbf{A}(\alpha,\phi))\,\delta\phi_1 + \mathbf{A}(\alpha,\phi)\,\delta\phi_2, \qquad (8.143)$$

where

$$\mathbf{A}(\alpha,\phi) = \alpha\,\mathbf{J}(\alpha\phi)\mathbf{J}(\phi)^{-1}. \qquad (8.144)$$

We see that this has a very nice form that mirrors the usual linear interpolation scheme. Notably, when ϕ is small, then $\mathbf{A}(\alpha,\phi) \approx \alpha\,\mathbf{1}$.

Although we have a means of computing $\mathbf{A}(\alpha,\phi)$ in closed form (via $\mathbf{J}(\cdot)$), we can work out a series expression for it as well. In terms of our series expressions for $\mathbf{J}(\cdot)$ and its inverse, we have

$$\mathbf{A}(\alpha,\phi) = \alpha\,\underbrace{\left(\sum_{k=0}^{\infty}\frac{1}{(k+1)!}\alpha^k\left(\phi^{\wedge}\right)^k\right)}_{\mathbf{J}(\alpha\phi)}\underbrace{\left(\sum_{\ell=0}^{\infty}\frac{B_\ell}{\ell!}\left(\phi^{\wedge}\right)^\ell\right)}_{\mathbf{J}(\phi)^{-1}}. \qquad (8.145)$$

Baron Augustin-Louis Cauchy (1789–1857) was a French mathematician who pioneered the study of continuity in terms of infinitesimals, almost singlehandedly founded complex analysis, and initiated the study of permutation groups in abstract algebra.

We can use a discrete convolution, or *Cauchy product* (of two series), to rewrite this as

$$\mathbf{A}(\alpha,\phi) = \sum_{n=0}^{\infty}\frac{F_n(\alpha)}{n!}\left(\phi^{\wedge}\right)^n, \qquad (8.146)$$

where

$$F_n(\alpha) = \frac{1}{n+1}\sum_{m=0}^{n}\binom{n+1}{m}B_m\alpha^{n+1-m} = \sum_{\beta=0}^{\alpha-1}\beta^n, \qquad (8.147)$$

Johann Faulhaber (1580–1635) was a German mathematician whose major contribution involved calculating the sums of powers of integers. Jakob Bernoulli makes references to Faulhaber in his *Ars Conjectandi*.

is a version of *Faulhaber's formula*. The first few Faulhaber coefficients (as we will call them) are

$$F_0(\alpha) = \alpha, \quad F_1(\alpha) = \frac{\alpha(\alpha-1)}{2},$$

$$F_2(\alpha) = \frac{\alpha(\alpha-1)(2\alpha-1)}{6},$$

$$F_3(\alpha) = \frac{\alpha^2(\alpha-1)^2}{4}, \ldots \qquad (8.148)$$

Putting these back into $\mathbf{A}(\alpha,\phi)$, we have

$$\mathbf{A}(\alpha,\phi) = \alpha\,\mathbf{1} + \frac{\alpha(\alpha-1)}{2}\phi^{\wedge} + \frac{\alpha(\alpha-1)(2\alpha-1)}{12}\phi^{\wedge}\phi^{\wedge}$$
$$+ \frac{\alpha^2(\alpha-1)^2}{24}\phi^{\wedge}\phi^{\wedge}\phi^{\wedge} + \cdots, \qquad (8.149)$$

where we likely would not need many terms if ϕ is small.

Alternate Interpretation of Perturbed Rotations

Technically speaking, the last sum on the far right of (8.147) does not make much sense since $\alpha \in [0,1]$, but we can also get to this another way. Let us pretend for the moment that α is in fact a positive integer. Then we can expand the exponentiated part of our interpolation formula according to

$$\left(\exp\left(\delta\phi^\wedge\right)\mathbf{C}\right)^\alpha = \underbrace{\exp\left(\delta\phi^\wedge\right)\mathbf{C}\cdots\exp\left(\delta\phi^\wedge\right)\mathbf{C}}_{\alpha}, \qquad (8.150)$$

where $\mathbf{C} = \exp\left(\phi^\wedge\right)$. We can then move all of the $\delta\phi$ terms to the far left so that

$$\left(\exp\left(\delta\phi^\wedge\right)\mathbf{C}\right)^\alpha = \exp\left(\delta\phi^\wedge\right)\exp\left(\left(\mathbf{C}\,\delta\phi\right)^\wedge\right)\cdots\exp\left(\left(\mathbf{C}^{\alpha-1}\delta\phi\right)^\wedge\right)\mathbf{C}^\alpha, \qquad (8.151)$$

where we have not yet made any approximations. Expanding each of the exponentials, multiplying out, and keeping only terms first-order in $\delta\phi$ leaves us with

$$\left(\exp\left(\delta\phi^\wedge\right)\mathbf{C}\right)^\alpha \approx \left(\mathbf{1} + \left(\left(\sum_{\beta=0}^{\alpha-1}\mathbf{C}^\beta\right)\delta\phi\right)^\wedge\right)\mathbf{C}^\alpha$$

$$= \left(\mathbf{1} + \left(\mathbf{A}(\alpha,\phi)\,\delta\phi\right)^\wedge\right)\mathbf{C}^\alpha, \qquad (8.152)$$

where

$$\mathbf{A}(\alpha,\phi) = \sum_{\beta=0}^{\alpha-1}\mathbf{C}^\beta = \sum_{\beta=0}^{\alpha-1}\exp\left(\beta\phi^\wedge\right) = \sum_{\beta=0}^{\alpha-1}\sum_{n=0}^{\infty}\frac{1}{n!}\beta^n\left(\phi^\wedge\right)^n$$

$$= \sum_{n=0}^{\infty}\frac{1}{n!}\underbrace{\left(\sum_{\beta=0}^{\alpha-1}\beta^n\right)}_{F_n(\alpha)}\left(\phi^\wedge\right)^n = \sum_{n=0}^{\infty}\frac{F_n(\alpha)}{n!}\left(\phi^\wedge\right)^n, \qquad (8.153)$$

which is the same as (8.146). Some examples of Faulhaber's coefficients are:

$$F_0(\alpha) = 0^0 + 1^0 + 2^0 + \cdots + (\alpha-1)^0 = \alpha, \qquad (8.154a)$$

$$F_1(\alpha) = 0^1 + 1^1 + 2^1 + \cdots + (\alpha-1)^1 = \frac{\alpha(\alpha-1)}{2}, \qquad (8.154b)$$

$$F_2(\alpha) = 0^2 + 1^2 + 2^2 + \cdots + (\alpha-1)^2 = \frac{\alpha(\alpha-1)(2\alpha-1)}{6}, \qquad (8.154c)$$

$$F_3(\alpha) = 0^3 + 1^3 + 2^3 + \cdots + (\alpha-1)^3 = \frac{\alpha^2(\alpha-1)^2}{4}, \qquad (8.154d)$$

which are the same as what we had before. Interestingly, these expressions work even when $\alpha \in [0,1]$.

Poses

Interpolation for elements of $SE(3)$ parallels the $SO(3)$ case. We define the interpolation scheme as the following:

$$\mathbf{T} = \left(\mathbf{T}_2\mathbf{T}_1^{-1}\right)^\alpha\mathbf{T}_1, \quad \alpha \in [0,1]. \qquad (8.155)$$

Again, this scheme ensures that $\mathbf{T} = \exp\left(\zeta^\wedge\right) \in SE(3)$ as long as $\mathbf{T}_1 = \exp\left(\boldsymbol{\xi}_1^\wedge\right), \mathbf{T}_2 = \exp\left(\boldsymbol{\xi}_2^\wedge\right) \in SE(3)$. Let $\mathbf{T}_{21} = \mathbf{T}_2\mathbf{T}_1^{-1} = \exp\left(\boldsymbol{\xi}^\wedge\right)$, so that

$$\boldsymbol{\zeta} = \ln\left(\mathbf{T}\right)^\vee = \ln\left(\left(\mathbf{T}_2\mathbf{T}_1^{-1}\right)^\alpha \mathbf{T}_1\right)^\vee = \ln\left(\exp\left(\alpha\,\boldsymbol{\xi}^\wedge\right)\exp\left(\boldsymbol{\xi}_1^\wedge\right)\right)^\vee$$
$$\approx \alpha\,\boldsymbol{\mathcal{J}}(\boldsymbol{\xi}_1)^{-1}\boldsymbol{\xi} + \boldsymbol{\xi}_1, \qquad (8.156)$$

where the approximation on the right holds if $\boldsymbol{\xi}$ is small. When $\mathbf{T}_1 = \mathbf{1}$, the scheme becomes

$$\mathbf{T} = \mathbf{T}_2^\alpha, \quad \boldsymbol{\zeta} = \alpha\,\boldsymbol{\xi}_2, \qquad (8.157)$$

with no approximation.

Perturbed Poses

As in the $SO(3)$ case, it will be useful to investigate what happens to $\mathbf{T}$ if we perturb $\mathbf{T}_1$ and/or $\mathbf{T}_2$ a little bit. Suppose now that $\mathbf{T}', \mathbf{T}_1', \mathbf{T}_2' \in SE(3)$ are the perturbed transformation matrices with the (left) differences given as

$$\delta\boldsymbol{\zeta} = \ln\left(\mathbf{T}'\mathbf{T}^{-1}\right)^\vee, \quad \delta\boldsymbol{\xi}_1 = \ln\left(\mathbf{T}_1'\mathbf{T}_1^{-1}\right)^\vee, \quad \delta\boldsymbol{\xi}_2 = \ln\left(\mathbf{T}_2'\mathbf{T}_2^{-1}\right)^\vee.$$
$$(8.158)$$

The interpolation scheme must hold for the perturbed transformation matrices:

$$\mathbf{T}' = \left(\mathbf{T}_2'\mathbf{T}_1'^{-1}\right)^\alpha \mathbf{T}_1', \quad \alpha \in [0,1]. \qquad (8.159)$$

We are interested in finding a relationship between $\delta\boldsymbol{\zeta}$ and $\delta\boldsymbol{\xi}_1, \delta\boldsymbol{\xi}_2$.

The derivation is very similar to $SO(3)$, so we will simply state the result:

$$\delta\boldsymbol{\zeta} = (1 - \boldsymbol{\mathcal{A}}(\alpha, \boldsymbol{\xi}))\,\delta\boldsymbol{\xi}_1 + \boldsymbol{\mathcal{A}}(\alpha, \boldsymbol{\xi})\,\delta\boldsymbol{\xi}_2, \qquad (8.160)$$

where

$$\boldsymbol{\mathcal{A}}(\alpha, \boldsymbol{\xi}) = \alpha\,\boldsymbol{\mathcal{J}}(\alpha\boldsymbol{\xi})\boldsymbol{\mathcal{J}}(\boldsymbol{\xi})^{-1}, \qquad (8.161)$$

and we note this is a 6×6 matrix. Again, we see this has a very nice form that mirrors the usual linear interpolation scheme. Notably, when $\boldsymbol{\xi}$ is small, then $\boldsymbol{\mathcal{A}}(\alpha, \boldsymbol{\xi}) \approx \alpha\,\mathbf{1}$. In series form, we have

$$\boldsymbol{\mathcal{A}}(\alpha, \boldsymbol{\xi}) = \sum_{n=0}^{\infty} \frac{F_n(\alpha)}{n!}\left(\boldsymbol{\xi}^\wedge\right)^n, \qquad (8.162)$$

where the $F_n(\alpha)$ are the Faulhaber coefficients discussed earlier.

8.1.8 Homogeneous Points

As discussed in Section 7.3.1, points in $\mathbb{R}^3$ can be represented using 4×1 *homogeneous coordinates* (Hartley and Zisserman, 2000), as follows:

$$\mathbf{p} = \begin{bmatrix} sx \\ sy \\ sz \\ s \end{bmatrix} = \begin{bmatrix} \boldsymbol{\varepsilon} \\ \eta \end{bmatrix},$$

where s is some real, non-zero scalar, $\boldsymbol{\varepsilon} \in \mathbb{R}^3$, and η is scalar. When s is zero, it is not possible to convert back to $\mathbb{R}^3$, as this case represents points that are infinitely far away. Thus, homogeneous coordinates can be used to describe near and distant landmarks with no singularities or scaling issues (Triggs et al., 2000). They are also a natural representation in that points may then be transformed from one frame to another very easily using transformation matrices (e.g., $\mathbf{p}_2 = \mathbf{T}_{21}\mathbf{p}_1$).

We will later make use of the following two operators[18] for manipulating 4×1 columns:

$$\begin{bmatrix} \boldsymbol{\varepsilon} \\ \eta \end{bmatrix}^{\odot} = \begin{bmatrix} \eta\mathbf{1} & -\boldsymbol{\varepsilon}^{\wedge} \\ \mathbf{0}^T & \mathbf{0}^T \end{bmatrix}, \quad \begin{bmatrix} \boldsymbol{\varepsilon} \\ \eta \end{bmatrix}^{\circledcirc} = \begin{bmatrix} \mathbf{0} & \boldsymbol{\varepsilon} \\ -\boldsymbol{\varepsilon}^{\wedge} & \mathbf{0} \end{bmatrix}, \tag{8.163}$$

which result in a 4×6 and 6×4, respectively. With these definitions, we have the following useful identities:

$$\boldsymbol{\xi}^{\wedge}\mathbf{p} \equiv \mathbf{p}^{\odot}\boldsymbol{\xi}, \qquad \mathbf{p}^T\boldsymbol{\xi}^{\wedge} \equiv \boldsymbol{\xi}^T\mathbf{p}^{\circledcirc}, \tag{8.164}$$

where $\boldsymbol{\xi} \in \mathbb{R}^6$ and $\mathbf{p} \in \mathbb{R}^4$, which will prove useful when manipulating expressions involving points and poses together. We also have the identity,

$$(\mathbf{T}\mathbf{p})^{\odot} \equiv \mathbf{T}\mathbf{p}^{\odot}\boldsymbol{\mathcal{T}}^{-1}, \tag{8.165}$$

which is similar to some others we have already seen.

8.1.9 Calculus and Optimization

Now that we have introduced homogeneous points, we formulate a bit of calculus to allow us to optimize functions of rotations and/or poses, sometimes in combination with three-dimensional points. As usual, we first study rotations and then poses. Absil et al. (2009) provides a much more detailed look at how to carry out optimization on matrix manifolds, exploring first-order, second-order, and trust-region methods. Boumal (2022) also provides an accessible introduction to optimization on smooth manifolds.

Rotations

We have already seen in Section 7.2.5 a preview of perturbing expressions in terms of their Euler angles. We first consider directly taking the Jacobian of a rotated point with respect to the Lie algebra vector representing the rotation:

$$\frac{\partial(\mathbf{C}\mathbf{v})}{\partial\boldsymbol{\phi}}, \tag{8.166}$$

where $\mathbf{C} = \exp(\boldsymbol{\phi}^{\wedge}) \in SO(3)$ and $\mathbf{v} \in \mathbb{R}^3$ is some arbitrary three-dimensional point.

To do this, we can start by taking the derivative with respect to a single element of $\boldsymbol{\phi} = (\phi_1, \phi_2, \phi_3)$. Applying the definition of a derivative along the $\mathbf{1}_i$ direction, we have

$$\frac{\partial(\mathbf{C}\mathbf{v})}{\partial\phi_i} = \lim_{h\to 0} \frac{\exp\left((\boldsymbol{\phi} + h\mathbf{1}_i)^{\wedge}\right)\mathbf{v} - \exp\left(\boldsymbol{\phi}^{\wedge}\right)\mathbf{v}}{h}, \tag{8.167}$$

---

[18] The $\odot$ operator for 4×1 columns is similar to the $\boxminus$ operator defined by Furgale (2011), which did not have the negative sign.

which we will refer to as a *directional derivative*. Since we are interested in the limit of h infinitely small, we can use the approximate BCH formula to write

$$\exp\left((\phi + h\mathbf{1}_i)^\wedge\right) \approx \exp\left((\mathbf{J}\,h\mathbf{1}_i)^\wedge\right)\exp\left(\phi^\wedge\right)$$
$$\approx \left(\mathbf{1} + h(\mathbf{J}\mathbf{1}_i)^\wedge\right)\exp\left(\phi^\wedge\right), \quad (8.168)$$

where $\mathbf{J}$ is the (left) Jacobian of $SO(3)$, evaluated at ϕ. Plugging this back into (8.167), we find that

$$\frac{\partial(\mathbf{Cv})}{\partial\phi_i} = (\mathbf{J}\mathbf{1}_i)^\wedge\,\mathbf{Cv} = -\left(\mathbf{Cv}\right)^\wedge\mathbf{J}\,\mathbf{1}_i. \quad (8.169)$$

Stacking the three directional derivatives alongside one another provides the desired Jacobian:

$$\frac{\partial(\mathbf{Cv})}{\partial\phi} = -\left(\mathbf{Cv}\right)^\wedge\mathbf{J}. \quad (8.170)$$

Moreover, if $\mathbf{Cv}$ appears inside another scalar function, $u(\mathbf{x})$, with $\mathbf{x} = \mathbf{Cv}$, then we have

$$\frac{\partial u}{\partial\phi} = \frac{\partial u}{\partial\mathbf{x}}\frac{\partial\mathbf{x}}{\partial\phi} = -\frac{\partial u}{\partial\mathbf{x}}\left(\mathbf{Cv}\right)^\wedge\mathbf{J}, \quad (8.171)$$

by the chain rule of differentiation. The result is the transpose of the gradient of u with respect to ϕ.

If we wanted to perform simple gradient descent of our function, we could take a step in the direction of the negative gradient, evaluated at our linearization point, $\mathbf{C}_{\text{op}} = \exp\left(\phi_{\text{op}}^\wedge\right)$:

$$\phi = \phi_{\text{op}} - \alpha\,\underbrace{\mathbf{J}^T\left(\mathbf{C}_{\text{op}}\mathbf{v}\right)^\wedge\left.\frac{\partial u}{\partial\mathbf{x}}\right|^T_{\mathbf{x}=\mathbf{C}_{\text{op}}\mathbf{v}}}_{\delta}, \quad (8.172)$$

where $\alpha > 0$ defines the step size.

We can easily see that stepping in this direction (by a small amount) will reduce the function value:

$$u\left(\exp\left(\phi^\wedge\right)\mathbf{v}\right) - u\left(\exp\left(\phi_{\text{op}}^\wedge\right)\mathbf{v}\right) \approx -\alpha\,\underbrace{\delta^T\left(\mathbf{J}\mathbf{J}^T\right)\delta}_{\geq 0}. \quad (8.173)$$

However, this is not the most streamlined way we could optimize u with respect to $\mathbf{C}$ because it requires that we store our rotation as a rotation vector, ϕ, which has singularities associated with it. Plus, we need to compute the Jacobian matrix, $\mathbf{J}$.

A cleaner way to carry out optimization is to find an update step for $\mathbf{C}$ in the form of a small rotation on the left[19] rather than directly on the Lie algebra rotation vector representing $\mathbf{C}$:

$$\mathbf{C} = \exp\left(\psi^\wedge\right)\mathbf{C}_{\text{op}}. \quad (8.174)$$

---

[19] A right-hand version is also possible.

The previous update can actually be cast in this form by using the approximate BCH formula once again:

$$\mathbf{C} = \exp\left(\boldsymbol{\phi}^\wedge\right) = \exp\left(\left(\boldsymbol{\phi}_{\mathrm{op}} - \alpha \mathbf{J}^T \boldsymbol{\delta}\right)^\wedge\right)$$

$$\approx \exp\left(-\alpha\left(\mathbf{J}\mathbf{J}^T\boldsymbol{\delta}\right)^\wedge\right)\mathbf{C}_{\mathrm{op}}, \tag{8.175}$$

or in other words, we could let $\boldsymbol{\psi} = -\alpha\mathbf{J}\mathbf{J}^T\boldsymbol{\delta}$ to accomplish the same thing as before, but this still requires that we compute $\mathbf{J}$. Instead, we can essentially just drop $\mathbf{J}\mathbf{J}^T > 0$ from the update and use

$$\boldsymbol{\psi} = -\alpha\boldsymbol{\delta}, \tag{8.176}$$

which still reduces the function,

$$u\left(\mathbf{C}\mathbf{v}\right) - u\left(\mathbf{C}_{\mathrm{op}}\mathbf{v}\right) \approx -\underbrace{\alpha\,\boldsymbol{\delta}^T\boldsymbol{\delta}}_{\geq 0}, \tag{8.177}$$

but takes a slightly different direction to do so.

Another way to look at this is that we are computing the Jacobian with respect to $\boldsymbol{\psi}$, where the perturbation is applied on the left.[20] Along the ψ_i direction, we have

$$\frac{\partial\left(\mathbf{C}\mathbf{v}\right)}{\partial\psi_i} = \lim_{h\to 0}\frac{\exp\left(h\mathbf{1}_i^\wedge\right)\mathbf{C}\mathbf{v} - \mathbf{C}\mathbf{v}}{h}$$

$$\approx \lim_{h\to 0}\frac{\left(1 + h\mathbf{1}_i^\wedge\right)\mathbf{C}\mathbf{v} - \mathbf{C}\mathbf{v}}{h} = -\left(\mathbf{C}\mathbf{v}\right)^\wedge\mathbf{1}_i. \tag{8.178}$$

Stacking the three directional derivatives together, we have

$$\frac{\partial\left(\mathbf{C}\mathbf{v}\right)}{\partial\boldsymbol{\psi}} = -\left(\mathbf{C}\mathbf{v}\right)^\wedge, \tag{8.179}$$

which is the same as our previous expression but without the $\mathbf{J}$.

An even simpler way to think about optimization is to skip the derivatives altogether and think in terms of perturbations. Choose a perturbation scheme,

$$\mathbf{C} = \exp\left(\boldsymbol{\psi}^\wedge\right)\mathbf{C}_{\mathrm{op}}, \tag{8.180}$$

where $\boldsymbol{\psi}$ is a small perturbation applied to an initial guess, $\mathbf{C}_{\mathrm{op}}$. When we take the product of the rotation and a point, $\mathbf{v}$, we can approximate the expression as follows:

$$\mathbf{C}\mathbf{v} = \exp\left(\boldsymbol{\psi}^\wedge\right)\mathbf{C}_{\mathrm{op}}\mathbf{v} \approx \mathbf{C}_{\mathrm{op}}\mathbf{v} - \left(\mathbf{C}_{\mathrm{op}}\mathbf{v}\right)^\wedge\boldsymbol{\psi}. \tag{8.181}$$

This is depicted graphically in Figure 8.3. Inserting this perturbation scheme into the function to be optimized, we have

$$u\left(\mathbf{C}\mathbf{v}\right) = u\left(\exp\left(\boldsymbol{\psi}^\wedge\right)\mathbf{C}_{\mathrm{op}}\mathbf{v}\right) \approx u\left(\left(1 + \boldsymbol{\psi}^\wedge\right)\mathbf{C}_{\mathrm{op}}\mathbf{v}\right)$$

$$\approx u(\mathbf{C}_{\mathrm{op}}\mathbf{v}) - \underbrace{\left.\frac{\partial u}{\partial\mathbf{x}}\right|_{\mathbf{x}=\mathbf{C}_{\mathrm{op}}\mathbf{v}}\left(\mathbf{C}_{\mathrm{op}}\mathbf{v}\right)^\wedge}_{\boldsymbol{\delta}^T}\boldsymbol{\psi} = u(\mathbf{C}_{\mathrm{op}}\mathbf{v}) + \boldsymbol{\delta}^T\boldsymbol{\psi}. \tag{8.182}$$

---

[20] This is sometimes called a (left) *Lie derivative*.

Figure 8.3 During optimization, we keep our nominal rotation, $\mathbf{C}_{\mathrm{op}}$, in the Lie group and consider a perturbation, $\boldsymbol{\psi}$, to take place in the Lie algebra, which is locally the tangent space of the group.

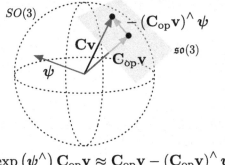

$$\mathbf{C}\mathbf{v} = \exp\left(\boldsymbol{\psi}^\wedge\right)\mathbf{C}_{\mathrm{op}}\mathbf{v} \approx \mathbf{C}_{\mathrm{op}}\mathbf{v} - (\mathbf{C}_{\mathrm{op}}\mathbf{v})^\wedge\,\boldsymbol{\psi}$$

Then pick a perturbation to decrease the function. For example, gradient descent suggests we would like to pick

$$\boldsymbol{\psi} = -\alpha\mathbf{D}\boldsymbol{\delta}, \tag{8.183}$$

In the parlance of manifold optimization, the exponential map is our *retraction* of our updated rotation back to the manifold.

with $\alpha > 0$ a small step size and $\mathbf{D} > 0$ any positive-definite matrix. Then apply the perturbation within the scheme to update the rotation,

$$\mathbf{C}_{\mathrm{op}} \leftarrow \exp\left(-\alpha\,(\mathbf{D}\boldsymbol{\delta})^\wedge\right)\mathbf{C}_{\mathrm{op}}, \tag{8.184}$$

and iterate to convergence. Our scheme guarantees $\mathbf{C}_{\mathrm{op}} \in SO(3)$ at each iteration.

The perturbation idea generalizes to more interesting optimization schemes than basic gradient descent, which can be quite slow. Consider the alternate derivation of the Gauss–Newton optimization method from Section 4.3.1. Suppose we have a general nonlinear, quadratic cost function of a rotation of the form,

$$J(\mathbf{C}) = \frac{1}{2}\sum_m \left(u_m(\mathbf{C}\mathbf{v}_m)\right)^2, \tag{8.185}$$

where $u_m(\cdot)$ are scalar nonlinear functions and $\mathbf{v}_m \in \mathbb{R}^3$ are three-dimensional points. We begin with an initial guess for the optimal rotation, $\mathbf{C}_{\mathrm{op}} \in SO(3)$, and then perturb this (on the left) according to

$$\mathbf{C} = \exp\left(\boldsymbol{\psi}^\wedge\right)\mathbf{C}_{\mathrm{op}}, \tag{8.186}$$

where $\boldsymbol{\psi}$ is the perturbation. We then apply our perturbation scheme inside each $u_m(\cdot)$ so that

$$u_m\left(\mathbf{C}\mathbf{v}_m\right) = u_m\left(\exp(\boldsymbol{\psi}^\wedge)\mathbf{C}_{\mathrm{op}}\mathbf{v}_m\right) \approx u_m\left(\left(\mathbf{1}+\boldsymbol{\psi}^\wedge\right)\mathbf{C}_{\mathrm{op}}\mathbf{v}_m\right)$$

$$\approx \underbrace{u_m(\mathbf{C}_{\mathrm{op}}\mathbf{v}_m)}_{\beta_m} \underbrace{-\left.\frac{\partial u_m}{\partial \mathbf{x}}\right|_{\mathbf{x}=\mathbf{C}_{\mathrm{op}}\mathbf{v}_m}(\mathbf{C}_{\mathrm{op}}\mathbf{v}_m)^\wedge\,\boldsymbol{\psi}}_{\boldsymbol{\delta}_m^T} \tag{8.187}$$

is a linearized version of $u_m(\cdot)$ in terms of our perturbation, $\boldsymbol{\psi}$. Inserting this back into our cost function, we have

$$J(\mathbf{C}) \approx \frac{1}{2}\sum_m \left(\boldsymbol{\delta}_m^T\boldsymbol{\psi} + \beta_m\right)^2, \tag{8.188}$$

which is exactly quadratic in $\boldsymbol{\psi}$. Taking the derivative of J with respect to $\boldsymbol{\psi}$, we have

$$\frac{\partial J}{\partial \boldsymbol{\psi}^T} = \sum_m \boldsymbol{\delta}_m \left(\boldsymbol{\delta}_m^T \boldsymbol{\psi} + \beta_m \right). \tag{8.189}$$

We can set the derivative to zero to find the optimal perturbation, $\boldsymbol{\psi}^\star$, that minimizes J:

$$\left(\sum_m \boldsymbol{\delta}_m \boldsymbol{\delta}_m^T \right) \boldsymbol{\psi}^\star = - \sum_m \beta_m \boldsymbol{\delta}_m. \tag{8.190}$$

This is a linear system of equations, which we can solve for $\boldsymbol{\psi}^\star$. We then apply this optimal perturbation to our initial guess, according to our perturbation scheme:

$$\mathbf{C}_{\text{op}} \leftarrow \exp\left(\boldsymbol{\psi}^{\star^\wedge} \right) \mathbf{C}_{\text{op}}, \tag{8.191}$$

which ensures that at each iteration, we have $\mathbf{C}_{\text{op}} \in SO(3)$. We iterate to convergence and then output $\mathbf{C}^\star = \mathbf{C}_{\text{op}}$ at the final iteration as our optimized rotation. This is exactly the Gauss–Newton algorithm, but adapted to work with the matrix Lie group, $SO(3)$, by exploiting the surjective-only property of the exponential map to define an appropriate perturbation scheme.

Poses

The same concepts can also be applied to poses. The Jacobian of a transformed point with respect to the Lie algebra vector representing the transformation is

$$\frac{\partial(\mathbf{Tp})}{\partial \boldsymbol{\xi}} = (\mathbf{Tp})^\odot \boldsymbol{\mathcal{J}}, \tag{8.192}$$

where $\mathbf{T} = \exp(\boldsymbol{\xi}^\wedge) \in SE(3)$ and $\mathbf{p} \in \mathbb{R}^4$ is some arbitrary three-dimensional point, expressed in homogeneous coordinates.

However, if we perturb the transformation matrix on the left,

$$\mathbf{T} \leftarrow \exp\left(\boldsymbol{\epsilon}^\wedge \right) \mathbf{T}, \tag{8.193}$$

then the Jacobian with respect to this perturbation (i.e., the (left) Lie derivative) is simply

$$\frac{\partial(\mathbf{Tp})}{\partial \boldsymbol{\epsilon}} = (\mathbf{Tp})^\odot, \tag{8.194}$$

which removes the need to calculate the $\boldsymbol{\mathcal{J}}$ matrix.

Finally, for optimization, suppose we have a general nonlinear, quadratic cost function of a transformation of the form

$$J(\mathbf{T}) = \frac{1}{2} \sum_m \left(u_m(\mathbf{Tp}_m) \right)^2, \tag{8.195}$$

where $u_m(\cdot)$ are nonlinear functions and $\mathbf{p}_m \in \mathbb{R}^4$ are three-dimensional points expressed in homogeneous coordinates. We begin with an initial guess for the optimal transformation, $\mathbf{T}_{\text{op}} \in SE(3)$, and then perturb this (on the left) according to

$$\mathbf{T} = \exp\left(\epsilon^\wedge\right)\mathbf{T}_{\text{op}},\tag{8.196}$$

where ϵ is the perturbation. We then apply our perturbation scheme inside each $u_m(\cdot)$ so that

$$u_m\left(\mathbf{T}\mathbf{p}_m\right) = u_m\left(\exp\left(\epsilon^\wedge\right)\mathbf{T}_{\text{op}}\mathbf{p}_m\right) \approx u_m\left((1+\epsilon^\wedge)\mathbf{T}_{\text{op}}\mathbf{p}_m\right)$$

$$\approx \underbrace{u_m(\mathbf{T}_{\text{op}}\mathbf{p}_m)}_{\beta_m} + \underbrace{\left.\frac{\partial u_m}{\partial \mathbf{x}}\right|_{\mathbf{x}=\mathbf{T}_{\text{op}}\mathbf{p}_m}(\mathbf{T}_{\text{op}}\mathbf{p}_m)^\odot\epsilon}_{\delta_m^T}\tag{8.197}$$

is a linearized version of $u_m(\cdot)$ in terms of our perturbation, ϵ. Inserting this back into our cost function, we have

$$J(\mathbf{T}) = \frac{1}{2}\sum_m\left(\delta_m^T\epsilon + \beta_m\right)^2,\tag{8.198}$$

which is exactly quadratic in ϵ. Taking the derivative of J with respect to ϵ, we have

$$\frac{\partial J}{\partial \epsilon^T} = \sum_m \delta_m\left(\delta_m^T\epsilon + \beta_m\right).\tag{8.199}$$

We can set the derivative to zero to find the optimal perturbation, $\epsilon^\star$, that minimizes J:

$$\left(\sum_m \delta_m\delta_m^T\right)\epsilon^\star = -\sum_m \beta_m\delta_m.\tag{8.200}$$

This is a linear system of equations, which we can solve for $\epsilon^\star$. We then apply this optimal perturbation to our initial guess, according to our perturbation scheme,

$$\mathbf{T}_{\text{op}} \leftarrow \exp\left(\epsilon^{\star\wedge}\right)\mathbf{T}_{\text{op}},\tag{8.201}$$

which ensures that at each iteration, we have $\mathbf{T}_{\text{op}} \in SE(3)$. We iterate to convergence and then output $\mathbf{T}^\star = \mathbf{T}_{\text{op}}$ at the final iteration as the optimal pose. This is exactly the Gauss–Newton algorithm, but adapted to work with the matrix Lie group, $SE(3)$, by exploiting the surjective-only property of the exponential map to define an appropriate perturbation scheme.

Gauss–Newton Discussion

This approach to Gauss–Newton optimization for our matrix Lie groups where we use a customized perturbation scheme has three key properties:

(i) We are storing our rotation or pose in a singularity-free format,

(ii) At each iteration we are performing unconstrained optimization,

(iii) Our manipulations occur at the matrix level so that we do not need to worry about taking the derivatives of a bunch of scalar trigonometric functions, which can easily lead to mistakes.

This makes implementation quite straightforward. We can also easily incorporate both of the practical patches to Gauss–Newton that were outlined in Section 4.3.1 (a line search and Levenberg–Marquardt) as well as the ideas from robust estimation described in 5.4.2.

8.1.10 Optimization on Riemannian Manifolds

In this section, we discuss how our optimization approach from the previous section is equivalent to optimization on a *Riemannian manifold*, a concept from differential geometry. Absil et al. (2009) and Boumal (2022) provide all the necessary background material; Ablin and Peyré (2021) provide a nice summary with 'left' tangent vectors matching our chosen convention. We will restrict our discussion to $SO(3)$ and $SE(3)$, but the concepts carry over to other matrix Lie groups.

Georg Friedrich Bernhard Riemann (1826–1866) was a German mathematician who made major contributions to analysis, number theory, and differential geometry. He is remembered most for the Riemann integral, Riemann surface, Riemann hypothesis, and laying the foundation of general relativity.

Rotations

When introducing $SO(3)$, we mentioned that it is a *smooth manifold*. Such manifolds have a well-defined *tangent space* at each point on the manifold, which is the same concept as the Lie algebra (at the identity element). Starting from the $SO(3)$ orthogonality constraint and taking the differential,

$$\mathbf{C}\mathbf{C}^T = \mathbf{1} \quad \Rightarrow \quad d\mathbf{C}\,\mathbf{C}^T + \mathbf{C}\,d\mathbf{C}^T = \mathbf{0}, \tag{8.202}$$

we have that the *tangent space* of $SO(3)$ at $\mathbf{C}$ comprises all vectors, $d\mathbf{C}$, satisfying the expression on the right. We see that all vectors of the form $d\mathbf{C} = \boldsymbol{\phi}^\wedge \mathbf{C}$ satisfy the condition:

$$\boldsymbol{\phi}^\wedge \mathbf{C}\mathbf{C}^T + \mathbf{C}\mathbf{C}^T \boldsymbol{\phi}^{\wedge^T} = \boldsymbol{\phi}^\wedge + \boldsymbol{\phi}^{\wedge^T} = \boldsymbol{\phi}^\wedge - \boldsymbol{\phi}^\wedge = \mathbf{0}. \tag{8.203}$$

Conveniently, we can move along any tangent vector and we will remain 'close' to the manifold. Adding a tangent vector, $\boldsymbol{\phi}^\wedge \mathbf{C}$, to $\mathbf{C}$, we have

$$\mathbf{C} + \boldsymbol{\phi}^\wedge \mathbf{C} = \left(\mathbf{1} + \boldsymbol{\phi}^\wedge\right)\mathbf{C}, \tag{8.204}$$

where we recognize $\mathbf{1} + \boldsymbol{\phi}^\wedge$ as a 'small' rotation matrix. The result is not quite in $SO(3)$ and to rectify this, we can use a *retraction*, $\mathbf{R}(\boldsymbol{\phi}^\wedge \mathbf{C}, \mathbf{C})$. There is an infinite number of such retractions possible for $SO(3)$ (Bauchau and Trainelli, 2003) (and $SE(3)$ (Barfoot et al., 2021)), but the most common for Lie groups is the *exponential map*:

$$\mathbf{R}(\boldsymbol{\phi}^\wedge \mathbf{C}, \mathbf{C}) = \exp\left(\boldsymbol{\phi}^\wedge\right)\mathbf{C}. \tag{8.205}$$

Now suppose we have a cost function, $f(\mathbf{C})$, and want to perform gradient descent on the $SO(3)$ manifold. This can be done using the *Riemannian gradient*, $\mathrm{grad} f(\mathbf{C})$, which is the unique vector that satisfies

$$\lim_{h \to 0} \frac{f(\mathbf{R}(h\phi^\wedge \mathbf{C}, \mathbf{C})) - f(\mathbf{C})}{h} = \langle \mathrm{grad} f(\mathbf{C}), \phi^\wedge \mathbf{C} \rangle_\mathbf{C}, \qquad (8.206)$$

for all tangent vectors, $\phi^\wedge \mathbf{C}$. This requires that the inner product, $\langle \cdot, \cdot \rangle_\mathbf{C}$, be defined for our tangent space (at $\mathbf{C}$), whereupon we can claim it to be a *Riemannian manifold*. We can use the inner product that we earlier defined in (8.107),

$$\langle \phi_1^\wedge \mathbf{C}, \phi_2^\wedge \mathbf{C} \rangle_\mathbf{C} = \frac{1}{2} \mathrm{tr} \left(\phi_1^\wedge \phi_2^{\wedge^T} \right) = \phi_1^T \phi_2. \qquad (8.207)$$

Then we have

$$\begin{aligned}
&\lim_{h \to 0} \frac{f(\mathbf{R}(h\phi^\wedge \mathbf{C}, \mathbf{C})) - f(\mathbf{C})}{h} \\
&= \lim_{h \to 0} \frac{f(\exp(h\phi^\wedge)\mathbf{C}) - f(\mathbf{C})}{h} \approx \lim_{h \to 0} \frac{f((\mathbf{1} + h\phi^\wedge)\mathbf{C}) - f(\mathbf{C})}{h} \\
&= \lim_{h \to 0} \frac{f(\mathbf{C}) + \mathrm{tr} \left(\frac{\partial f}{\partial \mathbf{C}} (h\phi^\wedge \mathbf{C})^T \right) - f(\mathbf{C})}{h} = \mathrm{tr} \left(\frac{\partial f}{\partial \mathbf{C}} (\phi^\wedge \mathbf{C})^T \right) \\
&= \frac{1}{2} \mathrm{tr} \left(\frac{\partial f}{\partial \mathbf{C}} \mathbf{C}^T \phi^{\wedge^T} + \phi^\wedge \mathbf{C} \frac{\partial f}{\partial \mathbf{C}}^T \right) \\
&= \frac{1}{2} \mathrm{tr} \left(\left(\frac{\partial f}{\partial \mathbf{C}} \mathbf{C}^T - \mathbf{C} \frac{\partial f}{\partial \mathbf{C}}^T \right) \phi^{\wedge^T} \right) \\
&= \underbrace{\left\langle \left(\frac{\partial f}{\partial \mathbf{C}} \mathbf{C}^T - \mathbf{C} \frac{\partial f}{\partial \mathbf{C}}^T \right) \mathbf{C}, \phi^\wedge \mathbf{C} \right\rangle_\mathbf{C}}_{\mathrm{grad} f(\mathbf{C})}, \qquad (8.208)
\end{aligned}$$

so that the Riemannian gradient is (Ablin and Peyré, 2021)

$$\mathrm{grad} f(\mathbf{C}) = \psi^\wedge \mathbf{C}, \quad \psi^\wedge = \frac{\partial f}{\partial \mathbf{C}} \mathbf{C}^T - \mathbf{C} \frac{\partial f}{\partial \mathbf{C}}^T, \qquad (8.209)$$

where $\frac{\partial f}{\partial \mathbf{C}}$ is the derivative of our cost with respect to $\mathbf{C}$, ignoring the fact that $\mathbf{C}$ lives on a manifold (this requires that f provides a *smooth extension* of the cost off the manifold). In essence, the Riemannian gradient is the projection of the unconstrained gradient onto the tangent space.

Once the Riemannian gradient is computed, we can then use it to perform gradient descent by taking a small step in the direction of the negative gradient and use our retraction to ensure the result remains on the manifold:

$$\mathbf{C}_{\mathrm{op}} \leftarrow \mathbf{R}(-\alpha \, \mathrm{grad} f(\mathbf{C}_{\mathrm{op}}), \mathbf{C}_{\mathrm{op}}), \qquad (8.210)$$

where $\alpha > 0$ and $\mathbf{C}_{op}$ is our current estimate of the rotation.

As an example, consider $f(\mathbf{C}) = \mathbf{u}^T \mathbf{C} \mathbf{v}$ with $\mathbf{u}$ and $\mathbf{v}$ known. We have

$$\frac{\partial f}{\partial \mathbf{C}} = \mathbf{u} \mathbf{v}^T, \tag{8.211}$$

so that the Riemannian gradient is

$$\mathrm{grad} f(\mathbf{C}) = \left(\mathbf{u} \mathbf{v}^T \mathbf{C}^T - \mathbf{C} \mathbf{v} \mathbf{u}^T \right) \mathbf{C} = \left((\mathbf{C} \mathbf{v})^\wedge \mathbf{u} \right)^\wedge \mathbf{C}, \tag{8.212}$$

and our gradient descent update equation becomes

$$\mathbf{C}_{op} \leftarrow \exp\left(-\alpha \left((\mathbf{C}_{op} \mathbf{v})^\wedge \mathbf{u} \right)^\wedge \right) \mathbf{C}_{op}, \tag{8.213}$$

where we have applied the retraction.

Using our perturbation approach from the last section, we can instead write

$$\begin{aligned} f(\mathbf{C}) = \mathbf{u}^T \mathbf{C} \mathbf{v} = \mathbf{u}^T \exp\left(\phi^\wedge \right) \mathbf{C}_{op} \mathbf{v} \approx \mathbf{u}^T \left(1 + \phi^\wedge \right) \mathbf{C}_{op} \mathbf{v} \\ = \mathbf{u}^T \mathbf{C}_{op} \mathbf{v} + \mathbf{u}^T \phi^\wedge \mathbf{C}_{op} \mathbf{v} = f(\mathbf{C}_{op}) - \mathbf{u}^T \left(\mathbf{C}_{op} \mathbf{v} \right)^\wedge \phi. \end{aligned} \tag{8.214}$$

To make the function decrease from one iteration to the next we can select

$$\phi = -\alpha \left(-\mathbf{u}^T \left(\mathbf{C}_{op} \mathbf{v} \right)^\wedge \right)^T = -\alpha \left(\mathbf{C}_{op} \mathbf{v} \right)^\wedge \mathbf{u}, \tag{8.215}$$

with $\alpha > 0$ so that $f(\mathbf{C}) - f(\mathbf{C}_{op}) = -\alpha^{-1} \phi^T \phi < 0$. Then, our update is

$$\mathbf{C}_{op} \leftarrow \exp\left(\phi^\wedge \right) \mathbf{C}_{op}, \tag{8.216}$$

which is identical to (8.213).

Poses

The same ideas carry over to $SE(3)$, but there are some subtleties that are worth spelling out. Tangent vectors for $SE(3)$ are of the form $\boldsymbol{\xi}^\wedge \mathbf{T}$ so that, if we add a tangent vector to a pose, $\mathbf{T}$, we have

$$\mathbf{T} + \boldsymbol{\xi}^\wedge \mathbf{T} = (1 + \boldsymbol{\xi}^\wedge) \mathbf{T}, \tag{8.217}$$

which is 'close' but not on $SE(3)$. We can again pick the exponential map as our retraction:

$$\mathbf{R}(\boldsymbol{\xi}^\wedge \mathbf{T}, \mathbf{T}) = \exp\left(\boldsymbol{\xi}^\wedge \right) \mathbf{T}, \tag{8.218}$$

which forces the result back onto $SE(3)$.

If we have a cost function, $f(\mathbf{T})$, and want to carry out gradient descent on the $SE(3)$ manifold, we can use the Riemannian gradient, $\mathrm{grad} f(\mathbf{T})$, which is the unique vector satisfying

$$\lim_{h \to 0} \frac{f(\mathbf{R}(h\boldsymbol{\xi}^\wedge \mathbf{T}, \mathbf{T})) - f(\mathbf{T})}{h} = \langle \text{grad} f(\mathbf{T}), \boldsymbol{\xi}^\wedge \mathbf{T} \rangle_{\mathbf{T}}, \qquad (8.219)$$

for all tangent vectors, $\boldsymbol{\xi}^\wedge \mathbf{T}$. We can define the inner product between two tangent vectors (at $\mathbf{T}$) as in (8.116a),

$$\langle \boldsymbol{\xi}_1^\wedge \mathbf{T}, \boldsymbol{\xi}_2^\wedge \mathbf{T} \rangle_{\mathbf{T}} = \text{tr}\left(\boldsymbol{\xi}_1^\wedge \begin{bmatrix} \frac{1}{2}\mathbf{1} & \mathbf{0} \\ \mathbf{0}^T & 1 \end{bmatrix} \boldsymbol{\xi}_2^{\wedge^T} \right) = \boldsymbol{\xi}_1^T \boldsymbol{\xi}_2, \qquad (8.220)$$

whereupon we have a Riemannian manifold.

To begin computing the Riemannian gradient, we note that

$$\lim_{h \to 0} \frac{f(\mathbf{R}(h\boldsymbol{\xi}^\wedge \mathbf{T}, \mathbf{T})) - f(\mathbf{T})}{h}$$

$$= \lim_{h \to 0} \frac{f(\exp(h\boldsymbol{\xi}^\wedge)\mathbf{T}) - f(\mathbf{T})}{h} \approx \lim_{h \to 0} \frac{f((\mathbf{1} + h\boldsymbol{\xi}^\wedge)\mathbf{T}) - f(\mathbf{T})}{h}$$

$$= \lim_{h \to 0} \frac{f(\mathbf{T}) + \text{tr}\left(\frac{\partial f}{\partial \mathbf{T}} \left(h\boldsymbol{\xi}^\wedge \mathbf{T} \right)^T \right) - f(\mathbf{T})}{h} = \text{tr}\left(\frac{\partial f}{\partial \mathbf{T}} \left(\boldsymbol{\xi}^\wedge \mathbf{T} \right)^T \right). \quad (8.221)$$

The gradient of our cost with respect to the pose (not accounting for the manifold constraints) can be broken down as[21]

$$\frac{\partial f}{\partial \mathbf{T}} = \begin{bmatrix} \frac{\partial f}{\partial \mathbf{C}} & \frac{\partial f}{\partial \mathbf{r}} \\ * & * \end{bmatrix}, \qquad (8.222)$$

where $*$ indicates a non-zero entry that we will not require. Then it is not hard to show that

$$\text{tr}\left(\frac{\partial f}{\partial \mathbf{T}} \left(\boldsymbol{\xi}^\wedge \mathbf{T} \right)^T \right) = \text{tr}\left(\boldsymbol{\epsilon}^\wedge \begin{bmatrix} \frac{1}{2}\mathbf{1} & \mathbf{0} \\ \mathbf{0}^T & 1 \end{bmatrix} \boldsymbol{\xi}^{\wedge^T} \right) = \langle \underbrace{\boldsymbol{\epsilon}^\wedge \mathbf{T}}_{\text{grad} f(\mathbf{T})}, \boldsymbol{\xi}^\wedge \mathbf{T} \rangle_{\mathbf{T}}, \quad (8.223)$$

with

$$\boldsymbol{\epsilon}^\wedge = \begin{bmatrix} \left(\frac{\partial f}{\partial \mathbf{C}}\mathbf{C}^T - \mathbf{C}\frac{\partial f}{\partial \mathbf{C}}^T \right) + \left(\frac{\partial f}{\partial \mathbf{r}}\mathbf{r}^T - \mathbf{r}\frac{\partial f}{\partial \mathbf{r}}^T \right) & \frac{\partial f}{\partial \mathbf{r}} \\ \mathbf{0}^T & 0 \end{bmatrix}, \qquad (8.224)$$

so that $\text{grad} f(\mathbf{T}) = \boldsymbol{\epsilon}^\wedge \mathbf{T}$ is the Riemannian gradient.

As an example, consider $f(\mathbf{T}) = \mathbf{q}^T \mathbf{T} \mathbf{p}$ with $\mathbf{q} = \begin{bmatrix} \mathbf{u} \\ 1 \end{bmatrix}$ and $\mathbf{p} = \begin{bmatrix} \mathbf{v} \\ 1 \end{bmatrix}$ known. We have

$$\frac{\partial f}{\partial \mathbf{T}} = \mathbf{q}\mathbf{p}^T = \begin{bmatrix} \mathbf{u}\mathbf{v}^T & \mathbf{u} \\ \mathbf{v}^T & 1 \end{bmatrix} \quad \Rightarrow \quad \frac{\partial f}{\partial \mathbf{C}} = \mathbf{u}\mathbf{v}^T, \ \frac{\partial f}{\partial \mathbf{r}} = \mathbf{u}. \quad (8.225)$$

With a bit of algebra,

---

[21] Here we note that $\frac{\partial f}{\partial \mathbf{r}}$ is a column to be consistent with the rest of the equation, but this is the opposite of our usual convention.

$$\text{grad} f(\mathbf{T}) = \boldsymbol{\epsilon}^{\wedge} \mathbf{T}, \quad \boldsymbol{\epsilon} = \begin{bmatrix} \mathbf{u} \\ (\mathbf{C}\mathbf{v} + \mathbf{r})^{\wedge} \mathbf{u} \end{bmatrix}, \tag{8.226}$$

and our gradient descent update equation becomes

$$\mathbf{T}_{op} \leftarrow \exp\left(-\alpha \begin{bmatrix} \mathbf{u} \\ (\mathbf{C}_{op}\mathbf{v} + \mathbf{r}_{op})^{\wedge} \mathbf{u} \end{bmatrix}^{\wedge}\right) \mathbf{T}_{op}, \tag{8.227}$$

where we have applied the retraction.

If we instead use the perturbation approach from the previous section, we have

$$\begin{aligned} f(\mathbf{T}) &= \mathbf{q}^T \mathbf{T} \mathbf{p} = \mathbf{q}^T \exp\left(\boldsymbol{\xi}^{\wedge}\right) \mathbf{T}_{op} \mathbf{p} \approx \mathbf{q}^T \left(\mathbf{1} + \boldsymbol{\xi}^{\wedge}\right) \mathbf{T}_{op} \mathbf{p} \\ &= \mathbf{q}^T \mathbf{T}_{op} \mathbf{p} + \mathbf{q}^T \boldsymbol{\xi}^{\wedge} \mathbf{T}_{op} \mathbf{p} = f(\mathbf{T}_{op}) + \mathbf{q}^T \left(\mathbf{T}_{op} \mathbf{p}\right)^{\odot} \boldsymbol{\xi}. \end{aligned} \tag{8.228}$$

To make the function decrease from one iteration to the next, we can select

$$\boldsymbol{\xi} = -\alpha \left(\mathbf{T}_{op} \mathbf{p}\right)^{\odot^T} \mathbf{q} = -\alpha \begin{bmatrix} \mathbf{u} \\ (\mathbf{C}_{op}\mathbf{v} + \mathbf{r}_{op})^{\wedge} \mathbf{u} \end{bmatrix} \tag{8.229}$$

with $\alpha > 0$ so that $f(\mathbf{T}) - f(\mathbf{T}_{op}) = -\alpha^{-1} \boldsymbol{\xi}^T \boldsymbol{\xi} < 0$. Then, our update is

$$\mathbf{T}_{op} \leftarrow \exp\left(\boldsymbol{\xi}^{\wedge}\right) \mathbf{T}_{op}, \tag{8.230}$$

which is identical to (8.227).

Summary

This shows that at least in the case of gradient descent our perturbation approach is, in fact, performing Riemannian gradient descent on the manifolds, $SO(3)$ and $SE(3)$. There is also the concept of a *Riemannian Hessian* that can be used to carry out Riemannian Newton's method on the manifold, but we will stick to the Gauss–Newton approach from the previous section.

In short, we can view our perturbation approach as providing a convenient shortcut to an elegant framework for carrying out unconstrained optimization on matrix Lie groups, which are also Riemannian manifolds.

8.1.11 Identities

We have seen many identities and expressions in this chapter related to our matrix Lie groups, $SO(3)$ and $SE(3)$. The next two pages summarize these. The first page provides identities for $SO(3)$ and the second for $SE(3)$.

$SO(3)$ Identities and Approximations

Lie Algebra

$$\mathbf{u}^\wedge = \begin{bmatrix} u_1 \\ u_2 \\ u_3 \end{bmatrix}^\wedge = \begin{bmatrix} 0 & -u_3 & u_2 \\ u_3 & 0 & -u_1 \\ -u_2 & u_1 & 0 \end{bmatrix}$$

$$(\alpha\mathbf{u} + \beta\mathbf{v})^\wedge \equiv \alpha\mathbf{u}^\wedge + \beta\mathbf{v}^\wedge$$

$$\mathbf{u}^{\wedge^T} \equiv -\mathbf{u}^\wedge$$

$$\mathbf{u}^\wedge\mathbf{v} \equiv -\mathbf{v}^\wedge\mathbf{u}$$

$$\mathbf{u}^\wedge\mathbf{u} \equiv \mathbf{0}$$

$$(\mathbf{Wu})^\wedge \equiv \mathbf{u}^\wedge(\mathrm{tr}(\mathbf{W})\mathbf{1} - \mathbf{W}) - \mathbf{W}^T\mathbf{u}^\wedge$$

$$\mathbf{u}^\wedge\mathbf{v}^\wedge \equiv -(\mathbf{u}^T\mathbf{v})\mathbf{1} + \mathbf{v}\mathbf{u}^T$$

$$\mathbf{u}^\wedge\mathbf{W}\mathbf{v}^\wedge \equiv (-\mathrm{tr}(\mathbf{v}\mathbf{u}^T)\mathbf{1} + \mathbf{v}\mathbf{u}^T)$$
$$\times(-\mathrm{tr}(\mathbf{W})\mathbf{1} + \mathbf{W}^T)$$
$$+ \mathrm{tr}(\mathbf{W}^T\mathbf{v}\mathbf{u}^T)\mathbf{1} - \mathbf{W}^T\mathbf{v}\mathbf{u}^T$$

$$\mathbf{u}^\wedge\mathbf{v}^\wedge\mathbf{u}^\wedge \equiv \mathbf{u}^\wedge\mathbf{u}^\wedge\mathbf{v}^\wedge + \mathbf{v}^\wedge\mathbf{u}^\wedge\mathbf{u}^\wedge + (\mathbf{u}^T\mathbf{u})\mathbf{v}^\wedge$$

$$(\mathbf{u}^\wedge)^3 + (\mathbf{u}^T\mathbf{u})\mathbf{u}^\wedge \equiv \mathbf{0}$$

$$\mathbf{u}^\wedge\mathbf{v}^\wedge\mathbf{v}^\wedge + \mathbf{v}^\wedge\mathbf{v}^\wedge\mathbf{u}^\wedge + 2(\mathbf{v}^T\mathbf{v})\mathbf{u}^\wedge \equiv (\mathbf{v}^\wedge\mathbf{u}^\wedge\mathbf{v})^\wedge$$

$$[\mathbf{u}^\wedge, \mathbf{v}^\wedge] \equiv \mathbf{u}^\wedge\mathbf{v}^\wedge - \mathbf{v}^\wedge\mathbf{u}^\wedge \equiv (\mathbf{u}^\wedge\mathbf{v})^\wedge$$

$$\underbrace{[\mathbf{u}^\wedge, [\mathbf{u}^\wedge, \dots [\mathbf{u}^\wedge, \mathbf{v}^\wedge] \dots]]}_{n} \equiv ((\mathbf{u}^\wedge)^n\mathbf{v})^\wedge$$

Lie Group

$$\mathbf{C} = \exp(\phi^\wedge) \equiv \sum_{n=0}^\infty \frac{1}{n!}(\phi^\wedge)^n$$
$$\equiv \cos\phi\,\mathbf{1} + (1-\cos\phi)\mathbf{aa}^T + \sin\phi\,\mathbf{a}^\wedge$$
$$\approx \mathbf{1} + \phi^\wedge$$

$$\mathbf{C}^{-1} \equiv \mathbf{C}^T \equiv \sum_{n=0}^\infty \frac{1}{n!}(-\phi^\wedge)^n \approx \mathbf{1} - \phi^\wedge$$
$$\phi = \phi\mathbf{a}$$
$$\mathbf{a}^T\mathbf{a} \equiv 1$$
$$\mathbf{C}^T\mathbf{C} \equiv \mathbf{1} \equiv \mathbf{C}\mathbf{C}^T$$
$$\mathrm{tr}(\mathbf{C}) \equiv 2\cos\phi + 1$$
$$\det(\mathbf{C}) \equiv 1$$
$$\mathbf{Ca} \equiv \mathbf{a}$$
$$\mathbf{C}\phi \equiv \phi$$
$$\mathbf{Ca}^\wedge \equiv \mathbf{a}^\wedge\mathbf{C}$$
$$\mathbf{C}\phi^\wedge \equiv \phi^\wedge\mathbf{C}$$
$$(\mathbf{Cu})^\wedge \equiv \mathbf{Cu}^\wedge\mathbf{C}^T$$
$$\exp((\mathbf{Cu})^\wedge) \equiv \mathbf{C}\exp(\mathbf{u}^\wedge)\mathbf{C}^T$$

(left) Jacobian

$$\mathbf{J} = \int_0^1 \mathbf{C}^\alpha\,d\alpha \equiv \sum_{n=0}^\infty \frac{1}{(n+1)!}(\phi^\wedge)^n$$
$$\equiv \frac{\sin\phi}{\phi}\mathbf{1} + \left(1 - \frac{\sin\phi}{\phi}\right)\mathbf{aa}^T + \frac{1-\cos\phi}{\phi}\mathbf{a}^\wedge$$
$$\approx \mathbf{1} + \frac{1}{2}\phi^\wedge$$

$$\mathbf{J}^{-1} \equiv \sum_{n=0}^\infty \frac{B_n}{n!}(\phi^\wedge)^n$$
$$\equiv \frac{\phi}{2}\cot\frac{\phi}{2}\mathbf{1} + \left(1 - \frac{\phi}{2}\cot\frac{\phi}{2}\right)\mathbf{aa}^T - \frac{\phi}{2}\mathbf{a}^\wedge$$
$$\approx \mathbf{1} - \frac{1}{2}\phi^\wedge$$

$$\exp((\phi + \delta\phi)^\wedge) \approx \exp((\mathbf{J}\delta\phi)^\wedge)\exp(\phi^\wedge)$$
$$\mathbf{C} \equiv \mathbf{1} + \phi^\wedge\mathbf{J}$$
$$\mathbf{J}(\phi) \equiv \mathbf{C}\mathbf{J}(-\phi)$$

$$(\exp(\delta\phi^\wedge)\mathbf{C})^\alpha \approx (\mathbf{1} + (\mathbf{A}(\alpha,\phi)\delta\phi)^\wedge)\mathbf{C}^\alpha$$
$$\mathbf{A}(\alpha,\phi) = \alpha\mathbf{J}(\alpha\phi)\mathbf{J}(\phi)^{-1} = \sum_{n=0}^\infty \frac{F_n(\alpha)}{n!}(\phi^\wedge)^n$$

$\alpha, \beta \in \mathbb{R}, \ \mathbf{u}, \mathbf{v}, \phi, \delta\phi \in \mathbb{R}^3, \ \mathbf{W}, \mathbf{A}, \mathbf{J} \in \mathbb{R}^{3\times3}, \ \mathbf{C} \in SO(3)$

$SE(3)$ Identities and Approximations

Lie Algebra	Lie Group	(left) Jacobian

Lie Group

$$\boldsymbol{\xi} = \begin{bmatrix} \boldsymbol{\rho} \\ \boldsymbol{\phi} \end{bmatrix}$$

$$\mathbf{T} = \exp(\boldsymbol{\xi}^\wedge) \equiv \sum_{n=0}^{\infty} \frac{1}{n!}(\boldsymbol{\xi}^\wedge)^n$$

$$\equiv \mathbf{1} + \boldsymbol{\xi}^\wedge + \left(\frac{1-\cos\phi}{\phi^2}\right)(\boldsymbol{\xi}^\wedge)^2 + \left(\frac{\phi-\sin\phi}{\phi^3}\right)(\boldsymbol{\xi}^\wedge)^3$$

$$\approx \mathbf{1} + \boldsymbol{\xi}^\wedge$$

$$\mathbf{T} \equiv \begin{bmatrix} \mathbf{C} & \mathbf{J}\boldsymbol{\rho} \\ \mathbf{0}^T & 1 \end{bmatrix}$$

$$\boldsymbol{\xi}^\wedge \equiv \mathrm{ad}(\boldsymbol{\xi}^\wedge)$$

$$\mathcal{T} = \exp(\boldsymbol{\xi}^\wedge) \equiv \sum_{n=0}^{\infty} \frac{1}{n!}(\boldsymbol{\xi}^\wedge)^n$$

$$\equiv \mathbf{1} + \left(\frac{3\sin\phi-\phi\cos\phi}{2\phi}\right)\boldsymbol{\xi}^\wedge + \left(\frac{4-\phi\sin\phi-4\cos\phi}{2\phi^2}\right)(\boldsymbol{\xi}^\wedge)^2 + \left(\frac{\sin\phi-\phi\cos\phi}{2\phi^3}\right)(\boldsymbol{\xi}^\wedge)^3 + \left(\frac{2-\phi\sin\phi-2\cos\phi}{2\phi^4}\right)(\boldsymbol{\xi}^\wedge)^4$$

$$\approx \mathbf{1} + \boldsymbol{\xi}^\wedge$$

$$\mathcal{T} = \mathrm{Ad}(\mathbf{T}) \equiv \begin{bmatrix} \mathbf{C} & (\mathbf{J}\boldsymbol{\rho})^\wedge \mathbf{C} \\ \mathbf{0} & \mathbf{C} \end{bmatrix}$$

$$\mathrm{tr}(\mathbf{T}) = 2\cos\phi + 2, \quad \det(\mathbf{T}) = 1$$

$$\mathrm{Ad}(\mathbf{T}_1\mathbf{T}_2) = \mathrm{Ad}(\mathbf{T}_1)\,\mathrm{Ad}(\mathbf{T}_2)$$

$$\mathbf{T}^{-1} = \exp(-\boldsymbol{\xi}^\wedge) \equiv \sum_{n=0}^{\infty} \frac{1}{n!}(-\boldsymbol{\xi}^\wedge)^n \approx \mathbf{1} - \boldsymbol{\xi}^\wedge$$

$$\mathbf{T}^{-1} \equiv \begin{bmatrix} \mathbf{C}^T & -\mathbf{C}^T\mathbf{r} \\ \mathbf{0}^T & 1 \end{bmatrix}$$

$$\mathcal{T}^{-1} = \exp(-\boldsymbol{\xi}^\wedge) \equiv \sum_{n=0}^{\infty} \frac{1}{n!}(-\boldsymbol{\xi}^\wedge)^n \approx \mathbf{1} - \boldsymbol{\xi}^\wedge$$

$$\mathcal{T}^{-1} \equiv \begin{bmatrix} \mathbf{C}^T & -\mathbf{C}^T(\mathbf{J}\boldsymbol{\rho})^\wedge \\ \mathbf{0} & \mathbf{C}^T \end{bmatrix}$$

$$\mathcal{T}\boldsymbol{\xi} = \boldsymbol{\xi}$$

$$\mathbf{T}\boldsymbol{\xi}^\wedge = \boldsymbol{\xi}^\wedge \mathbf{T}, \quad \mathcal{T}\boldsymbol{\xi}^\wedge = \boldsymbol{\xi}^\wedge \mathcal{T}$$

$$(\mathcal{T}\mathbf{x})^\wedge \equiv \mathbf{T}\mathbf{x}^\wedge\mathbf{T}^{-1}, \quad (\mathcal{T}\mathbf{x})^\wedge \equiv \mathcal{T}\mathbf{x}^\wedge\mathcal{T}^{-1}$$

$$\exp((\mathcal{T}\mathbf{x})^\wedge) \equiv \mathbf{T}\exp(\mathbf{x}^\wedge)\mathbf{T}^{-1}$$

$$\exp((\mathcal{T}\mathbf{x})^\wedge) \equiv \mathcal{T}\exp(\mathbf{x}^\wedge)\mathcal{T}^{-1}$$

$$(\mathbf{T}\mathbf{p})^\odot = \mathbf{T}\mathbf{p}^\odot\mathcal{T}^{-1}$$

$$(\mathbf{T}\mathbf{p})^{\odot T}(\mathbf{T}\mathbf{p}) \equiv \mathcal{T}^{-T}\mathbf{p}^{\odot T}\mathbf{p}^\odot\mathcal{T}^{-1}$$

(left) Jacobian

$$\mathcal{J} = \int_0^1 \mathcal{T}^\alpha d\alpha \equiv \sum_{n=0}^{\infty} \frac{1}{(n+1)!}(\boldsymbol{\xi}^\wedge)^n$$

$$= \mathbf{1} + \left(\frac{4-\phi\sin\phi-4\cos\phi}{2\phi^2}\right)\boldsymbol{\xi}^\wedge + \left(\frac{4\phi-5\sin\phi+\phi\cos\phi}{2\phi^3}\right)(\boldsymbol{\xi}^\wedge)^2 + \left(\frac{2-\phi\sin\phi-2\cos\phi}{2\phi^4}\right)(\boldsymbol{\xi}^\wedge)^3 + \left(\frac{2\phi-3\sin\phi+\phi\cos\phi}{2\phi^5}\right)(\boldsymbol{\xi}^\wedge)^4$$

$$\approx \mathbf{1} + \frac{1}{2}\boldsymbol{\xi}^\wedge$$

$$\mathcal{J} \equiv \begin{bmatrix} \mathbf{J} & \mathbf{Q} \\ \mathbf{0} & \mathbf{J} \end{bmatrix}$$

$$\mathcal{J}^{-1} \equiv \sum_{n=0}^{\infty} \frac{B_n}{n!}(\boldsymbol{\xi}^\wedge)^n \approx \mathbf{1} - \frac{1}{2}\boldsymbol{\xi}^\wedge$$

$$\mathcal{J}^{-1} \equiv \begin{bmatrix} \mathbf{J}^{-1} & -\mathbf{J}^{-1}\mathbf{Q}\mathbf{J}^{-1} \\ \mathbf{0} & \mathbf{J}^{-1} \end{bmatrix}$$

$$\mathbf{Q} = \sum_{n=0}^{\infty}\sum_{m=0}^{\infty} \frac{1}{(n+m+2)!}(\boldsymbol{\phi}^\wedge)^n \boldsymbol{\rho}^\wedge (\boldsymbol{\phi}^\wedge)^m$$

$$\equiv \frac{1}{2}\boldsymbol{\rho}^\wedge + \left(\frac{\phi-\sin\phi}{\phi^3}\right)(\boldsymbol{\phi}^\wedge\boldsymbol{\rho}^\wedge + \boldsymbol{\rho}^\wedge\boldsymbol{\phi}^\wedge + \boldsymbol{\phi}^\wedge\boldsymbol{\rho}^\wedge\boldsymbol{\phi}^\wedge)$$

$$+ \left(\frac{\phi^2+2\cos\phi-2}{2\phi^4}\right)(\boldsymbol{\phi}^\wedge\boldsymbol{\phi}^\wedge\boldsymbol{\rho}^\wedge + \boldsymbol{\rho}^\wedge\boldsymbol{\phi}^\wedge\boldsymbol{\phi}^\wedge - 3\boldsymbol{\phi}^\wedge\boldsymbol{\rho}^\wedge\boldsymbol{\phi}^\wedge)$$

$$+ \left(\frac{2\phi-3\sin\phi+\phi\cos\phi}{2\phi^5}\right)(\boldsymbol{\phi}^\wedge\boldsymbol{\rho}^\wedge\boldsymbol{\phi}^\wedge\boldsymbol{\phi}^\wedge + \boldsymbol{\phi}^\wedge\boldsymbol{\phi}^\wedge\boldsymbol{\rho}^\wedge\boldsymbol{\phi}^\wedge)$$

$$\exp((\boldsymbol{\xi}+\delta\boldsymbol{\xi})^\wedge) \approx \exp((\mathcal{J}\delta\boldsymbol{\xi})^\wedge)\exp(\boldsymbol{\xi}^\wedge)$$

$$\exp((\boldsymbol{\xi}+\delta\boldsymbol{\xi})^\wedge) \approx \exp((\mathcal{J}\delta\boldsymbol{\xi})^\wedge)\exp(\boldsymbol{\xi}^\wedge)$$

$$\mathcal{T} \equiv \mathbf{1} + \boldsymbol{\xi}^\wedge\mathcal{J}$$

$$\mathcal{J}\boldsymbol{\xi}^\wedge \equiv \boldsymbol{\xi}^\wedge\mathcal{J}$$

$$\mathcal{J}(\boldsymbol{\xi}) \equiv \mathcal{T}\mathcal{J}(-\boldsymbol{\xi})$$

$$(\exp(\delta\boldsymbol{\xi}^\wedge)\mathbf{T})^\alpha \approx (\mathbf{1} + (\mathcal{A}(\alpha,\boldsymbol{\xi})\delta\boldsymbol{\xi})^\wedge)\mathbf{T}^\alpha$$

$$\mathcal{A}(\alpha,\boldsymbol{\xi}) = \alpha\mathcal{J}(\alpha\boldsymbol{\xi})\mathcal{J}(\boldsymbol{\xi})^{-1} = \sum_{n=0}^{\infty} \frac{F_n(\alpha)}{n!}(\boldsymbol{\xi}^\wedge)^n$$

Lie Algebra

$$\mathbf{x}^\wedge = \begin{bmatrix} \mathbf{u} \\ \mathbf{v} \end{bmatrix}^\wedge = \begin{bmatrix} \mathbf{v}^\wedge & \mathbf{u} \\ \mathbf{0}^T & 0 \end{bmatrix}$$

$$\mathbf{x}^\wedge = \begin{bmatrix} \mathbf{u} \\ \mathbf{v} \end{bmatrix}^\wedge = \begin{bmatrix} \mathbf{v}^\wedge & \mathbf{u}^\wedge \\ \mathbf{0} & \mathbf{v}^\wedge \end{bmatrix}$$

$$(\alpha\mathbf{x} + \beta\mathbf{y})^\wedge \equiv \alpha\mathbf{x}^\wedge + \beta\mathbf{y}^\wedge$$

$$(\alpha\mathbf{x} + \beta\mathbf{y})^\wedge \equiv \alpha\mathbf{x}^\wedge + \beta\mathbf{y}^\wedge$$

$$\mathbf{x}^\wedge\mathbf{y} = -\mathbf{y}^\wedge\mathbf{x}$$

$$\mathbf{x}^\wedge\mathbf{x} = 0$$

$$(\mathbf{x}^\wedge)^4 + 2(\mathbf{v}^T\mathbf{v})(\mathbf{x}^\wedge)^3 + (\mathbf{v}^T\mathbf{v})^2(\mathbf{x}^\wedge)^2 \equiv 0$$

$$[\mathbf{x}^\wedge, \mathbf{y}^\wedge] \equiv \mathbf{x}^\wedge\mathbf{y}^\wedge - \mathbf{y}^\wedge\mathbf{x}^\wedge \equiv (\mathbf{x}^\wedge\mathbf{y})^\wedge$$

$$[\mathbf{x}^\wedge, \mathbf{y}^\wedge] \equiv \mathbf{x}^\wedge\mathbf{y}^\wedge - \mathbf{y}^\wedge\mathbf{x}^\wedge \equiv (\mathbf{x}^\wedge\mathbf{y})^\wedge$$

$$\underbrace{[\mathbf{x}^\wedge, [\dots, [\mathbf{x}^\wedge, \mathbf{y}^\wedge]\dots]]}_{n} \equiv ((\mathbf{x}^\wedge)^n\mathbf{y})^\wedge$$

$$\underbrace{[\mathbf{x}^\wedge, [\dots, [\mathbf{x}^\wedge, \mathbf{y}^\wedge]\dots]]}_{n} \equiv ((\mathbf{x}^\wedge)^n\mathbf{y})^\wedge$$

$$\mathbf{p}^\odot = \begin{bmatrix} \boldsymbol{\varepsilon} \\ \eta \end{bmatrix}^\odot = \begin{bmatrix} \eta\mathbf{1} & -\boldsymbol{\varepsilon}^\wedge \\ \mathbf{0}^T & \mathbf{0}^T \end{bmatrix}$$

$$\mathbf{p}^\odot = \begin{bmatrix} \boldsymbol{\varepsilon} \\ \eta \end{bmatrix}^\odot = \begin{bmatrix} \mathbf{0} & -\boldsymbol{\varepsilon}^\wedge \\ \boldsymbol{\varepsilon} & \mathbf{0} \end{bmatrix}$$

$$\mathbf{x}^\wedge\mathbf{p} \equiv \mathbf{p}^\odot\mathbf{x}$$

$$\mathbf{p}^T\mathbf{x}^\wedge \equiv \mathbf{x}^T\mathbf{p}^\odot$$

$\alpha, \beta \in \mathbb{R}$, $\mathbf{u}, \mathbf{v}, \boldsymbol{\phi}, \delta\boldsymbol{\phi} \in \mathbb{R}^3$, $\mathbf{p} \in \mathbb{R}^4$, $\mathbf{x}, \mathbf{y}, \boldsymbol{\xi}, \delta\boldsymbol{\xi} \in \mathbb{R}^6$, $\mathbf{C} \in SO(3)$, $\mathbf{J}, \mathbf{Q} \in \mathbb{R}^{3\times3}$, $\mathbf{T}, \mathbf{T}_1, \mathbf{T}_2 \in SE(3)$, $\mathcal{T} \in \mathrm{Ad}(SE(3))$, $\mathcal{J}, \mathcal{A} \in \mathbb{R}^{6\times6}$

8.2 Kinematics

We have seen how the geometry of a Lie group works. The next step is to allow the geometry to change over time. We will work out the *kinematics* associated with our two Lie groups, $SO(3)$ and $SE(3)$.

8.2.1 Rotations

We have already seen the kinematics of rotations in the previous chapter, but this was before we introduced Lie groups.

Lie Group

We know that a rotation matrix can be written as

$$\mathbf{C} = \exp\left(\boldsymbol{\phi}^\wedge\right), \qquad (8.231)$$

where $\mathbf{C} \in SO(3)$ and $\boldsymbol{\phi} = \phi\mathbf{a} \in \mathbb{R}^3$. The rotational kinematic equation relating angular velocity, $\boldsymbol{\omega}$, to rotation (i.e., Poisson's equation) is given by[22]

$$\dot{\mathbf{C}} = \boldsymbol{\omega}^\wedge\mathbf{C} \qquad \text{or} \qquad \boldsymbol{\omega}^\wedge = \dot{\mathbf{C}}\mathbf{C}^T. \qquad (8.232)$$

We will refer to this as kinematics of the Lie group; these equations are singularity-free since they are in terms of $\mathbf{C}$, but have the constraint that $\mathbf{C}\mathbf{C}^T = \mathbf{1}$. Owing to the surjective-only property of the exponential map from $\mathfrak{so}(3)$ to $SO(3)$, we can also work out the kinematics in terms of the Lie algebra.

Lie Algebra

To see the equivalent kinematics in terms of the Lie algebra, we need to differentiate $\mathbf{C}$:

$$\dot{\mathbf{C}} = \frac{d}{dt}\exp\left(\boldsymbol{\phi}^\wedge\right) = \int_0^1 \exp\left(\alpha\boldsymbol{\phi}^\wedge\right) \dot{\boldsymbol{\phi}}^\wedge \exp\left((1-\alpha)\boldsymbol{\phi}^\wedge\right) d\alpha, \qquad (8.233)$$

where the last relationship comes from the general expression for the time derivative of the matrix exponential:

$$\frac{d}{dt}\exp\left(\mathbf{A}(t)\right) = \int_0^1 \exp\left(\alpha\mathbf{A}(t)\right) \frac{d\mathbf{A}(t)}{dt} \exp\left((1-\alpha)\mathbf{A}(t)\right) d\alpha. \qquad (8.234)$$

From (8.233) we can rearrange to have

$$\dot{\mathbf{C}}\mathbf{C}^T = \int_0^1 \mathbf{C}^\alpha \dot{\boldsymbol{\phi}}^\wedge \mathbf{C}^{-\alpha} d\alpha = \int_0^1 \left(\mathbf{C}^\alpha \dot{\boldsymbol{\phi}}\right)^\wedge d\alpha$$

$$= \left(\int_0^1 \mathbf{C}^\alpha d\alpha\, \dot{\boldsymbol{\phi}}\right)^\wedge = \left(\mathbf{J}\,\dot{\boldsymbol{\phi}}\right)^\wedge, \qquad (8.235)$$

---

[22] Compared to (7.45) in our earlier development, this $\boldsymbol{\omega}$ is opposite in sign. This is because we have adopted the robotics convention described in Section 7.3.2 for the angle of rotation, and this leads to the form in (8.231); this in turn means we must use the angular velocity associated with that angle, and this is opposite in sign to the one we discussed earlier.

where $\mathbf{J} = \int_0^1 \mathbf{C}^\alpha \, d\alpha$ is the (left) Jacobian for $SO(3)$ that we saw earlier. Comparing (8.232) and (8.235), we have the pleasing result that

$$\boldsymbol{\omega} = \mathbf{J} \, \dot{\boldsymbol{\phi}}, \tag{8.236}$$

or

$$\dot{\boldsymbol{\phi}} = \mathbf{J}^{-1} \boldsymbol{\omega}, \tag{8.237}$$

which is an equivalent expression for the kinematics but in terms of the Lie algebra. Note that $\mathbf{J}^{-1}$ does not exist at $|\boldsymbol{\phi}| = 2\pi m$, where m is a non-zero integer, due to singularities of the 3×1 representation of rotation; the good news is that we no longer have constraints to worry about.

Numerical Integration

Because $\boldsymbol{\phi}$ has no constraints, we can use any numerical method we like to integrate (8.237). The same is not true if we want to integrate (8.232) directly, since we must enforce the constraint that $\mathbf{C}\mathbf{C}^T = \mathbf{1}$. There are a few simple strategies we can use to do this.

One approach is to assume that $\boldsymbol{\omega}(t)$ is piecewise constant. Suppose $\boldsymbol{\omega}$ is constant between two times, t_1 and t_2. In this case, (8.232) is a linear, time-invariant, ordinary differential equation, and we know the solution will be of the form

$$\mathbf{C}(t_2) = \underbrace{\exp\left(\boldsymbol{\omega}^\wedge \Delta t\right)}_{\mathbf{C}_{21} \in SO(3)} \mathbf{C}(t_1), \tag{8.238}$$

where $\Delta t = t_2 - t_1$ and we note that $\mathbf{C}_{21}$ is, in fact, in the correct form to be a rotation matrix. Let the rotation vector be

$$\boldsymbol{\phi} = \phi \, \mathbf{a} = \boldsymbol{\omega} \, \Delta t, \tag{8.239}$$

with angle, $\phi = |\boldsymbol{\phi}|$, and axis, $\mathbf{a} = \boldsymbol{\phi}/\phi$. Then construct the rotation matrix through our usual closed-form expression:

$$\mathbf{C}_{21} = \cos\phi \, \mathbf{1} + (1 - \cos\phi) \, \mathbf{a}\mathbf{a}^T + \sin\phi \, \mathbf{a}^\wedge. \tag{8.240}$$

The update then proceeds as

$$\mathbf{C}(t_2) = \mathbf{C}_{21} \, \mathbf{C}(t_1), \tag{8.241}$$

which mathematically guarantees that $\mathbf{C}(t_2)$ will be in $SO(3)$ since $\mathbf{C}_{21}, \mathbf{C}(t_1) \in SO(3)$. Repeating this over and over for many small time intervals allows us to integrate the equation numerically.

Another approach is to assume that $\boldsymbol{\omega}(t)$ varies linearly with time over the integration window:

$$\boldsymbol{\omega}(t) = \boldsymbol{\omega}_1 + \boldsymbol{\alpha}_1(t - t_1), \tag{8.242}$$

where $\boldsymbol{\alpha}_1 = \boldsymbol{\alpha}(t_1)$ is angular acceleration (assumed to be piecewise constant over the integration window) and $\boldsymbol{\omega}_1 = \boldsymbol{\omega}(t_1)$ is the angular velocity at the start of the integration window. We can then use the *Magnus expansion* (Magnus, 1954; Blanes et al., 2009) to write

$$\mathbf{C}(t_2) = \exp\left(\sum_{j=1}^{\infty} \phi_j(\Delta t)^\wedge\right) \mathbf{C}(t_1), \qquad (8.243)$$

where $\phi_j(t)$ are the terms of the expansion. In our case, the first three terms can be shown to be (Huber and Wollherr, 2020)

$$\phi_1(\Delta t) = \int_{t_1}^{t_2} \boldsymbol{\omega}(\tau_1)\, d\tau_1 = \boldsymbol{\omega}_1\,\Delta t + \frac{1}{2}\boldsymbol{\alpha}_1\,\Delta t^2, \qquad (8.244a)$$

$$\phi_2(\Delta t) = \frac{1}{2}\int_{t_1}^{t_2}\int_{t_1}^{\tau_1} \left([\boldsymbol{\omega}(\tau_1), \boldsymbol{\omega}(\tau_2)]\right)^\vee d\tau_2\, d\tau_1 = \frac{1}{12}\boldsymbol{\alpha}_1^\wedge\boldsymbol{\omega}_1\,\Delta t^3, \quad (8.244b)$$

$$\phi_3(\Delta t) = \frac{1}{6}\int_{t_1}^{t_2}\int_{t_1}^{\tau_1}\int_{t_1}^{\tau_2} \big([\boldsymbol{\omega}(\tau_1), [\boldsymbol{\omega}(\tau_2), \boldsymbol{\omega}(\tau_3)]]$$
$$+\, [\boldsymbol{\omega}(\tau_3), [\boldsymbol{\omega}(\tau_2), \boldsymbol{\omega}(\tau_1)]]\big)^\vee d\tau_3\, d\tau_2\, d\tau_1 = \frac{1}{240}\boldsymbol{\alpha}_1^\wedge\boldsymbol{\alpha}_1^\wedge\boldsymbol{\omega}_1\,\Delta t^5. \qquad (8.244c)$$

We see the first term matches the piecewise-constant angular velocity approach and the other terms are corrections. Although approximate, the Magnus expansion guarantees the resulting rotation matrix is a member of $SO(3)$,

$$\mathbf{C}(t_2) \approx \exp\left(\underbrace{\left(\boldsymbol{\omega}_1\,\Delta t + \frac{1}{2}\boldsymbol{\alpha}_1\,\Delta t^2 + \frac{1}{12}\boldsymbol{\alpha}_1^\wedge\boldsymbol{\omega}_1\,\Delta t^3 + \frac{1}{240}\boldsymbol{\alpha}_1^\wedge\boldsymbol{\alpha}_1^\wedge\boldsymbol{\omega}_1\,\Delta t^5\right)^\wedge}_{\text{rotation matrix}}\right) \mathbf{C}(t_1),$$
$$\qquad (8.245)$$

since the transition matrix is also a rotation matrix.

However, even if we do follow an integration approach (such as the ones shown earlier) that claims to keep the computed rotation in $SO(3)$, small numerical errors may eventually cause the result to depart $SO(3)$ through violation of the orthogonality constraint. A common solution is to periodically 'project' the computed rotation, $\mathbf{C} \notin SO(3)$, back onto $SO(3)$. In other words, we can try to find the rotation matrix, $\mathbf{R} \in SO(3)$, that is closest to $\mathbf{C}$ in some sense. We do this by solving the following optimization problem (Green, 1952):

$$\arg\max_{\mathbf{R}} J(\mathbf{R}), \quad J(\mathbf{R}) = \operatorname{tr}\left(\mathbf{C}\mathbf{R}^T\right) - \underbrace{\frac{1}{2}\sum_{i=1}^{3}\sum_{j=1}^{3}\lambda_{ij}\left(\mathbf{r}_i^T\mathbf{r}_j - \delta_{ij}\right)}_{\text{Lagrange multiplier terms}}, \quad (8.246)$$

where the Lagrange multiplier terms are necessary to enforce the $\mathbf{R}\mathbf{R}^T = 1$ constraint. Note that δ_{ij} is the Kronecker delta and

$$\mathbf{R}^T = \begin{bmatrix} \mathbf{r}_1 & \mathbf{r}_2 & \mathbf{r}_3 \end{bmatrix}, \qquad \mathbf{C}^T = \begin{bmatrix} \mathbf{c}_1 & \mathbf{c}_2 & \mathbf{c}_3 \end{bmatrix}. \qquad (8.247)$$

We also note that

$$\operatorname{tr}\left(\mathbf{C}\mathbf{R}^T\right) = \mathbf{r}_1^T\mathbf{c}_1 + \mathbf{r}_2^T\mathbf{c}_2 + \mathbf{r}_3^T\mathbf{c}_3. \qquad (8.248)$$

We then take the derivative of J with respect to the three rows of $\mathbf{R}$, revealing

$$\frac{\partial J}{\partial \mathbf{r}_i^T} = \mathbf{c}_i - \sum_{j=1}^{3} \lambda_{ij} \mathbf{r}_j, \qquad \forall i = 1 \dots 3. \qquad (8.249)$$

Setting this to zero, $\forall i = 1 \dots 3$, we have that

$$\underbrace{\begin{bmatrix} \mathbf{r}_1 & \mathbf{r}_2 & \mathbf{r}_3 \end{bmatrix}}_{\mathbf{R}^T} \underbrace{\begin{bmatrix} \lambda_{11} & \lambda_{12} & \lambda_{13} \\ \lambda_{21} & \lambda_{22} & \lambda_{23} \\ \lambda_{31} & \lambda_{32} & \lambda_{33} \end{bmatrix}}_{\mathbf{\Lambda}} = \underbrace{\begin{bmatrix} \mathbf{c}_1 & \mathbf{c}_2 & \mathbf{c}_3 \end{bmatrix}}_{\mathbf{C}^T}. \qquad (8.250)$$

Note, however, that $\mathbf{\Lambda}$ can be assumed to be symmetric owing to the symmetry of the Lagrange multiplier terms. Thus, what we know so far is that

$$\mathbf{\Lambda R} = \mathbf{C}, \qquad \mathbf{\Lambda} = \mathbf{\Lambda}^T, \qquad \mathbf{R}^T \mathbf{R} = \mathbf{R} \mathbf{R}^T = \mathbf{1}.$$

We can solve for $\mathbf{\Lambda}$ by noticing

$$\mathbf{\Lambda}^2 = \mathbf{\Lambda} \mathbf{\Lambda}^T = \mathbf{\Lambda} \underbrace{\mathbf{R} \mathbf{R}^T}_{\mathbf{1}} \mathbf{\Lambda}^T = \mathbf{C} \mathbf{C}^T \quad \Rightarrow \quad \mathbf{\Lambda} = \left(\mathbf{C} \mathbf{C}^T \right)^{\frac{1}{2}},$$

with $(\cdot)^{\frac{1}{2}}$ indicating a matrix square root. Finally,

$$\mathbf{R} = \left(\mathbf{C} \mathbf{C}^T \right)^{-\frac{1}{2}} \mathbf{C},$$

which simply looks like we are 'normalizing' $\mathbf{C}$. Computing the projection whenever the orthogonality constraint is not satisfied (to within some threshold) and then overwriting the integrated value,

$$\mathbf{C} \leftarrow \mathbf{R}, \qquad (8.251)$$

ensures that we do not stray too far from $SO(3)$.[23]

Transport Theorem

Once we know the rotational kinematics, it is not too difficult to relate the derivative of a vector quantity in one frame to that in another. Consider

$$\mathbf{v}_i = \mathbf{C}_{iv} \mathbf{v}_v, \qquad (8.252)$$

where $\mathbf{v}_i$ and $\mathbf{v}_v$ are coordinates of a vector in two frames (e.g., stationary and moving frames, respectively). By the product rule of differentiation we have

$$\dot{\mathbf{v}}_i = \dot{\mathbf{C}}_{iv} \mathbf{v}_v + \mathbf{C}_{iv} \dot{\mathbf{v}}_v. \qquad (8.253)$$

---

[23] Technically, this matrix square-root approach only works under certain conditions. For some pathological $\mathbf{C}$ matrices, it can produce an $\mathbf{R}$ where $\det \mathbf{R} = -1$ instead of $\det \mathbf{R} = 1$, as desired. This is because we have not enforced the $\det \mathbf{R} = 1$ constraint in our optimization properly. A more rigorous method that is based on singular-value decomposition and handles the more difficult cases, is presented later in Section 9.1.3. A sufficient test to know whether this matrix square-root approach will work is to check that $\det \mathbf{C} > 0$ before applying it. This should almost always be true in real situations where our integration step is small. If it is not true, the detailed method in Section 9.1.3 should be used.

Substituting a version of our rotational kinematics, $\dot{\mathbf{C}}_{iv} = -\mathbf{C}_{iv}\boldsymbol{\omega}_v^{iv^\wedge}$, and rearranging, we see that

$$\dot{\mathbf{v}}_i = \mathbf{C}_{iv}\left(\dot{\mathbf{v}}_v - \boldsymbol{\omega}_v^{iv^\wedge}\mathbf{v}_v\right), \qquad (8.254)$$

which is sometimes called the *transport theorem*. We saw another version of this earlier in (7.42).

8.2.2 Poses

There is an analogous approach to kinematics for $SE(3)$ that we will develop next.

Lie Group

We have seen that a transformation matrix can be written as

$$\mathbf{T} = \begin{bmatrix} \mathbf{C} & \mathbf{r} \\ \mathbf{0}^T & 1 \end{bmatrix} = \begin{bmatrix} \mathbf{C} & \mathbf{J}\rho \\ \mathbf{0}^T & 1 \end{bmatrix} = \exp\left(\boldsymbol{\xi}^\wedge\right), \qquad (8.255)$$

where

$$\boldsymbol{\xi} = \begin{bmatrix} \rho \\ \phi \end{bmatrix}.$$

Suppose the kinematics in terms of separated translation and rotation are given by

$$\dot{\mathbf{r}} = \boldsymbol{\omega}^\wedge\mathbf{r} + \boldsymbol{\nu}, \qquad (8.256a)$$

$$\dot{\mathbf{C}} = \boldsymbol{\omega}^\wedge\mathbf{C}, \qquad (8.256b)$$

where $\boldsymbol{\nu}$ and $\boldsymbol{\omega}$ are the translational and rotational velocities, respectively. Using transformation matrices, this can be written equivalently as

$$\dot{\mathbf{T}} = \boldsymbol{\varpi}^\wedge\mathbf{T} \qquad \text{or} \qquad \boldsymbol{\varpi}^\wedge = \dot{\mathbf{T}}\mathbf{T}^{-1}, \qquad (8.257)$$

where

$$\boldsymbol{\varpi} = \begin{bmatrix} \boldsymbol{\nu} \\ \boldsymbol{\omega} \end{bmatrix}$$

is the *generalized velocity*.[24] Again, these equations are singularity-free but still have the constraint that $\mathbf{C}\mathbf{C}^T = \mathbf{1}$.

Lie Algebra

Again, we can find an equivalent set of kinematics in terms of the Lie algebra. As in the rotation case, we have that

$$\dot{\mathbf{T}} = \frac{d}{dt}\exp\left(\boldsymbol{\xi}^\wedge\right) = \int_0^1 \exp\left(\alpha\boldsymbol{\xi}^\wedge\right)\dot{\boldsymbol{\xi}}^\wedge\exp\left((1-\alpha)\boldsymbol{\xi}^\wedge\right)d\alpha, \qquad (8.258)$$

or equivalently,

[24] We can also write the kinematics equivalently in 6×6 format:

$$\dot{\mathcal{T}} = \boldsymbol{\varpi}^\curlywedge\mathcal{T}.$$

$$\dot{\mathbf{T}}\mathbf{T}^{-1} = \int_0^1 \mathbf{T}^\alpha \, \dot{\boldsymbol{\xi}}^\wedge \, \mathbf{T}^{-\alpha} \, d\alpha = \int_0^1 \left(\boldsymbol{\mathcal{T}}^\alpha \dot{\boldsymbol{\xi}}\right)^\wedge d\alpha$$

$$= \left(\left(\int_0^1 \boldsymbol{\mathcal{T}}^\alpha \, d\alpha\right) \dot{\boldsymbol{\xi}}\right)^\wedge = \left(\boldsymbol{\mathcal{J}} \dot{\boldsymbol{\xi}}\right)^\wedge, \quad (8.259)$$

where $\boldsymbol{\mathcal{J}} = \int_0^1 \boldsymbol{\mathcal{T}}^\alpha \, d\alpha$ is the (left) Jacobian for $SE(3)$. Comparing (8.257) and (8.259), we have that

$$\boldsymbol{\varpi} = \boldsymbol{\mathcal{J}} \dot{\boldsymbol{\xi}} \qquad (8.260)$$

or

$$\dot{\boldsymbol{\xi}} = \boldsymbol{\mathcal{J}}^{-1} \boldsymbol{\varpi} \qquad (8.261)$$

for our equivalent kinematics in terms of the Lie algebra. Again, these equations are now free of constraints.

Hybrid

There is, however, another way to propagate the kinematics by noting that the equation for $\dot{\mathbf{r}}$ is actually linear in the velocity. By combining the equations for $\dot{\mathbf{r}}$ and $\dot{\boldsymbol{\phi}}$, we have

$$\begin{bmatrix} \dot{\mathbf{r}} \\ \dot{\boldsymbol{\phi}} \end{bmatrix} = \begin{bmatrix} \mathbf{1} & -\mathbf{r}^\wedge \\ \mathbf{0} & \mathbf{J}^{-1} \end{bmatrix} \begin{bmatrix} \boldsymbol{\nu} \\ \boldsymbol{\omega} \end{bmatrix}, \qquad (8.262)$$

which still has the singularities of $\mathbf{J}^{-1}$ but no longer requires us to evaluate $\mathbf{Q}$ and avoids the conversion $\mathbf{r} = \mathbf{J}\boldsymbol{\rho}$ after we integrate. This approach is also free of constraints. We can refer to this as a *hybrid* method, as the translation is kept in the usual space and the rotation is kept in the Lie algebra.

Numerical Integration

Similarly to the $SO(3)$ approach, we can integrate (8.261) without worrying about constraints, but integrating (8.257) takes a little more care.

Just as in the $SO(3)$ approach, we could assume that $\boldsymbol{\varpi}(t)$ is piecewise constant. With $\boldsymbol{\varpi}(t) = \boldsymbol{\varpi}$ constant between two times, t_1 and t_2, (8.257) is a linear, time-invariant, ordinary differential equation, and we know the solution will be of the form

$$\mathbf{T}(t_2) = \underbrace{\exp\left(\boldsymbol{\varpi}^\wedge \Delta t\right)}_{\mathbf{T}_{21} \in SE(3)} \mathbf{T}(t_1), \qquad (8.263)$$

where $\Delta t = t_2 - t_1$ and we note that $\mathbf{T}_{21}$ is in fact in the correct form to be a transformation matrix. Let

$$\boldsymbol{\xi} = \begin{bmatrix} \boldsymbol{\rho} \\ \boldsymbol{\phi} \end{bmatrix} = \begin{bmatrix} \boldsymbol{\nu} \, \Delta t \\ \boldsymbol{\omega} \, \Delta t \end{bmatrix} = \boldsymbol{\varpi} \, \Delta t, \qquad (8.264)$$

with angle, $\phi = |\boldsymbol{\phi}|$, and axis, $\mathbf{a} = \boldsymbol{\phi}/\phi$. Then construct the rotation matrix through our usual closed-form expression:

$$\mathbf{C} = \cos\phi \, \mathbf{1} + (1 - \cos\phi) \, \mathbf{a}\mathbf{a}^T + \sin\phi \, \mathbf{a}^\wedge. \qquad (8.265)$$

Build $\mathbf{J}$ and calculate $\mathbf{r} = \mathbf{J}\boldsymbol{\rho}$. Assemble $\mathbf{C}$ and $\mathbf{r}$ into

$$\mathbf{T}_{21} = \begin{bmatrix} \mathbf{C} & \mathbf{r} \\ \mathbf{0}^T & 1 \end{bmatrix}. \tag{8.266}$$

The update then proceeds as

$$\mathbf{T}(t_2) = \mathbf{T}_{21}\,\mathbf{T}(t_1), \tag{8.267}$$

which mathematically guarantees that $\mathbf{T}(t_2)$ will be in $SE(3)$ since $\mathbf{T}_{21}, \mathbf{T}(t_1) \in SE(3)$. Repeating this over and over for many small time intervals allows us to integrate the equation numerically.

We could also again use the *Magnus expansion* to integrate if our generalized velocity varies linearly with respect to time through the integration window:

$$\boldsymbol{\varpi}(t) = \boldsymbol{\varpi}_1 + \boldsymbol{\gamma}_1(t - t_1). \tag{8.268}$$

This results in an analogous approximation to the rotation case,

$$\mathbf{T}(t_2) \approx \exp\left(\underbrace{\left(\boldsymbol{\varpi}_1\,\Delta t + \frac{1}{2}\boldsymbol{\gamma}_1\,\Delta t^2 + \frac{1}{12}\boldsymbol{\gamma}_1^{\curlywedge}\boldsymbol{\varpi}_1\,\Delta t^3 + \frac{1}{240}\boldsymbol{\gamma}_1^{\curlywedge}\boldsymbol{\gamma}_1^{\curlywedge}\boldsymbol{\varpi}_1\,\Delta t^5\right)^{\wedge}}_{\text{transformation matrix}}\right)\mathbf{T}(t_1), \tag{8.269}$$

which mathematically ensures the result is in $SE(3)$ since the transition matrix is also a transformation matrix.

With either approach, we can also project the upper-left, rotation matrix part of $\mathbf{T}$ back onto $SO(3)$ periodically,[25] reset the lower-left block to $\mathbf{0}^T$, and reset the lower-right block to 1 to ensure $\mathbf{T}$ does not stray too far from $SE(3)$, numerically.

With Dynamics

We can augment our kinematic equation for pose with an equation for the translational/rotational dynamics (i.e., Newton's second law) as follows (D'Eleuterio, 1985):

$$\text{kinematics:} \quad \dot{\mathbf{T}} = \boldsymbol{\varpi}^{\wedge}\mathbf{T}, \tag{8.270a}$$

$$\text{dynamics:} \quad \dot{\boldsymbol{\varpi}} = -\boldsymbol{\mathcal{M}}^{-1}\boldsymbol{\varpi}^{\curlywedge^T}\boldsymbol{\mathcal{M}}\boldsymbol{\varpi} + \mathbf{a}, \tag{8.270b}$$

where $\mathbf{T} \in SE(3)$ is the pose, $\boldsymbol{\varpi} \in \mathbb{R}^6$ is the generalized velocity (in the body frame), $\mathbf{a} \in \mathbb{R}^6$ is a generalized applied force (per mass, in the body frame), and $\boldsymbol{\mathcal{M}} \in \mathbb{R}^{6\times6}$ is a generalized mass matrix of the form

$$\boldsymbol{\mathcal{M}} = \begin{bmatrix} m\mathbf{1} & -m\mathbf{c}^{\wedge} \\ m\mathbf{c}^{\wedge} & \mathbf{I} \end{bmatrix}, \tag{8.271}$$

with m the mass, $\mathbf{c} \in \mathbb{R}^3$ the center of mass, and $\mathbf{I} \in \mathbb{R}^{3\times3}$ the inertia matrix, all in the body frame.

---

[25] See the discussion in Section 8.2.1 for the details.

Transport Theorem

Once we know the $SE(3)$ kinematics, we can relate the derivative of a vector quantity in one frame to that in another. Consider

$$\mathbf{p}_i = \mathbf{T}_{iv}\mathbf{p}_v, \tag{8.272}$$

where $\mathbf{p}_i$ and $\mathbf{p}_v$ are homogeneous coordinates of a vector in two frames (e.g., stationary and moving frames, respectively). By the product rule of differentiation we have

$$\dot{\mathbf{p}}_i = \dot{\mathbf{T}}_{iv}\mathbf{p}_v + \mathbf{T}_{iv}\dot{\mathbf{p}}_v. \tag{8.273}$$

Substituting a version of our $SE(3)$ kinematics, $\dot{\mathbf{T}}_{iv} = -\mathbf{T}_{iv}\boldsymbol{\varpi}_v^{iv\wedge}$, and rearranging, we see that

$$\dot{\mathbf{p}}_i = \mathbf{T}_{iv}\left(\dot{\mathbf{p}}_v - \boldsymbol{\varpi}_v^{iv\wedge}\mathbf{p}_v\right), \tag{8.274}$$

which is sometimes called the *transport theorem*. We can also write this as

$$\dot{\mathbf{p}}_i = \mathbf{T}_{iv}\left(\dot{\mathbf{p}}_v - \mathbf{p}_v^\odot\boldsymbol{\varpi}_v^{iv}\right), \tag{8.275}$$

using the homogeneous point operator, $\odot$. If we are observing a static point in the stationary frame so that $\dot{\mathbf{p}}_i = \mathbf{0}$, then the point in the moving frame obeys

$$\dot{\mathbf{p}}_v = \mathbf{p}_v^\odot\boldsymbol{\varpi}_v^{iv}, \tag{8.276}$$

a tidy relation.

8.2.3 Linearized Rotations

Lie Group

We can also perturb our kinematics about some nominal solution (i.e., linearize), in both the Lie group and the Lie algebra. We begin with the Lie group. Consider the following perturbed rotation matrix, $\mathbf{C}' \in SO(3)$:

$$\mathbf{C}' = \exp\left(\delta\boldsymbol{\phi}^\wedge\right)\mathbf{C} \approx \left(1 + \delta\boldsymbol{\phi}^\wedge\right)\mathbf{C}, \tag{8.277}$$

where $\mathbf{C} \in SO(3)$ is the nominal rotation matrix and $\delta\boldsymbol{\phi} \in \mathbb{R}^3$ is a perturbation as a rotation vector. The perturbed kinematics equation, $\dot{\mathbf{C}}' = \boldsymbol{\omega}'^\wedge\mathbf{C}'$, becomes

$$\frac{d}{dt}\underbrace{\left(\left(1 + \delta\boldsymbol{\phi}^\wedge\right)\mathbf{C}\right)}_{\dot{\mathbf{C}}'} \approx \underbrace{\left(\boldsymbol{\omega} + \delta\boldsymbol{\omega}\right)^\wedge}_{\boldsymbol{\omega}'}\underbrace{\left(1 + \delta\boldsymbol{\phi}^\wedge\right)\mathbf{C}}_{\mathbf{C}'}, \tag{8.278}$$

after inserting our perturbation scheme. Dropping products of small terms, we can manipulate this into a pair of equations,

$$\text{nominal kinematics:} \quad \dot{\mathbf{C}} = \boldsymbol{\omega}^\wedge\mathbf{C}, \tag{8.279a}$$

$$\text{perturbation kinematics:} \quad \dot{\delta\boldsymbol{\phi}} = \boldsymbol{\omega}^\wedge\delta\boldsymbol{\phi} + \delta\boldsymbol{\omega}, \tag{8.279b}$$

which can be integrated separately and combined to provide the complete solution (approximately).

Lie Algebra

Perturbing the kinematics in the Lie algebra is more difficult but equivalent. In terms of quantities in the Lie algebra, we have

$$\phi' = \phi + \mathbf{J}(\phi)^{-1}\delta\phi, \tag{8.280}$$

where $\phi' = \ln(\mathbf{C}')^{\vee}$ is the perturbed rotation vector, $\phi = \ln(\mathbf{C})^{\vee}$ the nominal rotation vector, and $\delta\phi$ the same perturbation as in the Lie group case.

We start with the perturbed kinematics, $\dot{\phi}' = \mathbf{J}(\phi')^{-1}\omega'$, and then inserting our perturbation scheme, we have

$$\underbrace{\frac{d}{dt}\left(\phi + \mathbf{J}(\phi)^{-1}\delta\phi\right)}_{\dot{\phi}'} \approx \underbrace{\left(\mathbf{J}(\phi) + \delta\mathbf{J}\right)^{-1}}_{\mathbf{J}(\phi')}\underbrace{\left(\omega + \delta\omega\right)}_{\omega'}. \tag{8.281}$$

We obtain $\delta\mathbf{J}$ through a perturbation of $\mathbf{J}(\phi')$ directly:

$$\begin{aligned}
\mathbf{J}(\phi') &= \int_0^1 \mathbf{C}'^{\alpha}\,d\alpha = \int_0^1 \left(\exp\left(\delta\phi^{\wedge}\right)\mathbf{C}\right)^{\alpha}\,d\alpha \\
&\approx \int_0^1 \left(\mathbf{1} + \left(\mathbf{A}(\alpha,\phi)\,\delta\phi\right)^{\wedge}\right)\mathbf{C}^{\alpha}\,d\alpha \\
&= \underbrace{\int_0^1 \mathbf{C}^{\alpha}\,d\alpha}_{\mathbf{J}(\phi)} + \underbrace{\int_0^1 \alpha\left(\mathbf{J}(\alpha\phi)\mathbf{J}(\phi)^{-1}\,\delta\phi\right)^{\wedge}\mathbf{C}^{\alpha}\,d\alpha}_{\delta\mathbf{J}}, \tag{8.282}
\end{aligned}$$

where we have used the perturbed interpolation formula from Section 8.1.7. Manipulating the perturbed kinematics equation, we have

$$\begin{aligned}
\dot{\phi} - \mathbf{J}(\phi)^{-1}\dot{\mathbf{J}}(\phi)\mathbf{J}(\phi)^{-1}\delta\phi + \mathbf{J}(\phi)^{-1}\delta\dot{\phi} \\
\approx \left(\mathbf{J}(\phi)^{-1} - \mathbf{J}(\phi)^{-1}\,\delta\mathbf{J}\,\mathbf{J}(\phi)^{-1}\right)\left(\omega + \delta\omega\right) \tag{8.283}
\end{aligned}$$

Multiplying out, dropping the nominal solution, $\dot{\phi} = \mathbf{J}(\phi)^{-1}\omega$, as well as products of small terms, we have

$$\delta\dot{\phi} = \dot{\mathbf{J}}(\phi)\,\mathbf{J}(\phi)^{-1}\,\delta\phi - \delta\mathbf{J}\,\dot{\phi} + \delta\omega. \tag{8.284}$$

Substituting in the identity[26] (see Appendix B.2.1 for proof)

$$\dot{\mathbf{J}}(\phi) - \omega^{\wedge}\mathbf{J}(\phi) \equiv \frac{\partial\omega}{\partial\phi}, \tag{8.285}$$

we have

$$\delta\dot{\phi} = \omega^{\wedge}\,\delta\phi + \delta\omega + \underbrace{\frac{\partial\omega}{\partial\phi}\mathbf{J}(\phi)^{-1}\,\delta\phi - \delta\mathbf{J}\,\dot{\phi}}_{\text{extra term}}, \tag{8.286}$$

which is the same as the Lie group result for the perturbation kinematics, but with an extra term; it turns out this extra term is zero:

---

[26] This identity is well known in the dynamics literature (Hughes, 1986).

$$\frac{\partial \boldsymbol{\omega}}{\partial \boldsymbol{\phi}} \mathbf{J}(\boldsymbol{\phi})^{-1} \delta \boldsymbol{\phi} = \left(\frac{\partial}{\partial \boldsymbol{\phi}} \left(\mathbf{J}(\boldsymbol{\phi}) \, \dot{\boldsymbol{\phi}} \right) \right) \mathbf{J}(\boldsymbol{\phi})^{-1} \delta \boldsymbol{\phi}$$

$$= \left(\frac{\partial}{\partial \boldsymbol{\phi}} \int_0^1 \mathbf{C}^\alpha \, \dot{\boldsymbol{\phi}} \, d\alpha \right) \mathbf{J}(\boldsymbol{\phi})^{-1} \delta \boldsymbol{\phi}$$

$$= \int_0^1 \frac{\partial}{\partial \boldsymbol{\phi}} \left(\mathbf{C}^\alpha \, \dot{\boldsymbol{\phi}} \right) d\alpha \, \mathbf{J}(\boldsymbol{\phi})^{-1} \delta \boldsymbol{\phi}$$

$$= - \int_0^1 \alpha \left(\mathbf{C}^\alpha \, \dot{\boldsymbol{\phi}} \right)^\wedge \mathbf{J}(\alpha \boldsymbol{\phi}) \, d\alpha \, \mathbf{J}(\boldsymbol{\phi})^{-1} \delta \boldsymbol{\phi}$$

$$= \underbrace{\int_0^1 \alpha \left(\mathbf{J}(\alpha \boldsymbol{\phi}) \mathbf{J}(\boldsymbol{\phi})^{-1} \delta \boldsymbol{\phi} \right)^\wedge \mathbf{C}^\alpha \, d\alpha}_{\delta \mathbf{J}} \, \dot{\boldsymbol{\phi}} = \delta \mathbf{J} \, \dot{\boldsymbol{\phi}}, \quad (8.287)$$

where we have used an identity derived back in Section 7.2.5 for the derivative of a rotation matrix times a vector with respect to a three-parameter representation of rotation. Thus, our pair of equations is

$$\text{nominal kinematics:} \quad \dot{\boldsymbol{\phi}} = \mathbf{J}(\boldsymbol{\phi})^{-1} \boldsymbol{\omega}, \quad (8.288a)$$

$$\text{perturbation kinematics:} \quad \delta \dot{\boldsymbol{\phi}} = \boldsymbol{\omega}^\wedge \delta \boldsymbol{\phi} + \delta \boldsymbol{\omega}, \quad (8.288b)$$

which can be integrated separately and combined to provide the complete solution (approximately).

Solutions Commute

It is worth asking whether integrating the full solution is (approximately) equivalent to integrating the nominal and perturbation equations separately and then combining them. We show this for the Lie group kinematics. The perturbed solution will be given by

$$\mathbf{C}'(t) = \mathbf{C}'(0) + \int_0^t \boldsymbol{\omega}'(s)^\wedge \mathbf{C}'(s) \, ds. \quad (8.289)$$

Breaking this into nominal and perturbation parts, we have

$$\mathbf{C}'(t) \approx \left(1 + \delta \boldsymbol{\phi}(0)^\wedge \right) \mathbf{C}(0) + \int_0^t \left(\boldsymbol{\omega}(s) + \delta \boldsymbol{\omega}(s) \right)^\wedge \left(1 + \delta \boldsymbol{\phi}(s)^\wedge \right) \mathbf{C}(s) \, ds$$

$$\approx \underbrace{\mathbf{C}(0) + \int_0^t \boldsymbol{\omega}(s)^\wedge \mathbf{C}(s) \, ds}_{\mathbf{C}(t)}$$

$$+ \underbrace{\delta \boldsymbol{\phi}(0)^\wedge \mathbf{C}(0) + \int_0^t \left(\boldsymbol{\omega}(s)^\wedge \delta \boldsymbol{\phi}(s)^\wedge \mathbf{C}(s) + \delta \boldsymbol{\omega}(s)^\wedge \mathbf{C}(s) \right) ds}_{\delta \boldsymbol{\phi}(t)^\wedge \mathbf{C}(t)}$$

$$\approx \left(1 + \delta \boldsymbol{\phi}(t)^\wedge \right) \mathbf{C}(t), \quad (8.290)$$

which is the desired result. The rightmost integral on the second line can be computed by noting that

$$\frac{d}{dt}\left(\delta\phi^\wedge \mathbf{C}\right) = \dot{\delta\phi}^\wedge \mathbf{C} + \delta\phi^\wedge \dot{\mathbf{C}} = \underbrace{\left(\boldsymbol{\omega}^\wedge \delta\phi + \delta\boldsymbol{\omega}\right)^\wedge \mathbf{C}}_{\text{perturbation}} + \delta\phi^\wedge \underbrace{\left(\boldsymbol{\omega}^\wedge \mathbf{C}\right)}_{\text{nom.}}$$

$$= \boldsymbol{\omega}^\wedge \delta\phi^\wedge \mathbf{C} - \delta\phi^\wedge \boldsymbol{\omega}^\wedge \mathbf{C} + \delta\boldsymbol{\omega}^\wedge \mathbf{C} + \delta\phi^\wedge \boldsymbol{\omega}^\wedge \mathbf{C}$$

$$= \boldsymbol{\omega}^\wedge \delta\phi^\wedge \mathbf{C} + \delta\boldsymbol{\omega}^\wedge \mathbf{C}, \tag{8.291}$$

where we have used the nominal and perturbation kinematics.

Integrating the Solutions

In this section, we make some observations about integrating the nominal and perturbation kinematics. The nominal equation is nonlinear and can be integrated numerically (using either the Lie group or Lie algebra equations). The perturbation kinematics,

$$\dot{\delta\phi}(t) = \boldsymbol{\omega}(t)^\wedge \delta\phi(t) + \delta\boldsymbol{\omega}(t), \tag{8.292}$$

is a LTV equation of the form

$$\dot{\mathbf{x}}(t) = \mathbf{A}(t)\,\mathbf{x}(t) + \mathbf{B}(t)\,\mathbf{u}(t). \tag{8.293}$$

The general solution to the initial value problem is given by

$$\mathbf{x}(t) = \boldsymbol{\Phi}(t,0)\,\mathbf{x}(0) + \int_0^t \boldsymbol{\Phi}(t,s)\,\mathbf{B}(s)\,\mathbf{u}(s)\,ds, \tag{8.294}$$

where $\boldsymbol{\Phi}(t,s)$ is called the *state transition matrix* and satisfies

$$\dot{\boldsymbol{\Phi}}(t,s) = \mathbf{A}(t)\,\boldsymbol{\Phi}(t,s),$$
$$\boldsymbol{\Phi}(t,t) = \mathbf{1}.$$

The state transition matrix always exists and is unique, but it cannot always be found analytically. Fortunately, for our particular perturbation equation, we can express the 3×3 state transition matrix analytically:[27]

$$\boldsymbol{\Phi}(t,s) = \mathbf{C}(t)\mathbf{C}(s)^T. \tag{8.295}$$

The solution is therefore given by

$$\delta\phi(t) = \mathbf{C}(t)\mathbf{C}(0)^T\,\delta\phi(0) + \mathbf{C}(t)\int_0^t \mathbf{C}(s)^T\,\delta\boldsymbol{\omega}(s)\,ds. \tag{8.296}$$

We need the solution to the nominal equation, $\mathbf{C}(t)$, but this is readily available. To see this is indeed the correct solution, we can differentiate:

$$\dot{\delta\phi}(t) = \dot{\mathbf{C}}(t)\mathbf{C}(0)^T\,\delta\phi(0) + \dot{\mathbf{C}}(t)\int_0^t \mathbf{C}(s)^T\,\delta\boldsymbol{\omega}(s)\,ds + \mathbf{C}(t)\,\mathbf{C}(t)^T\,\delta\boldsymbol{\omega}(t)$$

$$= \boldsymbol{\omega}(t)^\wedge \underbrace{\left(\mathbf{C}(t)\mathbf{C}(0)^T\,\delta\phi(0) + \mathbf{C}(t)\int_0^t \mathbf{C}(s)^T\,\delta\boldsymbol{\omega}(s)\,ds\right)}_{\delta\phi(t)} + \delta\boldsymbol{\omega}(t)$$

$$= \boldsymbol{\omega}(t)^\wedge\delta\phi(t) + \delta\boldsymbol{\omega}(t), \tag{8.297}$$

---

[27] The nominal rotation matrix, $\mathbf{C}(t)$, is the *fundamental matrix* of the state transition matrix.

which is the original differential equation for $\delta\phi(t)$. We also see that our state transition matrix satisfies the required conditions:

$$\underbrace{\frac{d}{dt}\left(\mathbf{C}(t)\mathbf{C}(s)^T\right)}_{\dot{\Phi}(t,s)} = \dot{\mathbf{C}}(t)\mathbf{C}(s)^T = \boldsymbol{\omega}(t)^\wedge \underbrace{\mathbf{C}(t)\mathbf{C}(s)^T}_{\Phi(t,s)}, \quad \text{(8.298a)}$$

$$\underbrace{\mathbf{C}(t)\mathbf{C}(t)^T}_{\Phi(t,t)} = \mathbf{1}. \quad \text{(8.298b)}$$

Thus, we have everything we need to integrate the perturbation kinematics as long as we can also integrate the nominal kinematics.

8.2.4 Linearized Poses

We will only briefly summarize the perturbed kinematics for $SE(3)$, as they are quite similar to the $SO(3)$ case.

Lie Group

We will use the perturbation,

$$\mathbf{T}' = \exp\left(\delta\boldsymbol{\xi}^\wedge\right)\mathbf{T} \approx \left(\mathbf{1} + \delta\boldsymbol{\xi}^\wedge\right)\mathbf{T}, \quad \text{(8.299)}$$

with $\mathbf{T}', \mathbf{T} \in SE(3)$, and $\delta\boldsymbol{\xi} \in \mathbb{R}^6$. The perturbed kinematics,

$$\dot{\mathbf{T}}' = \boldsymbol{\varpi}'^\wedge \mathbf{T}', \quad \text{(8.300)}$$

can then be broken into nominal and perturbation kinematics:

$$\text{nominal kinematics:} \quad \dot{\mathbf{T}} = \boldsymbol{\varpi}^\wedge \mathbf{T}, \quad \text{(8.301a)}$$

$$\text{perturbation kinematics:} \quad \dot{\delta\boldsymbol{\xi}} = \boldsymbol{\varpi}^{\curlywedge} \delta\boldsymbol{\xi} + \delta\boldsymbol{\varpi}, \quad \text{(8.301b)}$$

where $\boldsymbol{\varpi}' = \boldsymbol{\varpi} + \delta\boldsymbol{\varpi}$. These can be integrated separately and combined to provide the complete solution (approximately).

Integrating the Solutions

The 6×6 transition matrix for the perturbation equation is

$$\boldsymbol{\Phi}(t,s) = \boldsymbol{\mathcal{T}}(t)\,\boldsymbol{\mathcal{T}}(s)^{-1}, \quad \text{(8.302)}$$

where $\boldsymbol{\mathcal{T}} = \text{Ad}(\mathbf{T})$. The solution for $\delta\boldsymbol{\xi}(t)$ is

$$\delta\boldsymbol{\xi}(t) = \boldsymbol{\mathcal{T}}(t)\,\boldsymbol{\mathcal{T}}(0)^{-1}\delta\boldsymbol{\xi}(0) + \boldsymbol{\mathcal{T}}(t)\int_0^t \boldsymbol{\mathcal{T}}(s)^{-1}\,\delta\boldsymbol{\varpi}(s)\,ds. \quad \text{(8.303)}$$

Differentiating recovers the perturbation kinematics, where we require the 6×6 version of the nominal kinematics in the derivation:

$$\dot{\boldsymbol{\mathcal{T}}}(t) = \boldsymbol{\varpi}(t)^{\curlywedge}\boldsymbol{\mathcal{T}}(t), \quad \text{(8.304)}$$

which is equivalent to the 4×4 version.

With Dynamics

We can also perturb the joint kinematics/dynamics equations in (8.270). We consider perturbing all of the quantities around some operating points as follows:

$$\mathbf{T}' = \exp\left(\delta\boldsymbol{\xi}^\wedge\right)\mathbf{T}, \qquad \boldsymbol{\varpi}' = \boldsymbol{\varpi} + \delta\boldsymbol{\varpi}, \qquad \mathbf{a}' = \mathbf{a} + \delta\mathbf{a}, \qquad (8.305)$$

so that the kinematics/dynamics are

$$\dot{\mathbf{T}}' = \boldsymbol{\varpi}'^\wedge\mathbf{T}', \qquad (8.306a)$$

$$\dot{\boldsymbol{\varpi}}' = -\boldsymbol{\mathcal{M}}^{-1}\boldsymbol{\varpi}'^{\wedge^T}\boldsymbol{\mathcal{M}}\boldsymbol{\varpi}' + \mathbf{a}'. \qquad (8.306b)$$

If we think of $\delta\mathbf{a}$ as an unknown noise input, then we would like to know how this turns into uncertainty on the pose and velocity variables through the chain of dynamics and kinematics. Substituting the perturbations into the motion models, we can separate them into a (nonlinear) nominal motion model,

$$\text{nominal kinematics:} \quad \dot{\mathbf{T}} = \boldsymbol{\varpi}^\wedge\mathbf{T}, \qquad (8.307a)$$

$$\text{nominal dynamics:} \quad \dot{\boldsymbol{\varpi}} = -\boldsymbol{\mathcal{M}}^{-1}\boldsymbol{\varpi}^{\wedge^T}\boldsymbol{\mathcal{M}}\boldsymbol{\varpi} + \mathbf{a}, \qquad (8.307b)$$

and a (linear) perturbation motion model,

$$\text{perturbation kinematics:} \quad \delta\dot{\boldsymbol{\xi}} = \boldsymbol{\varpi}^\wedge\,\delta\boldsymbol{\xi} + \delta\boldsymbol{\varpi}, \qquad (8.308a)$$

$$\text{perturbation dynamics:} \quad \delta\dot{\boldsymbol{\varpi}} = \boldsymbol{\mathcal{M}}^{-1}\left((\boldsymbol{\mathcal{M}}\boldsymbol{\varpi})^{\wedge^T} - \boldsymbol{\varpi}^\wedge\boldsymbol{\mathcal{M}}\right)\delta\boldsymbol{\varpi} + \delta\mathbf{a}, \qquad (8.308b)$$

which we can write in combined matrix form:

$$\begin{bmatrix}\delta\dot{\boldsymbol{\xi}}\\\delta\dot{\boldsymbol{\varpi}}\end{bmatrix} = \begin{bmatrix}\boldsymbol{\varpi}^\wedge & \mathbf{1}\\\mathbf{0} & \boldsymbol{\mathcal{M}}^{-1}\left((\boldsymbol{\mathcal{M}}\boldsymbol{\varpi})^{\wedge^T} - \boldsymbol{\varpi}^\wedge\boldsymbol{\mathcal{M}}\right)\end{bmatrix}\begin{bmatrix}\delta\boldsymbol{\xi}\\\delta\boldsymbol{\varpi}\end{bmatrix} + \begin{bmatrix}\mathbf{0}\\\delta\mathbf{a}\end{bmatrix}. \qquad (8.309)$$

Finding the transition matrix for this LTV *stochastic differential equation (SDE)* may be difficult, but it can be integrated numerically.

8.3 Probability and Statistics

We have seen throughout this chapter that elements of matrix Lie groups do not satisfy some basic operations that we normally take for granted. This theme continues when working with random variables. For example, we often work with Gaussian random variables, which typically take the form

$$\mathbf{x} \sim \mathcal{N}(\boldsymbol{\mu}, \boldsymbol{\Sigma}), \qquad (8.310)$$

where $\mathbf{x} \in \mathbb{R}^N$ (i.e., $\mathbf{x}$ lives in a vector space). An equivalent way to look at this is that $\mathbf{x}$ comprises a 'large', noise-free component, $\boldsymbol{\mu}$, and a 'small', noisy component, $\boldsymbol{\epsilon}$, that is zero-mean:

$$\mathbf{x} = \boldsymbol{\mu} + \boldsymbol{\epsilon}, \quad \boldsymbol{\epsilon} \sim \mathcal{N}(\mathbf{0}, \boldsymbol{\Sigma}). \qquad (8.311)$$

This arrangement works because all the quantities involved are vectors and the vector space is closed under the $+$ operation. Unfortunately, our matrix Lie groups are not closed under this type of addition, and so we need to think of a different way of defining random variables.

This section will introduce our definitions of random variables and *probability density functions (PDFs)* for rotations and poses, and then present some examples of using our new probability and statistics. We follow the approach outlined by Barfoot and Furgale (2014), which is a practical method when uncertainty on rotation does not become too large. This approach was inspired by and builds on the works of Su and Lee (1991, 1992), Chirikjian and Kyatkin (2001), Smith et al. (2003), Wang and Chirikjian (2006, 2008), Chirikjian (2009), Wolfe et al. (2011), Long et al. (2012), and Chirikjian and Kyatkin (2016). It must be noted that Chirikjian and Kyatkin (2001) (and the revision in Chirikjian and Kyatkin, 2016) explain how to represent and propagate PDFs on groups even when the uncertainty becomes large, whereas the discussion here is relevant only when uncertainty is reasonably small.

8.3.1 Gaussian Random Variables and PDFs

We will discuss general random variables and PDFs briefly, and then focus on Gaussians. We frame the main discussion in terms of rotations and then state the results for poses afterward.

Rotations

We have seen several times the dual nature of rotations/poses in the sense that they can be described in terms of a Lie group or a Lie algebra, each having advantages and disadvantages. Lie groups are nice because they are free of singularities but have constraints; this is also the form that is usually required in order to rotate/transform something in the real world. Lie algebras are nice because we can treat them as vector spaces (for which there are many useful mathematical tools),[28] and they are free of constraints, but we need to worry about singularities.

It seems logical to exploit the vector space character of a Lie algebra in defining our random variables for rotations and poses. In this way, we can leverage all the usual tools from probability and statistics, rather than starting over. Given this decision, and using (8.311) for inspiration, there are three possible ways to define a random variable for $SO(3)$ based on the different perturbation options:

	$SO(3)$	$\mathfrak{so}(3)$
left	$\mathbf{C} = \exp\left(\boldsymbol{\epsilon}_\ell^\wedge\right)\bar{\mathbf{C}}$	$\boldsymbol{\phi} \approx \boldsymbol{\mu} + \mathbf{J}_\ell^{-1}(\boldsymbol{\mu})\,\boldsymbol{\epsilon}_\ell$
middle	$\mathbf{C} = \exp\left((\boldsymbol{\mu} + \boldsymbol{\epsilon}_m)^\wedge\right)$	$\boldsymbol{\phi} = \boldsymbol{\mu} + \boldsymbol{\epsilon}_m$
right	$\mathbf{C} = \bar{\mathbf{C}}\exp\left(\boldsymbol{\epsilon}_r^\wedge\right)$	$\boldsymbol{\phi} \approx \boldsymbol{\mu} + \mathbf{J}_r^{-1}(\boldsymbol{\mu})\,\boldsymbol{\epsilon}_r$

where $\boldsymbol{\epsilon}_\ell, \boldsymbol{\epsilon}_m, \boldsymbol{\epsilon}_r \in \mathbb{R}^3$ are random variables in the usual (vector space) sense, $\boldsymbol{\mu} \in \mathbb{R}^3$ is a constant, and $\mathbf{C} = \exp(\boldsymbol{\phi}^\wedge)$, $\bar{\mathbf{C}} = \exp\left(\boldsymbol{\mu}^\wedge\right) \in SO(3)$. In each of these three cases, we know through the surjective-only property of the exponential map and the closure property of Lie groups that we will ensure that

---

[28] Including probability and statistics.

$\mathbf{C} = \exp\left(\phi^\wedge\right) \in SO(3)$. This idea of mapping a random variable onto a Lie group through the exponential map is sometimes informally referred to as 'injecting' noise onto the group, but this is misleading.[29]

Looking to the Lie algebra versions of the perturbations, we can see the usual relationships between the left, middle, right: $\epsilon_m \approx \mathbf{J}_\ell^{-1}(\boldsymbol{\mu}) \epsilon_\ell \approx \mathbf{J}_r^{-1}(\boldsymbol{\mu}) \epsilon_r$. Based on this, we might conclude that all the options are equally good. However, in the middle option, we must keep the nominal component of the variable in the Lie algebra as well as the perturbation, which means we will have to contend with the associated singularities. On the other hand, both the left and right perturbation approaches allow us to keep the nominal component of the variable in the Lie group. By convention, we will choose the left perturbation approach, but one could just as easily pick the right.

This approach to defining random variables for rotations/poses in some sense gets the best of both worlds. We can avoid singularities for the large, nominal part by keeping it in the Lie group, but we can exploit the constraint-free, vector space character of the Lie algebra for the small, noisy part. Since the noisy part is assumed to be small, it will tend to stay away from the singularities associated with the rotation-vector parameterization.[30]

Thus, for $SO(3)$, a random variable, $\mathbf{C}$, will be of the form[31]

$$\mathbf{C} = \exp\left(\epsilon^\wedge\right) \bar{\mathbf{C}}, \tag{8.312}$$

where $\bar{\mathbf{C}} \in SO(3)$ is a 'large', noise-free, nominal rotation and $\epsilon \in \mathbb{R}^3$ is a 'small', noisy component (i.e., it is just a regular, random variable from a vector space). This means that we can simply define a PDF for ϵ, and this will induce a PDF on $SO(3)$:

$$p(\epsilon) \;\rightarrow\; p(\mathbf{C}). \tag{8.313}$$

We will mainly be concerned with Gaussian PDFs in our estimation problems, and in this case we let

$$p(\epsilon) = \frac{1}{\sqrt{(2\pi)^3 \det(\boldsymbol{\Sigma})}} \exp\left(-\frac{1}{2}\epsilon^T \boldsymbol{\Sigma}^{-1} \epsilon\right), \tag{8.314}$$

or $\epsilon \sim \mathcal{N}(\mathbf{0}, \boldsymbol{\Sigma})$. Note that we can now think of $\bar{\mathbf{C}}$ as the 'mean' rotation and $\boldsymbol{\Sigma}$ as the associated covariance.

By definition, $p(\epsilon)$ is a valid PDF, and so

$$\int p(\epsilon)\, d\epsilon = 1. \tag{8.315}$$

---

[29] Mathematically, *injection* means that at most one element of the Lie algebra should map to each element of the Lie group. As we have seen, the exponential map linking the Lie algebra to the Lie group is *surjective-only*, which means every element of the Lie algebra maps to some element of the Lie group and every element of the Lie group is mapped to from many elements of the Lie algebra. If we limit the rotation angle magnitude, $|\phi| < \pi$, then the exponential map is *bijective*, meaning both surjective and injective (i.e., one-to-one and onto). However, we may not want to impose this limit, whereupon the injective property does not hold.

[30] This approach works reasonably well as long as the perturbation is small. If this is not the case, a more global approach to defining a random variable on Lie groups is required, but these are less well explored (Chirikjian and Kyatkin, 2001, 2016; Lee et al., 2008).

[31] We will drop the ℓ subscript from here to keep things clean.

We deliberately avoid making the integration limits explicit because we have defined ϵ to be Gaussian, which means it has probability mass out to infinity in all directions. However, we assume that most of the probability mass is encompassed in $|\epsilon| < \pi$ for this to make sense. Referring back to Section 8.1.6, we know that we can relate an infinitesimal volume element in the Lie algebra to an infinitesimal volume element in the Lie group according to

$$dC = |\det(\mathbf{J}(\epsilon))|\, d\epsilon, \qquad (8.316)$$

where we note that due to our choice of using the left perturbation, the Jacobian, $\mathbf{J}$, is evaluated at ϵ (which will hopefully be small) rather than at ϕ (which could be large); this will hopefully keep $\mathbf{J}$ very close to $\mathbf{1}$. We can use this to now work out the PDF that is induced on $\mathbf{C}$. We have that

$$1 = \int p(\epsilon)\, d\epsilon \qquad (8.317)$$

$$= \int \frac{1}{\sqrt{(2\pi)^3 \det(\boldsymbol{\Sigma})}} \exp\left(-\frac{1}{2}\epsilon^T \boldsymbol{\Sigma}^{-1} \epsilon\right) d\epsilon \qquad (8.318)$$

$$= \int \underbrace{\frac{1}{\sqrt{(2\pi)^3 \det(\boldsymbol{\Sigma})}} \exp\left(-\frac{1}{2}\ln\left(\mathbf{C}\bar{\mathbf{C}}^T\right)^{\vee^T} \boldsymbol{\Sigma}^{-1} \ln\left(\mathbf{C}\bar{\mathbf{C}}^T\right)^{\vee}\right) \frac{1}{|\det(\mathbf{J})|}}_{p(\mathbf{C})}\, d\mathbf{C},$$

$$(8.319)$$

where we indicate the induced $p(\mathbf{C})$. It is important to realize that $p(\mathbf{C})$ looks like this due to our choice to define $p(\epsilon)$ directly.[32]

A common method of defining the *mean rotation*, $\mathbf{M} \in SO(3)$, is the unique solution of the equation

$$\int \ln\left(\mathbf{C}\mathbf{M}^T\right)^{\vee} p(\mathbf{C})\, d\mathbf{C} = \mathbf{0}. \qquad (8.320)$$

Switching variables from $\mathbf{C}$ to ϵ, this is equivalent to

$$\int \ln\left(\exp\left(\epsilon^{\wedge}\right)\bar{\mathbf{C}}\mathbf{M}^T\right)^{\vee} p(\epsilon)\, d\epsilon = \mathbf{0}. \qquad (8.321)$$

Taking $\mathbf{M} = \bar{\mathbf{C}}$, we see that

$$\int \ln\left(\exp\left(\epsilon^{\wedge}\right)\bar{\mathbf{C}}\mathbf{M}^T\right)^{\vee} p(\epsilon)\, d\epsilon = \int \ln\left(\exp\left(\epsilon^{\wedge}\right)\bar{\mathbf{C}}\bar{\mathbf{C}}^T\right)^{\vee} p(\epsilon)\, d\epsilon$$

$$= \int \epsilon\, p(\epsilon)\, d\epsilon = E[\epsilon] = \mathbf{0}, \quad (8.322)$$

which validates our logic in referring to $\bar{\mathbf{C}}$ as the mean earlier.

---

[32] It is also possible to work in the other direction by first defining $p(\mathbf{C})$ (Chirikjian, 2009).

Figure 8.4
Graphical depiction of our approach to representing uncertainty on Lie groups. We define the mean in the Lie group, the uncertainty in the Lie algebra, and combine them to produce random variables in the Lie group.

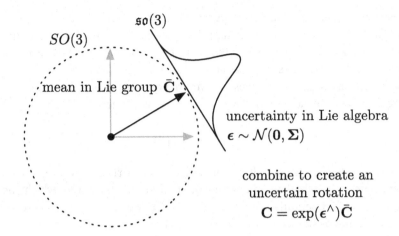

mean in Lie group $\bar{\mathbf{C}}$

uncertainty in Lie algebra
$\epsilon \sim \mathcal{N}(\mathbf{0}, \mathbf{\Sigma})$

combine to create an
uncertain rotation
$\mathbf{C} = \exp(\epsilon^\wedge)\bar{\mathbf{C}}$

The corresponding *covariance*, $\mathbf{\Sigma}$, computed about $\mathbf{M}$, can be defined as

$$\mathbf{\Sigma} = \int \ln\left(\exp\left(\epsilon^\wedge\right)\bar{\mathbf{C}}\mathbf{M}^T\right)^\vee \ln\left(\exp\left(\epsilon^\wedge\right)\bar{\mathbf{C}}\mathbf{M}^T\right)^{\vee^T} p(\epsilon)\,d\epsilon$$

$$= \int \ln\left(\exp\left(\epsilon^\wedge\right)\bar{\mathbf{C}}\bar{\mathbf{C}}^T\right)^\vee \ln\left(\exp\left(\epsilon^\wedge\right)\bar{\mathbf{C}}\bar{\mathbf{C}}^T\right)^{\vee^T} p(\epsilon)\,d\epsilon$$

$$= \int \epsilon\epsilon^T\, p(\epsilon)\,d\epsilon = E[\epsilon\epsilon^T], \tag{8.323}$$

which implies that choosing $\epsilon \sim \mathcal{N}(\mathbf{0}, \mathbf{\Sigma})$ is a reasonable thing to do and matches nicely with the noise 'injection' procedure. In fact, all higher-order statistics defined in an analogous way will produce the statistics associated with ϵ as well. Figure 8.4 provides a graphical depiction of how we are defining uncertainty for Lie groups.

As another advantage to this approach to representing random variables for rotations, consider what happens to our rotation random variables under a pure (deterministic) rotation mapping. Let $\mathbf{R} \in SO(3)$ be a constant rotation matrix that we apply to $\mathbf{C}$ to create a new random variable, $\mathbf{C}' = \mathbf{R}\,\mathbf{C}$. With no approximation we have

$$\mathbf{C}' = \mathbf{R}\,\mathbf{C} = \mathbf{R}\exp\left(\epsilon^\wedge\right)\bar{\mathbf{C}} = \exp\left((\mathbf{R}\epsilon)^\wedge\right)\mathbf{R}\,\bar{\mathbf{C}} = \exp\left(\epsilon'^\wedge\right)\bar{\mathbf{C}}', \tag{8.324}$$

where

$$\bar{\mathbf{C}}' = \mathbf{R}\,\bar{\mathbf{C}}, \quad \epsilon' = \mathbf{R}\,\epsilon \sim \mathcal{N}\left(\mathbf{0}, \mathbf{R}\,\mathbf{\Sigma}\,\mathbf{R}^T\right). \tag{8.325}$$

This is very appealing, as it allows us to carry out this common operation exactly. Related to this is the notion of continuous symmetry, which is discussed at the end of the chapter in Section 8.4.

Poses

Similarly to the rotation case, we choose to define a Gaussian random variable for poses as

$$\mathbf{T} = \exp\left(\epsilon^\wedge\right)\bar{\mathbf{T}}, \tag{8.326}$$

where $\bar{\mathbf{T}} \in SE(3)$ is a 'large' mean transformation and $\epsilon \in \mathbb{R}^6 \sim \mathcal{N}\left(\mathbf{0}, \mathbf{\Sigma}\right)$ is a 'small' Gaussian random variable (i.e., in a vector space).

The *mean transformation*, $\mathbf{M} \in SE(3)$, is the unique solution of the following equation:

$$\int \ln \left(\exp \left(\epsilon^{\wedge} \right) \bar{\mathbf{T}} \mathbf{M}^{-1} \right)^{\vee} p(\epsilon) \, d\epsilon = \mathbf{0}. \tag{8.327}$$

Taking $\mathbf{M} = \bar{\mathbf{T}}$, we see that

$$\int \ln \left(\exp \left(\epsilon^{\wedge} \right) \bar{\mathbf{T}} \mathbf{M}^{-1} \right)^{\vee} p(\epsilon) \, d\epsilon = \int \ln \left(\exp \left(\epsilon^{\wedge} \right) \bar{\mathbf{T}} \bar{\mathbf{T}}^{-1} \right)^{\vee} p(\epsilon) \, d\epsilon$$

$$= \int \epsilon \, p(\epsilon) \, d\epsilon = E[\epsilon] = \mathbf{0}, \tag{8.328}$$

which validates our logic in referring to $\bar{\mathbf{T}}$ as the mean.

The corresponding covariance, $\boldsymbol{\Sigma}$, computed about $\mathbf{M}$, can be defined as

$$\boldsymbol{\Sigma} = \int \ln \left(\exp \left(\epsilon^{\wedge} \right) \bar{\mathbf{T}} \mathbf{M}^{-1} \right)^{\vee} \ln \left(\exp \left(\epsilon^{\wedge} \right) \bar{\mathbf{T}} \mathbf{M}^{-1} \right)^{\vee^T} p(\epsilon) \, d\epsilon$$

$$= \int \ln \left(\exp \left(\epsilon^{\wedge} \right) \bar{\mathbf{T}} \bar{\mathbf{T}}^{-1} \right)^{\vee} \ln \left(\exp \left(\epsilon^{\wedge} \right) \bar{\mathbf{T}} \bar{\mathbf{T}}^{-1} \right)^{\vee^T} p(\epsilon) \, d\epsilon$$

$$= \int \epsilon \epsilon^T \, p(\epsilon) \, d\epsilon = E[\epsilon \epsilon^T], \tag{8.329}$$

which implies that choosing $\epsilon \sim \mathcal{N}(\mathbf{0}, \boldsymbol{\Sigma})$ is a reasonable thing to do and matches nicely with the noise 'injection' procedure. In fact, all higher-order statistics defined in an analogous way will produce the statistics associated with ϵ as well.

Again, consider what happens to our transformation random variables under a pure (deterministic) transformation mapping. Let $\mathbf{R} \in SE(3)$ be a constant transformation matrix that we apply to $\mathbf{T}$ to create a new random variable, $\mathbf{T}' = \mathbf{R}\,\mathbf{T}$. With no approximation we have

$$\mathbf{T}' = \mathbf{R}\,\mathbf{T} = \mathbf{R} \exp \left(\epsilon^{\wedge} \right) \bar{\mathbf{T}} = \exp \left((\boldsymbol{\mathcal{R}} \epsilon)^{\wedge} \right) \mathbf{R}\, \bar{\mathbf{T}} = \exp \left(\epsilon'^{\wedge} \right) \bar{\mathbf{T}}', \tag{8.330}$$

where

$$\bar{\mathbf{T}}' = \mathbf{R}\, \bar{\mathbf{T}}, \quad \epsilon' = \boldsymbol{\mathcal{R}}\, \epsilon \sim \mathcal{N} \left(\mathbf{0}, \boldsymbol{\mathcal{R}}\, \boldsymbol{\Sigma}\, \boldsymbol{\mathcal{R}}^T \right), \tag{8.331}$$

and $\boldsymbol{\mathcal{R}} = \mathrm{Ad}(\mathbf{R})$.

8.3.2 Uncertainty on a Rotated Vector

Consider the simple mapping from rotation to position given by

$$\mathbf{y} = \mathbf{C}\mathbf{x}, \tag{8.332}$$

where $\mathbf{x} \in \mathbb{R}^3$ is a constant and

$$\mathbf{C} = \exp \left(\epsilon^{\wedge} \right) \bar{\mathbf{C}}, \quad \epsilon \sim \mathcal{N}(\mathbf{0}, \boldsymbol{\Sigma}). \tag{8.333}$$

Figure 8.5
Depiction of
uncertainty on a
vector
$\mathbf{y} = \mathbf{C}\mathbf{x} \in \mathbb{R}^3$,
where $\mathbf{x}$ is constant
and $\mathbf{C} =$
$\exp{(\boldsymbol{\epsilon}^{\wedge})}\,\bar{\mathbf{C}}, \boldsymbol{\epsilon} \sim$
$\mathcal{N}(\mathbf{0}, \boldsymbol{\Sigma})$ is a random
variable. The dots
show samples of the
resulting density
over $\mathbf{y}$. The contours
(of varying
darkness) show one,
two, and three
standard deviations
of the equiprobable
contours of $\boldsymbol{\epsilon}$
mapped to $\mathbf{y}$. The
solid black line is the
noisefree vector,
$\bar{\mathbf{y}} = \bar{\mathbf{C}}\mathbf{x}$. The grey,
dashed, dotted, and
dash-dotted lines
show various
estimates of $E[\mathbf{y}]$
using brute-force
sampling, the
sigmapoint
transformation, a
second-order
method, and a
fourth-order method.

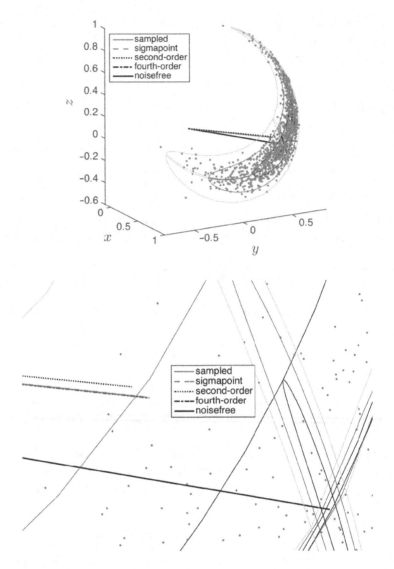

Figure 8.5 shows what the resulting density over $\mathbf{y}$ looks like for some particular values of $\bar{\mathbf{C}}$ and $\boldsymbol{\Sigma}$. We see that, as expected, the samples live on a sphere whose radius is $|\mathbf{x}|$ since rotations preserve length.

We might be interested in computing $E[\mathbf{y}]$ in the vector space $\mathbb{R}^3$ (i.e., not exploiting special knowledge that $\mathbf{y}$ must have length $|\mathbf{x}|$). We can imagine three ways of doing this:

(i) Drawing a large number of random samples and then averaging.

(ii) Using the sigmapoint transformation.

(iii) An analytical approximation.

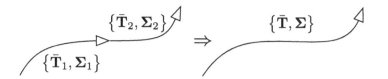

Figure 8.6
Combining a chain
of two poses into a
single compound
pose.

For (iii), we consider expanding $\mathbf{C}$ in terms of ϵ so that

$$\mathbf{y} = \mathbf{C}\mathbf{x} = \left(\mathbf{1} + \epsilon^\wedge + \frac{1}{2}\epsilon^\wedge\epsilon^\wedge + \frac{1}{6}\epsilon^\wedge\epsilon^\wedge\epsilon^\wedge + \frac{1}{24}\epsilon^\wedge\epsilon^\wedge\epsilon^\wedge\epsilon^\wedge + \cdots\right)\bar{\mathbf{C}}\mathbf{x}.$$
(8.334)

Since ϵ is Gaussian, the odd terms average to zero such that

$$E[\mathbf{y}] = \left(\mathbf{1} + \frac{1}{2}E\left[\epsilon^\wedge\epsilon^\wedge\right] + \frac{1}{24}E\left[\epsilon^\wedge\epsilon^\wedge\epsilon^\wedge\epsilon^\wedge\right] + \cdots\right)\bar{\mathbf{C}}\mathbf{x}.$$
(8.335)

Going term by term, we have

$$E\left[\epsilon^\wedge\epsilon^\wedge\right] = E\left[-(\epsilon^T\epsilon)\mathbf{1} + \epsilon\epsilon^T\right] = -\operatorname{tr}\left(E\left[\epsilon\epsilon^T\right]\right)\mathbf{1} + E\left[\epsilon\epsilon^T\right]$$
$$= -\operatorname{tr}\left(\mathbf{\Sigma}\right)\mathbf{1} + \mathbf{\Sigma},$$
(8.336)

and

$$\begin{aligned}
E\left[\epsilon^\wedge\epsilon^\wedge\epsilon^\wedge\epsilon^\wedge\right] &= E\left[-(\epsilon^T\epsilon)\,\epsilon^\wedge\epsilon^\wedge\right]\\
&= E\left[-(\epsilon^T\epsilon)\left(-(\epsilon^T\epsilon)\mathbf{1} + \epsilon\epsilon^T\right)\right]\\
&= \operatorname{tr}\left(E\left[(\epsilon^T\epsilon)\,\epsilon\epsilon^T\right]\right)\mathbf{1} - E\left[(\epsilon^T\epsilon)\,\epsilon\epsilon^T\right]\\
&= \operatorname{tr}\left(\mathbf{\Sigma}\left(\operatorname{tr}\left(\mathbf{\Sigma}\right)\mathbf{1} + 2\mathbf{\Sigma}\right)\right)\mathbf{1} - \mathbf{\Sigma}\left(\operatorname{tr}\left(\mathbf{\Sigma}\right)\mathbf{1} + 2\mathbf{\Sigma}\right)\\
&= \left((\operatorname{tr}\left(\mathbf{\Sigma}\right))^2 + 2\operatorname{tr}\left(\mathbf{\Sigma}^2\right)\right)\mathbf{1} - \mathbf{\Sigma}\left(\operatorname{tr}\left(\mathbf{\Sigma}\right)\mathbf{1} + 2\mathbf{\Sigma}\right), \quad (8.337)
\end{aligned}$$

where we have used the multivariate version of Isserlis' theorem. Higher-order
terms are also possible, but to fourth order in ϵ, we have

$$\begin{aligned}
E[\mathbf{y}] \approx \Big(\mathbf{1} &+ \frac{1}{2}\left(-\operatorname{tr}\left(\mathbf{\Sigma}\right)\mathbf{1} + \mathbf{\Sigma}\right)\\
&+ \frac{1}{24}\left(\left((\operatorname{tr}\left(\mathbf{\Sigma}\right))^2 + 2\operatorname{tr}\left(\mathbf{\Sigma}^2\right)\right)\mathbf{1} - \mathbf{\Sigma}\left(\operatorname{tr}\left(\mathbf{\Sigma}\right)\mathbf{1} + 2\mathbf{\Sigma}\right)\right)\Big)\bar{\mathbf{C}}\mathbf{x}.
\end{aligned}$$
(8.338)

We refer to the method keeping terms to second order in ϵ as 'second-order' and
the method keeping terms to fourth order in ϵ as 'fourth-order' in Figure 8.5. The
fourth-order method is very comparable to the sigmapoint method and random
sampling.

8.3.3 Compounding Poses

In this section, we investigate the problem of compounding two poses, each with
associated uncertainty, as depicted in Figure 8.6.

Theory

Consider two noisy poses, $\mathbf{T}_1$ and $\mathbf{T}_2$; we keep track of their nominal values and associated uncertainties:

$$\{\bar{\mathbf{T}}_1, \boldsymbol{\Sigma}_1\}, \quad \{\bar{\mathbf{T}}_2, \boldsymbol{\Sigma}_2\}. \tag{8.339}$$

Suppose now we let

$$\mathbf{T} = \mathbf{T}_1 \mathbf{T}_2, \tag{8.340}$$

as depicted in Figure 8.6. What is $\{\bar{\mathbf{T}}, \boldsymbol{\Sigma}\}$? Under our perturbation scheme we have

$$\exp\left(\boldsymbol{\epsilon}^\wedge\right)\bar{\mathbf{T}} = \exp\left(\boldsymbol{\epsilon}_1^\wedge\right)\bar{\mathbf{T}}_1 \exp\left(\boldsymbol{\epsilon}_2^\wedge\right)\bar{\mathbf{T}}_2. \tag{8.341}$$

Moving all the uncertain factors to the left side, we have

$$\exp\left(\boldsymbol{\epsilon}^\wedge\right)\bar{\mathbf{T}} = \exp\left(\boldsymbol{\epsilon}_1^\wedge\right)\exp\left(\left(\bar{\mathcal{T}}_1 \boldsymbol{\epsilon}_2\right)^\wedge\right)\bar{\mathbf{T}}_1\bar{\mathbf{T}}_2, \tag{8.342}$$

where $\bar{\mathcal{T}}_1 = \text{Ad}\left(\bar{\mathbf{T}}_1\right)$. If we let

$$\bar{\mathbf{T}} = \bar{\mathbf{T}}_1\bar{\mathbf{T}}_2, \tag{8.343}$$

we are left with

$$\exp\left(\boldsymbol{\epsilon}^\wedge\right) = \exp\left(\boldsymbol{\epsilon}_1^\wedge\right)\exp\left(\left(\bar{\mathcal{T}}_1 \boldsymbol{\epsilon}_2\right)^\wedge\right). \tag{8.344}$$

Letting $\boldsymbol{\epsilon}_2' = \bar{\mathcal{T}}_1 \boldsymbol{\epsilon}_2$, we can apply the BCH formula to find

$$\boldsymbol{\epsilon} = \boldsymbol{\epsilon}_1 + \boldsymbol{\epsilon}_2' + \frac{1}{2}\boldsymbol{\epsilon}_1^\wedge \boldsymbol{\epsilon}_2' + \frac{1}{12}\boldsymbol{\epsilon}_1^\wedge \boldsymbol{\epsilon}_1^\wedge \boldsymbol{\epsilon}_2' + \frac{1}{12}\boldsymbol{\epsilon}_2'^\wedge \boldsymbol{\epsilon}_2'^\wedge \boldsymbol{\epsilon}_1 - \frac{1}{24}\boldsymbol{\epsilon}_2'^\wedge \boldsymbol{\epsilon}_1^\wedge \boldsymbol{\epsilon}_1^\wedge \boldsymbol{\epsilon}_2' + \cdots. \tag{8.345}$$

For our approach to hold, we require that $E\left[\boldsymbol{\epsilon}\right] = \mathbf{0}$. Assuming that $\boldsymbol{\epsilon}_1 \sim \mathcal{N}\left(\mathbf{0}, \boldsymbol{\Sigma}_1\right)$ and $\boldsymbol{\epsilon}_2' \sim \mathcal{N}\left(\mathbf{0}, \boldsymbol{\Sigma}_2'\right)$ are uncorrelated with one another, we have

$$E\left[\boldsymbol{\epsilon}\right] = -\frac{1}{24}E\left[\boldsymbol{\epsilon}_2'^\wedge \boldsymbol{\epsilon}_1^\wedge \boldsymbol{\epsilon}_1^\wedge \boldsymbol{\epsilon}_2'\right] + O\left(\boldsymbol{\epsilon}^6\right), \tag{8.346}$$

since everything except the fourth-order term has zero mean. Thus, to third order, we can safely assume that $E\left[\boldsymbol{\epsilon}\right] = \mathbf{0}$, and thus (8.343) seems to be a reasonable way to compound the mean transformations.[33]

---

[33] It is also possible to show that the fourth-order term has zero mean, $E\left[\boldsymbol{\epsilon}_2'^\wedge \boldsymbol{\epsilon}_1^\wedge \boldsymbol{\epsilon}_1^\wedge \boldsymbol{\epsilon}_2'\right] = \mathbf{0}$, if $\boldsymbol{\Sigma}_1$ is of the special form

$$\boldsymbol{\Sigma}_1 = \begin{bmatrix} \boldsymbol{\Sigma}_{1,\rho\rho} & \mathbf{0} \\ \mathbf{0} & \sigma_{1,\phi\phi}^2 \mathbf{1} \end{bmatrix},$$

where the ρ and ϕ subscripts indicate a partitioning of the covariance into the translation and rotation components, respectively. This is a common situation for $\boldsymbol{\Sigma}_1$ when we are, for example, propagating uncertainty on velocity through the kinematics equations presented for $SE(3)$; from (8.263) we have $\mathbf{T}_1 = \exp\left((t_2 - t_1)\boldsymbol{\varpi}^\wedge\right)$, where $\boldsymbol{\varpi}$ is the (noisy) generalized velocity. In this case, we are justified in assuming $E\left[\boldsymbol{\epsilon}\right] = \mathbf{0}$ all the way out to fifth order (and possibly further).

The next task is to compute $\boldsymbol{\Sigma} = E\left[\boldsymbol{\epsilon}\boldsymbol{\epsilon}^T\right]$. Multiplying out to fourth order, we have

$$
\begin{aligned}
E\left[\boldsymbol{\epsilon}\boldsymbol{\epsilon}^T\right] \approx E\bigg[& \boldsymbol{\epsilon}_1\boldsymbol{\epsilon}_1^T + \boldsymbol{\epsilon}_2'\boldsymbol{\epsilon}_2'^T + \frac{1}{4}\boldsymbol{\epsilon}_1^\wedge\left(\boldsymbol{\epsilon}_2'\boldsymbol{\epsilon}_2'^T\right)\boldsymbol{\epsilon}_1^{\wedge T} \\
& + \frac{1}{12}\left(\left(\boldsymbol{\epsilon}_1^\wedge\boldsymbol{\epsilon}_1^\wedge\right)\left(\boldsymbol{\epsilon}_2'\boldsymbol{\epsilon}_2'^T\right) + \left(\boldsymbol{\epsilon}_2'\boldsymbol{\epsilon}_2'^T\right)\left(\boldsymbol{\epsilon}_1^\wedge\boldsymbol{\epsilon}_1^\wedge\right)^T\right. \\
& \left. + \left(\boldsymbol{\epsilon}_2'^\wedge\boldsymbol{\epsilon}_2'^\wedge\right)\left(\boldsymbol{\epsilon}_1\boldsymbol{\epsilon}_1^T\right) + \left(\boldsymbol{\epsilon}_2'^\wedge\boldsymbol{\epsilon}_2'^\wedge\right)\left(\boldsymbol{\epsilon}_1\boldsymbol{\epsilon}_1^T\right)\right)\bigg],
\end{aligned}
\tag{8.347}
$$

where we have omitted showing any terms that have an odd power in either $\boldsymbol{\epsilon}_1$ or $\boldsymbol{\epsilon}_2'$ since these will by definition have expectation zero. This expression may look daunting, but we can take it term by term. To save space, we define and make use of the following two linear operators:

$$
\langle\!\langle\mathbf{A}\rangle\!\rangle = -\operatorname{tr}\left(\mathbf{A}\right)\mathbf{1} + \mathbf{A},
\tag{8.348a}
$$

$$
\langle\!\langle\mathbf{A}, \mathbf{B}\rangle\!\rangle = \langle\!\langle\mathbf{A}\rangle\!\rangle\langle\!\langle\mathbf{B}\rangle\!\rangle + \langle\!\langle\mathbf{B}\mathbf{A}\rangle\!\rangle,
\tag{8.348b}
$$

with $\mathbf{A}, \mathbf{B} \in \mathbb{R}^{n\times n}$. These provide the useful identity,

$$
-\mathbf{u}^\wedge\mathbf{A}\mathbf{v}^\wedge \equiv \langle\!\langle\mathbf{v}\mathbf{u}^T, \mathbf{A}^T\rangle\!\rangle,
\tag{8.349}
$$

where $\mathbf{u}, \mathbf{v} \in \mathbb{R}^3$, and $\mathbf{A} \in \mathbb{R}^{3\times 3}$. Making use of this repeatedly, we have out to fourth order,

$$
E\left[\boldsymbol{\epsilon}_1\boldsymbol{\epsilon}_1^T\right] = \boldsymbol{\Sigma}_1 = \begin{bmatrix} \boldsymbol{\Sigma}_{1,\rho\rho} & \boldsymbol{\Sigma}_{1,\rho\phi} \\ \boldsymbol{\Sigma}_{1,\rho\phi}^T & \boldsymbol{\Sigma}_{1,\phi\phi} \end{bmatrix},
\tag{8.350a}
$$

$$
E\left[\boldsymbol{\epsilon}_2'\boldsymbol{\epsilon}_2'^T\right] = \boldsymbol{\Sigma}_2' = \begin{bmatrix} \boldsymbol{\Sigma}_{2,\rho\rho}' & \boldsymbol{\Sigma}_{2,\rho\phi}' \\ \boldsymbol{\Sigma}_{2,\rho\phi}'^T & \boldsymbol{\Sigma}_{2,\phi\phi}' \end{bmatrix} = \bar{\mathcal{T}}_1\boldsymbol{\Sigma}_2\bar{\mathcal{T}}_1^T,
\tag{8.350b}
$$

$$
E\left[\boldsymbol{\epsilon}_1^\wedge\boldsymbol{\epsilon}_1^\wedge\right] = \boldsymbol{\mathcal{A}}_1 = \begin{bmatrix} \langle\!\langle\boldsymbol{\Sigma}_{1,\phi\phi}\rangle\!\rangle & \langle\!\langle\boldsymbol{\Sigma}_{1,\rho\phi} + \boldsymbol{\Sigma}_{1,\rho\phi}^T\rangle\!\rangle \\ \mathbf{0} & \langle\!\langle\boldsymbol{\Sigma}_{1,\phi\phi}\rangle\!\rangle \end{bmatrix},
\tag{8.350c}
$$

$$
E\left[\boldsymbol{\epsilon}_2'^\wedge\boldsymbol{\epsilon}_2'^\wedge\right] = \boldsymbol{\mathcal{A}}_2' = \begin{bmatrix} \langle\!\langle\boldsymbol{\Sigma}_{2,\phi\phi}'\rangle\!\rangle & \langle\!\langle\boldsymbol{\Sigma}_{2,\rho\phi}' + \boldsymbol{\Sigma}_{2,\rho\phi}'^T\rangle\!\rangle \\ \mathbf{0} & \langle\!\langle\boldsymbol{\Sigma}_{2,\phi\phi}'\rangle\!\rangle \end{bmatrix},
\tag{8.350d}
$$

$$
E\left[\boldsymbol{\epsilon}_1^\wedge\left(\boldsymbol{\epsilon}_2'\boldsymbol{\epsilon}_2'^T\right)\boldsymbol{\epsilon}_1^{\wedge T}\right] = \boldsymbol{\mathcal{B}} = \begin{bmatrix} \mathbf{B}_{\rho\rho} & \mathbf{B}_{\rho\phi} \\ \mathbf{B}_{\rho\phi}^T & \mathbf{B}_{\phi\phi} \end{bmatrix},
\tag{8.350e}
$$

where

$$
\begin{aligned}
\mathbf{B}_{\rho\rho} = {} & \langle\!\langle\boldsymbol{\Sigma}_{1,\phi\phi}, \boldsymbol{\Sigma}_{2,\rho\rho}'\rangle\!\rangle + \langle\!\langle\boldsymbol{\Sigma}_{1,\rho\phi}^T, \boldsymbol{\Sigma}_{2,\rho\phi}'\rangle\!\rangle \\
& + \langle\!\langle\boldsymbol{\Sigma}_{1,\rho\phi}, \boldsymbol{\Sigma}_{2,\rho\phi}'^T\rangle\!\rangle + \langle\!\langle\boldsymbol{\Sigma}_{1,\rho\rho}, \boldsymbol{\Sigma}_{2,\phi\phi}'\rangle\!\rangle,
\end{aligned}
\tag{8.351a}
$$

$$
\mathbf{B}_{\rho\phi} = \langle\!\langle\boldsymbol{\Sigma}_{1,\phi\phi}, \boldsymbol{\Sigma}_{2,\rho\phi}'^T\rangle\!\rangle + \langle\!\langle\boldsymbol{\Sigma}_{1,\rho\phi}^T, \boldsymbol{\Sigma}_{2,\phi\phi}'\rangle\!\rangle,
\tag{8.351b}
$$

$$
\mathbf{B}_{\phi\phi} = \langle\!\langle\boldsymbol{\Sigma}_{1,\phi\phi}, \boldsymbol{\Sigma}_{2,\phi\phi}'\rangle\!\rangle.
\tag{8.351c}
$$

The resulting covariance is then

$$\mathbf{\Sigma}_{4\text{th}} \approx \underbrace{\mathbf{\Sigma}_1 + \mathbf{\Sigma}_2'}_{\mathbf{\Sigma}_{2\text{nd}}} + \underbrace{\frac{1}{4}\mathcal{B} + \frac{1}{12}\left(\mathcal{A}_1\mathbf{\Sigma}_2' + \mathbf{\Sigma}_2'\mathcal{A}_1^T + \mathcal{A}_2'\mathbf{\Sigma}_1 + \mathbf{\Sigma}_1\mathcal{A}_2'^T\right)}_{\text{additional fourth-order terms}},$$

(8.352)

correct to fourth order.[34] This result is essentially the same as that of Wang and Chirikjian (2008) but worked out for our slightly different PDF; it is important to note that while our method is fourth order in the perturbation variables, it is only second order in the covariance (same as Wang and Chirikjian, 2008). Chirikjian and Kyatkin (2016) provide helpful insight on the relationship between these results. In summary, to compound two poses, we propagate the mean using (8.343) and the covariance using (8.352).

Sigmapoint Method

We can also make use of the sigmapoint transformation (Julier and Uhlmann, 1996) to pass uncertainty through the compound pose change. In this section, we tailor this to our specific type of $SE(3)$ perturbation. Our approach to handling sigmapoints is quite similar to that taken by Hertzberg et al. (2013) and also Brookshire and Teller (2012). In our case, we begin by approximating the joint input Gaussian using a finite number of samples, $\{\mathbf{T}_{1,\ell}, \mathbf{T}_{2,\ell}\}$:

$$\mathbf{L}\mathbf{L}^T = \text{diag}(\mathbf{\Sigma}_1, \mathbf{\Sigma}_2), \quad \text{(Cholesky decomposition; } \mathbf{L} \text{ lower-triangular)}$$

$$\boldsymbol{\psi}_\ell = \sqrt{\lambda}\,\text{col}_\ell\mathbf{L}, \quad \ell = 1\ldots L,$$

$$\boldsymbol{\psi}_{\ell+L} = -\sqrt{\lambda}\,\text{col}_\ell\mathbf{L}, \quad \ell = 1\ldots L,$$

$$\begin{bmatrix}\boldsymbol{\epsilon}_{1,\ell} \\ \boldsymbol{\epsilon}_{2,\ell}\end{bmatrix} = \boldsymbol{\psi}_\ell, \quad \ell = 1\ldots 2L,$$

$$\mathbf{T}_{1,\ell} = \exp\left(\boldsymbol{\epsilon}_{1,\ell}^\wedge\right)\bar{\mathbf{T}}_1, \quad \ell = 1\ldots 2L,$$

$$\mathbf{T}_{2,\ell} = \exp\left(\boldsymbol{\epsilon}_{2,\ell}^\wedge\right)\bar{\mathbf{T}}_2, \quad \ell = 1\ldots 2L,$$

where λ is a user-definable scaling constant[35] and $L = 12$. We then pass each of these samples through the compound pose change and compute the difference from the mean:

$$\boldsymbol{\epsilon}_\ell = \ln\left(\mathbf{T}_{1,\ell}\mathbf{T}_{2,\ell}\bar{\mathbf{T}}^{-1}\right)^\vee, \quad \ell = 1\ldots 2L.$$

(8.353)

These are combined to create the output covariance according to

$$\mathbf{\Sigma}_{\text{sp}} = \frac{1}{2\lambda}\sum_{\ell=1}^{2L}\boldsymbol{\epsilon}_\ell\boldsymbol{\epsilon}_\ell^T.$$

(8.354)

Note, we have assumed that the output sigmapoint samples have zero mean in this formula, to be consistent with our mean propagation. Interestingly, this turns out to be algebraically equivalent to the second-order method (from the previous

---

[34] The sixth-order terms require a lot more work, but it is possible to compute them using Isserlis' theorem.

[35] For all experiments in this section, we used $\lambda = 1$; we need to ensure that the sigmapoints associated with the rotational degrees of freedom have length less than π to avoid numerical problems.

section) for this particular nonlinearity since the noise sources on $\mathbf{T}_1$ and $\mathbf{T}_2$ are assumed to be uncorrelated.

Simple Compound Example

In this section, we present a simple qualitative example of pose compounding and in Section 8.3.3 we carry out a more quantitative study on a different setup. To see the qualitative difference between the second- and fourth-order methods, let us consider the case of compounding transformations many times in a row:

$$\exp\left(\epsilon_K^\wedge\right)\bar{\mathbf{T}}_K = \left(\prod_{k=1}^{K}\exp\left(\epsilon^\wedge\right)\bar{\mathbf{T}}\right)\exp\left(\epsilon_0^\wedge\right)\bar{\mathbf{T}}_0. \tag{8.355}$$

As discussed earlier, this can be viewed as a discrete-time integration of the $SE(3)$ kinematic equations as in (8.263). To keep things simple, we make the following assumptions:

$$\bar{\mathbf{T}}_0 = \mathbf{1}, \quad \epsilon_0 \sim \mathcal{N}(\mathbf{0},\mathbf{0}), \tag{8.356a}$$

$$\bar{\mathbf{T}} = \begin{bmatrix}\bar{\mathbf{C}} & \bar{\mathbf{r}}\\ \mathbf{0}^T & 1\end{bmatrix}, \quad \epsilon \sim \mathcal{N}(\mathbf{0},\mathbf{\Sigma}), \tag{8.356b}$$

$$\bar{\mathbf{C}} = \mathbf{1}, \quad \bar{\mathbf{r}} = \begin{bmatrix}r\\0\\0\end{bmatrix}, \quad \mathbf{\Sigma} = \mathrm{diag}\left(0,0,0,0,0,\sigma^2\right). \tag{8.356c}$$

Although this example uses our three-dimensional tools, it is confined to a plane for the purpose of illustration and ease of plotting; it corresponds to a rigid body moving along the x-axis but with some uncertainty only on the rotational velocity about the z-axis. This could model a unicycle robot driving in the plane with constant translational speed and slightly uncertain rotational speed (centered about zero). We are interested in how the covariance matrix fills in over time.

According to the second-order scheme, we have

$$\bar{\mathbf{T}}_K = \begin{bmatrix}1 & 0 & 0 & Kr\\0 & 1 & 0 & 0\\0 & 0 & 1 & 0\\0 & 0 & 0 & 1\end{bmatrix}, \tag{8.357a}$$

$$\mathbf{\Sigma}_K = \begin{bmatrix}0 & 0 & 0 & 0 & 0 & 0\\0 & \frac{K(K-1)(2K-1)}{6}r^2\sigma^2 & 0 & 0 & 0 & -\frac{K(K-1)}{2}r\sigma^2\\0 & 0 & 0 & 0 & 0 & 0\\0 & 0 & 0 & 0 & 0 & 0\\0 & 0 & 0 & 0 & 0 & 0\\0 & -\frac{K(K-1)}{2}r\sigma^2 & 0 & 0 & 0 & K\sigma^2\end{bmatrix}, \tag{8.357b}$$

where we see that the top-left entry of $\mathbf{\Sigma}_K$, corresponding to uncertainty in the x-direction, does not have any growth of uncertainty. However, in the fourth-order scheme, the fill-in pattern is such that the top-left entry is non-zero. This happens for several reasons, but mainly through the $\mathbf{B}_{\rho\rho}$ submatrix of $\boldsymbol{\mathcal{B}}$. This

Figure 8.7 Example of compounding $K = 100$ uncertain transformations (Section 8.3.3). The light grey lines and grey dots show 1000 individual sampled trajectories starting from $(0,0)$ and moving nominally to the right at constant translational speed, but with some uncertainty on rotational velocity. The gray 1-sigma covariance ellipse is simply fitted to the samples to show what keeping xy-covariance relative to the start looks like. The black dotted (second-order) and dash-dotted (fourth-order) lines are the principal great circles of the 1-sigma covariance ellipsoid, given by Σ_K, mapped to the xy-plane. Looking to the area $(95, 0)$, corresponding to straight ahead, the fourth-order scheme has some non-zero uncertainty (as do the samples), whereas the second-order scheme does not. We used $r = 1$ and $\sigma = 0.03$.

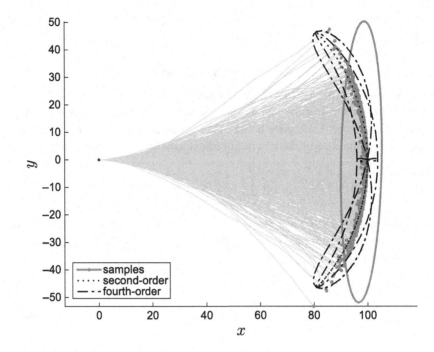

leaking of uncertainty into an additional degree of freedom cannot be captured by keeping only the second-order terms. Figure 8.7 provides a numerical example of this effect. It shows that both the second- and fourth-order schemes do a good job of representing the 'banana'-like density over poses, as discussed by Long et al. (2012). However, the fourth-order scheme has some finite uncertainty in the straight-ahead direction (as do the sampled trajectories), while the second-order scheme does not.

Compound Experiment

To quantitatively evaluate the pose-compounding techniques, we ran a second numerical experiment in which we compounded two poses, including their associated covariance matrices:

$$\bar{\mathbf{T}}_1 = \exp\left(\bar{\boldsymbol{\xi}}_1^\wedge\right), \quad \bar{\boldsymbol{\xi}}_1 = \begin{bmatrix} 0 & 2 & 0 & \pi/6 & 0 & 0 \end{bmatrix}^T,$$

$$\boldsymbol{\Sigma}_1 = \alpha \times \mathrm{diag}\left\{10, 5, 5, \frac{1}{2}, 1, \frac{1}{2}\right\}, \tag{8.358a}$$

$$\bar{\mathbf{T}}_2 = \exp\left(\bar{\boldsymbol{\xi}}_2^\wedge\right), \quad \bar{\boldsymbol{\xi}}_2 = \begin{bmatrix} 0 & 0 & 1 & 0 & \pi/4 & 0 \end{bmatrix}^T,$$

$$\boldsymbol{\Sigma}_2 = \alpha \times \mathrm{diag}\left\{5, 10, 5, \frac{1}{2}, \frac{1}{2}, 1\right\}, \tag{8.358b}$$

where $\alpha \in [0, 1]$ is a scaling parameter that increases the magnitude of the input covariances parametrically.

We compounded these two poses according to (8.341), which results in a mean of $\bar{\mathbf{T}} = \bar{\mathbf{T}}_1 \bar{\mathbf{T}}_2$. The covariance, $\boldsymbol{\Sigma}$, was computed using four methods:

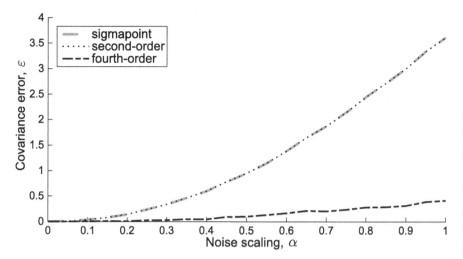

Figure 8.8 Results from Compound Experiment: error, ε, in computing covariance associated with compounding two poses using three methods, as compared to Monte Carlo. The sigmapoint and second-order methods are algebraically equivalent for this problem and thus appear the same on the plot. The input covariances were gradually scaled up via the parameter, α, highlighting the improved performance of the fourth-order method.

(i) *Monte Carlo*: We drew a large number, $M = 1{,}000{,}000$, of random samples ($\boldsymbol{\epsilon}_{m_1}$ and $\boldsymbol{\epsilon}_{m_2}$) from the input covariance matrices, compounded the resulting transformations, and computed the covariance as $\boldsymbol{\Sigma}_{\mathrm{mc}} = \frac{1}{M} \sum_{m=1}^{M} \boldsymbol{\epsilon}_m \boldsymbol{\epsilon}_m^T$ with $\boldsymbol{\epsilon}_m = \ln \left(\mathbf{T}_m \bar{\mathbf{T}}^{-1} \right)^\vee$ and $\mathbf{T}_m = \exp \left(\boldsymbol{\epsilon}_{m_1}^\wedge \right) \bar{\mathbf{T}}_1 \exp \left(\boldsymbol{\epsilon}_{m_2}^\wedge \right) \bar{\mathbf{T}}_2$. This slow-but-accurate approach served as our benchmark to which the other three much faster methods were compared.

(ii) *Second-Order*: We used the second-order method described earlier to compute $\boldsymbol{\Sigma}_{\mathrm{2nd}}$.

(iii) *Fourth-Order*: We used the fourth-order method described earlier to compute $\boldsymbol{\Sigma}_{\mathrm{4th}}$.

(iv) *Sigmapoint*: We used the sigmapoint transformation described earlier to compute $\boldsymbol{\Sigma}_{\mathrm{sp}}$.

We compared each of the last three covariance matrices to the Monte Carlo one using the *Frobenius norm*:

$$\varepsilon = \sqrt{\mathrm{tr} \left(\left(\boldsymbol{\Sigma} - \boldsymbol{\Sigma}_{\mathrm{mc}} \right)^T \left(\boldsymbol{\Sigma} - \boldsymbol{\Sigma}_{\mathrm{mc}} \right) \right)}.$$

Figure 8.8 shows that for small input covariance matrices (i.e., α small) there is very little difference between the various methods and the errors are all low compared to our benchmark. However, as we increase the magnitude of the input covariances, all the methods get worse, with the fourth-order method faring the best by about a factor of seven based on our error metric. Note that since α is scaling the covariance, the applied noise is increasing quadratically.

The second-order method and the sigmapoint method have indistinguishable performance, as they are algebraically equivalent. The fourth-order method goes beyond both of these by considering higher-order terms in the input covariance matrices. We did not compare the computational costs of the various methods, as they are all extremely efficient as compared to Monte Carlo.

It is also worth noting that our ability to correctly keep track of uncertainties on $SE(3)$ decreases with increasing uncertainty. This can be seen directly in

Figure 8.8, as error increases with increasing uncertainty. This suggests that it may be wise to use only relative pose variables to keep uncertainties small.

8.3.4 Inverse Pose

Suppose we have an uncertain pose,

$$\mathbf{T} = \exp(\boldsymbol{\xi}^\wedge)\bar{\mathbf{T}}, \quad \boldsymbol{\xi} \sim \mathcal{N}(\mathbf{0}, \boldsymbol{\Sigma}). \tag{8.359}$$

What is the uncertainty on the inverse pose? The inverse is of the form

$$\mathbf{T}^{-1} = \left(\exp(\boldsymbol{\xi}^\wedge)\bar{\mathbf{T}}\right)^{-1} = \bar{\mathbf{T}}^{-1}\exp(-\boldsymbol{\xi}^\wedge) = \exp\left(\left(\underbrace{-\bar{\mathcal{T}}^{-1}\boldsymbol{\xi}}_{\boldsymbol{\xi}'}\right)^\wedge\right)\bar{\mathbf{T}}^{-1},$$
$$\tag{8.360}$$

where $\bar{\mathcal{T}} = \mathrm{Ad}(\bar{\mathbf{T}})$. Since this is the form of a left perturbation already, we can compute the statistics of $\boldsymbol{\xi}'$:

$$E[\boldsymbol{\xi}'] = E\left[-\bar{\mathcal{T}}^{-1}\boldsymbol{\xi}\right] = -\bar{\mathcal{T}}^{-1}\underbrace{E[\boldsymbol{\xi}]}_{\mathbf{0}} = \mathbf{0}, \tag{8.361a}$$

$$E[\boldsymbol{\xi}'\boldsymbol{\xi}'^T] = E\left[\bar{\mathcal{T}}^{-1}\boldsymbol{\xi}\boldsymbol{\xi}^T\bar{\mathcal{T}}^{-T}\right] = \bar{\mathcal{T}}^{-1}\underbrace{E\left[\boldsymbol{\xi}\boldsymbol{\xi}^T\right]}_{\boldsymbol{\Sigma}}\bar{\mathcal{T}}^{-T} = \bar{\mathcal{T}}^{-1}\boldsymbol{\Sigma}\bar{\mathcal{T}}^{-T},$$
$$\tag{8.361b}$$

so finally we can say that

$$\mathbf{T}^{-1} = \exp\left(\boldsymbol{\xi}'^\wedge\right)\bar{\mathbf{T}}^{-1}, \quad \boldsymbol{\xi}' \sim \mathcal{N}\left(\mathbf{0}, \bar{\mathcal{T}}^{-1}\boldsymbol{\Sigma}\bar{\mathcal{T}}^{-T}\right). \tag{8.362}$$

Notably, we have not made any approximations in this derivation.

8.3.5 Compounding and Differencing Correlated Poses

In Section 8.3.3 on compounding two poses, we assumed that the poses were statistically independent. With

$$\mathbf{T}_1 = \exp(\boldsymbol{\xi}_1^\wedge)\bar{\mathbf{T}}_1, \quad \boldsymbol{\xi}_1 \sim \mathcal{N}(\mathbf{0}, \boldsymbol{\Sigma}_1), \tag{8.363a}$$
$$\mathbf{T}_2 = \exp(\boldsymbol{\xi}_2^\wedge)\bar{\mathbf{T}}_2, \quad \boldsymbol{\xi}_2 \sim \mathcal{N}(\mathbf{0}, \boldsymbol{\Sigma}_2), \tag{8.363b}$$

and $\boldsymbol{\xi}_1$ statistically independent of $\boldsymbol{\xi}_2$, we found that

$$\mathbf{T} = \mathbf{T}_1\mathbf{T}_2 = \exp(\boldsymbol{\xi}^\wedge)\bar{\mathbf{T}}_1\bar{\mathbf{T}}_2, \quad \boldsymbol{\xi} \sim \mathcal{N}(\mathbf{0}, \boldsymbol{\Sigma}), \tag{8.364}$$

where $\boldsymbol{\Sigma} \approx \boldsymbol{\Sigma}_1 + \bar{\mathcal{T}}_1\boldsymbol{\Sigma}_2\bar{\mathcal{T}}_1^T$ and $\bar{\mathcal{T}}_1 = \mathrm{Ad}(\bar{\mathbf{T}}_1)$, correct to second order.

If the two poses are not statistically independent, we can capture this by correlating $\boldsymbol{\xi}_1$ and $\boldsymbol{\xi}_2$ (Mangelson et al., 2020):

$$\begin{bmatrix} \boldsymbol{\xi}_1 \\ \boldsymbol{\xi}_2 \end{bmatrix} \sim \mathcal{N}\left(\begin{bmatrix} \mathbf{0} \\ \mathbf{0} \end{bmatrix}, \begin{bmatrix} \boldsymbol{\Sigma}_1 & \boldsymbol{\Sigma}_{12} \\ \boldsymbol{\Sigma}_{12}^T & \boldsymbol{\Sigma}_2 \end{bmatrix}\right). \tag{8.365}$$

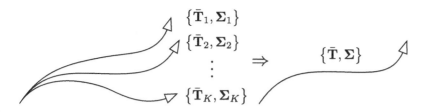

Figure 8.9
Combining K pose
estimates into a
single fused
estimate.

Accounting for the correlations, the covariance of the compounded pose is now approximately

$$\boldsymbol{\Sigma} \approx \boldsymbol{\Sigma}_1 + \bar{\boldsymbol{\mathcal{T}}}_1 \boldsymbol{\Sigma}_2 \bar{\boldsymbol{\mathcal{T}}}_1^T + \boldsymbol{\Sigma}_{12} \bar{\boldsymbol{\mathcal{T}}}_1^T + \bar{\boldsymbol{\mathcal{T}}}_1 \boldsymbol{\Sigma}_{12}^T, \tag{8.366}$$

correct to second order.

We may also want to take the 'difference' of two poses to create a relative pose according to $\mathbf{T} = \mathbf{T}_1 \mathbf{T}_2^{-1}$. This is distributed as

$$\mathbf{T} = \mathbf{T}_1 \mathbf{T}_2^{-1} = \exp(\boldsymbol{\xi}^\wedge)\bar{\mathbf{T}}_1 \bar{\mathbf{T}}_2^{-1}, \quad \boldsymbol{\xi} \sim \mathcal{N}(\mathbf{0}, \boldsymbol{\Sigma}), \tag{8.367}$$

with

$$\boldsymbol{\Sigma} \approx \boldsymbol{\Sigma}_1 + \bar{\boldsymbol{\mathcal{T}}} \boldsymbol{\Sigma}_2 \bar{\boldsymbol{\mathcal{T}}}^T - \boldsymbol{\Sigma}_{12} \bar{\boldsymbol{\mathcal{T}}}^T - \bar{\boldsymbol{\mathcal{T}}} \boldsymbol{\Sigma}_{12}^T, \tag{8.368}$$

and where $\boldsymbol{\mathcal{T}} = \text{Ad}(\bar{\mathbf{T}}_1 \bar{\mathbf{T}}_2^{-1})$. This is again correct to second order.

We leave derivations of these correlated expressions as exercises for the reader.

8.3.6 Fusing Poses

This section will investigate a different type of nonlinearity, the fusing of several pose estimates, as depicted in Figure 8.9. We will approach this as an estimation problem, our first involving quantities from a matrix Lie group. We will use the optimization ideas introduced in Section 8.1.9.

Theory

Suppose that we have K estimates of a pose and associated uncertainties:

$$\left\{\bar{\mathbf{T}}_1, \boldsymbol{\Sigma}_1\right\}, \left\{\bar{\mathbf{T}}_2, \boldsymbol{\Sigma}_2\right\}, \ldots, \left\{\bar{\mathbf{T}}_K, \boldsymbol{\Sigma}_K\right\}. \tag{8.369}$$

If we think of these as uncertain (pseudo)-measurements of the true pose, $\mathbf{T}_{\text{true}}$, how can we optimally combine these into a single estimate, $\{\bar{\mathbf{T}}, \boldsymbol{\Sigma}\}$?

As we have seen in the first part of this book, vector space solution to fusion is straightforward and can be found exactly in closed form:

$$\bar{\mathbf{x}} = \boldsymbol{\Sigma} \sum_{k=1}^{K} \boldsymbol{\Sigma}_k^{-1} \bar{\mathbf{x}}_k, \quad \boldsymbol{\Sigma} = \left(\sum_{k=1}^{K} \boldsymbol{\Sigma}_k^{-1}\right)^{-1}. \tag{8.370}$$

The situation is somewhat more complicated when dealing with $SE(3)$, and we shall resort to an iterative scheme.

We define the error (that we will seek to minimize) as $\mathbf{e}_k(\mathbf{T})$, which occurs between the individual measurement and the optimal estimate, $\mathbf{T}$, so that

$$\mathbf{e}_k(\mathbf{T}) = \ln\left(\bar{\mathbf{T}}_k \mathbf{T}^{-1}\right)^\vee. \tag{8.371}$$

We use our approach to pose optimization outlined earlier,[36] wherein we start with an initial guess, $\mathbf{T}_{\text{op}}$, and perturb this (on the left) by a small amount, ϵ, so that

$$\mathbf{T} = \exp\left(\epsilon^{\wedge}\right) \mathbf{T}_{\text{op}}. \qquad (8.372)$$

Inserting this into the error expression, we have

$$\mathbf{e}_k(\mathbf{T}) = \ln\left(\bar{\mathbf{T}}_k \mathbf{T}^{-1}\right)^{\vee} = \ln\left(\underbrace{\bar{\mathbf{T}}_k \mathbf{T}_{\text{op}}^{-1}}_{\text{small}} \exp\left(-\epsilon^{\wedge}\right)\right)^{\vee}$$

$$= \ln\left(\exp\left(\mathbf{e}_k(\mathbf{T}_{\text{op}})^{\wedge}\right)\exp\left(-\epsilon^{\wedge}\right)\right)^{\vee} = \mathbf{e}_k(\mathbf{T}_{\text{op}}) - \mathbf{G}_k\,\epsilon, \qquad (8.373)$$

where $\mathbf{e}_k(\mathbf{T}_{\text{op}}) = \ln\left(\bar{\mathbf{T}}_k \mathbf{T}_{\text{op}}^{-1}\right)^{\vee}$ and $\mathbf{G}_k = \mathcal{J}\left(-\mathbf{e}_k(\mathbf{T}_{\text{op}})\right)^{-1}$. We have used the approximate BCH formula from (8.105) to arrive at the final expression. Since $\mathbf{e}_k(\mathbf{T}_{\text{op}})$ is fairly small, this series will converge rapidly and we can get away with keeping just a few terms. With our iterative scheme, ϵ will (hopefully) converge to zero, and hence we are justified in keeping only terms linear in this quantity.

We define the cost function that we want to minimize as

$$J(\mathbf{T}) = \frac{1}{2}\sum_{k=1}^{K} \mathbf{e}_k(\mathbf{T})^T \boldsymbol{\Sigma}_k^{-1} \mathbf{e}_k(\mathbf{T})$$

$$\approx \frac{1}{2}\sum_{k=1}^{K} \left(\mathbf{e}_k(\mathbf{T}_{\text{op}}) - \mathbf{G}_k\,\epsilon\right)^T \boldsymbol{\Sigma}_k^{-1} \left(\mathbf{e}_k(\mathbf{T}_{\text{op}}) - \mathbf{G}_k\,\epsilon\right), \qquad (8.374)$$

which is already (approximately) quadratic in ϵ. It is, in fact, a squared *Mahalanobis distance* (Mahalanobis, 1936) since we have chosen the weighting matrices to be the inverse covariance matrices; thus minimizing J with respect to ϵ is equivalent to maximizing the joint likelihood of the individual estimates. It is worth noting that because we are using a constraint-sensitive perturbation scheme, we do not need to worry about enforcing any constraints on our state variables during the optimization procedure. Taking the derivative with respect to ϵ and setting to zero results in the following system of linear equations for the optimal value of ϵ:

$$\left(\sum_{k=1}^{K} \mathbf{G}_k^T \boldsymbol{\Sigma}_k^{-1} \mathbf{G}_k\right) \epsilon^{\star} = \sum_{k=1}^{K} \mathbf{G}_k^T \boldsymbol{\Sigma}_k^{-1}\, \mathbf{e}_k(\mathbf{T}_{\text{op}}). \qquad (8.375)$$

While this may appear strange compared to (8.370), the Jacobian terms appear because our choice of error definition is, in fact, nonlinear owing to the presence of the matrix exponentials. We then apply this optimal perturbation to our current guess,

$$\mathbf{T}_{\text{op}} \leftarrow \exp\left(\epsilon^{\star\wedge}\right) \mathbf{T}_{\text{op}}, \qquad (8.376)$$

---

[36] It is worth mentioning that we are using our constraint-sensitive perturbations for matrix Lie groups in two distinct ways in this section. First, the perturbations are used as a means of injection noise on the Lie group so that probability and statistics can be defined. Second, we are using a perturbation to carry out iterative optimization.

which ensures $\mathbf{T}_{op}$ remains in $SE(3)$, and iterate to convergence. At the last iteration, we take $\bar{\mathbf{T}} = \mathbf{T}_{op}$ as the mean of our fused estimate and

$$\mathbf{\Sigma} = \left(\sum_{k=1}^{K} \mathbf{G}_k^T \mathbf{\Sigma}_k^{-1} \mathbf{G}_k \right)^{-1} \tag{8.377}$$

for the covariance matrix. This approach has the form of a Gauss–Newton method as discussed in Section 8.1.9.

This fusion problem is similar to one investigated by Smith et al. (2003), but they only discuss the $K = 2$ case. Our approach is closer to that of Long et al. (2012), who discuss the $N = 2$ case and derive closed-form expressions for the fused mean and covariance for an arbitrary number of individual measurements, K; however, they do not iterate their solution and they are tracking a slightly different PDF. Wolfe et al. (2011) also discuss fusion at length, albeit again using a slightly different PDF than us. They discuss non-iterative methods of fusion for arbitrary K and show numerical results for $K = 2$. We believe our approach generalizes all of these previous works by (i) allowing the number of individual estimates, K, to be arbitrary, (ii) keeping an arbitrary number of terms in the approximation of the inverse Jacobian, N, and (iii) iterating to convergence via a Gauss–Newton style optimization method. Our approach may also be simpler to implement than some of these previous methods.

Fusion Experiment

To validate the pose fusion method from the previous subsection, we used a true pose given by

$$\mathbf{T}_{true} = \exp\left(\boldsymbol{\xi}_{true}^\wedge\right), \quad \boldsymbol{\xi}_{true} = \begin{bmatrix} 1 & 0 & 0 & 0 & 0 & \pi/6 \end{bmatrix}^T, \tag{8.378}$$

and then generated three random pose measurements,

$$\bar{\mathbf{T}}_1 = \exp\left(\boldsymbol{\epsilon}_1^\wedge\right)\mathbf{T}_{true}, \quad \bar{\mathbf{T}}_2 = \exp\left(\boldsymbol{\epsilon}_2^\wedge\right)\mathbf{T}_{true}, \quad \bar{\mathbf{T}}_3 = \exp\left(\boldsymbol{\epsilon}_3^\wedge\right)\mathbf{T}_{true}, \tag{8.379}$$

where

$$\boldsymbol{\epsilon}_1 \sim \mathcal{N}\left(\mathbf{0}, \operatorname{diag}\left\{10, 5, 5, \frac{1}{2}, 1, \frac{1}{2}\right\}\right),$$

$$\boldsymbol{\epsilon}_2 \sim \mathcal{N}\left(\mathbf{0}, \operatorname{diag}\left\{5, 15, 5, \frac{1}{2}, \frac{1}{2}, 1\right\}\right),$$

$$\boldsymbol{\epsilon}_3 \sim \mathcal{N}\left(\mathbf{0}, \operatorname{diag}\left\{5, 5, 25, 1, \frac{1}{2}, \frac{1}{2}\right\}\right). \tag{8.380}$$

We then solved for the pose using our Gauss–Newton technique (iterating until convergence), using the initial condition, $\mathbf{T}_{op} = \mathbf{1}$. We repeated this for $N = 1 \ldots 6$, the number of terms kept in $\mathbf{G}_k = \boldsymbol{\mathcal{J}}(-\mathbf{e}_k(\mathbf{T}_{op}))^{-1}$. We also used the closed-form expression to compute $\boldsymbol{\mathcal{J}}$ analytically (and then inverted numerically), and this is denoted by '$N = \infty$'.

Figure 8.10 plots two performance metrics. First, it plots the final converged value of the cost function, J_m, averaged over $M = 1000$ random trials,

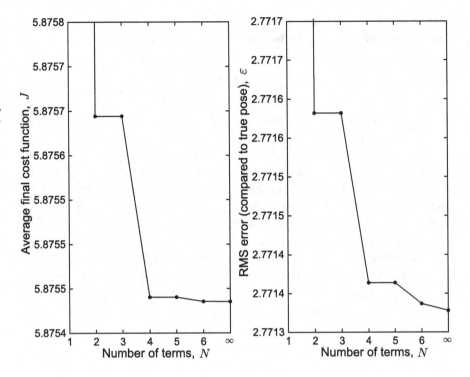

Figure 8.10 Results from Fusion Experiment: (left) average final cost function, J, as a function of the number of terms, N, kept in $\mathcal{J}^{-1}$; (right) same for the root-mean-square pose error with respect to the true pose. Both plots show that there is benefit in keeping more than one term in $\mathcal{J}^{-1}$. The data point denoted '∞' uses the analytical expression to keep all the terms in the expansion.

$J = \frac{1}{M} \sum_{m=1}^{M} J_m$. Second, it plots the root-mean-square pose error (with respect to the true pose), of our estimate, $\bar{\mathbf{T}}_m$, again averaged over the same M random trials:

$$\varepsilon = \sqrt{\frac{1}{M} \sum_{m=1}^{M} \varepsilon_m^T \varepsilon_m}, \quad \varepsilon_m = \ln\left(\mathbf{T}_{\text{true}} \bar{\mathbf{T}}_m^{-1}\right)^{\vee}.$$

The plots show that both measures of error are monotonically reduced with increasing N. Moreover, we see that for this example almost all of the benefit is gained with just four terms (or possibly even two). The results for $N = 2, 3$ are identical as are those for $N = 4, 5$. This is because in the Bernoulli number sequence, $B_3 = 0$ and $B_5 = 0$, so these terms make no additional contribution to $\mathcal{J}^{-1}$. It is also worth stating that if we make the rotational part of the covariances in (8.380) any bigger, we end up with a lot of samples that have rotated by more than angle π, and this can be problematic for the performance metrics we are using.

Figure 8.11 shows the convergence history of the cost, J, for a single random trial. The left side shows the strong benefit of iterating over the solution, while the right side shows that the cost converges to a lower value by keeping more terms in the approximation of $\mathcal{J}^{-1}$ (cases $N = 2, 4, \infty$ shown). It would seem that taking $N = 4$ for about seven iterations gains most of the benefit, for this example.

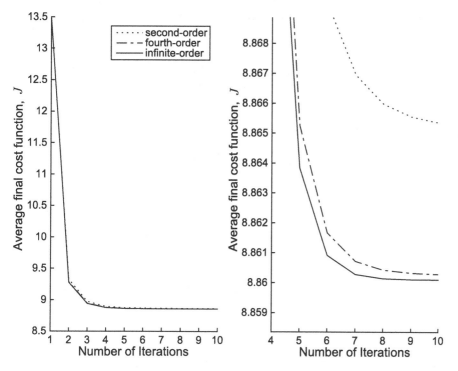

Figure 8.11 Results from Fusion Experiment: (left) convergence of the cost function, J, with successive Gauss–Newton iterations. This is for just one of the M trials used to generate Figure 8.10; (right) same as left, but zoomed in to show that the $N = 2, 4, \infty$ solutions do converge to progressively lower costs.

8.3.7 Propagating Uncertainty through a Nonlinear Camera Model

In estimation problems, we are often faced with passing uncertain quantities through nonlinear measurement models to produce expected measurements. Typically this is carried out via linearization (Matthies and Shafer, 1987). Sibley (2007) shows how to carry out a second-order propagation for a stereo camera model accounting for landmark uncertainty, but not pose uncertainty. Here we derive the full second-order expression for the mean (and covariance) and compare this with Monte Carlo, the sigmapoint transformation, and linearization. We begin by discussing our representation of points and then present the Taylor-series expansion of the measurement (camera) model followed by an experiment.

Perturbing Homogeneous points

As we have seen in Section 8.1.8, points in $\mathbb{R}^3$ can be represented using 4×1 *homogeneous coordinates* as follows:

$$\mathbf{p} = \begin{bmatrix} sx \\ sy \\ sz \\ s \end{bmatrix},\tag{8.381}$$

where s is some real, nonnegative scalar.

To perturb points in homogeneous coordinates we will operate directly on the xyz components by writing

$$\mathbf{p} = \bar{\mathbf{p}} + \mathbf{D}\,\zeta,\tag{8.382}$$

where $\zeta \in \mathbb{R}^3$ is the perturbation and $\mathbf{D}$ is a dilation matrix given by

$$\mathbf{D} = \begin{bmatrix} 1 & 0 & 0 \\ 0 & 1 & 0 \\ 0 & 0 & 1 \\ 0 & 0 & 0 \end{bmatrix}. \tag{8.383}$$

We thus have that $E[\mathbf{p}] = \bar{\mathbf{p}}$ and

$$E[(\mathbf{p} - \bar{\mathbf{p}})(\mathbf{p} - \bar{\mathbf{p}})^T] = \mathbf{D}\, E[\zeta\zeta^T]\, \mathbf{D}^T, \tag{8.384}$$

with no approximation.

Taylor-Series Expansion of Camera Model

It is common to linearize a nonlinear observation model for use in pose estimation. In this section, we show how to do a more general Taylor-series expansion of such a model and work out the second-order case in detail. Our camera model will be

$$\mathbf{y} = \mathbf{g}(\mathbf{T}, \mathbf{p}), \tag{8.385}$$

where $\mathbf{T}$ is the pose of the camera and $\mathbf{p}$ is the position of a landmark (as a homogeneous point). Our task will be to pass a Gaussian representation of the pose and landmark, given by $\{\bar{\mathbf{T}}, \bar{\mathbf{p}}, \boldsymbol{\Xi}\}$ where $\boldsymbol{\Xi}$ is a 9×9 covariance for both quantities, through the camera model to produce a mean and covariance for the measurement,[37] $\{\mathbf{y}, \mathbf{R}\}$.

We can think of this as the composition of two nonlinearities, one to transfer the landmark into the camera frame, $\mathbf{z}(\mathbf{T}, \mathbf{p}) = \mathbf{T}\mathbf{p}$, and one to produce the observations from the point in the camera frame, $\mathbf{y} = \mathbf{s}(\mathbf{z})$. Thus we have

$$\mathbf{g}(\mathbf{T}, \mathbf{p}) = \mathbf{s}(\mathbf{z}(\mathbf{T}, \mathbf{p})). \tag{8.386}$$

We will treat each one in turn. If we change the pose of the camera and/or the position of the landmark a little bit, we have

$$\mathbf{z} = \mathbf{T}\mathbf{p} = \exp\left(\epsilon^\wedge\right) \bar{\mathbf{T}}\left(\bar{\mathbf{p}} + \mathbf{D}\zeta\right) \approx \left(1 + \epsilon^\wedge + \frac{1}{2}\epsilon^\wedge\epsilon^\wedge\right) \bar{\mathbf{T}}\left(\bar{\mathbf{p}} + \mathbf{D}\zeta\right), \tag{8.387}$$

where we have kept the first two terms in the Taylor series for the pose perturbation. If we multiply out and continue to keep only those terms that are second-order or lower in ϵ and ζ, we have

$$\mathbf{z} \approx \bar{\mathbf{z}} + \mathbf{Z}\theta + \frac{1}{2}\sum_{i=1}^{4}\underbrace{\theta^T \boldsymbol{\mathcal{Z}}_i \theta}_{\text{scalar}} \mathbf{1}_i, \tag{8.388}$$

---

[37] In this example, the only sources of uncertainty come from the pose and the point and we neglect inherent measurement noise, but this could be incorporated as additive Gaussian noise, if desired.

where $\mathbf{1}_i$ is the ith column of the 4×4 identity matrix and

$$\bar{\mathbf{z}} = \bar{\mathbf{T}}\bar{\mathbf{p}}, \tag{8.389a}$$

$$\mathbf{Z} = \begin{bmatrix} (\bar{\mathbf{T}}\bar{\mathbf{p}})^{\odot} & \bar{\mathbf{T}}\mathbf{D} \end{bmatrix}, \tag{8.389b}$$

$$\boldsymbol{\mathcal{Z}}_i = \begin{bmatrix} \mathbf{1}_i^{\odot} (\bar{\mathbf{T}}\bar{\mathbf{p}})^{\odot} & \mathbf{1}_i^{\odot}\bar{\mathbf{T}}\mathbf{D} \\ (\mathbf{1}_i^{\odot}\bar{\mathbf{T}}\mathbf{D})^T & \mathbf{0} \end{bmatrix}, \tag{8.389c}$$

$$\boldsymbol{\theta} = \begin{bmatrix} \boldsymbol{\epsilon} \\ \boldsymbol{\zeta} \end{bmatrix}. \tag{8.389d}$$

Arriving at these expressions requires repeated application of the identities from Section 8.1.8.

To then apply the nonlinear camera model, we use the chain rule (for first and second derivatives), so that

$$\mathbf{g}\left(\mathbf{T}, \mathbf{p}\right) \approx \bar{\mathbf{g}} + \mathbf{G}\,\boldsymbol{\theta} + \frac{1}{2}\sum_j \underbrace{\boldsymbol{\theta}^T \boldsymbol{\mathcal{G}}_j\, \boldsymbol{\theta}}_{\text{scalar}}\, \mathbf{1}_j, \tag{8.390}$$

correct to second order in $\boldsymbol{\theta}$, where

$$\bar{\mathbf{g}} = \mathbf{s}(\bar{\mathbf{z}}), \tag{8.391a}$$

$$\mathbf{G} = \mathbf{S}\mathbf{Z}, \qquad \mathbf{S} = \left.\frac{\partial \mathbf{s}}{\partial \mathbf{z}}\right|_{\bar{\mathbf{z}}}, \tag{8.391b}$$

$$\boldsymbol{\mathcal{G}}_j = \mathbf{Z}^T \boldsymbol{\mathcal{S}}_j\, \mathbf{Z} + \sum_{i=1}^{4} \underbrace{\mathbf{1}_j^T \mathbf{S}\, \mathbf{1}_i}_{\text{scalar}}\, \boldsymbol{\mathcal{Z}}_i, \tag{8.391c}$$

$$\boldsymbol{\mathcal{S}}_j = \left.\frac{\partial^2 s_j}{\partial \mathbf{z}\, \partial \mathbf{z}^T}\right|_{\bar{\mathbf{z}}}, \tag{8.391d}$$

j is an index over the rows of $\mathbf{s}(\cdot)$, and $\mathbf{1}_j$ is the jth column of the identity matrix. The Jacobian of $\mathbf{s}(\cdot)$ is $\mathbf{S}$ and the Hessian of the jth row, $s_j(\cdot)$, is $\boldsymbol{\mathcal{S}}_j$.

If we only care about the first-order perturbation, we simply have

$$\mathbf{g}\left(\mathbf{T}, \mathbf{p}\right) = \bar{\mathbf{g}} + \mathbf{G}\,\boldsymbol{\theta}, \tag{8.392}$$

where $\bar{\mathbf{g}}$ and $\mathbf{G}$ are unchanged from the preceding.

These perturbed measurement equations can then be used within any estimation scheme we like; in the next subsection we will use these with a stereo camera model to show the benefit of the second-order terms.

Propagating Gaussian Uncertainty Through the Camera

Suppose that the input uncertainties, embodied by $\boldsymbol{\theta}$, are zero-mean, Gaussian,

$$\boldsymbol{\theta} \sim \mathcal{N}\left(\mathbf{0}, \boldsymbol{\Xi}\right), \tag{8.393}$$

where we note that in general there could be correlations between the pose, $\mathbf{T}$, and the landmark, $\mathbf{p}$.

Then, to first order, our measurement is given by

$$\mathbf{y}_{1\text{st}} = \bar{\mathbf{g}} + \mathbf{G}\,\boldsymbol{\theta}, \tag{8.394}$$

and $\bar{\mathbf{y}}_{1\mathrm{st}} = E[\mathbf{y}_{1\mathrm{st}}] = \bar{\mathbf{g}}$ since $E[\boldsymbol{\theta}] = \mathbf{0}$ by assumption. The (second-order) covariance associated with the first-order camera model is given by

$$\mathbf{R}_{2\mathrm{nd}} = E\left[(\mathbf{y}_{1\mathrm{st}} - \bar{\mathbf{y}}_{1\mathrm{st}})(\mathbf{y}_{1\mathrm{st}} - \bar{\mathbf{y}}_{1\mathrm{st}})^T\right] = \mathbf{G}\,\boldsymbol{\Xi}\,\mathbf{G}^T. \tag{8.395}$$

For the second-order camera model, we have

$$\mathbf{y}_{2\mathrm{nd}} = \bar{\mathbf{g}} + \mathbf{G}\,\boldsymbol{\theta} + \frac{1}{2}\sum_j \boldsymbol{\theta}^T\,\boldsymbol{\mathcal{G}}_j\,\boldsymbol{\theta}\,\mathbf{1}_j, \tag{8.396}$$

and consequently,

$$\bar{\mathbf{y}}_{2\mathrm{nd}} = E[\mathbf{y}_{2\mathrm{nd}}] = \bar{\mathbf{g}} + \frac{1}{2}\sum_j \mathrm{tr}\left(\boldsymbol{\mathcal{G}}_j\,\boldsymbol{\Xi}\right)\mathbf{1}_j, \tag{8.397}$$

which has an extra non-zero term as compared to the first-order camera model. The larger the input covariance $\boldsymbol{\Xi}$ is, the larger this term can become, depending on the nonlinearity. For a linear camera model, $\boldsymbol{\mathcal{G}}_j = \mathbf{0}$ and the second- and first-order camera model means are identical.

We will also compute a (fourth-order) covariance, but with just second-order terms in the camera model expansion. To do this properly, we should expand the camera model to third order as there is an additional fourth-order covariance term involving the product of first- and third-order camera-model terms; however, this would involve a complicated expression employing the third derivative of the camera model. As such, the approximate fourth-order covariance we will use is given by

$$\mathbf{R}_{4\mathrm{th}} \approx E\left[(\mathbf{y}_{2\mathrm{nd}} - \bar{\mathbf{y}}_{2\mathrm{nd}})(\mathbf{y}_{2\mathrm{nd}} - \bar{\mathbf{y}}_{2\mathrm{nd}})^T\right]$$

$$= \mathbf{G}\,\boldsymbol{\Xi}\,\mathbf{G}^T - \frac{1}{4}\left(\sum_{i=1}^{J} \mathrm{tr}\left(\boldsymbol{\mathcal{G}}_i\,\boldsymbol{\Xi}\right)\mathbf{1}_i\right)\left(\sum_{j=1}^{J} \mathrm{tr}\left(\boldsymbol{\mathcal{G}}_j\,\boldsymbol{\Xi}\right)\mathbf{1}_j\right)^T$$

$$+ \frac{1}{4}\sum_{i,j=1}^{J}\sum_{k,\ell,m,n=1}^{9} \mathcal{G}_{ik\ell}\mathcal{G}_{jmn}\left(\Xi_{k\ell}\Xi_{mn} + \Xi_{km}\Xi_{\ell n} + \Xi_{kn}\Xi_{\ell m}\right), \tag{8.398}$$

where $\mathcal{G}_{ikl}$ is the $k\ell$th element of $\boldsymbol{\mathcal{G}}_i$ and $\Xi_{k\ell}$ is the $k\ell$th element of $\boldsymbol{\Xi}$. The first- and third-order terms in the covariance expansion are identically zero owing to the symmetry of the Gaussian density. The last term in the preceding makes use of *Isserlis' theorem* for Gaussian variables.

Sigmapoint Method

Finally, we can also make use of the sigmapoint transformation to pass uncertainty through the nonlinear camera model. As in the pose compounding problem, we tailor this to our specific type of $SE(3)$ perturbation. We begin by approximating the input Gaussian using a finite number of samples, $\{\mathbf{T}_\ell, \mathbf{p}_\ell\}$:

$$\mathbf{L}\mathbf{L}^T = \boldsymbol{\Xi}, \quad \text{(Cholesky decomposition; } \mathbf{L} \text{ lower-triangular)} \quad (8.399a)$$

$$\boldsymbol{\theta}_\ell = \mathbf{0}, \quad (8.399b)$$

$$\boldsymbol{\theta}_\ell = \sqrt{L + \kappa}\, \mathrm{col}_\ell \mathbf{L}, \quad \ell = 1 \ldots L, \quad (8.399c)$$

$$\boldsymbol{\theta}_{\ell+L} = -\sqrt{L + \kappa}\, \mathrm{col}_\ell \mathbf{L}, \quad \ell = 1 \ldots L, \quad (8.399d)$$

$$\begin{bmatrix} \boldsymbol{\epsilon}_\ell \\ \boldsymbol{\zeta}_\ell \end{bmatrix} = \boldsymbol{\theta}_\ell, \quad (8.399e)$$

$$\mathbf{T}_\ell = \exp\left(\boldsymbol{\epsilon}_\ell^\wedge\right) \bar{\mathbf{T}}, \quad (8.399f)$$

$$\mathbf{p}_\ell = \bar{\mathbf{p}} + \mathbf{D}\, \boldsymbol{\zeta}_\ell, \quad (8.399g)$$

where κ is a user-definable constant[38] and $L = 9$. We then pass each of these samples through the nonlinear camera model:

$$\mathbf{y}_\ell = \mathbf{s}\left(\mathbf{T}_\ell\, \mathbf{p}_\ell\right), \quad \ell = 0 \ldots 2L. \quad (8.400)$$

These are combined to create the output mean and covariance according to

$$\bar{\mathbf{y}}_{\mathrm{sp}} = \frac{1}{L + \kappa}\left(\kappa\, \mathbf{y}_0 + \frac{1}{2}\sum_{\ell=1}^{2L} \mathbf{y}_\ell\right), \quad (8.401a)$$

$$\mathbf{R}_{\mathrm{sp}} = \frac{1}{L + \kappa}\left(\kappa\,(\mathbf{y}_0 - \bar{\mathbf{y}}_{\mathrm{sp}})(\mathbf{y}_0 - \bar{\mathbf{y}}_{\mathrm{sp}})^T \right.$$
$$\left. + \frac{1}{2}\sum_{\ell=1}^{2L}(\mathbf{y}_\ell - \bar{\mathbf{y}}_{\mathrm{sp}})(\mathbf{y}_\ell - \bar{\mathbf{y}}_{\mathrm{sp}})^T\right). \quad (8.401b)$$

The next section will provide the details for a specific nonlinear camera model, $\mathbf{s}(\cdot)$, representing a stereo camera.

Stereo Camera Model

To demonstrate the propagation of uncertainty through a nonlinear measurement model, $\mathbf{s}(\cdot)$, we will employ our midpoint stereo camera model given by

$$\mathbf{s}(\boldsymbol{\rho}) = \mathbf{M}\frac{1}{z_3}\mathbf{z}, \quad (8.402)$$

where

$$\mathbf{s} = \begin{bmatrix} s_1 \\ s_2 \\ s_3 \\ s_4 \end{bmatrix}, \quad \mathbf{z} = \begin{bmatrix} \boldsymbol{\rho} \\ 1 \end{bmatrix} = \begin{bmatrix} z_1 \\ z_2 \\ z_3 \\ z_4 \end{bmatrix}, \quad \mathbf{M} = \begin{bmatrix} f_u & 0 & c_u & f_u\frac{b}{2} \\ 0 & f_v & c_v & 0 \\ f_u & 0 & c_u & -f_u\frac{b}{2} \\ 0 & f_v & c_v & 0 \end{bmatrix}, \quad (8.403)$$

and f_u, f_v are the horizontal, vertical focal lengths (in pixels), (c_u, c_v) is the optical center of the images (in pixels), and b is the separation between the cameras (in metres). The optical axis of the camera is along the z_3, direction.

---

[38] For all experiments in this section, we used $\kappa = 0$.

The Jacobian of this measurement model is given by

$$
\frac{\partial \mathbf{s}}{\partial \mathbf{z}} = \mathbf{M} \frac{1}{z_3} \begin{bmatrix} 1 & 0 & -\frac{z_1}{z_3} & 0 \\ 0 & 1 & -\frac{z_2}{z_3} & 0 \\ 0 & 0 & 0 & 0 \\ 0 & 0 & -\frac{z_4}{z_3} & 1 \end{bmatrix},
\tag{8.404}
$$

and the Hessian is given by

$$
\frac{\partial^2 s_1}{\partial \mathbf{z} \partial \mathbf{z}^T} = \frac{f_u}{z_3^2} \begin{bmatrix} 0 & 0 & -1 & 0 \\ 0 & 0 & 0 & 0 \\ -1 & 0 & \frac{2z_1 + bz_4}{z_3} & -\frac{b}{2} \\ 0 & 0 & -\frac{b}{2} & 0 \end{bmatrix},
$$

$$
\frac{\partial^2 s_2}{\partial \mathbf{z} \partial \mathbf{z}^T} = \frac{\partial^2 s_4}{\partial \mathbf{z} \partial \mathbf{z}^T} = \frac{f_v}{z_3^2} \begin{bmatrix} 0 & 0 & 0 & 0 \\ 0 & 0 & -1 & 0 \\ 0 & -1 & \frac{2z_2}{z_3} & 0 \\ 0 & 0 & 0 & 0 \end{bmatrix},
$$

$$
\frac{\partial^2 s_3}{\partial \mathbf{z} \partial \mathbf{z}^T} = \frac{f_u}{z_3^2} \begin{bmatrix} 0 & 0 & -1 & 0 \\ 0 & 0 & 0 & 0 \\ -1 & 0 & \frac{2z_1 - bz_4}{z_3} & \frac{b}{2} \\ 0 & 0 & \frac{b}{2} & 0 \end{bmatrix},
\tag{8.405}
$$

where we have shown each component separately.

Camera Experiment

We used the following methods to pass a Gaussian uncertainty on camera pose and landmark position through the nonlinear stereo camera model:

(i) *Monte Carlo*: We drew a large number, $M = 1{,}000{,}000$, of random samples from the input density, passed these through the camera model, and then computed the mean, $\bar{\mathbf{y}}_{\mathrm{mc}}$, and covariance, $\mathbf{R}_{\mathrm{mc}}$. This slow-but-accurate approach served as our benchmark to which the other three much faster methods were compared.

(ii) *First/Second-Order*: We used the first-order camera model to compute $\bar{\mathbf{y}}_{1\mathrm{st}}$ and $\mathbf{R}_{2\mathrm{nd}}$, as described earlier.

(iii) *Second/Fourth-Order*: We used the second-order camera model to compute $\bar{\mathbf{y}}_{2\mathrm{nd}}$ and $\mathbf{R}_{4\mathrm{th}}$, as described earlier.

(iv) *Sigmapoint*: We used the sigmapoint method described earlier to compute $\bar{\mathbf{y}}_{\mathrm{sp}}$ and $\mathbf{R}_{\mathrm{sp}}$.

The camera parameters were

$$
b = 0.25 \text{ m}, \quad f_u = f_v = 200 \text{ pixels}, \quad c_u = c_v = 0 \text{ pixels}.
$$

We used the camera pose $\mathbf{T} = \mathbf{1}$ and let the landmark be located at $\mathbf{p} = \begin{bmatrix} 10 & 10 & 10 & 1 \end{bmatrix}^T$. For the combined pose/landmark uncertainty, we used an input covariance of

$$
\mathbf{\Xi} = \alpha \times \mathrm{diag}\left\{ \frac{1}{10}, \frac{1}{10}, \frac{1}{10}, \frac{1}{100}, \frac{1}{100}, \frac{1}{100}, 1, 1, 1 \right\},
$$

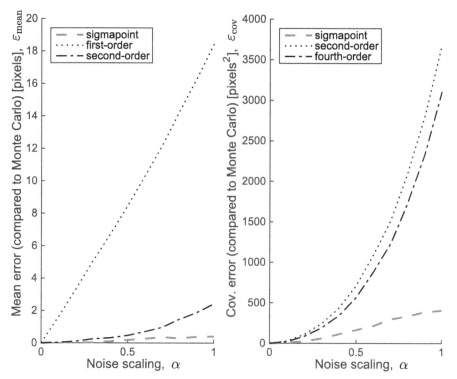

Figure 8.12 Results from Stereo Camera Experiment: (left) mean and (right) covariance errors, $\varepsilon_{\text{mean}}$ and ε_{cov}, for three methods of passing a Gaussian uncertainty through a nonlinear stereo camera model, as compared to Monte Carlo. The parameter, α, scales the magnitude of the input covariance matrix.

where $\alpha \in [0, 1]$ is a scaling parameter that allowed us to parametrically increase the magnitude of the uncertainty.

To gauge performance, we evaluated both the mean and covariance of each method by comparing the results to those of the Monte Carlo simulation according to the following metrics:

$$\varepsilon_{\text{mean}} = \sqrt{(\bar{\mathbf{y}} - \bar{\mathbf{y}}_{\text{mc}})^T (\bar{\mathbf{y}} - \bar{\mathbf{y}}_{\text{mc}})},$$

$$\varepsilon_{\text{cov}} = \sqrt{\text{tr}\left((\mathbf{R} - \mathbf{R}_{\text{mc}})^T (\mathbf{R} - \mathbf{R}_{\text{mc}})\right)},$$

where the latter is the *Frobenius norm*.

Figure 8.12 shows the two performance metrics, $\varepsilon_{\text{mean}}$ and ε_{cov}, for each of the three techniques over a wide range of noise scalings, α. We see that the sigmapoint technique does the best on both mean and covariance. The second-order technique does reasonably well on the mean, but the corresponding fourth-order technique does poorly on the covariance (due to our inability to compute a fully fourth-order-accurate covariance, as explained earlier).

Figure 8.13 provides a snapshot of a portion of the left image of the stereo camera with the mean and one-standard-deviation covariance ellipses shown for all techniques. We see that the sigmapoint technique does an excellent job on both the mean and the covariance, while the others do not fare as well.

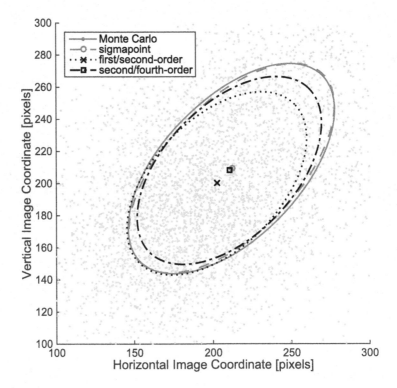

Figure 8.13 Results from Stereo Camera Experiment: A portion of the left image of a stereo camera showing the mean and covariance (as a one-standard-deviation ellipse) for four methods of imaging a landmark with Gaussian uncertainty on the camera's pose and the landmark's position. This case corresponds to the $\alpha = 1$ data point in Figure 8.12.

8.4 Symmetry, Invariance, and Equivariance

As we close this chapter on Lie groups, we reveal another of their core advantages: the notion of *continuous symmetry*. Continuous symmetry is roughly the idea of viewing symmetry as a continuous motion, in contrast to a discrete symmetry such as a reflection about a line. What this means for us in the context of the Lie groups representing rotations and poses is that regardless of what coordinate frame we use to express our state estimation problems, the answers should remain interchangeable/consistent in a sense.

Invariance

One type of symmetry can be established if we can show that a function is *invariant* to the action of a group. In the case of $SE(3)$, if we can show that

$$f(\mathbf{Tp}) = f(\mathbf{p}), \tag{8.406}$$

we say that the function f is invariant to the action of the group and $SE(3)$ is a symmetry of f.

As a concrete example, consider a function, $J^\star$, of the form

$$J^\star(\mathbf{p}_j) = \min_{\mathbf{T}_1 \in SE(3)} \frac{1}{2} \sum_j \left(\boldsymbol{y}_j - \mathbf{T}_1 \mathbf{p}_j\right)^T \left(\boldsymbol{y}_j - \mathbf{T}_1 \mathbf{p}_j\right), \tag{8.407}$$

where $\mathbf{p}_j$ are the (homogeneous) coordinates of some landmarks expressed in a stationary frame, $\boldsymbol{y}_j$ are the (noisy) observations of those landmarks in a frame attached to a robot, and $\mathbf{T}_1$ is our to-be-determined estimate of the transformation from the stationary frame to the robot frame. This is a preview of a localization problem we will discuss in depth in the next chapter; we want to localize a robot by matching landmark observations to a map of those landmarks. The function $J^\star$ is the lowest cost we can achieve over all possible robot poses, $\mathbf{T}_1 \in SE(3)$. Now consider expressing the landmarks in a different frame by transforming them by $\mathbf{T}_{12}$. Our minimal cost now becomes

$$J^\star(\mathbf{T}_{12}\mathbf{p}_j) = \min_{\mathbf{T}_1 \in SE(3)} \frac{1}{2} \sum_j \left(\boldsymbol{y}_j - \mathbf{T}_1\mathbf{T}_{12}\mathbf{p}_j\right)^T \left(\boldsymbol{y}_j - \mathbf{T}_1\mathbf{T}_{12}\mathbf{p}_j\right). \quad (8.408)$$

However, if we let $\mathbf{T}_2 = \mathbf{T}_1\mathbf{T}_{12}$, then we have

$$J^\star(\mathbf{T}_{21}\mathbf{p}_j) = \min_{\mathbf{T}_2 \in SE(3)} \frac{1}{2} \sum_j \left(\boldsymbol{y}_j - \mathbf{T}_2\mathbf{p}_j\right)^T \left(\boldsymbol{y}_j - \mathbf{T}_2\mathbf{p}_j\right), \quad (8.409)$$

whereupon it is easy to see that

$$J^\star(\mathbf{T}_{12}\mathbf{p}_j) = J^\star(\mathbf{p}_j). \quad (8.410)$$

In other words, the minimal cost that we can achieve in this optimization problem does not depend on the frame in which we express the landmarks' positions. Therefore we can say that $J^\star$ is invariant under a coordinate transformation and $SE(3)$ is a symmetry of $J^\star$.

Equivariance

Another related function that we can define is

$$\mathbf{T}^\star(\mathbf{p}_j) = \mathrm{argmin}_{\mathbf{T}_1 \in SE(3)} \frac{1}{2} \sum_j \left(\boldsymbol{y}_j - \mathbf{T}_1\mathbf{p}_j\right)^T \left(\boldsymbol{y}_j - \mathbf{T}_1\mathbf{p}_j\right), \quad (8.411)$$

which is the actual pose that minimizes the cost function. Now if we express the landmarks in a different frame, we have

$$\mathbf{T}^\star(\mathbf{T}_{12}\mathbf{p}_j) = \mathrm{argmin}_{\mathbf{T}_1 \in SE(3)} \frac{1}{2} \sum_j \left(\boldsymbol{y}_j - \mathbf{T}_1\mathbf{T}_{12}\mathbf{p}_j\right)^T \left(\boldsymbol{y}_j - \mathbf{T}_{12}\mathbf{T}_1\mathbf{p}_j\right)$$

$$= \mathrm{argmin}_{\mathbf{T}_2 \in SE(3)} \frac{1}{2} \sum_j \left(\boldsymbol{y}_j - \mathbf{T}_2\mathbf{p}_j\right)^T \left(\boldsymbol{y}_j - \mathbf{T}_2\mathbf{p}_j\right)$$

$$= \mathbf{T}^\star(\mathbf{p}_j)\,\mathbf{T}_{12}. \quad (8.412)$$

In words, the optimal pose of the robot depends on the frame in which we express the map of landmarks. However, it depends in a very predictable way, which is that we have to account for the change of the map coordinate frame to relate the two answers. This is another type of symmetry called *equivariance*. In this case, the optimal pose $\mathbf{T}^\star$ is equivariant since $\mathbf{T}^\star(\mathbf{T}_{12}\mathbf{p}_j) = \mathbf{T}^\star(\mathbf{p}_j)\,\mathbf{T}_{12}$ for any change of the map coordinate frame, $\mathbf{T}_{12}$. It ultimately means that it does not matter in which coordinate frame we express this state estimation problem since we can convert the answer to another frame with ease.

In general we can say that a matrix function of compatible dimensions, $\mathbf{F}(\mathbf{p})$, is *right-equivariant* if

$$\mathbf{F}(\mathbf{Tp}) = \mathbf{F}(\mathbf{p})\,\mathbf{T}, \qquad (8.413)$$

where $\mathbf{T} \in SE(3)$ and *left-equivariant* if

$$\mathbf{F}(\mathbf{Tp}) = \mathbf{T}\,\mathbf{F}(\mathbf{p}). \qquad (8.414)$$

In both cases we can say that $SE(3)$ is a symmetry of $\mathbf{F}$.

Invariant Errors

Bonnabel et al. (2008) introduced the idea of symmetry-preserving observers. The key insight is that when defining errors for a particular matrix Lie group, we would like the group to be a symmetry of the error. For example, when working with $SE(3)$, we would like to define an error of the form:

$$\mathbf{e}_v = \ln\left(\mathbf{T}_{vi}\tilde{\mathbf{T}}_{vi}^{-1}\right)^\vee = \ln\left(\mathbf{T}_{iv}^{-1}\tilde{\mathbf{T}}_{iv}\right)^\vee, \qquad (8.415)$$

which is a member of $\mathfrak{se}(3)$ and where $\mathbf{T}_{vi} = \mathbf{T}_{iv}^{-1}$ is the to-be-determined pose and $\tilde{\mathbf{T}}_{iv} = \tilde{\mathbf{T}}_{vi}^{-1}$ is a measurement of the pose obtained from some sensor. We can see that the error here is defined in $\overrightarrow{\mathcal{F}}_v$, the vehicle (moving) frame. It is also possible to define the error in $\overrightarrow{\mathcal{F}}_i$, the inertial (stationary) frame:

$$\mathbf{e}_i = \ln\left(\mathbf{T}_{vi}^{-1}\tilde{\mathbf{T}}_{vi}\right)^\vee = \ln\left(\mathbf{T}_{iv}\tilde{\mathbf{T}}_{iv}^{-1}\right)^\vee. \qquad (8.416)$$

All of these errors are invariant to the choice of stationary frame since they are relative quantities. Sometimes the labels *left-invariant error* and *right-invariant error* are used to distinguish between (8.415) and (8.416), but this can be confusing as it depends on whether $\mathbf{T}_{vi}$ or $\mathbf{T}_{iv}$ is being estimated. We will refer to (8.415) as a *moving-frame invariant error* and (8.416) as a *stationary-frame invariant error*. Throughout the last part of the book, we will always work with moving-frame invariant errors, regardless of whether we are estimating $\mathbf{T}_{vi}$ (most of the time) or $\mathbf{T}_{iv}$ (in the inertial navigation section).

Based on the notion of invariant errors, Barrau and Bonnabel (2017) introduced the *invariant* extended Kalman filter (EKF), which has been used widely in robotics. When filtering, they advocate for a particular choice of invariant error to be able to claim key properties of the filter, particularly stability; we discuss the *invariant EKF* in a bit more detail at the end of Section 9.2.4 and Appendix C.4. Recently, Mahony and Trumpf (2021) introduced the *equivariant filter (EqF)*, which allows any kinematic system on a Lie group to be set up in a way to exploit equivariance in the design of a filter.

In the next part of the book, we will look at a number of different estimation problems. When starting from a cost function, we will always set it up so that it has the symmetry properties discussed here. In other words, it will not be important in which stationary frame we express each problem, as the minimal cost will be invariant to the choice and the optimal solution will be equivariant to a change in the stationary frame.

8.5 Summary

The main takeaway points from this chapter are as follows:

1. While rotations and poses cannot be described using vector spaces, we can describe them using the matrix Lie groups, $SO(3)$ and $SE(3)$.
2. We can perturb both rotations and poses conveniently by using the exponential map, which (surjective-only) maps $\mathbb{R}^3$ and $\mathbb{R}^6$ to $SO(3)$ and $SE(3)$, respectively. We can use this mapping for two different purposes within state estimation:

   (i) to adjust a point estimate (i.e., mean or MAP) of rotation or pose by a little bit during an optimal estimation procedure.
   (ii) to define Gaussian-like PDFs for rotations and poses by mapping Gaussian noise onto $SO(3)$ and $SE(3)$ through the exponential map.
3. Our ability to represent uncertainty for rotations and poses using the methods in this chapter is limited to only small amounts. We cannot represent uncertainty globally on $SO(3)$ and $SE(3)$ using our Gaussian-like PDFs; for this, refer to Chirikjian and Kyatkin (2016). However, these methods are good enough to allow us to modify the estimation techniques from the first part of the book for use with rotations and poses.

The last part of the book will bring together these matrix-Lie-group tools with the estimation techniques from the first part of the book in order to carry out state estimation for practical robotics problems.

8.6 Exercises

8.1 Prove that

$$(\mathbf{C}\mathbf{u})^\wedge \equiv (2\cos\phi + 1)\mathbf{u}^\wedge - \mathbf{u}^\wedge\mathbf{C} - \mathbf{C}^T\mathbf{u}^\wedge.$$

8.2 Prove that

$$\exp\left((\mathbf{C}\mathbf{u})^\wedge\right) \equiv \mathbf{C}\exp\left(\mathbf{u}^\wedge\right)\mathbf{C}^T.$$

8.3 Prove that

$$(\boldsymbol{\mathcal{T}}\mathbf{x})^\wedge \equiv \mathbf{T}\mathbf{x}^\wedge\mathbf{T}^{-1}.$$

8.4 Prove that

$$\exp\left((\boldsymbol{\mathcal{T}}\mathbf{x})^\wedge\right) \equiv \mathbf{T}\exp\left(\mathbf{x}^\wedge\right)\mathbf{T}^{-1}.$$

8.5 Work out the expression for $\mathbf{Q}_\ell(\boldsymbol{\xi})$ in (8.91a).

8.6 Prove that

$$\mathbf{x}^\wedge\mathbf{p} \equiv \mathbf{p}^\odot\mathbf{x}.$$

8.7   Prove that

$$\mathbf{p}^T \mathbf{x}^\wedge \equiv \mathbf{x}^T \mathbf{p}^\odot.$$

8.8   Prove that

$$\int_0^1 \alpha^n (1 - \alpha)^m \, d\alpha \equiv \frac{n! \, m!}{(n + m + 1)!}.$$

Hint: use integration by parts.

8.9   Prove the identity

$$\dot{\mathbf{J}}(\phi) - \omega^\wedge \mathbf{J}(\phi) \equiv \frac{\partial \omega}{\partial \phi},$$

where

$$\omega = \mathbf{J}(\phi) \, \dot{\phi}$$

are the rotational kinematics expressed in $\mathfrak{so}(3)$. Hint: it can be shown one term at a time by writing out each quantity as a series.

8.10 Show that

$$(\mathbf{Tp})^\odot \equiv \mathbf{Tp}^\odot \mathcal{T}^{-1}.$$

8.11 Show that

$$(\mathbf{Tp})^{\odot^T} (\mathbf{Tp})^\odot \equiv \mathcal{T}^{-T} \mathbf{p}^{\odot^T} \mathbf{p}^\odot \mathcal{T}^{-1}.$$

8.12 Starting from the $SE(3)$ kinematics,

$$\dot{\mathbf{T}} = \boldsymbol{\varpi}^\wedge \mathbf{T},$$

show that the kinematics can also be written using the adjoint quantities:

$$\dot{\mathcal{T}} = \boldsymbol{\varpi}^\curlywedge \mathcal{T}.$$

8.13 Show that it is possible to work with a modified version of the homogeneous-point representation when using the adjoint quantities:

$$\underbrace{\mathrm{Ad}\big(\overbrace{\mathbf{Tp}}^{4 \times 1}\big)}_{6 \times 3} = \underbrace{\mathrm{Ad}(\mathbf{T})}_{6 \times 6} \underbrace{\mathrm{Ad}(\mathbf{p})}_{6 \times 3},$$

where we abuse notation and define an adjoint operator for a homogeneous point as

$$\mathrm{Ad}\left(\begin{bmatrix} \mathbf{c} \\ 1 \end{bmatrix}\right) = \begin{bmatrix} \mathbf{c}^\wedge \\ 1 \end{bmatrix},$$

$$\mathrm{Ad}^{-1}\left(\begin{bmatrix} \mathbf{A} \\ \mathbf{B} \end{bmatrix}\right) = \begin{bmatrix} (\mathbf{A}\mathbf{B}^{-1})^\vee \\ 1 \end{bmatrix},$$

with $\mathbf{c}$ a 3×1 and $\mathbf{A}, \mathbf{B}$ both 3×3.

8.14 Verify the second-order covariance for compounded poses that are correlated in (8.366):

$$\boldsymbol{\Sigma} \approx \boldsymbol{\Sigma}_1 + \bar{\boldsymbol{\mathcal{T}}}_1\boldsymbol{\Sigma}_2\bar{\boldsymbol{\mathcal{T}}}_1^T + \boldsymbol{\Sigma}_{12}\bar{\boldsymbol{\mathcal{T}}}_1^T + \bar{\boldsymbol{\mathcal{T}}}_1\boldsymbol{\Sigma}_{12}^T.$$

8.15 Verify the second-order covariance for compounded poses that are differenced in (8.368):

$$\boldsymbol{\Sigma} \approx \boldsymbol{\Sigma}_1 + \bar{\boldsymbol{\mathcal{T}}}\boldsymbol{\Sigma}_2\bar{\boldsymbol{\mathcal{T}}}^T - \boldsymbol{\Sigma}_{12}\bar{\boldsymbol{\mathcal{T}}}^T - \bar{\boldsymbol{\mathcal{T}}}\boldsymbol{\Sigma}_{12}^T.$$

8.16 Suppose that $\mathbf{C} = \exp(\boldsymbol{\phi}^\wedge)\bar{\mathbf{C}}$ with $\boldsymbol{\phi} \sim \mathcal{N}(\mathbf{0}, \mathbf{1})$. Calculate the following:

$$\boldsymbol{\mu} = E\left[\ln\left(\left(\mathbf{C}\bar{\mathbf{C}}^{-1}\right)^2\right)^\vee\right],$$

$$\boldsymbol{\Sigma} = E\left[\left(\ln\left(\left(\mathbf{C}\bar{\mathbf{C}}^{-1}\right)^2\right)^\vee - \boldsymbol{\mu}\right)\left(\ln\left(\left(\mathbf{C}\bar{\mathbf{C}}^{-1}\right)^2\right)^\vee - \boldsymbol{\mu}\right)^T\right].$$

8.17 Suppose that $\mathbf{T} = \exp\left(\boldsymbol{\xi}^\wedge\right)$. Show that $\boldsymbol{\xi}$ is an eigenvector of $\mathrm{Ad}(\mathbf{T})$ corresponding to an eigenvalue of 1.

8.18 Suppose that we perturb a pose according to $\mathbf{T} = \exp(\boldsymbol{\xi}^\wedge)\mathbf{T}_{\mathrm{op}}$. Using this perturbation, provide a second-order Taylor expansion of the function $f(\mathbf{T}) = (\mathbf{Tp})^T(\mathbf{Tp})$ in terms of the perturbation, $\boldsymbol{\xi}$. Assume that $\mathbf{p}$ is a point in homogeneous form.

8.19 A stereo camera measurement model is given by

$$\mathbf{y} = \begin{bmatrix} u_\ell \\ v_\ell \\ u_r \\ v_r \end{bmatrix} = \underbrace{\begin{bmatrix} f_u & 0 & c_u & f_u\frac{b}{2} \\ 0 & f_v & c_v & 0 \\ f_u & 0 & c_u & -f_u\frac{b}{2} \\ 0 & f_v & c_v & 0 \end{bmatrix}}_{\mathbf{M}} \frac{1}{z}\begin{bmatrix} x \\ y \\ z \\ 1 \end{bmatrix}, \qquad \begin{bmatrix} x \\ y \\ z \\ 1 \end{bmatrix} = \mathbf{Tp},$$

with $\mathbf{T} \in SE(3)$ and $\mathbf{p}$ a static point in a world frame (in homogenous representation). Consider now that we perturb the pose of the camera according to

$$\mathbf{T} = \exp\left(\boldsymbol{\xi}^\wedge\right)\bar{\mathbf{T}}.$$

Provide an approximation for $\mathbf{y}$ that is linear in $\boldsymbol{\xi}$.

8.20 Consider matrices of the form

$$\mathbf{T} = \begin{bmatrix} \cos\theta & -\sin\theta & x \\ \sin\theta & \cos\theta & y \\ 0 & 0 & 1 \end{bmatrix},$$

which represent poses restricted to a plane. Show that the set of all such matrices is a matrix Lie group; it is called $SE(2)$.

8.21 Consider the following 5×5 *extended pose* matrix,

$$\mathbf{T} = \begin{bmatrix} \mathbf{C} & \mathbf{r} & \mathbf{v} \\ \mathbf{0}^T & 1 & 0 \\ \mathbf{0}^T & 0 & 1 \end{bmatrix},$$

which now also includes velocity, $\mathbf{v}$. Show that the set of all such matrices is a matrix Lie group; the group is called $SE_2(3)$ and we will make use of it in Section 9.4 on inertial navigation.

8.22 Consider a satellite that is orbiting the Earth and whose orientation is described by $\mathbf{C} \in SO(3)$. We will seek to estimate the attitude using a Kalman filter adapted to work over the group of rotations. The proposed motion and observation models are

$$\text{motion model:} \quad \mathbf{C}_k = \exp\left(\left(\boldsymbol{\omega}_k h + \mathbf{w}_k\right)^\wedge\right) \mathbf{C}_{k-1},$$
$$\text{observation model:} \quad \mathbf{y}_k = \mathbf{C}_k \mathbf{v} + \mathbf{n}_k,$$

where $\boldsymbol{\omega}_k$ is angular velocity, $\mathbf{w}_k \sim \mathcal{N}(\mathbf{0}, \mathbf{Q})$ is process noise, $\mathbf{y}_k$ is a measurement of a star vector, $\mathbf{v}$ is the true star vector, $\mathbf{n}_k \sim \mathcal{N}(\mathbf{0}, \mathbf{R})$ is measurement noise, h is the discrete-time step, and k is the discrete-time index.

(i) Let our Gaussian estimate at time $k - 1$ be given by

$$p(\mathbf{x}_{k-1}|\mathbf{y}_{0:k}, \boldsymbol{\omega}_{0:k-1}) = \mathcal{N}\left(\hat{\mathbf{C}}_{k-1}, \hat{\mathbf{P}}_{k-1}\right),$$

where $\mathbf{C}_{k-1} = \exp\left(\boldsymbol{\phi}_{k-1}^\wedge\right) \hat{\mathbf{C}}_{k-1}$ and $\boldsymbol{\phi}_{k-1} \sim \mathcal{N}\left(\mathbf{0}, \hat{\mathbf{P}}_{k-1}\right)$ define our usual way of representing uncertainty on $SO(3)$. Show that we can accomplish the prediction step of the Kalman filter using

$$\text{mean:} \quad \check{\mathbf{C}}_k = \exp\left(\boldsymbol{\omega}_k^\wedge h\right) \hat{\mathbf{C}}_{k-1},$$
$$\text{covariance:} \quad \check{\mathbf{P}}_k = \exp\left(\boldsymbol{\omega}_k^\wedge h\right) \hat{\mathbf{P}}_{k-1} \exp\left(-\boldsymbol{\omega}_k^\wedge h\right) + \mathbf{Q}.$$

(ii) Construct an (approximate) joint Gaussian likelihood of the latest measurement and state, using the prediction from (a) as the prior for the state:

$$p(\mathbf{x}_k, \mathbf{y}_k|\mathbf{y}_{0:k-1}, \boldsymbol{\omega}_{0:k}) = \mathcal{N}\left(\begin{bmatrix} \check{\mathbf{C}}_k \\ ? \end{bmatrix}, \begin{bmatrix} \check{\mathbf{P}}_k & ? \\ ? & ? \end{bmatrix}\right),$$

where ? indicates a block that you should fill in. Note, we are abusing notation slightly here since $\check{\mathbf{C}}_k$ is actually 3×3 whereas the block below it will be 3×1. All the covariance blocks should be 3×3.

(iii) Complete our two-step approach to Bayesian inference by using the blocks from (b) to determine

$$p(\mathbf{x}_k|\mathbf{y}_{0:k}, \boldsymbol{\omega}_{0:k}) = \mathcal{N}\left(\hat{\mathbf{C}}_k, \hat{\mathbf{P}}_k\right)$$

where you should compute $\hat{\mathbf{C}}_k = ?$ and $\hat{\mathbf{P}}_k = ?$.

(iv) Given that we are only repeatedly observing the same star at each timestep, how do you expect this filter to perform?

Part III

Applications

9

Pose Estimation Problems

In this last part of the book, we will address some key three-dimensional estimation problems from robotics. We will bring together the ideas from Part I on classic state estimation with the three-dimensional machinery of Part II.

This chapter will start by looking at a key problem, aligning two point-clouds (i.e., collections of points) using the principle of least squares. We will then return to the EKF and batch state estimators and adjust these to work with rotation and pose variables, in the context of a specific pose estimation problem. Our focus will be on localization of a vehicle when the geometry of the world is known. The next chapter will address the more difficult scenario of unknown world geometry.

9.1 Point-Cloud Alignment

In this section, we will study a classic result in pose estimation. Specifically, we present the solution for aligning two sets of three-dimensional points, or *point-clouds*, while minimizing a least-squares cost function. The caveat is that the weights associated with each term in the cost function must be *scalars*, not matrices; this can be referred to as *ordinary* least squares.[1]

This result is used commonly in the popular *iterative closest point (ICP)* (Besl and McKay, 1992) algorithm for aligning three-dimensional points to a three-dimensional model. It is also used inside outlier rejection schemes, such as RANSAC (Fischler and Bolles, 1981) (see Section 5.4.1), for rapid pose determination using a minimal set of points.

We will present the solution using three different parameterizations of the rotation/pose variable: unit-length quaternions, rotation matrices, and then transformation matrices. The (non-iterative) quaternion approach comes down to solving an eigenproblem, while the (non-iterative) rotation-matrix approach turns into a singular-value decomposition. Finally, the iterative transformation matrix approach only involves solving a system of linear equations.

9.1.1 Problem Setup

We will use the setup in Figure 9.1. There are two reference frames, one non-moving, $\underrightarrow{\mathcal{F}}_i$, and one attached to a moving vehicle, $\underrightarrow{\mathcal{F}}_{v_k}$. In particular, we have

---

[1] This problem finds its origin in spacecraft attitude determination, with the famous *Wahba's problem* (Wahba, 1965).

Figure 9.1
Definition of
reference frames for
a point-cloud
alignment problem.
There is a stationary
reference frame and
a moving reference
frame, attached to a
vehicle. A collection
of points, P_j, is
observed in both
frames, and the goal
is to determine the
relative pose of the
moving frame with
respect to the
stationary one by
aligning the two
point-clouds.

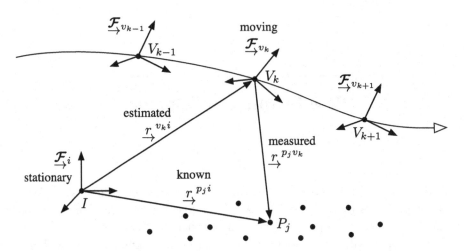

M measurements, $\mathbf{r}_{v_k}^{p_j v_k}$, where $j = 1 \dots M$, of points from the vehicle (expressed in the moving frame $\underset{\rightarrow}{\mathcal{F}}_{v_k}$). We assume these measurements could have been corrupted by noise.

Let us assume that we know $\mathbf{r}_i^{p_j i}$, the position of each point, P_j, located and expressed in the non-moving frame, $\underset{\rightarrow}{\mathcal{F}}_i$. For example, in the ICP algorithm, these points are determined by finding the closest point on the model to each observed point. Thus, we seek to align a collection of M points expressed in two different references frames. In other words, we want to find the translation and rotation that best align the two point-clouds.[2] Note that in this first problem we are only carrying out the alignment at a single time, k. We will consider a point-cloud tracking problem later in the chapter.

9.1.2 Unit-Length Quaternion Solution

We will present the unit-length quaternion approach to aligning point-clouds first.[3] This solution was first studied by Davenport (1965) in the aerospace world and later by Horn (1987b) in robotics. We will use our quaternion notation defined earlier in Section 7.2.3. The quaternion approach has an advantage over the rotation-matrix case (to be described in the next section) because the constraints required to produce a valid rotation are easier for unit-length quaternions.

To work with quaternions, we define the following 4×1 homogeneous versions of our points:

$$\mathbf{y}_j = \begin{bmatrix} \mathbf{r}_{v_k}^{p_j v_k} \\ 1 \end{bmatrix}, \quad \mathbf{p}_j = \begin{bmatrix} \mathbf{r}_i^{p_j i} \\ 1 \end{bmatrix}, \tag{9.1}$$

where we have dropped the sub- and superscripts, except for j, the point index.

We would like to find the translation, $\mathbf{r}$, and rotation, $\mathbf{q}$, that best align these points, thereby giving us the relative pose between $\underset{\rightarrow}{\mathcal{F}}_{v_k}$ and $\underset{\rightarrow}{\mathcal{F}}_i$. We note that the relationships between the quaternion versions of the translation, $\mathbf{r}$, and

---

[2] An unknown *scale* between the two point-clouds is also sometimes folded into the problem; we will assume the two point-clouds have the same scale.

[3] Our focus in this book is on the use of rotation matrices, but this is an example of a problem where unit-length quaternions make things easier, and therefore we include the derivation.

rotation, $\mathbf{q}$, and our usual 3×1 translation, $\mathbf{r}_i^{v_k i}$, and 3×3 rotation matrix, $\mathbf{C}_{v_k i}$ are defined by

$$\underbrace{\begin{bmatrix} \mathbf{r}_{v_k}^{p_j v_k} \\ 1 \end{bmatrix}}_{\mathbf{y}_j} = \underbrace{\begin{bmatrix} \mathbf{C}_{v_k i} & \mathbf{0} \\ \mathbf{0}^T & 1 \end{bmatrix}}_{\mathbf{q}^{-1^+}\mathbf{q}^{\oplus}} \left(\underbrace{\begin{bmatrix} \mathbf{r}_i^{p_j i} \\ 1 \end{bmatrix}}_{\mathbf{p}_j} - \underbrace{\begin{bmatrix} \mathbf{r}_i^{v_k i} \\ 0 \end{bmatrix}}_{\mathbf{r}} \right), \tag{9.2}$$

which is just an expression of the geometry of the problem in the absence of any noise corrupting the measurements. Using the identity in (7.19), we can rewrite this as

$$\mathbf{y}_j = \mathbf{q}^{-1^+} (\mathbf{p}_j - \mathbf{r})^+ \mathbf{q}, \tag{9.3}$$

which again is in the absence of any noise.

Referring to (9.3), we could form an error quaternion for point P_j as

$$\mathbf{e}_j = \mathbf{y}_j - \mathbf{q}^{-1^+} (\mathbf{p}_j - \mathbf{r})^+ \mathbf{q}, \tag{9.4}$$

but instead we can manipulate the preceding to generate an error that appears linear in $\mathbf{q}$:

$$\mathbf{e}'_j = \mathbf{q}^+ \mathbf{e}_j = \left(\mathbf{y}_j^{\oplus} - (\mathbf{p}_j - \mathbf{r})^+ \right) \mathbf{q}. \tag{9.5}$$

We will define the total objective function (to minimize), J, as

$$J(\mathbf{q}, \mathbf{r}, \lambda) = \frac{1}{2} \sum_{j=1}^{M} w_j \mathbf{e}'^T_j \mathbf{e}'_j - \underbrace{\frac{1}{2}\lambda \left(\mathbf{q}^T \mathbf{q} - 1 \right)}_{\text{Lagrange multiplier term}}, \tag{9.6}$$

where the w_j are unique scalar weights assigned to each of the point pairs. We have included the Lagrange multiplier term on the right to ensure the unit-length constraint on the rotation quaternion. It is also worth noting that selecting $\mathbf{e}'_j$ over $\mathbf{e}_j$ has no effect on our objective function since

$$\mathbf{e}'^T_j \mathbf{e}'_j = \left(\mathbf{q}^+ \mathbf{e}_j \right)^T \left(\mathbf{q}^+ \mathbf{e}_j \right) = \mathbf{e}_j^T \mathbf{q}^{+^T} \mathbf{q}^+ \mathbf{e}_j = \mathbf{e}_j^T \left(\mathbf{q}^{-1^+} \mathbf{q} \right)^+ \mathbf{e}_j = \mathbf{e}_j^T \mathbf{e}_j. \tag{9.7}$$

Inserting the expression for $\mathbf{e}'_j$ into the objective function, we see

$$J(\mathbf{q}, \mathbf{r}, \lambda) = \frac{1}{2} \sum_{j=1}^{M} w_j \mathbf{q}^T \left(\mathbf{y}_j^{\oplus} - (\mathbf{p}_j - \mathbf{r})^+ \right)^T \left(\mathbf{y}_j^{\oplus} - (\mathbf{p}_j - \mathbf{r})^+ \right) \mathbf{q}$$

$$- \frac{1}{2} \lambda \left(\mathbf{q}^T \mathbf{q} - 1 \right). \tag{9.8}$$

Taking the derivative of the objective function with respect to $\mathbf{q}$, $\mathbf{r}$, and λ, we find

$$\frac{\partial J}{\partial \mathbf{q}^T} = \sum_{j=1}^{M} w_j \left(\mathbf{y}_j{}^{\oplus} - (\mathbf{p}_j - \mathbf{r})^+ \right)^T \left(\mathbf{y}_j{}^{\oplus} - (\mathbf{p}_j - \mathbf{r})^+ \right) \mathbf{q} - \lambda \mathbf{q}, \quad (9.9a)$$

$$\frac{\partial J}{\partial \mathbf{r}^T} = \mathbf{q}^{-1\oplus} \sum_{j=1}^{M} w_j \left(\mathbf{y}_j{}^{\oplus} - (\mathbf{p}_j - \mathbf{r})^+ \right) \mathbf{q}, \quad (9.9b)$$

$$\frac{\partial J}{\partial \lambda} = -\frac{1}{2} \left(\mathbf{q}^T \mathbf{q} - 1 \right). \quad (9.9c)$$

Setting the second to zero, we find

$$\mathbf{r} = \mathbf{p} - \mathbf{q}^+ \mathbf{y}^+ \mathbf{q}^{-1}, \quad (9.10)$$

where $\mathbf{p}$ and $\mathbf{y}$ are defined below. Thus, the optimal translation is the difference of the centroids of the two point-clouds, in the stationary frame.

Substituting $\mathbf{r}$ into the first and setting to zero, we can show

$$\mathbf{W}\mathbf{q} = \lambda \mathbf{q}, \quad (9.11)$$

where

$$\mathbf{W} = \frac{1}{w} \sum_{j=1}^{M} w_j \left((\mathbf{y}_j - \mathbf{y})^{\oplus} - (\mathbf{p}_j - \mathbf{p})^+ \right)^T \left((\mathbf{y}_j - \mathbf{y})^{\oplus} - (\mathbf{p}_j - \mathbf{p})^+ \right),$$
$$(9.12a)$$

$$\mathbf{y} = \frac{1}{w} \sum_{j=1}^{M} w_j \mathbf{y}_j, \quad \mathbf{p} = \frac{1}{w} \sum_{j=1}^{M} w_j \mathbf{p}_j, \quad w = \sum_{j=1}^{M} w_j. \quad (9.12b)$$

We can see this is just an eigenproblem.[4] If the eigenvalues are positive and the smallest eigenvalue is distinct (i.e., not repeated), then finding the smallest eigenvalue and the corresponding unique eigenvector will yield $\mathbf{q}$ to within a multiplicative constant and our constraint that $\mathbf{q}^T \mathbf{q} = 1$ makes the solution unique.

To see that we want the smallest eigenvalue, we first note that $\mathbf{W}$ is both symmetric and positive-semidefinite. Positive-semidefiniteness implies that all the eigenvalues of $\mathbf{W}$ are nonnegative. Next, we can set (9.9a) to zero so that an equivalent expression for $\mathbf{W}$ is

$$\mathbf{W} = \sum_{j=1}^{M} w_j \left(\mathbf{y}_j{}^{\oplus} - (\mathbf{p}_j - \mathbf{r})^+ \right)^T \left(\mathbf{y}_j{}^{\oplus} - (\mathbf{p}_j - \mathbf{r})^+ \right). \quad (9.13)$$

Substituting this into the objective function in (9.8), we immediately see that

$$J(\mathbf{q}, \mathbf{r}, \lambda) = \frac{1}{2} \mathbf{q}^T \underbrace{\mathbf{W}\mathbf{q}}_{\lambda\mathbf{q}} - \frac{1}{2} \lambda \left(\mathbf{q}^T \mathbf{q} - 1 \right) = \frac{1}{2} \lambda. \quad (9.14)$$

---

[4] The *eigenproblem* associated with an $N \times N$ matrix, $\mathbf{A}$, is defined by the equation $\mathbf{A}\mathbf{x} = \lambda \mathbf{x}$. The N (not necessarily distinct) *eigenvalues*, λ_i, are found by solving for the roots of $\det(\mathbf{A} - \lambda \mathbf{1}) = 0$ and then for each eigenvalue the corresponding *eigenvector*, $\mathbf{x}_i$, is found (to within a multiplicative constant) through substitution of the eigenvalue into the original equation and appropriate manipulation. The case of non-distinct eigenvalues is tricky and requires advanced linear algebra.

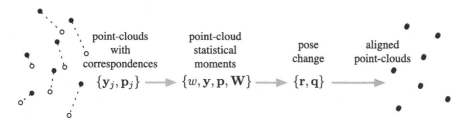

Figure 9.2 Steps involved in aligning two point-clouds.

Thus, picking the smallest possible value for λ will minimize the objective function.

However, there are some complications if $\mathbf{W}$ is singular or the smallest eigenvalue is not distinct. Then there can be multiple choices for the eigenvector corresponding to the smallest eigenvalue, and therefore the solution may not be unique. We will forgo discussing this further for the quaternion method as it would require advanced linear algebra techniques (e.g., Jordan normal form) and instead return to this issue in the next section when using rotation matrices.

Note, we have not made any approximations or linearizations in our technique, but this depends heavily on the fact that the weights are scalar not matrices. Figure 9.2 shows the process to align two point-clouds. Once we have the $\mathbf{r}$ and $\mathbf{q}$, we can construct the final estimates of the rotation matrix, $\hat{\mathbf{C}}_{v_k i}$, and translation, $\hat{\mathbf{r}}_i^{v_k i}$, from

$$\begin{bmatrix} \hat{\mathbf{C}}_{v_k i} & \mathbf{0} \\ \mathbf{0}^T & 1 \end{bmatrix} = \mathbf{q}^{-1+} \mathbf{q}^{\oplus}, \qquad \begin{bmatrix} \hat{\mathbf{r}}_i^{v_k i} \\ 0 \end{bmatrix} = \mathbf{r}, \qquad (9.15)$$

and then we can construct an estimated transformation matrix according to

$$\hat{\mathbf{T}}_{v_k i} = \begin{bmatrix} \hat{\mathbf{C}}_{v_k i} & -\hat{\mathbf{C}}_{v_k i} \hat{\mathbf{r}}_i^{v_k i} \\ \mathbf{0}^T & 1 \end{bmatrix}, \qquad (9.16)$$

which combines our rotation and translation into a single answer for the best alignment of the point-clouds. Referring back to Section 7.3.2, we may actually be interested in $\hat{\mathbf{T}}_{i v_k}$, which can be recovered using

$$\hat{\mathbf{T}}_{i v_k} = \hat{\mathbf{T}}_{v_k i}^{-1} = \begin{bmatrix} \hat{\mathbf{C}}_{i v_k} & \hat{\mathbf{r}}_i^{v_k i} \\ \mathbf{0}^T & 1 \end{bmatrix}. \qquad (9.17)$$

Both forms of the transformation matrix are useful, depending on how the solution will be used.

9.1.3 Rotation Matrix Solution

The rotation-matrix case was originally studied outside of robotics by Green (1952) and Wahba (1965) and later within robotics by Horn (1987a) and Arun et al. (1987) and later by Umeyama (1991) considering the $\det \mathbf{C} = 1$ constraint. We follow the approach of de Ruiter and Forbes (2013), which captures all of the cases in which $\mathbf{C}$ can be determined uniquely. We also identify how many global and local solutions can exist for $\mathbf{C}$ when there is not a single global solution.

The point-cloud alignment problem is often referred to as *Wahba's problem* when there is no unknown translation. With translation, we can refer to it as the *extended Wahba's problem*. Grace Wahba (1934–present) is an American statistician known for methods of smoothing noisy data and cross-validation, as well as the problem bearing her name.

As in the previous section, we will use some simplified notation to avoid repeating sub- and superscripts:

$$\mathbf{y}_j = \mathbf{r}_{v_k}^{p_j v_k}, \quad \mathbf{p}_j = \mathbf{r}_i^{p_j i}, \quad \mathbf{r} = \mathbf{r}_i^{v_k i}, \quad \mathbf{C} = \mathbf{C}_{v_k i}. \tag{9.18}$$

Also, we define

$$\mathbf{y} = \frac{1}{w} \sum_{j=1}^{M} w_j \mathbf{y}_j, \quad \mathbf{p} = \frac{1}{w} \sum_{j=1}^{M} w_j \mathbf{p}_j, \quad w = \sum_{j=1}^{M} w_j, \tag{9.19}$$

where the w_j are scalar weights for each point. Note that, as compared to the last section, some of the symbols are now 3×1 rather than 4×1.

We define an error term for each point:

$$\mathbf{e}_j = \mathbf{y}_j - \mathbf{C}(\mathbf{p}_j - \mathbf{r}). \tag{9.20}$$

Our estimation problem is then to globally minimize the cost function,

$$J(\mathbf{C}, \mathbf{r}) = \frac{1}{2} \sum_{j=1}^{M} w_j \mathbf{e}_j^T \mathbf{e}_j = \frac{1}{2} \sum_{j=1}^{M} w_j \left(\mathbf{y}_j - \mathbf{C}(\mathbf{p}_j - \mathbf{r}) \right)^T \left(\mathbf{y}_j - \mathbf{C}(\mathbf{p}_j - \mathbf{r}) \right), \tag{9.21}$$

subject to $\mathbf{C} \in SO(3)$ (i.e., $\mathbf{C}\mathbf{C}^T = \mathbf{1}$ and $\det \mathbf{C} = 1$).

Before carrying out the optimization, we will make a change of variables for the translation parameter. Define

$$\mathbf{d} = \mathbf{r} + \mathbf{C}^T \mathbf{y} - \mathbf{p}, \tag{9.22}$$

which is easy to isolate for $\mathbf{r}$ if all the other quantities are known. In this case, we can rewrite our cost function as

$$J(\mathbf{C}, \mathbf{d}) = \underbrace{\frac{1}{2} \sum_{j=1}^{M} w_j \left((\mathbf{y}_j - \mathbf{y}) - \mathbf{C}(\mathbf{p}_j - \mathbf{p}) \right)^T \left((\mathbf{y}_j - \mathbf{y}) - \mathbf{C}(\mathbf{p}_j - \mathbf{p}) \right)}_{\text{depends only on } \mathbf{C}}$$

$$+ \underbrace{\frac{1}{2} \mathbf{d}^T \mathbf{d}}_{\text{depends only on } \mathbf{d}}, \tag{9.23}$$

which is the sum of two positive-semidefinite terms, the first depending only on $\mathbf{C}$ and the second only on $\mathbf{d}$. We can minimize the second trivially by taking $\mathbf{d} = \mathbf{0}$, which in turn implies that

$$\mathbf{r} = \mathbf{p} - \mathbf{C}^T \mathbf{y}. \tag{9.24}$$

As in the quaternion case, this is simply the difference of the centroids of the two point-clouds, expressed in the stationary frame.

What is left is to minimize the first term with respect to $\mathbf{C}$. We note that if we multiply out each smaller term within the first large term, only one part actually depends on $\mathbf{C}$:

$$((\mathbf{y}_j - \mathbf{y}) - \mathbf{C}(\mathbf{p}_j - \mathbf{p}))^T ((\mathbf{y}_j - \mathbf{y}) - \mathbf{C}(\mathbf{p}_j - \mathbf{p}))$$

$$= \underbrace{(\mathbf{y}_j - \mathbf{y})^T (\mathbf{y}_j - \mathbf{y})}_{\text{independent of } \mathbf{C}} - 2 \underbrace{((\mathbf{y}_j - \mathbf{y})^T \mathbf{C}(\mathbf{p}_j - \mathbf{p}))}_{\text{tr}(\mathbf{C}(\mathbf{p}_j - \mathbf{p})(\mathbf{y}_j - \mathbf{y})^T)} + \underbrace{(\mathbf{p}_j - \mathbf{p})^T (\mathbf{p}_j - \mathbf{p})}_{\text{independent of } \mathbf{C}}.$$

$$(9.25)$$

Summing this middle term over all the (weighted) points, we have

$$\frac{1}{w} \sum_{j=1}^M w_j \left((\mathbf{y}_j - \mathbf{y})^T \mathbf{C}(\mathbf{p}_j - \mathbf{p}) \right) = \frac{1}{w} \sum_{j=1}^M w_j \mathrm{tr} \left(\mathbf{C}(\mathbf{p}_j - \mathbf{p})(\mathbf{y}_j - \mathbf{y})^T \right)$$

$$= \mathrm{tr} \left(\mathbf{C} \frac{1}{w} \sum_{j=1}^M w_j (\mathbf{p}_j - \mathbf{p})(\mathbf{y}_j - \mathbf{y})^T \right) = \mathrm{tr} \left(\mathbf{C} \mathbf{W}^T \right), \quad (9.26)$$

where

$$\mathbf{W} = \frac{1}{w} \sum_{j=1}^M w_j (\mathbf{y}_j - \mathbf{y})(\mathbf{p}_j - \mathbf{p})^T. \quad (9.27)$$

This $\mathbf{W}$ matrix plays a similar role to the one in the quaternion section, by capturing the spread of the points (similar to an inertia matrix in dynamics), but it is not exactly the same. Therefore, we can define a new cost function that we seek to minimize with respect to $\mathbf{C}$ as

$$J(\mathbf{C}, \boldsymbol{\Lambda}, \gamma) = -\mathrm{tr}(\mathbf{C} \mathbf{W}^T) + \underbrace{\mathrm{tr} \left(\boldsymbol{\Lambda}(\mathbf{C} \mathbf{C}^T - \mathbf{1}) \right) + \gamma(\det \mathbf{C} - 1)}_{\text{Lagrange multiplier terms}}, \quad (9.28)$$

where $\boldsymbol{\Lambda}$ and γ are Lagrange multipliers associated with the two terms on the right; these are used to ensure that the resulting $\mathbf{C} \in SO(3)$. Note that when $\mathbf{C} \mathbf{C}^T = \mathbf{1}$ and $\det \mathbf{C} = 1$, these terms have no effect on the resulting cost. It is also worth noting that $\boldsymbol{\Lambda}$ is symmetric since we only need to enforce six orthogonality constraints. This new cost function will be minimized by the same $\mathbf{C}$ as our original one.

Taking the derivative of $J(\mathbf{C}, \boldsymbol{\Lambda}, \gamma)$ with respect to $\mathbf{C}$, $\boldsymbol{\Lambda}$, and γ, we have[5]

$$\frac{\partial J}{\partial \mathbf{C}} = -\mathbf{W} + 2\boldsymbol{\Lambda}\mathbf{C} + \gamma \underbrace{\det \mathbf{C}}_{1} \underbrace{\mathbf{C}^{-T}}_{\mathbf{C}} = -\mathbf{W} + \mathbf{L}\mathbf{C}, \quad (9.29\text{a})$$

$$\frac{\partial J}{\partial \boldsymbol{\Lambda}} = \mathbf{C}\mathbf{C}^T - \mathbf{1}, \quad (9.29\text{b})$$

$$\frac{\partial J}{\partial \gamma} = \det \mathbf{C} - 1, \quad (9.29\text{c})$$

where we have lumped together the Lagrange multipliers as $\mathbf{L} = 2\boldsymbol{\Lambda} + \gamma \mathbf{1}$. Setting the first equation to zero, we find that

$$\mathbf{L}\mathbf{C} = \mathbf{W}. \quad (9.30)$$

---

[5] We require these useful facts to take the derivatives:
$\frac{\partial}{\partial \mathbf{A}} \det \mathbf{A} = \det(\mathbf{A}) \mathbf{A}^{-T}$,
$\frac{\partial}{\partial \mathbf{A}} \mathrm{tr}(\mathbf{A}\mathbf{B}^T) = \mathbf{B}$,
$\frac{\partial}{\partial \mathbf{A}} \mathrm{tr}(\mathbf{B}\mathbf{A}\mathbf{A}^T) = (\mathbf{B} + \mathbf{B}^T)\mathbf{A}$.

At this point, our explanation can proceed in a simplified or detailed manner, depending on the level of fidelity we want to capture.

Before moving forward, we show that it is possible to arrive at (9.30) using our Lie group tools without the use of Lagrange multipliers. We consider a perturbation of the rotation matrix of the form

$$\mathbf{C}' = \exp\left(\boldsymbol{\phi}^\wedge\right)\mathbf{C}, \tag{9.31}$$

and then take the derivative of the objective function with respect to $\boldsymbol{\phi}$ and set this to zero for a critical point. For the derivative with respect to the ith element of $\boldsymbol{\phi}$ we have

$$
\begin{aligned}
\frac{\partial J}{\partial \phi_i} &= \lim_{h \to 0} \frac{J(\mathbf{C}') - J(\mathbf{C})}{h} \\
&= \lim_{h \to 0} \frac{-\mathrm{tr}(\mathbf{C}'\mathbf{W}^T) + \mathrm{tr}(\mathbf{C}\mathbf{W}^T)}{h} \\
&= \lim_{h \to 0} \frac{-\mathrm{tr}(\exp(h\mathbf{1}_i^\wedge)\mathbf{C}\mathbf{W}^T) + \mathrm{tr}(\mathbf{C}\mathbf{W}^T)}{h} \\
&\approx \lim_{h \to 0} \frac{-\mathrm{tr}((\mathbf{1} + h\mathbf{1}_i^\wedge)\mathbf{C}\mathbf{W}^T) + \mathrm{tr}(\mathbf{C}\mathbf{W}^T)}{h} \\
&= \lim_{h \to 0} \frac{-\mathrm{tr}(h\mathbf{1}_i^\wedge\mathbf{C}\mathbf{W}^T)}{h} \\
&= -\mathrm{tr}\left(\mathbf{1}_i^\wedge\mathbf{C}\mathbf{W}^T\right).
\end{aligned}
\tag{9.32}
$$

Setting this to zero, we require

$$(\forall i)\ \mathrm{tr}\big(\mathbf{1}_i^\wedge \underbrace{\mathbf{C}\mathbf{W}^T}_{\mathbf{L}}\big) = 0. \tag{9.33}$$

Owing to the skew-symmetric nature of the $\wedge$ operator, this implies that $\mathbf{L} = \mathbf{C}\mathbf{W}^T$ is a symmetric matrix for a critical point. Taking the transpose and right-multiplying by $\mathbf{C}$, we come back to (9.30). We now continue with the main derivation.

Simplified Explanation

If we somehow knew that $\det \mathbf{W} > 0$, then we could proceed as follows. First, we postmultiply (9.30) by itself transposed to find

$$\mathbf{L}\underbrace{\mathbf{C}\mathbf{C}^T}_{\mathbf{1}}\mathbf{L}^T = \mathbf{W}\mathbf{W}^T. \tag{9.34}$$

Since $\mathbf{L}$ is symmetric, we have that

$$\mathbf{L} = \left(\mathbf{W}\mathbf{W}^T\right)^{\frac{1}{2}}, \tag{9.35}$$

which we see involves a matrix square root. Substituting this back into (9.30), the optimal rotation is

$$\mathbf{C} = \left(\mathbf{W}\mathbf{W}^T\right)^{-\frac{1}{2}}\mathbf{W}. \tag{9.36}$$

This has the same form as the projection onto $SO(3)$ discussed in Section 8.2.1.

Unfortunately, this approach does not tell the entire story since it relies on assuming something about $\mathbf{W}$, and therefore does not capture all of the subtleties of the problem. With lots of non-coplanar points, this method will typically work well. However, there are some difficult cases for which we need a more detailed analysis. A common situation in which this problem occurs is when carrying out alignments using just three pairs of noisy points in the RANSAC algorithm discussed earlier. The next section provides a more thorough analysis of the solution that handles the difficult cases.

Detailed Explanation

The detailed explanation begins by first carrying out a singular-value decomposition (SVD)[6] on the (square, real) matrix, $\mathbf{W}$, so that

$$\mathbf{W} = \mathbf{U}\mathbf{D}\mathbf{V}^T, \tag{9.37}$$

where $\mathbf{U}$ and $\mathbf{V}$ are square, orthogonal matrices and $\mathbf{D} = \text{diag}(d_1, d_2, d_3)$ is a diagonal matrix of singular values, $d_1 \geq d_2 \geq d_3 \geq 0$.

Returning to (9.30), we can substitute in the SVD of $\mathbf{W}$ so that

$$\mathbf{L}^2 = \mathbf{L}\mathbf{L}^T = \mathbf{L}\mathbf{C}\mathbf{C}^T\mathbf{L}^T = \mathbf{W}\mathbf{W}^T = \mathbf{U}\mathbf{D}\underbrace{\mathbf{V}^T\mathbf{V}}_{1}\mathbf{D}^T\mathbf{U}^T = \mathbf{U}\mathbf{D}^2\mathbf{U}^T. \tag{9.38}$$

Taking the matrix square root, we can write that

$$\mathbf{L} = \mathbf{U}\mathbf{M}\mathbf{U}^T, \tag{9.39}$$

where $\mathbf{M}$ is the symmetric, matrix square root of $\mathbf{D}^2$. In other words,

$$\mathbf{M}^2 = \mathbf{D}^2. \tag{9.40}$$

It can be shown (de Ruiter and Forbes, 2013) that every real, symmetric $\mathbf{M}$ satisfying this condition can be written in the form

$$\mathbf{M} = \mathbf{Y}\mathbf{D}\mathbf{S}\mathbf{Y}^T, \tag{9.41}$$

where $\mathbf{S} = \text{diag}(s_1, s_2, s_3)$ with $s_i = \pm 1$ and $\mathbf{Y}$ an orthogonal matrix (i.e., $\mathbf{Y}^T\mathbf{Y} = \mathbf{Y}\mathbf{Y}^T = 1$). An obvious example of this is $\mathbf{Y} = 1$ with $s_i = \pm 1$ and any values for d_i; a less obvious example that is a possibility when $d_1 = d_2$ is

$$\mathbf{M} = \begin{bmatrix} d_1 \cos\theta & d_1 \sin\theta & 0 \\ d_1 \sin\theta & -d_1 \cos\theta & 0 \\ 0 & 0 & d_3 \end{bmatrix}$$

$$= \underbrace{\begin{bmatrix} \cos\frac{\theta}{2} & -\sin\frac{\theta}{2} & 0 \\ \sin\frac{\theta}{2} & \cos\frac{\theta}{2} & 0 \\ 0 & 0 & 1 \end{bmatrix}}_{\mathbf{Y}} \underbrace{\begin{bmatrix} d_1 & 0 & 0 \\ 0 & -d_1 & 0 \\ 0 & 0 & d_3 \end{bmatrix}}_{\mathbf{DS}} \underbrace{\begin{bmatrix} \cos\frac{\theta}{2} & -\sin\frac{\theta}{2} & 0 \\ \sin\frac{\theta}{2} & \cos\frac{\theta}{2} & 0 \\ 0 & 0 & 1 \end{bmatrix}^T}_{\mathbf{Y}^T}, \tag{9.42}$$

---

[6] The *singular-value decomposition* of a real $M \times N$ matrix, $\mathbf{A}$, is a factorization of the form $\mathbf{A} = \mathbf{U}\mathbf{D}\mathbf{V}^T$ where $\mathbf{U}$ is an $M \times M$ real, orthogonal matrix (i.e., $\mathbf{U}^T\mathbf{U} = 1$), $\mathbf{D}$ is an $M \times N$ matrix with real entries $d_i \geq 0$ on the main diagonal (all other entries zero), and $\mathbf{V}$ is an $N \times N$ real, orthogonal matrix (i.e., $\mathbf{V}^T\mathbf{V} = 1$). The d_i are called the *singular values* and are typically ordered from largest to smallest along the diagonal of $\mathbf{D}$. Note that the SVD is not unique.

for any value of the free parameter, θ. This illustrates an important point, that the structure of $\mathbf{Y}$ can become more complex in correspondence with repeated singular values (i.e., we cannot just pick any $\mathbf{Y}$). Related to this, we always have that

$$\mathbf{D} = \mathbf{YDY}^T, \tag{9.43}$$

due to the relationship between the block structure of $\mathbf{Y}$ and the multiplicity of the singular values in $\mathbf{D}$.

Now, we can manipulate the objective function that we want to minimize as follows:

$$J = -\mathrm{tr}(\mathbf{CW}^T) = -\mathrm{tr}(\mathbf{WC}^T) = -\mathrm{tr}(\mathbf{L}) = -\mathrm{tr}(\mathbf{UYDSY}^T\mathbf{U}^T)$$
$$= -\mathrm{tr}(\underbrace{\mathbf{Y}^T\mathbf{U}^T\mathbf{UY}}_{1}\mathbf{DS}) = -\mathrm{tr}(\mathbf{DS}) = -(d_1 s_1 + d_2 s_2 + d_3 s_3). \tag{9.44}$$

There are now several cases to consider.

Case (i): $\det \mathbf{W} \neq 0$

Here we have that all of the singular values are positive. From (9.30) and (9.39) we have that

$$\det \mathbf{W} = \det \mathbf{L} \underbrace{\det \mathbf{C}}_{1} = \det \mathbf{L} = \det(\mathbf{UYDSY}^T\mathbf{U}^T)$$
$$= \underbrace{\det(\mathbf{Y}^T\mathbf{U}^T\mathbf{UY})}_{1} \det \mathbf{D} \det \mathbf{S} = \underbrace{\det \mathbf{D}}_{>0} \det \mathbf{S}. \tag{9.45}$$

Since the singular values are positive, we have that $\det \mathbf{D} > 0$. Or in other words, the signs of the determinants of $\mathbf{S}$ and $\mathbf{W}$ must be the same, which implies that

$$\det \mathbf{S} = \mathrm{sgn}\,(\det \mathbf{S}) = \mathrm{sgn}\,(\det \mathbf{W}) = \mathrm{sgn}\,(\det(\mathbf{UDV}^T))$$
$$= \mathrm{sgn}\big(\underbrace{\det \mathbf{U}}_{\pm 1} \underbrace{\det \mathbf{D}}_{>0} \underbrace{\det \mathbf{V}}_{\pm 1}\big) = \det \mathbf{U} \det \mathbf{V} = \pm 1. \tag{9.46}$$

Note that we have $\det \mathbf{U} = \pm 1$ since $(\det \mathbf{U})^2 = \det(\mathbf{U}^T\mathbf{U}) = \det \mathbf{1} = 1$ and the same for $\mathbf{V}$. There are now four subcases to consider:

Subcase (i-a): $\det \mathbf{W} > 0$

Since $\det \mathbf{W} > 0$ by assumption, we must also have $\det \mathbf{S} = 1$ and therefore to uniquely minimize J in (9.44) we must pick $s_1 = s_2 = s_3 = 1$ since all of the d_i are positive. $\mathbf{Y}$ is some orthogonal matrix allowing (9.41). Thus, from (9.30) we have

$$\mathbf{C} = \mathbf{L}^{-1}\mathbf{W} = \left(\mathbf{UYDSY}^T\mathbf{U}^T\right)^{-1}\mathbf{UDV}^T$$
$$= \mathbf{UY}\underbrace{\mathbf{S}^{-1}}_{\mathbf{S}}\mathbf{D}^{-1}\mathbf{Y}^T\underbrace{\mathbf{U}^T\mathbf{U}}_{1}\mathbf{DV}^T = \mathbf{UYSD}^{-1}\underbrace{\mathbf{Y}^T\mathbf{D}}_{\mathbf{DY}^T}\mathbf{V}^T$$
$$= \mathbf{UYSY}^T\mathbf{V}^T = \mathbf{USV}^T, \tag{9.47}$$

with $\mathbf{S} = \mathrm{diag}(1,1,1) = \mathbf{1}$, which is equivalent to the solution provided in our 'simplified explanation' in the last section.

Subcase (i-b): det $\mathbf{W} < 0$, $d_1 \geq d_2 > d_3 > 0$

Since $\det \mathbf{W} < 0$ by assumption, we have $\det \mathbf{S} = -1$, which means exactly one of the s_i must be negative. In this case, we can uniquely minimize J in (9.44) since the minimum singular value, d_3, is distinct, whereupon we must pick $s_1 = s_2 = 1$ and $s_3 = -1$ for the minimum. Since $s_1 = s_2 = 1$, we must have $\mathbf{Y}$ be one of

$$\mathbf{Y} = \mathrm{diag}(\pm 1, \pm 1, \pm 1), \quad \mathbf{Y} = \begin{bmatrix} \pm\cos\frac{\theta}{2} & \mp\sin\frac{\theta}{2} & 0 \\ \pm\sin\frac{\theta}{2} & \pm\cos\frac{\theta}{2} & 0 \\ 0 & 0 & \pm 1 \end{bmatrix}, \qquad (9.48)$$

depending on the values of d_1 and d_2 and where θ is a free parameter. Similar to the last subcase, from (9.30) and the fact that $\mathbf{Y}\mathbf{S}\mathbf{Y}^T = \mathbf{S}$ for this subcase, we have that

$$\mathbf{C} = \mathbf{U}\mathbf{S}\mathbf{V}^T, \qquad (9.49)$$

with $\mathbf{S} = \mathrm{diag}(1,1,-1)$.

Subcase (i-c): det $\mathbf{W} < 0$, $d_1 > d_2 = d_3 > 0$

As in the last subcase, we have $\det \mathbf{S} = -1$, which means exactly one of the s_i must be negative. Looking to (9.44), since $d_2 = d_3$ we can pick either $s_2 = -1$ or $s_3 = -1$ and end up with the same value for J. With these values for the s_i we can pick any of the following for $\mathbf{Y}$:

$$\mathbf{Y} = \mathrm{diag}(\pm 1, \pm 1, \pm 1), \quad \mathbf{Y} = \begin{bmatrix} \pm 1 & 0 & 0 \\ 0 & \pm\cos\frac{\theta}{2} & \mp\sin\frac{\theta}{2} \\ 0 & \pm\sin\frac{\theta}{2} & \pm\cos\frac{\theta}{2} \end{bmatrix}, \qquad (9.50)$$

where θ is a free parameter. We can plug any of these $\mathbf{Y}$ in to find minimizing solutions for $\mathbf{C}$ using (9.30):

$$\mathbf{C} = \mathbf{U}\mathbf{Y}\mathbf{S}\mathbf{Y}^T\mathbf{V}^T, \qquad (9.51)$$

with $\mathbf{S} = \mathrm{diag}(1,1,-1)$ or $\mathbf{S} = \mathrm{diag}(1,-1,1)$. Since θ can be anything, this means there is an infinite number of solutions that minimize the objective function.

Subcase (i-d): det $\mathbf{W} < 0$, $d_1 = d_2 = d_3 > 0$

As in the last subcase, we have $\det \mathbf{S} = -1$, which means exactly one of the s_i must be negative. Looking to (9.44), since $d_1 = d_2 = d_3$ we can pick $s_1 = -1$ or $s_2 = -1$ or $s_3 = -1$ and end up with the same value for J, implying there is an infinite number of minimizing solutions.

Case (ii): det $\mathbf{W} = 0$

This time there are three subcases to consider depending on how many singular values are zero.

Subcase (ii-a): rank $\mathbf{W} = 2$

In this case, we have $d_1 \geq d_2 > d_3 = 0$. Looking back to (9.44) we see that we can uniquely minimize J by picking $s_1 = s_2 = 1$ and since $d_3 = 0$, the value of s_3 does not affect J and thus it is a free parameter. Again looking to (9.30) we have

$$(\mathbf{UYDSY}^T\mathbf{U}^T)\mathbf{C} = \mathbf{UDV}^T. \tag{9.52}$$

Multiplying by $\mathbf{U}^T$ from the left and $\mathbf{V}$ from the right, we have

$$\mathbf{D}\underbrace{\mathbf{U}^T\mathbf{CV}}_{\mathbf{Q}} = \mathbf{D}, \tag{9.53}$$

since $\mathbf{DS} = \mathbf{D}$ due to $d_3 = 0$ and then $\mathbf{YDY}^T = \mathbf{D}$ from (9.43). The matrix, $\mathbf{Q}$, will be orthogonal since $\mathbf{U}$, $\mathbf{C}$, and $\mathbf{V}$ are all orthogonal. Since $\mathbf{DQ} = \mathbf{D}$, $\mathbf{D} = \mathrm{diag}(d_1, d_2, 0)$, and $\mathbf{QQ}^T = \mathbf{1}$, we know that $\mathbf{Q} = \mathrm{diag}(1, 1, q_3)$ with $q_3 = \pm 1$. We also have that

$$q_3 = \det\mathbf{Q} = \det\mathbf{U}\underbrace{\det\mathbf{C}}_{1}\det\mathbf{V} = \det\mathbf{U}\det\mathbf{V} = \pm 1, \tag{9.54}$$

and therefore rearranging (and renaming $\mathbf{Q}$ as $\mathbf{S}$), we have

$$\mathbf{C} = \mathbf{USV}^T, \tag{9.55}$$

with $\mathbf{S} = \mathrm{diag}(1, 1, \det\mathbf{U}\det\mathbf{V})$.

Subcase (ii-b): rank $\mathbf{W} = 1$

In this case, we have $d_1 > d_2 = d_3 = 0$. We let $s_1 = 1$ to minimize J and now s_2 and s_3 do not affect J and are free parameters. Similarly to the last subcase, we end up with an equation of the form

$$\mathbf{DQ} = \mathbf{D}, \tag{9.56}$$

which, along with $\mathbf{D} = \mathrm{diag}(d_1, 0, 0)$ and $\mathbf{QQ}^T = \mathbf{1}$, implies that $\mathbf{Q}$ will have one of the following forms:

$$\mathbf{Q} = \underbrace{\begin{bmatrix} 1 & 0 & 0 \\ 0 & \cos\theta & -\sin\theta \\ 0 & \sin\theta & \cos\theta \end{bmatrix}}_{\det\mathbf{Q}=1} \quad \text{or} \quad \mathbf{Q} = \underbrace{\begin{bmatrix} 1 & 0 & 0 \\ 0 & \cos\theta & \sin\theta \\ 0 & \sin\theta & -\cos\theta \end{bmatrix}}_{\det\mathbf{Q}=-1}, \tag{9.57}$$

with $\theta \in \mathbb{R}$ a free parameter. This means there are infinitely many minimizing solutions. Since

$$\det\mathbf{Q} = \det\mathbf{U}\underbrace{\det\mathbf{C}}_{1}\det\mathbf{V} = \det\mathbf{U}\det\mathbf{V} = \pm 1, \tag{9.58}$$

we have (renaming $\mathbf{Q}$ as $\mathbf{S}$) that

$$\mathbf{C} = \mathbf{USV}^T, \tag{9.59}$$

with

$$
\mathbf{S} = \begin{cases} \begin{bmatrix} 1 & 0 & 0 \\ 0 & \cos\theta & -\sin\theta \\ 0 & \sin\theta & \cos\theta \end{bmatrix} & \text{if } \det\mathbf{U}\det\mathbf{V} = 1 \\[20pt] \begin{bmatrix} 1 & 0 & 0 \\ 0 & \cos\theta & \sin\theta \\ 0 & \sin\theta & -\cos\theta \end{bmatrix} & \text{if } \det\mathbf{U}\det\mathbf{V} = -1 \end{cases} . \tag{9.60}
$$

Physically, this case corresponds to all of the points being collinear (in at least one of the frames) so that rotating about the axis formed by the points through any angle, θ, does not alter the objective function J.

Subcase (ii-c): rank $\mathbf{W} = 0$

This case corresponds to there being no points or all the points coincident and so any $\mathbf{C} \in SO(3)$ will produce the same value of the objective function, J.

Summary:

We have provided all of the solutions for $\mathbf{C}$ in our point-alignment problem; depending on the properties of $\mathbf{W}$, there can be one or infinitely many global solutions. Looking back through all the cases and subcases, we can see that if there is a unique global solution for $\mathbf{C}$, it is always of the form

$$
\mathbf{C} = \mathbf{U}\mathbf{S}\mathbf{V}^T, \tag{9.61}
$$

with $\mathbf{S} = \mathrm{diag}(1, 1, \det\mathbf{U}\det\mathbf{V})$ and $\mathbf{W} = \mathbf{U}\mathbf{D}\mathbf{V}^T$ is a singular-value decomposition of $\mathbf{W}$. The necessary and sufficient conditions for this unique global solution to exist are:

(i) $\det\mathbf{W} > 0$, or
(ii) $\det\mathbf{W} < 0$ and minimum singular value distinct: $d_1 \geq d_2 > d_3 > 0$, or
(iii) rank $\mathbf{W} = 2$.

If none of these conditions is true, there will be infinite solutions for $\mathbf{C}$. However, these cases are fairly pathological and do not occur frequently in practical situations.

Once we have solved for the optimal rotation matrix, we take $\hat{\mathbf{C}}_{v_k i} = \mathbf{C}$ as our estimated rotation. We build the estimated translation as

$$
\hat{\mathbf{r}}_i^{v_k i} = \mathbf{p} - \hat{\mathbf{C}}_{v_k i}^T \mathbf{y} \tag{9.62}
$$

and, if desired, combine the translation and rotation into an estimated transformation matrix,

$$
\hat{\mathbf{T}}_{v_k i} = \begin{bmatrix} \hat{\mathbf{C}}_{v_k i} & -\hat{\mathbf{C}}_{v_k i}\hat{\mathbf{r}}_i^{v_k i} \\ \mathbf{0}^T & 1 \end{bmatrix}, \tag{9.63}
$$

that provides the optimal alignment of the two point-clouds in a single quantity. Again, as mentioned in Section 7.3.2, we may actually be interested in $\hat{\mathbf{T}}_{iv_k}$, which can be recovered using

$$\hat{\mathbf{T}}_{iv_k} = \hat{\mathbf{T}}_{v_k i}^{-1} = \begin{bmatrix} \hat{\mathbf{C}}_{iv_k} & \hat{\mathbf{r}}_i^{v_k i} \\ \mathbf{0}^T & 1 \end{bmatrix}. \tag{9.64}$$

Both forms of the transformation matrix are useful, depending on how the solution will be used.

Example 9.1   We provide an example of *subcase (i-b)* to make things tangible. Consider the following two point-clouds that we wish to align, each consisting of six points:

$$\mathbf{p}_1 = 3 \times \mathbf{1}_1, \ \mathbf{p}_2 = 2 \times \mathbf{1}_2, \ \mathbf{p}_3 = \mathbf{1}_3, \ \mathbf{p}_4 = -3 \times \mathbf{1}_1,$$
$$\mathbf{p}_5 = -2 \times \mathbf{1}_2, \ \mathbf{p}_6 = -\mathbf{1}_3,$$
$$\mathbf{y}_1 = -3 \times \mathbf{1}_1, \ \mathbf{y}_2 = -2 \times \mathbf{1}_2, \ \mathbf{y}_3 = -\mathbf{1}_3, \ \mathbf{y}_4 = 3 \times \mathbf{1}_1,$$
$$\mathbf{y}_5 = 2 \times \mathbf{1}_2, \ \mathbf{y}_6 = \mathbf{1}_3,$$

where $\mathbf{1}_i$ is the ith column of the 3×3 identity matrix. The points in the first point-cloud are the centers of the faces of a rectangular prism and each point is associated with a point in the second point-cloud on the opposite face of another prism (that happens to be in the same location as the first).[7]

Using these points, we have the following:

$$\mathbf{p} = \mathbf{0}, \quad \mathbf{y} = \mathbf{0}, \quad \mathbf{W} = \frac{1}{6}\text{diag}(-18, -8, -2), \tag{9.65}$$

which means the centroids are already on top of one another so we only need to rotate to align the point-clouds.

Using the 'simplified approach', we have

$$\mathbf{C} = \left(\mathbf{W}\mathbf{W}^T\right)^{-\frac{1}{2}} \mathbf{W} = \text{diag}(-1, -1, -1). \tag{9.66}$$

Unfortunately, we can easily see that $\det \mathbf{C} = -1$ and so $\mathbf{C} \notin SO(3)$, which indicates this approach has failed.

For the more rigorous approach, a singular-value decomposition of $\mathbf{W}$ is

$$\mathbf{W} = \mathbf{U}\mathbf{D}\mathbf{V}^T, \quad \mathbf{U} = \text{diag}(1, 1, 1), \quad \mathbf{D} = \frac{1}{6}\text{diag}(18, 8, 2),$$
$$\mathbf{V} = \text{diag}(-1, -1, -1). \tag{9.67}$$

We have $\det \mathbf{W} = -4/3 < 0$ and see that there is a unique minimum singular value, so we need to use the solution from *subcase (i-b)*. The minimal solution is therefore of the form $\mathbf{C} = \mathbf{U}\mathbf{S}\mathbf{V}^T$ with $\mathbf{S} = \text{diag}(1, 1, -1)$. Plugging this in, we find

$$\mathbf{C} = \text{diag}(-1, -1, 1), \tag{9.68}$$

---

[7] As a physical interpretation, imagine joining each of the six point pairs by rubber bands. Finding the $\mathbf{C}$ that minimizes our cost metric is the same as finding the rotation that minimizes the amount of elastic energy stored in the rubber bands.

so that $\det \mathbf{C} = 1$. This is a rotation about the $\mathbf{1}_3$ axis through an angle π, which brings the error on four of the points to zero and leaves two of the points with non-zero error. This brings the objective function down to its minimum of $J = 4$.

Testing for Local Minima

In the previous section, we searched for global minima to the point-alignment problem and found there could be one or infinitely many. We did not, however, identify whether it was possible for local minima to exist, which we study now. Looking back to (9.30), this is the condition for a critical point in our optimization problem and therefore any solution that satisfies this criterion could be a minimum, a maximum, or a saddle point of the objective function, J.

If we have a solution, $\mathbf{C} \in SO(3)$, that satisfies (9.30), and we want to characterize it, we can try perturbing the solution slightly and see whether the objective function goes up or down (or both). Consider a perturbation of the form

$$\mathbf{C}' = \exp\left(\boldsymbol{\phi}^\wedge\right)\mathbf{C}, \tag{9.69}$$

where $\boldsymbol{\phi} \in \mathbb{R}^3$ is a perturbation in an arbitrary direction, but constrained to keep $\mathbf{C}' \in SO(3)$. The change in the objective function δJ by applying the perturbation is

$$\delta J = J(\mathbf{C}') - J(\mathbf{C}) = -\text{tr}(\mathbf{C}'\mathbf{W}^T) + \text{tr}(\mathbf{C}\mathbf{W}^T) = -\text{tr}\left((\mathbf{C}' - \mathbf{C})\mathbf{W}^T\right), \tag{9.70}$$

where we have neglected the Lagrange multiplier terms by assuming the perturbation keeps $\mathbf{C}' \in SO(3)$.

Now, approximating the perturbation out to second order, since this will tell us about the nature of the critical points, we have

$$\delta J \approx -\text{tr}\left(\left(\left(\mathbf{1} + \boldsymbol{\phi}^\wedge + \frac{1}{2}\boldsymbol{\phi}^\wedge\boldsymbol{\phi}^\wedge\right)\mathbf{C} - \mathbf{C}\right)\mathbf{W}^T\right)$$

$$= -\text{tr}\left(\boldsymbol{\phi}^\wedge\mathbf{C}\mathbf{W}^T\right) - \frac{1}{2}\text{tr}\left(\boldsymbol{\phi}^\wedge\boldsymbol{\phi}^\wedge\mathbf{C}\mathbf{W}^T\right). \tag{9.71}$$

Then, plugging in the conditions for a critical point from (9.30), we have

$$\delta J = -\text{tr}\left(\boldsymbol{\phi}^\wedge\mathbf{U}\mathbf{Y}\mathbf{D}\mathbf{S}\mathbf{Y}^T\mathbf{U}^T\right) - \frac{1}{2}\text{tr}\left(\boldsymbol{\phi}^\wedge\boldsymbol{\phi}^\wedge\mathbf{U}\mathbf{Y}\mathbf{D}\mathbf{S}\mathbf{Y}^T\mathbf{U}^T\right). \tag{9.72}$$

It turns out that the first term is zero (because it is a critical point), which we can see from

$$\text{tr}\left(\boldsymbol{\phi}^\wedge\mathbf{U}\mathbf{Y}\mathbf{D}\mathbf{S}\mathbf{Y}^T\mathbf{U}^T\right) = \text{tr}\left(\mathbf{Y}^T\mathbf{U}^T\boldsymbol{\phi}^\wedge\mathbf{U}\mathbf{Y}\mathbf{D}\mathbf{S}\right)$$

$$= \text{tr}\left(\left(\mathbf{Y}^T\mathbf{U}^T\boldsymbol{\phi}\right)^\wedge\mathbf{D}\mathbf{S}\right) = \text{tr}\left(\boldsymbol{\varphi}^\wedge\mathbf{D}\mathbf{S}\right) = 0, \tag{9.73}$$

where

$$\boldsymbol{\varphi} = \begin{bmatrix}\varphi_1 \\ \varphi_2 \\ \varphi_3\end{bmatrix} = \mathbf{Y}^T\mathbf{U}^T\boldsymbol{\phi}, \tag{9.74}$$

and owing to the properties of a skew-symmetric matrix (zeros on the diagonal). For the second term, we use the identity $\mathbf{u}^\wedge \mathbf{u}^\wedge = -\mathbf{u}^T\mathbf{u}\,\mathbf{1} + \mathbf{u}\mathbf{u}^T$ to write

$$
\begin{aligned}
\delta J &= -\frac{1}{2}\text{tr}\left(\phi^\wedge\phi^\wedge\mathbf{UYDSY}^T\mathbf{U}^T\right)\\
&= -\frac{1}{2}\text{tr}\left(\mathbf{Y}^T\mathbf{U}^T\left(-\phi^T\phi\,\mathbf{1} + \phi\phi^T\right)\mathbf{UYDS}\right)\\
&= -\frac{1}{2}\text{tr}\left(\left(-\varphi^2\,\mathbf{1} + \varphi\varphi^T\right)\mathbf{DS}\right),
\end{aligned}
\tag{9.75}
$$

where $\varphi^2 = \varphi^T\varphi = \varphi_1^2 + \varphi_2^2 + \varphi_3^2$.

Manipulating a little further, we have

$$
\begin{aligned}
\delta J &= \frac{1}{2}\varphi^2\text{tr}(\mathbf{DS}) - \frac{1}{2}\varphi^T\mathbf{DS}\varphi\\
&= \frac{1}{2}\left(\varphi_1^2(d_2s_2 + d_3s_3) + \varphi_2^2(d_1s_1 + d_3s_3) + \varphi_3^2(d_1s_1 + d_2s_2)\right),
\end{aligned}
\tag{9.76}
$$

the sign of which depends entirely on the nature of $\mathbf{DS}$.

We can verify the ability of this expression to test for a minimum using the unique global minima identified in the previous section. For *subcase (i-a)*, where $d_1 \geq d_2 \geq d_3$ and $s_1 = s_2 = s_3$, we have

$$
\delta J = \frac{1}{2}\left(\varphi_1^2(d_2 + d_3) + \varphi_2^2(d_1 + d_3) + \varphi_3^2(d_1 + d_2)\right) > 0
\tag{9.77}
$$

for all $\varphi \neq \mathbf{0}$, confirming a minimum. For *subcase (i-b)* where $d_1 \geq d_2 > d_3 > 0$ and $s_1 = s_2 = 1$, $s_3 = -1$, we have

$$
\delta J = \frac{1}{2}\left(\varphi_1^2\underbrace{(d_2 - d_3)}_{>0} + \varphi_2^2\underbrace{(d_1 - d_3)}_{>0} + \varphi_3^2(d_1 + d_2)\right) > 0,
\tag{9.78}
$$

for all $\varphi \neq \mathbf{0}$, again confirming a minimum. Finally, for *subcase (ii-a)* where $d_1 \geq d_2 > d_3 = 0$ and $s_1 = s_2 = 1$, $s_3 = \pm 1$, we have

$$
\delta J = \frac{1}{2}\left(\varphi_1^2 d_2 + \varphi_2^2 d_1 + \varphi_3^2(d_1 + d_2)\right) > 0,
\tag{9.79}
$$

for all $\varphi \neq \mathbf{0}$, once again confirming a minimum.

The more interesting question is whether there are any other local minima to worry about or not. This will become important when we use iterative methods to optimize rotation and pose variables. For example, let us consider *subcase (i-a)* a little further in the case that $d_1 > d_2 > d_3 > 0$. There are some other ways to satisfy (9.30) and generate a critical point. For example, we could pick $s_1 = s_2 = -1$ and $s_3 = 1$ so that $\det \mathbf{S} = 1$. In this case we have

$$
\delta J = \frac{1}{2}\left(\varphi_1^2\underbrace{(d_3 - d_2)}_{<0} + \varphi_2^2\underbrace{(d_3 - d_1)}_{<0} + \varphi_3^2\underbrace{(-d_1 - d_2)}_{<0}\right) < 0,
\tag{9.80}
$$

which corresponds to a maximum since any $\varphi \neq \mathbf{0}$ will decrease the objective function. The other two cases, $\mathbf{S} = \text{diag}(-1, 1, -1)$ and $\mathbf{S} = \text{diag}(1, -1, -1)$, turn out to be saddle points since, depending on the direction of the perturbation, the objective function can go up or down. Since there are no other critical points, we can conclude there are no local minima other than the global one.

Similarly for *subcase (i-b)*, we need $\det \mathbf{S} = -1$ and can show that $\mathbf{S} = \text{diag}(-1, -1, -1)$ is a maximum and that $\mathbf{S} = \text{diag}(-1, 1, 1)$ and $\mathbf{S} = \text{diag}(1, -1, 1)$ are saddle points. Again, since there are no other critical points, we can conclude there are no local minima other than the global one.

Also, for *subcase (ii-a)* we in general have

$$\delta J = \frac{1}{2} \left(\varphi_1^2 d_2 s_2 + \varphi_2^2 d_1 s_1 + \varphi_3^2 (d_1 s_1 + d_2 s_2) \right), \qquad (9.81)$$

and so the only way to create a local minimum is to pick $s_1 = s_2 = 1$, which is the global minimum we have discussed earlier. Thus, again there are no additional local minima.

Iterative Approach

We can also consider using an iterative approach to solve for the optimal rotation matrix, $\mathbf{C}$. We will use our $SO(3)$-sensitive scheme to do this. Importantly, the optimization we carry out is unconstrained, thereby avoiding the difficulties of the previous two approaches.[8] Technically, the result is not valid globally, only locally, as we require an initial guess that is refined from one iteration to the next; typically only a few iterations are needed. However, based on our discussion of local minima in the last section, we know that in all the important situations where there is a unique global minimum, there are no additional local minima to worry about.

Starting from the cost function where the translation has been eliminated,

$$J(\mathbf{C}) = \frac{1}{2} \sum_{j=1}^{M} w_j \left((\mathbf{y}_j - \mathbf{y}) - \mathbf{C}(\mathbf{p}_j - \mathbf{p}) \right)^T \left((\mathbf{y}_j - \mathbf{y}) - \mathbf{C}(\mathbf{p}_j - \mathbf{p}) \right),$$

$$(9.82)$$

we can insert the $SO(3)$-sensitive perturbation,

$$\mathbf{C} = \exp\left(\boldsymbol{\psi}^\wedge \right) \mathbf{C}_{\text{op}} \approx \left(\mathbf{1} + \boldsymbol{\psi}^\wedge \right) \mathbf{C}_{\text{op}}, \qquad (9.83)$$

where $\mathbf{C}_{\text{op}}$ is the current guess and $\boldsymbol{\psi}$ is the perturbation; we will seek an optimal value to update the guess (and then iterate). Inserting the approximate perturbation scheme into the cost function turns it into a quadratic in $\boldsymbol{\psi}$ for which the minimizing value, $\boldsymbol{\psi}^\star$, is given by the solution to

$$\mathbf{C}_{\text{op}} \underbrace{\left(-\frac{1}{w} \sum_{j=1}^{M} w_j (\mathbf{p}_j - \mathbf{p})^\wedge (\mathbf{p}_j - \mathbf{p})^\wedge \right)}_{\text{constant}} \mathbf{C}_{\text{op}}^T \boldsymbol{\psi}^\star$$

$$= -\frac{1}{w} \sum_{j=1}^{M} w_j (\mathbf{y}_j - \mathbf{y})^\wedge \mathbf{C}_{\text{op}} (\mathbf{p}_j - \mathbf{p}). \quad (9.84)$$

---

[8] The iterative approach does not require solving either an eigenproblem or carrying out a singular-value decomposition.

At first glance, the right-hand side appears to require recalculation using the individual points at each iteration. Fortunately, we can manipulate it into a more useful form. The right-hand side is a 3×1 column, and its ith row is given by

$$\mathbf{1}_i^T \left(-\frac{1}{w} \sum_{j=1}^{M} w_j (\mathbf{y}_j - \mathbf{y})^{\wedge} \mathbf{C}_{\mathrm{op}} (\mathbf{p}_j - \mathbf{p}) \right)$$

$$= \frac{1}{w} \sum_{j=1}^{M} w_j (\mathbf{y}_j - \mathbf{y})^T \mathbf{1}_i^{\wedge} \mathbf{C}_{\mathrm{op}} (\mathbf{p}_j - \mathbf{p})$$

$$= \frac{1}{w} \sum_{j=1}^{M} w_j \mathrm{tr} \left(\mathbf{1}_i^{\wedge} \mathbf{C}_{\mathrm{op}} (\mathbf{p}_j - \mathbf{p})(\mathbf{y}_j - \mathbf{y})^T \right)$$

$$= \mathrm{tr} \left(\mathbf{1}_i^{\wedge} \mathbf{C}_{\mathrm{op}} \mathbf{W}^T \right), \quad (9.85)$$

where

$$\mathbf{W} = \frac{1}{w} \sum_{j=1}^{M} w_j (\mathbf{y}_j - \mathbf{y})(\mathbf{p}_j - \mathbf{p})^T, \quad (9.86)$$

which we already saw in the non-iterative solution. Letting

$$\mathbf{I} = -\frac{1}{w} \sum_{j=1}^{M} w_j (\mathbf{p}_j - \mathbf{p})^{\wedge} (\mathbf{p}_j - \mathbf{p})^{\wedge}, \quad (9.87a)$$

$$\mathbf{b} = \left[\mathrm{tr} \left(\mathbf{1}_i^{\wedge} \mathbf{C}_{\mathrm{op}} \mathbf{W}^T \right) \right]_i, \quad (9.87b)$$

the optimal update can be written in closed form as

$$\boldsymbol{\psi}^{\star} = \mathbf{C}_{\mathrm{op}} \mathbf{I}^{-1} \mathbf{C}_{\mathrm{op}}^T \mathbf{b}. \quad (9.88)$$

We apply this to the initial guess,

$$\mathbf{C}_{\mathrm{op}} \leftarrow \exp \left(\boldsymbol{\psi}^{\star \wedge} \right) \mathbf{C}_{\mathrm{op}}, \quad (9.89)$$

and iterate to convergence, taking $\hat{\mathbf{C}}_{v_k i} = \mathbf{C}_{\mathrm{op}}$ at the final iteration as our rotation estimate. After convergence, the translation is given as in the non-iterative scheme:

$$\hat{\mathbf{r}}_i^{v_k i} = \mathbf{p} - \hat{\mathbf{C}}_{v_k i}^T \mathbf{y}. \quad (9.90)$$

Notably, both $\mathbf{I}$ and $\mathbf{W}$ can be computed in advance, and therefore we do not require the original points during execution of the iterative scheme.

Three Noncollinear Points Required

Clearly, to solve uniquely for $\boldsymbol{\psi}^{\star}$, we need $\det \mathbf{I} \neq 0$. A sufficient condition is to have $\mathbf{I}$ positive-definite, which implies that for any $\mathbf{x} \neq \mathbf{0}$, we must have

$$\mathbf{x}^T \mathbf{I} \mathbf{x} > 0. \quad (9.91)$$

We then notice that

$$\mathbf{x}^T \mathbf{I} \mathbf{x} = \mathbf{x}^T \left(-\frac{1}{w} \sum_{j=1}^{M} w_j (\mathbf{p}_j - \mathbf{p})^\wedge (\mathbf{p}_j - \mathbf{p})^\wedge \right) \mathbf{x}$$

$$= \frac{1}{w} \sum_{j=1}^{M} w_j \underbrace{\left((\mathbf{p}_j - \mathbf{p})^\wedge \mathbf{x} \right)^T \left((\mathbf{p}_j - \mathbf{p})^\wedge \mathbf{x} \right)}_{\geq 0} \geq 0. \quad (9.92)$$

Since each term in the sum is nonnegative, the total must be nonnegative. The only way to have the total be zero is if *every* term in the sum is also zero, or

$$(\forall j) \ (\mathbf{p}_j - \mathbf{p})^\wedge \mathbf{x} = \mathbf{0}. \quad (9.93)$$

In other words, we must have $\mathbf{x} = \mathbf{0}$ (not true by assumption), $\mathbf{p}_j = \mathbf{p}$, or $\mathbf{x}$ parallel to $\mathbf{p}_j - \mathbf{p}$. The last two conditions are never true as long as there are at least three points and they are not collinear.

Note that having three non-collinear points only provides a sufficient condition for a unique solution for $\psi^\star$ at each iteration, and does not tell us about the number of possible global solutions to minimize our objective function in general. This was discussed at length in the previous sections, where we learned there could be one or infinitely many global solutions. Moreover, if there is a unique global minimum, there are no local minima to worry about.

9.1.4 Transformation Matrix Solution

Finally, for completeness, we also can provide an iterative approach to solving for the pose change using transformation matrices and their relationship to the exponential map.[9] As in the previous two sections, we will use some simplified notation to avoid repeating sub- and super-scripts:

$$\boldsymbol{y}_j = \begin{bmatrix} \mathbf{y}_j \\ 1 \end{bmatrix} = \begin{bmatrix} \mathbf{r}_{v_k}^{p_j v_k} \\ 1 \end{bmatrix}, \quad \boldsymbol{p}_j = \begin{bmatrix} \mathbf{p}_j \\ 1 \end{bmatrix} = \begin{bmatrix} \mathbf{r}_i^{p_j i} \\ 1 \end{bmatrix},$$

$$\mathbf{T} = \mathbf{T}_{v_k i} = \begin{bmatrix} \mathbf{C}_{v_k i} & -\mathbf{C}_{v_k i} \mathbf{r}_i^{v_k i} \\ \mathbf{0}^T & 1 \end{bmatrix}. \quad (9.94)$$

We have used a different font for the homogeneous representations of the points; we will be making connections back to the previous section on rotation matrices so we also keep the non-homogeneous point representations around for convenience.

We define our error term for each point as

$$\mathbf{e}_j = \boldsymbol{y}_j - \mathbf{T} \boldsymbol{p}_j, \quad (9.95)$$

and our objective function as

$$J(\mathbf{T}) = \frac{1}{2} \sum_{j=1}^{M} w_j \mathbf{e}_j^T \mathbf{e}_j = \frac{1}{2} \sum_{j=1}^{M} w_j \left(\boldsymbol{y}_j - \mathbf{T} \boldsymbol{p}_j \right)^T \left(\boldsymbol{y}_j - \mathbf{T} \boldsymbol{p}_j \right), \quad (9.96)$$

---

[9] We will use the optimization approach outlined in Section 8.1.9.

where $w_j > 0$ are the usual scalar weights. We seek to minimize J with respect to $\mathbf{T} \in SE(3)$. Notably, this objective function is equivalent to the ones for the unit-quaternion and rotation-matrix parameterizations, so the minima should be the same.

To do this, we use our $SE(3)$-sensitive perturbation scheme,

$$\mathbf{T} = \exp\left(\boldsymbol{\epsilon}^\wedge\right) \mathbf{T}_{\text{op}} \approx \left(1 + \boldsymbol{\epsilon}^\wedge\right) \mathbf{T}_{\text{op}}, \qquad (9.97)$$

where $\mathbf{T}_{\text{op}}$ is some initial guess (i.e., operating point of our linearization) and $\boldsymbol{\epsilon}$ is a small perturbation to that guess. Inserting this into the objective function, we then have

$$J(\mathbf{T}) \approx \frac{1}{2} \sum_{j=1}^{M} w_j \left((\boldsymbol{y}_j - \boldsymbol{z}_j) - \boldsymbol{z}_j^\odot \boldsymbol{\epsilon}\right)^T \left((\boldsymbol{y}_j - \boldsymbol{z}_j) - \boldsymbol{z}_j^\odot \boldsymbol{\epsilon}\right), \qquad (9.98)$$

where $\boldsymbol{z}_j = \mathbf{T}_{\text{op}}\boldsymbol{p}_j$ and we have used that

$$\boldsymbol{\epsilon}^\wedge \boldsymbol{z}_j = \boldsymbol{z}_j^\odot \boldsymbol{\epsilon}, \qquad (9.99)$$

which was explained in Section 8.1.8.

Our objective function is now exactly quadratic in $\boldsymbol{\epsilon}$, and therefore we can carry out a simple, *unconstrained* optimization for $\boldsymbol{\epsilon}$. Taking the derivative, we find

$$\frac{\partial J}{\partial \boldsymbol{\epsilon}^T} = -\sum_{j=1}^{M} w_j \boldsymbol{z}_j^{\odot^T} \left((\boldsymbol{y}_j - \boldsymbol{z}_j) - \boldsymbol{z}_j^\odot \boldsymbol{\epsilon}\right). \qquad (9.100)$$

Setting this to zero, we have the following system of equations for the optimal $\boldsymbol{\epsilon}^\star$:

$$\left(\frac{1}{w} \sum_{j=1}^{M} w_j \boldsymbol{z}_j^{\odot^T} \boldsymbol{z}_j^\odot\right) \boldsymbol{\epsilon}^\star = \frac{1}{w} \sum_{j=1}^{M} w_j \boldsymbol{z}_j^{\odot^T} (\boldsymbol{y}_j - \boldsymbol{z}_j). \qquad (9.101)$$

While we could use this to compute the optimal update, both the left- and right-hand sides require construction from the original points at each iteration. As in the previous section on the iterative solution using rotation matrices, it turns out we can manipulate both sides into forms that do not require the original points.

Looking to the left-hand side first, we can show that

$$\frac{1}{w} \sum_{j=1}^{M} w_j \boldsymbol{z}_j^{\odot^T} \boldsymbol{z}_j^\odot = \underbrace{\boldsymbol{\mathcal{T}}_{\text{op}}^{-T}}_{>0} \underbrace{\left(\frac{1}{w} \sum_{j=1}^{M} w_j \boldsymbol{p}_j^{\odot^T} \boldsymbol{p}_j^\odot\right)}_{\boldsymbol{\mathcal{M}}} \underbrace{\boldsymbol{\mathcal{T}}_{\text{op}}^{-1}}_{>0}, \qquad (9.102)$$

where

$$\boldsymbol{\mathcal{T}}_{\text{op}} = \mathrm{Ad}(\mathbf{T}_{\text{op}}), \quad \boldsymbol{\mathcal{M}} = \begin{bmatrix} 1 & 0 \\ \mathbf{p}^\wedge & 1 \end{bmatrix} \begin{bmatrix} 1 & 0 \\ 0 & \mathbf{I} \end{bmatrix} \begin{bmatrix} 1 & -\mathbf{p}^\wedge \\ 0 & 1 \end{bmatrix},$$

$$w = \sum_{j=1}^{M} w_j, \quad \mathbf{p} = \frac{1}{w} \sum_{j=1}^{M} w_j \mathbf{p}_j, \quad \mathbf{I} = -\frac{1}{w} \sum_{j=1}^{M} w_j (\mathbf{p}_j - \mathbf{p})^\wedge (\mathbf{p}_j - \mathbf{p})^\wedge.$$

$$(9.103)$$

The 6×6 matrix, $\mathcal{M}$, has the form of a *generalized mass matrix* (Murray et al., 1994) with the weights as surrogates for masses. Notably, it is only a function of the points in the stationary frame and is therefore a constant.

Looking to the right-hand side, we can also show that

$$\mathbf{a} = \frac{1}{w} \sum_{j=1}^{M} w_j \mathbf{z}_j^{\odot^T} (\mathbf{y}_j - \mathbf{z}_j) = \begin{bmatrix} \mathbf{y} - \mathbf{C}_{\mathrm{op}}(\mathbf{p} - \mathbf{r}_{\mathrm{op}}) \\ \mathbf{b} - \mathbf{y}^\wedge \mathbf{C}_{\mathrm{op}}(\mathbf{p} - \mathbf{r}_{\mathrm{op}}) \end{bmatrix}, \qquad (9.104)$$

where

$$\mathbf{b} = \left[\mathrm{tr} \left(\mathbf{1}_i^\wedge \mathbf{C}_{\mathrm{op}} \mathbf{W}^T \right) \right]_i, \quad \mathbf{T}_{\mathrm{op}} = \begin{bmatrix} \mathbf{C}_{\mathrm{op}} & -\mathbf{C}_{\mathrm{op}} \mathbf{r}_{\mathrm{op}} \\ \mathbf{0}^T & 1 \end{bmatrix}, \qquad (9.105)$$

$$\mathbf{W} = \frac{1}{w} \sum_{j=1}^{M} w_j (\mathbf{y}_j - \mathbf{y})(\mathbf{p}_j - \mathbf{p})^T, \quad \mathbf{y} = \frac{1}{w} \sum_{j=1}^{M} w_j \mathbf{y}_j. \qquad (9.106)$$

Both $\mathbf{W}$ and $\mathbf{y}$ we have seen before and can be computed in advance from the points and then used at each iteration of the scheme.

Once again, we can write the solution for the optimal update down in closed form:

$$\boldsymbol{\epsilon}^\star = \mathcal{T}_{\mathrm{op}} \mathcal{M}^{-1} \mathcal{T}_{\mathrm{op}}^T \mathbf{a}. \qquad (9.107)$$

Once computed, we simply update our operating point,

$$\mathbf{T}_{\mathrm{op}} \leftarrow \exp\left(\boldsymbol{\epsilon}^{\star^\wedge} \right) \mathbf{T}_{\mathrm{op}}, \qquad (9.108)$$

and iterate the procedure to convergence. The estimated transformation is then $\hat{\mathbf{T}}_{v_k i} = \mathbf{T}_{\mathrm{op}}$ at the final iteration. Alternatively, $\hat{\mathbf{T}}_{i v_k} = \hat{\mathbf{T}}_{v_k i}^{-1}$ may be the output of interest.

Note, applying the optimal perturbation through the exponential map ensures that $\mathbf{T}_{\mathrm{op}}$ remains in $SE(3)$ at each iteration. Also, looking back to Section 4.3.1, we can see that our iterative optimization of $\mathbf{T}$ is exactly in the form of a Gauss–Newton style estimator, but adapted to work with $SE(3)$.

Three Non-collinear Points Required

It is interesting to consider when (9.101) has a unique solution. It immediately follows from (9.103) that

$$\det \mathcal{M} = \det \mathbf{I}. \qquad (9.109)$$

Therefore, to uniquely solve for $\boldsymbol{\epsilon}^\star$, we need $\det \mathbf{I} \neq 0$. A sufficient condition is to have $\mathbf{I}$ positive-definite, which (we saw in the previous section on rotation matrices) is true as long as there are at least three points and they are not collinear.

9.2 Point-Cloud Tracking

In this section, we study a problem very much related to point-cloud alignment, namely, point-cloud tracking. In the alignment problem, we simply wanted to align two point-clouds to determine the vehicle's pose at a single time. In the tracking problem, we want to estimate the pose of an object over time through a combination of measurements and a prior (with inputs). Accordingly, we will set up motion and observation models and then show how we can use these in both recursive (i.e., EKF) and batch (i.e., Gauss–Newton) solutions.

9.2.1 Problem Setup

We will continue to use the situation depicted in Figure 9.1. The state of the vehicle comprises

$\mathbf{r}_i^{v_k i}$: translation vector from I to V_k, expressed in $\underset{\rightarrow}{\mathcal{F}}_i$

$\mathbf{C}_{v_k i}$: rotation matrix from $\underset{\rightarrow}{\mathcal{F}}_i$ to $\underset{\rightarrow}{\mathcal{F}}_{v_k}$

or alternatively,

$$\mathbf{T}_k = \mathbf{T}_{v_k i} = \begin{bmatrix} \mathbf{C}_{v_k i} & -\mathbf{C}_{v_k i}\mathbf{r}_i^{v_k i} \\ \mathbf{0}^T & 1 \end{bmatrix}, \tag{9.110}$$

as a single transformation matrix. We use the shorthand

$$\mathbf{x} = \{\mathbf{T}_0, \mathbf{T}_1, \ldots, \mathbf{T}_K\}, \tag{9.111}$$

for the entire trajectory of poses. Our motion prior/inputs and measurements for this problem are as follows:

(i) Motion Prior/Inputs:

– We might assume the known inputs are the initial pose (with uncertainty),

$$\check{\mathbf{T}}_0, \tag{9.112}$$

as well as the translational velocity, $\boldsymbol{\nu}_{v_k}^{iv_k}$, and angular velocity of the vehicle, $\boldsymbol{\omega}_{v_k}^{iv_k}$, which we note are expressed in the vehicle frame. We combine these as

$$\boldsymbol{\varpi}_k = \begin{bmatrix} \boldsymbol{\nu}_{v_k}^{iv_k} \\ \boldsymbol{\omega}_{v_k}^{iv_k} \end{bmatrix}, \quad k = 1 \ldots K, \tag{9.113}$$

at a number of discrete times (we will assume the inputs are piecewise-constant in time). Together, the inputs can be written using the shorthand,

$$\mathbf{v} = \{\check{\mathbf{T}}_0, \boldsymbol{\varpi}_1, \boldsymbol{\varpi}_2, \ldots, \boldsymbol{\varpi}_K\}. \tag{9.114}$$

(ii) Measurements:

– We assume we are capable of measuring the position of a particular stationary point, P_j, in the vehicle frame, $\mathbf{r}_{v_k}^{p_j v_k}$. We assume the position of the point is known in the stationary frame, $\mathbf{r}_i^{p_j i}$. Note that there could also be measurements of multiple points, hence the subscript j. We will write

$$\mathbf{y}_{jk} = \mathbf{r}_{v_k}^{p_j v_k} \tag{9.115}$$

for the observation of point P_j at discrete time k. Together, the measurements can be written using the shorthand,

$$\mathbf{y} = \{\mathbf{y}_{11}, \ldots, \mathbf{y}_{M1}, \ldots, \mathbf{y}_{1K}, \ldots \mathbf{y}_{MK}\}. \qquad (9.116)$$

This pose estimation problem is fairly generic and could be used to describe a variety of situations.

9.2.2 Motion Priors

We will derive a general discrete-time, kinematic motion prior that can be used within a number of different estimation algorithms. We will start in continuous time and then move to discrete time.

Continuous Time

We will start with the $SE(3)$ kinematics,[10]

$$\dot{\mathbf{T}} = \boldsymbol{\varpi}^{\wedge}\mathbf{T}, \qquad (9.117)$$

where the quantities involved are perturbed by process noise according to

$$\mathbf{T} = \exp\left(\delta\boldsymbol{\xi}^{\wedge}\right)\bar{\mathbf{T}}, \qquad (9.118a)$$

$$\boldsymbol{\varpi} = \bar{\boldsymbol{\varpi}} + \delta\boldsymbol{\varpi}. \qquad (9.118b)$$

We can separate these into nominal and perturbation kinematics as in (8.301):

$$\text{nominal kinematics:} \quad \dot{\bar{\mathbf{T}}} = \bar{\boldsymbol{\varpi}}^{\wedge}\bar{\mathbf{T}}, \qquad (9.119a)$$

$$\text{perturbation kinematics:} \quad \delta\dot{\boldsymbol{\xi}} = \bar{\boldsymbol{\varpi}}^{\curlywedge}\delta\boldsymbol{\xi} + \delta\boldsymbol{\varpi}, \qquad (9.119b)$$

where we will think of $\delta\boldsymbol{\varpi}(t)$ as process noise that corrupts the nominal kinematics. Thus, integrating the perturbed kinematic equation allows us to track uncertainty in the pose of the system. While we could do this in continuous time, we will next move to discrete time to prepare to use this kinematic model in the EKF and batch, discrete-time MAP estimators.

Discrete Time

If we assume quantities remain constant between discrete times, then we can use the ideas from Section 8.2.2 to write

$$\text{nominal kinematics:} \quad \bar{\mathbf{T}}_k = \underbrace{\exp\left(\Delta t_k \bar{\boldsymbol{\varpi}}_k^{\wedge}\right)}_{\boldsymbol{\Xi}_k}\bar{\mathbf{T}}_{k-1}, \qquad (9.120a)$$

$$\text{perturbation kinematics:} \quad \delta\boldsymbol{\xi}_k = \underbrace{\exp\left(\Delta t_k \bar{\boldsymbol{\varpi}}_k^{\curlywedge}\right)}_{\mathrm{Ad}(\boldsymbol{\Xi}_k)}\delta\boldsymbol{\xi}_{k-1} + \mathbf{w}_k, \quad (9.120b)$$

with $\Delta t_k = t_k - t_{k-1}$ for the nominal and perturbation kinematics in discrete time. The process noise is now $\mathbf{w}_k = \mathcal{N}(\mathbf{0}, \mathbf{Q}_k)$.

---

[10] To be clear, $\mathbf{T} = \mathbf{T}_{v_k i}$ in this equation and $\boldsymbol{\varpi}$ is the generalized velocity expressed in $\underrightarrow{\mathcal{F}}_{v_k}$.

9.2.3 *Measurement Model*

We next develop a measurement model and then linearize it.

Nonlinear

Our 3×1 measurement model can be compactly written as

$$\mathbf{y}_{jk} = \mathbf{D}^T \mathbf{T}_k \mathbf{p}_j + \mathbf{n}_{jk}, \tag{9.121}$$

where the position of the known points on the moving vehicle are expressed in 4×1 homogeneous coordinates (bottom row equal to 1),

$$\mathbf{p}_j = \begin{bmatrix} \mathbf{r}_i^{p_j i} \\ 1 \end{bmatrix}, \tag{9.122}$$

and

$$\mathbf{D}^T = \begin{bmatrix} 1 & 0 & 0 & 0 \\ 0 & 1 & 0 & 0 \\ 0 & 0 & 1 & 0 \end{bmatrix} \tag{9.123}$$

is a projection matrix used to ensure the measurements are indeed 3×1 by removing the 1 on the bottom row. We have also now included $\mathbf{n}_{jk} \sim \mathcal{N}(\mathbf{0}, \mathbf{R}_{jk})$, which is Gaussian measurement noise.

Linearized

We linearize (9.121) in much the same way as the motion model through the use of perturbations:

$$\mathbf{T}_k = \exp\left(\delta \boldsymbol{\xi}_k^\wedge\right) \bar{\mathbf{T}}_k, \tag{9.124a}$$

$$\mathbf{y}_{jk} = \bar{\mathbf{y}}_{jk} + \delta \mathbf{y}_{jk}. \tag{9.124b}$$

Substituting these into the measurement model, we have

$$\bar{\mathbf{y}}_{jk} + \delta \mathbf{y}_{jk} = \mathbf{D}^T \left(\exp\left(\delta \boldsymbol{\xi}_k^\wedge\right) \bar{\mathbf{T}}_k\right) \mathbf{p}_j + \mathbf{n}_{jk}. \tag{9.125}$$

Subtracting off the nominal solution (i.e., the operating point in our linearization),

$$\bar{\mathbf{y}}_{jk} = \mathbf{D}^T \bar{\mathbf{T}}_k \mathbf{p}_j, \tag{9.126}$$

we are left with

$$\delta \mathbf{y}_{jk} \approx \mathbf{D}^T \left(\bar{\mathbf{T}}_k \mathbf{p}_j\right)^\odot \delta \boldsymbol{\xi}_k + \mathbf{n}_{jk}, \tag{9.127}$$

correct to first order. This perturbation measurement model relates small changes in the input to the measurement model to small changes in the output, in an $SE(3)$-constraint-sensitive manner.

Nomenclature

To match the notation used in our derivations of our nonlinear estimators, we define the following symbols:

$\hat{\mathbf{T}}_k$: 4×4 corrected estimate of pose at time k

$\hat{\mathbf{P}}_k$: 6×6 covariance of corrected estimate at time k
    (for both translation and rotation)

$\check{\mathbf{T}}_k$: 4×4 predicted estimate of pose at time k

$\check{\mathbf{P}}_k$: 6×6 covariance of predicted estimate at time k
    (for both translation and rotation)

$\check{\mathbf{T}}_0$: 4×4 prior input as pose at time 0

$\boldsymbol{\varpi}_k$: 6×1 prior input as generalized velocity at time k

$\mathbf{Q}_k$: 6×6 covariance of process noise
    (for both translation and rotation)

$\mathbf{y}_{jk}$: 3×1 measurement of point j from vehicle at time k

$\mathbf{R}_{jk}$: 3×3 covariance of measurement j at time k

We will use these in two different estimators, the EKF and batch discrete-time MAP estimation.

9.2.4 EKF Solution

In this section, we seek to estimate the pose of our vehicle using the classic EKF, but carefully applied to our situation involving rotations.

Prediction Step

Predicting the mean forward in time is not difficult in the case of the EKF; we simply pass our prior estimate and latest input through the nominal kinematics model in (9.120):

$$\check{\mathbf{T}}_k = \underbrace{\exp\left(\Delta t_k \, \boldsymbol{\varpi}_k^\wedge\right)}_{\boldsymbol{\Xi}_k} \hat{\mathbf{T}}_{k-1}. \tag{9.128}$$

To predict the covariance of the estimate,

$$\check{\mathbf{P}}_k = E\left[\delta\check{\boldsymbol{\xi}}_k \delta\check{\boldsymbol{\xi}}_k^T\right], \tag{9.129}$$

we require the perturbation kinematics model in (9.120),

$$\delta\check{\boldsymbol{\xi}}_k = \underbrace{\exp\left(\Delta t_k \, \boldsymbol{\varpi}_k^\wedge\right)}_{\mathbf{F}_{k-1} = \mathrm{Ad}(\boldsymbol{\Xi}_k)} \delta\hat{\boldsymbol{\xi}}_{k-1} + \mathbf{w}_k. \tag{9.130}$$

Thus, in this case, the coefficient matrix of the linearized motion model is

$$\mathbf{F}_{k-1} = \exp\left(\Delta t_k \, \boldsymbol{\varpi}_k^\wedge\right), \tag{9.131}$$

which depends only on the input and not the state due to our convenient choice of representing uncertainty via the exponential map. The covariance prediction proceeds in the usual EKF manner as

$$\check{\mathbf{P}}_k = \mathbf{F}_{k-1}\hat{\mathbf{P}}_{k-1}\mathbf{F}_{k-1}^T + \mathbf{Q}_k. \tag{9.132}$$

The correction step is where we must pay particular attention to the pose variables.

Correction Step

Looking back to (9.127) for the perturbation measurement model,

$$\delta\mathbf{y}_{jk} = \underbrace{\mathbf{D}^T \left(\check{\mathbf{T}}_k\mathbf{p}_j\right)^\odot}_{\mathbf{G}_{jk}} \delta\hat{\boldsymbol{\xi}}_k + \mathbf{n}_{jk}, \tag{9.133}$$

we see that the coefficient matrix of the linearized measurement model is

$$\mathbf{G}_{jk} = \mathbf{D}^T \left(\check{\mathbf{T}}_k\mathbf{p}_j\right)^\odot, \tag{9.134}$$

which is evaluated at the predicted mean pose, $\check{\mathbf{T}}_k$.

To handle the case in which there are M observations of points on the vehicle, we can stack the quantities as follows:

$$\mathbf{y}_k = \begin{bmatrix} \mathbf{y}_{1k} \\ \vdots \\ \mathbf{y}_{Mk} \end{bmatrix}, \quad \mathbf{G}_k = \begin{bmatrix} \mathbf{G}_{1k} \\ \vdots \\ \mathbf{G}_{Mk} \end{bmatrix}, \quad \mathbf{R}_k = \mathrm{diag}\left(\mathbf{R}_{1k}, \ldots, \mathbf{R}_{Mk}\right). \tag{9.135}$$

The Kalman gain and covariance update equations are then unchanged from the generic case:

$$\mathbf{K}_k = \check{\mathbf{P}}_k\mathbf{G}_k^T \left(\mathbf{G}_k\check{\mathbf{P}}_k\mathbf{G}_k^T + \mathbf{R}_k\right)^{-1}, \tag{9.136a}$$

$$\hat{\mathbf{P}}_k = \left(\mathbf{1} - \mathbf{K}_k\mathbf{G}_k\right)\check{\mathbf{P}}_k. \tag{9.136b}$$

Note that we must be careful to interpret the EKF corrective equations properly since

$$\hat{\mathbf{P}}_k = E\left[\delta\hat{\boldsymbol{\xi}}_k\delta\hat{\boldsymbol{\xi}}_k^T\right]. \tag{9.137}$$

In particular, for the mean update, we rearrange the equation as follows:

$$\epsilon_k = \underbrace{\ln\left(\hat{\mathbf{T}}_k\check{\mathbf{T}}_k^{-1}\right)^\vee}_{\text{update}} = \mathbf{K}_k \underbrace{\left(\mathbf{y}_k - \check{\mathbf{y}}_k\right)}_{\text{innovation}}, \tag{9.138}$$

where $\epsilon_k = \ln\left(\hat{\mathbf{T}}_k\check{\mathbf{T}}_k^{-1}\right)^\vee$ is the difference of the corrected and predicted means and $\check{\mathbf{y}}_k$ is the nonlinear, nominal measurement model evaluated at the predicted mean:

$$\check{\mathbf{y}}_k = \begin{bmatrix} \check{\mathbf{y}}_{1k} \\ \vdots \\ \check{\mathbf{y}}_{Mk} \end{bmatrix}, \qquad \check{\mathbf{y}}_{jk} = \mathbf{D}^T \check{\mathbf{T}}_k\mathbf{p}_j, \tag{9.139}$$

where we have again accounted for the fact that there could be M observations of points on the vehicle. Once we have computed the mean correction, ϵ_k, we apply it according to

$$\hat{\mathbf{T}}_k = \exp\left(\epsilon_k^\wedge\right)\check{\mathbf{T}}_k, \tag{9.140}$$

which ensures the mean stays in $SE(3)$.

Summary

Putting the pieces from the last two sections together, we have our canonical five EKF equations for this system:

$$\text{predictor:} \quad \begin{aligned} \check{\mathbf{P}}_k &= \mathbf{F}_{k-1}\hat{\mathbf{P}}_{k-1}\mathbf{F}_{k-1}^T + \mathbf{Q}_k, & \text{(9.141a)} \\ \check{\mathbf{T}}_k &= \boldsymbol{\Xi}_k\,\hat{\mathbf{T}}_{k-1}, & \text{(9.141b)} \end{aligned}$$

$$\text{Kalman gain:} \quad \mathbf{K}_k = \check{\mathbf{P}}_k\mathbf{G}_k^T\left(\mathbf{G}_k\check{\mathbf{P}}_k\mathbf{G}_k^T + \mathbf{R}_k\right)^{-1}, \tag{9.141c}$$

$$\text{corrector:} \quad \begin{aligned} \hat{\mathbf{P}}_k &= \left(\mathbf{1} - \mathbf{K}_k\mathbf{G}_k\right)\check{\mathbf{P}}_k, & \text{(9.141d)} \\ \hat{\mathbf{T}}_k &= \exp\left(\left(\mathbf{K}_k\left(\mathbf{y}_k - \check{\mathbf{y}}_k\right)\right)^\wedge\right)\check{\mathbf{T}}_k. & \text{(9.141e)} \end{aligned}$$

We have essentially modified the EKF so that all the mean calculations occur in $SE(3)$, the Lie group, and all of the covariance calculations occur in $\mathfrak{se}(3)$, the Lie algebra. As usual, we must initialize the filter at the first timestep using $\check{\mathbf{T}}_0$. Although we do not show it, we could easily turn this into an iterated EKF by relinearizing about the latest estimate and iterating over the correction step. Finally, the algorithm has $\hat{\mathbf{T}}_{v_k i} = \hat{\mathbf{T}}_k$ so we can compute $\hat{\mathbf{T}}_{i v_k} = \hat{\mathbf{T}}_k^{-1}$ if desired.

Relationship to Invariant EKF

In the book, we generally always use left perturbations when defining distributions over Lie groups and performing optimization over the same; this usually means perturbations on the 'moving frame' (i.e., vehicle) side of a quantity such as $\mathbf{T}_{vi}$. However, this choice is arbitrary and we could just as easily choose right perturbations/errors to derive our algorithms. In some situations, there can be a benefit to choosing one over the other.

An excellent example of choosing left versus right wisely is the *invariant EKF*[11] (Barrau and Bonnabel, 2017). If the motion and measurement models fit a particular form, Barrau and Bonnabel (2017) show it is possible to set up an EKF on Lie groups that closely mirrors the linear *Kalman filter (KF)* when it comes to its error dynamics (recall Section 3.3.6). In particular, Jacobians with respect to the state, $\mathbf{F}_{k-1}$ and $\mathbf{G}_k$, do not depend on the current state estimate. This additional structure makes analysis of the invariant EKF tractable to the point that it can be shown to be a *stable observer* under appropriate conditions. In this framework, the choice of left versus right depends on the specific form of the measurement model.

---

[11] Barrau and Bonnabel (2017) refer to the *invariant EKF* as 'IEKF' but we have already used this acronym for the *iterated extended Kalman filter (IEKF)* in this book, so we will simply write 'invariant'.

Looking through the invariant EKF lens, our EKF in (9.141) does not quite fit the template. For example, while our motion model Jacobian, $\mathbf{F}_{k-1}$ does not depend on the current state estimate, our measurement model Jacobian, $\mathbf{G}_k = \mathbf{D}^T \left(\check{\mathbf{T}}_k \mathbf{p}_j \right)^{\odot}$, does. However, in this particular case, it is possible to algebraically manipulate our EKF into the invariant EKF form. Alternatively, had we chosen right perturbations from the beginning (for this particular measurement model) we would arrive at the invariant EKF form more directly. So as not to interrupt the main flow of this section, we devote Appendix C.4 to showing the connection between (9.141) and the invariant EKF in further detail.

9.2.5 Batch Maximum a Posteriori Solution

In this section, we return to the discrete-time, batch estimation approach to see how this works on our pose tracking problem.

Error Terms and Objective Function

As usual for batch MAP problems, we begin by defining an error term for each of our inputs and measurements. For the inputs, $\check{\mathbf{T}}_0$ and $\boldsymbol{\varpi}_k$, we have

$$\mathbf{e}_{v,k}(\mathbf{x}) = \begin{cases} \ln \left(\check{\mathbf{T}}_0 \mathbf{T}_0^{-1} \right)^{\vee} & k = 0 \\ \ln \left(\boldsymbol{\Xi}_k \mathbf{T}_{k-1} \mathbf{T}_k^{-1} \right)^{\vee} & k = 1 \ldots K \end{cases}, \tag{9.142}$$

where $\boldsymbol{\Xi}_k = \exp \left(\Delta t_k \, \boldsymbol{\varpi}_k^{\wedge} \right)$ and we have used the convenient shorthand, $\mathbf{x} = \{ \mathbf{T}_0, \ldots, \mathbf{T}_K \}$. For the measurements, $\mathbf{y}_{jk}$, we have

$$\mathbf{e}_{y,jk}(\mathbf{x}) = \mathbf{y}_{jk} - \mathbf{D}^T \mathbf{T}_k \mathbf{p}_j. \tag{9.143}$$

Next we examine the noise properties of these errors.

Taking the Bayesian point of view, we consider that the true pose variables are drawn from the prior (see Section 4.1.1) so that

$$\mathbf{T}_k = \exp \left(\delta \boldsymbol{\xi}_k^{\wedge} \right) \check{\mathbf{T}}_k, \tag{9.144}$$

where $\delta \boldsymbol{\xi}_k \sim \mathcal{N} \left(\mathbf{0}, \check{\mathbf{P}}_k \right)$.

For the first input error, we have

$$\mathbf{e}_{v,0}(\mathbf{x}) = \ln \left(\check{\mathbf{T}}_0 \mathbf{T}_0^{-1} \right)^{\vee} = \ln \left(\check{\mathbf{T}}_0 \check{\mathbf{T}}_0^{-1} \exp \left(-\delta \boldsymbol{\xi}_0^{\wedge} \right) \right)^{\vee} = -\delta \boldsymbol{\xi}_0, \tag{9.145}$$

so that

$$\mathbf{e}_{v,0}(\mathbf{x}) \sim \mathcal{N} \left(\mathbf{0}, \check{\mathbf{P}}_0 \right). \tag{9.146}$$

For the later input errors, we have

$$\begin{aligned} \mathbf{e}_{v,k}(\mathbf{x}) &= \ln \left(\boldsymbol{\Xi}_k \mathbf{T}_{k-1} \mathbf{T}_k^{-1} \right)^{\vee} \\ &= \ln \left(\boldsymbol{\Xi}_k \exp \left(\delta \boldsymbol{\xi}_{k-1}^{\wedge} \right) \check{\mathbf{T}}_{k-1} \check{\mathbf{T}}_k^{-1} \exp \left(-\delta \boldsymbol{\xi}_k^{\wedge} \right) \right)^{\vee} \\ &= \ln \Big(\underbrace{\boldsymbol{\Xi}_k \check{\mathbf{T}}_{k-1} \check{\mathbf{T}}_k^{-1}}_{1} \exp \left(\left(\mathrm{Ad}(\boldsymbol{\Xi}_k) \, \delta \boldsymbol{\xi}_{k-1} \right)^{\wedge} \right) \exp \left(-\delta \boldsymbol{\xi}_k^{\wedge} \right) \Big)^{\vee} \\ &\approx \mathrm{Ad}(\boldsymbol{\Xi}_k) \, \delta \boldsymbol{\xi}_{k-1} - \delta \boldsymbol{\xi}_k \\ &= -\mathbf{w}_k, \end{aligned} \tag{9.147}$$

so that

$$\mathbf{e}_{v,k}(\mathbf{x}) \sim \mathcal{N}(\mathbf{0}, \mathbf{Q}_k). \tag{9.148}$$

For the measurement model, we consider that the measurements are generated by evaluating the noise-free versions (based on the true pose variables) and then corrupted by noise so that

$$\mathbf{e}_{y,jk}(\mathbf{x}) = \mathbf{y}_{jk} - \mathbf{D}^T \mathbf{T}_k \mathbf{p}_j = \mathbf{n}_{jk}, \tag{9.149}$$

and

$$\mathbf{e}_{y,jk}(\mathbf{x}) \sim \mathcal{N}(\mathbf{0}, \mathbf{R}_{jk}). \tag{9.150}$$

These noise properties allow us to next construct the objective function that we want to minimize in our batch MAP problem:

$$J_{v,k}(\mathbf{x}) = \begin{cases} \frac{1}{2}\mathbf{e}_{v,0}(\mathbf{x})^T \check{\mathbf{P}}_0^{-1} \mathbf{e}_{v,0}(\mathbf{x}) & k = 0 \\ \frac{1}{2}\mathbf{e}_{v,k}(\mathbf{x})^T \mathbf{Q}_k^{-1} \mathbf{e}_{v,k}(\mathbf{x}) & k = 1 \ldots K \end{cases}, \tag{9.151a}$$

$$J_{y,k}(\mathbf{x}) = \frac{1}{2}\mathbf{e}_{y,k}(\mathbf{x})^T \mathbf{R}_k^{-1} \mathbf{e}_{y,k}(\mathbf{x}), \tag{9.151b}$$

where we have stacked the M point quantities together according to

$$\mathbf{e}_{y,k}(\mathbf{x}) = \begin{bmatrix} \mathbf{e}_{y,1k}(\mathbf{x}) \\ \vdots \\ \mathbf{e}_{y,Mk}(\mathbf{x}) \end{bmatrix}, \qquad \mathbf{R}_k = \mathrm{diag}\left(\mathbf{R}_{1k}, \ldots, \mathbf{R}_{Mk}\right). \tag{9.152}$$

The overall objective function that we will seek to minimize is then

$$J(\mathbf{x}) = \sum_{k=0}^{K} \left(J_{v,k}(\mathbf{x}) + J_{y,k}(\mathbf{x})\right). \tag{9.153}$$

The next section will look at linearizing our error terms in order to carry out Gauss–Newton optimization.

Linearized Error Terms

It is fairly straightforward to linearize our error terms (in order to carry out Gauss–Newton optimization) just as we earlier linearized our motion and observation models. We will linearize about an operating point for each pose, $\mathbf{T}_{\mathrm{op},k}$, which we can think of as our current trajectory guess that will be iteratively improved. Thus, we will take

$$\mathbf{T}_k = \exp\left(\boldsymbol{\epsilon}_k^\wedge\right) \mathbf{T}_{\mathrm{op},k}, \tag{9.154}$$

where $\boldsymbol{\epsilon}_k$ will be the perturbation to the current guess that we seek to optimize at each iteration. We will use the shorthand

$$\mathbf{x}_{\mathrm{op}} = \{\mathbf{T}_{\mathrm{op},1}, \mathbf{T}_{\mathrm{op},2}, \ldots, \mathbf{T}_{\mathrm{op},K}\}, \tag{9.155}$$

for the operating point of the entire trajectory.

For the first input error, we have

$$\mathbf{e}_{v,0}(\mathbf{x}) = \ln\left(\check{\mathbf{T}}_0\mathbf{T}_0^{-1}\right)^\vee = \ln\Big(\underbrace{\check{\mathbf{T}}_0\mathbf{T}_{\mathrm{op},0}^{-1}}_{\exp(\mathbf{e}_{v,0}(\mathbf{x}_{\mathrm{op}})^\wedge)}\exp\left(-\epsilon_0^\wedge\right)\Big)^\vee$$

$$\approx \mathbf{e}_{v,0}(\mathbf{x}_{\mathrm{op}}) - \underbrace{\mathcal{J}\left(-\mathbf{e}_{v,0}(\mathbf{x}_{\mathrm{op}})\right)^{-1}}_{\mathbf{E}_0}\epsilon_0, \quad (9.156)$$

where $\mathbf{e}_{v,0}(\mathbf{x}_{\mathrm{op}}) = \ln\left(\check{\mathbf{T}}_0\mathbf{T}_{\mathrm{op},0}^{-1}\right)^\vee$ is the error evaluated at the operating point.
For the input errors at the later times, we have

$$\mathbf{e}_{v,k}(\mathbf{x}) = \ln\left(\boldsymbol{\Xi}_k\mathbf{T}_{k-1}\mathbf{T}_k^{-1}\right)^\vee$$

$$= \ln\left(\boldsymbol{\Xi}_k\exp\left(\epsilon_{k-1}^\wedge\right)\mathbf{T}_{\mathrm{op},k-1}\mathbf{T}_{\mathrm{op},k}^{-1}\exp\left(-\epsilon_k^\wedge\right)\right)^\vee$$

$$= \ln\Big(\underbrace{\boldsymbol{\Xi}_k\mathbf{T}_{\mathrm{op},k-1}\mathbf{T}_{\mathrm{op},k}^{-1}}_{\exp(\mathbf{e}_{v,k}(\mathbf{x}_{\mathrm{op}})^\wedge)}\exp\left(\left(\mathrm{Ad}\left(\mathbf{T}_{\mathrm{op},k}\mathbf{T}_{\mathrm{op},k-1}^{-1}\right)\epsilon_{k-1}\right)^\wedge\right)\exp\left(-\epsilon_k^\wedge\right)\Big)^\vee$$

$$\approx \mathbf{e}_{v,k}(\mathbf{x}_{\mathrm{op}}) + \underbrace{\mathcal{J}\left(-\mathbf{e}_{v,k}(\mathbf{x}_{\mathrm{op}})\right)^{-1}\mathrm{Ad}\left(\mathbf{T}_{\mathrm{op},k}\mathbf{T}_{\mathrm{op},k-1}^{-1}\right)}_{\mathbf{F}_{k-1}}\epsilon_{k-1}$$

$$- \underbrace{\mathcal{J}\left(-\mathbf{e}_{v,k}(\mathbf{x}_{\mathrm{op}})\right)^{-1}}_{\mathbf{E}_k}\epsilon_k,$$

$$= \mathbf{e}_{v,k}(\mathbf{x}_{\mathrm{op}}) + \mathbf{F}_{k-1}\epsilon_{k-1} - \mathbf{E}_k\epsilon_k, \quad (9.157)$$

where $\mathbf{e}_{v,k}(\mathbf{x}_{\mathrm{op}}) = \ln\left(\boldsymbol{\Xi}_k\mathbf{T}_{\mathrm{op},k-1}\mathbf{T}_{\mathrm{op},k}^{-1}\right)^\vee$ is the error evaluated at the operating point.
For the measurement errors, we have

$$\mathbf{e}_{y,jk}(\mathbf{x}) = \mathbf{y}_{jk} - \mathbf{D}^T\mathbf{T}_k\mathbf{p}_j$$

$$= \mathbf{y}_{jk} - \mathbf{D}^T\exp\left(\epsilon_k^\wedge\right)\mathbf{T}_{\mathrm{op},k}\mathbf{p}_j$$

$$\approx \mathbf{y}_{jk} - \mathbf{D}^T\left(1 + \epsilon_k^\wedge\right)\mathbf{T}_{\mathrm{op},k}\mathbf{p}_j$$

$$= \underbrace{\mathbf{y}_{jk} - \mathbf{D}^T\mathbf{T}_{\mathrm{op},k}\mathbf{p}_j}_{\mathbf{e}_{y,jk}(\mathbf{x}_{\mathrm{op}})} - \underbrace{\left(\mathbf{D}^T\left(\mathbf{T}_{\mathrm{op},k}\mathbf{p}_j\right)^\odot\right)}_{\mathbf{G}_{jk}}\epsilon_k. \quad (9.158)$$

We can stack all of the point measurement errors at time k together so that

$$\mathbf{e}_{y,k}(\mathbf{x}) \approx \mathbf{e}_{y,k}(\mathbf{x}_{\mathrm{op}}) - \mathbf{G}_k\epsilon_k, \quad (9.159)$$

where

$$\mathbf{e}_{y,k}(\mathbf{x}) = \begin{bmatrix} \mathbf{e}_{y,1k}(\mathbf{x}) \\ \vdots \\ \mathbf{e}_{y,Mk}(\mathbf{x}) \end{bmatrix}, \quad \mathbf{e}_{y,k}(\mathbf{x}_{\mathrm{op}}) = \begin{bmatrix} \mathbf{e}_{y,1k}(\mathbf{x}_{\mathrm{op}}) \\ \vdots \\ \mathbf{e}_{y,Mk}(\mathbf{x}_{\mathrm{op}}) \end{bmatrix}, \quad \mathbf{G}_k = \begin{bmatrix} \mathbf{G}_{1k} \\ \vdots \\ \mathbf{G}_{Mk} \end{bmatrix}.$$

$$(9.160)$$

Next, we will insert these approximations into our objective function to complete the Gauss–Newton derivation.

Gauss–Newton Update

To set up the Gauss–Newton update, we define the following stacked quantities:

$$
\delta\mathbf{x} = \begin{bmatrix} \boldsymbol{\epsilon}_0 \\ \boldsymbol{\epsilon}_1 \\ \boldsymbol{\epsilon}_2 \\ \vdots \\ \boldsymbol{\epsilon}_K \end{bmatrix}, \quad
\mathbf{H} = \left[\begin{array}{c|c}
\begin{matrix} \mathbf{E}_0 & & & & \\ -\mathbf{F}_0 & \mathbf{E}_1 & & & \\ & -\mathbf{F}_1 & \ddots & & \\ & & \ddots & \mathbf{E}_{K-1} & \\ & & & -\mathbf{F}_{K-1} & \mathbf{E}_K \end{matrix} \\ \hline
\begin{matrix} \mathbf{G}_0 & & & & \\ & \mathbf{G}_1 & & & \\ & & \mathbf{G}_2 & & \\ & & & \ddots & \\ & & & & \mathbf{G}_K \end{matrix}
\end{array}\right],
$$

$$
\mathbf{e}(\mathbf{x}_{\mathrm{op}}) = \left[\begin{array}{c}
\mathbf{e}_{v,0}(\mathbf{x}_{\mathrm{op}}) \\
\mathbf{e}_{v,1}(\mathbf{x}_{\mathrm{op}}) \\
\vdots \\
\mathbf{e}_{v,K-1}(\mathbf{x}_{\mathrm{op}}) \\
\mathbf{e}_{v,K}(\mathbf{x}_{\mathrm{op}}) \\
\hline
\mathbf{e}_{y,0}(\mathbf{x}_{\mathrm{op}}) \\
\mathbf{e}_{y,1}(\mathbf{x}_{\mathrm{op}}) \\
\vdots \\
\mathbf{e}_{y,K-1}(\mathbf{x}_{\mathrm{op}}) \\
\mathbf{e}_{y,K}(\mathbf{x}_{\mathrm{op}})
\end{array}\right], \tag{9.161}
$$

and

$$
\mathbf{W} = \operatorname{diag}\left(\check{\mathbf{P}}_0, \mathbf{Q}_1, \ldots, \mathbf{Q}_K, \mathbf{R}_0, \mathbf{R}_1, \ldots, \mathbf{R}_K\right), \tag{9.162}
$$

which are identical in structure to the matrices in the nonlinear version. The quadratic (in terms of the perturbation, $\delta\mathbf{x}$) approximation to the objective function is then

$$
J(\mathbf{x}) \approx J(\mathbf{x}_{\mathrm{op}}) - \mathbf{b}^T \delta\mathbf{x} + \frac{1}{2}\delta\mathbf{x}^T \mathbf{A}\, \delta\mathbf{x}, \tag{9.163}
$$

where

$$
\mathbf{A} = \underbrace{\mathbf{H}^T \mathbf{W}^{-1} \mathbf{H}}_{\text{block-tridiagonal}}, \quad \mathbf{b} = \mathbf{H}^T \mathbf{W}^{-1} \mathbf{e}(\mathbf{x}_{\mathrm{op}}). \tag{9.164}
$$

Minimizing with respect to $\delta\mathbf{x}$, we have

$$
\mathbf{A}\, \delta\mathbf{x}^\star = \mathbf{b}, \tag{9.165}
$$

for the optimal perturbation,

$$\delta \mathbf{x}^\star = \begin{bmatrix} \epsilon_0^\star \\ \epsilon_1^\star \\ \vdots \\ \epsilon_K^\star \end{bmatrix}. \tag{9.166}$$

Once we have the optimal perturbation, we update our operating point through the original perturbation scheme,

$$\mathbf{T}_{\mathrm{op},k} \leftarrow \exp\left(\epsilon_k^{\star^\wedge}\right) \mathbf{T}_{\mathrm{op},k}, \tag{9.167}$$

which ensures that $\mathbf{T}_{\mathrm{op},k}$ stays in $SE(3)$. We then iterate the entire scheme to convergence. As a reminder we note that at the final iteration we have $\hat{\mathbf{T}}_{v_k i} = \mathbf{T}_{\mathrm{op},k}$ as our estimate, but if we prefer we can compute $\hat{\mathbf{T}}_{i v_k} = \hat{\mathbf{T}}_{v_k i}^{-1}$.

Once again, the main concept that we have used to derive this Gauss–Newton optimization problem involving pose variables is to compute the update in the Lie algebra, $\mathfrak{se}(3)$, but store the mean in the Lie group, $SE(3)$.

9.3 Pose-Graph Relaxation

Another classic problem worth investigating in our framework is that of *pose-graph relaxation*. Here we do not explicitly measure any points in the stationary frame, but instead begin directly with a set of relative pose 'measurements' (aka pseudomeasurements) that may have come from some form of dead reckoning. The situation is depicted in Figure 9.3, where we can consider each white triangle to be a reference frame in three dimensions. We refer to this diagram as a *pose graph* in that it only involves poses and no points.

Importantly, pose graphs can contain closed loops (as well as leaf nodes), but unfortunately, the relative pose measurements are uncertain and do not necessarily compound to identity around any loop. Therefore, our task is to 'relax' the pose graph with respect to one (arbitrarily selected) pose, called pose 0. In other words, we will determine an optimal estimate for each pose relative to pose 0, given all of the relative pose measurements.

9.3.1 Problem Setup

There is an implicit reference frame, $\underrightarrow{\mathcal{F}}_k$, located at pose k in Figure 9.3. We will use a transformation matrix to denote the pose change from $\underrightarrow{\mathcal{F}}_0$ to $\underrightarrow{\mathcal{F}}_k$:

$\mathbf{T}_k$: transformation matrix representing pose of $\underrightarrow{\mathcal{F}}_k$ relative to $\underrightarrow{\mathcal{F}}_0$.

Our task will be to estimate this transformation for all the poses (other than pose 0).

As mentioned earlier, the measurements will be a set of relative pose changes between nodes in the pose graph. The measurements will be assumed to be Gaussian (on $SE(3)$) and thus have a mean and a covariance given by

$$\left\{ \bar{\mathbf{T}}_{k\ell}, \mathbf{\Sigma}_{k\ell} \right\}. \tag{9.168}$$

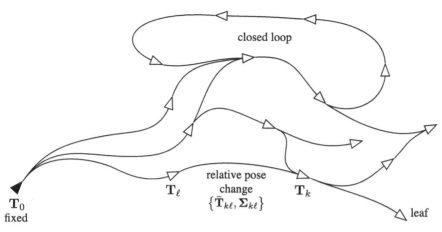

Figure 9.3 In the pose-graph relaxation problem, only relative pose change 'measurements' are provided, and the task is to determine where each pose is in relation to one privileged pose, labelled 0, which is fixed. We cannot simply compound the relative transforms due to the presence of closed loops, around which the relative transforms may not compound to identity.

Explicitly, a random sample, $\mathbf{T}_{k\ell}$, is drawn from this Gaussian density according to

$$\mathbf{T}_{k\ell} = \exp\left(\boldsymbol{\xi}_{k\ell}^{\wedge}\right)\bar{\mathbf{T}}_{k\ell}, \tag{9.169}$$

where

$$\boldsymbol{\xi}_{k\ell} \sim \mathcal{N}\left(\mathbf{0}, \boldsymbol{\Sigma}_{k\ell}\right). \tag{9.170}$$

Measurements of this type can arise from a lower-level dead-reckoning method such as wheel odometry, visual odometry, or inertial sensing. Not all pairs of poses will have relative measurements, making the problem fairly sparse in practice.

9.3.2 Batch Maximum Likelihood Solution

We will follow a batch *maximum likelihood (ML)* approach very similar to the pose-fusion problem described in Section 8.3.6. As usual, for each measurement we will formulate an error term,

$$\mathbf{e}_{k\ell}(\mathbf{x}) = \ln\left(\bar{\mathbf{T}}_{k\ell}\left(\mathbf{T}_k\mathbf{T}_\ell^{-1}\right)^{-1}\right)^{\vee} = \ln\left(\bar{\mathbf{T}}_{k\ell}\mathbf{T}_\ell\mathbf{T}_k^{-1}\right)^{\vee}, \tag{9.171}$$

where we have used the shorthand

$$\mathbf{x} = \{\mathbf{T}_1, \dots, \mathbf{T}_K\}, \tag{9.172}$$

for the state to be estimated. We will adopt the usual $SE(3)$-sensitive perturbation scheme,

$$\mathbf{T}_k = \exp\left(\boldsymbol{\epsilon}_k^{\wedge}\right)\mathbf{T}_{\mathrm{op},k}, \tag{9.173}$$

where $\mathbf{T}_{\mathrm{op},k}$ is the operating point and $\boldsymbol{\epsilon}_k$ the small perturbation. Inserting this into the error expression, we have

$$\mathbf{e}_{k\ell}(\mathbf{x}) = \ln\left(\bar{\mathbf{T}}_{k\ell}\exp\left(\boldsymbol{\epsilon}_\ell^{\wedge}\right)\mathbf{T}_{\mathrm{op},\ell}\mathbf{T}_{\mathrm{op},k}^{-1}\exp\left(-\boldsymbol{\epsilon}_k^{\wedge}\right)\right)^{\vee}. \tag{9.174}$$

We can pull the $\boldsymbol{\epsilon}_\ell$ factor over to the right without approximation:

$$\mathbf{e}_{k\ell}(\mathbf{x}) = \ln\left(\underbrace{\bar{\mathbf{T}}_{k\ell}\mathbf{T}_{\mathrm{op},\ell}\mathbf{T}_{\mathrm{op},k}^{-1}}_{\text{small}}\exp\left(\left(\boldsymbol{\mathcal{T}}_{\mathrm{op},k}\boldsymbol{\mathcal{T}}_{\mathrm{op},\ell}^{-1}\boldsymbol{\epsilon}_\ell\right)^{\wedge}\right)\exp\left(-\boldsymbol{\epsilon}_k^{\wedge}\right)\right)^{\vee}, \tag{9.175}$$

where $\mathcal{T}_{\mathrm{op},k} = \mathrm{Ad}(\mathbf{T}_{\mathrm{op},k})$. Since both ϵ_ℓ and ϵ_k will be converging toward zero, we can combine these approximately and write

$$\mathbf{e}_{k\ell}(\mathbf{x}) \approx \ln\left(\exp\left(\mathbf{e}_{k\ell}(\mathbf{x}_{\mathrm{op}})^\wedge\right)\exp\left(\left(\mathcal{T}_{\mathrm{op},k}\mathcal{T}_{\mathrm{op},\ell}^{-1}\epsilon_\ell - \epsilon_k\right)^\wedge\right)\right)^\vee, \quad (9.176)$$

where we have also defined

$$\mathbf{e}_{k\ell}(\mathbf{x}_{\mathrm{op}}) = \ln\left(\bar{\mathbf{T}}_{k\ell}\mathbf{T}_{\mathrm{op},\ell}\mathbf{T}_{\mathrm{op},k}^{-1}\right)^\vee, \qquad (9.177a)$$

$$\mathbf{x}_{\mathrm{op}} = \{\mathbf{T}_{\mathrm{op},1}, \ldots, \mathbf{T}_{\mathrm{op},K}\}. \qquad (9.177b)$$

Finally, we can use the BCH approximation in (8.105) to write our linearized error as

$$\mathbf{e}_{k\ell}(\mathbf{x}) \approx \mathbf{e}_{k\ell}(\mathbf{x}_{\mathrm{op}}) - \mathbf{G}_{k\ell}\,\delta\mathbf{x}_{k\ell}, \qquad (9.178)$$

where

$$\mathbf{G}_{k\ell} = \left[-\mathcal{J}\left(-\mathbf{e}_{k\ell}(\mathbf{x}_{\mathrm{op}})\right)^{-1}\mathcal{T}_{\mathrm{op},k}\mathcal{T}_{\mathrm{op},\ell}^{-1} \quad \mathcal{J}\left(-\mathbf{e}_{k\ell}(\mathbf{x}_{\mathrm{op}})\right)^{-1}\right], \quad (9.179a)$$

$$\delta\mathbf{x}_{k\ell} = \begin{bmatrix}\epsilon_\ell \\ \epsilon_k\end{bmatrix}. \qquad (9.179b)$$

We may choose to approximate $\mathcal{J} \approx \mathbf{1}$ to keep things simple, but as we saw in Section 8.3.6, keeping the full expression has some benefit. This is because, even after convergence, $\mathbf{e}_{k\ell}(\mathbf{x}_{\mathrm{op}}) \neq \mathbf{0}$; these are the non-zero residual errors for this least-squares problem.

With our linearized error expression in hand, we can now define the ML objective function as

$$J(\mathbf{x}) = \frac{1}{2}\sum_{k,\ell}\mathbf{e}_{k\ell}(\mathbf{x})^T\mathbf{\Sigma}_{k\ell}^{-1}\mathbf{e}_{k\ell}(\mathbf{x}), \qquad (9.180)$$

where we note that there will be one term in the sum for each relative pose measurement in the pose graph. Inserting our approximate error expression, we have

$$J(\mathbf{x}) \approx \frac{1}{2}\sum_{k,\ell}\left(\mathbf{e}_{k\ell}(\mathbf{x}_{\mathrm{op}}) - \mathbf{G}_{k\ell}\mathbf{P}_{k\ell}\,\delta\mathbf{x}\right)^T\mathbf{\Sigma}_{k\ell}^{-1}\left(\mathbf{e}_{k\ell}(\mathbf{x}_{\mathrm{op}}) - \mathbf{G}_{k\ell}\mathbf{P}_{k\ell}\,\delta\mathbf{x}\right),$$

$$(9.181)$$

or

$$J(\mathbf{x}) \approx J(\mathbf{x}_{\mathrm{op}}) - \mathbf{b}^T\,\delta\mathbf{x} + \frac{1}{2}\delta\mathbf{x}^T\mathbf{A}\,\delta\mathbf{x}, \qquad (9.182)$$

where

$$\mathbf{b} = \sum_{k,\ell}\mathbf{P}_{k\ell}^T\mathbf{G}_{k\ell}^T\mathbf{\Sigma}_{k\ell}^{-1}\mathbf{e}_{k\ell}(\mathbf{x}_{\mathrm{op}}), \qquad (9.183a)$$

$$\mathbf{A} = \sum_{k,\ell}\mathbf{P}_{k\ell}^T\mathbf{G}_{k\ell}^T\mathbf{\Sigma}_{k\ell}^{-1}\mathbf{G}_{k\ell}\mathbf{P}_{k\ell}, \qquad (9.183b)$$

$$\delta\mathbf{x}_{k\ell} = \mathbf{P}_{k\ell}\,\delta\mathbf{x}, \qquad (9.183c)$$

and $\mathbf{P}_{k\ell}$ is a projection matrix to pick out the $k\ell$th perturbation variables from the full perturbation state,

$$\delta\mathbf{x} = \begin{bmatrix} \boldsymbol{\epsilon}_1 \\ \vdots \\ \boldsymbol{\epsilon}_K \end{bmatrix}. \tag{9.184}$$

Our approximate objective function is now exactly quadratic and we minimize $J(\mathbf{x})$ with respect to $\delta\mathbf{x}$ by taking the derivative:

$$\frac{\partial J(\mathbf{x})}{\partial\,\delta\mathbf{x}^T} = -\mathbf{b} + \mathbf{A}\,\delta\mathbf{x}. \tag{9.185}$$

Setting this to zero, the optimal perturbation, $\delta\mathbf{x}^\star$, is the solution to the following linear system:

$$\mathbf{A}\,\delta\mathbf{x}^\star = \mathbf{b}. \tag{9.186}$$

As usual, the procedure iterates between solving (9.186) for the optimal perturbation,

$$\delta\mathbf{x}^\star = \begin{bmatrix} \boldsymbol{\epsilon}_1^\star \\ \vdots \\ \boldsymbol{\epsilon}_K^\star \end{bmatrix}, \tag{9.187}$$

and updating the nominal quantities using the optimal perturbations according to our original scheme,

$$\mathbf{T}_{\mathrm{op},k} \leftarrow \exp\left(\boldsymbol{\epsilon}_k^{\star\wedge}\right)\mathbf{T}_{\mathrm{op},k}, \tag{9.188}$$

which ensures that $\mathbf{T}_{\mathrm{op},k} \in SE(3)$. We continue until some convergence criterion is met. Once converged, we set $\hat{\mathbf{T}}_{k0} = \mathbf{T}_{\mathrm{op},k}$ at the last iteration as the final estimates for the vehicle poses relative to pose 0.

9.3.3 Initialization

There are several ways to initialize the operating point, $\mathbf{x}_{\mathrm{op}}$, at the start of the Gauss–Newton procedure. A common method is to find a spanning tree as in Figure 9.4; the initial values of the pose variables can be found by compounding (a subset of) the relative pose measurements outward from the chosen privileged node 0. Note, the spanning tree is not unique and as such different initialization can be computed. A shallow spanning tree is preferable over a deep one so that as little uncertainty as possible is accumulated to any given node.

9.3.4 Exploiting Sparsity

There is inherent sparsity in pose graphs, and this can be exploited to make the pose-graph relaxation procedure more computationally efficient.[12] As shown in

---

[12] The method in this section should be viewed as an approximation to the brute-force approach in the previous section, owing to the fact that it is a nonlinear system.

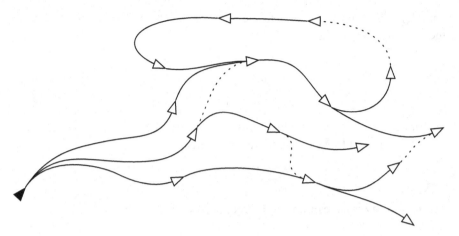

Figure 9.5, some nodes (shown as open triangles) in the pose graph have either
one or two edges, creating two types of *local chains*:

    (i) Constrained: both ends of the chain have a junction (closed-triangle)
       node and thus the chain's measurements are important to the rest of the
       pose graph.

   (ii) Cantilevered: only one end of the chain has a junction (closed-triangle)
       node and thus the chain's measurements do not affect the rest of the
       pose graph.

We can use any of the pose-compounding methods from Section 8.3.3 to combine
the relative pose measurements associated with the constrained local chains and
then treat this as a new relative pose measurement that replaces its constituents.
Once this is done, we can use the pose-graph relaxation approach to solve for the
reduced pose graph formed from only the junction (shown as closed-triangle)
nodes.

    Afterwards, we can treat all the junction nodes as fixed, and solve for the
local chain (open-triangle) nodes. For those nodes in cantilevered local chains,
we can simply use one of the pose-compounding methods from Section 8.3.3 to
compound outward from the one junction (closed-triangle) node associated with
the chain. The cost of this compounding procedure is linear in the length of the
local chain (and iteration is not required).

    For each constrained local chain, we can run a smaller pose-graph relaxa-
tion just for that chain to solve for its nodes. In this case, the two bounding
junction (closed-triangle) nodes will be fixed. If we order the variables sequentially along the local chain, the $\mathbf{A}$ matrix for this pose-graph relaxation will be
block-tridiagonal and thus the cost of each iteration will be linear in the length
of the chain (i.e., sparse Cholesky decomposition followed by forward-backward
passes).

    This two-phased approach to pose-graph relaxation is not the only way to
exploit the inherent sparsity in order to gain computational efficiency. A good
sparse solver should be able to exploit the sparsity in the $\mathbf{A}$ matrix for the full
system as well, avoiding the need to identify and bookkeep all of the local chains.

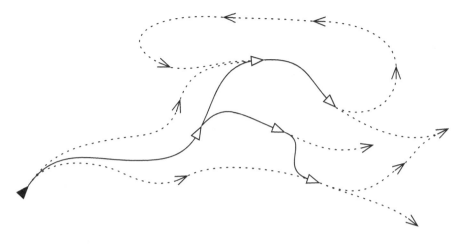

Figure 9.5 The pose-graph relaxation method can be sped up by exploiting the inherent sparsity in the pose graph. The open-triangle nodes only have one or two edges and thus do not need to be solved for initially. Instead, the relative measurements passing through the open-triangle nodes (dotted) are combined, allowing the closed-triangle nodes to be solved for much more efficiently. The open-triangle nodes also can be solved for afterwards.

9.3.5 Chain Example

It is worthwhile to provide an example of pose-graph relaxation for the short constrained chain in Figure 9.6. We only need to solve for poses 1, 2, 3, and 4 since 0 and 5 are fixed. The $\mathbf{A}$ matrix for this example is given by

$$
\mathbf{A} = \begin{bmatrix} \mathbf{A}_{11} & \mathbf{A}_{12} & & \\ \mathbf{A}_{12}^T & \mathbf{A}_{22} & \mathbf{A}_{23} & \\ & \mathbf{A}_{23}^T & \mathbf{A}_{33} & \mathbf{A}_{34} \\ & & \mathbf{A}_{34}^T & \mathbf{A}_{44} \end{bmatrix}
$$

$$
= \begin{bmatrix} \boldsymbol{\Sigma}_{10}^{\prime -1} + \boldsymbol{\mathcal{T}}_{21}^T \boldsymbol{\Sigma}_{21}^{\prime -1} \boldsymbol{\mathcal{T}}_{21} & -\boldsymbol{\mathcal{T}}_{21}^T \boldsymbol{\Sigma}_{21}^{\prime -1} & & \\ -\boldsymbol{\Sigma}_{21}^{\prime -1} \boldsymbol{\mathcal{T}}_{21} & \boldsymbol{\Sigma}_{21}^{\prime -1} + \boldsymbol{\mathcal{T}}_{32}^T \boldsymbol{\Sigma}_{32}^{\prime -1} \boldsymbol{\mathcal{T}}_{32} & -\boldsymbol{\mathcal{T}}_{32}^T \boldsymbol{\Sigma}_{32}^{\prime -1} & \\ & -\boldsymbol{\Sigma}_{32}^{\prime -1} \boldsymbol{\mathcal{T}}_{32} & \boldsymbol{\Sigma}_{32}^{\prime -1} + \boldsymbol{\mathcal{T}}_{43}^T \boldsymbol{\Sigma}_{43}^{\prime -1} \boldsymbol{\mathcal{T}}_{43} & -\boldsymbol{\mathcal{T}}_{43}^T \boldsymbol{\Sigma}_{43}^{\prime -1} \\ & & -\boldsymbol{\Sigma}_{43}^{\prime -1} \boldsymbol{\mathcal{T}}_{43} & \boldsymbol{\Sigma}_{43}^{\prime -1} + \boldsymbol{\mathcal{T}}_{54}^T \boldsymbol{\Sigma}_{54}^{\prime -1} \boldsymbol{\mathcal{T}}_{54} \end{bmatrix}
$$

$$(9.189)$$

where

$$
\boldsymbol{\Sigma}_{k\ell}^{\prime -1} = \boldsymbol{\mathcal{J}}_{k\ell}^{-T} \boldsymbol{\Sigma}_{k\ell}^{-1} \boldsymbol{\mathcal{J}}_{k\ell}^{-1}, \tag{9.190a}
$$

$$
\boldsymbol{\mathcal{T}}_{k\ell} = \boldsymbol{\mathcal{T}}_{\mathrm{op},k} \boldsymbol{\mathcal{T}}_{\mathrm{op},\ell}^{-1}, \tag{9.190b}
$$

$$
\boldsymbol{\mathcal{J}}_{k\ell} = \boldsymbol{\mathcal{J}}\left(-\mathbf{e}_{k\ell}(\mathbf{x}_{\mathrm{op}})\right). \tag{9.190c}
$$

The $\mathbf{b}$ matrix is given by

$$
\mathbf{b} = \begin{bmatrix} \mathbf{b}_1 \\ \mathbf{b}_2 \\ \mathbf{b}_3 \\ \mathbf{b}_4 \end{bmatrix} = \begin{bmatrix} \boldsymbol{\mathcal{J}}_{10}^{-T} \boldsymbol{\Sigma}_{10}^{-1} \mathbf{e}_{10}(\mathbf{x}_{\mathrm{op}}) - \boldsymbol{\mathcal{T}}_{21}^T \boldsymbol{\mathcal{J}}_{21}^{-T} \boldsymbol{\Sigma}_{21}^{-1} \mathbf{e}_{21}(\mathbf{x}_{\mathrm{op}}) \\ \boldsymbol{\mathcal{J}}_{21}^{-T} \boldsymbol{\Sigma}_{21}^{-1} \mathbf{e}_{21}(\mathbf{x}_{\mathrm{op}}) - \boldsymbol{\mathcal{T}}_{32}^T \boldsymbol{\mathcal{J}}_{32}^{-T} \boldsymbol{\Sigma}_{32}^{-1} \mathbf{e}_{32}(\mathbf{x}_{\mathrm{op}}) \\ \boldsymbol{\mathcal{J}}_{32}^{-T} \boldsymbol{\Sigma}_{32}^{-1} \mathbf{e}_{32}(\mathbf{x}_{\mathrm{op}}) - \boldsymbol{\mathcal{T}}_{43}^T \boldsymbol{\mathcal{J}}_{43}^{-T} \boldsymbol{\Sigma}_{43}^{-1} \mathbf{e}_{43}(\mathbf{x}_{\mathrm{op}}) \\ \boldsymbol{\mathcal{J}}_{43}^{-T} \boldsymbol{\Sigma}_{43}^{-1} \mathbf{e}_{43}(\mathbf{x}_{\mathrm{op}}) - \boldsymbol{\mathcal{T}}_{54}^T \boldsymbol{\mathcal{J}}_{54}^{-T} \boldsymbol{\Sigma}_{54}^{-1} \mathbf{e}_{54}(\mathbf{x}_{\mathrm{op}}) \end{bmatrix}. \tag{9.191}
$$

We can see that, for this chain example, $\mathbf{A}$ is block-tridiagonal and we can therefore solve the $\mathbf{A}\,\delta\mathbf{x}^{\star} = \mathbf{b}$ equation quite efficiently using a sparse Cholesky decomposition as follows. Let

$$
\mathbf{A} = \mathbf{U}\mathbf{U}^T, \tag{9.192}
$$

Figure 9.6 Example
pose-graph
relaxation problem
for a constrained
chain of poses. Here
the black poses are
fixed and we must
solve for the white
poses, given all the
relative pose
measurements.

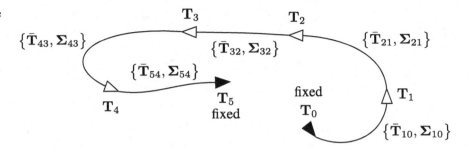

Figure 9.6 Example pose-graph relaxation problem for a constrained chain of poses. Here the black poses are fixed and we must solve for the white poses, given all the relative pose measurements.

where $\mathbf{U}$ is an upper-triangular matrix of the form

$$
\mathbf{U} = \begin{bmatrix}
\mathbf{U}_{11} & \mathbf{U}_{12} & & \\
& \mathbf{U}_{22} & \mathbf{U}_{23} & \\
& & \mathbf{U}_{33} & \mathbf{U}_{34} \\
& & & \mathbf{U}_{44}
\end{bmatrix}. \tag{9.193}
$$

The blocks of $\mathbf{U}$ can be solved for as follows:

$$\mathbf{U}_{44}\mathbf{U}_{44}^{T} = \mathbf{A}_{44} :\ \text{solve for } \mathbf{U}_{44} \text{ using Cholesky decomposition,}$$
$$\mathbf{U}_{34}\mathbf{U}_{44}^{T} = \mathbf{A}_{34} :\ \text{solve for } \mathbf{U}_{34} \text{ using linear algebra solver,}$$
$$\mathbf{U}_{33}\mathbf{U}_{33}^{T} + \mathbf{U}_{34}\mathbf{U}_{34}^{T} = \mathbf{A}_{33} :\ \text{solve for } \mathbf{U}_{33} \text{ using Cholesky decomposition,}$$
$$\mathbf{U}_{23}\mathbf{U}_{33}^{T} = \mathbf{A}_{23} :\ \text{solve for } \mathbf{U}_{23} \text{ using linear algebra solver,}$$
$$\mathbf{U}_{22}\mathbf{U}_{22}^{T} + \mathbf{U}_{23}\mathbf{U}_{23}^{T} = \mathbf{A}_{22} :\ \text{solve for } \mathbf{U}_{22} \text{ using Cholesky decomposition,}$$
$$\mathbf{U}_{12}\mathbf{U}_{22}^{T} = \mathbf{A}_{12} :\ \text{solve for } \mathbf{U}_{12} \text{ using linear algebra solver,}$$
$$\mathbf{U}_{11}\mathbf{U}_{11}^{T} + \mathbf{U}_{12}\mathbf{U}_{12}^{T} = \mathbf{A}_{11} :\ \text{solve for } \mathbf{U}_{11} \text{ using Cholesky decomposition.}$$

Then we can carry out a backward pass followed by a forward pass to solve for $\delta\mathbf{x}^{\star}$:

$$
\begin{array}{cc}
\text{backward pass} & \text{forward pass} \\
\mathbf{U}\mathbf{c} = \mathbf{b} & \mathbf{U}^{T}\delta\mathbf{x}^{\star} = \mathbf{c}
\end{array}
$$

$$
\begin{array}{cc}
\mathbf{U}_{44}\mathbf{c}_{4} = \mathbf{b}_{4} & \mathbf{U}_{11}^{T}\boldsymbol{\epsilon}_{1}^{\star} = \mathbf{c}_{1} \\
\mathbf{U}_{33}\mathbf{c}_{3} + \mathbf{U}_{34}\mathbf{c}_{4} = \mathbf{b}_{3} & \mathbf{U}_{12}^{T}\boldsymbol{\epsilon}_{1}^{\star} + \mathbf{U}_{22}^{T}\boldsymbol{\epsilon}_{2}^{\star} = \mathbf{c}_{2} \\
\mathbf{U}_{22}\mathbf{c}_{2} + \mathbf{U}_{23}\mathbf{c}_{3} = \mathbf{b}_{2} & \mathbf{U}_{23}^{T}\boldsymbol{\epsilon}_{2}^{\star} + \mathbf{U}_{33}^{T}\boldsymbol{\epsilon}_{3}^{\star} = \mathbf{c}_{3} \\
\mathbf{U}_{11}\mathbf{c}_{1} + \mathbf{U}_{12}\mathbf{c}_{2} = \mathbf{b}_{1} & \mathbf{U}_{34}^{T}\boldsymbol{\epsilon}_{3}^{\star} + \mathbf{U}_{44}^{T}\boldsymbol{\epsilon}_{4}^{\star} = \mathbf{c}_{4}
\end{array}
$$

First we proceed down the left column solving for $\mathbf{c}_4$, $\mathbf{c}_3$, $\mathbf{c}_2$, and $\mathbf{c}_1$. Then we proceed down the right column solving for $\boldsymbol{\epsilon}_1^{\star}$, $\boldsymbol{\epsilon}_2^{\star}$, $\boldsymbol{\epsilon}_3^{\star}$, and $\boldsymbol{\epsilon}_4^{\star}$. The cost of solving for each of $\mathbf{U}$, $\mathbf{c}$, and finally $\delta\mathbf{x}^{\star}$ is linear in the length of the chain. Once we solve for $\delta\mathbf{x}^{\star}$, we update the operating points of each pose variable,

$$
\mathbf{T}_{\text{op},k} \leftarrow \exp\left(\boldsymbol{\epsilon}_{k}^{\star\wedge}\right)\mathbf{T}_{\text{op},k}, \tag{9.194}
$$

and iterate the entire procedure to convergence. For this short chain, exploiting the sparsity may not be worthwhile, but for very long constrained chains the benefits are obvious.

9.4 Inertial Navigation

Inertial navigation based on data from accelerometers and gyroscopes has been a critical tool in state estimation since the Apollo program in the 1960s and 1970s; for example, an IMU was part of the Apollo Guidance Computer used in the Lunar Module (LM) during its descent to the lunar surface. The ability to dead reckon position and orientation of a vehicle is still critical in aerospace engineering and other fields today and plays a key role in some robotic state estimation. We introduced the basic sensor model for IMUs in Section 7.4.4. In this section, we will look into the details of how we can incorporate IMU data into state estimation.

Charles Stark 'Doc' Draper (1901–1987) is known as the 'father of inertial navigation'. An MIT professor, he led the development of the Apollo Guidance Computer that used *inertial measurement unit (IMU)* data (plus radar and other sensors) in an EKF to estimate the position/velocity of the Command Module on the way to the Moon and the LM state during descent to the surface.

9.4.1 Problem Setup

To recap, an *inertial measurement unit (IMU)* can measure three linear accelerations and three angular rates. If we assume that the IMU sensor frame and the vehicle frame are the same, $\underrightarrow{\mathcal{F}}_s = \underrightarrow{\mathcal{F}}_v$, we can use a simplified version of (7.154) as the IMU model:

$$\begin{bmatrix} \tilde{\mathbf{a}} \\ \tilde{\boldsymbol{\omega}} \end{bmatrix} = \begin{bmatrix} \mathbf{C}_{vi}(\mathbf{a}_i^{vi} - \mathbf{g}_i) \\ \boldsymbol{\omega}_v^{vi} \end{bmatrix}, \tag{9.195}$$

where $\tilde{\mathbf{a}}$ is measured acceleration in the vehicle frame, $\tilde{\boldsymbol{\omega}}$ is measured angular velocity in the vehicle frame, $\mathbf{g}_i$ is gravitational acceleration in the inertial frame, $\mathbf{a}_i^{vi}$ is acceleration in the inertial frame, $\mathbf{C}_{vi}$ is rotation, and $\boldsymbol{\omega}_v^{vi}$ is angular velocity in the vehicle frame.

It is very common to assume that the measured acceleration and angular rate are corrupted by slowly changing biases, $\mathbf{b}$, plus Gaussian process noise, $\mathbf{w}$, so that our overall model becomes

$$\begin{bmatrix} \tilde{\mathbf{a}} \\ \tilde{\boldsymbol{\omega}} \end{bmatrix} = \begin{bmatrix} \mathbf{C}_{iv}^T(\mathbf{a}_i^{vi} - \mathbf{g}_i) \\ \boldsymbol{\omega}_v^{vi} \end{bmatrix} + \underbrace{\begin{bmatrix} \mathbf{b}_a \\ \mathbf{b}_\omega \end{bmatrix}}_{\mathbf{b}} + \underbrace{\begin{bmatrix} \mathbf{w}_a \\ \mathbf{w}_\omega \end{bmatrix}}_{\mathbf{w}}. \tag{9.196}$$

We will take a look at incorporating these IMU measurements in filtering and batch estimation. In both cases we will have to consider that the state we are estimating at time k, $\mathbf{x}_k$, comprises the pose, the translational velocity, and the IMU biases. Whether or not we can estimate the biases from the measurements we have is a question of *observability*; see Section 5.2 for a general discussion of bias estimation.

9.4.2 Extended Poses

Because we are measuring linear acceleration with an IMU, it will become necessary to include linear velocity, $\mathbf{v}$, in our state to be estimated. The most elegant way to handle this is to extend the group of poses, $SE(3)$, to include velocity so that we have an *extended pose* of the form

$$\mathbf{T} = \begin{bmatrix} \mathbf{C} & \mathbf{r} & \mathbf{v} \\ \mathbf{0}^T & 1 & 0 \\ \mathbf{0}^T & 0 & 1 \end{bmatrix}. \tag{9.197}$$

The set of such 5×5 matrices forms another matrix Lie group called $SE_2(3)$. We will avoid formally establishing $SE_2(3)$ as it operates in a similar manner to $SE(3)$; we refer the reader to Barrau (2015), Barrau and Bonnabel (2018b), and Brossard et al. (2021) for further details on this useful group. A summary of the results we require follows.

There is, of course, a Lie algebra, $\mathfrak{se}_2(3)$, associated with this group, and an element from the algebra, $\boldsymbol{\xi} \in \mathfrak{se}_2(3)$, can once again be mapped to an element of the group, $\mathbf{T} \in SE_2(3)$, using the exponential map:

$$
\begin{aligned}
\mathbf{T} = \exp\left(\boldsymbol{\xi}^\wedge\right) = \exp\left(\begin{bmatrix} \boldsymbol{\rho} \\ \boldsymbol{\nu} \\ \boldsymbol{\phi} \end{bmatrix}^\wedge\right) &= \exp\left(\begin{bmatrix} \boldsymbol{\phi}^\wedge & \boldsymbol{\rho} & \boldsymbol{\nu} \\ \mathbf{0}^T & 0 & 0 \\ \mathbf{0}^T & 0 & 0 \end{bmatrix}\right) \\
&= \begin{bmatrix} \mathbf{C} & \mathbf{J}(\boldsymbol{\phi})\boldsymbol{\rho} & \mathbf{J}(\boldsymbol{\phi})\boldsymbol{\nu} \\ \mathbf{0}^T & 1 & 0 \\ \mathbf{0}^T & 0 & 1 \end{bmatrix} = \begin{bmatrix} \mathbf{C} & \mathbf{r} & \mathbf{v} \\ \mathbf{0}^T & 1 & 0 \\ \mathbf{0}^T & 0 & 1 \end{bmatrix},
\end{aligned} \tag{9.198}
$$

where $\mathbf{J}(\cdot)$ is the left Jacobian of $SO(3)$ and we have extended the $\wedge$ operator for $\mathfrak{se}_2(3)$ appropriately. Naturally, the mapping is again surjective only.

The 9×9 adjoint for $SE_2(3)$ is given by

$$
\begin{aligned}
\boldsymbol{\mathcal{T}} = \mathrm{Ad}(\mathbf{T}) = \exp\left(\boldsymbol{\xi}^\curlywedge\right) = \exp\left(\begin{bmatrix} \boldsymbol{\rho} \\ \boldsymbol{\nu} \\ \boldsymbol{\phi} \end{bmatrix}^\curlywedge\right) &= \exp\left(\begin{bmatrix} \boldsymbol{\phi}^\wedge & \mathbf{0} & \boldsymbol{\rho}^\wedge \\ \mathbf{0} & \boldsymbol{\phi}^\wedge & \boldsymbol{\nu}^\wedge \\ \mathbf{0} & \mathbf{0} & \boldsymbol{\phi}^\wedge \end{bmatrix}\right) \\
&= \begin{bmatrix} \mathbf{C} & \mathbf{0} & (\mathbf{J}(\boldsymbol{\phi})\boldsymbol{\rho})^\wedge\mathbf{C} \\ \mathbf{0} & \mathbf{C} & (\mathbf{J}(\boldsymbol{\phi})\boldsymbol{\nu})^\wedge\mathbf{C} \\ \mathbf{0} & \mathbf{0} & \mathbf{C} \end{bmatrix} = \begin{bmatrix} \mathbf{C} & \mathbf{0} & \mathbf{r}^\wedge\mathbf{C} \\ \mathbf{0} & \mathbf{C} & \mathbf{v}^\wedge\mathbf{C} \\ \mathbf{0} & \mathbf{0} & \mathbf{C} \end{bmatrix},
\end{aligned} \tag{9.199}
$$

where we have extended the $\curlywedge$ operator for $\mathrm{ad}(\mathfrak{se}_2(3))$. The identities,

$$
\begin{aligned}
(\boldsymbol{\mathcal{T}}\boldsymbol{\xi})^\wedge &= \mathbf{T}\boldsymbol{\xi}^\wedge\mathbf{T}^{-1}, & \text{(9.200a)} \\
(\boldsymbol{\mathcal{T}}\boldsymbol{\xi})^\curlywedge &= \boldsymbol{\mathcal{T}}\boldsymbol{\xi}^\curlywedge\boldsymbol{\mathcal{T}}^{-1}, & \text{(9.200b)} \\
\exp\left((\boldsymbol{\mathcal{T}}\boldsymbol{\xi})^\wedge\right) &= \mathbf{T}\exp\left(\boldsymbol{\xi}^\wedge\right)\mathbf{T}^{-1}, & \text{(9.200c)} \\
\exp\left((\boldsymbol{\mathcal{T}}\boldsymbol{\xi})^\curlywedge\right) &= \boldsymbol{\mathcal{T}}\exp\left(\boldsymbol{\xi}^\curlywedge\right)\boldsymbol{\mathcal{T}}^{-1}, & \text{(9.200d)}
\end{aligned}
$$

still hold for $SE_2(3)$.

The inverses of $\mathbf{T}$ and $\boldsymbol{\mathcal{T}}$ are

$$
\mathbf{T}^{-1} = \begin{bmatrix} \mathbf{C}^T & -\mathbf{C}^T\mathbf{r} & -\mathbf{C}^T\mathbf{v} \\ \mathbf{0}^T & 1 & 0 \\ \mathbf{0}^T & 0 & 1 \end{bmatrix}, \quad \boldsymbol{\mathcal{T}}^{-1} = \begin{bmatrix} \mathbf{C}^T & \mathbf{0} & -\mathbf{C}^T\mathbf{r}^\wedge \\ \mathbf{0} & \mathbf{C}^T & -\mathbf{C}^T\mathbf{v}^\wedge \\ \mathbf{0} & \mathbf{0} & \mathbf{C}^T \end{bmatrix}. \tag{9.201}
$$

The (left) Jacobian of $SE_2(3)$, $\boldsymbol{\mathcal{J}}$, is given by

$$
\boldsymbol{\mathcal{J}}(\boldsymbol{\xi}) = \begin{bmatrix} \mathbf{J}(\boldsymbol{\phi}) & \mathbf{0} & \mathbf{Q}(\boldsymbol{\phi}, \boldsymbol{\rho}) \\ \mathbf{0} & \mathbf{J}(\boldsymbol{\phi}) & \mathbf{Q}(\boldsymbol{\phi}, \boldsymbol{\nu}) \\ \mathbf{0} & \mathbf{0} & \mathbf{J}(\boldsymbol{\phi}) \end{bmatrix}, \tag{9.202}
$$

where $\mathbf{Q}(\cdot, \cdot)$ is provided in (8.91a) and should not be confused with further uses of $\mathbf{Q}$ in the following sections to mean process-noise covariance.

9.4.3 Motion Model

Although we could treat the IMU data as measurements of our state obtained through an observation model, it is more common to treat them as inputs to a motion model (Lupton and Sukkarieh, 2012; Forster et al., 2015). Typically, the translation and velocity variables are stored in the global frame when working with an IMU. As such, the continuous-time motion model that we will use is

$$\dot{\mathbf{C}}_{iv} = \mathbf{C}_{iv}\boldsymbol{\omega}_v^{vi^\wedge}, \tag{9.203a}$$

$$\dot{\mathbf{r}}_i^{vi} = \mathbf{v}_i^{vi}, \tag{9.203b}$$

$$\dot{\mathbf{v}}_i^{vi} = \mathbf{a}_i^{vi}. \tag{9.203c}$$

We note that the state variables can be combined into an extended pose:

$$\mathbf{T}_{iv} = \begin{bmatrix} \mathbf{C}_{iv} & \mathbf{r}_i^{vi} & \mathbf{v}_i^{vi} \\ \mathbf{0}^T & 1 & 0 \\ \mathbf{0}^T & 0 & 1 \end{bmatrix} \in SE_2(3). \tag{9.204}$$

We usually work with the inverse of this (extended) pose in this book, $\mathbf{T}_{vi}$, but we can easily reconcile these two approaches and will show how to do this later on.

Dropping the subscripts and inserting the specifics from (9.196), we have the following continuous-time motion model:

$$\dot{\mathbf{C}} = \mathbf{C}\left(\tilde{\boldsymbol{\omega}} - \mathbf{b}_\omega - \mathbf{w}_\omega\right)^\wedge, \tag{9.205a}$$

$$\dot{\mathbf{r}} = \mathbf{v}, \tag{9.205b}$$

$$\dot{\mathbf{v}} = \mathbf{C}\left(\tilde{\mathbf{a}} - \mathbf{b}_a - \mathbf{w}_a\right) + \mathbf{g}, \tag{9.205c}$$

$$\dot{\mathbf{b}}_\omega = \mathbf{w}_{b,\omega}, \tag{9.205d}$$

$$\dot{\mathbf{b}}_a = \mathbf{w}_{b,a}, \tag{9.205e}$$

where we also model the biases as a random walk. Following our approach to perturbing Lie groups, we consider a perturbation in $\mathfrak{se}_2(3)$ for the extended pose part of the state and additive perturbations for the biases:

$$\underbrace{\begin{bmatrix} \mathbf{C} & \mathbf{r} & \mathbf{v} \\ \mathbf{0}^T & 1 & 0 \\ \mathbf{0}^T & 0 & 1 \end{bmatrix}}_{\mathbf{T}} = \underbrace{\begin{bmatrix} \bar{\mathbf{C}} & \bar{\mathbf{r}} & \bar{\mathbf{v}} \\ \mathbf{0}^T & 1 & 0 \\ \mathbf{0}^T & 0 & 1 \end{bmatrix}}_{\bar{\mathbf{T}}} \underbrace{\begin{bmatrix} \exp\left(\delta\boldsymbol{\phi}^\wedge\right) & \mathbf{J}(\delta\boldsymbol{\phi})\delta\boldsymbol{\rho} & \mathbf{J}(\delta\boldsymbol{\phi})\delta\boldsymbol{\nu} \\ \mathbf{0}^T & 1 & 0 \\ \mathbf{0}^T & 0 & 1 \end{bmatrix}}_{\exp(\delta\boldsymbol{\xi}^\wedge)}, \tag{9.206a}$$

$$\mathbf{b}_\omega = \bar{\mathbf{b}}_\omega + \delta\mathbf{b}_\omega, \quad \mathbf{b}_a = \bar{\mathbf{b}}_a + \delta\mathbf{b}_a. \tag{9.206b}$$

This is the only place where we do a right-hand perturbation in the book, and it therefore serves as a good example thereof; this is consistent with our earlier approach since we have always kept the perturbations on the 'vehicle' side of the pose and we are now working with $\mathbf{T}_{iv}$ rather than $\mathbf{T}_{vi}$, as this is the most appropriate way to express the IMU motion model.

Using these perturbations and following the approach first introduced in Section 8.2.3, we can separate the motion model into a nominal component,

$$\underbrace{\begin{bmatrix} \dot{\bar{\mathbf{C}}} & \dot{\bar{\mathbf{r}}} & \dot{\bar{\mathbf{v}}} \\ \mathbf{0}^T & 0 & 0 \\ \mathbf{0}^T & 0 & 0 \end{bmatrix}}_{\dot{\bar{\mathbf{T}}}} = \underbrace{\begin{bmatrix} \bar{\mathbf{C}} & \bar{\mathbf{r}} & \bar{\mathbf{v}} \\ \mathbf{0}^T & 1 & 0 \\ \mathbf{0}^T & 0 & 1 \end{bmatrix}}_{\bar{\mathbf{T}}} \underbrace{\begin{bmatrix} \bar{\boldsymbol{\omega}}^\wedge & \mathbf{0} & \bar{\mathbf{a}} \\ \mathbf{0}^T & 0 & 0 \\ \mathbf{0}^T & 1 & 0 \end{bmatrix}}_{\Omega} + \underbrace{\begin{bmatrix} \mathbf{0} & \mathbf{0} & \mathbf{g} \\ \mathbf{0}^T & 0 & 0 \\ \mathbf{0}^T & -1 & 0 \end{bmatrix}}_{\Gamma}, \quad (9.207a)$$

$$\dot{\bar{\mathbf{b}}}_\omega = \mathbf{0}, \quad \dot{\bar{\mathbf{b}}}_a = \mathbf{0}, \quad (9.207b)$$

and a perturbation component,

$$\underbrace{\begin{bmatrix} \delta\dot{\boldsymbol{\rho}} \\ \delta\dot{\boldsymbol{\nu}} \\ \delta\dot{\boldsymbol{\phi}} \\ \delta\dot{\mathbf{b}}_\omega \\ \delta\dot{\mathbf{b}}_a \end{bmatrix}}_{\delta\dot{\mathbf{x}}} = \underbrace{\begin{bmatrix} -\bar{\boldsymbol{\omega}}^\wedge & 1 & 0 & 0 & 0 \\ 0 & -\bar{\boldsymbol{\omega}}^\wedge & -\bar{\mathbf{a}}^\wedge & 0 & -1 \\ 0 & 0 & -\bar{\boldsymbol{\omega}}^\wedge & -1 & 0 \\ 0 & 0 & 0 & 0 & 0 \\ 0 & 0 & 0 & 0 & 0 \end{bmatrix}}_{A} \underbrace{\begin{bmatrix} \delta\boldsymbol{\rho} \\ \delta\boldsymbol{\nu} \\ \delta\boldsymbol{\phi} \\ \delta\mathbf{b}_\omega \\ \delta\mathbf{b}_a \end{bmatrix}}_{\delta\mathbf{x}} + \underbrace{\begin{bmatrix} 0 & 0 & 0 & 0 \\ 0 & -1 & 0 & 0 \\ -1 & 0 & 0 & 0 \\ 0 & 0 & 1 & 0 \\ 0 & 0 & 0 & 1 \end{bmatrix}}_{L} \underbrace{\begin{bmatrix} \mathbf{w}_\omega \\ \mathbf{w}_a \\ \mathbf{w}_{b,\omega} \\ \mathbf{w}_{b,a} \end{bmatrix}}_{\mathbf{w}},$$

$$(9.208)$$

where $\bar{\boldsymbol{\omega}} = \tilde{\boldsymbol{\omega}} - \bar{\mathbf{b}}_\omega$ and $\bar{\mathbf{a}} = \tilde{\mathbf{a}} - \bar{\mathbf{b}}_a$. The nominal model appears to be a LTV system but is actually nonlinear due to the fact that the biases are contained in $\bar{\boldsymbol{\omega}}$ and $\bar{\mathbf{a}}$. The perturbation model is a LTV system. These two models will be key to our development in the next sections. We will use the nominal model to propagate the mean and the perturbation model to propagate uncertainty, as we have done several times throughout the book.

9.4.4 Propagating the Mean

IMUs can produce data at a very high rate (e.g., hundreds or thousands of times per second). We will thus make two key assumptions: (i) the IMU measurements are piecewise constant and thus constant over a small interval, (τ_{j-1}, τ_j), and (ii) the biases are constant over this same interval (and possibly an even larger interval). Our goal in this section is to integrate (9.207) from τ_{j-1} to τ_j.

The biases are trivial to integrate. We simply have that $\bar{\mathbf{b}}_\omega(\tau_j) = \bar{\mathbf{b}}_\omega(\tau_{j-1})$ and $\bar{\mathbf{b}}_a(\tau_j) = \bar{\mathbf{b}}_a(\tau_{j-1})$, which matches our assumption that the biases are constant over an interval larger than our integration interval.

With both the biases and the IMU measurements constant over our integration interval, $\bar{\boldsymbol{\omega}}$ and $\bar{\mathbf{a}}$ are constant and thus the extended-pose dynamics in (9.207a) become a LTI system. The solution will be of the form (see Appendix C.3)

$$\bar{\mathbf{T}}(\tau_j) = \bar{\mathbf{T}}(\tau_{j-1})\bar{\boldsymbol{\Phi}}(\tau_{j-1}, \tau_j) + \underbrace{\int_{\tau_{j-1}}^{\tau_j} \Gamma\, \bar{\boldsymbol{\Phi}}(t, \tau_j)\, dt}_{\Lambda(\Delta\tau_j)}, \quad (9.209)$$

where the transition function for this (right-hand) LTI system is

$$
\begin{aligned}
\bar{\boldsymbol{\Phi}}(\tau_{j-1}, \tau_j) &= \exp\left(\boldsymbol{\Omega}(\tau_j)\,\Delta\tau_j\right) \\
&= \begin{bmatrix} \exp\left(\Delta\tau_j\,\bar{\boldsymbol{\omega}}_j^\wedge\right) & \frac{1}{2}\Delta\tau_j^2\,\mathbf{N}(\Delta\tau_j\,\bar{\boldsymbol{\omega}}_j)\,\bar{\mathbf{a}}_j & \Delta\tau_j\,\mathbf{J}(\Delta\tau_j\,\bar{\boldsymbol{\omega}}_j)\,\bar{\mathbf{a}}_j \\ \mathbf{0}^T & 1 & 0 \\ \mathbf{0}^T & \Delta\tau_j & 1 \end{bmatrix}, \quad (9.210)
\end{aligned}
$$

and where $\Delta\tau_j = \tau_j - \tau_{j-1}$, $\boldsymbol{\Omega}(\tau_j)$ is evaluated at $\bar{\boldsymbol{\omega}}_j = \tilde{\boldsymbol{\omega}}(\tau_j) - \mathbf{b}_\omega$ and $\bar{\mathbf{a}}_j = \tilde{\mathbf{a}}(\tau_j) - \mathbf{b}_a$, and $\tilde{\boldsymbol{\omega}}(\tau_j)$ and $\tilde{\mathbf{a}}(\tau_j)$ are the constant IMU measurements over the interval (τ_{j-1}, τ_j).

The matrix, $\mathbf{J}(\cdot)$, is the left Jacobian of $SO(3)$ and $\mathbf{N}(\cdot)$ is a new matrix function that is in general given by

$$
\begin{aligned}
\mathbf{N}(\phi\mathbf{a}) &= 2\int_0^1 \alpha\,\mathbf{J}(\alpha\phi\mathbf{a})\,d\alpha = 2\sum_{n=0}^\infty \frac{1}{(n+2)!}\,(\phi\mathbf{a}^\wedge)^n \\
&= 2\frac{1-\cos\phi}{\phi^2}\mathbf{1} + \left(1 - 2\frac{1-\cos\phi}{\phi^2}\right)\mathbf{a}\mathbf{a}^T + 2\frac{\phi-\sin\phi}{\phi^2}\mathbf{a}^\wedge, \quad (9.211)
\end{aligned}
$$

where ϕ is an angle and $\mathbf{a}$ is a unit-length axis of rotation.

The remaining integral in (9.209) is also easily evaluated as

$$
\begin{aligned}
\boldsymbol{\Lambda}(\Delta\tau_j) &= \int_{\tau_{j-1}}^{\tau_j} \boldsymbol{\Gamma}\,\bar{\boldsymbol{\Phi}}(t, \tau_j)\,dt = \int_{\tau_{j-1}}^{\tau_j} \begin{bmatrix} \mathbf{0} & (\tau_j - t)\mathbf{g} & \mathbf{g} \\ \mathbf{0}^T & 0 & 0 \\ \mathbf{0}^T & -1 & 0 \end{bmatrix} dt \\
&= \begin{bmatrix} \mathbf{0} & \frac{1}{2}\Delta\tau_j^2\,\mathbf{g} & \Delta\tau_j\,\mathbf{g} \\ \mathbf{0}^T & 0 & 0 \\ \mathbf{0}^T & -\Delta\tau_j & 0 \end{bmatrix}. \quad (9.212)
\end{aligned}
$$

Finally, we can reassemble all the pieces of (9.209) and summarize the resulting discrete-time update as

$$
\bar{\mathbf{C}}(\tau_j) = \bar{\mathbf{C}}(\tau_{j-1}) \exp\left(\Delta\tau_j\,\bar{\boldsymbol{\omega}}_j^\wedge\right), \tag{9.213a}
$$

$$
\bar{\mathbf{r}}(\tau_j) = \bar{\mathbf{r}}(\tau_{j-1}) + \Delta\tau_j\,\bar{\mathbf{v}}(\tau_{j-1}) + \frac{1}{2}\Delta\tau_j^2\left(\boldsymbol{\alpha}_r(\tau_j) + \mathbf{g}\right), \tag{9.213b}
$$

$$
\bar{\mathbf{v}}(\tau_j) = \bar{\mathbf{v}}(\tau_{j-1}) + \Delta\tau_j\left(\boldsymbol{\alpha}_v(\tau_j) + \mathbf{g}\right), \tag{9.213c}
$$

where

$$
\boldsymbol{\alpha}_r(\tau_j) = \bar{\mathbf{C}}(\tau_{j-1})\,\mathbf{N}\left(\Delta\tau_j\,\bar{\boldsymbol{\omega}}_j\right)\bar{\mathbf{a}}_j, \tag{9.214a}
$$

$$
\boldsymbol{\alpha}_v(\tau_j) = \bar{\mathbf{C}}(\tau_{j-1})\,\mathbf{J}\left(\Delta\tau_j\,\bar{\boldsymbol{\omega}}_j\right)\bar{\mathbf{a}}_j, \tag{9.214b}
$$

with the biases constant. We next turn our attention to propagating the covariance.

9.4.5 Propagating the Covariance

We will use the perturbation model in (9.208) to propagate uncertainty through our motion model. In continuous time, we assume that the perturbation variables will be distributed according to a joint zero-mean, Gaussian process:

$$\delta\mathbf{x}(t) \sim \mathcal{GP}\left(\mathbf{0}, \check{\mathbf{P}}(t,t')\right), \qquad (9.215)$$

with $\check{\mathbf{P}}(t,t') = E\left[\delta\mathbf{x}(t)\,\delta\mathbf{x}(t')^T\right]$. This will be true under the assumption that the (linear) perturbation model is driven by white noise, $\mathbf{w}(t) \sim \mathcal{GP}(\mathbf{0}, \mathbf{Q}\delta(t-t'))$, with $\mathbf{Q}$ a power-spectral-density matrix (see Section 3.4.2 for further discussion of Gaussian processes).

The covariance between times $t > t_0$ and $t' > t_0$ can be obtained by stochastically integrating the perturbation model from (9.208):

$$\check{\mathbf{P}}(t,t') = \mathbf{\Phi}(t,t_0)\check{\mathbf{P}}(t_0,t_0)\mathbf{\Phi}(t',t_0)^T + \int_{t_0}^{\min(t,t')} \mathbf{\Phi}(t,s)\mathbf{L}\mathbf{Q}\mathbf{L}^T\mathbf{\Phi}(t',s)^T\,ds, \qquad (9.216)$$

where $\mathbf{\Phi}(t,t_0)$ is the transition function for our (left-hand) LTV system and $\check{\mathbf{P}}(t_0,t_0)$ is the initial covariance. If we are interested in integrating from τ_{j-1} to τ_j where the IMU measurements and biases are constant (see previous section), then we actually have a LTI system and then the transition function is simply

$$\mathbf{\Phi}(\tau_j,\tau_{j-1}) = \exp\left(\mathbf{A}_j\,\Delta\tau_j\right), \qquad (9.217)$$

where $\mathbf{A}_j = \mathbf{A}(\tau_j)$ sets $\bar{\boldsymbol{\omega}}_j = \tilde{\boldsymbol{\omega}}(\tau_j) - \bar{\mathbf{b}}_\omega$ and $\bar{\mathbf{a}}_j = \tilde{\mathbf{a}}(\tau_j) - \bar{\mathbf{b}}_a$. Then

$$\check{\mathbf{P}}(\tau_j,\tau_j) = \mathbf{\Phi}(\tau_j,\tau_{j-1})\check{\mathbf{P}}(\tau_{j-1},\tau_{j-1})\mathbf{\Phi}(\tau_j,\tau_{j-1})^T + \mathbf{Q}(\tau_j,\tau_{j-1}), \quad (9.218)$$

where

$$\mathbf{Q}(\tau_j,\tau_{j-1}) = \int_{\tau_{j-1}}^{\tau_j} \mathbf{\Phi}(\tau_j,t)\mathbf{L}\mathbf{Q}\mathbf{L}^T\mathbf{\Phi}(\tau_j,t)^T\,dt, \qquad (9.219)$$

which can be evaluated numerically with the approximation that $\Delta\tau_j$ is small (see also Appendix C.3). For example, if we approximate $\mathbf{\Phi}(\tau_j,t) \approx 1 + \mathbf{A}_j(\tau_j - t) + \cdots$, insert into (9.219), and integrate, we have

$$\mathbf{Q}(\tau_j,\tau_{j-1}) \approx \Delta\tau_j\,\mathbf{L}\mathbf{Q}\mathbf{L}^T + \frac{1}{2}\Delta\tau_j^2\left(\mathbf{A}_j\mathbf{L}\mathbf{Q}\mathbf{L}^T + \mathbf{L}\mathbf{Q}\mathbf{L}^T\mathbf{A}_j^T\right)$$
$$+ \frac{1}{6}\Delta\tau_j^3\left(2\mathbf{A}_j\mathbf{L}\mathbf{Q}\mathbf{L}^T\mathbf{A}_j^T + \mathbf{A}_j^2\mathbf{L}\mathbf{Q}\mathbf{L}^T + \mathbf{L}\mathbf{Q}\mathbf{L}^T\mathbf{A}_j^{2^T}\right), \qquad (9.220)$$

correct to $O(\Delta\tau_j^3)$[13]. This completes our propagation of the covariance.

It is worth mentioning here that

$$E\left[\left(\mathbf{\Phi}(\tau_j,\tau_{j-1})\delta\mathbf{x}(\tau_{j-1}) - \delta\mathbf{x}(\tau_j)\right)\left(\mathbf{\Phi}(\tau_j,\tau_{j-1})\delta\mathbf{x}(\tau_{j-1}) - \delta\mathbf{x}(\tau_j)\right)^T\right]$$
$$= \mathbf{Q}(\tau_j,\tau_{j-1}), \quad (9.221)$$

a result we will employ later when using IMUs for batch estimation.

---

[13] It seems we might need to keep this many terms numerically to keep $\mathbf{Q}(\tau_j,\tau_{j-1})$ positive definite.

9.4.6 Filtering

With our discrete-time motion model now in hand, we can now apply it to state estimation. In this section, we consider the filtering situation. We previously presented the EKF for a point-cloud tracking problem in (9.141). We can replace the motion model used there with the IMU one that we developed in the preceding sections.

Our state to be estimated is now

$$\mathbf{x} = \left\{ \mathbf{T}_{iv} = \begin{bmatrix} \mathbf{C}_{iv} & \mathbf{r}_i^{vi} & \mathbf{v}_i^{vi} \\ \mathbf{0}^T & 1 & 0 \\ \mathbf{0}^T & 0 & 1 \end{bmatrix}, \mathbf{b} = \begin{bmatrix} \mathbf{b}_\omega \\ \mathbf{b}_a \end{bmatrix} \right\}. \tag{9.222}$$

The estimated mean quantities at time k will be written as

$$\mathbf{x}_k = \left\{ \hat{\mathbf{T}}_k, \hat{\mathbf{b}}_k \right\}, \tag{9.223}$$

and the 15×15 covariance matrix as $\hat{\mathbf{P}}_k$, where the perturbations in (9.206) are used.

Similarly to Section 9.2.4, the EKF update equations are now as follows:

prediction step:
$$\check{\mathbf{P}}_{j=0} = \hat{\mathbf{P}}_{k-1}, \tag{9.224a}$$
$$\check{\mathbf{T}}_{j=0} = \hat{\mathbf{T}}_{k-1}, \tag{9.224b}$$
$$(j = 1 \dots J)$$
$$\check{\mathbf{P}}_j = \mathbf{F}_{j-1}\check{\mathbf{P}}_{j-1}\mathbf{F}_{j-1}^T + \mathbf{Q}_j, \tag{9.224c}$$
$$\check{\mathbf{T}}_j = \check{\mathbf{T}}_{j-1}\bar{\boldsymbol{\Phi}}_j + \boldsymbol{\Lambda}_j, \tag{9.224d}$$
$$\check{\mathbf{P}}_k = \check{\mathbf{P}}_{j=J}, \tag{9.224e}$$
$$\check{\mathbf{T}}_k = \check{\mathbf{T}}_{j=J}, \tag{9.224f}$$

correction step:
$$\mathbf{K}_k = \check{\mathbf{P}}_k\mathbf{G}_k^T \left(\mathbf{G}_k\check{\mathbf{P}}_k\mathbf{G}_k^T + \mathbf{R}_k \right)^{-1}, \tag{9.224g}$$
$$\hat{\mathbf{P}}_k = (\mathbf{1} - \mathbf{K}_k\mathbf{G}_k)\check{\mathbf{P}}_k, \tag{9.224h}$$
$$\begin{bmatrix} \boldsymbol{\epsilon}_k \\ \boldsymbol{\beta}_k \end{bmatrix} = \mathbf{K}_k (\mathbf{y}_k - \check{\mathbf{y}}_k), \tag{9.224i}$$
$$\hat{\mathbf{T}}_k = \check{\mathbf{T}}_k \exp(\boldsymbol{\epsilon}_k^\wedge), \tag{9.224j}$$
$$\hat{\mathbf{b}}_k = \hat{\mathbf{b}}_{k-1} + \boldsymbol{\beta}_k, \tag{9.224k}$$

which requires some explanation.

In the prediction step, we let $\mathbf{F}_{j-1} = \boldsymbol{\Phi}(\tau_j, \tau_{j-1})$, $\mathbf{Q}_j = \mathbf{Q}(\tau_j, \tau_{j-1})$, $\bar{\boldsymbol{\Phi}}_j = \bar{\boldsymbol{\Phi}}(\tau_{j-1}, \tau_j)$, and $\boldsymbol{\Lambda}_j = \boldsymbol{\Lambda}(\Delta\tau_j)$ (see the previous two sections for details). We use j as a local time index to allow for the fact that the prediction step will be run many times for each execution of the correction step owing to the fact that IMU data arrive at a high frequency. The prediction step uses the mean and covariance propagation developed in the previous two sections. It is worth noting that there is no prediction update for the mean of the biases, as we will assume these are constant over the interval of the prediction step.

In the correction step, the Kalman gain and posterior covariance are calculated as normal. The correction is computed as the Kalman gain times the innovation and then unstacked into the portion associated with the extended pose, ϵ_k, and the portion associated with the biases, β_k. Each part of the state is then updated using its portion of the correction. The extended pose is updated on the right (since we are using $\mathbf{T}_{iv}$) using our chosen perturbation scheme. It is important to mention that the biases will change slowly over time because they become correlated with the extended pose; when the correction step adjusts the extended pose, it also adjusts the biases through these correlations.

9.4.7 Time Machines

In this section, we introduce a set of helper matrices for $SE_2(3)$ that we will refer to as *time machines*. Consider a 5×5 matrix, $\mathbf{\Delta}$, of the form

$$\mathbf{\Delta} = \begin{bmatrix} 1 & 0 & 0 \\ \mathbf{0}^T & 1 & 0 \\ \mathbf{0}^T & \tau & 1 \end{bmatrix}, \tag{9.225}$$

where $\tau \in \mathbb{R}$ represents a time increment. The set of such matrices forms another matrix group, $\mathbb{T}$, as can be easily verified by establishing the usual properties. For example, we have an identity ($\mathbf{1} \in \mathbb{T}$), an inverse,

$$\mathbf{\Delta}^{-1} = \begin{bmatrix} 1 & 0 & 0 \\ \mathbf{0}^T & 1 & 0 \\ \mathbf{0}^T & \tau & 1 \end{bmatrix}^{-1} = \begin{bmatrix} 1 & 0 & 0 \\ \mathbf{0}^T & 1 & 0 \\ \mathbf{0}^T & -\tau & 1 \end{bmatrix} \in \mathbb{T}, \tag{9.226}$$

closure,

$$\mathbf{\Delta}_1 \mathbf{\Delta}_2 = \begin{bmatrix} 1 & 0 & 0 \\ \mathbf{0}^T & 1 & 0 \\ \mathbf{0}^T & \tau_1 & 1 \end{bmatrix} \begin{bmatrix} 1 & 0 & 0 \\ \mathbf{0}^T & 1 & 0 \\ \mathbf{0}^T & \tau_2 & 1 \end{bmatrix} = \begin{bmatrix} 1 & 0 & 0 \\ \mathbf{0}^T & 1 & 0 \\ \mathbf{0}^T & \tau_1 + \tau_2 & 1 \end{bmatrix} \in \mathbb{T}, \tag{9.227}$$

and associativity easily follows from the properties of matrix multiplication. There is an exponential-map generator for $\mathbb{T}$ so that

$$\mathbf{\Delta} = \exp\left(\begin{bmatrix} 0 & 0 & 0 \\ \mathbf{0}^T & 0 & 0 \\ \mathbf{0}^T & \tau & 0 \end{bmatrix} \right). \tag{9.228}$$

We can also define a 9×9 version of the group with an associated exponential-map generator,

$$\mathcal{D}(\mathbf{\Delta}) = \begin{bmatrix} 1 & \tau\mathbf{1} & 0 \\ 0 & 1 & 0 \\ 0 & 0 & 1 \end{bmatrix} = \exp\left(\begin{bmatrix} 0 & \tau\mathbf{1} & 0 \\ 0 & 0 & 0 \\ 0 & 0 & 0 \end{bmatrix} \right). \tag{9.229}$$

We can now take a look at how these time machines help our IMU situation.

Inspired by Brossard et al. (2021), we can now write the discrete-time mean propagation from (9.209) exactly as follows:

$$\mathbf{T}_j = \mathbf{T}_{g,j} \boldsymbol{\Delta}_j^{-1} \mathbf{T}_{j-1} \boldsymbol{\Delta}_j \boldsymbol{\Xi}_j, \tag{9.230}$$

where $\mathbf{T}_j = \bar{\mathbf{T}}(\tau_j)$ and

$$\mathbf{T}_{g,j} = \begin{bmatrix} \mathbf{1} & \frac{1}{2}\Delta\tau_j^2\,\mathbf{g} & \Delta\tau_j\,\mathbf{g} \\ \mathbf{0}^T & 1 & 0 \\ \mathbf{0}^T & 0 & 1 \end{bmatrix}, \quad \boldsymbol{\Delta}_j = \begin{bmatrix} \mathbf{1} & \mathbf{0} & \mathbf{0} \\ \mathbf{0}^T & 1 & 0 \\ \mathbf{0}^T & \Delta\tau_j & 1 \end{bmatrix},$$

$$\boldsymbol{\Xi}_j = \begin{bmatrix} \exp\left(\Delta\tau_j\,\bar{\boldsymbol{\omega}}_j^\wedge\right) & \frac{1}{2}\Delta\tau_j^2\,\mathbf{N}_j\bar{\mathbf{a}}_j & \Delta\tau_j\,\mathbf{J}_j\bar{\mathbf{a}}_j \\ \mathbf{0}^T & 1 & 0 \\ \mathbf{0}^T & 0 & 1 \end{bmatrix}, \tag{9.231}$$

with $\mathbf{N}_j = \mathbf{N}(\Delta\tau_j\,\bar{\boldsymbol{\omega}}_j)$ and $\mathbf{J}_j = \mathbf{J}(\Delta\tau_j\,\bar{\boldsymbol{\omega}}_j)$. This is an important manipulation since now our mean propagation is the product of three elements of $SE_2(3)$: $\mathbf{T}_{g,j}$, $\boldsymbol{\Delta}_j^{-1}\mathbf{T}_{j-1}\boldsymbol{\Delta}_j$, and $\boldsymbol{\Xi}_j$. The matrix $\boldsymbol{\Delta}_j^{-1}\mathbf{T}_{j-1}\boldsymbol{\Delta}_j$ has the form

$$\boldsymbol{\Delta}_j^{-1}\mathbf{T}_{j-1}\boldsymbol{\Delta}_j = \begin{bmatrix} \mathbf{C}_j & \mathbf{r}_j + \Delta\tau_j\,\mathbf{v}_j & \mathbf{v}_j \\ \mathbf{0}^T & 1 & 0 \\ \mathbf{0}^T & 0 & 1 \end{bmatrix}, \tag{9.232}$$

which we see is indeed an element of $SE_2(3)$. The matrix, $\boldsymbol{\Xi}_j$, can also be written as

$$\boldsymbol{\Xi}_j = \exp\left(\begin{bmatrix} \frac{1}{2}\Delta\tau_j^2\,\mathbf{J}_j^{-1}\mathbf{N}_j\,\bar{\mathbf{a}}_j \\ \Delta\tau_j\,\bar{\mathbf{a}}_j \\ \Delta\tau_j\,\bar{\boldsymbol{\omega}}_j \end{bmatrix}^\wedge\right), \tag{9.233}$$

which will be helpful when linearizing expressions involving the biases that are embedded in $\bar{\boldsymbol{\omega}}_j$ and $\bar{\mathbf{a}}_j$.

A very useful connection between $SE_2(3)$ and $\mathbb{T}$ is the following identity:

$$(\mathcal{D}(\boldsymbol{\Delta})\,\boldsymbol{\xi})^\wedge = \boldsymbol{\Delta}^{-1}\boldsymbol{\xi}^\wedge\boldsymbol{\Delta}, \tag{9.234}$$

where $\boldsymbol{\Delta} \in \mathbb{T}$ and $\boldsymbol{\xi} \in \mathfrak{se}_2(3)$. We therefore also have that

$$\exp\left((\mathcal{D}(\boldsymbol{\Delta})\,\boldsymbol{\xi})^\wedge\right) = \boldsymbol{\Delta}^{-1}\exp\left(\boldsymbol{\xi}^\wedge\right)\boldsymbol{\Delta} \in SE_2(3), \tag{9.235}$$

which can be verified easily by a series expansion and an application of (9.234) to each term.

The connection between $SE_2(3)$ and $\mathbb{T}$ allows us to manipulate our expressions quite freely. Consider the compounding of (9.230) over two timesteps:

$$\mathbf{T}_{j+1} = \underbrace{\mathbf{T}_{g,j+1}\boldsymbol{\Delta}_{j+1}^{-1}\mathbf{T}_{g,j}\boldsymbol{\Delta}_j^{-1}}_{\text{combine}}\mathbf{T}_{j-1}\boldsymbol{\Delta}_j\boldsymbol{\Xi}_j\boldsymbol{\Delta}_{j+1}\boldsymbol{\Xi}_{j+1}. \tag{9.236}$$

We see there is an interleaving of elements from $SE_2(3)$ and $\mathbb{T}$. We can use (9.235) to shift elements around to simplify the expression. For example, it is not hard to show that we can combine all the gravity-related elements together as

$$\mathbf{T}_{g,j+1}\boldsymbol{\Delta}_{j+1}^{-1}\mathbf{T}_{g,j}\boldsymbol{\Delta}_j^{-1} = \mathbf{T}_{g,j+1:j-1}\boldsymbol{\Delta}_{j+1:j-1}^{-1}, \tag{9.237}$$

where

$$\mathbf{T}_{g,j:\ell} = \exp \left(\begin{bmatrix} \frac{1}{2}(\tau_j - \tau_\ell)^2 \mathbf{g} \\ (\tau_j - \tau_\ell) \mathbf{g} \\ \mathbf{0} \end{bmatrix}^\wedge \right), \tag{9.238a}$$

$$\mathbf{\Delta}_{j:\ell} = \begin{bmatrix} 1 & \mathbf{0} & 0 \\ \mathbf{0}^T & 1 & 0 \\ \mathbf{0}^T & \tau_j - \tau_\ell & 1 \end{bmatrix}, \tag{9.238b}$$

and where τ_j and τ_ℓ are any two timestamps. This same process can be repeated to combine as many of these gravity elements as we like, which can reduce the number of matrix products needed to propagate the mean update over several timesteps. In the next section, we will rely heavily on our time machines to carry out further manipulations on the mean propagation update.

9.4.8 Pre-Integration for Batch Estimation

In addition to filtering, we would like to make use of IMU data in batch estimation. However, because we are now optimizing the whole trajectory at once, we would like to avoid putting a state variable at the frequency of the IMU data. Instead, we can pre-integrate a larger sequence of IMU measurements into a single MAP cost term to keep the number of state variables manageable (Lupton and Sukkarieh, 2012; Forster et al., 2015). Our approach is based on Brossard et al. (2021), who show how to exploit $SE_2(3)$ for this problem.

Error Definition

As we did in filtering, we use the local times for the pre-integration window to be $\tau_0, \tau_1, \ldots, \tau_j, \ldots, \tau_J$. We will only be estimating states at the two endpoints of the pre-integration window, τ_0 and τ_J. We can begin by defining the error that we want to minimize as

$$\mathbf{e} = \begin{bmatrix} \mathbf{e}_T \\ \mathbf{e}_b \end{bmatrix}, \tag{9.239}$$

where $\mathbf{e}_T$ is a 9×1 error for the extended pose part of the state and $\mathbf{e}_b$ is a 6×1 error for the bias part of the state given by

$$\mathbf{e}_T = \ln \left(\mathbf{T}_J^{-1} \mathbf{T}_{g,J:0} \mathbf{\Delta}_{J:0}^{-1} \mathbf{T}_0 \prod_{j=1}^{J} \mathbf{\Delta}_j \mathbf{\Xi}_j \right)^\vee, \tag{9.240a}$$

$$\mathbf{e}_b = \begin{bmatrix} \mathbf{b}_{\omega,0} - \mathbf{b}_{\omega,J} \\ \mathbf{b}_{a,0} - \mathbf{b}_{a,J} \end{bmatrix}, \tag{9.240b}$$

where $\vee$ undoes the $\wedge$ operator for $SE_2(3)$. The previous section provides the definitions of the symbols. The errors are essentially the difference between the state at the end of the window and a prediction of the same state propagated from the state at the start of the window using the IMU measurements. For the extended pose part of the state this 'difference' is computed in our now-familiar Lie group sense. We also amalgamated all of the gravity elements together based on the discussion in the previous section. It is important to mention that Ξ_j depends only on the bias part of the state and the IMU measurements.

Perturbing the Extended Poses

After having done a lot of preparation, it will come as some relief that linearizing our extended-pose error with respect to the extended poses at the start and end of the pre-integration window is straightforward. To be consistent with the rest of this section, we perform right-hand perturbations of the form

$$\mathbf{T}_j = \mathbf{T}_{\mathrm{op},j} \exp\left(\epsilon_j^\wedge\right), \tag{9.241}$$

where $\mathbf{T}_{\mathrm{op}}$ is the operating point of our linearization and ϵ_j is the perturbation. Inserting these into the error expression we see that

$$\mathbf{e}_T = \ln\left(\exp\left(-\epsilon_J^\wedge\right) \mathbf{T}_{\mathrm{op},J}^{-1} \mathbf{T}_{g,J:0} \mathbf{\Delta}_{J:0}^{-1} \mathbf{T}_{\mathrm{op},0} \exp\left(\epsilon_0^\wedge\right) \prod_{j=1}^{J} \mathbf{\Delta}_j \Xi_j\right)^\vee. \tag{9.242}$$

Using (9.200) and (9.235), we can move ϵ_0 to the left side so that

$$\mathbf{e}_T \approx \ln\left(\exp\left((\mathbf{V}_0\epsilon_0 - \epsilon_J)^\wedge\right) \mathbf{T}_{\mathrm{op},J}^{-1} \mathbf{T}_{g,J:0} \mathbf{\Delta}_{J:0}^{-1} \mathbf{T}_{\mathrm{op},0} \prod_{j=1}^{J} \mathbf{\Delta}_j \Xi_j\right)^\vee, \tag{9.243}$$

where we assume both ϵ_0 and ϵ_J are small and define

$$\mathbf{V}_0 = \mathcal{T}_{\mathrm{op},J}^{-1} \mathcal{T}_{g,J:0} \, \mathcal{D}_{J:0} \mathcal{T}_{\mathrm{op},0}, \tag{9.244}$$

with $\mathcal{T}_{\mathrm{op},J} = \mathrm{Ad}\left(\mathbf{T}_{\mathrm{op},J}\right)$ and $\mathcal{T}_{\mathrm{op},0} = \mathrm{Ad}\left(\mathbf{T}_{\mathrm{op},0}\right)$ are evaluated at the operating points, $\mathcal{D}_{J:0} = \mathcal{D}\left(\mathbf{\Delta}_{J:0}\right)$, and $\mathcal{T}_{g,J:0} = \mathrm{Ad}\left(\mathbf{T}_{g,J:0}\right)$ is a constant.

Perturbing the Biases

Unfortunately, linearizing the errors with respect to the biases is more involved, but still achievable. We only need to perturb the biases at $j = 0$ since we consider them to be held constant at these values throughout the pre-integration window. We will use the following perturbations:

$$\mathbf{b}_{\omega,0} = \mathbf{b}_{\mathrm{op},\omega,0} + \boldsymbol{\beta}_{\omega,0}, \quad \mathbf{b}_{a,0} = \mathbf{b}_{\mathrm{op},a,0} + \boldsymbol{\beta}_{a,0}, \tag{9.245}$$

where $\mathbf{b}_{\mathrm{op},\omega,0}$ and $\mathbf{b}_{\mathrm{op},a,0}$ are the operating points and $\boldsymbol{\beta}_{\omega,0}$ and $\boldsymbol{\beta}_{a,0}$ are the perturbations, respectively.

As the biases are only contained inside the Ξ_j quantities, we can begin by perturbing just one of these. We can write $\Xi_j = \exp\left(\xi_j^\wedge\right)$ with

$$\xi_j = \begin{bmatrix} \frac{1}{2}\Delta\tau_j^2 \mathbf{J}_j^{-1} \mathbf{N}_j \, \bar{\mathbf{a}}_j \\ \Delta\tau_j \, \bar{\mathbf{a}}_j \\ \Delta\tau_j \, \bar{\boldsymbol{\omega}}_j \end{bmatrix}. \tag{9.246}$$

It is only the first row that presents some challenge when perturbing with respect to the bias since both $\mathbf{J}_j$ and $\mathbf{N}_j$ depend on it. We can show in general that

$$\mathbf{J}(\phi)^{-1}\mathbf{N}(\phi) = \left(\sum_{n=0}^{\infty} \frac{B_n}{n!}(\phi^{\wedge})^n\right)\left(2\sum_{m=0}^{\infty}\frac{1}{(m+2)!}(\phi^{\wedge})^m\right)$$

$$= 2\sum_{n=0}^{\infty}\sum_{m=0}^{\infty}\frac{B_n}{n!(m+2)!}(\phi^{\wedge})^{n+m}$$

$$= 1 - \frac{1}{6}\phi^{\wedge} + \frac{1}{360}\phi^{\wedge^3} - \frac{1}{15120}\phi^{\wedge^5} + \cdots. \quad (9.247)$$

Thus, if we keep terms out to $\phi^{\wedge^3}$, we have that

$$\mathbf{J}_j^{-1}\mathbf{N}_j\,\bar{\mathbf{a}}_j \approx \underbrace{\left(1 - \frac{1}{6}\Delta\tau_j\bar{\boldsymbol{\omega}}_{\mathrm{op},j}^{\wedge} + \frac{1}{360}\Delta\tau_j^3\bar{\boldsymbol{\omega}}_{\mathrm{op},j}^{\wedge^3}\right)\bar{\mathbf{a}}_{\mathrm{op},j} - \frac{1}{6}\Delta\tau_j\bar{\mathbf{a}}_{\mathrm{op},j}^{\wedge}\boldsymbol{\beta}_{\omega,0}}_{\approx\,\mathbf{J}_{\mathrm{op},j}^{-1}\mathbf{N}_{\mathrm{op},j}}$$

$$+ \frac{1}{360}\Delta\tau_j^3\underbrace{\left(\bar{\boldsymbol{\omega}}_{\mathrm{op},j}^{\wedge^2}\bar{\mathbf{a}}_{\mathrm{op},j}^{\wedge} + \bar{\boldsymbol{\omega}}_{\mathrm{op},j}^{\wedge}(\bar{\boldsymbol{\omega}}_{\mathrm{op},j}^{\wedge}\bar{\mathbf{a}}_{\mathrm{op},j})^{\wedge} + (\bar{\boldsymbol{\omega}}_{\mathrm{op},j}^{\wedge^2}\bar{\mathbf{a}}_{\mathrm{op},j})^{\wedge}\right)}_{\mathbf{W}_j}\boldsymbol{\beta}_{\omega,0}$$

$$- \mathbf{J}_{\mathrm{op},j}^{-1}\mathbf{N}_{\mathrm{op},j}\boldsymbol{\beta}_{a,0}, \quad (9.248)$$

where $\mathbf{J}_{\mathrm{op},j} = \mathbf{J}(\Delta\tau_j\,\bar{\boldsymbol{\omega}}_{\mathrm{op},j})$, $\mathbf{N}_{\mathrm{op},j} = \mathbf{N}(\Delta\tau_j\,\bar{\boldsymbol{\omega}}_{\mathrm{op},j})$, $\bar{\boldsymbol{\omega}}_{\mathrm{op},j} = \tilde{\boldsymbol{\omega}}(\tau_j) - \mathbf{b}_{\mathrm{op},\omega,0}$, and $\bar{\mathbf{a}}_{\mathrm{op},j} = \tilde{\mathbf{a}}(\tau_j) - \mathbf{b}_{\mathrm{op},a,0}$. This expression is correct to first order in $\boldsymbol{\beta}_{\omega,0}$ and $\boldsymbol{\beta}_{a,0}$ and third order in $\Delta\tau_j\bar{\boldsymbol{\omega}}_{\mathrm{op},j}$.

Using this result, we have that

$$\boldsymbol{\xi}_j \approx \boldsymbol{\xi}_{\mathrm{op},j} + \mathbf{B}_j\boldsymbol{\beta}_0, \quad (9.249)$$

where

$$\boldsymbol{\xi}_{\mathrm{op},j} = \begin{bmatrix}\frac{1}{2}\Delta\tau_j^2\,\mathbf{J}_{\mathrm{op},j}^{-1}\mathbf{N}_{\mathrm{op},j}\,\bar{\mathbf{a}}_{\mathrm{op},j} \\ \Delta\tau_j\,\bar{\mathbf{a}}_{\mathrm{op},j} \\ \Delta\tau_j\,\bar{\boldsymbol{\omega}}_{\mathrm{op},j}\end{bmatrix}, \quad \boldsymbol{\beta}_0 = \begin{bmatrix}\boldsymbol{\beta}_{\omega,0} \\ \boldsymbol{\beta}_{a,0}\end{bmatrix}, \quad (9.250\mathrm{a})$$

$$\mathbf{B}_j = \begin{bmatrix}-\frac{1}{12}\Delta\tau_j^3\bar{\mathbf{a}}_{\mathrm{op},j}^{\wedge} + \frac{1}{720}\Delta\tau_j^5\mathbf{W}_j & -\frac{1}{2}\Delta\tau_j^2\,\mathbf{J}_{\mathrm{op},j}^{-1}\mathbf{N}_{\mathrm{op},j} \\ \mathbf{0} & -\Delta\tau_j\,\mathbf{1} \\ -\Delta\tau_j\,\mathbf{1} & \mathbf{0}\end{bmatrix}. \quad (9.250\mathrm{b})$$

To save computations, we could likely neglect the $\Delta\tau_j^3$ and $\Delta\tau_j^5$ quantities as a further approximation. We can then write that

$$\boldsymbol{\Xi}_j \approx \exp\left((\boldsymbol{\xi}_{\mathrm{op},j} + \mathbf{B}_j\boldsymbol{\beta}_0)^{\wedge}\right) \approx \underbrace{\exp(\boldsymbol{\xi}_{\mathrm{op},j}^{\wedge})}_{\boldsymbol{\Xi}_{\mathrm{op},j}}\exp\left((\boldsymbol{\mathcal{J}}(-\boldsymbol{\xi}_{\mathrm{op},j})\mathbf{B}_j\boldsymbol{\beta}_0)^{\wedge}\right),$$
$$(9.251)$$

where $\boldsymbol{\mathcal{J}}(\cdot)$ is the left Jacobian of $SE_2(3)$ provided in (9.202).

Returning to (9.243), we can use (9.200) and (9.235) to write the part on the right as

$$\prod_{j=1}^{J} \boldsymbol{\Delta}_j \boldsymbol{\Xi}_j \approx \prod_{j=1}^{J} \boldsymbol{\Delta}_j \boldsymbol{\Xi}_{\mathrm{op},j} \exp\left(\left(\boldsymbol{\mathcal{J}}(-\boldsymbol{\xi}_{\mathrm{op},j})\,\mathbf{B}_j \boldsymbol{\beta}_0\right)^{\wedge}\right)$$

$$\approx \exp\left((\mathbf{B}_0 \boldsymbol{\beta}_0)^{\wedge}\right) \prod_{j=1}^{J} \boldsymbol{\Delta}_j \boldsymbol{\Xi}_{\mathrm{op},j}, \qquad (9.252)$$

where

$$\mathbf{B}_0 = \sum_{j=1}^{J} \left(\prod_{\ell=1}^{j} \boldsymbol{\mathcal{D}}_\ell^{-1} \mathrm{Ad}(\boldsymbol{\Xi}_{\mathrm{op},\ell}) \right) \boldsymbol{\mathcal{J}}(-\boldsymbol{\xi}_{\mathrm{op},j})\,\mathbf{B}_j. \qquad (9.253)$$

We next assemble the linearized error.

Assembling the Linearized Error

Inserting (9.252) back into (9.243), and moving the bias perturbation all the way to the left, we have

$$\mathbf{e}_T \approx \ln\left(\exp\left((\mathbf{V}_0 \boldsymbol{\epsilon}_0 - \boldsymbol{\epsilon}_J + \mathbf{V}_0 \mathbf{B}_0 \boldsymbol{\beta}_0)^{\wedge}\right) \exp\left(\mathbf{e}_{\mathrm{op},T}\right)^{\wedge}\right)^{\vee}, \qquad (9.254)$$

where

$$\mathbf{e}_{\mathrm{op},T} = \ln\left(\mathbf{T}_{\mathrm{op},J}^{-1} \mathbf{T}_{g,J:0} \boldsymbol{\Delta}_{J:0}^{-1} \mathbf{T}_{\mathrm{op},0} \prod_{j=1}^{J} \boldsymbol{\Delta}_j \boldsymbol{\Xi}_{\mathrm{op},j} \right)^{\vee}. \qquad (9.255)$$

Finally then we can write

$$\mathbf{e}_T \approx \mathbf{e}_{\mathrm{op},T} + \boldsymbol{\mathcal{J}}\left(\mathbf{e}_{\mathrm{op},T}\right)^{-1} \left(\mathbf{V}_0 \boldsymbol{\epsilon}_0 - \boldsymbol{\epsilon}_J + \mathbf{V}_0 \mathbf{B}_0 \boldsymbol{\beta}_0\right) \qquad (9.256)$$

as our linearized extended-pose error expression. Combining this with the bias error expression we have

$$\underbrace{\begin{bmatrix} \mathbf{e}_T \\ \mathbf{e}_b \end{bmatrix}}_{\mathbf{e}} = \underbrace{\begin{bmatrix} \mathbf{e}_{\mathrm{op},T} \\ \mathbf{e}_{\mathrm{op},b} \end{bmatrix}}_{\mathbf{e}_{\mathrm{op}}} + \underbrace{\begin{bmatrix} \boldsymbol{\mathcal{J}}\left(\mathbf{e}_{\mathrm{op},T}\right)^{-1} \mathbf{V}_0 & \boldsymbol{\mathcal{J}}\left(\mathbf{e}_{\mathrm{op},T}\right)^{-1} \mathbf{V}_0 \mathbf{B}_0 \\ \mathbf{0} & \mathbf{1} \end{bmatrix}}_{\mathbf{F}_0} \underbrace{\begin{bmatrix} \boldsymbol{\epsilon}_0 \\ \boldsymbol{\beta}_0 \end{bmatrix}}_{\boldsymbol{\varepsilon}_0}$$

$$- \underbrace{\begin{bmatrix} \boldsymbol{\mathcal{J}}\left(\mathbf{e}_{\mathrm{op},T}\right)^{-1} & \mathbf{0} \\ \mathbf{0} & \mathbf{1} \end{bmatrix}}_{\mathbf{E}_J} \underbrace{\begin{bmatrix} \boldsymbol{\epsilon}_J \\ \boldsymbol{\beta}_J \end{bmatrix}}_{\boldsymbol{\varepsilon}_J}, \qquad (9.257)$$

which is correct to first order in $\boldsymbol{\varepsilon}_0$ and $\boldsymbol{\varepsilon}_J$.

Constructing the Full Motion Prior

To use our IMU pre-integrated cost term in batch MAP estimation, we can replace the endpoint timestamps of our pre-integration window, τ_0 and τ_J, with global timestamps, t_{k-1} and t_k. Then (9.257) can be written as

$$\mathbf{e}_{v,k}(\mathbf{x}) = \mathbf{e}_{v,k}(\mathbf{x}_{\mathrm{op}}) + \mathbf{F}_{k-1} \boldsymbol{\varepsilon}_{k-1} - \mathbf{E}_k \boldsymbol{\varepsilon}_k, \qquad (9.258)$$

which is of the same form as (9.157).

In addition to the IMU measurements, we may have some initial state knowledge of the form

$$\left\{ \check{\mathbf{T}}_0, \check{\mathbf{b}}_0 \right\},$$ (9.259)

and an associated 15×15 covariance, $\check{\mathbf{P}}_0$. The linearized error for t_0 is of the form

$$\mathbf{e}_{v,0}(\mathbf{x}) = \underbrace{\begin{bmatrix} \mathbf{e}_{v,T,0}(\mathbf{x}_{\mathrm{op}}) \\ \mathbf{e}_{v,b,0}(\mathbf{x}_{\mathrm{op}}) \end{bmatrix}}_{\mathbf{e}_{v,0}(\mathbf{x}_{\mathrm{op}})} - \underbrace{\begin{bmatrix} \boldsymbol{\mathcal{J}}\left(\mathbf{e}_{v,T,0}(\mathbf{x}_{\mathrm{op}})\right)^{-1} & \mathbf{0} \\ \mathbf{0} & \mathbf{1} \end{bmatrix}}_{\mathbf{E}_0} \underbrace{\begin{bmatrix} \boldsymbol{\epsilon}_0 \\ \boldsymbol{\beta}_0 \end{bmatrix}}_{\boldsymbol{\varepsilon}_0} \qquad (9.260)$$

where $\mathbf{e}_{v,T,0}(\mathbf{x}_{\mathrm{op}}) = \ln\left(\mathbf{T}_{\mathrm{op},0}^{-1}\check{\mathbf{T}}_0\right)^{\vee}$ and $\mathbf{e}_{v,b,0}(\mathbf{x}_{\mathrm{op}}) = \check{\mathbf{b}}_0 - \mathbf{b}_{\mathrm{op},0}$.

We can then define the stacked quantities

$$\mathbf{e}_v(\mathbf{x}_{\mathrm{op}}) = \begin{bmatrix} \mathbf{e}_{v,0}(\mathbf{x}_{\mathrm{op}}) \\ \mathbf{e}_{v,1}(\mathbf{x}_{\mathrm{op}}) \\ \vdots \\ \mathbf{e}_{v,K}(\mathbf{x}_{\mathrm{op}}) \end{bmatrix}, \quad \mathbf{Q} = \mathrm{diag}\left(\check{\mathbf{P}}_0, \mathbf{Q}_1, \ldots, \mathbf{Q}_K\right), \qquad (9.261)$$

and

$$\mathbf{F}^{-1} = \begin{bmatrix} \mathbf{E}_0 & & & & \\ -\mathbf{F}_0 & \mathbf{E}_1 & & & \\ & -\mathbf{F}_1 & \mathbf{E}_2 & & \\ & & \ddots & \ddots & \\ & & & -\mathbf{F}_{K-1} & \mathbf{E}_K \end{bmatrix}, \quad \delta\mathbf{x} = \begin{bmatrix} \boldsymbol{\varepsilon}_0 \\ \boldsymbol{\varepsilon}_1 \\ \boldsymbol{\varepsilon}_2 \\ \vdots \\ \boldsymbol{\varepsilon}_K \end{bmatrix}, \qquad (9.262)$$

where we use the symbol $\mathbf{F}^{-1}$ to remain consistent with our previous motion-prior setups from earlier chapters. Then finally our quadratic approximation of the cost term for the motion prior can be written as

$$J_v \approx \frac{1}{2}\left(\mathbf{e}_v(\mathbf{x}_{\mathrm{op}}) - \mathbf{F}^{-1}\delta\mathbf{x}\right)^T \mathbf{Q}^{-1}\left(\mathbf{e}_v(\mathbf{x}_{\mathrm{op}}) - \mathbf{F}^{-1}\delta\mathbf{x}\right), \qquad (9.263)$$

which can be combined with cost terms associated with any type of measurements we like to form a full estimation problem. For example, we could replace the motion model from Section 9.2.5 with the IMU one developed here to perform point-cloud tracking; see the next section for some hints on doing so.

The covariances, $\mathbf{Q}_k$, are constructed by computing (9.219) over each pre-integration window. From t_{k-1} to t_k there may be many IMU measurements so the covariance must be compounded over all the small increments to get an overall $\mathbf{Q}_k$. Each $\mathbf{Q}_k$ depends on the biases at that time and the IMU measurements in the window, but not on the extended pose part of the state. Typically, the $\mathbf{Q}_k$ are recalculated at each iteration of the batch estimation procedure, using the value of the biases from the previous iteration.

Naturally, at each iteration of the batch procedure we must update the state using our chosen perturbation schemes:

$$\mathbf{T}_{\text{op},k} \leftarrow \mathbf{T}_{\text{op},k} \exp\left(\boldsymbol{\epsilon}_k^{\star\wedge}\right), \tag{9.264a}$$

$$\mathbf{b}_{\text{op},k} \leftarrow \mathbf{b}_{\text{op},k} + \boldsymbol{\beta}_k^{\star}, \tag{9.264b}$$

where

$$\boldsymbol{\varepsilon}_k^{\star} = \begin{bmatrix} \boldsymbol{\epsilon}_k^{\star} \\ \boldsymbol{\beta}_k^{\star} \end{bmatrix} \tag{9.265}$$

is the optimal solution for the perturbation to the state at time k. We iterate the whole procedure to convergence.

9.4.9 Relating Left to Right

It is worth noting that in relation to our usual approach of perturbing a regular pose on the left we have that

$$\left(\mathbf{T}_{\text{op},iv} \exp(\boldsymbol{\epsilon}^{\wedge})\right)^{-1} = \exp(-\boldsymbol{\epsilon}^{\wedge})\mathbf{T}_{\text{op},vi}. \tag{9.266}$$

Notably, both types of perturbations occur on the vehicle side of the pose. This means that it is easy to convert one type of perturbation to the other; it is merely a matter of changing the sign. For example, in Section 9.2.3 on point-cloud tracking using an EKF, we used a measurement model of the form

$$\mathbf{y} = \mathbf{D}^T \mathbf{T}_{vi} \mathbf{p} = \mathbf{D}^T \mathbf{T}_{iv}^{-1} \mathbf{p}, \tag{9.267}$$

where $\mathbf{p}$ is a three-dimensional landmark. Because we are working with extended poses in this section we can let

$$\mathbf{D}^T = \begin{bmatrix} 1 & 0 & 0 & 0 & 0 \\ 0 & 1 & 0 & 0 & 0 \\ 0 & 0 & 1 & 0 & 0 \end{bmatrix}, \quad \mathbf{p} = \begin{bmatrix} x \\ y \\ z \\ 1 \\ 0 \end{bmatrix}, \tag{9.268}$$

to ensure we are ignoring the presence of the velocity in the extended pose correctly. If we do a right-hand perturbation, $\mathbf{T}_{iv} = \mathbf{T}_{\text{op},iv} \exp(\boldsymbol{\epsilon}_r^{\wedge})$, then

$$\mathbf{y} = \mathbf{D}^T \mathbf{T}_{\text{op},iv}^{-1} \mathbf{p} \underbrace{- \mathbf{D}^T \left(\mathbf{T}_{\text{op},iv}^{-1} \mathbf{p}\right)^{\odot}}_{\mathbf{G}_r} \boldsymbol{\epsilon}_r \tag{9.269}$$

is our linearized observation model with Jacobian, $\mathbf{G}_r$. The $\odot$ operator that allows $\boldsymbol{\epsilon}^{\wedge}\mathbf{p} = \mathbf{p}^{\odot}\boldsymbol{\epsilon}$, must also be modified for extended poses,

$$\mathbf{p}^{\odot} = \begin{bmatrix} \mathbf{q} \\ 1 \\ 0 \end{bmatrix}^{\odot} = \begin{bmatrix} \mathbf{1} & -\mathbf{q}^{\wedge} & \mathbf{0} \\ \mathbf{0}^T & \mathbf{0}^T & \mathbf{0}^T \\ \mathbf{0}^T & \mathbf{0}^T & \mathbf{0}^T \end{bmatrix}, \tag{9.270}$$

which now correctly ignores the velocity component. If we do a left-hand perturbation, $\mathbf{T}_{vi} = \exp(\boldsymbol{\epsilon}_\ell^\wedge)\mathbf{T}_{\mathrm{op},vi}$, then

$$\mathbf{y} = \mathbf{D}^T \mathbf{T}_{\mathrm{op},vi}\mathbf{p} + \underbrace{\mathbf{D}^T \left(\mathbf{T}_{\mathrm{op},vi}\mathbf{p}\right)^\odot}_{\mathbf{G}_\ell} \boldsymbol{\epsilon}_\ell \qquad (9.271)$$

is our linearized observation model with Jacobian, $\mathbf{G}_\ell$. Since $\boldsymbol{\epsilon}_r = -\boldsymbol{\epsilon}_\ell$, we have that $\mathbf{G}_r = -\mathbf{G}_\ell$, meaning that if we have worked out the Jacobian for one perturbation, we can easily determine the other.

10

Pose-and-Point Estimation Problems

In this chapter of the book, we will address one of the most fundamental problems in mobile robotics, estimating the trajectory of a robot and the structure of the world around it (i.e., point landmarks) together. In robotics, this is called the *simultaneous localization and mapping (SLAM)* problem. However, in computer vision an almost identical problem came to prominence through the application of aligning aerial photographs into a mosaic; the classic solution to this problem is called *bundle adjustment (BA)*. We will look at BA through the lens of our $SE(3)$ estimation techniques.

10.1 Bundle Adjustment

Photogrammetry, the process of aerial map building, has been in use since the 1920s (Dyce, 2013). It involves flying an airplane along a route, taking hundreds or thousands of pictures of the terrain below, and then stitching these together into a mosaic. In the early days, photogrammetry was a highly laborious process; printed photographs were spread out on a large surface and aligned by hand. From the late 1920s until the 1960s, clever projectors called *multiplex stereoplotters* were used to more precisely align photos, but it was still a painstaking, manual process. The first automated stitching of photos occurred in the 1960s with the advent of computers and an algorithm called bundle adjustment (Brown, 1958). Starting around the 1970s, aerial map making was gradually replaced by satellite-based mapping (e.g., the US Landsat program), but the basic algorithms for image stitching remain the same (Triggs et al., 2000). It is worth noting that the robustness of automated photogrammetry was increased significantly with the invention of modern feature detectors in computer vision, starting with the work of Lowe (2004). Today, commercial software packages exist that automate the photogrammetry process well, and they all essentially use BA for alignment.

10.1.1 Problem Setup

Figure 10.1 shows the setup for our bundle adjustment problem. The state that we wish to estimate is

$$\mathbf{T}_k = \mathbf{T}_{v_k i} : \text{ transformation matrix representing the pose}$$
$$\text{of the vehicle at time } k$$

Figure 10.1
Definition of
reference frames for
the bundle
adjustment problem.
There is a stationary
reference frame and
a moving reference
frame, attached to a
vehicle. A collection
of points, P_j, are
observed by the
moving vehicle
(using a camera) and
the goal is to
determine the
relative pose of the
moving frame with
respect to the
stationary one (at all
of the times of
interest) as well as
the positions of all of
the points in the
stationary frame.

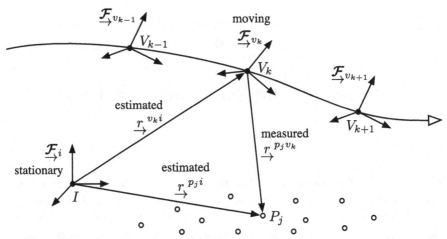

$$\mathbf{p}_j = \begin{bmatrix} \mathbf{r}_i^{p_j i} \\ 1 \end{bmatrix} : \text{ homogeneous point representing the position}$$

$$\text{of landmark } j$$

where $k = 1 \dots K$ and $j = 1 \dots M$ and we will use the cleaner version of the notation to avoid writing out all the sub- and super-scripts throughout the derivation. We will use the shorthand,

$$\mathbf{x} = \{\mathbf{T}_1, \dots, \mathbf{T}_K, \mathbf{p}_1, \dots, \mathbf{p}_M\}, \tag{10.1}$$

to indicate the entire state that we wish to estimate as well as $\mathbf{x}_{jk} = \{\mathbf{T}_k, \mathbf{p}_j\}$ to indicate the subset of the state including the kth pose and jth landmark. Notably, we exclude $\mathbf{T}_0$ from the state to be estimated, as the system is otherwise unobservable; recall the discussion in Section 5.2.3 about unknown measurement bias.

10.1.2 Measurement Model

There are two main differences between the problem treated here and the one from the previous chapter. First, we are now estimating the point positions in addition to the poses. Second, we will introduce a nonlinear sensor model (e.g., a camera) such that we have a more complicated measurement than simply the point expressed in the vehicle frame.

Nonlinear Model

The measurement, $\mathbf{y}_{jk}$, will correspond to some observation of point j from pose k (i.e., some function of $\mathbf{r}_{v_k}^{p_j v_k}$). The measurement model for this problem will be of the form

$$\mathbf{y}_{jk} = \mathbf{g}(\mathbf{x}_{jk}) + \mathbf{n}_{jk}, \tag{10.2}$$

where $\mathbf{g}(\cdot)$ is the nonlinear model and $\mathbf{n}_{jk} \sim \mathcal{N}(\mathbf{0}, \mathbf{R}_{jk})$ is additive Gaussian noise. We can use the shorthand

$$\mathbf{y} = \{\mathbf{y}_{10}, \dots \mathbf{y}_{M0}, \dots, \mathbf{y}_{1K}, \dots, \mathbf{y}_{MK}\} \tag{10.3}$$

to capture all the measurements that we have available.

As discussed in Section 8.3.7, we can think of the overall observation model as the composition of two nonlinearities: one to transform the point into the vehicle frame and one to turn that point into the actual sensor measurement through a camera (or other sensor) model. Letting

$$\mathbf{z}(\mathbf{x}_{jk}) = \mathbf{T}_k \mathbf{p}_j, \tag{10.4}$$

we can write

$$\mathbf{g}(\mathbf{x}_{jk}) = \mathbf{s}(\mathbf{z}(\mathbf{x}_{jk})), \tag{10.5}$$

where $\mathbf{s}(\cdot)$ is the nonlinear camera model.[1] In other words, we have $\mathbf{g} = \mathbf{s} \circ \mathbf{z}$, in terms of the composition of functions.

Perturbed Model

We will go one step beyond simply linearizing our model and work out the perturbed model to second order. This could be used, for example, to estimate the bias in using ML estimation, as discussed in Section 4.3.3.

We define the following perturbations to our state variables:

$$\mathbf{T}_k = \exp\left(\epsilon_k^\wedge\right) \mathbf{T}_{\mathrm{op},k} \approx \left(\mathbf{1} + \epsilon_k^\wedge + \frac{1}{2}\epsilon_k^\wedge \epsilon_k^\wedge\right) \mathbf{T}_{\mathrm{op},k}, \tag{10.6a}$$

$$\mathbf{p}_j = \mathbf{p}_{\mathrm{op},j} + \mathbf{D}\,\boldsymbol{\zeta}_j, \tag{10.6b}$$

where

$$\mathbf{D} = \begin{bmatrix} 1 & 0 & 0 \\ 0 & 1 & 0 \\ 0 & 0 & 1 \\ 0 & 0 & 0 \end{bmatrix} \tag{10.7}$$

is a dilation matrix so that our landmark perturbation, $\boldsymbol{\zeta}_j$, is 3×1. We will use the shorthand $\mathbf{x}_{\mathrm{op}} = \{\mathbf{T}_{\mathrm{op},1}, \ldots, \mathbf{T}_{\mathrm{op},K}, \mathbf{p}_{\mathrm{op},1}, \ldots, \mathbf{p}_{\mathrm{op},M}\}$ to indicate the entire trajectory's linearization operating point as well as $\mathbf{x}_{\mathrm{op},jk} = \{\mathbf{T}_{\mathrm{op},k}, \mathbf{p}_{\mathrm{op},j}\}$ to indicate the subset of the operating point including the kth pose and jth landmark. The perturbations will be denoted

$$\delta\mathbf{x} = \begin{bmatrix} \epsilon_1 \\ \vdots \\ \epsilon_K \\ \hline \boldsymbol{\zeta}_1 \\ \vdots \\ \boldsymbol{\zeta}_M \end{bmatrix}, \tag{10.8}$$

with the pose quantities on top and the landmark quantities on the bottom. We will also use

$$\delta\mathbf{x}_{jk} = \begin{bmatrix} \epsilon_k \\ \boldsymbol{\zeta}_j \end{bmatrix} \tag{10.9}$$

---

[1] See Section 7.4 for several possibilities for the camera (or sensor) model.

to indicate just the perturbations associated with the kth pose and the jth land-mark.

Using the preceding perturbation schemes, we have that

$$
\begin{aligned}
\mathbf{z}(\mathbf{x}_{jk}) &\approx \left(\mathbf{1} + \boldsymbol{\epsilon}_k^\wedge + \frac{1}{2}\boldsymbol{\epsilon}_k^\wedge\boldsymbol{\epsilon}_k^\wedge\right)\mathbf{T}_{\mathrm{op},k}\left(\mathbf{p}_{\mathrm{op},j} + \mathbf{D}\,\boldsymbol{\zeta}_j\right) \\
&\approx \mathbf{T}_{\mathrm{op},k}\mathbf{p}_{\mathrm{op},j} + \boldsymbol{\epsilon}_k^\wedge\mathbf{T}_{\mathrm{op},k}\mathbf{p}_{\mathrm{op},j} + \mathbf{T}_{\mathrm{op},k}\mathbf{D}\,\boldsymbol{\zeta}_j \\
&\quad + \frac{1}{2}\boldsymbol{\epsilon}_k^\wedge\boldsymbol{\epsilon}_k^\wedge\mathbf{T}_{\mathrm{op},k}\mathbf{p}_{\mathrm{op},j} + \boldsymbol{\epsilon}_k^\wedge\mathbf{T}_{\mathrm{op},k}\mathbf{D}\,\boldsymbol{\zeta}_j \\
&= \mathbf{z}(\mathbf{x}_{\mathrm{op},jk}) + \mathbf{Z}_{jk}\,\delta\mathbf{x}_{jk} + \frac{1}{2}\sum_i \mathbf{1}_i\,\underbrace{\delta\mathbf{x}_{jk}^T\boldsymbol{\mathcal{Z}}_{ijk}\,\delta\mathbf{x}_{jk}}_{\text{scalar}}, \quad (10.10)
\end{aligned}
$$

correct to second order, where

$$
\begin{aligned}
\mathbf{z}(\mathbf{x}_{\mathrm{op},jk}) &= \mathbf{T}_{\mathrm{op},k}\mathbf{p}_{\mathrm{op},j}, && (10.11a) \\
\mathbf{Z}_{jk} &= \left[(\mathbf{T}_{\mathrm{op},k}\mathbf{p}_{\mathrm{op},j})^\odot \quad \mathbf{T}_{\mathrm{op},k}\mathbf{D}\right], && (10.11b) \\
\boldsymbol{\mathcal{Z}}_{ijk} &= \begin{bmatrix} \mathbf{1}_i^\odot\,(\mathbf{T}_{\mathrm{op},k}\mathbf{p}_{\mathrm{op},j})^\odot & \mathbf{1}_i^\odot\mathbf{T}_{\mathrm{op},k}\mathbf{D} \\ (\mathbf{1}_i^\odot\mathbf{T}_{\mathrm{op},k}\mathbf{D})^T & \mathbf{0} \end{bmatrix}, && (10.11c)
\end{aligned}
$$

and i is an index over the rows of $\mathbf{z}(\cdot)$, and $\mathbf{1}_i$ is the ith column of the identity matrix, $\mathbf{1}$.

To then apply the nonlinear camera model, we use the chain rule (for first and second derivatives), so that

$$
\begin{aligned}
\mathbf{g}(\mathbf{x}_{jk}) &= \mathbf{s}\left(\mathbf{z}(\mathbf{x}_{jk})\right) \\
&\approx \mathbf{s}\Bigg(\underbrace{\mathbf{z}_{\mathrm{op},jk} + \mathbf{Z}_{jk}\,\delta\mathbf{x}_{jk} + \frac{1}{2}\sum_m \mathbf{1}_m\,\delta\mathbf{x}_{jk}^T\boldsymbol{\mathcal{Z}}_{mjk}\,\delta\mathbf{x}_{jk}}_{\delta\mathbf{z}_{jk}}\Bigg) \\
&\approx \mathbf{s}(\mathbf{z}_{\mathrm{op},jk}) + \mathbf{S}_{jk}\,\delta\mathbf{z}_{jk} + \frac{1}{2}\sum_i \mathbf{1}_i^T\,\delta\mathbf{z}_{jk}^T\boldsymbol{\mathcal{S}}_{ijk}\,\delta\mathbf{z}_{jk} \\
&= \mathbf{s}(\mathbf{z}_{\mathrm{op},jk}) \\
&\quad + \sum_i \mathbf{1}_i\left(\mathbf{1}_i^T\mathbf{S}_{jk}\right)\left(\mathbf{Z}_{jk}\,\delta\mathbf{x}_{jk} + \frac{1}{2}\sum_m \mathbf{1}_m\,\delta\mathbf{x}_{jk}^T\boldsymbol{\mathcal{Z}}_{mjk}\,\delta\mathbf{x}_{jk}\right) \\
&\quad + \frac{1}{2}\sum_i \mathbf{1}_i\left(\mathbf{Z}_{jk}\,\delta\mathbf{x}_{jk} + \frac{1}{2}\sum_m \mathbf{1}_m\,\delta\mathbf{x}_{jk}^T\boldsymbol{\mathcal{Z}}_{mjk}\,\delta\mathbf{x}_{jk}\right)^T \\
&\qquad\qquad \times \boldsymbol{\mathcal{S}}_{ijk}\left(\mathbf{Z}_{jk}\,\delta\mathbf{x}_{jk} + \frac{1}{2}\sum_m \mathbf{1}_m\,\delta\mathbf{x}_{jk}^T\boldsymbol{\mathcal{Z}}_{mjk}\,\delta\mathbf{x}_{jk}\right) \\
&\approx \mathbf{g}(\mathbf{x}_{\mathrm{op},jk}) + \mathbf{G}_{jk}\,\delta\mathbf{x}_{jk} + \frac{1}{2}\sum_i \mathbf{1}_i\,\underbrace{\delta\mathbf{x}_{jk}^T\boldsymbol{\mathcal{G}}_{ijk}\,\delta\mathbf{x}_{jk}}_{\text{scalar}}, \quad (10.12)
\end{aligned}
$$

correct to second order, where

$$\mathbf{g}(\mathbf{x}_{\mathrm{op},jk}) = \mathbf{s}(\mathbf{z}(\mathbf{x}_{\mathrm{op},jk})), \tag{10.13a}$$

$$\mathbf{G}_{jk} = \mathbf{S}_{jk}\mathbf{Z}_{jk}, \tag{10.13b}$$

$$\mathbf{S}_{jk} = \left.\frac{\partial \mathbf{s}}{\partial \mathbf{z}}\right|_{\mathbf{z}(\mathbf{x}_{\mathrm{op},jk})}, \tag{10.13c}$$

$$\boldsymbol{\mathcal{G}}_{ijk} = \mathbf{Z}_{jk}^T \boldsymbol{\mathcal{S}}_{ijk} \mathbf{Z}_{jk} + \sum_m \underbrace{\mathbf{1}_i^T \mathbf{S}_{jk} \mathbf{1}_m}_{\text{scalar}} \boldsymbol{\mathcal{Z}}_{mjk}, \tag{10.13d}$$

$$\boldsymbol{\mathcal{S}}_{ijk} = \left.\frac{\partial^2 s_i}{\partial \mathbf{z}\,\partial \mathbf{z}^T}\right|_{\mathbf{z}(\mathbf{x}_{\mathrm{op},jk})}, \tag{10.13e}$$

and i is an index over the rows of $\mathbf{s}(\cdot)$, and $\mathbf{1}_i$ is the ith column of the identity matrix, $\mathbf{1}$.

If we only care about the linearized (i.e., first-order) model, then we can simply use

$$\mathbf{g}(\mathbf{x}_{jk}) \approx \mathbf{g}(\mathbf{x}_{\mathrm{op},jk}) + \mathbf{G}_{jk}\,\delta\mathbf{x}_{jk} \tag{10.14}$$

for our approximate observation model.

10.1.3 Maximum Likelihood Solution

We will set up the bundle adjustment problem using the ML framework described in Section 4.3.3, which means we will not use a motion prior.[2]

For each observation of a point from a pose, we define an error term as

$$\mathbf{e}_{y,jk}(\mathbf{x}) = \mathbf{y}_{jk} - \mathbf{g}\left(\mathbf{x}_{jk}\right), \tag{10.15}$$

where $\mathbf{y}_{jk}$ is the measured quantity and $\mathbf{g}$ is our observation model described above. We seek to find the values of $\mathbf{x}$ to minimize the following objective function:

$$J(\mathbf{x}) = \frac{1}{2}\sum_{j,k} \mathbf{e}_{y,jk}(\mathbf{x})^T \mathbf{R}_{jk}^{-1} \mathbf{e}_{y,jk}(\mathbf{x}), \tag{10.16}$$

where $\mathbf{x}$ is the full state that we wish to estimate (all poses and landmarks) and $\mathbf{R}_{jk}$ is the symmetric, positive-definite covariance matrix associated with the jkth measurement. If a particular landmark is not actually observed from a particular pose, we can simply delete the appropriate term from the objective function. The usual approach to this estimation problem is to apply the Gauss–Newton method. Here we will derive the full Newton's method and then approximate to arrive at Gauss–Newton.

Newton's Method

Approximating the error function, we have

$$\mathbf{e}_{y,jk}(\mathbf{x}) \approx \underbrace{\mathbf{y}_{jk} - \mathbf{g}(\mathbf{x}_{\mathrm{op},jk})}_{\mathbf{e}_{y,jk}(\mathbf{x}_{\mathrm{op}})} - \mathbf{G}_{jk}\delta\mathbf{x}_{jk} - \frac{1}{2}\sum_i \mathbf{1}_i\,\delta\mathbf{x}_{jk}^T\,\boldsymbol{\mathcal{G}}_{ijk}\,\delta\mathbf{x}_{jk}, \quad (10.17)$$

---

[2] In robotics, when a motion prior or odometry smoothing terms are introduced, we typically call this SLAM.

and thus for the perturbed objective function, we have

$$J(\mathbf{x}) \approx J(\mathbf{x}_{\mathrm{op}}) - \mathbf{b}^T \, \delta\mathbf{x} + \frac{1}{2}\delta\mathbf{x}^T \, \mathbf{A} \, \delta\mathbf{x}, \qquad (10.18)$$

correct to second order, where

$$\mathbf{b} = \sum_{j,k} \mathbf{P}_{jk}^T \mathbf{G}_{jk}^T \mathbf{R}_{jk}^{-1} \mathbf{e}_{y,jk}(\mathbf{x}_{\mathrm{op}}), \qquad (10.19a)$$

$$\mathbf{A} = \sum_{j,k} \mathbf{P}_{jk}^T \left(\mathbf{G}_{jk}^T \mathbf{R}_{jk}^{-1} \mathbf{G}_{jk} - \overbrace{\sum_i \underbrace{\mathbf{1}_i^T \mathbf{R}_{jk}^{-1} \mathbf{e}_{y,jk}(\mathbf{x}_{\mathrm{op}})}_{\text{scalar}} \mathcal{G}_{ijk}}^{\text{Gauss–Newton neglects this term}} \right) \mathbf{P}_{jk},$$
$$(10.19b)$$

$$\delta\mathbf{x}_{jk} = \mathbf{P}_{jk}\,\delta\mathbf{x}, \qquad (10.19c)$$

where $\mathbf{P}_{jk}$ is an appropriate projection matrix to pick off the jkth components of the overall perturbed state, $\delta\mathbf{x}$.

It is worth noting that $\mathbf{A}$ is symmetric, positive-definite. We can see the term that Gauss–Newton normally neglects in the Hessian of J. When $\mathbf{e}_{y,jk}(\mathbf{x}_{\mathrm{op}})$ is small, this new term has little effect (and this is the usual justification for its neglect). However, far from the minimum, this term will be more significant and could improve the rate and region of convergence.[3] We will consider the Gauss–Newton approximation in the next section.

We now minimize $J(\mathbf{x})$ with respect to $\delta\mathbf{x}$ by taking the derivative:

$$\frac{\partial J(\mathbf{x})}{\partial\,\delta\mathbf{x}^T} = -\mathbf{b} + \mathbf{A}\,\delta\mathbf{x}. \qquad (10.20)$$

Setting this to zero, the optimal perturbation, $\delta\mathbf{x}^\star$, is the solution to the following linear system:

$$\mathbf{A}\,\delta\mathbf{x}^\star = \mathbf{b}. \qquad (10.21)$$

As usual, the procedure iterates between solving (10.21) for the optimal perturbation,

$$\delta\mathbf{x}^\star = \left[\begin{array}{c} \boldsymbol{\epsilon}_1^\star \\ \vdots \\ \boldsymbol{\epsilon}_K^\star \\ \hline \boldsymbol{\zeta}_1^\star \\ \vdots \\ \boldsymbol{\zeta}_M^\star \end{array} \right], \qquad (10.22)$$

and updating the nominal quantities using the optimal perturbations according to our original schemes,

$$\mathbf{T}_{\mathrm{op},k} \leftarrow \exp\left(\boldsymbol{\epsilon}_k^{\star\wedge} \right) \mathbf{T}_{\mathrm{op},k}, \qquad (10.23a)$$

$$\mathbf{p}_{\mathrm{op},j} \leftarrow \mathbf{p}_{\mathrm{op},j} + \mathbf{D}\,\boldsymbol{\zeta}_j^\star, \qquad (10.23b)$$

which ensure that $\mathbf{T}_{\mathrm{op},k} \in SE(3)$ and $\mathbf{p}_{\mathrm{op},j}$ keeps its bottom (fourth) entry equal to 1. We continue until some convergence criterion is met. Once converged, we

---

[3] In practice, including this extra term sometimes makes the numerical stability of the whole procedure worse, so it should be added with caution.

set $\hat{\mathbf{T}}_{v_k i} = \mathbf{T}_{\text{op},k}$ and $\hat{\mathbf{p}}_i^{p_j i} = \mathbf{p}_{\text{op},j}$ at the last iteration as the final estimates for the vehicle poses and landmark positions of interest.

Gauss–Newton Method

Typically in practice, the Gauss–Newton approximation to the Hessian is taken so that at each iteration we solve the linear system

$$\mathbf{A}\, \delta\mathbf{x}^\star = \mathbf{b}, \tag{10.24}$$

with

$$\mathbf{b} = \sum_{j,k} \mathbf{P}_{jk}^T \mathbf{G}_{jk}^T \mathbf{R}_{jk}^{-1} \mathbf{e}_{y,jk}(\mathbf{x}_{\text{op}}), \tag{10.25a}$$

$$\mathbf{A} = \sum_{j,k} \mathbf{P}_{jk}^T \mathbf{G}_{jk}^T \mathbf{R}_{jk}^{-1} \mathbf{G}_{jk} \mathbf{P}_{jk}, \tag{10.25b}$$

$$\delta\mathbf{x}_{jk} = \mathbf{P}_{jk}\, \delta\mathbf{x}. \tag{10.25c}$$

This has the significant advantage of not requiring the second derivative of the measurement model to be computed. Assembling the linear system, we find it has the form

$$\underbrace{\mathbf{G}^T \mathbf{R}^{-1} \mathbf{G}}_{\mathbf{A}}\, \delta\mathbf{x}^\star = \underbrace{\mathbf{G}^T \mathbf{R}^{-1} \mathbf{e}_y(\mathbf{x}_{\text{op}})}_{\mathbf{b}}, \tag{10.26}$$

with

$$\mathbf{G}_{jk} = \begin{bmatrix} \mathbf{G}_{1,jk} & \mathbf{G}_{2,jk} \end{bmatrix},$$
$$\mathbf{G}_{1,jk} = \mathbf{S}_{jk}\left(\mathbf{T}_{\text{op},k}\mathbf{p}_{\text{op},j}\right)^{\odot}, \quad \mathbf{G}_{2,jk} = \mathbf{S}_{jk}\mathbf{T}_{\text{op},k}\mathbf{D}, \tag{10.27}$$

using the definitions from earlier.

In the case of $K = 3$ free poses (plus fixed pose 0) and $M = 2$ landmarks, the matrices have the form

$$\mathbf{G} = \begin{bmatrix} \mathbf{G}_1 \mid \mathbf{G}_2 \end{bmatrix} = \left[\begin{array}{cccccc|cccc} & & & & & & \mathbf{G}_{2,10} & & & \\ & & & & & & & \mathbf{G}_{2,20} & & \\ \mathbf{G}_{1,11} & & & & & & \mathbf{G}_{2,11} & & & \\ \mathbf{G}_{1,21} & & & & & & & \mathbf{G}_{2,21} & & \\ & & \mathbf{G}_{1,12} & & & & \mathbf{G}_{2,12} & & & \\ & & \mathbf{G}_{1,22} & & & & & \mathbf{G}_{2,22} & & \\ & & & & \mathbf{G}_{1,13} & & \mathbf{G}_{2,13} & & & \\ & & & & \mathbf{G}_{1,23} & & & \mathbf{G}_{2,23} & & \end{array} \right],$$

$$\mathbf{e}_y(\mathbf{x}_{\text{op}}) = \begin{bmatrix} \mathbf{e}_{y,10}(\mathbf{x}_{\text{op}}) \\ \mathbf{e}_{y,20}(\mathbf{x}_{\text{op}}) \\ \mathbf{e}_{y,11}(\mathbf{x}_{\text{op}}) \\ \mathbf{e}_{y,21}(\mathbf{x}_{\text{op}}) \\ \mathbf{e}_{y,12}(\mathbf{x}_{\text{op}}) \\ \mathbf{e}_{y,22}(\mathbf{x}_{\text{op}}) \\ \mathbf{e}_{y,13}(\mathbf{x}_{\text{op}}) \\ \mathbf{e}_{y,23}(\mathbf{x}_{\text{op}}) \end{bmatrix},$$

$$\mathbf{R} = \text{diag}\left(\mathbf{R}_{10}, \mathbf{R}_{20}, \mathbf{R}_{11}, \mathbf{R}_{21}, \mathbf{R}_{12}, \mathbf{R}_{22}, \mathbf{R}_{13}, \mathbf{R}_{23}\right), \tag{10.28}$$

under one particular ordering of the measurements.

In general, multiplying out the left-hand side, $\mathbf{A} = \mathbf{G}^T\mathbf{R}^{-1}\mathbf{G}$, we see that

$$\mathbf{A} = \begin{bmatrix} \mathbf{A}_{11} & \mathbf{A}_{12} \\ \mathbf{A}_{12}^T & \mathbf{A}_{22} \end{bmatrix}, \tag{10.29}$$

where

$$\mathbf{A}_{11} = \mathbf{G}_1^T\mathbf{R}^{-1}\mathbf{G}_1 = \mathrm{diag}\left(\mathbf{A}_{11,1}, \dots, \mathbf{A}_{11,K}\right), \tag{10.30a}$$

$$\mathbf{A}_{11,k} = \sum_{j=1}^{M} \mathbf{G}_{1,jk}^T\mathbf{R}_{jk}^{-1}\mathbf{G}_{1,jk}, \tag{10.30b}$$

$$\mathbf{A}_{12} = \mathbf{G}_1^T\mathbf{R}^{-1}\mathbf{G}_2 = \begin{bmatrix} \mathbf{A}_{12,11} & \cdots & \mathbf{A}_{12,M1} \\ \vdots & \ddots & \vdots \\ \mathbf{A}_{12,1K} & \cdots & \mathbf{A}_{12,MK} \end{bmatrix}, \tag{10.30c}$$

$$\mathbf{A}_{12,jk} = \mathbf{G}_{1,jk}^T\mathbf{R}_{jk}^{-1}\mathbf{G}_{2,jk}, \tag{10.30d}$$

$$\mathbf{A}_{22} = \mathbf{G}_2^T\mathbf{R}^{-1}\mathbf{G}_2 = \mathrm{diag}\left(\mathbf{A}_{22,1}, \dots, \mathbf{A}_{22,M}\right), \tag{10.30e}$$

$$\mathbf{A}_{22,j} = \sum_{k=0}^{K} \mathbf{G}_{2,jk}^T\mathbf{R}_{jk}^{-1}\mathbf{G}_{2,jk}. \tag{10.30f}$$

The fact that both $\mathbf{A}_{11}$ and $\mathbf{A}_{22}$ are block-diagonal means this system has a very special sparsity pattern that can be exploited to efficiently solve for $\delta\mathbf{x}^\star$ at each iteration. This will be discussed in detail in the next section.

10.1.4 Exploiting Sparsity

Whether we choose to use Newton's method or Gauss–Newton, we are faced with solving a system of the following form at each iteration:

$$\underbrace{\begin{bmatrix} \mathbf{A}_{11} & \mathbf{A}_{12} \\ \mathbf{A}_{12}^T & \mathbf{A}_{22} \end{bmatrix}}_{\mathbf{A}} \underbrace{\begin{bmatrix} \delta\mathbf{x}_1^\star \\ \delta\mathbf{x}_2^\star \end{bmatrix}}_{\delta\mathbf{x}^\star} = \underbrace{\begin{bmatrix} \mathbf{b}_1 \\ \mathbf{b}_2 \end{bmatrix}}_{\mathbf{b}}, \tag{10.31}$$

where the state, $\delta\mathbf{x}^\star$, has been partitioned into parts corresponding to (1) the pose perturbation, $\delta\mathbf{x}_1^\star = \boldsymbol{\epsilon}^\star$, and (2) the landmark perturbations, $\delta\mathbf{x}_2^\star = \boldsymbol{\zeta}^\star$.

It turns out that the Hessian of the objective function, $\mathbf{A}$, has a very special sparsity pattern as depicted in Figure 10.2; it is sometimes referred to as an *arrowhead* matrix. This pattern is due to the presence of the projection matrices, $\mathbf{P}_{jk}$, in each term of $\mathbf{A}$; they embody the fact that each measurement involves just one pose variable and one landmark.

As seen in Figure 10.2, we have that $\mathbf{A}_{11}$ and $\mathbf{A}_{22}$ are both block-diagonal because each measurement involves only one pose and one landmark at a time. We can exploit this sparsity to efficiently solve (10.21) for $\delta\mathbf{x}^\star$; this is sometimes referred to as *sparse bundle adjustment*. There are a few different ways to do this; we will discuss the Schur complement and a Cholesky technique.

Schur Complement

Typically, the Schur complement is used to manipulate (10.31) into a form that is more efficiently solved. This can be seen by premultiplying both sides by

$$\mathbf{A} = $$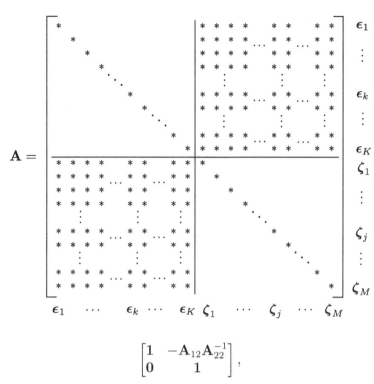

Figure 10.2
Sparsity pattern of
$\mathbf{A}$. Non-zero entries
are indicated by *.
This structure is
often referred to as
an *arrowhead*
matrix, because the
ζ part is large
compared to the ϵ
part.

$$\begin{bmatrix} \mathbf{1} & -\mathbf{A}_{12}\mathbf{A}_{22}^{-1} \\ \mathbf{0} & \mathbf{1} \end{bmatrix},$$

so that

$$\begin{bmatrix} \mathbf{A}_{11} - \mathbf{A}_{12}\mathbf{A}_{22}^{-1}\mathbf{A}_{12}^T & \mathbf{0} \\ \mathbf{A}_{12}^T & \mathbf{A}_{22} \end{bmatrix} \begin{bmatrix} \delta\mathbf{x}_1^\star \\ \delta\mathbf{x}_2^\star \end{bmatrix} = \begin{bmatrix} \mathbf{b}_1 - \mathbf{A}_{12}\mathbf{A}_{22}^{-1}\mathbf{b}_2 \\ \mathbf{b}_2 \end{bmatrix},$$

which has the same solution as (10.31). We may then easily solve for $\delta\mathbf{x}_1^\star$ and since $\mathbf{A}_{22}$ is block-diagonal, $\mathbf{A}_{22}^{-1}$ is cheap to compute. Finally, $\delta\mathbf{x}_2^\star$ (if desired) can also be efficiently computed through back-substitution, again owing to the sparsity of $\mathbf{A}_{22}$. This procedure brings the complexity of each solve down from $O\left((K + M)^3\right)$ without sparsity to $O\left(K^3 + K^2M\right)$ with sparsity, which is most beneficial when $K \ll M$.

A similar procedure can be had by exploiting the sparsity of $\mathbf{A}_{11}$, but in robotics problems we may also have some additional measurements that perturb this structure and, more importantly, $\delta\mathbf{x}_2^\star$ is usually much larger than $\delta\mathbf{x}_1^\star$ in bundle adjustment. While the Schur complement method works well, it does not directly provide us with an explicit method of computing $\mathbf{A}^{-1}$, the covariance matrix associated with $\delta\mathbf{x}^\star$, should we desire it. The Cholesky approach is better suited to this end.

Cholesky Decomposition

Every symmetric positive-definite matrix, including $\mathbf{A}$, can be factored as follows through a Cholesky decomposition:

$$\underbrace{\begin{bmatrix} \mathbf{A}_{11} & \mathbf{A}_{12} \\ \mathbf{A}_{12}^T & \mathbf{A}_{22} \end{bmatrix}}_{\mathbf{A}} = \underbrace{\begin{bmatrix} \mathbf{U}_{11} & \mathbf{U}_{12} \\ \mathbf{0} & \mathbf{U}_{22} \end{bmatrix}}_{\mathbf{U}} \underbrace{\begin{bmatrix} \mathbf{U}_{11}^T & \mathbf{0} \\ \mathbf{U}_{12}^T & \mathbf{U}_{22}^T \end{bmatrix}}_{\mathbf{U}^T}, \qquad (10.32)$$

where $\mathbf{U}$ is an upper-triangular matrix. Multiplying this out reveals

$$\mathbf{U}_{22}\mathbf{U}_{22}^T = \mathbf{A}_{22} : \text{ cheap to compute } \mathbf{U}_{22} \text{ via Cholesky}$$
$$\text{due to } \mathbf{A}_{22} \text{ block-diagonal,}$$

$$\mathbf{U}_{12}\mathbf{U}_{22}^T = \mathbf{A}_{12} : \text{ cheap to solve for } \mathbf{U}_{12}$$
$$\text{due to } \mathbf{U}_{22} \text{ block-diagonal,}$$

$$\mathbf{U}_{11}\mathbf{U}_{11}^T + \mathbf{U}_{12}\mathbf{U}_{12}^T = \mathbf{A}_{11} : \text{ cheap to compute } \mathbf{U}_{11} \text{ via Cholesky}$$
$$\text{due to small size of } \delta\mathbf{x}_1^\star,$$

so that we have a procedure to very efficiently compute $\mathbf{U}$, owing to the sparsity of $\mathbf{A}_{22}$. Note that $\mathbf{U}_{22}$ is also block-diagonal.

If all we cared about was efficiently solving (10.31), then after computing the Cholesky decomposition we can do so in two steps. First, solve

$$\mathbf{U}\mathbf{c} = \mathbf{b}, \tag{10.33}$$

for a temporary variable, $\mathbf{c}$. This can be done very quickly since $\mathbf{U}$ is upper-triangular and so can be solved from the bottom to the top through substitution and exploiting the additional known sparsity of $\mathbf{U}$. Second, solve

$$\mathbf{U}^T \delta\mathbf{x}^\star = \mathbf{c}, \tag{10.34}$$

for $\delta\mathbf{x}^\star$. Again, since $\mathbf{U}^T$ is lower-triangular we can solve quickly from the top to the bottom through substitution and exploiting the sparsity.

Alternatively, we can invert $\mathbf{U}$ directly so that

$$\begin{bmatrix} \mathbf{U}_{11} & \mathbf{U}_{12} \\ \mathbf{0} & \mathbf{U}_{22} \end{bmatrix}^{-1} = \begin{bmatrix} \mathbf{U}_{11}^{-1} & -\mathbf{U}_{11}^{-1}\mathbf{U}_{12}\mathbf{U}_{22}^{-1} \\ \mathbf{0} & \mathbf{U}_{22}^{-1} \end{bmatrix}, \tag{10.35}$$

which can again be computed efficiently due to the fact that $\mathbf{U}_{22}$ is block-diagonal and $\mathbf{U}_{11}$ is small and in upper-triangular form. Then we have that

$$\mathbf{U}^T \delta\mathbf{x}^\star = \mathbf{U}^{-1}\mathbf{b}, \tag{10.36}$$

or

$$\begin{bmatrix} \mathbf{U}_{11}^T & \mathbf{0} \\ \mathbf{U}_{12}^T & \mathbf{U}_{22}^T \end{bmatrix} \begin{bmatrix} \delta\mathbf{x}_1^\star \\ \delta\mathbf{x}_2^\star \end{bmatrix} = \begin{bmatrix} \mathbf{U}_{11}^{-1}(\mathbf{b}_1 - \mathbf{U}_{12}\mathbf{U}_{22}^{-1}\mathbf{b}_2) \\ \mathbf{U}_{22}^{-1}\mathbf{b}_2 \end{bmatrix}, \tag{10.37}$$

which allows us to compute $\delta\mathbf{x}_1^\star$ and then back-substitute for $\delta\mathbf{x}_2^\star$, similarly to the Schur complement method.

However, unlike the Schur complement method, $\mathbf{A}^{-1}$ is now computed easily:

$$\mathbf{A}^{-1} = \left(\mathbf{U}\mathbf{U}^T\right)^{-1} = \mathbf{U}^{-T}\mathbf{U}^{-1} = \mathbf{L}\mathbf{L}^T$$

$$= \underbrace{\begin{bmatrix} \mathbf{U}_{11}^{-T} & \mathbf{0} \\ -\mathbf{U}_{22}^{-T}\mathbf{U}_{12}^T\mathbf{U}_{11}^{-T} & \mathbf{U}_{22}^{-T} \end{bmatrix}}_{\mathbf{L}} \underbrace{\begin{bmatrix} \mathbf{U}_{11}^{-1} & -\mathbf{U}_{11}^{-1}\mathbf{U}_{12}\mathbf{U}_{22}^{-1} \\ \mathbf{0} & \mathbf{U}_{22}^{-1} \end{bmatrix}}_{\mathbf{L}^T}$$

$$= \begin{bmatrix} \mathbf{U}_{11}^{-T}\mathbf{U}_{11}^{-1} & -\mathbf{U}_{11}^{-T}\mathbf{U}_{11}^{-1}\mathbf{U}_{12}\mathbf{U}_{22}^{-1} \\ -\mathbf{U}_{22}^{-T}\mathbf{U}_{12}^T\mathbf{U}_{11}^{-T}\mathbf{U}_{11}^{-1} & \mathbf{U}_{22}^{-T}\left(\mathbf{U}_{12}^T\mathbf{U}_{11}^{-T}\mathbf{U}_{11}^{-1}\mathbf{U}_{12} + 1\right)\mathbf{U}_{22}^{-1} \end{bmatrix}, \tag{10.38}$$

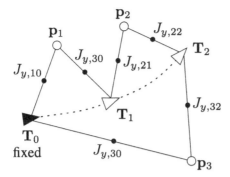

Figure 10.3 A BA problem with only three (non-collinear) point landmarks and two free poses (1 and 2). Pose 0 is fixed. It turns out this problem does not have a unique solution as there are too few landmarks to constrain the two free poses. There is one term in the cost function, $J_{y,jk}$, for each measurement, as shown; these are depicted as black dots, sometimes called *factors*.

where we see additional room for efficiency through repeated products inside the final matrix.

10.1.5 Interpolation Example

It will be instructive to work out the details for the small BA problem in Figure 10.3. There are three (non-collinear) point landmarks and two free poses (1 and 2). We will assume pose 0 is fixed to make the problem observable. We will also assume that the measurements of our point landmarks are three-dimensional; thus the sensor could be either a stereo camera or a range-azimuth-elevation sensor, for example. Unfortunately, there is not enough information present to uniquely solve for the two free poses as well as the positions of the three landmarks. This type of situation arises in rolling-shutter cameras and scanning-while-moving laser sensors.

In the absence of any measurements of additional landmarks, our only recourse is to assume something about the trajectory the vehicle has taken. There are essentially two possibilities:

(i) Penalty Term: we can take a *maximum a posteriori (MAP)* approach that assumes a prior density over trajectories and encourages the solver to select a likely trajectory that is compatible with the measurements by introducing a penalty term in the cost function. This is essentially the *simultaneous localization and mapping (SLAM)* approach and will be treated in the next section.

(ii) Constraint: we can stick with a *maximum likelihood (ML)* approach, but constrain the trajectory to be of a particular form. Here we will do this by assuming the vehicle has a constant six-degree-of-freedom velocity between poses 0 and 2 so that we can use pose interpolation for pose 1. This reduces the number of free pose variables from two to one and provides a unique solution.

We will first set up the equations as though it were possible to solve for both poses 1 and 2 and then introduce the pose-interpolation scheme.

The state variables to be estimated are

$$\mathbf{x} = \{\mathbf{T}_1, \mathbf{T}_2, \mathbf{p}_1, \mathbf{p}_2, \mathbf{p}_3\}. \tag{10.39}$$

We use the usual perturbation schemes,

$$\mathbf{T}_k = \exp\left(\boldsymbol{\epsilon}_k^\wedge\right)\mathbf{T}_{\text{op},k}, \qquad \mathbf{p}_j = \mathbf{p}_{\text{op},j} + \mathbf{D}\boldsymbol{\zeta}_j, \tag{10.40}$$

and stack our perturbation variables as

$$\delta\mathbf{x} = \begin{bmatrix} \epsilon_1 \\ \epsilon_2 \\ \hline \zeta_1 \\ \zeta_2 \\ \zeta_3 \end{bmatrix}. \tag{10.41}$$

At each iteration, the optimal perturbation variables should be the solution to the linear system,

$$\mathbf{A}\,\delta\mathbf{x}^\star = \mathbf{b}, \tag{10.42}$$

where the $\mathbf{A}$ and $\mathbf{b}$ matrices for this problem have the form

$$\mathbf{A} = \left[\begin{array}{ccc|ccc} \mathbf{A}_{11} & & & \mathbf{A}_{13} & \mathbf{A}_{14} & \\ & \mathbf{A}_{22} & & & \mathbf{A}_{24} & \mathbf{A}_{25} \\ \hline \mathbf{A}_{13}^T & & & \mathbf{A}_{33} & & \\ \mathbf{A}_{14}^T & \mathbf{A}_{24}^T & & & \mathbf{A}_{44} & \\ & \mathbf{A}_{25}^T & & & & \mathbf{A}_{55} \end{array} \right], \qquad \mathbf{b} = \begin{bmatrix} \mathbf{b}_1 \\ \mathbf{b}_2 \\ \mathbf{b}_3 \\ \mathbf{b}_4 \\ \mathbf{b}_5 \end{bmatrix}, \tag{10.43}$$

with

$$\mathbf{A}_{11} = \mathbf{G}_{1,11}^T \mathbf{R}_{11}^{-1} \mathbf{G}_{1,11} + \mathbf{G}_{1,21}^T \mathbf{R}_{21}^{-1} \mathbf{G}_{1,21},$$

$$\mathbf{A}_{22} = \mathbf{G}_{1,22}^T \mathbf{R}_{22}^{-1} \mathbf{G}_{1,22} + \mathbf{G}_{1,32}^T \mathbf{R}_{32}^{-1} \mathbf{G}_{1,32},$$

$$\mathbf{A}_{33} = \mathbf{G}_{2,10}^T \mathbf{R}_{10}^{-1} \mathbf{G}_{2,10} + \mathbf{G}_{2,11}^T \mathbf{R}_{11}^{-1} \mathbf{G}_{2,11},$$

$$\mathbf{A}_{44} = \mathbf{G}_{2,21}^T \mathbf{R}_{21}^{-1} \mathbf{G}_{2,21} + \mathbf{G}_{2,22}^T \mathbf{R}_{22}^{-1} \mathbf{G}_{2,22},$$

$$\mathbf{A}_{55} = \mathbf{G}_{2,30}^T \mathbf{R}_{30}^{-1} \mathbf{G}_{2,30} + \mathbf{G}_{2,32}^T \mathbf{R}_{32}^{-1} \mathbf{G}_{2,32},$$

$$\mathbf{A}_{13} = \mathbf{G}_{1,11}^T \mathbf{R}_{11}^{-1} \mathbf{G}_{2,11},$$

$$\mathbf{A}_{14} = \mathbf{G}_{1,21}^T \mathbf{R}_{21}^{-1} \mathbf{G}_{2,21},$$

$$\mathbf{A}_{24} = \mathbf{G}_{1,22}^T \mathbf{R}_{22}^{-1} \mathbf{G}_{2,22},$$

$$\mathbf{A}_{25} = \mathbf{G}_{1,32}^T \mathbf{R}_{32}^{-1} \mathbf{G}_{2,32},$$

and

$$\mathbf{b}_1 = \mathbf{G}_{1,11}^T \mathbf{R}_{11}^{-1} \mathbf{e}_{y,11}(\mathbf{x}_{op}) + \mathbf{G}_{1,21}^T \mathbf{R}_{21}^{-1} \mathbf{e}_{y,21}(\mathbf{x}_{op}),$$

$$\mathbf{b}_2 = \mathbf{G}_{1,22}^T \mathbf{R}_{22}^{-1} \mathbf{e}_{y,22}(\mathbf{x}_{op}) + \mathbf{G}_{1,32}^T \mathbf{R}_{32}^{-1} \mathbf{e}_{y,32}(\mathbf{x}_{op}),$$

$$\mathbf{b}_3 = \mathbf{G}_{2,10}^T \mathbf{R}_{10}^{-1} \mathbf{e}_{y,10}(\mathbf{x}_{op}) + \mathbf{G}_{2,11}^T \mathbf{R}_{11}^{-1} \mathbf{e}_{y,11}(\mathbf{x}_{op}),$$

$$\mathbf{b}_4 = \mathbf{G}_{2,21}^T \mathbf{R}_{21}^{-1} \mathbf{e}_{y,21}(\mathbf{x}_{op}) + \mathbf{G}_{2,22}^T \mathbf{R}_{22}^{-1} \mathbf{e}_{y,22}(\mathbf{x}_{op}),$$

$$\mathbf{b}_5 = \mathbf{G}_{2,30}^T \mathbf{R}_{30}^{-1} \mathbf{e}_{y,30}(\mathbf{x}_{op}) + \mathbf{G}_{2,32}^T \mathbf{R}_{32}^{-1} \mathbf{e}_{y,32}(\mathbf{x}_{op}).$$

Unfortunately, $\mathbf{A}$ is not invertible in this situation, which means that we cannot solve for $\delta\mathbf{x}^\star$ at any iteration.

To remedy the problem we will assume that the vehicle has followed a constant-velocity trajectory so that we can write $\mathbf{T}_1$ in terms of $\mathbf{T}_2$ using the pose-interpolation scheme of Section 8.1.7. To do this, we require the times corresponding to each pose:

$$t_0, t_1, t_2. \tag{10.44}$$

We then define the interpolation variable,

$$\alpha = \frac{t_1 - t_0}{t_2 - t_0}, \tag{10.45}$$

so that we can write

$$\mathbf{T}_1 = \mathbf{T}^\alpha, \tag{10.46}$$

where $\mathbf{T} = \mathbf{T}_2$. Our usual perturbation scheme is

$$\mathbf{T} = \exp\left(\boldsymbol{\epsilon}^\wedge\right) \mathbf{T}_{\mathrm{op}} \approx \left(1 + \boldsymbol{\epsilon}^\wedge\right) \mathbf{T}_{\mathrm{op}}, \tag{10.47}$$

and for the interpolated variable we have

$$\mathbf{T}^\alpha = \left(\exp\left(\boldsymbol{\epsilon}^\wedge\right) \mathbf{T}_{\mathrm{op}}\right)^\alpha \approx \left(1 + \left(\boldsymbol{\mathcal{A}}(\alpha, \boldsymbol{\xi}_{\mathrm{op}})\boldsymbol{\epsilon}\right)^\wedge\right) \mathbf{T}_{\mathrm{op}}^\alpha, \tag{10.48}$$

where $\boldsymbol{\mathcal{A}}$ is the interpolation Jacobian and $\boldsymbol{\xi}_{\mathrm{op}} = \ln(\mathbf{T}_{\mathrm{op}})^\vee$. Using this pose-interpolation scheme, we can write the old stacked perturbation variables in terms of a new reduced set:

$$\underbrace{\begin{bmatrix} \boldsymbol{\epsilon}_1 \\ \boldsymbol{\epsilon}_2 \\ \hline \boldsymbol{\zeta}_1 \\ \boldsymbol{\zeta}_2 \\ \boldsymbol{\zeta}_3 \end{bmatrix}}_{\delta\mathbf{x}} = \underbrace{\left[\begin{array}{c|ccc} \boldsymbol{\mathcal{A}}(\alpha, \boldsymbol{\xi}_{\mathrm{op}}) & & & \\ 1 & & & \\ \hline & 1 & & \\ & & 1 & \\ & & & 1 \end{array} \right]}_{\mathbf{I}} \underbrace{\begin{bmatrix} \boldsymbol{\epsilon} \\ \hline \boldsymbol{\zeta}_1 \\ \boldsymbol{\zeta}_2 \\ \boldsymbol{\zeta}_3 \end{bmatrix}}_{\delta\mathbf{x}'}, \tag{10.49}$$

where we will call $\mathbf{I}$ the *interpolation matrix*. Our new set of state variables to be estimated is

$$\mathbf{x}' = \{\mathbf{T}, \mathbf{p}_1, \mathbf{p}_2, \mathbf{p}_3\}, \tag{10.50}$$

now that we have eliminated $\mathbf{T}_1$ as a free variable. Returning to our original ML cost function, we can now rewrite it as

$$J(\mathbf{x}') \approx J(\mathbf{x}'_{\mathrm{op}}) - \mathbf{b}'^T \delta\mathbf{x}' + \frac{1}{2}\delta\mathbf{x}'^T \mathbf{A}' \, \delta\mathbf{x}', \tag{10.51}$$

where

$$\mathbf{A}' = \mathbf{I}^T \mathbf{A} \, \mathbf{I}, \qquad \mathbf{b}' = \mathbf{I}^T \mathbf{b}. \tag{10.52}$$

The optimal perturbation (that minimizes the cost function), $\delta\mathbf{x}'^*$, is now the solution to

$$\mathbf{A}' \, \delta\mathbf{x}'^* = \mathbf{b}'. \tag{10.53}$$

We update all the operating points in

$$\mathbf{x}'_{\mathrm{op}} = \{\mathbf{T}_{\mathrm{op}}, \mathbf{p}_{\mathrm{op},1}, \mathbf{p}_{\mathrm{op},2}, \mathbf{p}_{\mathrm{op},3}\}, \tag{10.54}$$

using the usual schemes,

$$\mathbf{T}_{\mathrm{op}} \leftarrow \exp\left(\boldsymbol{\epsilon}^{\star\wedge}\right) \mathbf{T}_{\mathrm{op}}, \qquad \mathbf{p}_{\mathrm{op},j} \leftarrow \mathbf{p}_{\mathrm{op},j} + \mathbf{D}\boldsymbol{\zeta}_j^\star, \tag{10.55}$$

and iterate to convergence.

Importantly, applying the interpolation matrix on either side of $\mathbf{A}$ to create $\mathbf{A}'$ does not completely destroy the sparsity. In fact, the bottom-right block corresponding to the landmarks remains block-diagonal, and thus $\mathbf{A}'$ is still an arrowhead matrix:

$$\mathbf{A}' = \begin{bmatrix} * & * & * & * \\ * & * & & \\ * & & * & \\ * & & & * \end{bmatrix}, \tag{10.56}$$

where $*$ indicates a non-zero block. This means that we can still exploit the sparsity using the methods of the previous section, while interpolating poses.

It turns out that we can use this interpolation scheme (and others) for more complicated BA problems as well. We just need to decide which pose variables we want to keep in the state and which to interpolate, then build the appropriate interpolation matrix, $\mathbf{I}$.

10.2 Simultaneous Localization and Mapping

The SLAM problem is essentially the same as BA, except that we also typically know something about how the vehicle has moved (i.e., a motion model) and can therefore include inputs, $\mathbf{v}$, in the problem. Logistically, we only need to augment the BA cost function with additional terms corresponding to the inputs (Sibley, 2006). Smith et al. (1990) is the classic reference on SLAM and Durrant-Whyte and Bailey (2006); Bailey and Durrant-Whyte (2006) provide a detailed survey of the area. The difference is essentially that BA is a *maximum likelihood (ML)* problem and SLAM is a *maximum a posteriori (MAP)* problem. Our approach is a batch-SLAM method (Lu and Milios, 1997) similar to the Graph SLAM approach of Thrun and Montemerlo (2005), but using our method of handling pose variables in three-dimensional space.

10.2.1 Problem Setup

Another minor difference is that by including inputs/priors, we can also assume that we have a prior on the initial state, $\mathbf{T}_0$, so that it can be included in the estimation problem (unlike BA).[4] Our state to be estimated is thus

$$\mathbf{x} = \{\mathbf{T}_0, \ldots, \mathbf{T}_K, \mathbf{p}_1, \ldots, \mathbf{p}_M\}. \tag{10.57}$$

We assume the same measurement model as the BA problem, and the measurements are given by

$$\mathbf{y} = \{\mathbf{y}_{10}, \ldots \mathbf{y}_{M0}, \ldots, \mathbf{y}_{1K}, \ldots, \mathbf{y}_{MK}\}. \tag{10.58}$$

We will adopt the motion model from Section 9.2 and the inputs are given by

$$\mathbf{v} = \{\check{\mathbf{T}}_0, \varpi_1, \varpi_2, \ldots, \varpi_K\}. \tag{10.59}$$

We will next set up the batch MAP problem.

---

[4] We could also choose not to estimate it and simply hold it fixed, which is very common.

10.2.2 Batch Maximum a Posteriori Solution

We define the following matrices:

$$\delta \mathbf{x} = \begin{bmatrix} \delta \mathbf{x}_1 \\ \delta \mathbf{x}_2 \end{bmatrix}, \quad \mathbf{H} = \begin{bmatrix} \mathbf{F}^{-1} & 0 \\ \mathbf{G}_1 & \mathbf{G}_2 \end{bmatrix}, \quad \mathbf{W} = \begin{bmatrix} \mathbf{Q} & 0 \\ 0 & \mathbf{R} \end{bmatrix},$$

$$\mathbf{e}(\mathbf{x}_{\mathrm{op}}) = \begin{bmatrix} \mathbf{e}_v(\mathbf{x}_{\mathrm{op}}) \\ \mathbf{e}_y(\mathbf{x}_{\mathrm{op}}) \end{bmatrix}, \tag{10.60}$$

where

$$\delta \mathbf{x}_1 = \begin{bmatrix} \boldsymbol{\epsilon}_0 \\ \boldsymbol{\epsilon}_1 \\ \vdots \\ \boldsymbol{\epsilon}_K \end{bmatrix}, \quad \delta \mathbf{x}_2 = \begin{bmatrix} \boldsymbol{\zeta}_1 \\ \boldsymbol{\zeta}_2 \\ \vdots \\ \boldsymbol{\zeta}_M \end{bmatrix},$$

$$\mathbf{e}_v(\mathbf{x}_{\mathrm{op}}) = \begin{bmatrix} \mathbf{e}_{v,0}(\mathbf{x}_{\mathrm{op}}) \\ \mathbf{e}_{v,1}(\mathbf{x}_{\mathrm{op}}) \\ \vdots \\ \mathbf{e}_{v,K}(\mathbf{x}_{\mathrm{op}}) \end{bmatrix}, \quad \mathbf{e}_y(\mathbf{x}_{\mathrm{op}}) = \begin{bmatrix} \mathbf{e}_{y,10}(\mathbf{x}_{\mathrm{op}}) \\ \mathbf{e}_{y,20}(\mathbf{x}_{\mathrm{op}}) \\ \vdots \\ \mathbf{e}_{y,MK}(\mathbf{x}_{\mathrm{op}}) \end{bmatrix},$$

$$\mathbf{Q} = \mathrm{diag}\left(\check{\mathbf{P}}_0, \mathbf{Q}_1, \ldots, \mathbf{Q}_K\right), \quad \mathbf{R} = \mathrm{diag}\left(\mathbf{R}_{10}, \mathbf{R}_{20}, \ldots, \mathbf{R}_{MK}\right),$$

$$\mathbf{F}^{-1} = \begin{bmatrix} \mathbf{E}_0 & & & & \\ -\mathbf{F}_0 & \mathbf{E}_1 & & & \\ & -\mathbf{F}_1 & \ddots & & \\ & & \ddots & \mathbf{E}_{K-1} & \\ & & & -\mathbf{F}_{K-1} & \mathbf{E}_K \end{bmatrix}, \tag{10.61}$$

$$\mathbf{G}_1 = \begin{bmatrix} \mathbf{G}_{1,10} & & & & \\ \vdots & & & & \\ \mathbf{G}_{1,M0} & & & & \\ & \mathbf{G}_{1,11} & & & \\ & \vdots & & & \\ & \mathbf{G}_{1,M1} & & & \\ & & \ddots & & \\ & & & \ddots & \\ & & & & \mathbf{G}_{1,1K} \\ & & & & \vdots \\ & & & & \mathbf{G}_{1,MK} \end{bmatrix}, \quad \mathbf{G}_2 = \begin{bmatrix} \mathbf{G}_{2,10} & & & \\ & \ddots & & \\ & & \mathbf{G}_{2,M0} \\ \mathbf{G}_{2,11} & & & \\ & \ddots & & \\ & & \mathbf{G}_{2,M1} \\ \vdots & & & \\ \vdots & & & \\ \mathbf{G}_{2,1K} & & & \\ & \ddots & & \\ & & \mathbf{G}_{2,MK} \end{bmatrix}.$$

From Sections 9.2.5 for the motion priors and 10.1.3 for the measurements, the detailed blocks are

$$\mathbf{E}_k = \boldsymbol{\mathcal{J}}\left(-\mathbf{e}_{v,k}(\mathbf{x}_{\mathrm{op}})\right)^{-1}, \quad k = 0 \ldots K,$$

$$\mathbf{F}_{k-1} = \boldsymbol{\mathcal{J}}\left(-\mathbf{e}_{v,k}(\mathbf{x}_{\mathrm{op}})\right)^{-1} \mathrm{Ad}\left(\mathbf{T}_{\mathrm{op},k}\mathbf{T}_{\mathrm{op},k-1}^{-1}\right), \quad k = 1 \ldots K,$$

$$\mathbf{e}_{v,k}(\mathbf{x}_{\mathrm{op}}) = \begin{cases} \ln\left(\check{\mathbf{T}}_0 \mathbf{T}_{\mathrm{op},0}^{-1}\right)^{\vee} & k = 0 \\ \ln\left(\exp\left((t_k - t_{k-1})\boldsymbol{\varpi}_k^{\wedge}\right)\mathbf{T}_{\mathrm{op},k-1}\mathbf{T}_{\mathrm{op},k}^{-1}\right)^{\vee} & k = 1\ldots K \end{cases},$$

$$(10.62)$$

$$\mathbf{G}_{1,jk} = \mathbf{S}_{jk}\left(\mathbf{T}_{\mathrm{op},k}\mathbf{p}_{\mathrm{op},j}\right)^{\odot}, \quad \mathbf{G}_{2,jk} = \mathbf{S}_{jk}\mathbf{T}_{\mathrm{op},k}\mathbf{D},$$
$$\mathbf{e}_{y,jk}(\mathbf{x}_{\mathrm{op}}) = \mathbf{y}_{jk} - \mathbf{s}\left(\mathbf{T}_{\mathrm{op},k}\mathbf{p}_{\mathrm{op},j}\right).$$

Finally, the objective function can be written as usual as

$$J(\mathbf{x}) \approx J(\mathbf{x}_{\mathrm{op}}) - \mathbf{b}^T\,\delta\mathbf{x} + \frac{1}{2}\delta\mathbf{x}^T\mathbf{A}\,\delta\mathbf{x}, \qquad (10.63)$$

where

$$\mathbf{A} = \mathbf{H}^T\mathbf{W}^{-1}\mathbf{H}, \quad \mathbf{b} = \mathbf{H}^T\mathbf{W}^{-1}\mathbf{e}(\mathbf{x}_{\mathrm{op}}), \qquad (10.64)$$

whereupon the minimizing perturbations, $\delta\mathbf{x}^{\star}$, are the solutions to

$$\mathbf{A}\,\delta\mathbf{x}^{\star} = \mathbf{b}. \qquad (10.65)$$

We solve for $\delta\mathbf{x}^{\star}$, then update our operating points according to

$$\mathbf{T}_{\mathrm{op},k} \leftarrow \exp\left(\boldsymbol{\epsilon}_k^{\star\wedge}\right)\mathbf{T}_{\mathrm{op},k}, \qquad \mathbf{p}_{\mathrm{op},j} \leftarrow \mathbf{p}_{\mathrm{op},j} + \mathbf{D}\boldsymbol{\zeta}_j^{\star}, \qquad (10.66)$$

and iterate to convergence. As in the BA case, once converged we set $\hat{\mathbf{T}}_{v_k i} = \mathbf{T}_{\mathrm{op},k}$ and $\hat{\mathbf{p}}_i^{p_j i} = \mathbf{p}_{\mathrm{op},j}$ at the last iteration as the final estimates for the vehicle poses and landmark positions of interest.

10.2.3 Exploiting Sparsity

Introducing the motion priors does not destroy the nice sparsity of the original BA problem. We can see this by noting that

$$\mathbf{A} = \begin{bmatrix} \mathbf{A}_{11} & \mathbf{A}_{12} \\ \mathbf{A}_{12}^T & \mathbf{A}_{22} \end{bmatrix} = \mathbf{H}^T\mathbf{W}^{-1}\mathbf{H}$$
$$= \begin{bmatrix} \mathbf{F}^{-T}\mathbf{Q}^{-1}\mathbf{F}^{-1} + \mathbf{G}_1^T\mathbf{R}^{-1}\mathbf{G}_1 & \mathbf{G}_1^T\mathbf{R}^{-1}\mathbf{G}_2 \\ \mathbf{G}_2^T\mathbf{R}^{-1}\mathbf{G}_1 & \mathbf{G}_2^T\mathbf{R}^{-1}\mathbf{G}_2 \end{bmatrix}. \qquad (10.67)$$

Compared to the BA problem, blocks $\mathbf{A}_{12}$ and $\mathbf{A}_{22}$ have not changed at all, showing that $\mathbf{A}$ is still an arrowhead matrix with $\mathbf{A}_{22}$ block-diagonal. We can thus exploit this sparsity to solve for the perturbations at each iteration efficiently using either the Schur or Cholesky methods.

While block $\mathbf{A}_{11}$ is now different than the BA problem,

$$\mathbf{A}_{11} = \underbrace{\mathbf{F}^{-T}\mathbf{Q}^{-1}\mathbf{F}^{-1}}_{\text{prior}} + \underbrace{\mathbf{G}_1^T\mathbf{R}^{-1}\mathbf{G}_1}_{\text{measurements}}, \qquad (10.68)$$

we have seen previously (e.g., Section 9.2.5) that it is block-tridiagonal. Thus, we could choose to exploit the sparsity of $\mathbf{A}_{11}$ rather than $\mathbf{A}_{22}$, if the number of poses were large compared to the number of landmarks, for example. In this case, the Cholesky method is preferred over the Schur one as we do not need

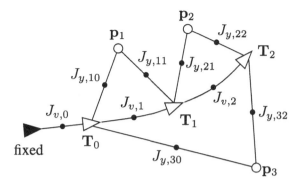

Figure 10.4 A SLAM problem with only three (non-collinear) point landmarks and three free poses. Pose 0 is not fixed as we have some prior information about it. There is one term in the cost function for each measurement, $J_{y,jk}$, and motion prior, $J_{v,k}$, as shown; these are depicted as black dots, sometimes called *factors*.

to construct $\mathbf{A}_{11}^{-1}$, which is actually dense. Kaess et al. (2008, 2012) provide incremental methods of updating the batch-SLAM solution that exploit sparsity beyond the primary block structure discussed here.

10.2.4 SLAM Example

Figure 10.4 shows a simple SLAM problem with three point landmarks and three free poses. In contrast to the BA example of Figure 10.3, we now allow $\mathbf{T}_0$ to be estimated as we have some prior information about it, $\{\check{\mathbf{T}}_0, \check{\mathbf{P}}_0\}$, in relation to an external reference frame (shown as the black, fixed pose). We have shown graphically all of the terms in the objective function,[5] one for each measurement and input, totalling nine terms:

$$ J = \underbrace{J_{v,0} + J_{v,1} + J_{v,2}}_{\text{prior terms}} + \underbrace{J_{y,10} + J_{y,30} + J_{y,11} + J_{y,21} + J_{y,22} + J_{y,32}}_{\text{measurement terms}}. $$

(10.69)

Also, with the motion priors we have used, $\mathbf{A}$ is always well conditioned and will provide a solution for the trajectory, even without any measurements.

---

[5] Sometimes this type of diagram is called a *factor graph* with each 'factor' from the posterior likelihood over the states becoming a 'term' in the objective function, which is really just the negative log likelihood of the posterior over states.

11

Continuous-Time Estimation

All of our examples in this last part of the book have been in discrete time, which is sufficient for many applications. However, it is worth investigating how we might make use of the continuous-time estimation tools from Sections 3.4 and 4.4 when working with state variables in $SE(3)$. To this end, we show one way to start from a specific nonlinear, stochastic differential equation and build motion priors that encourage trajectory smoothness.[1] We then show where these motion priors could be used within a trajectory estimation problem. Finally, we show how to interpolate and extrapolate for query poses at times between and after the main solution times.

11.1 Motion Prior

We will begin by discussing how to represent a motion prior on $SE(3)$. We will do this in the context of a specific nonlinear, stochastic differential equation, which we approximate as a sequence of local GPs to make the solution tractable.

11.1.1 Stochastic Differential Equations

Ideally, we would like to use the following system of nonlinear, stochastic, differential equations to build our motion prior:[2]

$$\dot{\mathbf{T}}(t) = \boldsymbol{\varpi}(t)^\wedge \mathbf{T}(t), \tag{11.1a}$$

$$\dot{\boldsymbol{\varpi}}(t) = \mathbf{w}'(t), \tag{11.1b}$$

$$\mathbf{w}'(t) \sim \mathcal{GP}\left(\mathbf{0}, \mathbf{Q}'_C \, \delta(t - t')\right). \tag{11.1c}$$

To use this to build our motion priors, we will need to estimate the pose, $\mathbf{T}(t)$, and the body-centric, generalized velocity, $\boldsymbol{\varpi}(t)$, at some times of interest: t_0, $t_1, \ldots, t_K$. White noise, $\mathbf{w}'(t)$, enters the system through the generalized angular acceleration; in the absence of noise, the body-centric, generalized velocity is constant. This is sometimes referred to as the 'white-noise-on-acceleration' or 'constant-velocity' prior. The trouble with using this model directly in continuous time is that it is nonlinear and the state is of the form $\{\mathbf{T}(t), \boldsymbol{\varpi}(t)\}$

---

[1] See Furgale et al. (2015) for a survey of continuous-time methods.

[2] It is this model that we approximated as a discrete-time system in the previous two chapters in order to build discrete-time motion priors.

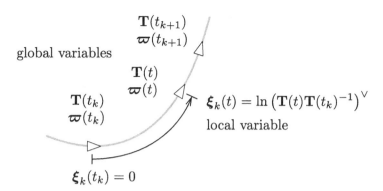

Figure 11.1 We can approximate a continuous-time trajectory as a sequence of local GPs by introducing local variables, $\boldsymbol{\xi}_k$, that stitch together our global variables.

$\in SE(3) \times \mathbb{R}^6$. Even the nonlinear tools from Section 4.4 do not directly apply in this situation.

11.1.2 Local SDEs

One practical route to using our GP approach to continuous-time trajectory estimation (see Section 3.4) is to introduce a sequence of local variables that stitch together our global variables.

The challenge with (11.1) is that the kinematics are nonlinear, which is necessary to allow for large robot displacements. This makes it fairly difficult to stochastically integrate these models to produce a simple-to-use motion prior. To overcome this problem, we will employ the same approach as Anderson and Barfoot (2015) and Anderson (2016) by using a series of local GPs that are stitched together. Figure 11.1 depicts the idea. We start by selecting times, t_k, along the trajectory at which we initialize each of these local GPs. We define local pose variables in the Lie algebra, $\boldsymbol{\xi}_k(t) \in \mathfrak{se}(3)$, such that between two times we have

$$\mathbf{T}(t) = \underbrace{\exp\left(\boldsymbol{\xi}_k(t)^\wedge\right)}_{\in SE(3)} \mathbf{T}(t_k). \tag{11.2}$$

The local variable is essentially compounded onto its associated global pose. This allows us to convert back and forth between the global pose, $\mathbf{T}(t)$, and the local pose, $\boldsymbol{\xi}_k(t)$. As long as the rotational motion of this local variable does not become too large, it will be a very good representation of the global pose in its local region.

We now choose to define our GP indirectly through a linear, time-invariant stochastic differential equation on the local variables (as opposed to the global ones):

$$\ddot{\boldsymbol{\xi}}_k(t) = \mathbf{w}_k(t), \qquad \mathbf{w}_k(t) \sim \mathcal{GP}(\mathbf{0}, \boldsymbol{Q}(t - t')). \tag{11.3}$$

In other words, we corrupt the second derivative of pose with a zero-mean, white-noise Gaussian process. We reorganize this into a first-order stochastic differential equation as

$$\frac{d}{dt}\begin{bmatrix} \boldsymbol{\xi}_k(t) \\ \boldsymbol{\psi}_k(t) \end{bmatrix} = \begin{bmatrix} \mathbf{0} & \mathbf{1} \\ \mathbf{0} & \mathbf{0} \end{bmatrix} \underbrace{\begin{bmatrix} \boldsymbol{\xi}_k(t) \\ \boldsymbol{\psi}_k(t) \end{bmatrix}}_{\boldsymbol{\gamma}_k(t)} + \begin{bmatrix} \mathbf{0} \\ \mathbf{1} \end{bmatrix} \mathbf{w}_k(t), \tag{11.4}$$

where $\psi_k(t) = \dot{\xi}_k(t)$; while $\psi_k(t)$ is the derivative of local pose, it is not exactly the same as the generalized velocity, $\varpi(t)$. Next, we need to (stochastically) integrate this equation once in order to calculate a GP for the Markovian state, $\gamma_k(t)$.

The local variable equation (11.4) is linear and stochastic integration can be done in closed form (see Section 3.4); this was, in fact, the point of switching to the local variables:

$$\gamma_k(t) \sim \mathcal{GP}\big(\underbrace{\mathbf{\Phi}(t, t_k)\check{\gamma}_k(t_k)}_{\text{mean function}}, \underbrace{\mathbf{\Phi}(t, t_k)\check{\mathbf{P}}(t_k)\mathbf{\Phi}(t, t_k)^T + \mathbf{Q}(t - t_k)}_{\text{covariance function}}\big), \quad (11.5)$$

where $\mathbf{\Phi}(t, t')$ is the transition function,

$$\mathbf{\Phi}(t, t') = \begin{bmatrix} \mathbf{1} & (t - t')\mathbf{1} \\ \mathbf{0} & \mathbf{1} \end{bmatrix}, \qquad t \geq t', \tag{11.6}$$

$\mathbf{Q}(t - t')$ is the covariance accumulated between two times,

$$\mathbf{Q}(t - t') = \begin{bmatrix} \frac{1}{3}(t - t')^3 \mathbf{Q} & \frac{1}{2}(t - t')^2 \mathbf{Q} \\ \frac{1}{2}(t - t')^2 \mathbf{Q} & (t - t')\mathbf{Q} \end{bmatrix}, \qquad t \geq t', \tag{11.7}$$

and $\check{\gamma}_k(t_k)$ and $\check{\mathbf{P}}(t_k)$ are the initial mean and covariance at $t = t_k$, the starting point of the local variable.

11.1.3 Error Terms and Cost Function

As we will be setting up our estimation problem as an MAP optimization, we will need to turn our motion prior into a cost term that represents the negative log-likelihood of a trajectory. Normally in GP regression we would build a *kernel matrix* between all pairs of unique states to be estimated (i.e., all pairs of times whose states are to be estimated). However, because we have built our GP prior from a stochastic differential equation, it has an inherently sparse structure deriving from the Markovian property of the equation and we only need to evaluate the kernel between sequential states along the robot trajectory (Barfoot et al., 2014). We define the error at the first time and between two sequential values of the time as

$$\mathbf{e}_{v,k} = \begin{cases} \begin{bmatrix} -\ln\left(\mathbf{T}(t_0)\check{\mathbf{T}}_0^{-1}\right)^{\vee} \\ \check{\varpi}_0 - \varpi(t_0) \end{bmatrix} & k = 0 \\ \mathbf{\Phi}(t_k, t_{k-1})\left(\gamma_{k-1}(t_{k-1}) - \check{\gamma}_{k-1}(t_{k-1})\right) \\ \qquad - \left(\gamma_{k-1}(t_k) - \check{\gamma}_{k-1}(t_k)\right) & k > 0 \end{cases}. \tag{11.8}$$

We can construct a cost term for this error as

$$J_{v,k} = \frac{1}{2}\mathbf{e}_{v,k}^T \mathbf{Q}_k^{-1}\mathbf{e}_{v,k}, \tag{11.9}$$

where $\mathbf{Q}_k = \mathbf{Q}(t_k - t_{k-1})$ for $k > 0$; for $k = 0$ we use the initial covariance on the state, $\check{\mathbf{P}}_0$. The cost term represents the negative log-likelihood of the error, or in other words (the negative log of) how likely the two consecutive states are at this point on the robot trajectory; the further away the two states are from what

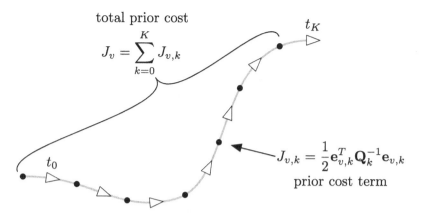

total prior cost

$$J_v = \sum_{k=0}^{K} J_{v,k}$$

t_K

$J_{v,k} = \frac{1}{2} \mathbf{e}_{v,k}^T \mathbf{Q}_k^{-1} \mathbf{e}_{v,k}$

prior cost term

t_0

Figure 11.2 The prior for the entire robot state can be broken down into a sequence of binary *factors* (black dots), each of which represents a squared error term for how that pair of states is related. High cost is associated with poses and velocities that deviate from the prior mean (i.e., constant-velocity trajectory).

the prior mean indicates, the less likely, and this will be traded off against any measurements of the state we also have. Finally, we can sum all the individual errors between consecutive states along the trajectory to create the total prior cost as

$$J_v = \sum_{k=0}^{K} J_{v,k}. \qquad (11.10)$$

Figure 11.2 depicts the cost terms as a *factor graph*; each black dot represents one of the squared-error cost terms and the sum of these is our overall prior cost term. The first prior term is a *unary factor*, meaning it only connects to the first state while the subsequent terms are *binary* factors.

The last detail we need to work out is how to swap out the local variables in the error (11.8) for the original global variables, since these are the ones we actually want to estimate. We can isolate for $\boldsymbol{\xi}_k(t)$ in (11.2) so that

$$\boldsymbol{\xi}_k(t) = \ln\left(\mathbf{T}(t)\mathbf{T}(t_k)^{-1}\right)^{\vee}, \qquad (11.11)$$

where $\ln(\cdot)$ is the matrix logarithm. We can also write the kinematics of (11.1) using the local variable as

$$\boldsymbol{\psi}_k(t) = \dot{\boldsymbol{\xi}}_k(t) = \boldsymbol{\mathcal{J}}\left(\boldsymbol{\xi}_k(t)\right)^{-1} \boldsymbol{\varpi}(t), \qquad (11.12)$$

where $\boldsymbol{\mathcal{J}}$ is the left Jacobian of $SE(3)$. Inserting (11.11) and (11.12) into the error (11.8), we can rewrite it as (Anderson and Barfoot, 2015)

$$\mathbf{e}_{v,k} = \begin{cases} \begin{bmatrix} -\ln\left(\mathbf{T}(t_0)\check{\mathbf{T}}_0^{-1}\right)^{\vee} \\ \check{\boldsymbol{\varpi}}_0 - \boldsymbol{\varpi}(t_0) \end{bmatrix} & k = 0 \\ \begin{bmatrix} (t_k - t_{k-1})\boldsymbol{\varpi}(t_{k-1}) - \ln\left(\mathbf{T}(t_k)\mathbf{T}(t_{k-1})^{-1}\right)^{\vee} \\ \boldsymbol{\varpi}(t_{k-1}) - \boldsymbol{\mathcal{J}}\left(\ln\left(\mathbf{T}(t_k)\mathbf{T}(t_{k-1})^{-1}\right)^{\vee}\right)^{-1} \boldsymbol{\varpi}(t_k) \end{bmatrix} & k > 0 \end{cases}, \qquad (11.13)$$

which is now only in terms of the global variables, $\{\mathbf{T}(t_k), \boldsymbol{\varpi}(t_k)\}$.

Another way to think about the development of the prior in this section is that we defined uncertainty affecting our state in the Lie algebra of the pose, where we can avoid the need to worry about the constraints on the variables. While this development is somewhat involved, the result is quite simple. We use (11.13) inside (11.9) to build a bunch of squared-error terms (aka factors) for the states at a number of discrete positions along the arclength of the robot, as depicted in

Figure 11.2. The *hyperparameters* of our prior are the initial state, $\{\check{\mathbf{T}}_0, \check{\boldsymbol{\varpi}}_0\}$, the initial covariance, $\check{\mathbf{P}}_0$, and the power spectral density, $\mathbf{Q}$, which controls smoothness in six degrees of freedom.

11.1.4 Linearized Error Terms

With an eye towards using Gauss–Newton to solve our continuous-time estimation problem, we can now linearize our error expression from (11.13). We will use our now-standard approach to perturbing poses,

$$\mathbf{T}_k = \exp(\boldsymbol{\epsilon}_k^\wedge)\mathbf{T}_{\mathrm{op},k}, \tag{11.14}$$

where $\mathbf{T}_k = \mathbf{T}(t_k)$ is a shorthand, $\boldsymbol{\epsilon}_k$ is our perturbation, and $\mathbf{T}_{\mathrm{op},k}$ is the operating point. We will perturb the velocity variables using a standard additive perturbation:

$$\boldsymbol{\varpi}_k = \boldsymbol{\varpi}_{\mathrm{op},k} + \boldsymbol{\eta}_k, \tag{11.15}$$

where $\boldsymbol{\varpi}_k = \boldsymbol{\varpi}(t_k)$ is a shorthand, $\boldsymbol{\eta}_k$ is our perturbation, and $\boldsymbol{\varpi}_{\mathrm{op},k}$ is the operating point.

We will need to work in steps. Consider the expression, $\ln\left(\mathbf{T}_k \mathbf{T}_{k-1}^{-1}\right)^\vee$. Inserting our perturbations, we see that

$$\begin{aligned}
\ln\left(\mathbf{T}_k \mathbf{T}_{k-1}^{-1}\right)^\vee &= \ln\left(\exp(\boldsymbol{\epsilon}_k^\wedge)\mathbf{T}_{\mathrm{op},k}\mathbf{T}_{\mathrm{op},k-1}^{-1}\exp(-\boldsymbol{\epsilon}_{k-1}^\wedge)\right)^\vee \\
&= \ln\left(\exp\left((\boldsymbol{\epsilon}_k - \boldsymbol{\mathcal{T}}_{\mathrm{op},k,k-1}\boldsymbol{\epsilon}_{k-1})^\wedge\right)\mathbf{T}_{\mathrm{op},k}\mathbf{T}_{\mathrm{op},k-1}^{-1}\right)^\vee \\
&\approx \ln\left(\mathbf{T}_{\mathrm{op},k}\mathbf{T}_{\mathrm{op},k-1}^{-1}\right)^\vee + \boldsymbol{\mathcal{J}}_{\mathrm{op},k,k-1}^{-1}\left(\boldsymbol{\epsilon}_k - \boldsymbol{\mathcal{T}}_{\mathrm{op},k,k-1}\boldsymbol{\epsilon}_{k-1}\right), \quad (11.16)
\end{aligned}$$

where we have assumed that $\boldsymbol{\epsilon}_k - \boldsymbol{\mathcal{T}}_{\mathrm{op},k,k-1}\boldsymbol{\epsilon}_{k-1}$ is small and defined

$$\boldsymbol{\mathcal{T}}_{\mathrm{op},k,k-1} = \boldsymbol{\mathcal{T}}_{\mathrm{op},k}\boldsymbol{\mathcal{T}}_{\mathrm{op},k-1}^{-1}, \quad \boldsymbol{\mathcal{J}}_{\mathrm{op},k,k-1} = \boldsymbol{\mathcal{J}}\left(\ln\left(\mathbf{T}_{\mathrm{op},k}\mathbf{T}_{\mathrm{op},k-1}^{-1}\right)^\vee\right), \tag{11.17}$$

and $\boldsymbol{\mathcal{T}}_{\mathrm{op},k} = \mathrm{Ad}(\mathbf{T}_{\mathrm{op},k})$.

We can now turn our attention to $\boldsymbol{\mathcal{J}}\left(\ln\left(\mathbf{T}(t_k)\mathbf{T}(t_{k-1})^{-1}\right)^\vee\right)^{-1}$, which looks more daunting. However, we have already linearized the part on the inside in the previous paragraph so that

$$\begin{aligned}
\boldsymbol{\mathcal{J}}&\left(\ln\left(\mathbf{T}(t_k)\mathbf{T}(t_{k-1})^{-1}\right)^\vee\right)^{-1} \\
&\approx \boldsymbol{\mathcal{J}}\left(\ln\left(\mathbf{T}_{\mathrm{op},k}\mathbf{T}_{\mathrm{op},k-1}^{-1}\right)^\vee + \boldsymbol{\mathcal{J}}_{\mathrm{op},k,k-1}^{-1}\left(\boldsymbol{\epsilon}_k - \boldsymbol{\mathcal{T}}_{\mathrm{op},k,k-1}\boldsymbol{\epsilon}_{k-1}\right)\right)^{-1} \\
&\approx \boldsymbol{\mathcal{J}}_{\mathrm{op},k,k-1}^{-1} - \frac{1}{2}\left(\boldsymbol{\mathcal{J}}_{\mathrm{op},k,k-1}^{-1}\left(\boldsymbol{\epsilon}_k - \boldsymbol{\mathcal{T}}_{\mathrm{op},k,k-1}\boldsymbol{\epsilon}_{k-1}\right)\right)^\wedge, \quad (11.18)
\end{aligned}$$

where we have exploited again that $\boldsymbol{\epsilon}_k - \boldsymbol{\mathcal{T}}_{\mathrm{op},k,k-1}\boldsymbol{\epsilon}_{k-1}$ is small and carried out a first-order Taylor expansion of the general expression for the inverse left Jacobian, $\boldsymbol{\mathcal{J}}^{-1}(\mathbf{x}) \approx \mathbf{1} - \frac{1}{2}\mathbf{x}^\wedge$.

We can now insert (11.16) and (11.18) into (11.13) to see that our linearized error expression becomes

$$\mathbf{e}_{v,k}(\mathbf{x}) \approx \mathbf{e}_{v,k}(\mathbf{x}_{\mathrm{op}}) + \mathbf{F}_{k-1}\boldsymbol{\varepsilon}_{k-1} - \mathbf{E}_k\boldsymbol{\varepsilon}_k, \tag{11.19}$$

where $\varepsilon_k = \begin{bmatrix} \epsilon_k \\ \eta_k \end{bmatrix}$,

$$\mathbf{F}_{k-1} = \begin{cases} \mathbf{0} & k = 0 \\ \begin{bmatrix} \boldsymbol{\mathcal{J}}_{\mathrm{op},k,k-1}^{-1} \boldsymbol{\mathcal{T}}_{\mathrm{op},k,k-1} & (t_k - t_{k-1})\mathbf{1} \\ \frac{1}{2}\boldsymbol{\varpi}_{\mathrm{op},k}^{\wedge} \boldsymbol{\mathcal{J}}_{\mathrm{op},k,k-1}^{-1} \boldsymbol{\mathcal{T}}_{\mathrm{op},k,k-1} & \mathbf{1} \end{bmatrix} & k > 0 \end{cases},$$

(11.20)

and

$$\mathbf{E}_k = \begin{cases} \begin{bmatrix} \boldsymbol{\mathcal{J}}\left(\ln\left(\mathbf{T}_{\mathrm{op},0}\check{\mathbf{T}}_0^{-1}\right)^{\vee}\right)^{-1} & \mathbf{0} \\ \mathbf{0} & \mathbf{1} \end{bmatrix} & k = 0 \\ \begin{bmatrix} \boldsymbol{\mathcal{J}}_{\mathrm{op},k,k-1}^{-1} & \mathbf{0} \\ \frac{1}{2}\boldsymbol{\varpi}_{\mathrm{op},k}^{\wedge} \boldsymbol{\mathcal{J}}_{\mathrm{op},k,k-1}^{-1} & \boldsymbol{\mathcal{J}}_{\mathrm{op},k,k-1}^{-1} \end{bmatrix} & k > 0 \end{cases}.$$

(11.21)

We can then define the stacked quantities

$$\mathbf{e}_v(\mathbf{x}_{\mathrm{op}}) = \begin{bmatrix} \mathbf{e}_{v,0}(\mathbf{x}_{\mathrm{op}}) \\ \mathbf{e}_{v,1}(\mathbf{x}_{\mathrm{op}}) \\ \vdots \\ \mathbf{e}_{v,K}(\mathbf{x}_{\mathrm{op}}) \end{bmatrix}, \quad \mathbf{Q} = \mathrm{diag}\left(\check{\mathbf{P}}_0, \mathbf{Q}_1, \ldots, \mathbf{Q}_K\right),$$

(11.22)

and

$$\mathbf{F}^{-1} = \begin{bmatrix} \mathbf{E}_0 & & & & \\ -\mathbf{F}_0 & \mathbf{E}_1 & & & \\ & -\mathbf{F}_1 & \mathbf{E}_2 & & \\ & & \ddots & \ddots & \\ & & & -\mathbf{F}_{K-1} & \mathbf{E}_K \end{bmatrix}, \quad \delta\mathbf{x}_1 = \begin{bmatrix} \boldsymbol{\varepsilon}_0 \\ \boldsymbol{\varepsilon}_1 \\ \boldsymbol{\varepsilon}_2 \\ \vdots \\ \boldsymbol{\varepsilon}_K \end{bmatrix},$$

(11.23)

where we use the symbol $\mathbf{F}^{-1}$ to remain consistent with several of our previous motion-prior setups from earlier chapters. Then finally our quadratic approximation of the cost term for the motion prior can be written as

$$J_v \approx \frac{1}{2}\left(\mathbf{e}_v(\mathbf{x}_{\mathrm{op}}) - \mathbf{F}^{-1}\delta\mathbf{x}_1\right)^T \mathbf{Q}^{-1}\left(\mathbf{e}_v(\mathbf{x}_{\mathrm{op}}) - \mathbf{F}^{-1}\delta\mathbf{x}_1\right),$$

(11.24)

which can be combined with cost terms associated with any type of measurements we like to form a full estimation problem. The next section will investigate the case of combining the motion prior with observations of landmarks.

11.2 Simultaneous Trajectory Estimation and Mapping

Using the motion prior from the previous section to smooth the solution, we can set up a batch MAP estimation problem that involves additional measurements. Figure 11.3 shows some possibilities. For example, we can set up a *simultaneous trajectory estimation and mapping (STEAM)* problem if we are able to observe some landmarks whose positions must also be estimated. STEAM is just a variant of *simultaneous localization and mapping (SLAM)*, where we have the ability to inherently query the robot's underlying continuous-time trajectory at any time of interest, not just the measurement times (Anderson and Barfoot, 2015).

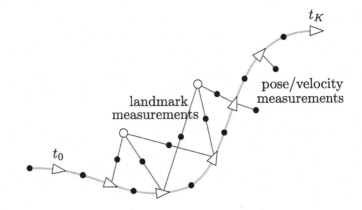

In this section we show first how to solve for the state at the measurement times. The next section will show how to use Gaussian process interpolation (and extrapolation) to solve for the state (and covariance) at other query times.

11.2.1 Problem Setup

The use of our continuous-time motion prior is a fairly straightforward modification of the discrete-time approach from Section 10.2.2. The state to be estimated is now

$$\mathbf{x} = \{\mathbf{T}_0, \boldsymbol{\varpi}_0, \dots, \mathbf{T}_K, \boldsymbol{\varpi}_K, \mathbf{p}_1, \dots, \mathbf{p}_M\}, \qquad (11.25)$$

which includes the poses, the generalized velocity variables, and the landmark positions in homogeneous coordinates, $\mathbf{p}_j$. The measurement times are $t_0, t_1, \dots, t_K$ and the measurements available in our problem are

$$\mathbf{y} = \{\mathbf{y}_{10}, \dots \mathbf{y}_{M0}, \dots, \mathbf{y}_{1K}, \dots, \mathbf{y}_{MK}\}, \qquad (11.26)$$

which remain the same as the discrete-time SLAM case. Each measurement is of the form

$$\mathbf{y}_{jk} = \mathbf{s}(\mathbf{T}_k \mathbf{p}_j) + \mathbf{n}_{jk}, \quad \mathbf{n}_{jk} \sim \mathcal{N}(\mathbf{0}, \mathbf{R}_{jk}), \qquad (11.27)$$

where $\mathbf{s}(\cdot)$ is a nonlinear sensor model (e.g., a stereo camera).

11.2.2 Measurement Model

Although we use the same measurement model as the discrete-time SLAM case, we must modify some of the block matrices to account for the fact that the estimated state now includes the $\boldsymbol{\varpi}_k$ quantities, which are not required in the measurement error terms. We continue to use the usual perturbation scheme for the landmark positions:

$$\mathbf{p}_j = \mathbf{p}_{\mathrm{op},j} + \mathbf{D}\boldsymbol{\zeta}_j, \qquad (11.28)$$

where $\mathbf{p}_{\mathrm{op},j}$ is the operating point and $\boldsymbol{\zeta}_j$ is the perturbation.

To build the part of the objective function associated with the measurements, we define the following matrices:

$$\delta\mathbf{x}_2 = \begin{bmatrix} \boldsymbol{\zeta}_1 \\ \boldsymbol{\zeta}_2 \\ \vdots \\ \boldsymbol{\zeta}_M \end{bmatrix}, \quad \mathbf{e}_y(\mathbf{x}_{\mathrm{op}}) = \begin{bmatrix} \mathbf{e}_{y,10}(\mathbf{x}_{\mathrm{op}}) \\ \mathbf{e}_{y,20}(\mathbf{x}_{\mathrm{op}}) \\ \vdots \\ \mathbf{e}_{y,MK}(\mathbf{x}_{\mathrm{op}}) \end{bmatrix},$$

$$\mathbf{R} = \mathrm{diag}\left(\mathbf{R}_{10}, \mathbf{R}_{20}, \ldots, \mathbf{R}_{MK}\right), \qquad (11.29)$$

and

$$\mathbf{G}_1 = \begin{bmatrix} \mathbf{G}_{1,10} \\ \vdots \\ \mathbf{G}_{1,M0} \\ & \mathbf{G}_{1,11} \\ & \vdots \\ & \mathbf{G}_{1,M1} \\ & & \ddots \\ & & & \ddots \\ & & & & \mathbf{G}_{1,1K} \\ & & & & \vdots \\ & & & & \mathbf{G}_{1,MK} \end{bmatrix}, \quad \mathbf{G}_2 = \begin{bmatrix} \mathbf{G}_{2,10} \\ & \ddots \\ & & \mathbf{G}_{2,M0} \\ \mathbf{G}_{2,11} \\ & \ddots \\ & & \mathbf{G}_{2,M1} \\ \vdots \\ \vdots \\ \mathbf{G}_{2,1K} \\ & \ddots \\ & & \mathbf{G}_{2,MK} \end{bmatrix}.$$

$$(11.30)$$

The detailed blocks are

$$\mathbf{G}_{1,jk} = \begin{bmatrix} \mathbf{S}_{jk}\left(\mathbf{T}_{\mathrm{op},k}\mathbf{p}_{\mathrm{op},j}\right)^{\odot} & \mathbf{0} \end{bmatrix}, \quad \mathbf{G}_{2,jk} = \mathbf{S}_{jk}\mathbf{T}_{\mathrm{op},k}\mathbf{D},$$

$$\mathbf{e}_{y,jk}(\mathbf{x}_{\mathrm{op}}) = \mathbf{y}_{jk} - \mathbf{s}\left(\mathbf{T}_{\mathrm{op},k}\mathbf{p}_{\mathrm{op},j}\right),$$

where we see that the only change from the SLAM case is that the $\mathbf{G}_{1,jk}$ matrix has a padding $\mathbf{0}$ to account for the fact that the $\boldsymbol{\psi}_k$ perturbation variable (associated with $\boldsymbol{\varpi}_k$) is not involved in the observation of landmark j from pose k. The part of the objective function associated with the measurements is then approximately

$$J_y(\mathbf{x}) \approx \frac{1}{2}\left(\mathbf{e}_y(\mathbf{x}_{\mathrm{op}}) - \mathbf{G}_1\,\delta\mathbf{x}_1 - \mathbf{G}_2\,\delta\mathbf{x}_2\right)^T \mathbf{R}^{-1}$$

$$\times\left(\mathbf{e}_y(\mathbf{x}_{\mathrm{op}}) - \mathbf{G}_1\,\delta\mathbf{x}_1 - \mathbf{G}_2\,\delta\mathbf{x}_2\right), \quad (11.31)$$

which is again quadratic in the perturbation variables, $\delta\mathbf{x}_1$ and $\delta\mathbf{x}_2$. See the previous section on the motion prior for the definition of $\delta\mathbf{x}_1$.

11.2.3 Batch Maximum a Posteriori Solution

With both the motion prior and the measurement terms in hand, we can write the full MAP objective function as

$$J(\mathbf{x}) = J_v(\mathbf{x}) + J_y(\mathbf{x}) \approx J(\mathbf{x}_{\mathrm{op}}) - \mathbf{b}^T\,\delta\mathbf{x} + \delta\mathbf{x}^T\mathbf{A}\,\delta\mathbf{x}, \qquad (11.32)$$

with

$$\mathbf{A} = \mathbf{H}^T\mathbf{W}^{-1}\mathbf{H}, \quad \mathbf{b} = \mathbf{H}^T\mathbf{W}^{-1}\mathbf{e}(\mathbf{x}_{\mathrm{op}}), \qquad (11.33)$$

Figure 11.4
Example STEAM
posterior solution
with 30 states (pose
and velocity) and 10
landmarks. The
motion prior
preferred
straight-ahead
motion, but based on
the landmark
measurements the
correct
three-dimensional
corkscrew motion is
estimated. Notably,
each pose only
observes a single
landmark making
the motion prior
critical to solving the
problem.

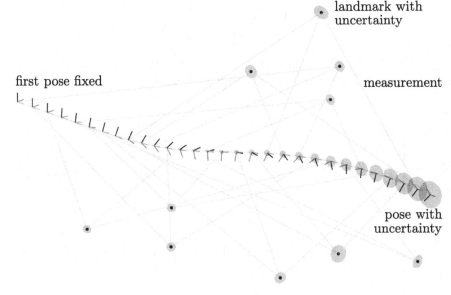

and

$$\delta\mathbf{x} = \begin{bmatrix} \delta\mathbf{x}_1 \\ \delta\mathbf{x}_2 \end{bmatrix}, \quad \mathbf{H} = \begin{bmatrix} \mathbf{F}^{-1} & \mathbf{0} \\ \mathbf{G}_1 & \mathbf{G}_2 \end{bmatrix}, \quad \mathbf{W} = \begin{bmatrix} \mathbf{Q} & \mathbf{0} \\ \mathbf{0} & \mathbf{R} \end{bmatrix},$$

$$\mathbf{e}(\mathbf{x}_{\mathrm{op}}) = \begin{bmatrix} \mathbf{e}_v(\mathbf{x}_{\mathrm{op}}) \\ \mathbf{e}_y(\mathbf{x}_{\mathrm{op}}) \end{bmatrix}. \tag{11.34}$$

The minimizing perturbation, $\delta\mathbf{x}^\star$, is the solution to

$$\mathbf{A}\,\delta\mathbf{x}^\star = \mathbf{b}. \tag{11.35}$$

As usual, we solve for $\delta\mathbf{x}^\star$, then apply the optimal perturbations using the appropriate schemes,

$$\mathbf{T}_{\mathrm{op},k} \leftarrow \exp\left(\boldsymbol{\epsilon}_k^{\star\wedge}\right)\mathbf{T}_{\mathrm{op},k}, \tag{11.36a}$$

$$\boldsymbol{\varpi}_{\mathrm{op},k} \leftarrow \boldsymbol{\varpi}_{\mathrm{op},k} + \boldsymbol{\eta}_k^\star, \tag{11.36b}$$

$$\mathbf{p}_{\mathrm{op},j} \leftarrow \mathbf{p}_{\mathrm{op},j} + \mathbf{D}\boldsymbol{\zeta}_j^\star, \tag{11.36c}$$

and iterate to convergence. Similarly to the SLAM case, once converged we set $\hat{\mathbf{T}}_{v_k i} = \mathbf{T}_{\mathrm{op},k}$, $\hat{\boldsymbol{\varpi}}_{v_k}^{v_k i} = \boldsymbol{\varpi}_{\mathrm{op},k}$, and $\hat{\mathbf{p}}_i^{p_j i} = \mathbf{p}_{\mathrm{op},j}$ at the last iteration as the final estimates for the vehicle poses, generalized velocity, and landmark positions of interest at the measurement times. Figure 11.4 provides an example STEAM posterior solution based on the methods in this chapter.

11.2.4 Exploiting Sparsity

Introducing the continuous-time motion priors does not destroy the nice sparsity of the discrete-time SLAM problem. We can see this by noting that

$$\mathbf{A} = \begin{bmatrix} \mathbf{A}_{11} & \mathbf{A}_{12} \\ \mathbf{A}_{12}^T & \mathbf{A}_{22} \end{bmatrix} = \mathbf{H}^T\mathbf{W}^{-1}\mathbf{H}$$

$$= \begin{bmatrix} \mathbf{F}^{-T}\mathbf{Q}^{-1}\mathbf{F}^{-1} + \mathbf{G}_1^T\mathbf{R}^{-1}\mathbf{G}_1 & \mathbf{G}_1^T\mathbf{R}^{-1}\mathbf{G}_2 \\ \mathbf{G}_2^T\mathbf{R}^{-1}\mathbf{G}_1 & \mathbf{G}_2^T\mathbf{R}^{-1}\mathbf{G}_2 \end{bmatrix}. \tag{11.37}$$

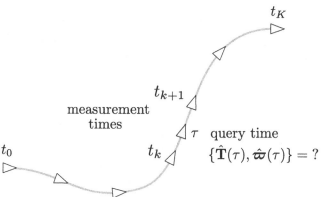

Figure 11.5 The major advantage of setting up our state estimation problem using a continuous-time motion prior is that once we have solved for the state at the measurement times, we can query the trajectory at another time of interest, τ. In this case, the query involves interpolating the posterior solution.

Compared to the SLAM problem, blocks $\mathbf{A}_{12}$ and $\mathbf{A}_{22}$ have not changed at all, showing that $\mathbf{A}$ is still an arrowhead matrix with $\mathbf{A}_{22}$ block-diagonal. We can thus exploit this sparsity to solve for the perturbations at each iteration efficiently using either the Schur or Cholesky methods.

The block $\mathbf{A}_{11}$ looks very similar to the discrete-time SLAM case,

$$\mathbf{A}_{11} = \underbrace{\mathbf{F}^{-T}\mathbf{Q}^{-1}\mathbf{F}^{-1}}_{\text{prior}} + \underbrace{\mathbf{G}_1^T\mathbf{R}^{-1}\mathbf{G}_1}_{\text{measurements}}, \qquad (11.38)$$

but recall that the $\mathbf{G}_1$ matrix is slightly different due to the fact that we are estimating both pose and generalized velocity at each measurement time. Nevertheless, $\mathbf{A}_{11}$ is still block-tridiagonal. Thus, we could choose to exploit the sparsity of $\mathbf{A}_{11}$ rather than $\mathbf{A}_{22}$, if the number of poses were large compared to the number of landmarks, for example. In this case, the Cholesky method is preferred over the Schur one as we do not need to construct $\mathbf{A}_{11}^{-1}$, which is actually dense. Yan et al. (2014) explain how to use the sparse-GP method within the incremental approach of Kaess et al. (2008, 2012).

11.3 Interpolation and Extrapolation

After we have solved for the state at the measurement times, we can also now use our Gaussian process framework to interpolate for the state at one or more query times. The situation is depicted in Figure 11.5, where our goal is to interpolate the posterior pose (and generalized velocity) at query time, τ.

11.3.1 Interpolating the Mean

Because we have deliberately estimated a Markovian state for our chosen *stochastic differential equation (SDE)* defining the prior, $\{\mathbf{T}_k, \boldsymbol{\varpi}_k\}$, we know that to interpolate at time τ, we need only consider the two measurement times on either side. Without loss of generality, we assume

$$t_k \leq \tau < t_{k+1}, \qquad (11.39)$$

which means we can work directly with the local variables for a single GP.

The generic GP interpolation equations from (3.209a) are then

$$\hat{\boldsymbol{\gamma}}_k(\tau) = \check{\boldsymbol{\gamma}}_k(\tau) + \begin{bmatrix}\boldsymbol{\Lambda}(\tau) & \boldsymbol{\Psi}(\tau)\end{bmatrix}\left(\begin{bmatrix}\hat{\boldsymbol{\gamma}}_k(t_k) \\ \hat{\boldsymbol{\gamma}}_k(t_{k+1})\end{bmatrix} - \begin{bmatrix}\check{\boldsymbol{\gamma}}_k(t_k) \\ \check{\boldsymbol{\gamma}}_k(t_{k+1})\end{bmatrix}\right), \quad (11.40)$$

where

$$\Lambda(\tau) = \Phi(\tau, t_k) - \mathbf{Q}_\tau \Phi(t_{k+1}, \tau)^T \mathbf{Q}_{k+1}^{-1} \Phi(t_{k+1}, t_k), \quad (11.41a)$$
$$\Psi(\tau) = \mathbf{Q}_\tau \Phi(t_{k+1}, \tau)^T \mathbf{Q}_{k+1}^{-1}, \quad (11.41b)$$

and $\mathbf{Q}_\tau = \mathbf{Q}(\tau - t_k)$. It is not too difficult to verify that

$$\check{\gamma}_k(\tau) = \Lambda(\tau)\check{\gamma}_k(t_k) + \Psi(\tau)\check{\gamma}_k(t_{k+1}) \quad (11.42)$$

by exploiting the fact that $\check{\gamma}_k(t) = \Phi(t, t_k)\check{\gamma}_k(t_k)$. The posterior interpolation equations then reduce to

$$\hat{\gamma}_k(\tau) = \Lambda(\tau)\hat{\gamma}_k(t_k) + \Psi(\tau)\hat{\gamma}_k(t_{k+1}), \quad (11.43)$$

where

$$\hat{\gamma}_k(\tau) = \begin{bmatrix} \ln\left(\hat{\mathbf{T}}(\tau)\hat{\mathbf{T}}_k^{-1}\right)^\vee \\ \mathcal{J}\left(\ln\left(\hat{\mathbf{T}}(\tau)\hat{\mathbf{T}}_k^{-1}\right)^\vee\right)^{-1}\hat{\varpi}(\tau) \end{bmatrix}, \quad \hat{\gamma}_k(t_k) = \begin{bmatrix} \mathbf{0} \\ \hat{\varpi}_k \end{bmatrix},$$

$$\hat{\gamma}_k(t_{k+1}) = \begin{bmatrix} \ln\left(\hat{\mathbf{T}}_{k+1}\hat{\mathbf{T}}_k^{-1}\right)^\vee \\ \mathcal{J}\left(\ln\left(\hat{\mathbf{T}}_{k+1}\hat{\mathbf{T}}_k^{-1}\right)^\vee\right)^{-1}\hat{\varpi}_{k+1} \end{bmatrix}, \quad (11.44)$$

and we note that the posterior values at the two measurement times come from the operating point values at the last iteration of the main MAP solution: $\left\{\hat{\mathbf{T}}_k, \hat{\varpi}_k\right\} = \{\mathbf{T}_{\mathrm{op},k}, \varpi_{\mathrm{op},k}\}$. Rearranging, we have for the interpolated posterior pose and generalized velocity,

$$\hat{\mathbf{T}}(\tau) = \exp\left((\Lambda_1(\tau)\hat{\gamma}_k(t_k) + \Psi_1(\tau)\hat{\gamma}_k(t_{k+1}))^\wedge\right)\hat{\mathbf{T}}_k, \quad (11.45a)$$
$$\hat{\varpi}(\tau) = \mathcal{J}\left(\ln\left(\hat{\mathbf{T}}(\tau)\hat{\mathbf{T}}_k^{-1}\right)^\vee\right)(\Lambda_2(\tau)\hat{\gamma}_k(t_k) + \Psi_2(\tau)\hat{\gamma}_k(t_{k+1})), \quad (11.45b)$$

where we have partitioned $\Lambda(\tau)$ and $\Psi(\tau)$ as

$$\Lambda(\tau) = \begin{bmatrix} \Lambda_1(\tau) \\ \Lambda_2(\tau) \end{bmatrix}, \quad \Psi(\tau) = \begin{bmatrix} \Psi_1(\tau) \\ \Psi_2(\tau) \end{bmatrix}. \quad (11.46)$$

The cost of this trajectory query is $O(1)$ since it only involves two measurement times in the interpolation equation. We can repeat this as many times as we like for different values of τ. The next section discusses how to interpolate the covariance at the query time.

11.3.2 Interpolating the Covariance

Interpolating the covariance is a bit more involved. Once we have a converged solution to the MAP estimation problem,

$$\underbrace{\mathbf{H}^T\mathbf{W}^{-1}\mathbf{H}}_{\hat{\mathbf{P}}^{-1}}\delta\mathbf{x}^\star = \mathbf{H}^T\mathbf{W}^{-1}\mathbf{e}(\mathbf{x}_{\mathrm{op}}), \quad (11.47)$$

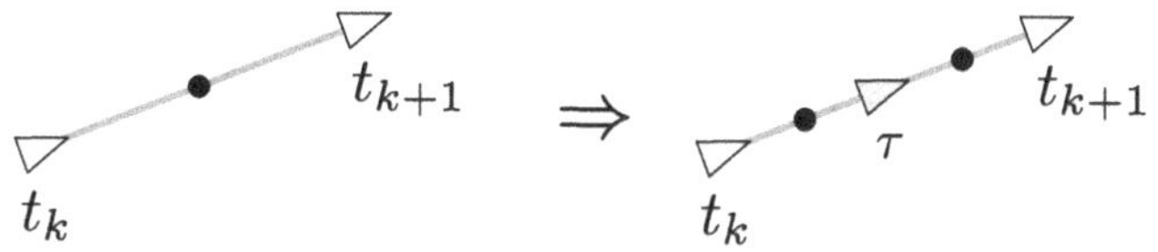

Figure 11.6 To interpolate the covariance, we replace the single factor between the bracketing times with two motion-prior factors to connect the state at the query time.

the left-hand side coefficient matrix is the inverse covariance of the full-trajectory estimate, $\hat{\mathbf{P}}$; this is the Laplace approximation (see Section 4.3.1). To interpolate the covariance at the query time, we only require the marginal of $\hat{\mathbf{P}}$ corresponding to the two pose/velocity states bracketing the query time,

$$\text{cov}(\delta\mathbf{x}^\star_{k:k+1}) = \begin{bmatrix} \hat{\mathbf{P}}(t_k, t_k) & \hat{\mathbf{P}}(t_k, t_{k+1}) \\ \hat{\mathbf{P}}(t_{k+1}, t_k) & \hat{\mathbf{P}}(t_{k+1}, t_{k+1}) \end{bmatrix}, \tag{11.48}$$

which we can extract efficiently by exploiting the arrowhead structure of $\hat{\mathbf{P}}^{-1}$ in (2.61).

Once we have this marginal covariance for the two bracketing states, there are a few possible ways to interpolate for the covariance. Anderson (2016) uses the built-in GP covariance interpolation, requiring a few approximations to adapt it to $SE(3)$. Here we offer an alternative covariance interpolation that exploits the building blocks that we already have for the motion prior.

Without loss of generality, we assume again that $t_k < \tau < t_{k+1}$. We can imagine setting up a small estimation problem with just the states associated with these three times involved. Figure 11.6 depicts the situation; we replace the original motion prior connecting the two times with a new one that is chained through the desired query time. If we use the MAP solution for the states at t_k and t_{k+1} as a prior, the inverse joint covariance for this small estimation problem, $\mathbf{P}^{-1}_{\text{interp}}$, will be of the form

$$\hat{\mathbf{P}}^{-1}_{\text{interp}} = \underbrace{\begin{bmatrix} 1 & 0 \\ 0 & 0 \\ 0 & 1 \end{bmatrix} \begin{bmatrix} \hat{\mathbf{P}}(t_k, t_k) & \hat{\mathbf{P}}(t_k, t_{k+1}) \\ \hat{\mathbf{P}}(t_{k+1}, t_k) & \hat{\mathbf{P}}(t_{k+1}, t_{k+1}) \end{bmatrix}^{-1} \begin{bmatrix} 1 & 0 & 0 \\ 0 & 0 & 1 \end{bmatrix}}_{\text{from main estimation problem}}$$

$$+ \underbrace{\begin{bmatrix} -\mathbf{F}^T_{\tau,k} & 0 \\ \mathbf{E}^T_{\tau,k} & -\mathbf{F}^T_{k+1,\tau} \\ 0 & \mathbf{E}^T_{k+1,\tau} \end{bmatrix} \begin{bmatrix} \mathbf{Q}_{\tau,k} & 0 \\ 0 & \mathbf{Q}_{k+1,\tau} \end{bmatrix}^{-1} \begin{bmatrix} -\mathbf{F}_{\tau,k} & \mathbf{E}_{\tau,k} & 0 \\ 0 & -\mathbf{F}_{k+1,\tau} & \mathbf{E}_{k+1,\tau} \end{bmatrix}}_{\text{add motion prior to connect query time}}$$

$$- \underbrace{\begin{bmatrix} -\mathbf{F}^T_k \\ 0 \\ \mathbf{E}^T_{k+1} \end{bmatrix} \mathbf{Q}^{-1}_{k+1} \begin{bmatrix} -\mathbf{F}_k & 0 & \mathbf{E}_{k+1} \end{bmatrix}}_{\text{remove original motion prior}}, \tag{11.49}$$

where $\mathbf{F}_{\tau,k}$ and $\mathbf{E}_{\tau,k}$ have the same form as (11.20) and (11.21) but with times τ and k, and $\mathbf{F}_{k+1,\tau}$ and $\mathbf{E}_{k+1,\tau}$ are the same for times $k+1$ and τ. Also, $\mathbf{Q}_{\tau,k} = \mathbf{Q}(\tau - t_k)$ and $\mathbf{Q}_{k+1,\tau} = \mathbf{Q}(t_{k+1} - \tau)$ are from (11.7). Since we already interpolated for the mean in the previous section, we do not need to form the full estimation problem and iterate, just set up the inverse covariance that would be

Figure 11.7
Example STEAM
posterior solution
with 10 states (pose
and velocity) and
five landmarks in the
main solution. After
the main MAP
solution converged,
the trajectory was
queried at nine
additional times
between two of the
primary states; a
zoom-in of this
portion of the
trajectory shows the
interpolated poses
and position
covariances.

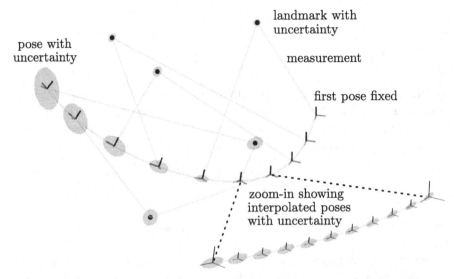

the left-hand side in one of our Gauss–Newton iterations; the reason is that we are only after the Laplace approximation of the covariance at the interpolated time, τ.

The inverse joint covariance, $\mathbf{P}_{\text{interp}}^{-1}$, is actually a 36×36 matrix since it is associated with the three states at t_k, τ, and t_{k+1}. Since we are only interested in the interpolated covariance at τ, we can use the approach of Section 2.2.5 to marginalize out the states at t_k and t_{k+1}, which reveals

$$
\begin{aligned}
\hat{\mathbf{P}}(\tau,\tau)^{-1} = & \ \mathbf{E}_{\tau,k}^T \mathbf{Q}_{\tau,k}^{-1} \mathbf{E}_{\tau,k} + \mathbf{F}_{k+1,\tau}^T \mathbf{Q}_{k+1,\tau}^{-1} \mathbf{F}_{k+1,\tau} \\
& - \begin{bmatrix} \mathbf{F}_{\tau,k}^T \mathbf{Q}_{\tau,k}^{-1} \mathbf{E}_{\tau,k} \\ \mathbf{E}_{k+1,\tau}^T \mathbf{Q}_{k+1,\tau}^{-1} \mathbf{F}_{k+1,\tau} \end{bmatrix}^T \left(\begin{bmatrix} \hat{\mathbf{P}}(t_k,t_k) & \hat{\mathbf{P}}(t_k,t_{k+1}) \\ \hat{\mathbf{P}}(t_{k+1},t_k) & \hat{\mathbf{P}}(t_{k+1},t_{k+1}) \end{bmatrix}^{-1} \right. \\
& \quad + \begin{bmatrix} \mathbf{F}_{\tau,k}^T \mathbf{Q}_{\tau,k}^{-1} \mathbf{F}_{\tau,k} & \mathbf{0} \\ \mathbf{0} & \mathbf{E}_{k+1,\tau}^T \mathbf{Q}_{k+1,\tau}^{-1} \mathbf{E}_{k+1,\tau} \end{bmatrix} \\
& \quad \left. - \begin{bmatrix} \mathbf{F}_k^T \mathbf{Q}_{k+1}^{-1} \mathbf{F}_k & -\mathbf{F}_k^T \mathbf{Q}_{k+1}^{-1} \mathbf{E}_{k+1} \\ -\mathbf{E}_{k+1}^T \mathbf{Q}_{k+1}^{-1} \mathbf{F}_k & \mathbf{E}_{k+1}^T \mathbf{Q}_{k+1}^{-1} \mathbf{E}_{k+1} \end{bmatrix} \right)^{-1} \begin{bmatrix} \mathbf{F}_{\tau,k}^T \mathbf{Q}_{\tau,k}^{-1} \mathbf{E}_{\tau,k} \\ \mathbf{E}_{k+1,\tau}^T \mathbf{Q}_{k+1,\tau}^{-1} \mathbf{F}_{k+1,\tau} \end{bmatrix},
\end{aligned}
$$

$$(11.50)$$

which we can invert for $\hat{\mathbf{P}}(\tau,\tau)$, our desired interpolated posterior covariance at τ. The cost of a single covariance query is also $O(1)$ since we only need to use the two bracketing states at t_k and t_{k+1}.

Figure 11.7 provides a STEAM example with 10 states (pose and velocity) and five landmarks in the main solution. After iterating the main solution to convergence, the methods of the previous and current sections were used to interpolate for nine additional states between each of the original states. A zoom-in of one section of the trajectory shows the interpolated poses and associated position covariances, which both vary smoothly over the interval from t_k to t_{k+1}.

11.3.3 Extrapolating the Mean and Covariance

Fortunately, extrapolating beyond the last timestamp of the main solve is easier than interpolating. Figure 11.8 depicts the situation; we have $t_K < \tau$. Since we

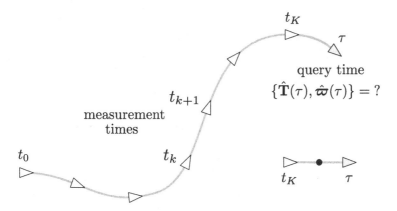

t_K

query time

$\{\hat{\mathbf{T}}(\tau), \hat{\boldsymbol{\varpi}}(\tau)\} = ?$

measurement
times

t_{k+1}

t_0

t_k

t_K τ

Figure 11.8
Sometimes we may want to query the trajectory after the last measurement time, t_K. In other words, we want to extrapolate beyond the measurements or predict a future state. To do this we consider only the small estimation problem in the bottom-right of the figure, where the motion prior is used to 'cantilever' off the last state.

are essentially 'cantilevering' off the state at time t_K, the mean extrapolation at time τ is simply

$$\hat{\mathbf{T}}(\tau) = \exp\left((\tau - t_K)\hat{\boldsymbol{\varpi}}(t_K)^\wedge\right)\hat{\mathbf{T}}(t_K), \tag{11.51a}$$

$$\hat{\boldsymbol{\varpi}}(\tau) = \hat{\boldsymbol{\varpi}}(t_K). \tag{11.51b}$$

In other words, the generalized velocity is constant for all times beyond t_K.

For covariance extrapolation, we can follow a similar approach to the previous section. We consider a small estimation problem over just two times, t_K and τ (see bottom-right of Figure 11.8). The inverse joint covariance for these two times, $\hat{\mathbf{P}}_{\text{extrap}}^{-1}$, will be

$$\hat{\mathbf{P}}_{\text{extrap}}^{-1} = \begin{bmatrix} \hat{\mathbf{P}}(t_K, t_K)^{-1} + \mathbf{F}_{\tau,K}^T \mathbf{Q}_{\tau,K}^{-1} \mathbf{F}_{\tau,K} & -\mathbf{F}_{\tau,K}^T \mathbf{Q}_{\tau,K}^{-1} \mathbf{E}_{\tau,K} \\ -\mathbf{E}_{\tau,K}^T \mathbf{Q}_{\tau,K}^{-1} \mathbf{F}_{\tau,K} & \mathbf{E}_{\tau,K}^T \mathbf{Q}_{\tau,K}^{-1} \mathbf{E}_{\tau,K} \end{bmatrix}, \tag{11.52}$$

where $\hat{\mathbf{P}}(t_K, t_K)$ is the posterior covariance at time K, $\mathbf{F}_{\tau,K}$ and $\mathbf{E}_{\tau,K}$ have the same form as (11.20) and (11.21) but with times τ and K, and $\mathbf{Q}_{\tau,K} = \mathbf{Q}(\tau - t_K)$ is from (11.7).

The inverse joint covariance is 24×24 since it is for the two times, t_K and τ. If we only want the covariance at τ, we can marginalize out the state at t_K using the approach in Section 2.2.5, leaving

$$\hat{\mathbf{P}}(\tau, \tau)^{-1} = \mathbf{E}_{\tau,K}^T \mathbf{Q}_{\tau,K}^{-1} \mathbf{E}_{\tau,K} - \mathbf{E}_{\tau,K}^T \mathbf{Q}_{\tau,K}^{-1} \mathbf{F}_{\tau,K}$$
$$\times \left(\hat{\mathbf{P}}(t_K, t_K)^{-1} + \mathbf{F}_{\tau,K}^T \mathbf{Q}_{\tau,K}^{-1} \mathbf{F}_{\tau,K} \right)^{-1} \mathbf{F}_{\tau,K}^T \mathbf{Q}_{\tau,K}^{-1} \mathbf{E}_{\tau,K}. \tag{11.53}$$

Applying one of the SMW identities, this becomes

$$\hat{\mathbf{P}}(\tau, \tau)^{-1} = \mathbf{E}_{\tau,K}^T \left(\mathbf{F}_{\tau,K} \hat{\mathbf{P}}(t_K, t_K) \mathbf{F}_{\tau,K}^T + \mathbf{Q}_{\tau,K} \right)^{-1} \mathbf{E}_{\tau,K}, \tag{11.54}$$

or

$$\hat{\mathbf{P}}(\tau, \tau) = \mathbf{E}_{\tau,K}^{-1} \left(\mathbf{F}_{\tau,K} \hat{\mathbf{P}}(t_K, t_K) \mathbf{F}_{\tau,K}^T + \mathbf{Q}_{\tau,K} \right) \mathbf{E}_{\tau,K}^{-T}, \tag{11.55}$$

which is reminiscent of the covariance prediction in the EKF, but adapted for our $SE(3) \times \mathbb{R}^6$ state.

11.4 Discussion

It is worth pointing out that while our underlying approach in this chapter considers a trajectory that is continuous in time, we are still discretizing it in order to carry out the batch MAP solution at the measurement times and also the interpolation at the query times. The point is that we have a principled way to query the trajectory at any time of interest, not just the measurement times. Moreover, the interpolation scheme is chosen up front and provides the abilities to (i) smooth the solution based on a physically motivated prior and, (ii) carry out interpolation/extrapolation at any time of interest.

One thing related to interpolation that we left out in the interest of space is that it is actually possible to reduce the number of states in the main solution by using the fact that we can interpolate. This offers the possibility of having three separate sets of timestamps: (i) the measurement times, (ii) the estimation times, and (iii) the query times. Decoupling the roles of these different timestamps offers many possibilities when it comes to efficient continuous-time estimation setups. Typically, the numbers of measurement and query times will be large compared to the number of estimation times.

It is also worth noting that the Gaussian process approach taken in this chapter is quite different from the interpolation approach taken in Section 10.1.5. There we forced the motion between measurement times to have constant body-centric generalized velocity: it was a constraint-based interpolation method. Here we are defining a whole distribution of possible trajectories and encouraging the solution to find one that balances the prior with the measurements: this is a penalty-term approach. Both approaches have their merits.

Although we worked through the details of this chapter for the specific case of 'white-noise-on-acceleration' for the local SDEs, this is not the only possibility. 'White-noise-on-jerk' (Tang et al., 2019) and the Singer model (Wong et al., 2020) are two higher-order SDEs that have been explored in this overall framework.

Finally, the ideas from continuous-time trajectory estimation carry over very nicely to *continuum robot* state estimation (Lilge et al., 2022). A continuum robot is a long, flexible beam that can be actuated to perform manipulation tasks. If we replace 'time' with 'arclength', then much of our discussion in this chapter can be applied directly to the continuum robot domain, where a simplified Cosserat rod prior is very similar to the white-noise-on-acceleration trajectory prior.

Part IV

Appendices

Appendix A

Matrix Primer

This appendix provides some background information on matrix algebra and matrix calculus that may serve as a useful primer and/or reference when approaching this book and state estimation more generally. Magnus and Neudecker (2019) is an excellent reference as is Petersen et al. (2008).

A.1 Matrix Algebra

In this section we lay out the basics of matrix algebra. A *matrix*, $\mathbf{A}$, is a two-dimensional array of numbers,

$$\mathbf{A} = \begin{bmatrix} a_{11} & a_{12} & \cdots & a_{1N} \\ a_{21} & a_{22} & \cdots & a_{2N} \\ \vdots & \vdots & \ddots & \vdots \\ a_{M1} & a_{M2} & \cdots & a_{MN} \end{bmatrix}. \tag{A.1}$$

There are M rows and N columns and the entries, a_{ij}, are real numbers.[1] The entries $a_{11}, a_{22}, a_{33}, \ldots$ sit along the *main diagonal* of the matrix.

We call the set of all such matrices, $\mathbb{R}^{M \times N}$:

$$\mathbb{R}^{M \times N} = \left\{ \mathbf{A} = \begin{bmatrix} a_{11} & \cdots & a_{1N} \\ \vdots & \ddots & \vdots \\ a_{M1} & \cdots & a_{MN} \end{bmatrix} \, \middle| \, (\forall i, j) \, a_{ij} \in \mathbb{R} \right\}. \tag{A.2}$$

The $(\forall i, j)$ notation means 'for each i and j' and the $\in$ symbol means 'is a member of'.

If we only have a single column we write this as

$$\mathbf{a} = \begin{bmatrix} a_1 \\ a_2 \\ \vdots \\ a_N \end{bmatrix} \in \mathbb{R}^N. \tag{A.3}$$

The term *matrix* was first introduced by James Sylvester in the nineteenth century. However, it was his friend and fellow English mathematician, Arthur Cayley (1821–1895) who recognized matrices obeyed a number of properties similar to regular numbers, such as addition and scalar multiplication, and went on to lay the foundations of modern linear algebra. Cayley also postulated the Cayley–Hamilton theorem and was the first to define the notion of a mathematical group, amongst other achievements.

---

[1] We could have defined things in terms of complex entries, but as our goal is to be tutorial we restrict ourselves to real matrices.

Throughout this book, we use $\mathbf{A}$ to be a matrix, $\mathbf{a}$ to be a column, and a to be a scalar.

A.1.1 Vector Space

Addition of matrices $\mathbf{A}, \mathbf{B} \in \mathbb{R}^{M \times N}$ is defined as

$$
\mathbf{A} + \mathbf{B} = \begin{bmatrix} a_{11} & \cdots & a_{1N} \\ \vdots & \ddots & \vdots \\ a_{M1} & \cdots & a_{MN} \end{bmatrix} + \begin{bmatrix} b_{11} & \cdots & b_{1N} \\ \vdots & \ddots & \vdots \\ b_{M1} & \cdots & b_{MN} \end{bmatrix}
$$

$$
= \begin{bmatrix} a_{11} + b_{11} & \cdots & a_{1N} + b_{1N} \\ \vdots & \ddots & \vdots \\ a_{M1} + b_{M1} & \cdots & a_{MN} + b_{MN} \end{bmatrix}. \tag{A.4}
$$

Scalar multiplication of matrix $\mathbf{A} \in \mathbb{R}^{M \times N}$ by scalar $\alpha \in \mathbb{R}$ is defined as

$$
\alpha \mathbf{A} = \alpha \begin{bmatrix} a_{11} & \cdots & a_{1N} \\ \vdots & \ddots & \vdots \\ a_{M1} & \cdots & a_{MN} \end{bmatrix} = \begin{bmatrix} \alpha a_{11} & \cdots & \alpha a_{1N} \\ \vdots & \ddots & \vdots \\ \alpha a_{M1} & \cdots & \alpha a_{MN} \end{bmatrix}. \tag{A.5}
$$

Our set of matrices, $\mathbb{R}^{M \times N}$, is a *vector space* over the field $\mathbb{R}$ under these definitions of addition and scalar multiplication. The *dimension* of this vector space is $M \times N$.

This requires showing the following properties hold. For all $\mathbf{A}, \mathbf{B}, \mathbf{C} \in \mathbb{R}^{M \times N}$ and $\alpha, \beta \in \mathbb{R}$,

$$
\begin{aligned}
\mathbf{A} + \mathbf{B} &\in \mathbb{R}^{M \times N} && \text{(additive closure)} \\
\mathbf{A} + \mathbf{B} &= \mathbf{B} + \mathbf{A} && \text{(additive commutativity)} \\
(\mathbf{A} + \mathbf{B}) + \mathbf{C} &= \mathbf{A} + (\mathbf{B} + \mathbf{C}) && \text{(additive associativity)} \\
\mathbf{A} + \mathbf{0} &= \mathbf{A} && \text{(additive zero)} \\
\mathbf{A} + (-\mathbf{A}) &= \mathbf{0} && \text{(additive inverse)} \\
\alpha \mathbf{A} &\in \mathbb{R}^{M \times N} && \text{(scalar mult. closure)} \\
\alpha(\beta \mathbf{A}) &= (\alpha \beta)\mathbf{A} && \text{(scalar mult. associativity)} \\
1\mathbf{A} &= \mathbf{A} && \text{(scalar mult. identity)} \\
(\alpha + \beta)\mathbf{A} &= \alpha \mathbf{A} + \beta \mathbf{A} && \text{(scalar mult. distributivity)} \\
\alpha(\mathbf{A} + \mathbf{B}) &= \alpha \mathbf{A} + \alpha \mathbf{B} && \text{(additive distributivity)}
\end{aligned}
$$

We note that the additive inverse is $-\mathbf{A} = (-1)\mathbf{A}$ and the *zero matrix*, $\mathbf{0}$, has all zero entries. We will leave the proof of these properties as an exercise.

A.1.2 Associative Algebra

Matrix multiplication of $\mathbf{A} \in \mathbb{R}^{M \times N}$ and $\mathbf{B} \in \mathbb{R}^{N \times P}$ is defined as

$$
\mathbf{AB} = \begin{bmatrix} a_{11} & a_{12} & \cdots & a_{1N} \\ a_{21} & a_{22} & \cdots & a_{2N} \\ \vdots & \vdots & \ddots & \vdots \\ a_{M1} & a_{M2} & \cdots & a_{MN} \end{bmatrix} \begin{bmatrix} b_{11} & b_{12} & \cdots & b_{1P} \\ b_{21} & b_{22} & \cdots & b_{2P} \\ \vdots & \vdots & \ddots & \vdots \\ b_{N1} & b_{N2} & \cdots & a_{NP} \end{bmatrix}
$$

$$
= \begin{bmatrix} \sum_{n=1}^{N} a_{1n}b_{n1} & \sum_{n=1}^{N} a_{1n}b_{n2} & \cdots & \sum_{n=1}^{N} a_{1n}b_{nP} \\ \sum_{n=1}^{N} a_{2n}b_{n1} & \sum_{n=1}^{N} a_{2n}b_{n2} & \cdots & \sum_{n=1}^{N} a_{2n}b_{nP} \\ \vdots & \vdots & \ddots & \vdots \\ \sum_{n=1}^{N} a_{Mn}b_{n1} & \sum_{n=1}^{N} a_{Mn}b_{n2} & \cdots & \sum_{n=1}^{N} a_{Mn}b_{nP} \end{bmatrix},
$$

$$(A.6)$$

which is an element of $\mathbb{R}^{M \times P}$.

The vector space, $\mathbb{R}^{N \times N}$, together with matrix multiplication defined earlier is an *associative algebra* that we will refer to as *matrix algebra*. This requires showing the following properties hold. For all $\mathbf{A}, \mathbf{B}, \mathbf{C} \in \mathbb{R}^{N \times N}$ and $\alpha, \beta \in \mathbb{R}$,

$$\mathbf{AB} \in \mathbb{R}^{N \times N} \qquad \text{(matrix mult. closure)}$$
$$\mathbf{A}(\mathbf{B} + \mathbf{C}) = \mathbf{AB} + \mathbf{AC} \qquad \text{(matrix mult. left distributivity)}$$
$$(\mathbf{A} + \mathbf{B})\mathbf{C} = \mathbf{AC} + \mathbf{BC} \qquad \text{(matrix mult. right distributivity)}$$
$$(\alpha\mathbf{A})(\beta\mathbf{B}) = (\alpha\beta)(\mathbf{AB}) \qquad \text{(multiplicative compatibility)}$$
$$(\mathbf{AB})\mathbf{C} = \mathbf{A}(\mathbf{BC}) \qquad \text{(matrix mult. associativity)}$$

We leave the proof of these as an exercise. These properties can also be shown to hold when the matrices are not square so long as their dimensions are compatible with the given operations.

Matrix algebra also has the following:

$$\mathbf{A0} = \mathbf{0A} = \mathbf{0} \qquad \text{(matrix mult. zero)}$$
$$\mathbf{A1} = \mathbf{1A} = \mathbf{A} \qquad \text{(matrix mult. identity)}$$
$$\mathbf{AA}^{-1} = \mathbf{A}^{-1}\mathbf{A} = \mathbf{1} \qquad \text{(matrix mult. inverse)}$$

where $\mathbf{0}$ is again the zero matrix and $\mathbf{1}$ is the *identity matrix* (ones on the main diagonal and zeros elsewhere). The *multiplicative inverse*, $\mathbf{A}^{-1}$, does not always exist and we will return to this later.

Importantly, commutativity does not generally hold for matrix multiplication:

$$\mathbf{AB} \neq \mathbf{BA}. \qquad (A.7)$$

It does hold when $\mathbf{A}$ and $\mathbf{B}$ are *diagonal matrices* (square with only non-zero entries on the main diagonal).

A.1.3 Transpose and Trace

Consider a matrix,

$$\mathbf{A} = \begin{bmatrix} a_{11} & a_{12} & \cdots & a_{1N} \\ a_{21} & a_{22} & \cdots & a_{2N} \\ \vdots & \vdots & \ddots & \vdots \\ a_{M1} & a_{M2} & \cdots & a_{MN} \end{bmatrix} \in \mathbb{R}^{M \times N}. \tag{A.8}$$

The *transpose*, $(\cdot)^T$, of this matrix is defined as

$$\mathbf{A}^T = \begin{bmatrix} a_{11} & a_{21} & \cdots & a_{M1} \\ a_{12} & a_{22} & \cdots & a_{M2} \\ \vdots & \vdots & \ddots & \vdots \\ a_{1N} & a_{2N} & \cdots & a_{MN} \end{bmatrix} \in \mathbb{R}^{N \times M}. \tag{A.9}$$

In other words, we 'flip' the matrix about its main diagonal. Transpose has some useful properties. For all $\mathbf{A}, \mathbf{B} \in \mathbb{R}^{M \times N}$, $\mathbf{C} \in \mathbb{R}^{N \times P}$, and $\alpha \in \mathbb{R}$,

$$\begin{aligned} (\mathbf{A}^T)^T &= \mathbf{A} && \text{(transpose self-inverse)} \\ (\mathbf{A} + \mathbf{B})^T &= \mathbf{A}^T + \mathbf{B}^T && \text{(transpose addition)} \\ (\alpha \mathbf{A})^T &= \alpha \mathbf{A}^T && \text{(transpose scalar mult.)} \\ (\mathbf{AC})^T &= \mathbf{C}^T \mathbf{A}^T && \text{(transpose matrix mult.)} \end{aligned}$$

A (square) matrix where $\mathbf{A}^T = \mathbf{A}$ is called *symmetric*. A (square) matrix where $\mathbf{A}^T = -\mathbf{A}$ is called *skew-symmetric*.

The *trace*, $\text{tr}(\cdot)$, of square matrix $\mathbf{A} \in \mathbb{R}^{N \times N}$ is defined as

$$\text{tr}\mathbf{A} = \sum_{n=1}^{N} a_{nn}. \tag{A.10}$$

It is the sum of the entries on the main diagonal (a scalar number). Trace also has some useful properties. For all $\mathbf{A}, \mathbf{B} \in \mathbb{R}^{M \times N}$ and $\alpha \in \mathbb{R}$,

$$\begin{aligned} \text{tr}(\mathbf{A} + \mathbf{B}) &= \text{tr}\mathbf{A} + \text{tr}\mathbf{B} && \text{(trace addition)} \\ \text{tr}(\alpha \mathbf{A}) &= \alpha \text{tr}\mathbf{A} && \text{(trace scalar mult.)} \\ \text{tr}(\mathbf{A}^T) &= \text{tr}\mathbf{A} && \text{(trace transpose)} \\ \text{tr}(\mathbf{A}^T \mathbf{B}) &= \text{tr}(\mathbf{B}\mathbf{A}^T) && \text{(trace matrix mult.)} \end{aligned}$$

From these it can be shown that, with appropriately sized matrices, trace is invariant under *cyclic permutations*:

$$\text{tr}(\mathbf{ABC}) = \text{tr}(\mathbf{BCA}) = \text{tr}(\mathbf{CAB}). \tag{A.11}$$

Notably, trace does not distribute over matrix multiplication: $\text{tr}(\mathbf{AB}) \neq \text{tr}\mathbf{A} \, \text{tr}\mathbf{B}$.

A.1.4 Inner-Product Space and Norms

The *inner product*, $\langle \cdot, \cdot \rangle$, for two matrices, $\mathbf{A}, \mathbf{B} \in \mathbb{R}^{M \times N}$ is defined as

$$\langle \mathbf{A}, \mathbf{B} \rangle = \text{tr}(\mathbf{A}^T \mathbf{B}), \tag{A.12}$$

which is also known as the *Frobenius inner product*. The result of the inner product is a single scalar number. In the case of two columns, $\mathbf{a}, \mathbf{b} \in \mathbb{R}^N$, the inner product is the same as the *dot product*:

$$\langle \mathbf{a}, \mathbf{b} \rangle = \text{tr}(\mathbf{a}^T \mathbf{b}) = \mathbf{a}^T \mathbf{b}. \tag{A.13}$$

With this definition of the inner product, vector space $\mathbb{R}^{M \times N}$ is also an *inner-product space* (aka a pre-Hilbert space). To establish this requires showing the following properties for all $\mathbf{A}, \mathbf{B}, \mathbf{C} \in \mathbb{R}^{M \times N}$ and $\alpha, \beta \in \mathbb{R}$:

$$\langle \mathbf{A}, \mathbf{B} \rangle = \langle \mathbf{B}, \mathbf{A} \rangle \qquad \text{(inner prod. commutativity)}$$
$$\langle \alpha \mathbf{A} + \beta \mathbf{B}, \mathbf{C} \rangle = \alpha \langle \mathbf{A}, \mathbf{C} \rangle + \beta \langle \mathbf{B}, \mathbf{C} \rangle \qquad \text{(inner prod. linearity)}$$
$$\langle \mathbf{A}, \mathbf{A} \rangle \geq 0 \qquad \text{(inner prod. positivity)}$$

where in the last property $\langle \mathbf{A}, \mathbf{A} \rangle = 0$ if and only if $\mathbf{A} = \mathbf{0}$. When $\langle \mathbf{A}, \mathbf{B} \rangle = 0$, we say that $\mathbf{A}$ and $\mathbf{B}$ are *orthogonal* to one another.[2]

Every inner-product space has a *norm*, $|| \cdot ||$, sometimes called its *canonical norm*, defined as

$$||\mathbf{A}|| = \sqrt{\langle \mathbf{A}, \mathbf{A} \rangle} = \sqrt{\text{tr}(\mathbf{A}^T \mathbf{A})}. \tag{A.14}$$

For our inner product, this is called the *Frobenius norm*, sometimes denoted $|| \cdot ||_F$. In the case of a column, $\mathbf{a} \in \mathbb{R}^N$, the norm is

$$a = ||\mathbf{a}|| = \sqrt{\mathbf{a}^T \mathbf{a}}, \tag{A.15}$$

which is simply the Euclidean length of the column, sometimes denoted $|| \cdot ||_2$ for '2-norm'. There are also other norms, not all of which come from an inner product, but we do not require them here.

Norms come along with a number of useful general properties. For example, for all $\mathbf{A}, \mathbf{B} \in \mathbb{R}^{M \times N}$ and $\alpha \in \mathbb{R}$,

$$||\mathbf{A}|| \geq 0 \qquad \text{(norm positivity)}$$
$$||\alpha \mathbf{A}|| = |\alpha| \, ||\mathbf{A}|| \qquad \text{(norm absolute homogeneity)}$$
$$||\mathbf{A} + \mathbf{B}|| \leq ||\mathbf{A}|| + ||\mathbf{B}|| \qquad \text{(triangle inequality)}$$
$$|\langle \mathbf{A}, \mathbf{B} \rangle| \leq ||\mathbf{A}|| \, ||\mathbf{B}|| \qquad \text{(Cauchy–Schwarz inequality)}$$
$$||\mathbf{A} - \mathbf{B}||^2 = ||\mathbf{A}||^2 + ||\mathbf{B}||^2 - 2 \langle \mathbf{A}, \mathbf{B} \rangle \qquad \text{(law of cosines)}$$

where $| \cdot |$ denotes *absolute value*. In the first, equality occurs if and only if $\mathbf{A} = \mathbf{0}$. Equality in Cauchy–Schwarz occurs only when $\mathbf{A} = \alpha \mathbf{B}$ for some α (linear dependence). In the law of cosines, when $\mathbf{A}$ and $\mathbf{B}$ are orthogonal we have *Pythagoras' theorem*; for example, for $\mathbf{a}, \mathbf{b}, \mathbf{c} = \mathbf{a} - \mathbf{b} \in \mathbb{R}^N$ we see

$$\underbrace{||\mathbf{c}||^2}_{c^2} = \underbrace{||\mathbf{a}||^2}_{a^2} + \underbrace{||\mathbf{b}||^2}_{b^2} - 2 \underbrace{\mathbf{a}^T \mathbf{b}}_{ab\cos\phi}, \tag{A.16}$$

with ϕ being the angle between $\mathbf{a}$ and $\mathbf{b}$, which will be zero when they are orthogonal.

---

[2] Not to be confused with the concept of an *orthogonal matrix*, $\mathbf{A} \in \mathbb{R}^{N \times N}$, which requires $\mathbf{A}^T \mathbf{A} = \mathbf{A} \mathbf{A}^T = \mathbf{1}$.

Ferdinand Georg Frobenius (1849–1917) was a German mathematician who worked on a variety of mathematical topics including elliptic functions, differential equations, and group theory. Notably, he was the first to give a full proof of the Cayley–Hamilton theorem.

David Hilbert (1862–1943) was a German mathematician who was considered one of the most influential mathematicians of his time, touching on many topics including commutative algebra, geometry, and the foundations of mathematics. In 1900 he posed 23 unsolved problems that greatly influenced the course of twentieth-century mathematics.

A.1.5 Linear Independence and Bases

We have discussed that the set of $M \times N$ matrices, $\mathbb{R}^{M \times N}$, is a vector space of dimension $M \times N$. A powerful tool that comes along with a vector space is the notion of a *basis*, which is a set of members (the number equal to the dimension of the space) that can be used to construct every element in the space through a *linear combination*. For example, for each $\mathbf{A} \in \mathbb{R}^{M \times N}$, we can write it as a linear combination,

$$\mathbf{A} = \sum_{m=1}^{M} \sum_{n=1}^{N} a_{mn} \mathbf{1}_{mn}, \tag{A.17}$$

where $\mathbf{1}_{mn}$ is a *single-entry matrix* with 1 in the (m, n) entry and zeros elsewhere. The set of all $M \times N$ single-entry matrices, $\{(\forall m, n) \, \mathbf{1}_{mn}\}$, is a basis for $\mathbb{R}^{M \times N}$ and $a_{mn} \in \mathbb{R}$ are the *coordinates* of $\mathbf{A}$ in this basis. We can also write that

$$\mathbb{R}^{M \times N} = \mathrm{span} \left\{ (\forall m, n) \, \mathbf{1}_{mn} \right\}, \tag{A.18}$$

which says that our vector space is *spanned* by the basis and means that every $\mathbf{A} \in \mathbb{R}^{M \times N}$ can be written as a unique linear combination of the basis vectors. In general, $\mathrm{span} \{\cdot\}$ produces all possible linear combinations of a set of vectors.

Our example basis above is not unique. Any set of $M \times N$ *linearly independent* members of a vector space of dimension $M \times N$ constitutes a basis. Suppose we have a set of $M \times N$ matrices, $\{(\forall m, n) \, \mathbf{A}_{mn}\}$, from $\mathbb{R}^{M \times N}$. The set of matrices is *linearly independent* if the condition

$$\sum_{m=1}^{M} \sum_{n=1}^{N} \alpha_{mn} \mathbf{A}_{mn} = \mathbf{0} \tag{A.19}$$

can only be satisfied when $(\forall m, n) \, \alpha_{mn} = 0$. In other words, the only way to build a linear combination that adds up to zero is when each coefficient is zero. If we can satisfy the condition with at least one $\alpha_{mn} \neq 0$, we say the set is *linearly dependent*.

A special type of basis is an *orthogonal basis*. In such a basis, all the basis vectors are orthogonal to one another. Specifically, if $\{(\forall m, n) \, \mathbf{A}_{mn}\}$ is our basis, it is orthogonal if

$$(\forall mn \neq pq) \quad \langle \mathbf{A}_{mn}, \mathbf{A}_{pq} \rangle = 0. \tag{A.20}$$

For example, the basis $\{(\forall m, n) \, \mathbf{1}_{mn}\}$ is orthogonal. If we start with a basis that is not orthogonal we can use it to construct one that is by using a procedure called Gram–Schmidt orthogonalization.

We furthermore call an orthogonal basis *orthonormal* if the inner product of each basis vector with itself is equal to 1:

$$(\forall mn) \quad \langle \mathbf{A}_{mn}, \mathbf{A}_{mn} \rangle = 1. \tag{A.21}$$

The basis $\{(\forall m, n) \, \mathbf{1}_{mn}\}$ is also orthonormal. As we will see in the next section, having an orthonormal basis is desirable as it makes projections simpler.

A.1.6 Subspaces, Projections, Nullspace, Rank

Another important concept that comes along with a vector space is a *subspace*. A subspace is itself a vector space that is contained inside another vector space. A subset, $\mathcal{S} \subseteq \mathbb{R}^{M \times N}$, must satisfy three properties to be a subspace. For all $\mathbf{A}, \mathbf{B} \in \mathcal{S}$ and $\alpha \in \mathbb{R}$ we require

$$\mathbf{0} \in \mathcal{S} \qquad \text{(subspace contains zero)}$$
$$\mathbf{A} + \mathbf{B} \in \mathcal{S} \qquad \text{(subspace additive closure)}$$
$$\alpha \mathbf{A} \in \mathcal{S} \qquad \text{(subspace scalar mult. closure)}$$

In other words, all linear combinations of elements in the subset must also be in the subset, including the zero matrix.

For example, the set of all *diagonal matrices* (only non-zero entries are on the main diagonal) is a subspace of all square matrices $\mathbb{R}^{N \times N}$. Since a subspace is itself a vector space we must be able to find a basis for it. Continuing the example, the set of diagonal matrices, $\mathcal{D}$, has as a basis all the single-entry matrices that have a 1 on the diagonal, $\{(\forall n) \, \mathbf{1}_{nn}\}$:

$$\mathcal{D} = \text{span} \left\{ (\forall n) \, \mathbf{1}_{nn} \right\}. \tag{A.22}$$

The number of basis vectors is N, so the dimension of $\mathcal{D}$ is also N.

We can also work the other way around. If we start with a set of linearly independent vectors in a vector space, the span of that set will be a subspace. For example consider the linearly independent set $\{\mathbf{1}_1, \mathbf{1}_2\}$ where $\mathbf{1}_n \in \mathbb{R}^N$ is a *single-entry column* (a column with a 1 in row n and zeros otherwise). If $N = 3$, then we are working in familiar three-dimensional Euclidean space, $\mathbb{R}^3$. The subspace $\text{span}\{\mathbf{1}_1, \mathbf{1}_2\}$ is then a plane within $\mathbb{R}^3$. Each member of this two-dimensional subspace can be written as $x\mathbf{1}_1 + y\mathbf{1}_2$ for some coordinates (x, y).

It is sometimes useful to start with a member in one vector space and project it onto an associated subspace. The simplest case is when the subspace is one-dimensional. Imagine we have a subspace, $\mathcal{B} = \text{span} \{\mathbf{B}\}$ with $\mathbf{B} \in \mathbb{R}^{M \times N}$. Then, if we start with any $\mathbf{A} \in \mathbb{R}^{M \times N}$, the *projection* of $\mathbf{A}$ onto subspace $\mathcal{B}$ is

$$\text{proj}_{\mathcal{B}} \mathbf{A} = \frac{\langle \mathbf{B}, \mathbf{A} \rangle}{\langle \mathbf{B}, \mathbf{B} \rangle} \, \mathbf{B}. \tag{A.23}$$

For a B-dimensional subspace, for example, $\mathcal{B} = \text{span} \{\mathbf{B}_1, \mathbf{B}_2, \ldots, \mathbf{B}_B\}$ with $(\forall i) \, \mathbf{B}_i \in \mathbb{R}^{M \times N}$, the projection of $\mathbf{A}$ onto $\mathcal{B}$ is

$$\text{proj}_{\mathcal{B}} \mathbf{A} = \sum_{i=1}^{B} \beta_i \mathbf{B}_i, \tag{A.24}$$

where

$$\begin{bmatrix} \beta_1 \\ \beta_2 \\ \vdots \\ \beta_B \end{bmatrix} = \begin{bmatrix} \langle \mathbf{B}_1, \mathbf{B}_1 \rangle & \langle \mathbf{B}_1, \mathbf{B}_2 \rangle & \cdots & \langle \mathbf{B}_1, \mathbf{B}_B \rangle \\ \langle \mathbf{B}_2, \mathbf{B}_1 \rangle & \langle \mathbf{B}_2, \mathbf{B}_2 \rangle & \cdots & \langle \mathbf{B}_2, \mathbf{B}_B \rangle \\ \vdots & \vdots & \ddots & \vdots \\ \langle \mathbf{B}_B, \mathbf{B}_1 \rangle & \langle \mathbf{B}_B, \mathbf{B}_2 \rangle & \cdots & \langle \mathbf{B}_B, \mathbf{B}_B \rangle \end{bmatrix}^{-1} \begin{bmatrix} \langle \mathbf{B}_1, \mathbf{A} \rangle \\ \langle \mathbf{B}_2, \mathbf{A} \rangle \\ \vdots \\ \langle \mathbf{B}_B, \mathbf{A} \rangle \end{bmatrix}. \tag{A.25}$$

In the case that $\{\mathbf{B}_1, \mathbf{B}_2, \ldots, \mathbf{B}_B\}$ is an orthonormal basis, the matrix of inner products whose inverse we must take becomes $\mathbf{1}$, whereupon we simply have that $\beta_i = \langle \mathbf{B}_i, \mathbf{A} \rangle$.

Projections become notationally simpler in the case of columns rather than matrices. Suppose we have a B-dimensional subspace of $\mathbb{R}^N$ given by $\mathcal{B} = \mathrm{span}\,\{\mathbf{b}_1, \mathbf{b}_2, \ldots, \mathbf{b}_B\}$ with $(\forall i)\,\mathbf{b}_i \in \mathbb{R}^N$ as the basis. Then the projection of $\mathbf{a} \in \mathbb{R}^N$ onto $\mathcal{B}$ is

$$\mathrm{proj}_{\mathcal{B}} \mathbf{a} = \underbrace{\mathbf{B} \left(\mathbf{B}^T \mathbf{B}\right)^{-1} \mathbf{B}^T}_{\mathbf{P}} \mathbf{a}, \tag{A.26}$$

where $\mathbf{B} = \begin{bmatrix} \mathbf{b}_1 & \mathbf{b}_2 & \cdots & \mathbf{b}_B \end{bmatrix}$. The matrix $\mathbf{P} \in \mathbb{R}^{N \times N}$ is known as a *projection matrix* (for $\mathcal{B}$) and we see that to project $\mathbf{a}$ onto $\mathcal{B}$ we need only carry out a matrix multiplication. In the case that the basis is orthonormal, the projection matrix simplifies to $\mathbf{P} = \mathbf{B}\mathbf{B}^T$ since $\mathbf{B}^T \mathbf{B} = \mathbf{1}$. Projection matrices are square, symmetric, and examples of *idempotent* matrices, meaning $\mathbf{P}^2 = \mathbf{P}$.

This is also a convenient place to introduce the notion of *nullspace* of a matrix. The nullspace, $\mathrm{null}(\cdot)$, of matrix $\mathbf{A} \in \mathbb{R}^{M \times N}$ is defined as

$$\mathrm{null}(\mathbf{A}) = \left\{ \mathbf{x} \in \mathbb{R}^N \mid \mathbf{A}\mathbf{x} = \mathbf{0} \right\}. \tag{A.27}$$

In other words, it is the set of all columns that when premultiplied by $\mathbf{A}$ produce $\mathbf{0}$. Other important spaces associated with $\mathbf{A}$ are the *rowspace* (span of the rows of $\mathbf{A}$), *columnspace* (span of the columns of $\mathbf{A}$), and *left nullspace* (nullspace of $\mathbf{A}^T$); these four spaces can all be shown to be subspaces of the larger spaces in which they reside. While general, these concepts are perhaps best understood in the context of projections. Consider again projecting $\mathbf{a} \in \mathbb{R}^N$ onto $\mathcal{B}$ as defined earlier. The part of $\mathbf{a}$ that is left over after the projection, $\mathbf{a} - \mathrm{proj}_{\mathcal{B}} \mathbf{a}$, called the *orthogonal complement*, must lie in the nullspace of the projection matrix, $\mathbf{P}$:

$$\mathbf{P}\mathbf{a} = \mathbf{P}\left(\mathbf{a} - \mathrm{proj}_{\mathcal{B}} \mathbf{a} + \mathrm{proj}_{\mathcal{B}} \mathbf{a}\right) = \underbrace{\mathbf{P}\left(\mathbf{a} - \mathrm{proj}_{\mathcal{B}} \mathbf{a}\right)}_{0} + \mathbf{P}\left(\mathrm{proj}_{\mathcal{B}} \mathbf{a}\right) = \mathrm{proj}_{\mathcal{B}} \mathbf{a}.$$
$$\tag{A.28}$$

Another way to say this is that the component of $\mathbf{A}$ in the nullspace of the projection matrix is orthogonal to the subspace to which we are projecting, while the resulting projection is 'parallel' and contained therein.

For matrix $\mathbf{A} \in \mathbb{R}^{M \times N}$ the *rank* of a matrix is the dimension of the columnspace (number of linearly independent columns) or equivalently the dimension of the rowspace (number of linearly independent rows). The *nullity* is the dimension of the nullspace. The *rank-nullity theorem* then tells us that

$$\mathrm{rank}(\mathbf{A}) + \mathrm{nullity}(\mathbf{A}) = N. \tag{A.29}$$

In the case of a projection matrix, $\mathbf{P}$, the rank is equal to the dimension of the subspace to which we are projecting and the nullity is the dimension of the space whose members result in zero when projected.

A.1.7 Determinant and Inverse

The *determinant*, $\det(\cdot)$, of a square matrix, $\mathbf{A} \in \mathbb{R}^{N \times N}$, can be defined in terms of the *Laplace expansion*:

$$\det(\mathbf{A}) = \sum_{j=1}^{N} (-1)^{i+j} a_{ij} M_{ij}, \tag{A.30}$$

where a_{ij} is the (i, j) entry of $\mathbf{A}$ and M_{ij} is the ijth *minor* of $\mathbf{A}$; the minor is calculated by taking the determinant of $\mathbf{A}$ with its ith row and jth column removed. This recursive definition takes determinants of smaller and smaller matrices until we need to take the determinant of a scalar, which is defined to just be the number itself: $\det(a) = a$. The result of the determinant is a scalar number that tells us something about the degeneracy of the matrix. Sometimes the notation $|\cdot|$ is used to denote the determinant, but this can be easily confused with absolute value and is problematic for a scalar quantity where the results can disagree.

We earlier introduced the *inverse* of a matrix, but we can say more about it here. The inverse, $\mathbf{A}^{-1} \in \mathbb{R}^{N \times N}$, of matrix, $\mathbf{A} \in \mathbb{R}^{N \times N}$, is the unique matrix (if it exists) such that

$$\mathbf{A}\mathbf{A}^{-1} = \mathbf{A}^{-1}\mathbf{A} = \mathbf{1}. \tag{A.31}$$

However, the inverse of a matrix does not always exist. There are several ways to check if the inverse exists, but the most practical are

$$\mathbf{A}^{-1} \text{ exists} \iff \det(\mathbf{A}) \neq 0 \iff \text{rank}(\mathbf{A}) = N. \tag{A.32}$$

When the inverse exists, we say that a matrix is *invertible*.

The inverse (provided it exists) has some useful properties. For all $\mathbf{A}, \mathbf{B} \in \mathbb{R}^{N \times N}$ and $\alpha \in \mathbb{R}$ we have

$$\begin{aligned}
(\mathbf{A}^{-1})^{-1} &= \mathbf{A} && \text{(inverse inverse)} \\
(\mathbf{A}^{T})^{-1} &= (\mathbf{A}^{-1})^{T} && \text{(inverse transpose)} \\
(\alpha\mathbf{A})^{-1} &= \tfrac{1}{\alpha}\mathbf{A}^{-1} && \text{(inverse scalar mult.)} \\
(\mathbf{A}\mathbf{B})^{-1} &= \mathbf{B}^{-1}\mathbf{A}^{-1} && \text{(inverse matrix mult.)}
\end{aligned}$$

And for the determinant we have

$$\begin{aligned}
\det(\mathbf{A}^{T}) &= \det(\mathbf{A}) && \text{(determinant transpose)} \\
\det(\alpha\mathbf{A}) &= \alpha^{N}\det(\mathbf{A}) && \text{(determinant scalar mult.)} \\
\det(\mathbf{A}\mathbf{B}) &= \det(\mathbf{A})\det(\mathbf{B}) && \text{(determinant matrix mult.)} \\
\det(\mathbf{A}^{-1}) &= 1/\det(\mathbf{A}) && \text{(determinant inverse)}
\end{aligned}$$

In the last of these we see that, if $\det(\mathbf{A}) = 0$, then $\det(\mathbf{A}^{-1})$ will be undefined, which is exactly when $\mathbf{A}^{-1}$ does not exist.

A.1.8 Linear Systems of Equations and Partitions

This section is one of the most important in practice. In many cases, we use matrix algebra to express relationships between different unknown variables in the form of *linear systems of equations*. Most commonly, these are of the form

$$\mathbf{A}\mathbf{x} = \mathbf{b}, \tag{A.33}$$

where $\mathbf{A} \in \mathbb{R}^{M \times N}$, $\mathbf{x} \in \mathbb{R}^{N}$, and $\mathbf{b} \in \mathbb{R}^{M}$. Typically $\mathbf{A}$ and $\mathbf{b}$ are known while $\mathbf{x}$ is unknown. Each of the M rows of this system of equations provides a scalar relationship between the N unknown variables contained in $\mathbf{x}$. There are three cases to discuss:

- *underspecified (M < N)*: we have less equations than unknowns and there can be zero or infinitely many solutions (values for $\mathbf{x}$) to the linear system of equations; we deliberately avoid this situation in state estimation
- *square (M = N)*: we have an equal number of equations and unknowns, and now there can be zero, one, or infinitely many solutions
- *overspecified (M > N)*: we have more equations than unknowns, but there can still be zero, one, or infinitely many solutions

The last two cases are of the most interest to us in state estimation. In the square case, we often want to know when a unique solution exists; this is precisely when $\mathbf{A}$ is invertible, whereupon

$$\mathbf{x} = \mathbf{A}^{-1}\mathbf{b}, \tag{A.34}$$

although in practice there are better ways to compute the answer than to invert $\mathbf{A}$.

In the overspecified case, the most common situation in state estimation is when there are no exact solutions, whereupon we often turn to the *least-squares* solution,

$$\mathbf{x} = \underbrace{\left(\mathbf{A}^{T}\mathbf{A}\right)^{-1}\mathbf{A}^{T}}_{\mathbf{A}^{+}}\mathbf{b} = \mathbf{A}^{+}\mathbf{b}, \tag{A.35}$$

where we employ the *(Moore–Penrose) pseudoinverse*, $\mathbf{A}^{+}$. Notably, in the square case the inverse and the pseudoinverse are the same.

Worth bringing up in this section is the idea of solving *partitioned* linear systems of equations. We can partition (i.e., subdivide) the matrices in a square linear system of equations such that

$$\underbrace{\begin{bmatrix} \mathbf{A}_{11} & \mathbf{A}_{12} \\ \mathbf{A}_{21} & \mathbf{A}_{22} \end{bmatrix}}_{\mathbf{A}} \underbrace{\begin{bmatrix} \mathbf{x}_{1} \\ \mathbf{x}_{2} \end{bmatrix}}_{\mathbf{x}} = \underbrace{\begin{bmatrix} \mathbf{b}_{1} \\ \mathbf{b}_{2} \end{bmatrix}}_{\mathbf{b}}. \tag{A.36}$$

The sizes of the partition blocks, sometimes called *submatrices*, must be compatible since multiplying this out means $\mathbf{A}_{11}\mathbf{x}_{1} + \mathbf{A}_{12}\mathbf{x}_{2} = \mathbf{b}_{1}$ and $\mathbf{A}_{21}\mathbf{x}_{1} + \mathbf{A}_{22}\mathbf{x}_{2} = \mathbf{b}_{2}$. Suppose now that we only want to solve for $\mathbf{x}_{1}$ and do not care at all about $\mathbf{x}_{2}$. We could solve the full system of linear equations and discard the part we do not want, but this could be wasteful in some situations. Instead, we can use the *Schur complement* to help us. The idea is to left-multiply both sides of the system of equations by a specially constructed invertible matrix:

$$\begin{bmatrix} 1 & -\mathbf{A}_{12}\mathbf{A}_{22}^{-1} \\ 0 & 1 \end{bmatrix} \begin{bmatrix} \mathbf{A}_{11} & \mathbf{A}_{12} \\ \mathbf{A}_{21} & \mathbf{A}_{22} \end{bmatrix} \begin{bmatrix} \mathbf{x}_{1} \\ \mathbf{x}_{2} \end{bmatrix} = \begin{bmatrix} 1 & -\mathbf{A}_{12}\mathbf{A}_{22}^{-1} \\ 0 & 1 \end{bmatrix} \begin{bmatrix} \mathbf{b}_{1} \\ \mathbf{b}_{2} \end{bmatrix}. \tag{A.37}$$

The solutions to this new system will be the same as those from the original. Multiplying out a bit we see

$$\begin{bmatrix} \mathbf{A}_{11} - \mathbf{A}_{12}\mathbf{A}_{22}^{-1}\mathbf{A}_{21} & \mathbf{0} \\ \mathbf{A}_{21} & \mathbf{A}_{22} \end{bmatrix} \begin{bmatrix} \mathbf{x}_1 \\ \mathbf{x}_2 \end{bmatrix} = \begin{bmatrix} \mathbf{b}_1 - \mathbf{A}_{21}\mathbf{A}_{22}^{-1}\mathbf{b}_2 \\ \mathbf{b}_2 \end{bmatrix}. \tag{A.38}$$

This last system is useful to us because of the $\mathbf{0}$ block, which makes the first block-row become

$$\underbrace{\left(\mathbf{A}_{11} - \mathbf{A}_{12}\mathbf{A}_{22}^{-1}\mathbf{A}_{21}\right)}_{\mathbf{A}/\mathbf{A}_{22}} \mathbf{x}_1 = \mathbf{b}_1 - \mathbf{A}_{21}\mathbf{A}_{22}^{-1}\mathbf{b}_2, \tag{A.39}$$

and now only involves $\mathbf{x}_1$. The Schur complement is denoted $\mathbf{A}/\mathbf{A}_{22}$. A similar approach can be used to solve for only $\mathbf{x}_2$. A nice corollary to the Schur complement is that $\det(\mathbf{A}) = \det(\mathbf{A}_{22})\det(\mathbf{A}/\mathbf{A}_{22})$.

A.1.9 Eigenproblem and Diagonalization

Perhaps the second-most common problem in matrix algebra after the linear system of equations is the *eigenproblem*. In short, the goal is to find the values of $\mathbf{x} \neq \mathbf{0} \in \mathbb{C}^N$ and $\lambda \in \mathbb{C}$ so that

$$\mathbf{A}\mathbf{x} = \lambda\mathbf{x} \tag{A.40}$$

for a given $\mathbf{A} \in \mathbb{R}^{N \times N}$. Even if $\mathbf{A}$ is a real matrix, the eigenvalues can be (and are often) complex numbers of the form $\lambda = a + ib$ where $i = \sqrt{-1}$. The eigenvectors can also have complex (rather than real) entries. We use $\mathbb{C}$ to indicate complex and $\mathbb{R}$ to indicate real.[3]

Equivalently to (A.40), we must have

$$(\mathbf{A} - \lambda\mathbf{1})\mathbf{x} = \mathbf{0}, \tag{A.41}$$

or in other words $\mathbf{x}$ must be in the nullspace of $\mathbf{A} - \lambda\mathbf{1}$. If the determinant of $\mathbf{A} - \lambda\mathbf{1}$ is not zero, it will be invertible and then $\mathbf{x} = \mathbf{0}$ is the only solution, which is not what we seek. This means we are looking for the values of λ so that

$$\det(\mathbf{A} - \lambda\mathbf{1}) = 0. \tag{A.42}$$

This is called the *characteristic equation* for $\mathbf{A}$ and its solutions are the *eigenvalues* of $\mathbf{A}$. Solving the characteristic equation involves finding the roots of a Nth order polynomial, which is often left to a computer but can be done by hand for simple cases.

Once we have the N eigenvalues, we solve for the corresponding values of $\mathbf{x}$ that satisfy (A.41), which are called the *eigenvectors*. They are not unique in that any non-zero scalar multiple of an eigenvector is also an eigenvector; often they are selected to have unit length. In the case of repeated eigenvalues, there are some subtleties that we will not go into.[4] Let us assume for now that for each eigenvalue, λ_n, we can compute an eigenvector, $\mathbf{v}_n$, and the set of all eigenvectors, $\{\mathbf{v}_1, \ldots, \mathbf{v}_N\}$, is linearly independent (we will come back to this a bit later).

David Hilbert first introduced the prefix *eigen* in 1904, which was adopted from German to mean 'special', 'inherent', or 'characteristic'. The eigenproblem was studied by an ensemble cast of characters over the years from Euler and Lagrange (for rigid-body motion), Cauchy (for quadric surfaces), Fourier (for the heat equation), and Hilbert (for operator theory). Eigendecomposition or diagonalization has much to do with finding a special coordinate system in which some problems become simpler to solve.

---

[3] In our development of matrix algebra we assumed everything was real, but all the same concepts can be extended to the complex case.

[4] *Jordan decomposition* handles the general case.

We can then write our N solutions in the form

$$\mathbf{A} \underbrace{\begin{bmatrix} \mathbf{v}_1 & \mathbf{v}_2 & \cdots & \mathbf{v}_N \end{bmatrix}}_{\mathbf{V}} = \underbrace{\begin{bmatrix} \mathbf{v}_1 & \mathbf{v}_2 & \cdots & \mathbf{v}_N \end{bmatrix}}_{\mathbf{V}} \underbrace{\begin{bmatrix} \lambda_1 & 0 & \cdots & 0 \\ 0 & \lambda_2 & \cdots & 0 \\ \vdots & \vdots & \ddots & \vdots \\ 0 & 0 & \cdots & \lambda_N \end{bmatrix}}_{\mathbf{D}}.$$

$$(A.43)$$

If our eigenvectors form a linearly independent set, it means also that the columns of $\mathbf{V}$ are linearly independent and therefore $\mathbf{V}$ is invertible. Thus, we can write that

$$\mathbf{A} = \mathbf{VDV}^{-1}, \qquad (A.44)$$

which we refer to as an *eigendecomposition* or *diagonalization* of $\mathbf{A}$. The matrix $\mathbf{D}$ is a diagonal matrix with the eigenvalues along the main diagonal, sometimes denoted $\mathbf{D} = \mathrm{diag}\,(\lambda_1, \lambda_2, \ldots, \lambda_N)$. It is not always possible to diagonalize a matrix; the condition essentially comes down to being able to find a set of N linearly independent eigenvectors. A sufficient (but not necessary) condition for this to be true is to have all the eigenvalues be distinct.

If diagonalization of $\mathbf{A}$ is possible, we can use this to help simplify the solution of other problems. The classic example is computing powers of matrix $\mathbf{A}$; suppose we want to compute $\mathbf{A}^M = \underbrace{\mathbf{AA}\cdots\mathbf{A}}_{M}$. Then we can do as follows:

$$\mathbf{A}^M = \left(\mathbf{VDV}^{-1}\right)^M = \mathbf{VD}\underbrace{\mathbf{V}^{-1}\mathbf{V}}_{1}\mathbf{DV}^{-1}\cdots\mathbf{VDV}^{-1} = \mathbf{VD}^M\mathbf{V}^{-1},$$

$$(A.45)$$

where $\mathbf{D}^M = \mathrm{diag}\,(\lambda_1^M, \lambda_2^M, \ldots, \lambda_N^M)$. In other words, we can exploit the fact that it is much easier to compute powers of a diagonal matrix than the original one.

A few other important facts regarding the eigenvalues of a matrix, $\mathbf{A} \in \mathbb{R}^{N \times N}$:

William Rowan
Hamilton
(1805–1865) was an
Irish mathematician
who is particularly
known for
Hamiltonian
mechanics and
quaternions, but also
contributed to many
other areas.

$$\mathrm{tr}(\mathbf{A}) = \sum_{i=1}^N \lambda_i \qquad \text{(eigenvalue trace)}$$
$$\det(\mathbf{A}) = \prod_{i=1}^N \lambda_i \qquad \text{(eigenvalue determinant)}$$
$$\mathbf{A}^{-1} \text{ exists} \iff (\forall i)\, \lambda_i \neq 0 \qquad \text{(eigenvalues non-zero for inverse)}$$

The third statement follows from the second since, for the inverse to exist, we want $\det(\mathbf{A}) \neq 0$, which means none of the eigenvalues can be zero.

Finally, the *Cayley–Hamilton theorem* tells us that every square matrix satisfies its own characteristic equation; in other words, we can replace every copy of λ with $\mathbf{A}$ in the characteristic equation and it will still hold.

A.1.10 Symmetric and Definite Matrices

Certain classes of matrices come up frequently in state estimation, particularly *symmetric* matrices and *definite* matrices. For example, *covariance* matrices that are key parameters in multivariate Gaussian distributions are symmetric, positive-definite matrices.

We have already seen that a square matrix, $\mathbf{A} \in \mathbb{R}^{N \times N}$, is called symmetric if and only if $\mathbf{A}^T = \mathbf{A}$. It can be shown that the set of all symmetric matrices is a subspace of $\mathbb{R}^{N \times N}$, which naturally comes along with the usual subspace properties. Also, the inverse of a symmetric matrix, if it exists, is also symmetric. An important result is that every real, symmetric $\mathbf{A}$ is diagonalizable according to

$$\mathbf{A} = \mathbf{V}\mathbf{D}\mathbf{V}^T, \tag{A.46}$$

where $\mathbf{D}$ is the diagonal matrix of real eigenvalues and $\mathbf{V}$ is a real, orthogonal matrix (i.e., $\mathbf{V}^{-1} = \mathbf{V}^T$) whose columns are the corresponding eigenvectors.

A *positive-definite matrix*, $\mathbf{A} \in \mathbb{R}^{N \times N}$, is a square matrix such that for all $\mathbf{x} \neq \mathbf{0} \in \mathbb{R}^N$

$$\mathbf{x}^T \mathbf{A} \mathbf{x} > 0. \tag{A.47}$$

Notationally, we write $\mathbf{A} > 0$ to mean positive-definite. A *positive-semidefinite* matrix ($\mathbf{A} \geq 0$) requires $\mathbf{x}^T \mathbf{A} \mathbf{x} \geq 0$, a *negative-definite* matrix ($\mathbf{A} < 0$) requires $\mathbf{x}^T \mathbf{A} \mathbf{x} < 0$, and a *negative-semidefinite* matrix ($\mathbf{A} \leq 0$) requires $\mathbf{x}^T \mathbf{A} \mathbf{x} \leq 0$. Technically, these conditions do not require $\mathbf{A}$ to also be symmetric but it is generally implied to be the case.

The definiteness of a matrix is correlated with the allowable range for its eigenvalues. It can be shown in general that

$$\lambda_{\min} \leq \frac{\mathbf{x}^T \mathbf{A} \mathbf{x}}{\mathbf{x}^T \mathbf{x}} \leq \lambda_{\max}, \tag{A.48}$$

for all $\mathbf{x} \neq \mathbf{0}$ where $\lambda_{\min}$ is the smallest eigenvalue of $\mathbf{A}$ and $\lambda_{\max}$ the largest. The quantity in the center is known as the *Rayeigh quotient* and takes on its minimal value when $\mathbf{x}$ is the eigenvector associated with $\lambda_{\min}$ and its maximal value when $\mathbf{x}$ is the eigenvector associated with $\lambda_{\max}$. From this we can discern that positive-definite matrices have positive eigenvalues, positive-semidefinite matrices have nonnegative eigenvalues, negative-definite matrices have negative eigenvalues, and negative-semidefinite matrices have nonpositive eigenvalues.

Finally, it is worth mentioning what happens when we form linear combinations of definite matrices. Consider $\mathbf{A}, \mathbf{B}, \mathbf{C} \in \mathbb{R}^{N \times N}$ with $\mathbf{A} > 0$, $\mathbf{B} \geq 0$, and $\mathbf{C} \geq 0$. For all $\alpha, \beta \in \mathbb{R}$ with $\alpha > 0$ and $\beta > 0$ we have

$$\alpha \mathbf{A} + \beta \mathbf{B} > 0 \quad \text{(positive semipositive sum)}$$
$$\alpha \mathbf{C} + \beta \mathbf{B} \geq 0 \quad \text{(semipositive semipositive sum)}$$

Similar conditions hold for linear combinations of negative-definite and negative-semidefinite matrices.

John William Strutt, 3rd Baron Rayleigh (1842–1919) was a Cambridge mathematician and physicist who won the 1904 Nobel Prize in Physics. He made extensive contributions to several areas including fluids, waves, optics, and black-body radiation.

A.1.11 Triangular Matrices and Cholesky Decomposition

In the previous section, we learned that real, symmetric matrices can always be diagonalized. If we restrict ourselves to symmetric, positive-definite matrices,

André-Louis
Cholesky
(1875–1918) was a
French military
officer and
mathematician. He is
primarily remembered
for this particular
decomposition of
matrices, which he
used in his military
map-making work.

we can also carry out *Cholesky decomposition* (aka Cholesky factorization or triangular factorization).

Let $\mathbf{A} \in \mathbb{R}^{N \times N}$ be symmetric, positive-definite. Then we can uniquely decompose it as

$$\mathbf{A} = \mathbf{L}\mathbf{L}^T, \tag{A.49}$$

where $\mathbf{L}$ is a real, square, lower-triangular matrix with positive diagonal entries. A *lower-triangular* matrix has all zero entries above the main diagonal. $\mathbf{L}^T$ is therefore an *upper-triangular matrix*, which has all zero entries below the main diagonal.

As a simple example of carrying out Cholesky decomposition, consider a symmetric, positive-definite $\mathbf{A} \in \mathbb{R}^{3 \times 3}$ and its Cholesky factor:

$$\mathbf{A} = \begin{bmatrix} a_{11} & a_{21} & a_{31} \\ a_{21} & a_{22} & a_{32} \\ a_{31} & a_{32} & a_{33} \end{bmatrix}, \quad \mathbf{L} = \begin{bmatrix} \ell_{11} & 0 & 0 \\ \ell_{21} & \ell_{22} & 0 \\ \ell_{31} & \ell_{32} & \ell_{33} \end{bmatrix}. \tag{A.50}$$

When we multiply out, we have

$$\mathbf{A} = \mathbf{L}\mathbf{L}^T = \begin{bmatrix} \ell_{11}^2 & \ell_{11}\ell_{21} & \ell_{11}\ell_{31} \\ \ell_{11}\ell_{21} & \ell_{21}^2 + \ell_{22}^2 & \ell_{21}\ell_{31} + \ell_{22}\ell_{32} \\ \ell_{11}\ell_{31} & \ell_{21}\ell_{31} + \ell_{22}\ell_{32} & \ell_{31}^2 + \ell_{32}^2 + \ell_{33}^2 \end{bmatrix}. \tag{A.51}$$

Comparing the two versions of $\mathbf{A}$, we can solve for the entries of $\mathbf{L}$:

$$\ell_{11} = \sqrt{a_{11}}, \quad \ell_{21} = a_{21}/\ell_{11}, \quad \ell_{22} = \sqrt{a_{22} - \ell_{21}^2}, \quad \ell_{31} = a_{31}/\ell_{11},$$

$$\ell_{32} = (a_{32} - \ell_{21}\ell_{31})/\ell_{22}, \quad \ell_{33} = \sqrt{a_{33} - \ell_{31}^2 - \ell_{32}^2}. \tag{A.52}$$

The pattern naturally extends to matrices of any size.

One application of the Cholesky decomposition is solving linear systems of equations of the form $\mathbf{A}\mathbf{x} = \mathbf{b}$. Rather than inverting $\mathbf{A}$, we could perform a Cholesky decomposition, $\mathbf{A} = \mathbf{L}\mathbf{L}^T$, and then solve the following two systems of equations :

$$\mathbf{L}\mathbf{z} = \mathbf{b} \qquad \text{(solve for } \mathbf{z}) \tag{A.53a}$$

$$\mathbf{L}^T\mathbf{x} = \mathbf{z} \qquad \text{(solve for } \mathbf{x}) \tag{A.53b}$$

Because $\mathbf{L}$ is lower-triangular, we can solve the first of these equations using a procedure called *forward substitution*. Consider

$$\underbrace{\begin{bmatrix} \ell_{11} & 0 & 0 & \cdots & 0 \\ \ell_{21} & \ell_{22} & 0 & \cdots & 0 \\ \ell_{31} & \ell_{32} & \ell_{33} & \cdots & 0 \\ \vdots & \vdots & \vdots & \ddots & \vdots \\ \ell_{N1} & \ell_{N2} & \ell_{N3} & \cdots & \ell_{NN} \end{bmatrix}}_{\mathbf{L}} \underbrace{\begin{bmatrix} z_1 \\ z_2 \\ z_3 \\ \vdots \\ z_N \end{bmatrix}}_{\mathbf{z}} = \underbrace{\begin{bmatrix} b_1 \\ b_2 \\ b_3 \\ \vdots \\ b_N \end{bmatrix}}_{\mathbf{b}}. \tag{A.54}$$

From the first row we simply have that $z_1 = b_1/\ell_{11}$. Then, from the second row we have $z_2 = (b_2 - \ell_{21}z_1)/\ell_{22}$ with the value of z_1 already known. We can continue this pattern all the way down to z_N, substituting in the values of the variables we already know.

To solve the second system in (A.53), we go the other way with *backward substitution*. This time

$$\underbrace{\begin{bmatrix} \ell_{11} & \cdots & \ell_{N-2,1} & \ell_{N-1,1} & \ell_{N1} \\ \vdots & \ddots & \vdots & \vdots & \vdots \\ 0 & \cdots & \ell_{N-2,N-2} & \ell_{N-1,N-2} & \ell_{N,N-2} \\ 0 & \cdots & 0 & \ell_{N-1,N-1} & \ell_{N,N-1} \\ 0 & \cdots & 0 & 0 & \ell_{NN} \end{bmatrix}}_{\mathbf{L}^T} \underbrace{\begin{bmatrix} x_1 \\ \vdots \\ x_{N-2} \\ x_{N-1} \\ x_N \end{bmatrix}}_{\mathbf{x}} = \underbrace{\begin{bmatrix} z_1 \\ \vdots \\ z_{N-2} \\ z_{N-1} \\ z_N \end{bmatrix}}_{\mathbf{z}}. \quad \text{(A.55)}$$

From the last row we have $x_N = z_N/\ell_{NN}$. Then, from the second-last row we have $x_{N-1} = (z_{N-1} - \ell_{N,N-1}x_N)/\ell_{N-1,N-1}$ with the value of x_N already known. We can again continue this pattern all the way up to x_1, substituting in the values of the variables we already know. Once the forward and backward passes are complete, we have solved the original $\mathbf{Ax} = \mathbf{b}$ system for $\mathbf{x}$.

The advantage of solving linear systems this way is revealed when the $\mathbf{A}$ matrix (and the corresponding Cholesky factor, $\mathbf{L}$) has an exploitable *sparsity pattern* (some, often many, of its entries are zero). We then refer to the technique as *sparse Cholesky decomposition*. A good example of this, which is exploited heavily in this book, is the case of a tridiagonal matrix. A *tridiagonal matrix* is one that has non-zero entries only on the main diagonal and one diagonal above and below. For example, a symmetric, positive-definite, tridiagonal $\mathbf{A} \in \mathbb{R}^{5 \times 5}$ and the corresponding Cholesky factor have the patterns

$$\mathbf{A} = \begin{bmatrix} a_{11} & a_{21} & 0 & 0 & 0 \\ a_{21} & a_{22} & a_{32} & 0 & 0 \\ 0 & a_{32} & a_{33} & a_{43} & 0 \\ 0 & 0 & a_{43} & a_{44} & a_{54} \\ 0 & 0 & 0 & a_{54} & a_{55} \end{bmatrix}, \quad \mathbf{L} = \begin{bmatrix} \ell_{11} & 0 & 0 & 0 & 0 \\ \ell_{21} & \ell_{22} & 0 & 0 & 0 \\ 0 & \ell_{32} & \ell_{33} & 0 & 0 \\ 0 & 0 & \ell_{43} & \ell_{44} & 0 \\ 0 & 0 & 0 & \ell_{54} & \ell_{55} \end{bmatrix}.$$

(A.56)

When we carry out the forward and backward substitutions, it will be very efficient due to the sparsity of $\mathbf{L}$. In general we can solve a system of equations with a symmetric, tridiagonal, positive-definite $\mathbf{A} \in \mathbb{R}^{N \times N}$ in a number of operations proportional to N (including the Cholesky decomposition itself).

In this book, we will also make use of Cholesky decomposition at the block (i.e., partitioned matrix) level, where similar ideas can be applied.

A.1.12 Singular-Value Decomposition

A related topic to eigendecomposition is *singular-value decomposition (SVD)*. While eigendecomposition applies only to square matrices and diagonalization is only possible some of the time, an SVD can always be computed even when the matrix is not square. The SVD is not unique.

The SVD of matrix $\mathbf{A} \in \mathbb{R}^{M \times N}$ is the decomposition

$$\mathbf{A} = \mathbf{U \Sigma V}^T, \quad \text{(A.57)}$$

where $\mathbf{U} \in \mathbb{R}^{N \times N}$, $\boldsymbol{\Sigma} \in \mathbb{R}^{M \times N}$, and $\mathbf{V} \in \mathbb{R}^{M \times M}$. The $\mathbf{U}$ and $\mathbf{V}$ are *orthogonal matrices*, meaning $\mathbf{U}^{-1} = \mathbf{U}^T$ and $\mathbf{V}^{-1} = \mathbf{V}^T$. The matrix $\boldsymbol{\Sigma}$ has on its diagonal the nonnegative, real *singular values* and zeros elsewhere. For example, with $M < N$ we have

$$\boldsymbol{\Sigma} = \begin{bmatrix} \sigma_1 & 0 & 0 & \cdots & 0 \\ 0 & \sigma_2 & 0 & \cdots & 0 \\ \vdots & \vdots & \ddots & \ddots & \vdots \\ 0 & \cdots & 0 & \sigma_M & 0 \end{bmatrix}, \tag{A.58}$$

where $\sigma_1 \geq \sigma_2 \geq \cdots \geq \sigma_M \geq 0$ are the singular values. The number of non-zero singular values is equal to $\text{rank}(\mathbf{A})$.

To compute the SVD, we consider the two eigenproblems

$$\mathbf{A}^T \mathbf{A} \mathbf{v} = \lambda \mathbf{v}, \tag{A.59a}$$

$$\mathbf{A} \mathbf{A}^T \mathbf{u} = \lambda \mathbf{u}. \tag{A.59b}$$

Because both $\mathbf{A}^T \mathbf{A}$ and $\mathbf{A} \mathbf{A}^T$ are square, real, positive-semidefinite matrices, their eigenvalues are real (and nonnegative) and their eigenvectors are also real. We can select either of these two eigenproblems and solve for the eigenvalues and eigenvectors. Without loss of generality, consider that $M \leq N$. Since $\mathbf{A} \mathbf{A}^T$ is smaller or the same in size as $\mathbf{A}^T \mathbf{A}$, we solve the second eigenproblem for the eigenvalues, λ_i, and associated eigenvectors, $\mathbf{u}_i$. We arrange the eigenvectors as

$$\mathbf{U} = \begin{bmatrix} \mathbf{u}_1 & \mathbf{u}_2 & \cdots & \mathbf{u}_M \end{bmatrix}, \tag{A.60}$$

where $\mathbf{U}$ is an orthogonal matrix (because $\mathbf{A} \mathbf{A}^T$ is symmetric); the ordering is typically chosen to go from largest eigenvalue to smallest. Because

$$\mathbf{A} \mathbf{A}^T = \mathbf{U} \boldsymbol{\Sigma} \underbrace{\mathbf{V}^T \mathbf{V}}_{1} \boldsymbol{\Sigma}^T \mathbf{U}^T = \mathbf{U} \underbrace{\boldsymbol{\Sigma} \boldsymbol{\Sigma}^T}_{D} \mathbf{U}^T, \tag{A.61}$$

we see that the (real, nonnegative) singular values are just the square roots of the (real, nonnegative) eigenvalues: $\sigma_i = \sqrt{\lambda_i}$. The last piece of the puzzle is to solve for

$$\mathbf{V} = \begin{bmatrix} \mathbf{v}_1 & \mathbf{v}_2 & \cdots & \mathbf{v}_N \end{bmatrix}, \tag{A.62}$$

which is also an orthogonal matrix (because $\mathbf{A}^T \mathbf{A}$ is symmetric). We note that

$$\mathbf{A}^T \mathbf{u}_i = \mathbf{V} \boldsymbol{\Sigma}^T \underbrace{\mathbf{U}^T \mathbf{u}_i}_{1_i} = \mathbf{V} \boldsymbol{\Sigma}^T 1_i = \sigma_i \mathbf{V} 1_i = \sigma_i \mathbf{v}_i. \tag{A.63}$$

Therefore, for all the non-zero singular values, we can take $\mathbf{v}_i = \frac{1}{\sigma_i} \mathbf{A}^T \mathbf{u}_i$. For the remaining $N - \text{rank}(\mathbf{A})$ columns of $\mathbf{V}$, we simply need to select the $\mathbf{v}_i$ so that the complete set, $\{(\forall i) \mathbf{v}_i\}$, is orthogonal.

In the case that $M > N$ we can either start with the other eigenproblem and solve for $\mathbf{V}$ first, or we can compute the SVD of $\mathbf{A}^T$ and then take the transpose of the result.

A.1.13 Sparse Matrices

In previous sections, we already encountered diagonal, tridiagonal, and triangular matrices; these are all examples of *sparse matrices*. Sparse matrices have a particular pattern of entries that are zeros. The main types of sparse matrices encountered in this book are

- *diagonal matrix*: a matrix where the only non-zero entries are on the main diagonal
- *tridiagonal matrix*: a matrix where the only non-zero entries are on the main diagonal and the one diagonal immediately above and below the main diagonal
- *triangular matrix*: a lower-triangular matrix has all the entries above the main diagonal equal to zero; an upper-triangular matrix has all the entries below the main diagonal equal to zero
- *arrowhead matrix*: a matrix partitioned into a 2×2 pattern of submatrices with the top-left and bottom-right submatrices having a (tri)diagonal pattern; this comes up frequently in formulations of the *bundle adjustment (BA)* and *simultaneous localization and mapping (SLAM)* problems

Often we encounter these sparsity patterns at the block level. Examples of block-diagonal, block-tridiagonal, block-lower-triangular, and block-arrowhead matrices are, respectively,

$$
\begin{bmatrix}
\mathbf{A}_{11} & & & \\
& \mathbf{A}_{22} & & \\
& & \mathbf{A}_{33} & \\
& & & \mathbf{A}_{44}
\end{bmatrix},
\begin{bmatrix}
\mathbf{A}_{11} & \mathbf{A}_{12} & & \\
\mathbf{A}_{21} & \mathbf{A}_{22} & \mathbf{A}_{23} & \\
& \mathbf{A}_{32} & \mathbf{A}_{33} & \mathbf{A}_{34} \\
& & \mathbf{A}_{43} & \mathbf{A}_{44}
\end{bmatrix},
$$

$$
\begin{bmatrix}
\mathbf{A}_{11} & & & \\
\mathbf{A}_{21} & \mathbf{A}_{22} & & \\
\mathbf{A}_{31} & \mathbf{A}_{32} & \mathbf{A}_{33} & \\
\mathbf{A}_{41} & \mathbf{A}_{42} & \mathbf{A}_{43} & \mathbf{A}_{44}
\end{bmatrix},
\left[
\begin{array}{cc|cc}
\mathbf{A}_{11} & & \mathbf{A}_{13} & \mathbf{A}_{14} \\
& \mathbf{A}_{22} & \mathbf{A}_{23} & \mathbf{A}_{24} \\
\hline
\mathbf{A}_{31} & \mathbf{A}_{32} & \mathbf{A}_{33} & \\
\mathbf{A}_{41} & \mathbf{A}_{42} & & \mathbf{A}_{44}
\end{array}
\right]. \quad (A.64)
$$

Note, in this book we typically leave the zero entries as blanks to avoid clutter. The solid lines in the last example indicate partitions (visual guides only) of the matrix into submatrices.

A.1.14 Vectorization and Kronecker Product

Sometimes when working with a matrix it becomes convenient to turn it into a single tall column by stacking up all the individual columns. This can be done with the (linear) *vectorization* operator, $\mathrm{vec}(\cdot)$. Consider $\mathbf{A} = \begin{bmatrix} \mathbf{a}_1 & \mathbf{a}_2 & \cdots & \mathbf{a}_N \end{bmatrix} \in \mathbb{R}^{M \times N}$ with $(\forall n)\ \mathbf{a}_n \in \mathbb{R}^M$ as its columns. Then the vectorization of $\mathbf{A}$ is

$$
\mathrm{vec}(\mathbf{A}) = \begin{bmatrix} \mathbf{a}_1 \\ \mathbf{a}_2 \\ \vdots \\ \mathbf{a}_N \end{bmatrix} \in \mathbb{R}^{MN}. \quad (A.65)
$$

We shall also define the $\text{vec}^{-1}(\cdot)$ operator to mean the inverse of the $\text{vec}(\cdot)$ operator; in other words it unstacks the columns back into the original matrix, whose original size is presumably remembered somehow. Thus

$$\text{vec}^{-1}\left(\text{vec}\left(\mathbf{A}\right)\right) = \mathbf{A}. \tag{A.66}$$

Leopold Kronecker (1823–1891) was a German mathematician who made contributions to number theory, algebra, and logic.

We also can define a special product between two matrices called the *Kronecker product*, denoted $\otimes$. If $\mathbf{A} \in \mathbb{R}^{M \times N}$ and $\mathbf{B} \in \mathbb{R}^{P \times Q}$, then the Kronecker product is

$$\mathbf{A} \otimes \mathbf{B} = \begin{bmatrix} a_{11}\mathbf{B} & a_{12}\mathbf{B} & \cdots & a_{1N}\mathbf{B} \\ a_{21}\mathbf{B} & a_{22}\mathbf{B} & \cdots & a_{2N}\mathbf{B} \\ \vdots & \vdots & \ddots & \vdots \\ a_{M1}\mathbf{B} & a_{M2}\mathbf{B} & \cdots & a_{MN}\mathbf{B} \end{bmatrix} \in \mathbb{R}^{MP \times NQ}, \tag{A.67}$$

where the a_{ij} are the individual entries of $\mathbf{A}$. Some basic properties of vectorization and the Kronecker product for all $\mathbf{A}, \mathbf{B} \in \mathbb{R}^{M \times N}$, $\mathbf{C} \in \mathbb{R}^{P \times Q}$, and $\alpha \in \mathbb{R}$ are

$$\begin{aligned} \text{vec}(\mathbf{A} + \mathbf{B}) &= \text{vec}(\mathbf{A}) + \text{vec}(\mathbf{B}) & \text{(vec. addition)} \\ \text{vec}(\alpha\mathbf{A}) &= \alpha\,\text{vec}(\mathbf{A}) & \text{(vec. scalar mult.)} \\ (\mathbf{A} + \mathbf{B}) \otimes \mathbf{C} &= \mathbf{A} \otimes \mathbf{C} + \mathbf{B} \otimes \mathbf{C} & \text{(kron. left distributivity)} \\ \mathbf{C} \otimes (\mathbf{A} + \mathbf{B}) &= \mathbf{C} \otimes \mathbf{A} + \mathbf{C} \otimes \mathbf{B} & \text{(kron. right distributivity)} \\ (\alpha\mathbf{A}) \otimes \mathbf{C} &= \alpha(\mathbf{A} \otimes \mathbf{C}) = \mathbf{A} \otimes (\alpha\mathbf{C}) & \text{(kron. scalar mult.)} \\ \mathbf{A} \otimes \mathbf{0} &= \mathbf{0} \otimes \mathbf{A} = \mathbf{0} & \text{(kron. zero)} \end{aligned}$$

Additional useful identities involving the Kronecker product and the vectorization operator include

$$\text{vec}(\mathbf{a}) = \mathbf{a} \tag{A.68a}$$

$$\text{vec}(\mathbf{a}\mathbf{b}^T) = \mathbf{b} \otimes \mathbf{a} \tag{A.68b}$$

$$\text{vec}(\mathbf{A}\mathbf{B}\mathbf{C}) = (\mathbf{C}^T \otimes \mathbf{A})\,\text{vec}(\mathbf{B}) \tag{A.68c}$$

$$\text{vec}(\mathbf{A})^T\text{vec}(\mathbf{B}) = \text{tr}(\mathbf{A}^T\mathbf{B}) \tag{A.68d}$$

$$(\mathbf{A} \otimes \mathbf{B})(\mathbf{C} \otimes \mathbf{D}) = (\mathbf{A}\mathbf{C}) \otimes (\mathbf{B}\mathbf{D}) \tag{A.68e}$$

$$(\mathbf{A} \otimes \mathbf{B})^{-1} = \mathbf{A}^{-1} \otimes \mathbf{B}^{-1} \tag{A.68f}$$

$$(\mathbf{A} \otimes \mathbf{B})^T = \mathbf{A}^T \otimes \mathbf{B}^T \tag{A.68g}$$

$$|\mathbf{A}_{N \times N} \otimes \mathbf{B}_{M \times M}| = |\mathbf{A}|^M |\mathbf{B}|^N \tag{A.68h}$$

$$\text{rank}(\mathbf{A} \otimes \mathbf{B}) = \text{rank}(\mathbf{A})\,\text{rank}(\mathbf{B}) \tag{A.68i}$$

$$\text{tr}(\mathbf{A} \otimes \mathbf{B}) = \text{tr}(\mathbf{A})\,\text{tr}(\mathbf{B}) \tag{A.68j}$$

$$\mathbf{a}^T\mathbf{B}\mathbf{C}\mathbf{B}^T\mathbf{d} = \text{vec}(\mathbf{B})^T(\mathbf{C} \otimes \mathbf{d}\mathbf{a}^T)\text{vec}(\mathbf{B}) \tag{A.68k}$$

where the sizes of the various quantities can be inferred from context.

A.1.15 Parameterizing Symmetric Matrices without Duplication

Often in state estimation we are working with symmetric matrices, particularly covariance matrices. Sometimes it is useful to parameterize these uniquely to avoid redundancy. We follow the approach of Magnus and Neudecker (2019, §18).

We begin by introducing the *half-vectorization* operator, $\mathrm{vech}(\cdot)$, that stacks up the elements in a matrix, excluding all the elements above the main diagonal. Then, we define the *duplication matrix*, $\mathbf{D}$, that allows us to build the full symmetric matrix from its unique parts:

$$\mathrm{vec}(\mathbf{A}) = \mathbf{D}\,\mathrm{vech}(\mathbf{A}) \qquad \text{(for symmetric } \mathbf{A}\text{)}. \qquad (A.69)$$

It is useful to consider a simple 2×2 example:

$$\mathbf{A} = \begin{bmatrix} a & b \\ b & c \end{bmatrix}, \quad \mathrm{vec}(\mathbf{A}) = \begin{bmatrix} a \\ b \\ b \\ c \end{bmatrix}, \quad \mathbf{D} = \begin{bmatrix} 1 & 0 & 0 \\ 0 & 1 & 0 \\ 0 & 1 & 0 \\ 0 & 0 & 1 \end{bmatrix}, \quad \mathrm{vech}(\mathbf{A}) = \begin{bmatrix} a \\ b \\ c \end{bmatrix}.$$

$$(A.70)$$

If we want to convert back to a matrix, it is useful to define a corresponding $\mathrm{vech}^{-1}(\cdot)$ operator so that

$$\mathrm{vech}^{-1}(\mathrm{vech}(\mathbf{A})) = \mathrm{vec}^{-1}(\mathbf{D}\,\mathrm{vech}(\mathbf{A}))$$
$$= \mathrm{vec}^{-1}(\mathrm{vec}(\mathbf{A})) = \mathbf{A}, \quad \text{(for symmetric } \mathbf{A}\text{)}. \quad (A.71)$$

The Moore–Penrose pseudoinverse of $\mathbf{D}$ will be denoted $\mathbf{D}^+$ and is given by

$$\mathbf{D}^+ = \left(\mathbf{D}^T\mathbf{D}\right)^{-1}\mathbf{D}^T. \qquad (A.72)$$

We can then use $\mathbf{D}^+$ to calculate the unique vector from the nonunique vector:

$$\mathrm{vech}(\mathbf{A}) = \mathbf{D}^+\mathrm{vec}(\mathbf{A}) \qquad \text{(for symmetric } \mathbf{A}\text{)}. \qquad (A.73)$$

For our 2×2 example we have

$$\mathbf{D}^+ = \begin{bmatrix} 1 & 0 & 0 & 0 \\ 0 & \frac{1}{2} & \frac{1}{2} & 0 \\ 0 & 0 & 0 & 1 \end{bmatrix}. \qquad (A.74)$$

Useful identities involving $\mathbf{D}$ are then

$$\mathbf{D}^+\mathbf{D} = \mathbf{1} \qquad (A.75a)$$
$$\mathbf{D}^{+T}\mathbf{D}^T = \mathbf{D}\mathbf{D}^+ \qquad (A.75b)$$
$$\mathbf{D}\mathbf{D}^+\mathrm{vec}(\mathbf{A}) = \mathrm{vec}(\mathbf{A}) \qquad \text{(for symmetric } \mathbf{A}\text{)} \quad (A.75c)$$
$$\mathbf{D}\mathbf{D}^+\left(\mathbf{A} \otimes \mathbf{A}\right)\mathbf{D} = \left(\mathbf{A} \otimes \mathbf{A}\right)\mathbf{D} \qquad \text{(for any } \mathbf{A}\text{)} \quad (A.75d)$$

which can be found in Magnus and Neudecker (1980). We can also define the *symmetricize operator*, $\mathrm{sym}(\cdot)$, as

$$\mathrm{sym}(\mathbf{A}) = \mathbf{A} + \mathbf{A}^T - \mathbf{A} \circ \mathbf{1}, \qquad (A.76)$$

with $\circ$ the *Hadamard (elementwise) product*. Then we can relate the $\mathrm{sym}(\cdot)$ operator to the duplication matrix as follows:

$$\mathbf{D}\mathbf{D}^T\mathrm{vec}(\mathbf{A}) = \mathrm{vec}\left(\mathrm{sym}(\mathbf{A})\right), \qquad (A.77)$$

which holds for any $\mathbf{A}$.

A.2 Matrix Calculus

In this book, will often require taking derivatives of quantities not just with respect to scalar quantities but also columns and matrices. This section outlines our approach and notation around this important topic.

A.2.1 Column/Matrix Derivative Definitions

We assume that we know how to take the derivative of a scalar function of a scalar variable, $f(x)$, with respect to that scalar variable, x:

$$\frac{\partial f(x)}{\partial x}.\tag{A.78}$$

We would like to extend this to columns and matrices. We define the derivative of a scalar function of a column variable, $f(\mathbf{x})$, with respect to that column variable, $\mathbf{x} \in \mathbb{R}^N$, as a row:

$$\frac{\partial f(\mathbf{x})}{\partial \mathbf{x}} = \begin{bmatrix} \frac{\partial f(\mathbf{x})}{\partial x_1} & \frac{\partial f(\mathbf{x})}{\partial x_2} & \cdots & \frac{\partial f(\mathbf{x})}{\partial x_N} \end{bmatrix} \in \mathbb{R}^{1 \times N},\tag{A.79}$$

where the x_n are the entries of $\mathbf{x}$. If we want to turn this into a column we can take the transpose and write

$$\left(\frac{\partial f(\mathbf{x})}{\partial \mathbf{x}} \right)^T \quad \text{or} \quad \frac{\partial f(\mathbf{x})}{\partial \mathbf{x}^T}.\tag{A.80}$$

Defining the derivative with respect to a column this way[5] makes it easy to extend to other important cases. We define the derivative of a column of functions of a scalar variable, $\mathbf{f}(x) \in \mathbb{R}^M$, with respect to that scalar variable, x, as

$$\frac{\partial \mathbf{f}(x)}{\partial x} = \begin{bmatrix} \frac{\partial f_1(x)}{\partial x} \\ \frac{\partial f_2(x)}{\partial x} \\ \vdots \\ \frac{\partial f_M(x)}{\partial x} \end{bmatrix} \in \mathbb{R}^M,\tag{A.81}$$

where the $f_m(x)$ are the individual rows of $\mathbf{f}(x)$. Finally, we define the derivative of a column of functions of a column variable, $\mathbf{f}(\mathbf{x}) \in \mathbb{R}^M$, with respect to that column variable, $\mathbf{x} \in \mathbb{R}^N$, as

$$\frac{\partial \mathbf{f}(\mathbf{x})}{\partial \mathbf{x}} = \begin{bmatrix} \frac{\partial f_1(\mathbf{x})}{\partial x_1} & \frac{\partial f_1(\mathbf{x})}{\partial x_2} & \cdots & \frac{\partial f_1(\mathbf{x})}{\partial x_N} \\ \frac{\partial f_2(\mathbf{x})}{\partial x_1} & \frac{\partial f_2(\mathbf{x})}{\partial x_2} & \cdots & \frac{\partial f_2(\mathbf{x})}{\partial x_N} \\ \vdots & \vdots & \ddots & \vdots \\ \frac{\partial f_M(\mathbf{x})}{\partial x_1} & \frac{\partial f_M(\mathbf{x})}{\partial x_2} & \cdots & \frac{\partial f_M(\mathbf{x})}{\partial x_N} \end{bmatrix} \in \mathbb{R}^{M \times N}.\tag{A.82}$$

This last expression generalizes all the other ones discussed so far.

We define the derivative of a scalar function of a matrix variable, $f(\mathbf{X})$, with respect to that matrix variable, $\mathbf{X} \in \mathbb{R}^{M \times N}$, as

---

[5] Sometimes the transpose of our definition is used.

$$
\frac{\partial f(\mathbf{X})}{\partial \mathbf{X}} =
\begin{bmatrix}
\frac{\partial f(\mathbf{X})}{\partial x_{11}} & \frac{\partial f(\mathbf{X})}{\partial x_{12}} & \cdots & \frac{\partial f(\mathbf{X})}{\partial x_{1N}} \\
\frac{\partial f(\mathbf{X})}{\partial x_{21}} & \frac{\partial f(\mathbf{X})}{\partial x_{22}} & \cdots & \frac{\partial f(\mathbf{X})}{\partial x_{2N}} \\
\vdots & \vdots & \ddots & \vdots \\
\frac{\partial f(\mathbf{X})}{\partial x_{M1}} & \frac{\partial f(\mathbf{X})}{\partial x_{M2}} & \cdots & \frac{\partial f(\mathbf{X})}{\partial x_{MN}}
\end{bmatrix}
\in \mathbb{R}^{M \times N}.
\tag{A.83}
$$

Unfortunately, there is no way to make all of our derivative definitions perfectly consistent, as one would hope that when $\mathbf{X}$ is a column in (A.83) we would recover (A.79). Had we instead defined (A.79) to be consistent with (A.83), it would no longer be consistent with (A.82).

A.2.2 Column Derivatives Using Differentials

To take derivatives of expressions involving columns, we follow the approach of Magnus and Neudecker (2019, §18).

We will introduce the idea of *differentials* in taking derivatives. Consider first a simple scalar case. We would like to take the derivative of a $f(x) = x^2$ with respect to x. One way to think about this is to apply the product rule of differentiation as follows:

$$
df = dx \cdot x + x \cdot dx = 2x \cdot dx \quad \rightarrow \quad \frac{\partial f}{\partial x} = 2x,
\tag{A.84}
$$

where df is the differential of f and dx is the differential of x.

We can do a similar thing when working with columns. Consider taking the derivative of scalar function $f(\mathbf{x}) = \mathbf{x}^T \mathbf{A} \mathbf{x}$ with respect to $\mathbf{x}$ where $\mathbf{A}$ is some known square matrix:

$$
df = d\mathbf{x}^T \mathbf{A} \mathbf{x} + \mathbf{x}^T \mathbf{A} d\mathbf{x} = \mathbf{x}^T (\mathbf{A} + \mathbf{A}^T) \, d\mathbf{x} \quad \rightarrow \quad \frac{\partial f}{\partial \mathbf{x}} = \mathbf{x}^T (\mathbf{A} + \mathbf{A}^T).
\tag{A.85}
$$

We simply treat the column like a scalar variable, apply the usual rules of differentiation, then rearrange to produce the desired derivative.

Some other common examples include

$$
\frac{\partial}{\partial \mathbf{x}} \mathbf{A} \mathbf{x} = \mathbf{A}
\tag{A.86a}
$$

$$
\frac{\partial}{\partial \mathbf{x}} (\mathbf{A}\mathbf{x} - \mathbf{b})^T \mathbf{C} (\mathbf{A}\mathbf{x} - \mathbf{b}) = (\mathbf{A}\mathbf{x} - \mathbf{b})^T (\mathbf{C} + \mathbf{C}^T) \mathbf{A}
\tag{A.86b}
$$

$$
\frac{\partial}{\partial \mathbf{x}} \mathbf{f}(\mathbf{x})^T \mathbf{C} \, \mathbf{f}(\mathbf{x}) = \mathbf{f}(\mathbf{x})^T (\mathbf{C} + \mathbf{C}^T) \frac{\partial \mathbf{f}}{\partial \mathbf{x}}
\tag{A.86c}
$$

Things get slightly more complicated in the case of matrices.

A.2.3 Matrix Derivatives Using Differentials

To take derivatives of expressions involving matrices, we again follow the approach of Magnus and Neudecker (2019, §18). This section discusses (unconstrained) differentials before moving on to how to handle symmetric matrices. Some of the results that we often make use of include

$$d\,\mathrm{tr}(\mathbf{X}) = \mathrm{tr}(d\mathbf{X}) \tag{A.87a}$$

$$d\det(\mathbf{X}) = \det(\mathbf{X})\,\mathrm{tr}\left(\mathbf{X}^{-1}\,d\mathbf{X}\right) \tag{A.87b}$$

$$d\ln\det(\mathbf{X}) = \mathrm{tr}\left(\mathbf{X}^{-1}\,d\mathbf{X}\right) \tag{A.87c}$$

$$d\mathbf{X}^{-1} = -\mathbf{X}^{-1}\,d\mathbf{X}\,\mathbf{X}^{-1} \tag{A.87d}$$

$$df(\mathbf{X}) = \mathrm{tr}\left(\left(\frac{\partial f}{\partial \mathbf{X}}\right)^{T} d\mathbf{X}\right) \tag{A.87e}$$

All of the usual linear operations for differentials apply as well. From the last relationship, we see that if we can manipulate our differential into the form

$$df(\mathbf{X}) = \mathrm{tr}\left(\mathbf{A}^{T}\,d\mathbf{X}\right), \tag{A.88}$$

we can read the derivative,

$$\mathbf{A} = \frac{\partial f}{\partial \mathbf{X}}, \tag{A.89}$$

directly. Another way to see this is to make use of vectorization. We can rewrite the differential as

$$df(\mathbf{X}) = \mathrm{vec}\left(\mathbf{A}\right)^{T}\mathrm{vec}\left(d\mathbf{X}\right) = d\mathrm{vec}\left(\mathbf{X}\right)^{T}\mathrm{vec}\left(\mathbf{A}\right), \tag{A.90}$$

so that

$$\frac{\partial f(\mathbf{X})}{\partial \mathrm{vec}\left(\mathbf{X}\right)^{T}} = \mathrm{vec}\left(\mathbf{A}\right). \tag{A.91}$$

Then, converting back to a matrix, we have

$$\frac{\partial f}{\partial \mathbf{X}} = \mathrm{vec}^{-1}\left(\frac{\partial f(\mathbf{X})}{\partial \mathrm{vec}\left(\mathbf{X}\right)^{T}}\right) = \mathrm{vec}^{-1}\left(\mathrm{vec}\left(\mathbf{A}\right)\right) = \mathbf{A}. \tag{A.92}$$

These expressions can be used recursively to calculate second differentials as well. The main idea is to minimize tedious calculations by first building all the differentials, then using the vectorization tools to assemble them into the desired quantities.

A.2.4 Symmetric Matrix Derivatives Using Differentials

We can also calculate derivatives of functions of symmetric matrices, which have two copies of all variables not on the main diagonal. The key idea is to reparameterize the symmetric matrices to avoid duplication:

$$\mathrm{vec}(\mathbf{A}) = \mathbf{D}\,\mathrm{vech}(\mathbf{A}). \tag{A.93}$$

Taking the differential of this we have

$$d\mathrm{vec}(\mathbf{A}) = \mathbf{D}\,d\mathrm{vech}(\mathbf{A}). \tag{A.94}$$

We can insert this whenever we have a differential involving a symmetric matrix:

$$df(\mathbf{X}) = d\mathrm{vec}\left(\mathbf{X}\right)^{T}\mathrm{vec}\left(\frac{\partial f}{\partial \mathbf{X}}\right) = d\mathrm{vech}\left(\mathbf{X}\right)^{T}\mathbf{D}^{T}\mathrm{vec}\left(\frac{\partial f}{\partial \mathbf{X}}\right), \tag{A.95}$$

so that

$$\frac{\partial f(\mathbf{X})}{\partial \text{vech}\,(\mathbf{X})^T} = \mathbf{D}^T \text{vec}\left(\frac{\partial f}{\partial \mathbf{X}}\right). \qquad (A.96)$$

What the extra $\mathbf{D}^T$ effectively does is add together the unconstrained elements of the derivative corresponding to the same element above and below the main diagonal and then maps this to a single parameter in the unique representation.

If we define $\eth$ to indicate a partial derivative with respect to a full symmetric matrix (where we have accounted for the symmetry) we can write

$$\frac{\eth f}{\eth \mathbf{X}} = \text{vech}^{-1}\left(\frac{\partial f(\mathbf{X})}{\partial \text{vech}\,(\mathbf{X})^T}\right)$$

$$= \text{vec}^{-1}\left(\mathbf{D}\frac{\partial f(\mathbf{X})}{\partial \text{vech}\,(\mathbf{X})^T}\right) = \text{vec}^{-1}\left(\mathbf{D}\mathbf{D}^T \text{vec}\left(\frac{\partial f}{\partial \mathbf{X}}\right)\right)$$

$$= \text{vec}^{-1}\left(\text{vec}\left(\text{sym}\left(\frac{\partial f}{\partial \mathbf{X}}\right)\right)\right) = \text{sym}\left(\frac{\partial f}{\partial \mathbf{X}}\right), \quad (A.97)$$

which is now in terms of the $\text{sym}(\cdot)$ operator.

Appendix B

Rotation and Pose Extras

This appendix provides some extra details for those specifically interested in the details of rotations and poses.

B.1 Lie Group Tools

B.1.1 Ad(SE(3)) Derivative

On occasion, we may want to take the derivative of the product of a 6×6 transformation matrix and a 6×1 column, with respect to the 6×1 pose variable.

To do this, we can start by taking the derivative with respect to a single element of $\boldsymbol{\xi} = (\xi_1, \xi_2, \xi_3, \xi_4, \xi_5, \xi_6)$. Applying the definition of a derivative along the $\mathbf{1}_i$ direction, we have

$$\frac{\partial(\boldsymbol{\mathcal{T}}(\boldsymbol{\xi})\mathbf{x})}{\partial \xi_i} = \lim_{h \to 0} \frac{\exp\left((\boldsymbol{\xi} + h\mathbf{1}_i)^\wedge\right)\mathbf{x} - \exp\left(\boldsymbol{\xi}^\wedge\right)\mathbf{x}}{h}, \tag{B.1}$$

which we previously referred to as a *directional derivative*. Since we are interested in the limit of h infinitely small, we can use the approximate BCH formula to write

$$\exp\left((\boldsymbol{\xi} + h\mathbf{1}_i)^\wedge\right) \approx \exp\left((\boldsymbol{\mathcal{J}}(\boldsymbol{\xi})\, h\mathbf{1}_i)^\wedge\right) \exp\left(\boldsymbol{\xi}^\wedge\right)$$
$$\approx (1 + h(\boldsymbol{\mathcal{J}}(\boldsymbol{\xi})\mathbf{1}_i)^\wedge)\exp\left(\boldsymbol{\xi}^\wedge\right), \tag{B.2}$$

where $\boldsymbol{\mathcal{J}}(\boldsymbol{\xi})$ is the (left) Jacobian of $SE(3)$, evaluated at $\boldsymbol{\xi}$. Plugging this back into (B.1), we find that

$$\frac{\partial(\boldsymbol{\mathcal{T}}(\boldsymbol{\xi})\mathbf{x})}{\partial \xi_i} = (\boldsymbol{\mathcal{J}}(\boldsymbol{\xi})\mathbf{1}_i)^\wedge \boldsymbol{\mathcal{T}}(\boldsymbol{\xi})\mathbf{x} = -\left(\boldsymbol{\mathcal{T}}(\boldsymbol{\xi})\mathbf{x}\right)^\wedge \boldsymbol{\mathcal{J}}(\boldsymbol{\xi})\, \mathbf{1}_i. \tag{B.3}$$

Stacking the six directional derivatives alongside one another provides the desired Jacobian:

$$\frac{\partial(\boldsymbol{\mathcal{T}}(\boldsymbol{\xi})\mathbf{x})}{\partial \boldsymbol{\xi}} = -\left(\boldsymbol{\mathcal{T}}(\boldsymbol{\xi})\mathbf{x}\right)^\wedge \boldsymbol{\mathcal{J}}(\boldsymbol{\xi}). \tag{B.4}$$

B.2 Kinematics

B.2.1 SO(3) Jacobian Identity

An important identity that is used frequently in rotational kinematics is

$$\dot{\mathbf{J}}(\boldsymbol{\phi}) - \boldsymbol{\omega}^\wedge \mathbf{J}(\boldsymbol{\phi}) \equiv \frac{\partial \boldsymbol{\omega}}{\partial \boldsymbol{\phi}}, \tag{B.5}$$

where the relationship between angular velocity and the rotational parameter derivative is

$$\omega = \mathbf{J}(\phi)\dot{\phi}. \tag{B.6}$$

Beginning with the right-hand side, we have

$$\frac{\partial \omega}{\partial \phi} = \frac{\partial}{\partial \phi}\left(\mathbf{J}(\phi)\dot{\phi}\right) = \frac{\partial}{\partial \phi}\left(\underbrace{\int_0^1 \mathbf{C}(\phi)^\alpha d\alpha}_{\mathbf{J}(\phi)} \dot{\phi}\right)$$

$$= \int_0^1 \frac{\partial}{\partial \phi}\left(\mathbf{C}(\alpha\phi)\dot{\phi}\right) d\alpha = -\int_0^1 \left(\mathbf{C}(\alpha\phi)\dot{\phi}\right)^\wedge \alpha\mathbf{J}(\alpha\phi)\, d\alpha. \tag{B.7}$$

Noting that

$$\frac{d}{d\alpha}\left(\alpha\mathbf{J}(\alpha\phi)\right) = \mathbf{C}(\alpha\phi), \qquad \int \mathbf{C}(\alpha\phi) d\alpha = \alpha\mathbf{J}(\alpha\phi), \tag{B.8}$$

we can then integrate by parts to see that

$$\frac{\partial \omega}{\partial \phi} = -\underbrace{\left(\alpha\mathbf{J}(\alpha\phi)\dot{\phi}\right)^\wedge \alpha\mathbf{J}(\alpha\phi)\Big|_{\alpha=0}^{\alpha=1}}_{\omega^\wedge \mathbf{J}(\phi)} + \int_0^1 \left(\alpha\mathbf{J}(\alpha\phi)\dot{\phi}\right)^\wedge \underbrace{\mathbf{C}(\alpha\phi)}_{\dot{\mathbf{C}}(\alpha\phi)}\, d\alpha$$

$$= -\omega^\wedge\mathbf{J}(\phi) + \frac{d}{dt}\underbrace{\int_0^1 \mathbf{C}(\phi)^\alpha d\alpha}_{\mathbf{J}(\phi)} = \dot{\mathbf{J}}(\phi) - \omega^\wedge\mathbf{J}(\phi), \tag{B.9}$$

which is the desired result.

B.2.2 SE(3) Jacobian Identity

We can derive a similar identity for pose kinematics:

$$\dot{\boldsymbol{\mathcal{J}}}(\boldsymbol{\xi}) - \boldsymbol{\varpi}^\curlywedge\boldsymbol{\mathcal{J}}(\boldsymbol{\xi}) \equiv \frac{\partial \boldsymbol{\varpi}}{\partial \boldsymbol{\xi}}, \tag{B.10}$$

where the relationship between generalized velocity and the pose parameter derivative is

$$\boldsymbol{\varpi} = \boldsymbol{\mathcal{J}}(\boldsymbol{\xi})\dot{\boldsymbol{\xi}}. \tag{B.11}$$

Beginning with the right-hand side, we have

$$\frac{\partial \boldsymbol{\varpi}}{\partial \boldsymbol{\xi}} = \frac{\partial}{\partial \boldsymbol{\xi}}\left(\boldsymbol{\mathcal{J}}(\boldsymbol{\xi})\dot{\boldsymbol{\xi}}\right) = \frac{\partial}{\partial \boldsymbol{\xi}}\left(\underbrace{\int_0^1 \boldsymbol{\mathcal{T}}(\boldsymbol{\xi})^\alpha d\alpha}_{\boldsymbol{\mathcal{J}}(\boldsymbol{\xi})} \dot{\boldsymbol{\xi}}\right)$$

$$= \int_0^1 \frac{\partial}{\partial \boldsymbol{\xi}}\left(\boldsymbol{\mathcal{T}}(\alpha\boldsymbol{\xi})\dot{\boldsymbol{\xi}}\right) d\alpha = -\int_0^1 \left(\boldsymbol{\mathcal{T}}(\alpha\boldsymbol{\xi})\dot{\boldsymbol{\xi}}\right)^\curlywedge \alpha\boldsymbol{\mathcal{J}}(\alpha\boldsymbol{\xi})\, d\alpha. \tag{B.12}$$

Noting that

$$\frac{d}{d\alpha}\left(\alpha\boldsymbol{\mathcal{J}}(\alpha\boldsymbol{\xi})\right) = \boldsymbol{\mathcal{T}}(\alpha\boldsymbol{\xi}), \qquad \int \boldsymbol{\mathcal{T}}(\alpha\boldsymbol{\xi}) d\alpha = \alpha\boldsymbol{\mathcal{J}}(\alpha\boldsymbol{\xi}), \tag{B.13}$$

we can then integrate by parts to see that

$$\frac{\partial \boldsymbol{\varpi}}{\partial \boldsymbol{\xi}} = - \underbrace{\left(\alpha \boldsymbol{\mathcal{J}}(\alpha \boldsymbol{\xi}) \dot{\boldsymbol{\xi}} \right)^{\wedge} \alpha \boldsymbol{\mathcal{J}}(\alpha \boldsymbol{\xi}) \Big|_{\alpha=0}^{\alpha=1}}_{\boldsymbol{\varpi}^{\wedge} \boldsymbol{\mathcal{J}}(\boldsymbol{\xi})} + \int_0^1 \underbrace{\left(\alpha \boldsymbol{\mathcal{J}}(\alpha \boldsymbol{\xi}) \dot{\boldsymbol{\xi}} \right)^{\wedge} \boldsymbol{\mathcal{T}}(\alpha \boldsymbol{\xi})}_{\dot{\boldsymbol{\mathcal{T}}}(\alpha \boldsymbol{\xi})} \, d\alpha$$

$$= -\boldsymbol{\varpi}^{\wedge} \boldsymbol{\mathcal{J}}(\boldsymbol{\xi}) + \frac{d}{dt} \underbrace{\int_0^1 \boldsymbol{\mathcal{T}}(\boldsymbol{\xi})^{\alpha} d\alpha}_{\boldsymbol{\mathcal{J}}(\boldsymbol{\xi})} = \dot{\boldsymbol{\mathcal{J}}}(\boldsymbol{\xi}) - \boldsymbol{\varpi}^{\wedge} \boldsymbol{\mathcal{J}}(\boldsymbol{\xi}), \quad \text{(B.14)}$$

which is the desired result.

B.3 Decompositions

Given the importance of rotation and pose matrices in our estimation theory, it is worth understanding these quantities a little better. Here we look at eigen decomposition for rotations and the more general Jordan decomposition for poses. Key results of these decompositions are the *minimal polynomials* for rotations, poses, and adjoint poses that we use heavily in the main body of the book. This section is based on the development of D'Eleuterio and Barfoot (2022).

The *minimal polynomial* of a matrix, $\mathbf{A}$, is the monic polynomial, p, of least degree such that $p(\mathbf{A}) = \mathbf{0}$. It always divides the *characteristic polynomial* and sometimes the two are equal.

B.3.1 SO(3) Eigen Decomposition

In this section, we seek to provide a canonical *eigen decomposition* of a rotation, both in the Lie algebra and the Lie group (via the exponential map).

To begin, an element of the Lie algebra, $\boldsymbol{\phi}^{\wedge} \in \mathfrak{so}(3)$, given by

$$\boldsymbol{\phi}^{\wedge} = \begin{bmatrix} \phi_1 \\ \phi_2 \\ \phi_3 \end{bmatrix}^{\wedge} = \begin{bmatrix} 0 & -\phi_3 & \phi_2 \\ \phi_3 & 0 & -\phi_1 \\ -\phi_2 & \phi_1 & 0 \end{bmatrix}, \quad \text{(B.15)}$$

has the following *characteristic polynomial*:

$$\det\left(\lambda \mathbf{1} - \boldsymbol{\phi}^{\wedge} \right) = \lambda (\lambda^2 + \underbrace{\phi_1^2 + \phi_2^2 + \phi_3^2}_{\phi^2}) = \lambda^3 + \phi^2 \lambda = 0. \quad \text{(B.16)}$$

The eigenvalues, the (complex) roots of the characteristic polynomial, are in general $i\theta$, $-i\theta$, and 0, where $i = \sqrt{-1}$. Recall that $\boldsymbol{\phi} = \phi \mathbf{a}$ where ϕ is the angle of rotation and $\mathbf{a}$ the axis. From an eigenvalue perspective, there are two cases to consider.

Special Case: $\phi = 0$

This case is almost trivial since when the angle of rotation is zero, $\phi = 0$, then $\boldsymbol{\phi}^{\wedge} = \mathbf{0}$ and it is already diagonalized with three eigenvalues equal to zero. From the exponential map we have $\mathbf{C} = \exp(\mathbf{0}) = \mathbf{1}$, which is also diagonalized, having three unit eigenvalues.

General Case

When $\phi \neq 0$, the eigenvalues are distinct, so we know that $\phi^\wedge$ can still be diagonalized. To handle $\phi = 0$, the axis of rotation can be taken to be anything we like in what follows.

A matrix of (orthonormal) eigenvectors, $\mathbf{V}$, can be verified to be

$$\mathbf{V} = \left[\tfrac{1}{\sqrt{2}} (\mathbf{b} - i\mathbf{c}) \quad \tfrac{1}{\sqrt{2}} (\mathbf{b} + i\mathbf{c}) \quad \mathbf{a} \right], \tag{B.17}$$

where $\mathbf{b}$ and $\mathbf{c}$ are unit vectors selected such that $(\mathbf{a}, \mathbf{b}, \mathbf{c})$ form a *dextral* orthonormal frame; in other words: $\mathbf{a}^\wedge \mathbf{b} = \mathbf{c}$, $\mathbf{b}^\wedge \mathbf{c} = \mathbf{a}$, $\mathbf{c}^\wedge \mathbf{a} = \mathbf{b}$.

If we further define $\mathbf{D} = \operatorname{diag}(i\theta, -i\theta, 0)$, then the eigen decomposition of $\phi^\wedge$ can be written as

$$\phi^\wedge = \mathbf{V}\mathbf{D}\mathbf{V}^H, \tag{B.18}$$

where $\mathbf{V}^H$ denotes the *conjugate transpose* and is equal to $\mathbf{V}^{-1}$ in this case. It is noteworthy that $\mathbf{D}$ depends only on the rotation angle, ϕ, while $\mathbf{V}$ depends only on the rotation axis, $\mathbf{a}$.

While we could directly seek an eigen decomposition of a rotation matrix, $\mathbf{C}$, we may leverage the connection to the Lie algebra via the exponential map:

$$\mathbf{C} = \exp(\phi^\wedge) = \sum_{n=0}^\infty \frac{1}{n!} (\phi^\wedge)^n = \sum_{n=0}^\infty \frac{1}{n!} (\mathbf{V}\mathbf{D}\mathbf{V}^H)^n$$

$$= \mathbf{V} \left(\sum_{n=0}^\infty \frac{1}{n!} \mathbf{D}^n \right) \mathbf{V}^H = \mathbf{V} \exp(\mathbf{D}) \mathbf{V}^H, \tag{B.19}$$

which provides the desired decomposition. The diagonal matrix of eigenvalues for $\mathbf{C}$ is

$$\exp(\mathbf{D}) = \operatorname{diag}(\exp(i\theta), \exp(-i\theta), \exp(0))$$

$$= \operatorname{diag}(\cos\theta + i\sin\theta, \cos\theta - i\sin\theta, 1), \tag{B.20}$$

where we have employed *Euler's formula*. From here we can immediately see that the trace (sum of the eigenvalues) and determinant (product of the eigenvalues) of $\mathbf{C}$ are

$$\operatorname{tr}\mathbf{C} = (\cos\theta + i\sin\theta) + (\cos\theta - i\sin\theta) + (1) = 2\cos\theta + 1,$$

$$\det\mathbf{C} = (\cos\theta + i\sin\theta)(\cos\theta - i\sin\theta)(1) = \cos^2\theta + \sin^2\theta = 1,$$

which are familiar results.

We can also recover Euler's classic expression for the rotation matrix in terms of the axis and angle by simply multiplying out the factors in the eigen decomposition. To start,

$$\mathbf{C} = \mathbf{V} \exp(\mathbf{D}) \mathbf{V}^H = \frac{1}{2}(\cos\theta + i\sin\theta)(\mathbf{b} - i\mathbf{c})(\mathbf{b} - i\mathbf{c})^H$$

$$+ \frac{1}{2}(\cos\theta - i\sin\theta)(\mathbf{b} + i\mathbf{c})(\mathbf{b} + i\mathbf{c})^H + \mathbf{a}\mathbf{a}^T, \tag{B.21}$$

where we have leveraged the orthonormality of the columns of $\mathbf{V}$. Multiplying this out a little further, we have

$$\mathbf{C} = \cos\theta \underbrace{\left(\mathbf{b}\mathbf{b}^T + \mathbf{c}\mathbf{c}^T\right)}_{\mathbf{1}-\mathbf{a}\mathbf{a}^T} + \sin\theta \underbrace{\left(\mathbf{c}\mathbf{b}^T - \mathbf{b}\mathbf{c}^T\right)}_{\mathbf{a}^\wedge} + \mathbf{a}\mathbf{a}^T, \qquad (B.22)$$

where the expressions in the underbraces can be gleaned by exploiting that $(\mathbf{a}, \mathbf{b}, \mathbf{c})$ form a dextral frame. Finally, we can rearrange to arrive at

$$\mathbf{C} = \cos\theta\,\mathbf{1} + (1 - \cos\theta)\,\mathbf{a}\mathbf{a}^T + \sin\theta\,\mathbf{a}^\wedge, \qquad (B.23)$$

which is Euler's classic result.

Minimal Polynomial

According to the *Cayley–Hamilton theorem*, every matrix must satisfy its own characteristic polynomial and thus we have immediately the identity

$$\phi^{\wedge^3} + \phi^2\phi^\wedge = \mathbf{0}, \qquad (B.24)$$

of which we often make use. The characteristic polynomial also happens to be the *minimal polynomial* for $\phi^\wedge$. We can verify the above identity by making use of our eigen decomposition as follows:

$$\phi^{\wedge^3} + \phi^2\phi^\wedge = \left(\mathbf{V}\mathbf{D}\mathbf{V}^H\right)^3 + \phi^2\mathbf{V}\mathbf{D}\mathbf{V}^H = \mathbf{V}\left(\mathbf{D}^3 + \phi^2\mathbf{D}\right)\mathbf{V}^H$$

$$= \mathbf{V}\begin{bmatrix} (i\phi)^3 + \phi^2(i\phi) & 0 & 0 \\ 0 & (-i\phi)^3 + \phi^2(-i\phi) & 0 \\ 0 & 0 & 0 \end{bmatrix}\mathbf{V}^H = \mathbf{0}, \quad (B.25)$$

where we make a note that $\mathbf{D}^3 + \phi^2\mathbf{D} = \mathbf{0}$ for later use.

Since $\exp(\mathbf{D})$ contains the eigenvalues for $\mathbf{C}$, we can easily construct its characteristic polynomial as

$$(\lambda - 1)(\lambda - \cos\phi - i\sin\phi)(\lambda - \cos\phi + i\sin\phi)$$
$$= \lambda^3 - \underbrace{(2\cos\phi + 1)}_{\text{tr}\,\mathbf{C}}\lambda^2 + \underbrace{(2\cos\phi + 1)}_{\text{tr}\,\mathbf{C}}\lambda - 1 = 0, \quad (B.26)$$

which is also its minimal polynomial since the eigenvalues are distinct (unless $\phi = 0$). We thus have

$$\mathbf{C}^3 - (\text{tr}\,\mathbf{C})\,\mathbf{C}^2 + (\text{tr}\,\mathbf{C})\,\mathbf{C} - \mathbf{1} = \mathbf{0} \qquad (B.27)$$

as an interesting identity.

B.3.2 SE(3) Jordan Decomposition

Following on to the previous section, we can attempt to decompose poses in a similar way. As we will see, however, the analysis becomes more involved due to the fact that we cannot always diagonalize elements of the Lie algebra or Lie group associated with poses and must make use of a *Jordan decomposition* instead.

To begin, an element of the Lie algebra for poses, $\boldsymbol{\xi}^\wedge \in \mathfrak{se}(3)$, given by

$$\boldsymbol{\xi}^\wedge = \begin{bmatrix} \boldsymbol{\rho} \\ \boldsymbol{\phi} \end{bmatrix}^\wedge = \begin{bmatrix} \boldsymbol{\phi}^\wedge & \boldsymbol{\rho} \\ \mathbf{0}^T & 0 \end{bmatrix}, \tag{B.28}$$

has a characteristic polynomial given by

$$\det\left(\lambda \mathbf{1} - \boldsymbol{\xi}^\wedge\right) = \det\left(\begin{bmatrix} \lambda \mathbf{1} - \boldsymbol{\phi}^\wedge & -\boldsymbol{\rho} \\ \mathbf{0}^T & \lambda \end{bmatrix}\right) = \lambda^2 \left(\lambda^2 + \phi^2\right) = 0. \tag{B.29}$$

The four eigenvalues are $i\theta$, $-i\theta$, 0, and 0. These are the same eigenvalues as the rotation matrix case plus an extra copy of $\lambda = 0$. Because the eigenvalues are no longer distinct, it may or may not be that $\boldsymbol{\xi}^\wedge$ can be diagonalized; it turns out not to be possible in every case. We start with the general case, then discuss two special cases afterwards.

General Case

In general, we are unable to diagonalize $\boldsymbol{\xi}^\wedge$ and $\mathbf{T} = \exp\left(\boldsymbol{\xi}^\wedge\right)$ in this case and turn to a Jordan decomposition.

We must again analyze $\lambda = 0$ in detail since we have an algebraic multiplicity of two. Any eigenvectors, $\mathbf{u} = \begin{bmatrix} \mathbf{v} \\ w \end{bmatrix}$, for $\lambda = 0$ must satisfy

$$\left(\boldsymbol{\xi}^\wedge - \lambda\mathbf{1}\right)\mathbf{u} = \boldsymbol{\xi}^\wedge\mathbf{u} = \begin{bmatrix} \boldsymbol{\phi}^\wedge & \boldsymbol{\rho} \\ \mathbf{0}^T & 0 \end{bmatrix}\begin{bmatrix} \mathbf{v} \\ w \end{bmatrix} = \begin{bmatrix} \boldsymbol{\phi}^\wedge\mathbf{v} + w\boldsymbol{\rho} \\ 0 \end{bmatrix} = \mathbf{0}. \tag{B.30}$$

We can verify easily that

$$\mathbf{u}_3 = \begin{bmatrix} \mathbf{a} \\ 0 \end{bmatrix}, \tag{B.31}$$

is a (unit) eigenvector. However, in general there is no second linearly independent eigenvector; this follows from the fact that $\boldsymbol{\phi}^\wedge\mathbf{v}$ is orthogonal to $\boldsymbol{\phi}$ and $\boldsymbol{\rho}$ is not guaranteed to be in this direction, which is required to satisfy (B.30). This means that we cannot diagonalize $\boldsymbol{\xi}^\wedge$; instead we turn to computing its Jordan decomposition.

To proceed, we would like to compute a generalized eigenvector for the eigenvalue $\lambda = 0$. Because our algebraic multiplicity is two, we seek to find a vector, $\mathbf{u}$, that satisfies

$$\left(\boldsymbol{\xi}^\wedge - \lambda\mathbf{1}\right)^2\mathbf{u} = \boldsymbol{\xi}^{\wedge^2}\mathbf{u} = \begin{bmatrix} \boldsymbol{\phi}^\wedge\boldsymbol{\phi}^\wedge & \boldsymbol{\phi}^\wedge\boldsymbol{\rho} \\ \mathbf{0}^T & 0 \end{bmatrix}\begin{bmatrix} \mathbf{v} \\ w \end{bmatrix} = \begin{bmatrix} \boldsymbol{\phi}^\wedge\boldsymbol{\phi}^\wedge\mathbf{v} + w\boldsymbol{\phi}^\wedge\boldsymbol{\rho} \\ 0 \end{bmatrix} = \mathbf{0}. \tag{B.32}$$

We can select

$$\mathbf{u}_4 = \begin{bmatrix} \mathbf{v}_4 \\ w_4 \end{bmatrix} = \begin{bmatrix} \phi^{-1}\mathbf{a}^\wedge\boldsymbol{\rho} \\ 1 \end{bmatrix}, \tag{B.33}$$

whereupon

$$\boldsymbol{\xi}^{\wedge^2}\mathbf{u}_4 = \begin{bmatrix} \boldsymbol{\phi}^\wedge\boldsymbol{\phi}^\wedge & \boldsymbol{\phi}^\wedge\boldsymbol{\rho} \\ \mathbf{0}^T & 0 \end{bmatrix}\begin{bmatrix} \frac{1}{\phi}\mathbf{a}^\wedge\boldsymbol{\rho} \\ 1 \end{bmatrix} = \begin{bmatrix} \phi^{-2}\left(\boldsymbol{\phi}^{\wedge^3} + \phi^2\boldsymbol{\phi}^\wedge\right)\boldsymbol{\rho} \\ 0 \end{bmatrix} = \mathbf{0}. \tag{B.34}$$

We have made use of (B.24) to claim the last step. We can also verify that

$$\mathbf{u}_3 = \boldsymbol{\xi}^\wedge \mathbf{u}_4 \neq \mathbf{0}, \tag{B.35}$$

allowing us to use $\mathbf{u}_3$ and $\mathbf{u}_4$ as two linearly independent eigenvectors for $\lambda = 0$.

The eigenvectors for $\lambda = i\theta$ and $\lambda = -i\theta$ can again be chosen analogously to the rotation case:

$$\mathbf{u}_1 = \begin{bmatrix} \frac{1}{\sqrt{2}}(\mathbf{b} - i\mathbf{c}) \\ 0 \end{bmatrix}, \quad \mathbf{u}_2 = \begin{bmatrix} \frac{1}{\sqrt{2}}(\mathbf{b} + i\mathbf{c}) \\ 0 \end{bmatrix}, \tag{B.36}$$

respectively.

Assembling all the eigenvectors into the columns of a matrix,

$$\begin{aligned} \mathbf{U} = \begin{bmatrix} \mathbf{u}_1 & \mathbf{u}_2 & \mathbf{u}_3 & \mathbf{u}_4 \end{bmatrix} &= \begin{bmatrix} \mathbf{V} & \mathbf{v}_4 \\ \mathbf{0}^T & 1 \end{bmatrix} \\ &= \begin{bmatrix} \frac{1}{\sqrt{2}}(\mathbf{b} - i\mathbf{c}) & \frac{1}{\sqrt{2}}(\mathbf{b} + i\mathbf{c}) & \mathbf{a} & \phi^{-1}\mathbf{a}^\wedge\boldsymbol{\rho} \\ 0 & 0 & 0 & 1 \end{bmatrix}, \end{aligned} \tag{B.37}$$

and defining the *Jordan matrix*,

$$\mathbf{E} = \begin{bmatrix} \mathbf{D} & r\mathbf{1}_3 \\ \mathbf{0}^T & 0 \end{bmatrix} = \begin{bmatrix} i\theta & 0 & 0 & 0 \\ 0 & -i\theta & 0 & 0 \\ 0 & 0 & 0 & r \\ 0 & 0 & 0 & 0 \end{bmatrix}, \tag{B.38}$$

with $\mathbf{1}_3$ the third column of the 3×3 identity matrix and $r = \mathbf{a}^T\boldsymbol{\rho}$, we have the Jordan decomposition of $\boldsymbol{\xi}^\wedge$ as

$$\boldsymbol{\xi}^\wedge = \mathbf{U}\mathbf{E}\mathbf{U}^{-1}, \tag{B.39}$$

where $\mathbf{V}$ and $\mathbf{D}$ are the same as the rotation case. The inverse of the (block upper-triangular) eigenvector matrix can be verified to be

$$\mathbf{U}^{-1} = \begin{bmatrix} \mathbf{V}^H & -\mathbf{V}^H\mathbf{v}_4 \\ \mathbf{0}^T & 1 \end{bmatrix}. \tag{B.40}$$

It is again noteworthy that $\mathbf{E}$ depends only on the rotation angle, ϕ, but unlike the rotation case the eigenvectors do not exclusively depend on the rotation axis, $\mathbf{a}$, since ϕ also makes an appearance.

We can again make use of the connection between a Lie group and its Lie algebra via the exponential map to calculate the Jordan decomposition of a transformation matrix, $\mathbf{T}$:

$$\mathbf{T} = \exp\left(\boldsymbol{\xi}^\wedge\right) = \mathbf{U}\exp\left(\mathbf{E}\right)\mathbf{U}^{-1}. \tag{B.41}$$

Due to the Jordan structure of $\mathbf{E}$, it is not too difficult to see that

$$\exp\left(\mathbf{E}\right) = \begin{bmatrix} \exp\left(\mathbf{D}\right) & r\mathbf{1}_3 \\ \mathbf{0}^T & 1 \end{bmatrix} = \begin{bmatrix} \cos\theta + i\sin\theta & 0 & 0 & 0 \\ 0 & \cos\theta - i\sin\theta & 0 & 0 \\ 0 & 0 & 1 & r \\ 0 & 0 & 0 & 1 \end{bmatrix}, \tag{B.42}$$

which is also a Jordan matrix, resulting from having two unit eigenvalues.

We can recover the standard expression for a transformation matrix by multiplying out the Jordan factors:

$$
\mathbf{T} = \mathbf{U} \exp\left(\mathbf{E}\right) \mathbf{U}^{-1} = \begin{bmatrix} \mathbf{V} & \mathbf{v}_4 \\ \mathbf{0}^T & 1 \end{bmatrix} \begin{bmatrix} \exp\left(\mathbf{D}\right) & r\mathbf{1}_3 \\ \mathbf{0}^T & 1 \end{bmatrix} \begin{bmatrix} \mathbf{V}^H & -\mathbf{V}^H \mathbf{v}_4 \\ \mathbf{0}^T & 1 \end{bmatrix}
$$

$$
= \begin{bmatrix} \mathbf{V}\exp(\mathbf{D})\mathbf{V}^H & -\mathbf{V}\exp(\mathbf{D})\mathbf{V}^H\mathbf{v}_4 + r\mathbf{V}\mathbf{1}_3 + \mathbf{v}_4 \\ \mathbf{0}^T & 1 \end{bmatrix}
$$

$$
= \begin{bmatrix} \mathbf{C} & (\mathbf{1} - \mathbf{C})\,\mathbf{v}_4 + r\mathbf{a} \\ \mathbf{0}^T & 1 \end{bmatrix}. \tag{B.43}
$$

Using the identities $\mathbf{C} = \mathbf{1} + \phi \mathbf{J}\mathbf{a}^\wedge$ and $\mathbf{J}\mathbf{a} = \mathbf{a}$, with $\mathbf{J}$ the left Jacobian of $SO(3)$, the upper-right block can be written as

$$
(\mathbf{1} - \mathbf{C})\,\mathbf{v}_4 + r\mathbf{a} = (-\phi \mathbf{J}\mathbf{a}^\wedge)(\phi^{-1}\mathbf{a}^\wedge \rho) + \mathbf{J}\mathbf{a}(\mathbf{a}^T \rho)
$$

$$
= \mathbf{J}\underbrace{\left(-\mathbf{a}^\wedge \mathbf{a}^\wedge + \mathbf{a}\mathbf{a}^T\right)}_{\mathbf{1}}\rho = \mathbf{J}\rho, \tag{B.44}
$$

whereupon

$$
\mathbf{T} = \begin{bmatrix} \mathbf{C} & \mathbf{J}\rho \\ \mathbf{0}^T & 1 \end{bmatrix}, \tag{B.45}
$$

the usual expression.

Special Case: $\phi = 0$

This case corresponds to pure translation and is handled by the general case if we choose the (arbitrary) rotation axis to be $\mathbf{a} = \rho^{-1}\rho$. Then we have

$$
\mathbf{E} = \begin{bmatrix} \mathbf{0} & \rho\mathbf{1}_3 \\ \mathbf{0}^T & 0 \end{bmatrix}, \quad \mathbf{U} = \begin{bmatrix} \mathbf{V} & \mathbf{0} \\ \mathbf{0}^T & 1 \end{bmatrix}, \tag{B.46}
$$

and

$$
\mathbf{T} = \begin{bmatrix} \mathbf{1} & \rho \\ \mathbf{0}^T & 1 \end{bmatrix}, \tag{B.47}
$$

as expected. This case is not diagonalizable unless $\rho = \mathbf{0}$ (i.e., no motion at all).

Special Case: $\phi \neq 0, \mathbf{a}^T \rho = 0$

This case corresponds to motion in a plane since the axis of rotation is perpendicular to the translation. Then we have $r = \mathbf{a}^T \rho = 0$ so that

$$
\mathbf{E} = \begin{bmatrix} \mathbf{D} & \mathbf{0} \\ \mathbf{0}^T & 0 \end{bmatrix}, \tag{B.48}
$$

with $\mathbf{U}$ and $\mathbf{T}$ the same as the general case. Since $\mathbf{E}$ is now diagonal it means that $\boldsymbol{\xi}^\wedge$ is diagonalizable in this case and so is $\mathbf{T}$.

Minimal Polynomial

Again, it is worth mentioning that according to the Cayley–Hamilton theorem, $\boldsymbol{\xi}^\wedge$ must satisfy its own characteristic polynomial resulting in the identity

$$\boldsymbol{\xi}^{\wedge^4} + \phi^2 \boldsymbol{\xi}^{\wedge^2} = \mathbf{0}. \tag{B.49}$$

The characteristic polynomial also happens to be the minimal polynomial for $\boldsymbol{\xi}^\wedge$, which is determined by the case $\phi \neq 0$, $\mathbf{a}^T \boldsymbol{\rho} \neq 0$, since the sizes of the Jordan blocks for the different eigenvalues are equal to the associated algebraic multiplicities. We can verify the preceding identity using our Jordan decomposition:

$$
\begin{aligned}
\boldsymbol{\xi}^{\wedge^4} + \phi^2 \boldsymbol{\xi}^{\wedge^2} &= \left(\mathbf{UEU}^{-1}\right)^4 + \phi^2 \left(\mathbf{UEU}^{-1}\right)^2 = \mathbf{U}\left(\mathbf{E}^4 + \phi^2 \mathbf{E}^2\right)\mathbf{U}^{-1} \\
&= \mathbf{U}\left(\begin{bmatrix} \mathbf{D} & r\mathbf{1}_3 \\ \mathbf{0}^T & 0 \end{bmatrix}^4 + \phi^2 \begin{bmatrix} \mathbf{D} & r\mathbf{1}_3 \\ \mathbf{0}^T & 0 \end{bmatrix}^2\right)\mathbf{U}^{-1} \\
&= \mathbf{U}\begin{bmatrix} \mathbf{D} & r\mathbf{1}_3 \\ \mathbf{0}^T & 0 \end{bmatrix}\begin{bmatrix} \mathbf{D}^3 + \phi^2 \mathbf{D} & \phi^2 r\mathbf{1}_3 \\ \mathbf{0}^T & 0 \end{bmatrix}\mathbf{U}^{-1} \\
&= \mathbf{U}\begin{bmatrix} \mathbf{D} & r\mathbf{1}_3 \\ \mathbf{0}^T & 0 \end{bmatrix}\begin{bmatrix} \mathbf{0} & \phi^2 r\mathbf{1}_3 \\ \mathbf{0}^T & 0 \end{bmatrix}\mathbf{U}^{-1} = \mathbf{0}, \quad (\text{B.50})
\end{aligned}
$$

where we use that $r\mathbf{D1}_3 = \mathbf{0}$ and $\mathbf{D}^3 + \phi^2 \mathbf{D} = \mathbf{0}$, from the rotation case.

B.3.3 Ad(SE(3)) Jordan Decomposition

Following on the two previous sections, we seek a Jordan decomposition for pose adjoints. An element of the Lie algebra adjoint vector space, $\boldsymbol{\xi}^\curlywedge \in \text{ad}\left(\mathfrak{se}(3)\right)$, given by

$$\boldsymbol{\xi}^\curlywedge = \begin{bmatrix} \boldsymbol{\rho} \\ \boldsymbol{\phi} \end{bmatrix}^\curlywedge = \begin{bmatrix} \boldsymbol{\phi}^\wedge & \boldsymbol{\rho}^\wedge \\ \mathbf{0} & \boldsymbol{\phi}^\wedge \end{bmatrix}, \tag{B.51}$$

has the following characteristic polynomial:

$$
\begin{aligned}
\det\left(\lambda\mathbf{1} - \boldsymbol{\xi}^\curlywedge\right) &= \det\left(\begin{bmatrix} \lambda\mathbf{1} - \boldsymbol{\phi}^\wedge & -\boldsymbol{\rho}^\wedge \\ \mathbf{0}^T & \lambda\mathbf{1} - \boldsymbol{\phi}^\wedge \end{bmatrix}\right) \\
&= \left(\det\left(\lambda\mathbf{1} - \boldsymbol{\phi}^\wedge\right)\right)^2 = \lambda^2\left(\lambda^2 + \phi^2\right)^2 = 0. \quad (\text{B.52})
\end{aligned}
$$

The six eigenvalues are $i\theta$, $-i\theta$, 0, $i\theta$, $-i\theta$, and 0. These are the same eigenvalues as the rotation matrix case except that there are two copies of each. Because the eigenvalues are no longer distinct, it may or may not be that $\boldsymbol{\xi}^\curlywedge$ can be diagonalized; it turns out not to be possible in every situation. Similarly to the previous section, we consider the general case followed by some special ones.

General Case

Paralleling the $SE(3)$ case, we are unable to diagonalize $\boldsymbol{\xi}^\curlywedge$ and $\boldsymbol{\mathcal{T}} = \exp\left(\boldsymbol{\xi}^\curlywedge\right)$ in general and instead satisfy ourselves with a Jordan decomposition.

For the two copies of $\lambda = i\phi$, we seek eigenvectors, $\mathbf{u} = \begin{bmatrix} \mathbf{v} \\ \mathbf{w} \end{bmatrix}$, that satisfy

$$
\begin{aligned}
\left(\boldsymbol{\xi}^\curlywedge - i\phi\mathbf{1}\right)\mathbf{u} &= \begin{bmatrix} \boldsymbol{\phi}^\wedge - i\phi\mathbf{1} & \boldsymbol{\rho}^\wedge \\ \mathbf{0} & \boldsymbol{\phi}^\wedge - i\phi\mathbf{1} \end{bmatrix}\begin{bmatrix} \mathbf{v} \\ \mathbf{w} \end{bmatrix} \\
&= \begin{bmatrix} \left(\boldsymbol{\phi}^\wedge - i\phi\mathbf{1}\right)\mathbf{v} + \boldsymbol{\rho}^\wedge\mathbf{w} \\ \left(\boldsymbol{\phi}^\wedge - i\phi\mathbf{1}\right)\mathbf{w} \end{bmatrix} = \mathbf{0}. \quad (\text{B.53})
\end{aligned}
$$

We can show that

$$\mathbf{u}_1 = \frac{1}{\sqrt{2}} \begin{bmatrix} \mathbf{b} - i\mathbf{c} \\ \mathbf{0} \end{bmatrix} \tag{B.54}$$

meets the requirements. Unfortunately, there is not a second linearly independent eigenvector again in this case.

We must instead seek a generalized eigenvector, $\mathbf{u} = \begin{bmatrix} \mathbf{v} \\ \mathbf{w} \end{bmatrix}$, for $\lambda = i\phi$ that satisfies

$$\begin{aligned} \left(\boldsymbol{\xi}^{\curlywedge} - i\phi\mathbf{1} \right)^2 \mathbf{u} \\ = \begin{bmatrix} \left(\phi^{\wedge} - i\phi\mathbf{1} \right)^2 & \left(\phi^{\wedge} - i\phi\mathbf{1} \right) \rho^{\wedge} + \rho^{\wedge} \left(\phi^{\wedge} - i\phi\mathbf{1} \right) \\ \mathbf{0} & \left(\phi^{\wedge} - i\phi\mathbf{1} \right)^2 \end{bmatrix} \begin{bmatrix} \mathbf{v} \\ \mathbf{w} \end{bmatrix} = \mathbf{0}. \end{aligned} \tag{B.55}$$

We can verify that the choice

$$\mathbf{u}_4 = \frac{1}{\sqrt{2}} \begin{bmatrix} i\phi^{-1} \left(\mathbf{b} + i\mathbf{c} \right)^{\wedge} \rho \\ \mathbf{b} - i\mathbf{c} \end{bmatrix}, \tag{B.56}$$

meets this requirement. We also note that

$$\mathbf{u}_1 = \left(\boldsymbol{\xi}^{\curlywedge} - i\phi\mathbf{1} \right) \mathbf{u}_4 \neq \mathbf{0}. \tag{B.57}$$

Thus we can pick $\mathbf{u}_1$ and $\mathbf{u}_4$ as two linearly independent eigenvectors for $\lambda = i\phi$, resulting in one Jordan block of size two.

We have a similar outcome for the two copies of $\lambda = -i\phi$. There are two linearly independent eigenvectors,

$$\mathbf{u}_2 = \frac{1}{\sqrt{2}} \begin{bmatrix} \mathbf{b} + i\mathbf{c} \\ \mathbf{0} \end{bmatrix}, \quad \mathbf{u}_5 = \frac{1}{\sqrt{2}} \begin{bmatrix} -i\phi^{-1} \left(\mathbf{b} - i\mathbf{c} \right)^{\wedge} \rho \\ \mathbf{b} + i\mathbf{c} \end{bmatrix}, \tag{B.58}$$

tied together in one Jordan block of size two.

For the two copies of $\lambda = 0$, we can easily see that

$$\mathbf{u}_3 = \begin{bmatrix} \mathbf{a} \\ \mathbf{0} \end{bmatrix}, \quad \mathbf{u}_6 = \begin{bmatrix} \phi^{-1}\rho \\ \mathbf{a} \end{bmatrix} \tag{B.59}$$

are two linearly independent eigenvectors satisfying $\left(\boldsymbol{\xi}^{\curlywedge} - \lambda\mathbf{1} \right) \mathbf{u} = \boldsymbol{\xi}^{\curlywedge}\mathbf{u} = \mathbf{0}$. In this case there are two Jordan blocks of size one.

The (slightly permuted) Jordan decomposition for $\boldsymbol{\xi}^{\curlywedge}$ is therefore

$$\boldsymbol{\xi}^{\curlywedge} = \mathbf{U}\mathbf{E}\mathbf{U}^{-1}, \tag{B.60}$$

where

$$\mathbf{U} = \begin{bmatrix} \mathbf{u}_1 & \mathbf{u}_2 & \mathbf{u}_3 & \mathbf{u}_4 & \mathbf{u}_5 & \mathbf{u}_6 \end{bmatrix} = \begin{bmatrix} \mathbf{V} & \mathbf{Y} \\ \mathbf{0} & \mathbf{V} \end{bmatrix},$$

$$\mathbf{E} = \begin{bmatrix} \mathbf{D} & \mathbf{H} \\ \mathbf{0} & \mathbf{D} \end{bmatrix}, \quad \mathbf{U}^{-1} = \begin{bmatrix} \mathbf{V}^H & -\mathbf{V}^H\mathbf{Y}\mathbf{V}^H \\ \mathbf{0} & \mathbf{V}^H \end{bmatrix}, \tag{B.61}$$

and with $\mathbf{V}$, $\mathbf{D}$ from the now familiar rotation case, and

$$\mathbf{H} = \begin{bmatrix} ir & 0 & 0 \\ 0 & -ir & 0 \\ 0 & 0 & 0 \end{bmatrix}, \quad \mathbf{Y} = \phi^{-1} \left[i\tfrac{1}{\sqrt{2}}(\mathbf{b} - i\mathbf{c})^\wedge \rho \quad -i\tfrac{1}{\sqrt{2}}(\mathbf{b} + i\mathbf{c})^\wedge \rho \quad \rho \right].$$

(B.62)

We see $\mathbf{H}$ contains the off-diagonal Jordan entries, due to our choice to order the eigenvalues in a nonstandard way to exploit the structure from the rotation case.

To verify the decomposition, we can simply multiply out the factors:

$$\boldsymbol{\xi}^\wedge = \begin{bmatrix} \mathbf{VDV}^H & (\mathbf{YD} - \mathbf{VDV}^H\mathbf{Y} + \mathbf{VH})\,\mathbf{V}^H \\ 0 & \mathbf{VDV}^H \end{bmatrix}$$

$$= \begin{bmatrix} \phi^\wedge & (\mathbf{YD} - \phi^\wedge\mathbf{Y} + \mathbf{VH})\,\mathbf{V}^H \\ 0 & \phi^\wedge \end{bmatrix}. \quad (\text{B.63})$$

Note that

$$\mathbf{YD} - \phi^\wedge\mathbf{Y} + \mathbf{VH}$$

$$= \left[-\tfrac{1}{\sqrt{2}}(\mathbf{b} - i\mathbf{c})^\wedge \rho \quad -\tfrac{1}{\sqrt{2}}(\mathbf{b} + i\mathbf{c})^\wedge \rho \quad 0 \right]$$

$$- \left[\tfrac{1}{\sqrt{2}}(\mathbf{c} + i\mathbf{b})\,\mathbf{a}^T \rho \quad \tfrac{1}{\sqrt{2}}(\mathbf{c} - i\mathbf{b}) \quad \mathbf{a}^\wedge \rho \right]$$

$$+ i\mathbf{a}^T\rho \left[\tfrac{1}{\sqrt{2}}(\mathbf{b} - i\mathbf{c}) \quad -\tfrac{1}{\sqrt{2}}(\mathbf{b} + i\mathbf{c}) \quad 0 \right]$$

$$= \rho^\wedge \left[\tfrac{1}{\sqrt{2}}(\mathbf{b} - i\mathbf{c}) \quad \tfrac{1}{\sqrt{2}}(\mathbf{b} + i\mathbf{c}) \quad \mathbf{a} \right] = \rho^\wedge\mathbf{V}. \quad (\text{B.64})$$

Then

$$\left(\mathbf{YD} - \phi^\wedge\mathbf{Y} + \mathbf{VH}\right)\mathbf{V}^H = \rho^\wedge\mathbf{VV}^H = \rho^\wedge, \quad (\text{B.65})$$

whereupon

$$\boldsymbol{\xi}^\wedge = \begin{bmatrix} \phi^\wedge & \rho^\wedge \\ 0 & \phi^\wedge \end{bmatrix}, \quad (\text{B.66})$$

as expected.

We can again produce a decomposition for the Lie group through the exponential map:

$$\mathcal{T} = \exp\left(\boldsymbol{\xi}^\wedge\right) = \mathbf{U}\exp\left(\mathbf{E}\right)\mathbf{U}^{-1}, \quad (\text{B.67})$$

where

$$\exp\left(\mathbf{E}\right) = \begin{bmatrix} \exp\left(\mathbf{D}\right) & \exp\left(\mathbf{D}\right)\mathbf{H} \\ 0 & \exp\left(\mathbf{D}\right) \end{bmatrix}. \quad (\text{B.68})$$

Multiplying out the factors, we have

$$\mathcal{T} = \begin{bmatrix} \mathbf{V}\exp\left(\mathbf{D}\right)\mathbf{V}^H & \mathbf{X} \\ 0 & \mathbf{V}\exp\left(\mathbf{D}\right)\mathbf{V}^H \end{bmatrix} = \begin{bmatrix} \mathbf{C} & \mathbf{X} \\ 0 & \mathbf{C} \end{bmatrix}, \quad (\text{B.69})$$

where the upper-right block is given by

$$\mathbf{X} = \mathbf{Y}\mathbf{V}^H\mathbf{C} - \mathbf{C}\mathbf{Y}\mathbf{V}^H + \mathbf{V}\mathbf{H}\mathbf{V}^H\mathbf{C}. \tag{B.70}$$

With a little effort, this can be shown to be $\mathbf{X} = (\mathbf{J}\rho)^\wedge \mathbf{C}$. Returning this result to (B.69), we arrive at

$$\mathcal{T} = \begin{bmatrix} \mathbf{C} & (\mathbf{J}\rho)^\wedge \mathbf{C} \\ \mathbf{0} & \mathbf{C} \end{bmatrix}, \tag{B.71}$$

the usual result.

Special Case: $\phi = 0$

This case corresponds to pure translation and is handled by the general case if we choose the rotation axis to be $\mathbf{a} = \rho^{-1}\rho$. Then we have

$$\mathbf{E} = \begin{bmatrix} \mathbf{0} & \mathbf{H} \\ \mathbf{0} & \mathbf{0} \end{bmatrix}, \tag{B.72}$$

with $\mathbf{U}$ from the general case and

$$\mathbf{T} = \begin{bmatrix} \mathbf{1} & \rho^\wedge \\ \mathbf{0} & \mathbf{1} \end{bmatrix}, \tag{B.73}$$

as expected. This case is not diagonalizable unless $\rho = \mathbf{0}$ (i.e., no motion at all).

Special Case: $\phi \neq 0, \mathbf{a}^T\rho = 0$

This case corresponds to motion in a plane since the axis of rotation is perpendicular to the translation. Then we have $r = \mathbf{a}^T\rho = 0$ so that

$$\mathbf{E} = \begin{bmatrix} \mathbf{D} & \mathbf{0} \\ \mathbf{0} & \mathbf{D} \end{bmatrix}, \tag{B.74}$$

with $\mathbf{U}$ and $\mathbf{T}$ the same as the general case. Since $\mathbf{E}$ is now diagonal it means that $\xi^\wedge$ is diagonalizable in this case.

Minimal Polynomial

The general case determines the most general minimal polynomial for $\xi^\wedge$. Eigenvalue $\lambda = 0$ had both algebraic and geometric multiplicities of two. The other two eigenvalues, $\lambda = i\phi$ and $\lambda = -i\phi$, had algebraic multiplicities of two but geometric multiplicities of one, each eigenvalue thus resulting in a Jordan block of size two. The Jordan structure thus allows us to see that the minimal polynomial will be

$$\lambda(\lambda^2 + \phi^2)^2 = 0, \tag{B.75}$$

which is a factor of the characteristic polynomial, the other being λ. The minimal polynomial drops this factor of λ because the largest Jordan block associated with the two copies of $\lambda = 0$ was size one. We can verify that $\xi^\wedge$ satisfies this minimal polynomial using our Jordan decomposition:

$$\boldsymbol{\xi}^{\wedge}\left(\boldsymbol{\xi}^{\wedge^{2}}+\phi^{2}\mathbf{1}\right)^{2}=\mathbf{UEU}^{-1}\left(\mathbf{UEU}^{-1}\mathbf{UEU}^{-1}+\phi^{2}\mathbf{1}\right)^{2}$$

$$=\mathbf{UE}\left(\mathbf{E}^{2}+\phi^{2}\mathbf{1}\right)^{2}\mathbf{U}^{-1}=\mathbf{U}\begin{bmatrix}\mathbf{D}&\mathbf{H}\\\mathbf{0}&\mathbf{D}\end{bmatrix}\begin{bmatrix}\mathbf{D}^{2}+\phi^{2}\mathbf{1}&2\mathbf{DH}\\\mathbf{0}&\mathbf{D}^{2}+\phi^{2}\mathbf{1}\end{bmatrix}^{2}\mathbf{U}^{-1}$$

$$\mathbf{U}\begin{bmatrix}\mathbf{D}&\mathbf{H}\\\mathbf{0}&\mathbf{D}\end{bmatrix}\begin{bmatrix}\phi^{2}(\mathbf{D}^{2}+\phi^{2}\mathbf{1})&\mathbf{0}\\\mathbf{0}&\phi^{2}(\mathbf{D}^{2}+\phi^{2}\mathbf{1})\end{bmatrix}\mathbf{U}^{-1}=\mathbf{0},\quad\text{(B.76)}$$

where we utilized $\mathbf{D}=\frac{\phi}{r}\mathbf{H}$ and $\mathbf{D}^{3}+\phi^{2}\mathbf{D}=\mathbf{0}$ from the characteristic polynomial for the rotation case.

Appendix C

Miscellaneous Extras

C.1 Fisher Information Matrix for a Multivariate Gaussian

In Sections 2.1.10 and 2.2.14 we discussed the *Cramér–Rao lower bound (CRLB)* and in Section 6.2.3, we showed that our variational inference approach to state estimation could be interpreted as carrying out *natural gradient descent (NGD)*. Both of these topics required an expression for the *Fisher information matrix (FIM)*, $\mathcal{I}_\theta$, of a multivariate Gaussian. There are several useful ways to parameterize a Gaussian, each with its own FIM, so we will show a few. First we will derive the general expression.

C.1.1 Derivation

A multivariate Gaussian *probability density function (PDF)* takes the form

$$q(\mathbf{x}) = \mathcal{N}(\boldsymbol{\mu}, \boldsymbol{\Sigma}) = \frac{1}{\sqrt{(2\pi)^N |\boldsymbol{\Sigma}|}} \exp\left(-\frac{1}{2}(\mathbf{x} - \boldsymbol{\mu})^T \boldsymbol{\Sigma}^{-1}(\mathbf{x} - \boldsymbol{\mu})\right), \quad \text{(C.1)}$$

which has been parameterized using mean, $\boldsymbol{\mu}$, and covariance, $\boldsymbol{\Sigma}$.

We will use the *Kullback–Leibler (KL)* divergence (Kullback and Leibler, 1951) to define the *Fisher information matrix (FIM)* (Fisher, 1922). The KL divergence between two Gaussians, q and q', can be expressed as

$$\text{KL}(q||q') = -\int q(\mathbf{x}) \ln\left(\frac{q'(\mathbf{x})}{q(\mathbf{x})}\right) d\mathbf{x} = E_q\left[\ln q(\mathbf{x}) - \ln q'(\mathbf{x})\right]. \quad \text{(C.2)}$$

If we suppose that q and q' are infinitesimally close to one another in some parameter space, then

$$\ln q'(\mathbf{x}) \approx \ln q(\mathbf{x}) + d\ln q(\mathbf{x}) + \frac{1}{2}d^2 \ln q(\mathbf{x}), \quad \text{(C.3)}$$

and so

$$\text{KL}(q||q') \approx E_q\left[-d\ln q(\mathbf{x}) - \frac{1}{2}d^2 \ln q(\mathbf{x})\right], \quad \text{(C.4)}$$

out to second order in the differentials. For Gaussians (and some other distributions) the first term is in fact zero. To see this, we write the negative log-likelihood of $q(\mathbf{x})$ as

$$-\ln q(\mathbf{x}) = \frac{1}{2}(\mathbf{x} - \boldsymbol{\mu})^T \boldsymbol{\Sigma}^{-1}(\mathbf{x} - \boldsymbol{\mu}) + \frac{1}{2}\ln|\boldsymbol{\Sigma}| + \text{constant}. \quad \text{(C.5)}$$

The first differential is

$$-d\ln q(\mathbf{x}) = -d\boldsymbol{\mu}^T\boldsymbol{\Sigma}^{-1}(\mathbf{x}-\boldsymbol{\mu})+\frac{1}{2}(\mathbf{x}-\boldsymbol{\mu})^T d\boldsymbol{\Sigma}^{-1}(\mathbf{x}-\boldsymbol{\mu})+\frac{1}{2}\mathrm{tr}\left(\boldsymbol{\Sigma}^{-1}\,d\boldsymbol{\Sigma}\right)$$

$$= -d\boldsymbol{\mu}^T\boldsymbol{\Sigma}^{-1}(\mathbf{x}-\boldsymbol{\mu})+\frac{1}{2}\mathrm{tr}\left((\boldsymbol{\Sigma}^{-1}-\boldsymbol{\Sigma}^{-1}(\mathbf{x}-\boldsymbol{\mu})(\mathbf{x}-\boldsymbol{\mu})^T\boldsymbol{\Sigma}^{-1})\,d\boldsymbol{\Sigma}\right),$$

$$\text{(C.6)}$$

and so

$$E_q\left[-d\ln q(\mathbf{x})\right] = -d\boldsymbol{\mu}^T\boldsymbol{\Sigma}^{-1}\underbrace{E[\mathbf{x}-\boldsymbol{\mu}]}_{\mathbf{0}}$$

$$+\frac{1}{2}\mathrm{tr}\left(((\boldsymbol{\Sigma}^{-1}-\boldsymbol{\Sigma}^{-1}\underbrace{E\left[(\mathbf{x}-\boldsymbol{\mu})(\mathbf{x}-\boldsymbol{\mu})^T\right]}_{\boldsymbol{\Sigma}}\boldsymbol{\Sigma}^{-1}))\,d\boldsymbol{\Sigma}\right) = \mathbf{0}. \quad \text{(C.7)}$$

Turning the differentials into partial derivatives, we can rewrite (C.4) as

$$\mathrm{KL}(q\|q') \approx E_q\left[-\frac{1}{2}d^2\ln q(\mathbf{x})\right] = \frac{1}{2}\delta\boldsymbol{\theta}^T\underbrace{E_q\left[\frac{\partial^2(-\ln q(\mathbf{x}))}{\partial\boldsymbol{\theta}^T\partial\boldsymbol{\theta}}\right]}_{\mathcal{I}_{\boldsymbol{\theta}}}\delta\boldsymbol{\theta}, \quad \text{(C.8)}$$

for some parameterization, $\boldsymbol{\theta}$, of a Gaussian. The matrix,

$$\mathcal{I}_{\boldsymbol{\theta}} = E_q\left[\frac{\partial^2(-\ln q(\mathbf{x}))}{\partial\boldsymbol{\theta}^T\partial\boldsymbol{\theta}}\right], \quad \text{(C.9)}$$

is called the *Fisher information matrix (FIM)* and defines a Riemannian metric tensor for the parameters, $\boldsymbol{\theta}$. When using the KL divergence as a cost functional, we can use the FIM as an approximation of the Hessian to build a Newton-like optimizer; see Section 6.2.3. We will next work out the FIM for a few common parameterizations of multivariate Gaussians.

C.1.2 Canonical Parameters

We begin with the most obvious parameterization, the mean and (vectorized) covariance:

$$\boldsymbol{\theta} = \begin{bmatrix} \boldsymbol{\mu} \\ \mathrm{vec}(\boldsymbol{\Sigma}) \end{bmatrix}, \quad \text{(C.10)}$$

which we will refer to as the *canonical parameterization*. To calculate the FIM, we need the second differential, which we can obtain by taking the differential of (C.6):

$$-d^2\ln q(\mathbf{x}) = d\boldsymbol{\mu}^T\boldsymbol{\Sigma}^{-1}\,d\boldsymbol{\mu} - 2d\boldsymbol{\mu}^T\boldsymbol{\Sigma}^{-1}(\mathbf{x}-\boldsymbol{\mu})$$

$$+\frac{1}{2}\mathrm{tr}\left(\boldsymbol{\Sigma}^{-1}\,d^2\boldsymbol{\Sigma}\,\boldsymbol{\Sigma}^{-1}\left(\boldsymbol{\Sigma}-(\mathbf{x}-\boldsymbol{\mu})(\mathbf{x}-\boldsymbol{\mu})^T\right)\right)$$

$$+\frac{1}{2}\mathrm{tr}\left(\boldsymbol{\Sigma}^{-1}\,d\boldsymbol{\Sigma}\,\boldsymbol{\Sigma}^{-1}\,d\boldsymbol{\Sigma}\,\boldsymbol{\Sigma}^{-1}\left(2(\mathbf{x}-\boldsymbol{\mu})(\mathbf{x}-\boldsymbol{\mu})^T-\boldsymbol{\Sigma}\right)\right). \quad \text{(C.11)}$$

The expected value of the second differential over $q(\mathbf{x})$ is

$$-E_q\left[d^2 \ln q(\mathbf{x})\right] = d\boldsymbol{\mu}^T \boldsymbol{\Sigma}^{-1} d\boldsymbol{\mu} + \frac{1}{2} \mathrm{tr}\left(\boldsymbol{\Sigma}^{-1} d\boldsymbol{\Sigma}\,\boldsymbol{\Sigma}^{-1} d\boldsymbol{\Sigma}\right). \qquad (C.12)$$

Vectorizing $\boldsymbol{\Sigma}$, we have the nice result

$$-E_q\left[d^2 \ln q(\mathbf{x})\right] = d\boldsymbol{\theta}^T \underbrace{\begin{bmatrix} \boldsymbol{\Sigma}^{-1} & \mathbf{0} \\ \mathbf{0} & \frac{1}{2}\left(\boldsymbol{\Sigma}^{-1} \otimes \boldsymbol{\Sigma}^{-1}\right) \end{bmatrix}}_{\mathcal{I}_\theta} d\boldsymbol{\theta}, \qquad (C.13)$$

so the FIM is

$$\mathcal{I}_\theta = \begin{bmatrix} \boldsymbol{\Sigma}^{-1} & \mathbf{0} \\ \mathbf{0} & \frac{1}{2}\left(\boldsymbol{\Sigma}^{-1} \otimes \boldsymbol{\Sigma}^{-1}\right) \end{bmatrix}. \qquad (C.14)$$

The inverse FIM is simply

$$\mathcal{I}_\theta^{-1} = \begin{bmatrix} \boldsymbol{\Sigma} & \mathbf{0} \\ \mathbf{0} & 2\left(\boldsymbol{\Sigma} \otimes \boldsymbol{\Sigma}\right) \end{bmatrix}. \qquad (C.15)$$

The trouble is that we have not accounted for the symmetric nature of $\boldsymbol{\Sigma}$.

C.1.3 Canonical Parameters with Symmetry

To account for the symmetric nature of $\boldsymbol{\Sigma}$, we define the symmetry-aware parameterization as

$$\boldsymbol{\gamma} = \begin{bmatrix} \boldsymbol{\gamma}_1 \\ \boldsymbol{\gamma}_2 \end{bmatrix} = \begin{bmatrix} \boldsymbol{\mu} \\ \mathrm{vech}(\boldsymbol{\Sigma}) \end{bmatrix}, \qquad (C.16)$$

where the half-vectorization operator, $\mathrm{vech}(\cdot)$, removes the redundant entries of $\boldsymbol{\Sigma}$. Then we have

$$d\boldsymbol{\mu} = d\boldsymbol{\gamma}_1, \quad \mathrm{vec}\left(d\boldsymbol{\Sigma}\right) = \mathbf{D}\, d\boldsymbol{\gamma}_2, \qquad (C.17)$$

or

$$d\boldsymbol{\theta} = \begin{bmatrix} \mathbf{1} & \mathbf{0} \\ \mathbf{0} & \mathbf{D} \end{bmatrix} d\boldsymbol{\gamma}. \qquad (C.18)$$

Substituting this into (C.13), we have

$$-E_q\left[d^2 \ln q(\mathbf{x})\right] = d\boldsymbol{\gamma}^T \underbrace{\begin{bmatrix} \boldsymbol{\Sigma}^{-1} & \mathbf{0} \\ \mathbf{0} & \frac{1}{2}\mathbf{D}^T\left(\boldsymbol{\Sigma}^{-1} \otimes \boldsymbol{\Sigma}^{-1}\right)\mathbf{D} \end{bmatrix}}_{\mathcal{I}_\gamma} d\boldsymbol{\gamma}. \qquad (C.19)$$

The inverse FIM is given by

$$\mathcal{I}_\gamma^{-1} = \begin{bmatrix} \boldsymbol{\Sigma} & \mathbf{0} \\ \mathbf{0} & 2\mathbf{D}^+\left(\boldsymbol{\Sigma} \otimes \boldsymbol{\Sigma}\right)\mathbf{D}^{+^T} \end{bmatrix}, \qquad (C.20)$$

corresponding to Magnus and Neudecker (2019, §18).

C.1.4 Hybrid Parameters

In many real large-scale problems, the inverse covariance matrix is sparse so that it is much more desirable to work with it directly. We call this the *hybrid* parameterization as the mean is as before while we use the inverse covariance:

$$\boldsymbol{\alpha} = \begin{bmatrix} \boldsymbol{\alpha}_1 \\ \boldsymbol{\alpha}_2 \end{bmatrix} = \begin{bmatrix} \boldsymbol{\mu} \\ \mathrm{vec}(\boldsymbol{\Sigma}^{-1}) \end{bmatrix}. \tag{C.21}$$

We then have

$$d\boldsymbol{\mu} = d\boldsymbol{\alpha}_1, \quad \mathrm{vec}\left(d\boldsymbol{\Sigma}^{-1}\right) = d\boldsymbol{\alpha}_2. \tag{C.22}$$

Expanding the second of these, we see

$$d\boldsymbol{\alpha}_2 = \mathrm{vec}\left(d\boldsymbol{\Sigma}^{-1}\right) = \mathrm{vec}\left(-\boldsymbol{\Sigma}^{-1}\,d\boldsymbol{\Sigma}\,\boldsymbol{\Sigma}^{-1}\right) = -\left(\boldsymbol{\Sigma}^{-1} \otimes \boldsymbol{\Sigma}^{-1}\right)\mathrm{vec}\left(d\boldsymbol{\Sigma}\right), \tag{C.23}$$

and so

$$\mathrm{vec}\left(d\boldsymbol{\Sigma}\right) = -\left(\boldsymbol{\Sigma} \otimes \boldsymbol{\Sigma}\right)d\boldsymbol{\alpha}_2. \tag{C.24}$$

We therefore have

$$d\boldsymbol{\theta} = \begin{bmatrix} 1 & 0 \\ 0 & -\left(\boldsymbol{\Sigma} \otimes \boldsymbol{\Sigma}\right) \end{bmatrix} d\boldsymbol{\alpha}. \tag{C.25}$$

Substituting this into (C.13), we have

$$-E_q\left[d^2 \ln q(\mathbf{x})\right] = d\boldsymbol{\alpha}^T \underbrace{\begin{bmatrix} \boldsymbol{\Sigma}^{-1} & 0 \\ 0 & \frac{1}{2}\left(\boldsymbol{\Sigma} \otimes \boldsymbol{\Sigma}\right) \end{bmatrix}}_{\boldsymbol{\mathcal{I}}_{\alpha}} d\boldsymbol{\alpha}. \tag{C.26}$$

The inverse FIM is given by

$$\boldsymbol{\mathcal{I}}_{\alpha}^{-1} = \begin{bmatrix} \boldsymbol{\Sigma} & 0 \\ 0 & 2\left(\boldsymbol{\Sigma}^{-1} \otimes \boldsymbol{\Sigma}^{-1}\right) \end{bmatrix}, \tag{C.27}$$

which follows a similar form to the previous section.

C.1.5 Hybrid Parameters with Symmetry

If we want to account for symmetry, we choose

$$\boldsymbol{\beta} = \begin{bmatrix} \boldsymbol{\beta}_1 \\ \boldsymbol{\beta}_2 \end{bmatrix} = \begin{bmatrix} \boldsymbol{\mu} \\ \mathrm{vech}(\boldsymbol{\Sigma}^{-1}) \end{bmatrix}. \tag{C.28}$$

Similarly to how we convert to the symmetry-aware version of the canonical representation, we have

$$d\boldsymbol{\beta} = \begin{bmatrix} 1 & 0 \\ 0 & \mathbf{D} \end{bmatrix} d\boldsymbol{\alpha}. \tag{C.29}$$

Substituting this into (C.13), we have

$$-E_q\left[d^2 \ln q(\mathbf{x})\right] = d\boldsymbol{\beta}^T \underbrace{\begin{bmatrix} \boldsymbol{\Sigma}^{-1} & 0 \\ 0 & \frac{1}{2}\mathbf{D}^T\left(\boldsymbol{\Sigma} \otimes \boldsymbol{\Sigma}\right)\mathbf{D} \end{bmatrix}}_{\boldsymbol{\mathcal{I}}_{\beta}} d\boldsymbol{\beta}. \tag{C.30}$$

The inverse FIM is given by

$$
\mathcal{I}_\beta^{-1} = \begin{bmatrix} \boldsymbol{\Sigma} & \mathbf{0} \\ \mathbf{0} & 2\mathbf{D}^+ \left(\boldsymbol{\Sigma}^{-1} \otimes \boldsymbol{\Sigma}^{-1} \right) \mathbf{D}^{+^T} \end{bmatrix}, \tag{C.31}
$$

which follows a similar form to the previous section.

C.1.6 Natural Parameters

Somewhat confusingly named,[1] the *natural parameters* for a Gaussian can be defined as

$$
\boldsymbol{\eta} = \begin{bmatrix} \boldsymbol{\Sigma}^{-1}\boldsymbol{\mu} \\ \mathrm{vec}\left(\boldsymbol{\Sigma}^{-1} \right) \end{bmatrix}. \tag{C.32}
$$

This is also sometimes called the *inverse covariance form* of a Gaussian. The derivation for these parameters is somewhat more involved, as the FIM is no longer block diagonal, making this choice somewhat *unnatural*.

We will build off the hybrid parameterization, as it already deals with the inverse covariance matrix and so the covariance parameter differentials are the same, $d\boldsymbol{\eta}_2 = d\boldsymbol{\alpha}_2$. The differential for the mean is

$$
d\boldsymbol{\eta}_1 = d\boldsymbol{\Sigma}^{-1}\boldsymbol{\mu} + \boldsymbol{\Sigma}^{-1} d\boldsymbol{\mu} = \boldsymbol{\Sigma}^{-1} d\boldsymbol{\alpha}_1 + \left(\boldsymbol{\mu}^T \otimes \mathbf{1} \right) d\boldsymbol{\alpha}_2, \tag{C.33}
$$

which takes a bit of manipulation. Stacking these we have

$$
d\boldsymbol{\eta} = \begin{bmatrix} \boldsymbol{\Sigma}^{-1} & \left(\boldsymbol{\mu}^T \otimes \mathbf{1} \right) \\ \mathbf{0} & \mathbf{1} \end{bmatrix} d\boldsymbol{\alpha}, \tag{C.34}
$$

which is the reverse relationship from what we want, but we will need this coefficient matrix when computing the inverse FIM. Inverting we have

$$
d\boldsymbol{\alpha} = \begin{bmatrix} \boldsymbol{\Sigma} & -\boldsymbol{\Sigma}\left(\boldsymbol{\mu}^T \otimes \mathbf{1} \right) \\ \mathbf{0} & \mathbf{1} \end{bmatrix} d\boldsymbol{\eta}. \tag{C.35}
$$

The FIM is then

$$
\begin{aligned}
\mathcal{I}_\eta &= \begin{bmatrix} \boldsymbol{\Sigma} & -\boldsymbol{\Sigma}\left(\boldsymbol{\mu}^T \otimes \mathbf{1} \right) \\ \mathbf{0} & \mathbf{1} \end{bmatrix}^T \mathcal{I}_\alpha \begin{bmatrix} \boldsymbol{\Sigma} & -\boldsymbol{\Sigma}\left(\boldsymbol{\mu}^T \otimes \mathbf{1} \right) \\ \mathbf{0} & \mathbf{1} \end{bmatrix} \\
&= \begin{bmatrix} \boldsymbol{\Sigma} & -\boldsymbol{\Sigma}\left(\boldsymbol{\mu}^T \otimes \mathbf{1} \right) \\ -\left(\boldsymbol{\mu} \otimes \mathbf{1} \right) \boldsymbol{\Sigma} & \frac{1}{2}\left(\boldsymbol{\Sigma} \otimes \boldsymbol{\Sigma} \right) + \left(\boldsymbol{\mu} \otimes \mathbf{1} \right) \boldsymbol{\Sigma} \left(\boldsymbol{\mu}^T \otimes \mathbf{1} \right) \end{bmatrix}.
\end{aligned} \tag{C.36}
$$

The inverse FIM is then

$$
\begin{aligned}
\mathcal{I}_\eta^{-1} &= \begin{bmatrix} \boldsymbol{\Sigma}^{-1} & \left(\boldsymbol{\mu}^T \otimes \mathbf{1} \right) \\ \mathbf{0} & \mathbf{1} \end{bmatrix} \mathcal{I}_\alpha^{-1} \begin{bmatrix} \boldsymbol{\Sigma}^{-1} & \left(\boldsymbol{\mu}^T \otimes \mathbf{1} \right) \\ \mathbf{0} & \mathbf{1} \end{bmatrix}^T \\
&= \begin{bmatrix} \boldsymbol{\Sigma}^{-1} + 2\left(\boldsymbol{\mu} \otimes \mathbf{1} \right) \left(\boldsymbol{\Sigma}^{-1} \otimes \boldsymbol{\Sigma}^{-1} \right) \left(\boldsymbol{\mu}^T \otimes \mathbf{1} \right) & 2\left(\boldsymbol{\mu}^T \otimes \mathbf{1} \right) \left(\boldsymbol{\Sigma}^{-1} \otimes \boldsymbol{\Sigma}^{-1} \right) \\ 2\left(\boldsymbol{\Sigma}^{-1} \otimes \boldsymbol{\Sigma}^{-1} \right) \left(\boldsymbol{\mu} \otimes \mathbf{1} \right) & 2\left(\boldsymbol{\Sigma}^{-1} \otimes \boldsymbol{\Sigma}^{-1} \right) \end{bmatrix} \\
&= \begin{bmatrix} \left(1 + 2\boldsymbol{\mu}^T\boldsymbol{\Sigma}^{-1}\boldsymbol{\mu} \right)\boldsymbol{\Sigma}^{-1} & 2\left(\boldsymbol{\mu}^T\boldsymbol{\Sigma}^{-1} \otimes \boldsymbol{\Sigma}^{-1} \right) \\ 2\left(\boldsymbol{\Sigma}^{-1}\boldsymbol{\mu} \otimes \boldsymbol{\Sigma}^{-1} \right) & 2\left(\boldsymbol{\Sigma}^{-1} \otimes \boldsymbol{\Sigma}^{-1} \right) \end{bmatrix}, \tag{C.37}
\end{aligned}
$$

---

[1] There does not seem to be a connection with *natural* gradient descent.

where it is worth noting that all of the expressions can be easily built from $\boldsymbol{\eta}$. We will not pursue the symmetry-aware version of the natural parameters, but it would be straightforward to do so using the same approach as the other parameterizations.

C.2 Derivation of Stein's Lemma

We begin with a key identity. Let $\mathbf{f}(\cdot)$ be a column of Lipschitz continuous and differentiable functions and $q(\mathbf{z}) = \mathcal{N}(\boldsymbol{\mu}, \boldsymbol{\Sigma})$ is a Gaussian PDF for $\mathbf{z}$. Then we can show that

$$\int_{-\infty}^{\infty} \frac{\partial \mathbf{f}(\mathbf{z})}{\partial \mathbf{z}} q(\mathbf{z}) \, d\mathbf{z} + \int_{-\infty}^{\infty} \mathbf{f}(\mathbf{z}) \frac{\partial q(\mathbf{z})}{\partial \mathbf{z}} \, d\mathbf{z} = \mathbf{0}. \tag{C.38}$$

To see this, consider just the first row,

$$\int_{-\infty}^{\infty} \frac{\partial f_1(\mathbf{z})}{\partial \mathbf{z}} q(\mathbf{z}) \, d\mathbf{z} = \int \left[\frac{\partial f_1(\mathbf{z})}{\partial z_1} q(\mathbf{z}) \quad \cdots \quad \frac{\partial f_1(\mathbf{z})}{\partial z_N} q(\mathbf{z}) \right] d\mathbf{z}$$

$$= \left[\int \frac{\partial f_1(\mathbf{z})}{\partial z_1} q(\mathbf{z}) \, d\mathbf{z} \quad \cdots \quad \int \frac{\partial f_1(\mathbf{z})}{\partial z_N} q(\mathbf{z}) \, d\mathbf{z} \right]. \tag{C.39}$$

Examining the first entry of this, we have

$$\int \frac{\partial f_1(\mathbf{z})}{\partial z_1} q(\mathbf{z}) \, d\mathbf{z} = \int \cdots \int \int \frac{\partial f_1(\mathbf{z})}{\partial z_1} q(\mathbf{z}) \, dz_1 \, dz_2 \cdots dz_N$$

$$= \int \cdots \int \left(\underbrace{f_1(\mathbf{z}) q(\mathbf{z}) \Big|_{-\infty}^{\infty}}_{0} - \int f_1(\mathbf{z}) \frac{\partial q(\mathbf{z})}{\partial z_1} \, dz_1 \right) dz_2 \cdots dz_N$$

$$= - \int f_1(\mathbf{z}) \frac{\partial q(\mathbf{z})}{\partial z_1} \, d\mathbf{z},$$

where we used integration by parts in the middle line. Putting this back into (C.39), we have

$$\int_{-\infty}^{\infty} \frac{\partial f_1(\mathbf{z})}{\partial \mathbf{z}} q(\mathbf{z}) \, d\mathbf{z} = - \int f_1(\mathbf{z}) \frac{\partial q(\mathbf{z})}{\partial \mathbf{z}} \, d\mathbf{z}. \tag{C.40}$$

Then (C.38) follows by applying the same process to each row of $\mathbf{f}(\mathbf{z})$.

Now, we can compute that

$$\frac{\partial q(\mathbf{z})}{\partial \mathbf{z}} = - (\mathbf{z} - \boldsymbol{\mu})^T \boldsymbol{\Sigma}^{-1} q(\mathbf{z}). \tag{C.41}$$

Inserting this into (C.38), we have

$$\int_{-\infty}^{\infty} \frac{\partial \mathbf{f}(\mathbf{z})}{\partial \mathbf{z}} q(\mathbf{z}) \, d\mathbf{z} = \int_{-\infty}^{\infty} \mathbf{f}(\mathbf{z}) (\mathbf{z} - \boldsymbol{\mu})^T \boldsymbol{\Sigma}^{-1} q(\mathbf{z}) \, d\mathbf{z}. \tag{C.42}$$

Converting the integrals to expectations, we have

$$E_q \left[\frac{\partial \mathbf{f}(\mathbf{z})}{\partial \mathbf{z}} \right] = E_q \left[\mathbf{f}(\mathbf{z}) (\mathbf{z} - \boldsymbol{\mu})^T \right] \boldsymbol{\Sigma}^{-1}. \tag{C.43}$$

Right-multiplying by $\boldsymbol{\Sigma}$ and taking the transpose, we have Stein's lemma (Stein, 1981):

$$E_q\left[(\mathbf{z} - \boldsymbol{\mu})\mathbf{f}(\mathbf{z})^T\right] = \boldsymbol{\Sigma}\, E_q\left[\left(\frac{\partial \mathbf{f}(\mathbf{z})}{\partial \mathbf{z}}\right)^T\right]. \tag{C.44}$$

If the function is scalar, $f(\mathbf{z})$, it becomes

$$E_q\left[(\mathbf{z} - \boldsymbol{\mu})f(\mathbf{z})\right] = \boldsymbol{\Sigma}\, E_q\left[\frac{\partial f(\mathbf{z})}{\partial \mathbf{z}^T}\right], \tag{C.45}$$

which is (2.125).

Suppose now that we partition $\mathbf{z}$ into $\mathbf{x}$ and $\mathbf{y}$ so that

$$q(\mathbf{x}, \mathbf{y}) = \mathcal{N}\left(\begin{bmatrix} \boldsymbol{\mu}_x \\ \boldsymbol{\mu}_y \end{bmatrix}, \begin{bmatrix} \boldsymbol{\Sigma}_{xx} & \boldsymbol{\Sigma}_{xy} \\ \boldsymbol{\Sigma}_{yx} & \boldsymbol{\Sigma}_{yy} \end{bmatrix}\right). \tag{C.46}$$

Then Stein's lemma tells us that

$$E_q\left[\begin{bmatrix} \mathbf{x} - \boldsymbol{\mu}_x \\ \mathbf{y} - \boldsymbol{\mu}_y \end{bmatrix} \mathbf{f}(\mathbf{x}, \mathbf{y})^T\right] = \begin{bmatrix} \boldsymbol{\Sigma}_{xx} & \boldsymbol{\Sigma}_{xy} \\ \boldsymbol{\Sigma}_{yx} & \boldsymbol{\Sigma}_{yy} \end{bmatrix} E_q\left[\begin{bmatrix} \left(\frac{\partial \mathbf{f}(\mathbf{x},\mathbf{y})}{\partial \mathbf{x}}\right)^T \\ \left(\frac{\partial \mathbf{f}(\mathbf{x},\mathbf{y})}{\partial \mathbf{y}}\right)^T \end{bmatrix}\right]. \tag{C.47}$$

If the function only depends on $\mathbf{x}$ and not $\mathbf{y}$, we have

$$E_q\left[\begin{bmatrix} \mathbf{x} - \boldsymbol{\mu}_x \\ \mathbf{y} - \boldsymbol{\mu}_y \end{bmatrix} \mathbf{f}(\mathbf{x})^T\right] = \begin{bmatrix} \boldsymbol{\Sigma}_{xx} & \boldsymbol{\Sigma}_{xy} \\ \boldsymbol{\Sigma}_{yx} & \boldsymbol{\Sigma}_{yy} \end{bmatrix} E_q\left[\begin{bmatrix} \left(\frac{\partial \mathbf{f}(\mathbf{x})}{\partial \mathbf{x}}\right)^T \\ \mathbf{0} \end{bmatrix}\right]. \tag{C.48}$$

The second block row of this is

$$E_q\left[(\mathbf{y} - \boldsymbol{\mu}_y)\mathbf{f}(\mathbf{x})^T\right] = \boldsymbol{\Sigma}_{yx} E_q\left[\left(\frac{\partial \mathbf{f}(\mathbf{x})}{\partial \mathbf{x}}\right)^T\right], \tag{C.49}$$

or in the scalar function case

$$E_q\left[(\mathbf{y} - \boldsymbol{\mu}_y)f(\mathbf{x})\right] = \boldsymbol{\Sigma}_{yx} E_q\left[\frac{\partial f(\mathbf{x})}{\partial \mathbf{x}^T}\right], \tag{C.50}$$

which is the same as (2.127).

Finally we can create a double application of Stein's lemma by using (C.44) with $\mathbf{f}(\mathbf{z}) = (\mathbf{z} - \boldsymbol{\mu})g(\mathbf{z})$ for another Lipschitz continuous and twice-differentiable function, $g(\cdot)$. We note that

$$\frac{\partial \mathbf{f}(\mathbf{z})}{\partial \mathbf{z}} = g(\mathbf{z})\mathbf{1} + (\mathbf{z} - \boldsymbol{\mu})\frac{\partial g(\mathbf{z})}{\partial \mathbf{z}}. \tag{C.51}$$

Substituting $\mathbf{f}(\mathbf{z})$ and $\frac{\partial \mathbf{f}(\mathbf{z})}{\partial \mathbf{z}}$ into (C.44), we have

$$E_q\left[(\mathbf{z} - \boldsymbol{\mu})(\mathbf{z} - \boldsymbol{\mu})^T g(\mathbf{z})\right] = \boldsymbol{\Sigma}\, \underbrace{E_q\left[\frac{\partial g(\mathbf{z})}{\partial \mathbf{z}^T}(\mathbf{z} - \boldsymbol{\mu})^T\right]}_{E_q\left[\frac{\partial^2 g(\mathbf{z})}{\partial \mathbf{z}^T \partial \mathbf{z}}\right]\boldsymbol{\Sigma}} + \boldsymbol{\Sigma}\, E_q\left[g(\mathbf{z})\right]. \tag{C.52}$$

We can apply Stein's lemma again as indicated in the underbrace, so finally

$$E_q \left[(\mathbf{z} - \boldsymbol{\mu})(\mathbf{z} - \boldsymbol{\mu})^T g(\mathbf{z}) \right] = \boldsymbol{\Sigma} \, E_q \left[\frac{\partial^2 g(\mathbf{z})}{\partial \mathbf{z}^T \partial \mathbf{z}} \right] \boldsymbol{\Sigma} + \boldsymbol{\Sigma} \, E_q \left[g(\mathbf{z}) \right], \quad \text{(C.53)}$$

which is the same as (2.126).

C.3 Temporally Discretizing Motion Models

Several times in the book we are faced with turning a continuous-time motion model into a discrete-time one for use in our estimation problems. Here we discuss doing so for linear motion models.

Linear Time-Varying Models

We start by considering *linear time-varying (LTV)* continuous-time models of the form

$$\dot{\mathbf{x}}(t) = \mathbf{A}(t)\mathbf{x}(t) + \mathbf{B}(t)\mathbf{u}(t) + \mathbf{L}(t)\mathbf{w}(t), \quad \text{(C.54)}$$

with

$$\mathbf{w}(t) \sim \mathcal{GP}(\mathbf{0}, \mathbf{Q}\,\delta(t - t')), \quad \text{(C.55)}$$

a (stationary) zero-mean *Gaussian process (GP)* with (symmetric, positive-definite) *power spectral density matrix*, $\mathbf{Q}$. The general solution for this LTV stochastic differential equation is

$$\underbrace{\mathbf{x}(t_k)}_{\mathbf{x}_k} = \underbrace{\boldsymbol{\Phi}(t_k, t_{k-1})}_{\mathbf{A}_{k-1}} \underbrace{\mathbf{x}(t_{k-1})}_{\mathbf{x}_{k-1}} + \underbrace{\int_{t_{k-1}}^{t_k} \boldsymbol{\Phi}(t_k, s)\mathbf{B}(s)\mathbf{u}(s)\, ds}_{\mathbf{v}_k}$$

$$+ \underbrace{\int_{t_{k-1}}^{t_k} \boldsymbol{\Phi}(t, s)\mathbf{L}(s)\mathbf{w}(s)\, ds}_{\mathbf{w}_k}, \quad \text{(C.56)}$$

which is now in a discrete-time form. The discrete-time process noise is $\mathbf{w}_k \sim \mathcal{N}(\mathbf{0}, \mathbf{Q}_k)$ where the covariance is

$$\mathbf{Q}_k = \int_{t_{k-1}}^{t_k} \boldsymbol{\Phi}(t_k, s)\mathbf{L}(s)\mathbf{Q}\mathbf{L}(s)^T \boldsymbol{\Phi}(t_k, s)^T\, ds. \quad \text{(C.57)}$$

The matrix $\boldsymbol{\Phi}(t, s)$ is known as the *transition function* and has the following properties:

$$\boldsymbol{\Phi}(t, t) = \mathbf{1}, \quad \text{(C.58)}$$

$$\dot{\boldsymbol{\Phi}}(t, s) = \mathbf{A}(t)\boldsymbol{\Phi}(t, s), \quad \text{(C.59)}$$

$$\boldsymbol{\Phi}(t, s) = \boldsymbol{\Phi}(t, r)\boldsymbol{\Phi}(r, s). \quad \text{(C.60)}$$

It is often straightforward to work out the transition function for systems in practice, but there is no general formula for the LTV case.

Linear Time-Invariant Models

When the system is *linear time-invariant (LTI)* so that

$$\dot{\mathbf{x}}(t) = \boldsymbol{A}\mathbf{x}(t) + \boldsymbol{B}\mathbf{u}(t) + \boldsymbol{L}\mathbf{w}(t), \tag{C.61}$$

with $\boldsymbol{A}$, $\boldsymbol{B}$, and $\boldsymbol{L}$ constant, the situation is somewhat simpler. The transition matrix can now be written in terms of a matrix exponential:

$$\boldsymbol{\Phi}(t, s) = \exp\left(\boldsymbol{A}\left(t - s\right)\right). \tag{C.62}$$

Then we have

$$\mathbf{x}_k = \mathbf{A}_{k-1}\mathbf{x}_{k-1} + \mathbf{v}_k + \mathbf{w}_k, \quad \mathbf{w}_k \sim \mathcal{N}(\mathbf{0}, \mathbf{Q}_k), \tag{C.63}$$

where

$$\mathbf{A}_{k-1} = \exp\left(\boldsymbol{A}\,\Delta t_k\right), \tag{C.64a}$$

$$\mathbf{Q}_k = \int_0^{\Delta t_k} \exp\left(\boldsymbol{A}\left(\Delta t_k - s\right)\right) \boldsymbol{L}\boldsymbol{Q}\boldsymbol{L}^T \exp\left(\boldsymbol{A}\left(\Delta t_k - s\right)\right)^T ds, \tag{C.64b}$$

and $\Delta t_k = t_k - t_{k-1}$.

If we further assume the input is held constant from t_{k-1} to t_k at $\mathbf{u}(t) = \mathbf{u}_k$, then we can write

$$\mathbf{x}_k = \mathbf{A}_{k-1}\mathbf{x}_{k-1} + \mathbf{B}_k\mathbf{u}_k + \mathbf{w}_k, \quad \mathbf{w}_k \sim \mathcal{N}(\mathbf{0}, \mathbf{Q}_k), \tag{C.65}$$

where $\mathbf{A}_{k-1}$ and $\mathbf{Q}_k$ are as in (C.64) and

$$\mathbf{B}_k = \int_0^{\Delta t_k} \exp\left(\boldsymbol{A}\left(\Delta t_k - s\right)\right) ds\,\boldsymbol{B}. \tag{C.66}$$

Next, we look at a convenient way of computing $\mathbf{A}_{k-1}$, $\mathbf{B}_k$, and $\mathbf{Q}_k$ using the matrix exponential.

Exponential Map Calculation

The exponential map provides a tidy way to carry out the integrals for LTI motion models (Farrell, 2008; Van Loan, 1978). We can use the results,

$$\begin{bmatrix} \mathbf{A}_{k-1} & \mathbf{B}_k \\ \mathbf{0} & \mathbf{1} \end{bmatrix} = \exp\left(\begin{bmatrix} \boldsymbol{A} & \boldsymbol{B} \\ \boldsymbol{0} & \boldsymbol{0} \end{bmatrix} \Delta t_k\right), \tag{C.67a}$$

$$\begin{bmatrix} \mathbf{A}_{k-1} & \mathbf{Q}_k\mathbf{A}_{k-1}^{-T} \\ \mathbf{0} & \mathbf{A}_{k-1}^{-T} \end{bmatrix} = \exp\left(\begin{bmatrix} \boldsymbol{A} & \boldsymbol{L}\boldsymbol{Q}\boldsymbol{L}^T \\ \boldsymbol{0} & -\boldsymbol{A}^T \end{bmatrix} \Delta t_k\right), \tag{C.67b}$$

to compute the desired discrete-time quantities.[2] If the operand of the matrix exponential is not nilpotent, we can approximate by keeping only a few terms in a series expansion since typically Δt_k is small.

The result in (C.67a) can be seen by carrying out a series expansion:

$$\exp\left(\begin{bmatrix} \boldsymbol{A} & \boldsymbol{B} \\ \boldsymbol{0} & \boldsymbol{0} \end{bmatrix} \Delta t_k\right) = \begin{bmatrix} \sum_{n=0}^{\infty} \frac{\Delta t_k^n}{n!} \boldsymbol{A}^n & \sum_{n=0}^{\infty} \frac{\Delta t_k^{n+1}}{(n+1)!} \boldsymbol{A}^n \boldsymbol{B} \\ \mathbf{0} & \mathbf{1} \end{bmatrix}. \tag{C.68}$$

---

[2] The result in (C.67b) was provided (as a personal communication) by Steven Dahdah and James Forbes from McGill University.

The top-left entry is $\mathbf{A}_{k-1} = \exp(\boldsymbol{A}\,\Delta t_k)$. The top-right entry is

$$\sum_{n=0}^{\infty} \frac{\Delta t_k^{n+1}}{(n+1)!} \mathbf{A}^n \mathbf{B} = \sum_{n=0}^{\infty} \frac{1}{n!} \int_0^{\Delta t_k} (\Delta t_k - s)^n \, ds \, \mathbf{A}^n \mathbf{B}$$

$$= \int_0^{\Delta t_k} \underbrace{\left(\sum_{n=0}^{\infty} \frac{(\Delta t_k - s)^n}{n!} \boldsymbol{A}^n \right)}_{\exp(\boldsymbol{A}(\Delta t_k - s))} ds \, \mathbf{B} = \mathbf{B}_k. \quad \text{(C.69)}$$

Furthermore, the result in (C.67b) can be seen by carrying out another series expansion:

$$\exp\left(\begin{bmatrix} \boldsymbol{A} & \boldsymbol{L}\boldsymbol{Q}\boldsymbol{L}^T \\ \boldsymbol{0} & -\boldsymbol{A}^T \end{bmatrix} \Delta t_k \right)$$

$$= \begin{bmatrix} \sum_{n=0}^{\infty} \frac{\Delta t_k^n}{n!} \boldsymbol{A}^n & \sum_{n=0}^{\infty} \sum_{m=0}^{\infty} \frac{(-1)^m \Delta t_k^{n+m+1}}{(n+m+1)!} \boldsymbol{A}^n \boldsymbol{L}\boldsymbol{Q}\boldsymbol{L}(\boldsymbol{A}^m)^T \\ \boldsymbol{0} & \sum_{n=0}^{\infty} \frac{(-\Delta t_k)^n}{n!} (\boldsymbol{A}^n)^T \end{bmatrix}. \quad \text{(C.70)}$$

The top-left and bottom-right entries are clearly $\mathbf{A}_{k-1} = \exp(\boldsymbol{A}\,\Delta t_k)$ and $\mathbf{A}_{k-1}^{-T} = \exp(-\boldsymbol{A}^T\,\Delta t_k)$, respectively. The top-right entry takes a little more work:

$$\sum_{n=0}^{\infty} \sum_{m=0}^{\infty} (-1)^m \Delta t_k^{n+m+1} \underbrace{\frac{1}{(n+m+1)!}}_{\frac{1}{n!m!} \int_0^1 (1-\alpha)^n \alpha^m \, d\alpha} \boldsymbol{A}^n \boldsymbol{L}\boldsymbol{Q}\boldsymbol{L}(\boldsymbol{A}^m)^T$$

$$= \sum_{n=0}^{\infty} \sum_{m=0}^{\infty} \frac{1}{n!m!} \int_0^{\Delta t_k} (\Delta t_k - s)^n (-s)^m \, ds \, \boldsymbol{A}^n \boldsymbol{L}\boldsymbol{Q}\boldsymbol{L}(\boldsymbol{A}^m)^T$$

$$= \int_0^{\Delta t_k} \underbrace{\left(\sum_{n=0}^{\infty} \frac{(\Delta t_k - s)^n}{n!} \boldsymbol{A}^n \right)}_{\exp(\boldsymbol{A}(\Delta t_k - s))} \boldsymbol{L}\boldsymbol{Q}\boldsymbol{L}^T \underbrace{\left(\sum_{m=0}^{\infty} \frac{(-s)^m}{m!} \boldsymbol{A}^m \right)}_{\exp(-\boldsymbol{A}s)} ds$$

$$= \mathbf{Q}_k \mathbf{A}_{k-1}^{-T}. \quad \text{(C.71)}$$

C.4 Invariant EKF

In Section 9.2.4, we introduced an *extended Kalman filter (EKF)* tailored to work on the Lie group, $SE(3)$. At the end of that section, we introduced the concept of the *invariant EKF* (Barrau and Bonnabel, 2017), which enjoys error dynamics akin to the linear *Kalman filter (KF)*; in particular, the motion model Jacobian, $\mathbf{F}_{k-1}$, and observation model Jacobian, $\mathbf{G}_k$, do not depend on the current state estimate, which makes analysis of the error dynamics significantly simpler. We refer to Barrau and Bonnabel (2017) for the general derivation of the invariant EKF, but use this section to show how we can algebraically manipulate our EKF in (9.141) into the required form.

C.4.1 Setup

To keep the discussion as clear as possible, we will assume that we have the same motion model as Section 9.2.4, but we will simplify our observation model slightly to be

$$\mathbf{y}_k = \mathbf{T}_k \mathbf{p} + \mathbf{n}_k, \quad \mathbf{n}_k \sim \mathcal{N}(\mathbf{0}, \mathbf{R}_k), \tag{C.72}$$

where $\mathbf{y}_k$ is now in 4×1 homogenous form, removing the need for the projection matrix, $\mathbf{D}^T$. We will also consider just a single landmark (and therefore drop the j landmark index) but the argument can be extended to many. Using our left perturbations, the observation model Jacobian is then

$$\mathbf{G}_k = (\check{\mathbf{T}}_k \mathbf{p})^{\odot}, \tag{C.73}$$

which is the same as Section 9.2.4 without the $\mathbf{D}^T$.

C.4.2 Prediction Step

Our motion model already has a Jacobian, $\mathbf{F}_{k-1}$, that does not depend on the state. However, to make the connection to the invariant EKF, we need to manipulate it a bit. Our mean prediction equation from (9.141) is

$$\check{\mathbf{T}}_k = \boldsymbol{\Xi}_k \, \hat{\mathbf{T}}_{k-1}, \tag{C.74}$$

which we will leave the same. From (9.141) our covariance prediction equation is

$$\check{\mathbf{P}}_k = \underbrace{\mathbf{F}_{k-1}}_{\check{\mathcal{T}}_k \hat{\mathcal{T}}_{k-1}^{-1}} \hat{\mathbf{P}}_{k-1} \underbrace{\mathbf{F}_{k-1}^T}_{\hat{\mathcal{T}}_{k-1}^{-T} \check{\mathcal{T}}_k^T} + \mathbf{Q}_k, \tag{C.75}$$

where we see that $\mathbf{F}_{k-1} = \mathrm{Ad}(\boldsymbol{\Xi}_k) = \check{\mathcal{T}}_k \hat{\mathcal{T}}_{k-1}^{-1}$. Rearranging the covariance prediction, we have

$$\underbrace{\check{\mathcal{T}}_k^{-1} \check{\mathbf{P}}_k \check{\mathcal{T}}_k^{-T}}_{\check{\mathbf{P}}_k'} = \underbrace{\hat{\mathcal{T}}_{k-1}^{-1} \hat{\mathbf{P}}_{k-1} \hat{\mathcal{T}}_{k-1}^{-T}}_{\hat{\mathbf{P}}_{k-1}'} + \underbrace{\check{\mathcal{T}}_k^{-1} \mathbf{Q}_k \check{\mathcal{T}}_k^{-T}}_{\mathbf{Q}_k'}, \tag{C.76}$$

or in terms of the new symbols defined in the underbraces,

$$\check{\mathbf{P}}_k' = \mathbf{F}_{k-1}' \hat{\mathbf{P}}_{k-1}' \mathbf{F}_{k-1}'^T + \mathbf{Q}_k', \tag{C.77}$$

with $\mathbf{F}_{k-1}' = \mathbf{1}$. We have essentially rewritten the covariance prediction in terms of covariances stored in the stationary frame rather than the moving frame. Using these new covariances, the Jacobians with respect to the state are identity. There is now a dependence on the state estimate embedded in the definition of $\mathbf{Q}_{k-1}'$, but this is acceptable for what we are trying to achieve.

C.4.3 Correction Step

The Kalman gain from (9.141) is

$$\mathbf{K}_k = \check{\mathbf{P}}_k \mathbf{G}_k^T \left(\mathbf{G}_k \check{\mathbf{P}}_k \mathbf{G}_k^T + \mathbf{R}_k \right)^{-1}. \tag{C.78}$$

Substituting our Jacobian, $\mathbf{G}_k$, this becomes

$$\mathbf{K}_k = \check{\mathbf{P}}_k \left(\check{\mathbf{T}}_k \mathbf{p}\right)^{\odot^T} \left(\left(\check{\mathbf{T}}_k \mathbf{p}\right)^{\odot} \check{\mathbf{P}}_k \left(\check{\mathbf{T}}_k \mathbf{p}\right)^{\odot^T} + \mathbf{R}_k\right)^{-1}. \qquad (C.79)$$

If we then use that $\left(\check{\mathbf{T}}_k \mathbf{p}\right)^{\odot} = \check{\mathbf{T}}_k \mathbf{p}^{\odot} \check{\boldsymbol{\mathcal{T}}}_k^{-1}$, we can manipulate this into

$$\mathbf{K}_k = \check{\boldsymbol{\mathcal{T}}}_k \underbrace{\check{\boldsymbol{\mathcal{T}}}_k^{-1} \check{\mathbf{P}}_k \check{\boldsymbol{\mathcal{T}}}_k^{-T}}_{\check{\mathbf{P}}'_k} \mathbf{p}^{\odot^T} \left(\mathbf{p}^{\odot} \underbrace{\check{\boldsymbol{\mathcal{T}}}_k^{-1} \check{\mathbf{P}}_k \check{\boldsymbol{\mathcal{T}}}_k^{-T}}_{\check{\mathbf{P}}'_k} \mathbf{p}^{\odot^T} + \underbrace{\check{\mathbf{T}}_k^{-1} \mathbf{R}_k \check{\mathbf{T}}_k^{-T}}_{\mathbf{R}'_k}\right)^{-1} \check{\mathbf{T}}_k^{-1},$$

$$(C.80)$$

where we see our new predicted covariance, $\check{\mathbf{P}}'_k$, appearing and define $\mathbf{R}'_k$, which does depend now on the current state estimate, similarly to $\mathbf{Q}'_k$. In terms of the simpler quantities we thus have

$$\mathbf{K}_k = \check{\boldsymbol{\mathcal{T}}}_k \underbrace{\check{\mathbf{P}}'_k \mathbf{p}^{\odot^T} \left(\mathbf{p}^{\odot} \check{\mathbf{P}}'_k \mathbf{p}^{\odot^T} + \mathbf{R}'_k\right)^{-1}}_{\mathbf{K}'_k} \check{\mathbf{T}}_k^{-1}, \qquad (C.81)$$

where we define a new Kalman gain, $\mathbf{K}'_k$.

Our mean correction update from (9.141) is then

$$\hat{\mathbf{T}}_k = \exp\left(\left(\mathbf{K}_k \left(\mathbf{y}_k - \check{\mathbf{y}}_k\right)\right)^{\wedge}\right) \check{\mathbf{T}}_k = \exp\left(\left(\check{\boldsymbol{\mathcal{T}}}_k \mathbf{K}'_k \check{\mathbf{T}}_k^{-1} \left(\mathbf{y}_k - \check{\mathbf{y}}_k\right)\right)^{\wedge}\right) \check{\mathbf{T}}_k$$

$$= \check{\mathbf{T}}_k \exp\left(\left(\mathbf{K}'_k \check{\mathbf{T}}_k^{-1} \left(\mathbf{y}_k - \check{\mathbf{y}}_k\right)\right)^{\wedge}\right), \quad (C.82)$$

which is in the standard form of the *left-invariant EKF*. The quantity, $\check{\mathbf{T}}_k^{-1} \left(\mathbf{y}_k - \check{\mathbf{y}}_k\right)$, is known as the *left-invariant innovation*. We can think of it as a pseudomeasurement model that replaces that of the original $\mathbf{y}_k$. Importantly, the Jacobian of this model is $\mathbf{G}'_k = \mathbf{p}^{\odot}$, which now does not depend on the current state estimate and is in fact a constant in this case. The new Kalman gain that we defined earlier can then also be written as

$$\mathbf{K}'_k = \check{\mathbf{P}}'_k \mathbf{G}'^T_k \left(\mathbf{G}'_k \check{\mathbf{P}}'_k \mathbf{G}'^T_k + \mathbf{R}'_k\right)^{-1}, \qquad (C.83)$$

which has the standard form of a Kalman gain. A similar derivation for this part can be found in Barrau and Bonnabel (2018a, Remark 2).

Finally, we need to manipulate the covariance correction update from (9.141). We have

$$\hat{\mathbf{P}}_k = \left(\mathbf{1} - \mathbf{K}_k \mathbf{G}_k\right) \check{\mathbf{P}}_k = \left(\mathbf{1} - \check{\boldsymbol{\mathcal{T}}}_k \mathbf{K}'_k \underbrace{\check{\mathbf{T}}_k^{-1} \check{\mathbf{T}}_k}_{\mathbf{1}} \underbrace{\mathbf{p}^{\odot} \check{\boldsymbol{\mathcal{T}}}_k^{-1}}_{\mathbf{G}'_k}\right) \check{\mathbf{P}}_k$$

$$= \check{\boldsymbol{\mathcal{T}}}_k \left(\mathbf{1} - \mathbf{K}'_k \mathbf{G}'_k\right) \check{\boldsymbol{\mathcal{T}}}_k^{-1} \check{\mathbf{P}}_k. \quad (C.84)$$

Here we are forced to approximate $\check{\boldsymbol{\mathcal{T}}}_k^{-1} \check{\mathbf{P}}_k \check{\boldsymbol{\mathcal{T}}}_k^{-T} \approx \hat{\mathbf{P}}'_k$, such that the covariance update is

$$\hat{\mathbf{P}}'_k = \left(\mathbf{1} - \mathbf{K}'_k \mathbf{G}'_k\right) \check{\mathbf{P}}'_k, \qquad (C.85)$$

which is again in standard form. We could also avoid making an approximation by substituting (C.82), but this is less elegant and does not result in the standard form. Other than this one approximation, we have shown the EKF of (9.141) can be exactly manipulated into the invariant EKF form.

C.4.4 Summary

Gathering the (left-)invariant EKF equations together, we have

$$\text{predictor:} \qquad \check{\mathbf{P}}'_k = \mathbf{F}'_{k-1} \hat{\mathbf{P}}'_{k-1} \mathbf{F}'^T_{k-1} + \mathbf{Q}'_k, \qquad \text{(C.86a)}$$

$$\check{\mathbf{T}}_k = \boldsymbol{\Xi}_k \, \hat{\mathbf{T}}_{k-1}, \qquad \text{(C.86b)}$$

$$\text{Kalman gain:} \qquad \mathbf{K}'_k = \check{\mathbf{P}}'_k \mathbf{G}'^T_k \left(\mathbf{G}'_k \check{\mathbf{P}}'_k \mathbf{G}'^T_k + \mathbf{R}'_k \right)^{-1}, \qquad \text{(C.86c)}$$

$$\hat{\mathbf{P}}'_k = \left(\mathbf{1} - \mathbf{K}'_k \mathbf{G}'_k \right) \check{\mathbf{P}}'_k, \qquad \text{(C.86d)}$$

$$\text{corrector:} \qquad \hat{\mathbf{T}}_k = \check{\mathbf{T}}_k \exp \left(\left(\mathbf{K}'_k \check{\mathbf{T}}_k^{-1} \left(\mathbf{y}_k - \check{\mathbf{y}}_k \right) \right)^\wedge \right). \qquad \text{(C.86e)}$$

In appearance, they look very similar to (9.141). The advantage of this form is that now $\mathbf{F}'_{k-1} = \mathbf{1}$ and $\mathbf{G}'_k = \mathbf{p}^\odot$ are both constants (i.e., they do not depend on the state estimate). Under certain conditions, the stability properties of the filter can now be analyzed cleanly along the lines of Section 3.3.6. We defer to Barrau and Bonnabel (2017) for further details on the properties of the invariant EKF.

Finally, a more direct route to the invariant EKF would have been to use right-hand perturbations in our original derivation; this is actually what the invariant EKF approach prescribes given the observation model we have. A left-invariant error/perturbation should be used with a left-invariant measurement model, which we have in this case. Somewhat confusingly, left-invariant errors correspond to perturbations on the right (and vice versa). Taking this more direct approach avoids the one approximation we made in linking to the invariant EKF.

Appendix D

Solutions to Exercises

D.1 Chapter 2: Primer on Probability Theory

2.1 We can do this brute force to see how it works:

$$\operatorname{tr}\left(\mathbf{v}\mathbf{u}^T\right) = \operatorname{tr}\left(\begin{bmatrix} v_1 \\ v_2 \\ v_3 \end{bmatrix} \begin{bmatrix} u_1 \\ u_2 \\ u_3 \end{bmatrix}^T\right) = \operatorname{tr}\left(\begin{bmatrix} v_1u_1 & v_1u_2 & v_1u_3 \\ v_2u_1 & v_2u_2 & v_3u_3 \\ v_3u_1 & v_3u_2 & v_3u_3 \end{bmatrix}\right)$$

$$= v_1u_1 + v_2u_2 + v_3u_3 = \mathbf{u}^T\mathbf{v}.$$

But, it is easier to use the cyclic property of trace: $\operatorname{tr}\left(\mathbf{v}\mathbf{u}^T\right) = \operatorname{tr}\left(\mathbf{u}^T\mathbf{v}\right) = \mathbf{u}^T\mathbf{v}$.

2.2 Apply the definition of Shannon information and manipulate:

$$H(\mathbf{x}, \mathbf{y}) = -\iint p(\mathbf{x}, \mathbf{y}) \ln p(\mathbf{x}, \mathbf{y}) \, d\mathbf{x} \, d\mathbf{y}$$

$$= -\iint p(\mathbf{x})p(\mathbf{y}) \ln (p(\mathbf{x})p(\mathbf{y})) \, d\mathbf{x} \, d\mathbf{y}$$

$$= -\iint p(\mathbf{x})p(\mathbf{y}) (\ln p(\mathbf{x}) + \ln p(\mathbf{y})) \, d\mathbf{x} \, d\mathbf{y}$$

$$= -\int p(\mathbf{x}) \ln p(\mathbf{x}) \, d\mathbf{x} \underbrace{\int p(\mathbf{y}) \, d\mathbf{y}}_{1} - \underbrace{\int p(\mathbf{x}) \, d\mathbf{x}}_{1} \int p(\mathbf{y}) \ln p(\mathbf{y}) \, d\mathbf{y}$$

$$= H(\mathbf{x}) + H(\mathbf{y}).$$

2.3 Complete the square:

$$E[\mathbf{x}\mathbf{x}^T] = E[(\mathbf{x} - \boldsymbol{\mu})(\mathbf{x} - \boldsymbol{\mu})^T] + \boldsymbol{\mu}E[\mathbf{x}]^T + E[\mathbf{x}]\boldsymbol{\mu}^T - \boldsymbol{\mu}\boldsymbol{\mu}^T = \boldsymbol{\Sigma} + \boldsymbol{\mu}\boldsymbol{\mu}^T.$$

2.4 See previous question for $E[\mathbf{x}\mathbf{x}^T]$. Then

$$E[\mathbf{x}^T\mathbf{x}] = E[\operatorname{tr}(\mathbf{x}\mathbf{x}^T)] = \operatorname{tr}(E[\mathbf{x}\mathbf{x}^T]) = \operatorname{tr}(\boldsymbol{\Sigma} + \boldsymbol{\mu}\boldsymbol{\mu}^T) = \operatorname{tr}(\boldsymbol{\Sigma}) + \boldsymbol{\mu}^T\boldsymbol{\mu}.$$

2.5 Marginals are simply $p(\mathbf{x}) = \mathcal{N}(\boldsymbol{\mu}_x, \boldsymbol{\Sigma}_{xx})$ and $p(\mathbf{y}) = \mathcal{N}(\boldsymbol{\mu}_y, \boldsymbol{\Sigma}_{yy})$; see Section 2.2.5. For $p(\mathbf{x}, \mathbf{y}) = p(\mathbf{x})p(\mathbf{y})$ we require $\boldsymbol{\Sigma}_{xy} = \boldsymbol{\Sigma}_{yx}^T = \mathbf{0}$.

2.6 Use the even- and oddness of functions about $\mathbf{x} - \boldsymbol{\mu}$:

$$\int_{-\infty}^{\infty} \mathbf{x}\, p(\mathbf{x}) \, d\mathbf{x} = \int_{-\infty}^{\infty} \underbrace{(\mathbf{x} - \boldsymbol{\mu})}_{\text{odd}} \underbrace{p(\mathbf{x})}_{\text{even}} \, d\mathbf{x} + \int_{-\infty}^{\infty} \boldsymbol{\mu}\, p(\mathbf{x}) \, d\mathbf{x}$$

$$= \mathbf{0} + \boldsymbol{\mu} \underbrace{\int_{-\infty}^{\infty} p(\mathbf{x}) \, d\mathbf{x}}_{1} = \boldsymbol{\mu}.$$

2.7 The easiest way is using Stein's lemma with $\mathbf{f}(\mathbf{x}) = \mathbf{x} - \boldsymbol{\mu}$:

$$E[(\mathbf{x} - \boldsymbol{\mu})(\mathbf{x} - \boldsymbol{\mu})^T] = E[\mathbf{f}(\mathbf{x})(\mathbf{x} - \boldsymbol{\mu})^T] = E\left[\frac{\partial \mathbf{f}(\mathbf{x})}{\partial \mathbf{x}}\right]\boldsymbol{\Sigma}$$

$$= E[\mathbf{1}]\,\boldsymbol{\Sigma} = \boldsymbol{\Sigma}.$$

See Appendix C.2 for the derivation of Stein's lemma.

2.8 Hint: use the fact that the product of exponentials is the exponential of a sum, then complete the square.

2.9 It must be that

$$p(\mathbf{x}) = \sum_{k=1}^{K} w_k p_k(\mathbf{x}),$$

where $p_k(\mathbf{x})$ is the PDF for $\mathbf{x}_k$. Then

$$\int p(\mathbf{x})\,d\mathbf{x} = \int \sum_{k=1}^{K} w_k p_k(\mathbf{x})\,d\mathbf{x} = \sum_{k=1}^{K} w_k \underbrace{\int p_k(\mathbf{x})\,d\mathbf{x}}_{1} = \sum_{k=1}^{K} w_k = 1.$$

Finally,

$$\boldsymbol{\mu} = \int \mathbf{x}\,p(\mathbf{x})\,d\mathbf{x} = \int \mathbf{x}\sum_{k=1}^{K} w_k p_k(\mathbf{x})\,d\mathbf{x}$$

$$= \sum_{k=1}^{K} w_k \int \mathbf{x}\,p_k(\mathbf{x})\,d\mathbf{x} = \sum_{k=1}^{K} w_k \boldsymbol{\mu}_k.$$

2.10 For the mean:

$$E[y] = E[\mathbf{x}^T\mathbf{x}] = \mathrm{tr}(\boldsymbol{\Sigma}) + \boldsymbol{\mu}^T\boldsymbol{\mu} = \mathrm{tr}(\mathbf{1}) = K.$$

For the variance use Isserlis' theorem:

$$E[(y - K)^2] = E[\mathbf{x}^T\mathbf{x}\mathbf{x}^T\mathbf{x}] - 2KE[\mathbf{x}^T\mathbf{x}] + K^2$$

$$= \mathrm{tr}(E[\mathbf{x}\mathbf{x}^T\mathbf{x}\mathbf{x}^T]) - K^2 = \mathrm{tr}(\boldsymbol{\Sigma}(\mathrm{tr}(\boldsymbol{\Sigma})\mathbf{1} + 2\boldsymbol{\Sigma})) - K^2$$

$$= \mathrm{tr}(\mathbf{1}(\mathrm{tr}(\mathbf{1})\mathbf{1} + 2\mathbf{1})) - K^2 = 2K + K^2 - K^2 = 2K.$$

2.11 For the mean,

$$E[y] = E[(\mathbf{x} - \boldsymbol{\mu})^T\boldsymbol{\Sigma}^{-1}(\mathbf{x} - \boldsymbol{\mu})] = \mathrm{tr}(\boldsymbol{\Sigma}^{-1}E[(\mathbf{x} - \boldsymbol{\mu})(\mathbf{x} - \boldsymbol{\mu})^T])$$

$$= \mathrm{tr}(\boldsymbol{\Sigma}^{-1}\boldsymbol{\Sigma}) = \mathrm{tr}(\mathbf{1}) = K.$$

For the variance use Isserlis' theorem:

$$E[(y - K)^2] = E[(\mathbf{x} - \boldsymbol{\mu})^T\boldsymbol{\Sigma}^{-1}(\mathbf{x} - \boldsymbol{\mu})(\mathbf{x} - \boldsymbol{\mu})^T\boldsymbol{\Sigma}^{-1}(\mathbf{x} - \boldsymbol{\mu})]$$

$$\quad - 2KE[(\mathbf{x} - \boldsymbol{\mu})^T\boldsymbol{\Sigma}^{-1}(\mathbf{x} - \boldsymbol{\mu})] + K^2$$

$$= \mathrm{tr}(\boldsymbol{\Sigma}^{-1}E[(\mathbf{x} - \boldsymbol{\mu})(\mathbf{x} - \boldsymbol{\mu})^T\boldsymbol{\Sigma}^{-1}(\mathbf{x} - \boldsymbol{\mu})(\mathbf{x} - \boldsymbol{\mu})^T]) - K^2$$

$$= \mathrm{tr}(\boldsymbol{\Sigma}^{-1}\boldsymbol{\Sigma}(\mathrm{tr}(\boldsymbol{\Sigma}^{-1}\boldsymbol{\Sigma})\mathbf{1} + 2\boldsymbol{\Sigma})) - K^2$$

$$= \mathrm{tr}(\mathbf{1}(\mathrm{tr}(\mathbf{1})\mathbf{1} + 2\mathbf{1})) - K^2 = 2K + K^2 - K^2 = 2K.$$

2.12 Insert the definition of a Gaussian PDF into KL and manipulate:

$$\mathrm{KL}(p_1||p_2) = E_{p_2}[\ln p_2 - \ln p_1]$$

$$= E_{p_2}\left[-\frac{1}{2}(\mathbf{x} - \boldsymbol{\mu}_2)^T\boldsymbol{\Sigma}_2^{-1}(\mathbf{x} - \boldsymbol{\mu}_2) - \frac{1}{2}\ln((2\pi)^N|\boldsymbol{\Sigma}_2|)\right]$$

$$-E_{p_2}\left[-\frac{1}{2}(\mathbf{x} - \boldsymbol{\mu}_1)^T\boldsymbol{\Sigma}_1^{-1}(\mathbf{x} - \boldsymbol{\mu}_1) - \frac{1}{2}\ln((2\pi)^N|\boldsymbol{\Sigma}_1|)\right]$$

$$= E_{p_2}\left[\frac{1}{2}\mathbf{x}^T\boldsymbol{\Sigma}^{-1}\mathbf{x}\right] - 2E_{p_2}\left[\frac{1}{2}\mathbf{x}^T\boldsymbol{\Sigma}^{-1}\boldsymbol{\mu}_1\right] + \frac{1}{2}\boldsymbol{\mu}_1^T\boldsymbol{\Sigma}_1^{-1}\boldsymbol{\mu}_1$$

$$+ \frac{1}{2}\ln|\boldsymbol{\Sigma}_1| - \frac{1}{2}N - \frac{1}{2}\ln|\boldsymbol{\Sigma}_2|$$

$$= \frac{1}{2}\mathrm{tr}\left(\boldsymbol{\Sigma}_1^{-1}E_{p_2}[\mathbf{x}\mathbf{x}^T]\right) - \boldsymbol{\mu}_2^T\boldsymbol{\Sigma}_1^{-1}\boldsymbol{\mu}_1 + \frac{1}{2}\boldsymbol{\mu}_1^T\boldsymbol{\Sigma}_1^{-1}\boldsymbol{\mu}_1$$

$$+ \frac{1}{2}\ln|\boldsymbol{\Sigma}_1| - \frac{1}{2}N - \frac{1}{2}\ln|\boldsymbol{\Sigma}_2|$$

$$= \frac{1}{2}\left((\boldsymbol{\mu}_2 - \boldsymbol{\mu}_1)^T\boldsymbol{\Sigma}_1^{-1}(\boldsymbol{\mu}_2 - \boldsymbol{\mu}_1) + \ln|\boldsymbol{\Sigma}_1\boldsymbol{\Sigma}_2^{-1}| + \mathrm{tr}(\boldsymbol{\Sigma}_1^{-1}\boldsymbol{\Sigma}_2) - N\right).$$

2.13 For the mean:

$$\boldsymbol{\mu}_k = E[\mathbf{x}_k] = E[\mathbf{A}\mathbf{x}_{k-1} + \mathbf{w}_k] = \mathbf{A}E[\mathbf{x}_{k-1}] + E[\mathbf{w}_k] = \mathbf{A}\boldsymbol{\mu}_{k-1}.$$

For the variance:

$$E[(\mathbf{x}_k - \boldsymbol{\mu}_k)(\mathbf{x}_k - \boldsymbol{\mu}_k)^T]$$

$$= E[(\mathbf{A}\mathbf{x}_{k-1} + \mathbf{w}_k - \mathbf{A}\boldsymbol{\mu}_{k-1})(\mathbf{A}\mathbf{x}_{k-1} + \mathbf{w}_k - \mathbf{A}\boldsymbol{\mu}_{k-1})^T]$$

$$= \mathbf{A}E[(\mathbf{x}_{k-1} - \boldsymbol{\mu}_{k-1})(\mathbf{x}_{k-1} - \boldsymbol{\mu}_{k-1})^T]\mathbf{A}^T + E[\mathbf{w}_k\mathbf{w}_k^T]$$

$$+ \mathbf{A}\underbrace{E[(\mathbf{x}_{k-1} - \boldsymbol{\mu}_{k-1})\mathbf{w}_k^T]}_{0} + \underbrace{E[\mathbf{w}_k(\mathbf{x}_{k-1} - \boldsymbol{\mu}_{k-1})^T]}_{0}\mathbf{A}^T$$

$$= \mathbf{A}\boldsymbol{\Sigma}_{k-1}\mathbf{A}^T + \mathbf{Q}.$$

2.14 This is one way, with η a normalization constant:

$$p(\mathbf{x}) = \frac{p(\mathbf{x}, \mathbf{y})}{p(\mathbf{y}|\mathbf{x})}$$

$$= \eta\exp\left(-\frac{1}{2}\left(\begin{bmatrix}\mathbf{x}\\\mathbf{y}\end{bmatrix} - \begin{bmatrix}\boldsymbol{\mu}_x\\\boldsymbol{\mu}_y\end{bmatrix}\right)^T\begin{bmatrix}\boldsymbol{\Sigma}_{xx} & \boldsymbol{\Sigma}_{xy}\\\boldsymbol{\Sigma}_{yx} & \boldsymbol{\Sigma}_{yy}\end{bmatrix}^{-1}\left(\begin{bmatrix}\mathbf{x}\\\mathbf{y}\end{bmatrix} - \begin{bmatrix}\boldsymbol{\mu}_x\\\boldsymbol{\mu}_y\end{bmatrix}\right)\right)$$

$$\bigg/ \exp\left(-\frac{1}{2}\left(\mathbf{y} - \boldsymbol{\mu}_y - \boldsymbol{\Sigma}_{yx}\boldsymbol{\Sigma}_{xx}^{-1}(\mathbf{x} - \boldsymbol{\mu}_x)\right)^T\left(\boldsymbol{\Sigma}_{yy} - \boldsymbol{\Sigma}_{yx}\boldsymbol{\Sigma}_{xx}^{-1}\boldsymbol{\Sigma}_{xy}\right)^{-1}\right.$$

$$\left. \times \left(\mathbf{y} - \boldsymbol{\mu}_y - \boldsymbol{\Sigma}_{yx}\boldsymbol{\Sigma}_{xx}^{-1}(\mathbf{x} - \boldsymbol{\mu}_x)\right)\right)$$

$$= \eta\exp\left(-\frac{1}{2}(\mathbf{x} - \boldsymbol{\mu}_x)^T\boldsymbol{\Sigma}_{xx}^{-1}(\mathbf{x} - \boldsymbol{\mu}_x)\right) = \mathcal{N}(\boldsymbol{\mu}_x, \boldsymbol{\Sigma}_{xx}).$$

2.15 We have that:

$$\begin{bmatrix}\mathbf{A}_{xx} & \mathbf{A}_{xy}\\\mathbf{A}_{yx} & \mathbf{A}_{yy}\end{bmatrix}\begin{bmatrix}\boldsymbol{\Sigma}_{xx} & \boldsymbol{\Sigma}_{xy}\\\boldsymbol{\Sigma}_{yx} & \boldsymbol{\Sigma}_{yy}\end{bmatrix} = \begin{bmatrix}\mathbf{A}_{xx}\boldsymbol{\Sigma}_{xx} + \mathbf{A}_{xy}\boldsymbol{\Sigma}_{yx} & *\\\mathbf{A}_{yx}\boldsymbol{\Sigma}_{xx} + \mathbf{A}_{yy}\boldsymbol{\Sigma}_{yx} & *\end{bmatrix} = \begin{bmatrix}\mathbf{1} & \mathbf{0}\\\mathbf{0} & \mathbf{1}\end{bmatrix},$$

where $*$ is an entry we will not need. From the bottom-left, $\boldsymbol{\Sigma}_{yx}\boldsymbol{\Sigma}_{xx}^{-1} = -\mathbf{A}_{yy}^{-1}\mathbf{A}_{yx}$, and plugging this into the top-left gives $\boldsymbol{\Sigma}_{xx}^{-1} = \mathbf{A}_{xx} - \mathbf{A}_{xy}\mathbf{A}_{yy}^{-1}\mathbf{A}_{yx}$. Then, from

$$\begin{bmatrix} \boldsymbol{\mu}_x \\ \boldsymbol{\mu}_y \end{bmatrix} = \begin{bmatrix} \boldsymbol{\Sigma}_{xx} & \boldsymbol{\Sigma}_{xy} \\ \boldsymbol{\Sigma}_{yx} & \boldsymbol{\Sigma}_{yy} \end{bmatrix} \begin{bmatrix} \mathbf{b}_x \\ \mathbf{b}_y \end{bmatrix} = \begin{bmatrix} \boldsymbol{\Sigma}_{xx}\mathbf{b}_x + \boldsymbol{\Sigma}_{xy}\mathbf{b}_y \\ * \end{bmatrix},$$

we have

$$\boldsymbol{\Sigma}_{xx}^{-1}\boldsymbol{\mu}_x = \mathbf{b}_x + \boldsymbol{\Sigma}_{xx}^{-1}\boldsymbol{\Sigma}_{xy}\mathbf{b}_y = \mathbf{b}_x - \mathbf{A}_{xy}\mathbf{A}_{yy}^{-1}\mathbf{b}_y.$$

2.16 For (i) we have $p(\mathbf{y}|\mathbf{x}) = \mathcal{N}(\mathbf{Cx}, \mathbf{R})$, and for (ii):

$$p(\mathbf{x}, \mathbf{y}) = p(\mathbf{y}|\mathbf{x})p(\mathbf{x}) = \mathcal{N}\left(\begin{bmatrix} \boldsymbol{\mu} \\ \mathbf{C}\boldsymbol{\mu} \end{bmatrix}, \begin{bmatrix} \boldsymbol{\Sigma} & \boldsymbol{\Sigma}\mathbf{C}^T \\ \mathbf{C}\boldsymbol{\Sigma} & \mathbf{C}\boldsymbol{\Sigma}\mathbf{C}^T + \mathbf{R} \end{bmatrix}\right).$$

For (iii):

$$p(\mathbf{x}|\mathbf{y}) = \mathcal{N}\left(\boldsymbol{\mu} + \boldsymbol{\Sigma}\mathbf{C}^T(\mathbf{C}\boldsymbol{\Sigma}\mathbf{C}^T + \mathbf{R})^{-1}(\mathbf{y} - \mathbf{C}\boldsymbol{\mu}),\right.$$

$$\left. \boldsymbol{\Sigma} - \boldsymbol{\Sigma}\mathbf{C}^T(\mathbf{C}\boldsymbol{\Sigma}\mathbf{C}^T + \mathbf{R})^{-1}\mathbf{C}\boldsymbol{\Sigma}\right),$$

$$p(\mathbf{y}) = \mathcal{N}\left(\mathbf{C}\boldsymbol{\mu}, \mathbf{C}\boldsymbol{\Sigma}\mathbf{C}^T + \mathbf{R}\right).$$

For (iv) $\boldsymbol{\Sigma} - \boldsymbol{\Sigma}\mathbf{C}^T(\mathbf{C}\boldsymbol{\Sigma}\mathbf{C}^T + \mathbf{R})^{-1}\mathbf{C}\boldsymbol{\Sigma}$ is 'smaller' than $\boldsymbol{\Sigma}$.

D.2 Chapter 3: Linear-Gaussian Estimation

3.1 Linear system of equations for $\hat{\mathbf{x}}$ is

$$\mathbf{H}^T\mathbf{W}^{-1}\mathbf{H}\hat{\mathbf{x}} = \mathbf{H}^T\mathbf{W}^{-1}\mathbf{z},$$

with

$$\mathbf{C} = 1, \quad \mathbf{H} = \begin{bmatrix} \mathbf{A}^{-1} \\ \mathbf{C} \end{bmatrix}, \quad \mathbf{z} = \begin{bmatrix} \mathbf{v} \\ \mathbf{y} \end{bmatrix}, \quad \mathbf{W} = \begin{bmatrix} \mathbf{Q} & \mathbf{0} \\ \mathbf{0} & \mathbf{R} \end{bmatrix},$$

$$\mathbf{A}^{-1} = \begin{bmatrix} -1 & 1 & 0 & 0 & 0 & 0 \\ 0 & -1 & 1 & 0 & 0 & 0 \\ 0 & 0 & -1 & 1 & 0 & 0 \\ 0 & 0 & 0 & -1 & 1 & 0 \\ 0 & 0 & 0 & 0 & -1 & 1 \end{bmatrix}, \quad \mathbf{v} = \begin{bmatrix} v_1 \\ v_2 \\ v_3 \\ v_4 \\ v_5 \end{bmatrix}, \quad \mathbf{y} = \begin{bmatrix} y_0 \\ y_1 \\ y_2 \\ y_3 \\ y_4 \\ y_5 \end{bmatrix},$$

$$\mathbf{Q} = \mathrm{diag}(Q, Q, Q, Q, Q), \quad \mathbf{R} = \mathrm{diag}(R, R, R, R, R, R).$$

3.2 This is simply a matter of plugging in the numbers. The sparsity pattern for $\mathbf{L}$ will be such that only the main diagonal and the one below have non-zero entries.

3.3 In this case we have

$$\mathbf{R} = \begin{bmatrix} R & R/2 & R/4 & 0 & 0 & 0 \\ R/2 & R & R/2 & R/4 & 0 & 0 \\ R/4 & R/2 & R & R/2 & R/4 & 0 \\ 0 & R/4 & R/2 & R & R/2 & R/4 \\ 0 & 0 & R/4 & R/2 & R & R/2 \\ 0 & 0 & 0 & R/4 & R/2 & R \end{bmatrix}.$$

For $R > 0$ this matrix is full rank and thus $\mathbf{R} > 0$. Then

$$\mathbf{H}^T\mathbf{W}^{-1}\mathbf{H} = \underbrace{\mathbf{A}^{-T}\mathbf{Q}^{-1}\mathbf{A}}_{\geq 0} + \underbrace{\mathbf{R}^{-1}}_{>0},$$

so $\mathbf{H}^T\mathbf{W}^{-1}\mathbf{H} > 0$ and thus the solution will be unique.

3.4 The Kalman filter covariance equations are

$$\check{P}_k = \hat{P}_{k-1} + Q,$$
$$K_k = \check{P}_k(\check{P}_k + R)^{-1},$$
$$\hat{P}_k = (1 - K_k)\check{P}_k.$$

At steady state $\hat{P}_k = \hat{P}_{k-1} = \hat{P}$ and $\check{P}_k = \check{P}_{k-1} = \check{P}$. Substituting the steady-state values into the KF equations and rearranging gives the required expressions. Each quadratic has a positive and a negative root. Since variance is positive, only the positive root is physically meaningful.

3.5 Follow the hint in the question by setting up the problem as a small batch estimator.

3.6 The easiest way is just to multiply $\mathbf{A}$ by the proposed $\mathbf{A}^{-1}$ to see that the result is the identity matrix.

3.7 While $\mathbf{L}$ is sparse, $\mathbf{L}^{-1}$ is actually a dense lower-triangular matrix. So, unfortunately, the cost of computing $\hat{\mathbf{P}}$ this way is ultimately cubic in the size of the matrix. However, if only select entries of $\hat{\mathbf{P}}$ are required, these can be computed more efficiently; see, for example, Section 6.3.2.

3.8 (i) $e_k = d_k - (x_k - x_{k-1}), \quad e_{k,\ell} = e_{k,\ell} - (m_\ell - x_k)$

(ii) $\mathbf{e} = \mathbf{y} - \mathbf{A}\mathbf{x}$ with $\mathbf{A} = \begin{bmatrix} 1 & 0 & 0 & 0 & 0 \\ -1 & 1 & 0 & 0 & 0 \\ 0 & -1 & 1 & 0 & 0 \\ 0 & 0 & 0 & 1 & 0 \\ 0 & -1 & 0 & 1 & 0 \\ -1 & 0 & 0 & 0 & 1 \\ 0 & -1 & 0 & 0 & 1 \\ 0 & 0 & -1 & 0 & 1 \end{bmatrix}$

(iii) $J = \frac{1}{2}(\mathbf{y} - \mathbf{A}\mathbf{x})^T(\mathbf{y} - \mathbf{A}\mathbf{x})$

(iv) $\frac{\partial J}{\partial \mathbf{x}^T} = -\mathbf{A}^T(\mathbf{y} - \mathbf{A}\mathbf{x}^\star) = \mathbf{0} \quad \Rightarrow \quad \mathbf{x}^\star = (\mathbf{A}^T\mathbf{A})^{-1}\mathbf{A}^T\mathbf{y}$

(v) $\mathbf{A}^T\mathbf{A}$ is full rank so invertible and thus the solution is unique.

3.9 (i) The first landmark measurement model can be rearranged as $m_0 = y_0 + p_0 - n_0$. The required expectations are then

$$\hat{m}_0 = E[y_0 + p_0 - n_0] = y_0 + E[p_0] - E[n_0] = y_0,$$
$$E[((y_0 + p_0 - n_0) - y_0)^2] = E[p_0^2] - 2E[p_0 n_0] + E[n_0^2] = 1,$$
$$E[((y_0 + p_0 - n_0)(p_0 - 0)] = E[p_0^2] - E[p_0 n_0] = 0,$$

so that

$$\hat{\mathbf{x}}_0 = \begin{bmatrix} 0 \\ y_0 \end{bmatrix}, \quad \hat{\mathbf{P}}_0 = \begin{bmatrix} 0 & 0 \\ 0 & 1 \end{bmatrix}.$$

(ii) We have

$$\check{\mathbf{x}}_K = \begin{bmatrix} 0 \\ y_0 \end{bmatrix} + \sum_k \begin{bmatrix} d_k \\ 0 \end{bmatrix} = \begin{bmatrix} \sum_k d_k \\ y_0 \end{bmatrix},$$
$$\check{\mathbf{P}}_K = \begin{bmatrix} 0 & 0 \\ 0 & 1 \end{bmatrix} + \begin{bmatrix} 1 \\ 0 \end{bmatrix} \begin{bmatrix} 1 \\ 0 \end{bmatrix}^T \sum_k \frac{2}{K} = \begin{bmatrix} 2 & 0 \\ 0 & 1 \end{bmatrix}.$$

(iii) Kalman gain with $\mathbf{c}^T = \begin{bmatrix} -1 & 1 \end{bmatrix}$ and $R = 1$ is

$$\mathbf{k} = \check{\mathbf{P}}_K \mathbf{c} \left(\mathbf{c}^T \check{\mathbf{P}}_K \mathbf{c} + R \right)^{-1} = \frac{1}{4} \begin{bmatrix} -2 \\ 1 \end{bmatrix},$$

so then the final estimate is

$$\hat{\mathbf{x}}_K = \check{\mathbf{x}}_K + \mathbf{k}(y_K - \mathbf{c}^T \check{\mathbf{x}}_K) = \begin{bmatrix} \frac{1}{2}(\sum_k d_k - y_K + y_0) \\ \frac{1}{4}(\sum_k d_k + y_K) + \frac{3}{4} y_0 \end{bmatrix},$$

$$\hat{\mathbf{P}}_K = (\mathbf{1} - \mathbf{k}\mathbf{c}^T)\check{\mathbf{P}}_K = \begin{bmatrix} 1 & \frac{1}{2} \\ \frac{1}{2} & \frac{3}{4} \end{bmatrix}.$$

(iv) The answer would be the same since we use the same measurements in both cases.

3.10   (i) We can choose $\hat{p}_{k,k-1} = y_{k-1,k} - y_{k,k}$.

     (ii) Then have

$$E[\hat{p}_{k,k-1}] = E[y_{k-1,k}] - E[y_{k,k}] = E[m_k - p_{k-1} + n_{k-1,k}]$$
$$- E[m_k - p_k + n_{k,k}] = p_k - p_{k-1},$$
$$E[([\hat{p}_{k,k-1} - (p_k - p_{k-1}))^2] = E[(n_{k-1,k} - n_k)^2]$$
$$= \underbrace{E[n_{k-1}^2]}_{\sigma^2} - 2\underbrace{E[n_{k-1,k} n_{k,k}]}_{0} + \underbrace{E[n_{k,k}^2]}_{\sigma^2} = 2\sigma^2,$$

where we have used independence of all the measurement noises.

    (iii) We can choose $\hat{p}_{K,0} = \sum_{k=1}^{K} \hat{p}_{k,k-1}$.

    (iv) Then we have

$$E[\hat{p}_{K,0}] = \sum_{k=1}^{K} E[\hat{p}_{k,k-1}] = \sum_{k=1}^{K}(p_k - p_{k-1}) = p_K - p_0,$$

$$E[(\hat{p}_{K,0} - (p_K - p_0))^2] = E\left[\left(\sum_{k=1}^{K}(n_{k,k} - n_{k-1,k}) \right)^2 \right]$$

$$= \sum_{k-1}^{K} 2\sigma^2 = 2K\sigma^2,$$

where we have again used independence of all the measurement noises.

    (v) In inverse-covariance form, the correction step of the KF (fusing two Gaussians) gives us

$$\hat{P}^{-1} = \check{P}^{-1} + \frac{1}{\sigma^2},$$
$$\hat{P}^{-1}\hat{x} = \check{P}^{-1}\check{x} + \frac{1}{\sigma^2} y_{K0},$$

where $\check{x} = \hat{p}_{K,0}$ and $\check{P} = 2K\sigma^2$.

    (vi) The variance of our estimator is

$$\hat{P} = \left(\check{P}^{-1} + \frac{1}{\sigma^2} \right)^{-1} = \left(\frac{1}{2K\sigma^2} + \frac{1}{\sigma^2} \right) = \frac{2K}{2K+1}\sigma^2.$$

In the limit $K \to \infty$, the variance will be simply σ^2, which is the variance of the direct measurement alone since the odometry adds no further value.

D.3 Chapter 4: Nonlinear Non-Gaussian Estimation

4.1 For the motion model we have

$$\mathbf{F}_{k-1} = \begin{bmatrix} 1 & 0 & -v_k T \sin\theta_{k-1} \\ 0 & 1 & v_k T \cos\theta_{k-1} \\ 0 & 0 & 1 \end{bmatrix},$$

$$\mathbf{Q}'_k = T^2 \begin{bmatrix} \cos\theta_{k-1} & 0 \\ \sin\theta_{k-1} & 0 \\ 0 & 1 \end{bmatrix} \mathbf{Q} \begin{bmatrix} \cos\theta_{k-1} & 0 \\ \sin\theta_{k-1} & 0 \\ 0 & 1 \end{bmatrix}^T.$$

For the observation model we have

$$\mathbf{G}_k = \begin{bmatrix} \frac{x_k}{\sqrt{x_k^2+y_k^2}} & \frac{y_k}{\sqrt{x_k^2+y_k^2}} & 0 \\ \frac{-y_k}{\sqrt{x_k^2+y_k^2}} & \frac{x_k}{\sqrt{x_k^2+y_k^2}} & -1 \end{bmatrix}, \quad \mathbf{R}'_k = \mathbf{R}.$$

4.2 We have for $y = x^3$ that

Monte Carlo: $y \sim \mathcal{N}\left(\mu_x^3 + 3\mu_x\sigma_x^2, \; 9\mu_x^4\sigma_x^2 + 36\mu_x^2\sigma_x^4 + 15\sigma_x^6\right)$

linearization: $y \sim \mathcal{N}\left(\mu_x^3, \; 9\mu_x^4\sigma_x^2\right)$

sigmapoint: $y \sim \mathcal{N}\left(\mu_x^3 + 3\mu_x\sigma_x^2, \right.$
$$\left. 9\mu_x^4\sigma_x^2 + (15\kappa + 6)\mu_x^2\sigma_x^4 + (\kappa+1)^2\sigma_x^6\right)$$

If we pick $\kappa = 2$, the sigmapoint variance matches Monte Carlo on the first two terms.

4.3 We have for $y = x^4$ that

Monte Carlo: $y \sim \mathcal{N}\left(\mu_x^4 + 6\mu_x^2\sigma_x^2 + 3\sigma_x^4, \right.$
$$\left. 16\mu_x^6\sigma_x^2 + 168\mu_x^4\sigma_x^4 + 384\mu_x^2\sigma_x^6 + 96\sigma_x^8\right)$$

linearization: $y \sim \mathcal{N}\left(\mu_x^4, \; 16\mu_x^6\sigma_x^2\right)$

sigmapoint: $y \sim \mathcal{N}\left(\mu_x^4 + 6\mu_x^2\sigma_x^2 + (1+\kappa)\sigma_x^4, \right.$
$$16\mu_x^6\sigma_x^2 + (68\kappa + 32)\mu_x^4\sigma_x^4$$
$$\left. + (\kappa+1)(28\kappa + 16)\mu_x^2\sigma_x^6 + \kappa(1+\kappa)^2\sigma_x^8\right)$$

If we pick $\kappa = 2$, the sigmapoint mean matches Monte Carlo, and the variance match on the first two terms.

4.4 (i) Using similar triangles in the diagram, we have

$$\frac{u+n}{f} = \frac{x+b}{z}, \quad \frac{v+m}{f} = \frac{x-b}{z}.$$

Isolating for u and v and arranging in matrix form gives the required result:

$$\begin{bmatrix} u \\ v \end{bmatrix} = \underbrace{\begin{bmatrix} f & 0 & fb \\ f & 0 & -fb \end{bmatrix}}_{\mathbf{K}} \frac{1}{z} \begin{bmatrix} x \\ z \\ 1 \end{bmatrix} - \begin{bmatrix} n \\ m \end{bmatrix}.$$

(ii) Multiplying the similar-triangle equations through, we have

$$z(u+n) = f(x+b), \quad z(v+m) = f(x-b),$$

which is a linear system of two equations that can be solved for x and z.

(iii) The required Jacobians are

$$\mathbf{A} = \begin{bmatrix} \frac{\partial g}{\partial u}\big|_{u,v} & \frac{\partial g}{\partial v}\big|_{u,v} \\ \frac{\partial h}{\partial u}\big|_{u,v} & \frac{\partial h}{\partial v}\big|_{u,v} \end{bmatrix} = \begin{bmatrix} \frac{-2bv}{(u-v)^2} & \frac{2bu}{(u-v)^2} \\ \frac{-2fb}{(u-v)^2} & \frac{2fb}{(u-v)^2} \end{bmatrix}.$$

(iv) For the mean we have

$$E \begin{bmatrix} x \\ z \end{bmatrix} = \begin{bmatrix} g(u, v) \\ h(u, v) \end{bmatrix} = \frac{b}{u - v} \begin{bmatrix} u + v \\ 2fb \end{bmatrix}.$$

For the covariance we have

$$\mathrm{cov}\left(\begin{bmatrix} x \\ z \end{bmatrix}\right) = \mathbf{A} \begin{bmatrix} \sigma^2 & 0 \\ 0 & \sigma^2 \end{bmatrix} \mathbf{A}^T.$$

Inserting the details and multiplying out gives the required result.

(v) On the optical axis means $x = 0$, so $u = fb/2$ and $v = -fb/2$. Inserting these into the covariance expression from (iv), the top-left entry is the variance in the x direction and the bottom-right is the variance in the z direction. Taking the square roots of these provide the requested standard deviations.

4.5 This one follows from the general result that

$$\mathbf{A}\mathbf{A}^T = \begin{bmatrix} \mathbf{a}_1 & \mathbf{a}_2 & \cdots \mathbf{a}_N \end{bmatrix} \begin{bmatrix} \mathbf{a}_1^T \\ \mathbf{a}_2^T \\ \vdots \\ \mathbf{a}_N^T \end{bmatrix} = \mathbf{a}_1 \mathbf{a}_1^T + \mathbf{a}_2 \mathbf{a}_2^T + \cdots \mathbf{a}_N \mathbf{a}_N^T.$$

4.6 You are on your own for this one; the solution is quite long.

4.7 (i) From the generic EKF prediction step equations:

$$\check{P}_k = F_{k-1}\hat{P}_{k-1}F_{k-1} + Q'_k = (1)\hat{P}_{k-1}(1) + Q = \hat{P}_{k-1} + Q,$$
$$\check{x}_k = f(\hat{x}_{k-1}, u_k, 0) = \hat{x}_{k-1} + u_k.$$

(ii) From the generic Kalman gain expression:

$$K_k = \frac{\check{P}_k G_k}{G_k \check{P}_k G_k + R'_k} = \frac{\check{P}_k(-1)}{(-1)\check{P}_k(-1) + R} = -\frac{\check{P}_k}{\check{P}_k + R}.$$

(iii) From the generic EKF correction step equations:

$$\hat{P}_k = (1 - K_k G_k)\check{P}_k = \frac{R}{\check{P}_k + R}\check{P}_k$$

$$\hat{x}_k = \check{x}_k + K_k(y_k - g(\check{x}_k, 0)) = \frac{R}{\check{P}_k + R}\check{x}_k + \frac{\check{P}_k}{\check{P}_k + R}(\ell - y_k).$$

(iv) Since $\frac{R}{\check{P}_k + R} + \frac{\check{P}_k}{\check{P}_k + R} = 1$, we can interpret the expression as a weighted average between the prediction, $\check{x}_k$, and measured position, $\ell - y_k$. If the uncertainty of the measured position, R, is larger than the uncertainty of the prediction, $\check{P}_k$, the EKF trusts the prediction term more and applies to it a larger weight, $\frac{R}{\check{P}_k + R} > \frac{\check{P}_k}{\check{P}_k + R}$. Consequently, the opposite is also true. If the uncertainty of the measured position, R, is smaller than the uncertainty of the prediction, $\check{P}_k$, the EKF trusts the prediction term less and applies to it a smaller weight, $\frac{R}{\check{P}_k + R} < \frac{\check{P}_k}{\check{P}_k + R}$.

4.8 (i) $\check{P}_0 = 0, \check{x}_0 = 0, G_0 = 0, K_0 = 0, \hat{P}_0 = 0, \hat{x}_0 = 0$

(ii) $\check{P}_1 = 1, \check{x}_1 = 1, G_1 = 1/\sqrt{2}, K_1 = 1/\sqrt{2}, \hat{P}_1 = 1/2, \hat{x}_1 = 1$

(iii) $\check{P}_2 = 3/2, \check{x}_2 = 2, G_2 = 2/\sqrt{5}, K_2 = 6\sqrt{5}/17, \hat{P}_2 = 15/34, \hat{x}_2 = (6\sqrt{30}+4)/17$

(iv) From $k = 1$ to $k = 2$, $\hat{P}_k$ decreases slightly from $1/2$ to $15/34$. If the cart moves far away from the flagpole, the measurement model will become approximately linear: $y_k = \sqrt{x_k^2 + h^2} + n_k \approx x_k + n_k$. Since the system is approximately linear, the variance $\hat{P}_k$ should approach a steady-state value.

D.4 Chapter 5: Handling Nonidealities in Estimation

5.1 The augmented system is

$$\begin{bmatrix} x_k \\ \bar{v}_k \end{bmatrix} = \underbrace{\begin{bmatrix} 1 & 1 \\ 0 & 1 \end{bmatrix}}_{\mathbf{A}'} \begin{bmatrix} x_{k-1} \\ \bar{v}_{k-1} \end{bmatrix} + \begin{bmatrix} 1 \\ 0 \end{bmatrix} v_k,$$

$$y_k = \underbrace{\begin{bmatrix} 1 & 0 \end{bmatrix}}_{\mathbf{C}'} \begin{bmatrix} x_k \\ \bar{v}_k \end{bmatrix}.$$

The observability matrix is

$$\mathcal{O} = \begin{bmatrix} \mathbf{C}' \\ \mathbf{C}'\mathbf{A}' \end{bmatrix} = \begin{bmatrix} 1 & 0 \\ 1 & 1 \end{bmatrix},$$

which has rank 2, making the augmented system observable.

5.2 The augmented system is

$$\begin{bmatrix} x_k \\ v_k \\ \bar{d}_k \end{bmatrix} = \underbrace{\begin{bmatrix} 1 & 1 & 0 \\ 0 & 1 & 0 \\ 0 & 0 & 1 \end{bmatrix}}_{\mathbf{A}'} \begin{bmatrix} x_{k-1} \\ v_{k-1} \\ \bar{d}_{k-1} \end{bmatrix} + \begin{bmatrix} 0 \\ 1 \\ 0 \end{bmatrix} a_k,$$

$$\begin{bmatrix} d_{1,k} \\ d_{2,k} \end{bmatrix} = \underbrace{\begin{bmatrix} 1 & 0 & 0 \\ 1 & 0 & 1 \end{bmatrix}}_{\mathbf{C}'} \begin{bmatrix} x_k \\ v_k \\ \bar{d}_k \end{bmatrix}.$$

The observability matrix is

$$\mathcal{O} = \begin{bmatrix} \mathbf{C}' \\ \mathbf{C}'\mathbf{A}' \\ \mathbf{C}'\mathbf{A}'^2 \end{bmatrix} = \begin{bmatrix} 1 & 0 & 0 \\ 1 & 0 & 1 \\ 1 & 1 & 0 \\ 1 & 1 & 1 \\ 1 & 2 & 0 \\ 1 & 2 & 1 \end{bmatrix},$$

which has rank 3, making the augmented system observable.

5.3 Based on the formula, $k = \frac{\ln(1-p)}{\ln(1-w^n)} = \frac{\ln(1-0.999)}{\ln(1-0.1^3)} = 6904.3$, so we can use 6905 iterations.

5.4 Based on the formula, $k = \frac{\ln(1-p)}{\ln(1-w^n)} = \frac{\ln(1-0.99999)}{\ln(1-0.75^2)} = 13.9267$, so we can use 14 iterations.

5.5 Plot the two different cost functions to see the difference. The new one sits above Geman-McClure, which will mean it is less strict at rejecting outliers and behaves exactly as $\frac{1}{2}u^2$ for $u^2 < 1$.

D.5 Chapter 7: Primer on Three-Dimensional Geometry

7.1 We can do this one brute force:

$$\mathbf{u}^\wedge \mathbf{v} = \begin{bmatrix} 0 & -u_3 & u_2 \\ u_3 & 0 & -u_1 \\ -u_2 & u_1 & 0 \end{bmatrix} \begin{bmatrix} v_1 \\ v_2 \\ v_3 \end{bmatrix} = \begin{bmatrix} -u_3 v_2 + u_2 v_3 \\ u_3 v_1 - u_1 v_3 \\ -u_2 v_1 + u_1 v_2 \end{bmatrix}$$

$$= \begin{bmatrix} 0 & v_3 & -v_2 \\ -v_3 & 0 & v_1 \\ v_2 & -v_1 & 0 \end{bmatrix} \begin{bmatrix} u_1 \\ u_2 \\ u_3 \end{bmatrix} = -\mathbf{v}^\wedge \mathbf{u}.$$

7.2 We can multiply out:

$$\mathbf{C}\mathbf{C}^T = \left(\cos\theta \mathbf{1} + (1 - \cos\theta)\mathbf{a}\mathbf{a}^T + \sin\theta\,\mathbf{a}^\wedge \right)$$

$$\times \left(\cos\theta \mathbf{1} + (1 - \cos\theta)\mathbf{a}\mathbf{a}^T + \sin\theta\,\mathbf{a}^\wedge \right)^T$$

$$= \cos^2\theta \mathbf{1} + 2\cos\theta(1 - \cos\theta)\mathbf{a}\mathbf{a}^T + (1 - \cos\theta)^2 \mathbf{a}\underbrace{\mathbf{a}^T\mathbf{a}}_{1}\mathbf{a}^T$$

$$+ \sin^2\theta \underbrace{\mathbf{a}^\wedge \mathbf{a}^{\wedge^T}}_{1 - \mathbf{a}\mathbf{a}^T} + \sin\theta(1 - \cos\theta)(\underbrace{\mathbf{a}^\wedge \mathbf{a}\mathbf{a}^T}_{0} + \underbrace{\mathbf{a}\mathbf{a}^T\mathbf{a}^{\wedge^T}}_{0})$$

$$+ \cos\theta \sin\theta \underbrace{(\mathbf{a}^\wedge + \mathbf{a}^{\wedge^T})}_{0}$$

$$= \underbrace{(\cos^2\theta + \sin^2\theta)}_{1} \mathbf{1}$$

$$+ \underbrace{(2\cos\theta - 2\cos^2\theta + 1 - 2\cos\theta + \cos^2\theta - \sin^2\theta)}_{0} \mathbf{a}\mathbf{a}^T = \mathbf{1},$$

which shows that $\mathbf{C}^T = \mathbf{C}^{-1}$.

7.3 Let $\mathbf{C}^T = \begin{bmatrix} \mathbf{a} & \mathbf{b} & \mathbf{c} \end{bmatrix}$ where the columns form a right-hand coordinate system such that $\mathbf{a}^\wedge \mathbf{b} = \mathbf{c}$, $\mathbf{b}^\wedge \mathbf{c} = \mathbf{a}$, $\mathbf{c}^\wedge \mathbf{a} = \mathbf{b}$. Then we have

$$\mathbf{C}\mathbf{v}^\wedge \mathbf{C}^T = \begin{bmatrix} \mathbf{a}^T \\ \mathbf{b}^T \\ \mathbf{c}^T \end{bmatrix} \mathbf{v}^\wedge \begin{bmatrix} \mathbf{a} & \mathbf{b} & \mathbf{c} \end{bmatrix} = -\begin{bmatrix} \mathbf{v}^T \mathbf{a}^\wedge \\ \mathbf{v}^T \mathbf{b}^\wedge \\ \mathbf{v}^T \mathbf{c}^\wedge \end{bmatrix} \begin{bmatrix} \mathbf{a} & \mathbf{b} & \mathbf{c} \end{bmatrix}$$

$$= -\begin{bmatrix} \mathbf{v}^T \mathbf{a}^\wedge \mathbf{a} & \mathbf{v}^T \mathbf{a}^\wedge \mathbf{b} & \mathbf{v}^T \mathbf{a}^\wedge \mathbf{c} \\ \mathbf{v}^T \mathbf{b}^\wedge \mathbf{a} & \mathbf{v}^T \mathbf{b}^\wedge \mathbf{b} & \mathbf{v}^T \mathbf{b}^\wedge \mathbf{c} \\ \mathbf{v}^T \mathbf{c}^\wedge \mathbf{a} & \mathbf{v}^T \mathbf{c}^\wedge \mathbf{b} & \mathbf{v}^T \mathbf{c}^\wedge \mathbf{c} \end{bmatrix} = \begin{bmatrix} 0 & -\mathbf{v}^T \mathbf{c} & \mathbf{v}^T \mathbf{b} \\ \mathbf{v}^T \mathbf{c} & 0 & -\mathbf{v}^T \mathbf{a} \\ -\mathbf{v}^T \mathbf{b} & \mathbf{v}^T \mathbf{a} & 0 \end{bmatrix}$$

$$= \begin{bmatrix} \mathbf{a}^T \mathbf{v} \\ \mathbf{b}^T \mathbf{v} \\ \mathbf{c}^T \mathbf{v} \end{bmatrix}^\wedge = \left(\begin{bmatrix} \mathbf{a}^T \\ \mathbf{b}^T \\ \mathbf{c}^T \end{bmatrix} \mathbf{v} \right)^\wedge = (\mathbf{C}\mathbf{v})^\wedge .$$

7.4 We already know that

$$\dot{\mathbf{T}}_{vi} = \boldsymbol{\varpi}^\wedge \mathbf{T}_{vi}, \quad \boldsymbol{\varpi}^\wedge = \begin{bmatrix} 0 & v\kappa & 0 & -v \\ -v\kappa & 0 & v\tau & 0 \\ 0 & -v\tau & 0 & 0 \\ 0 & 0 & 0 & 0 \end{bmatrix}.$$

Then, $\dot{\mathbf{T}}_{vi} = (\dot{\mathbf{T}_{iv}^{-1}}) = -\mathbf{T}_{iv}^{-1}\dot{\mathbf{T}}_{iv}\mathbf{T}_{iv}^{-1} = \boldsymbol{\varpi}^\wedge \mathbf{T}_{vi}$. Left- and right-multiplying by $\mathbf{T}_{iv}$ provides $\dot{\mathbf{T}}_{iv} = -\mathbf{T}_{iv}\boldsymbol{\varpi}^\wedge$, which is the desired result.

7.5 We have $\dot{\mathbf{T}}_{iv} = -\mathbf{T}_{iv}\boldsymbol{\varpi}^\wedge$ with

$$\mathbf{T}_{vi} = \begin{bmatrix} \cos\theta_{vi} & -\sin\theta_{vi} & 0 & x \\ \sin\theta_{vi} & \cos\theta_{vi} & 0 & y \\ 0 & 0 & 1 & 0 \\ 0 & 0 & 0 & 1 \end{bmatrix}, \quad \boldsymbol{\varpi}^\wedge = \begin{bmatrix} 0 & \omega & 0 & -v \\ -\omega & 0 & 0 & 0 \\ 0 & 0 & 0 & 0 \\ 0 & 0 & 0 & 0 \end{bmatrix}.$$

The kinematics then become

$$\underbrace{\begin{bmatrix} -\dot{\theta}_{vi}\sin\theta_{vi} & -\dot{\theta}_{vi}\cos\theta_{vi} & 0 & \dot{x} \\ \dot{\theta}_{vi}\cos\theta_{vi} & -\dot{\theta}_{vi}\sin\theta_{vi} & 0 & \dot{y} \\ 0 & 0 & 0 & 0 \\ 0 & 0 & 0 & 0 \end{bmatrix}}_{\dot{\mathbf{T}}_{iv}}$$

$$= \underbrace{\begin{bmatrix} -\omega\sin\theta_{vi} & -\omega\cos\theta_{vi} & 0 & v\cos\theta_{vi} \\ \omega\cos\theta_{vi} & -\omega\sin\theta_{vi} & 0 & v\sin\theta_{vi} \\ 0 & 0 & 0 & 0 \\ 0 & 0 & 0 & 0 \end{bmatrix}}_{-\mathbf{T}_{iv}\boldsymbol{\varpi}^\wedge}.$$

Comparing the left and right sides provides the desired result.

7.6 A line between two points in image space will have the form

$$\begin{bmatrix} \frac{x}{z} \\ \frac{y}{z} \end{bmatrix} = (1-\beta)\begin{bmatrix} \frac{x_1}{z_1} \\ \frac{y_1}{z_1} \end{bmatrix} + \beta\begin{bmatrix} \frac{x_2}{z_2} \\ \frac{y_2}{z_2} \end{bmatrix},$$

where $\beta \in [0,1]$. Multiplying through by z gives

$$\begin{bmatrix} x \\ y \end{bmatrix} = \underbrace{(1-\beta)\frac{z}{z_1}}_{1-\alpha}\begin{bmatrix} x_1 \\ y_1 \end{bmatrix} + \underbrace{\beta\frac{z}{z_2}}_{\alpha}\begin{bmatrix} x_2 \\ y_2 \end{bmatrix},$$

where α is a new interpolation variable such that

$$(1-\beta)z = (1-\alpha)z_1, \quad \beta z = \alpha z_2.$$

Adding these reveals $z = (1-\alpha)z_1 + \alpha z_2$, which together with the x and y interpolations shows every straight line in image space comes from a straight line in Euclidean space and vice versa.

7.7 We can invert directly:

$$\mathbf{H}_{ba}^{-1} = \left(\frac{z_a}{z_b}\mathbf{C}_{ba}\left(1 + \frac{1}{d_a}\mathbf{r}_a^{ba}\mathbf{n}_a^T\right)\right)^{-1} = \frac{z_b}{z_a}\left(1 + \frac{1}{d_a}\mathbf{r}_a^{ba}\mathbf{n}_a^T\right)^{-1}\mathbf{C}_{ab}$$

$$= \frac{z_b}{z_a}\left(1 - \mathbf{r}_a^{ba}\underbrace{(d_a + \mathbf{n}_a^T\mathbf{r}_a^{ba})^{-1}}_{d_b}\mathbf{n}_a^T\right)\mathbf{C}_{ab} = \frac{z_b}{z_a}\mathbf{C}_{ab}\left(1 + \frac{1}{d_b}\mathbf{r}_b^{ab}\mathbf{n}_b^T\right) = \mathbf{H}_{ab},$$

where we used an SMW identity in the middle.

7.8 Stereo model with sensor frame at right camera:

$$\begin{bmatrix} u_\ell \\ v_\ell \\ u_r \\ v_r \end{bmatrix} = \begin{bmatrix} f_u & 0 & c_u & f_u b \\ 0 & f_v & c_v & 0 \\ f_u & 0 & c_u & 0 \\ 0 & f_v & c_v & 0 \end{bmatrix}\frac{1}{z}\begin{bmatrix} x \\ y \\ z \\ 1 \end{bmatrix}.$$

7.9 Isolate for x, y, and z from the camera model:

$$x = \frac{b}{u_\ell - u_r}\left(\frac{u_\ell + u_r}{2} - c_u\right) + \frac{b}{2},$$

$$y = \frac{f_u}{f_v}\frac{b}{u_\ell - u_r}\left(\frac{v_\ell + v_r}{2} - c_v\right),$$

$$z = \frac{f_u b}{u_\ell - u_r}.$$

7.10 (i) The required poses are

$$\mathbf{T}_{2,0} = \begin{bmatrix} 1 & 0 & 3 \\ 0 & 1 & 2 \\ 0 & 0 & 1 \end{bmatrix}, \quad \mathbf{T}_{0,3} = \begin{bmatrix} 0 & 1 & 5 \\ -1 & 0 & 2 \\ 0 & 0 & 1 \end{bmatrix},$$

$$\mathbf{T}_{0,4} = \begin{bmatrix} 0 & 1 & 5 \\ -1 & 0 & 0 \\ 0 & 0 & 1 \end{bmatrix}, \quad \mathbf{T}_{0,5} = \begin{bmatrix} -1 & 0 & 0 \\ 0 & -1 & 0 \\ 0 & 0 & 1 \end{bmatrix}.$$

(ii) See the figure below.

(iii) See the dotted parts in the figure below.

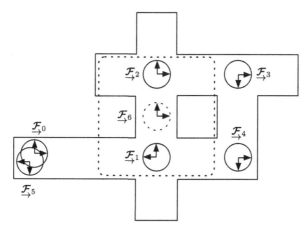

(iv) Yes, it will always be possible to uniquely determine the robot's pose because every possible pose in this map has a unique laser rangefinder reading.

7.11 You are on your own for this one; take a look at other resources in the literature.

D.6 Chapter 8: Matrix Lie Groups

8.1 Using $\mathbf{C} = \cos\theta\mathbf{1} + (1 - \cos\theta)\mathbf{a}\mathbf{a}^T + \sin\theta\,\mathbf{a}^\wedge$, we have

$$
\begin{aligned}
(\mathbf{C}\mathbf{u})^\wedge &= \cos\theta\mathbf{u}^\wedge + (1 - \cos\theta)\mathbf{u}^T\mathbf{a}\mathbf{a}^\wedge + \sin\theta\,(\mathbf{a}^\wedge\mathbf{u})^\wedge \\
&= \cos\theta\mathbf{u}^\wedge + (1 - \cos\theta)(\mathbf{a}\mathbf{u}^T - \mathbf{u}^\wedge\mathbf{a}^\wedge)\mathbf{a}^\wedge + \sin\theta\,(\mathbf{a}^\wedge\mathbf{u}^\wedge - \mathbf{u}^\wedge\mathbf{a}^\wedge) \\
&= \cos\theta\mathbf{u}^\wedge + (1 - \cos\theta)(-\mathbf{a}\mathbf{a}^T\mathbf{u}^\wedge + \mathbf{u}^\wedge - \mathbf{u}^\wedge\mathbf{a}\mathbf{a}^T) + \sin\theta\,(\mathbf{a}^\wedge\mathbf{u}^\wedge - \mathbf{u}^\wedge\mathbf{a}^\wedge) \\
&= (1 + 2\cos\theta)\mathbf{u}^\wedge - \mathbf{u}^\wedge\underbrace{\left(\cos\theta\mathbf{1} + (1 - \cos\theta)\mathbf{a}\mathbf{a}^T + \sin\theta\,\mathbf{a}^\wedge\right)}_{\mathbf{C}} \\
&\quad - \underbrace{\left(\cos\theta\mathbf{1} + (1 - \cos\theta)\mathbf{a}\mathbf{a}^T - \sin\theta\,\mathbf{a}^\wedge\right)}_{\mathbf{C}^T}\mathbf{u}^\wedge.
\end{aligned}
$$

8.2 Use a series form of the exponential:

$$\exp\left((\mathbf{Cu})^\wedge\right) = \sum_{n=0}^{\infty} \frac{1}{n!} \left((\mathbf{Cu})^\wedge\right)^n = \sum_{n=0}^{\infty} \frac{1}{n!} \left(\mathbf{Cu}^\wedge \mathbf{C}^T\right)^n$$

$$= 1 + \mathbf{Cu}^\wedge \mathbf{C}^T + \frac{1}{2} \mathbf{Cu}^\wedge \underbrace{\mathbf{C}^T \mathbf{C}}_{1} \mathbf{u}^\wedge \mathbf{C}^T$$

$$+ \frac{1}{6} \mathbf{Cu}^\wedge \underbrace{\mathbf{C}^T \mathbf{C}}_{1} \mathbf{u}^\wedge \underbrace{\mathbf{C}^T \mathbf{C}}_{1} \mathbf{u}^\wedge \mathbf{C}^T + \cdots$$

$$= \mathbf{C} \left(\sum_{n=0}^{\infty} \frac{1}{n!} (\mathbf{u}^\wedge)^n\right) \mathbf{C}^T = \mathbf{C} \exp\left(\mathbf{u}^\wedge\right) \mathbf{C}^T.$$

8.3 We have

$$(\boldsymbol{\mathcal{T}}\mathbf{x})^\wedge = \left(\begin{bmatrix} \mathbf{C} & \mathbf{r}^\wedge \mathbf{C} \\ \mathbf{0} & \mathbf{C} \end{bmatrix} \begin{bmatrix} \mathbf{u} \\ \mathbf{v} \end{bmatrix}\right)^\wedge = \begin{bmatrix} \mathbf{Cu} + \mathbf{r}^\wedge \mathbf{Cv} \\ \mathbf{Cv} \end{bmatrix}^\wedge$$

$$= \begin{bmatrix} (\mathbf{Cv})^\wedge & \mathbf{Cu} + \mathbf{r}^\wedge \mathbf{Cv} \\ \mathbf{0}^T & 0 \end{bmatrix} = \begin{bmatrix} \mathbf{Cv}^\wedge \mathbf{C}^T & \mathbf{Cu} + \mathbf{r}^\wedge \mathbf{Cv} \\ \mathbf{0}^T & 0 \end{bmatrix}$$

$$= \begin{bmatrix} \mathbf{C} & \mathbf{r} \\ \mathbf{0}^T & 1 \end{bmatrix} \begin{bmatrix} \mathbf{v}^\wedge & \mathbf{u} \\ \mathbf{0}^T & 0 \end{bmatrix} \begin{bmatrix} \mathbf{C}^T & -\mathbf{C}^T \mathbf{r} \\ \mathbf{0}^T & 1 \end{bmatrix} = \mathbf{Tx}^\wedge \mathbf{T}^{-1}.$$

8.4 Follow the same steps as Exercise 8.6.2, using the result of Exercise 8.6.3.

8.5 You are on your own for this one; the solution is quite long.

8.6 We have

$$\mathbf{x}^\wedge \mathbf{p} = \begin{bmatrix} \mathbf{u} \\ \mathbf{v} \end{bmatrix}^\wedge \begin{bmatrix} \boldsymbol{\varepsilon} \\ \eta \end{bmatrix} = \begin{bmatrix} \mathbf{v}^\wedge & \mathbf{u} \\ \mathbf{0}^T & 0 \end{bmatrix} \begin{bmatrix} \boldsymbol{\varepsilon} \\ \eta \end{bmatrix} = \begin{bmatrix} \mathbf{v}^\wedge \boldsymbol{\varepsilon} + \eta \mathbf{u} \\ 0 \end{bmatrix} = \begin{bmatrix} \eta \mathbf{u} - \boldsymbol{\varepsilon}^\wedge \mathbf{v} \\ 0 \end{bmatrix}$$

$$= \begin{bmatrix} \eta \mathbf{1} & -\boldsymbol{\varepsilon}^\wedge \\ \mathbf{0}^T & \mathbf{0}^T \end{bmatrix} \begin{bmatrix} \mathbf{u} \\ \mathbf{v} \end{bmatrix} = \mathbf{p}^\odot \mathbf{x}.$$

8.7 We have

$$\mathbf{p}^T \mathbf{x}^\wedge = \begin{bmatrix} \boldsymbol{\varepsilon}^T & \eta \end{bmatrix} \begin{bmatrix} \mathbf{u} \\ \mathbf{v} \end{bmatrix}^\wedge = \begin{bmatrix} \boldsymbol{\varepsilon}^T & \eta \end{bmatrix} \begin{bmatrix} \mathbf{v}^\wedge & \mathbf{u} \\ \mathbf{0}^T & 0 \end{bmatrix} = \begin{bmatrix} \boldsymbol{\varepsilon}^T \mathbf{v}^\wedge & \boldsymbol{\varepsilon}^T \mathbf{u} \end{bmatrix}$$

$$= \begin{bmatrix} -\mathbf{v}^T \boldsymbol{\varepsilon}^\wedge & \mathbf{u}^T \boldsymbol{\varepsilon} \end{bmatrix} = \begin{bmatrix} \mathbf{u}^T & \mathbf{v}^T \end{bmatrix} \begin{bmatrix} \mathbf{0} & \boldsymbol{\varepsilon} \\ -\boldsymbol{\varepsilon}^\wedge & 0 \end{bmatrix} = \mathbf{x}^T \mathbf{p}^\odot.$$

8.8 This can be done by integrating by parts n times. The first time:

$$\int_0^1 \underbrace{\alpha^n}_{u} \underbrace{(1-\alpha)^m}_{dv} d\alpha = \underbrace{\frac{-\alpha^n(1-\alpha)^{m+1}}{m+1}}_{uv}\Big|_0^1$$

$$- \int_0^1 \underbrace{\frac{-n(1-\alpha)^{m+1}}{m+1}}_{v} \underbrace{\alpha^{n-1} d\alpha}_{du} = \frac{n\,m!}{(m+1)!} \int_0^1 \alpha^{n-1}(1-\alpha)^{m+1}\,d\alpha.$$

After the second time, then the nth time:

$$= \frac{n(n-1)\,m!}{(m+2)!} \int_0^1 \alpha^{n-2}(1-\alpha)^{m+2}\,d\alpha = \cdots$$

$$= \frac{n!\,m!}{(m+n+1)!} \underbrace{\int_0^1 (1-\alpha)^{m+n}\,d\alpha}_{1} = \frac{n!\,m!}{(m+n+1)!}.$$

8.9 This one is proved in Appendix B.2.1.

8.10 We have

$$(\mathbf{Tp})^{\odot} = \left(\begin{bmatrix} \mathbf{C} & \mathbf{r} \\ \mathbf{0}^T & 1 \end{bmatrix} \begin{bmatrix} \boldsymbol{\varepsilon} \\ \eta \end{bmatrix}\right)^{\odot} = \begin{bmatrix} \mathbf{C}\boldsymbol{\varepsilon} + \eta\mathbf{r} \\ \eta \end{bmatrix}^{\odot}$$

$$= \begin{bmatrix} \eta\mathbf{1} & -(\mathbf{C}\boldsymbol{\varepsilon} + \eta\mathbf{r})^{\wedge} \\ \mathbf{0}^T & \mathbf{0}^T \end{bmatrix} = \begin{bmatrix} \eta\mathbf{1} & -\mathbf{C}\boldsymbol{\varepsilon}^{\wedge}\mathbf{C}^T - \eta\mathbf{r}^{\wedge} \\ \mathbf{0}^T & \mathbf{0}^T \end{bmatrix}$$

$$= \begin{bmatrix} \mathbf{C} & \mathbf{r} \\ \mathbf{0}^T & 1 \end{bmatrix} \begin{bmatrix} \eta\mathbf{1} & -\boldsymbol{\varepsilon}^{\wedge} \\ \mathbf{0}^T & \mathbf{0}^T \end{bmatrix} \begin{bmatrix} \mathbf{C}^T & -\mathbf{C}^T\mathbf{r}^{\wedge} \\ \mathbf{0} & \mathbf{C}^T \end{bmatrix} = \mathbf{Tp}^{\odot}\boldsymbol{\mathcal{T}}^{-1}.$$

8.11 Using the result from the previous exercise, we have

$$(\mathbf{Tp})^{\odot^T} (\mathbf{Tp})^{\odot} = \boldsymbol{\mathcal{T}}^{-T} \mathbf{p}^{\odot^T} \mathbf{T}^T \mathbf{Tp}^{\odot}\boldsymbol{\mathcal{T}}^{-1}$$

$$= \boldsymbol{\mathcal{T}}^{-T} \begin{bmatrix} \eta\mathbf{1} & \mathbf{0} \\ \boldsymbol{\varepsilon}^{\wedge} & \mathbf{0} \end{bmatrix} \begin{bmatrix} \mathbf{C}^T & \mathbf{0} \\ \mathbf{r}^T & 1 \end{bmatrix} \begin{bmatrix} \mathbf{C} & \mathbf{r} \\ \mathbf{0}^T & 1 \end{bmatrix} \begin{bmatrix} \eta\mathbf{1} & -\boldsymbol{\varepsilon}^{\wedge} \\ \mathbf{0}^T & \mathbf{0}^T \end{bmatrix} \boldsymbol{\mathcal{T}}^{-1}$$

$$= \boldsymbol{\mathcal{T}}^{-T} \begin{bmatrix} \eta^2\mathbf{1} & -\eta\boldsymbol{\varepsilon}^{\wedge} \\ \eta\boldsymbol{\varepsilon}^{\wedge} & \mathbf{0} \end{bmatrix} \boldsymbol{\mathcal{T}}^{-1} = \boldsymbol{\mathcal{T}}^{-T} \begin{bmatrix} \eta\mathbf{1} & \mathbf{0} \\ \boldsymbol{\varepsilon}^{\wedge} & \mathbf{0} \end{bmatrix} \begin{bmatrix} \eta\mathbf{1} & -\boldsymbol{\varepsilon}^{\wedge} \\ \mathbf{0}^T & \mathbf{0}^T \end{bmatrix} \boldsymbol{\mathcal{T}}^{-1}$$

$$= \boldsymbol{\mathcal{T}}^{-T} \mathbf{p}^{\odot^T} \mathbf{p}^{\odot} \boldsymbol{\mathcal{T}}^{-1}.$$

8.12 Starting from $\dot{\mathbf{T}} = \boldsymbol{\varpi}^{\wedge}\mathbf{T}$, we have

$$\begin{bmatrix} \dot{\mathbf{C}} & \dot{\mathbf{r}} \\ \mathbf{0}^T & 0 \end{bmatrix} = \begin{bmatrix} \boldsymbol{\omega}^{\wedge} & \mathbf{v} \\ \mathbf{0}^T & 0 \end{bmatrix} \begin{bmatrix} \mathbf{C} & \mathbf{r} \\ \mathbf{0}^T & 1 \end{bmatrix} = \begin{bmatrix} \boldsymbol{\omega}^{\wedge}\mathbf{C} & \mathbf{v} + \boldsymbol{\omega}^{\wedge}\mathbf{r} \\ \mathbf{0}^T & 0 \end{bmatrix},$$

so $\dot{\mathbf{C}} = \boldsymbol{\omega}^{\wedge}\mathbf{C}$ and $\dot{\mathbf{r}} = \mathbf{v} + \boldsymbol{\omega}^{\wedge}\mathbf{r}$. For the adjoint kinematics, we have

$$\dot{\boldsymbol{\mathcal{T}}} = \begin{bmatrix} \mathbf{C} & \mathbf{r}^{\wedge}\mathbf{C} \\ \mathbf{0} & \mathbf{C} \end{bmatrix}^{\cdot} = \begin{bmatrix} \dot{\mathbf{C}} & \dot{\mathbf{r}}^{\wedge}\mathbf{C} + \mathbf{r}^{\wedge}\dot{\mathbf{C}} \\ \mathbf{0} & \dot{\mathbf{C}} \end{bmatrix}$$

$$= \begin{bmatrix} \boldsymbol{\omega}^{\wedge}\mathbf{C} & (\mathbf{v}^{\wedge} + (\boldsymbol{\omega}^{\wedge}\mathbf{r})^{\wedge})\mathbf{C} + \mathbf{r}^{\wedge}\boldsymbol{\omega}^{\wedge}\mathbf{C} \\ \mathbf{0} & \boldsymbol{\omega}^{\wedge}\mathbf{C} \end{bmatrix} = \begin{bmatrix} \boldsymbol{\omega}^{\wedge}\mathbf{C} & \mathbf{v}^{\wedge}\mathbf{C} + \boldsymbol{\omega}^{\wedge}\mathbf{r}^{\wedge}\mathbf{C} \\ \mathbf{0} & \boldsymbol{\omega}^{\wedge}\mathbf{C} \end{bmatrix}$$

$$= \begin{bmatrix} \boldsymbol{\omega}^{\wedge} & \mathbf{v}^{\wedge} \\ \mathbf{0} & \boldsymbol{\omega}^{\wedge} \end{bmatrix} \begin{bmatrix} \mathbf{C} & \mathbf{r}^{\wedge}\mathbf{C} \\ \mathbf{0} & \mathbf{C} \end{bmatrix} = \boldsymbol{\varpi}^{\curlywedge}\boldsymbol{\mathcal{T}}.$$

8.13 Using the provided adjoint definition, the right-hand side is

$$\text{Ad}(\mathbf{T})\text{Ad}(\mathbf{p}) = \begin{bmatrix} \mathbf{C} & \mathbf{r}^{\wedge}\mathbf{C} \\ \mathbf{0} & \mathbf{C} \end{bmatrix} \begin{bmatrix} \boldsymbol{\rho}^{\wedge} \\ \mathbf{1} \end{bmatrix} = \begin{bmatrix} \mathbf{C}\boldsymbol{\rho}^{\wedge} + \mathbf{r}^{\wedge}\mathbf{C} \\ \mathbf{C} \end{bmatrix}.$$

Then applying the provided inverse adjoint, we have

$$\text{Ad}^{-1}\left(\text{Ad}(\mathbf{T})\text{Ad}(\mathbf{p})\right) = \begin{bmatrix} (\mathbf{C}\boldsymbol{\rho}^{\wedge}\mathbf{C}^T + \mathbf{r}^{\wedge})^{\vee} \\ 1 \end{bmatrix} = \begin{bmatrix} \mathbf{C}\boldsymbol{\rho} + \mathbf{r} \\ 1 \end{bmatrix}$$

$$= \begin{bmatrix} \mathbf{C} & \mathbf{r} \\ \mathbf{0}^T & 1 \end{bmatrix} \begin{bmatrix} \boldsymbol{\rho} \\ 1 \end{bmatrix} = \mathbf{Tp}.$$

8.14 Given

$$\begin{matrix} \mathbf{T}_1 = \exp(\boldsymbol{\xi}_1)\bar{\mathbf{T}}_1 \\ \mathbf{T}_2 = \exp(\boldsymbol{\xi}_2)\bar{\mathbf{T}}_2 \end{matrix}, \quad \begin{bmatrix} \boldsymbol{\xi}_1 \\ \boldsymbol{\xi}_2 \end{bmatrix} \sim \mathcal{N}\left(\begin{bmatrix} \mathbf{0} \\ \mathbf{0} \end{bmatrix}, \begin{bmatrix} \boldsymbol{\Sigma}_1 & \boldsymbol{\Sigma}_{12} \\ \boldsymbol{\Sigma}_{12}^T & \boldsymbol{\Sigma}_2 \end{bmatrix}\right),$$

we want

$$\mathbf{T} = \mathbf{T}_1\mathbf{T}_2 = \exp(\boldsymbol{\xi}^{\wedge})\bar{\mathbf{T}}_1\bar{\mathbf{T}}_2, \quad \boldsymbol{\xi} \sim \mathcal{N}(\mathbf{0}, \boldsymbol{\Sigma}).$$

Inserting the perturbations, we have

$$\mathbf{T}_1\mathbf{T}_2 = \exp(\boldsymbol{\xi}_1)\bar{\mathbf{T}}_1\exp(\boldsymbol{\xi}_2)\bar{\mathbf{T}}_2 \approx \exp\left((\boldsymbol{\xi}_1 + \bar{\mathcal{T}}_1\boldsymbol{\xi}_2)^\wedge\right)\bar{\mathbf{T}}_1\bar{\mathbf{T}}_2.$$

Therefore

$$E[\boldsymbol{\xi}\boldsymbol{\xi}^T] = E[(\boldsymbol{\xi}_1 + \bar{\mathcal{T}}_1\boldsymbol{\xi}_2)(\boldsymbol{\xi}_1 + \bar{\mathcal{T}}_1\boldsymbol{\xi}_2)^T] = E[\boldsymbol{\xi}_1\boldsymbol{\xi}_1^T] + E[\boldsymbol{\xi}_1\boldsymbol{\xi}_2^T]\bar{\mathcal{T}}_1^T$$
$$+ \bar{\mathcal{T}}_1 E[\boldsymbol{\xi}_2\boldsymbol{\xi}_1^T] + \bar{\mathcal{T}}_1 E[\boldsymbol{\xi}_2\boldsymbol{\xi}_2^T]\bar{\mathcal{T}}_1^T = \boldsymbol{\Sigma}_1 + \boldsymbol{\Sigma}_{12}\bar{\mathcal{T}}_1^T + \bar{\mathcal{T}}_1\boldsymbol{\Sigma}_{12}^T + \bar{\mathcal{T}}_1\boldsymbol{\Sigma}_2\bar{\mathcal{T}}_1^T.$$

8.15 Similarly to the previous exercise, we want

$$\mathbf{T} = \mathbf{T}_1\mathbf{T}_2^{-1} = \exp(\boldsymbol{\xi}^\wedge)\bar{\mathbf{T}}_1\bar{\mathbf{T}}_2^{-1}, \quad \boldsymbol{\xi} \sim \mathcal{N}(\mathbf{0}, \boldsymbol{\Sigma}).$$

Inserting the perturbations we have

$$\mathbf{T}_1\mathbf{T}_2^{-1} = \exp(\boldsymbol{\xi}_1)\bar{\mathbf{T}}_1\bar{\mathbf{T}}_2^{-1}\exp(-\boldsymbol{\xi}_2)$$
$$\approx \exp\left((\boldsymbol{\xi}_1 - \bar{\mathcal{T}}_1\bar{\mathcal{T}}_2^{-1}\boldsymbol{\xi}_2)^\wedge\right)\bar{\mathbf{T}}_1\bar{\mathbf{T}}_2^{-1}.$$

Therefore

$$E[\boldsymbol{\xi}\boldsymbol{\xi}^T] = E[(\boldsymbol{\xi}_1 - \bar{\mathcal{T}}\boldsymbol{\xi}_2)(\boldsymbol{\xi}_1 - \bar{\mathcal{T}}\boldsymbol{\xi}_2)^T] = E[\boldsymbol{\xi}_1\boldsymbol{\xi}_1^T] - E[\boldsymbol{\xi}_1\boldsymbol{\xi}_2^T]\bar{\mathcal{T}}^T$$
$$- \bar{\mathcal{T}}E[\boldsymbol{\xi}_2\boldsymbol{\xi}_1^T] + \bar{\mathcal{T}}E[\boldsymbol{\xi}_2\boldsymbol{\xi}_2^T]\bar{\mathcal{T}}^T = \boldsymbol{\Sigma}_1 - \boldsymbol{\Sigma}_{12}\bar{\mathcal{T}}^T - \bar{\mathcal{T}}\boldsymbol{\Sigma}_{12}^T + \bar{\mathcal{T}}\boldsymbol{\Sigma}_2\bar{\mathcal{T}}^T,$$

where $\bar{\mathcal{T}} = \bar{\mathcal{T}}_1\bar{\mathcal{T}}_2^{-1}$.

8.16 For the mean,

$$\boldsymbol{\mu} = E\left[\ln\left((\mathbf{C}\bar{\mathbf{C}}^{-1})^2\right)^\vee\right] = E\left[\ln\left((\exp(\boldsymbol{\phi}^\wedge)\bar{\mathbf{C}}\bar{\mathbf{C}}^{-1})^2\right)^\vee\right]$$
$$= E\left[\ln\left(\exp(2\boldsymbol{\phi}^\wedge)\right)^\vee\right] = E[2\boldsymbol{\phi}] = 2E[\boldsymbol{\phi}] = \mathbf{0}.$$

For the covariance,

$$\boldsymbol{\Sigma} = E\left[\left(\ln\left((\mathbf{C}\bar{\mathbf{C}}^{-1})^2\right)^\vee - \boldsymbol{\mu}\right)\left(\ln\left((\mathbf{C}\bar{\mathbf{C}}^{-1})^2\right)^\vee - \boldsymbol{\mu}\right)^T\right]$$
$$= E\left[\left(\ln\left((\exp(\boldsymbol{\phi}^\wedge)\bar{\mathbf{C}}\bar{\mathbf{C}}^{-1})^2\right)^\vee\right)\left(\ln\left((\exp(\boldsymbol{\phi}^\wedge)\bar{\mathbf{C}}\bar{\mathbf{C}}^{-1})^2\right)^\vee\right)^T\right]$$
$$= E\left[\ln\left(\exp(2\boldsymbol{\phi}^\wedge)\right)^\vee \ln\left(\exp(2\boldsymbol{\phi}^\wedge)\right)^{\vee^T}\right] = 4E[\boldsymbol{\phi}\boldsymbol{\phi}^T] = 4\mathbf{1}.$$

8.17 To be an eigenvector corresponding to an eigenvalue of 1 we must have that $\text{Ad}(\mathbf{T})\boldsymbol{\xi} = \boldsymbol{\xi}$:

$$\text{Ad}(\mathbf{T})\boldsymbol{\xi} = \exp(\boldsymbol{\xi}^\wedge)\boldsymbol{\xi} = \left(\mathbf{1} + \boldsymbol{\xi}^\wedge + \frac{1}{2}\boldsymbol{\xi}^\wedge\boldsymbol{\xi}^\wedge + \cdots\right)\boldsymbol{\xi}$$
$$= \boldsymbol{\xi} + \underbrace{\boldsymbol{\xi}^\wedge\boldsymbol{\xi}}_{0} + \frac{1}{2}\boldsymbol{\xi}^\wedge\underbrace{\boldsymbol{\xi}^\wedge\boldsymbol{\xi}}_{0} + \cdots = \boldsymbol{\xi}.$$

8.18 We start with a second-order perturbation, $\mathbf{T} = \exp(\boldsymbol{\xi}^\wedge)\mathbf{T}_{\text{op}} \approx (\mathbf{1} + \boldsymbol{\xi}^\wedge + \frac{1}{2}\boldsymbol{\xi}^\wedge\boldsymbol{\xi}^\wedge)\mathbf{T}_{\text{op}}$. The function is then

$$\mathbf{p}^T\mathbf{T}^T\mathbf{T}\mathbf{p} \approx \mathbf{p}^T\mathbf{T}_{\text{op}}^T(\mathbf{1} + \boldsymbol{\xi}^\wedge + \frac{1}{2}\boldsymbol{\xi}^\wedge\boldsymbol{\xi}^\wedge)^T(\mathbf{1} + \boldsymbol{\xi}^\wedge + \frac{1}{2}\boldsymbol{\xi}^\wedge\boldsymbol{\xi}^\wedge)\mathbf{T}_{\text{op}}\mathbf{p}$$
$$\approx \mathbf{p}^T\mathbf{T}_{\text{op}}^T\left(\mathbf{1} + \boldsymbol{\xi}^\wedge + \boldsymbol{\xi}^{\wedge^T} + \boldsymbol{\xi}^{\wedge^T}\boldsymbol{\xi}^\wedge + \frac{1}{2}\boldsymbol{\xi}^\wedge\boldsymbol{\xi}^\wedge + \frac{1}{2}\boldsymbol{\xi}^{\wedge^T}\boldsymbol{\xi}^{\wedge^T}\right)\mathbf{T}_{\text{op}}\mathbf{p},$$

where we keep only products of $\boldsymbol{\xi}$ up to quadratic. This can be manipulated into the form

$$\mathbf{p}^T \mathbf{T}^T \mathbf{T} \mathbf{p} \approx \mathbf{p}^T \mathbf{T}_{\mathrm{op}}^T \mathbf{T}_{\mathrm{op}} \mathbf{p} + \underbrace{2 \mathbf{p}^T \mathbf{T}_{\mathrm{op}}^T \left(\mathbf{T}_{\mathrm{op}} \mathbf{p} \right)^{\odot}}_{\text{Jacobian}} \boldsymbol{\xi}$$

$$+ \frac{1}{2} \boldsymbol{\xi}^T \underbrace{\left(2 \left(\mathbf{T}_{\mathrm{op}} \mathbf{p} \right)^{\odot^T} \left(\mathbf{T}_{\mathrm{op}} \mathbf{p} \right)^{\odot} + 2 \left(\mathbf{T}_{\mathrm{op}} \mathbf{p} \right)^{\circledcirc} \left(\mathbf{T}_{\mathrm{op}} \mathbf{p} \right)^{\odot} \right)}_{\text{Hessian}} \boldsymbol{\xi}.$$

8.19 Let the stereo camera model be $\mathbf{y} = \mathbf{g}(\mathbf{T}\mathbf{p})$. Then we have

$$\mathbf{y} = \mathbf{g}(\mathbf{T}\mathbf{p}) = \mathbf{g}\left(\exp(\boldsymbol{\xi}^{\wedge}) \mathbf{T}_{\mathrm{op}} \mathbf{p} \right) \approx \mathbf{g}\left((1 + \boldsymbol{\xi}^{\wedge}) \mathbf{T}_{\mathrm{op}} \mathbf{p} \right)$$

$$= \mathbf{g}\left(\mathbf{T}_{\mathrm{op}} \mathbf{p} + \left(\mathbf{T}_{\mathrm{op}} \mathbf{p} \right)^{\odot} \boldsymbol{\xi} \right) \approx \mathbf{g}\left(\mathbf{T}_{\mathrm{op}} \mathbf{p} \right) + \underbrace{\left. \frac{\partial \mathbf{g}}{\partial \mathbf{x}} \right|_{\mathbf{x} = \mathbf{T}_{\mathrm{op}} \mathbf{p}} \left(\mathbf{T}_{\mathrm{op}} \mathbf{p} \right)^{\odot}}_{\text{Jacobian}} \boldsymbol{\xi}.$$

8.20 We must show the usual four properties. The identity element is just the identity matrix, which is clearly in the set. For closure,

$$\begin{bmatrix} \cos\theta_1 & -\sin\theta_1 & x_1 \\ \sin\theta_1 & \cos\theta_1 & y_1 \\ 0 & 0 & 1 \end{bmatrix} \begin{bmatrix} \cos\theta_2 & -\sin\theta_2 & x_2 \\ \sin\theta_2 & \cos\theta_2 & y_2 \\ 0 & 0 & 1 \end{bmatrix}$$

$$= \begin{bmatrix} \cos(\theta_1 + \theta_2) & -\sin(\theta_1 + \theta_2) & x_1 + x_2 \cos\theta_1 - y_2 \sin\theta_1 \\ \sin(\theta_1 + \theta_2) & \cos(\theta_1 + \theta_2) & y_1 + x_2 \sin\theta_1 + y_2 \cos\theta_1 \\ 0 & 0 & 1 \end{bmatrix},$$

which is still in the set. The inverse of a member is

$$\begin{bmatrix} \cos\theta & -\sin\theta & x \\ \sin\theta & \cos\theta & y \\ 0 & 0 & 1 \end{bmatrix}^{-1} = \begin{bmatrix} \cos(-\theta) & -\sin(-\theta) & -x\cos\theta - y\sin\theta \\ \sin(-\theta) & \cos(-\theta) & x\sin\theta - y\cos\theta \\ 0 & 0 & 1 \end{bmatrix},$$

which is still in the set. Associativity follows from standard matrix multiplication. Therefore, it is a group.

8.21 We must show the usual four properties. The identity element is just the identity matrix, which is clearly in the set. For closure,

$$\begin{bmatrix} \mathbf{C}_1 & \mathbf{r}_1 & \mathbf{v}_1 \\ \mathbf{0}^T & 1 & 0 \\ \mathbf{0}^T & 0 & 1 \end{bmatrix} \begin{bmatrix} \mathbf{C}_2 & \mathbf{r}_2 & \mathbf{v}_2 \\ \mathbf{0}^T & 1 & 0 \\ \mathbf{0}^T & 0 & 1 \end{bmatrix} = \begin{bmatrix} \mathbf{C}_1 \mathbf{C}_2 & \mathbf{C}_1 \mathbf{r}_2 + \mathbf{r}_1 & \mathbf{C}_1 \mathbf{v}_2 + \mathbf{v}_1 \\ \mathbf{0}^T & 1 & 0 \\ \mathbf{0}^T & 0 & 1 \end{bmatrix},$$

which is still in the set since $\mathbf{C}_1 \mathbf{C}_2 \in SO(3)$. The inverse of a member is

$$\begin{bmatrix} \mathbf{C} & \mathbf{r} & \mathbf{v} \\ \mathbf{0}^T & 1 & 0 \\ \mathbf{0}^T & 0 & 1 \end{bmatrix}^{-1} = \begin{bmatrix} \mathbf{C}^T & -\mathbf{C}^T \mathbf{r} & -\mathbf{C}^T \mathbf{v} \\ \mathbf{0}^T & 1 & 0 \\ \mathbf{0}^T & 0 & 1 \end{bmatrix},$$

which is still in the set since $\mathbf{C}^T \in SO(3)$. Associativity follows from standard matrix multiplication. Therefore, it is a group.

8.22 This question could be attempted after reading Chapter 9, or used as a good preview.

(i) We can separate the kinematics into two parts:

$$\text{nominal kinematics:} \quad \mathbf{C}_k = \exp(\boldsymbol{\omega}_k^{\wedge} h) \mathbf{C}_{k-1}$$

$$\text{perturbation kinematics:} \quad \boldsymbol{\phi}_k = \exp(\boldsymbol{\omega}_k^{\wedge} h) \boldsymbol{\phi}_{k-1} + \mathbf{w}_k.$$

We propagate the mean of our estimate using the nominal kinematics:

$$\check{\mathbf{C}}_k = \exp(\boldsymbol{\omega}_k^{\wedge} h)\hat{\mathbf{C}}_{k-1}.$$

We propagate the covariance using the perturbation kinematics:

$$\check{\mathbf{P}} = E\left[\left(\exp(\boldsymbol{\omega}_k^{\wedge} h)\boldsymbol{\phi}_{k-1} + \mathbf{w}_k\right)\left(\exp(\boldsymbol{\omega}_k^{\wedge} h)\boldsymbol{\phi}_{k-1} + \mathbf{w}_k\right)^T\right]$$
$$= \exp(\boldsymbol{\omega}_k^{\wedge} h)\hat{\mathbf{P}}_{k-1}\exp(\boldsymbol{\omega}_k^{\wedge} h)^T + \mathbf{Q}.$$

(ii) We can perturb the measurement model as follows:

$$\mathbf{y}_k = \mathbf{C}_k\mathbf{v} + \mathbf{n}_k = \exp(\boldsymbol{\psi}_k^{\wedge})\check{\mathbf{C}}_k\mathbf{v} + \mathbf{n}_k \approx (1 + \boldsymbol{\psi}_k^{\wedge})\check{\mathbf{C}}_k\mathbf{v} + \mathbf{n}_k$$
$$= \check{\mathbf{C}}_k\mathbf{v} - \left(\check{\mathbf{C}}_k\mathbf{v}\right)^{\wedge}\boldsymbol{\psi}_k + \mathbf{n}_k,$$

where $\boldsymbol{\psi}_k \sim \mathcal{N}(\mathbf{0}, \check{\mathbf{P}}_k)$. We can then work out the requested expectations,

$$E[\mathbf{y}_k] = \check{\mathbf{C}}_k\mathbf{v},$$
$$E[(\mathbf{y}_k - E[\mathbf{y}_k])(\mathbf{y}_k - E[\mathbf{y}_k])^T] = \left(\check{\mathbf{C}}_k\mathbf{v}\right)^{\wedge}\check{\mathbf{P}}_k\left(\check{\mathbf{C}}_k\mathbf{v}\right)^{\wedge^T} + \mathbf{R},$$
$$E[\boldsymbol{\psi}_k(\mathbf{y}_k - E[\mathbf{y}_k])^T] = -\check{\mathbf{P}}_k\left(\check{\mathbf{C}}_k\mathbf{v}\right)^{\wedge^T},$$

so that

$$p(\mathbf{x}_k, \mathbf{y}_k | \mathbf{y}_{0:k-1}, \boldsymbol{\omega}_{0:k})$$
$$= \mathcal{N}\left(\begin{bmatrix} \check{\mathbf{C}}_k \\ \check{\mathbf{C}}_k\mathbf{v} \end{bmatrix}, \begin{bmatrix} \check{\mathbf{P}}_k & -\check{\mathbf{P}}_k\left(\check{\mathbf{C}}_k\mathbf{v}\right)^{\wedge^T} \\ -\left(\check{\mathbf{C}}_k\mathbf{v}\right)^{\wedge}\check{\mathbf{P}}_k & \left(\check{\mathbf{C}}_k\mathbf{v}\right)^{\wedge}\check{\mathbf{P}}_k\left(\check{\mathbf{C}}_k\mathbf{v}\right)^{\wedge^T} + \mathbf{R} \end{bmatrix}\right),$$

where we have abused notation slightly since the means are not dimensionally consistent, but the covariances are.

(iii) Generically, we can use (2.52) to write

$$p(\mathbf{x}|\mathbf{y}) = \mathcal{N}\left(\boldsymbol{\mu}_x + \underbrace{\boldsymbol{\Sigma}_{xy}\boldsymbol{\Sigma}_{yy}^{-1}(\mathbf{y} - \boldsymbol{\mu}_y)}_{\delta\mathbf{x}}, \boldsymbol{\Sigma}_{xx} - \boldsymbol{\Sigma}_{xy}\boldsymbol{\Sigma}_{yy}^{-1}\boldsymbol{\Sigma}_{yx}\right).$$

Because we are working with $SO(3)$, we adapt the mean update to use our $SO(3)$ perturbation scheme so that

$$\hat{\mathbf{C}}_k = \exp\left(\delta\mathbf{x}^{\wedge}\right)\check{\mathbf{C}}_k.$$

with

$$\delta\mathbf{x} = -\check{\mathbf{P}}_k\left(\check{\mathbf{C}}_k\mathbf{v}\right)^{\wedge^T}\left(\left(\check{\mathbf{C}}_k\mathbf{v}\right)^{\wedge}\check{\mathbf{P}}_k\left(\check{\mathbf{C}}_k\mathbf{v}\right)^{\wedge^T} + \mathbf{R}\right)^{-1}\left(\mathbf{y}_k - \check{\mathbf{C}}_k\mathbf{v}\right).$$

The updated covariance is then

$$\hat{\mathbf{P}}_k = \check{\mathbf{P}}_k - \check{\mathbf{P}}_k\left(\check{\mathbf{C}}_k\mathbf{v}\right)^{\wedge^T}\left(\left(\check{\mathbf{C}}_k\mathbf{v}\right)^{\wedge}\check{\mathbf{P}}_k\left(\check{\mathbf{C}}_k\mathbf{v}\right)^{\wedge^T} + \mathbf{R}\right)^{-1}$$
$$\times \left(\check{\mathbf{C}}_k\mathbf{v}\right)^{\wedge}\check{\mathbf{P}}_k.$$

(iv) Because this estimator is only observing a single star, rotating the estimate about this vector does not change the measurement. Therefore, not all degrees of freedom can be corrected and the estimator will drift from the ground truth.

References

Ablin, P., and Peyré, G. 2021. Fast and Accurate Optimization on the Orthogonal Manifold without Retraction. (arXiv:2102.07432).

Absil, P. A., Mahony, R., and Sepulchre, R. 2009. *Optimization on Matrix Manifolds*. Princeton University Press.

Ala-Luhtala, J., Särkkä, S. and Piché, R. 2015. Gaussian Filtering and Variational Approximations for Bayesian Smoothing in Continuous-Discrete Stochastic Dynamic Systems. *Signal Processing*, **111**(Jun), 124–136.

Amari, S.-I. 1998. Natural Gradient Works Efficiently in Learning. *Neural Computation*, **10**(2), 251–276.

Anderson, S., and Barfoot, T. D. 2015. Full STEAM Ahead: Exactly Sparse Gaussian Process Regression for Batch Continuous-Time Trajectory Estimation on SE(3). Pages 157–164 of *Proceedings of the IEEE/RSJ International Conference on Intelligent Robots and Systems (IROS)*. doi: https://doi.org/10.1109/IROS.2015.7353368.

Anderson, S., Barfoot, T. D., Tong, C. H. and Särkkä, S. 2015. Batch Nonlinear Continuous-Time Trajectory Estimation as Exactly Sparse Gaussian Process Regression. *Autonomous Robots,* special issue on "Robotics Science and Systems," **39**(3), 221–238.

Anderson, S. W. 2016. Batch Continuous-Time Trajectory Estimation. Ph.D. Thesis, University of Toronto.

Arasaratnam, I., and Haykin, S. 2009. Cubature Kalman Filters. *IEEE Transactions on Automatic Control*, **54**(6), 1254–1269.

Arun, K. S., Huang, T. S. and Blostein, S. D. 1987. Least-Squares Fitting of Two 3D Point Sets. *IEEE Transactions on Pattern Analysis and Machine Intelligence*, **9**(5), 698–700.

Bailey, T., and Durrant-Whyte, H. 2006. Simultaneous Localisation and Mapping (SLAM): Part II State of the Art. *IEEE Robotics and Automation Magazine*, **13**(3), 108–117.

Barfoot, T. D., Forbes, J. R. and Furgale, P. T. 2011. Pose Estimation Using Linearized Rotations and Quaternion Algebra. *Acta Astronautica*, **68**(1–2), 101–112.

Barfoot, T. D., Tong, C. H. and Särkkä, S. 2014. Batch Continuous-Time Trajectory Estimation as Exactly Sparse Gaussian Process Regression. *Autonomous Robots*, **39**, 221–238.

Barfoot, T. D., Forbes, J. R. and Yoon, D. J. 2020. Exactly Sparse Gaussian Variational Inference with Application to Derivative-Free Batch Nonlinear State Estimation. *International Journal of Robotics Research (IJRR)*, **39**(13), 1473–1502. (arXiv:1911.08333 [cs.RO]).

Barfoot, T. D., Forbes, J. R. and D'Eleuterio, G. M. T. 2021. Vectorial Parameterizations of Pose. *Robotica*, **40**(7), 2409–2427. (arXiv:2103.07309 [cs.RO]).

Barfoot, T. D., and Furgale, P. T. 2014. Associating Uncertainty with Three-Dimensional Poses for Use in Estimation Problems. *IEEE Transactions on Robotics*, **30**(3), 679–693.

Barrau, A. 2015. Non-linear State Error Based Extended Kalman Filters with Applications to Navigation. Ph.D. thesis, MINES ParisTech.

Barrau, A., and Bonnabel, S. 2017. The Invariant Extended Kalman Filter as a Stable Observer. *IEEE Transactions on Automatic Control*, **62**(4), 1797–1812.

Barrau, A., and Bonnabel, S. 2018a. Invariant Kalman Filtering. *Annual Review of Control, Robotics, and Autonomous Systems*, **1**(1), 237–257.

Barrau, A., and Bonnabel, S. 2018b. *Linear Observation Systems on Groups (I)*. Technical Report. MINES ParisTech.

Barron, J. T. 2019. A General and Adaptive Robust Loss Function. Pages 4331–4339 of *Proceedings of the IEEE/CVF Conference on Computer Vision and Pattern Recognition*. doi: https://doi.org/10.1109/CVPR.2019.00446.

Bar-Shalom, Y., Li, X. R. and Kirubarajan, T. 2001. *Estimation with Applications to Tracking and Navigation: Theory Algorithms and Software*. John Wiley & Sons.

Bauchau, O. A., and Trainelli, L. 2003. The Vectorial Parameterization of Rotation. *Nonlinear Dynamics*, **32**(1), 71–92.

Baum, L., and Petrie, T. 1966. Statistical Inference for Probabilistic Functions of Finite State Markov Chains. *Annals of Mathematical Statistics*, **37**(6), 1554–1563.

Bayes, T. 1764. Essay towards Solving a Problem in the Doctrine of Chances. *Philosophical Transactions of the Royal Society of London*, **53**, 370–418.

Besl, P. J., and McKay, N. D. 1992. A Method for Registration of 3-D Shapes. *IEEE Transactions on Pattern Analysis and Machine Intelligence*, **14**(2), 239–256.

Bierman, G. J. 1974. Sequential Square Root Filtering and Smoothing of Discrete Linear Systems. *Automatica*, **10**(2), 147–158.

Bishop, C. M. 2006. *Pattern Recognition and Machine Learning*. Springer.

Bjorck, A. 1996. *Numerical Methods for Least Squares Problems*. Society for Industrial and Applied Mathematics.

Black, M. J., and Rangarajan, A. 1996. On the Unification of Line Processes, Outlier Rejection, and Robust Statistics with Applications in Early Vision. *International Journal of Computer Vision*, **19**(1), 57–91.

Blanes, S., Casas, F., Oteo, J.-A. and Ros, J. 2009. The Magnus Expansion and Some of Its Applications. *Physics Reports*, **470**(5–6), 151–238.

Bonnabel, S., Martin, P., and Rouchon, P.. 2008. Symmetry-Preserving Observers. *IEEE Transactions on Automatic Control*, **53**(11), 2514–2526.

Boumal, N. 2022. *An Introduction to Optimization on Smooth Manifolds*. Cambridge University Press. doi: https://doi.org/10.1017/9781009166164.

Box, M. J. 1971. Bias in Nonlinear Estimation. *Journal of the Royal Statistical Society, Series B*, **33**(2), 171–201.

Brookshire, J., and Teller, S. 2012. Extrinsic Calibration from Per-Sensor Egomotion. Pages 25–32 of *Proceedings of Robotics: Science and Systems VIII*. Massachusetts Institute of Technology Press.

Brossard, M., Barrau, A., Chauchat, P. and Bonnabel, S. 2021. Associating Uncertainty to Extended Poses for on Lie Group IMU Preintegration with Rotating Earth. *IEEE Transactions on Robotics*, **38**(2), 998–1015.

Broussolle, F. 1978. State Estimation in Power Systems: Detecting Bad Data through the Sparse Inverse Matrix Method. *IEEE Transactions on Power Apparatus and Systems*, **PAS-97**(3), 678–682.

Brown, D. C. 1958. *A Solution to the General Problem of Multiple Station Analytical Stereotriangulation*. RCA-MTP Data Reduction Technical Report No. 43 (or AFMTC TR 58-8). Patrick Airforce Base, Florida.

Bryson, A. E. 1975. *Applied Optimal Control: Optimization, Estimation and Control*. Taylor and Francis.

Chen, C. S., Hung, Y. P. and Cheng, J. B. 1999. RANSAC-based DARCES: a New Approach to Fast Automatic Registration of Partially Overlapping Range Images. *IEEE Transactions on Pattern Analysis and Machine Intelligence*, **21**(11), 1229–1234.

Chen, Z., Heckman, C., Julier, S. and Ahmed, N. 2018. Weak in the NEES?: Auto-tuning Kalman Filters with Bayesian Optimization. Pages 1072–1079 of *21st International Conference on Information Fusion (FUSION)*. Institute of Electrical and Electronics Engineers.

Chirikjian, G. S. 2009. *Stochastic Models, Information Theory, and Lie Groups: Classical Results and Geometric Methods*. Vol. 1–2. Applied and Numerical Harmonic Analysis. Birkhauser.

Chirikjian, G. S., and Kyatkin, A. B. 2001. *Engineering Applications of Noncommutative Harmonic Analysis: with Emphasis on Rotation and Motion Groups*. CRC Press.

Chirikjian, G. S., and Kyatkin, A. B. 2016. *Harmonic Analysis for Engineers and Applied Scientists: Updated and Expanded Edition*. Dover Publications.

Cools, R. 1997. Constructing Cubature Formulae: the Science behind the Art. *Acta Numerica*, **6**, 1–54.

Corke, P. 2011. *Robotics, Vision, and Control*. Springer Tracts in Advanced Robotics 73. Springer.

Davenport, P. B. 1965. *A Vector Approach to the Algebra of Rotations with Applications*. Technical Report X-546-65-437. National Aeronautics and Space Administration.

de Ruiter, A. H. J., and Forbes, J. R. 2013. On the Solution of Wahba's Problem on SO(n). *Journal of the Astronautical Sciences*, **60**(1), 1–31.

D'Eleuterio, G. M. T. 1985. *Multibody Dynamics for Space Station Manipulators: Recursive Dynamics of Topological Chains*. Technical Report SS-3. Dynacon Enterprises Ltd.

D'Eleuterio, G. M. T., and Barfoot, T. D. 2022. On the Eigenstructure of Rotations and Poses: Commonalities and Peculiarities. *Royal Society Proceedings A*, **478**, n. pag.

Devlin, K. 2008. *The Unfinished Game: Pascal, Fermat, and the Seventeenth-Century Letter that Made the World Modern*. Basic Books.

Dudek, G., and Jenkin, M. 2010. *Computational Principles of Mobile Robotics*. Cambridge University Press.

Durrant-Whyte, H., and Bailey, T. 2006. Simultaneous Localisation and Mapping (SLAM): Part I The Essential Algorithms. *IEEE Robotics and Automation Magazine*, **11**(3), 99–110.

Dyce, M. 2013. Canada between the Photograph and the Map: Aerial Photography, Geographical Vision and the State. *Journal of Historical Geography*, **39**, 69–84.

Erisman, A. M., and Tinney, W. F. 1975. On Computing Certain Elements of the Inverse of a Sparse Matrix. *Communununications of the ACM*, **18**(3), 177–179.

Farrell, J. 2008. *Aided Navigation: GPS with High Rate Sensors*. McGraw-Hill, Inc.

Fischler, M., and Bolles, R. 1981. Random Sample Consensus: a Paradigm for Model Fitting with Applications to Image Analysis and Automated Cartography. *Communications of ACM*, **24**(6), 381–395.

Fisher, R. A. 1922. On the Mathematical Foundations of Theoretical Statistics. *Philosophical Transactions of the Royal Society of London. Series A, Containing Papers of a Mathematical or Physical Character*, **222**(594–604), 309–368.

Forster, C., Carlone, L., Dellaert, F., and Scaramuzza, D. 2015. IMU Preintegration on Manifold for Efficient Visual-Inertial Maximum-a-Posteriori Estimation. Pages 6–15 of *Proceedings of Robotics: Science and Systems*. Georgia Institute of Technology.

Furgale, P. T. 2011. Extensions to the Visual Odometry Pipeline for the Exploration of Planetary Surfaces. Ph.D. thesis, University of Toronto.

Furgale, P. T., Tong, C. H., Barfoot, T. D. and Sibley, G. 2015. Continuous-Time Batch Trajectory Estimation Using Temporal Basis Functions. *International Journal of Robotics Research*, **34**(14), 1688–1710.

García-Fernández, A. F., Svensson, L., Morelande, M. R., and Särkkä, S. 2015. Posterior Linearization Filter: Principles and Implementation Using Sigma Points. *IEEE Transactions on Signal Processing*, **63**(20), 5561–5573.

Gašperin, M., and Juričić, D. 2011. Application of Unscented Transformation in Nonlinear System Identification. *IFAC Proceedings Volumes*, **44**(1), 4428–4433.

Gauss, C. F. 1809. *Theoria motus corporum coelestium*. Perthes and Besser, Hamburg.

Gauss, C. F. 1821. Theoria combinationis observationum erroribus minimis obnoxiae, pars prior. *Werke, IV, Koniglichen Gesellschaft der Wissenschaften zu Gottingen*, 1–26.

Gauss, C. F. 1823. Theoria combinationis observationum erroribus minimis obnoxiae, pars posterior. *Werke, IV, Koniglichen Gesellschaft der Wissenschaften zu Gottingen*, 27–53.

Ghahramani, Z., and Hinton, G. E. 1996. *Parameter Estimation for Linear Dynamical Systems*. Technical Report CRG-TR-96-2. University of Toronto.

Ghahramani, Z., and Roweis, S. T. 1999. Learning nonlinear dynamical systems using an EM algorithm. Pages 431–437 of *NIPS'98: Proceedings of the 11th International Conference on Neural Information Processing Systems*. Massachusetts Institute of Technology.

Golub, H. G., and Van Loan, C. F. 1996. *Matrix Computations*. Johns Hopkins University Press.

Goudar, A., Zhao, W., Barfoot, T. D., and Schoellig, A. P. 2022. Gaussian Variational Inference with Covariance Constraints Applied to Range-Only Localization. Pages 2872–2879 of *Proceedings of the IEEE/RSJ International Conference on Intelligent Robot Systems (IROS)*. doi: https://doi.org/10.1109/IROS47612.2022.9981520.

Green, B. F. 1952. The Orthogonal Approximation of an Oblique Structure in Factor Analysis. *Psychometrika*, **17**(4), 429–440.

Hartley, R., and Zisserman, A. 2000. *Multiple View Geometry in Computer Vision*. Cambridge University Press.

Hertzberg, C., Wagner, R., Frese, U. and Schröder, L. 2013. Integrating Generic Sensor Fusion Algorithms with Sound State Representations through Encapsulation of Manifolds. *Information Fusion*, **14**(1), 57–77.

Hoffman, M. D., Blei, D. M., Wang, C. and Paisley, J. 2013. Stochastic Variational Inference. *The Journal of Machine Learning Research*, **14**(1), 1303–1347.

Holland, P. W., and Welsch, R. E. 1977. Robust Regression Using Iteratively Reweighted Least-Squares. *Communications in Statistics – Theory and Methods*, **6**(9), 813–827.

Horn, B. K. P. 1987a. Closed-Form Solution of Absolute Orientation using Orthonormal Matrices. *Journal of the Optical Society of America A*, **5**(7), 1127–1135.

Horn, B. K. P. 1987b. Closed-Form Solution of Absolute Orientation using Unit Quaternions. *Journal of the Optical Society of America A*, **4**(4), 629–642.

Huber, G., and Wollherr, D. 2020. An Online Trajectory Generator on SE (3) for Human–Robot Collaboration. *Robotica*, **38**(10), 1756–1777.

Hughes, P. C. 1986. *Spacecraft Attitude Dynamics*. Dover.

Ito, K., and Xiong, K. 2000. Gaussian Filters for Nonlinear Filtering Problems. *IEEE Transactions on Automatic Control*, **45**(5), 910–927.

Jazwinski, A. H. 1970. *Stochastic Processes and Filtering Theory*. Academic.

Jensen, J. L. W. V. 1906. Sur les fonctions convexes et les inégalités entre les valeurs moyennes. *Acta Mathematica*, **30**, 175–193.

Jia, B., Xin, M., and Cheng, Y. 2013. High-Degree Cubature Kalman Filter. *Automatica*, **49**(2), 510–518.

Jordan, M. I., Ghahramani, Z., Jaakkola, T. and Saul, L. K. 1999. An Introduction to Variational Methods for Graphical Models. *Machine Learning*, **37**(2), 183–233.

Julier, S., and Uhlmann, J. 1996. *A General Method for Approximating Nonlinear Transformations of Probability Distributions*. Technical Report. Robotics Research Group, University of Oxford.

Kaess, M., Ranganathan, A., and Dellaert, R. 2008. iSAM: Incremental Smoothing and Mapping. *IEEE Transactions on Robotics*, **24**(6), 1365–1378.

Kaess, M., Johannsson, H., Roberts, R. et al. 2012. iSAM2: Incremental Smoothing and Mapping Using the Bayes Tree. *International Journal of Robotics Research*, **31**(2), 217–236.

Kaess, M., and Dellaert, F. 2009. Covariance Recovery from a Square Root Information Matrix for Data Association. *Robotics and Autonomous Systems*, **57**(12), 1198–1210.

Kalman, R. E. 1960a. Contributions to the Theory of Optimal Control. *Boletin de la Sociedad Matematica Mexicana*, **5**, 102–119.

Kalman, R. E. 1960b. A New Approach to Linear Filtering and Prediction Problems. *Journal of Basic Engineering*, **82**(1), 35–45.

Kalman, R. E., and Bucy, R. S. 1961. New Results in Linear Filtering and Prediction Theory. *Journal of Basic Engineering*, **83**(1), 95–108.

Kelly, A. 2013. *Mobile Robotics: Mathematics, Models, and Methods*. Cambridge University Press.

Klarsfeld, S., and Oteo, J. A. 1989. The Baker–Campbell–Hausdorff Formula and the Convergence of the Magnus Expansion. *Journal of Physics A: Mathematical and Theoretical*, **22**(21), 4565–4572.

Kokkala, J., Solin, A. and Särkkä, S. 2014. Expectation Maximization Based Parameter Estimation by Sigma-Point and Particle Smoothing. Pages 1–8 of *17th International Conference on Information Fusion (FUSION)*. Institute of Electrical and Electronics Engineers.

Kokkala, J., Solin, A. and Särkkä, S. 2016. Sigma-Point Filtering and Smoothing Based Parameter Estimation in Nonlinear Dynamic Systems. *Journal of Advances in Information Fusion*, **11**(1), 15–30.

Kullback, S., and Leibler, R. A. 1951. On Information and Sufficiency. *The Annals of Mathematical Statistics*, **22**(1), 79–86.

Larson, N. 2019. *The Bernoulli Numbers: a Brief Primer*. Whitman College.

Lee, T., Leok, M., and McClamroch, N. H. 2008. Global Symplectic Uncertainty Propagation on SO(3). Pages 61–66 of *Proceedings of the 47th IEEE Conference on Decision and Control*. doi: https//doi.org/10.1109/CDC.2008.4739058.

Lilge, S., Barfoot, T. D., and Burgner-Kahrs, J. 2022. Continuum Robot State Estimation Using Gaussian Process Regression on SE(3). *International Journal of Robotics Research (IJRR)*, **41**(13–14): 027836492211288. doi: https://doi.org/10.1177/02783649221128843.

Long, A. W., Wolfe, K. C., Mashner, M. J. and Chirikjian, G. S. 2012. The Banana Distribution Is Gaussian: a Localization Study with Exponential Coordinates. Pages 265–272 of *Proceedings of Robotics: Science and Systems VIII*. Massachusetts Institute of Technology Press.

Lowe, D. G. 2004. Distinctive Image Features from Scale-Invariant Keypoints. *International Journal of Computer Vision*, **60**(2), 91–110.

Lu, F., and Milios, E. 1997. Globally Consistent Range Scan Alignment for Environment Mapping. *Autonomous Robots*, **4**(4), 333–349.

Lupton, T., and Sukkarieh, S. 2012. Visual-Inertial-Aided Navigation for High-Dynamic Motion in Built Environments without Initial Conditions. *IEEE Transactions on Robotics*, **28**(1), 61–76.

MacTavish, K. A., and Barfoot, T. D. 2015 (3–5 June). At All Costs: a Comparison of Robust Cost Functions for Camera Correspondence Outliers. Pages 62–69 of *Proceedings of the 12th Conference on Computer and Robot Vision (CRV)*. IEEE Computer Society, USA.

Madow, W. F. 1949. On the Theory of Systematic Sampling, II. *Annals of Mathematical Statistics*, **30**, 333–354.

Magnus, J. R., and Neudecker, H. 1980. The Elimination Matrix: Some Lemmas and Applications. *SIAM Journal on Algebraic Discrete Methods*, **1**(4), 422–449.

Magnus, J. R., and Neudecker, H. 2019. *Matrix Differential Calculus with Applications in Statistics and Econometrics*. John Wiley & Sons.

Magnus, W. 1954. On the Exponential Solution of Differential Equations for a Linear Operator. *Communications on Pure and Applied Mathematics*, **7**(4), 649–673.

Mahalanobis, P. 1936. On the Generalized Distance in Statistics. Pages 49–55 of *Proceedings of the National Institute of Science*, vol. 2.

Mahony, R., and Trumpf, J. 2021. Equivariant Filter Design for Kinematic Systems on Lie Groups. *IFAC-PapersOnLine*, **54**(9), 253–260.

Mangelson, J. G., Ghaffari, M., Vasudevan, R. and Eustice, R. M. 2020. Characterizing the Uncertainty of Jointly Distributed Poses in the Lie Algebra. *IEEE Transactions on Robotics*, **36**(5), 1371–1388.

Markov, A. A. 1912. *Wahrscheinlichkeitsrechnung*. Teubner.

Matthies, L., and Shafer, S. A. 1987. Error Modeling in Stereo Navigation. *IEEE Journal of Robotics and Automation*, **3**(3), 239–248.

Maybeck, P. S. 1994. *Stochastic Models, Estimation and Control*. Navtech Book and Software Store.

McGee, L. A., and Schmidt, S. F. 1985 (November). *Discovery of the Kalman Filter as a Practical Tool for Aerospace and Industry*. Technical Report NASA-TM-86847. NASA.

Meurant, G. 1992. A Review on the Inverse of Symmetric Tridiagonal and Block Tridiagonal Matrices. *SIAM Journal of Matrix Analysis and Applications*, **13**(3), 707–728.

Murray, R. M., Li, Z., and Sastry, S. 1994. *A Mathematical Introduction to Robotic Manipulation*. CRC Press.

Neal, R. M., and Hinton, G. E. 1998. A view of the EM algorithm that justifies incremental, sparse, and other variants. Pages 355–368 of *Learning in Graphical Models*. Springer.

O'Hagan, A. 1991. Bayes–Hermite Quadrature. *Journal of Statistical Planning and Inference*, **29**(3), 245–260.

Opper, M., and Archambeau, C. 2009. The Variational Gaussian Approximation Revisited. *Neural Computation*, **21**(3), 786–792.

Papoulis, A. 1965. *Probability, Random Variables, and Stochastic Processes*. McGraw-Hill Book Company.

Peretroukhin, V., Vega-Brown, W., Roy, N., and Kelly, J. 2016 (16–21 May). PROBE-GK: Predictive Robust Estimation Using Generalized Kernels. Pages 817–824 of *Proceedings of the IEEE International Conference on Robotics and Automation (ICRA)*. IEEE Press.

Petersen, K. B., and Pedersen, M. S. 2008. The Matrix Cookbook. *Technical University of Denmark*, **7**(15), 510.

Press, W. H., Teukolsky, S. A., Vetterling, W. T., and Flannery, B. P. 2007. *Numerical Recipes: the Art of Scientific Computing*. Cambridge University Press.

Rasmussen, C. E., and Williams, C. K. I. 2006. *Gaussian Processes for Machine Learning*. Massachusetts Institute of Technology Press.

Rauch, H. E., Tung, F. and Striebel, C. T. 1965. Maximum Likelihood Estimates of Linear Dynamic Systems. *AIAA Journal*, **3**(8), 1445–1450.

Särkkä, S. 2006. Recursive Bayesian Inference on Stochastic Differential Equations. Ph.D. thesis, Helsinki University of Technology.

Särkkä, S. 2013. *Bayesian Filtering and Smoothing*. Cambridge University Press.

Särkkä, S, Hartikainen, J., Svensson, L., and Sandblom, F. 2016. On the Relation between Gaussian Process Quadratures and Sigma-Point Methods. *Journal of Advances in Information Fusion*, **11**(1), 31–46.

Sarmavuori, J., and Särkkä, S. 2012. Fourier–Hermite Kalman Filter. *IEEE Transactions on Automatic Control*, **57**(6), 1511–1515.

Sastry, S. 1999. *Nonlinear Systems: Analysis, Stability, and Control*. Springer.

Schön, T. B., Wills, A. and Ninness, B. 2011. System Identification of Nonlinear State-Space Models. *Automatica*, **47**(1), 39–49.

Shannon, C. E. 1948. A Mathematical Theory of Communication. *The Bell System Technical Journal*, **27**, 379–423, 623–656.

Sherman, J., and Morrison, W. J. 1949. Adjustment of an Inverse Matrix Corresponding to Changes in the Elements of a Given Column or Given Row of the Original Matrix. *Annals of Mathematics and Statistics*, **20**, 621.

Sherman, J., and Morrison, W. J. 1950. Adjustment of an Inverse Matrix Corresponding to a Change in One Element of a Given Matrix. *Annals of Mathematics and Statistics*, **21**, 124–127.

Shumway, R. H., and Stoffer, D. S. 1982. An Approach to Time Series Smoothing and Forecasting Using the EM Algorithm. *Journal of Time Series Analysis*, **3**(4), 253–264.

Sibley, G. 2006. *A Sliding Window Filter for SLAM*. Technical Report. University of Southern California.

Sibley, G., Sukhatme, G. and Matthies, L. 2006. The Iterated Sigma Point Kalman Filter with Applications to Long-Range Stereo. In *Proceedings of Robotics: Science and Systems*. www.roboticsproceedings.org/rss02/index.html.

Sibley, G. 2007. Long Range Stereo Data-Fusion From Moving Platforms. Ph.D. thesis, University of Southern California.

Simon, D. 2006. *Optimal State Estimation: Kalman, H Infinity, and Nonlinear Approaches*. Wiley-Interscience.

Smith, P., Drummond, T., and Roussopoulos, K. 2003. Computing MAP Trajectories by Representing, Propagating, and Combining PDFs over Groups. In *Proceedings of the IEEE International Conference on Computer Vision*. https://ieeexplore.ieee.org/xpl/conhome/8769/proceeding.

Smith, R. C., Self, M., and Cheeseman, P. 1990. Estimating Uncertain Spatial Relationships in Robotics. Pages 167–193 of Cox, I. J., and Wilfong, G. T. (eds.), *Autonomous Robot Vehicles*. Springer.

Solà Ortega, J., Deray, J. and Atchuthan, D. 2018. *A Micro Lie Theory for State Estimation in Robotics*. arXiv:1812.01537v9.

Stein, C. M. 1981. Estimation of the Mean of a Multivariate Normal Distribution. *Annals of Statistics*, **9**(6), 1135–1151.

Stengel, R. F. 1994. *Optimal Control and Estimation*. Dover Publications.

Stillwell, J. 2008. *Naive Lie Theory*. Springer.

Stuelpnagel, J. 1964. On the Parameterization of the Three-Dimensional Rotation Group. *SIAM Review*, **6**(4), 422–430.

Su, S. F., and Lee, C. S. G. 1991. Uncertainty Manipulation and Propagation and Verification of Applicability of Actions in Assembly Tasks. Pages 2471–2476 of *Proceedings of the IEEE International Conference on Robotics and Automation*, vol. 3. https://ieeexplore.ieee.org/xpl/conhome/347/proceeding.

Su, S. F., and Lee, C. S. G. 1992. Manipulation and Propagation of Uncertainty and Verification of Applicability of Actions in Assembly Tasks. *IEEE Transactions on Systems, Man and Cybernetics*, **22**(6), 1376–1389.

Takahashi, K., Fagan, J. and Chen, M.-S. 1973. A Sparse Bus Impedance Matrix and Its Application to Short Circuit Study. In *Proceedings of the PICA Conference*. IEEE.

Tang, T. Y., Yoon, D. J., and Barfoot, T. D. 2019. A White-Noise-On-Jerk Motion Prior for Continuous-Time Trajectory Estimation on SE(3). *IEEE Robotics and Automation Letters*, **4**(2), 594–601. (arXiv:1809.06518 [cs.RO]), presented at ICRA 2019.

Thrun, S., and Montemerlo, M. 2005. The GraphSLAM Algorithm with Applications to Large-Scale Mapping of Urban Structures. *International Journal on Robotics Research*, **25**(5/6), 403–430.

Thrun, S., Burgard, W., and Fox, D. 2006. *Probabilistic Robotics*. Massachusetts Institute of Technology Press.

Thrun, S., Fox, D., Burgard, W. and Dellaert, F. 2001. Robust Monte Carlo Localization for Mobile Robots. *Artificial Intelligence*, **128**(1–2), 99–141.

Tong, C. H., Furgale, P. T., and Barfoot, T. D. 2013. Gaussian Process Gauss–Newton for Non-parametric Simultaneous Localization and Mapping. *International Journal of Robotics Research*, **32**(5), 507–525.

Triggs, W., McLauchlan, P., Hartley, R., and Fitzgibbon, A. 2000. Bundle Adjustment: a Modern Synthesis. Pages 298–375 of Triggs, W., Zisserman, A., and Szeliski, R. (eds.), *Vision Algorithms: Theory and Practice*. LNCS. Springer.

Umeyama, S. 1991. Least-Squares Estimation of Transformation Parameters between Two Point Patterns. *IEEE Transactions on Pattern Analysis and Machine Intelligence*, **13**(4), 376–380.

Van Loan, C. 1978. Computing Integrals Involving the Matrix Exponential. *IEEE Transactions on Automatic Control*, **23**(3), 395–404.

Wahba, G. 1965. A Least-Squares Estimate of Spacecraft Attitude. *SIAM Review*, **7**(3), 409.

Wang, Y., and Chirikjian, G. S. 2006. Error Propagation on the Euclidean Group with Applications to Manipulator Kinematics. *IEEE Transactions on Robotics*, **22**(4), 591–602.

Wang, Y., and Chirikjian, G. S. 2008. Nonparametric Second-Order Theory of Error Propagation on Motion Groups. *International Journal of Robotics Research*, **27**(11), 1258–1273.

Wolfe, K., Mashner, M., and Chirikjian, G. 2011. Bayesian Fusion on Lie Groups. *Journal of Algebraic Statistics*, **2**(1), 75–97.

Wong, J. N., Yoon, D. J., Schoellig, A. P. and Barfoot, T. D. 2020. A Data-Driven Motion Prior for Continuous-Time Trajectory Estimation on SE(3). *IEEE Robotics and Automation Letters (RAL)*, **5**(2), 1429–1436. presented at ICRA 2020.

Woodbury, M. A. 1950. *Inverting Modified Matrices*. Technical Report 42. Statistical Research Group, Princeton University.

Wu, Y., Hu, D., Wu, M., and Hu, X. 2006. Gaussian Filters for Nonlinear Filtering Problems. *IEEE Transactions on Signal Processing*, **54**(8), 2910–2921.

Yan, X., Indelman, V., and Boots, B. 2014. Incremental Sparse GP Regression for Continuous-time Trajectory Estimation and Mapping. Pages 20–132 of *Proceedings of the NIPS Workshop on Autonomously Learning Robots*, vol. 87. doi: https://doi.org/10.48550/arXiv.1504.02696.

Yang, H., Antonante, P., Tzoumas, V., and Carlone, L. 2020. Graduated Non-convexity for Robust Spatial Perception: from Non-minimal Solvers to Global Outlier Rejection. *IEEE Robotics and Automation Letters*, **5**(2), 1127–1134.

Zhang, Z. 1997. Parameter Estimation Techniques: a Tutorial with Application to Conic Fitting. *Image and Vision Computing*, **15**(1), 59–76.

Index

Printed in the United States
by Baker & Taylor Publisher Services